P9-CUK-432

The 1996 World Book

YEAR BOOK

The Annual Supplement to The World Book Encyclopedia

▪▪▪ A REVIEW OF THE EVENTS OF 1995 ▪▪▪

World Book, Inc.

a Scott Fetzer company

Chicago ▪ London ▪ Sydney ▪ Toronto

© 1996 World Book, Inc. All rights reserved. This volume may not be reproduced in whole or in part in any form without prior written permission from the publisher. Portions of the material contained in this volume are taken from *The World Book Encyclopedia* © 1996 and from *The World Book Dictionary* © 1996 World Book, Inc.

World Book, Inc.
525 W. Monroe
Chicago, IL 60661

ISBN 0-7166-0496-5
ISSN 0084-1439
Library of Congress Catalog Card Number: 62-4818

Printed in the United States of America.

The 1996 World Book

YEAR BOOK

The Annual Supplement to The World Book Encyclopedia

■ ■ ■ **A REVIEW OF THE EVENTS OF 1995** ■ ■ ■

World Book, Inc.

a Scott Fetzer company

Chicago ■ London ■ Sydney ■ Toronto

© 1996 World Book, Inc. All rights reserved. This volume may not be reproduced in whole or in part in any form without prior written permission from the publisher. Portions of the material contained in this volume are taken from *The World Book Encyclopedia* © 1996 and from *The World Book Dictionary* © 1996 World Book, Inc.

World Book, Inc.
525 W. Monroe
Chicago, IL 60661

ISBN 0-7166-0496-5
ISSN 0084-1439
Library of Congress Catalog Card Number: 62-4818

Printed in the United States of America.

Staff

■ EDITORIAL

Executive Editor
Darlene R. Stille

Managing Editor
David Dreier

Senior Editors
Mary Carvlin
Mark Dunbar
Carol L. Hanson
Patricia Ohlenroth

Staff Editor
Susan Cassidy

Contributing Editors
Jinger Hoop
Karin C. Rosenberg

Editorial Assistant
Ethel Matthews

Cartographic Services
H. George Stoll, Head
Wayne K. Pichler

Index Services
David Pofelski, Head

Permissions Editor
Janet Peterson

Statistical Services
Thomas J. Wrobel, Head

■ ART

Executive Director
Roberta Dimmer

Senior Designer, Year Book
Brenda B. Tropinski

Senior Designers
Cari L. Biamonte
Melanie J. Lawson

Designer
Don DiSante

Senior Photographs Editor
Sandra M. Dyrlund

Art Production Assistant
Stephanie Tunney

■ RESEARCH SERVICES

Director
Mary Norton

Researchers
Karen McCormack
Kristina Vaicikonis

Library Services
Mary Ann Urbashich,
Head

■ PRODUCTION

Daniel N. Bach,
Vice President

Manufacturing/Pre-Press
Sandra Van den Broucke,
Director
Barbara Podczerwinski
Joann Seastrom
Aldo Pacini

Proofreaders
Anne Dillon
Karen Lenburg

Text Processing
Curley Hunter
Gwendolyn Johnson

■ EDITOR IN CHIEF
W. Richard Dell

■ PUBLISHER EMERITUS
William H. Nault

■ PRESIDENT, WORLD BOOK PUBLISHING
John E. Frere

World Book Advisory Board

Bonnie J. Brunkhorst, Professor of Science Education and Geology, California State University, San Bernardino;

Lynn A. Fontana, President, Fountain Communications, Inc., and Research Associate Professor, Instructional Development Office, George Mason University;

Ruth A. Vinz, Associate Professor of English Education, Teachers College, Columbia University;

Scott L. Waugh, Dean of Social Sciences and Professor of History, University of California, Los Angeles;

Robert Wedgeworth, University Librarian, University of Illinois at Urbana-Champaign.

Contributors

Contributors not listed on these pages are members of *The World Book Year Book* editorial staff.

- **ALEXIOU, ARTHUR G.**, B.S.E.E., M.S.E.E.; Assistant Secretary, Committee on Climatic Changes and Ocean. [Ocean]

- **ANDREWS, PETER J.**, B.A., M.S.; Free-lance writer; biochemist. [Chemistry]

- **APSELOFF, MARILYN FAIN**, B.A., M.A.; Associate Professor of English, Kent State University. [Literature for children]

- **ARNDT, RANDOLPH C.**, Media Relations Director, National League of Cities. [City]

- **BARBER, PEGGY**, B.A., M.L.S.; Associate Executive Director for Public Policy and Programs, American Library Association. [Library]

- **BARNHART, BILL**, B.A., M.S.T., M.B.A.; Financial markets columnist, *Chicago Tribune*. [Stocks and bonds]

- **BERGER, JIM**, B.A., M.P.A.; Editor/Publisher, *Washington Trade Daily*. [International trade]

- **BLACKADAR, ALFRED K.**, A.B., Ph.D.; Professor Emeritus, Pennsylvania State University. [Weather]

- **BOWER, BRUCE**, M.A.; Behavioral Sciences Editor, *Science News* magazine. [Psychology]

- **BOYD, JOHN D.**, B.S.; Economics/Corporate Reporter, *Knight-Ridder Financial News*. [Economics]

- **BRADSHER, HENRY S.**, A.B., B.J.; Foreign affairs analyst. [Asia and Asian country articles]

- **BRETT, CARLTON E.**, B.A., M.S., Ph.D.; Professor of Geological Sciences, University of Rochester. [Paleontology]

- **BRODY, HERB**, B.S.; Senior Editor, *Technology Review* magazine. [Telecommunications Special Report: Wired to the World]

- **BUERKLE, TOM**, B.A.; Correspondent, *International Herald Tribune*. [Europe and Western European country articles]

- **CAMPBELL, GEOFFREY A.**, B.J.; Free-lance writer. [Civil rights Special Report: Affirmative Action: Opportunity or Obstacle?; Civil rights; Courts; Supreme Court of the United States]

- **CAMPBELL, LINDA P.**, B.A., M.S.L.; Senior reporter, *Fort Worth Star-Telegram*. [Civil rights; Courts; Supreme Court of the United States]

- **CARDINALE, DIANE P.**, B.A.; Assistant Communications Director, Toy Manufacturers of America. [Toys and games]

- **CARMODY, DEIRDRE**, Media reporter, *The New York Times*. [Magazine]

- **CASEY, MICHAEL T.**, B.A. M.A.; Auto writer, *The Detroit News*. [Automobile]

- **CORNELL, VINCENT J.**, B.A., M.A., Ph.D.; Andrew W. Mellon Assistant Professor of Religion, Duke University. [Islam]

- **CROMIE, WILLIAM J.**, B.S., M.S.; Science writer, Harvard University. [Space exploration]

- **DeFRANK, THOMAS M.**, B.A., M.A.; White House Correspondent, *Newsweek* magazine. [Armed forces]

- **DeLANCEY, MARK W.**, B.A., M.A., Ph.D.; Professor of Government and International Studies, University of South Carolina. [Africa and African country articles]

- **DIAMOND, PETER A.**, Ph.D.; Professor of Economics, Massachusetts Institute of Technology. [Social Security Special Report: Social Security's Insecure Future]

- **DILLON, DAVID**, B.A., M.A., Ph.D.; Architecture critic, *The Dallas Morning News*. [Architecture]

- **DIRDA, MICHAEL**, B.A., M.A., Ph.D.; Writer and editor, *The Washington Post Book World*. [Poetry]

- **EATON, WILLIAM J.**, B.S.J., M.S.J.; Curator, Humphrey Fellows Program, University of Maryland. [U.S. government articles]

- **ELLIS, GAVIN**, Assistant Editor, *New Zealand Herald*. [New Zealand]

- **FARR, DAVID M. L.**, M.A., D.Phil.; Professor Emeritus of History, Carleton University, Ottawa. [Canada; Canadian provinces]

- **FISHER, ROBERT W.**, B.A., M.A.; Free-lance writer; formerly a Senior Economist/Editor, U.S. Bureau of Labor Statistics. [Labor]

- **FITZGERALD, MARK**, B.A.; Midwest Editor, *Editor & Publisher* magazine. [Newspaper]

- **FIXICO, DONALD L.**, B.A., M.A., Ph.D.; Professor of History, Western Michigan University. [Indian, American]

- **FOX, THOMAS C.**, B.A., M.A.; Editor/Associate Publisher, *National Catholic Reporter*. [Roman Catholic Church]

- **FRICKER, KAREN**, B.A., M.A.; Senior Editor, *Stagebill* magazine. [Theater]

- **FRIEDMAN, EMILY**, B.A.; Health policy columnist, *Journal of the American Medical Association*. [Health care issues]

- **GARVIE, MAUREEN**, B.A., B.Ed., M.A.; Teacher and free-lance editor and writer, Queen's University. [Canadian literature]

- **GATTY, BOB**, Editor, Periodicals News Service. [Food]

- **GIBSON, ERIC**, Executive Editor, *ART news*. [Art]

- **GOLDEN, CARON**, B.A.; Free-lance writer and editor. [San Diego]

- **GOLDNER, NANCY**, B.A.; Dance critic, *The Philadelphia Inquirer*. [Dancing]

- **HANNA, JACK**, B.A.; Director Emeritus, Columbus Zoological Park. [World Book Supplement: Zoo]

- **HARAKAS, STANLEY SAMUEL**, B.A., B.D., Th.D.; Archbishop Iakovos Professor of Orthodox Theology, Emeritus, Hellenic College, Holy Cross Greek Orthodox School of Theology. [Eastern Orthodox Churches]

- **HAVERSTOCK, NATHAN A.**, A.B.; Affiliate Scholar, Oberlin College. [Latin America and Latin American country articles]

- **HELMS, CHRISTINE**, B.A., Ph.D.; Foreign affairs analyst; author. [Middle East and Middle Eastern country articles; North African country articles]

- **HILLGREN, SONJA**, B.J., M.A.; Editor, *Farm Journal*. [Farm and farming]

- **HOLMES, BOB**, B.Sc., Ph.D., U.S. Correspondent, *New Scientist* magazine. [Conservation Special Report: Have We Fished Out the Sea?]

- **HOWELL, LEON**, A.B., M.Div.; Editor and Publisher, *Christianity and Crisis*. [Religion]

- **JOHANSON, DONALD C.**, B.S., M.A., Ph.D.; President, Institute of Human Origins. [Anthropology]

- **JONES, TIM**, B.S.; Media writer, *Chicago Tribune*. [Telecommunications]

- **KILGORE, MARGARET**, B.A., M.B.A.; Editor, Phillips-Van Buren, Inc. [Los Angeles]

- **KING, MIKE**, Reporter, *The Montreal Gazette*. [Montreal]

- **KISOR, HENRY**, B.A., M.S.J.; Book Editor, *Chicago Sun-Times*. [Literature; Literature, American]

KISTE, ROBERT C., Ph.D.; Director and Professor, Center for Pacific Islands Studies, University of Hawaii. **[Pacific Islands]**

KLOBUCHAR, LISA, B.A.; Free-lance editor and writer. **[Biographies]**

KOLGRAF, RONALD, B.A., M.A.; Publisher, *Adweek/New England* magazine. **[Manufacturing]**

KORMAN, RICHARD, Associate Editor, *Engineering News-Record*. **[Building and construction Special Report: Designing for Disasters; Building and construction]**

LAWRENCE, AL, B.A., M.A., M.Ed.; Executive Director, United States Chess Federation. **[Chess]**

LEWIS, DAVID C., M.D.; Professor of Medicine and Community Health, Brown University. **[Drug abuse]**

LITSKY, FRANK, B.S.; Sportswriter, *The New York Times*. **[Sports articles]**

MARCH, ROBERT H., A.B., S.M., Ph.D.; Professor of Physics, University of Wisconsin at Madison. **[Physics]**

MARSCHALL, LAURENCE A., Ph.D.; Professor of Physics, Gettysburg College. **[Astronomy]**

MARTY, MARTIN E., Ph.D.; Fairfax M. Cone Distinguished Service Professor, University of Chicago. **[Protestantism]**

MATHER, IAN J., B.A., M.A.; Diplomatic Editor, *The European*, London. **[Northern Ireland Special Report: The Pursuit of Peace in Northern Ireland; Ireland; Northern Ireland; United Kingdom]**

MAUGH, THOMAS H., II, Ph.D.; Science writer, *Los Angeles Times*. **[Biology]**

MAYES, BARBARA A., B.A.; Free-lance editor and writer. **[Nobel Prizes; Pulitzer Prizes; Washington, D.C.]**

McLEESE, DON, B.A., M.A.; Columnist/critic-at-large, *Austin American-Statesman*. **[Popular music]**

MERLINE, JOHN W., B.A.; Washington Correspondent, *Investor's Business Daily*. **[Consumerism]**

MORITZ, OWEN, B.A.; Free-lance writer. **[New York City]**

MORRIS, BERNADINE, B.A., M.A.; Free-lance fashion writer. **[Fashion]**

MULLINS, HENRY T., B.S., M.S., Ph.D.; Professor of Geology, Syracuse University. **[Geology]**

NGUYEN, J. TUYET, B.A.; Bureau manager, United Nations Correspondent, United Press International. **[Population; United Nations]**

PENNISI, ELIZABETH, B.S., M.S.; Free-lance science writer. **[Biology]**

PRIESTAF, IRIS, B.A., M.A., Ph.D.; Geographer and Vice President, David Keith Todd Consulting Engineers, Incorporated. **[Water]**

RALOFF, JANET, B.S.J., M.S.J.; Senior Editor, *Science News* magazine. **[Environmental pollution]**

RAPHAEL, M. L., B.A., M.A., Ph.D.; Gimenick Professor of Judaic Studies, College of William and Mary. **[Judaism]**

REARDON, PATRICK T., B.A.; Urban affairs writer, *Chicago Tribune*. **[Chicago]**

ROSE, MARK J., B.A., M.A., Ph.D.; Managing Editor, *Archaeology* magazine. **[Archaeology]**

RUBENSTEIN, RICHARD E., B.A., M.A., J.D.; Professor of Conflict Resolution and Public Affairs, George Mason University. **[Terrorism Special Report: The Terrorist Agenda]**

SAVAGE, IAN, B.A., M.A., Ph.D.; Assistant Professor of Economics and Transportation, Northwestern University. **[Aviation; Transportation]**

SEGAL, TROY, B.A.; Free-lance writer. **[Television]**

SHAPIRO, HOWARD S., B.S.; Cultural Arts Editor, *The Philadelphia Inquirer*. **[Philadelphia]**

SOLNICK, STEVEN L., B.A., M.A., Ph.D.; Professor of Political Science, Columbia University. **[Baltic states and other former Soviet republic articles]**

STEIN, DAVID LEWIS, B.A., M.S.; Urban affairs columnist, *The Toronto Star*. **[Toronto]**

STUART, ELAINE, B.A.; Managing Editor, Council of State Governments. **[State government]**

SUMMERS, DAVID, Ph.D., Professor of the History of Art, University of Virginia. **[World Book Supplement: Leonardo da Vinci; Michelangelo]**

TANNER, JAMES C., B.S.J.; Senior energy correspondent, *The Wall Street Journal*. **[Petroleum and gas]**

TATUM, HENRY K., B.A.; Associate Editorial Page Editor, *The Dallas Morning News*. **[Dallas]**

THOMAS, PAULETTE, B.A.; Reporter, *The Wall Street Journal*. **[Bank]**

TOCH, THOMAS W., B.A., M.A.; Associate editor and education correspondent, *U.S. News & World Report*. **[Education]**

TONRY, MICHAEL, A.B., LL.B.; Sonosky Professor of Law and Public Policy, University of Minnesota Law School. **[Prison]**

TRENT, KIMBERLY, B.A.; Free-lance writer. **[Detroit]**

TUCK, JAMES A., Ph.D.; Professor of Archaeology, Memorial University of Newfoundland. **[World Book Supplement: Inuit]**

von RHEIN, JOHN, B.A., M.A.; Music critic, *Chicago Tribune*. **[Classical music]**

WALLECHINSKY, DAVID, Chief Executive Officer, Almanac Researchers. **[World Book Supplement: Olympic Games]**

WALTER, EUGENE J., Jr., B.A.; Free-lance writer. **[Comic strips Special Report: 100 Years of Comics; Conservation; Zoos]**

WATSON, BURKE, B.A.; Assistant suburban editor, *Houston Chronicle*. **[Houston]**

WEINTRAUB, SIDNEY, Ph.D.; William E. Simon Chair, Center for Strategic and International Studies. **[Mexico Special Report: Crisis in Mexico]**

WILLIAMS, SUSAN G., B.A.; Free-lance journalist, Sydney, Australia. **[Australia]**

WILSON, MARY ELIZABETH, A.B., M.D.; Chief, Infectious Diseases, Mount Auburn Hospital; Assistant Professor, Harvard School of Public Health. **[Public health Special Report: Emerging Diseases]**

WOLCHIK, SHARON L., B.A., M.A., Ph.D.; Director, Russian and East European Studies, George Washington University. **[Eastern European country articles]**

WOODS, MICHAEL, B.S.; Science Editor, *The* (Toledo, Ohio) *Blade*. **[AIDS; Computer; Drugs; Electronics; Energy supply; Medicine; Mental health; Public health; Safety]**

WUNTCH, PHILIP, B.A.; Film critic, *The Dallas Morning News*. **[Motion pictures]**

ZIMBALIST, ANDREW, B.A., M.A., Ph.D.; Professor of Economics, Smith College. **[Sports Special Report: Are Professional Team Sports Striking Out?]**

Contents

▲ Page 458

▲ Page 12

The major world events of 1995 are reported in more than 265 alphabetically arranged articles—from "Africa" and "Europe" to "Motion pictures" and "Zoos." Included are Special Reports that provide an in-depth focus on especially noteworthy developments.

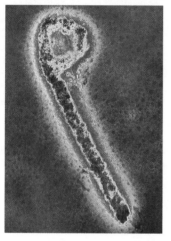
▼ Page 125

The Year's
Major News Stories

From such tragedies as the bombing of a U.S. federal building and the assassination of a world leader to such triumphs as the beginnings of peace in Northern Ireland and Bosnia, 1995 was a year filled with momentous events. On these two pages are stories that *Year Book* editors picked as the most memorable, exciting, or important of the year, along with details on where to find information about them in *The World Book Year Book.*   *The Editors*

Rabin Assassinated ▶
Israeli Prime Minister Yitzhak Rabin was assassinated after a peace rally in November by an Israeli extremist who opposed Rabin's plans for making peace with the Palestinians. See **Israel,** page 248; **Middle East,** page, 294.

Republican Congress
In January 1995, Republicans took control of both the Senate and the U.S. House of Representatives for the first time in 40 years and battled all year long with Democratic President Bill Clinton over ways to cut the federal budget deficit. See **Congress of the United States,** page 164; **Republican Party,** page 356.

▲ Alfred P. Murrah Federal Building in Oklahoma bombed
The Oklahoma City federal building lies in ruins after a truck bomb exploded on April 19, killing 168 occupants. See **Crime,** page 186; **Terrorism:** Special Report: **The Terrorist Agenda,** page 424.

Bosnian peace agreement

Leaders of Bosnia, Croatia, and Serbia, meeting at a military base near Dayton, Ohio, in November, initial an agreement to end civil war in the Balkans. See **Bosnia-Herzegovina,** page 82; **Croatia,** page 188; **Europe,** page 216.

▼

Women's conferences in China

About 36,000 women representing governments and nongovernmental agencies arrived in Beijing in September for conferences on removing obstacles to the advancement of women. First Lady Hillary Rodham Clinton in a speech reprimanded China for human rights abuses. **China,** page 123; **United Nations,** page 444.

Million Man March

Hundreds of thousands of African American men converged on Washington, D.C., on October 16 for a day of reconciliation, unity, and atonement for past neglect of family and community. The event was organized by controversial Nation of Islam leader Louis Farrakhan. See **Civil Rights,** page 130; **Washington, D.C.,** page 452.

◀ **O. J. acquitted**

Former football star O. J. Simpson reacts with triumphant joy after a Los Angeles jury on October 3 unanimously found him not guilty of the murders of his former wife Nicole Brown Simpson and her friend Ronald L. Goldman. See **Courts,** page 184.

Earthquake in Kobe, Japan. ▶

Crumbled buildings line the streets of Kobe after a quake struck the area on Jan. 17, 1995. See **Building and construction:** Special Report: **Designing for Disasters,** page 88; **Japan,** page 251.

AEOLOGY ■ ARCHITECTURE ■ ARGENTINA ■ ARMED FORCES ■ ARMENIA ■ ART

BILE RACING ■ AVIATION ■ BAHRAIN ■ BANGLADESH ■ BANK ■ BASEBALL ■

DING AND CONSTRUCTIO

GO ■ CHILE ■ CHINA

PUTER ■ CONSERVATIO

DETROIT ■ DISABLED

EL SALVADOR ■ ELEC

N ■ FINLAND ■ FOC

■ HORSE RACING ■

■ ITALY ■ JAPAN ■

TIN AMERICA ■ LATVI

BA ■ MANUFACTURIN

W YORK CITY

WEST TERRITORIES

TROLEUM AN

OSTAL CE ■ PRINC

1995

THE YEAR IN BRIEF

A month-by-month listing of the most significant world events that occurred during 1995.

STOCKS AND BOND

COMM

FIELD ■ TRAN

■ UKRAINE ■ UNITED KINGDOM ■ UNITED NATIONS ■ UNITED STATES GOVER

WELFARE ■ YUGOSLAVIA ■ YUKON TERRITORY ■ ZAIRE ■ ZAMB ■ ZOOS

S	M	T	W	TH	F	S
January 1995						
1	2	3	4	5	6	7
8	9	10	11	12	13	14
15	16	17	18	19	20	21
22	23	24	25	26	27	28
29	30	31				

1   **Russia's Defense Minister Pavel Grachev** claims control of the central part of Grozny, capital of the breakaway republic of Chechnya. But Chechen rebels the next day oust Russian forces from the center of the city in fierce street fighting.

Brazil's new president, Fernando Henrique Cardoso, is inaugurated in ceremonies at Brasília, the capital. Cardoso succeeds President Itamar Franco.

4   **The first session of the 104th Congress** of the United States convenes in Washington, D.C., with Republicans holding a majority in both the House of Representatives and the Senate for the first time in 40 years.

9   **Jury selection begins in New York City** in the trial of Muslim leader Sheik Omar Abdel Rahman and 11 other defendants accused of conspiring to bomb the World Trade Center and other landmarks in 1993.

10   **Heavy flooding in California,** the result of a major storm system pushing out of the Pacific Ocean, prompts United States President Bill Clinton to issue a disaster declaration for 24 counties. By January 14, 10 other counties were declared disaster areas, qualifying them for federal aid.

11   **National Hockey League (NHL)** player and owner representatives reach a tentative contract agreement to end the owners' lockout and salvage the 1994-1995 NHL season. The season is set to begin on January 20.

17   **A devastating earthquake strikes Kobe, Japan,** a port city of 1.5 million people, killing more than 5,400 people, injuring about 26,000 others, and leaving over 300,000 people homeless. It was Japan's highest death toll from an earthquake since a 1923 quake destroyed Tokyo.

18   **The discovery of Stone Age paintings** in an underground cave in southern France is reported by France's Minister of Culture Jacques Toubon, who described the find as having "exceptional value because of its size and variety and because it was found undisturbed."

19   **Russian troops capture the presidential palace** in the center of Grozny after weeks of constant shelling and rocket attacks.

22   **Two Palestinian suicide bombers** kill 19 Israelis, most of them Israeli soldiers, at a bus stop north of Tel Aviv, Israel. The bombers are believed to be members of Hamas, a militant Islamic fundamentalist group.

29   **The San Francisco 49ers win Super Bowl XXIX** in Miami, Florida, defeating the San Diego Chargers, 49-26, as 49ers quarterback Steve Young throws six touchdown passes, a Super Bowl record, to win the game's Most Valuable Player award.

31   **A $50-billion loan package for Mexico** is arranged by President Clinton, who bypasses Congress and uses his emergency authority to help rescue the failing Mexican economy.

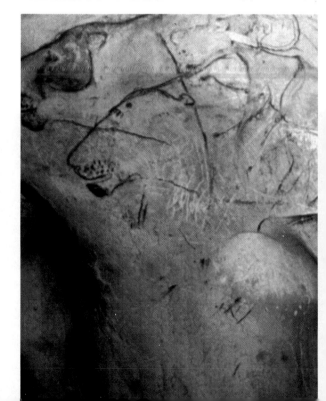

12

A section of a freeway in Kobe, Japan, lies toppled on its side after an earthquake struck the city on January 17, killing more than 5,400 people.

Quarterback Steve Young drops back for a pass during the San Francisco 49ers 49-26 victory over the San Diego Chargers in Super Bowl XXIX on January 29. Young was named the Most Valuable Player.
▼

The discovery of Stone Age cave paintings, exquisitely preserved in southern France, is announced on January 18 by France's minister of culture.

S	M	T	W	TH	F	S
February 1995						
			1	2	3	4
5	6	7	8	9	10	11
12	13	14	15	16	17	18
19	20	21	22	23	24	25
26	27	28				

1,2 **More than 250,000 Dutch residents** flee their homes to escape rising floodwaters in the Netherlands's largest peacetime evacuation.

4 **United States President Bill Clinton threatens** to impose more than $1 billion in punitive tariffs on Chinese imports in retaliation for copyright infringements. But a trade war is averted on February 26, when China agrees to crack down on copyright violations, averting what would have been the harshest trade sanctions in U.S. history.

5 **A German neo-Nazi group** takes responsibility for a bomb blast that killed four people outside a gypsy (Romany) settlement in Oberwart, Germany.

7 **Poland's coalition government** names Jozef Oleksy, a former Communist, to become Poland's next premier. Poland's President Lech Walesa approves the nomination the next day.

8 **The United Nations Security Council** votes to send a peacekeeping force of 7,000 soldiers to Angola to police a 1994 accord that ended 19 years of civil war in the southern African nation.

12 **Mexico's conservative National Action Party** sweeps elections in the state of Jalisco, winning the gubernatorial election and the mayoralty of Guadalajara and handing the ruling Institutional Revolutionary Party its worst defeat since it was founded in 1929.

19 **Serbian President Slobodan Milošević rejects an offer** by five major countries to lift trade sanctions on Serbia in exchange for Serbia's recognition of Bosnia-Herzegovina and Croatia.

22 **British Prime Minister John Major** and Ireland's Prime Minister John Bruton present a peace plan for Northern Ireland that would create a legislative assembly free of Protestant domination and would allow for Northern Ireland's unification with the Republic of Ireland based on majority approval.

France accuses four U.S. diplomats and a private U.S. citizen of political and economic espionage and asks them to leave the country.

Algerian security forces put down a rebellion in an Algiers prison where Muslim militants killed four guards. Algerian officials said 96 inmates died in the crackdown, but Muslim fundamentalists said at least 200 inmates were killed.

24-28 **The Mexican government makes several arrests** in connection with the 1994 assassinations of two PRI leaders. On February 28, the older brother of former Mexican President Carlos Salinas de Gotari was charged with ordering the murder of top PRI official José Francisco Ruíz Massieu. Earlier, on February 24, Mexico's attorney general announced the arrests of two men with links to the PRI in connection with the assassination of PRI presidential candidate Luis Donaldo Colosio Murrieta. The attorney general said the 1994 investigation of Colosio's death, which concluded he was slain by a lone gunman, was a cover-up.

▲
Floodwaters bury farmland in the Netherlands as a result of rainstorms that forced more than 250,000 Dutch residents to evacuate their homes on February 1 and 2.

British Prime Minister John Major, left, shakes hands with John Bruton, prime minister of Ireland, after the ▶ two leaders reached an agreement on February 22 on a framework for peace talks on Northern Ireland.

S	M	T	W	TH	F	S
			1	2	3	4
5	6	7	8	9	10	11
12	13	14	15	16	17	18
19	20	21	22	23	24	25
26	27	28	29	30	31	

March 1995

2 **A proposed constitutional amendment** requiring the United States government to balance its budget fails in the U.S. Senate by a vote of 66 to 34.

3 **A former Argentine Navy commander** reveals that he took part in "death flights" in 1977 in which political prisoners, after being tortured and then sedated, were thrown into the ocean from navy aircraft. The commander estimated that about 2,000 political prisoners were killed in this manner in 1977 and 1978.

The last United Nations (UN) forces in Somalia depart from the airport at Mogadishu, the capital, as the UN ends its peacekeeping mission in the strife-torn African nation.

5 **In Estonia, a coalition led by former Communists** wins a majority of seats in parliamentary elections, ousting from power the reformist-minded Fatherland Party.

13 **United States President Bill Clinton** declares more than half of California a federal disaster area due to flooding caused by a series of rainstorms. At least 14 people died in the flooding, which left thousands homeless and ruined vast areas of cropland.

14 **The United Kingdom withdraws a regiment** of 400 soldiers from Northern Ireland, the largest reduction of British troops there in 10 years.

Baseball owners violated labor laws by walking out of contract negotiations with the players' union in December 1994, the counsel for the National Labor Relations Board rules, in announcing that he will seek an injunction against the owners.

Astronaut Norman E. Thagard becomes the first American to enter space aboard a Russian rocket as he and two cosmonauts take off from the Baikonur Space Center in Kazakhstan en route to Russia's orbiting space station, Mir.

19 **Basketball superstar Michael Jordan** ends his retirement and returns to the National Basketball Association in a game with the Indiana Pacers, scoring 19 points and grabbing headlines from Beijing to Paris.

20, 22 **A poison gas attack in Tokyo's subway system** kills 12 people and hospitalizes more than 5,500 others during the morning rush hour. On March 22, Japanese police raid the training compound of a religious cult and find equipment and chemicals for making poison gas.

23 **Turkish officials say they will establish a buffer zone** in northern Iraq to prevent raids by Kurdish rebels based there.

The U.S. Senate passes legislation that gives the President the line-item veto (the power to veto specific items in the federal budget), an unprecedented expansion of presidential power.

31 **United States forces in Haiti** turn over their peacekeeping duties to a United Nations force as President Clinton praises the restoration of democracy during a ceremony in Port-au-Prince, the Haitian capital.

◄ Two women care for a Tokyo subway passenger who was felled by a poison gas attack that killed 12 people and hospitalized more than 5,500 others during the morning rush hour on March 20.

▲
Basketball superstar Michael Jordan returns to the court on March 19 after ending his retirement from the National Basketball Association.

S	M	T	W	TH	F	S
April 1995						
						1
2	3	4	5	6	7	8
9	10	11	12	13	14	15
16	17	18	19	20	21	22
23	24	25	26	27	28	29
30						

2 **Major league baseball owners** in the United States and Canada accept a players' offer to return to work under the terms of their old contract after a federal district court judge ruled that the owners had violated labor laws. An abbreviated 144-game schedule was set to begin April 25.

2,3 **The University of Connecticut's women's basketball** team wins the National Collegiate Athletic Association (NCAA) national title, defeating Tennessee, 70 to 64, and ending the season undefeated with 35 victories. On April 3, the University of California at Los Angeles wins the men's NCAA title for the 11th time with an 89-78 victory over defending champion Arkansas.

3 **Diplomats report the massacre** of about 400 Hutus, mostly women and children, in northeastern Burundi, raising fears that central Africa will again become embroiled in genocidal warfare.

9 **Ben Crenshaw wins the 59th Masters golf tournament** at Augusta, Georgia, with a 14-under-par 274, the lowest score at the Masters since 1976.

Peruvian President Alberto Fujimoro wins reelection by an overwhelming margin, capturing 64 percent of the vote.

Former U.S. Defense Secretary Robert S. McNamara stirs controversy when it is revealed that he describes the Vietnam War as "wrong, terribly wrong" in his soon-to-be-published book.

10 **Robert Dole, the U.S. Senate majority leader,** formally announces his candidacy for the 1996 Republican presidential nomination.

13 **Finland's new prime minister,** Paavo Lipponen, takes the oath of office after his Social Democratic Party won a plurality in parliamentary elections in March.

16 **Canada and the European Union reach an agreement** on fishing rights that ends a six-week dispute between Canada and Spain over fishing for turbot off Newfoundland.

19,21 **A powerful truck bomb destroys** the Alfred P. Murrah Federal Building in Oklahoma City, Oklahoma, killing 168 people, including 19 children who were in a day-care center on the building's second floor. A nurse also died during rescue efforts. On April 21, federal authorities arrest Timothy McVeigh and hold two other men as material witnesses.

24 **Federal authorities link the "Unabomber"** to the death of the chief lobbyist for the California Forestry Association who is killed when a mail bomb explodes in his Sacramento office.

30 **An expanded trade embargo against Iran** is announced by United States President Bill Clinton who says Iran is attempting to acquire nuclear weapons and is continuing to support terrorism. Clinton suspends all U.S. trade with Iran.

The Alfred P. Murrah Federal Building in Oklahoma City, Oklahoma, lies in utter ruin after a truck-bomb explosion on April 19 collapsed most of the building, killing 168 people. A nurse who died during rescue efforts brought the final death toll to 169.

S	M	T	W	TH	F	S
		1	2	3	4	5	6

May 1995

S	M	T	W	TH	F	S
		1	2	3	4	5	6
7	8	9	10	11	12	13
14	15	16	17	18	19	20
21	22	23	24	25	26	27
28	29	30	31			

1-3 **Croatian forces attack the Serb-held Krajina region** of central Croatia, seizing a section of a vital highway between Zagreb, the capital of Croatia, and Belgrade, the capital of Serb-dominated Yugoslavia. On May 2 and 3, Serb forces retaliate with rocket attacks on Zagreb that kill six people and injure 175 others.

7 **French voters elect conservative Jacques Chirac** to the presidency by a margin of 53 percent to 47 percent for Socialist candidate Lionel Jospin. The victory ended the Socialists' 14-year hold on the French presidency.

8 **The 50th anniversary of V-E Day** (Victory in Europe), the unconditional surrender of Nazi Germany to Allied forces during World War II (1939-1945), is commemorated at a ceremony in Berlin, Germany, with several world leaders, including German Chancellor Helmut Kohl, taking part.

9 **Most Western leaders,** including United States President Bill Clinton, protest Russian military actions in Chechnya by boycotting a military parade commemorating the end of World War II in Moscow's Red Square.

11 **A deadly outbreak of the Ebola virus** is reported in Zaire by scientists with the Centers for Disease Control and Prevention in the United States and the World Health Organization.

14 **Argentine President Carlos Saúl Menem** is easily reelected, garnering 50 percent of the vote, more than enough to avoid a runoff election.

15 **The discovery of what may be the largest burial tomb** ever excavated in Egypt is reported by archaeologists. The 3,000-year-old tomb contains at least 67 chambers and is believed to hold the remains of some 50 sons of Pharaoh Ramses II.

Dow Corning Company, maker of a silicone breast implant, files for bankruptcy, throwing into doubt the outcome of hundreds of thousands of lawsuits filed against the company by women who claimed the implant was defective.

16 **Japanese police arrest the leader of the Aum Shinrikyo** religious cult and charge him with organizing the March 20 nerve gas attack on the Tokyo subway system that killed 12 people.

22 **The U.S. Supreme Court rules** that state efforts to limit congressional terms of office are unconstitutional, making term-limit provisions in 23 states null and void.

25 **In a milestone vote, the U.S. Senate approves a bill** that would cut federal spending by $1 trillion in a move intended to balance the federal budget by the year 2000.

28 **Bosnian Serb forces shoot down a helicopter** carrying Bosnia's foreign minister, who is killed in the attack. The Serbs also take 41 United Nations peacekeepers as hostages, bringing the total number of peacekeepers held hostage to more than 300.

▲

A statue of the Egyptian god Osiris presides over the ruins of a burial chamber for the sons of Pharaoh Ramses II. Archaeologists reported the discovery of what may be the largest burial tomb ever excavated in Egypt on May 15.

The newly elected president of France, Jacques Chirac, left, accompanies his predecessor, François Mitterrand, at inauguration ceremonies in Paris on May 17. ▶

	S	M	T	W	TH	F	S
June 1995						1	2	3
	4	5	6	7	8	9	10
	11	12	13	14	15	16	17
	18	19	20	21	22	23	24
	25	26	27	28	29	30	

2 **A United States F-16C jet fighter is shot down** near Mrkonjic Grad in Bosnia-Herzegovina by Bosnian Serb forces. On June 8, U.S. marines rescue the pilot, Scott F. O'Grady, who had managed to remain hidden in an area controlled by Bosnian Serbs.

7 **United States President Bill Clinton** issues the first veto of his presidential tenure, overriding spending cuts in education and job training that amounted to $16.4 billion. Republicans lacked the votes needed to override the veto.

8 **Canada's Progressive Conservative Party** sweeps Ontario's provincial elections, capturing the premiership for party leader Michael Harris and winning 82 of the provincial assembly's 130 seats.

12 **The U.S. Supreme Court makes two major rulings** on issues concerning racial equality. In a 5-to-4 decision, the court ruled that affirmative action programs are constitutional only when they address specific acts of past discrimination, thereby imposing a more exacting standard on such programs. In a second 5-to-4 decision, the court rejected a sweeping school desegregation plan in Kansas City, Missouri.

14 **The Houston Rockets,** led by center Hakeem Olajuwon, win their second consecutive National Basketball Association championship, defeating the Orlando Magic 113-101 to sweep the series in four games.

18 **Russia's Prime Minister Victor Chernomyrdin** agrees to halt all military activities in the southern republic of Chechnya and to hold peace talks with Chechen rebels in return for the release of hostages held by Chechen forces in the Russian town of Budennovsk.

20 **The Southern Baptist Convention,** the largest Protestant denomination in the United States, apologizes for the church's past support of slavery and for "condoning . . . systematic racism in our lifetime."

22 **The nomination of Henry W. Foster, Jr.,** as U.S. surgeon general is blocked by a Senate filibuster mounted by Republicans who objected to the fact that Foster, an obstetrician/gynecologist, had performed abortions.

28 **Japan and the United States reach a trade accord** on automobiles and automotive parts, ending a U.S. threat to impose sanctions that would have curtailed imports of Japanese luxury cars such as the Lexus.

29 **The Atlantis space shuttle and the Russian Mir** space station link up in space to form the largest spacecraft ever to orbit Earth.

The U.S. Supreme Court in a narrow 5-to-4 decision rules that congressional districts drawn to increase minority representation in Congress are unconstitutional unless they meet strict judicial standards. The ruling, called a "blow" to the 1965 Voting Rights Act, is expected to reduce minority representation in Congress.

▲

Houston Rockets center Hakeem Olajuwon goes up over the Orlando Magic's Dennis Scott and Shaquille O'Neal on June 14 as Houston wins its second consecutive National Basketball Association championship.

United States pilot Scott O'Grady arrives on the deck of the U.S.S. *Kearsage* on June 8 after being rescued from Bosnia-Herzegovina, where his plane was shot down by Bosnian Serbs.
▼

U.S. astronaut Robert L. Gibson, right, shakes hands with Russian cosmonaut Vladimir N. Dezhurov on June 29 as the Atlantis space shuttle hooks up with Russia's Mir space station, forming the largest spacecraft ever to orbit the Earth.
▼

	S	M	T	W	TH	F	S
July 1995							1
	2	3	4	5	6	7	8
	9	10	11	12	13	14	15
	16	17	18	19	20	21	22
	23	24	25	26	27	28	29
	30	31					

1 **The government of Russian President Boris Yeltsin** survives a no-confidence vote in the State Duma, the lower house of Russia's parliament.

3 **Rioting erupts in Belfast and Londonderry,** Northern Ireland, in response to the release of a British soldier who had been sentenced to life imprisonment for the murder in 1990 of a Roman Catholic teen-ager.

4 **Britain's Prime Minister John Major** easily wins reelection as leader of the ruling Conservative Party in a confidence vote meant to stifle a rebellion by the party's right wing.

5 **Turkey renews its attacks on Kurdish guerrillas** in northern Iraq, sending 3,000 troops with support from warplanes and heavy artillery into the region.

8,9 **American Pete Sampras** on July 9 wins the Wimbledon men's singles title in England, defeating Boris Becker, 6-7, 6-2, 6-4, 6-2. The previous day, Steffi Graf of Germany won the women's title, beating Arantxa Sánchez Vicario of Spain, 4-6, 6-1, 7-5.

10 **Burma's military junta lifts the house arrest** imposed on opposition leader Aung San Suu Kyi, the 1991 Nobel Peace Prize winner who was sentenced to house arrest in 1989 as a result of her campaign for democracy.

11 **Bosnian Serbs capture the town of Srebrenica,** an ethnic enclave under the protection of the United Nations (UN), in one of the most humiliating defeats for UN forces in their three years of peacekeeping in Bosnia-Herzegovina.

United States President Bill Clinton extends diplomatic recognition to Vietnam, 20 years after Communist forces captured Saigon, now Ho Chi Minh City.

23 **Japan's Social Democratic Party suffers a setback** in elections to the upper house of parliament, winning only 16 of the 22 seats it hoped to win, but Prime Minister Tomiichi Murayama insists the setback is not severe enough to cause his resignation.

25 **A terrorist bomb explodes in Paris** near Notre Dame Cathedral, killing 7 people and injuring about 80 others on a crowded commuter train.

The UN's Yugoslav War Crimes Tribunal in The Hague, the Netherlands, indicts Bosnian Serb leader Radovan Karadzic and Bosnian Serb military commander General Ratko Mladic for war crimes committed during fighting in Bosnia.

27 **Three of the largest labor unions** in the United States, representing steelworkers, autoworkers, and machinists, plan to merge to form the largest industrial union in the country.

31 **Walt Disney Company says it will buy** Capital Cities/ABC Inc. in a $19-billion deal that will create one of the world's largest entertainment companies.

Bosnian Muslim refugees from the town of Srebrenica gaze through the razor-wire emplacements of a United Nations (UN) refugee camp after Bosnian Serb forces captured the town on October 11. Srebrenica had been under UN protection.

	S	M	T	W	TH	F	S
August 1995			1	2	3	4	5
	6	7	8	9	10	11	12
	13	14	15	16	17	18	19
	20	21	22	23	24	25	26
	27	28	29	30	31		

4 **A conference on world fishing,** sponsored by the United Nations (UN), reaches agreement on the first treaty ever to regulate fishing on the high seas in an effort to stem a serious decline in global fish stocks. The pact was approved by more than 90 countries.

5 **Croatian troops seize the town of Knin,** routing rebel Croatian Serb forces in an all-out offensive against the self-proclaimed Serb Republic of Krajina, a region of Croatia that borders Bosnia-Herzegovina. By August 7, the Croatian forces have recaptured all of the Krajina region.

10 **A federal grand jury in Oklahoma City** indicts Timothy McVeigh and Terry Nichols for the April 19 bombing of the Alfred P. Murrah Federal Building, in which 168 people were killed. Related but lesser charges are filed against Michael Fortier, who is expected to be the government's chief witness.

15 **On the 50th anniversary** of the end of World War II in the Pacific, Japan's Prime Minister Tomiichi Murayama offers his "heartfelt apology" for the suffering Japan caused "to the people of many countries, particularly to those of Asian nations." Japan's first frank apology for its World War II role drew both praise and criticism. In June, the lower house of Japan's "parliament" had expressed remorse for Japan's actions in the war but refused to apologize for them.

16 **Anthropologists report the discovery** in Kenya of the fossilized bones of a new human ancestor that lived about 4 million years ago. The new hominid species, which represents the earliest direct evidence of upright walking, is named Australopithecus anamensis.

24 **China expels American human rights activist** Harry Wu after convicting him of espionage. Chinese officials apparently sought to improve relations with the United States by expelling Wu rather than sentencing him to prison. After his release, Wu returned to the United States.

28 **The Chemical Banking Corporation** says it will acquire the Chase Manhattan Corporation to create the largest bank in the United States, with assets of $297 billion. The merged bank was to be called Chase Manhattan. Chemical Banking Chairman Walter V. Shipley, who was named to head the new bank, said the merger would result in about 12,000 layoffs out of a work force of 75,000.

Two mortar shells land in Sarajevo's central market, killing 38 people in the worst attack on the Bosnian capital since February 1994. Blaming Bosnian Serbs for the attack, NATO warplanes and artillery on August 30 begin a massive retaliation against Bosnian Serb positions.

30 **More than 15,000 women** from private organizations assemble in Huairou, China, outside Beijing, to attend a nongovernmental forum on women's issues.

◄ Smoke rises from an ammunition dump in the Bosnian Serb stronghold of Pale on August 30 as North Atlantic Treaty Organization (NATO) planes carry out air strikes against the Serbs in retaliation for an August 28 mortar attack on the city of Sarajevo.

▲
U.S. human rights activist Harry Wu faces spy charges in China on August 24. He was convicted and then expelled from China.

S	M	T	W	TH	F	S
September 1995					1	2
3	4	5	6	7	8	9
10	11	12	13	14	15	16
17	18	19	20	21	22	23
24	25	26	27	28	29	30

1   **French commandos seize** two Greenpeace vessels that attempted to lead an international flotilla into waters of the South Pacific to protest French underground nuclear tests there. France conducted the first of a series of tests on September 5, despite worldwide protests.

2   **President Bill Clinton speaks** during ceremonies at Pearl Harbor in Hawaii commemorating the 50th anniversary of V-J Day (Victory over Japan), the date of the formal surrender of Japan at the end of World War II (1939-1945).

5   **First Lady Hillary Rodham Clinton** lectures China on human rights abuses in an address to the United Nations Fourth World Conference on Women in Beijing.

6   **Baltimore Orioles shortstop Cal Ripken, Jr.,** plays in his 2,131st consecutive game, breaking a 56-year-old record set by the New York Yankees Lou Gehrig, who was known as the "Iron Horse" because of his endurance.

The United States Senate's Ethics Committee votes unanimously to recommend the expulsion of Senator Bob Packwood (R., Oregon), charging him with sexual misconduct. On September 7, Packwood says he will resign his Senate seat.

20   **The AT&T Corporation,** the world's largest telecommunications company, announces plans to split up into three separate companies. The breakup would be the largest in U.S. corporate history.

22   **Time Warner Inc. agrees to purchase** the Turner Broadcasting System for about $7 billion in stock, a merger that would create the world's largest entertainment and media conglomerate.

24   **An agreement between Israel** and the Palestine Liberation Organization (PLO) provides for the expansion of Palestinian self-rule in the West Bank and the withdrawal of Israeli troops. The accord, reached after marathon negotiations, represents the second stage of the Israeli-PLO peace process, which began in September 1993. The agreement is signed on September 28 at the White House in Washington, D.C.

25   **Dallas billionaire Ross Perot** announces the formation of a third political party, the Independence Party (later renamed the Reform Party), aimed at capturing independent voters in the 1996 presidential race. Perot says the party, in addition to fielding a presidential candidate in 1996, will endorse Democratic and Republican candidates in congressional races.

26   **Bosnian Serb, Croat, and Muslim leaders** agree on a framework for a postwar government, but the accord, reached after intense negotiations at the United Nations in New York City, does not include a cease-fire or internal boundaries.

28   **The president of Comoros,** an island nation off the east coast of Africa, is held hostage by foreign mercenaries who staged a coup attempt by attacking the presidential palace and seizing the main army compound.

UNITED NATIONS
FOURTH WORLD CONFERENCE ON
BEIJING, 4-15 SEPTEMBER 1

Baltimore Orioles shortstop Cal Ripken, Jr., takes to the field at Baltimore's Camden Yards ballpark on September 6 as he sets a new record for consecutive games played—2,131.

▲
First Lady Hillary Rodham Clinton addresses a special session of the United Nations Fourth World Conference on Women in Beijing, China, on September 5, where she made an impassioned call for human rights and freedom of expression.

S	M	T	W	TH	F	S

October 1995

1	2	3	4	5	6	7
8	9	10	11	12	13	14
15	16	17	18	19	20	21
22	23	24	25	26	27	28
29	30	31				

1 **Muslim fundamentalist leader** Sheik Omar Abdel Rahman and nine other defendants on trial for conspiring to carry out a terrorist campaign of bombings and assassinations are found guilty on 48 of 50 charges by a federal jury in New York City.

2 **Portugal's Socialist Party** wins the most seats in parliamentary elections held October 1 but concedes that it lacks a majority and will have to form a governing coalition.

3 **Former football star O. J. Simpson** is found not guilty by a Los Angeles jury of the murders of his former wife Nicole Brown Simpson and her friend Ronald L. Goldman.

4 **Pope John Paul II begins a five-day papal visit** to the United States, arriving at Newark (New Jersey) International Airport, where he is greeted by President Bill Clinton.

Florida and Alabama are battered by Hurricane Opal, which causes at least 20 deaths and leaves more than 1 million people without electric power.

9 **An Amtrak train carrying 268 people derails** in the Arizona desert, killing 1 person and injuring 78. Investigators said the track had been sabotaged and that copies of a note found near the accident site claimed a group calling itself the Sons of Gestapo was responsible.

12 **A fragile truce takes effect** between the government of Bosnia-Herzegovina and Bosnian Serbs after the two sides, warring since 1992, sign a cease-fire agreement.

15 **More than 8 million Iraqis go to the polls** to vote in a referendum on the rule of President Saddam Hussein. According to the government, more than 99 percent of the voters cast ballots in support of Saddam.

16 **An estimated 400,000 black men** from around the nation gather in Washington, D.C., to express racial solidarity in the Million Man March, organized by Nation of Islam leader Louis Farrakhan.

23 **President Clinton and Russian President** Boris N. Yeltsin meet in Hyde Park, New York, and pledge continued friendship and cooperation between the United States and Russia. Yeltsin says Russia will help keep peace in the Balkans.

24 **The United Nations (UN)** celebrates its 50th anniversary. Among the heads of state speaking at commemoration ceremonies was Cuba's President Fidel Castro, who addressed the UN General Assembly in New York City on October 22.

25 **John J. Sweeney,** long-time president of the Service Employees International Union is elected the new president of the American Federation of Labor and Congress of Industrial Organizations (AFL-CIO).

30 **Voters in Quebec** by a narrow margin reject a proposal for Quebec to become separate from Canada.

▲

African American men from throughout the United States converge on Washington, D.C., on October 16 to participate in the Million Man March, a demonstration of racial solidarity organized by Louis Farrakhan, leader of the Nation of Islam.

Former football star O.J. Simpson reacts to the jury's verdict in a Los Angeles courtroom on October 3 as he is acquitted of the murder of his wife Nicole Brown Simpson and her friend Ronald L. Goldman.

S	M	T	W	TH	F	S

November 1995

S	M	T	W	TH	F	S
			1	2	3	4
5	6	7	8	9	10	11
12	13	14	15	16	17	18
19	20	21	22	23	24	25
26	27	28	29	30		

4 **Israel's Prime Minister Yitzhak Rabin,** who had pursued peace with Israel's long-time Palestinian enemies, is assassinated by a lone gunman after addressing a rally of his supporters in Tel Aviv. Rabin's self-confessed assailant—Yigal Amir, a 25-year-old Israeli law student—was taken into police custody. Amir said he was following the will of God in assassinating Rabin because of the prime minister's policy of trading away land in return for peace with the Arabs. Although Amir claimed that he had acted alone, the Israeli government would make several more arrests and assert that the assassination was part of a right wing conspiracy.

8 **General Colin L. Powell,** the retired chairman of the Joint Chiefs of Staff and coordinator of the Persian Gulf War (1991), announces that he will not seek the presidency in 1996. Giving his reason for declining to join the presidential race despite being urged by many people to run, Powell says that life in the political arena "requires a calling that I do not yet hear."

17 **Nigeria's military regime** hangs nine political activists, including a noted playwright, Ken Saro-Wiwa. The nine had been convicted of the murder of four progovernment Ogoniland chiefs in May 1994, but critics of the Nigerian leadership contended that the charges were trumped up. The true purpose of the executions, they asserted, was to make people fearful of taking part in antigovernment activities.

12 **Croatian Serbs** in the Eastern Slavonia region of Croatia, who had been rebelling against the central government, agree to avoid war and rejoin Croatia. The peace agreement preserves the multiethnic makeup of the disputed area.

13 **A bomb explodes** at a U.S.-run military training center in Riyadh, Saudi Arabia, killing seven people—five of them Americans—and injuring about 60 others. The bomb was thought to have been planted by Saudi militants who want to end the American presence in Saudi Arabia.

14 **The Republican-controlled U.S. Congress** and President Bill Clinton fail to agree on a short-term spending bill. As a result, the government runs out of money to pay its employees, and 800,000 federal workers are laid off until an agreement can be reached. The impasse will last until November 19, when the President and Congress reach a compromise.

19 **President Lech Walesa of Poland** fails in a bid for reelection to a second five-year term, losing narrowly to Alexander Kwasniewski, a former Communist. With Kwasniewski's victory, former Communists have successfully completed a campaign to take control of the entire government.

21 **The presidents of Bosnia-Herzegovina,** Croatia, and Serbia, meeting at Wright-Patterson Air Force Base near Dayton, Ohio, sign an agreement to bring peace to the war-torn Balkan region. The pact calls for Bosnia-Herzegovina to be divided into a Bosnian-Croat federation and a Serb republic. Some 60,000 NATO troops, including 20,000 from the United States, are to enforce the peace.

A huge crowd, including many world leaders, surrounds the flag-draped casket of Yitzhak Rabin in Jerusalem on November 6 as the slain Israeli prime minister is laid to rest. Rabin was killed by a right wing Jewish zealot on November 4 in Tel Aviv, Israel.

S	M	T	W	TH	F	S
					1	2
3	4	5	6	7	8	9
10	11	12	13	14	15	16
17	18	19	20	21	22	23
24	25	26	27	28	29	30
31						

December 1995

4 **The first of 60,000** North Atlantic Treaty Organization (NATO) troops begin arriving in Bosnia-Herzegovina to enforce a peace agreement worked out in November in the United States. The next day at a meeting in Brussels, Belgium, foreign and defense ministers representing the 16 NATO nations give their approval to the intervention—the largest military deployment in the history of the Western alliance. The formal signing of the peace agreement took place on December 14 in Paris.

Prosecutors in Israel file murder charges against Yigal Amir, the confessed killer of Prime Minister Yitzhak Rabin. Two other men, including Amir's brother, Hagai, are indicted for conspiracy in the assassination, and an army sergeant is charged with supplying arms and ammunition. Amir's trial opened on December 19 but was then suspended until January 23, 1996, to give the defense additional time to study the case.

Former South Korean President Roh Tae Woo is indicted for allegedly accepting at least $370 million in corporate bribes. Three of Roh's aides and 24 business executives are also indicted.

6 **President Bill Clinton** vetoes a Republican plan to balance the federal budget in seven years, saying the plan goes too far in cutting Medicare, Medicaid, and education and contains an unacceptable rollback of environmental protection. The next day, the White House offers its own plan, but it in turn is attacked by Republican congressional leaders, who dismiss it as inadequate.

7 **The Galileo spacecraft** reaches Jupiter and goes into orbit around the giant planet. A probe released earlier from Galileo plunges into Jupiter's dense atmosphere and sends back data for about 75 minutes before being destroyed by pressure and heat.

16 **Hundreds of thousands of workers** demonstrate in Paris and other French cities on the last day of a three-week strike called to protest government cutbacks in social welfare benefits.

With still no budget decided on, the U.S. government partially shuts down for the second time in two months, and about 265,000 employees are furloughed.

17 **Russian citizens go to the polls** to vote in parliamentary elections. The Communist Party ends up with 158 of the 450 seats in the lower house of parliament.

In Haiti, voters choose René Préval, candidate of the Lavalas Party, to succeed Jean-Bertrand Aristide as president when Aristide's term expires in February 1996.

25 **Turkey's Prime Minister Tansu Ciller** resigns after her True Path Party is defeated in parliamentary elections by the Welfare Party, a Muslim organization. Ciller is expected to continue in office until a new government can be formed. The Welfare Party's victory is the first win by a Muslim party in Turkey's 72-year history as a secular state.

A U.S. soldier arriving in Tuzla, Bosnia-Herzegovina in early December is greeted by children at a refugee camp. Some 20,000 Amercan troops were scheduled to be sent to Bosnia-Herzegovina as part of 60,000-troop North Atlantic Treaty Organization deployment to enforce a peace pact between warring factions in that Baltic nation.

1995

WORLD BOOK
YEAR BOOK UPDATE

The major events of 1995 are summarized in more than 265 alphabetically arranged articles, from "Adams" to "Zoos." In most cases, the article titles are the same as those of the articles in *The World Book Encyclopedia* that they update. Included are Special Reports that offer in-depth looks at subjects, ranging from the 100th anniversary of the comic strip to the public health threat of newly emerging diseases. The Special Reports can be found on the following pages under their respective Update article titles.

Adams, Gerry (1948-), the president of Sinn Féin, the political wing of the Irish Republican Army (IRA), the underground military group fighting for Northern Ireland's independence from Great Britain, was one of Northern Ireland's most prominent leaders in 1995. Adams was a chief architect of an IRA cease-fire announced in August 1994.

Adams was born Oct. 6, 1948, in the working-class Catholic community of West Belfast, Northern Ireland. His father was an IRA member, and his mother's family included prominent Irish activists.

Adams joined Sinn Féin in the mid-1960's. By the early 1970's, according to British Intelligence sources, he had risen to the IRA's commanding ranks. He was imprisoned without trial during the 1970's for anti-British activities. In 1983, he became president of Sinn Féin. From 1983 to 1992, he represented West Belfast in the British Parliament, though in accord with Sinn Féin tradition he did not take his seat.

Beginning in 1988, Adams took part in a series of peace talks that eventually led to the August 1994 cease-fire. Earlier in 1994, the Adminstration of President Bill Clinton, against Great Britain's wishes, allowed Adams to visit the United States to speak at a foreign policy conference. Adams visited the United States again in March 1995, making numerous public appearances and conducting fund-raising activities.

Adams is the author of five books. He is married and has three children. □ Lisa Klobuchar

Afghanistan. With stunning speed, a new force known as the Taliban captured the southwestern half of Afghanistan in 1995 and more than once nearly took over the capital, Kabul. There, Burhanuddin Rabbani presided as president, despite the fact that his term had expired in December 1994. The Taliban vowed to fight until Rabbani stepped down. The Taliban blamed him for the civil war that had killed thousands of people since it erupted in 1992, when the nation's Communist regime fell.

The Taliban, whose name means Seekers of Knowledge and refers to Muslim students, rose abruptly in late 1994 under the loose leadership of an Muslim teacher, Muhammad Umar. The group subdued local factions to take control of the main southern city of Qandahar. The Taliban rallied students, former guerrillas, and former Communist soldiers from the nation's Pushtun ethnic majority. The group scored victories mainly by persuading or paying war-weary local commanders to join them. In areas they controlled, the Taliban imposed strict Islamic laws that banned women from public jobs, prohibited coeducation, and forbade most sports.

The Taliban advanced northward toward Kabul for the first time in February 1995. Gulbuddin Hikmatyar, Rabbani's main rival, had troops south of the city. He had been trying since 1992 to defeat Rabbani's military commander defending Kabul, Ahmad Shah Massoud, and seize the government. By

1995, Hikmatyar's artillery and rocket attacks had destroyed much of the city and had killed some 30,000 residents. But in mid-February, Hikmatyar retreated in the face of the Taliban advance.

Upon approaching Kabul, the Taliban forces insisted they were a neutral force to whom Rabbani should yield power. But Massoud's forces defeated the inexperienced Taliban troops in early March, driving them out of artillery range and giving the capital its first peaceful period in years.

In April, the Taliban moved northwest against Ismael Khan, an ally of Rabbani's who controlled most of western Afghanistan from the city of Herat. Ismael Khan drove the Taliban off with heavy casualties. On August 28, Ismael Khan's troops, plus soldiers dispatched by Massoud, drove the Taliban to within 120 miles (190 kilometers) of Qandahar.

Taliban resurgence. But on September 4 , in the most dramatic upset of the civil war, the Taliban captured Herat, aided by defectors from Ismael Khan's army. Ismael Khan fled across the border to Iran.

Strengthened by the victory, the Taliban then refocused on Kabul. In mid-September, they pushed Massoud back into the city suburbs. Kabul once again came under artillery and rocket attack. Fierce fighting continued in October, but on November 5, Rabbani forces repulsed the Taliban attack. Nevertheless, Rabbani again promised to step down.

Peace efforts. Over the summer, seven separate peacemakers attempted to find a settlement satisfactory to all the fighting factions. United Nations envoy Mahmoud Mestiri tried to put together an interim leadership until elections could be held. The Organization of the Islamic Conference and various countries also tried to broker peace. But none succeeded.

Other nations played major roles in the 1995 civil war, as they had in the nation's Communist era, from 1978 to 1992. Pakistan had supported Rabbani's government, but then, tired of the ongoing civil war, it turned against him. Rabbani charged that Pakistan helped create the Taliban and gave it military support. He said the Taliban's appearance coincided with Pakistan's efforts to open a trade route across Afghanistan to central Asian nations. Repeatedly, Pakistani Prime Minister Benazir Bhutto denied that her country supported any faction. Pakistan accused India and Iran of giving Rabbani military aid and political support. India, in turn, accused Pakistan of backing a Taliban effort to establish a fundamentalist Islamic state in Afghanistan.

Embassy burned. On September 6, a crowd burned the Pakistan embassy in Kabul. One Pakistani was killed and at least 23 others were injured. Retaliating, Pakistan expelled Afghan diplomats and began to restrict Afghan trade. □ Henry S. Bradsher

See also **Asia** (Facts in brief table). In *World Book,* see **Afghanistan.**

Rwandan refugees wander among makeshift dwellings at a camp in Zaire. Some 1.5 million Rwandans who fled the 1994 civil war were living in such camps in 1995.

Africa

Some African countries, most notably South Africa, continued to make progress toward democratic rule in 1995, but definite setbacks occurred in several other African nations, including Nigeria and Kenya. In still others, the democracy movement seemed to have stalled, as authoritarian governments found ways to stay in power while putting up a facade of democracy. Peace was restored or maintained in several countries that had experienced severe internal turmoil in the past, including Angola, Liberia, and Mozambique. Sierra Leone and Rwanda, however, seemed no closer to resolving their internal conflicts,

and Burundi remained on the brink of civil war.

Economic improvement on the continent as a whole remained elusive in 1995, though some southern African countries reported substantial progress. Drought, war, and refugee problems remained major impediments to economic growth and development. The AIDS epidemic was claiming 70 percent of its victims from Africa, health officials said. And an outbreak of the deadly Ebola virus in Zaire raised the terrifying prospect of a widespread epidemic.

Progress in South Africa. The international reputation of South Africa's government, headed by Nelson R. Mandela, continued to grow in 1995. Negotiations on a new constitution began in earnest, and the government successfully conducted local

39

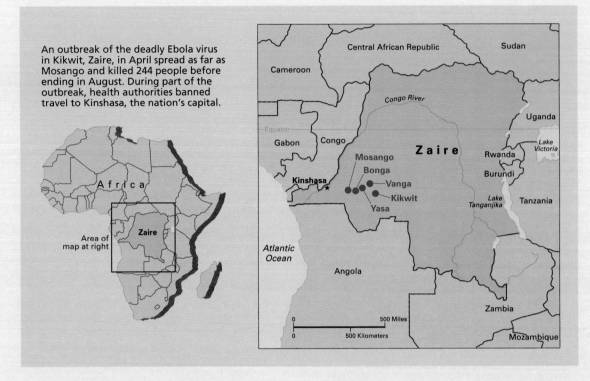

An outbreak of the deadly Ebola virus in Kikwit, Zaire, in April spread as far as Mosango and killed 244 people before ending in August. During part of the outbreak, health authorities banned travel to Kinshasa, the nation's capital.

elections on November 1. Mandela took office as president in 1994, after South Africa's first parliamentary elections in which people of all races were allowed to vote.

The changeover from a system of *apartheid* (racial separation) to a more inclusive, democratic government was not without conflict, however. One example was the uproar among white South Africans that followed the November 1995 arrest of 11 senior military officers from the previous regime, including the former minister of defense. The officers were charged with involvement in killings that took place during the struggle against apartheid. But the government moved ahead on several difficult issues. Those issues included a plan for land redistribution to give blacks a larger share and the integration of the military forces, especially the units that had fought each other in the struggle against apartheid.

South Africa's economy improved as investment money came in from abroad. But a drought harmed crops, and many observers worried about the possibility of unrest stemming from the government's failure to fulfill immediately the expectations of poverty-stricken black South Africans for improved housing and education and more jobs.

Elections in Ethiopia. Ethiopia successfully conducted its first multiparty parliamentary elections in May and June. Although some political parties urged voters to boycott the elections amid charges that the process favored the ruling party, foreign observers declared the elections fair. Relations with the newly independent Eritrea, formerly a part of Ethiopia, improved during the year as the two countries seemed headed toward the formation of an economic union.

Abuses in Nigeria. The most disappointing political news out of Africa in 1995 came from Nigeria, where the military rule of General Sani Abacha became more repressive than ever. Abacha throttled all opposition, arrested numerous potential opponents, and kept the elected President, Moshood Abiola, in prison. A low point was reached on November 10, when the government executed playwright Ken Saro-Wiwa and eight other human rights activists only days after their hasty conviction by a military court for inciting the murder of four rural leaders. Saro-Wiwa said he had been framed.

Most Nigerians greeted with cynicism an announcement by Abacha on October 1 that he would give up power in three years. Outside Nigeria, pressure began to build for instituting economic *sanctions* (bans) against the country in an effort to promote better government. Some countries ordered a stop to military sales to Nigeria, but none seemed willing to institute a boycott of Nigerian petroleum, the one weapon that government opponents felt might prove effective. Nigeria's economy continued to deteriorate, reducing this oil-rich country to one of the poorest in Africa.

Political oppression in Kenya. Even though Kenya's 1997 presidential elections seemed far off, a new opposition party, Safina, led by anthropologist Richard E. F. Leakey, became quite active during 1995. The party warned the government not to try to rig the upcoming election. Kenyan President Daniel arap Moi, apparently unsure of his hold on the presidency, struck back. The government's bitter attacks included the accusation that Safina was linked to the Ku Klux Klan. In August, Leakey and several other members of Safina were assaulted.

Setbacks to democracy. Democratic movements foundered or suffered setbacks in several other countries as well. In Cameroon, for example, President Paul Biya continued to postpone local elections while promoting disunity among opposition movements. Although several countries held elections, outside observers did not view the elections as progress toward democracy.

In Ivory Coast, presidential elections took place on October 22. The government candidate, Henri Konan Bédié, won as expected, but the main opposition parties boycotted the election, charging that the voting was rigged.

Most candidates and parties withdrew from Tanzania's elections on October 29 after widespread charges of fraud. The government called new elections, but the opposition parties boycotted them.

In Zimbabwe, where presidential elections were planned for early 1996, President Robert Mugabe had his main opponent, clergyman Ndabaningi Sithole, arrested on Oct. 14, 1995. Sithole was charged with conspiring to overthrow the government and murder the president. The arrest was difficult to understand as Mugabe's party had won an overwhelming victory in parliamentary elections in April and was not expected to face a close challenge in the upcoming presidential contest.

A new constitution took effect in Uganda on October 8. It contained a provision preventing political parties from holding rallies or putting up candidates for elections. And in Zambia, President Frederick Chiluba tried to have former President Kenneth Kaunda deported as an illegal alien in an effort to prevent the growth of an opposition movement around Kaunda. After riots protesting this action broke out, the government abandoned the attempt.

Government takeovers were attempted in Comoros and in Saõ Tomé and Príncipe in 1995. In both cases, the government was eventually returned to power, by negotiation in Saõ Tomé and by French paratroopers in Comoros. The Comoros coup was led by a French citizen, Bob Denard, and a small band of European *mercenaries* (hired soldiers). Denard had a long and ugly history as a mercenary involved in numerous African conflicts, including the Nigerian civil war of the late 1960's and a previous attempt to overthrow the government of Comoros.

A South African government representative in July urges black people to pay their rent and utility bills—payments many blacks had long refused to make.

Facts in brief on African political units

Country	Population	Government	Monetary unit*	Foreign trade (million U.S.$) Exports†	Imports†
Algeria	29,350,000	President Liamine Zeroual; Prime Minister Mokdad Sifi	dinar (50.59 = $1)	11,137	8,648
Angola	11,440,000	President José Eduardo dos Santos	readj. kwanza (5,692.00 = $1)	2,989	1,140
Benin	5,560,000	President Nicephore Soglo	CFA franc (487.95 = $1)	97	207
Botswana	1,532,000	President Sir Ketumile Masire	pula (2.80 = $1)	1,800	1,800
Burkina Faso	10,628,000	Popular Front Chairman, Head of State, & Head of Government Blaise Compaoré	CFA franc (487.95 = $1)	105	536
Burundi	6,510,000	President Sylvestre Ntibantunganya; Prime Minister Antoine Nduwayo	franc (251.23 = $1)	106	224
Cameroon	13,651,000	President Paul Biya	CFA franc (487.95 = $1)	1,815	1,175
Cape Verde	430,000	President Antonio Mascarenhas Monteiro; Prime Minister Carlos Alberto Wahnon de Carvalho Veiga	escudo (82.97 = $1)	4	154
Central African Republic	3,026,000	President Ange Patasse	CFA franc (487.95 = $1)	124	165
Chad	6,537,000	President Idriss Deby	CFA franc (487.95 = $1)	151	228
Comoros	676,000	President Said Mohamed Djohar	franc (365.96 = $1)	22	69
Congo	2,662,000	President Pascal Lissouba; Prime Minister Jacques Joachim Yhombi-Opango	CFA franc (487.95 = $1)	1,277	587
Djibouti	526,000	President Hassan Gouled Aptidon; Prime Minister Barkat Gourad Hamadou	franc (177.72 = $1)	16	219
Egypt	59,713,000	President Hosni Mubarak; Prime Minister Atef Sedky	pound (3.40 = $1)	2,243	8,176
Equatorial Guinea	410,000	President Teodoro Obiang Nguema Mbasogo; Prime Minister Silvestre Siale Bileka	CFA franc (487.95 = $1)	62	60
Eritrea	3,920,000	President Isaias Afworki	Ethiopian birr	no statistics available	
Ethiopia	55,279,000	President Negasso Gidada	birr (6.29 = $1)	169	707
Gabon	1,115,000	President El Hadj Omar Bongo; Prime Minister Paulin Obame	CFA franc (487.95 = $1)	2,329	886
Gambia	1,106,000	Chairman, Armed Forces Provisional Ruling Council, & Head of State Yahya Jammeh	dalasi (9.65 = $1)	66	232
Ghana	17,959,000	President Jerry John Rawlings	cedi (1,362.00 = $1)	1,020	1,277
Guinea	6,897,000	President Lansana Conté	franc (985.20 = $1)	622	768
Guinea-Bissau	1,096,000	President João Bernardo Vieira	peso (18,036.00 = $1)	33	63
Ivory Coast	14,891,000	President Henri Konan Bédié	CFA franc (487.95 = $1)	6,221	5,347
Kenya	28,794,000	President Daniel T. arap Moi	shilling (55.52 = $1)	1,523	2,119
Lesotho	2,025,000	King Moshoeshoe II; Prime Minister Ntsu Mokhehle	maloti (3.64 = $1)	109	964
Liberia	3,136,000	Transitional government led by a Council of State	dollar (1 = $1)	396	272
Libya	5,587,000	Leader of the Revolution Muammar Muhammad al-Qadhafi; General People's Committee Secretary (Prime Minister) Abd al Majid al-Qa'ud	dinar (0.36 = $1)	11,213	5,356

| Country | Population | Government | Monetary unit* | Foreign trade (million U.S.$) | |
				Exports†	Imports†
Madagascar	13,309,000	President Albert Zafy; Prime Minister Francisque Ravony	franc (4,450.00 = $1)	261	434
Malawi	11,552,000	President Muluzi Bakili	kwacha (15.32 = $1)	319	545
Mali	11,124,000	President Alpha Oumar Konare; Prime Minister Ibrahima Boubacar Keita	CFA franc (487.95 = $1)	247	340
Mauritania	2,399,000	President Maaouya Ould Sid Ahmed Taya	ouguiya (130.59 = $1)	437	222
Mauritius	1,140,000	President Sir Cassam Uteem; Prime Minister Sir Anerood Jugnauth	rupee (17.84 = $1)	1,326	1,897
Morocco	28,913,000	King Hassan II; Prime Minister Abdellatif Filali	dirham (8.35 = $1)	4,013	7,211
Mozambique	16,923,000	President Joaquím Alberto Chissano; Prime Minister Pascoal Mocumbi	metical (9,900.00 = $1)	132	955
Namibia	1,739,000	President Sam Nujoma; Prime Minister Hage Geingob	rand (3.64 = $1)	1,300	1,100
Niger	9,386,000	President Mahamane Ousmane; Prime Minister Hama Amadou	CFA franc (487.95 = $1)	312	355
Nigeria	108,320,000	Head of State Sani Abacha	naira (22.00 = $1)	9,596	7,508
Rwanda	8,000,000	President Pasteur Bizimungu	franc (220.00 = $1)	68	288
São Tomé and Príncipe	136,000	President Miguel Trovoada	dobra (1,480.74 = $1)	6	32
Senegal	8,610,000	President Abdou Diouf; Prime Minister Habib Thiam	CFA franc (487.95 = $1)	683	1,172
Seychelles	75,000	President France Albert René	rupee (4.82 = $1)	52	191
Sierra Leone	4,863,000	Supreme Council of State Chairman Valentine E. M. Strasser	leone (835.00 = $1)	116	150
Somalia	6,872,000	No functioning government	shilling (2,620 = $1)	104	132
South Africa	43,715,000	State President Nelson Mandela	rand (3.64 = $1)	24,070	22,478
Sudan	27,061,000	President Umar Hasan Ahmad al-Bashir	pound (800.00 = $1)	509	1,060
Swaziland	882,000	King Mswati III; Prime Minister Prince Jameson Mbilini Dlamini	lilangeni (3.64 = $1)	632	734
Tanzania	31,698,000	President Ali Hassan Mwinyi; Prime Minister Cleopa David Msuya	shilling (613.00 = $1)	349	1,127
Togo	4,264,000	President Gnassingbé Eyadéma	CFA franc (487.95 = $1)	162	222
Tunisia	9,095,000	President Zine El Abidine Ben Ali; Prime Minister Hamed Karoui	dinar (0.93 = $1)	4,584	6,484
Uganda	19,278,000	President Yoweri Kaguta Museveni; Prime Minister Kintu Musoke	shilling (1,075.00 = $1)	399	858
Zaire	45,142,000	President Mobutu Sese Seko	new zaire (10,624.00 = $1)	421	383
Zambia	9,623,000	President Frederick Chiluba	kwacha (947.00 = $1)	1,095	908
Zimbabwe	11,845,000	Executive President Robert Mugabe	dollar (9.20 = $1)	1,438	2,213

*Exchange rates as of Oct. 27, 1995, or latest available data.   †Latest available data.

Fighting in Sierra Leone. Violence continued for most of 1995 in Sierra Leone, Rwanda, and Somalia. Fighting began in Sierra Leone when a civil war in neighboring Liberia spread. The rural areas of Sierra Leone sank into political chaos as government control shrank to an ever-smaller area around the capital, Freetown. Some observers believed that elements of the army were working with the rebels, enabling each group to plunder portions of the country. Reports coming out of Sierra Leone said that foreign mercenaries, including Gurkhas (highly trained soldiers from Nepal) and whites from South Africa, were assisting the government forces.

In January, the Revolutionary United Front, Sierra Leone's main rebel group led by Foday Sankoh, kidnapped several Roman Catholic nuns and held them until late March. Reports of widespread starvation surfaced in September. In October, a group of government troops rebelled and attempted to overthrow the country's military ruler, Captain Valentine E. M. Strasser. The troops opposed Strasser's plan to restore civilian rule to Sierra Leone in elections planned for February 1996.

Tension in Rwanda. Although there were no major outbreaks of violence in Rwanda in 1995, the situation remained extremely tense following the 1994 civil war. The split between the country's two major ethnic groups, the Hutu and the Tutsi, was not resolved, and most of the Hutu remained in refugee camps in neighboring Zaire, Tanzania, and Uganda. With so much of the population absent, it was difficult to get the economy going again. And constant reports of Hutu militia training to reconquer the country stoked fears of renewed bloodshed.

In late November 1995, former United States President Jimmy Carter sponsored talks in Cairo, the capital of Egypt, with representatives from Rwanda and from the countries hosting the refugees. The purpose of the talks was to find a means of safely returning hundreds of thousands of displaced Rwandans to their homeland. The accord they reached proposed that 10,000 refugees return a day. By December, hostility between Hutu and Tutsi in neighboring Burundi was near the boiling point, making civil war appear imminent.

Withdrawal from Somalia. In late February, U.S. Marines landed in Somalia to aid in the scheduled withdrawal of the last members of the United Nations (UN) peacekeeping force in early March. The peacekeepers had failed to achieve their goal of installing a stable government, and their withdrawal left the country without a central government for the rest of the year. Talks between the major clan and militia leaders made little progress toward resolving the questions of who would rule or how the country would be governed. Local rule by clan elders was in effect in much of rural Somalia, and some reports suggested these rulers were developing ways to work together. The economy showed improvement in the so-called Somaliland Republic to the north, a region that declared its independence from Somalia in 1991.

The political situation in Liberia offered more hope, though economic conditions remained extremely difficult at the end of 1995. After prolonged negotiations, the civil war that began in 1989 came to an end, but not until more than 150,000 people had been killed and most of the country's inhabitants had become refugees. On Sept. 1, 1995, a new governing council consisting of representatives from the major warring groups took power. The economy was in terrible shape at year's end, with most of the country's infrastructure destroyed and the main sources of employment out of operation.

Events in Mozambique took a positive turn during 1995. A UN peacekeeping mission withdrew early in the year, having overseen the implementation of a peace accord reached in 1992 between the country's two warring factions—the Front for the Liberation of Mozambique (Frelimo) and the Mozambique Resistance Movement (Renamo). More than 1.5 million refugees returned to Mozambique from Malawi, South Africa, and other nearby countries, under the supervision of United Nations High Commissioner for Refugees. Although there was little work for the returnees in the war-torn land, the government planned to undertake huge reform projects in an effort to restart the economy.

Prospects for Angola also improved greatly in 1995. Angola, like Mozambique, is a former Portuguese colony torn by years of civil war. A cease-fire negotiated in 1994 remained in effect throughout 1995, and a UN peacekeeping force moved into the country to enforce the cease-fire and to merge the rebel forces of the National Union for the Total Liberation of Angola (UNITA), led by Jonas Savimbi, with the government army. Savimbi, however, had not yet decided by year's end whether to join the proposed coalition government, and distrust ran high between his followers and supporters of the government.

Angola's economy, destroyed by years of fighting, showed little sign of recovery. The inflation rate reached more than 1,000 percent per year. Moreover, the government had difficulty determining where petroleum revenues were going. And Angola's President, José Eduardo dos Santos, complained that diamond smuggling had cost the country several hundred million dollars in lost revenue. Huge numbers of land mines dotted the countryside, left behind from the war. The location of the mines was not known, which led to a slow and painstaking search for them and to numerous civilian injuries from explosions.

Economic growth and debt. The UN reported that Africa's annual rate of economic growth would probably reach 3 percent in 1995, an improvement over 1994's 2.1 percent and the highest rate in six years. Cereal production increased, and prices rose for the major export crops—coffee and cocoa. Foreign aid, however, continued to decline, and the debt problem worsened. In 1994, Africa's foreign debt reached $211 billion, according to the World Bank, an agency of the United Nations. Drought in southern Africa badly hurt harvests in at least 11 countries, and war and refugee problems also damaged economies. Although foreign investment in Africa rose, the increase was smaller than that in other developing areas of the world.

Health reports from Africa brought mixed news in 1995. The best news came late in the year, when another UN agency, the World Health Organization (WHO), announced that a major African health problem, the Guinea worm, was on the verge of eradication. The worm's larvae enter the body in contaminated water, and mature worms emerge a year later through painful skin blisters.

On the negative side was the still-spreading epidemic of AIDS and an outbreak in Zaire of a deadly disease caused by the Ebola virus. The Ebola outbreak killed 244 people before WHO declared that it had ended in August. In December, Ebola was reported to have erupted in war-torn Liberia. But WHO experts determined that those deaths had actually resulted from cholera.   □ Mark DeLancey

See also the various African country articles. In *World Book,* see **Africa.**

AIDS. A panel of scientific experts recommended in July 1995 that the United States Food and Drug Administration (FDA) allow Jeff Getty, an AIDS patient at San Francisco, to receive a transplant of bone marrow cells from a baboon. Physicians hoped that the baboon marrow cells, which cannot be infected by the AIDS virus, would restore Getty's immune system by producing infection-fighting blood cells. The panel also proposed guidelines for future transplants of animal cells and organs into humans.

The FDA in May had refused to approve such procedures, termed xenotransplants, because of public health concerns. Some experts believe that xenotransplants might infect patients with dangerous animal viruses that could spread throughout the population. They note that the human immunodeficiency virus (HIV), which causes AIDS, probably originated in a monkey. But the expert panel said that risk of spreading a virus contracted from a xenotransplant could be minimized if patients followed certain precautions, including practicing safe sex.

The FDA approved the procedure in August, and the transplant took place in December at the University of California at San Francisco.

Pregnancy and HIV. Testing for infection with HIV and counseling about treatment for those found to be infected should be a routine part of health care for all pregnant women, the U.S. Centers for Disease Control and Prevention (CDC) urged in new guidelines issued on July 7. Women who test positive should be offered treatment with the drug zidovudine, also known as AZT, the CDC said.

The agency based its recommendation on a 1994 study that showed that HIV-infected pregnant women who take AZT can reduce the chances of transmitting the virus to their babies by about two-thirds. AZT therapy is most effective when begun by the 14th week of pregnancy and continued through labor and delivery. The newborn infant also must receive AZT for the first six weeks of life. About 7,000 HIV-infected women give birth each year, and 15 to 30 percent of them pass the infection on to their newborn infants.

AIDS in America. In a report issued Feb. 10, 1995, the CDC said that AIDS cases among women continued to rise rapidly in 1994. About 18 percent—or 14,081—of the 79,674 new AIDS cases reported in 1994 occurred in women, compared with only 7 percent of cases in 1985. Of the new cases in women, about 41 percent occurred through intravenous drug use; 38 percent through heterosexual contact with an infected person; and 2 percent through contaminated blood. No specific risk factor was cited by the remaining 19 percent.

The CDC in January 1995 said that in 1994 AIDS became the leading cause of death among Americans aged 25 to 44. Accidents fell to second place, followed by cancer, heart disease, homicide, and sui-

The percentage of new AIDS cases traced to heterosexual sex and intravenous drug use is on the rise, United States health authorities report in 1995.

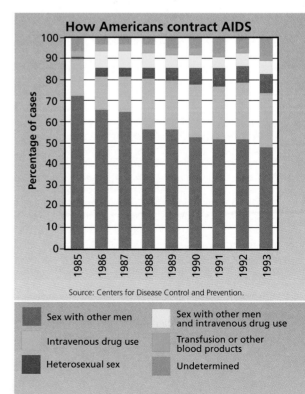

How Americans contract AIDS

Percentage of cases

1985 1986 1987 1988 1989 1990 1991 1992 1993

Source: Centers for Disease Control and Prevention.

Sex with other men

Intravenous drug use

Heterosexual sex

Sex with other men and intravenous drug use

Transfusion or other blood products

Undetermined

cide. In October 1995, the CDC reported that 476,899 people in the United States had been diagnosed with AIDS and 295,473 of them had died since the disease first was recognized in 1981.

AIDS and TB. The World Health Organization (WHO) announced in June 1995 that it would intensify efforts to battle AIDS and tuberculosis (TB) in developing countries of Africa and Southeast Asia. WHO, an agency of the United Nations, said that interrelated epidemics of AIDS and TB were taking an enormous toll on human life in developing countries, with each epidemic making the other more difficult to control. Infection with HIV weakens the immune system, making people more vulnerable to TB. By the end of the 1990's, WHO predicted, TB would contribute to about 1 in every 3 AIDS deaths.

Infection with a relatively mild form of HIV, HIV-2, seems to protect some people from infection with the more serious HIV-1, which has caused most deaths, according to a June 1995 report by researchers from the Harvard School of Public Health in Boston and from Dakar, Senegal, in west Africa. HIV-2 is common in west Africa but rare elsewhere. AIDS experts said the finding could help in developing AIDS vaccines, much as the cowpox virus was used as the basis for a smallpox vaccine. The cowpox and smallpox viruses are related, but only the latter virus causes a deadly disease.　　　　　　　□ Michael Woods

See also **Drugs.** In *World Book,* see **AIDS.**

Albania. Albanian President Sali Berisha reiterated his commitment to economic and political reform in 1995. After his defeat in a referendum on a new Constitution in November 1994, Berisha replaced many cabinet ministers. In early 1995, he launched an aggressive anticorruption campaign. Disputes between Berisha and Eduard Selami, the leader of Berisha's Democratic Party of Albania, led to Selami's dismissal as party leader in March.

Opposition. Members of the Socialist Party staged a protest in August to demand the release of their leader, Fatos Nano. Nano was sentenced in April 1994 to 12 years in prison for misappropriating humanitarian aid and falsifying government papers.

Privatization. The government in 1995 planned to issue privatization bonds in state-owned companies to all Albanians who were age 18 or older as of August 1991. Parliament also drafted a law to privatize land. Yet many Albanians continued to suffer as the country shifted to a market economy. The capital, Tiranë, had more than 7,000 homeless families in early 1995. Miners and workers in state-owned bread shops and textile factories staged hunger strikes. Trade unions threatened to strike when the government refused to increase the wages of state workers by 35 percent.　　　　　□ Sharon L. Wolchik

See also **Europe** (Facts in brief table). In *World Book,* see **Albania.**

Alberta. See **Canadian provinces.**

Alexander, Lamar (1940-　), former governor of Tennessee and secretary of education in the Cabinet of President George Bush, declared his candidacy for the Republican presidential nomination on Feb. 28, 1995. Although generally considered a moderate, Alexander blasted the federal government as an "arrogant empire" and called for billions of dollars in spending to be returned to the states.

Andrew Lamar Alexander was born on July 3, 1940, in Maryville, Tennessee. He enrolled in Vanderbilt University in 1958, where, as editor of the university newspaper, he supported the cause of desegregation. He then went on to earn his law degree from New York University School of Law in 1965. For the next several years he worked on various Republican election campaigns and served in the Administration of President Richard M. Nixon.

In 1974, Alexander waged an unsuccessful bid for governorship of Tennessee, but a second attempt four years later was successful. He won reelection in 1982. As governor, Alexander pushed through a number of educational reforms and attracted industrial investment to the state. He was chairman of the National Governor's Association from 1985 to 1986.

After his term in office ended in 1987, Alexander became president of the University of Tennessee. He was U.S. secretary of education from 1991 to 1992.

Alexander married Leslee Kathryn Buhler in 1969. They have four children.　　　　　　□ Lisa Klobuchar

Algeria was wracked by violence in 1995 as Muslim militants continued to resist the nation's military regime. The crisis, which had claimed an estimated 40,000 lives by late 1995, began in January 1992 when the military seized power to prevent a parliamentary victory by the Islamic Salvation Front (FIS).

Politics. Liamine Zeroual, who headed Algeria's military-backed government, won the presidential election on Nov. 16, 1995, with 61 percent of the vote. Zeroual's majority win was seen as an affirmation of the public's desire to end the violence. Some 65 percent of Algeria's 16 million voters ignored threats by Muslim militants and went to the polls.

Sheik Mahfoud Nahnah, a Muslim opposed to violence, collected 23 percent of the vote. Zeroual indicated after the election that Muslim moderates such as the sheik were the legitimate representatives of political Islam. Zeroual had tried in 1994 and 1995 to negotiate with jailed members of FIS but failed.

Major opposition parties had claimed that the election would not be fair and called for a boycott. Eight parties, including the FIS, had proposed early in the year that they and the government form a transitional administration to pave the way for multiparty elections. But they demanded as a precondition that the army end its involvement in politics and release political detainees, who numbered more than 10,000. The government rejected the proposal,

An Algerian woman holds an Algerian flag and a photo of a slain victim of Islamic fundamentalist violence at a protest march in Paris in February.

Muslim militants killed more than 100 foreigners from September 1993, when they declared foreigners to be targets, through July 1995. Nearly one-third of those slain were French. France, which controlled Algeria from 1914 to 1962, has been sympathetic to the Zeroual regime. Militants also killed civilians in France in 1995.

The militants also caused serious damage to Algeria's basic infrastructure, such as transportation and electricity systems. On July 10, a gas pipeline near Algiers was blown up. In addition, the slaying of five foreign oil workers on May 5 alarmed officials, since 90 percent of Algeria's foreign revenues came from oil and gas exports.

Algeria's neighbors worried about the violence spilling over their borders. Libyan leader Muammar Muhammed al-Qadhafi agreed in January to precisely mark Libya's 500-mile (800-kilometer) desert border with Algeria to thwart any destabilizing movement of goods and people. In the past, Qadhafi had rejected such an action because he opposed divisions within the Arab world. Algerian extremists claimed to have killed seven Tunisian border guards in February as a warning to the Tunisians not to aid the Algerian regime. □ Christine Helms

See also **Africa** (Facts in brief table). In **World Book**, see **Algeria**.

Angola. See Africa.

Animal. See Conservation; Zoology; Zoos.

as did two militant Muslim factions: the Armed Islamic Group and the Islamic Salvation Army.

Violent incidents continued through 1995 as fundamentalists attacked and the government responded. The government, which appeared to gain the upper hand, was assisted to some extent by an increasing division among the Islamic groups over the use of violence.

A suicide bomber attacked a police station in the capital, Algiers, on January 30, killing at least 42 people and injuring 286. In February alone, according to reports, more than 500 politicians, security personnel, lawyers, judges, intellectuals, and cultural figures were slain in multiple attacks. Militants often targeted journalists, whom they viewed as government sympathizers. These threatening conditions caused restricted news coverage as the media avoided sending reporters to Algeria. More than 60 Algerian newspeople had been killed since the violence began, half of them in 1995.

The government responded harshly. Security forces in Algiers reportedly killed at least 95 prisoners on February 22 in crushing a prison revolt that began when Muslim militants killed four guards. In late March, the government sent air and ground forces into an area west of Algiers, reportedly killing over 300 people. In June, a court condemned to death an army officer for the June 1992 assassination of Algeria's head of state, Mohammed Boudiaf.

Anthropology. Four-million-year-old fossils discovered in northern Kenya may belong to the oldest known humanlike species. That finding was reported in August 1995 by anthropologist Meave G. Leakey of the National Museums of Kenya in Nairobi; anthropologist Alan Walker of Pennsylvania State University in University Park; geologist Craig Feibel of Rutgers University in New Brunswick, New Jersey; and geologist Ian McDougall of the Australian National University in Canberra. The team said the fossils represent a new species of hominid, which they named *Australopithecus anamensis*. (Hominids are members of the group of species that includes human beings and our close prehuman ancestors.)

The fossils were found near Kenya's Lake Turkana at two sites, Kanapoi and Allia Bay. The Kanapoi finds consist of a skull fragment, isolated teeth, upper and lower jaws, and portions of a shinbone. The majority of the specimens came from a geological zone dated to 4.2 million years ago. Fragments of jaws and isolated teeth from Allia Bay were dated to 3.9 million years ago.

In the report, Leakey and Walker stressed numerous similarities between the fossils from Lake Turkana and those of a slightly more recent hominid species, *Australopithecus afarensis. A. afarensis,* best known from the fossil skeleton discovered in 1974 and dubbed "Lucy," has been found at sites dated to between 3.9 million and 3 million years ago. *A. ana-*

Clues to the evolution of upright walking

Four foot bones, *right,* may provide insight into the locomotion of early members of the human family. According to a July report, the 3.5-million-year-old bones show that prehuman ancestors both walked on the ground and climbed in trees.

In their report, South African anthropologists compared the four connected foot bones with the anatomy of modern chimpanzee feet, *below right,* and modern human feet, *bottom right.*

According to the anthropologists, the anatomical comparison showed that the 3.5-million-year-old prehuman foot, *above,* had a weight-bearing heel, needed for walking on the ground, as well as a splayed-out big toe, useful for grasping tree branches.

mensis was classified as a new species because its teeth and jaws are slightly more primitive than those of *A. afarensis.* Hence, the discoverers considered the Lake Turkana specimens to be prime candidates for a direct ancestor to Lucy's species.

The anatomical details of the newly discovered shinbone indicate that the species was capable of *bipedal* (two-legged) walking. Leakey and her colleagues said this finding pushed back the date for the earliest known example of bipedalism. However, critics noted that the shinbone is younger than the other fossils found at Kanapoi, perhaps by as much as 500,000 years. If the bone is only 3.7 million years old, it would be about the same age as a previously known example of evidence indicating upright walking—fossil footprints found at Laetoli, Tanzania.

The Lake Turkana specimens prompted a reexamination of a group of 4.4-million-year-old hominid fossils whose discovery in Aramis, Ethiopia, had been announced in 1994. The fossils were first dubbed *Australopithecus ramidus,* but in 1995 the discoverers changed the name to *Ardipithecus ramidus.* The fossils exhibit chimplike anatomical features, and Leakey and Walker argued that the species may represent a side branch rather than a direct ancestor on the hominid family tree.

Feet for walking and grasping. Four hominid foot bones from the cave site of Sterkfontein in South Africa give clues to the transition from apelike

Oldest prehuman ancestor?

Four-million-year-old fossils found in Kenya appear to belong to the oldest known *hominid* (a member of the group of species that includes human beings and their close prehuman ancestors). Scientists reported the discovery in August and named the species *Australopithecus anamensis.*

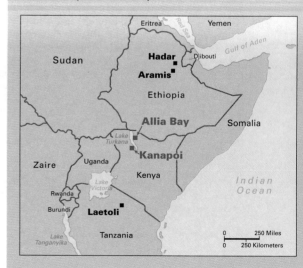

tree-climbing to upright walking. That was the conclusion of a July 1995 report by anthropologists Ronald J. Clarke and Phillip V. Tobias of the University of the Witwatersrand in Johannesburg, South Africa. The bones presumably belong to a species of *Australopithecus* and may be up to 3.5 million years old.

The ankle bone resembles that of a modern human, but the bones along the instep show a more apelike anatomy, with the big toe splayed out and very mobile. Clarke and Tobias concluded that while the foot belonged to an upright-walking hominid, the divergent big toe could have been used for grasping branches while climbing in trees.

Long-lived Neanderthals. An autumn 1995 report suggested that Neanderthals may not have died out in Europe by 35,000 years ago, as many anthropologists had believed. The report was based on an international scientific team's discovery of a 30,000-year-old Neanderthal lower jaw in a cave in southern Spain. Because *Homo sapiens* (the species to which modern human beings belong) entered Europe roughly 40,000 years ago, the finding suggests that Neanderthals existed alongside *Homo sapiens* for nearly 10,000 years. Southern Spain is a geographic cul-de-sac in the European land mass, so the discovery may indicate that *Homo sapiens* pushed Neanderthals into peripheral areas, where they survived for a considerable time. □ Donald C. Johanson

In *World Book*, see **Anthropology.**

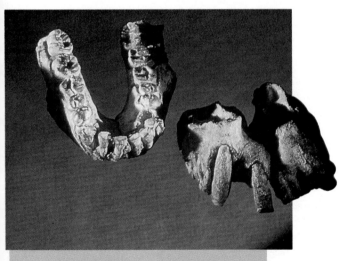

Among the fossils discovered were an upper jaw and lower jaw dated to about 4.2 million years ago, *above.* These fossils—along with a skull fragment, isolated teeth, and parts of a shinbone—were found at a site called Kanapoi near Kenya's Lake Turkana, *left.* At another site, Allia Bay, scientists discovered fragments of jaws and isolated teeth dated to 3.9 million years ago.

Archaeology. The discovery in Zaire of 80,000-year-old bone points used for hunting and fishing suggests that human beings in Africa were making and using tools thousands of years before tool use developed elsewhere. The finding was reported in April 1995 by archaeologists Alison Brooks of George Washington University and John Yellen of the National Science Foundation, both in Washington, D.C.

The bones, from three sites in Zaire's Semliki River Valley, included barbed and unbarbed points and a flat dagger-shaped object with rounded edges. Found near the points were the remains of fish and mammals.

By dating sand overlying the deposits and hippo teeth found with the points, the scientists estimated the age of the site at 80,000 to 90,000 years. Similar tools have been discovered throughout Europe and Asia, but they are only 12,000 to 14,000 years old.

Oldest cave paintings. Chauvet cave, a spectacular decorated cave found in southern France in December 1994, contains the world's oldest known cave paintings, according to a June 1995 report by French and British archaeologists. The cave is located near Vallon-Pont-d'Arc on the Ardeche River, a tributary of the Rhône.

The cave is decorated with hundreds of paintings and engravings, including an unusually large number of depictions of rhinos, lions, and bears. One figure, which archaeologists called "the sorcerer," is a composite creature standing upright on human legs but with the head and humped back of a bison.

The art was initially dated to about 22,000 years ago based on the sophistication of the artistic techniques. Those techniques include perspective, shading, and the use of overlapping images to convey a sense of movement. But a dating technique using charcoal samples from the cave drawings of two rhinos and a bison yielded ages of 30,340 and 32,410 years.

Previously, the oldest dated cave painting was a 27,000-year-old stencil of a hand. By comparison, the more sophisticated rock art of Lascaux in France is generally dated at about 17,000 years. If the new dates for the Chauvet cave are confirmed, experts say, our understanding of the development of prehistoric art must change radically.

Ramses' family tombs. The 3,200-year-old tomb of Egyptian queen Nefertari, wife of the pharaoh Ramses II, was reopened in 1995 following an intensive conservation program. The tomb, located in the Valley of the Queens in West Thebes, had been closed soon after its discovery in 1902 because of the fragility of its paintings. Nefertari was the first wife of Ramses II, who ruled Egypt from 1279 to 1212 B.C. She died in approximately 1255 B.C., having given birth to the pharaoh's first son and heir.

An international project to save the tomb began in 1986 and was completed 1992. Afterward, the tomb was kept closed while experts monitored the

Uncovering a princely tomb

In May 1995, archaeologists announced that they had opened what appeared to be the largest royal tomb ever found in Egypt. The tomb was built for the sons of Ramses II, who ruled during the New Kingdom period of ancient Egypt.

The tomb was discovered in an area called the Valley of the Kings, *bottom,* site of the burial places of Tutankhamen—the boy king whose intact tomb was discovered in 1922—and other Egyptian royalty. The valley is near the Nile River, about 315 miles (500 kilometers) south of Cairo, *below.*

Major periods of ancient Egypt

Early Dynastic Period	Old Kingdom
3100 B.C.	2686 B.C.

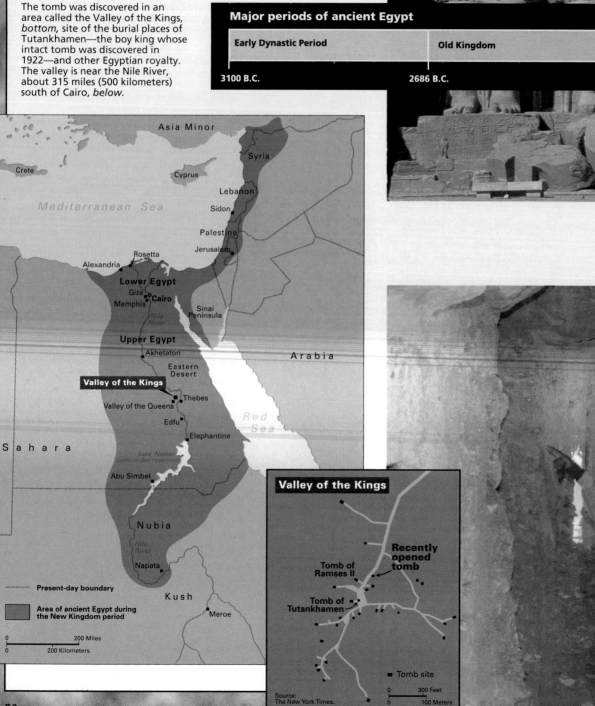

Crete

Asia Minor

Syria

Cyprus

Mediterranean Sea

Lebanon

Sidon

Palestine

Rosetta

Jerusalem

Alexandria

Lower Egypt

Giza **Cairo**

Memphis

Sinai Peninsula

Nile River

Upper Egypt

Akhetaton

Arabia

Eastern Desert

Valley of the Kings

Thebes

Valley of the Queens

Edfu

Red Sea

Elephantine

S a h a r a

Lake Nasser (present-day reservoir)

Abu Simbel

N u b i a

Nile River

Napata

— — — Present-day boundary

▨ Area of ancient Egypt during the New Kingdom period

K u s h

Meroe

| 0 | 200 Miles |
| 0 | 200 Kilometers |

Valley of the Kings

Recently opened tomb

Tomb of Ramses II

Tomb of Tutankhamen

■ Tomb site

| 0 | 300 Feet |
| 0 | 100 Meters |

Source: The New York Times.

A stone statue depicts Ramses II, who ruled Egypt from 1279 to 1212 B.C., during the time of the exodus of the Israelites from Egypt. Ramses II claimed to have fathered more than 100 children, including 52 sons. Archaeologists believe that most of those sons are buried in the newly opened tomb.

Carved figures and inscriptions adorn a wall of the tomb, *below.* Although the tomb was plundered in ancient times, inscriptions, pottery, jewelry, furniture, and some other artifacts remained.

	First Intermediate Period	Middle Kingdom	Second Intermediate Period	New Kingdom	
	2181 B.C.	1991 B.C.	1786 B.C.	1554 B.C.	1070 B.C.

An Egyptian archaeologist, *below,* examines one of the dozens of funeral chambers discovered in the tomb. Illuminated on the far wall is a statue of Osiris, the ancient Egyptian god of the underworld.

environment to determine whether the tomb could be opened to the public.

In May 1995, archaeologists from the American University in Cairo, Egypt, reported their explorations of the largest tomb ever found in Egypt's Valley of the Kings. The tomb was a mausoleum for many of the 100 or more children of Ramses II.

The scientists examined 67 rooms, many decorated with wall paintings, and said there were more rooms on the tomb's unexcavated lower levels. It is unlikely that the tomb holds any great treasures, however, because it was plundered in 1150 B.C. To archaeologists, the chief importance of the mausoleum is what it can tell them about the family burials and tomb designs of Egyptian royalty.

White Horse of Uffington. In February 1995, archaeologists finally dated the 300-foot (91-meter) abstract figure of a horse outlined in chalk on a grassy hillside near Uffington in southern England. Previously, no one knew just when the White Horse, one of Britain's best-known landmarks, was created. According to local legend, the horse was cut into the hillside to commemorate a victory of Alfred the Great, king of Wessex, in the year 870. Archaeologists, on the other hand, had believed the figure was much older, based on similarities between it and abstract horses on Celtic coins made 2,000 years ago.

Scientists analyzed the site using a dating technique that determines how long it has been since a layer of sediment was exposed to light. The results indicated the horse was made far earlier than anyone had expected—between 1400 B.C. and 600 B.C.

Tombs of Maya rulers. The excavation of remains believed to be those of Popol Kinich, a ruler of the Maya city of Copán in the A.D. 400's, was completed in spring 1995 by archaeologists from the University of Pennsylvania Museum in Philadelphia. The excavation, which began in Honduras in 1993, required extreme care, because the Maya had painted the bones a brilliant red using cinnabar, a poisonous mercury ore. The decoration was perhaps meant to symbolize the high status of the dead man.

In April, the excavators discovered another tomb at a lower level in an adjacent structure. A remote-controlled camera revealed the remains of a human body laid out on a slab, but debris obscured any offerings that may have been interred with it. Because of the unstable condition of the masonry in this structure, investigation was put off until 1996. The burial is believed to be that of Popol Kinich's father, the founder of Copán.

Inca sacrifices. High in the Andes Mountains in Peru, scientists in September and October 1995 discovered the frozen remains of three victims of Inca human sacrifice rituals. The remains were dated to approximately A.D. 1500. (See **Newsmakers.**)

☐ Mark Rose

See also **Anthropology; Geology.** In *World Book*, see **Archaeology**.

Architecture. The most touted building of 1995 was the Rock and Roll Hall of Fame and Museum in Cleveland, designed by I. M. Pei. The museum in the $92-million structure, which opened in September, surveys the history of rock and roll from blues to heavy metal, with displays of costumes, instruments, advertising, and performances. The Hall of Fame perches atop a tower overlooking Lake Erie.

The building appeared to be more popular with rock fans than with architectural critics, who pointed to the incongruity of what many people consider subversive art being housed in a slick steel-and-glass building designed by the premier establishment architect. The complex was a key element in the revitalization of downtown Cleveland, which in 1994 opened a new basketball arena and a ball park.

Coors Field in Denver, which opened in April 1995, was the latest in a series of neotraditional baseball parks featuring natural grass, an asymmetrical outfield, and no roof. Finished in brick, stone, and steel, Coors Field—home of the Colorado Rockies baseball team—makes a strong addition to downtown Denver. Its entrances line up with major streets, its architectural details are crisp, and it even has a pub beneath the right-field grandstand.

Awards. The American Institute of Architects in January presented its gold medal for lifetime achievement to Cesar Pelli. Born in Argentina, Pelli came to the United States to work with architect Eero Saarinen, from whom he acquired both his lyrical feeling for structure and materials and a strong sense of civic responsibility. His major buildings, from the early Pacific Design Center in Los Angeles to the World Financial Center in New York City, reflect a deep understanding of urban life.

Tadao Ando of Japan in April won the $100,000 Pritzker Prize, given annually to a living architect who has contributed significantly to the art of design. His work combines the power of classic geometric forms with exquisite craftsmanship in concrete, steel, and glass. Ando views his buildings as sanctuaries from the chaos of modern urban life. Among his best-known works are the Japanese Pavilion at Expo '92 in Seville, Spain, and the Church on the Water in Hokkaido, Japan.

A library boom, unrivaled since the 1930's, continued unabated in 1995. But the new libraries, unlike their predecessors, function as community centers and communication hubs as well.

Michael Graves's Denver Central Library, which opened in March, has a blazing copper crown, a *campanile* (bell tower) for an entrance, and a reading room with a two-story oil derrick in the center. These exotic elements are balanced, however, by simple maple paneling and classic furniture that create a mood of reflective calm.

The Phoenix Central Library, which opened in May, rises next to a downtown freeway like a piece of minimalist sculpture. Architect Will Bruder wrapped curved copper panels around a crystalline core of stacks, offices, and meeting rooms. A grand reading room on the top two floors offers patrons spectacular views of nearby mountains.

The most colorful library was Ricardo Legorreta's San Antonio Central Library. Decked out in combinations of yellow, blue, purple, and chili red, the library houses more than 750,000 books, plus a restaurant, shop, rooftop terraces, and exhibition gallery. With its opening in May, the library not only became the city's new cultural center but also revitalized its sense of color. Yellow doors and chili-red walls popped up all over town.

The library boom spilled over into Canada. Library Square in Vancouver, designed by Moshe Safdie, combines an eight-story shelf area for books with a monumental circular reading room reminiscent of the Colosseum in Rome. Safdie's radical scheme attracted its share of critics, some of whom showed up in togas for the June opening. But the library made a valuable contribution to the revival of a depressed section of downtown Vancouver.

Museums. San Francisco's $60-million Museum of Modern Art opened in January. Designed by Swiss architect Mario Botta, it blends Bauhaus simplicity with postmodern theatrics. A huge circular skylight decorated with black-and-white stripes tops its stair-stepping brick facade. Arrayed below is the second-largest collection of modern art in the United States—after that of New York City's Museum of Modern Art.

The Cy Twombly Gallery in Houston, designed by Italian architect Renzo Piano, opened in February. A veritable jewel box of a building, it is one of the few American museums devoted to the work of one artist. It consists of nine cube-shaped rooms containing some 50 paintings, drawings and sculptures by Twombly, a master of abstraction. The museum's most dramatic feature is a "floating" solar roof.

The New England Holocaust Memorial, architect Stanley Saitowitz's small but moving tribute to the millions of European Jews and other victims who were murdered by the Nazis during World War II (1939-1945), opened in Boston in October. The memorial features six 54-foot (16-meter) glass-and-steel towers inscribed with 6 million numbers representing the Jewish victims of the Holocaust. Beneath the towers are steel grates that cover simulated glowing embers, a reminder of the ovens used to cremate concentration camp victims.

Celebrating the land. One of 1995's most provocative projects was the Lady Bird Johnson National Wildflower Research Center in Austin, designed by Overland Partners of San Antonio. The 42-acre (17-hectare) center, which opened in April, explores the ecology, economics, and esthetic value of native plants.   □ David Dillon

See also **Art.** In *World Book,* see **Architecture.**

A building by Japanese architect Tadao Ando in Hyogo, Japan, reveals the imaginative use of concrete that helped earn him the 1995 Pritzker Prize.

Argentina

Argentina. President Carlos Saúl Menem of the Justicialist (Peronist) Party, was sworn in for a second term on July 8, 1995. Due to a 1994 change in Argentina's Constitution that allowed Menem to seek another term, he became only the second Argentine president in the 1900's to serve a second term. (Juan Domingo Perón was president from 1946 to 1955, and from 1973 to 1974.)

Record unemployment. To win reelection on May 14, 1995, Menem had to persuade Argentines that despite record unemployment—12.2 percent on election eve—his free-market policies represented the best hope for economic stability. On March 13, Menem received a big boost from the World Bank, the Inter-American Development Bank, and the International Monetary Fund, which lent Argentina $11.4 billion to shore up its troubled banking system.

But despite this help and solid support for Menem's policies from both foreign and national business communities, Argentina turned in a disappointing economic performance in 1995. According to economists, the estimated growth rate for the year ranged from zero to less than 1 percent.

When unemployment surged in late September to 18.6 percent, labor unions called for the resignation of Economic Minister Domingo Cavallo. Typically, Jorge Blanco Villegas, head of the Argentine Industrial Union, blamed Cavallo for the loss of hundreds of thousands of union jobs, saying Cavallo had opened up the economy to international competition too quickly.

Labor unrest. As 1995 progressed, there was also rising dissatisfaction among workers in the public sector. On June 23, 100 people were injured in Córdoba, the country's second-largest city, when protesters attacked banks and shopping centers. The Menem administration touched off the protest by withholding the pay of government workers in an attempt to force local authorities to privatize the province's banks and utilities. On July 6, the province's governor, who had led the fight against privatization, was forced to resign.

"Dirty War" admissions. High-ranking military officers publicly admitted for the first time that the nation's armed forces had tortured and killed dissidents during the so-called "Dirty War" from 1976 to 1983. In an interview published on March 3, 1995, a former naval officer, Commander Adolfo Francisco Scilingo, said that 1,500 to 2,000 political prisoners had been tortured before being dropped into the Atlantic Ocean from helicopters. In a television interview on April 25, Lieutenant General Martín Balza, army chief of staff, confirmed that the military had indeed "employed illegitimate methods, including the suppression of life, to obtain information."

Argentine President Carlos Saúl Menem gestures to supporters in May after winning reelection to a second term.

Falklands oil and gas. In a surprising development, Argentina and the United Kingdom announced a tentative agreement in September to share in profits from the exploitation of oil and natural gas around the disputed Falkland Islands, which lie about 400 miles (640 kilometers) off Argentina's coast. The two countries both claim the islands and fought a 10-week war over them in 1982. The agreement notwithstanding, Argentine foreign minister Guido di Tella told reporters in London in June 1995 that Argentina would never give up its claim to the Falkland Islands.

Evita's corpse. In July, Argentines rushed to buy *Santa Evita*, a book by Tomás Eloy Martínez. The book was a fictional account of the exile and long journey home of the body of Eva Duarte de Perón, who died in 1952. She was the charismatic second wife of President Juan Domingo Perón.

Military officers who seized power in 1955 had the body buried in Italy under a false name, and it was not returned until Perón's third wife, Isabel, became president in November 1974. When Isabel was overthrown in 1976, the nation's new military dictators reburied Evita's body in her family's Buenos Aires tomb. □ Nathan A. Haverstock

See also **Latin America** (Facts in brief table). In *World Book,* see **Argentina.**

Arizona. See State government.

Arkansas. See State government.

Armed forces. The radical restructuring of United States military forces to reflect the reduction in superpower tensions and an increase in regional conflicts continued in 1995. During the year, U.S. troops participated in a variety of peacekeeping and humanitarian operations throughout the globe despite more cuts in manpower and base closings.

Bosnia. U.S. military involvement escalated sharply in the Balkan conflict in August when North Atlantic Treaty Organization (NATO) warplanes launched the heaviest air strikes of the three-year war in Bosnia-Herzegovina (often called Bosnia). The majority of air attacks against Bosnian Serb military targets came from U.S. planes based in Italy and on the aircraft carrier *Theodore Roosevelt* in the Adriatic Sea. NATO commanders approved the strikes in retaliation for the August 28 Serb shelling of Sarajevo and in an effort to force a diplomatic settlement to the war. On September 10, the U.S. cruiser *Normandy* launched 13 Tomahawk cruise missiles against Bosnian Serb surface-to-air missile sites. The action marked the heaviest combat use of the lethal cruise missiles since the 1991 Persian Gulf War against Iraq. NATO halted the bombing campaign on Sept. 14, 1995, after Bosnian Serbs agreed to take part in peace talks.

The signing of a Bosnian peace agreement on December 14 in Paris renewed debate over the use of U.S. ground forces in Bosnia. President Bill Clinton committed the United States to sending 20,000 troops to the region as part of a 60,000-member NATO deployment to enforce the peace pact. Many Americans and members of Congress expressed opposition to sending U.S. troops to Bosnia. Nonetheless, the deployment went ahead as planned.

U.S. Air Force Captain Scott F. O'Grady was rescued by U.S. Marines on June 8 after his F-16 fighter was shot down on June 2 over Serb-occupied Bosnia. O'Grady, who was stationed at a NATO air base in Italy, had been on a routine patrol over a Bosnian *no-fly zone* (an area closed to hostile aircraft). After being shot down, he eluded Serb forces for six days. A Pentagon investigation disclosed that U.S. intelligence had discovered the existence of the surface-to-air missile site that shot O'Grady down, but a communications error prevented the transmission of that information to the pilot.

Somalia and Haiti. More than 1,800 Marines provided security for the withdrawal of the last United Nation (UN) peacekeepers from Somalia in March, ending an ill-fated U.S. military involvement in that country. American troops had entered Somalia in December 1992 to assist the UN's humanitarian relief efforts. They soon became involved in fighting between Somalia's warring clans, and a fierce fire-fight in October 1993 left 18 U.S. soldiers dead.

U.S. peacekeeping operations were more successful in Haiti, where the September 1994 deployment of U.S. troops had restored democracy. UN forces took over peacekeeping responsibilities in the Caribbean nation from U.S. troops on March 31, 1995. By the end of 1995, about 2,400 U.S. troops remained in Haiti from an original deployment of more than 20,000.

The escalating cost of these operations prompted Congress to enact a $3-billion supplemental defense appropriations bill in April to fund peacekeeping and humanitarian operations in Haiti, Bosnia-Herzegovina, Cuba, South Korea, Somalia, and Kuwait.

Friendly-fire acquittal. An Air Force tribunal found Captain James Wang not guilty on June 20 of criminal charges in the April 1994 friendly-fire incident over Iraq that killed 26 people, including 15 Americans. Wang was a supervisor on a U.S. radar plane patrolling the skies over Iraq when two U.S. F-15 jet fighters enforcing a no-fly zone over Iraq shot down two unarmed U.S. helicopters that they mistook for Iraqi helicopters.

A Pentagon investigation of the incident was sharply critical of several individuals involved in the incident. Nonetheless, charges against five officers, including the two pilots who shot down the helicopters, were dropped, leaving Wang as the only individual to be charged. Stung by allegations that Wang had been made a scapegoat to protect the fighter pilots and senior officers, the Air Force disclosed that several personnel had received letters of reprimand that effectively barred them from promotions.

Strategic developments. Over the objections of the Clinton Administration, Congress sought to revive plans for a defense system to protect the country against a ballistic missile attack. The Senate approved legislation in September directing the Pentagon to develop a system that could be operational by the year 2003 to protect against an accidental nuclear missile launch or a limited nuclear missile attack. In February, Congress rejected a far more ambitious plan similar to the "Star Wars" initiative proposed in the 1980's. The Clinton Administration opposed the Senate's scaled-down version on the grounds that it might violate a 1972 antiballistic-missile treaty with the former Soviet Union and could also jeopardize negotiations with Russia and former Soviet republics over the destruction of thousands of nuclear missile warheads.

Retrenchment. The rapid downsizing of the U.S. armed forces in the post-Cold War environment continued. By the end of 1995, U.S. troop strength in Europe had dropped to 100,000, a reduction of 40,000 soldiers from the previous year and less than one-third of the 340,000 who were there in 1990. The number of U.S. Army forces in Europe fell to 65,000—a 70 percent reduction from the 213,000 in 1990.

Congressional action on Sept. 8, 1995, cleared the way for a new round of base closings recommended by the nonpartisan Defense Base Closure and Re-

Armed forces

alignment Commission. In June, the commission had recommended closing 79 bases and realigning 26 others for an estimated saving of $19.3 billion over 20 years. Among the major bases ordered closed were Kelly Air Force Base in Texas and McClellan Air Force Base in California. To ease the economic impact, the base closings would be implemented over six years. Another notable closing was that of the Philadelphia Naval Shipyard, which ceased operations on September 15 after 194 years of service.

Weapons systems. Despite substantial cutbacks in weapons procurement, development continued on a handful of new weapons systems. The largest such program was the Air Force's F-22 jet fighter. Development also began on a new generation of nuclear attack submarines and continued on a new air-to-surface missile being developed by the Air Force and Navy.

The Marine Corps disclosed that it might be forced to purchase fewer V-22 Osprey tilt-rotor aircraft than the 425 it wanted because of a total program cost of more than $46 billion. But the Air Force, reversing an earlier decision, said it was satisfied with the performance of the C-17 transport jet and ordered 80 more planes on November 3.

Vietnam mistake. Former U.S. Secretary of Defense Robert S. McNamara, one of the architects of the Vietnam War (1957-1975), asserted in April 1995 that U.S. involvement in that war had been a mis-

take. In a new book, *In Retrospect: The Tragedy and Lessons of Vietnam*, McNamara reflected on the controversial and divisive conflict that took the lives of about 58,000 Americans and as many as 2 million Vietnamese, McNamara admitted that he and other U.S. officials had been "wrong, terribly wrong" to have pursued the war and that the United States should have withdrawn its forces in the mid-1960's instead of escalating its involvement. McNamara's remarks ignited a firestorm in many quarters, particularly among veterans' groups.

On July 11, 1995, President Clinton established full diplomatic ties with Vietnam, citing increased cooperation from the Vietnamese government to resolve the fate of nearly 4,000 U.S. military personnel still listed as missing in action from the war.

Personnel. Four soldiers training to be U.S. Army Rangers died from *hypothermia* (severe loss of body heat) in February during a field exercise in a Florida swamp. The deaths were the worst incident in the 44-year history of the elite Ranger training program. The soldiers died after wading for several hours in water estimated at 52 °F (11 °C). An investigation revealed that the soldiers had been allowed to remain in the chilly water several hours longer than the prescribed limits.

Shannon Faulkner's fight of more than two years to become the first woman in the cadet corps of The Citadel, a military college in Charleston, South Carolina, took a bizarre twist. After the U.S. Supreme Court on August 11 rejected a last-minute appeal from The Citadel to block her admission, Faulkner began military training with other first-year cadets on August 14. On August 18, however, she abruptly dropped out, citing emotional stress and hostility from other students. Faulkner had spent five days in the school's infirmary after collapsing from heat exhaustion during the first day of cadet training.

A federal judge on March 30 ruled that the Clinton Administration's controversial "don't ask, don't tell" policy concerning homosexuals in the military was unconstitutional. The ruling affected only six servicemen who had challenged the policy in March of 1994 and was appealed by the government. Other court challenges to the policy were in various stages of litigation during 1995.

In June, Rebecca E. Marier became the first female cadet in the 193-year-history of the U.S. Military Academy to graduate first in her class.

Defense budget. The Clinton Administration's defense budget for the 1996 fiscal year, released on Feb. 6, 1995, requested spending authority of $261.4 billion, a $10.2-billion decrease from the previous year's projected spending. After adjusting for inflation, defense spending would decline for the 11th consecutive year and would be nearly 40 percent less than the budget for fiscal year 1985. The budget request sharply curtailed weapons spending for the second straight year and increased funding

U.S. Air Force Captain Scott O'Grady waves to well-wishers in Italy in June after being rescued in Bosnia, where his plane had been shot down.

for peacekeeping operations, combat readiness, ballistic missile defense, and nuclear threat reduction.

The single largest request was $2.9 billion for a variety of ballistic missile defense programs. The Pentagon also requested $2.6 billion for 6 C-17 jet cargo planes, $2.4 billion for two Aegis missile cruisers, $2.2 billion for the F-22 advanced tactical fighter, $1.8 billion for F/A-18 Hornet jet fighters, $1.7-billion for a Seawolf attack submarine, and $987 million for the B-2 stealth bomber.

Congress passed a $243.3-billion defense spending bill on September 25. On November 30, President Clinton signed the bill, but announced that in early 1996 he would ask Congress to rescind approximately $7 billion in weapons spending that the Pentagon believed was unnecessary.

Command changes. John M. Deutch, deputy secretary of defense, was named director of the Central Intelligence Agency in May. In June, General Dennis J. Reimer became Army chief of staff, and General Charles C. Krulak was named commandant of the Marine Corps. Marcelite Jordan Harris of the Air Force became the military's first black female two-star general in March. Les Aspin, Jr., President Clinton's first secretary of defense and former chairman of the House Armed Services Committee, died on May 21. □ Thomas M. DeFrank

In *World Book*, see the articles on the branches of the armed forces.

Armenia continued to occupy about 20 percent of neighboring Azerbaijan during 1995, but a fragile cease-fire negotiated in May 1994 held. Armenia consolidated its hold over the ethnic Armenian enclave of Nagorno-Karabakh, which it seized from Azerbaijan in 1993, by building roads linking Armenia and the enclave. Peace talks held in Moscow under the auspices of the Conference on Security and Cooperation in Europe failed to resolve differences over the fate of occupied Azerbaijani territory.

In May 1995, Armenian Prime Minister Hrant Bagratyan and Iran signed a 20-year pact under which Iran will supply Armenia with natural gas through a specially constructed pipeline. Armenia's energy supply had been crippled for the previous three years by repeated sabotage of a pipeline carrying gas from central Asia.

In July, the ruling Armenian National Movement and its allies won parliamentary elections, but international observers condemned restrictions on opposition campaigning. The leaders of one opposition group, the Armenian Revolutionary Federation (Dashnak), were arrested on charges of terrorism. In the election, voters also approved a new Constitution that strengthened the presidency. President Levon Ter-Petrosyan scheduled a presidential election for September 1996. □ Steven L. Solnick

See also **Asia** (Facts in brief table); **Azerbaijan.** In *World Book,* see **Armenia.**

Armey, Richard K. (1940-), a United States congressman from Texas, served as the majority leader of the U.S. House of Representatives in 1995. Armey was the first Republican majority leader in the House since the 1950's. An ultraconservative, Armey opposed abortion, the ban on assault weapons, and federal aid to education. He advocated replacing the current federal income tax code with a 17 percent flat tax.

Armey was born in Cando, North Dakota, on July 7, 1940. He earned a doctorate in economics at the University of Oklahoma in Norman in 1968. For the next 16 years, he taught economics, first at Austin College in Sherman, Texas, and then at North Texas State University in Denton.

In 1984, Armey was elected to Congress, narrowly upsetting a popular Democratic incumbent congressman. As a legislator, Armey became known for making inflammatory statements and for putting ideology before pragmatism, but he gradually developed into a consensus-builder.

In 1988, Armey drafted legislation that closed hundreds of obsolete military bases, and in 1990, he got a bill passed to cut farm subsidies. In 1994, he was coauthor, with Speaker of the House Newt Gingrich, of the Republicans' 10-point program of conservative legislation, the "Contract with America."

Armey is the author of several books. He and his wife, Susan, have five children. □ Lisa Klobuchar

Art. Unlike previous years, when the art market dominated news of the art world, 1995 was the year of the museum. Two events early in the year summarized the current state of United States art museums. On January 18, the San Francisco Museum of Modern Art opened a new $60-million, 225,000-square-foot (21,000-square-meter) facility designed by Swiss architect Mario Botta. The building replaced the museum's previous quarters—two floors of the city's War Memorial Veterans Building, which it had occupied since 1935.

Like many museums built since the 1960's, the new building was not so much a museum as an architectural statement. The structure consists of a mammoth central tower surrounded by a three-tiered, stepped-back, brick-clad exterior. Punctuating the building is a zebra-striped, stone-clad cylinder sliced at a 45-degree angle that contains a skylight 130 feet (40 meters) high. Critics generally disapproved of the building's imposing monolithic exterior while praising the airy, light-filled interior.

Selling to save. In a highly unusual attempt to stave off bankruptcy, New York City's New-York Historical Society raised nearly $18 million by auctioning a total of 183 objects and works of art from its collection in January and October. The proceeds were earmarked for renovations and an endowment. By law, museums normally may sell works only to buy others. But severe financial problems and the failure of merger negotiations with several city institutions left the historical society few alternatives.

The New York attorney general's office, which oversees the financial operations of that state's nonprofit institutions, permitted the auction on the condition that museums and other nonprofit institutions in New York receive preferential treatment. That is, these institutions were given one week after the auctions to override winning bids from collectors and dealers and to buy items at slightly discounted prices. This unprecedented arrangement was intended to keep the works in New York state. As a result, the Metropolitan Museum of Art and the Brooklyn Museum, both in New York City, and Vassar College in Poughkeepsie acquired important works of art. At year's end, however, the historical society was still struggling with financial problems, and New York City again had begun trying to arrange a merger, raising questions as to whether the historical society's artworks had been needlessly sacrificed.

Barnes controversy. The Barnes Foundation in Merion, Pennsylvania, reopened to the public in November after a 32-month, $12-million renovation. The foundation includes an art school and museum housing the greatest group of impressionist, post-impressionist and early modern paintings acquired by an American collector—Albert C. Barnes, who died in 1951.

The renovation of the 70-year-old foundation was undertaken in an attempt to resolve financial problems that had made its future uncertain. Many of these problems had resulted from the tightly drawn charter, based on Barnes's will, that had established the foundation. Under the terms of the charter, for example, the museum's holdings could be viewed only by appointment. In addition, the charter banned fund-raising activities at the foundation and the loan or sale of the museum's paintings. In the early 1990's, the trustees attempted to alter the charter in order, they argued, to modernize the museum and place it on a sound financial footing. But critics heatedly opposed these efforts, contending that the plans were contrary to Barnes's vision.

Central to the board's fund-raising efforts for the renovation and endowment was a seven-city international tour of 80 paintings from the collection. (A 1993 court decision allowed the trustees to stage the show.) The tour, one of the most successful ever mounted by any museum, concluded in November 1995 and raised $17 million.

Yet even as the Barnes reopened, uncertainties remained. Shortly before the reopening, a Pennsylvania judge ruled that the foundation could not raise its admission fee to $10 from the $1 established by a 1961 court ruling, but could charge only $5. Claiming the lower figure would prevent them from meeting their financial obligations, the trustees threatened to close the institution completely if their appeal was not granted.

Hidden treasures revealed. In March 1995, the Hermitage Museum in St. Petersburg, Russia, opened "Hidden Treasures Revealed: Impressionist Masterpieces and Other Important French Paintings Preserved by the State Hermitage Museum." The show displayed 74 paintings that had been presumed lost or destroyed during World War II (1939-1945) until *ARTnews* magazine in 1991 revealed their presence at the Hermitage Museum.

The paintings represent a fraction of the estimated 500,000 works of art, books, and other cultural objects that the Soviet Army stole from Nazi Germany at the end of World War II in retaliation for the Nazis' destruction and theft of Soviet cultural property. Russia contended that the Nazis took an equal number of artworks from the Soviet Union.

The fate of the paintings in the Hermitage show remained uncertain at year-end as negotiations between the Hermitage and Russian government and the heirs of the paintings' original owners remained at an impasse. Complicating the negotiations was the fate of the stolen Soviet art, most of which is in private hands outside the former Soviet Union.

Exhibiting errors. Another unique exhibition in 1995 was "Rembrandt/Not Rembrandt," staged by the Metropolitan Museum of Art. The museum displayed about 100 paintings, drawings, and prints known or once thought to have been painted by the Dutch master of the 1600's. Wall panels, X rays, and other materials were used to explain how the museum authenticated some works and concluded that other works had, in fact, been painted by others. Museums seldom admit error; even less often do they explain their methods to the public.

Reality check. Perhaps the most unusual show of 1995 was "Willem de Kooning: The Late Paintings, the 1980's," which opened at the San Francisco Museum of Modern Art in October on the first leg of a five-city international tour. The exhibited works of the highly influential abstract expressionist artist have posed problems for critics and scholars since they were first exhibited in commercial galleries in the 1980's. In the late 1980's, de Kooning was diagnosed as suffering from Alzheimer's disease or a similar neurological disorder. Critics debated whether the work produced during that period constituted a valid artistic statement or represented the scrawlings of a man out of touch with reality. The point of the show was to confront that issue head-on.

Wrapped at last. The most spectacular artistic display in 1995 was in the open air. In June, the artist Christo—known for draping things with fabric—and his wife, Jeanne-Claude, wrapped Berlin's historic Reichstag (parliament building) in about 1 million square feet (100,000 square meters) of silvery fabric and more than 10 miles (16 kilometers) of blue rope. The $10-million display ended a 20-year quest to wrap the building, which was nearly destroyed in World War II.

Berlin's Reichstag (parliament building) was encased in silvery fabric and blue rope in June by the artist Christo and his artist wife, Jeanne-Claude.

Technology. In October, the National Gallery of Art in Washington, D.C., opened its Micro Gallery, a room with interactive workstations at which visitors can view digitized images of the 1,700 works in the museum's collection and call up information about them. (In digitizing, paintings or photographs are scanned by a computer that converts the image into a numerical code then re-creates the image for viewing on the computer screen.)

Also in October, the Corbis Corporation, the digital image licensing company founded by William H. Gates, the chief executive officer of the Microsoft Corporation in Redmond, Washington, bought the Bettmann Archive, one of the world's largest photographic collections, for an undisclosed amount. Bettmann, which owns 17 million images, had long been a prime resource for publishers. Corbis had previously obtained the digital rights to paintings and other artworks owned by a number of museums, including the National Gallery in London and the Barnes Foundation. In November, Corbis bought the digital rights to the 3 million works of art owned by the Hermitage Museum. Corbis planned to market the digital images not only to publishers but also to owners of home computers.

Moving into cyberspace. In 1995, the Association of Art Museum Directors (AAMD) set up a World Wide Web site on the Internet, a global web of computer networks that operate over telephone lines. The World Wide Web is a portion of the Internet that has graphics, animation, and sound capabilities as well as text. The AAMD site lists member museums along with such information as hours and current exhibitions. The site also offers access to individual museums on the Internet.

Split decision in L.A. The Los Angeles County Museum of Art, without a director since 1993, divided the director's responsibilities between two positions. In November 1995, Andrea Rich, executive vice-chancellor of the University of California in Los Angeles became president and chief executive officer. She was to be responsible for planning and fund-raising, while a new director, still unnamed in late 1995, was to be the curator.

Debated, even in death. In April 1995, a New York Surrogate Court judge ruled that Edward W. Hayes, the former attorney for the estate of pop icon Andy Warhol, was entitled to $7.45 million in legal fees. This ruling followed a 1994 decision by the judge that Warhol's estate was worth $509.9-million in 1991 when the estate was transferred to the Andy Warhol Foundation for the Visual Arts in New York City. The figure was more than twice that proposed by the foundation and the New York attorney general. The foundation vowed to appeal the ruling on Hayes's fee. □ Eric Gibson

See also **Architecture.** In *World Book,* see **Art and the arts; Painting; Sculpture.**

Asia

Asia led the world in economic growth during 1995, raising the living standards of many people, though millions of Asians remained in poverty. The Asian Development Bank, an affiliate of the United Nations (UN), said in April that the economies of Asian countries expanded at an average annual rate of more than 7 percent—fast enough to double individual incomes in just 11 years. Sustained growth, the bank said, depended on keeping inflation and budget deficits low and increasing the level of education in order to upgrade workers' skills.

Growing pains. The bank predicted that by the year 2020 Asia would have 17 cities with more than 10 million inhabitants, more than double the number in 1995. The bank projected that metropolitan Tokyo and Bombay, India, would approach 30 million people, and Shanghai; Jakarta, Indonesia; and Karachi, Pakistan would exceed 20 million. The bank also warned that social and environmental problems would accompany the growth.

In September, the World Bank said that east and Southeast Asia alone needed to spend up to $1.5-trillion over the next decade to meet rising demand for clean drinking water, sanitation systems, electricity, telephones, and transportation. The bank said Asian nations needed foreign capital to finance such huge projects.

However, investing in Asia was complicated. Several countries imposed taxes, set interest limits, and imposed other measures to limit profits on projects in an effort to curb excessive returns to foreign investors. The low fixed returns coupled with excessive regulation by local bureaucracies discouraged investors from financing some essential projects.

Workers and jobs migrate. Throughout Asia in 1995, people left rural poverty to look for work in cities. China had the largest number of such workers within its borders, but millions elsewhere crossed international borders in search of employment, particularly in construction. Indonesians worked on office buildings in Malaysia, Bangladeshis built bridges in Japan, Burmese labored on a stadium in Thailand, Vietnamese built Taiwanese factories, and Nepalis worked on South Korean sewers. Millions of people from Sri Lanka, Bangladesh, and the Philippines left home to work as domestics in other Asian nations or in the Persian Gulf states.

Many migrants entered those countries illegally—about 55,000 out of 85,000 in South Korea, for example—attracted by the relatively high pay scales. Still, they were paid only a fraction of what the local people earned. Stories of employers and labor contractors abusing migrant laborers were common, and some workers were cheated out of their pay.

Jobs also migrated in 1995, as well. Thailand and Malaysia, which had begun their industrial booms

producing simple things for Japanese and Western companies, moved up to the production of more-sophisticated products. In 1995, many companies looked to Vietnam, the Philippines, Burma, and other less-developed countries as sites for the manufacture of labor-intensive products. China continued to attract foreign investment in factories, despite rising wages in its booming coastal areas.

Aging populations. Asia's labor market was also affected by the aging of its population. People were living longer and having fewer children. According to the UN, a person born in east Asia in 1960 could expect to live to age 51, but a person born there in the 1990's could expect to live beyond age 70. In the 1960's, women in east Asia had an average of more than five children, but in the early 1990's, the average number of children had fallen to about two. The UN predicted that by the year 2025, almost

A woman stands dazed amid the rubble of Kobe, Japan, after an earthquake devastated the city in January, killing more than 5,400 people.

20 percent of east Asia's population would be age 60 or older, and for south Asia, the percentage would be only slightly lower. Thus, there would be fewer workers to pay taxes to support necessary services for a growing number of older people.

Corruption. The business community in 1995 rated Asia as one of the more corrupt parts of the world in which to operate, according to several opinion surveys. A German research group found that the most corrupt countries were Indonesia, China, Pakistan, the Philippines, India, and Thailand. An Asian business magazine found that more than a third of the business leaders in Malaysia, Indonesia, South Korea, and Thailand said they would rather bribe a customer than lose a big sale.

In 1995, China conducted a campaign against corruption that caught a member of the ruling Communist party's top leadership plus many lesser officials.

In South Korea, India, and other countries probes into political slush funds and illegal "black money" payments implicated senior politicians and businessmen. Many big contracts signed in Japan, Taiwan, and other places reportedly were finalized only with the help of bribes or "commissions" to officials.

Boat people. Vietnam agreed in March to simplify procedures to repatriate Vietnamese "boat people" living in camps in other countries. Almost 1 million Vietnamese had fled by sea after the Communist takeover of Vietnam in 1975. Some 43,000 remained in Asian camps because they were considered jobseekers, not political refugees. Under a UN plan, all the Vietnamese except those in Hong Kong would be sent home by the end of 1995. Hong Kong was given a few more months because it had the largest number of boat people, 23,000 Vietnamese.

News of the plan led to riots in some boat people

Country	Population	Government	Monetary unit*	Foreign trade (million U.S.$)	
				Exports†	Imports†
Afghanistan	19,494,000	President Burhanuddin Rabbani	afghani (4,442.00 = $1)	188	616
Armenia	3,816,000	President Levon Ter-Petrosyan	dram (not available)	29	85
Australia	18,058,000	Governor General Bill Hayden; Prime Minister Paul Keating	dollar (1.32 = $1)	47,556	53,414
Azerbaijan	7,507,000	President Heydar A. Aliyev	manat (4,435.00 = $1)	625	727
Bangladesh	117,944,000	President Abdur Rahman Biswas; Prime Minister Khaleda Ziaur Rahman	taka (41.28 = $1)	2,650	4,701
Bhutan	1,769,000	King Jigme Singye Wangchuck	ngultrum (35.78 = $1)	67	98
Brunei	294,000	Sultan Sir Hassanal Bolkiah	dollar (1.41 = $1)	2,198	1,201
Burma (Myanmar)	47,502,000	State Law and Order Restoration Council Chairman Than Shwe	kyat (5.63 = $1)	764	878
Cambodia (Kampuchea)	9,661,000	King Norodom Sihanouk; Prime Minister Prince Norodom Ranariddh; Prime Minister Hun Sen	riel (2,300.00 = $1)	284	479
China	1,252,188,000	Communist Party General Secretary and President Jiang Zemin; Premier Li Peng	yuan (8.31 = $1)	121,014	115,671
Georgia	5,478,000	Parliament Chairman Eduard Shevardnadze	lari (not available)	209	330
India	947,803,000	President Shankar Dayal Sharma; Prime Minister P. V. Narasimha Rao	rupee (35.78 = $1)	25,053	26,764
Indonesia	204,660,000	President Suharto; Vice President Try Sutrisno	rupiah (2,267.50 = $1)	36,825	28,086
Iran	64,073,000	Leader of the Islamic Revolution Ali Hoseini Khamenei; President Ali Akbar Hashemi Rafsanjani	rial (3,000.00 = $1)	16,000	18,000
Japan	126,320,000	Emperor Akihito; Prime Minister Tomiichi Murayama	yen (101.30 = $1)	397,373	275,548
Kazakhstan	17,575,000	President Nursultan Nazarbayev	tenge (not available)	1,095	514
Korea, North	24,307,000	Premier Kang Song-San	won (2.15 = $1)	1,020	1,640
Korea, South	45,516,000	President Kim Yong-Sam; Prime Minister Yi Hong-Ku	won (765.70 = $1)	95,893	102,198
Kyrgyzstan	4,754,000	President Askar Akayev	som (not available)	112	112

*Exchange rates as of Oct. 27, 1995, or latest available data.   †Latest available data.

camps. In the Philippines and in Hong Kong, where the people lived in virtual prison camps, hundreds threatened to commit suicide if they were sent home. Those in Thailand staged hunger strikes rather than leave the camps.

The situation became more explosive when the United States House of Representatives voted on May 25 to give up to 20,000 camp residents priority to immigrate to the United States. The bill did not become law, but it touched off bigger riots in the camps by people who refused to go home as long as hope flickered of settling abroad. Hundreds of officials and local police were injured in Hong Kong and Malaysia while trying to quell the riots. By year-end, the UN goal of clearing the camps was unmet.

Spratly Islands. The ongoing dispute over ownership of the Spratly Islands in the South China Sea flared anew in February 1995. The sea floor in the region is potentially rich in oil and natural gas. The Philippines said that China had built a naval installation on Mischief Reef, which is part of the Spratlys, in an area that the Philippines claims as its territorial waters. Brunei, Malaysia, Taiwan, and Vietnam also had overlapping claims to various atolls and reefs making up the Spratlys.

At a July meeting in Brunei of the Association of Southeast Asian Nations (ASEAN), China's foreign minister said China had "indisputable sovereignty" over the Spratlys, but was willing to negotiate disputes by rules of international and maritime law.

Country	Population	Government	Monetary unit*	Foreign trade (million U.S.$)	
				Exports†	Imports†
Laos	5,015,000	President Nouhak Phoumsavan; Prime Minister Khamtai Siphandon	kip (920.00 = $1)	81	162
Malaysia	20,532,000	Paramount Ruler Tuanku Ja'afar ibni Al-Marhum Tuanku Abdul Rahman; Prime Minister Mahathir bin Mohamad	ringgit (2.54 = $1)	58,755	39,580
Maldives	255,000	President Maumoon Abdul Gayoom	rufiyaa (11.77 = $1)	35	191
Mongolia	2,560,000	President Punsalmaagiyn Ochirbat; Prime Minister Puntsagiyn Jasray	tugrik (460.18 = $1)	360	361
Nepal	20,813,000	King Birendra Bir Bikram Shah Dev; Prime Minister Mana Mohan Adhikari	rupee (51.75 = $1)	391	880
New Zealand	3,583,000	Governor General Dame Catherine Tizard; Prime Minister James B. Bolger	dollar (1.52 = $1)	12,184	11,902
Pakistan	138,672,000	President Farooq Leghari; Prime Minister Benazir Bhutto	rupee (31.93 = $1)	7,294	8,829
Papua New Guinea	4,443,000	Governor General Sir Wiwa Korowi; Prime Minister Sir Julius Chan	kina (1.32 = $1)	2,484	1,299
Philippines	70,559,000	President Fidel Ramos	peso (25.98 = $1)	12,930	17,271
Russia	150,638,000	President Boris Yeltsin	C.I.S. ruble (4,504.00 = $1)	63,243	38,650
Singapore	2,877,000	President Ong Teng Cheong; Prime Minister Goh Chok Tong	dollar (1.41 = $1)	96,749	102,590
Sri Lanka	18,559,000	President Chandrika Kumaratunga; Prime Minister Sirimavo Bandaranaike	rupee (52.48 = $1)	3,192	4,482
Taiwan	21,709,000	President Li Teng-hui; Premier Lien Chan	dollar (26.96 = $1)	93,000	85,100
Tajikistan	6,155,000	President Emomili Rakhmonov; National Assembly Chairman Safarali Rajabov	C.I.S. ruble (4,504.00 = $1)	356	328
Thailand	58,836,000	King Phumiphon Adunyadet; Prime Minister Banhan Sinlapa-acha	baht (25.13 = $1)	37,173	46,058
Turkmenistan	4,260,000	President Saparmurad Niyazov	manat (not available)	1,049	501
Uzbekistan	23,308,000	President Islam Karimov	som (not available)	1,006	1,127
Vietnam	75,280,000	Communist Party General Secretary Do Muoi; President Le Duc Anh; Prime Minister Vo Van Kiet	dong (10,985.00 = $1)	1,970	1,900

China rejected discussions concerning the Spratlys with ASEAN as a whole, insisting on separate talks with separate claimants. On August 9, China agreed with the Philippines to resolve the dispute under provisions of a 1982 United Nations sea rule.

Growing economic cooperation. Nations of the lower Mekong River—Cambodia, Laos, Thailand, and Vietnam—agreed on April 5, 1995, to set up a Mekong River Commission to regulate use of the river, including the building of dams. In October, the four nations plus China and Burma on the upper Mekong agreed under the auspices of the Asian Development Bank on a regional development strategy, to cost $40 billion.

Another regional grouping, the South Asian As-sociation for Regional Cooperation (SAARC), agreed on May 4 in New Delhi to give preference to trade among themselves. However, the SAARC members—Bangladesh, Bhutan, India, the Maldives, Nepal, Pakistan, and Sri Lanka—would cut tariffs on only a small proportion of their total trade.

On December 6, China, North Korea, South Korea, Mongolia, and Russia signed agreements for the Tumen River Area Development Program formed to boost trade and investment along the Tumen River, where North Korea, China, and Russia have a common border. The United Nations Development Program encouraged the creation of the new industrial area on the delta, but the project had been making only slow progress.

ASEAN admitted its seventh member, Vietnam, on July 28, 1995, and Burma, Cambodia, and Laos were candidates for membership. ASEAN was established by Indonesia, Malaysia, the Philippines, Singapore, and Thailand in 1967 as a bulwark against Communism. Brunei joined later. But the threat of Communism was fading, and Vietnam, with its Communist government, joined for economic reasons. In 1995, ASEAN was working toward setting up what could be the world's largest free-trade zone by the year 2000.

Nepal ended 10 months of Communist government on Sept. 12, 1995, when Sher Bahadur Deuba of the Nepali Congress Party (NPC) was sworn in as prime minister. Deuba's new coalition invited private investment in infrastructure development.

Deuba's NPC had governed Nepal before parliamentary elections in November 1994 brought to power a coalition of the Nepal Communist Party-United Marxist Leninist (UML). By June 1995, disaffection between coalition partners endangered the UML's majority, and King Birendra Bir Bikram Shah Dev dissolved parliament, calling for new elections. But on August 28, Nepal's Supreme Court ruled that dissolving parliament was unconstitutional. It reconvened and voted to oust the UML government, giving power to Deuba.   □ Henry S. Bradsher

See also the articles on the individual Asian nations. In *World Book,* see **Asia.**

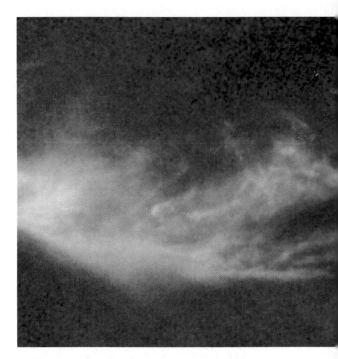

A gaseous jet that formed as a by-product of the birth of a star extends 3 trillion miles (5 trillion kilometers) into space in the Gum Nebula. The Hubble Space Telescope captured the image in June.

Astronomy. In 1995, astronomers discovered tiny moons that orbit Saturn and a bright new comet. Looking beyond our solar system, they found new evidence of distant planets, black holes, and the mysterious dark matter that fills the universe.

Saturn's new moons. On May 22, astronomers Amanda Bosh and Andrew Rivkin of the Lowell Observatory in Flagstaff, Arizona, used the Hubble Space Telescope to photograph what appeared to be 4 additions to Saturn's known contingent of 18 moons. The new satellites orbit just outside Saturn's rings. Because the moons are too small and faint to be seen over the glare of the rings in normal viewing conditions, Bosh and Rivkin photographed them when the rings were oriented edge-on to Earth. The thin rings seem to disappear from that perspective.

Further Hubble observations of Saturn on August 10, when the rings were again edge-on, revealed three more new satellites. The three appeared elongated rather than spherical, however, and it is possible that they were actually clouds of shattered debris produced by collisions between the orbiting icy chunks that make up Saturn's rings. The four moons first seen in May were also evident, but two of them appeared surprisingly bright—too bright to have been missed during the 1980 flyby by the Voyager I spacecraft. A third moon was recognized as Prometheus, which was discovered in 1980.

Another set of observations planned for Feb. 11,

1996, when the rings would again be edge-on, was expected to contribute additional information. Until then, the question of whether Saturn has 20 moons, 22 moons, or even more remains open. There should be plenty of time for debate, because Saturn's rings will not again be visible edge-on until 2038.

Bright future for a new comet. On July 22, 1995, when amateur American astronomers Alan Hale and Thomas Bopp first spotted a comet that now bears their name, it was just a fuzzy spot in the constellation Sagittarius. At the time of discovery, Comet Hale-Bopp was over 500 million miles (800 million kilometers) away and could be seen only with a large telescope. But by year-end, astronomers were predicting that Comet Hale-Bopp would soon become one of the most spectacular comets of the century. If it continues to brighten as expected, in 1997, when it reaches its closest approach to the sun, Hale-Bopp should be one of the brightest objects in the night sky, resembling the Great Comet of 1811, whose tail spanned over a third of the sky.

A planet orbiting 51 Pegasi. In October 1995, astronomer Michel Mayor of the Geneva Observatory in Switzerland reported the discovery of the first known planet orbiting a star similar to the sun. Previously, scientists had detected only planets orbiting a pulsar, the dense remnant of a dead star.

The newly discovered planet travels around its star, called 51 Pegasi, in a close orbit every 4.2 days.

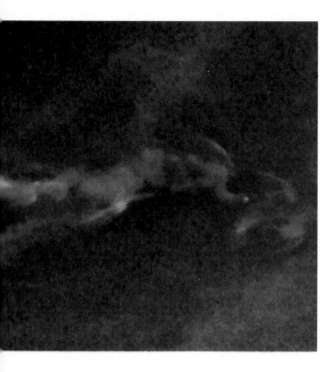

mysterious stuff that astronomers believe accounts for 90 to 98 percent of the matter in the universe. Dark matter does not glow like ordinary stars and so it cannot be seen from Earth, but its gravitational effects can be detected by observing the orbital speed of stars in the outer regions of distant galaxies.

Physicist Kem Cook of the Lawrence Livermore National Laboratory in California reported in April that his team's observations appeared to rule out one strong candidate for dark matter, MACHO's (*Massive Compact Halo Objects*). These are any dark objects smaller than normal stars, including neutron stars, planets, or dim stars called white dwarfs. For more than three years, several groups of astronomers looked for these dark objects by seeing what happens when they pass in front of stars that lie well outside the Milky Way. The gravity of the MACHO can bend and focus the light from the distant object, causing it to brighten in a phenomenon called gravitational lensing. So few of these events have been seen, however, that astronomers estimated that less than 20 percent of the mass of our Galaxy's outer region can be in the form of these solid objects.

Further observations may help pin down the nature of the dark matter. The present evidence suggests that it must be something more unfamiliar than stars or planets, perhaps some sort of exotic subatomic particle.   ☐ Laurence A. Marschall

In **World Book**, see *Astronomy*.

The star heats the planet's surface to about 1800 °F (1000 °C), so experts say it is not likely to support life.

Best evidence for a black hole. A team of radio astronomers led by James Moran of the Harvard-Smithsonian Center for Astrophysics in Cambridge, Massachusetts, reported in January that they had detected a black hole containing as much matter as 40 million suns at the center of the galaxy NGC 4258. Black holes, objects whose gravity is so strong that even light cannot escape them, have long been sought by astronomers, but previous findings had been far less convincing than this one.

Because black holes do not emit light, they can be detected only by observing their gravitational pull on adjacent objects. To detect the black hole in NGC 4258, the team of astronomers employed the Very Long Baseline Array (VLBA), a network of 10 radio telescopes spread across North America, which together have the ability to see extraordinarily fine detail. The VLBA enabled astronomers to pinpoint the position and velocity of gases circling the center of the galaxy at speeds of up to 560 miles (900 kilometers) per second. The high speed indicates that an enormous amount of matter is packed into a very small region of the galaxy core—too much matter to be accounted for by individual stars or star clusters.

Dark-matter mystery deepens. Hubble Space Telescope observations in 1995 seemed to eliminate dim, cool stars as candidates for dark matter, the

Aung San Suu Kyi, Daw (1945-   ), leader of the Burmese democracy movement and winner of the Nobel Peace Prize in 1991, was released from confinement on July 10, 1995. She cofounded the National League for Democracy, Burma's most powerful opposition party. The military government had held her under house arrest since 1989.

Aung San Suu Kyi (ong san SOO chee) was born in Rangoon, Burma, on June 19, 1945. Her father, a leader of the nationalist movement that challenged the United Kingdom's control of Burma, was assassinated shortly before the nation achieved independence in 1948. No strong civilian leader emerged, and Burma fell into the hands of the military in 1962. Aung San Suu Kyi earned a B.A. from Oxford University in 1967 and in 1972 married Michael Aris, a British academic. For the next several years she raised her two sons and pursued scholarly research.

Aung San Suu Kyi became involved with the Burmese democracy movement in 1988 in response to the army's murder of thousands of prodemocracy demonstrators. In late 1988, the government set up an authoritarian State Law and Order Restoration Council (SLORC) as the supreme political power, and in July 1989 it arrested Aung San Suu Kyi. SLORC permitted the formation of rival political parties, and free elections were held in 1990. Aung San Suu Kyi's party won 80 percent of the vote, but the government refused to cede power.   ☐ Lisa Klobuchar

Australia. A sharp increase in exports helped the national economy achieve a 3.75 percent growth rate during 1995. The Treasury predicted the economy would continue to grow at that rate for the next three years. Unemployment fell to 8.3 percent from 9.5 percent in 1994. Low inflation—3 percent—prompted the head of the Reserve Bank of Australia to announce in October 1995 that interest rates would stay at 7.5 percent for the next six months.

Monetary issues. On May 9, Treasurer Ralph Willis handed down a budget with an unexpected surplus of $718 million, largely a result of the federal government's sale of its interest in the Commonwealth Bank. (All monetary figures in this article are in Australian dollars. One Australian dollar equaled about U.S. $0.74 in 1995.) The bank was the last large holding sold in the government's program of selling state assets to reduce the federal deficit.

Australia's foreign debt grew by 10 percent in 1995 to $180 billion, which represented nearly 40 percent of the *gross domestic product* (GDP), the total value of goods and services produced within a country. Although the nation's debt is mainly private, conservative opposition leader John Howard, who came to office on January 30, criticized the ruling Labor Party government for allowing the foreign debt to soar since 1993, when it was about 14 percent of GDP. He argued that the large foreign debt and the budget deficit kept domestic interest rates high. He also said the foreign debt made Australia susceptible to international pressures and restricted flexibility in economic management.

Drought eases. Australia's crippling five-year drought eased in mid-September 1995 as rains brought relief to farmers in the southeast. But some agriculture experts estimated that the protracted drought was responsible for reducing the nation's agricultural production by 47 percent. The drought was expected to force 20 percent of the farmers in the hard-hit state of New South Wales to sell their land. The September rains produced a record crop of winter wheat. Meanwhile, Australian wheat fetched record prices on the international market as global wheat supplies continued to dwindle. The International Grains Council predicted in September that world wheat supplies would hit their lowest level in 20 years.

In New South Wales, the Labor Party won parliamentary elections on March 17, and party leader Bob Carr became state premier. Carr introduced legislation that mandated a life sentence for anyone convicted of trafficking 2.2 pounds (1 kilogram) or more of heroin or cocaine.

In September, a government commission began investigating allegations of corruption in the state's federal police force. Reportedly, senior officers had received bribes from drug dealers and participated in theft, perjury, fabrication of evidence, and extortion. The commission report was due January 1996.

The state's first legal gambling casino, a joint Australian-United States venture, opened in Sydney on Sept. 13, 1995. Parliament had awarded the contract in late December 1994, after completing a five-month inquiry into allegations that the American company, Showboat, Inc., had links to organized crime. No such links were proved.

Queensland reelected the Labor government of Premier Wayne Goss to a third parliamentary term on July 15, 1995, in one of the nation's tightest elections ever. The Labor Party won in Mundingburra by just 16 votes, which gave Goss a one-seat majority in parliament.

The tight election was seen as an omen for federal Prime Minister Paul Keating, who must call for elections by May 1996. Polls indicated that the public perceived Goss and Keating as arrogant and unconcerned about issues worrying most Australians.

The Northern Territory. The parliament of the Northern Territory in May 1995 enacted landmark legislation allowing terminally ill people to end their lives. Under the law, terminally ill Australians can travel to the region for assisted suicide, but they must meet strict criteria, including a diagnosis of incurable disease from two doctors. However, religious, medical, and right-to-life groups backed a bill to repeal the law, and parliament had the measure under consideration at year-end.

Media. Optus Vision became the nation's first cable television provider on September 20, when it began telecasting sports, news, movies, and general entertainment programs to two areas of Sydney, the nation's largest city. Backed by Kerry Packer, Australia's richest man, Optus aimed to provide service to 250,000 subscribers by year-end. In October, Foxtel, backed by media mogul Rupert Murdoch, started a competing cable service in Sydney and planned to provide programming for 1 million homes by December. But the conservative opposition in the Senate challenged the government's plan to allow the two companies exclusive access to pay-TV for two years. The senators said the plan was at odds with the established open-access policy for telecommunications.

In May, the federal Cabinet (senior government ministers) imposed a ceiling of 20 percent on cross-media ownership to ensure that companies cannot gain large holdings in both television and newspapers. The limitation was seen as a block to the attempt by Kerry Packer to win control of John Fairfax Holdings, a newspaper group. In September, the government announced that it would allow up to 49 percent foreign ownership of provincial and suburban newspapers, but it kept a limit of 30 percent foreign ownership for major metropolitan papers.

Native land rights upheld. On March 16, the High Court rejected a law passed in 1993 by Western Australia concerning land rights of the *Aborigines* (native people). The court said the law discriminated against the Aborigines and conflicted with the federal Native Title Act of 1993. The act clarified the conditions under which Aborigines could claim ownership of land they traditionally held before Europeans began arriving in the late 1700's.

Western Australia had sought to confirm the validity of non-Aboriginal land titles. The state law had been passed largely in response to miners in Western Australia who were concerned that the federal act would deter them from exploring and mining large areas of public land with rich deposits of valuable minerals. Many Aborigines also live on this land. The High Court rejected the state law, ruling that it gave non-Aboriginal titles priority over Aboriginal rights.

Australians protested against France's nuclear tests on an atoll in the Pacific Ocean in September. In response, French President Jacques Chirac threatened to ban sales of Australian uranium to France. Chirac claimed Australia's real motivation was to oust France from the Pacific, which Australia denied.

Republic of Australia. On June 7, Prime Minister Keating unveiled a plan for the nation to become the Republic of the Commonwealth of Australia by 2001. The plan called for a president to replace the British monarch as head of the nation. Keating said a referendum would be held in 1998 or 1999. □ Susan G. Williams

See also **Asia** (Facts in brief table). In *World Book,* see **Australia.**

Austria entered the European Union (EU) with enthusiasm on Jan. 1, 1995. But the austerity demanded of EU members left many Austrians disillusioned and the political establishment divided.

The coalition government of Austrian Chancellor Franz Vranitzky collapsed on October 12 after the two sides—the center-left Social Democratic Party and the conservative People's Party—failed to agree on ways to reduce the nation's budget deficit. Both parties agreed that the deficit needed to be cut by about 10 percent for fiscal 1996 in order to meet the strict economic guidelines for joining the European monetary union in 1999. But the People's Party demanded deep cuts in the country's welfare system. The Social Democrats refused such cuts and argued instead for higher taxes and the sale of state-owned companies.

The collapse of the government triggered an election nearly three years early, on Dec. 17, 1995. In the election, the Social Democrats won about 38 percent of the vote. The Freedom Party, led by Jörg Haider, garnered just 22 percent. President Thomas Klestil asked Vranitzky to form a new government, and the chancellor was expected to renew the coalition with the People's Party, an alliance that had governed Austria since 1986.

EU popularity slides. Surveys showed a sharp reversal in public opinion toward the EU in 1995, with fewer than 40 percent of Austrians expressing

People hold candles during a memorial vigil near Vienna, Austria, for four Gypsies killed in February by a bomb allegedly planted by neo-Nazis.

support for membership, down from 66 percent in 1994. The chief reason for the decline in support was the failure of prices for food and consumer goods to fall as much as EU supporters had predicted.

Roman Catholic controversy. In March 1995, a former schoolboy accused Hans Hermann Cardinal Groer, archbishop of Vienna, of molesting him 20 years earlier. The allegation shook many Austrians' confidence in the Roman Catholic Church, and thousands of members quit the church. About half of the country's 1 million regular Catholic churchgoers signed a petition in July demanding reforms. Groer retired in September.

Fund for Nazi victims. The government voted on June 2 to create a $50-million fund to compensate Austrian victims of Nazi persecution during World War II or their families. Those to be compensated included some 200,000 Jews who perished in concentration camps or fled abroad.

Letter bombs. The Austrian police were criticized for incompetence after two neo-Nazi activists were acquitted on December 21 of involvement in a series of letter bombs that had killed four people and injured more than a dozen others since December 1993. Two more bombs went off on Oct. 16, 1995, injuring a doctor and a 71-year-old woman who helped political refugees.   □ Tom Buerkle

See also **Europe** (Facts in brief table). In *World Book,* see **Austria; European Union.**

Automobile. Analysts had expected American automobile sales in 1995 to continue the strong momentum of 1994 and predicted near-record sales of 16 million vehicles. But their forecasts were far too optimistic. After a disastrous start, sales of cars and light trucks recovered in the second half of 1995 to reach an estimated 14.8 million units. Automakers increased rebates and provided more attractive lease incentives to lure customers to showrooms. They tried to put the best face on the disappointing sales figures, saying that sales of nearly 15 million vehicles represented a decent year and were preferable to the industry's usual boom-or-bust cycle.

Company officials attributed slow sales to rising interest rates in early 1995 and fears of a recession. Declining interest rates later in 1995 sparked the sales recovery, they said. But some analysts reported that rising vehicle costs had put a new car or truck out of the reach of many Americans. The National Automobile Dealers Association said that 26.7 weeks of median family income were needed to buy an average-priced new vehicle in 1995, compared with 24 weeks in 1991. However, automakers expected sales to improve by 1 to 2 percent in 1996 due to declining interest rates and a strong economy.

Big Three hold market share. The Big Three automakers—General Motors Corporation (GM), Ford Motor Company, and Chrysler Corporation—took 73 percent of the American light-vehicle mar-

ket in 1995, the same percentage they held in 1994. But financial results of the three companies for the first nine months of 1995 were mixed. Chrysler's net earnings were $1.1 billion, compared with $2.5 billion for the same period in 1994. The company attributed lower earnings to the expenses of retooling a plant and repairing minivan rear latches. Ford earned $3.5 billion for the first nine months of 1995, compared with $3.7 billion for the same period in 1994. Company officials said the drop in earnings was due to slow sales in Europe, start-up costs for new models, and higher vehicle incentives. Ford was in the midst of an ambitious plan to launch new versions of the Ford Escort and F-series trucks in 1996.

GM, however, continued its financial turnaround, posting a net income of $5 billion for the first nine months of 1995, compared with $3.3 billion in 1994. Profits would have been greater, GM executives said, had the company not experienced delays with launching new cars.

Trade dispute. Unproductive trade talks between the United States and Japan in 1995 led the Administration of President Bill Clinton to threaten to apply 100 percent import duties on Japanese luxury cars. Automobiles and automobile parts accounted for more than half of the U.S.-Japan trade deficit and the Clinton Administration had pledged to boost American auto exports to Japan. U.S. automakers and auto parts suppliers supported the President, claiming that Japanese trade and business practices had shut them out of the Japanese market. The Japanese government responded that it was open to U.S. competition and pointed out that U.S. companies produced few right-hand-drive vehicles for the Japanese market. Some economists feared the threatened $5.9 billion in tariffs would cause a full-scale trade war.

U.S. trade representative Mickey Kantor met with Japanese trade representative Ryutaro Hashimoto in Geneva, Switzerland, in June. The two reached an agreement under which the Japanese government would encourage Japanese auto dealers to sell more American cars and auto parts. The Clinton Administration praised the pact as a step toward increasing exports to Japan. Some observers, however, called the agreement's wording vague and wondered if Japanese consumers would buy American-made cars. Domestic automakers said they hoped to increase sales of American automobiles in Japan to 300,000—compared with 38,000 in 1994—by the end of the 1990's.

Truck sales increase. Strong demand continued in the United States for sport utility vehicles and light trucks, such as the Ford Explorer, Chevrolet Blazer, and Dodge Ram pickup. Trucks accounted for 41 percent of light-vehicle sales in 1995, compared with 34 percent in 1991. Automakers added features to make trucks feel and handle more like cars.

Ford boosted Explorer output and GM increased

Blazer production for 1995 sales. GM also planned to stop making large rear-wheel-drive cars at its Arlington, Texas, plant. The company expected to switch the facility to building light trucks at the end of the 1996 model year.

Japanese automakers in 1995 continued to be hurt by the high yen, which made Japanese imports more expensive in the United States. Japan lost 0.05 percent of its share of the U.S. market, while European companies gained 0.05 percent.

To avoid problems created by the yen, Japanese automakers increased production in the United States in order to limit imports. Honda boosted production of its popular Civic and Accord models at assembly plants in Ohio and planned to sell an Ohio-produced Acura luxury model in 1996. And Nissan planned to build a $30-million engine facility in Tennessee as part of its assembly operations there.

Chrysler takeover attempt. In April 1995, billionaire Kirk Kerkorian, with the assistance of retired Chrysler chairman Lee Iacocca, announced plans for a $22.8-billion buyout of the Chrysler Corporation, asserting that Chrysler shareholders were not getting their money's worth. Chrysler resisted the takeover, which failed due to lack of financing and shareholder interest. But Kerkorian's associates kept the possibility of a takeover alive.

New models. Motorists saw several new models in 1995. Ford perhaps took the biggest risk, with the Taurus, the most popular car in the country, and its "sister" vehicle, the Mercury Sable. Ford changed the cars' "jellybean" shape to a more radical, elliptical look. GM's Saturn received a more modest facelift, with engineers concentrating on making the small car quieter. Chrysler gave its minivan a sleeker look and easier-to-remove seats. By 1995, the company had sold 5 million of the minivans, which were introduced in 1983. And the Honda Civic was given a more aerodynamic appearance, a more powerful engine, and better fuel economy in 1995.

Labor issues. Stephen P. Yokich was elected president of the United Automobile Workers (UAW) to replace Owen Bieber, who retired in 1995. The 800,000-member union represents workers at GM, Ford, and Chrysler, as well as employees in other auto-related industries. Yokich pledged to increase organizing efforts for the union, which has lost 700,000 members since 1979. The UAW planned to organize workers at nonunion Japanese and German auto plants in the United States and in several other industries.

Recalls. A National Highway Traffic Safety Administration investigation led in 1995 to the recall of 8.8 million vehicles made by 11 auto companies, due to defects in a Japanese supplier's seat belts. Investigators found that the belts deteriorated with age and had caused 90 injuries, but no deaths.

□ Mike Casey

In *World Book,* see **Automobile.**

Automobile racing. Controversy struck the world's richest auto race, the Indianapolis 500, in 1995, allowing one Canadian driver, Jacques Villeneuve, to win and collect the $8,063,000 prize at the expense of another, Scott Goodyear. Controversy also threatened to strip the 1996 race of most of the major drivers and owners.

The surprises started when car owner Roger Penske, who had won the race 10 times and the starting pole 11 times in 27 years, failed to qualify any of his three cars for the field of 33.

The 500-mile (800-kilometer), 200-lap race was run on May 28 at the Indianapolis Motor Speedway in Indianapolis. On an early lap, Villeneuve received a black penalty flag because, as the race leader, he did not get behind the pace car when a yellow caution flag came out after an accident. He was penalized two laps, which meant he had to drive an extra 5 miles (8 kilometers).

Villeneuve patiently made up ground. Meanwhile, Goodyear was leading on the 196th lap when another yellow flag came out. Race officials said Goodyear ignored it and failed to make a mandatory pit stop, for which they stopped scoring his laps. That put the 24-year-old Villeneuve, in only his second Indy 500, in the lead again, and he won by 2.481 seconds. Goodyear placed 14th.

IndyCar. The Indianapolis 500 was the showcase of the IndyCar circuit. Villeneuve and Al Unser, Jr., each won 4 of the 17 oval and road races, and Villeneuve won the series title with 172 points to Unser's 161.

But a new racing league threatened the IndyCar circuit in 1995. In March 1994, Indianapolis Motor Speedway president Tony George founded the Indy Racing League, an alternative organization that planned to launch a circuit of five oval-track races in 1996. The 500 was to be the third of the five races.

Most car owners, while planning to stay with IndyCar, had also been planning to enter the 500. However, they became angry when George said that 25 of the 33 starting spots in the race would be reserved for cars from the new circuit, meaning that only 8 spots would remain for IndyCar regulars. To retaliate, IndyCar owners said in December 1995 that they woud run a race of their own in Michigan on the same day as the 1996 Indianapolis 500.

NASCAR. Jeff Gordon of Pittsboro, Indiana, only 24 years old, dominated the National Association for Stock Car Racing's Winston Cup series for late-model sedans. Including a season-ending bonus of $1.3 million, he earned $4.3 million for the year, a record for the sport.

Gordon won the driving title with 4,614 points to 4,580 for Dale Earnhardt of Kannapolis, North Carolina. Each drove a Chevrolet Monte Carlo. Of the 32 races, Gordon won seven and Earnhardt five.

Of the two richest races in NASCAR history, Earnhardt won one and almost the other. In the $3.2-mil-

Automobile racing

lion Daytona 500 on Feb. 19, 1995, in Daytona Beach, Florida, Sterling Marlin, in a Chevrolet, defeated Earnhardt by six car lengths. Earnhardt won the $4.5-million Brickyard 400 on August 5 in Indianapolis. In September, Ernie Irvan, injured so badly in a crash 13 months before that he was given only a 10 percent chance to survive, returned to racing.

Other races. Michael Schumacher of Germany won the Formula One international series for the second straight year. He compiled 102 points, to 69 for Damon Hill of the United Kingdom. Schumacher, in his Benetton-Renault, won 9 of the 17 races.

In endurance racing, a McLaren BMW F1 GTR won the world's leading race, the 24 Hours of Le Mans June 17 and 18 in France. America's most important race for these cars was the 24 Hours of Daytona on February 4 and 5 in Daytona Beach, Florida. The winner was a prototype Porsche Spyder K8, but more attention went to a less-powerful Ford Mustang Cobra that finished first in its class and third overall because one of its four alternating drivers was Paul Newman, the 70-year-old actor.

The season champions in the National Hot Rod Association's 19-race series included Scott Kalitta in the top-fuel class for the second consecutive year, John Force in funny cars for the fifth time in six years, and Warren Johnson in pro stock for the third time.   □ Frank Litsky

In *World Book,* see **Automobile racing.**

Aviation. Denver International Airport, located 23 miles (37 kilometers) northeast of downtown Denver, opened for business on Feb. 28, 1995. The 53-square-mile (137-square-kilometer) airport's opening came amid complaints about cost overruns and delays due to a malfunctioning automated baggage system. The facility replaced Stapleton International Airport and became the first new airport built in the United States since the 1970's.

Air traffic control problems. The Federal Aviation Administration (FAA) continued with plans to reorganize air traffic control (ATC) services in the United States into a federally owned corporation that derives revenues from user fees. ATC services were still funded by the U.S. Department of Transportation in 1995. The change would help free the ATC system of government restrictions that had impeded the purchase of new equipment at ATC centers.

The need for new ATC equipment in the United States was highlighted in 1995 by a series of failures of the 30-year-old computer system at the ATC center in Aurora, Illinois, which controls air traffic for Chicago's O'Hare International and Midway airports. FAA officials said Aurora was scheduled to receive a new main computer in 1997.

In June 1995, the ATC centers in Denver, Seattle, and Salt Lake City, Utah, received digital communications equipment that replaced equipment using

Driver Stan Fox's car breaks apart in a crash at the Indianapolis 500 in May that left him seriously injured. Jacques Villeneuve of Canada won the race.

The $4.9-billion Denver International Airport opened for business in February.
Its multipeaked roofline was designed to evoke the nearby Rocky Mountains.

outdated vacuum-tube technology. The upgrade at the three ATC centers was part of a $5.4-billion program to phase out vacuum-tube technology in air-traffic control by the year 2000.

The federal government also announced in April 1995 that the 21 busiest U.S. airports would start to receive ground radar to help controllers keep track of taxiing aircraft and prevent runway collisions. That decision was prompted by the collision in November 1994 of a jet airliner with a small, taxiing private plane at Lambert-St. Louis International Airport in St. Louis, Missouri.

Economic ups . . . The aviation industry showed signs in 1995 of coming out of the economic slump of the early 1990's. In October, the International Air Transport Association reported that the world's airlines would post a $5.7-billion profit in 1995 compared with a loss of $15.6 billion from 1990 to 1993.

. . . And downs. Not all carriers saw improved finances in 1995. Trans World Airlines (TWA) of St. Louis filed for Chapter 11 bankruptcy protection on June 30 for the second time in four years. It re-emerged on August 23 with rescheduled debts and a new marketing campaign. Also, the FAA grounded in March and August two of the industry's low-cost competitors—Arrow Air of Miami, Florida, and Mark Air of Denver—for not maintaining all of their aircraft according to FAA standards.

USAir for sale? In late 1995, USAir Group Incorporated of Arlington, Virginia, unsuccessfully tried to negotiate an alliance or a merger with one of the nation's two largest airlines—Chicago-based United Airlines and American Airlines of Fort Worth, Texas. The news came after reports in early 1995 that USAir was in dire financial straits.

Reducing travel agent commissions. On February 10, several major airlines followed the lead of Delta Air Lines of Atlanta, Georgia, and reduced the commission paid to travel agents for making airline reservations. The companies all lowered the maximum commission to $50 per domestic ticket. Despite considerable opposition by travel agents, only TWA broke ranks—on May 9, it restored the 10 percent commission on all tickets.

Ticketless travel. In September, United made available ticketless travel on all domestic flights. The new system allowed passengers to make reservations over the telephone and then just show a photo identification at the boarding gate to receive a boarding pass for the airplane. The system had been successfully used by United's West Coast operations and by Dallas-based Southwest Airlines.

International travel liberalization. The United States sought greater access to markets in Canada and Europe in 1995. In February, the United States and Canada signed a bilateral treaty that greatly expanded air service between the two countries, in-

71

cluding more nonstop flights, better service to small Canadian cities, and more frequent flights.

The United States also in 1995 made "open skies" agreements with several European countries. The agreements would eliminate quotas on air service and give U.S. carriers the right to fly passengers to additional cities in Europe. In return, the European airlines would acquire similar rights in the United States. Controversy about the agreements arose within the European Union (EU) because some EU member nations had acted on their own in negotiating with the United States rather than taking part in a continent-wide effort.

New aircraft. On June 7, United Airlines introduced the Boeing 777 into service on transatlantic and Chicago-Denver routes. The airliner, which was equipped with the latest electronic cockpit controls, was the world's largest twin-engine jet. The 777 also featured a twin-aisle passenger cabin designed to promote a feeling of spaciousness, expanded overhead baggage storage, larger bathrooms with changing tables for infants, and color-display terminals for video and computer games built into the back of each seat.

Accident investigation. The French-Italian aircraft makers ATR (Avion de Transport Régional) redesigned the anti-icing equipment on the wings of their commuter aircraft after ice buildup was found to be the cause of the fatal crash of an ATR commuter flight in Indiana in October 1994. The FAA had banned flight of the aircraft when icy conditions were present.

No cause had been identified in 1995 for the fatal crash of USAir flight 427 in Pennsylvania in September 1994. Despite much speculation concerning a malfunctioning rudder on the plane—a Boeing 737—no evidence of mechanical problems had been found. In September 1995, tests were conducted to find out whether wake turbulence from a Boeing 727 that flew about 4 miles (6.4 kilometers) ahead of the ill-fated aircraft might have caused the USAir jet to spin out of control.

Airline privatization. The global trend to privatize national airlines continued in 1995. In July, the Australian government sold its 75 percent in Qantas Airways. The remaining 25 percent continued to be owned by British Airways PLC. Some Australians expressed concern after the stock sale that over 50 percent of the airline was owned by non-Australians.

On July 25, Swissair purchased 49.5 percent of Belgium's Sabena Belgian World Airlines. Although the airlines were to continue using their own names, the integration of aircraft maintenance and various airline services was expected to bring considerable savings. The German government also announced plans in 1995 to reduce its holding in its national carrier, Lufthansa German Airlines, from 50 percent to 20 percent. □ Ian Savage

In *World Book,* see **Aviation.**

Azerbaijan. Azerbaijan's President Heydar A. Aliyev survived a coup attempt in March 1995. Insurgents led by Deputy Interior Minister Rovshan Dzhavadov clashed for several days with government forces in the capital, Baku, before being put down on March 17. Hundreds of alleged conspirators were arrested.

On November 12, Aliyev's New Azerbaijan party won a decisive majority of 125 seats in parliament. European observers said the election was marked by "clear cases of fraud."

During the year, a September 1994 multinational agreement to develop the Azeri oil fields, which lie beneath the Caspian Sea, was a matter of contention with Russia. Under a compromise reached in October 1995, oil from the fields will flow through two pipelines, one through Georgia and the other through Russia.

A cease-fire in the war with Armenia over the the disputed ethnic Armenian enclave of Nagorno-Karabakh continued in 1995. Peace talks in Moscow made little progress.

On October 28, more than 300 people died when a fire swept through a five-car train in a subway in Baku. Investigators said the fire was caused by an electrical malfunction. □ Steven L. Solnick

See also **Armenia; Asia** (Facts in brief table). In *World Book,* see **Azerbaijan.**

Bahamas. See **West Indies.**

Bahrain. Violent prodemocracy demonstrations near Bahrain's capital, Manama, killed at least 10 civilians and 3 policemen in early 1995. The ruling Al Khalifa family, Arab sheiks of the small Persian Gulf island nation, blamed the violence on "infiltrators" spreading Iran's Islamic revolutionary ideology. The Al Khalifas are Sunni Muslims, but at least 60 percent of Bahrain's people belong to the Shiah sect, which is also the dominant sect in Iran.

In June, a reshuffling of the 16-member cabinet increased Shiite members from two to five. But the change helped little since influential Sunni members remained. In spite of secret talks between the Al Khalifa family and opposition groups in late summer, many people remained jailed for political dissent. Bahrain also expelled several leading Shiite clerics in 1995 and arrested others. The unrest started in December 1994 after a large number of Bahrainis—Sunni as well as Shiah—signed a petition calling for the restoration of the national parliament, which the ruling family dissolved in 1975. Bahrainis also complained that the government had failed to find more jobs for its citizens. At least 130,000 foreigners worked in Bahrain, though Bahrainis numbered only about 578,000. Shiites have been barred from serving in the police or military. □ Christine Helms

See also **Middle East** (Facts in brief table). In *World Book,* see **Bahrain.**

Ballet. See **Dancing.**

Bangladesh suffered political turmoil throughout 1995. Repeated general strikes sparked violence, caused economic disruptions, and discouraged foreign investment needed for economic progress.

The strikes throughout the year were organized by the Awami League (AL), a major opposition party in coalition with two smaller political parties. AL leader Hasina Wajed, with the support of her coalition parties, demanded that Prime Minister Khaleda Ziaur Rahman (known as Zia) resign immediately and let the Supreme Court's chief justice organize new parliamentary elections.

In 1994, Zia, who led her Bangladesh Nationalist Party (BNP) to victory in 1991 elections, said that rather than step down immediately she would do so 30 days before the next elections. But Hasina would not accept that compromise. Her rejection was widely viewed as showing a desire for power without offering any new policies.

Political maneuvers and strikes. In an attempt to bring pressure on Zia, 142 opposition members of Parliament resigned in December 1994. The resignations were initially rejected on a technicality, but on Aug. 6, 1995, all 142 seats were declared vacant because the members had failed to attend sessions.

On November 24, Parliament was dissolved, and new parliamentary elections were scheduled for Feb. 7, 1996. However, Hasina continued to call for strikes.

Two general strikes disrupted Bangladesh in September. Both led to clashes between police and opposition demonstrators who were trying to enforce a complete shutdown of all urban activity. Hundreds of people were injured in the violence, and several people were reportedly killed.

Economic activity suffered from the strikes, costing Hasina support in the business community. But Zia came in for her own share of criticism. Early in the year she had been given credit for reducing inflation, increasing exports, and building up foreign exchange reserves. By midyear, however, a combination of political disruption, drought, and floods increased grain prices. Moreover, both domestic and foreign investment, needed to improve living conditions, were below expectations.

The government was also blamed for a fertilizer shortage in early 1995. Bangladesh normally produces more fertilizer than it needs and exports some, but official bungling led to excessive exports. As a result, rice crops in Bangladesh were below normal and farmers' incomes suffered.

The worst floods since 1988 inundated the area around the capital, Dhaka, in July. They affected some 15 million people, destroyed nearly 70,000 homes, and caused more than 200 deaths. Many of those deaths resulted from bites of poisonous snakes fleeing the floods. □ Henry S. Bradsher

See also **Asia** (Facts in brief table). In *World Book,* see **Bangladesh.**

Bank. Some of the nation's oldest banks announced mergers in 1995. In June, First Union Corporation of Charlotte, North Carolina, announced that it would acquire First Fidelity Bancorp of Newark, New Jersey, for $5.4 billion. In July, PNC Corporation of Pittsburgh, Pennsylvania, said it would acquire Midlantic Bank Corporation of Edison, New Jersey, for $3 billion, and First Chicago Corporation and NBD Bancorp of Detroit announced that they had agreed to a merger valued at about $5 billion. The latter would create an organization called First Chicago NBD Corporation. And in August came the news of the largest bank merger in United States history: Chemical Bank Corporation announced that it would acquire Chase Manhattan Corporation for $10 billion. The combined bank would retain the Chase Manhattan name and would form the nation's largest bank, with assets of $297 billion.

Industry analysts said the wave of mergers was related to the industry's drive to make more banking services and products available through electronic banking systems operated via the telephone lines. Many of the nation's banks believed that by merging, they would be in a better financial position to make the large investments necessary to convert to electronic systems. Though few of the nation's bank customers managed their money by electronic banking in 1995, many experts believed that most retail banking services and such products as loans would soon be available through electronic banking. Experts said that the familiar branch banking system, where customers conduct business at teller windows, would eventually become obsolete.

Another factor that contributed to the acquisition fever of 1995 was the robust health of the industry. In the first half of the year, the nation's 10,168 banks earned record profits of $23.2 billion, more than $930 million higher than the profits earned at the same time in 1994. And the nation's 2,081 savings and loans (S&L's) in mid-1995 posted earnings of about $3.6 billion. The high earnings drove up the value of bank and thrift stocks and gave financial institutions the buying power to make large acquisitions.

Economic health. The Federal Reserve Board kept interest rates steady in 1995, apparently satisfied that inflation was in check. The federal funds rate, which is the interest rate that member banks of the Federal Reserve charge each other for short-term loans, remained between 5.5 and 6 percent for most of the year.

RTC closes shop. One of the worst chapters in banking history drew to a close in late 1995 as the Resolution Trust Corporation (RTC), the federal agency formed to sell the assets of failed savings and loans, wound up its operations one year ahead of schedule. The government agency was established in 1989 after more than 1,000 thrifts failed as a result of poor government regulation of the industry, mismanagement and fraud, and competition from other types of financial institutions. The widespread failure of savings and loans bankrupted the Federal Savings and Loan Insurance Corporation (FSLIC), the fund that insured deposits in savings and loans. In 1989, Congress dissolved the FSLIC, gave responsibility for insuring savings and loans to the Federal Deposit Insurance Corporation (FDIC), and created the RTC as part of the FDIC.

By the time the RTC closed its doors, it had taken control of $450 billion in assets, including loans, mortgages, real estate, and securities, from 747 savings and loans. It sold them to investors for $359 billion. The difference—about $90 billion plus interest—was made up with taxpayer dollars by the U.S. Department of the Treasury. At the end of 1995, about $8 billion worth of assets that had not been sold were folded into the FDIC.

S&L owners win appeal. On August 30, a U. S. Circuit Court of Appeals ruled 9-2 that federal regulators had reneged on promises to help some struggling savings and loans in the 1980's. The promises were part of a federal plan to salvage failed S&L's in the 1980's that predated the 1989 bailout.

Regulators at the FSLIC in the late 1980's had encouraged healthy thrifts to purchase failed S&L's by promising that if they bought the money-losing S&L's, they could use special accounting rules that made them appear more profitable. But in 1989, Congress passed the Financial Institutions Reform, Recovery and Enforcement Act, which wiped out the special accounting rules. The rules allowed them to inflate their net worth with such noncash items as the perceived value of their franchise. Many of the S&L's that had acquired the failed thrifts under the FSLIC promise were then declared insolvent and seized by the government. The court ruling in August could make the government liable to thrifts for as much as $20 billion for reneging on promises.

Derivatives scandal. Another scandal hit the banking world in October 1995 when, in documents of taped conversations made public for the first time, employees at Bankers Trust New York Corporation, one of the most powerful and profitable banks in the world, talked about using deceptive sales practices to market derivatives. Derivatives are high-risk bonds that pay interest rates based on the performance of interest rates overseas, currency fluctuations, and other financial changes.

In a lawsuit filed in 1994, consumer products giant Procter & Gamble Company (P&G) of Cincinnati, Ohio, accused Bankers Trust of fraud. P&G claimed that it was misled when Bankers Trust, one of the most powerful and profitable banks in the world, sold it complex derivatives that eventually caused P&G to lose $195.5 million. The case took a twist in October 1995 when court documents revealed taped conversations of Bankers Trust employees, in which the employees discussed deceptive practices. The

employees indicated that the derivatives were so complex that customers did not understand what they were buying. If P&G were to win its lawsuit in federal court, it would stand to to regain the millions it lost on its derivative investments.

Community Reinvestment Act revised. Bankers continued to battle federal regulators in 1995 over how much banks should lend to poorer consumers in the wake of government studies showing that it is easier for whites to get mortgages than minorities of similar income levels.

In the spring of 1995, federal regulators unveiled new regulations for the Community Reinvestment Act, which was instituted in 1977 to ensure that a bank met the credit needs of its community before it was allowed to open a new branch or merge with another bank. The aim of the new guidelines, which were less rigorous than the original, was to reduce the amount of paperwork for banks. The new regulations were scheduled to take effect Jan. 1, 1996.

Glass-Steagall Act. Many bankers in 1995 believed that the Glass-Steagall Banking Act of 1933, which created barriers between commercial and investment banking, would fall. But the legislation in Congress stalled in November, primarily due to a dispute over whether banks would be allowed to merge with insurance companies.

☐ Paulette Thomas

In *World Book,* see **Bank.**

Baseball. Despite all its positives—marvelous regular seasons for the Cleveland Indians and the Atlanta Braves, a World Series win for the Braves, and Cal Ripken, Jr.'s besting of a supposedly unbreakable record—the 1995 baseball season was almost a disaster.

The season started late, and it started only because a federal judge ended the longest strike in major professional sports history, effectively preventing a threatened lockout by the owners. At year's end, there was still no collective-bargaining agreement. Fan interest diminished, attendance was down, and television ratings fell.

Strike. The 234-day strike began on Aug. 12, 1994, when major-league players refused to accept a team salary cap, thus spoiling the club owners' plan for richer clubs to share some revenues with poorer clubs. The strike wiped out the last 52 days of the 1994 regular season and the 1994 World Series, which had been played every year since 1905.

The owners sought a salary cap of 50 percent of their revenue. When the players resisted, the owners tried to control large salaries by proposing a luxury tax on teams with high payrolls, with the tax money to be given largely to teams with lower payrolls. When the players resisted the tax as well, the owners planned to start the season with replacement players. United States President Bill Clinton and his labor mediator, William Usery, Jr., intervened with limited success. Finally, on March 31, 1995, federal judge Sonia Sotomayor issued an injunction barring the owners from unilaterally eliminating such practices as salary arbitration and individual contract bargaining.

The players offered to return to work while still negotiating a new agreement. On April 2, the owners abandoned their plan to use replacement players and agreed to let the players return and the season begin. On April 25, the season started, 23 days later than scheduled, with each team playing 144 games rather than 162. No further meaningful negotiations took place until November.

The season. This was the first year of expanded play-offs. Each league was split into three divisions, with the division winners and the second-place team with the best record advancing to the play-offs.

In the National League, Atlanta won the Eastern Division by 21 games; the Cincinnati Reds, the Central Division by 9 games; and the Los Angeles Dodgers, the Western Division by 1 game over the Colorado Rockies. Colorado became the wild-card team.

In the first round of the play-offs, Atlanta eliminated Colorado, 3 games to 1, while Cincinnati beat Los Angeles, 3 games to 0. In the league championship series, Atlanta routed Cincinnati, 4 games to 0.

The American League's division winners were Cleveland by the huge margin of 30 games in the Central Division, and the Boston Red Sox by 7 games

Final standings in major league baseball

American League

Eastern Division

	W.	L.	Pct.	G.B.
Boston Red Sox	86	58	.597	
New York Yankees*	79	65	.549	7
Baltimore Orioles	71	73	.493	15
Detroit Tigers	60	84	.417	26
Toronto Blue Jays	56	88	.389	30

Central Division

	W.	L.	Pct.	G.B.
Cleveland Indians	100	44	.694	
Kansas City Royals	70	74	.486	30
Chicago White Sox	68	76	.472	32
Milwaukee Brewers	65	79	.451	35
Minnesota Twins	56	88	.389	44

Western Division

	W.	L.	Pct.	G.B.
Seattle Mariners	79	66	.545	
California Angels	78	67	.538	1
Texas Rangers	74	70	.514	4½
Oakland Athletics	67	77	.465	11½

American League champions—Cleveland Indians (defeated the Mariners, 4 games to 2)

World Series champions—Atlanta Braves (defeated the Indians, 4 games to 2)

Offensive leaders

Batting average—Edgar Martinez, Seattle	.356
Runs scored—Albert Belle, Cleveland	121
Home runs—Albert Belle, Cleveland	50
Runs batted in—Albert Belle, Cleveland; Mo Vaughn, Boston (tie)	126
Hits—Lance Johnson, Chicago	186
Stolen bases—Kenny Lofton, Cleveland	54
Slugging percentage—Albert Belle, Cleveland	.690

Leading pitchers

Games won—Mike Mussina, Baltimore	19
Win average (15 decisions or more)—Randy Johnson, Seattle (18-2)	.900
Earned run average (144 or more innings)— Randy Johnson, Seattle	2.48
Strikeouts—Randy Johnson, Seattle	294
Saves—José Mesa, Cleveland	46
Shut-outs—Mike Mussina, Baltimore	4

Awards[†]

Most Valuable Player—Mo Vaughn, Boston
Cy Young—Randy Johnson, Seattle
Rookie of the Year—Marty Cordova, Minnesota
Manager of the Year—Lou Piniella, Seattle

National League

Eastern Division

	W.	L.	Pct.	G.B.
Atlanta Braves	90	54	.625	
New York Mets	69	75	.479	21
Philadelphia Phillies	69	75	.479	21
Florida Marlins	67	76	.469	22½
Montreal Expos	66	78	.458	24

Central Division

	W.	L.	Pct.	G.B.
Cincinnati Reds	85	59	.590	
Houston Astros	76	68	.528	9
Chicago Cubs	73	71	.507	12
St. Louis Cardinals	62	81	.434	22½
Pittsburgh Pirates	58	86	.403	27

Western Division

	W.	L.	Pct.	G.B.
Los Angeles Dodgers	78	66	.542	
Colorado Rockies*	77	67	.535	1
San Diego Padres	70	74	.486	8
San Francisco Giants	67	77	.465	11

National League champions—Atlanta Braves (defeated the Reds, 4 games to 0)

Offensive leaders

Batting average—Tony Gwynn, San Diego	.368
Runs scored—Craig Biggio, Houston	123
Home runs—Dante Bichette, Colorado	40
Runs batted in—Dante Bichette, Colorado	128
Hits—Dante Bichette, Colorado	197
Stolen bases—Quilvio Veras, Florida	56
Slugging percentage—Dante Bichette, Colorado	.620

Leading pitchers

Games won—Greg Maddux, Atlanta	19
Win average (15 decisions or more)—Greg Maddux, Atlanta, (19-2)	.905
Earned run average (144 or more innings)— Greg Maddux, Atlanta	1.63
Strikeouts—Hideo Nomo, Los Angeles	236
Saves—Randy Myers, Chicago	38
Shut-outs—Hideo Nomo, Los Angeles; Greg Maddux, Atlanta (tie)	3

Awards[†]

Most Valuable Player—Barry Larkin, Cincinnati
Cy Young—Greg Maddux, Atlanta
Rookie of the Year—Hideo Nomo, Los Angeles
Manager of the Year—Don Baylor, Colorado

*Qualified for wild-card play-off spot.
[†]Selected by the Baseball Writers Association of America.

Baseball

over the New York Yankees in the Eastern Division. The Yankees won the wild-card play-off spot. The Seattle Mariners and the California Angels tied for the Western Division title, and in a one-game play-off on October 2 in Seattle, the Mariners won, 9-1, on Randy Johnson's three-hit pitching.

In the American League play-offs, Cleveland blanked Boston, 3 games to 0, and Seattle won the last three games to defeat the Yankees, 3 games to 2. In the championship series, Cleveland beat Seattle, 4 games to 2.

World Series. The opponents in the World Series were Cleveland (100-44) and Atlanta (90-54), the teams with the year's best records. Atlanta combined pitching, power, defense, and experience. Cleveland, in its first World Series in 41 years, led the major leagues in batting, home runs, and scoring and had a veteran pitching staff.

The Series ran from October 21 to 28. The Braves won, 4 games to 2, earning their first World Series title since 1957, when the team was based in Milwaukee, Wisconsin. Atlanta won the last game, 1-0, on David Justice's home run and Tommy Glavine's one-hit pitching over eight innings. Glavine, with a 2-0 record and a 1.29 earned-run average in the World Series, was voted the Most Valuable Player.

Stars. From 1925 to 1939, until he was stopped by the illness that came to bear his name, the Yankees' first baseman, Lou Gehrig, played in 2,130 con-

secutive games. On Sept. 6, 1995, in a streak that began 13½ seasons earlier, Ripken, the 35-year-old shortstop of the Baltimore Orioles, broke the record. At season's end, his streak had reached 2,153. The next longest current streak was 259 games by Frank Thomas of the Chicago White Sox.

The Cy Young Awards for best pitching went to Greg Maddux of Atlanta for the fourth consecutive year in the National League and Johnson of Seattle in the American. Maddux led the major leagues in won-lost record (19-2), earned-run average (1.63), and complete games (10). Johnson led the American League in won-lost record (18-2), earned-run average (2.48), and strikeouts (294).

Shortstop Barry Larkin of Cincinnati in the National League and first baseman Mo Vaughn of Boston in the American League won the Most Valuable Player awards. With a batting average of .319, 15 home runs, 66 runs batted in, and 51 stolen bases, Larkin edged out outfielder Dante Bichette of Colorado (128 runs batted in, 40 home runs, .620 slugging percentage) and Maddux. Vaughn (39 home runs, 126 runs batted in) outpolled outfielder Albert Belle of Cleveland, who led the major leagues in home runs (50), total bases (377), and slugging percentage (.690).

Outfielder Tony Gwynn of the San Diego Padres (.368) won his sixth National League batting title. Los Angeles Dodgers rookie Hideo Nomo, a pitcher

David Justice of the Atlanta Braves hits the game-winning home run in the final game of the World Series in October as the Braves defeat the Cleveland Indians, 4 games to 2.

from Japan, struck out 236 batters and was voted National League Rookie of the Year.

On June 30, Eddie Murray, Cleveland's first baseman/designated hitter, became the 20th player to record 3,000 major-league hits. Manager George (Sparky) Anderson of the Detroit Tigers retired in October after 17 years with the Tigers and 9 with Cincinnati. Anderson's 2,194 victories were third all-time behind Connie Mack and John McGraw.

Other. On June 22, ABC and NBC quit the Baseball Network, a joint television venture with Major League Baseball that paid each team about $7 million in 1995. On November 6, NBC, Fox, and the cable networks ESPN and Liberty Media agreed to a $1.7-billion, five-year package that would pay each team $12 million in 1996.

In January 1995, third baseman Mike Schmidt, who hit 548 home runs for the Philadelphia Phillies between 1972 and 1989, was elected to the Baseball Hall of Fame. In March, the Hall of Fame veterans committee elected outfielder Richie Ashburn, pitchers Vic Willis and Leon Day, and the National League founder, William Hulbert.

In March 1995, the major leagues expanded to 30 teams by adding the Arizona Diamondbacks and the Tampa Bay Devil Rays. The teams were to begin play in 1998, but their leagues were not determined.

□ Frank Litsky

In *World Book,* see **Baseball.**

Basketball. The National Basketball Association (NBA), whose 1994-1995 season escaped the labor shutdowns that hurt major-league baseball and hockey, locked out its players after the season because of little progress toward a collective-bargaining agreement. Before the lockout, the Houston Rockets won their second consecutive championship. The UCLA men and the undefeated Connecticut (35-0) women were the college champions.

Professional. Uncertainties involving the National Basketball Players' Association—the players' union—created obstacles to labor peace in the NBA. On June 22, Michael Jordan, Patrick Ewing, Scottie Pippen, and 14 other players petitioned the National Labor Relations Board to decertify the players' union on grounds that it was not informing players adequately concerning negotiations with team owners over a new collective-bargaining agreement. Hours later, the NBA and the union agreed on a six-year contract. The owners approved the contract, but the union postponed a vote because many of its players, encouraged by agents who felt they would lose money with the new pact, had signed decertification petitions. The team owners responded by locking out the players on June 30.

There was a movement to decertify the union if a new collective-bargaining agreement was not reached by midnight August 8. An hour before that deadline, management and labor agreed on a con-

National Basketball Association standings

Eastern Conference

Atlantic Division	W.	L.	Pct.	G.B.
Orlando Magic*	57	25	.695	
New York Knicks*	55	27	.671	2
Boston Celtics*	35	47	.427	22
Miami Heat	32	50	.390	25
New Jersey Nets	30	52	.366	27
Philadelphia 76ers	24	58	.293	33
Washington Bullets	21	61	.256	36

Central Division				
Indiana Pacers*	52	30	.634	
Charlotte Hornets*	50	32	.610	2
Chicago Bulls*	47	35	.573	5
Cleveland Cavaliers*	43	39	.524	9
Atlanta Hawks*	42	40	.512	10
Milwaukee Bucks	34	48	.415	18
Detroit Pistons	28	54	.341	24

Western Conference

Midwest Division	W.	L.	Pct.	G.B.
San Antonio Spurs*	62	20	.756	
Utah Jazz*	60	22	.732	2
Houston Rockets*	47	35	.573	15
Denver Nuggets*	41	41	.500	21
Dallas Mavericks	36	46	.439	26
Minnesota Timberwolves	21	61	.256	41

Pacific Division				
Phoenix Suns*	59	23	.720	
Seattle SuperSonics*	57	25	.695	2
Los Angeles Lakers*	48	34	.585	11
Portland Trail Blazers*	44	38	.537	15
Sacramento Kings	39	43	.476	20
Golden State Warriors	26	56	.317	33
Los Angeles Clippers	17	65	.207	42

*Made play-offs.

NBA champions—Houston Rockets (defeated Orlando Magic, 4 games to 0)

Individual leaders

Scoring	G.	F.G.	F.T.	Pts.	Avg.
Shaquille O'Neal, Orlando	79	930	455	2,315	29.3
Hakeem Olajuwon, Houston	72	798	406	2,005	27.8
David Robinson, San Antonio	81	788	656	2,238	27.6
Karl Malone, Utah	82	830	516	2,187	26.7
Jamal Mashburn, Dallas	80	683	447	1,926	24.1
Patrick Ewing, New York	79	730	420	1,886	23.9
Charles Barkley, Phoenix	68	554	379	1,561	23.0
Mitch Richmond, Sacramento	82	668	375	1,867	22.8
Glenn Rice, Miami	82	667	312	1,831	22.3
Glenn Robinson, Milwaukee	80	636	397	1,755	21.9

Rebounding	G.	Tot.	Avg.
Dennis Rodman, San Antonio	49	823	16.8
Dikembe Mutombo, Denver	82	1,029	12.5
Shaquille O'Neal, Orlando	79	901	11.4
Patrick Ewing, New York	79	867	11.0
Shawn Kemp, Seattle	82	893	10.9
Tyrone Hill, Cleveland	70	765	10.9

tract that eliminated the sore point among many players, a luxury tax on teams with high payrolls. The players voted on August 30 and September 7 to retain the union, and the new season began on schedule.

1994-1995 season. From November 1994 to April 1995, the 27 teams played 82 games each, with 16 teams advancing to the play-offs. The division champions were the San Antonio Spurs (62-20), the Phoenix Suns (59-23), the Orlando Magic (57-25), and the Indiana Pacers (52-30).

The 1994-1995 college basketball season

College tournament champions

NCAA	(Men)	Division I: UCLA
		Division II: Southern Indiana
		Division III: Wisconsin-Platteville
NCAA	(Women)	Division I: Connecticut
		Division II: North Dakota State
		Division III: Capital (Ohio)
NAIA	(Men)	Division I: Birmingham-Southern (Ala.)
		Division II: Bethel (Ind.)
	(Women)	Division I: Southern Nazarene (Okla.)
		Division II: Western Oregon
NIT	(Men)	Virginia Tech
Junior College	(Men)	Division I: Okaloosa-Walton (Fla.)
		Division II: North Iowa Area
		Division III: Sullivan County (N.Y.)
	(Women)	Division I: Westark (Ark.)
		Division II: Kankakee (Ill.)
		Division III: Rainy River (Minn.)

Men's college champions

Conference	School
American West	Southern Utah*
Atlantic Coast	Maryland—North Carolina—Virginia—Wake Forest (tie; reg. season)
	Wake Forest (tournament)
Atlantic Ten	Massachusetts*
Big East	Connecticut (reg. season)
	Villanova (tournament)
Big Eight	Kansas (reg. season)
	Oklahoma State (tournament)
Big Sky	Montana—Weber State (tie; reg. season)
	Weber State (tournament)
Big South	North Carolina-Greenville (reg. season)
	Charleston Southern (tournament)
Big Ten	Purdue (reg. season)
Big West	Utah State (reg. season)
	Long Beach State (tournament)
Colonial	Old Dominion*
Great Midwest	Memphis (reg. season)
	Cincinnati (tournament)
Ivy League	Pennsylvania (reg. season)
Metropolitan	North Carolina-Charlotte (reg. season)
	Louisville (tournament)
Metro Atlantic	Manhattan (reg. season)
	Saint Peter's (tournament)
Mid-American	Miami (Ohio) (reg. season)
	Ball State (tournament)
Mid-Continent	Valparaiso*
Mid-Eastern	Coppin State (reg. season)
	North Carolina A&T (tournament)
Midwestern	Xavier (Ohio) (reg. season)
	Wisconsin-Green Bay (tournament)
Missouri Valley	Tulsa (reg. season)
	Southern Illinois (tournament)
North Atlantic	Drexel*
Northeast	Rider (reg. season)
	Mount Saint Mary's (tournament)
Ohio Valley	Murray State—Tennessee State (tie; reg. season)
	Murray State (tournament)
Pacific Ten	UCLA (reg. season)
Patriot League	Bucknell—Colgate (tie; reg. season)
	Colgate (tournament)
Southeastern	Kentucky (tournament)
Eastern Division	Kentucky (reg. season)
Western Division	Arkansas—Mississippi State (tie; reg. season)
Southern	Tennessee-Chattanooga (tournament)
North Division	Marshall (reg. season)
South Division	Tennessee-Chattanooga (reg. season)
Southland	Nicholls State*
Southwest	Texas*
Southwestern	Texas Southern*
Sun Belt	Western Kentucky*
Trans America	Charleston (S. Caro.) (reg. season)
	Florida International (tournament)
West Coast	Santa Clara (reg. season)
	Gonzaga (tournament)
Western Athletic	Utah*

*Regular season and conference tournament champions.

UCLA's Ed O'Bannon puts up 2 of the 30 points he scored in the NCAA championship game that UCLA won over Arkansas in April.

Because Houston (47-35) finished sixth in the west, it seemed likely to be eliminated in the first round of the play-offs by the Utah Jazz, whose 60-22 record was the second best in the league. Instead, Houston eliminated Utah, 3 games to 2. The talented but undisciplined Seattle SuperSonics (57-25) lost in the first round for the second consecutive season, this time to the Los Angeles Lakers, 3 games to 1.

Houston upset three favorites—Utah after trailing by 2-1; Phoenix by 4-3 after trailing by 3-1; and San Antonio by 4-2. Yet Houston advanced to the final as underdogs.

Orlando had two 23-year-old stars in center Shaquille O'Neal and point guard Anfernee (Penny) Hardaway. But Houston had play-off experience and toughness and swept the finals in four games. Center Hakeem Olajuwon of Houston was voted the Most Valuable Player of the play-offs.

Center David Robinson of San Antonio, third in scoring (27.6 points per game) and seventh in rebounds (10.8 per game), was voted the NBA's regular-season Most Valuable Player. Del Harris of Los Angeles was the coach of the year. The all-star team comprised Karl Malone of Utah and Pippen of Chicago at forward, Robinson at center, and John Stockton of Utah and Hardaway at guard.

On March 9, 1995, Michael Jordan, one of basketball's most glamorous players, returned to the Chicago Bulls. In October 1993, Jordan had quit basketball to play minor-league baseball. Lenny Wilkens of the Atlanta Hawks broke Red Auerbach's NBA coaching record of 938 victories in January, and Stockton broke Earvin (Magic) Johnson's career record of 9,921 assists in February.

College men. Arkansas, Connecticut, Kansas, Massachusetts, North Carolina, and UCLA held the top ranking in the national polls at various times during the season. When the regular season ended, the Associated Press poll of writers and broadcasters ranked UCLA (25-2) first, Kentucky (25-4) second, Wake Forest (24-5) third, North Carolina (24-5) fourth, Kansas (23-5) fifth, and Arkansas (27-6) sixth.

In the National Collegiate Athletic Association's (NCAA) 64-team tournament, the regional winners were UCLA, North Carolina, Arkansas, and Oklahoma State (seeded only fourth in the East). They advanced to the Final Four April 1 and 3 in Seattle.

In the semifinals there, UCLA whipped Oklahoma State, 74-61, and Arkansas eliminated North Carolina, 75-68. That put Arkansas in position to win its second consecutive title, but UCLA won the championship game, 89-78. Power forward Ed O'Bannon had 30 points and 17 rebounds for UCLA and was voted the outstanding player in the Final Four.

O'Bannon, center Joe Smith of Maryland, and forward Jerry Stackhouse of North Carolina won various player-of-the-year awards. They made the AP All-America team with guards Shawn Respert of Michigan State and Damon Stoudamire of Arizona.

College women. Women's college basketball reached new heights in 1995. For the first time, there was a preseason National Invitational Tournament, the AP picked its first women's All-America team, and for the first time there were two national weekly polls involving major colleges. Attendance at major college games rose 9 percent to almost 4 million.

Poll leaders after the regular season were Connecticut (29-0), Colorado (27-2), Tennessee (29-2), Stanford (26-2), and Texas Tech (30-3). Connecticut was ranked number one for the second half of the season after a 77-66 victory over Tennessee. Connecticut won its regular-season games by an average of 33.2 points—the most among major colleges.

The Final Four began April 1 in Minneapolis, Minnesota, with Connecticut routing Stanford, 87-60, and Tennessee whipping Georgia, 73-51. In the championship game the next day, Connecticut trailed with less than two minutes remaining before rallying for a 70-64 victory. Its final record of 35-0 was the best ever for a men's or women's national champion.

Rebecca Lobo, Connecticut's 6-foot-4-inch (193-centimeter) forward/center, was voted the outstanding player in the Final Four. She was a unanimous choice as Player of the Year, and Geno Auriemma of Connecticut was voted Coach of the Year.

International. Ten NBA stars were named in July to the United States men's team for the 1996 Olympics in Atlanta, Georgia. They were Hakeem Olajuwon, Shaquille O'Neal, and David Robinson at center; Karl Malone, Scottie Pippen, Grant Hill, and Glenn Robinson at forward, and John Stockton, Anfernee (Penny) Hardaway, and Reggie Miller at guard. Two players were to be added in 1996. Lenny Wilkens was named coach. Eleven players, including Rebecca Lobo, Teresa Edwards, and Sheryl Swoopes, were named to the United States national team that will become the core of the Olympic women's team.

Yugoslavia defeated Lithuania, 96-90, on July 2, 1995, to win the European championship in Athens, Greece.   □ Frank Litsky

In *World Book*, see **Basketball.**

Belarus. On Jan. 6, 1995, Russia and Belarus agreed to form a customs union removing all trade barriers between them. The agreement put the two countries on the road to closer economic integration but was bitterly opposed by nationalists in Belarus, who claimed it threatened Belarussian sovereignty.

Belarussian President Alexander Lukashenko responded to the critics by putting Russia-Belarus relations to a national vote. On May 14, an overwhelming majority of voters ratified his policies, including making Russian the second official language of Belarus, pursuing closer economic integration with Russia, and restoring Soviet-era flags and symbols.

Belarussian ratification of the customs-union treaty was stalled by a stalemate between Lukashenko and the parliament. In the May election, low voter turnout resulted in only 86 of 260 parliamentary seats being filled. Because the new parliament lacked a quorum, the outgoing parliament refused to relinquish power and tried to limit the powers of the president.

New elections were scheduled for November, and parliament reluctantly lowered the minimum voter turnout necessary for the elections to be valid. Lukashenko threatened to institute direct presidential rule if the November elections failed to elect a parliament.   □ Steven L. Solnick

See also **Europe** (Facts in brief table). In *World Book*, see **Belarus.**

Belgium. The government of Prime Minister Jean-Luc Dehaene overcame political scandal and public discontent with budget austerity and unemployment to retain its control in elections held on May 21, 1995. Dehaene's Christian Democratic Party of Flanders, the Dutch-speaking region of Belgium, beat back a challenge from the Liberal Party of Flanders to win a leading 29 seats in the 150-seat Chamber of Representatives, Belgium's lower parliamentary house. Dehaene quickly reestablished his four-party coalition government.

Regional assemblies elected. Voters in May also elected regional assemblies in Flanders, French-speaking Wallonia, the capital district of Brussels, and the small German-speaking community in the East. They were the first such elections under constitutional reforms by which the federal government delegated significant powers to the regions. The ballots produced Christian Democratic-Socialist coalitions in all but Brussels, which elected a Liberal-Socialist coalition.

Economic news. Dehaene on October 3 unveiled a package of tax increases and spending cuts designed to reduce the government's budget deficit and the national debt so that Belgium can link its monetary system to a single European currency in 1999. Belgium's debt stood at nearly 140 percent of the gross domestic product (GDP) in 1995, the largest in the European Union. The Maastricht treaty, which set the standards for the European monetary union, limits gross public debt to 60 percent of the GDP.

Bribery scandal continues. The Socialist Party was rocked in 1995 by a continuing investigation into allegations that Italian helicopter maker Agusta paid bribes to Belgian government officials to win a large government contract in 1988. On March 8, a retired air force chief, General Jacques Lefebvre, was found dead in an apparent suicide after he became implicated in the scandal. The scandal later led to the resignations of Franck Vandenbroucke, Belgium's foreign minister, and Willy Claes, NATO's secretary-general, who was Belgium's economics minister at the time of the contract. Though Vandenbroucke and Claes were implicated in the scandal, they denied any wrongdoing.

Companies sold. Belgium in 1995 became the first major European country to cede effective control of its telephone company and airline. The government sold 49.5 percent of the Belgian airline Sabena to Swissair for $225 million in May and sold 49 percent of the Belgacom phone system to a group led by Ameritech of the United States for $2.6 billion in December. □ Tom Buerkle

See also **Europe** (Facts in brief table). In *World Book,* see **Belgium; European Union.**
Belize. See **Latin America.**
Benin. See **Africa.**
Bhutan. See **Asia.**

Biology. California scientists reported in May 1995 that they had successfully revived 25 million-year-old bacteria and thus produced the oldest living organisms. The bacteria, which were identified as an ancient strain of *Bacillus sphaericus*, were isolated from the abdomen of a honey bee that had been encased in amber for 25 million to 40 million years before being discovered in a mine in the Dominican Republic. The scientific team, from California Polytechnic University in San Luis Obispo, carefully sterilized the exterior of the amber, opened it, and placed the contents in a specially prepared nutrient solution, where the bacteria began to grow again.

The bacteria species was of a type that produces *spores* (cells capable of developing into new bacteria) as a survival tactic when faced with a lack of food or water. Such spores are quite durable, able to persist in extreme heat and cold and even in a vacuum. The California researchers theorize that the spores they studied survived because the amber kept them dry. However, critics said that the bacteria were probably present-day microbes that contaminated the sample. The team disagreed, saying they took adequate measures against contamination.

Ancient seed germinates. Plant physiologist Jane Shen-Miller at the University of California in Los Angeles reported in November that she and her colleagues had forced a 1,300-year-old lotus plant seed to sprout. The seed, one of several brought to California from the Beijing Institute of Botany in China, may have been the oldest known seed to germinate.

Viral genes and human pregnancy. A virus whose genes were incorporated into human genes in ancient times may help prevent a mother's immune system from rejecting the placenta during pregnancy. British and American researchers reported in August that cells in the wall of the placenta contain a protein produced by a previously discovered virus called ERV-3 and that the protein is not found elsewhere in the body. The scientists said that ERV-3 is similar to other viruses known to suppress immunity. ERV-3 may thus help prevent the maternal immune system from attacking the fetus. Because half of a fetus's genes come from the father, a fetus could be seen by the immune system as "foreign" tissue. Without the ERV-3 protein, the scientists said, the fetus would be much more likely to be spontaneously aborted.

Rock-growing bacteria. Geologists have long known that as much as 10 percent of all sedimentary rock on the Earth's surface is *dolomite* (calcium magnesium carbonate). How the dolomite was formed, however, was a puzzle. An important clue came in September, when a scientific team with the Swiss Federal Institute of Technology in Zurich reported that the rock builder could have been a species of bacterium. The scientists made the discovery after placing bacteria from a lagoon in Brazil in a growth medium in test tubes. After a year, the test tubes

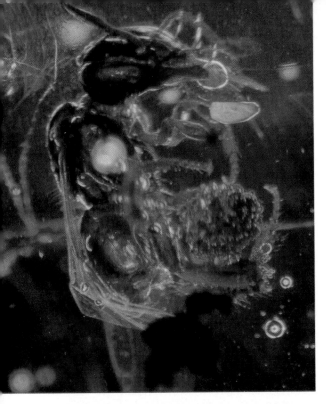

A honey bee encased in amber 25 million to 40 million years ago contains ancient bacteria that California scientists claimed in May they were able to revive.

1995. While at the University of Wyoming in Laramie, Hayes discovered that when prairie rattlesnakes catch small mice, they inject less venom through their hollow fangs than when they snare larger prey. In his study, Hayes studied seven 18-month-old snakes as they attacked small, medium, or large mice. During their first feedings, the snakes did not adjust their venom to fit the size of the mouse. But the second time the snakes encountered a big mouse, they increased the venom accordingly.

Aquatic pheromones. For the first time, scientists in 1995 discovered that a microscopic seagoing animal uses the same kinds of chemical cues to find mates as some insects, mammals, and birds do. In September, Terry W. Snell and several colleagues at the Georgia Institute of Technology in Atlanta reported isolating one of these chemicals, called a sex pheromone, from a tiny aquatic animal called a rotifer.

The Georgia biologists found the chemical by purifying the proteins in the bodies of female rotifers and testing the reactions of male rotifers to the compounds. The scientists discovered that males are on the lookout for a particular compound of a group known as glycoproteins. That type of recognition system is very similar to the one used by a sperm cell to recognize the egg it seeks to fertilize.

☐ Thomas H. Maugh II and Elizabeth Pennisi
In *World Book,* see Biology; Botany; Zoology.

contained crystals of dolomite. Tubes containing the growth medium but no bacteria had no dolomite.

Diet and viral disease. Biologists have long speculated about why some viruses are harmless while closely related viruses cause disease and death. New evidence reported in May indicates that the diet of the virus's host may play a key role in converting some harmless viruses into harmful ones. Scientists at the University of North Carolina at Chapel Hill found that one normally benign virus is transformed into a deadly form in mice whose diet is deficient in the trace element selenium.

The virus, called coxsackie virus B3, normally causes no damage to the mice it infects. But when the team injected it into mice fed a selenium-deficient diet, they found that within a week the virus *mutated* (changed) into a form that caused heart disease in the animals. Furthermore, the mutated virus then caused heart disease when it was injected into mice fed a selenium-rich diet, indicating that the virus—and not the selenium deficiency—was the cause of the heart illness. A similar mutation in a monkey virus might have created the human AIDS virus, the researchers noted, because the virus was first observed in people in selenium-poor regions of Africa.

Doling out the venom. At least one kind of snake delivers a measured amount of venom in each bite, zoologist William K. Hayes, now at Southern College in Collegedale, Tennessee, reported in July

Boating. In 1995, for only the second time in the 144-year history of the America's Cup, the United States lost yachting's most treasured trophy. In the finals of the five-of-nine-race challenge series off San Diego, a New Zealand boat swept away the U.S. defender in five consecutive races.

The competition involved sloops of the International America's Cup Class—75 feet (23 meters) long, weighing 37,000 pounds (17,000 kilograms), and able to sail more than 20 knots in a strong wind. Each boat used a crew of at least 16 people.

From January through April off San Diego, there were two sets of trials. One set involved three potential U.S. defenders—*Stars & Stripes*, *Young America*, and *America³* (pronounced America cubed). The other set attracted seven challenging syndicates—two each from New Zealand and Australia, and one each from France, Spain, and Japan.

There were many oddities. *America³* began the trials with the only all-female crew in cup history, but it later added a male strategist. One challengers' race was postponed when the U.S. Navy's nuclear-powered aircraft carrier *Abraham Lincoln* wandered onto the race course during a heavy fog. Another race was aborted when the yacht *One Australia* broke in half in 20-knot winds and sank in two minutes. The 17 crewmen swam safely to other boats.

On April 4, the day before *Stars & Stripes* or *America³* would have been eliminated in the semifinals of the trials, the three American groups agreed that all would advance to the defender final. Dennis Conner won that final in *Stars & Stripes*, then chartered the slightly faster *Young America* for the cup final. It made little difference.

Black Magic 2 of New Zealand won the challengers' eliminations with a 36-4 record, and three of its four losses were on technicalities. In the cup final May 6 to 13 over an 18.55-nautical-mile (34-kilometer) course, Russell Coutts sailed the syndicate's older boat, *Black Magic 1*, to five easy victories.

Solo. On April 27, Christophe Auguin, a 35-year-old Frenchman, won the BOC Challenge as he did in 1991, the last time the 27,000-nautical-mile (50,000-kilometer) round-the-world solo race was held. The race started and ended in Charleston, South Carolina. Auguin's winning time in his 60-foot (18-meter) sloop, *Sceta Calberson*, was 121 days 17 hours 11 minutes. Of the 20 starters, 12 finished. One, 70-year-old Harry Mitchell of the United Kingdom, was lost at sea. The only woman in the race, 38-year-old Isabelle Autissier of France, easily won the opening leg from Charleston to Cape Town, South Africa, but a huge wave rolled her boat and dislodged its mast on the next leg. She was rescued.　□ Frank Litsky

In *World Book,* see **Boating; Sailing.**
Bolivia. See **Latin America.**
Books. See **Canadian literature; Literature; Literature, American; Literature for children.**

Bosnia-Herzegovina. In 1995, international negotiators brought about agreement on a plan to end the nation's civil war. The plan called for dividing Bosnia (as the nation is often called) into two entities, one dominated by a Muslim-Croat federation and the other by Bosnian Serbs. Details were worked out in peace talks that opened on November 1 in Dayton, Ohio, between Bosnian President Alija Izetbegovic, Serbian President Slobodan Milošević, and Croatian President Franjo Tudjman. The agreement, signed in Paris on December 14, called for a cease-fire to be policed by 60,000 North Atlantic Treaty Organiziation (NATO) troops, including 20,000 from the United States.

The war. A cease-fire between the Bosnian government and Bosnian Serbs negotiated in December 1994 held for the first four months of 1995. Bosnia had been at war since soon after it declared its independence from the Yugoslav federation in March 1992. The government had intended Bosnia to be a multiethnic state, but Bosnian Serbs and Croats sought separate ethnic states. That led to conflict between those groups and the Muslim-dominated government. Despite the cease-fire, there was continued fighting in many parts of the country. NATO planes bombed Bosnian Serb ammunition dumps on May 25 and 26, 1995, after repeated Serb shelling of Sarajevo from within the 12-mile (19-kilometer) "exclusion zone" established by the United Nations

Bosnian Muslim refugees are evacuated from the vicinity of Srebrenica in July after Serb forces overran the town.

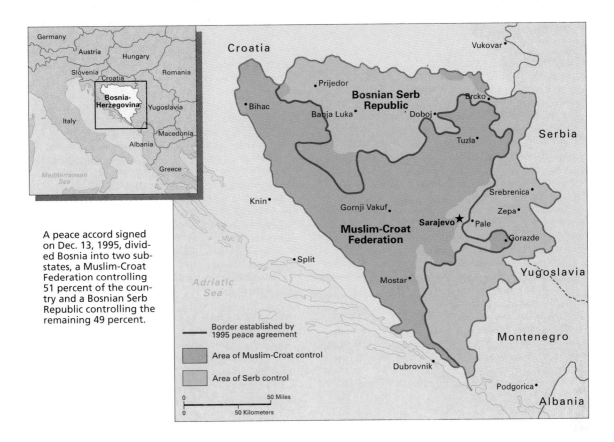

Croatia

Vukovar

Bosnia-Herzegovina

Germany
Austria
Hungary
Slovenia
Croatia
Romania
Italy
Yugoslavia
Macedonia
Albania
Greece
Mediterranean Sea

Prijedor

Bosnian Serb Republic

Brcko

Bihac

Banja Luka

Doboj

Serbia

Tuzla

Knin

Gornji Vakuf

Srebrenica

Zepa

Sarajevo ★ Pale

Muslim-Croat Federation

Gorazde

Split

Yugoslavia

A peace accord signed on Dec. 13, 1995, divided Bosnia into two substates, a Muslim-Croat Federation controlling 51 percent of the country and a Bosnian Serb Republic controlling the remaining 49 percent.

Adriatic Sea

Mostar

Montenegro

Border established by 1995 peace agreement

Area of Muslim-Croat control

Area of Serb control

Dubrovnik

0   50 Miles
0   50 Kilometers

Podgorica

Albania

(UN). In retaliation, Bosnian Serbs took about 370 UN peacekeepers hostage in late May, but released them in June after pressure from Milošević.

Fall of "safe areas." In July, Bosnian Serbs overran the UN "safe areas" of Srebrenica and Zepa in northeastern Bosnia. An estimated 2,000 Muslim men of military age were killed and buried in a mass grave in Srebrenica. The massacre outraged many people outside the country, but divisions between Russia and the United States, Germany, France, and the United Kingdom prevented a concerted response from the international community.

A stronger response came when a Serb shell killed 38 people in a Sarajevo marketplace on August 28. NATO launched massive bombing raids on August 30 against Bosnian Serb positions, mainly near Sarajevo, Tuzla, Gorazde, Mostar, and Pale.

Peace plan. Also on August 30, Milošević and the Bosnian Serbs agreed to form a united team to negotiate peace. On September 8, the foreign ministers of Croatia, Bosnia, and Yugoslavia agreed to accept the principles of a U.S.-crafted plan. According to the plan, Bosnia would remain a single nation composed of two substates. A Muslim-Croat federation would control 51 percent of the country and the Bosnian Serbs 49 percent. NATO suspended its airstrikes against Bosnian Serbs on September 14.

An agreement on the constitutional framework of a new Bosnia followed on September 26. The

agreement specified that Bosnia would hold free elections and restore basic human rights, including the right of refugees to return home or be compensated for their property. The Muslim-Croat federation and the Bosnian Serbs would contribute two-thirds and one-third of delegates respectively to the state's parliament and a collective presidency. A constitutional court would also be established. The agreement did not address some issues, including control of key government positions, the establishment of a currency, passports, and citizenship.

A cease-fire went into effect October 12, and the final agreement was signed on December 14 in Paris.

Bosnian federation. In February, Bosnian Croats and Muslims asked the United States to arbitrate disagreements concerning the federation they established in 1994. Croat and Muslim leaders signed a military pact and a plan to strengthen the federation in early 1995.

Reconstruction plan. European Union (EU) officials developed a $4-billion plan for rebuilding Bosnia, aiding refugees, and creating links between the EU and countries of the former Yugoslavia. The EU pledged to pay one-third of reconstruction costs.

☐ Sharon L. Wolchik

See also **Croatia; Europe** (Facts in brief table); **United Nations; Yugoslavia.** In *World Book,* see Bosnia-Herzegovina.

Botswana. See Africa.

Bowling. In the United States, where 80 million people bowl, the men's Professional Bowlers Association (PBA) tour continued to struggle in 1995. One bowler who did well was Mike Aulby, who won two of the four most important tournaments and led the tour in earnings and scoring average.

The American Broadcasting Companies (ABC), which had televised the men's tour for 33 years, had been paying $3.52 million for 24 tournaments. In 1995, ABC cut its financial support to $700,000 for 14 tournaments.

Since 1993, a handful of tournaments had stimulated public interest by installing four lanes in large sports arenas and moving tournament finals there from the traditional bowling establishments. This change made it possible for thousands of spectators to attend, rather than just a few hundred. The final of the United States Open on April 8, 1995, in Detroit attracted 7,212 people.

PBA tour. The 30 tournaments paid $5,145,000 in prize money. Aulby earned $216,492, and second-place Dave D'Entremont picked up $180,625. Aulby's season scoring average of 225.37 broke Walter Ray Williams's 1993 record of 223.98.

In the triple-crown tournaments, Aulby won the $300,000 Tournament of Champions in April 1995, Scott Alexander the $200,000 PBA national championship in February, and Dave Husted the $250,000 United States Open. Then Aulby won the American Bowling Congress Masters in May, becoming not only the fourth bowler to win every triple-crown title in his career but also the first to win those three tournaments plus the Masters.

Senior. This tour for bowlers 50 and older comprised 12 tournaments worth a total of $1.2 million. Tommy Evans won three tournaments but finished third in earnings. John Handegard was the leading earner with $63,132 and attained two distinctions. At 57, he became the oldest bowler to win on the regular tour and the first to win on the regular and senior tours in the same year.

Women. The Ladies Professional Bowlers Tour benefited from the three-year, $4-million umbrella sponsorship of Sam's Town, a combination hotel, casino, and bowling center in Las Vegas, Nevada. The tour's 22 tournaments paid $1,832,000 in prize money.

The leading money winners were Tish Johnson with $115,190, Anne Marie Duggan with $112,497, and Cheryl Daniels with $106,391—the first time three women had earned more than $100,000 in one year. In the major competitions, Sandy Postma won the $100,000 Women's International Bowling Congress Queens tournament in May, Daniels the $100,000 United States Open in October, Duggan the $105,000 Hammer Players Championship in November, and Michelle Mullen the $107,000 Sam's Town Invitational in November. □ Frank Litsky

In *World Book,* see **Bowling.**

Boxing. After serving three years and six weeks of a six-year sentence for rape, Mike Tyson was released from an Indiana prison on March 25, 1995, and stepped into a confused heavyweight picture.

On August 19 in Las Vegas, Nevada, in his first fight in four years, Tyson knocked down Peter McNeeley twice before McNeeley's manager climbed into the ring and told the referee to stop the fight. The referee did. The fight lasted 89 seconds.

Tyson then prepared for a November 4 fight against Buster Mathis, Jr. That bout and one between Riddick Bowe and Evander Holyfield were scheduled the same night in Las Vegas. Tyson-Mathis was moved to free television. But four days before the bout, Tyson broke his right thumb and called off the fight. The fight was rescheduled for December 16 in Philadelphia, and Tyson knocked out Mathis in the third round.

Tyson's next fight was scheduled for March 1996 against Frank Bruno of the United Kingdom (UK), the World Boxing Council (WBC) champion. Meanwhile, the federal trial of Tyson's promoter, Don King, on charges of filing a false insurance claim for $350,000, ended in a mistrial on November 16 because the jury was deadlocked.

Heavyweight champions. Oliver McCall, who started the year as WBC champion, outpointed 45-year-old Larry Holmes April 8 in Las Vegas, only to lose the title on points to Bruno on September 2. The World Boxing Association (WBA) stripped 46-year-old George Foreman of its version of the title when he fought Axel Schulz of Germany rather than Tony Tucker, the number-one contender. Bruce Seldon won the vacant title by stopping Tucker in seven rounds on April 8 in Las Vegas.

The International Boxing Federation (IBF) still recognized Foreman as champion, but when he took a beating April 22 in Las Vegas from the unheralded Schulz and escaped with a controversial majority decision, the IBF ordered a rematch. Foreman declined, and the IBF stripped him of the title. Schulz and Frans Botha of South Africa fought for the title on December 9, with Botha winning by decision.

The upstart World Boxing Organization (WBO) had the most respected champion in Bowe. He won the title in six rounds March 11 from Herbie Hide of the UK, stopped Cuban-born Jorge Luis Gonzalez in six rounds in a June 17 defense, and stopped Holyfield in eight rounds in a nontitle bout.

Other. The best young fighters were super middleweight Roy Jones, Jr., welterweight Felix Trinidad of Puerto Rico, and lightweight Oscar De La Hoya. Terry Norris regained the WBC super-welterweight title in August from Luis Santana after being disqualified in two previous title bouts against Santana.

Amateur. Cuba won 4 of the 12 gold medals in the world championships in May 1995 in Berlin, Germany. □ Frank Litsky

In *World Book,* see **Boxing.**

World champion boxers

World Boxing Association

Division	Champion	Country	Date won
Heavyweight	George Foreman	U.S.A.	1994
	Vacant		
	Bruce Seldon	U.S.A.	April '95
Light heavyweight	Virgil Hill	U.S.A.	1992
Middleweight	Jorge Castro	Argentina	1994
	Shinji Takahara	Japan	Dec. '95
Welterweight	Ike Quartey	Ghana	1994
Lightweight	Orzubek Nazarov	Russia	1993
Featherweight	Eloy Rojas	Venezuela	1993
Bantamweight	Daorung Chuwatana	Thailand	1994
	Veerapol Sahaprom	Thailand	Sept. '95
Flyweight	Saen Sor Ploenchit	Thailand	1994

World Boxing Council

Division	Champion	Country	Date won
Heavyweight	Oliver McCall	U.S.A.	1994
	Frank Bruno	Great Britain	Sept. '95
Light heavyweight	Mike McCallum	U.S.A.	1994
	Fabrice Tiozzo	France	June '95
Middleweight	Gerald McClellan	U.S.A.	1993
	Vacant		
	Julian Jackson	U.S. Virgin Islands	March '95
	Quincy Taylor	U.S.A.	August '95
Welterweight	Pernell Whitaker	U.S.A.	1993
Lightweight	Miguel Gonzalez	Mexico	1992
Featherweight	Kevin Kelley	U.S.A.	1993
	Alejandro Gonzalez	Mexico	Jan. '95
	Manuel Medina	Mexico	Sept. '95
	Luisito Espinoza	Philippines	Dec. '95
Bantamweight	Yashuei Yakushiji	Japan	1994
	Wayne McCullough	Ireland	July '95
Flyweight	Yuri Arbachakov	Russia	1992

Brazil. On Jan. 1, 1995, Fernando Henrique Cardoso, 63, of the Brazilian Social Democratic Party was sworn in as president. In accord with a change to the Constitution approved in 1994, Cardoso was to serve a four-year term and was ineligible for reelection.

Foreign investment. Cardoso quickly made good on his pledge to reverse a half-century of state control of the Brazilian economy and welcome foreign investment. On Feb. 13, 1995, he signed a new law permitting private companies to build highways, hydroelectric dams, and water and sewer systems—jobs previously reserved for the government. On February 16, he introduced legislation that would allow foreigners to invest in Brazilian oil, mining, and telecommunications ventures.

The measures prompted an immediate flurry of big project announcements by multinational business firms. In early March, the General Electric Company of the United States unveiled an ambitious $5.6-billion plan to build 16 coal-burning electric power plants in southern Brazil. Foreign and domestic business giants geared up to bid on some 27 state-run hydroelectric facilities, scheduled for privatization.

In his first fight since being released from jail, Mike Tyson knocks down Peter NcNeeley in August in Las Vegas, Nevada. Tyson won in 89 seconds.

Later in the month, Brazil's four largest auto-makers announced plans for expansions at their Brazilian factories. Ford and General Motors said they would each invest $2 billion, Volkswagen $3-billion, and Fiat $1 billion to help Brazil reach its national goal of doubling automotive production by the year 2000.

Oil strike. Cardoso returned from an official visit to the United States on April 21 to find Brazil's labor unions angry about his plans to end the government's oil monopoly. On April 28, he fired José Machado Sobrinho, president of Petrobrás, the state-owned oil monopoly, for criticizing the government's plan to privatize the industry. When a month-long strike by 48,000 oil workers showed no sign of resolution, Cardoso ordered troops to seize four state oil refineries in São Paulo and Paraná states on May 24. Despite the labor unrest, the nation's Chamber of Deputies voted June 7 to end the state monopoly of the oil sector.

Slave labor. In June, President Cardoso appointed a commission to investigate growing reports of serflike conditions for many workers. Reports surfaced of unscrupulous companies that had lured between 25,000 and 85,000 workers to Brazil's interior with promises of desirable jobs, only to force them into slum housing and keep them indebted to company stores.

Westward movement. South of the Amazon Basin, Brazilian cities in the west continued to grow faster than established metropolitan centers in 1995. Typically, the population of Ribeirão Prêto, four hours by road north of São Paulo, had nearly doubled since 1985 to half a million people. About the same distance west of São Paulo, the town of Presidente Prudente had grown to a quarter of a million people thanks to the region's growing cattle industry. In 1995, municipal authorities hired world-renowned Oscar Niemeyer, architect of Brazil's capital, Brasília, to design a 35,000-seat arena for the favorite local entertainment, American-style rodeos.

Railroad into the interior. To support the westward movement, Olacyr de Morães, a multibillionaire producer of soybeans and owner of Brazil's third-largest construction company, embarked in 1995 on the construction of a railroad at a cost of $2.5 billion. When tied into existing systems, his railroad will facilitate commerce more than 1,000 miles (1,600 kilometers) into the interior of the continent.

The railroad was expected to cut in half the price of transporting soybeans, beef, grain, and lumber to the port of Santos. On return trips it was to carry fuel, fertilizer, and general cargo to towns as far west as Cuiabá, capital of the huge state of Mato Grosso. ☐ Nathan A. Haverstock

See also **Latin America** (Facts in brief table). In *World Book,* see Brazil.

British Columbia. See **Canadian provinces.**

Brunei. See **Asia.**

Building and construction. The pace of construction in the United States slowed in 1995 compared to the rapid gains of 1994. The decrease stemmed partly from interest rate increases that the Federal Reserve System (the Fed), the nation's central bank, ordered in 1994 to put the brakes on rapid economic growth. A total of 990 thousand single-family homes went up in 1995, about 8 percent fewer than in 1994, according to F. W. Dodge, a forecasting company based in New York City.

Other types of construction performed better in 1995. With excess office space slowly filling, construction of office buildings increased 14 percent. In the manufacturing sector, factory construction went up 5 percent. Public works projects grew only slightly as Congress tried to limit government spending.

Union blues. Hourly union pay scales grew little in 1995. A 20-city survey conducted by *Engineering News-Record,* an industry magazine, showed increases ranging from 2 percent to 4 percent for most building trades.

Trade union leaders faced many challenges in 1995. For the first time in his 21-year tenure, Robert A. Georgine, president of the AFL-CIO's Building and Construction Trades department faced a challenger, A. L. Mike Monroe, president of the International Brotherhood of Painters and Allied Trades. Monroe and his followers claimed that union members felt estranged from their elected leaders and that the trades needed to return to grassroots organizing. Construction unions have been losing members and work since the 1970's as nonunion contractors have grown. Monroe withdrew, and Georgine unanimously won another five-year term in an August election.

The nation's largest construction union, the 500,000-member United Brotherhood of Carpenters and Joiners, got a new leader in 1995. Sigurd Lucassen retired after serving seven years as president, and union members selected one of the union's vice presidents, Douglas J. McCarron, to succeed him.

In the Laborers' International Union, president Arthur A. Coia faced a challenge from the U.S. Justice Department, which had been investigating corruption and alleged ties to organized crime at numerous local unions. But no charges were filed against Coia, and on February 15, union leaders and the Justice Department reached an agreement under which the leaders would take a more active role in rooting out corruption. Over a number of years, the Justice Department has prosecuted more than 80 laborers' union officials on federal criminal charges.

Construction of stadiums continued at a feverish pace in 1995, falling just short of 1994's record $1.5 billion, according to F. W. Dodge. In addition to construction for the 1996 Olympic Games in Atlanta, Georgia, several stadiums were being replaced by new facilities or were undergoing major renovations. They included the Gator Bowl in Jacksonville,

Florida, and in California, the Los Angeles Coliseum, the Oakland Coliseum, and San Diego's Jack Murphy Stadium. In Phoenix, construction began on a new domed stadium. In Boston, crews put the finishing touches on a new home for the Bruins hockey team and Celtics basketball team in September. The much-loved but aged Boston Garden was soon to be razed.

Affirmative action. On June 12, the U.S. Supreme Court ruled on a case involving a construction contractor to issue an important affirmative action decision. In the case of *Adarand Constructors, Inc. v. Peña*, the court ruled in favor of a contractor in Colorado who sued the federal government. He claimed his constitutional rights had been violated when an affirmative action program caused his company to lose a subcontract to install guardrails on a U.S. highway. The subcontract was awarded to a firm whose owners were Hispanic even though Adarand had submitted a lower bid. The court decision scaled back the federal government's ability to give special consideration to minorities and women when awarding construction contracts.

The 1995 Supreme Court ruling expanded a 1989 decision, *City of Richmond v. Croson,* in which the court ruled that a state or local government must apply a standard referred to as *strict scrutiny* before enacting an affirmative action program for the awarding of construction contracts. Strict scrutiny requires the government to find proof of prior discrim-ination. In *Adarand v. Peña,* the court ruled that federal agencies also must apply strict scrutiny.

The structural collapse of the Sampoong Department Store complex in Seoul, South Korea, on June 29 was the worst of 1995. Korean prosecutors charged 25 people in connection with the disaster, which was blamed on illegal alterations made to the building. At least 501 people died when the five-story structure fell. The concrete-frame structure had shown signs of impending collapse, including cracks in its roof and sagging of the upper floors, but the owners did not shut the complex.

The Morrison Knudsen Corporation of Boise, Idaho, one of the biggest U.S. construction firms, struggled in 1995 after reporting a $350-million loss for 1994. The company announced its financial problems on Feb. 1, 1995, and said that chairman and chief executive William Agee would retire within a year. Some shareholders sued Morrison Knudsen for having misrepresented its financial condition. As the scope of the company's problems became clear, Agee left on February 10. Agee had steered the company into ventures that lost heavily. The company finally worked out a deal with their banks and insurers to get through 1996, and they gave Agee a $100,000-a-year pension.   □ Richard Korman

See also **Building and construction** Special Report: **Designing for Disasters.** In *World Book,* see **Building construction.**

The world's longest cable-stayed suspension bridge (2,808 feet [856 meters]) opened in January in France, spanning the Seine River at its mouth.

The destruction caused by earthquakes and hurricanes can be minimized with good design and solid construction.

Designing for Disasters

By Richard Korman

The earthquake that devastated the Japanese city of Kobe on Jan. 17, 1995, was Japan's worst natural disaster in more than 50 years. The quake killed more than 5,400 people, injured another 26,000, and destroyed or heavily damaged more than 56,000 buildings. The destruction was compounded by hundreds of fires that erupted soon after the shaking had ceased. Surveying the damage, one young Japanese engineer remarked, "We used to say that Japan's earthquake engineering was the best in the world. I don't think we'll be saying that anymore."

The Kobe earthquake was the latest in a series of natural disasters that have jolted engineers, insurance companies, and public officials into a new awareness of nature's ability to tear down what human beings have erected. A year to the day before the Kobe quake, the ground shook in the Los Angeles area, collapsing several expressway overpasses, damaging thousands of other structures, and killing 57 people. An earthquake in the San Francisco Bay Area of California in October 1989 caused similar destruction and 63 deaths.

Ranking high among nature's other furies are hurricanes. In August 1992, Hurricane Andrew, one of the fiercest storms ever to hit the United States, battered the Florida coast, killing 13 people and damaging or flattening about 72,000 homes.

These and other calamities revealed multiple weaknesses in the human-built environment. Inadequate building codes, the minimal or nonexistent enforcement of such codes, shoddy construction techniques, and the vulnerability of older structures built in dangerous locations to out-of-date standards all contributed to making the U.S. and Japanese disasters so destructive and costly.

Engineers and architects in both countries are now striv-

Glossary

Base isolation: The installation of large shock-absorbing mechanisms at a building's base to greatly reduce the amount of earthquake movements that are transmitted upward into the building.

Compressive strength: The ability of a material to bear loads that squeeze or press down on it.

Ductility: The capability of a material to be stretched or bent without fracturing.

Liquefaction: The transformation of loose, wet, sandy soils to the temporary consistency of quicksand during an earthquake.

Reinforced concrete: Concrete that has been strengthened by being formed around steel rods.

Reinforced masonry: Brickwork that has been reinforced with vertical and horizontal steel rods.

Tensile strength: The ability of a material to resist forces acting to pull it apart.

The author

Richard Korman is associate editor of *Engineering News-Record* magazine.

ing to learn why buildings and other structures fail under stress, and they are developing new construction methods aimed at limiting the destruction and loss of life caused by future disasters. One solution for protecting against earthquakes involves installing large shock absorbers at the base of buildings to limit the shaking and swaying that occurs during a quake. Another is redesigning the columns supporting bridges and elevated roadways so that even if the columns are damaged the structure will continue to stand. Safeguarding houses against hurricanes is less dependent on new technologies and building techniques than on strict adherence to solid construction aimed at strengthening roofs, windows, walls, and doors.

Aside from the deaths, injuries, and homelessness they cause, earthquakes and hurricanes exact a steep economic price. And as population densities increase in disaster-prone regions, the dollar costs of natural disasters escalate. Clearing rubble; repairing or rebuilding homes, buildings, and expressways; providing disaster relief; and paying off insurance claims all cost a lot of money. Since 1989, a year that included the devastating Hurricane Hugo as well as the San Francisco-area quake, federal disaster relief alone has totalled more than $67 billion, according to a report from the University of Colorado in Boulder. The cost of cleanup and repairs after the Kobe earthquake was estimated at $147 billion.

Projected economic costs for The Big One that *seismologists* (earthquake experts) predict will someday hit California—a quake measuring 8.0 or greater on the magnitude scale—are higher yet. According to one scenario, an 8.3 quake in San Francisco would cause 3,000 to 8,000 deaths, insured losses of $80 billion to $105 billion, and total economic losses of $170 billion to $225 billion. The lion's share of the bill for those losses would be presented to insurance companies and the taxpayers.

Much of the high economic cost, many experts believe, could be avoided by improving building designs and codes in disaster-prone areas. The patterns of destruction in earthquakes and hurricanes show that it is possible to limit the damage that occurs. Often, similar structures in the same area—even ones right next to each other—will suffer wildly different amounts of damage, depending on how they were constructed.

The destructive force of earthquakes

Earthquakes are the biggest challenge, because a major quake exerts destructive forces on buildings and other structures that no hurricane can match. An earthquake generally exerts violent *lateral* (side-to-side) forces on a building. These movements, which can be combined with a lesser degree of up-and-down shaking, impose severe stresses on a building. The walls of old brick buildings bulge, crack, and collapse. In taller concrete or steel-frame buildings, windows and stone panels on the outer wall fracture or shatter.

More dangerously, tall buildings sway excessively in an earthquake, and their frames can shift out of alignment. When that happens, connections between the vertical columns and horizontal beams may break apart, removing support for a floor and sending it crashing down onto the one below. This type of collapse, known as *pancaking,* is the most dangerous form of construction failure in a quake.

The sideways shaking that characterizes most earthquakes can also play havoc with bridges and elevated highways. Roadbeds and beams get pushed off their columns or supports, columns shear, and sometimes the motions are so violent, the entire structure gets toppled onto its side.

Buildings situated on loose or wet soils can be particularly vulnerable during an earthquake because such types of ground move more than dense soil or rock. Buildings on wet, sandy soils can even end up tilted or lying on their side when an earthquake phenomenon known as *liquefaction* occurs. In liquefaction, ground shaking breaks up the soft soil into loosely organized particles saturated with water, turning the ground temporarily into something resembling quicksand. A building sitting on liquefying soil will suddenly be without any solid underlying support.

The damage in California and Kobe

These various kinds of destruction were seen in the California and Kobe earthquakes. The collapse of an elevated highway in Oakland accounted for most of the deaths in the San Francisco-area earthquake of 1989. The quake, centered 50 miles (80 kilometers) south of downtown San Francisco in the Loma Prieta area of the Santa Cruz mountains, had a magnitude of 7.1.

The collapsed freeway, which caused 42 of the 63 fatalities, was located in an area of loose soil. Damage from the Loma Prieta tremor was concentrated in parts of Oakland and San Francisco where the subsoil consisted of landfill, including mud dredged from the bay and debris from previous earthquakes. Some of those areas were also affected by liquefaction, which contributed to the destruction. In San Francisco, most of the damage was sustained by old apartment buildings, many of them brick, erected years before the introduction of modern building codes and construction practices. The buildings lacked any support elements tying the walls together to prevent them from pulling apart or buckling.

What happens when the earth moves

An earthquake causes violent *lateral* (side-to-side) and vertical ground movements. These motions exert tremendous stresses on buildings and other structures that can damage or destroy them in a matter of seconds.

As the base of a building is jerked to the left by a ground motion, the lower floors move with it, but the upper floors lag behind.

Within moments, the upper stories of the building are also moving to the left.

Suddenly, the ground and the building's base move back toward the right, but the top floors are still moving to the left.

By the time the ground motions stop, the building has been seriously deformed and may collapse.

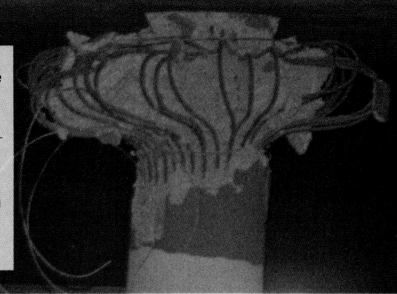

When concrete becomes rubble

A column holding up an elevated express-way in Los Angeles is a mass of broken con-crete and twisted steel after the Jan-uary 1994 quake in southern California. Such damage showed the necessity of strongly reinforcing concrete support structures.

To make concrete columns resistant to quake-generated forces that can stretch and fracture them, engineers have learned, the columns must con-tain a large number of horizontal and vertical steel reinforcing rods. When a column is constructed, the wet concrete is poured around a dense circular grouping of vertical steel rods that are enclosed by narrowly spaced horizontal hoops of steel, *below, left.* To reinforce existing columns against stretching forces, engineers jacket the entire column with large pieces of curved steel, *below, right.*

Damage in the 1994 Los Angeles earthquake, too, revealed deficiencies in the older building codes under which many buildings were con-structed. Centered in Northridge, a subdivision of Los Angeles, the 6.7-magnitude quake caused extensive damage to many concrete and steel-frame buildings.

Concrete buildings proved particularly trou-blesome. Many older concrete buildings lacked *ductility* in their joints. Ductility is the ability of a joint or structural element to deform without breaking apart. Under California codes in place until 1976, concrete buildings did not need to be ductile. Structural engineers now believe those pre-1976 buildings are dangerous in a quake. Steel buildings also had structural problems, to the surprise of many architects and engineers. Buildings with welded frames—common among high-rise structures in the Los Angeles area and elsewhere—had been considered extremely strong and largely immune to the dangers of earthquakes. Such buildings remained standing and apparently unharmed in the Los Angeles quake, but inspections about a month later revealed cracks in the steel frames near the welds used to connect beams to columns. Such cracks had been found in more than 120 buildings as of June 1995, and the Los Angeles city govern-ment was asking the owners of hundreds of other buildings to search for and repair cracked welds. Meanwhile, architects, engineers, and contractors argued about whether this problem was caused by poor design, poor construction, or both.

The destruction in the Kobe earthquake far surpassed that caused by the two California quakes. More than 300,000 people in Kobe were left homeless after their houses collapsed. Most houses in the city were older wood-frame structures built in the traditional Japanese style, with lightly constructed walls and heavy tile roofs. The walls of many thousands of those houses quickly gave way during the 6.8-magnitude quake, causing the roofs to come crashing down.

But among the thousands of larger structures that were ruined in the Kobe disaster, the causes of damage were much the same as in the California quakes. Weaknesses in older concrete buildings, vulnerable welded connections in steel-frame high-rises, and foundations situated on soft soils all contributed to the extensive destruction. One of the most dramatic sights from the quake was a long section of the elevated Hanshin Expressway that fell over on its side when 15 concrete columns broke off at the base.

In some cases, the damage presented a more complex picture of the seismic forces acting on a structure. For example, many mid-rise buildings

From brick wall to brick pile

A brick building in Nepal lies in ruins after an earthquake. Unreinforced brickwork is highly vulnerable to earthquakes and can be quickly shaken to pieces by ground movements.

All building codes in parts of the United States where earthquakes are common now require brick buildings to be constructed with reinforced masonry. In this method of construction, vertical and horizontal steel reinforcing bars are set into brickwork as the bricks are laid. The steel gives considerable strength to the walls, enabling them to make it through an earthquake without buckling.

Lessons on the limits of steel

A badly deformed steel-frame building in Kobe was just one of many steel buildings that suffered damage in the strong earthquake that hit the Japanese city in January 1995. The Kobe and southern California earthquakes both demonstrated that many steel-frame buildings that architects and engineers had thought were relatively quake resistant were in fact highly vulnerable.

One cause of earthquake damage in many steel buildings has been overly rigid joints in the frame. A possible solution being considered by engineers, *below*, involves inserting a nickel plate between structural parts that are being bolted together. The nickel would help the joints absorb twisting motions during a quake.

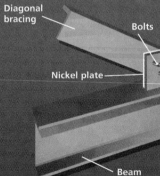

Column

Diagonal bracing

Bolts

Nickel plate

Beam

Engineers are also experimenting with other new ways of constructing steel-frame buildings to make them more resistant to earthquakes. At a Chicago engineering company, the strength of a three-story test structure consisting of a twist-resistant steel frame reinforced with diagonal steel bracing is mounted on a platform that simulates earthquake movements, *left*.

pancaked at a midlevel floor. This apparently occurred, engineers concluded, because columns in the lower portion of the buildings were encased in concrete, making them more rigid than upper-story columns, which were not surrounded by concrete. As a result of this mode of construction, the lower part of the building's frame was stiffer than the upper part, preventing the building from swaying as a unit in response to ground motions.

Earthquake-resistant design

The good news from Kobe was that most of the city's newer buildings came through the quake unscathed. Here was convincing evidence that modern building codes—particularly when combined with new technologies aimed at insulating buildings from ground motions—can protect most buildings from the ravages of a major earthquake.

Engineering earthquake resistance into many buildings is largely a matter of reinforcing them. An older masonry building, for instance, can be reinforced by attaching a strong wire mesh to the bricks to hold them together. The mesh gives a brick wall increased *tensile strength,* the ability to resist stretching forces acting to pull it apart. Other work might include installing braces, anchors, and other devices to strengthen the walls and foundation. Such measures to improve the survivability of an existing building are known as *retrofitting.* After the Northridge quake, California ordered the retrofitting of thousands of unreinforced brick buildings in the state.

A much better way to strengthen a brick building, however, is with the addition of vertical and horizontal steel rods running through mortar-filled cavities between some of the bricks. But this solution is only practical with new buildings. Today, building codes in U.S. earthquake zones require all new masonry to be constructed with steel reinforcing rods.

The tensile strength of reinforced concrete structures can also be increased with additional steel. Although plain concrete has great

Workers in San Francisco install a *base-isolation* system consisting of large energy-absorbing bearings under support columns of the U.S. Court of Appeals building. Base isolation is the use of bearings, rubber pads, springs, or other devices at the base of a building to prevent ground movements in an earthquake from being transferred to the upper part of the building. Base isolation has proven effective in protecting buildings from major earthquake damage.

95

compressive strength (the ability to bear loads that squeeze or press down on it), it is not good at withstanding stretching forces. To provide concrete columns with tensile strength, wet concrete is poured around a grouping of vertical steel rods that are enclosed within hoops of horizontal steel rods. When the concrete hardens, the steel allows it to resist forces that would ordinarily stretch and fracture it.

But there must be a liberal use of steel in a column for it to resist an earthquake. Examining the rubble left by the Northridge quake, engineers found that some columns crumbled because they contained too few horizontal steel hoops. That, for example, is what caused the partial collapse of the five-story Kaiser Permanente medical office building in Granada Hills, a suburb not far from Northridge.

Engineers are looking at ways to increase the ductility of joints in steel buildings. Some think that rather than welding the connections between columns and beams, it may be better to go back to the old method of just bolting them together, but with one additional element: a plate of nickel between the two structural members to absorb twisting forces. But this idea is new and has not yet been tested.

Preventing buildings from swaying

Another method for protecting large buildings from the excessive swaying and twisting that can tear them apart—and one that has shown its effectiveness—is called *base isolation.* This technology involves isolating the above-ground frame of a building from its foundation by inserting giant rubber pads, springs, or other shock-absorbing mechanisms at the base of the building to absorb the energy of a quake. Tests show that the system limits motion significantly, and the evidence from Kobe is impressive. There, the largest base-isolated building in the world, the six-story West Japan Building, was untouched by the 1995 earthquake. Neighboring buildings of similar size and design suffered damage, though most of it was nonstructural, such as broken windows.

Base-isolation systems are being retrofitted to a number of older buildings. Both Oakland and Los Angeles decided to protect their city halls in this way after their respective earthquakes. The Los Angeles project, still in the planning stage in 1995, called for cutting out sections at the bottoms of 435 columns and installing shock absorbers.

Engineers are applying base-isolation technology to all kinds of structures. Engineers constructing an addition to a wharf in Los Angeles in 1995 were installing 46 sliding bearings, each 4 feet (1.2 meters) on a side, to act as base isolators between the wharf's surface and its foundation. In each bearing, three layers of steel plates alternate with three layers of Teflon pads bonded to other steel plates. The Teflon pads can slide 8 inches (20 centimeters), absorbing that much lateral movement from a quake.

Japanese researchers have been among the most ambitious in promoting earthquake safety, but in some cases they have used technologies that some American engineers consider somewhat questionable. For example, the Japanese have equipped quite a few buildings with *mass dampers,* large computer-controlled weights that shift position to limit the swaying of a building from a quake, or even from the wind. Whichever way the building sways, the computer—receiving information from motion sensors—orders the weight to move in the opposite direction. Some U.S. engineers regard mass damping technology warily because, they say, the disruption of a city's electrical supply during a quake could cause the computer guiding the damper to malfunction. A number of buildings, however, have been equipped with backup power supplies to prevent that from happening.

Other engineering approaches

One of the biggest questions remaining after the Kobe earthquake was whether Japanese engineers would change their approach to designing bridges and highways, which suffered severe damage in the quake. Engineers in both Japan and the United States design elevated roadways to be ductile, but the Japanese follow a "bigger is better" approach, using larger concrete columns with more vertical steel reinforcing bars to reduce the chance of damage. But they also used fewer horizontal steel hoops in each column to interlock with the vertical steel bars. That approach did not work in Kobe.

When the ground turns to quicksand

Several apartment buildings in Niigata, Japan, are tilted or lying on their side after a 1964 earthquake that caused *liquefaction* of the ground beneath their foundations, *above.* In liquefaction, the shaking of the ground causes wet, sandy soils to become loosely organized and saturated with water, temporarily giving them a consistency similar to quicksand. A building constructed on ground that could liquefy during an earthquake should be supported by long, heavy *piles* (steel or concrete columns) driven down to firm soil or bedrock, *below.*

Wet, sandy soil

Piles

Firm soil

The power of wind

Houses in South Dade County, Florida, are in various stages of ruin after being pummeled by Hurricane Andrew in August 1992, *top.* Hurricane-force winds can cause damage in several ways. As the wind exerts pressure on one side of a house, *above, left,* the protected side experiences relatively low pressure, and the house can be pushed off its foundation. Wind rushing over the top of a house, *above,* center, speeds up, creating a low-pressure area above the house that can pull the roof away from its moorings. If the wind breaks into a house through a door or window, *above,* right, pressure builds up inside the house like air in an inflating balloon, exerting an outward force on the walls and roof that can make the house collapse.

California structural engineers don't try to fend off damage to roadways as zealously as the Japanese do. They have been designing expressway columns in the Golden State to deform, but not collapse, in an earthquake so that repairs can be made. The columns are not as big as those on Japanese roadways, but they are bolstered with more horizontal reinforcing hoops, which are more closely spaced.

At the same time, the California engineers are trying to estimate how much damage to roadways will occur. Researchers at the California Department of Transportation (Caltrans), for example, have developed a computer program to determine how much a column or beam and the bolts and welds that tie them together can deform or rotate without causing the structure to collapse. With such information in hand, Caltrans engineers may be able to reduce by more than a third the cost of a planned renovation of an elevated expressway in Santa Monica, a project that had been expected to cost $50 million. One saving will come from reducing the number of columns that need to be retrofitted with steel reinforcing jackets.

Engineers can save even more money when, rather than retrofitting, they build effective earthquake resistance into the initial design. In a new steel-frame building that costs $10 million to build, for instance, a base-isolation system can add $500,000 to construction costs. But strengthening the joints in a building after it is completed can cost far more. For one five-story building in Los Angeles in which 86 connections had to be upgraded, the owners spent $3 million. They also lost $1 million in rent during the three months when the work was being done. Still, if a building is vulnerable to an earthquake, retrofitting is usually the only solution.

The cost of protecting other types of buildings from earthquakes varies depending on the kind of building and its location. For example, the cost of rehabilitating an unreinforced brick building of 11,000 square feet (1,022 square meters) in Los Angeles is between $70,000 and $80,000, according to the Federal Emergency Management Agency, an independent U.S. agency that coordinates disaster relief. The cost for a seismic rehabilitation of a 10,000-square-foot (930-square-meter) concrete building is about $150,000.

Hurricane damage and how to prevent it

While earthquakes can destroy any structure that has not been built to the highest standards, hurricanes do most of their worst damage to houses and other smaller buildings. Hurricanes, like earthquakes, attack structures mainly from the sides. But there are significant differences between the stresses exerted by short-lived ground motions and those created by the relentless pressure of hurricane-force winds. The wind shoves a building again and again, sometimes pushing its frame out of alignment or even lifting it off its foundation. It jabs at openings along the surface, such as windows and doors, nibbling at weak points until it finds a way to get in. And it picks up debris and hurls it with great force at walls and windows.

When a high wind blows directly against the side of a typical wood-frame house, it exerts intense pressure on that side, the wind-

Weak spots that invite destruction

A hurricane batters a house relentlessly for hours, and any deficiencies of design or construction are potential trouble spots. Once the wind has created an opening in a house, damage can multiply rapidly.

Inferior workmanship in constructing the roof and fastening it securely to the house can be disastrous. If the roof goes, the house may be entirely destroyed.

Gable vents are often structurally weak and are apt to be blown out by heavy winds.

Many garage doors are not designed to withstand hurricanes and may give the wind easy entry into the house.

If the framework of the house is not securely fastened to the foundation, the wind could lift the entire house and move it.

ward side, and creates a low-pressure area on the opposite side, the leeward side. Thus, walls and windows on the windward side of the house are in danger of being pushed in, while on the leeward side they may be sucked right off the house. And the moment the wind breaks in through a window or door, the sudden pressure buildup inside the house can cause doors and other weak places on the leeward side to pop right out. The wind then combines with rain to destroy the interior of the house and all its contents.

Roofs, windows, and doors proved to be the weak points of houses when Hurricane Andrew plowed through Dade County in south Florida in 1992. With winds of 140 miles (225 kilometers) per hour and peak gusts of nearly 165 miles (265 kilometers) per hour, Andrew turned out to be the costliest natural disaster ever to strike the United States. Insurers counted $16.5 billion in covered losses, and estimates of total home and business losses exceeded $30 billion.

Dade County's many mobile homes, in particular, proved no

A hurricane-resistant house

Making a house resistant to hurricane damage is largely a matter of solid construction. A house that meets or exceeds building codes for hurricane-prone regions stands a very good chance of making it through a hurricane without serious damage.

Roof shingles should be securely nailed to the roof and the framing of the roof should be reinforced and connected to the walls with heavy nails and metal straps.

Storm shutters and windows with shatter-resistant plastic-laminated glass will make a tight seal against the wind and prevent wind-blown objects from crashing through windows.

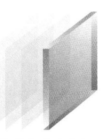

Plastic-laminated glass

Metal straps

Reinforced frame

Construction throughout the house ought to be of the highest quality and all structural parts should be solidly connected to one another with strong nails and metal strapping. The bottom of the frame should be bolted securely to the foundation.

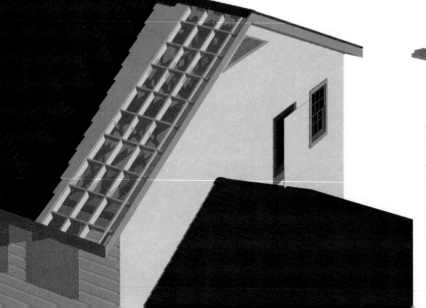

match for Andrew's fierce winds, and most were smashed to pieces. But thousands of standard houses, too, were wrecked or badly damaged. Investigators discovered that many of those houses, especially ones erected in recent years, had not been constructed in accordance with the South Florida Building Code, which had been adopted in Dade County. Moreover, county building inspectors reportedly had turned a blind eye to such infractions.

Homebuilders had cut corners in several ways. Often, the investigators found, builders hammered in fewer nails than were needed to securely hold the plywood sheets that covered the roof frame. Door frames also were found to have too few nails holding them in place. Investigators cited numerous examples of houses that could have been saved if a few extra boards had been installed to brace a roof overhang or if some extra metal straps had been used to better tie together the parts of the house.

In addition to being ignored in Dade County, the South Florida Building Code had fallen behind other, more sophisticated construction codes. In the two years following Hurricane Andrew, the county commissioners passed amendments to the code that increased the standards for the wind pressures and peak gusts that buildings must withstand. The new code also called for windows to be able to resist a 2 x 4 board crashing into them at 34 miles (55 kilometers) per hour. Homebuilders can meet the latter requirement by equipping a house with either steel shutters or plastic-laminated glass.

Besides being equipped with storm shutters or shatter-resistant windows, a house can be strengthened against hurricanes in a number of ways. The entire house should be tightly bolted to its foundation, and the roof framing should be reinforced and connected solidly to the walls with strong nails and metal straps. Heavy nails and strapping should be used throughout the frame to hold all members together securely. And exterior wall siding should be securely nailed to sheets of plywood connected to the frame. A house built in this way possesses in spades the overall strength that architects and engineers call structural integrity.

Structural integrity is the key to protecting our built environment in regions where hurricanes and earthquakes are an ever-present threat. Engineers believe that we now have the knowledge and technology to protect ourselves from these calamities of nature—perhaps not completely but to a far greater extent than we have in the past. Strengthening our homes and cities against the day when the winds blow or the ground shakes costs money, but it is money well spent. The alternative, if the effort isn't made, is to risk another, and probably more costly, cycle of destruction. ▪ ▪ ▪

For further reading:

Levy, Matthys, and Salvadori, Mario. *Why Buildings Fall Down: How Structures Fail.* W.W. Norton & Co., 1992.

Fisher, David E. *The Scariest Place on Earth: Eye to Eye with Hurricanes.* Random House, 1994.

Bulgaria. On Jan. 25, 1995, a new government headed by Prime Minister Zhan Videnov, chairman of the Bulgarian Socialist Party, took office. The installation of the new government followed December 1994 elections in which the Socialist Party—formerly the Communist Party—in coalition with two other leftist parties, won 43.5 percent of the vote and 125 of 240 parliamentary seats.

Government and media. In June 1995, parliament voted to replace the directors of the state radio, television, and telegraph services. The government claimed the action was necessary because newscasts lacked objectivity and distorted the government's work. Members of the opposition charged that the government was trying to restrict the media. Opposition parties also protested an anticrime bill that allowed government wiretapping. But in September, a vote of no confidence in Videnov was defeated by a margin of 28 votes—130 to 102.

Privatizing industry. The government in May announced plans for a mass privatization program based on the one in Czechoslovakia. The program aimed at selling up to 200 large, state-owned enterprises to private buyers. President Zhelyu Zhelev vetoed a privatization measure requiring farmers to offer their land for sale to the state before making it available to other buyers. In June, the Constitutional Court declared the measure unconstitutional.

The Bulgarian economy continued to struggle. Inflation dropped to 15.2 percent in the first half of 1995, but experts anticipated a sharp rise by the end of the year. The price of fuel, energy, and other essential items increased dramatically. The government reported that 73 percent of Bulgarians lived in poverty. Unemployment fell slightly to 13 percent in the first half of 1995, due to the recovery of certain industries and growth in the service sector. Industrial production grew by 2 percent in the first half of 1995.

Foreign relations. Bulgaria became an associate member of the European Union (EU) in February. The government restated Bulgaria's commitment to joining both the EU and the North Atlantic Treaty Organization (NATO). But in May, parliament failed to adopt a common position on NATO membership after Russia objected to NATO expansion. In September, however, Bulgaria participated in NATO naval maneuvers in the Black Sea.

In February, the International Monetary Fund (IMF) and the World Bank, agencies of the United Nations, agreed to extend Bulgaria a $93-million loan to improve its power-generating capabilities. Distribution of those funds by the IMF was delayed, however, until the Bulgarian government prepared a program to cut the country's domestic debt.

◻ Sharon L. Wolchik

See also **Europe** (Facts in brief table). In *World Book,* see Bulgaria.

Burkina Faso. See Africa.

Burma. The ruling military junta of Burma (officially named Myanmar) released democratic opposition leader Daw Aung San Suu Kyi from house arrest on July 10, 1995. Aung San Suu Kyi had been confined for six years, since July 1989, despite the 1990 election victory of the National League for Democracy, which she headed. The league had won 392 out of 485 seats in a parliament that the junta never allowed to convene. In 1991, Aung San Suu Kyi won the Nobel Peace Prize, but the junta kept her from accepting it.

The junta gave no explanation for the release. However, many countries had been applying political and economic pressure on Burma to persuade the junta to free Aung San Suu Kyi. At her release, Japan

Dissident leader Daw Aung San Suu Kyi speaks to supporters applauding her release in July from a six-year house arrest enforced by Burma's ruling military junta.

and other countries said they would resume humanitarian and economic aid to Burma. Although Burma is rich in natural resources, its economy had withered during 33 years of military rule.

Conciliatory role. In a statement the day following her release, Aung San Suu Kyi told waiting crowds outside her house that the junta had asked her to help achieve peace and stability. She also said she would continue to be politically active, and she called for dialogue and national reconciliation.

Aung San Suu Kyi began consultations with other league leaders, including chairman Tin Oo, a former military officer who had broken with the army after soldiers had killed thousands of civilians in suppressing prodemocracy demonstrations in 1988. Tin Oo had been a political prisoner until the junta freed him in March 1995.

On November 28, the junta reconvened a constitutional convention packed with its supporters. The next day, Aung San Suu Kyi announced that the league would boycott the convention because it was "not heading toward democracy." As the atmosphere in the capital, Rangoon, became more tense, the junta continued to work toward a constitution that would preserve military control.

Ethnic strife. The Burmese army scored successes in 1995 against minority ethnic groups that had been fighting for separate states since shortly after Burma gained independence from the United Kingdom in 1948. Several groups had established bases along the jungle border with Thailand in order to obtain supplies through that country.

On Jan. 26, 1995, the strongest rebel army, the Karen National Union, burned its headquarters at Manerplaw as it retreated into Thailand to escape Burmese troop advances. Thousands of Karen civilians also fled into Thailand, joining an estimated 60,000 other refugees, mainly Karens, who had fled from previous government strikes. Refugee camps were strung out all along the Thai border.

On April 28, the Thai government complained that Burmese troops were crossing into Thailand and burning the camps in order to force refugees back across the border. Thai officials said as many as 12,000 refugees had fled Burma in the latest wave. In a strong letter to Burma, Thailand warned of "appropriate retaliatory action in the strongest form."

Opium war. Burma's army also tried to destroy Khun Sa, an opium-producing warlord with his base on the Thai border. But Burmese authorities allowed the Wa tribe and others to ship opium and its derivative, heroin, to the outside world.

U Nu, Burma's last elected prime minister, died in obscurity on February 14 at age 87. He had won the support of most Burmese in the years after 1948, when Burma won independence from Britain. But the army ousted him in 1962. □ Henry S. Bradsher

See also **Asia** (Facts in brief); **Aung San Suu Kyi, Daw.** In *World Book*, see **Burma.**

A young Rwandan Hutu woman holds a crying baby after arriving in April at a temporary refugee camp in northern Burundi.

Burundi teetered on the brink of total collapse in 1995. The country's ethnic groups, the majority Hutu and the minority Tutsi, parallel those of Rwanda, and violent conflict between these groups has characterized the history of both countries. Since the mid-1970's, fighting between Hutu and Tutsi had caused an estimated 200,000 deaths in Burundi. The memories of past battles and the turmoil in neighboring Rwanda stimulated widespread fears of further fighting in Burundi.

Warfare in Burundi in 1993 caused over 150,000 deaths, the flight of more than 600,000 refugees to Rwanda, Tanzania, and Zaire, and the internal displacement of about 1 million people. Fighting in Rwanda in 1994 caused thousands of refugees to flow into Burundi, increasing economic problems and political tensions.

There was at least a facade of power-sharing in Burundi in 1995. The Tutsi were dominant in the military and the Hutu were dominant in the government, albeit with Tutsi participation. The President of Burundi, Sylvestre Ntibantunganya, was Hutu, but the prime minister was Tutsi. However, the military did not always follow the government's directives, and there were powerful ethnic militias both inside and outside of the country. A Hutu group led by Leonard Nyangoma, a former Cabinet minister in the Burundian government, had attacked from Zaire in 1994 and in 1995 controlled a small part of Burundi.

In late March, attacks by the Tutsi-dominated army against Hutu in Bujumbura, Burundi's capital, caused 50,000 Hutu to flee the city. Bujumbura in late 1995 was almost purely Tutsi in its population. Massacres of Hutu were reported in April in several rural areas. More fighting occurred in Bujumbura in November and December. It appeared that the Tutsi military was forcing the few remaining Hutu out of the city, an action many observers predicted would lead to reprisals by the Hutu militia.

□ Mark DeLancey

See also **Africa** (Facts in brief table). In *World Book,* see **Burundi.**

Bus. See Transit.

Business. See Bank; Economics; Manufacturing.

Cabinet, U.S. Ethics problems plagued two members of President Bill Clinton's Cabinet in 1995, but they remained in their posts with strong backing from the White House. Attorney General Janet Reno asked federal judges to appoint an independent counsel to investigate allegations against Secretary of Commerce Ronald H. Brown and Henry G. Cisneros, secretary of the Department of Housing and Urban Development (HUD). Reno exonerated another Cabinet member, Secretary of Transportation Federico F. Peña, of conflict-of-interest charges relating to his former investment firm.

The inquiry involving Cisneros centered on whether he lied to federal investigators in 1993 about the amount of money he paid to Linda Medlar, a woman with whom he had an extramarital affair in the late 1980's while he was mayor of San Antonio. In seeking appointment of an independent counsel on March 14, Reno said that Cisneros made false statements but that it was not clear whether he violated the law or sought to influence his confirmation as HUD secretary.

Cisneros asserted his innocence and vowed to "stay and fight" against Republican-led attempts to make large cuts in federal housing programs. Cisneros and Medlar settled out of court for $49,000, ending her lawsuit charging him with breach of contract. Medlar had sought $256,000, claiming that Cisneros had failed to give her the financial help he

had promised. As part of the settlement, both parties agreed to stop publicly discussing their affair.

Washington, D.C., attorney David M. Barrett was named independent counsel in the Cisneros investigation on May 24. A former Republican fund-raiser and federal prosecutor, Barrett had once served as special counsel to the House Ethics Committee.

Brown under investigation. Commerce Secretary Brown, former Democratic National Committee chairman and the highest-ranking African American in the Clinton Administration, was the subject of an independent inquiry into his personal finances and his partnership with businesswoman Nolanda Hill. Brown said he did not invest money in First International Communications Corporation, which he and Hill founded in 1990. He also stated that he was not personally involved in another Hill-owned firm, Corridor Broadcasting Corporation, which defaulted on federal loans totaling $40 million. Brown reported that he had sold Hill his share of First International Communications on Dec. 15, 1993, for over $400,000.

Reno sought the appointment of a special counsel on May 18, 1995, to investigate whether Hill's payments to Brown were in violation of federal law. Reno said the counsel should determine whether Brown made false statements on his annual financial disclosure forms. She also requested an investigation into Brown's 1993 purchase of a townhouse for a friend, Lillian Madsen, to see if Brown concealed the fact that he made the down payment with money given to him by Madsen, who had borrowed it from a friend. Dan Pearson, a prominent Miami attorney and former federal prosecutor, was named independent counsel in the Brown investigation on July 6.

CIA director appointed. The President in March appointed John M. Deutch, a former deputy secretary of defense, to head the Central Intelligence Agency, and gave that job Cabinet-level status. Clinton's first choice, retired Air Force General Michael P.C. Carns, withdrew following disclosures that he had violated immigration laws by bringing a Philippine resident to the United States. Deutch was confirmed by the Senate on May 9.

New secretaries of treasury, agriculture. In January, former Wall Street investment banker Robert E. Rubin replaced Lloyd M. Bentsen as secretary of the Treasury. Rubin, who had served as chairman of the National Economic Council, was approved by the Senate on January 10. In March, Dan Glickman, a former Kansas congressman, succeeded Mike Espy as secretary of agriculture. Espy resigned in October 1994 amid charges that he had accepted gifts from companies subject to regulation by the Department of Agriculture. Glickman, who lost his bid for reelection to Congress in 1994, was endorsed by the Senate on March 30, 1995. □ William J. Eaton

In *World Book,* see **Cabinet.**

California. See Los Angeles; San Diego; State government.

Cambodia slumped more deeply into corrupt, inefficient, and autocratic government in 1995. First Prime Minister Norodom Ranariddh said in August that "the Western brand of democracy and freedom of the press is not applicable to Cambodia." Only after millions of the nation's rural poor have the basic necessities could democracy be preached, he said.

Ranariddh's statement followed the visit on August 4 of United States Secretary of State Warren Christopher to the capital, Phnom Penh. It was the first visit of a U.S. chief diplomat in 40 years. Christopher warned that "the survival of Cambodian democracy cannot be taken for granted."

The Khmer Rouge threat. Deputy Prime Minister Sar Kheng said in March that unless government corruption lessened, the Communist Khmer Rouge would regain strength. The Khmer Rouge had boycotted Cambodia's democratic elections in 1993, which brought Ranariddh to power. In 1995, Khmer Rouge guerrillas based along the borders with Thailand fought sporadically with government troops in a civil war. The government claimed that defections were weakening the guerrillas, yet the Khmer Rouge terrorized villagers in much of the country.

Dissident ousted. Former Finance Minister Sam Rainsy continued to denounce official corruption after he was fired from his post in October 1994. Rainsy's party, the National United Front for an Independent, Neutral, Peaceful, and Cooperative Cambodia (known as FUNCINPEC) headed by Ranariddh, expelled him on May 23, 1995, over his intention to start a new political alliance. On June 22, Rainsy was expelled from the National Assembly without a vote, a debate, or charges being brought. Rainsy founded a new political party, Khmer Nation, on November 9, but the government refused to give it any official recognition.

Foreign observers said government repression had created a climate of fear among dissidents and journalists. Critics regularly received death threats.

Media problems. The government forcefully repressed critical reporting by the more than 30 daily newspapers in Phnom Penh. The government closed down one newspaper, dropped charges against a soldier accused of murdering a reporter investigating military corruption, and sentenced several editors to jail. An international organization, Human Rights Watch Asia, said on May 22 that these cases were "an all-out war on freedom of speech."

On July 18, the National Assembly passed a new press law that allowed the government to close newspapers without a hearing and levy heavy fines and jail sentences for publishing material that "affects national security and political stability." However, King Norodom Sihanouk, Ranariddh's father, refused to sign it into law. But on August 31, while the king was out of the country, National Assembly President Chea Sim, as acting head of state, signed the measure.

Sihanouk continued his battle with cancer in 1995. Cambodians respected the king, but he lacked much influence. FUNCINPEC had won the most votes in the 1993 elections because it was considered his party, but the Cambodian People's Party (CPP) of former Communists dominated the government.

Political plotting. On Nov. 21, 1995, Prince Norodom Sirivut, a half-brother of the king, was arrested on charges that he was plotting to assassinate Second Prime Minister Hun Sen, who led the CPP. The prince resigned as foreign minister in 1994, but he remained a senior member of FUNCINPEC and was regarded as a potential opposition candidate in National Assembly elections scheduled for 1998. Observers believed that the arrest, made over Ranariddh's objections, showed that Hun Sen dominated the government.

The economy included many illegal activities, such as a thriving heroin trade that critics charged was protected by some officials. In May, the government banned the export of logs in an effort to reduce the pillaging of forests and encourage wood processing as a way of creating jobs. Both the army and the Khmer Rouge guerrillas cut timber to sell in Thailand. Some legal logging produced revenue, as did foreign concessions, but foreign aid accounted for 40 percent of the budget. □ Henry S. Bradsher

See also **Asia** (Facts in brief table). In *World Book,* see **Cambodia.**

Cameroon. President Paul Biya outlasted his opponents in 1995, stalling demands for democracy. Biya used such tactics as postponing municipal elections to encourage divisions within the opposition. He also stalled talks for a new constitution, refusing the demands of the *Anglophone* (English-speaking) minority. In the Anglophone community, the split between the radical northwest and the conservative southwest provinces became more pronounced.

The Nigerian border crisis that began in January 1994 receded in importance in 1995. Nigeria and Cameroon had disputed rights to the petroleum-rich Bakassi area in the Gulf of Guinea, the loss of which would be a serious detriment to Cameroon's economy. The case was expected to be decided by the International Court of Justice.

In October, it was announced that Cameroon would join the Commonwealth, an organization of former British colonies. Cameroon's application had been held up by its undemocratic conditions.

Armed bandits became a significant problem in northern Cameroon in 1995. But the country's economy improved, partly due to increases in export prices. The government paid salaries on time, but continued to shrink the size of the civil service and sell shares of government-controlled companies in order to make ends meet. □ Mark DeLancey

See also **Africa** (Facts in brief table). In *World Book,* see **Cameroon.**

In one of the largest rallies in Canadian history, about 100,000 people from all over Canada join Quebecers in October to show support for national unity.

Canada

Canada moved to the brink of dissolution in October 1995 when voters in Quebec considered—then narrowly rejected—a referendum proposing separation from the Canadian federation. About 60 percent of French-speaking Quebecers voted to assert their identity in English-speaking North America through the creation of a sovereign state.

Campaign for independence. The separatist Parti Québécois (PQ) had promoted sovereignty for Quebec during its winning campaign for office in September 1994. Despite public opinion polls predicting that sovereignty would be defeated by a 60-to-40 percent vote—the results of an independence referendum in 1980—the PQ government of Premier

Jacques Parizeau pressed ahead with plans for a second referendum. In February 1995, the administration launched hearings in 223 Quebec communities to discuss a draft bill on sovereignty. The opposition Liberal Party refused to participate in the hearings, claiming they allowed no opportunity to discuss alternatives to separation. In an April report on the hearings, the Parizeau government recommended that Quebec declare sovereignty after popular approval, then negotiate a political and economic partnership with the federal government and the remaining nine provinces.

On June 12, Quebec's three separatist parties announced the formation of a coalition to work for approval of the referendum. The coalition consisted of the PQ; the Bloc Québécois (BQ), whose leader, Lu-

The campaign for the referendum generated little excitement at first. But the situation changed dramatically on October 7 when Parizeau named Bouchard as chief negotiator with Canada after a referendum victory and, thus, the leader of the "Yes" campaign. A magnetic orator and popular figure, Bouchard made light of any adverse economic consequences of separation. Instead, he extolled the advantages of a partnership with Canada and liberation from a wasteful and inefficient federal system. Bouchard's message, which also included an emotional appeal to Quebecers' self-esteem and confidence, gave the sovereignists a strong boost in public-opinion polls.

The opposition. The federalist side in the campaign was led by Daniel Johnson, the leader of the Liberal Party, who had served briefly as premier in 1994. A solid if uninspiring speaker, he emphasized the likely economic costs of separation, including a soaring budget deficit, higher interest rates, the flight of investment capital, and rising unemployment. But Johnson was vague about possible changes to Canada's constitution that could satisfy Quebec's demands for autonomy without secession.

At first, Canadian Prime Minister Jean Chrétien adopted a reassuring attitude, contending that the referendum was certain to fail. Canada was not interested in further constitutional talks, he said, but wanted the government to focus on strengthening the economy and promoting employment.

In the final weeks of the campaign, however, Chrétien realized that the momentum for separation had reached dangerous levels. He threw himself into the debate with strong speeches in Quebec and a national television address. On October 27, three days before the vote, he spoke at a gigantic rally in Montreal, where an estimated 100,000 Canadians, many from outside Quebec, converged to show their support for Quebec as a valued part of Canada. Chrétien also made vague promises about constitutional change. It was clear that Chrétien, a veteran of almost 30 years in Canadian politics, had seriously misjudged the mood in his native province.

The vote. About 93 percent of Quebec's eligible voters cast ballots on October 30. "Yes" votes for separation totaled 2,308,266 or 49.4 percent. "No" votes came to 2,360,714 or 50.5 percent. Only 52,448 votes, slightly more than 1 percent of the total, separated the two sides. The separatists captured 80 of Quebec's 125 voting districts—up from 22 districts won in 1980. But there were lopsided majorities supporting federalism on the island of Montreal, where most English-speaking Quebecers and almost all the province's ethnic minorities lived. The referendum was also soundly defeated in districts along the Ottawa River adjoining Ottawa, Canada's capital, and in the Eastern Townships near the United States border. The far north part of the province, home to the Cree Indians and the Inuit, also voted "No."

cien Bouchard, controlled 53 seats in Canada's House of Commons; and the Parti Action Démocratique, headed by Mario Dumont. The coalition also was to oversee negotiations with Canada if the referendum won approval.

On September 20, Quebec's assembly passed a bill authorizing a declaration of independence to be issued if the measure passed and setting forth the referendum question: Do you agree that Quebec should become sovereign, after having made a formal offer to Canada for a new economic and political partnership? The bill also authorized the drafting of a new constitution and promised self-government to Quebec's Indian and Inuit populations and protection for the province's English-speaking minority.

Federal spending in Canada
Estimated budget for fiscal 1995-1996*

Department or agency	Millions of dollars†
Agriculture and agri-food	1,765
Atlantic Canada Opportunities Agency	389
Canadian heritage	2,800
Citizenship and immigration	670
Environment	630
Finance	**59,400
Fisheries and oceans	897
Foreign affairs and international trade	3,565
Governor general	10
Health	8,754
Human resources development	33,561
Indian affairs and northern development	5,338
Industry	2,853
Justice	737
National defence	11,097
National revenue	2,137
Natural resources	1,152
Parliament	282
Privy Council	158
Public works and government services	4,096
Solicitor general	2,572
Transport	2,524
Treasury board	1,271
Veterans affairs	1,998
Western economic diversification	478
Total	**149,134**

* April 1, 1995, to March 31, 1996.
**Adjusted for nonbudgetary items
† Canadian dollars; $1 = U.S. $0.73 as of Dec. 18, 1995.

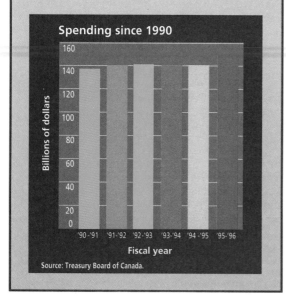

Spending since 1990

Fiscal year

Source: Treasury Board of Canada.

The large support for the referendum among French-speaking Quebecers, however, represented a resounding rejection of the role Quebec had played in Canada's political, economic, and cultural life since a united Canada was formed in 1867. The vision of a bilingual and bicultural Canada had been set aside.

The aftermath. The referendum's defeat gave the federal government time to devise a response to the crisis, which the vote hardly resolved. Facing the gravest test in his career, Chrétien had to reconcile Quebec's wish for a distinct status with the prevailing view in the rest of Canada that the country consisted of 10 equal provinces. One solution to the crisis—transferring more power to all the provinces—would inevitably weaken the central government.

On Dec. 11, 1995, the House of Commons approved a resolution, introduced by Chrétien, that recognized Quebec's distinct language, culture and civil law. On December 13, the House approved a Chretien proposal to grant a veto over constitutional changes to the provinces of Quebec, British Columbia and Ontario and to a prairie region composed of Alberta, Manitoba, and Saskatchewan, and an Atlantic region composed of New Brunswick, Newfoundland, Nova Scotia, and Prince Edward Island.

Budget cuts. The federal budget, released on Feb. 27, 1995, slashed government spending in an unprecedented manner. Driven by an overriding desire to reduce the federal deficit, the government reduced overall expenditures to $158.6 billion in fiscal year 1996-1997 from $162.9 billion in fiscal 1994-1995 (all figures are in Canadian dollars). Program spending was to fall 8.8 percent between fiscal year 1994-1995 and fiscal 1996-1997. Finance Minister Paul Martin estimated that with the cuts the deficit would fall from $37.9 billion to $24.3 billion by 1997. This reduction, he argued, would allow him to meet the Liberal government's promise to reduce the deficit to 3 percent of Canada's gross domestic product—the total value of all goods and services produced within the country—by that date.

The government cut $7 billion from transfers to the provinces for social programs, to be implemented in fiscal years 1996-1997 and 1997-1998. It also lumped together grants for health, welfare, and education, leaving the provinces free to spend the money as they desired. Critics attacked these moves as a betrayal by the governing Liberal Party of its historic commitment to social justice. Even some members of the Liberal caucus were restless with the party's apparent disregard of social policies in the harsh climate of fiscal restraint.

The cuts in expenditures fell heavily on public services, to be cut by 19 percent, or 45,000 jobs, over the next three years. The Department of National Defence was also targeted, with its expenditures slated for a 14 percent reduction by 1997. In addition, Martin eliminated a $560-million payment to

The Spanish fishing vessel *Estai* enters St. John's Harbor in Newfoundland after its seizure by Canadian officials in March for illegal fishing.

Canadian farmers for transporting grain to market by rail, started in 1867.

Martin refrained from raising personal income taxes, though he increased the excise tax on gasoline as well as some taxes on corporations. He claimed that he had cut expenditures by $7 for each $1 in new taxes. The government also announced it would sell its 70 percent stake in such state enterprises as Petro-Canada as well as its ownership of Canadian National Railways.

Legislation. The most controversial measure before Parliament in 1995 was a new Firearms Act introduced by Justice Minister Allan Rock in February. It called for the mandatory government registration of all firearms, including shotguns and rifles, by the year 2003 and a ban on 24 military and paramilitary weapons. Although the legislation won wide popular support, farmers, hunters, recreational-gun owners, and native people opposed it. They claimed that the plan would be costly to administer and ineffective in reducing violent crime.

The three Prairie Provinces along with the Northwest Territories and the Yukon announced their united opposition to the bill in September 1995 and promised a court challenge should it win approval. Nevertheless, the House of Commons passed the measure by a vote of 192 to 63 on June 13. The Senate approved the bill on November 22, and it became law on December 5, the eve of the anniversary of the fatal shootings of 14 women at the École Polytechnique in Montreal in 1989.

Cabinet. Chrétien made only one change in his Cabinet during 1995. On February 22, he named Liberal Lucienne Robillard, elected nine days earlier in a Montreal by-election, as minister of labor.

By-elections. The Liberals won two other by-elections on February 13. The victories left party standings in the House of Commons as: Liberals 177; Bloc Québécois 53; Reform Party 52; New Democratic Party 9; Progressive Conservative Party 2; and independents 2.

Governor general. A new Canadian representative of Queen Elizabeth II of Great Britain was installed in office. Romeo LeBlanc, the first member of New Brunswick's French-speaking Acadian community to be named governor general, took over the largely ceremonial post on February 8.

Economy. Economic conditions in 1995 were disappointing. Overall, the economy grew marginally in the first quarter, shrank in the second quarter and recovered slightly later in the year. The annual rate of increase was expected to settle at 2.5 percent. The midyear estimate of the gross domestic product was $777.2 billion. The slow economic performance of Canada's chief trading partner, the United States, hurt such major exports as automobiles. Trade across the Pacific expanded, with Japan the chief market. Interest rates, though lower than in 1994, were still

Members of the Canadian House of Commons

The House of Commons of the first session of the 35th Parliament convened on Jan. 17, 1994. As of Nov. 1, 1995, the House of Commons consisted of the following members: 177 Liberal Party, 53 Bloc Québécois, 52 Reform Party, 9 New Democratic Party, 2 Progressive Conservative Party, 1 Independent, and 1 Independent Liberal. This table shows each legislator and party affiliation. Asterisk (*) denotes those who served in the 34th Parliament.

Alberta
Diane Ablonczy, Ref.
Leon E. Benoit, Ref.
Judy Bethel, Lib.
Cliff Breitkreuz, Ref.
Jan Brown, Ref.
David Charters, Ref.
Ken Epp, Ref.
Deborah Grey, Ref.*
Art Hanger, Ref.
Hugh Hanrahan, Ref.
Stephen Harper, Ref.
Grant Hill, Ref.
Dale Johnston, Ref.
David Kilgour, Lib.*
John Loney, Lib.
Preston Manning, Ref.
Ian McClelland, Ref.
Anne McLellan, Lib.
Bob Mills, Ref.
Charles Penson, Ref.
Jack Ramsay, Ref.
Jim Silye, Ref.
Monte Solberg, Ref.
Ray Speaker, Ref.
Myron Thompson, Ref.
John Williams, Ref.

British Columbia
Jim Abbott, Ref.
David Anderson, Lib.
Margaret Bridgman, Ref.
Raymond Chan, Lib.
John Cummins, Ref.
Harbance Singh Dhaliwal, Lib.
John Duncan, Ref.
Paul E. Forseth, Ref.
Jack Frazer, Ref.
Hedy Fry, Lib.
Bill Gilmour, Ref.
Jim Gouk, Ref.
Herb Grubel, Ref.
Richard M. Harrison, Ref.
Jim Hart, Ref.
Sharon Hayes, Ref.
Jay Hill, Ref.
Daphne Jennings, Ref.
Keith Martin, Ref.
Philip Mayfield, Ref.
Ted McWhinney, Lib.
Val Meredith, Ref.
Nelson Riis, N.D.P.*
Bob Ringma, Ref.
Svend J. Robinson, N.D.P.*
Werner Schmidt, Ref.
Mike Scott, Ref.
Darrel Stinson, Ref.
Chuck Strahl, Ref.
Anna Terrana, Lib.
Randy White, Ref.
Ted White, Ref.

Manitoba
Reg Alcock, Lib.
Lloyd Axworthy, Lib.*

Bill Blaikie, N.D.P.*
Marlene Cowling, Lib.
Ronald J. Duhamel, Lib.*
Ron Fewchuck, Lib.
Jon Gerrard, Lib.
Elijah Harper, Lib.
John Harvard, Lib.*
Jake E. Hoeppner, Ref.
David Iftody, Lib.
Glen McKinnon, Lib.
Rey D. Pagtakhan, Lib.*
David Walker, Lib.*

New Brunswick
Guy H. Arseneault, Lib.*
Harold Culbert, Lib.
Charles Hubbard, Lib.
George S. Rideout, Lib.*
Pierrette Ringuette-Maltais, Lib.
Fernand Robichaud, Lib.
Andy Scott, Lib.
Elsie Wayne, P.C.
Douglas Young, Lib.*
Paul Zed, Lib.

Newfoundland
George S. Baker, Lib.*
Bonnie Hickey, Lib.
Fred Mifflin, Lib.*
Jean Payne, Lib.
Roger Simmons, Lib.*
Brian Tobin, Lib.*

Northwest Territories
Jack Iyerak Anawak, Lib.*
Ethel Blondin-Andrew, Lib.*

Nova Scotia
Dianne Brushett, Lib.
Mary Clancy, Lib.*
David Dingwall, Lib.*
Francis G. LeBlanc, Lib.*
Ron MacDonald, Lib.*
Russell MacLellan, Lib.*
John Murphy, Lib.
Geoff Regan, Lib.
Roseanne Skoke, Lib.
Harry Verran, Lib.
Derek Wells, Lib.

Ontario
Peter Adams, Lib.
Sarkis Assadourian, Lib.
Jean Augustine, Lib.
Sue Barnes, Lib.
Colleen Beaumier, Lib.
Reginald Belair, Lib.
Mauril Belanger, Lib.
Eugene Bellemare, Lib.*
Maurizio Bevilacqua, Lib.*
Jag Bhaduria, Ind. Lib.
Raymond Bonin, Lib.
Don Boudria, Lib.*

Bonnie Brown, Lib.
John Bryden, Lib.
Charles Caccia, Lib.*
Murray Calder, Lib.*
Barry Campbell, Lib.
John Cannis, Lib.
Marlene Catterall, Lib.*
Brenda Chamberlain, Lib.
Shaughnessy Cohen, Lib.
David M. Collenette, Lib.
Joe Comuzzi, Lib.*
Sheila Copps, Lib.*
Rex Crawford, Lib.*
Paul DeVillers, Lib.
Stan Dromisky, Lib.
Arthur C. Eggleton, Lib.
John English, Lib.
John Finlay, Lib.
Jesse Flis, Lib.*
Joe Fontana, Lib.*
Beryl Gaffney, Lib.*
Roger Gallaway, Lib.
John Godfrey, Lib.
Bill Graham, Lib.
Herb Gray, Lib.*
Ivan Grose, Lib.
Albina Guarnieri, Lib.*
Mac Harb, Lib.*
Ed Harper, Ref.
Leonard Hopkins, Lib.*
Tony Ianno, Lib.
Ron Irwin, Lib.
Ovid L. Jackson, Lib.
Jim Jordan, Lib.*
Jim Karygiannis, Lib.*
Stan Keyes, Lib.*
Bob Kilger, Lib.*
Gar Knutson, Lib.
Karen Kraft Sloan, Lib.
Walt Lastewka, Lib.
Derek Lee, Lib.*
Roy MacLaren, Lib.*
Gurbax Singh Malhi, Lib.
John Maloney, Lib.
John Manley, Lib.*
Sergio Marchi, Lib.*
Diane Marleau, Lib.*
Larry McCormick, Lib.
Dan McTeague, Lib.
Peter Milliken, Lib.*
Dennis J. Mills, Lib.*
Maria Minna, Lib.
Andy Mitchell, Lib.
Ian Murray, Lib.
Robert D. Nault, Lib.*
John Nunziata, Lib.*
Pat O'Brien, Lib.
John O'Reilly, Lib.
Gilbert Parent, Lib.*
Carolyn Parrish, Lib.
Janko Peric, Lib.
Douglas Peters, Lib.
Jim Peterson, Lib.*

Beth Phinney, Lib.*
Jerry Pickard, Lib.*
Gary Pillitteri, Lib.
Julian Reed, Lib.
John Richardson, Lib.
Allan Rock, Lib.
Benoît Serré, Lib.
Alex Shepherd, Lib.
Bob Speller, Lib.*
Brent St. Denis, Lib.
Paul Steckle, Lib.
Christine Stewart, Lib.*
Jane Stewart, Lib.
Paul Szabo, Lib.
Andrew Telegdi, Lib.
Peter Thalheimer, Lib.
Paddy Torsney, Lib.
Rose-Marie Ur, Lib.
Tony Valeri, Lib.
Lyle Vanclief, Lib.*
Joseph Volpe, Lib.
Tom Wappel, Lib.*
Susan Whelan, Lib.
Bob Wood, Lib.*

Prince Edward Island
Wayne Easter, Lib.
Lawrence MacAulay, Lib.*
Joe McGuire, Lib.*
George Proud, Lib.*

Quebec
Warren Allmand, Lib.*
Mark Assad, Lib.*
Gérard Asselin, B.Q.
Claude Bachand, B.Q.
Eleni Bakopanos, Lib.
Richard Bélisle, B.Q.
Michel Bellehumeur, B.Q.
Stéphane Bergeron, B.Q.
Maurice Bernier, B.Q.
Yvan Bernier, B.Q.
Gilles Bernier, Ind.*
Robert Bertrand, Lib.
Lucien Bouchard, B.Q.*
Pierre Brien, B.Q.
René Canuel, B.Q.
André Caron, B.Q.
Martin Cauchon, Lib.
Jean J. Charest, P.C.*
Jean Chrétien, Lib.*
Jean-Guy Chrétien, B.Q.
Paul Crête, B.Q.
Madeleine Dalphond-Guiral, B.Q.
Michel Daviault, B.Q.
Pierre de Savoye, B.Q.
Maud Debien, B.Q.
Bernard Deshaies, B.Q.
Nunzio Discepola, Lib.
Antoine Dubé, B.Q.
Gilles Duceppe, B.Q.*
Maurice Dumas, B.Q.
Michel Dupuy, Lib.

Gilbert Fillion, B.Q.
Sheila Finestone, Lib.*
Alfonso Gagliano, Lib.*
Christiane Gagnon, B.Q.
Patrick Gagnon, Lib.
Michel Gauthier, B.Q.
Maurice Godin, B.Q.
Monique Guay, B.Q.
Michel Guimond, B.Q.
Jean-Marc Jacob, B.Q.
Francine Lalonde, B.Q.
Jean Landry, B.Q.
François Langlois, B.Q.
René Laurin, B.Q.
Laurent Lavigne, B.Q.
Raymond Lavigne, Lib.
Ghislain Lebel, B.Q.
Nic Leblanc, B.Q.*
Réjean Lefebvre, B.Q.
Gaston Leroux, B.Q.
Jean H. Leroux, B.Q.
Clifford Lincoln, Lib.
Yvan Loubier, B.Q.
Shirley Maheu, Lib.*
Jean-Paul Marchand, B.Q.
Paul Martin, Lib.*
Marcel Massé, Lib.
Réal Ménard, B.Q.
Paul Mercier, B.Q.
Osvaldo Nunez, B.Q.
André Oueller, Lib.*
Denis Paradis, Lib.
Philippe Paré, B.Q.
Bernard Patry, Lib.
Pauline Picard, B.Q.
Louis Plamondon, B.Q.*
Roger Pomerleau, B.Q.
Lucienne Robillard, Lib.
Yves Rocheleau, B.Q.
Benoît Sauvageau, B.Q.
Bernard St-Laurent, B.Q.
Suzanne Tremblay, B.Q.
Benoît Tremblay, B.Q.
Pierrette Venne, B.Q.

Saskatchewan
Vic Althouse, N.D.P.*
Chris Axworthy, N.D.P.*
Morris Bodnar, Lib.
Garry Breitkreuz, Ref.
Bernie Collins, Lib.
Simon de Jong, N.D.P.*
Ralph E. Goodale, Lib.
Elwin Hermanson, Ref.
Allan Kerpan, Ref.
Gordon Kirkby, Lib.
Lee Morrison, Ref.
Georgette Sheridan, Lib.
John Solomon, N.D.P.
Len Taylor, N.D.P.*

Yukon Territory
Audrey McLaughlin, N.D.P.*

Members of the Canadian Senate

The Senate of the first session of the 35th Parliament convened on Jan. 17, 1994. As of Nov. 1, 1995, the Senate consisted of 51 Progressive Conservatives, 50 Liberals, and 3 Independents. The first date in each listing shows when the senator was appointed. The second date in each listing shows when the senator's term expires. A senator's term expires when the senator reaches the age of 75. Senators appointed before 1965 need not retire at the age of 75. An * denotes the two senators who were appointed before 1965. Though Orville H. Phillips was appointed in 1963, he has elected to retire at the age of 75. Thus, his end-of-term date of 1999 is indicated.

Province	Term
Alberta	
Joyce Fairbairn, Lib.	1984-2014
Ronald D. Ghitter, P.C.	1993-2010
Earl A. Hastings, P.C.	1966-1999
Daniel Hays, Lib.	1984-2014
H. A. Olson, Lib.	1977-2000
Walter Patrick Twinn, P.C.	1990-2009
British Columbia	
Jack Austin, Lib.	1975-2007
Pat Carney, P.C.	1990-2010
Edward M. Lawson, Ind.	1970-2004
Len Marchand, Lib.	1984-2008
Raymond J. Perrault, Lib.	1973-2001
Gerry St. Germain, P.C.	1993-2012
Manitoba	
Sharon Carstairs, Lib.	1994-2017
Duncan J. Jessiman, P.C.	1993-1998
Janis G. Johnson, P.C.	1990-2021
Gildas L. Molgat, Lib.	1970-2002
Mira Spivak, P.C.	1986-2009
Terrance R. Stratton, P.C.	1993-2013
New Brunswick	
John G. Bryden, Lib.	1994-2012
Erminie J. Cohen, P.C.	1993-2001
Eymard G. Corbin, Lib.	1984-2009
Mabel M. DeWare, P.C.	1990-2001
Noel A. Kinsella, P.C.	1990-2014
Rose-Marie Losier-Cool, Lib.	1995-2012
Brenda Robertson, P.C.	1984-2004
Louis J. Robichaud, Lib.	1973-2000
Jean-Maurice Simard, P.C.	1985-2006
L. Norbert Theriault, Lib.	1979-1996
Newfoundland	
Ethel M. Cochrane, P.C.	1986-2012
C. William Doody, P.C.	1979-2006
P. Derek Lewis, Lib.	1978-1999
Gerald R. Ottenheimer, P.C.	1987-2009
William J. Petten, Lib.	1968-1998
William Rompkey, Lib.	1995-2011
Northwest Territories	
Willie Adams, Lib.	1977-2009
Nova Scotia	
John M. Buchanan, P.C.	1990-2006
Gérald J. Comeau, P.C.	1990-2021
J. Michael Forrestall, P.C.	1990-2007
B. Alasdair Graham, Lib.	1972-2004
Michael Kirby, Lib.	1984-2016
Finlay MacDonald, P.C.	1984-1998
John M. Macdonald, P.C.*	1960-
Allan J. MacEachen, Lib.	1984-1996
Donald H. Oliver, Lib.	1990-2013
John B. Stewart, Lib.	1984-1999
Ontario	
Norman K. Atkins, P.C.	1986-2009
Peter Bosa, Lib.	1977-2002
Anne C. Cools, Lib.	1984-2018
D. Keith Davey, Lib.	1966-2001
Consiglio Di Nino, P.C.	1990-2013
Richard J. Doyle, P.C.	1985-1998

Province	Term
Ontario cont'd	
John T. Eyton, P.C.	1990-2009
Jean-Robert Gauthier, Lib.	1994-2004
Jerahmiel S. Grafstein, Lib.	1984-2010
Stanley Haidasz, Lib.	1978-1998
James F. Kelleher, P.C.	1990-2005
Wiliam M. Kelly, P.C.	1982-2000
Colin Kenny, Lib.	1984-2018
Wilbert Joseph Keon, P.C.	1990-2010
Marjory LeBreton, P.C.	1993-2015
Michael Arthur Meighen, P.C.	1990-2014
Lorna Milne, Lib.	1995-2009
Lowell Murray, P.C.	1979-2011
Landon Pearson, Lib.	1994-2005
P. Michael Pitfield, Ind.	1982-2012
Marie-P. Poulin, Lib.	1995-2009
Richard J. Stanbury, Lib.	1968-1998
Peter A. Stollery, Lib.	1981-2010
Andrew Thompson, Lib.	1967-1999
Prince Edward Island	
Doris M. Anderson, Lib.	1995-1997
M. Lorne Bonnell, Lib.	1971-1998
Orville H. Phillips, P.C.*	1963-1999
Eileen Rossiter, P.C.	1986-2004
Quebec	
W. David Angus, P.C.	1993-2012
Lise Bacon, Lib.	1994-2009
Gérald A. Beaudoin, P.C.	1988-2004
Roch Bolduc, P.C.	1988-2003
Guy Charbonneau, P.C.	1979-1997
Michel Cogger, P.C.	1986-2014
Pierre De Bané, Lib.	1984-2013
Philippe D. Gigantès, Lib.	1984-1998
Jacques Hébert, Lib.	1983-1998
Céline Hervieux-Payette, Lib.	1995-2016
Leo Kolber, Lib.	1983-2004
John Lynch-Staunton, P.C.	1990-2005
Pierre Claude Nolin, P.C.	1993-2025
Marcel Prud'homme, Ind.	1993-2009
Maurice Rlel, Lib.	1973-1997
Jean-Claude Rivest, P.C.	1993-2018
Pietro Rizzuto, Lib.	1976-2009
Fernand Roberge, P.C.	1993-2015
Jean-Louis Roux, Lib.	1994-1998
John Sylvain, P.C.	1990-1999
Charlie Watt, Lib.	1984-2019
Dalia Wood, Lib.	1979-1999
Quebec divisional	
Normand Grimard, P.C.	1990-2000
Thérèse Lavoie-Roux, P.C.	1990-2003
Saskatchewan	
Raynell Andreychuk, P.C.	1993-2019
James Balfour, P.C.	1979-2003
Eric A. Berntson, P.C.	1990-2016
Leonard J. Gustafson, P.C.	1993-2008
Herbert O. Sparrow, Lib.	1968-2005
David Tkachuk, P.C.	1993-2020
Yukon Territory	
Paul Lucier, Lib.	1975-2005

Canada

Canada, provinces, and territories population estimates

	1995 estimates
Alberta	2,748,300
British Columbia	3,764,200
Manitoba	1,138,000
New Brunswick	760,300
Newfoundland	575,600
Northwest Territories	65,500
Nova Scotia	938,200
Ontario	11,103,300
Prince Edward Island	136,200
Quebec	7,329,900
Saskatchewan	1,016,200
Yukon Territory	30,100
Canada	**29,606,100**

City and metropolitan populations

	Metropolitan area 1995 estimates	City 1991 census
Toronto, Ont.	4,306,300	635,395
Montreal, Que.	3,324,200	1,017,666
Vancouver, B.C.	1,828,100	471,844
Ottawa-Hull	1,024,600	
Ottawa, Ont.		313,987
Hull, Que.		60,707
Edmonton, Alta.	882,300	616,741
Calgary, Alta.	832,900	710,677
Quebec, Que.	689,900	167,517
Winnipeg, Man.	678,200	616,790
Hamilton, Ont.	647,300	318,499
London, Ont.	419,200	303,165
Kitchener, Ont.	396,900	168,282
St. Catharines-Niagara	390,500	
St. Catharines, Ont.		129,300
Niagara Falls, Ont.		75,399
Halifax, N.S.	340,300	114,455
Victoria, B.C.	313,200	71,228
Windsor, Ont.	286,600	191,435
Oshawa, Ont.	274,800	129,344
Saskatoon, Sask.	221,300	186,058
Regina, Sask.	198,800	179,178
St. John's, Nfld.	176,000	95,770
Chicoutimi-Jonquière	168,200	
Chicoutimi, Que.		62,670
Jonquière, Que.		57,933
Sudbury, Ont.	166,800	92,884
Sherbrooke, Que.	147,500	76,429
Trois-Rivières, Que.	141,700	49,426
Thunder Bay, Ont.	129,900	113,946
Saint John, N.B.	129,600	74,969

Source: Statistics Canada.

An estimated 10,000 jobseekers wait outside a General Motors plant near Toronto in January to fill out applications for 700 jobs.

high enough to limit growth. Consumer confidence was shaken by the debate over Quebec sovereignty.

Inflation remained under control, with the consumer price index in October 1995 up only 2.4 percent from the previous October. Unemployment stood in November at 9.4 percent. The Canadian dollar, battered by uncertainty over Canadian unity in foreign money markets, fluctuated between U.S. 70.5 cents and U.S. 75 cents during the year.

Foreign affairs. Canada began withdrawing most of its 2,000 soldiers in the United Nations (UN) peacekeeping force that had been stationed in war-torn Bosnia-Herzegovina (usually referred to as Bosnia) since 1992. In August 1995, the government announced that 800 ground troops in Croatia would

be called home. On October 5, the Cabinet revealed that nearly all the remaining 1,300 Canadian soldiers would be withdrawn by mid-November. The Chrétien government had been under increasing public pressure to withdraw Canadian forces from what was perceived as an impossible mission. Ten Canadian soldiers had been killed and several had been held hostage in Bosnia. Despite some opposition, however, the government in November said it would send additional troops to join the United States-led force that was being sent to Bosnia to enforce a peace agreement reached that month by the warring parties. On December 6, the government announced that it would send a 1,000-person force, half combat personnel and half support personnel.

Fish war. A confrontation between Canada and Spain erupted on the high seas of the North Atlantic Ocean in February as Canada continued its efforts to protect declining stocks of turbot. With the disappearance of cod in the waters of the Grand Banks off Newfoundland, turbot had become the most valuable remaining commercial catch. Canadian conservation measures were strictly enforced in this area within the 200-nautical-mile (370-kilometer) fishing zone over which Canada has jurisdiction. The turbot, however, is a straddling stock—that is, a fish that lives on either side of the line separating coastal waters from international waters. Canada had attempted to deal with the problem in May 1994 by passing

legislation asserting its authority to regulate the harvest of straddling stocks beyond the 200-mile limit.

In February 1995, the Northwest Atlantic Fisheries Organization (NAFO), a group of 15 countries that fish the North Atlantic, moved to protect turbot stocks by imposing a total allowable catch of 27,000 metric tons (29,700 tons) for the 1995 fishing season. The European Union (EU), which includes such traditional fishing nations as Spain and Portugal, endorsed the total catch limits but objected to its quota, which fell to 12 percent of the 1995 allocation, compared with 80 percent of the 1994 allocation. In February 1995, Spanish fishing trawlers entered the waters off the Grand Banks, declaring their intention to take turbot in defiance of both NAFO and Canadian regulations.

On March 9, Royal Canadian Mounted Police officers aboard a patrol boat chased the *Estai*, a Spanish vessel believed to be using illegal fishing methods, into international waters, boarded the ship, and then escorted it to St. John's, Newfoundland. The police subsequently reported finding a secret second hold in the ship containing undersized turbot taken with nets whose mesh size was smaller than that permitted. Canada charged the captain of the fishing boat with illegal fishing practices. The EU denied the charges and accused Canada of piracy on the high seas. Great Britain and several other EU members, however, blocked proposed sanctions against

The Ministry of Canada*

Jean Chrétien—prime minister
Herbert Eser Gray—solicitor general of Canada; leader of the government in the House of Commons
André Ouellet—minister of foreign affairs
Lloyd Axworthy—minister of human resources development; minister of Western economic diversification
David Michael Collenette—minister of national defence; minister of veterans affairs
Roy MacLaren—minister for international trade
David Anderson—minister of national revenue
Ralph E. Goodale—minister of agriculture and agri-food
David Charles Dingwall—minister of public works and government services; minister for the Atlantic Canada Opportunities Agency
Ron Irwin—minister of Indian affairs and Northern development
Brian Tobin—minister of fisheries and oceans
Joyce Fairbairn—leader of the government in the Senate; minister with special responsibility for literacy
Sheila Copps—deputy prime minister; minister of the environment
Sergio Marchi—minister of citizenship and immigration
John Manley—minister of industry
Diane Marleau—minister of health
Paul Martin—minister of finance; minister responsible for the Federal Office of Regional Development-Quebec
Douglas Young—minister of transport
Michel Dupuy—minister of Canadian heritage
Arthur C. Eggleton—president of the Treasury Board; minister responsible for infrastructure
Marcel Massé—president of the Queen's Privy Council for Canada; minister of intergovernmental affairs; minister responsible for public service renewal
Anne McLellan—minister of natural resources
Allan Rock—minister of justice; attorney general of Canada
Sheila Finestone—secretary of state (multiculturalism/status of women)
Fernand Robichaud—secretary of state (agriculture and agri-food, fisheries and oceans)
Ethel Blondin-Andrew—secretary of state (training and youth)
Lawrence MacAulay—secretary of state (veterans)
Christine Stewart—secretary of state (Latin America and Africa)
Raymond Chan—secretary of state (Asia-Pacific)
Jon Gerrard—secretary of state (science, research, and development)
Douglas Peters—secretary of state (international financial institutions)
Alfonso Gagliano—secretary of state (parliamentary affairs); deputy leader of the government in the House of Commons
Lucienne Robillard—minister of labor
*As of Dec. 31, 1995.

Premiers of Canadian provinces

Province	Premier
Alberta	Ralph Klein
British Columbia	Michael Harcourt
Manitoba	Gary A. Filmon
New Brunswick	Frank J. McKenna
Newfoundland	Clyde K. Wells
Nova Scotia	John Savage
Ontario	Mike Harris
Prince Edward Island	Catherine Callbeck
Quebec	Jacques Parizeau
Saskatchewan	Roy Romanow

Government leaders of territories

Northwest Territories	Nellie Cournoyea
Yukon Territory	John Ostashek

Canadian literature

Canada. While negotiations between Canada and the EU dragged on in Belgium, tensions between Spanish vessels and their Canadian observers grew.

On April 15, the two sides finally reached an agreement. Canada offered to give part of its turbot quota to Spain, drop its charges against the fishing captain, and rescind the law declaring control over the entire Grand Banks region when a UN convention on straddling stocks had been approved. Also, as of May 5, 1995, all Canadian and European vessels fishing turbot were required to have an independent observer aboard. The total catch of each boat as well as the fishing gear used were to be inspected at dockside.

In August, the UN negotiated a new convention on straddling stocks that laid down international controls on high-seas fishing. Included in the agreement were binding mechanisms for settling fishing disputes. And in September, NAFO agreed to new control measures, based on the April agreement between Canada and the EU, that included a ban on small-mesh nets that caught turbot too small to reproduce. Although Canada came under some criticism for acting outside international law, its action opened the way for the gradual recovery of a historic North Atlantic resource.　　□ David Farr

See also **Canadian provinces; Canadian territories; Chrétien, Jean; Montreal; Toronto.** In **World Book,** see **Canada; Quebec.**

Carol Shields, an American-born writer living in Canada, in April won the 1995 Pulitzer Prize for fiction for her novel *The Stone Diaries.*

Canadian literature. As Canada focused on an October 1995 referendum—narrowly defeated—that proposed Quebec's separation from the Canadian federation, Canadian writers reflected a preoccupation with the state of the nation. In *Nationalism Without Walls: The Unbearable Lightness of Being Canadian*, Richard Gwyn argued that an eroding commitment to egalitarianism threatened national cohesion. *All the King's Horses: Politics Among the Ruins* by Ron Graham depicted politicians and international money managers struggling to control Canada's agenda.

Linda McQuaig's *Shooting the Hippo* called the deficit crisis a destructive fiction, and *Straight Through the Heart: How the Liberals Abandoned the Just Society* by Maude Barlow and Bruce Campbell sounded an alarm about Canada's social network. More positively, Peter C. Newman's *The Canadian Revolution, 1985-1995: From Deference to Defiance* saw Canadian deference to authority give way as the result of a loss of faith in business, church, and the monarchy.

Other nonfiction. Lawrence Martin's *Chrétien: The Will to Win* was the first volume of a two-volume biography of Canada's Prime Minister Jean Chrétien. Richard Siklos's *Shades of Black: Conrad Black and the World's Fastest Growing Press Empire* told the story of a Canadian media magnate; and Heather Robertson's *Driving Force: The McLaughlin*

Family and the Age of the Car chronicled the family who founded General Motors of Canada. June Callwood's *Trial Without End* followed the case of a man charged with knowingly infecting at least 17 people with the AIDS virus, while *The Gift of Death* by Andre Picard probed the story of how Canada's blood supply became tainted with the AIDS virus. In *Our Kids, Our Teachers, Our Classrooms*, Ken Dryden critiqued Canada's education system. *Boys Don't Cry* by Darcy Henton with David McCann described the sexual abuse of boys at two Catholic schools.

Canadian primatologist Birute Galdikas recounted her life in the jungle in *Reflections of Eden: My Years with the Orangutans of Borneo.* Sid Marty argued for balance between nature and civilization in *Leaning on the Wind.* *The Manitous: The Spiritual World of the Ojibways* by Basil Johnson brought together sacred stories of tricksters, tree spirits, and giants. Paulette Jiles recalled her seven-year sojourn in northern Ontario in *North Spirit: Travels Among the Cree and Ojibway Nations and Their Star Maps.* And James Houston's *Confessions of an Igloo Dweller* recounted his introduction of Inuit art to the world.

Other notable titles. The 50th anniversary of the end of World War II (1939-1945) ushered in a boom of war memoirs, among them *Aftermath: Travels in a Post-War World*, an account of Farley Mowat's trip to European battle sites in 1953; and *Hilmar and Odette: Two Stories from the Nazi Era* by

Eric Koch, who fled his native Germany in the mid-1930's, then returned in the 1980's to probe his German-Jewish past.

Elma Softic's *Sarajevo Days, Sarajevo Nights* described the end of ordinary life in the besieged capital of Bosnia-Herzegovina. And in *The End of Days: A Story of Tolerance, Tyranny, and the Expulsion of the Jews from Spain*, Erna Paris found a context in medieval Spain for religious intolerance and anti-Semitism in later periods.

Books on sports included Paul Quarrington's *Fishing with My Old Guy* and William Humber's *Diamonds of the North: A Concise History of Baseball in Canada*. But hockey dominated the field: Stephen Cole's *The Last Hurrah: A Celebration of Hockey's Greatest Season '66/'67;* Roy MacGregor's *The Home Team;* and Dick Irvin's *In the Crease.*

The Arts. Charles Hill's *The Group of Seven: Art for a Nation,* based on a highly praised art exhibit, marked a landmark reappraisal of painters who attempted to create a distinct identity for Canadian art in the 1920's and 1930's. Margaret Atwood's *Strange Things: The Malevolent North in Canadian Literature* resumed her thematic exploration of the imaginative landscape. Rosemary Sullivan's *Shadow Maker: The Life of Gwendolyn MacEwan* reconstructed the life of that prolific poet. Jock Carroll's *Glenn Gould: Some Portraits of the Artist as a Young Man* commemorated a Bahamian sojourn early in an extraordinary musical career, and *Stompin' Tom Before the Fame* by Tom Connors summed up another Canadian music legend's turbulent youth.

Fiction. In *Mister Sandman* Barbara Gowdy told the story of a dysfunctional family, while Timothy Findley drew on his own ancestors in *The Piano Man's Daughter.* A child's viewpoint unified Greg Hollingshead's collection *The Roaring Girl.* Guy Gavriel Kay's *The Lions of Al-Rassan* featured a fantastic world modeled on Moorish Spain. Douglas Coupland's *Microserfs* followed computer nerds who left the Microsoft Corporation in Redmond, Washington, to start their own business. Rohinton Mistry's *A Fine Balance* portrayed four people sharing a Bombay apartment in 1970's India, and Richard B. Wright's *The Age of Longing* evoked small-town life in Ontario in the 1950's.

Poetry. Robert Bringhurst's *The Calling* brought together new and selected poems. *Morning in the Burned House* was Margaret Atwood's first book of poems in 10 years. Other notable titles included Anne Szumigalski's *Voice;* Di Brandt's *Jerusalem Beloved;* and Don Domanski's *Stations for the Left Hand.*

Children's literature. Diana Wieler's *RanVan: A Worthy Opponent* continued the saga of the knight of video arcades. In Tim Wynne-Jones's *The Maestro,* an encounter with a genius changes a boy's life, while Mordecai Richler's *Jacob Two-Two's First Spy Case* took on school injustice and bad lunches.

Awards. Winners of the 1995 Governor-General's Award for books in English included Greg Hollingshead for *The Roaring Girl* (fiction); Anne Szumigalski for *Voice* (poetry); Jason Sherman for *Three in the Back, Two in the Head* (drama); Rosemary Sullivan for *Shadow Maker* (nonfiction); Tim Wynne-Jones for *The Maestro* (children's literature—text); Ludmila Zeman for *The Last Quest of Gilgamesh* (children's literature—illustration); and David Homel for *Why Must a Black Writer Write About Sex?* (translation).

Winners for French-language books were Nicole Houde for *Les Oiseaux de Saint-John Perse* (fiction); Emile Martel for *Pour l'Orchestre et Poète Seul* (poetry); Carole Frechette for *Les Quatre Morts de Marie* (drama); Yvan Lamonde for *Louis-Antoine Dessaulles* (nonfiction); Sonia Sarfati for *Comme une Peau de Chagrin* (children's literature—text); Annouchka Gravel Galouchko for *Sho et les Dragons d'Eau* (children's literature—illustration); and Herve Juste for *Entre l'Ordre et la Liberté* (translation).

Rohinton Mistry's *A Fine Balance* won the Giller Prize, and Shyam Selvadurai took the Smith Books/ Books in Canada First Novel Award for *Funny Boy.*

Milestones. Three leading figures in Canadian literature—novelist Robertson Davies, poet Ralph Gustafson, and essayist George Woodcock—died in 1995 after long careers. ☐ Maureen McCallum Garvie

In *World Book,* see **Canadian literature.**

Canadian provinces in 1995 faced uncertain but far-reaching changes in Canada's federal system of government in the aftermath of Quebec's narrow rejection on October 30 of a proposal to form an independent state (see **Canada**).

Beyond the referendum, fiscal restraint, marked by cuts in government services, was the order of the day in 1995 with 7 of the 10 provinces predicting budget surpluses. In their politics, provincial governments were moderate or conservative. The trend to the right was illustrated by the resounding defeat in June of the socialist New Democratic Party (NDP) administration in Ontario by a government dedicated to giving market forces free rein.

Quebec. The debate over independence that dominated public affairs in Quebec before the October referendum showed no signs of abating after voters narrowly rejected the measure—50.5 percent to 49.4 percent. The day after the vote, Jacques Parizeau, Quebec's premier and the leader of the separatist Parti Québécois (PQ), resigned. In a remark that stirred widespread outrage, Parizeau blamed the referendum's defeat on "money and the ethnic vote," which was largely against the measure. On November 21, Lucien Bouchard, the leader of the separatist Bloc Québécois and of the campaign for sovereignty, announced he intended to run for the leadership of the PQ and so succeed Parizeau as premier of Quebec.

Gerald Regan, former premier of Nova Scotia and former federal Cabinet minister, was charged with 19 sex-related offenses in 1995.

Engaged in selling the "Yes" option for independence, Parizeau's government spared little attention for ordinary legislation. Reforms in the province's educational system, in the financial management of government departments, and in social policy—all promised when the PQ came to power in September 1994—had to be put aside.

The new government issued its first budget, one that promoted the sovereignty option, on May 9, 1995. Finance Minister Jean Campeau blamed the federal government for Quebec's financial problems and the federal system for hindering Quebec's economic growth. Campeau also predicted that Quebec residents would face steep tax increases because of cuts in the federal budget if they rejected the refer-

endum. But the budget was silent on the economic benefits that supposedly would flow from a sovereign Quebec.

The government made no changes in personal income taxes, though corporations were hit with a loss of valuable tax credits. The budget forecast a drop in the deficit to $3.9 billion in fiscal year 1995-1996 from $5.7 billion in fiscal 1994-1995 (all amounts in Canadian dollars). The estimate was based on a rosy economic growth rate of 3.3 percent, which would yield higher revenues. Financial observers, however, criticized the budget's failure to take stronger measures to restrain expenditures, as other provinces had done, and to reduce Quebec's overhanging debt of $74.4 billion.

Alberta. Premier Ralph Klein, a fiscal conservative, pressed ahead with drastic spending cuts introduced when his Progressive Conservative Party (PCP) assumed power in 1992. The budget, released on Feb. 21, 1995, posted an estimated surplus of $110-million in fiscal year 1994-1995 but predicted, based on a conservative estimate of oil and gas revenue, a deficit of $506 million for fiscal 1995-1996. The budget included $478 million in spending cuts, with more than half coming from health care. At the same time, the government planned to relax its plan to pay down the province's $32-billion debt to ease voter unhappiness with reductions in public services. The debt was to be lowered by average annual payments of $343 million over the next 25 years.

Several costly natural disasters struck Alberta in 1995. In the south, the worst floods in a century along the South Saskatchewan and Oldman rivers wreaked havoc in early June. Thousands of residents evacuated Medicine Hat as the South Saskatchewan crested 33 feet (10 meters) above its normal level. The flooding resulted from unusually heavy rains in the foothills of the Rocky Mountains combined with rapid snow melting at higher elevations. In the north, a hot, dry summer fueled forest fires that swept through a belt extending from British Columbia through Alberta to western Ontario. The fires destroyed nearly 20,000 square miles (50,000 square kilometers) of forest.

British Columbia. The NDP government of Premier Michael Harcourt on January 23 scuttled a plan by Alcan Aluminum Limited to add a 285-megawatt powerhouse to the massive Kemano hydroelectric project in northwest British Columbia on the grounds that the facility would threaten salmon runs in the Fraser River. That action won praise from environmentalists, as did a decision on July 6 to end clear-cutting by loggers in the Clayoquot Sound rain forest on Vancouver Island. (In clear-cutting, every tree in selected forest areas is cut down.) Opposition between environmentalists and loggers over the issue had led to angry confrontations in recent years. New standards calling for selective logging were expected to cut the harvest by nearly half.

The Harcourt government moved to erase its antibusiness image by agreeing on August 18 to pay $26 million to Royal Oak Mines in compensation for a 1993 decision to forbid a proposed mine in a remote northwest corner of the province, where the government had created a new park, Tatshenshini. The complicated deal committed the government to providing an additional $77.8 million over several years to help Royal Oak develop two new gold and silver mines.

The budget, issued on March 28, 1995, announced that the province's books had been balanced a year earlier than projected. A surplus of $114 million on total spending of $20.1 billion was forecast. The budget contained no new taxes because a growing economy had provided $500 million more in tax revenues than had been predicted. But the province's long-term debt was expected to grow by $956 million to $27.9 billion.

Disputes over native land claims continued to disturb the Pacific province. A master plan for negotiations, adopted by the Cabinet, revealed that the government was prepared to give up only 5 percent of the land area of the province to native groups. (The 5 percent figure reflected the aboriginal share of British Columbia's population.) In addition, all privately owned land would be left off the bargaining table. Discussion on the claims continued through 1995.

On November 15, Harcourt announced he would resign as premier to help the NDP win reelection in upcoming provincial elections, considered likely in 1996. The NDP's standing in public opinion polls had fallen as Harcourt had come under continuing attack by political opponents as well as by some members of his own party for failing to exert leadership in a number of matters. Harcourt was to remain as premier until the NDP selected a new leader in early 1996.

Manitoba. The PCP administration of Premier Gary Filmon won a third term in office on April 25, 1995, increasing its standing in the 57-seat legislature from 29 to 31 members. The opposition NDP gained two seats to control 22. The Liberal Party fell from six seats to three.

The provincial budget, announced on March 9, showed the cautious financial management of Filmon and his ministers. Manitoba's first operating surplus in 22 years—$48 million for fiscal 1995-1996—was forecast. The deficit for fiscal 1994-1995 had amounted to $218 million. Much of the turnaround came from the transfer of $145 million from government-run gambling operations. For the seventh year, there was no increase in personal income tax rates.

Implementation of a December 1994 agreement under which 60 aboriginal bands were to assume control of the Manitoba operations of the federal Department of Indian Affairs began in 1995. Under the agreement—the first of its kind with native people of a Canadian province—aboriginal institutions were to gain control of lands, water, resources, languages, culture, and social services.

New Brunswick, a small lumbering and fishing province heavily dependent on federal transfer payments, emerged in 1995 as a major Canadian center for customer service operations. The transformation began when the province set up the first telephone system in Canada with completely digitized services, using fiber-optic cables to transmit information at high speed. Low wages and a bilingual work force helped persuade a number of companies relying on telecommunications to move parts of their operations to New Brunswick. As a result of the changing economy, the province registered the highest percentage increase in employment in Canada in 1994.

Premier Frank McKenna's reward for attracting employers to his province was a third electoral victory for his Liberal Party on Sept. 11, 1995. The party, which had captured all the seats in the legislature when it first won office in 1987, took 46 seats, compared to 7 for the PCP and 1 for the NDP. The Confederation of Regions Party, an antibilingual organization that had been the official opposition since 1991, did not win a single seat. The PCP, rejuvenated under Bernard Valcourt, a former federal Cabinet minister, was expected be a strong opposition to McKenna.

Fiscal restraint marked the budget, announced on Feb. 21, 1995. Finance Minister Allan Maher forecast a $68-million surplus for fiscal year 1995-1996, the first surplus since 1980. The budget slashed $93-million from administration and programs. Four hundred public service jobs were to be cut as part of an ongoing process. The preelection budget contained no personal income tax increases.

Newfoundland. Economic prospects for Newfoundland, hard hit by the collapse of the cod-fishing industry, brightened in 1995 as prospectors and geologists rushed to Voisey Bay on the mainland coast of Labrador, where a rich deposit of nickel, cobalt, and copper was found in October 1994. Provincial officials expected that exploration and mining activities in the area, which is 6 miles (10 kilometers) from a deep-water harbor, would create thousands of jobs.

A referendum on Sept. 5, 1995, approved government plans to take control of publicly financed schools from the religious denominations that had been operating them for more than 100 years. The proposal was narrowly approved by a 54-to-46 percent vote. The government plan, intended to create a more effective and inexpensive educational system, would consolidate school boards and create interdenominational schools. Implementation of the plan, however, depended on approval by the federal Parliament of amendments to the 1949 Terms of Union between Newfoundland and Canada.

Canadian provinces

Nova Scotia. After two years of internal dissent, members of the governing Liberal Party voted on June 24, 1995, to continue their support for Premier John Savage, the party's leader. Had he been ousted, it would have been the first time in Canadian history that a party had rejected a leader who also was the head of government.

Savage had become the lightning rod for unhappiness within the party over such controversial decisions as hospital closures, reductions and freezes in public service salaries, budget cuts in education, and the opening of a casino in Halifax. Party members also criticized Savage for not replacing workers in government jobs with Liberal Party members when he became premier in 1993.

Many of the Savage government's measures were designed to further reduce a deficit on operating expenses that had been cut to $99 million in fiscal year 1994-1995. The budget, announced on April 11, 1995, forecast that additional cuts would reduce the deficit to $28 million for fiscal 1995-1996.

Ontario. Provincial elections on June 8, 1995, handed power to the PCP, which had promised the most sweeping changes in the role of government in Canada's most populous province since the end of World War II (1939-1945). The victorious PCP was led by Michael Harris, who campaigned vigorously on what he called a "common-sense revolution" of reducing the role and cost of government. He was sworn in as Ontario's 22nd premier on June 26.

Advocating deficit reduction and tax cuts, the PCP captured 82 seats in the 130-seat legislature and 45 percent of the popular vote. The NDP, which had held office since 1990, won only 17 seats, down from the 69 it had held at the dissolution of the chamber. The Liberal Party, which had gone into the campaign leading the polls, held on to only 30 seats but remained the official opposition.

The Harris government promised to reduce annual spending by $6 billion over three years and eliminate budget deficits within five years. To help accomplish this, the government on Oct. 1, 1995, cut welfare benefits by 21.6 percent for 400,000 recipients, about half of whom had dependent children. The Harris government also planned to eliminate 13,000 public service jobs over the next two years. It vowed to repeal NDP legislation banning the use of replacement workers by companies with striking employees, to end employment equity laws designed to favor women and minorities, and to privatize government liquor stores and parts of Ontario Hydro, the state-owned electrical utility. The government also promised to reduce personal income taxes by 30 percent over three years, the first half of the cut to come in spring 1996.

Prince Edward Island. The calm of Canada's smallest province was disturbed on April 20, 1995, when a bomb exploded outside historic Province House, the seat of the province's legislature and the

Michael Harris, and his wife, Janet, celebrate the landslide election victory that swept him into office as the new premier of Ontario on June 8.

site of a conference held in 1864 that led to the formation of the Canadian confederation, the first united Canada. The explosion slightly injured one person and caused superficial damage to the building. There was no apparent motive for the blast.

The province's budget, introduced on March 30, 1995, forecast a $2.7-million surplus for fiscal 1995-1996. Revenue increases, notably larger-than-expected federal transfer payments, were more significant than spending cuts in helping to balance the books.

A plan to raise a sunken oil barge that sank in the Gulf of St. Lawrence in 1970, was halted in August 1995 by a federal court on the grounds that the presence of toxic polychlorinated biphenyls (PCB's) in the vessel's heating system could pollute the environment. What was to have been the largest ocean salvage operation in Canadian history was postponed until 1996, by which time it was hoped environmental concerns could be answered.

Saskatchewan. The NDP government of Premier Roy Romanow swept to a solid electoral victory on June 21, 1995, winning a second majority in the legislature. The NDP took 42 seats in the 58-seat assembly and captured 48 percent of the popular vote. The Liberals moved ahead of the PCP to win 11 seats, a gain of 8 from the 3 seats held before the election. The PCP took only 5 seats, their image tarnished by charges of expense-account irregularities leveled against a dozen current and former members of the legislature.

The NDP government's reputation as a middle-of-the-road administration was exemplified in the province's first balanced budget in 12 years. In the budget, issued on February 16, Finance Minister Janice MacKinnon announced that the province had posted a surplus of $119 million for fiscal 1994-1995, to be followed by smaller surpluses for the years 1996 to 1999. These gains would allow the provincial debt to fall from its current $14.9 billion to $13.7 billion by 1999. The government also removed a deficit surtax applied in 1993 against personal income for low-income earners and cut the corporate income tax for small businesses. □ David M. L. Farr

In *World Book,* see the various province articles.

Canadian territories. The economic prospects of the Yukon Territory's 31,000 inhabitants brightened in 1995 with the reopening of the Faro mine, 125 miles (200 kilometers) northeast of Whitehorse. The mine, which produces silver, zinc, and lead, was formerly the Yukon's largest employer. It shut down in September 1993 after metal prices dropped. The Anvil Range Mining Corporation of Toronto, which bought the mine in late 1994, resumed ore shipments in August 1995, restoring at least 550 jobs. The owners predicted that the mine would yield about 555,000 tons (500,000 metric tons) of ore annually, with a value of about $200 million (Canadian dollars). Meanwhile, work at an open-pit gold mine at Brewery Creek, east of Dawson, continued in preparation for a 1996 reopening.

Treaties. Agreements with 4 of the Yukon's 14 native *bands* (groups) took effect on Feb. 14, 1995, climaxing a process that took 22 years. Under the agreements, the bands were to receive certain land titles, recognition of their aboriginal rights, and financial compensation to settle outstanding land claims. Negotiations continued during 1995 on similar agreements with the other groups.

New assembly. The Northwest Territories, which cover one-third of Canada's land mass, elected a new assembly on October 16. The 24 members of the assembly, which does not have political parties, planned to choose a speaker and a premier (leader

of the government) by secret ballot at a later date. The newly elected assembly was dominated by 15 newcomers, who replaced members who retired or were defeated at the polls because of unethical conduct. The election was expected to be the last before the eastern part of the Northwest Territories, largely populated by Inuit (Eskimos), becomes the self-governing region of Nunavut, an event scheduled for April 1999. The new assembly was to work out the details of the division.

An epic ski journey through the Northwest Territories to the North Pole and back without any outside help was completed on June 15, 1995, by a Canadian engineer and a Russian surgeon. They made the 930-mile (1,500-kilometer) trek in 122 days without air-dropped supplies, dogs, or snowmobiles, while carrying and pulling about 528 pounds (250 kilograms) of food and equipment.

Miner convicted. A miner was convicted of second-degree murder, with no eligibility for parole for at least 20 years, on January 20 for the 1992 bombing death of nine workers at the Giant gold mine in Yellowknife. The lesser sentence reflected the jury's belief that the defendant had not meant to kill anyone when he left an explosive device in one of the mine's tunnels during a strike. □ David Farr

In *World Book,* see **Northwest Territories; Yukon Territory.**

Cape Verde. See Africa.

Carrey, Jim (1962–), a Canadian-born actor and comedian, became one of the motion picture industry's most popular and highest-paid actors in 1995. Carrey's comedic style, as seen in *The Mask, Ace Ventura: Pet Detective,* and several other movies, is characterized by outrageous slapstick contortions and rubber-faced mugging.

Carrey was born in Ontario, Canada, on Jan. 17, 1962. He started his performing career as a stand-up comedian at Yuk Yuk's, a comedy club in Toronto, where he developed his unique brand of physical comedy. He moved to Los Angeles at age 19, supporting himself with small acting and comedy jobs.

A few years later, Carrey gained the attention of movie director Francis Ford Coppola, who cast him in a small role in his 1986 comedy, *Peggy Sue Got Married.* He later played a psychotic in *The Dead Pool* (1988) and an alien in *Earth Girls Are Easy* (1989). During the early 1990's, Carrey was part of the cast of the television comedy show "In Living Color."

Carrey was catapulted into superstardom in 1994 with his title role in *Ace Ventura: Pet Detective. Ace* was followed quickly by two other 1994 hits, *The Mask* and *Dumb and Dumber.* In 1995, he co-starred as the Riddler in *Batman Forever* and starred in an *Ace* sequel, *Ace Ventura: When Nature Calls.*

Carrey married actress Melissa Womer in 1987, but they separated in 1995. Carrey and Womer have a daughter, Jane. □ Lisa Klobuchar

Census. The number of people living in the United States in 1994 who were born in a foreign country was the highest since 1940, increasing to 8.7 percent of the U.S. population, from 7.9 percent in 1990. The U.S. Bureau of the Census reported these statistics on Aug. 29, 1995. The Census Bureau estimated that 22.6 million current U.S. residents had been born abroad, with about 4.5 million, or one in five, arriving in the United States between 1990 and 1994. California and New York had the most foreign-born residents—25 percent and 16 percent, respectively. The bureau's report appeared certain to fuel the debate over U.S. immigration policy, in both the U.S. Congress and the 1996 election campaign.

Before the release of the Census Bureau estimate, the Urban Institute of Washington, D.C., projected that the foreign-born population would reach 13 or 14 percent by 2045 if current trends continued. The historic peak was reached in 1910, when 14.7 percent of the population was foreign-born.

Changes in birth and death rates. The Census Bureau estimated on July 31 that the U.S. population at the start of 1995 was 261,638,000, an increase of 1 percent over the 1994 figure of 259,167,000. But the bureau also noted that the number of U.S. births fell in 1994 and a record number of residents died during the year. An estimated 3.949 million babies were born in 1994, a 2.2 percent decline from 1993 and the first time since 1988 that births fell below the 4-million mark. The number of recorded deaths in 1994 rose to 2.294 million, 1.2 percent more than the previous year's total of 2.267 million.

Census Bureau analysts attributed the changes to the aging of the U.S. population. *Baby boomers* (people born during the population surge after World War II) were reaching the ages when they were less likely to have children. At the same time, improvements in medical care had led to an increase in the percentage of elderly people in the population. The greatest increase in deaths in 1994 occurred among people over 85 years of age, and this increase led to the rise in total deaths.

Poverty rates. On October 5, the Census Bureau reported that the percentage of Americans living in poverty dropped in 1994, the first decline in five years. The poverty rate was 14.5 percent, down from 15.1 percent in 1993. A household was considered to be in poverty if its income was below the poverty line, fixed in 1994 at $15,141 for a family of four.

The poverty rate among Hispanics was 30.7 percent. The rate among blacks was 30.6 percent. For non-Hispanic whites, the poverty rate was 11.7 percent. People under 18 years of age had a poverty rate of 21.8 percent, the highest of any age group.

□ William J. Eaton

See also **Population.** In *World Book,* see **Census; Population.**

Central African Republic. See Africa.
Chad. See Africa.

Chemistry. New hope for insomniacs, at least those of the feline variety, was announced in June 1995. Chemist Richard A. Lerner and his colleagues at the Scripps Research Institute in La Jolla, California, reported that they had identified and synthesized a fatlike compound that induces sleep in cats.

The scientists found the chemical in the brain fluid of cats that had been kept awake and were thus ready for sleep. The compound was absent from the brain fluid of rested cats. Lerner and his colleagues then made a synthetic version of the chemical and injected it into cats and rats. Each animal quickly fell into a deep sleep. The scientists also discovered the chemical in human brains, so it may trigger sleep for human beings, too.

How agates got their shimmer. Agates are semiprecious stones whose bands of white and colored crystals make them popular in jewelry and desktop ornaments and as the traditional shooter for a game of marbles. But how did some agates get their iridescent shimmer? In September, geological chemist Andrew M. Davis of the University of Chicago and geologist Peter J. Heaney of Princeton University in New Jersey explained the mystery.

Agates form in the cracks of volcanic rock, which trap water with high concentrations of dissolved minerals. "Fibers" of growing quartz crystals bridge the cracks, and the stripes form as dissolved minerals in the water deposit layer after layer of crystals between the fibers, parallel with the rock walls.

The researchers examined agates using a transmission electron microscope and found that some bands contained quartz crystals that were about 100 times larger than the crystals in the adjacent band. The scientists determined that highly concentrated mineral solutions crystallize rapidly near the tip of a growing quartz fiber to form small crystals containing impurities. As the tip moves into a less-concentrated solution, crystallization proceeds more slowly, allowing larger, perfect crystals to form. When the tip moves into a mineral-rich solution, small, defective crystals form again. Light striking the different crystals in successive layers gives certain agate rocks their distinctive shimmer.

By deepening their understanding of the chemistry behind mineral patterns, the scientists hoped to gain insight into how the chemistry of biological systems forms structures such as seashells or bones. The research also yielded tips for materials scientists who want to mimic agates' patterns in new materials.

Chemical calculator. If scientists can study psychology by putting rats in mazes, what can they learn by allowing chemicals to react in a maze? They can find the answer to a mathematical puzzle, according to a February report by chemists at West Virginia University in Morgantown. Kenneth Showalter and his colleagues took advantage of the peculiar properties of a chemical reaction called the Belousov-Zhabotinsky (BZ) reaction to find the shortest distance between two points in a maze. BZ reactions produce fluctuating amounts of products as they proceed. If the products are colored, the progress of the reaction is visible as waves of changing colors.

The researchers fashioned their maze from a plastic membrane. They soaked reactant chemicals into the membrane and started the BZ reaction at one end. They captured the reaction in a sequence of 250 video images and then superimposed the images to create a "map" of the waves where the reactions were taking place. By analyzing the appearance of the waves traveling through the maze, the scientists could easily determine the shortest distance between the start of the maze and any point in it.

A computer programmed to find the shortest routes in a maze typically would find them by trial and error, checking every possibility one at a time. The chemical system works every possibility at once, a big advantage if the maze is highly complex.

A practical use for this chemical calculator might be to give robots delivering packages in huge warehouses immediate solutions on the shortest routes to take. And the robots would not have to carry little chemical-soaked membranes to get their answers. An *algorithm* (mathematical model) can be used to simulate the reaction in a computer and provide an equally good answer.

Stretchable polypropylene. Polypropylene is a hard plastic used in soda bottles, cups, carpets, and even clothing. To make the inexpensive *polymer* (chainlike molecule) more useful, chemists at Stanford University in California found a way to make it up to eight times stretchier. Chemists Geoffrey W. Coates and Robert M. Waymouth reported this finding in January.

Knitters know that if they vary their stitches— essentially the links of a chain—as they work with yarn and needles, they can have some control over the stretchiness of a sweater. To a certain extent, the same thing happens with polypropylene chains. If the links that make up the chain of the molecule are lined up just alike, the plastic is very stiff. Random arrangement of the chemical groups that hang off the links yields a molecule with more give to it.

To make polypropylene stretchier, Coates and Waymouth created a special *catalyst* (a chemical that speeds up a reaction without being changed by it). This catalyst varies its shape and, in doing so, it changes from being a template for ordered links to serving as one for random links. The chemists found that they could control which form of the catalyst creates most of the links by varying the pressure and temperature of the reaction.

In addition to extending polypropylene's usefulness, the scientists created the first practical rubberlike plastic that can be recycled. Unlike rubber, the new plastic can be melted and reused just as ordinary polypropylene can. □ Peter J. Andrews

In *World Book,* see **Chemistry.**

Chess. Two official world chess champions continued to reign in 1995 as the International Chess Federation (FIDE), founded in 1929, and the Professional Chess Association (PCA) founded in 1993, failed to agree on a plan to unify the title. Anatoly Karpov of Russia held the FIDE crown, while countryman Garry Kasparov was the PCA champion.

PCA world championship. Kasparov defended his PCA title against Viswanathan Anand of India beginning on Sept. 11, 1995, in one of the most widely publicized chess events ever. The match, held on the observation deck of New York City's World Trade Center, drew thousands of spectators from around the world who listened to live commentary from grand masters and viewed huge computer images of the ongoing games. Meanwhile, Kasparov and Anand played in a soundproof booth. On October 10, after 18 games, Kasparov won, 10.5 to 7.5, and went home with $900,000, while Anand settled for $450,000.

FIDE world championship. New York City's Gata Kamsky, 20, in February became the first United States player to challenge for the world championship since Bobby Fischer became world champion in 1972. Kamsky was due to play Karpov for his FIDE crown. After some uncertainty about whether the pair would attract the needed sponsorship, a Canadian promotional firm in late November 1995 pledged a $1-million prize fund for a match in Montreal, Canada, in 1996.

Tournaments. Julian Hodgson of the United Kingdom won the National Open on May 7, 1995, in Las Vegas, Nevada. Alex Yermolinsky of Euclid, Ohio, won the World Open in Philadelphia on July 4. On August 18 in Concord, California, Yermolinsky topped a field of 536 to become the U.S. Open champion. The U.S. Interplay Invitational Championship and separate Interplay Women's Invitational Championship were held simultaneously in Modesto, California. On December 4, Patrick Wolff of Somerville, Massachusetts, Nick deFirmian of New York City, and Alexander Ivanov of Brookline, Massachusetts, tied in the overall championship. Anjelina Belakovskaya of New York City and Sharon Burtman of Orange, California, tied in the women's event.

School players. Vinay Bhat of San Jose set a record in January 1995 by becoming, at age 10, the youngest U.S. grand master ever. On April 9, in Little Rock, Arkansas, Sharon School of Charlotte, North Carolina, won the National Elementary School Championship. St. Gregory College Prep of Tucson, Arizona, won the National Junior High School Championship on May 14 in Dearborn, Michigan. New York City's Dalton School won the National High School Championship on April 9 in Chicago. The three National Scholastic Championship tournaments drew a record 3,456 school players from all over the United States. □ Al Lawrence

Chicago's renovated Navy Pier opened in July, with attractions that included a 1,500-seat stage pavilion, a children's museum, and a giant Ferris wheel.

Chicago. Richard M. Daley won reelection as mayor of Chicago on April 4, 1995, with 60 percent of the vote. Former Illinois Attorney General Roland Burris, who ran as an independent, received 36 percent. Republican Ray Wardingley, a disabled veteran and former professional clown, received 3 percent. Lawrence Redmond, representing the Harold Washington Party, got only 1 percent.

Daley, elected mayor in a special election in April 1989 and reelected in 1991, had also easily won the Democratic primary on Feb. 28, 1995. He received 66 percent of the vote, compared with 33 percent for city water commissioner Joseph Gardner.

Aldermanic elections in February and April resulted in a 50-member City Council that for the first time was comprised mostly of minorities. Nineteen aldermen were African American, and seven were Hispanic. Thirteen council members were women.

U.S. Representative Mel Reynolds of Chicago was sentenced to five years in prison on September 28. Reynolds, a second-term Democrat, was convicted of having a sexual relationship in 1992 with campaign volunteer Beverly Heard, who was 16 years old at the time, and of soliciting sexually explicit photographs of another teen-age girl. Reynolds was also charged with obstructing the investigation into his actions. A criminal courts jury found Reynolds guilty on August 22 of criminal sexual assault, aggravated criminal sexual abuse, child pornography, and ob-

struction of justice. Heard, the key witness against Reynolds, contacted the police with her story in June 1994. She later recanted and spent 13 nights in jail before agreeing to testify about the relationship. Reynolds, who had represented portions of Chicago's Far South Side and southern suburbs, resigned from Congress on October 1. On December 12, Jesse L. Jackson, Jr., son of civil rights leader Jesse Jackson, was elected to succeed Reynolds.

Heat wave. In one of the worst heat waves in Chicago history, temperatures soared over 100° F (38° C) in July and contributed to the death of hundreds of people, many of them elderly. Mayor Daley initially criticized Cook County Medical Examiner Edmund Donoghue for attributing so many deaths to the heat, but Donoghue's assessment was later validated by the federal Centers for Disease Control and Prevention in Atlanta, Georgia. A Chicago Health Department study indicated that as many as 733 deaths in July may have been heat-related. On July 13, the temperature at Chicago's Midway Airport reached a record high of 106° F (41° C).

Public housing. The federal Department of Housing and Urban Development (HUD) took over the operation and management of Chicago public housing on May 30, citing the failure of the Chicago Housing Authority (CHA) to adequately shelter its 86,000 tenants. The move, approved by Mayor Daley, came as a surprise because longtime CHA chairman Vincent Lane had been praised as a public housing visionary by HUD Secretary Henry G. Cisneros.

Public schools. Mayor Daley on June 29 appointed a team of administrators and educators to run the Chicago public school system. Paul Vallas, Daley's former city budget director, was appointed chief executive officer, and Gery Chico, the mayor's former chief of staff, was named to head a new five-member school board. Vallas replaced Superintendent Argie Johnson, whose contract was bought out. Chico replaced D. Sharon Grant, who was sentenced to 30 months in prison on November 8 for failing to file income tax returns for 17 years.

Jordan returns. Seventeen months after retiring from basketball, Michael Jordan rejoined the Chicago Bulls line-up on March 19 in a 103-96 overtime loss to the Indiana Pacers in Indianapolis. Basketball fans in Chicago and throughout the world were euphoric over the return of the 32-year-old superstar. Although Jordan was out of practice after two years as a minor league baseball player, the Bulls won 12 of their final 14 games, defeating the Charlotte Hornets 3 games to 1 in the first round of the National Basketball Association play-offs. But on May 18, the Orlando Magic, led by former Jordan teammate Horace Grant, defeated the Bulls 4 games to 2 in the second round. □ Patrick T. Reardon

See also **City.** In *World Book,* see **Chicago.**

Children's books. See Literature for children.

Chile. Chile's economy grew by nearly 7 percent as 1995 closed. In the year's first quarter, the country more than tripled its trade surplus to $827 million compared with $238.8 million in 1994.

Negotiations aimed at bringing Chile into the North American Free Trade Agreement began in Toronto, Canada, on June 7, 1995. But hopes for Chile's quick entry into the pact, as pledged by United States President Clinton in December 1994, were dimmed by the economic crisis in Mexico. (See **Mexico** Special Report: **Crisis in Mexico.**)

Jail for military assassins. Chile's Supreme Court sentenced two high-level military officers to jail on May 30, 1995, for their role in a 1976 political murder. The court sentenced General Juan Manuel Contreras Sepulveda, the former head of Chile's secret military police, and his deputy, Brigadier General Pedro Espinoza Bravo, to seven and six years in jail, respectively. They had been convicted of complicity in the killing of Orlando Letelier, foreign minister under President Salvador Allende, with a car bomb in Washington, D.C.

Park controversy. On July 1, 1995, the government announced the purchase of a tract of forest-land in southern Chile to prevent Douglas Tompkins, a U.S. businessman, from creating a 750,000-acre (300,000-hectare) park. □ Nathan A. Haverstock

See also **Latin America** (Facts in brief table). In *World Book,* see **Chile.**

China. The ruling Communist Party in 1995 launched a largely unsuccessful campaign to end China's rampant corruption. The Chinese public increasingly resented the high lifestyle of party officials while they themselves earned meager wages. Reportedly, President Jiang Zemin feared that corruption might ignite public protests that could topple the Communist Party.

However, Jiang and other high officials also used the anticorruption campaign as a tool against others in the party hierarchy who struggled to consolidate power in preparation for the day the nation's failing 91-year-old leader, Deng Xiaoping, died. Although Jiang was Deng's hand-picked successor, twice in the 1980's men chosen by Deng to assume his authority were sidelined by rivals.

Beginning in 1993, officials slowly began to realize that widespread favoritism, nepotism, and bribery were damaging the Communist Party's image. In 1995, even some of Jiang's friends and protégés were caught in corrupt activities. And one of Deng's old comrades, Zhou Guanwu, abruptly retired from heading up a giant government steel conglomerate in Beijing after his son was arrested in February for

A boy plays with a figure of Mickey Mouse in February at a Beijing store licensed to sell Walt Disney products. Disney had ceased business with China over its piracy of trademarked products but returned in 1995.

"economic crimes." On Feb. 25, 1995, a dozen prominent Chinese intellectuals said in an unusual petition to the National People's Congress, China's parliament, that "corruption, in the form of trading power for money, has become the principal affliction causing great public resentment and is capable of leading to social upheaval." Nonetheless, corruption remained widespread, and relatives of party bosses continued to get rich.

Fighting corruption. The most politically damaging corruption case involved Wang Baosen, the deputy mayor of Beijing, China's capital, and business developers who wanted a prime downtown site that was occupied by a McDonald's restaurant. In late 1994, city officials gave McDonald's an eviction notice, despite its having a 20-year contract. An investigation pointed to payoffs by the developers to Wang and other city officials. More important, the case lifted the lid on other "economic crimes."

Wang was accused of embezzling $37 million in public funds, and on April 4, 1995, he committed suicide. After investigators found that he had spent the money on relatives, friends, and mistresses, the Communist Party declared that Wang "was morally degenerate and lived a rotten life."

On April 27, a few weeks after Wang's suicide, his superior, Chen Xitong, resigned from the powerful post of leader of the Communist Party of Beijing. Chen was also a member of the Politburo, the party's highest policy-making group. As a member, Chen had long been a rival of Jiang's. Chen reportedly had said in meetings that he was better qualified than Jiang to lead China.

On September 28, the party's Central Committee ousted Chen from his party posts, saying he had lived a "dissolute and extravagant life" and that he was responsible for Wang's wrongdoing. Chen was the highest-ranking official brought down in the anticorruption campaign. Investigators attempted to sort out how much of Wang's millions went to Chen.

The anticorruption drive spread to the provinces. In July, two women in Wuxi, near Shanghai, were accused of swindling state firms and government agencies in dozens of cities out of $380 million. Ostensibly, the money was to be invested in a fictional medical firm at a high interest rate for the investors. It was China's largest corruption scandal under Communism, and there were links to Beijing officials as well. In November, the women were executed.

Deng's health prompted constant speculation in 1995. Officials reportedly were unhappy when a newspaper published a picture in January taken three months earlier that showed Deng looking dazed, perhaps senile. His daughter, Xiao Rong, said in January that he could no longer stand or walk, and in February, she said, "Someday, he'll die." The Hong Kong stock market fell, reflecting widespread concern over China's future without Deng.

The only serious rival to Deng for influence, Chen Yun, died on April 10 at the age of 90. Chen, like Deng, was one of the so-called "eight immortals" of the 1990's—men who had played major roles beginning in the 1920's in bringing Communism to power in China in 1949. The architect of the nation's centrally planned economy, Chen had led those who opposed Deng's economic liberalization.

The only surviving "immortal" who possibly could inherit Deng's influence was former national president Yang Shangkun. But political analysts predicted that if Jiang succeeded in sufficiently consolidating his power to ensure that Deng's death would not lead to political turmoil, Yang's influence would be limited.

Leadership changes. The National People's Congress, a parliament that traditionally rubber-stamped Communist Party decisions, reflected the growing power struggle. On March 17, only 63 percent of the delegates voted to approve Jiang Chunyun as a vice premier. Such appointments usually passed with 90 percent approval. But Jiang, a member of the party Politburo and party Secretariat, had been criticized for failing to control corruption when he was a provincial boss.

At its September meeting, the party's Central Committee promoted two supporters of Jiang Zemin to vice chairmen of the party's Central Military Commission, which Jiang headed. They were Chi Haotian, the minister of national defense, and Zhang Wannian, the chief of the army general staff.

Economic plan—and plight. At the September meeting, the Central Committee also approved vague plans for economic development from 1996 to 2000. China hoped to keep up economic growth that had averaged 11.7 percent annually in recent years. Most growth occurred in new and unplanned private businesses. The 108,000 state-owned enterprises, most of which were overstaffed and lost money, accounted for 43 percent of the nation's industrial output in 1994, down from 78 percent in 1978.

Officials said 2.8 percent of China's urban working population lacked jobs, but a survey by the United Nations' International Labor Organization suggested that the true figure was 18 percent. China's State Planning Commission said the nation needed to create 180 million new jobs by 2000. In May, state enterprises reduced the workweek from six to five days in order to employ more people.

State planners worked to narrow the gap between the booming coastal areas and the underdeveloped interior regions. Most of China's 70 million people living below the poverty line—officially defined as earning $52 a year—were in the interior. But the coastal cities teemed with tens of millions of people from overcrowded farms seeking jobs.

Population problems. On February 15, China's population officially reached 1.2 billion. Chinese experts said that birth control efforts since the 1970's meant 300 million fewer babies had been born than

Women representing different world cultures hold a "peace torch" at the opening ceremonies of an international women's conference in Beijing in August.

otherwise would have been added to the population, but new ways were needed to encourage couples to have just one child. The population was still growing by 14 million a year. The experts warned that pollution, construction, overgrazing, and erosion had caused the amount of fertile farmland to drop below the minimum needed to maintain self-sufficiency in grain production. As a result, China was forced to begin importing grain in 1995, after years of exporting a surplus.

Tibet troubles. China celebrated the 30th anniversary of the founding of the Tibetan Autonomous Region on September 1. But exiled Tibetans rejected what they called the colonization of their homeland. China imposed tight security in Tibet's capital, Lhasa, to prevent the eruption of nationalist demonstrations.

On May 14, the Dalai Lama, the spiritual leader of Tibetan Buddhists, declared from exile in India that a 6-year-old boy living in Tibet was the incarnation of the Panchen Lama, who died in 1989. China contested the selection, saying its committee of monks had the right to decide on incarnations.

Relations with the United States were troubled throughout 1995. One problem was trade. On February 4, the United States imposed the largest trade sanctions ever on China because China violated U.S. copyright law by pirating computer software, videos, and other items. The issue was resolved on March 11, when China said it would improve laws against piracy and enforce them more thoroughly.

The United States was also concerned about China's restrictions on American imports, which resulted in a $30-billion annual trade surplus with the United States. And it opposed China's admission to the new World Trade Organization until China accepted free-trade principles. Relations became even chillier in June, when the United States issued a visa to Li Teng-hui, president of Taiwan, over which China claims sovereignty. (See **Taiwan.**)

Relations were further complicated by China's arrest on June 19 of Harry Wu, an American citizen of Chinese origin who had gone to China to investigate human rights abuses. Wu was sentenced to 15 years in jail for spying, but then he was expelled from China on August 24. Wu's release removed an obstacle that threatened to prevent U.S. First Lady Hillary Rodham Clinton from attending the Fourth United Nations Women's Conference in Beijing.

President Bill Clinton met Jiang Zemin in New York City on October 24 to try to repair the strained relationship. No specific agreements were reached but U.S. officials expressed confidence that relations would improve.

Record summer floods of the Yangtze River, China's longest, killed more than 1,200 people. Property losses reached $5 billion.   ☐ Henry S. Bradsher

See also **Asia** (Facts in brief table); **Taiwan.** In *World Book,* see **China.**

Chirac, Jacques (1932-   ), the mayor of Paris, was elected president of France on May 7, 1995, defeating the Socialist candidate, Lionel Jospin. Chirac, a conservative with strong nationalistic convictions, promised to work toward reducing France's double-digit unemployment rate and lower taxes. Later in the year, Chirac precipitated an international furor when he ordered resumption of French underground nuclear testing in the Pacific Ocean.

Jacques René Chirac was born in Paris on Nov. 29, 1932. He graduated from the Institute of Political Studies and then was drafted into the army. He served in France's war with Algeria, a French colony at the time, and was wounded in action. After his discharge in 1957, he enrolled in the École Nationale d'Administration, graduating in 1959.

Beginning in 1967, Chirac held a series of appointive governmental posts, culminating with his appointment as prime minister under President Valéry Giscard d'Estaing in 1974.

In 1977, Chirac was elected mayor of Paris. In that office, he undertook a program of urban renewal and established programs to assist working and single mothers, senior citizens, the handicapped, and the poor. He was reelected in 1983 and 1989. From 1986 to 1988, while continuing as mayor, he also served again as prime minister.

Chirac married Bernadette Chodron de Courcel in 1956. They have two daughters.   ☐ Lisa Klobuchar

Chrétien, Jean, who had enjoyed strong popularity as Canada's prime minister, saw his credibility slip with the razor-thin victory of the federalists in the Quebec independence referendum of Oct. 30, 1995. In repeatedly reassuring Canadians that the separatist movement did not represent the majority opinion in Quebec, Chrétien displayed an unfortunate lack of understanding of the political mood in his native province. Chrétien, who argued for a bilingual Canada in which the central government would promote Quebec's interests, had opposed previous attempts to grant more powers to Quebec.

Quick action by Chrétien's wife thwarted an armed intruder who entered the prime minister's residence in the early morning hours of November 5. Aline Chrétien spotted a man armed with a jackknife in an upstairs hallway. Quickly retreating to the bedroom, she locked the door and awakened her husband, who armed himself with an Inuit statue of a loon, and called the police.

But nearly 10 minutes passed before the Royal Canadian Mounted Police apprehended André Dallaire, 34, of Longueuil, who was later charged with attempted murder. The Mounties, under severe criticism for their lax response, admitted security at the residence was inadequate and suspended at least five officers.   ☐ David M. L. Farr

See also **Canada.** In *World Book,* see **Chrétien, Jean.**

Christo (1935-   ), a Bulgarian-born American artist famous for huge temporary artworks, completed his most ambitious project yet in 1995. In June, Christo and his wife and collaborator, Jeanne-Claude, unveiled *Wrapped Reichstag, Berlin, 1971–1995.* The two artists enclosed the building in more than 1 million square feet (100,000 square meters) of silver fabric. They had worked on *Wrapped Reichstag* since 1971 and raised most of its $10-million cost by selling renderings and collages of the project.

Christo was born Christo Javacheff in Gabrovo, Bulgaria, on June 13, 1935—the same day Jeanne-Claude was born in Casablanca, Morocco. He studied at the Fine Arts Academy in Sofia, Bulgaria, from 1953 to 1956 and moved to Paris in 1958. That year he married Jeanne-Claude, and they began working together. Their works include *Wrapped Kunsthalle, Berne, Switzerland* (1969) and *Running Fence, Sonoma and Marin Counties, California, 1972–76,* a shimmering wall of white fabric that stretched along the hills of northern California. Another important work was *The Umbrellas, Japan-U.S.A., 1984–91* (1991), a collection of 1,340 giant blue umbrellas installed north of Tokyo and 1,760 yellow umbrellas in the Tejon Pass in California.

Cristo and Jeanne-Claude have a son, Cyril, born in 1960.   ☐ Lisa Klobuchar

Churches. See **Eastern Orthodox Churches; Islam; Protestantism; Religion; Roman Catholic Church.**

City. Terrorist acts created scenes of horror in cities of the United States, Europe, the Middle East, and Asia in 1995 during a year of militant violence.

An enormous homemade bomb ripped through a federal office building in Oklahoma City on April 19, killing 168 people and wounding hundreds of others. The bomb had been concealed in a truck parked outside the Alfred P. Murrah Federal Building. The building was so badly damaged that it was demolished after the search for victims was concluded.

Timothy J. McVeigh, 27, and Terry Lynn Nichols, 40, were indicted in August on charges of conspiring to blow up the federal building. McVeigh and Nichols had met in the Army and shared extreme antigovernment views.

Concern over the potential danger of similar bombings in Washington, D.C., led in May to the closing of Pennsylvania Avenue on the north side of the White House. Several streets near congressional office buildings on Capitol Hill were also closed.

Terrorism in foreign cities. Hatred of government also seemed to be an important element in a series of bombings in France, Israel, and Pakistan and in several gas attacks in Japan. In Paris, several bombings in 1995 left at least 7 people dead and over 150 injured during a three-month period from July to October. The attacks occurred at rail and subway stations and other busy public areas, including the Arc de Triomphe. They were believed to be the work of militant Muslim groups in Algeria opposed to French support of the Algerian government.

Muslim militants opposed to Egypt's government claimed responsibility for an attack in Islamabad, Pakistan, in November. A suicide bomber killed himself and at least 15 others, and wounded some 60 people, by driving a truck loaded with explosives into the Egyptian embassy.

In Israel, a Palestinian suicide bomber killed himself and six others on a bus in Tel Aviv in July amid negotiations between Israeli and Palestinian leaders. Four months later, Israel's prime minister, Yitzhak Rabin, was assassinated by a young Israeli student from an ultraconservative faction.

Another terrorist bomb exploded in November at an American training camp in Riyadh, the capital of Saudi Arabia, killing 7 people and injuring about 60 others. Experts suspected that Saudi groups opposed to the government's ties with the West were responsible for the blast.

Nerve gas attacks. The subways of Tokyo, which carry nearly 6 million passengers each day, became the target of terrorists using a deadly nerve gas. Chemicals that react to form a toxic gas called sarin were planted in March on subway cars along three different routes. The attacks left 12 dead and more than 5,500 hospitalized. A Japanese religious cult was held responsible. A month later in Yokohama, a gas attack in the city's main train station left hundreds of people hospitalized.

50 largest cities in the world

Rank	Urban center*	Population
1.	Tokyo-Yokohama, Japan	28,447,000
2.	Mexico City, Mexico	23,913,000
3.	São Paulo, Brazil	21,539,000
4.	Seoul, South Korea	19,065,000
5.	New York City, U.S.	14,638,000
6.	Osaka-Kobe-Kyoto, Japan	14,060,000
7.	Bombay, India	13,532,000
8.	Calcutta, India	12,885,000
9.	Rio de Janeiro, Brazil	12,786,000
10.	Buenos Aires, Argentina	12,232,000
11.	Teheran, Iran	11,681,000
12.	Manila, Philippines	11,342,000
13.	Cairo, Egypt	11,155,000
14.	Jakarta, Indonesia	11,151,000
15.	Moscow, Russia	10,769,000
16.	Los Angeles, U.S.	10,414,000
17.	Delhi, India	10,105,000
18.	Lagos, Nigeria	9,799,000
19.	Karachi, Pakistan	9,350,000
20.	London, U.K.	8,897,000
21.	Paris, France	8,764,000
22.	Lima, Peru	7,853,000
23.	Istanbul, Turkey	7,624,000
24.	Taipei, Taiwan	7,477,000
25.	Essen, Germany	7,364,000
26.	Shanghai, China	7,194,000
27.	Bogotá, Colombia	6,801,000
28.	Bangkok, Thailand	6,657,000
29.	Madras, India	6,550,000
30.	Chicago, U.S.	6,541,000
31.	Beijing, China	5,865,000
32.	Hong Kong	5,841,000
33.	Santiago, Chile	5,812,000
34.	Pusan, South Korea	5,748,000
35.	Bangalore, India	5,644,000
36.	Dhaka, Bangladesh	5,296,000
37.	Tianjin, China	5,041,000
38.	Nagoya, Japan	5,017,000
39.	Lahore, Pakistan	4,986,000
40.	Milan, Italy	4,795,000
41.	Madrid, Spain	4,772,000
42.	St. Petersburg, Russia	4,694,000
43.	Baghdad, Iraq	4,566,000
44.	Kinshasa, Zaire	4,520,000
45.	Barcelona, Spain	4,492,000
46.	Shenyang, China	4,457,000
47.	Belo Horizonte, Brazil	4,373,000
48.	Ahmadabad, India	4,200,000
49.	Hyderabad, India	4,149,000
50.	San Francisco Bay Area, U.S.	4,104,000

*An urban center is a continuous built-up area, similar to a metropolitan area, having a population density of at least 5,000 persons per square mile (1,900 per square kilometer). Source: 1995 estimates from the U.S. Bureau of the Census.

50 largest cities in the United States

Rank	City	Population*	Percent change in population since 1990	Unemployment rate†	Mayor‡
1.	New York City	7,333,253	+0.1	7.5%	Rudolph W. Giuliani (R, 12/97)
2.	Los Angeles	3,448,613	-1.1	7.4	Richard J. Riordan (R, 6/97)
3.	Chicago	2,731,743	-1.9	4.2	Richard M. Daley (D, 4/99)
4.	Houston	1,702,086	+4.4	6.6	Bob Lanier (NP, 12/99)
5.	Philadelphia	1,524,249	-3.9	6.0	Edward G. Rendell (D, 1/00)
6.	San Diego	1,151,977	+3.7	6.8	Susan Golding (NP, 12/96)
7.	Phoenix	1,048,949	+6.6	4.0	Skip Rimsza (NP, 12/99)
8.	Dallas	1,022,830	+1.5	5.5	Ronald Kirk (NP, 5/99)
9.	San Antonio	998,905	+6.8	5.5	William E. Thornton (NP, 5/97)
10.	Detroit	992,038	-3.5	5.9	Dennis Archer (D, 1/98)
11.	San Jose	816,884	+4.4	5.4	Susan Hammer (NP, 12/98)
12.	Indianapolis	752,279	+2.9	3.9	Stephen Goldsmith (R, 12/99)
13.	San Francisco	734,676	+1.5	5.7	Frank M. Jordan (D, 1/96)
14.	Baltimore	702,979	-4.5	6.3	Kurt L. Schmoke (D, 12/99)
15.	Jacksonville, Fla.	665,070	+4.7	4.4	John A. Delaney (R, 7/99)
16.	Columbus, Ohio	635,913	+0.5	3.5	Gregory S. Lashutka (R, 12/99)
17.	Milwaukee	617,044	-1.8	3.8	John O. Norquist (D, 4/96)
18.	Memphis	614,289	-0.7	5.4	W. W. Herenton (D, 12/99)
19.	El Paso	579,307	+12.4	10.5	Larry Francis (NP, 7/97)
20.	Washington, D.C.	567,094	-6.6	4.5	Marion S. Barry, Jr. (D, 1/99)
21.	Boston	547,725	-4.6	5.1	Thomas M. Menino (D, 1/98)
22.	Seattle	520,947	+0.9	5.2	Norman B. Rice (NP, 12/97)
23.	Austin	514,013	+10.4	3.6	Bruce Todd (NP, 6/97)
24.	Nashville	504,505	+3.3	3.9	Philip Bredesen (D, 9/99)
25.	Denver	493,559	+5.5	3.9	Wellington E. Webb (D, 6/97)
26.	Cleveland	492,901	-2.5	4.6	Michael R. White (D, 12/97)
27.	New Orleans, La.	484,149	-2.6	7.8	Marc Morial (D, 5/98)
28.	Oklahoma City, Okla.	463,201	+4.2	3.8	Ronald J. Norick (NP, 4/98)
29.	Fort Worth, Tex.	451,814	+0.9	5.3	Kay Granger (NP, 5/97)
30.	Portland, Ore.	450,777	+2.7	4.2	Vera Katz (NP, 12/96)
31.	Kansas City, Mo.	443,878	+2.1	4.4	Emanuel Cleaver II (D, 4/99)
32.	Charlotte, N.C.	437,797	+10.6	3.8	Pat McCrory (R, 11/99)
33.	Tucson, Ariz.	434,726	+6.4	3.9	George Miller (D, 12/99)
34.	Long Beach, Calif.	433,852	+1.1	7.4	Beverly O'Neill (D, 6/98)
35.	Virginia Beach, Va.	430,295	+9.5	5.3	Meyera E. Oberndorf (NP, 6/96)
36.	Albuquerque, N. Mex.	411,994	+7.1	5.1	Martin J. Chavez (D, 11/97)
37.	Atlanta, Ga.	396,052	+0.5	4.8	Bill Campbell (D, 12/97)
38.	Fresno, Calif.	386,551	+9.2	13.1	Jim Patterson (NP, 3/97)
39.	Honolulu, Hawaii	385,881	+2.3	4.4	Jeremy Harris (D, 1/97)
40.	Tulsa, Okla.	374,851	+2.1	4.4	M. Susan Savage (D, 5/98)
41.	Sacramento, Calif.	373,964	+1.2	7.2	Joe Serna, Jr. (D, 11/96)
42.	Miami, Fla.	373,024	+4.0	7.1	Stephen P. Clark (D, 11/97)
43.	St. Louis, Mo.	368,215	-7.2	5.0	Freeman R. Bosley, Jr. (D, 4/97)
44.	Oakland, Calif.	366,926	-1.4	6.2	Elihu Mason Harris (NP, 12/98)
45.	Pittsburgh, Pa.	358,883	-3.0	6.0	Thomas Murphy (D, 12/97)
46.	Cincinnati, Ohio	358,170	-1.6	4.3	Roxanne Qualls (D, 11/97)
47.	Minneapolis, Minn.	354,590	-3.7	3.5	Sharon Sayles Belton (D, 12/97)
48.	Omaha, Nebr.	345,033	+2.8	2.8	Hal Daub (R, 6/97)
49.	Las Vegas, Nev.	327,878	+27.0	6.4	Jan Laverty Jones (D, 5/99)
50.	Toledo, Ohio	322,550	-3.1	4.9	Carlton Finkbeiner (D, 12/97)

*1994 estimates (source: U.S. Bureau of the Census).
†June 1995 unemployment figures are for metropolitan areas (source: U.S. Bureau of Labor Statistics).
‡The letters in parentheses represent the mayor's party, with *D* meaning Democrat, *R* Republican, *I* Independent, and *NP* nonpartisan. The date is when the term of office ends (source: mayors' offices).

Reactions to terrorist activities included heightened security at many government buildings as well as at commercial offices and public facilities. Airports imposed strict rules on baggage checking and passenger identification. Curbside traffic enforcement also increased. Organizers of the 1996 Olympic Games in Atlanta, Georgia, were planning to spend nearly $100 million on security systems.

Police misconduct. In New Orleans, Louisiana, police officer Antoinette Frank in March was convicted and sentenced to death on charges of robbery and murder. The victims were a brother and sister at a family-owned Vietnamese restaurant and a fellow police officer working there as a security guard.

Also during the year, six Atlanta police officers were charged with taking money seized during drug arrests and demanding payoffs in exchange for police protection. Six Philadelphia police officers were charged with falsifying records and planting evidence. Investigations of corruption in New York City's police department led to dismissals and reassignment of officers and supervisors. And in Pittsburgh, three police officers faced charges in the death of a motorist following an arrest.

Public security concerns. One response to the public anxiety over personal safety and security in 1995 was the steady growth of "gated" communities. A report by the Lincoln Institute of Land Policy listed Miami, Los Angeles, Houston, Phoenix, New York, and Chicago as cities where security had been augmented in new housing developments. "Gated" communities are closed-off areas, usually surrounded by walls or tall fences, in which residents pay an assessment for their own street maintenance, security, and other services.

Local government financial losses. The overall picture of municipal finances improved for most cities in 1995, according to the annual survey of city government finances conducted by the National League of Cities. But local government leaders got a scare about their fiscal security when public investment strategies backfired in several cities.

Orange County, California, a wealthy area near Los Angeles, plummeted into bankruptcy because of highly speculative financial transactions. Investment in high-risk securities led to the $1.7-billion collapse of the county's investment pool. About $7.5 billion had been contributed to the pool by nearly 200 cities, school districts, and agencies in Orange County and throughout the West.

In other fiscal debacles, a state-managed fund that handled investments for local governments in Wisconsin sustained losses of $95 million. And in Escambia County, Florida, financial mismanagement caused the value of a $44-million investment to shrink to $19 million. Such losses left enormous shortfalls in capital spending, forced layoffs and cutbacks in services, and left many communities with the need to borrow funds to meet their obligations.

The finances of the nation's capital also reached a crisis stage in 1995. With local revenues and the federal payment inadequate to cover an overspent budget, Congress imposed an independent financial control board to oversee and, if necessary, administer the District of Columbia's finances.

Congressional action. A different threat to the fiscal well-being of U.S. cities was reduced significantly by legislation to deter Congress from passing unfunded federal mandates. Opposition to the growing burden of mandates—federal laws and regulations imposed on cities and states without the money needed to implement them—found a positive response in the Republican leadership of the 104th Congress. In mid-March, Congress passed a bill designed to curb unfunded mandates. President Bill Clinton signed the bill on March 22.

Other federal policy initiatives moving through Congress aroused concern among city leaders, however. Proposals to end federal involvement in programs such as welfare, child assistance, Medicaid, and job training called for giving the states block grants to design and carry out those programs. City leaders wanted assurances that the states would attend to the needs of urban populations, and they wanted an assured role for local governments in designing and carrying out the decisions of state-administered programs.

Conference on local government. In November, the three organizations representing local governments throughout the United States—the National League of Cities, the National Association of Counties, and the United States Conference of Mayors—held a first-ever Conference of Local Governments in Chicago. The conference concluded with a call for a national summit on the roles of government at all levels. That meeting would examine functions and responsibilities to enable citizens to understand who is accountable for the policies and services affecting them.

Education. A similar debate over accountability and responsibility continued to bring changes in the nation's schools. In Chicago, Mayor Richard M. Daley in June gained policy control over the nation's third-largest school system. The existing structure of the problem-plagued school system was abolished by the state legislature, which gave the mayor authority to appoint new leaders but also left him with major funding problems.

In Seattle, where the mayor has little control over the local school board, the board itself struck out for change by hiring John Henry Stanford, a retired Army general, to serve as superintendent. In Ohio and New Jersey, the state stepped in to take over troubled school systems in Cleveland and Newark.

Alternative education enterprises continued to attract interest and spark disagreement in 1995. Two private firms—Education Alternatives Incorporated and The Edison Project, L.P.—were operating schools in 1995 in a number of cities, including Baltimore, Boston, and Wichita, Kansas. At year's end, many of these programs appeared to be faltering. The companies struggled to provide the services they had promised while still making a profit.

Many cities held elections in 1995, and most mayoral contests in major cities were won by incumbents. Among the new mayors elected in open contests, Democrat Ron Kirk became the first African American mayor of Dallas, and Scott King, a local attorney, became the first white candidate to win the mayoral election in Gary, Indiana, in 28 years. In another open contest, City Council member William Thornton won the mayoral election in San Antonio. In Georgia, the city of Augusta and surrounding Richmond County completed a consolidation to become the state's second-largest city, after Atlanta. The chairman of the county board of commissioners, Larry Sconyers, was elected to lead the new consolidated government.

Football teams relocate. The Raiders returned from Los Angeles to Oakland, their original city, in 1995. Also, the Los Angeles Rams relocated to St. Louis, Missouri.

Newspapers shut down. Three major daily newspapers went out of existence in 1995: the *Houston Post,* the *Baltimore Evening Sun,* and *New York Newsday.* □ Randolph C. Arndt

In **World Book,** see **City.**

Randy Pech stands by his construction firm's truck after the Supreme Court ruled in June that he should not have lost a contract bid to a minority-owned business.

Civil rights. Race relations in the United States during 1995 were buffeted by crosscurrents of hope, despair, and anxiety as Americans struggled to find common ground and goals on volatile racial issues. From the acquittal of former football star O.J. Simpson on double murder charges to the Million Man March by blacks to renewed debate over affirmative action both in Congress and in many states, issues of race dominated discussion and political debate through much of the year.

Simpson verdict. When Simpson was acquitted on October 3 by a jury whose 12 members included 9 blacks, the nation's racial divide became tangible. A CBS News poll conducted after the verdict was announced showed that 9 out of 10 blacks thought the jury reached the correct verdict while 6 out of 10 whites believed the jury was wrong. (See **Courts.**)

A massive gathering of African American men in Washington, D.C., on October 16 also polarized racial camps. Nation of Islam leader Louis Farrakhan organized what he called the Million Man March as a call to action to end the problems plaguing black communities, including violence, illiteracy, and the abandonment of families by fathers. Many blacks and whites applauded the goals of the march, but many avoided endorsing it because of Farrakhan's reportedly racist and anti-Semitic views. The U.S. Park Service estimated that 400,000 people attended. But Farrakhan accused the government of racial

bias in its count. An estimate by Boston University put the crowd at between 670,000 and 1 million.

Affirmative action. California led what became widespread debate about affirmative action in 1995, largely through Governor Pete Wilson, a candidate for the 1996 Presidential race until he quit in September 1995. Affirmative action refers to laws and policies that take race and gender into account in order to raise the numbers of women and minorities in the work force and in higher education.

On June 1, Wilson signed an order abolishing as many as 150 boards that advised California state agencies on policies for hiring minorities and women. On July 20, the controlling board of California's university system, of which Wilson was a member, voted to stop taking race and gender into account in admissions, hiring, and contracting. Finally, on August 10, Wilson sued his own state government to abolish affirmative action laws adopted by the legislature. During 1995, lawmakers in 14 other states considered limiting such programs or making them illegal, though most proposals did not become law.

Similar debate took place in Congress, where some Republicans talked about ending all federal affirmative action programs. President Bill Clinton responded by ordering a study of more than 100 federal programs. On July 19, with the study completed, Clinton defended affirmative action. However, he also ordered some changes in federal programs.

Supreme Court. On June 12, the U.S. Supreme Court ruled that Congress can authorize only affirmative action programs that are narrowly defined to remedy clear cases of past discrimination. The court ruled 5 to 4 in favor of a Colorado construction company owner, Randy Pech, who sued because he lost a contract that went to a minority-owned business even though Pech had submitted a lower bid. The ruling restricted federal agencies' ability to give special consideration to minorities and women competing for work on publicly funded projects.

The court dealt another blow to affirmative action on May 23 when the justices declined to consider reinstating a scholarship program for African American students at the University of Maryland. Because the program excluded nonblack applicants, an appeals court had struck it down as a violation of the Constitution's equal protection guarantees.

Voting. The Supreme Court also made it harder for lawmakers to use race in drawing new voting districts. On June 29, the court struck down a Georgia congressional district formed in 1992 to increase minority voting strength in the state. The justices said that drawing electoral districts solely on the basis of voters' race violates the Constitution's equal protection guarantees.

Desegregation. On June 12, 1995, the Supreme Court made it easier for public school districts to end court-ordered desegregation plans. The court ruled that Missouri did not have to continue special funding for the Kansas City, Missouri, school district simply because minority students in the district scored below the national average on standardized tests. The justices said that when lower courts are deciding whether a desegregation plan can be lifted, minorities' low scholastic achievement can be considered only if it is clearly due to past segregation.

Women and The Citadel. A debate over whether states can operate publicly funded single-sex colleges became more complicated in 1995. An April 13 court order allowed Shannon Faulkner, a 20-year-old South Carolina woman, to become the first female cadet at The Citadel, an all-male military academy in Charleston, South Carolina. After a 2½-year legal fight, Faulkner joined the cadet corps in early August. However, she became ill during the first week of training and withdrew from the school on August 18. She said emotional stress from her long fight to enter the college led her to resign.

The Citadel is one of only two public, all-male military colleges in the United States. The other is Virginia Military Institute in Lexington, Virginia . In 1993, Faulkner sued The Citadel for sex discrimination after being denied admission. By late 1995, Faulkner's lawyers had said that three other women planned to join the suit against The Citadel rather than let the challenge drop.

The Glass Ceiling Commission, set up by Congress in 1991 to explore the problem of invisible barriers that women and minorities hit as they approach the top of the corporate hierarchy, issued its report on March 15, 1995. Women and minorities rarely make it to the highest levels of U.S. businesses, the report stated. Because of barriers to advancement, 97 percent of the top managers at the country's largest companies are white and 95 to 97 percent are men, the commission said. The panel said that women and minorities are locked into low-paying, dead-end jobs far more often than white men. While women hold 48 percent of the management and professional jobs in the United States, the commission reported, they usually work for the government, health or social-welfare agencies, or in other areas that pay less than private corporations.

NAACP. Myrlie Evers-Williams, widow of slain civil rights leader Medgar Evers, became chair of the National Association for the Advancement of Colored People (NAACP) on February 18. She replaced William F. Gibson, chairman since 1985, who was accused of improper financial practices. An audit released by the NAACP on July 13 said that Gibson and former executive directors Benjamin Chavis and Benjamin L. Hooks had run up nearly $150,000 in questionable expenses as the NAACP ran nearly $4 million into debt. In December, Representative Kweisi Mfume (D., Md.) became the NAACP chief executive.

Sexual harassment. Del Laboratories of Farmingdale, New York, a major cosmetics maker, agreed in 1995 to pay 15 female workers a total of $1.2 million to settle a sexual harassment complaint against the company's president. The Equal Employment Opportunity Commission (EEOC) announced the settlement on August 3. It was the largest settlement ever won by the EEOC, a federal agency that investigates and prosecutes workplace discrimination.

Homosexual rights. On August 4, President Clinton issued an executive order saying that the federal government could no longer deny security clearances to homosexuals based only on their sexual orientation. Federal regulations already barred denying security clearances—which allow access to classified information—on the basis of race, sex, color, religion, national origin, or disability.

Amnesty International, a London-based human rights group, released its report on worldwide rights violations in July 1995. The report, which covered 1994, focused on abuse against women, saying, "In a world racked by violence, women face rape, mutilation, and death at the hands of armed men."

Amnesty International, which opposes the death penalty under all circumstances, reported that there were 2,870 people on death row in 35 U.S. states in 1994. States executed 31 prisoners in 1994, and three states executed their first prisoners in about 30 years.   □ Linda P. Campbell and Geoffrey A. Campbell

See also **Civil rights** Special Report: **Affirmative Action: Opportunity or Obstacle?** In *World Book,* see **Civil rights.**

Affirmative action: Opportunity or obstacle?

By Geoffrey A. Campbell

Affirmative action programs have enabled minorities and women to improve their job and educational opportunities. But have they erected barricades to others?

California often leads the United States in legal trends, and in 1995, the state sparked a nationwide scrutiny of civil rights practices by boldly moving to end several affirmative action programs. Affirmative action, the practice of taking race and gender into account in college admissions, job hiring, and other kinds of decisions, had become a much-used tool for helping women and minorities advance in higher education and the workplace. However, a rising voice of criticism argued that racial and gender preferences discriminate against white men and even work against the individuals they are intended to help.

California Governor Pete Wilson attacked affirmative action as part of his short-lived quest for the 1996 Republican nomination for U.S. President. "Almost every American can sense the tension and unfairness this system of racial spoils has produced," Wilson said in an open letter to the people of California on May 31, 1995. "The current system of special privilege based on race and gender is breeding resentment from those left standing on the sidelines."

The next day, June 1, Wilson signed an executive order eliminating as many as 150 boards that advised state agencies on hiring women and minorities. In his role as president of the University of California board of regents, he led a July 20 vote to scrap a policy of considering race and gender in admissions, hiring, and contracting at what is the largest public university system in the United States.

Riding the momentum of the regents' vote, Wilson in August sued his own state government to overturn existing affirmative action laws. Joining the movement, other opponents of those laws aimed to force a statewide vote on the issue in 1996. Wilson said that state laws providing for racial preferences "stigmatize the very people they purport to assist. . . . [and] maintain division within our increasingly and richly diverse state." Although no other state immediately followed California's aggressive lead, a countrywide renewal of soul-searching and political posturing began over what are the best ways to ensure equality for men and women of all races and ethnic groups.

A history of struggle

Civil rights in America took its first step into the modern world in June 1866, following the Civil War (1861-1865), when legislators added the 14th Amendment—often called the Civil Rights Amendment—to the Constitution of the United States. The amendment gave citizenship to African Americans and guaranteed that all federal and state laws would apply equally to blacks and whites. In 1869, Congress passed the 15th Amendment, which made it illegal to deny a person the right to vote on the basis of race. Women won the right to vote in every state with adoption of the 19th Amendment in 1920.

But after federal troops were removed from the South in 1877, many of the gains won by African Americans were reversed, including the right to vote. And despite the 19th Amendment, women continued to be excluded from certain professions, were usually paid less than men, and were denied such rights as property ownership.

Previous pages: In 1965, blacks march from Selma, Alabama, to the state capital, Montgomery, demanding voting rights. In 1995, Californians, *inset,* rally at their state capitol to demand that affirmative action programs not be cut.

The author

Geoffrey A. Campbell is a writer and regular contributor to *Year Book.*

These injustices continued with little relief until the mid-1900's, when the modern civil rights struggle erupted. In 1954, blacks won a major victory when the Supreme Court of the United States ruled that racially segregated schools violated the constitutional right to equal protection guaranteed by the 14th Amendment. The movement gained momentum in 1955, when a black seamstress named Rosa Parks refused to give a white man her seat at the front of a bus in Montgomery, Alabama, violating a city law. Police arrested Parks, which set off a boycott of buses and other protests around the country to force better treatment of African Americans. Eventually, protests led to the passage of the Civil Rights Act of 1964, a law that banned discrimination against individuals based on their race, sex, color, ethnicity, or national origin. The law prohibits discrimination in employment, voting, and access to public accommodations. It also forbids discrimination by any program that receives federal money.

Women's ongoing struggle for equal treatment gained momentum alongside this fight for racial equality. The Equal Rights Amendment (ERA) to the Constitution had first been proposed to Congress in 1923. The amendment read: "Equality of rights under the law shall not be denied or abridged by the United States or any state on account of sex." Congress finally passed the ERA in 1972. However, the amendment never entered the Constitution because it was ratified by only 35 of the 38 states required. Critics of the ERA said that women already had protection under the Constitution, as well as under the Civil Rights Act of 1964. But ERA proponents wanted an amendment that specifically barred discrimination on the basis of sex.

The history of affirmative action

The term *affirmative action* was first used in an executive order issued by President John F. Kennedy in 1961. The order required businesses with U.S. government contracts to treat their employees without regard to race, ethnic origin, religion, or sex. President Lyndon B. Johnson in 1965 also issued executive orders to boost minority employment at firms contracting with the federal government. Affirmative action soon developed into a complicated system of programs operated by the state and federal governments, private employers, and colleges and universities. Many affirmative action programs also broadened their focus to include people with disabilities and Vietnam veterans.

As a result of affirmative action orders, many employers began set-

---

What is affirmative action?

- Affirmative action consists of efforts to counteract past discrimination against minorities, women, people with disabilities, and Vietnam veterans in employment, education, and other areas.

- Some affirmative action programs encourage or recruit women and minorities to apply for contracts or employment.

- Other programs in such areas as employment, college admissions, and government contracts set goals to ensure that women or minorities are included in fair proportions.

- The federal government sets aside a fixed share of federal contracts for businesses owned by women or minorities. These are often referred to as set-asides.

- Many state and local governments as well as businesses and schools create their own affirmative-action programs.

The ups and downs of affirmative action

Affirmative action has never been without controversy. Its history is one of legislation and court decisions that have either reinforced it or modified it.

1961
President John F. Kennedy first uses the term *affirmative action* in an order that requires businesses with U.S. government contracts to treat their employees without regard to race, ethnic origin, religion, or sex.

1964
President Lyndon B. Johnson signs the Civil Rights Act of 1964, banning any discrimination against individuals based on race, sex, color, ethnicity, or national origin.

1965
President Johnson issues an executive order requiring firms with federal government contracts to actively undertake affirmative action. This order includes funding and enforcement measures.

1969-1971
The Administration of President Richard M. Nixon requires federal contractors to set specific goals and timetables for employing women and minorities.

1978
Allan Bakke sues the University of California, claiming that he was denied entrance to medical school because he was white. The Supreme Court of the United States rules that colleges and universities may not use quotas to achieve racial balance, but they may consider race as one factor in admissions.

1979
The Supreme Court rules in *United Steelworkers v. Weber* that private employers may have their own voluntary affirmative action plans.

1980's

1980
In the case of *Fullilove v. Klutznick,* the Supreme Court upholds minority set-aside contracts established by the U.S. Congress for federal programs.

1986
The Supreme Court rules in *Wygant v. Jackson Board of Education* that laying off senior white teachers to protect the jobs of newly hired black teachers was unconstitutional.

1987
In a case involving a female road-repair dispatcher in Santa Clara County, California, the Supreme Court upholds hiring minorities and women over comparably qualified white men in order to remedy past discrimination.

1989
The Supreme Court, in *City of Richmond v. Croson,* restricts the power of state and local governments to set aside public-works contracts for minority firms.

1990's

1994
California drafts the Civil Rights Initiative to go on the 1996 state ballot. The initiative calls for a ban on affirmative action in state colleges and universities, public employment, and government contracting.

1995
February: President Bill Clinton orders a five-month review of affirmative action programs.
May: The Supreme Court denies an appeal from the University of Maryland, in Baltimore, to reinstate a scholarship program for talented black students. A lower court had said the program discriminated against nonblacks.
June: In the case of *Adarand Constructors, Inc. v. Peña,* the Supreme Court restricts the power of the federal government to set aside public-works contracts for minority firms.
July 19: Clinton defends affirmative action. "Mend it, but don't end it," he says. He directs federal agencies to comply with the June Supreme Court decision.
July 20: The University of California becomes the first state university system voting to end affirmative action efforts in admission, hiring, and contracting.

ting goals for the numbers of women or minorities they would hire. Under another type of program, agencies set aside a percentage of public works contracts for minority-owned businesses or gave competing companies extra points for having a minority or female owner. These are referred to as set-asides. In a third common form of affirmative action, college scholarships were made available specifically for blacks and Hispanics.

Affirmative action met approval from those who considered it an important way to "level the playing field" for groups denied opportunities for so long that they lagged significantly behind. Some critics, however, warned that what they considered quotas could cause qualified white men to lose out to less-qualified minorities and women.

For many years, the Supreme Court turned back legal challenges to affirmative action. The key 1971 case of *Griggs v. Duke Power Co.* barred employers from using hiring exams that are not job-related because such tests tended to unfairly screen out blacks. In education, the court ruled in *Regents of the University of California v. Allan Bakke* in 1978 that "colleges and universities cannot set aside a specified number of places for minorities but can take race into consideration in admissions decisions." As the justices continued to uphold different forms of affirmative action, the practice spread among state and local governments as well as many private companies. After the 1980 case of *Fullilove v. Klutsnick,* in which the court allowed Congress to set aside a percentage of public contracts for minority businesses, that practice became standard for government agencies.

The gains that were made

In the years since the Civil Rights Act of 1964 became law, minorities and women have increased their share of jobs and raised their average income. In 1950, white men made up 65 percent of the labor force, while white women made up only 24 percent of the labor force. But white women reached nearly 36 percent of the labor force in 1990. In the same period, minority representation in the labor force doubled to more than 15 percent. In the early 1990's, white and nonwhite women totalled 47 percent of the workforce and accounted for at least half the enrollment in undergraduate colleges, law schools, medical schools, and other professional programs.

African Americans have moved into a range of professions that once excluded them and have joined the middle class in greater numbers. By 1994, blacks made up 12.4 percent of the American adult population and they reached nearly that percentage in some job categories. For example, according to the United States Bureau of Labor Statistics, blacks accounted for 12.2 percent of education administrators, 9 percent of accountants and auditors, 9.3 percent of registered nurses, 13.9 percent of clinical laboratory technologists and technicians, and 9.7 percent of firefighters.

The gaps that remain

Despite these gains, minorities and women still trail white men in average pay, access to well-paying management jobs, and educational opportunities. In 1993, the most recent year for which figures are available, women earned only 71.5 percent as much as men earned, and black men earned only 74 percent as much as white men, according to the U.S. Bureau of the Census. These wage gaps can be explained partly by the interplay between jobs and education levels. A study by the American Council on Education released in March 1995 showed that although increasing numbers of blacks and Hispanic Americans are going to college, white high school graduates are still the group most likely to earn college degrees. In 1993, 42 percent of white high school graduates aged 18 to 24 went to college, compared with 33 percent of blacks and 36 percent of Hispanics.

However, even with college degrees, minorities and women are likely to receive lower pay than white men with similar educational backgrounds, according to the National Committee on Pay Equity, a private coalition that works to end wage discrimination. In 1992, white men who graduated from college earned as much as $9,600 more than black and Hispanic men with college degrees and $11,700 more than all college-educated women, regardless of color. College-educated Hispanic women fared the worst, earning $820 less than white men who only had high school diplomas.

Although the American labor force had become increasingly diverse by the early 1990's, the wage and achievement gaps were still great. In spite of increased numbers in the work world, women and minorities hit invisible barriers as they approached the top of the corporate hierarchy. In 1991, Congress created the Federal Glass Ceiling Commission to explore this problem.

In March 1995, the commission issued an extensively researched report. One of the commission's most remarkable findings was that 97 percent of top managers at the largest American companies are white, and only 3 to 5 percent of top managers are women. The report also found wage disparities between men and women at mid-level managerial and professional positions. The explanation for this was that, even though women hold 48 percent of these positions, they usually work for the government, health or social welfare agencies, or in other areas that pay less than the private corporate world. The commission said that women and minorities disproportionately "are locked into low-wage, low-prestige and dead-end jobs."

United States Secretary of Labor Robert B. Reich said in the report, "In short, the fact-finding report tells us that the world at the top of the corporate hierarchy does not yet look anything like America. . . . Nor, ominously, does the population of today's executive suite resemble the workforce of America's future. Women and minority men will make up 62 percent of the workforce in the year 2005." Reich commented on a finding of the report that businesses with a diverse workforce experience better financial performance. Nevertheless, said Reich, "serious barriers to advancement remain—such as persistent stereotyping, erroneous beliefs that 'no qualified women or minorities are out there,' and plain old fear of change."

The current debate

These continuing inequities caused Americans in 1995 to grapple with the difficult questions of what to do about them. People asked whether the broad preferences allowed by the years of affirmative action had actually helped the disadvantaged. And they looked at what better alternatives might be available.

Dissent over affirmative action has always been present, and the debate heated up in the early 1990's. Critics, both white and black, have said that affirmative action causes racial hostility because some people believe it allows individuals to get jobs even if they are not qualified. The critics argue that members of the black middle class, rather than the working poor, are often the beneficiaries. Some say that racial preferences were supposed to be a temporary tool and that continuing them prevents the realization of a colorblind society.

Black author Shelby Steele in his 1990 book *The Content of Our Character* argued that affirmative action contributes to a "victim-focused identity." Preferential treatment, he wrote, "does not teach

Makeup of U.S. population in 1990

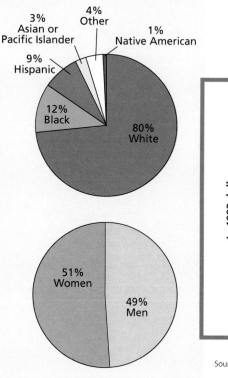

3%
Asian or
Pacific Islander

4%
Other

1%
Native American

9%
Hispanic

12%
Black

80%
White

51%
Women

49%
Men

Gaps in earnings and education

Although women and minorities have made many gains, disparities remain. Women make up 51 percent of the population, *left,* and 46 percent of the workforce, *opposite page.* Blacks make up 12 percent of the population and 10 percent of the workforce. In wages and education, *below and opposite,* significant gaps remain between white males and women and minorities.

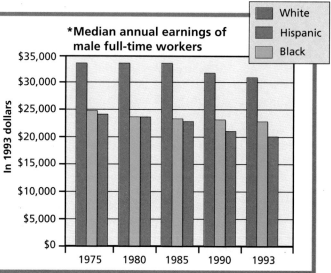

*Median annual earnings of male full-time workers

In 1993 dollars

Legend: White, Hispanic, Black

Source: U.S. Bureau of the Census.

Earnings for all women are below those of men. For example, white women in 1993 earned just above $20,000, while white men earned just above $30,000. Hispanic workers of both sexes had the lowest earnings. Because earnings, shown in 1993 dollars, have not kept up with inflation, the earnings reflect a decrease in the value of the dollar since 1975.

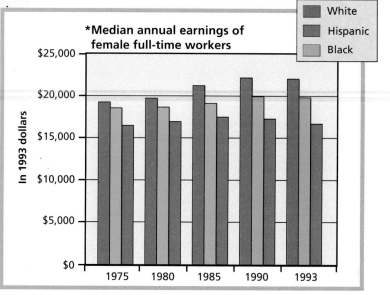

*Median annual earnings of female full-time workers

In 1993 dollars

Legend: White, Hispanic, Black

* Median earnings are a middle number at which half of the people earn more than that amount and half of the people earn less.

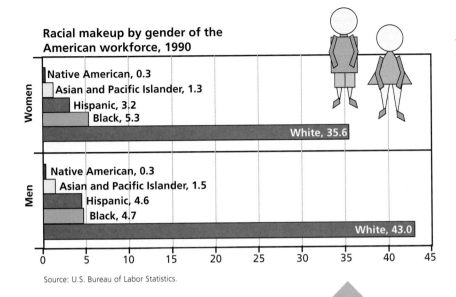

Racial makeup by gender of the American workforce, 1990

Women:
- Native American, 0.3
- Asian and Pacific Islander, 1.3
- Hispanic, 3.2
- Black, 5.3
- White, 35.6

Men:
- Native American, 0.3
- Asian and Pacific Islander, 1.5
- Hispanic, 4.6
- Black, 4.7
- White, 43.0

Source: U.S. Bureau of Labor Statistics.

The American workforce in 1990 consisted of about 46 percent women and 54 percent men, *left.* Women of all groups have increased their numbers since the mid-1900's. For example, in 1950, white women made up only 24 percent of the workforce. Education levels, *below,* have risen for all groups of people, though women and minorities lag behind white men.

skills, or educate, or instill motivation. It only passes out entitlement by color. . . ." Steele's book title comes from a speech by civil rights leader Martin Luther King, Jr., who said "I have a dream that my four little children will one day live in a nation where they will not be judged by the color of their skin but by the content of their character."

However, supporters of affirmative action counter that discrimination still lingers and that ending racial and gender preferences would cut off a broad range of opportunities for minorities and women. Because people feel most comfortable with those who look and act like themselves, they argue, it took affirmative action to counter this bias and to get white men to hire women and minorities for police and fire departments, admit them into law and medical schools, and give them a share of lucrative government contracts. And, in spite of progress, studies show that African Americans are still more likely than Anglo Americans to encounter racial bias when they apply for loans, seek jobs, or try to buy homes.

Mary Frances Berry, chair of the U.S. Commission on Civil Rights,

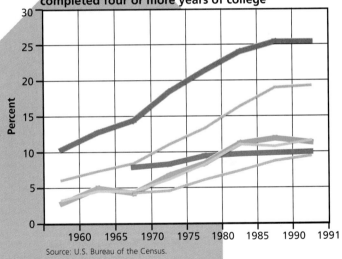

Percentage of adult Americans who have completed four or more years of college

Source: U.S. Bureau of the Census.

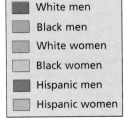

Legend:
- White men
- Black men
- White women
- Black women
- Hispanic men
- Hispanic women

Affirmative action: Save it or scrap it?

Although many people agree with the goal of ending discrimination, there is debate over how to achieve it. In 1995, the debate focused on the use of affirmative action programs as some lawmakers threatened to dismantle them.

Arguments against

- Affirmative action gives preferences to women and minorities solely because of their gender or race. Unqualified people are hired and promoted in order to fulfill affirmative action requirements.

- There are already laws against discrimination in employment. Affirmative action is not needed.

- Affirmative action results in reverse discrimination against white men.

- Affirmative action is no longer necessary in America. We have achieved a color-blind, nonsexist society.

- Affirmative action puts a strain on employers that hurts business.

- The positive effects of affirmative action are not measurable and thus cannot be proven.

- Giving preferences to minorities and women promotes their identity as victims.

Arguments for

- Affirmative action is necessary to remedy the ongoing effects of past discrimination.

- Affirmative action allows more people to compete on their own merits, without excluding qualified individuals due to their race, gender, or other secondary traits.

- Affirmative action is a necessary tool to open doors for qualified women and minorities who may not otherwise receive an equal opportunity.

- Many companies have affirmative action policies only because of government pressure. If government standards were to be relaxed, employers would revert to hiring only people of a gender or race that they favor.

- Affirmative action widens the labor pool and helps create a workforce that reflects the diversity of the marketplace.

- The increases in minority and female representation in the workplace since the 1960's show that affirmative action works.

wrote in *Emerge: Black America's Newsmagazine,* "The reason we need affirmative action is because we've had so much negative action throughout American history. Those negative actions began with slavery and have continued with African-Americans being treated as second-class citizens for more than two centuries."

The argument in favor of affirmative action at colleges and universities follows a domino theory. If race and ethnicity are not taken into account, many minority students would either be shut out of the nation's elite schools or not be accepted for college at all. Minorities often attend inferior schools in poorer neighborhoods and score lower, on average, than whites on the standardized tests that are important for college admission. And without that college education, the argument goes, individuals have little hope of gaining the key jobs that will improve their economic status.

The whittling away at affirmative action began with a 1989 Supreme Court decision, *City of Richmond v. Croson.* The ruling restricted the power of state and local governments to set aside public-works contracts for minority firms. It did not stop all such programs, but showed that they were vulnerable to attack.

By 1995, there were moves in at least 15 states to cut back or outlaw racial and gender preferences. Early in the year, pushed by Republicans in Congress wanting to end more than 100 federal affirmative action programs, President Bill Clinton ordered a five-month review of the programs in question. Before those results were in, affirmative action took a hit in May when the Supreme Court refused to hear an appeal from the University of Maryland, in Baltimore, which wanted to reinstate a scholarship program for talented black students. A lower court had abolished the program in 1994, saying it violated the Constitution by discriminating against nonblacks.

On June 12, 1995, a major Supreme Court decision further restricted affirmative action practices. In the case of *Adarand Constructors, Inc. v. Peña,* the court reduced Congress's power to order agencies to give preferences to women and minorities. The court said such programs must meet a standard of "strict scrutiny" and be specifically designed to benefit individuals who suffered actual discrimination in the past. Adarand, a construction company in Colorado, had gone to court after it lost out on a project that went to a Hispanic-owned company under a program that earmarked highway contracts for minorities.

Affirmative action survives, but for how long?

"Mend it, but don't end it, " President Clinton said about affirmative action on July 19 after the review he ordered was completed. Clinton defended government affirmative action programs, saying, "Affirmative action has not always been perfect, and affirmative action should not go on forever. . . . It should be changed now to take care of those things that are wrong, and it should be retired when its job is done. . . . I am resolved that that day will come, but the evidence suggests, indeed screams, that that day has not come. The job of ending discrimination in this country is not over." Clinton ordered all federal agencies to review their affirmative action programs and revise them to comply with the June 12 Supreme Court decision. They were advised to eliminate or reshape any programs that imposed quotas, created preferences for unqualified people, fostered reverse discrimination, or continued after their goals had been achieved. However, he also added a new category of preferences for federal contracts to go to companies located in poor communities.

The events of 1995 seemed to promise that the debate over affirmative action would continue near the top of America's political agenda. Aspiring presidential candidates began making affirmative action programs a key issue in their campaigns for the 1996 election. And political experts began discussing the idea of having social and economic disadvantage, rather than race, be the deciding factor in who should receive special assistance. Even after decades of debate and change, the nation that was founded on principles of equality and opportunity still struggled to define the exact scope of civil rights. ■ ■ ■

Classical music. One of the most talked-about operatic premieres of 1995 was that of *Harvey Milk*, based on the life and legacy of a gay San Francisco city supervisor who was murdered in 1978. Presented on Jan. 21, 1995, by the Houston Grand Opera, the work featured music by Stewart Wallace and a libretto by Michael Korie. The New York City Opera, which shared production costs with the Houston and San Francisco operas, gave three later performances in April.

The Woman at Otowi Crossing, also based on historical events and figures, received its first performance on June 15 by the Opera Theatre of St. Louis (Missouri). The Stephen Paulus work, adapted from a novel by Frank Waters, was set against the background of the United States government's Manhattan Project, which developed the first atomic bomb in the 1940's. John Ruskin, a British art critic, social reformer and theorist of the 1800's, was the subject of *Modern Painters,* premiered by the Santa Fe (New Mexico) Opera on July 29, 1995. David Lang wrote the music and Manuela Hoelterhoff provided the libretto.

Director Peter Sellars staged *I Was Looking at the Ceiling and Then I Saw the Sky,* a new song-play (or, as it was subtitled, an "earthquake/romance"). The work, with a text by poet June Jordan and a pop-influenced score by John Adams, premiered on May 12 in Berkeley, California.

Symphonic and chamber music. Perhaps the most unusual new-music premiere of 1995 was German composer Karlheinz Stockhausen's *Helicopter String Quartet,* presented in July at the Holland Festival in Amsterdam, the Netherlands. Members of the Arditti String Quartet performed while flying over the city in helicopters piloted by a Dutch helicopter team. The composer-narrator created the music, a blend of the sounds of the stringed instruments and rotor-blade noise, at an electronic console while the audience watched the performance on video screens.

Peter Maxwell Davies, perhaps the best-known living British composer, led four U.S. premieres of his works as conductor of the British Broadcasting Company (BBC) Philharmonic, which toured the United States in March and April. Presented were *The Beltane Fire,* Davies's score for a ballet based on the lore of Scotland's Orkney Islands, Symphony No. 5, Trumpet Concerto, and *Cross Lane Fair.*

The BBC Symphony Orchestra under Andrew Davis gave the first performances of American composer Elliott Carter's *Adagio Tenebroso* on September 13 and British composer Harrison Birtwistle's *Panic* on September 16 in London's Royal Albert Hall. The Arditti String Quartet presented a second Carter premiere, his String Quartet No. 5, on September 19 in Antwerp, Belgium.

The Emerson String Quartet presented the first performance of American composer Ned Rorem's String Quartet No. 4 on October 8 in Pittsfield, Massachusetts. Rorem's song cycle, *More Than a Day,* premiered on November 3 in Los Angeles. Countertenor Brian Asawa performed with the Los Angeles Chamber Orchestra conducted by Yoav Talmi.

Conductor Daniel Barenboim led the Chicago Symphony Orchestra in the premiere of German composer York Höller's *Aura* on October 12 in Chicago. American minimalist composer Steve Reich's *City Life* made its European debut in March in Metz, France, and its American debut in August at the Festival of Contemporary Music at Tanglewood in Lenox, Massachusetts.

Milestones. The year 1995 marked the 100th anniversary of the birth of the prolific German composer Paul Hindemith, who died in 1963; the 90th birthday of English composer Sir Michael Tippett; and the 80th birthday of the eminent Russian pianist Sviatoslav Richter. The year also saw the 50th anniversary of the deaths of Hungarian composer Béla Bartók and Austrian composer Anton Webern, two of the foremost voices in the music of this century.

Appointments. American conductor James Conlon was named principal conductor of the Paris National Opera in May. He succeeded Korean conductor Myung-Whun Chung, who was dismissed from the post in 1994. Dutch conductor Hans Vonk was named to succeed Leonard Slatkin as music director of the St. Louis Symphony Orchestra, beginning with

---

Grammy Award winners in 1995

Classical Album, *Bartók: Concerto for Orchestra; Four Orchestral Pieces (Op. 12),* Chicago Symphony Orchestra, Pierre Boulez, conductor.

Orchestral Performance, *Bartók: Concerto for Orchestra; Four Orchestral Pieces (Op. 12),* Chicago Symphony Orchestra, Pierre Boulez, conductor.

Opera Recording, *Floyd: Susannah,* Orchestra and Chorus of the Lyon Opera, Kent Nagano, conductor.

Choral Performance, *Berlioz: Messe Solennelle,* Orchestre Révolutionnaire et Romantique, Monteverdi Choir, and various artists, John Eliot Gardiner, choral director.

Classical Performance, Instrumental Solo with Orchestra, *The New York Album (Works of Albert, Bartók, Bloch),* Yo-Yo Ma, cello and alto violin, with the Baltimore Symphony Orchestra, David Zinman, conductor.

Classical Performance, Instrumental Solo Without Orchestra, *Haydn: Piano Sonatas Nos. 32, 47, 53, 59,* Emanuel Ax, piano.

Chamber Music Performance, *Beethoven/Mozart: Quintets,* Daniel Barenboim, piano; Dale Clevenger, horn; Larry Combs, clarinet; Daniele Damiano, bassoon; Hansjorg Schellenberger, oboe.

Classical Vocal Performance, *The Impatient Lover (Italian Songs by Beethoven, Schubert, Mozart, etc.),* Cecilia Bartoli, mezzo-soprano.

Classical Contemporary Composition, *Albert: Cello Concerto,* Stephen Albert, composer.

the 1996-1997 season. Slatkin was to become director of the National Symphony Orchestra in Washington, D.C.

Awards. Composer John Adams won the 1995 Grawemeyer Award for music composition, presented annually by the University of Louisville (Kentucky), for his Violin Concerto. *The Dreams and Prayers of Isaac the Blind,* a quintet for clarinet and strings by Argentine-born composer Osvaldo Golijov took first prize in the 18th Friedheim Awards for New Music presented by the John F. Kennedy Center for the Performing Arts in Washington, D.C.

Other news. The Metropolitan Opera in New York City, which had long resisted the use of projected English captions with opera performances, unveiled its $2.7-million seat-back translation system, Met Titles, in October. Nearly two years in the making, the system uses small electronic screens attached to the backs of seats. By 1995, every major U.S. opera theater that performs opera in foreign languages employed a form of projected titles.

The New York Public Library for the Performing Arts in January acquired the manuscripts of composer John Cage, a giant of avant-garde music in this century. Cage died in 1992. The collection obtained by the library includes nearly all of Cage's scores, sketches, and writings.

The Cleveland Quartet, one of the most respected American string quartets, disbanded after 26 years. As its swan song, the group toured about 12 North American cities, beginning in October 1995 in Toronto, Canada, where it premiered John Corigliano's String Quartet, written for this tour.

Deaths. Christopher Keene, 48, general director of the New York City Opera since 1989, died of AIDS-related lymphoma in October. Ulysses Kay, one of the most celebrated African American classical composers, died in May at 78. Mexican conductor Eduardo Mata, 52, who led the Dallas Symphony from 1977 to 1993, died in a plane crash in Mexico in January. German-born American conductor Max Rudolf, who led the Cincinnati (Ohio) Symphony Orchestra from 1958 to 1970, died at 92 in February. And Sir Alexander Gibson, former principal conductor of the Scottish Opera, died at 68 in January.

Russian-born American violinist Louis Krasner, who premiered the violin concertos by composers Alban Berg and Arnold Schoenberg, died at 91 in May. Also 91 at her passing in November was the Austrian-born violinist Erica Morini. Josef Gingold, one of the most influential violin teachers in the United States, died at 85 in January.

Italian pianist Arturo Benedetti Michelangeli, one of the premier keyboard artists of his time, died at 75 in June. And Ferrucio Tagliavini, an Italian lyric tenor popular with New York City audiences in the late 1940's, died at 81 in February.   □ John von Rhein

See also **Popular music.** In *World Book,* see **Classical music; Opera.**

Clinton, Bill. President Bill Clinton, besieged by the first Republican-controlled Congress in 40 years, wielded his veto pen in 1995 to protect Democratic programs while moving toward a balanced budget. A historic clash between the White House and Capitol Hill led to a partial shutdown of the United States government for six days in November. The President refused to accept Republican conditions on a temporary spending bill, forcing the furlough of 800,000 federal employees on November 14 until a compromise agreement on November 20 reopened the government.

While both sides claimed victory in the standoff, polls suggested that in terms of public opinion, President Clinton came out ahead. The skirmish paved the way for an even bigger battle over a bill, rejected by Clinton, that would slash spending, cut taxes, and reduce federal regulations to eliminate the United States deficit by the year 2002.

The President positioned himself as the defender of Medicare, Medicaid, education, and the environment from Republican assaults, while he joined the Grand Old Party (GOP) call for a balanced budget in seven years. But Republicans pressured Clinton to accept major reductions in government programs. In December, a second government shutdown occurred as Clinton and GOP leaders continued to negotiate.

Appointments. The Senate quickly confirmed Clinton's choices of Robert E. Rubin as secretary of the treasury and Dan Glickman as secretary of agriculture, replacing resigned Cabinet members Lloyd M. Bentsen and Mike Espy, respectively.

Foreign policy. While he was stymied on domestic issues, Clinton took bold action abroad. In August, he rejected a bill to lift the U.S. arms embargo against the former Yugoslavian republic of Bosnia-Herzegovina, saying that ending the embargo would undercut efforts to negotiate peace there. In November, Clinton ordered the deployment of 20,000 American troops to Bosnia-Herzegovina as part of a North Atlantic Treaty Organization (NATO) peacekeeping force of 60,000.

Clinton met in Moscow on May 10 with Russian President Boris N. Yeltsin. The two leaders reached only partial agreement on security in Europe and failed to iron out differences on other issues, including the 1994-1995 Russian war against the breakaway republic of Chechnya, Moscow's plan to sell nuclear reactors to Iran, and the expansion of NATO.

Facing strong opposition from Congress, Clinton used emergency powers on January 31 to provide a $20-billion U.S. loan to Mexico—part of a $49.5-billion international loan package to stabilize the faltering peso. His action received bipartisan backing from congressional leaders.

In other decisions, Clinton on July 11 reestablished normal diplomatic relations with Vietnam. And on May 8, he imposed a total U.S. trade embargo on Iran, accusing that nation of supporting terrorism and planning to acquire nuclear weapons.

On the domestic front. The Senate on June 22 blocked Clinton's choice of Henry W. Foster, Jr., for United States surgeon general because his supporters failed to obtain the 60 votes necessary to stop a Republican-led filibuster. Two 57-to-43 votes indicated that Foster, a black physician from Nashville, did not have enough backing to overcome antiabortion opposition.

President Clinton in June used his first veto to reject a measure to cut $16.4 billion from spending previously approved for the fiscal year ending September 30. He said the measure cut education and job-training programs too deeply. No other President in this century had been in office so long without using his veto power. Clinton later signed a bill that reduced outlays by $16.3 billion but restored some funds for programs he favored.

In July, Clinton accepted recommendations of the Defense Base Closure and Realignment Commission to close 79 military bases and consolidate 26 others, which would eliminate 43,742 military and civilian jobs and save an estimated $19.3 billion over a 20-year period. Clinton gave his approval only after the Pentagon made special arrangements to turn military functions at Kelly Air Force Base in Texas and McClellan Air Force Base in California over to private contractors in those politically important states.

Whitewater. Throughout 1995, Clinton was be-deviled by the fallout from the investment he and his wife, Hillary, had made in a real estate venture, the Whitewater Development Corporation. A special prosecutor and congressional investigators sought to determine whether the Clintons had benefited improperly from their partnership with James B. Mc-Dougal, owner of the Madison Guaranty Savings and Loan in Little Rock, Arkansas. The Clintons were interviewed on April 22 by Kenneth W. Starr, the independent prosecutor in the Whitewater affair.

In June, a report to the Resolution Trust Corporation—the federal agency that was charged with cleaning up the slew of failed savings-and-loan institutions in the late 1980's—upheld the Clintons' claim that they were only passive investors in the Whitewater venture. The report, written by former Republican prosecutor Jay B. Stephens, found no evidence that the Clintons were aware of a transfer of $58,000 from Madison Guaranty Savings to the Whitewater corporation. The study concluded that the Clintons lost about $42,000 on their investment.

A federal grand jury on August 17 indicted James B. McDougal and his ex-wife, Susan, on bank fraud and conspiracy charges. Arkansas Governor Jim Guy Tucker also was accused of fraud in the indictment. McDougal was accused of arranging fraudulent loans from Madison Guaranty Savings and through Capital Management Services, a Little Rock, Arkansas, investment firm. The Whitewater firm was not

President Clinton and Speaker of the House Newt Gingrich shake hands in June as they begin a public discussion of political issues at a New Hampshire senior citizens center.

mentioned in the indictment, which brought to 14 the number of people who had pleaded guilty or been accused of criminal activity in the Whitewater investigation since January 1994.

Republicans in the Senate and House of Representatives held further hearings on the Whitewater affair in 1995. Senate investigators focused on actions by Clinton aides after the 1993 death of deputy White House counsel Vincent W. Foster, Jr., who had handled some of the Clintons' personal legal affairs, including the Whitewater matter. Aides were accused of hiding some of Foster's papers from the police and the Justice Department. Controversy also surrounded a set of notes from a 1993 White House meeting at which aides and lawyers discussed Whitewater. On Dec. 22, 1995, Clinton turned over the notes to the Senate Whitewater committee after the committee voted to subpoena them.

Clinton associates face charges. On May 2, 1995, Neil Ainley, former president of a bank in Perryville, Arkansas, pleaded guilty to two misdemeanor violations related to cash contributions to Clinton's 1990 campaign for governor. At issue was whether Ainley had concealed the transfer of $52,500 from the bank to the Clinton campaign in violation of federal financial disclosure laws.

On June 8, 1995, former Clinton aide Stephen Smith pleaded guilty to misdemeanor charges of misusing federal loan funds he obtained from Capital Management Services.

Webster L. Hubbell, whom Clinton had appointed associate attorney general, was sentenced on June 28 to 21 months in prison for tax evasion and mail fraud for cheating on his former law firm's expense account.

Hillary Rodham Clinton, who had played a leading role in the Administration's losing battle for health-care legislation in 1994, kept a lower profile in 1995. However, the First Lady addressed a United Nations women's conference in Beijing in August and spoke at a United Nations conference on social issues in March in Copenhagen.

White House security. A man armed with an unloaded handgun jumped a fence and ran toward the White House on May 23. The man, Leland W. Modjeski, was shot and wounded by a Secret Service agent.

On April 4, a federal jury found a Colorado man, Francisco Martin Duran, guilty of trying to assassinate the President. On Oct. 29, 1994, Duran fired more than 25 shots at the White House. In May 1995, Clinton approved tighter security measures at the White House, such as closing off a section of Pennsylvania Avenue on the north side of the presidential residence. □ William J. Eaton

See also **Congress of the United States; United States, Government of the.** In *World Book,* see **Clinton, Bill.**

Clothing. See **Fashion.**

Colombia. Allegations that President Ernesto Samper Pizano knowingly financed his 1994 campaign with $5.9 million in contributions from a drug cartel centered in the city of Cali threatened Colombia's political stability in 1995. The allegations had dogged Samper since June 1994, but his troubles escalated when authorities arrested his campaign treasurer, Santiago Medina, on July 26, 1995, on charges of accepting money from Cali drug lords.

Medina testified to authorities that Samper had sent a thank-you note following one substantial donation from the Cali drug cartel. In the note, Medina said, Samper promised drug traffickers a lenient plea-bargain system and guarantees that they would be allowed to negotiate the terms of their sentences if they turned themselves in. Medina said that he signed receipts for contributions from drug lords and that Samper admonished him to "Do what has to be done, but don't let me know about it."

The Colombian newspaper *El Tiempo* reported on September 17 that the president's wife, Jacquin Strouss de Samper, was also involved in the drug scandal. The paper reported that a nonprofit foundation directed by the president's wife received at least $20,000 in checks from reputed drug lords.

A congressional panel appointed to investigate Samper's alleged involvement with drug traffickers dropped its inquiry in mid-December, however. The panel said that there was not enough evidence that Samper took drug money for his campaign.

Defense minister resigns. On August 2, the scandal involving Colombia's president claimed its highest-ranking victim with the resignation of Defense Minister Fernando Botero. Botero quit amid charges that he solicited millions of dollars in campaign contributions from drug lords when he worked as Samper's campaign manager. On Aug. 14, 1995, the police arrested Botero in connection with the charges.

Drug arrests. Bowing to pressure from the United States to step up his country's antidrug activities, Samper had staged a much-publicized crackdown on drug trafficking in June and July. Drug raids led to the indictments of more than a dozen congressmen and officials high in the Samper administration, including the the country's comptroller and attorney general. Police also arrested the head of the Cali cartel, Gilberto Rodríguez Orejuela, in Cali on June 9.

State of emergency. Samper declared a 90-day state of emergency on August 16, saying that the order was necessary to fight a wave of crime and violence that he blamed for 19,450 killings and more than 700 kidnappings in Colombia in 1995. Samper promised increased prison sentences for serious crimes and an immediate military offensive against rebels and drug traffickers. □ Nathan A. Haverstock

See also **Latin America.** (Facts in brief table). In *World Book,* see **Colombia.**

Colorado. See **State government.**

Eeek! Gasp! Wow! Years of Comics!

100

By Eugene J. Walter, Jr.

Artist Richard Outcault's Yellow Kid leads his rag-tag parade in an 1896 cartoon, *opposite page.* The Yellow Kid first appeared as Mickey Dugan in a cartoon panel "At the Circus in Hogan's Alley" in the *New York World* on May 5, 1895, marking the birth of the comic strip in the United States.

On Sunday, May 5, 1895, readers of the *New York World* opened the newspaper's color supplement to find a large panel cartoon titled "At the Circus in Hogan's Alley." It depicted rowdy antics of a bunch of ragged, slum-dwelling children, mostly poor Irish-Americans, and their mongrel pets. One youngster stood out, a sort of instant superstar: a bald, beady-eyed, buck-toothed, barefoot urchin wearing a nightshirt. His name was Mickey Dugan, and he came to be known as "The Yellow Kid."

That cartoon marked the birth of the comic strip in the United States, and in 1995, Americans celebrated the comics centennial. The Library of Congress in Washington, D.C., and several other institutions mounted exhibitions devoted to "the funnies," as they were dubbed early on. The U.S. Postal Service issued commemorative stamps featuring classic comic strip characters. *The New York Times*, one of America's most influential newspapers and one of the very few that does not carry comics, editorialized, "Humbly, we note that this is the centennial year of an institution known to readers of other newspapers as the comics. . . . We salute them—from a distance."

The comic strip is a uniquely American art form that captivated audiences from its first appearance. In the years that followed the debut of "The Yellow Kid," the medium branched out into a variety of categories. Comic strip artists turned their skills to depicting not only rough jokes and pranks, but glimpses of life, real and fantastic. For 100 years, comic strips have given people humor, artistic innovation, delightful slang expressions, and a host of characters with the power to pull people into their world. And that world quickly included radio, television, movies, and even the theater.

Two developments in the late 19th century set the stage for comic strips. First, in the 1880's, weekly humor magazines, such as *Puck*, *Judge*, *Truth*, and *St. Nicholas*, became extremely popular, amusing readers with a combination of political and gag cartoons and jokes. Second, the invention of the color printing press allowed publishers to offer readers a vivid new dimension on the printed page. In 1894,

Joseph Pulitzer, owner of the *New York World,* took advantage of both developments by introducing a four-page Sunday supplement in color that imitated the humor weeklies. Pulitzer hired Richard Felton Outcault, a technical artist for *Electrical World* magazine who had submitted his cartoons to the *New York World.* It was Outcault who created "Hogan's Alley" and its star urchin, Mickey Dugan.

Mickey's dialogue first appeared as captions under the drawing, but soon his crude street lingo was scrawled on his nightshirt. Originally, his shirt was blue, but that made the overprinted text difficult to read. A new yellow ink tried early in 1896 solved the problem, and Mickey Dugan turned into "The Yellow Kid." The *World*'s circulation rose steadily, and by midsummer of 1896, the Yellow Kid was a celebrity.

Outcault drew "Hogan's Alley" residents staging raucous versions of circuses, races, dog shows, parades, and weddings. Although most of the youngsters appeared to be in the 8- to 12-year age range, they were a rough crowd. Some smoked cigarettes and drank whiskey, and most of them brawled a lot, which drew criticism from ministers, teachers, and parents.

However, William Randolph Hearst, Pulitzer's chief rival, also noticed how the kids sold lots of newspapers. In the early years of comic strips, newspapers played a much larger role in the daily lives of average Americans than they do today. In addition to the news, newspapers provided affordable pop entertainment when movies and phonograph records were in their infancy. It would be years before radio—and still more years before television—would enter American homes. In the meantime, newspapers waged fierce wars to increase circulation, and the comic strip became potent ammunition in these wars.

In panels from a 1911 strip of the "The Katzenjammer Kids," Hans and Fritz, *top right,* delight in playing tricks, *above,* despite spankings for their pranks, *bottom right.* The rascally twins were still scheming in 1995, primarily in publications outside the United States.

Thus it was that in late 1896 Hearst hired Outcault away to work for his *New York Journal* at a higher salary. Pulitzer found another artist to draw "Hogan's Alley," resulting in two versions running simultaneously for several years.

In 1896, Hearst also beefed up the *Journal*'s color supplement, touting it as "eight pages of iridescent polychromous effulgence

The Author

Eugene J. Walter, Jr., is a free-lance writer.

that make the rainbow look like a lead pipe." Hearst's promotional effort included the premiere late in 1897 of the second great blockbuster among comic strips, "The Katzenjammer Kids." (Their name means "hangover" in colloquial German.) The artist, German-born Rudolph Dirks, patterned his kids after *Max und Moritz,* a book about a pair of rascally boys that was extremely popular with German immigrants. Indeed, Dirks's twin boys, Hans and Fritz, devised all manner of diabolical pranks, subjecting their Momma's star boarder, Der Captain, and his poker-playing pal, Der Inspector, to firecrackers under their chairs, lobsters in their britches, swarms of angry hornets, and much more. Readers found the mayhem hilarious.

In 1912, Dirks and Hearst quarreled bitterly. The artist moved his hellions to Pulitzer's *World* and sued for the rights to his characters. The court ruled that Dirks could keep them but not the strip's title. Hearst won the rights to use both. For this reason, two versions— "The Katzenjammer Kids" and "The Captain and the Kids"—ran simultaneously for more than half a century. In 1995, the Katzenjammers still pull their pranks but primarily in publications outside the United States.

Early strips emphasized slapstick humor, and most observers of the comics agree that no greater clown appeared than "Happy Hooligan," the creation of Frederick Burr Opper that premiered in 1900. Happy was a well-meaning Irish-American hobo and habitual loser, a bit of a fool, and a natural victim. For example, in a 1909 Sunday page, Happy emerges from a haberdashery proudly sporting a new outfit (but, as always, wearing his trademark tin-can hat). An escaped circus elephant named Nero grabs Happy with his trunk, drops him in an empty baby carriage, and pushes him through the middle of the annual policemen's parade. Nero dumps the pram off the end of a pier. The strip ends with angry cops fishing Happy from the river, their nightsticks poised to punish him for ruining the parade.

Opper, more than any other artist, defined the comic-strip format of today, earning from his peers the accolade of "dean of American cartoonists" for more than half a century. Among his innovations in "Happy Hooligan" were consistent reliance on a series of panels to tell a story and extensive use of dialogue balloons. Opper was also

A 1915 "Mutt and Jeff" strip depicts the two characters wagering at the races, *above,* a theme that artist "Bud" Fisher introduced when the strip debuted in 1907. "Mutt and Jeff" was the first strip to run regularly in daily newspapers. A lovable slapstick comedy, "Happy Hooligan," *below,* premiered in Sunday papers in 1900.

the first artist to experiment with to-be-continued, cliffhanger stories, a concept he introduced in "Alphonse and Gaston," a strip about overly polite Frenchmen that first appeared in 1902. His suspenseful approach eventually gave rise to a new category, adventure strips.

Opper and other early comic artists first appeared only on Sunday in a few big-city newspapers. But papers in other cities, noting soaring readerships generated by comics, clamored for funnies. Hearst and other publishers, sensing a potential for increased revenue, created syndicates that licensed the strips to run in other cities. By 1905, nearly every newspaper in America had to have a Sunday comic section to keep up with the competition.

Given the success of the Sunday funnies, it was only a matter of time before strips appeared in the daily papers. The strips had to be only in black-and-white, like the rest of the newspaper, and they ran only sporadically. But this changed in 1907, when Harry Conway "Bud" Fisher, a sports cartoonist at the *San Francisco Chronicle,* launched a strip about a lanky, horse-playing schemer named Augustus Mutt. In 1908, Mutt visited an insane asylum and left with a good-hearted little inmate named Jeff. "Mutt and Jeff," the Laurel and Hardy of the comics, ran daily and Sunday until 1982.

Buster Brown proudly displays his latest prank in a panel from a 1904 strip. It was a second big success for Yellow Kid creator, Richard Outcault, when Buster first appeared in 1902.

"Little Nemo in Slumberland" by Winsor McCay, *opposite page,* is regarded by many critics as the masterpiece of the comic strip as graphic art.

Evolution of comics categories

From the 1900's through the 1930's, comic strips developed into several major categories. Comics about kids were among the most popular, including Outcault's second big success, "Buster Brown," who debuted in 1902. Dressed in a Little Lord Fauntleroy sailor suit, hair cut in a pageboy bob, Buster was the genteel son of a well-to-do Victorian family. But he was no sissy. Accompanied by his bulldog, Tige (who spoke), Buster devised practical jokes that sometimes rivaled the Katzenjammers, yet each episode found him resolving to mend his ways.

Another kid classic, "Little Nemo in Slumberland," has been described by comic critics as "the supreme all-time masterpiece of the comic strip considered as a graphic art." Nemo flowed from the pencil of a brilliant illustrator, Winsor McCay, and appeared from 1905 to 1914 and again from 1924 to 1927. McCay used an elaborate Art Nouveau style with surrealistic tendencies—weird angles, distorted scale, and abnormal perspective—to chronicle the dream adventures of a little boy who usually ate too much before going to bed. In his sleep, Nemo met fantasy animals and people, always accompanied by his companion Flip, a green-faced imp who often got Nemo into trouble.

Buster Brown and Little Nemo have spiritual descendants in the 1990's, attesting to the ongoing popularity of kid subjects. Modern counterparts include Bill Watterson's "Calvin and Hobbes," Hank Ketcham's "Dennis the Menace," and Charles M. Schulz's "Peanuts." Charlie Brown and his Peanuts gang have more psychological hang-

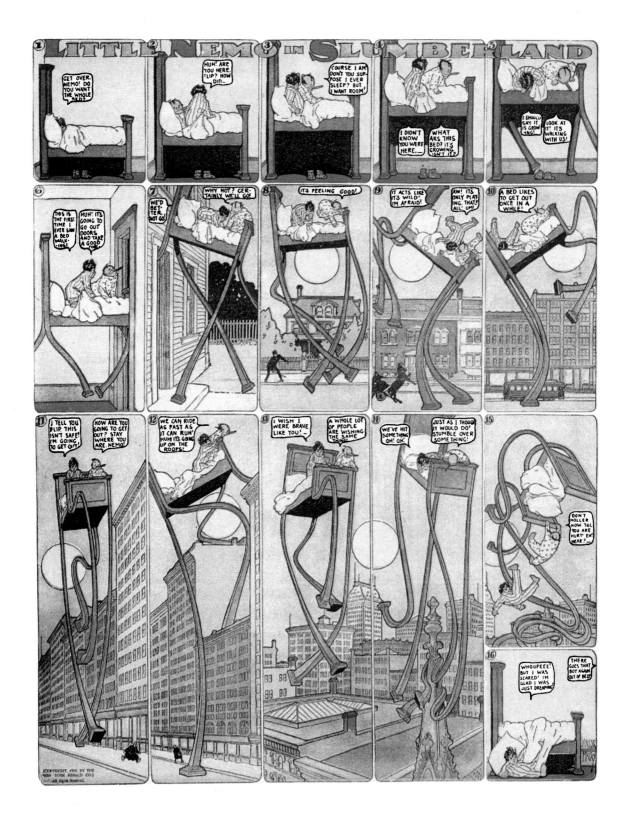

153

A 1937 strip of "Bringing Up Father" depicts the social-climbing nature of Maggie juxtaposed against the down-to-earth aspirations of Jiggs, a theme that originator George McManus introduced in the first episode in 1913.

ups than their predecessors, but apparently this quality appeals to modern readers, because "Peanuts" is the most widely distributed and most profitable strip of all time.

Comics about families are another popular category with great longevity. "Bringing Up Father," begun in 1913 by George McManus, was the first big family hit, and it was still running in 1995. Father is an Irish-American laborer named Jiggs who strikes it rich by winning the Irish sweepstakes and moves from a tenement to a mansion. His shrewish, social-climber wife, Maggie, loves to entertain the "upper crust," while down-to-earth Jiggs prefers to sneak out for a corned-beef-and-cabbage dinner with his working-class cronies at Dinty Moore's tavern. When he returns home, Jiggs is usually assaulted by Maggie with a barrage of china, rolling pins, and flat irons.

A less raucous family strip appeared in 1930, when Murat "Chic" Young introduced "Blondie." Blondie Boopadoop is the apple of Dagwood Bumstead's eye, and he is the son of a millionaire. After he marries the gorgeous, but decidedly not upper-class Blondie, his snooty family disinherits him. Nevertheless, Dagwood finds middle-class happiness with Blondie, raising two children while suffering the tyranny of his boss, Julius Dithers.

Family strips are more popular than ever today, and include Mort Walker and Dik Browne's "Hi and Lois," Bil Keane's "Family Circus," and Lynn Johnston's "For Better or For Worse." Even after 65 years, Blondie was still one of the five most popular strips, according to a 1992 survey commissioned by Metropolitan Sunday Newspapers, an advertising sales company. The 1995 Bumsteads appeared in 35 languages in more than 2,000 newspapers in 55 countries. The other four leaders were "Calvin and Hobbes," "Peanuts," Jim Davis's smartaleck cat "Garfield," and Garry Trudeau's "Doonesbury."

From the first, many comic strip artists mirrored cultural change in America, such as the growing number of women entering the labor force. Artists spun off characters from family strips into situation comedies about working women, invariably secretaries. Alfred E. Hayward started "Somebody's Stenog" in 1918, and the strip depicted her difficulties with bosses and boyfriends until 1941. By 1995, women's job possibilities had expanded beyond the typing pool, but Cathy Guisewite's "Cathy" faced the same dilemmas of career and romance as earlier in the century, only with a more neurotic slant.

Everyday life also evolved into soap opera strips. "Little Orphan Annie," a plucky, self-reliant waif, arrived in 1924 wearing a red dress and curls inspired by silent screen star Mary Pickford. An unwilling resident of a miserable orphanage, Annie was adopted by Oliver "Daddy" Warbucks, a self-made millionaire. Tear-jerking separations from Daddy were a regular event, but Annie always had the companionship of her faithful dog, Sandy. When the Great Depression hit the United States in 1929, Annie's artist-author, Harold Gray, used his heroine to voice his ultraconservative political philosophy. Annie's

sermonizing along with the behavior of plain, poor folks, whose hard work and decency triumphed over hard times, were intended to show that capitalism and free enterprise would rise again. Although her wardrobe has not improved, Annie continues to have adventures and to help poor folks, but without a political agenda.

Ageless Dagwood Bumstead, *top left,* is still married to "Blondie" 65 years after "Chic" Young introduced the strip in 1930. In a strip from 1935, *below left,* Dagwood is at his typical best, balking at the routine necessity that plagues middle class America—working for a living.

Satire was a vital aspect of the funnies even in the earliest days. But some cartoonists, such as Al Capp, relied on political and social commentary as dominant themes. In Capp's strip "Li'l Abner," created in 1934, Abner Yokum, the ultimate innocent yokel, lived in the village of Dogpatch with his Mammy, Pappy, and pet pig, Salomey. Initially a folksy, hillbilly comedy, the strip soon spoofed American fads, institutions, and personalities, lampooning politicians (personified by Senator Jack S. Phogbound), bureaucrats, industrialists, militarists, fashion designers, and popular media stars.

Capp's fertile imagination generated schmoos, balloon-shaped creatures who provided for all of humanity's needs. Capp invented Lower Slobbovia, the coldest, most miserable place on Earth and home of the world's ugliest woman, Lena the Hyena. He devised Sadie Hawkins Day, an annual Dogpatch event when single women could capture eligible bachelors and marry them. Every Sadie Hawkins Day, L'il Abner outraced a voluptuous blonde named Daisy Mae Scragg, but after more than 20 years, they married. Capp even kidded other comics with "Fearless Fosdick" (Abner's hero), a send-up of Dick Tracy.

A 1938 "Krazy Kat," *opposite page*, depicts the sketchy style and verbal playfulness of creator George Herriman, regarded by his fellow cartoonists as the foremost among them. Ignatz the mouse, *top right*, began hurling brick missiles at lovesick Krazy, *below*, in 1913. The strip ended in 1944.

Capp shifted from liberal to more conservative views in the 1960's strips. He lambasted "Women's Lip" and needled the counter culture with protest folksinger Joanie Phonie and an organization called S.W.I.N.E. (Students Wildly Indignant about Nearly Everything). L'il Abner bowed out in 1977.

Another social commentator originated in a 1942 comic book and then became a newspaper strip in 1948. His name was Pogo, an opossum. Most of the time, Pogo, Albert Alligator, Howland Owl, the turtle Churchy LaFemme, Porkypine, and others indulged in delightful whimsy and outrageous puns. In the 1950's, Pogo artist Walt Kelly's liberalism turned the strip toward political satire with irreverent caricatures of such figures as Communist-hunting Senator Joseph McCarthy and Presidents Richard Nixon and Lyndon Johnson. Pogo also was an early environmentalist. Viewing the trash polluting his swamp in 1971, he said, "We have met the enemy and he is us."

The late 20th century heir to L'il Abner and Pogo's often caustic tradition is "Doonesbury," which Garry Trudeau started drawing while he was a student at Yale University in New Haven, Connecticut, in 1968. Among his many unflattering characterizations, Trudeau depicted Speaker of the House Newt Gingrich as a bomb with a smoking fuse and President Bill Clinton as a waffle.

Pogo and his associates sprang from a long line of comic-strip animals with human attributes. One predecessor, "Krazy Kat," is revered by most cartoonists, past and present, as the greatest comic strip of all time. George Herriman brought Krazy Kat to life as a sort of footnote in "The Dingbat Family," a strip that appeared in 1910. Krazy became a separate feature in 1913 and lasted until 1944.

Herriman's long-running plot centered on an eternal triangle. Krazy Kat, the sweetest, most innocent of creatures, adores Ignatz the mouse. Ignatz can't stand Krazy and never misses an opportunity to fling a brick at the cat's head. Krazy views this as a gesture of love. Her typical response: "Ah-h li'l Ainjil in my hour of mellun-kolly he soothes me with a brick—missil of love and iffection." Officer B. Pupp, a canine cop, defender of law and order, loves Krazy and heaves Ignatz into jail regularly.

Herriman drew the characters in a sketchy style against a background of Grand Canyon country in Arizona. But his southwestern desert had a surrealistic twist. Characters stood still while mesas, cacti, and the like appeared and disappeared from panel to panel. Trees sometimes grew in decorative pots. Urban lampposts and fire plugs sprouted in the desert wilderness. Ships occasionally sailed past on waves of sand.

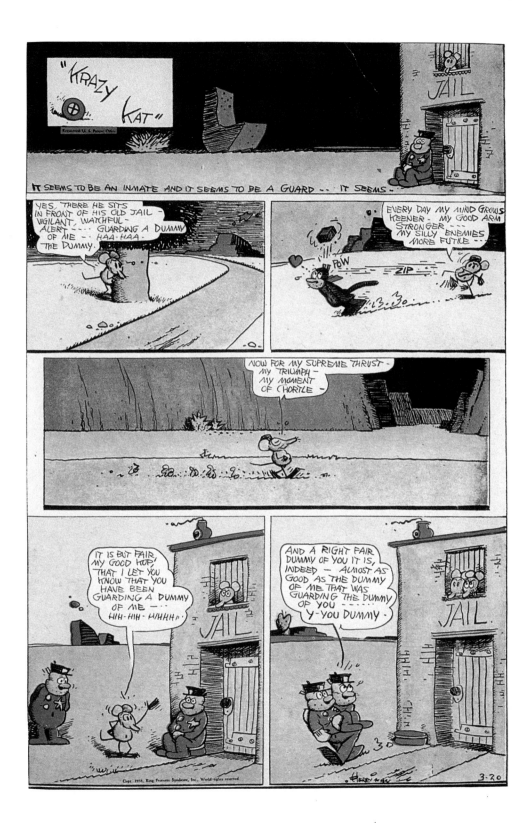

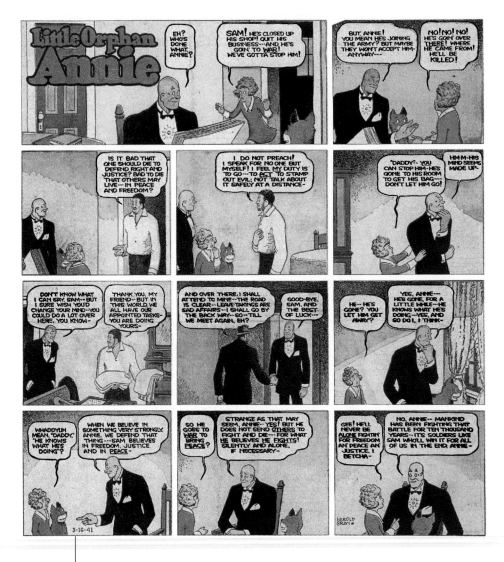

"Little Orphan Annie" and her millionaire step-father, Daddy Warbucks, often voiced artist Harold Gray's social and political views, including those on war in 1941, *above*. Annie debuted in newspapers in 1924 and continued to entertain readers in 1995.

Herriman was a master at verbal playfulness. Puns reminded some readers of the baroque wordplay in novels by Irish author James Joyce. Characters spoke a linguistic medley composed of everything from Elizabethan English to Brooklyn Yiddish and deep South dialects. For example, in a 1918 episode, Krazy asks Ignatz, "Can you unda-stend a Finn, or a Leplender, or a Oshkosher, huh?" Ignatz can't, and, pointing out that those people can't understand Ignatz either, Krazy concludes, "Then I would say, lenguage is that we may *mis*-unda-stend each udda."

Intellectuals and artists adored "Krazy Kat" and wrote scholarly papers about it. In his 1924 book *The Seven Lively Arts,* art critic Gilbert Seldes called Herriman's strip "the most amusing and fantastic and satisfactory work of art produced in America today." Poet E. E. Cummings

said Herriman was a "poet-painter." Abstract artists Pablo Picasso and Willem de Kooning were fans. Yet "Krazy Kat" never enjoyed the mass-market popularity of other leading strips of its era. Fortunately for Krazy's fans, Herriman's employer, William Randolph Hearst, was one of Krazy Kat's staunchest admirers.

For 1995 devotees of animals with human foibles, the star player is fat, lazy "Garfield," the feline creation of Jim Davis, who introduced the strip in 1978. Garfield enjoys a popularity Krazy never dreamed of. He appears in 2,400 newspapers in 83 countries.

In contrast with strips featuring talking animals, adventure strips were slow to evolve. Artists created the earliest versions as tongue-in-cheek tales of derring-do rendered in a cartoon style. The comics' first superhero showed up in 1929. This creation of artist Elzie C. Segar was a one-eyed, pipe-smoking sailor with enormous forearms, who first appeared as a supporting actor in Segar's 10-year-old strip "Thimble Theatre." But Popeye the sailor promptly took over. Accompanied by his bony sweetheart, Olive Oyl, and his shiftless, mooching sidekick, J. Wellington Wimpy, Popeye took on both earthly and otherworldly adversaries, such as the Sea Hag, last witch on Earth. Ageless, he was still punching in 1995.

Adventure strips acquired more serious storylines and artwork took on the realistic look of book illustrations in 1929, when Buck Rogers awoke in the 25th century after a 500-year-long nap. Buck was the first serious science fiction strip hero. His storyline came from Philip Nowlan, and artist Dick Calkins brought him to life. Rocketships operated by television, rocket bombs, armies of robots, radar, ray guns, voyages to Mars and other planets kept Buck busy. A 1939 episode exposed comics readers to the atomic bomb, six years before the first bomb exploded.

Popeye pummels a pirate in 1934, *top left,* though his battles began four years earlier with an appearance in a strip called "Thimble Theatre." Also brought to life in 1934 was a superhero far more handsome than the one-eyed sailor—Flash Gordon. Flash fought bizarre enemies from outer space, including an attack of hawkmen in 1935, *below.*

Pogo and Porkypine view their trash-filled swamp in a famous cartoon commemorating Earth Day 1971. Pogo's satirist creator, Walt Kelly, introduced the opossum and his pals in a 1942 comic book, and in 1948, newspapers started to carry the "Pogo" strip.

Artistically, however, Buck was not on the same planet as Flash Gordon, who landed in 1934. Flash, "Yale graduate and world-renowned polo player," had the same outer-space hardware as Buck, but he also had the advantage of the superior artistic talents of Alex Raymond. Raymond's style verged on photographic realism, and his action scenes influenced many other adventure-strip artists. He created characters who possessed movie-star beauty, exemplified by Flash's girlfriend, Dale Arden, as well as bizarre humanoid creatures, such as hawkmen and death dwarfs. The action occurs against a background of awesome fantasy cities, soaring castles, and weird wildernesses inhabited by extraterrestrial beasts capable of scaring any space voyager.

Somewhat more down-to-earth, "cops-and-robber" thrillers also blossomed in the 1930's. King of these was Chester Gould's "Dick Tracy," who started combatting criminals in 1931 and has never let up. Angered by real-life gangsters who openly ruled city streets in the 1930's, readers approved of the hawk-nosed Tracy's tendency to shoot first and ask questions later. The plainclothes cop was up against a rogue's gallery of some of the orneriest, most grotesque villains in comics history: Flattop, the Brain, Pruneface, Shaky, the Brow, Fly Face, Itchy, the Mole, B-B Eyes, and many others whose names were similarly descriptive.

Adventure strips about soldiers of fortune leaned toward foreign locales. The most universally acclaimed was "Terry and the Pirates," a 1934 entry. Captain Joseph Patterson of the *New York News* wanted a "blood-and-thunder" suspense strip "with a juvenile angle" and hired Milton Caniff to draw it. One of stripdom's immortals, according to comics experts, Caniff was a brilliant storyteller who created an amazing array of characters. The gifted artist's mastery of light and shadow veered between detailed realism and impressionism.

In the strip, Terry Lee inherits from his grandfather a map of an abandoned mine in China where treasure is buried. He begins to search for the treasure, accompanied by a handsome Irish-American bodyguard, Pat Ryan, and a Chinese comic-relief guide, George Webster Confucius, nicknamed Connie. The strip portrays China of the 1930's, a country filled with dangerous warlords ruling large territories and pirates lurking along rivers. One band of these brigands is led by archetypal femme fatale Lai Choi San, the Dragon Lady. She way-lays Terry and his pals two months into the story. "Luvva Pete! We're captured by a WOMAN!" Terry exclaims.

In the real world, Japanese troops invaded China in 1937, and by late 1939, Caniff's comic strip world focused on the war. Terry, a kid in knickers at the start, grows up to fight for his adopted country—eventually he becomes an American air force pilot—and even the Dragon Lady abandons thievery to lead a guerrilla army against the invaders. The strip continued until 1973, but Caniff departed in 1946 to create another adventurous aviator, "Steve Canyon." Terry made a comeback in 1995, hardly recognizable from his earlier life.

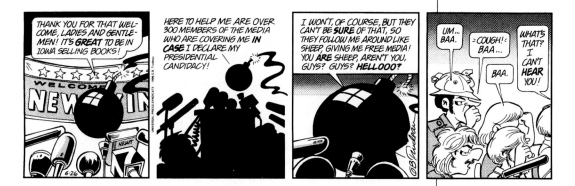

Within a few years of the establishment of comic sections in Sunday newspapers, collections of many of the most popular strips took on a second life as reprints in books with cardboard covers. In 1934, the first modern comic book in America premiered. But *Famous Funnies* also contained only reprints of well-known strips. Finally, in 1938, comic books got their own original hero, Superman. Teen-agers Jerry Siegel and Joe Shuster from Cleveland, Ohio, had conceived the Man of Steel as a newspaper strip in the early 1930's, but syndicates had rejected their brainchild. Superman leaped into a newspaper version in 1938. "Batman" first suited up to fight crime the next year.

Characters acquire voices—and influence

From the 1930's on, comic strip characters expanded their horizons into other entertainment media. "Blondie" thrived as a weekly, prime-time radio, then television, show. Beginning in 1938, a new Blondie movie appeared in theaters every six months for 10 years. Many of the adventure heroes, including Dick Tracy and Superman, had their own radio and television shows. They also starred in feature films, while Popeye and others performed in animated cartoons.

Some comic strip characters became stage-struck. Victor Herbert, one of the most famous composers in early musical theater, put Little Nemo in a musical comedy in 1908. The most successful by far was *Annie,* a Broadway musical version of the life and hard times of the spunky orphan.

In a 1995 "Doonesbury" strip, originator Garry Trudeau depicts Speaker of the House Newt Gingrich as a bomb with a lit fuse, *above.* Trudeau also has depicted President Bill Clinton as a waffle, thus carrying on the "Pogo" tradition of cartoon satire.

The most popular characters pitched products. The Yellow Kid sold whiskey and cigars, and Buster Brown promoted a line of children's shoes that still exists decades after the strip disappeared. And from the Yellow Kid to Peanuts, comic strip characters have generated millions of dollars in sales of toys, board games, coloring books, clothing, and wristwatches, to name a few items that depict their famous faces.

· From the Yellow Kid on, many people have dismissed comics as silly and trivial. Nevertheless, comic strips have reflected generations of readers' concerns and infatuations—wars, the Jazz Age, the Great Depression, immigration, automobiles and airplanes, feminism, and environmentalism. In the process, our language became enriched by a host of slang expressions: horsefeathers, baloney, piker, fall guy, dumbbell, ball and chain, hard-boiled, heebie-jeebies, meal ticket, barfly, bonehead, Bronx cheer, buttinsky, kibitzer, chew the fat, nickel nurser, windbag, and countless others. The expression "Rube Goldberg invention" is a reference to artist Rube Goldberg's cartoons of insanely complex devices designed to perform the simplest tasks, and the multilayered Dagwood sandwich first saw the light of day in the hands of Blondie's husband.

In the United States, more than 30 scholarly research centers are devoted to comic strips and other cartoons. The largest is the Cartoon Research Library at Ohio State University in Columbus with more than 200,000 pieces of original art and manuscript materials. Michigan

The "Peanuts" strip portrays the sophisticated style of creator Charles M. Schulz, who began it in 1950. In 1995, cartoonists, cartoon historians, and others voted "Peanuts" the best strip of all time in a poll conducted to commemorate the 100th anniversary of the comic strip.

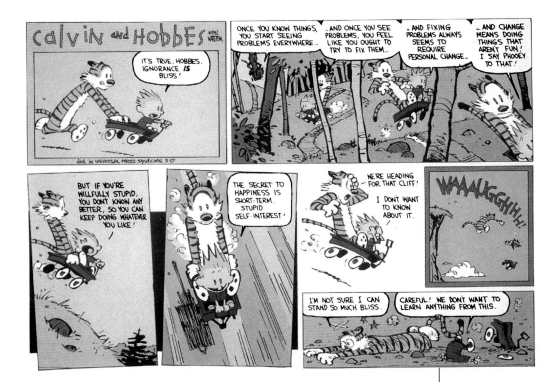

State University's library in East Lansing contains nearly 100,000 comic books. There are museums of comic art in Northampton, Massachusetts; Portland, Oregon; San Francisco; and Washington, D.C. The International Museum of Cartoon Art, the largest, was scheduled to open in Boca Raton, Florida, in 1996. Similar museums are located in cities throughout Europe, Asia, and Latin America.

Comic strip art attracts public and private collectors. The Louvre in Paris in the 1960's and the Whitney Museum of American Art in New York City in the 1980's mounted comic strip exhibitions. Original "Flash Gordon" and "Prince Valiant" drawings have fetched $35,000 to $40,000. In a 1995 auction at Sotheby's in New York City, a collector paid $75,100 for a copy of the first *Superman* comic book that originally cost 10 cents. The first *Batman* brought $68,500.

Since "The Yellow Kid" arrived, comic strips have undergone many changes, yet the audience is bigger than ever. A survey commissioned by Metropolitan Sunday Newspapers in 1992 found that 113 million Americans read the funnies regularly; 86 million of those people are over age 18. Comics created in the United States and other nations are read by millions more in Asia, Europe, and Latin America. As Little Orphan Annie would say, "Leapin' Lizards!!" ■ ■ ■

Calvin lives on the edge in a wonderland of imagination accompanied by his faithful toy tiger in a 1992 episode of "Calvin and Hobbes" that typifies artist-author Bill Watterson's style. The 100th year anniversary poll declared "Calvin and Hobbes" the best of all current comic strips.

For further reading:

Blackbeard, Bill. *Comic Strip Century,* 2 vols. Kitchen Sink Press, 1995.

Marschall, Richard. *America's Great Comic Strip Artists.* Abbeville Press, 1989.

Computer. Windows 95, a major new version of the operating system used on most of the world's personal computers, was introduced in August 1995 by the Microsoft Corporation of Redmond, Washington. Windows 95 was designed to upgrade Microsoft's existing operating systems, which are used on about 90 percent of all personal computers (PC's). An operating system consists of software that controls and coordinates a computer's most basic functions. It handles communication between the computer's hardware—the physical components such as disk drives—and the application programs.

Among the advanced features of Windows 95 was the ability to easily perform multiple tasks, dubbed "multitasking." An operating system with multitasking enables the computer to be used for more than one task at a time, so that a user can spell-check a report, for example, while a document is being printed. Another feature allowed different programs to share the information in a file. A user could add new figures to a financial spreadsheet, for instance, and a chart based on the spreadsheet in another document would be automatically updated.

Mac clones. The Power Computing Corporation, of Milpitas, California, in April introduced the first generic versions of the Macintosh computer. Several other firms said they planned to sell Mac-compatible computers. The Macintosh is made by Apple Computer, Incorporated, of Cupertino, California.

Apple Computer had previously refused to permit other manufacturers to use Mac technology. International Business Machines (IBM) of Armonk, New York, had followed a different strategy. Its personal computer technology was widely copied by other manufacturers, and experts cited the availability of IBM clones as one reason why PC's outsold Macs by a wide margin. Apple hoped allowing clones onto the market would encourage software firms to develop new Mac-compatible programs, which would increase interest in Macs and boost Apple's sales.

Supercomputing speed record. America recaptured the world speed record for supercomputing in January 1995, surpassing Japan's 1994 record by more than 50 percent. Scientists at Sandia National Laboratories in Albuquerque, New Mexico, and Intel Corporation's supercomputer facility in Beaverton, Oregon, set the new record. The researchers linked two of Intel's most powerful Paragon computers to establish a record 281 billion flops, eclipsing the 170.4 billion flops previously reached by a Japanese computer. (Flops are a standard measure of computing speed, the acronym for *f*loating-point *o*perations *p*er second.)

Sandia and Intel officials hailed the feat as a milestone for American supercomputing efforts that demonstrated the possibility of eventually building affordable computers with speeds in the *teraflop* (trillions of flops) range. Greater computing speed is critical for studying extremely complex scientific and technological problems such as learning how the ocean and atmosphere interact to influence climate.

World's most powerful computer. The United States Department of Energy in September announced a $45-million agreement with Intel to build the world's most powerful computer, which could perform 1.8 teraflops. The machine, expected to be in operation at Sandia by 1997, would use about 9,000 copies of Intel's newest microprocessor, called the Pentium Pro chip. The machine was the first to be ordered under an Energy Department program to speed the development of advanced computers.

Home computers may be changing the lifestyles of Americans in the 1990's, much as television did in the 1950's, according to a study reported in August. The national survey of 1,000 households was conducted in December 1994 by sociologist John Robinson at the University of Maryland in College Park. Robinson found that about 35 percent of Americans have a home computer, which they use an average of 10 hours per week. About 7.5 percent of households used the worldwide computer network called the Internet. The study also confirmed that most home users have limited technical knowledge about their machines. Some 62 percent did not know the capacity of their hard disk, and 66 percent did not know the speed of their modem.   □ Michael Woods

In *World Book,* see **Computer.**

Congo. See **Africa.**

Congress of the United States. With Republicans in control for the first time in four decades, Congress in 1995 clashed repeatedly with Democratic President Bill Clinton on the size and scope of the federal government. The confrontation led to a partial shutdown of government services in November and again in December as Republican congressional leaders and the White House failed to agree on terms of a bill extending government spending authority. The dispute idled hundreds of thousands of federal workers who were deemed to be nonessential until temporary agreements could be worked out to renew funding. Public-opinion polls indicated that Republicans in Congress received most of the blame for the impasse.

The deadlock occurred after Congress failed to pass all of its 13 regular appropriations bills by the start of the 1996 fiscal year, which began on Oct. 1, 1995. Instead, Congress approved legislation to continue spending through November 13 in hopes that it could get the work done by then. But Clinton vetoed the resolution, objecting to what he considered unnecessary provisions added to the measure, including an increase in premiums for Medicare, the federal insurance program for people over 65 and those with disabilities.

Congress, in turn, refused to remove the additional provisions, and the President went ahead with plans to close down all but essential parts of the federal government. Air traffic controllers stayed on the job but social security offices were closed. Pentagon employees reported for work, but the State Department stopped issuing passports. In all, some 800,000 federal workers were sent home in what was the longest interruption of government service in the nation's history. In the December shutdown, which lasted even longer, about 265,000 workers were idled.

With Speaker of the House Newt Gingrich (R., Ga.) in firm control of the relatively narrow Grand Old Party (GOP) majority in the House of Representatives, large tax and spending cuts won House approval as part of a seven-year plan to balance the federal budget. In the Senate, Majority Leader Bob Dole (R., Kan.) moved similar legislation.

Clinton, however, objected to the Republicans' budget bill and called for negotiations to produce a compromise plan that both he and the GOP-led Congress would accept. Political stakes were high for both sides. Clinton hoped to rally support as the defender of popular federal programs, while Republicans sought to show that they could dramatically reduce the size of government, lower taxes, and wipe out the deficit by 2002.

Gingrich, the first Republican Speaker since 1955, followed a bold agenda that he described as a "revolution." On the first day the House met in January, it abolished three standing committees, cut committee staffs by one-third, and set term limits for committee chairs and the Speaker as well. The Speaker said only the social security program, defense spending, and interest on the national debt would be spared in massive, across-the-board reductions in federal outlays. It became clear that Clinton would be forced to rely on his veto to stop or modify the radical changes favored by the political opposition.

Contract with America. By April, the House voted on all 10 items in the Contract with America that Gingrich advocated, approving 9 of them. Only a proposal to amend the Constitution to limit terms of House members was defeated. Another constitutional amendment to require a balanced federal budget was approved by the House but lost in the Senate, falling one vote shy of the required two-thirds majority. In February and March, the House and Senate passed differing versions of a bill to give the President the authority to veto individual items in a bill, but this so-called *line-item veto* measure got stalled in a Senate-House conference committee.

One item in the Contract with America got almost unanimous support. In January, Congress quickly passed and Clinton signed a bill to apply federal laws on minimum wages, disabilities, and job discrimination to the House and Senate and their members. In March, the President also approved of another widely backed bill to curb federal demands for state or local actions unless Congress also provided the money to pay for them.

Reining in lobbyists. Legislation designed to improve the monitoring of lobbyists also gained wide congressional support. On November 29, Congress gave final approval to a bill that would require lobbyists to report who pays them, how much they are paid, and what issues they try to influence. The House and and the Senate unanimously approved the measure, which was the most comprehensive rewrite of lobbying laws since 1946. Clinton indicated that he would sign the bill.

State of the Union. The President, placed on the defensive by the Republican landslide in 1994, offered few new proposals in his State of the Union message on Jan. 24, 1995. GOP leaders quickly rejected Clinton's call for an increase in the federal minimum wage to $5.15 from $4.25 an hour.

Cutting welfare. But Republicans followed up on Clinton's familiar call to "end welfare as we know it" as the House on March 24 approved a bill to slash spending on welfare by $66 billion over five years and end a 60-year-old federal guarantee of welfare aid for families with dependent children. The vote was 234 to 199, mainly along party lines. In September, the Senate approved a similar but less sweeping change in welfare laws. Clinton, however, indicated that he would veto a third version adopted by a Senate-House conference on grounds that it cut too deeply into social programs.

Budget battles. Republican majorities in the House and Senate approved a blueprint for balancing the budget by 2002. It would involve a total of $812 billion in spending reductions while at the same time providing tax cuts worth $245 billion. Clinton responded on June 13 with a revised budget with his own plan to eliminate the federal deficit in 10 years, by 2005, and threatened to veto the GOP version.

As part of their package, House Republicans pushed through a bill to overhaul the Medicare program for 37 million people over age 65 and the disabled. The vote was 231-201, along party lines. The measure would reduce payments to providers of health care, raise premiums for insurance covering doctors' bills, and charge higher premiums for high-income beneficiaries. In all, the GOP budget called for reducing Medicare outlays by $270 billion from projected spending levels by 2002. GOP leaders said the changes were needed to keep the Medicare program from going broke. They conceded that spending on the health program would continue to grow, but only at 7.2 percent a year, compared with the 10 percent annual growth that had been projected.

Medicaid, the federal health program for the poor, was to be turned over to the states under the Republican plan. Federal grants would be provided but the states would design the benefits, though coverage of poor children under age 13 and pregnant women in families at or below the poverty line would have to be provided.

The House of Representatives of the second session of the 104th Congress consisted of Democrats, Republicans, and 1 independent (not including representatives from American Samoa, the District of Columbia, Guam, Puerto Rico, and the Virgin Islands), when it convened on Jan. 22, 1996. There were 197 Democrats, 236 Republicans, 1 independent, and 1 vacancy when the first session of the 104th Congress convened. This table shows congressional district, legislator, and party affiliation. Asterisk (*) denotes those who served in the 103rd Congress; dagger (†) denotes "at large."

Alabama
1. Sonny Callahan, R.*
2. Terry Everett, R.*
3. Glen Browder, D.*
4. Tom Bevill, D.*
5. Bud Cramer, D.*
6. Spencer Bachus, R.*
7. Earl Hilliard, D.*

Alaska
† Donald E. Young, R.*

Arizona
1. Matt Salmon, R.
2. Ed Pastor, D.*
3. Bob Stump, R.*
4. John Shadegg, R.
5. Jim Kolbe, R.*
6. J. D. Hayworth, R.

Arkansas
1. Blanche L. Lincoln, D.*
2. Ray Thornton, D.*
3. Tim Hutchinson, R.*
4. Jay Dickey, R.*

California
1. Frank Riggs, R.
2. Wally Herger, R.*
3. Vic Fazio, D.*
4. John Doolittle, R.*
5. Robert T. Matsui, D.*
6. Lynn Woolsey, D.*
7. George E. Miller, D.*
8. Nancy Pelosi, D.*
9. Ronald V. Dellums, D.*
10. Bill Baker, R.*
11. Richard Pombo, R.*
12. Tom Lantos, D.*
13. Fortney H. (Peter) Stark, D.*
14. Anna Eshoo, D.*
15. Tom Campbell, R.
16. Zoe Lofgren, D.
17. Sam Farr, D.*
18. Gary Condit, D.*
19. George Radanovich, R.
20. Calvin Dooley, D.*
21. William M. Thomas, R.*
22. Andrea Seastrand, R.
23. Elton Gallegly, R.*
24. Anthony Beilenson, D.*
25. Howard McKeon, R.*
26. Howard L. Berman, D.*
27. Carlos J. Moorhead, R.*
28. David Dreier, R.*
29. Henry A. Waxman, D.*
30. Xavier Becerra, D.*
31. Matthew Martinez, D.*
32. Julian C. Dixon, D.*
33. Lucille Roybal-Allard, D.*
34. Esteban E. Torres, D.*
35. Maxine Waters, D.*
36. Jane Harman, D.*
37. Vacant
38. Steve Horn, R.*
39. Edward Royce, R.*
40. Jerry Lewis, R.*
41. Jay Kim, R.*

42. George E. Brown, Jr., D.*
43. Kenneth Calvert, R.*
44. Sonny Bono, R.
45. Dana Rohrabacher, R.*
46. Robert K. Dornan, R.*
47. C. Christopher Cox, R.*
48. Ronald C. Packard, R.*
49. Brian Bilbray, R.
50. Bob Filner, D.*
51. Randy (Duke) Cunningham, R.*
52. Duncan L. Hunter, R.*

Colorado
1. Patricia Schroeder, D.*
2. David E. Skaggs, D.*
3. Scott McInnis, R.*
4. Wayne Allard, R.*
5. Joel Hefley, R.*
6. Daniel Schaefer, R.*

Connecticut
1. Barbara B. Kennelly, D.*
2. Sam Gejdenson, D.*
3. Rosa DeLauro, D.*
4. Christopher Shays, R.*
5. Gary Franks, R.*
6. Nancy L. Johnson, R.*

Delaware
†Michael Castle, R.*

Florida
1. Joe Scarborough, R.
2. Pete Peterson, D.*
3. Corrine Brown, D.*
4. Tillie Fowler, R.*
5. Karen Thurman, D.*
6. Clifford B. Stearns, R.*
7. John Mica, R.*
8. Bill McCollum, R.*
9. Michael Bilirakis, R.*
10. C. W. Bill Young, R.*
11. Sam M. Gibbons, D.*
12. Charles Canady, R.*
13. Dan Miller, R.*
14. Porter J. Goss, R.*
15. Dave Weldon, R.
16. Mark Foley, R.
17. Carrie Meek, D.*
18. Ileana Ros-Lehtinen, R.*
19. Harry A. Johnston II, D.*
20. Peter Deutsch, D.*
21. Lincoln Diaz-Balart, R.*
22. E. Clay Shaw, Jr., R.*
23. Alcee Hastings, D.*

Georgia
1. Jack Kingston, R.*
2. Sanford Bishop, D.*
3. Mac Collins, R.*
4. John Linder, R.*
5. John Lewis, D.*
6. Newt Gingrich, R.*
7. Bob Barr, R.
8. Saxby Chambliss, R.
9. Nathan Deal, R.*
10. Charlie Norwood, R.
11. Cynthia McKinney, D.*

Hawaii
1. Neil Abercrombie, D.*
2. Patsy T. Mink, D.*

Idaho
1. Helen Chenoweth, R.
2. Michael Crapo, R.*

Illinois
1. Bobby Rush, D.*
2. Jesse L. Jackson, Jr., D.
3. William O. Lipinski, D.*
4. Luis Gutierrez, D.*
5. Michael Flanagan, R.
6. Henry J. Hyde, R.*
7. Cardiss Collins, D.*
8. Philip M. Crane, R.*
9. Sidney R. Yates, D.*
10. John Edward Porter, R.*
11. Gerald Weller, R.
12. Jerry F. Costello, D.*
13. Harris W. Fawell, R.*
14. J. Dennis Hastert, R.*
15. Thomas W. Ewing, R.*
16. Donald Manzullo, R.*
17. Lane A. Evans, D.*
18. Ray LaHood, R.
19. Glenn Poshard, D.*
20. Richard J. Durbin, D.*

Indiana
1. Peter J. Visclosky, D.*
2. David McIntosh, R.
3. Tim Roemer, D.*
4. Mark Souder, R.
5. Steve Buyer, R.*
6. Danny L. Burton, R.*
7. John T. Myers, R.*
8. John Hostettler, R.
9. Lee H. Hamilton, D.*
10. Andrew Jacobs, Jr., D.*

Iowa
1. Jim Leach, R.*
2. Jim Nussle, R.*
3. Jim Ross Lightfoot, R.*
4. Greg Ganske, R.
5. Tom Latham, R.

Kansas
1. Pat Roberts, R.*
2. Sam Brownback, R.
3. Jan Meyers, R.*
4. Todd Tiahrt, R.

Kentucky
1. Edward Whitfield, R.
2. Ron Lewis, R.*
3. Mike Ward, D.
4. Jim Bunning, R.*
5. Harold (Hal) Rogers, R.*
6. Scotty Baesler, D.*

Louisiana
1. Robert L. Livingston, Jr., R.*
2. William J. Jefferson, D.*
3. W. J. (Billy) Tauzin, R.*
4. Cleo Fields, D.*
5. Jim McCrery, R.*
6. Richard Hugh Baker, R.*
7. James A. (Jimmy) Hayes, R.*

Maine
1. James Longley, R.
2. John Baldacci, D.

Maryland
1. Wayne T. Gilchrest, R.*
2. Robert Ehrlich, Jr., R.
3. Benjamin L. Cardin, D.*
4. Albert Wynn, D.*
5. Steny H. Hoyer, D.*
6. Roscoe Bartlett, R.*
7. Kweisi Mfume, D.*
8. Constance A. Morella, R.*

Massachusetts
1. John W. Olver, D.*
2. Richard E. Neal, D.*
3. Peter Blute, R.*
4. Barney Frank, D.*
5. Martin Meehan, D.*
6. Peter Torkildsen, R.*
7. Edward J. Markey, D.*
8. Joseph P. Kennedy II, D.*
9. John Joseph Moakley, D.*
10. Gerry E. Studds, D.*

Michigan
1. Bart Stupak, D.*
2. Peter Hoekstra, R.*
3. Vernon Ehlers, R.*
4. Dave Camp, R.*
5. James Barcia, D.*
6. Frederick S. Upton, R.*
7. Nick Smith, R.*
8. Dick Chrysler, R.
9. Dale E. Kildee, D.*
10. David E. Bonior, D.*
11. Joseph Knollenberg, R.*
12. Sander M. Levin, D.*
13. Lynn Rivers, D.
14. John Conyers, Jr., D.*
15. Barbara-Rose Collins, D.*
16. John D. Dingell, D.*

Minnesota
1. Gil Gutknecht, R.
2. David Minge, D.*
3. Jim Ramstad, R.*
4. Bruce F. Vento, D.*
5. Martin O. Sabo, D.*
6. William P. Luther, D.
7. Collin C. Peterson, D.*
8. James L. Oberstar, D.*

Mississippi
1. Roger Wicker, R.
2. Bennie Thompson, D.*
3. G. V. (Sonny) Montgomery, D.*
4. Mike Parker, R.*
5. Gene Taylor, D.*

Missouri
1. William L. (Bill) Clay, D.*
2. James Talent, R.*
3. Richard A. Gephardt, D.*
4. Ike Skelton, D.*
5. Karen McCarthy, D.
6. Pat Danner, D.*
7. Mel Hancock, R.*
8. Bill Emerson, R.*
9. Harold L. Volkmer, D.*

Montana
† Pat Williams, D.*

Nebraska
1. Doug Bereuter, R.*
2. Jon Christensen, R.
3. Bill Barrett, R.*

Nevada
1. John Ensign, R.
2. Barbara F. Vucanovich, R.*

New Hampshire
1. Bill Zeliff, R.*
2. Charles Bass, R.

New Jersey
1. Robert E. Andrews, D.*
2. Frank LoBiondo, R.
3. H. James Saxton, R.*
4. Christopher H. Smith, R.*
5. Marge Roukema, R.*
6. Frank Pallone, Jr., D.*
7. Bob Franks, R.*
8. Bill Martini, R.
9. Robert G. Torricelli, D.*
10. Donald M. Payne, D.*
11. Rodney Frelinghuysen, R.
12. Richard A. Zimmer, R.*
13. Robert Menendez, D.*

New Mexico
1. Steven H. Schiff, R.*
2. Joe Skeen, R.*
3. William B. Richardson, D.*

New York
1. Michael Forbes, R.
2. Rick Lazio, R.*
3. Peter King, R.*
4. Daniel Frisa, R.
5. Gary L. Ackerman, D.*
6. Floyd H. Flake, D.*
7. Thomas J. Manton, D.*
8. Jerrold Nadler, D.*
9. Charles E. Schumer, D.*
10. Edolphus Towns, D.*
11. Major R. Owens, D.*
12. Nydia Velázquez, D.*
13. Susan Molinari, R.*
14. Carolyn Maloney, D.*

15. Charles B. Rangel, D.*
16. José E. Serrano, D.*
17. Eliot L. Engel, D.*
18. Nita M. Lowey, D.*
19. Sue Kelly, R.
20. Benjamin A. Gilman, R.*
21. Michael R. McNulty, D.*
22. Gerald B. Solomon, R.*
23. Sherwood L. Boehlert, R.*
24. John McHugh, R.*
25. James Walsh, R.*
26. Maurice Hinchey, D.*
27. William Paxon, R.*
28. Louise M. Slaughter, D.*
29. John J. LaFalce, D.*
30. Jack Quinn, R.*
31. Amory Houghton, Jr., R.*

North Carolina
1. Eva Clayton, D.*
2. David Funderburk, R.
3. Walter Jones, Jr., R.
4. Frederick Heineman, R.
5. Richard Burr, R.
6. Howard Coble, R.*
7. Charles Rose III, D.*
8. W. G. (Bill) Hefner, D.*
9. Sue Myrick, R.
10. Cass Ballenger, R.*
11. Charles H. Taylor, R.*
12. Melvin Watt, D.*

North Dakota
† Earl Pomeroy, D.*

Ohio
1. Steve Chabot, R.
2. Rob Portman, R.*
3. Tony P. Hall, D.*
4. Michael G. Oxley, R.*
5. Paul E. Gillmor, R.*
6. Frank Cremeans, R.
7. David L. Hobson, R.*
8. John A. Boehner, R.*
9. Marcy Kaptur, D.*
10. Martin Hoke, R.*
11. Louis Stokes, D.*
12. John R. Kasich, R.*
13. Sherrod Brown, D.*
14. Thomas C. Sawyer, D.*
15. Deborah Pryce, R.*
16. Ralph Regula, R.*
17. James A. Traficant, Jr., D.*
18. Bob Ney, R.
19. Steven LaTourette, R.

Oklahoma
1. Steve Largent, R.*
2. Tom Coburn, R.
3. Bill Brewster, D.*
4. J. C. Watts, R.
5. Ernest Jim Istook, R.*
6. Frank Lucas, R.*

Oregon
1. Elizabeth Furse, D.*
2. Wes Cooley, R.
3. Ron Wyden, D.*
4. Peter A. DeFazio, D.*
5. Jim Bunn, R.

Pennsylvania
1. Thomas M. Foglietta, D.*
2. Chaka Fattah, D.
3. Robert A. Borski, Jr., D.*
4. Ron Klink, D.*
5. William F. Clinger, Jr., R.*
6. Tim Holden, D.*
7. W. Curtis Weldon, R.*
8. Jim Greenwood, R.*
9. E. G. (Bud) Shuster, R.*
10. Joseph M. McDade, R.*
11. Paul E. Kanjorski, D.*
12. John P. Murtha, D.*
13. Jon Fox, R.
14. William J. Coyne, D.*
15. Paul McHale, D.*
16. Robert S. Walker, R.*
17. George W. Gekas, R.*
18. Michael Doyle, D.
19. William F. Goodling, R.*
20. Frank Mascara, D.
21. Philip English, R.

Rhode Island
1. Patrick Kennedy, D.
2. John F. Reed, D.*

South Carolina
1. Mark Sanford, R.
2. Floyd Spence, R.*
3. Lindsey Graham, R.
4. Bob Inglis, R.*
5. John M. Spratt, Jr., D.*
6. James Clyburn, D.*

South Dakota
† Tim Johnson, D.*

Tennessee
1. James H. Quillen, R.*
2. John J. Duncan, Jr., R.*
3. Zach Wamp, R.
4. Van Hilleary, R.
5. Bob Clement, D.*
6. Bart Gordon, D.*
7. Ed Bryant, R.
8. John S. Tanner, D.*
9. Harold E. Ford, D.*

Texas
1. Jim Chapman, D.*
2. Charles Wilson, D.*
3. Sam Johnson, R.*
4. Ralph M. Hall, D.*
5. John W. Bryant, D.*
6. Joe Barton, R.*
7. Bill Archer, R.*
8. Jack Fields, Jr., R.*
9. Steve Stockman, R.
10. Lloyd Doggett, D.*
11. Chet Edwards, D.*
12. Preston P. (Pete) Geren, D.*
13. William Thornberry, R.
14. Greg Laughlin, R.*
15. Eligio (Kika) de la Garza, D.*
16. Ronald D. Coleman, D.*
17. Charles W. Stenholm, D.*
18. Sheila Lee, D.
19. Larry Combest, R.*

20. Henry B. Gonzalez, D.*
21. Lamar S. Smith, R.*
22. Tom DeLay, R.*
23. Henry Bonilla, R.*
24. Martin Frost, D.*
25. Ken Bentsen, D.
26. Richard K. Armey, R.*
27. Solomon P. Ortiz, D.*
28. Frank Tejeda, D.*
29. Gene Green, D.*
30. Eddie Bernice Johnson, D.*

Utah
1. James V. Hansen, R.*
2. Enid Waldholtz, R.
3. William Orton, D.*

Vermont
† Bernard Sanders, Ind.*

Virginia
1. Herbert H. Bateman, R.*
2. Owen B. Pickett, D.*
3. Robert Scott, D.*
4. Norman Sisisky, D.*
5. Lewis F. Payne, Jr., D.*
6. Robert Goodlatte, R.*
7. Thomas J. (Tom) Bliley, Jr., R.*
8. James P. Moran, Jr., D.*
9. Frederick C. Boucher, D.*
10. Frank R. Wolf, R.*
11. Thomas Davis III, R.

Washington
1. Rick White, R.
2. Jack Metcalf, R.
3. Linda Smith, R.
4. Doc Hastings, R.
5. George Nethercutt, R.
6. Norman D. Dicks, D.*
7. Jim McDermott, D.*
8. Jennifer Dunn, R.*
9. Randy Tate, R.

West Virginia
1. Alan B. Mollohan, D.*
2. Robert E. Wise, Jr., D.*
3. Nick J. Rahall II, D.*

Wisconsin
1. Mark Neumann, R.
2. Scott Klug, R.*
3. Steven Gunderson, R.*
4. Gerald D. Kleczka, D.*
5. Thomas Barrett, D.*
6. Thomas E. Petri, R.*
7. David R. Obey, D.*
8. Toby Roth, R.*
9. F. James Sensenbrenner, Jr., R.*

Wyoming
† Barbara Cubin, R.

Nonvoting representatives
American Samoa
Eni F. H. Faleomavaega, D.*

District of Columbia
Eleanor Holmes Norton, D.*

Guam
Robert Underwood, D.*

Puerto Rico
Carlos Romero-Barceló, D.*

Virgin Islands
Victor O. Frazer, Ind.

Drastic changes for welfare were also included in the Republicans' budget bill. The measure would trim spending on food stamps, require adults on welfare to work after two years, and forbid any family to remain on welfare more than five years. States would be able to deny benefits to unwed teen-age mothers, and additional benefits would be denied for children born to women already on welfare.

The GOP plan would cut taxes by a total of $245-billion over seven years. Single parents earning up to $75,000 and couples making up to $110,000 a year would receive a $125 tax credit for each child under 18. The credit would increase to $500 per child in subsequent years. For gains on the sale of stocks and other capital assets, the maximum tax rate would drop from 28 percent to 19.8 percent. At the same time, a special tax break for the working poor would be cut back by $32.5 billion over seven years.

Clinton's budget. The President vetoed the GOP budget bill on Dec. 6, 1995, saying that the proposed spending cuts were too harsh. He also claimed that the Republicans were slashing Medicare in order to provide tax cuts for wealthy Americans. Clinton countered the GOP budget on December 7 with a budget proposal—his third of the year—that also called for eliminating the federal deficit by 2002.

Clinton's revised budget proposed spending cuts of $465 billion, $347 billion less than the GOP plan, and tax cuts of $98 billion, $147 billion less than the Republican budget. The scaled-down tax cut included a $300 tax credit for each child under age 13 in families with incomes under $60,000, rising to $500 each starting in 1999. Families with incomes between $60,000 and $75,000 would be eligible for smaller tax credits. At year-end, the budgetary impasse had still not been settled.

International issues. Domestic issues were at the core of confrontation between the White House and Congress, but foreign policy also played a part. Sensing congressional hostility toward a proposed loan to Mexico to bolster the plunging peso, the President used emergency powers in February 1995 to extend a $20-billion loan to Mexico and encouraged the International Monetary Fund and the Bank of International Settlements to contribute another $29.5 billion in aid to prop up the peso.

On Aug. 11, 1995, Clinton vetoed a bill to end U.S. participation in an arms embargo against the former Yugoslav republic of Bosnia-Herzegovina (often called Bosnia), where war had raged since 1991. Clinton contended that lifting the embargo would intensify the fighting there and hamper diplomatic efforts to settle the conflict.

The President also faced a difficult foreign policy task in getting congressional support for dispatching 20,000 U.S. troops to Bosnia, which Clinton had pledged as part of a peace agreement reached in November 1995 in Dayton, Ohio, among the leaders of Croatia, Bosnia, and Serbia to halt the war. On December 7, 201 House members, including 15 Democrats, signed a letter to Clinton opposing U.S. troop deployment in Bosnia. On December 13, the House and the Senate passed resolutions supporting the troops while criticizing the intervention.

At times, Clinton was under fire from Democrats in Congress who complained that he frequently shifted positions and did not consult members of his own party on Capitol Hill before taking major policy stands. Their morale also suffered when Senator Ben Nighthorse Campbell of Colorado switched from the Democratic to the Republican party in March, along with five House Democrats from southern states. Eight Democratic Senators also decided not to run for reelection in 1996, including such veterans as Sam Nunn (D.-Ga.), Bill Bradley (D.-N.J.), and Paul Simon (D.-Ill.). Four Republicans in the Senate—Hank Brown of Colorado, Nancy Kassebaum of Kansas, Alan Simpson of Wyoming, and Mark Hatfield of Oregon—said they would not seek another term.

With the political momentum apparently moving in their direction, many GOP candidates emerged to compete for their party's presidential nomination. Chief among them was Dole, the veteran legislator who had tried twice before and failed to win the nomination. Three other senators also entered the Republican race—Richard G. Lugar of Indiana, Phil Gramm of Texas, and Arlen Specter of Pennsylvania. By late November, however, Specter had dropped out, saying that his moderate stance on issues did not attract the financial backing he needed to be a contender. In the House, Robert K. Dornan (R.-Calif.) declared his candidacy in April.

Ethics problems plagued both chambers in 1995. On December 6, the House Ethics Committee voted to order an investigation into whether Gingrich misused tax-exempt donations to teach a college course in Georgia and whether he benefited improperly from his office in signing a lucrative book deal. Senator Bob Packwood (R.-Ore.) resigned on October 1 after the Senate Ethics committee recommended his expulsion from the Senate. Packwood was accused of making unwanted sexual advances to women on his staff, as well as to female campaign workers and lobbyists, and of altering parts of his personal diaries to cover up his actions.

In the House, Mel Reynolds (D.-Ill.) resigned on October 1 after he was convicted in a Chicago trial of sexual misconduct, soliciting child pornography, and obstruction of justice. He was sentenced to five years in prison. (On December 12, Jesse L. Jackson, Jr., son of civil rights leader Jesse Jackson, was elected to take Reynold's seat in Congress.) On December 15, Representative Walter Tucker (D., Calif.) also resigned his seat after he was convicted of extortion and tax evasion.   □ William J. Eaton

See also **United States, Government of the.** In *World Book,* see **Congress of the United States.**

Connecticut. See State government.

Members of the United States Senate

The Senate of the second session of the 104th Congress consisted of 46 Democrats and 53 Republicans plus 1 vacancy when it convened on January 3, 1996. Sen. Bob Packwood of Oregon resigned October 1, 1995. His seat was to be filled following a special election in January 1996. The first date in each listing shows when the senator's term began. The second date in each listing shows when the senator's term expires.

State	Term	State	Term	State	Term
Alabama		**Louisiana**		**Ohio**	
Howell T. Heflin, D.	1979-1997	J. Bennett Johnston, Jr., D.	1972-1997	John H. Glenn, Jr., D.	1974-1999
Richard C. Shelby, R.	1987-1999	John B. Breaux, D.	1987-1999	Mike DeWine, R.	1995-2001
Alaska		**Maine**		**Oklahoma**	
Theodore F. Stevens, R.	1968-1997	William S. Cohen, R.	1979-1997	Don Nickles, R.	1981-1999
Frank H. Murkowski, R.	1981-1999	Olympia Snowe, R.	1995-2001	James M. Inhofe, R.	1994-1997
Arizona		**Maryland**		**Oregon**	
John McCain III, R.	1987-1999	Paul S. Sarbanes, D.	1977-2001	Mark O. Hatfield, R.	1967-1997
Jon Kyl, R.	1995-2001	Barbara A. Mikulski, D.	1987-1999		
Arkansas		**Massachusetts**		**Pennsylvania**	
Dale Bumpers, D.	1975-1999	Edward M. Kennedy, D.	1962-2001	Arlen Specter, R.	1981-1999
David H. Pryor, D.	1979-1997	John F. Kerry, D.	1985-1997	Rick Santorum, R.	1995-2001
California		**Michigan**		**Rhode Island**	
Barbara Boxer, D.	1993-1999	Carl Levin, D.	1979-1997	Claiborne Pell, D.	1961-1997
Dianne Feinstein, D.	1993-2001	Spencer Abraham, R.	1995-2001	John H. Chafee, R.	1976-2001
Colorado		**Minnesota**		**South Carolina**	
Hank Brown, R.	1991-1997	Paul D. Wellstone, D.	1991-1997	Strom Thurmond, R.	1955-1997
Ben N. Campbell, R.	1993-1999	Rod Grams, R.	1995-2001	Ernest F. Hollings, D.	1966-1999
Connecticut		**Mississippi**		**South Dakota**	
Christopher J. Dodd, D.	1981-1999	Thad Cochran, R.	1978-1997	Larry Pressler, R.	1979-1997
Joseph I. Lieberman, D.	1989-2001	Trent Lott, R.	1989-2001	Thomas A. Daschle, D.	1987-1999
Delaware		**Missouri**		**Tennessee**	
William V. Roth, Jr., R.	1971-2001	Christopher S. (Kit) Bond, R.	1987-1999	Bill Frist, R.	1995-2001
Joseph R. Biden, Jr., D.	1973-1997	John Ashcroft, R.	1995-2001	Fred Thompson, R.	1994-2001
Florida		**Montana**		**Texas**	
Bob Graham, D.	1987-1999	Max Baucus, D.	1978-1997	Phil Gramm, R.	1985-1997
Connie Mack III, R.	1989-2001	Conrad Burns, R.	1989-2001	Kay Bailey Hutchison, R.	1993-2001
Georgia		**Nebraska**		**Utah**	
Sam Nunn, D.	1972-1997	J. James Exon, D.	1979-1997	Orrin G. Hatch, R.	1977-2001
Paul Coverdell, R.	1993-1999	J. Robert Kerrey, D.	1989-2001	Robert F. Bennett, R.	1993-1999
Hawaii		**Nevada**		**Vermont**	
Daniel K. Inouye, D.	1963-1999	Harry M. Reid, D.	1987-1999	Patrick J. Leahy, D.	1975-1999
Daniel K. Akaka, D.	1990-2001	Richard H. Bryan, D.	1989-2001	James M. Jeffords, R.	1989-2001
Idaho		**New Hampshire**		**Virginia**	
Larry E. Craig, R.	1991-1997	Robert C. Smith, R.	1990-1997	John W. Warner, R.	1979-1997
Dirk Kempthorne, R.	1993-1999	Judd Gregg, R.	1993-1999	Charles S. Robb, D.	1989-2001
Illinois		**New Jersey**		**Washington**	
Paul Simon, D.	1985-1997	Bill Bradley, D.	1979-1997	Slade Gorton, R.	1989-2001
Carol Moseley-Braun, D.	1993-1999	Frank R. Lautenberg, D.	1982-2001	Patty Murray, D.	1993-1999
Indiana		**New Mexico**		**West Virginia**	
Richard G. Lugar, R.	1977-2001	Pete V. Domenici, R.	1973-1997	Robert C. Byrd, D.	1959-2001
Dan R. Coats, R.	1989-1999	Jeff Bingaman, D.	1983-2001	John D. Rockefeller IV, D.	1985-1997
Iowa		**New York**		**Wisconsin**	
Charles E. Grassley, R.	1981-1999	Daniel P. Moynihan, D.	1977-2001	Herbert Kohl, D.	1989-2001
Tom Harkin, D.	1985-1997	Alfonse M. D'Amato, R.	1981-1999	Russell D. Feingold, D.	1993-1999
Kansas		**North Carolina**		**Wyoming**	
Robert J. Dole, R.	1969-1999	Jesse A. Helms, R.	1973-1997	Alan K. Simpson, R.	1979-1997
Nancy Landon Kassebaum, R.	1979-1997	Lauch Faircloth, R.	1993-1999	Craig Thomas, R.	1995-2001
Kentucky		**North Dakota**			
Wendell H. Ford, D.	1974-1999	Kent Conrad, D.	1987-2001		
Mitch McConnell, R.	1985-1997	Byron L. Dorgan, D.	1992-1999		

Conservation. Amid heated controversy, gray wolves returned to Yellowstone National Park in 1995, after an absence of nearly 70 years. In March, biologists from the U.S. Fish and Wildlife Service released 14 wolves as part of a program the service initiated in the 1970's to restore the natural ecosystem of the park. Ranchers had sued in a Wyoming federal district court in November 1994 to halt the wolf reintroduction, arguing that the wolves would leave the park to prey on cattle and sheep. Were that to occur, however, ranchers had the right to kill marauding wolves without penalty. In January 1995, a federal judge allowed the program to proceed.

Gray wolves were common throughout the Rocky Mountains when Yellowstone was established in 1872. As the West became more settled, ranchers, aided by the federal government, launched a program to eradicate gray wolves in order to protect their livestock. Park rangers killed the last two wolves in Yellowstone in 1926. Eventually the gray wolf was eliminated throughout the United States except in Alaska and Minnesota, and the species was designated as endangered.

Some conservationists felt that the gray wolf would have repopulated Yellowstone without help. For about 30 years, they had been crossing into the United States from Canada on their own. In the early 1990's, several had been sighted near the park. Had repopulation occurred naturally, someone caught killing a gray wolf would have been prosecuted under the Endangered Species Act, even if the wolf had preyed on livestock outside the park. The maximum penalty for anyone convicted of killing an endangered animal was two years in prison and a $150,000 fine.

But federal biologists said such natural reintroduction, if it occurred at all, would have taken many years. Further, they said, wolves are far more interested in elk, moose, mule deer, and other natural prey than in livestock. However, a few days after 15 wolves were released in a wilderness area of Idaho as part of the same reintroduction program, one animal apparently killed a calf on a ranch some 45 miles (72 kilometers) from the release site.

By late April, the wolves had formed packs that were preying on elk. Without predators, the park's elk population had exploded, seriously disrupting the ecological balance. The overgrazed land could not support the rising elk population, and consequently many starved to death. Biologists hoped that by the year 2002 wolves would number 100 to 150—about 10 packs—which could reduce the current elk population by 20 percent. Since wolves prey on weak and sick animals, the overall health of the elk could improve as well.

In early May, a female wolf gave birth to eight pups. Because of the stress of capture and captivity, biologists did not expect reproduction until 1996 at the earliest. Then a man shot and killed the female's mate, a criminal offense since it occurred inside the park.

Meanwhile, program coordinators planned to introduce more wolves into Yellowstone to assure a diverse gene pool. Ranchers continued to seek ways to stop reintroduction, and in July, the Senate Appropriations Committee approved a proposal introduced by Republican Senator Conrad Burns of Montana to cut funding for wolf restoration.

The Florida panther, down to about 30 to 50 animals, was one of America's most critically endangered animals in 1995. But over the next few years, the panther could be revitalized as a result of the introduction of eight female Texas cougars into panther habitat in 1995.

Until the 1920's, the panther ranged over the Southeastern United States. Hunters and motor vehicles killed off large numbers, and land development gradually reduced its habitat to an isolated section of south Florida. The steadily decreasing population meant that most mating occurred between close relatives—even members of the same litter. As a result the gene pool shrank, and offspring were increasingly affected with inherited physical problems. By 1995, the Florida panther as a subspecies was plagued by heart deformities, sterility, and a weakened immune system.

Panther researchers for the Florida Game and Fresh Water Fish Commission wanted to revitalize the subspecies and restore it as a viable breeding population. They chose Texas cougars because they are genetically linked to the Florida panther subspecies. The cougars were released during March and April, the breeding season, into the Fakahatchee Strand State Reserve, the Big Cypress National Preserve, and other wild sites in and around the Everglades.

Parrot project fails. In May, biologists abandoned a seven-year effort to reintroduce thick-billed parrots to the Chiricahua Mountain forests of Arizona. The species disappeared from the United States in the early 1900's, largely because of the illegal pet trade in parrots. The green and scarlet bird is one of only two parrots native to the United States. The other, the Carolina parakeet, became extinct in 1914.

Researchers found no evidence of the 88 parrots released during the seven-year program. The first 29 birds had been confiscated from smugglers, but most died as a result of drought and disease. The project also included parrots bred in captivity, but those birds lacked the survival instincts of wild parrots. Wild thick-bills congregate in large flocks, whether flying, feeding, or nesting. In flight this behavior confuses hawks and other predatory birds, thus protecting the group. In contrast, when the birds bred in captivity were released, they flew off singly, making no attempt to join the wild flock. Although the U.S. parrots did not survive, a healthy population of thick-bill parrots still exists in Mexico.

New national park in Spain. The Spanish parliament approved legislation in May 1995 that created a new national park, called Picos de Europa, in Spain's northern Cantabrian mountain range. Regional governments in the area fought the plan for the park for 10 years, fearing it would deter economic development. In fact, the legislation did set restrictions on commercial development in the region and strict controls on access to the preserve.

Picos de Europa protected many rare species native to this mountainous area. Those species included the chamois, a small goat-antelope that can leap nimbly across steep slopes; the brown bear, very scarce in Europe; the capercaillie, the largest wild grouse; and hundreds of other rare birds.

African elephants continued to decline in number in 1995, despite a worldwide ban on trading ivory, according to a report released in January by the United Nations, the United States, and private conservation organizations. No accurate count of African elephants exists, but the 1995 estimate of 600,000 was down from the 1990 count of 620,000, largely the result of poaching. The worldwide ivory ban began in 1990.

The report found that several African nations had growing stockpiles of government-held ivory. Further, they spent less on elephant protection than they had in 1990. The report also noted more inci-

dents of elephants killing people, as well as people killing elephants, across the African continent, an indicator of a growing human population intruding into wild-elephant habitat. The report concluded that the elephant population would not soon—or perhaps ever—rebound to its natural level.

Endangered species debate. The U.S. Supreme Court ruled on June 29, 1995, that under the Endangered Species Act of 1973, the prohibition against harming wildlife was not limited to outright killing. The court stated that harm included destruction of endangered-species habitat. Property-rights advocates had argued that the law should not mean that landowners were restricted from carrying on such activities as logging or farming on private property.

But on September 21, Congress completed negotiations on a $12-billion joint spending bill for the Department of the Interior. The bill gave landowners tax breaks and other incentives to encourage their voluntary protection of endangered species. The bill also required the government to compensate landowners if habitat protection reduced the value of their land, and it mandated a one-year moratorium on the listing of any new endangered species. Fiscal conservatives and environmentalists from both parties defeated the bill in both houses on September 29. At year-end, Congress was working on a compromise. □ Eugene J. Walter, Jr.

In *World Book,* see **Conservation.**

Wildlife officials watch as 1 of 15 gray wolves captured in Canada is set free in Idaho in January. Another 14 gray wolves from Canada were freed in Yellowstone National Park as part of a plan to restore wolves to the West.

Overfishing has severely depleted
the world's fish stocks and created
painful choices in the effort to rebuild
an essential natural resource.

Have We Fished
Out the Sea?

By Bob Holmes

The first treaty to regulate fishing in international waters was approved in August 1995 by 99 member nations of the United Nations (UN). Three years in the making, the Straddling Fish Stocks and Highly Migratory Fish Stocks agreement recognized that fisheries around the world were in serious trouble due to overfishing. After rising steadily since the late 1940's, the world catch of ocean fish has stagnated since 1989, despite an increasing number of fishing boats and more advanced technologies for finding fish. By 1995, populations of many of the most commercially valuable fish had fallen to dangerously low levels, and increasingly aggressive fishing practices threatened to worsen the problem.

Continued overfishing holds potentially serious consequences. Fish is the primary source of animal protein for more than 1 billion people, especially in such areas as the Philippines and western Africa. And in some island nations, fish is the only source of protein for most people. Any prolonged shortage of fish could therefore threaten the health of millions of people. Overfishing may also jeopardize the livelihood of as many as 90 percent of the world's *fishers* (people who catch fish as an occupation)—an estimated 14 million to 20 million people.

Problems related to overfishing made headlines throughout 1995. In March, Massachusetts Governor William F. Weld said he would ask that the state's fishing industry be declared a federal disaster area so that fishers could qualify for federal aid. The same month, the Canadian government provoked a heated international incident when it seized the Spanish trawler *Estai,* which had been fishing in international waters on the Grand Banks off the Canadian province of Newfoundland.

How bad has the overfishing problem become? Some of the most dramatic effects can be seen in waters off Canada. When the English explorer John Cabot first sailed over the Grand Banks in 1497, he found the waters teeming with cod. The fish were so numerous that sailors caught them by simply lowering baskets over the side of the ship. Great fleets of fishing schooners still worked the Grand Banks in the late 1800's, and as recently as the early 1990's, the cod fishery was one of the mainstays of Newfoundland's economy. But today, not a single cod fisher sails from the ports of Newfoundland. The cod of the Grand Banks are almost gone, reduced to less than 1 percent of their former abundance. To help the fishery recover, the Canadian government in 1992 ended all inshore fishing for cod off Newfoundland. But fisheries scientists say the cod population may not be able to support a fishing industry again until 2010, and some scientists fear that the cod may not return at all.

A global problem

Newfoundland's fishers are not alone in their misery. Fish populations in all the world's oceans are in trouble from overfishing. With too many boats chasing too few fish, the consequences—both economic and ecological—have often been ruinous. According to the Food and Agriculture Organization (FAO), a UN division that tracks fishing activity around the world, the catch in all but 2 of the world's 15 major marine fishing regions has fallen since 1989, resulting in the loss of more than 100,000 fishing jobs.

The peak catches of 18 common fish species declined by an average of 30 percent between 1964 and 1988, according to the FAO. The worst declines were in polar cod and South African pilchard, both popular food fish. By 1992, catches of these fish had fallen 94 percent from their peaks in the late 1960's and early 1970's. At the same time, catches of Atlantic herring fell 63 percent; silver hakes, 88 percent; and Atlantic cod, 69 percent. According to the FAO, 70 percent of the world's commercial fish species are at risk of decline or are already in decline from overfishing. In the United States, the National Marine Fisheries Service (NMFS), which tracks the status of ocean fisheries off U.S. coasts, found that fully 40 percent of all U.S. marine fish stocks whose status is known are now overfished.

Most fisheries experts agree that the North Atlantic cod and other bottom-dwelling fish such as haddock, flounder, and hake—collectively known as groundfish—represent the most dismal failure of fishery management in the world's oceans. In 1965, fishers harvested 844,000 short tons (766,000 metric tons) of groundfish off the coast of New England. By 1993, the annual take totalled only 122,000 short tons (111,000 metric tons), despite a huge increase in the number of boats during the 1970's and 1980's. For some species, the decline was even sharper: The harvest of red hakes, silver hakes, and haddock fell

The author

Bob Holmes is a U.S. correspondent for *New Scientist* magazine.

from 633,000 short tons (574,000 metric tons) in 1965 to only 26,500 short tons (24,000 metric tons) in 1993.

Groundfish are not the only ones in trouble. In 1980, the FAO estimated that populations of about 25 major fish species could safely support heavier fishing in the near future. The FAO warned, however, that 20 other species were already overfished. Only 10 years later, in 1990, the number of overfished species had risen to 50, and the number of species that could safely be fished more heavily had dropped to just 7. Many experts warn that the world's fishers are perilously close to jeopardizing these remaining healthy populations, as well.

Although populations of individual fish species have declined, the total marine catch has increased. This is partly because fishers began to catch other species they once didn't bother to pursue. The world's total marine fish catch rose steadily from 22 million tons (20 million metric tons) just after World War II (1939-1945) to a peak of more than 95 million tons (86 million metric tons) in 1989. Since then, yields have remained flat.

During the boom in ocean fisheries in the 1950's and 1960's, fishers concentrated on the most valuable species—cod, halibut, snapper, and other large, firm-fleshed fish prized for food. As the stocks of these prime species began to dwindle, however, fishers shifted their attention to less valuable fish in order to maintain their catches. By the mid-1990's, the bulk of the world's fish catch consisted of smaller, less valuable fish and squid, many of which go to factories to be ground into fish meal for animal food, instead of to the dinner table.

Boats and technology

Experts believe that the declines in fish stocks can be attributed to several factors, including an increase in the number of fishing boats, more effective nets, and technological advances, such as improved navigational systems and sonar. Environmental changes, such as pollution and encroachments on fish spawning grounds, have also contributed to the decline. Even faulty estimates of the size of fish stocks have played a role.

Most experts agree, however, that an excess of fishing boats is the biggest single cause of the declines in world fish stocks. An important change came after World War II, when surplus ships—and surplus workers newly discharged from the military—turned to fishing. This increase in the number of boats was accompanied by huge increases in fishing power. Larger, metal-hulled vessels replaced small, wooden boats. The first factory trawler set out from the United Kingdom in 1954. On-board freezers and larger holds meant that fishers no longer had to return to port before their catch spoiled.

The gross tonnage of the world's fishing fleet nearly doubled between 1970 and 1992. And while the world catch of marine fish increased 58 percent during that period, the stagnation in catch from 1989 through 1992 occurred despite a continued increase in the number of fishing vessels.

The Alaskan halibut fishery is perhaps the most extreme example

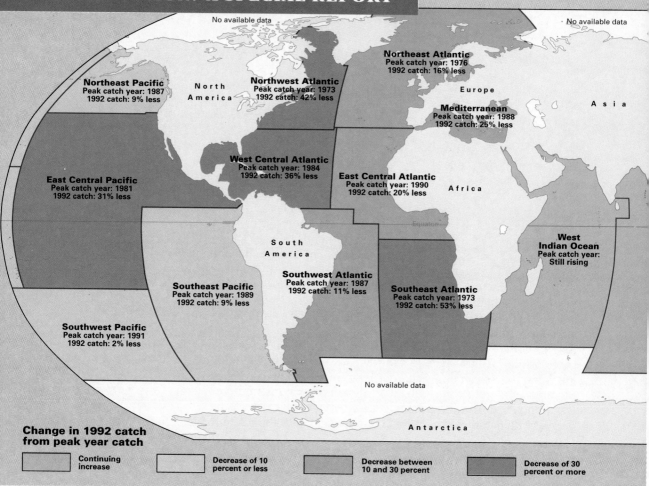

No available data

No available data

Northeast Pacific
Peak catch year: 1987
1992 catch: 9% less

North
America

Northwest Atlantic
Peak catch year: 1973
1992 catch: 42% less

Northeast Atlantic
Peak catch year: 1976
1992 catch: 16% less

Europe

Asia

Mediterranean
Peak catch year: 1988
1992 catch: 25% less

East Central Pacific
Peak catch year: 1981
1992 catch: 31% less

West Central Atlantic
Peak catch year: 1984
1992 catch: 36% less

East Central Atlantic
Peak catch year: 1990
1992 catch: 20% less

Africa

Equator

South
America

**West
Indian Ocean**
Peak catch year:
Still rising

Southeast Pacific
Peak catch year: 1989
1992 catch: 9% less

Southwest Atlantic
Peak catch year: 1987
1992 catch: 11% less

Southeast Atlantic
Peak catch year: 1973
1992 catch: 53% less

Southwest Pacific
Peak catch year: 1991
1992 catch: 2% less

No available data

Antarctica

**Change in 1992 catch
from peak year catch**

| | Continuing increase | | Decrease of 10 percent or less | | Decrease between 10 and 30 percent | | Decrease of 30 percent or more |

Catches in all but 2 of the world's 15 major fishing regions have declined since 1973. Only catches in the Indian Ocean were still rising in 1995.

of too many boats. Until 1995, fishery managers had set no restrictions on the number of participants in the fishery. The fishery became so overloaded with boats—as many as 6,000 by the early 1990's—that fishers hauled in the entire year's limit of fish in just one or two days.

Fishers also resorted to larger and more efficient nets. New nylon nets proved much lighter and cheaper than their traditional counterparts made of rope or twine, so fishers could set more of them. Fishers began to use radar and other navigational aids for finding good fishing spots and sonar for finding schools of fish.

In recent years, technology has improved still further. By the 1990's, advanced navigational systems allowed ship captains to return exactly to a good fishing spot—even out of sight of land—and work it again and again until they had caught all the fish. With modern sonar, fishers can locate ever-smaller schools of fish. And sonar mounted directly on trawl nets drives machinery that raises and lowers nets to dodge rocks, letting captains fish areas they had formerly avoided for fear of losing gear.

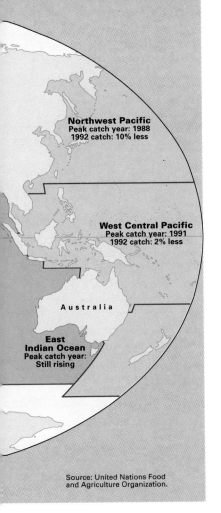

Northwest Pacific
Peak catch year: 1988
1992 catch: 10% less

West Central Pacific
Peak catch year: 1991
1992 catch: 2% less

Australia

**East
Indian Ocean**
Peak catch year:
Still rising

Source: United Nations Food
and Agriculture Organization.

Some experts claim that inexact estimates of fish populations indirectly contribute to the decline in fish stocks. Fisheries managers estimate fish populations based on the size of commercial catch and random surveys by research vessels—a process similar to guessing a city's population from the number of its murder victims. Scientists admit that estimates using this method may be off target by as much as 30 percent.

These inaccuracies can have serious results. For example, when Canadian fisheries biologists estimated the numbers for the commercial harvest of Atlantic cod in the late 1980's, they forgot to account for improvements in technology that made it easier to catch fish. As a result, biologists mistakenly thought the rising cod catch signalled a booming cod population, so they failed to set catch limits low enough to prevent the stocks from collapsing.

Environmental factors

Natural short-term fluctuations in the environment itself can also help deplete fish stocks by amplifying the effects of overfishing. Off the coast of Peru, the appearance of a warm ocean current called El Niño every three to seven years can disrupt anchovy populations by preventing the upwelling of nutrients that normally rise from colder, deeper water. Sardine populations also vary according to the amount of upwelling cold water along the west coast of the United States and South America. Such upwelling depends largely on wind direction and speed, since winds must push surface water away from land to allow deeper water to rise. Because of the variability of such atmospheric and ocean conditions, many fisheries scientists believe that blaming falling fish populations in some areas only on overfishing is too simplistic.

Environmental pollution and habitat changes also diminish some fish populations. About two-thirds of all marine fish begin their lives close to shore in shallow wetland areas and near the mouths of rivers. These coastal environments are among the most threatened habitats worldwide, as humans continue to drain and fill them for development. In addition, toxic runoff from industry and farm fields pollutes coastal areas.

Pacific salmon, which return to spawn in freshwater streams, have been hit especially hard by habitat changes. Throughout western

**World's top
fishing nations***

Nation	Percent of world catch
1. China	12
2. Peru	10
3. Chile	7
4. United States	7
5. Russia	4
6. Thailand	4
7. Indonesia	3
8. South Korea	3
9. Norway	3
10. India	3

*1993 Figures
Source: United Nations
Food and Agriculture
Organization.

North America, humans have dammed rivers and diverted water for irrigation. Clearcut logging has led to extensive soil erosion, clogging with silt the gravelly streams in which salmon like to spawn. These changes are the main cause of salmon declines. At least 320 spawning populations of Pacific salmon are now extinct or in danger of going extinct. As recently as 1987, a million chinook salmon entered the Columbia River to spawn each fall. In 1995, that number was expected to dwindle to an all-time low of fewer than 200,000.

Consequences of overfishing

Overfishing has set the stage for a variety of economic, health, and ecological problems. The economic consequences of overfishing are numerous. In 1989, an FAO survey found that the annual operating costs for fuel, maintenance, supplies, insurance, and labor of the world's fishing fleet topped $92 billion. The value of the catch that year was approximately $70 billion—$22 billion less than the fishers paid to catch them. When the FAO also factored in capital costs such as loan payments for the fishing vessels themselves, fishing's annual deficit ballooned to $54 billion. Government subsidies made up much of this shortfall.

Better fisheries management would improve this bleak economic picture by tens of billions of dollars annually, according to fisheries analysts. Fishers could probably catch an additional 22 million short tons (20 million metric tons) from the world's oceans if depleted fish stocks were allowed to recover to their former abundance. Even at current prices, the FAO calculates that this extra catch would boost earnings by $15 billion. A 1992 NMFS study estimated that if all depleted fish stocks in the United States were allowed to recover, total fish catch could increase by about 40 percent. The extra fish would earn fishers an additional $2.9 billion per year. In turn, the fishers' increased wealth could boost the national economy by $8 billion and add as many as 300,000 jobs.

In the short term, however, easing up on depleted fish stocks means under- or unemployment for people in the fishing industry. And this toll can exact a high price on a nation's economy. For example, more than 20,000 people were left unemployed by the closure of the Canadian cod fishery in 1992. And even if governments implement conservation measures, there is no guarantee that catches will ever return to peak levels in threatened areas. Fishery scientists say that even when groundfish stocks come back on Canada's Grand Banks, it is unlikely that a healthy, well-managed fishery could sustain anything like the old number of jobs that once existed.

Aside from economic considerations, the world's fishery crisis has health consequences. Average worldwide fish consumption per capita almost doubled between 1961 and 1989, according to the FAO. But fish prices have increased in many areas, depriving many of the urban poor in developing countries of their cheapest source of animal protein. For example, in Bangladesh—one of the world's poorest countries—the consumption of fish has been declining since the

Identifying the cause of fish declines

After increasing steadily since the 1950's, the total world catch of ocean fish leveled off in 1989 and had not recovered by the mid-1990's, *below*. A major reason for the decline was the continued increase in the number of fishing vessels, *right*.

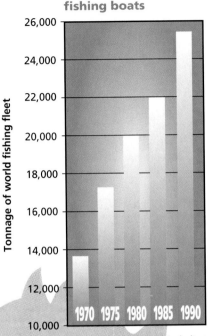

More and more fishing boats

Tonnage of world fishing fleet

1970 1975 1980 1985 1990

Source: Food and Agriculture Organization.

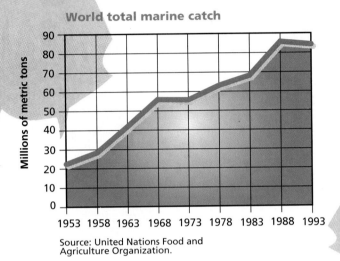

World total marine catch

Millions of metric tons

1953 1958 1963 1968 1973 1978 1983 1988 1993

Source: United Nations Food and Agriculture Organization.

The total weight of registered boats in the world fishing fleet has more than doubled since 1970, reflecting a surge in the number of operating fishing boats. As more boats take to the seas, the depletion of fish has become a crisis in some fisheries.

1970's. Many poor families can no longer afford to buy fish as often as they once did, and many researchers believe this will have an impact on their health.

Overfishing has had ecological impacts, as well. Whole ocean ecosystems have changed radically as fishers catch the large, long-lived fish, leaving room for more fish of smaller, faster-growing species. Off the coast of New England, for example, groundfish and skates made up more than 80 percent of the fish in the nets of NMFS research trawlers in 1963. In 1995, they made up barely 30 percent of the catch, which is now mostly dogfish and other fish few consumers will eat.

As high-quality fish become scarcer, fishers have to work harder to catch them. This, too, can result in severe ecological damage. For example, in the Gulf of Mexico, shrimp have become so scarce that shrimp trawlers' nets now contain 4 pounds (1.8 kilograms) of other fish for every pound of shrimp they catch. These fish are often juveniles of desirable species such as red snapper that would be a valuable catch if allowed to mature. Most of this so-called bycatch, however, is discarded and dies.

Destructive fishing methods have increased in some tropical countries as poor people use whatever means they can to try to eke out a living from depleted fisheries. Fishing with dynamite has become common, with more than 40 countries reporting its use. The

The consequences of overfishing

Overfishing around the world had seriously depleted stocks of many of the most desirable fish by the mid-1990's, *below*. Declining fish stocks result in idle fishing boats in British Columbia, Canada, *right*.

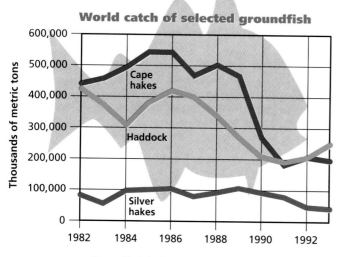

World catch of selected groundfish

Cape hakes

Haddock

Silver hakes

Thousands of metric tons

600,000
500,000
400,000
300,000
200,000
100,000
0

1982   1984   1986   1988   1990   1992

Source: The United Nations Food and Agriculture Organization.

Popular table fish such as Haddock, Cape hakes, and Silver hakes have suffered heavily from overfishing. Since the mid-1980's, the world catch of these three groundfish has fallen 40 to 60 percent.

blast kills the fish, which then rise to the surface. Likewise, some fishers now poison fish by squirting cyanide into crevices in a reef. Both techniques kill much more than the target fish.

A history of mismanagement

Of course, the world's fisheries didn't get into such a sorry state overnight. Human population growth and decades of poor management have compounded the present fisheries crisis. At the end of World War II, countries claimed as their national waters only a narrow strip—typically 3 or 12 nautical miles (5.6 or 22.2 kilometers)—along their coast. This left most of the rich continental shelf areas in international waters free of regulation by national governments. As a result, in the years after World War II a variety of international commissions, such as the International Commission on Northwest Atlantic Fisheries and the International Commission for the Conservation of Atlantic Tuna, were created to oversee fishing. Most experts today agree that these commissions did a good job of gathering data on fishing catches but did little or nothing to curb the swelling number of fishers.

As fishing intensified through the 1960's and 1970's, however, more and more nations began to claim the right to control all fishing as far as 200 nautical miles (370 kilometers) from their coastlines. These limited areas of fishing became known as exclusive economic

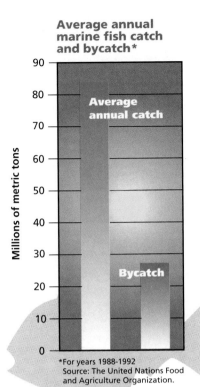

Average annual marine fish catch and bycatch*

Millions of metric tons

- 90
- 80 — Average annual catch
- 70
- 60
- 50
- 40
- 30
- 20 — Bycatch
- 10
- 0

*For years 1988-1992
Source: The United Nations Food and Agriculture Organization.

Worldwide, commercial fishers throw out more than 30 percent of their catch because it is not the type of fish they want. Such bycatch kills millions of tons of fish each year and contributes significantly to the depletion of fish stocks.

zones (EEZ's). In 1982, member nations of the UN approved the Law of the Sea Treaty, which recognized these 200-mile limits. The treaty went into effect in November 1994.

In theory, EEZ's should have brought overfishing under control by giving each country the authority to limit or exclude foreign fleets. These fleets roamed the world, often depleting one fishery and then moving on to another. Overfishing, however, continued with the EEZ's, which were now exploited by domestic rather than foreign fleets. In the United States, for example, Congress passed the Magnuson Fishery Conservation and Management Act in 1976. The Magnuson Act established a 200-mile EEZ and set up eight regional fishery management bodies to manage fishing in the expanded zones and prevent overfishing. Fishery managers promptly expelled most foreign fishing vessels, and the U.S. fishing industry—backed by government subsidies—launched a massive buildup. American fishers nearly doubled their catch between 1974 and 1992—more than double the rate of increase in the world catch.

Critics claim that the U.S. regional fishery councils did too little, too late to preserve fish stocks, partly due to the conflicting financial interests of some council members. The councils have the authority to set catch limits and impose other regulations on the industry. But that balance has proven difficult to find because many council members work in the fishing industry or hold financial stakes in the fish-

A fish farm floats in ocean water off the coast of Japan. In the 1990's, some nations began to rely more heavily on fish breeding and farming to counter falling ocean catches.

eries they regulate, and they feared that any catch limits would cost fishers money and even jobs. The same conflict has hand-cuffed fisheries managers around the world.

Working on solutions

But in the 1990's, nation after nation showed signs of finally getting serious about fishery conservation. The FAO, NMFS, and conservation organizations have reached a consensus that the world's fisheries somehow need to limit fishing. In December 1994, the United States closed some 6,000 square miles (15,500 square kilometers) of fishing grounds off the coast of Massachusetts to allow depleted fishing stocks there to recover from overfishing.

A less drastic remedy than closing fishing grounds involves issuing a limited number of fishing licenses for a particular fishery. Alaska, for example, has restricted the number of commercial salmon-fishing licenses for more than a decade. As a result, Alaskan salmon populations are healthier than those farther south. Even with a license system, however, managers may still need to impose some restriction on the total allowable catch to prevent overfishing the stock in vulnerable years.

Other major changes in fisheries management were planned for late 1995. The U.S. House of Representatives passed a revised version of the Magnuson Act in October 1995 that would require the regional fishery management councils to give greater weight to scientists' recommendations on ways to protect endangered fish stocks. The Senate was considering the revised bill as the year ended. Congress was also considering tightening regulations to minimize the number of unwanted fish accidentally caught in nets.

On the international front, the UN's August 1995 migratory fish treaty was an attempt to manage the fishing of migratory species, such as bluefin tuna and swordfish, which range so widely across the Atlantic that no single country can manage them effectively. The treaty also covers so-called "straddling stocks"—nonmigratory species that overlap the boundaries of EEZ's.

Resolving conflicts

Part of the Grand Banks of Newfoundland, for example, lies outside Canada's 200-mile EEZ. When Canada seized the Spanish trawler *Estai,* the Canadians charged that the Spanish vessel had caught more than its limit of Greenland halibut under a quota imposed by the Northwest Atlantic Fishing Organization (NAFO). They also said the *Estai* was using an illegal net with too small a mesh, and thus taking too many juvenile halibut. If this illegal fishing continued, the Canadians warned, Greenland halibut populations might crash throughout the Grand Banks. The Spanish said that the *Estai* was outside Canada's 200-mile EEZ and that the Canadians thus had no jurisdiction over the boat. The Spanish had also protested the NAFO halibut quotas since their imposition in 1991, claiming that the limits allowed Spanish fishers too few fish.

Canada and Spain settled the dispute in April, with the Canadians reassigning some of their halibut quota to the European Union and the Europeans agreeing to stricter enforcement of the quotas. The new UN treaty, if ratified, would provide an enforceable, uniform means to deal with such disputes.

The UN in late 1995 was also working to develop an international code of responsible fishing. Countries that adopt the code would agree to restrict the use of fishing techniques, such as dynamiting reefs, that damage ecosystems. They would also agree to abide by guidelines to ensure healthy fish populations. The code would apply to all fisheries, not just those in international waters. But unlike the straddling-stocks provision of the UN treaty, it would be voluntary, lacking the teeth of enforcement.

It remains to be seen whether the new climate of concern for fisheries conservation will lead to the recovery of depleted fish stocks around the world. Whatever the outcome, however, one thing seems certain: The old days when anyone with a boat and a net could make a living as a fisher are gone forever. ■ ■ ■

For further reading:

Safina, Carl. "The World's Imperiled Fish." *Scientific American,* November 1995, pp. 46-53.

Webb, Peter. *Net Loss: Fish, Jobs, and the Marine Environment.* Worldwatch Institute, 1994.

United Nations global fishing treaty

One hundred nations agreed to an accord in August 1995 designed to conserve dwindling stocks of ocean fish. The Straddling Fish Stocks and Highly Migratory Fish Stock agreement was the first international treaty to regulate fishing practices in international waters. The treaty will go into effect when the national legislatures of 30 of the signatories approve the agreement. Highlights of the treaty include:

- Limits on catches of fish that migrate to international waters from waters surrounding individual countries. Such fish include cod, tuna, swordfish, turbot, and marlin.

- Provisions to allow international inspectors on fishing vessels to monitor catch limits.

- Mandatory reporting by trawler captains to the UN of the size of their catches.

- Demands that countries attempt to limit the amount of unintended fish caught each year. Such bycatches waste millions of tons of fish.

Consumerism.

Consumerism. The United States economy slowed in 1995. Economists expected the *gross domestic product (GDP)* to grow close to 3 percent for the year. The GDP is the value of all goods and services produced in a country and is one of the most widely used measures of a nation's economic performance. The GDP in 1994 was about 4 percent.

Inflation remained modest in 1995. The government's official measure of the cost of living, the Consumer Price Index (CPI), rose 2.8 percent over a 12-month period ending in October. Inflation in the year ending October 1994 was about the same. However, a congressional panel reported on Sept. 15, 1995, that the CPI may overstate inflation by about 1 percent. This finding could affect how the government establishes tax brackets and cost-of-living increases for recipients of government benefits.

The Federal Reserve System, the nation's central bank, cut interest rates in July by 0.25 percent. The move was aimed at lowering borrowing costs for consumers and businesses, thereby spurring the economy and keeping it from a recession. Prior to the cut, the Federal Reserve had hiked rates seven times to prevent inflationary economic growth.

Consumer confidence in the economy continued to rise in 1995. A monthly survey, called the Consumer Confidence Index, asks consumers to forecast their financial status for the next six months. As of October 1995, the index stood at 97. A level of 100 represents the level of confidence in 1985, when the U.S. economy was growing steadily.

Telecommunications. The U.S. Congress considered a bill in the fall to sweep away more than 60 years of regulations controlling the nation's telecommunications industry. The bill aimed to increase competition among telephone, cable television, and other companies. The new rules included allowing local phone companies to compete for long-distance services and allowing competitors into local phone and cable TV markets, which have operated as monopolies. Supporters said the competition would improve services to consumers and lower prices. Opponents of the legislation, including President Bill Clinton, said it would increase the holdings of the largest communications companies. The bill was still pending at year-end.

Legislation. Congress in 1995 considered a bill to allow banks to sell insurance or stocks, activities that have been forbidden to banks for more than 60 years. Also, Congress reviewed a measure that would limit damage awards in product liability cases. Both bills were still pending at year's end.

Health. In October, the U.S. Food and Drug Administration (FDA) approved a procedure for correcting the eye condition called myopia, or near-sightedness. The procedure involved a laser device using powerful beams of light to sculpt the outer coating of the eyeball to better focus light on the retina. Consumers were warned, however, that the laser surgery caused some patients to see halos or glare.

Telemarketing. The Federal Trade Commission in August imposed rules designed to make it harder to commit telemarketing fraud. The rules, to take effect Jan. 1, 1996, require telemarketers to tell consumers right away that they are making a sales call. They must also identify themselves and the precise cost and terms of the products they are selling. The rules also could make prosecuting fraudulent telemarketers easier by allowing courts to impose nationwide injunctions against them.

Automobile safety. A report issued in July by the General Accounting Office, an investigative department of Congress, concluded that the U.S. Department of Transportation's auto crash-testing program may be unreliable. The report said the crash tests may differ from real accidents. In part, this is due to the fact that the government tests only front-end crashes of a single vehicle, which account for only about half of all injury-causing accidents.

The Ford Motor Company equipped its 1996 Ranger pickup truck with a switch that allowed owners to turn off the passenger-side air bag. The automaker included the switch because safety experts said that small children sitting in rear-facing car seats in the passenger seat could be killed by the force of an inflating air bag. □ John Merline

In *World Book*, see **Consumerism; Economics.**

Costa Rica. See Latin America.

Courts.

Courts. In one of the most sensational criminal trials of the 20th century, a Los Angeles jury on Oct. 3, 1995, found former football star O. J. Simpson not guilty of murdering his former wife, Nicole Brown Simpson, and her friend Ronald L. Goldman. The jury delivered its unanimous verdict after deliberating for less than four hours.

Nicole Simpson, who divorced O. J. Simpson in 1992, and Goldman, a waiter at an upscale restaurant, were stabbed to death outside her Los Angeles home on June 12, 1994. During the trial, the prosecution relied heavily on experts who testified that sophisticated genetic tests showed that blood found at the murder scene matched O. J. Simpson's. However, lawyers for the defense accused the Los Angeles police of making many mistakes in their investigation of the case. The defense also tried to damage the credibility of police detective Mark Fuhrman, a key witness, by showing he had used racial slurs and expressed bigoted views about blacks.

The trial, including jury selection, lasted one year and seven days and cost taxpayers $9 million. Because of Simpson's celebrity and the nature of the charges against him, the trial received unprecedented publicity, including live television coverage. Simpson had been a star running back for the University of Southern California and the Buffalo Bills.

Children's deaths. A jury in Union, South Carolina, sentenced Susan V. Smith to life in prison on

In a dramatic moment in June during his murder trial, O. J. Simpson has difficulty putting on a glove that prosecutors hoped would link him with the crime.

July 28, 1995, for murdering her two sons, Michael, aged 3, and Alexander, aged 14 months. Six days earlier, the jury had convicted Smith of drowning the children by rolling her car into a lake on Oct. 25, 1994, with the boys strapped into their car seats. Smith had prompted a massive search by claiming on national television that a carjacker had taken her car with the children inside. However, she eventually confessed to sending the car into the lake, though she said she was very depressed and had intended to go down with her children.

Terrorists convicted. On Oct. 1, 1995, a federal jury convicted Sheik Omar Abdel Rahman and nine other Muslim militants of conspiring to terrorize the United States through a series of violent acts. These acts included the bombing of the World Trade Center in New York City on Feb. 26, 1993, and the killing of Rabbi Meir Kahane, a right wing Israeli activist, in New York City on Nov. 5, 1990.

The government said the group also had planned to bomb several other New York City landmarks in an effort to change U.S. policies in the Middle East. Among the targets were the United Nations headquarters, automobile tunnels linking the borough of Manhattan to New Jersey, and the George Washington Bridge over the Hudson River. The defendants were to be sentenced in early 1996.

New York train shooting. Colin Ferguson, a native of Jamaica, was sentenced by a New York judge to six consecutive life terms in prison for fatally shooting six people on a crowded commuter train to Long Island on Dec. 7, 1993. Ferguson also was ordered to spend an additional 50 years in prison for wounding another 19 people in his rampage. Ferguson represented himself during the trial and said that an unknown man had shot the passengers.

Shabazz charges dropped. On May 1, 1995, federal prosecutors agreed to drop charges against Qubilah B. Shabazz for allegedly plotting to arrange the assassination of Nation of Islam leader Louis Farrakhan. She had been charged with the crime on January 12. The settlement averted what promised to be an ugly trial, with government testimony coming mainly from a paid informer. As part of the settlement, Shabazz agreed to undergo a two-year program of psychiatric and drug-abuse treatment.

Shabazz is a daughter of slain Black Muslim leader Malcolm X. Her mother, Betty Shabazz, had accused Farrakhan of involvement in Malcolm X's 1965 killing.

Microsoft settlement. A U.S. district judge on Aug. 21, 1995, approved a 1994 antitrust settlement between the Microsoft Corporation and the U.S. Department of Justice. The settlement required the computer software giant to change the way it licenses its products to makers of personal computers. The Justice Department had charged that the company's licensing practices forced computer manufacturers to use Microsoft products, stifling competition and raising retail prices. Federal investigators began looking at Microsoft's activities in 1990 to learn how the company grew to dominate the market with its Windows operating system, the most widely used software program for personal computers.

Microsoft averted an earlier showdown with the government on May 20, 1995, when it scuttled a planned purchase of Intuit, Incorporated. Intuit makes a popular personal-finance computer program known as *Quicken*. The Justice Department sued to halt the deal on April 28, claiming that the merger of the companies would increase prices for consumers and discourage innovation in personal-finance software.

Accepting bribes. Dennis R. Josleyn and John W. Billmyer, former executives of the American Honda Motor Company, were convicted on June 1 of accepting kickbacks from automobile dealers, who in return received preferential treatment in obtaining sought-after Honda and Acura cars and dealerships. Prosecutors described the trial as the largest commercial bribery case ever.

A federal jury also convicted Josleyn of racketeering and mail fraud for skimming money from sales-training and advertising programs. On Oct. 2, Billmyer was sentenced to 5 years in prison and fined $150,000, and Josleyn was sentenced to 6½ years in prison. Prosecutors said that a total of 18 former executives of Honda and its Acura division had been sentenced "for substantial imprisonment and total fines of about $1.5 million" for illegal dealings—dealings that involved payments of $15 million in cash and expensive gifts from dealers in more than 30 states during the period from 1979 to 1992.

Assisted suicide. The Ninth U.S. Circuit Court of Appeals on March 9, 1995, upheld a Washington state law that prohibits doctors from helping terminally ill patients take their own lives. The ruling overturned a lower-court decision that said the Washington law was unconstitutional. The Ninth Circuit also was considering whether to review a right-to-die law that Oregon voters approved in 1994. The Oregon law was the first in the nation to allow physician-assisted suicide, but a federal judge in December 1994 blocked its enforcement.

Immigration payments. Four states in 1995 appealed federal judges' rulings that dismissed 1994 lawsuits against the federal government. In the suits, the states sought to recover more than $4 billion spent on providing social services to illegal immigrants. In dismissing California's suit on Feb. 13, 1995, U.S. District Judge Judith Keep said that Congress and the President, not the courts, should decide immigration policies. Texas, Arizona, and New Jersey were fighting similar dismissals of their suits.

☐ Linda P. Campbell and Geoffrey A. Campbell

See also **Crime; Supreme Court of the United States.** In *World Book,* see **Court.**

Federal agents lead Timothy J. McVeigh out of court in April in Perry, Oklahoma. He was charged with bombing the Alfred P. Murrah Federal Building in Oklahoma City.

Crime. The United States experienced the worst terrorist attack in its history within its borders on April 19 when a truck packed with 4,800 pounds (2,200 kilograms) of explosives blew up outside the nine-story Alfred P. Murrah Federal Building in Oklahoma City, Oklahoma. The blast killed 168 people, including 19 children who were in a day-care center in the building when the bomb went off. A nurse who died during rescue efforts brought the final death toll to 169.

Immediately after the bombing, many people suspected that Middle Eastern terrorists were responsible for the attack. But on April 21, federal authorities arrested Timothy J. McVeigh, 27, a decorated U.S. Army veteran with links to antigovernment paramilitary groups, in connection with the bombing. Authorities claimed that McVeigh parked a rented truck packed with explosives outside the federal building, lit a slow-burning fuse, and drove off in another vehicle.

Federal authorities on April 21 also took into custody two brothers—Terry L. and James D. Nichols—with links to McVeigh and militia groups. The two were placed under arrest as material witnesses to the bombing and charged with conspiring to build bombs. Terry Nichols had served in the army with McVeigh, and the three shared a house for part of 1994 in Decker, Michigan. On May 10, prosecutors formally charged Terry Nichols with malicious dam-

age to a federal building and with helping to carry out the bombing. Authorities eventually dropped all charges against James Nichols.

According to prosecutors, McVeigh and Nichols planned the attack in retaliation for the April 1993 raid on the Branch Davidian cult compound in Waco, Texas. The Waco raid by members of the Bureau of Alcohol, Tobacco, and Firearms (ATF) resulted in the death of about 82 cult members, including many children. The Oklahoma City attack came on the second anniversary of the Waco raid, and authorities believed the bombers may have chosen the building partly because it housed ATF offices.

The bomb had been constructed with a combination of ammonium nitrate fertilizer and diesel oil, investigators said. According to prosecutors, Nichols bought the ammonium nitrate used to make the bomb and stored it in several Kansas towns. Nichols also allegedly helped McVeigh steal other bomb-making ingredients.

On Aug. 10, 1995, a federal grand jury indicted McVeigh and Nichols on 11 charges related to the bombing, including murder. The grand jury also indicted a third man—Michael J. Fortier, an army veteran who served with McVeigh and Nichols—on charges of hiding information about the plot to bomb the building. On August 15, McVeigh and Nichols pleaded not guilty to the charges against them.

Unabomber strikes again. On April 24, a mail bomb exploded and killed Gilbert B. Murray, a lobbyist for the California Forestry Association, in the group's offices in Sacramento, California. The Federal Bureau of Investigation (FBI) said the bomb was sent by the so-called Unabomber, who authorities believed was responsible for 15 other mail bombing incidents since 1978. With the April attack, the Unabomber had killed 3 men and wounded 23 other people.

According to the FBI, the mysterious mail bomber was probably a white man in his 40's. Authorities derived the bomber's nickname from a combination of "university" and "airline," because his original targets had been university researchers and airline executives.

On April 25, 1995, the FBI said that the Unabomber had sent four letters to news organizations just before his attack on the previous day. The Unabomber offered to stop his attacks if several publications with national circulations published a long paper he had written explaining his beliefs. In the letters, the bomber criticized scientists and engineers and described himself as an anarchist who wanted to destroy the "worldwide industrial system."

On September 19, *The Washington Post* published the document, entitled *Industrial Society and Its Future*. The *Post* split the publishing cost with *The New York Times*. On September 21, the *Oakland Tribune* also published the manifesto.

Japanese cult poison-gas attacks. Poison gas released from hidden canisters on subway trains in Tokyo killed 12 people and sickened about 5,500 on March 20. Authorities said the poison was sarin, a deadly nerve gas.

On March 22, the national police stormed offices of the religious cult Aum Shinrikyo, a group that reportedly mixed Buddhist and Hindu beliefs along with assorted theories about how the world would end. The police confiscated tons of chemicals, some of which they said could be used to make sarin, as well as literature predicting that 90 percent of people in the world's major cities would be victims of poison-gas attacks in the coming few years.

On March 16, the police arrested the cult's leader, 40-year-old Shoko Asahara, for masterminding and carrying out the subway gas attack. Several of Asahara's top followers were also arrested. The police said they suspected that the cult was also involved in a poison-gas attack that occurred in June 1994 in Matsumoto, Japan, in which seven people died.

Terrorist bombings in France. From July through October, an Algerian terrorist group went on a bombing spree in France that killed 7 people and injured at least 170. Most of the bombs went off in Paris. The most serious attack occurred on July 25, when a bomb exploded at a commuter train stop in Paris, killing 7 people and injuring at least 80.

In October, a group calling itself the Armed Islamic Group (AIG) claimed responsibility for the attacks. AIG members were Algerians reportedly upset at France's support for the Algerian government, which they opposed.

Amtrak train derailment. Saboteurs derailed an Amtrak train some 50 miles (80 kilometers) southwest of Phoenix on October 9, killing 1 person and injuring at least 100 others. Investigators found that 29 spikes holding the rail to supporting crossties had been pulled out, and a steel bar used to connect two sections of rail had been unbolted. They also said that a safety system designed to alert train engineers to damaged or missing sections of track had been disabled.

The investigators found two antigovernment notes near the accident site. The notes mentioned the 1993 Waco siege of the Branch Davidian compound and were signed "Sons of Gestapo," authorities said. Law-enforcement officials said they were unfamiliar with any antigovernment groups by that name, however, and were unable to determine the motive behind the attack.

Singer Selena killed. Popular Mexican-American singer Selena was shot to death on March 31 in a hotel in Corpus Christi, Texas. The singer, whose full name was Selena Quintanilla Perez, performed a style of music known as Tejano, which features accordion accompaniments and lyrics in Spanish and English. She had won a Grammy award for best Mexican-American album and was regarded by most observers as a rising star.

The police arrested Yolanda Saldivar, the founder and past president of Selena's fan club, for the murder. Saldivar was convicted of the murder on October 23 and later sentenced to life in prison.

Grisly Illinois murders. On November 17 or 18, in Addison, Illinois, a suburb of Chicago, assailants killed a woman who was nine months pregnant, cut her fetus from her womb, and murdered two of her children. On November 19, the police arrested a 22-year-old man, his 28-year-old girlfriend, and her 24-year-old cousin and charged them with the murders. Miraculously, the police found the newborn infant alive when they arrested the suspects. According to the police, the couple charged in the killings apparently wanted a child but were unable to have one.

Violence up among juveniles. A Justice Department report released in September 1995 showed a sharp increase in juvenile crime. The report, "Juvenile Offenders and Victims: A National Report," said that the arrest rate among juveniles for violent crimes jumped 100 percent between 1983 and 1993. And in November, the Justice Department reported that arrests of juveniles for weapons offenses rose by more than 100 percent from 1985 to 1993, compared with an increase of 30 percent for adults.

◻ Mark Dunbar

In *World Book,* see **Crime.**

Croatia. There was a resumption of conflict between government troops and Croatian Serbs in 1995. The two sides had observed an uneasy truce since the end of a 1991-1992 war between the newly independent Croatia, Serbia—one of two remaining republics in Yugoslavia—and Croatian Serbs. The Croatian government regained much of the territory it had lost to the rebels. In November, Croatia joined in talks in the United States aimed at bringing peace to the former Yugoslavia. Those talks resulted in a peace pact on November 12.

Dispute over peacekeepers. In January, Croatian President Franjo Tudjman demanded that the United Nations (UN) Protection Force leave Croatia when its mandate expired on March 31. The 14,000 UN troops came to Croatia in March 1992 to patrol buffer zones between government and Croatian Serb territory. Tudjman agreed on March 12 to allow about 5,000 UN troops to remain.

The war. A four-month regional cease-fire negotiated by former U.S. President Jimmy Carter in late 1994 expired on May 1. On May 2 and 3, Croatian troops recaptured the region of Western Slavonia, which had been held by Croatian Serbs. In retaliation, Serb forces launched rockets at the Croatian capital, Zagreb, from the Serb-held region of Krajina. Six people were killed and about 175 injured.

In August, the Croatian military recaptured Krajina from the Serbs, who had held the region since 1991. About 150,000 Croatian Serbs fled Krajina, the largest single migration of the war in the former Yugoslavia. The UN and international human-rights groups criticized alleged atrocities by Croatian forces in Krajina, including the killing of elderly Serbs.

Peace talks. On September 26, Croatian leaders agreed with Bosnian and Yugoslavian leaders on a new constitutional framework for Bosnia. Under the agreement, Bosnia would keep its existing borders but be divided into two substates, one controlled by a Muslim-Croat federation and the other by Bosnian Serbs. Each substate would have the right to form "special relationships" with neighboring countries. Details of the plan were to be worked out in talks among Tudjman, Bosnian President Alija Izetbegovic, and Serbian President Slobodan Milošević that opened November 1 in Dayton, Ohio.

At the talks, on November 12, the warring sides agreed on the subdivision of Bosnia. They further agreed that the Croatian Serbs would relinquish Eastern Slavonia, an oil-rich region along Croatia's border with Serbia. Eastern Slavonia was the last piece of Croatian territory held by rebel Serbs.

Elections. In October parliamentary elections, Tudjman's party received 44 percent of the vote, thereby increasing its representation in parliament from 31 to 42 seats. ☐ Sharon L. Wolchik

See also **Bosnia-Herzegovina; Europe** (Facts in brief table); **Yugoslavia.** In *World Book,* see **Croatia.**

Croatian President Franjo Tudjman joins the leaders of Bosnia and Serbia in signing a Balkan peace agreement in Dayton, Ohio, on November 12.

Cuba. Dressed like a businessman rather than in his usual military outfit, President Fidel Castro courted good will and foreign investment in 1995 during visits to France, Trinidad and Tobago, Colombia, Argentina, China, and the United States. While visiting New York City from October 22 to 26 to attend a meeting of the United Nations, Castro accepted invitations to meet with hundreds of U.S. executives anxious to learn more about the terms of some 212 joint ventures and other investment agreements Cuba had already signed with foreign companies.

Foreign investment approved. After a year-long debate, Cuba's National Assembly on September 5 approved a law allowing foreigners to own businesses and property in Cuba. The law would allow investors access to all businesses except those in the fields of defense, health care, and education.

The Cuban government also announced in late June that it would set up free-trade zones for foreign investment in plants that assemble goods in Cuba for export. The trade zones would offer tax advantages and reduced tariffs on imported goods used for manufacturing. The first free-trade zone was to be in the western port of Mariel.

Trade embargo. Unimpressed by Cuba's opening of its economy to capitalistic ventures, the U.S. Congress voted to tighten the 33-year-old U.S. trade embargo against Cuba. The new legislation, approved in the House of Representatives on September 21 and in the Senate on October 19, would deny U.S. visas to any foreigner who uses, manages, or profits from American-owned commercial properties that were confiscated when Castro seized power in 1959. The law would also permit U.S. citizens, including Cuban exiles who have become U.S. citizens, to sue in U.S. courts for damages arising out of the confiscations. At year-end, Congress had not yet passed a final version of the bill.

Cuban refugees. After secret negotiations with Cuba, the Clinton Administration announced on May 2 that it would end the long-standing U.S. policy of giving preferential treatment to Cubans seeking asylum in the United States. Under the agreement, the United States said that it would return to Cuba boat people intercepted trying to reach the United States. The agreement did, however, permit 21,000 Cuban refugees who had been confined at the U.S. naval base at Guantánamo Bay, Cuba, for almost a year to enter the United States.

Vesco arrest. On June 10, Cuban authorities said they had arrested fugitive U.S. financier Robert L. Vesco, wanted by U.S. courts for bilking investors of nearly a quarter of a billion dollars before he fled the country in 1971. Cuban authorities said they would not return Vesco to stand trial in the United States.   ☐ Nathan A. Haverstock

See also **Latin America** (Facts in brief table). In *World Book*, see **Cuba**.

Cyprus. See **Middle East**.

Czech Republic continued to enjoy stability in 1995. President Václav Havel won widespread approval, and most citizens supported the country's move toward an open-market economy.

Political divisions in the four-party coalition government came to the fore, however. Scandals within the Civic Democratic Alliance, one of the coalition parties, and charges of corruption against government agencies threatened the coalition. Coalition partners disagreed on whether property that had been seized from the Roman Catholic Church by former Communist governments should be returned. The coalition also sparred over reform of the social welfare system, which Prime Minister Václav Klaus identified as the key task of 1995.

Spending cuts. Parliament took steps to cut government spending. It introduced means testing for children's allowances, changed the pension system to gradually increase the retirement age, cut health services, and lowered education funding. These measures sparked a number of large demonstrations, including one organized by trade unions in March that drew between 60,000 and 90,000 protesters to Prague.

Scandals. The head of the country's privatization program, Jaroslav Lizner, faced charges in 1995 that he had accepted a $300,000 bribe. Lizner's arrest in November 1994 undermined support for Klaus and his government. Support for the opposition Czech Social Democratic Party and its leader, Milos Zeman, grew substantially in 1995.

The citizenship law continued to cause controversy. The law requires foreign nationals, including some 200,000 Romanies (Gypsies) who formerly lived in Slovakia, to have no criminal record for five years before they can become citizens of the Czech Republic. Klaus and the Constitutional Court continued to support the law, despite sharp criticism from the United States government and international human rights groups.

The Czech economy grew during the first six months of 1995. The nation's *gross domestic product* (the total value of goods and services produced in the nation) increased by 3.9 percent. Imports rose considerably, but exports declined. Inflation increased, reaching an annual rate of 10 percent by June. Unemployment stood at less than 3 percent. Wages for workers in industry increased by an average of 18 percent.

Foreign relations. Relations with Germany were complicated by the issue of ethnic Germans who were expelled from Czechoslovakia after World War II. Some of those expelled are seeking the return of their land or compensation. But on March 8, the Constitutional Court upheld 1945 government decrees that stripped 2.5 million ethnic Germans of their property and citizenship.   ☐ Sharon L. Wolchik

See also **Europe** (Facts in brief table). In *World Book*, see **Czech Republic**.

Ron Kirk, elected mayor of Dallas in May, celebrates his victory. Kirk became the first black mayor of a major Texas city.

Dallas. On May 6, 1995, former Texas Secretary of State Ron Kirk was elected mayor of Dallas. He was the first African American to be elected mayor of a major Texas city. Kirk received 62 percent of the vote, attorney Darrell Jordan received 23 percent, and City Councilman Domingo Garcia got 13 percent. During his campaign, Kirk had promised to bring unity to Dallas and promote business growth.

A severe thunderstorm swept rapidly through Dallas on May 5, killing 17 people and causing hundreds of millions of dollars in damage. The storm was one of the deadliest natural disasters ever to hit the city.

A $175-million municipal bond program was approved by Dallas voters on May 6. The capital improvements program, the city's first in 10 years, would enable the city to repair historic buildings at Fair Park, dredge White Rock Lake, open a new police headquarters building, and repair streets.

SMU names new president. R. Gerald Turner, the 49-year-old chancellor of the University of Mississippi, was selected on January 27 to be Southern Methodist University's 10th president. During his 11-year tenure at "Ole Miss," Turner increased the university's endowment from $8 million to $64 million, doubled minority enrollment, and raised academic standards. Turner succeeded A. Kenneth Pye, who resigned on June 22, 1994, and died of cancer three weeks later.

Trinity River plan. In February, a citizen's committee unveiled a 20-year plan for making the flood-prone Trinity River an economic and recreational asset. The multibillion-dollar program recommended developing a chain of lakes in the flood plains of the Trinity River, constructing a new freeway along the river levees, and setting aside land for parks and high-rise residential development. Project funding would come from local bond programs, the Texas Department of Transportation, the United States Army Corps of Engineers, and private investors.

Public housing controversy. Plans by the Dallas Housing Authority to build 75 public housing units in an affluent Far North Dallas neighborhood drew strong opposition in August. Residents complained that the federally subsidized apartments for low-income tenants would increase crime and reduce property values. The apartment proposal was part of a court-ordered agreement for the housing authority to build at least 474 public housing units in predominantly white North Dallas neighborhoods over the next three years.

Downtown real estate. In October, real estate brokers reported that an additional 285,000 square feet (26,477 square meters) of office space had been leased in downtown Dallas in 1995. In 1994, leased space had declined by over 1 million square feet (92,903 square meters). City officials credited $200-million in downtown improvements for the change.

School board member resigns. Dallas School Board member Dan Peavy resigned on October 5 following the release of secretly recorded tapes of his conversations, which included racist remarks and obscenities. Disclosure of the tapes prompted a Federal Bureau of Investigation probe into illegal wiretapping of school board members' telephones.

J. Erik Jonsson, a former Dallas mayor and the founder of Texas Instruments Corporation, died on August 31 at age 93. He was a key figure in improving the city's tarnished image after the assassination of President John F. Kennedy in Dallas in 1963. Jonsson established the Goals for Dallas program and led efforts to build Dallas/Fort Worth International Airport, the second busiest airport in the world.

Hall of Fame baseball star Mickey Mantle underwent liver transplant surgery at the Baylor University Medical Center in Dallas on June 8. Mantle died on August 13 from cancer that had spread to other parts of his body. His transplant increased public awareness of the need for more organ donors.

Sports. The National Football League (NFL) filed a $300-million lawsuit against Dallas Cowboys owner Jerry Jones on September 18 for alleged violations of NFL licensing rules. Jones had signed separate marketing agreements with Pepsi Cola, Nike, and American Express. Such sponsorships had been under the control of NFL Properties. □ Henry K. Tatum

See also **City.** In *World Book,* see **Dallas.**

Dancing. The plight of New York City's world-famous Joffrey Ballet in 1995 illustrated two major currents in the United States dance world. First, the Joffrey faced the monetary crisis that dance in general faced. And second, the Joffrey's attempt to leave New York City pointed to the decline of New York as the nation's dance capital.

Destination Chicago. No American dance company led a more precarious existence in the early 1990's than The Joffrey Ballet. Hope for a resolution of the 40-year-old troupe's financial problems came on Sept. 7, 1995, when Gerald Arpino, the Joffrey's cofounder and current artistic director, announced that his group was reorganizing as The Joffrey Ballet of Chicago. The troupe, named after the late Robert Joffrey, had always been based in New York City.

The announcement came on the heels of rumors that the Joffrey would fold altogether. The troupe had not performed since January, at Chicago's Auditorium Theater, and no other touring dates were scheduled. They had been negotiating a merger with Ballet Chicago, but that plan fell apart in July.

The new Joffrey Ballet of Chicago, with a budget of $5 million and a roster of thirty dancers, was more modest than its predecessor. By September, they had confirmed touring dates in December at the Kennedy Center in Washington, D.C., and the Dorothy Chandler Pavilion in Los Angeles. Despite those positive signs, however, future prosperity was

in question, because Chicago had never been a city to adequately support even such a small ballet troupe as Ballet Chicago. Observers wondered if the two groups could coexist.

Good-by New York. Because of rising rents for studio spaces and escalating production expenses for performances, several other New York-based groups pulled up stakes in 1995. Critically acclaimed *choreographer* (creator of dances) Susan Marshall left New York for an uncertain destination, and major avant-garde dance figure Laura Dean relocated her group of dancers and musicians to Salisbury, North Carolina.

The exodus from New York also influenced where companies from abroad chose to perform. In 1995, the hub of international dance life was the West Coast. The San Francisco Ballet mounted a festival called United We Dance to celebrate the 50-year anniversary of the signing of the United Nations charter. Between May 9 and 14, a dozen groups from such countries as Australia, Canada, China, Cuba, Denmark, the Netherlands, Russia, and Venezuela each presented a premiere at San Francisco's War Memorial Opera House. The host group, led by Helgi Tomasson, also offered a new work by Mark Morris.

The War Memorial Opera House also housed Britain's Royal Ballet the last week of June, after which the famous group danced in Los Angeles. The Royal Ballet performed several ballets by the late choreographer Frederick Ashton and a new piece by principal dancer Ashley Page. In May, the Royal Danish Ballet performed a radically revised version of the romantic masterpiece *La Sylphide* (1832) at the Orange County Performing Arts Center in Costa Mesa, California.

Financial woes caused the Lar Lubovitch Dance Company of New York City to suspend performances for 1996. However, other troupes collapsed altogether. In the summer of 1995, finances forced the leading exponent of modern dance on the West Coast, Bella Lewitzky, to fold her 30-year-old troupe. The 80-year-old choreographer only wanted to retire, but she could not secure funding for her company to be led by a successor. In the autumn, the highly regarded Ralph Lemon Company of New York also closed.

Twyla Tharp led the pace of choreographic productivity in 1995. She cemented her free-lance relationship with the American Ballet Theater (ABT) of New York City by creating three new works for them. *How Near Heaven,* the story of two women who are opposites, premiered on March 3 at the Kennedy Center for the Performing Arts in Washington, D.C. In contrast to that rather dark work, *Americans We* was a partly satirical, partly affectionate look at the American past, with music by Stephen Foster, Henry Fillmore, and other popular American composers. *Americans We*, along with a collaboration with jazz composer Wynton Marsalis, called *Jump Start,* opened on May 1 during ABT's two-month run at the Metropolitan Opera in New York City. Hubbard Street Dance Chicago performed another Tharp premiere on August 10 at the Jacob's Pillow Dance Festival in Becket, Massachusetts. Titled *I Remember Clifford,* it was a homage to trumpeter Clifford Brown, who died in the 1950's at the age of 26.

New realms. Several major choreographers and companies explored new territories in 1995. The normally experimental choreographer Trisha Brown went to classical musical sources in her choreography of German composer Johann Sebastian Bach's *Musical Offering* (1740's). The dance, titled *M.O.,* was as formally rigorous as Bach's music. It premiered in Brussels in May and had its American debut in New York City in July.

Paul Taylor, usually inspired by the likes of Bach, turned to the frothy French composer Jacques Offenbach for his *Offenbach Overtures,* which opened in October at New York City Center.

The Martha Graham Dance Company, which nearly always performs only the work of the late Graham, commissioned an hour-long piece by the multidisciplinary wizard Robert Wilson. Premiering November 2 at the Kennedy Center in Washington, D.C., Wilson's *Snow on the Mesa* was meant to capture the spiritual essence of Graham. *Snow on the Mesa* was set to Balinese and Balinese-inspired music, reflecting Graham's passion for Eastern art.

The smash hit of the year was also a surprise. It was *West Side Story Suite,* a compendium of dances from Jerome Robbins's choreography for the musical *West Side Story* (1957). The *Suite* was premiered on May 18 by the New York City Ballet during its annual spring season at the New York State Theater and proved as fresh and daring as when the musical first played on Broadway. The City Ballet dancers, famous for their elegant bearing, were unexpectedly adept at Robbins's rough-and-tumble style.

New dance groups. Two new groups debuted in 1995. John Clifford revived his Los Angeles Ballet following a hiatus of 11 years. Obtaining generous backing from a department store chain and other donors, Clifford promised a repertory that included *The Nutcracker* (1892). However, when Clifford failed to launch the production in 1995, he lost much of his funding.

On October 17, a troupe directed by Suzanne Farrell premiered in Washington, D.C., for a one-week run of a program that featured only works by the renowned Russian-American choreographer George Balanchine. Farrell, a favorite ballerina of the late Balanchine, had been openly critical of Peter Martins's direction of the New York City Ballet, the company Balanchine founded. ☐ Nancy Goldner

In *World Book,* see **Ballet; Dancing.**

Dancers face videotapes of deathly ill people talking in *Still/Here,* a dance by choreographer Bill T. Jones that stirred controversy in early 1995.

Deaths in 1995 included those listed below, who were Americans unless otherwise indicated.

Abbott, George F. (1887-January 31),
director, playwright, actor, and producer who was involved in more than
120 productions, including such hits
as *Pal Joey* (1940), *Pajama Game*
(1954), and *Damn Yankees* (1955).

Alfvén, Hannes Olof Gösta (1908-
April 2), Swedish physicist who shared
the Nobel Prize in physics in 1970 for
his studies in plasma physics.

Andrews, Maxine (1916-October 21),
one of the Andrews Sisters, a musical
trio who had one hit song after another in the 1940's.

Aspin, Les, Jr. (1938-May 21), Wisconsin congressman from 1970 to 1992
and former secretary of defense in
the Administration of President Bill
Clinton.

Ballantine, Ian (1916-March 9), publisher who helped introduce paper-
back books to the United States as
founder of Penguin U.S.A., Bantam
Books, and Ballantine Books.

Belladonna, Giorgio (1923?-May 12),
Italian bridge player regarded as one
of the greatest bridge players ever.

Bolt, Robert (1924-February 20), British
playwright and screenwriter who won
two Academy Awards for his screenplay adaptations for *Doctor Zhivago*
(1965) and *A Man for All Seasons* (1966).

Botvinnik, Mikhail (1911-May 5), Russian chess
grand master who held the title of world chess
champion during most of the 1950's.

Brett, Jeremy (Peter Jeremy Huggins) (1935-Septem-
ber 12), British stage and television actor known for
his portrayal of Sherlock Holmes.

Burger, Warren E. (1907-June 25), chief justice of
the United States Supreme Court from 1969 to
1986, known for helping to reverse the liberal
direction of the court under his predecessor, Earl
Warren.

Butenandt, Adolph (1903-January 18), German
scientist who did pioneering research on sex hormones. He shared the Nobel Prize in chemistry in
1939, but because of the Nazi regime, could not
claim it until after World War II (1939-1945).

Cahill, Margaret G. (1905?-October 1), winner of
the first Miss America beauty pageant in 1921.

Chandrasekhar, Subrahmanyan (1910-August 21),
astrophysicist who shared the Nobel Prize for physics in 1983 for his findings on how stars evolve.

Chen Yun (1906?-April 10), Chinese Communist
leader who was one of the founders of the People's
Republic of China.

Cook, Elisha, Jr. (1907-May 18), character actor

Doug McClure, television actor and rodeo star.

Elizabeth Montgomery, television actress.

Subrahmanyan Chandrasekhar, Nobel-winning astrophysicist.

Warren Burger, former U.S. chief justice.

known for his memorable roles in such film classics
as *The Maltese Falcon* (1941), *The Big Sleep* (1946),
The Killing (1956), and *Shane* (1953).

Cosell, Howard (Howard William Cohen) (1918-April
23), sports broadcaster best known for his announcing on television's "Monday Night Football."

Crosby, Gary (1933-August 24), singer and actor best
remembered for the duets he recorded with his
father, Bing Crosby.

Day, Leon (1916-March 13), baseball Hall of Famer
who was known as both an outstanding pitcher and
hitter in the Negro leagues in the 1930's and 1940's.

Delany, Annie Elizabeth "Bessie" (1891-Septem-
ber 25), co-author (with her sister Sarah Delaney)
of the best-selling memoir *Having Our Say: The
Delaney Sisters' First 100 Years* (1993), a memoir
about growing up black before the civil rights era.

Eisenstaedt, Alfred (1898-August 23), photographer
known for capturing spontaneous moments in history while working as a staff photographer for *Life*
magazine from 1936 until 1972.

Egan, Eddie (1930-November 4), New York City
Police detective, better known by his nickname,
Popeye Doyle, whose career inspired the 1971
motion picture *The French Connection*.

William Kunstler, noted defense lawyer.

Jonas Salk, famed medical researcher.

Selena, popular Tejano singer.

Mickey Mantle, New York Yankee slugger.

Gabor, Eva (1921-July 4), Hungarian-born television and motion-picture actress best known for her role in the TV series "Green Acres."

Garcia, Jerry (1942-August 9), guitarist and vocalist with the Grateful Dead, one of rock music's most popular and longest-lasting groups.

Godunov, Alexander (1949-May 18), Soviet ballet star who defected in 1979 while touring with the Bolshoi Ballet and later became a motion-picture actor, appearing in such films as *Witness* (1985) and *Die Hard* (1989).

Gonzales, Pancho (Richard Alonzo Gonzales) (1928-July 3), tennis professional considered one of the greatest players in the game's history.

Grinkov, Sergei (1967-November 20), figure-skating champion who, with his skating partner and wife, Ekaterina Gordeeva, won two Olympic gold medals.

Hazen, Lita Annenberg (1909-October 2), philanthropist who contributed to medical and scientific programs and cultural institutions.

Hemphill, Julius (1938?-April 2), jazz composer and saxophonist who helped found the World Saxophone Quartet.

Herriot, James (James Alfred Wight) (1916-February 23), Scottish-born author who wrote *All Creatures Great and Small* (1972) and other best-selling books about the life of a country veterinarian.

Hobby, Oveta Culp (1905-August 16), organizer of the Women's Auxiliary Army Corps (WAC's), during World War II; the first Secretary of Health, Education, and Welfare in the Cabinet of Dwight D. Eisenhower; and an executive at *The Houston Post.*

Holman, Nat (1896-February 12), basketball player and coach who was elected to the National Basketball Hall of Fame in 1964.

Home of the Hirsel, Lord (Sir Alec Douglas-Home) (1903-October 9), British prime minister in 1963 and 1964.

Hoon, Shannon (1967-October 21), lead singer for the rock group Blind Melon.

Horgan, Paul (1903-March 8), writer who won two Pulitzer Prizes for history and biography and wrote novels set in the Southwest.

Hunter, Howard W. (1907-March 3), religious leader who became president of the Church of Jesus Christ of Latter-day Saints in 1994.

Ives, Burl (1909-April 14), folk singer and actor known for his recordings of such songs as "The Blue Tail Fly" and "A Little Bitty Tear" and for his

Elkin, Stanley (1930-May 31), novelist and short-story writer known for such critically acclaimed works as *Criers and Kibitzers, Kibitzers and Criers* (1966) and *George Mills* (1982).

Ferrell, Rick (1905-July 27), baseball catcher elected to the Hall of Fame in 1984; held the American League record for most games caught for 41 years.

Finley, Murray H. (1922-July 31), textile union president known for his innovative campaign to organize the J. P. Stevens Company in the 1970's.

Finney, Jack (1911-November 16), science fiction writer whose novels included *Time After Time* and *The Body Snatchers*.

Flores, Lola (1923-March 16), Spanish singer and actress who helped popularize flamenco dancing.

Fowler, William A. (1911-March 14), astrophysicist who shared the Nobel Prize in physics in 1983 for his contribution to the theory that the heavy elements originated in the cores of stars as the stars evolved.

Fulbright, J. William (1905-February 9), United States Senator from Arkansas from 1945 to 1974 who was chairman of the Senate Foreign Relations Committee from 1959 to 1974. He sponsored the Fulbright Act of 1946, which established the Fulbright Scholarship.

Academy Award-winning role in *The Big Country* (1958).

Kennedy, Rose (1890-January 22), matriarch of the Kennedy family; the wife of multimillionaire investor Joseph P. Kennedy and the mother of John F. Kennedy, the 35th President of the United States, and Robert F. and Edward M. Kennedy, both of whom became U.S. senators.

Keyes, Jimmy (1930?-July 22), singer and songwriter who helped write "Sh-Boom," the song that made his group, the Chords, the first rhythm-and-blues group to reach pop music's Top 10.

Kirby, George (1924-September 30), Black comedian who was known for his impressions of many male and female celebrities.

Koch, Howard (1902-August 17), writer best known for winning the Academy Award in 1943 for his screenplay for *Casablanca* (1942) and his radio script for Orson Welles's broadcast adaptation of H. G. Wells's *War of the Worlds* (1938).

Köhler, Georges J. F. (1946-March 1), West German-born biochemist who shared the Nobel Prize in physiology or medicine in 1984 for developing a technique to produce clones of antibodies.

Kuhn, Maggie (1905-April 22), the founder of the Gray Panthers, an advocacy organization for the elderly.

Kunstler, William (1919-September 4), lawyer noted for representing political dissidents and unpopular criminal defendants.

Kurtz, Efrem (1900-June 27), Russian-born music director of the Houston Symphony,1948 to 1954, and of the Liverpool Symphony from 1955 to 1957.

Lamont, Corliss (1902-April 26), radical socialist author and former director of the American Civil Liberties Union and the National Emergency Civil Liberties Committee.

Lindfors, Viveca (1921-October 25), Swedish actress who had starring roles in a number of American films.

Lowe, Edward (1920-October 4), Multimillionaire whose fortune came from the invention of Kitty Litter.

Lubin, Arthur (1899?-May 11), director of Abbot and Costello comedies in the 1940's; "Francis the Talking Mule" films after World War II; and the television series, "Mr. Ed," in the early 1960's.

Lupino, Ida (1918-August 3), British-born motion-picture actress and director who starred in such films as *They Drive by Night* (1940) and *High Sierra* (1941) and later became one of Hollywood's first woman directors.

Mantle, Mickey (1931-August 13), baseball player who starred with the

New York Yankees from 1951 through 1968, retiring with 536 home runs in regular season play and a record 18 home runs in World Series play; voted into the National Baseball Hall of Fame in 1974.

Malle, Louis (1932-November 23), French New Wave motion-picture director who went on to direct films in the United States.

Martin, Dean (1917-December 25), pop crooner and motion-picture and television star who first hit it big in show business in the late 1940's after pairing up with comedian Jerry Lewis.

McClure, Doug (1935-February 5), rodeo bronco-buster and television actor who starred in the TV series "The Virginian."

McQueen, Butterfly (1911-December 22), black actress best known for her role as the slave Prissy in the movie *Gone with the Wind.*

Merrill, James (1926-February 6), Pulitzer Prize-winning poet, novelist, and playwright.

Monette, Paul (1945-February 10), author who won the National Book Award in 1992 for his autobiography *Becoming a Man: Half a Life Story.*

Montgomery, Elizabeth (1938-May 18), television actress who played a witch in the popular comedy series "Bewitched" from 1964 to 1972.

Pancho Gonzales, tennis star.

Lana Turner, motion-picture actress.

Donald Pleasence, British film, stage, and TV actor.

Jerry Garcia, rock-music legend.

Deaths

Nearing, Helen K. (1904?-September 17), author who with her husband, Scott, helped inspire the back-to-the-land movement of the 1970's.

Nelson, Lindsey (1919-June 10), sports broadcaster known for his play-by-play announcing of Notre Dame football and New York Mets baseball.

Okada, Eiji (1920?-September 14), Japanese motion-picture actor who starrred in several foreign films, including *Hiroshima Mon Amour* (1959).

Penick, Harvey (1904-April 2), golf instructor who authored a book on golf tips that became the best-selling sports book in history.

Perry, Frank (1930-August 29), motion-picture director best known for *David and Lisa* (1962).

Perry, Fred (1909-February 2), British tennis player who won the Wimbledon singles title in 1934, 1935, and 1936 and who became the first male player to win all four grand-slam titles, though not in the same year.

Pleasence, Donald (1919-February 2), British actor who won critical acclaim for his role in the Harold Pinter play *The Caretaker* (1960) and who was often cast as a villain in stage and film roles.

Pullen, Don (1942?-April 22), jazz pianist known for his avant-garde style.

Rabin, Yitzhak (1922-November 4), prime minister of Israel, who shared the Nobel Peace Prize in 1994 for achieving a peace accord with the Palestinian Liberation Organization.

Redenbacher, Orville (1907?-September 19), farmer and businessman who created a gourmet-popcorn company.

Reston, James B. (1909-December 6), long-time columnist and editor for *The New York Times*.

Rich, Charlie (1932-July 25), country music singer and songwriter known for his 1973 hits "Behind Closed Doors" and "The Most Beautiful Girl."

Richardson, Ron (1952-April 5), musical theater actor who won a Tony award in 1985 as best supporting actor in *Big River* (1985).

Riggs, Bobby (1918-October 25), tennis star of the 1930's and 1940's who made a famous comeback appearance against Billie Jean King at the Houston Astrodome in September 1973, a match he lost to her in straight sets.

Rodger, George (1908-July 25), British photojournalist known for his coverage of World War II for *Life* magazine and as a co-founder of the Magnum photo agency.

Rogers, Ginger (Virginia Katherine McMath) (1911-April 25), actress who won the Academy Award for best actress for her role in *Kitty Foyle* (1940) but was best known for her dancing collaboration with Fred Astaire in film musicals during the 1930's.

Rudolf, Max (1902-February 28), German-born conductor and teacher who was the music director of the Cincinnati Symphony in Ohio from 1958 to 1970.

Salk, Jonas E. (1914-June 23), research scientist celebrated for developing the first effective vaccine against poliomyelitis in the early 1950's.

Sarton, May (1912-July 16), Belgian-born American writer known for her novels, poetry, and personal memoirs which won her acclaim from feminists.

Scali, John A. (1918-October 9), former ABC News correspondent who, as a go-between, played a key role in resolving the Cuban missile crisis in 1962.

Scribner, Charles, Jr. (1921-November 11), head of the Charles Scribner's Sons publishing house from 1952 until its acquisition in 1984.

Selena (Selena Quintanilla Perez) (1971-March 31), singer who was regarded as one of the leading voices of Tejano music, a mixture of Mexican ranchera, polka, and country music.

William Fulbright, former U.S. senator.

Orville Redenbacher, popcorn magnate.

Burl Ives, folk singer and actor.

Ginger Rogers, dancer and movie actress.

Smith, Margaret Chase (1897-May 29), Maine Republican who became the first woman elected to both houses of Congress; she served in the House of Representatives from 1940 to 1948 and in the Senate from 1949 to 1972 where she was known as a staunch opponent of Senator Joseph McCarthy.

Souphanouvong, Prince (1902-January 9), Laotian leader who rejected the monarchy to become a leader of the Communist Pathet Lao guerrillas and was elected president of Laos in 1975.

Southern, Terry (1924-October 29), novelist and screenwriter whose film credits included the scripts for *Dr. Strangelove* and *Easy Rider*.

Spender, Sir Stephen (1909-July 16), English poet, critic, and novelist and one of the so-called Oxford poets, a group led by W. H. Auden.

Stennis, John C. (1901-April 23), Mississippi Democrat who served in the U.S. Senate for over 41 years, the second-longest Senate term in U.S. history.

Stoner, Arthur (1970?-March 17), the first African American to win the bronco riding championship of the International Professional Rodeo Association.

Rose Kennedy, matriarch of the Kennedy clan.

Howard Cosell, TV sportscaster.

Lord Harold Wilson, two-time UK prime minister.

Ida Lupino, British-born film actress.

Swayze, John Cameron (1906-August 15), news broadcaster who became one of television's first news anchors.

Towers, Robert (1923?-May 2), novelist best known for *The Necklace of Kali* (1960) and *The Summoning* (1983).

Turner, Lana (1920-June 29), motion-picture actress who won critical acclaim for her role in *The Postman Always Rings Twice* (1946).

Veach, Charles Lacy (1944-October 3), astronaut who participated in two space shuttle flights in 1991 and 1992.

Walker, Junior (Autry DeWalt, Jr.) (1942-November 23), saxophonist and leader of the Motown group Junior Walker and the All Stars.

Walton, Ernest Thomas Sinton (1903-June 25), Irish nuclear physicist who shared the Nobel Prize in physics in 1951 for his work on changing atomic nuclei by bombarding them with particles.

Wayne, David (Wayne McKeekan) (1914-February 9), stage, motion-picture, and television actor who received the first Tony Award for best actor for his role in *Finian's Rainbow* (1947).

White, Ronnie (1939-August 26), pop music singer who helped found the Motown group, Smokey Robinson and the Miracles, and co-author of the hit song "My Girl."

White, Slappy (Melvin White) (1921-November 7), African American comedian who was among the first group of black comics to perform before white audiences.

Whitten, Jamie (1910-September 9), congressman from Mississippi who served in the House of Representatives for 53 years, longer than any other member of congress.

Wigner, Eugene P. (1902-January 1), Hungarian-born physicist who shared the Nobel Prize in physics in 1963 for his contributions to the study of atomic nuclei and the complex behavior of electrons.

Wilson, Lord Harold (1916-May 24), prime minister of the United Kingdom from 1964 to 1970 and from 1974 to 1976 and leader of Britain's Labour Party from 1963 to 1976.

Wolfman Jack (Robert Smith) (1938?-July 1), legendary radio disk jockey immortalized in the 1973 motion picture *American Graffiti*.

Wood, Evelyn (1909-August 26), founder of the Evelyn Wood Reading Dynamics Institute known for teaching speed-reading techniques.

Woodcock, George (1912-January 28), Canadian author best known for his works on anarchism.

Yglesias, José (1920-November 7), novelist, journalist, and playwright who wrote extensively about Latin Americans caught up in revolutions.

Democratic Party

Democratic Party. The Democrats, struggling against Republican domination of Congress, suffered setbacks in 1995. Democrats groped for a successful strategy to counter congressional Republicans, who pushed through legislation to slash federal spending and cut taxes in carrying out their 1994 Contract with America. President Bill Clinton seemed eclipsed by Grand Old Party (GOP) leaders, who were in control of Congress for the first time in 40 years, but vowed to use his veto to protect Medicare and education programs from Republican budget cuts.

New party leaders. The Democratic Party selected new leaders in 1995 at a meeting on January 20 and 21 in Washington, D.C., the first gathering of top Democrats since the Republican avalanche at the polls the previous November. Senator Christopher Dodd of Connecticut, an articulate liberal, was selected as general chairman of the party. Donald Fowler, a former state party leader in South Carolina, was named national chairman and operating officer. The two men replaced David Wilhelm, who stepped down late in 1994 under fire for the party's poor election performance.

Nebraska Senator Bob Kerrey, a moderate Democrat, was named by Senate Minority Leader Thomas A. Daschle of South Dakota to run the Democratic Senatorial Campaign Committee and raise funds for the 1996 elections. A major debate surrounding the elections was whether the Democrats should stick to their past policies or move toward the political center in hopes of recapturing voters' loyalties. Massachusetts Senator Edward M. Kennedy, a leading liberal, said the Democrats should not abandon their basic beliefs. "If we become pale carbon copies of the opposition and try to act like Republicans, we will lose, and we will deserve to lose," he said on Jan. 11, 1995, at the National Press Club. However, President Clinton and other members of Congress read the 1994 election results as a call for more centrist policies.

Democratic defectors. Some Democrats decided to leave their party and join the Republicans in what many saw as a sign of political realignment, especially in the South and Southwest. Senator Ben Nighthorse Campbell of Colorado switched from Democrat to Republican, following the example of Richard Shelby of Alabama, who did the same in 1994. In the House of Representatives, Nathan Deal of Georgia, Greg Laughlin of Texas, Mike Parker of Mississippi, and James Hayes and W. J. (Billy) Tauzin of Louisiana all defected to the Republican Party.

Party resignations. In another sign of party disarray, eight Democrats in the Senate announced that they would not run for reelection in 1996. Among the dropouts were Senator Bill Bradley of New Jersey and Senator Sam Nunn of Georgia, both of whom were regarded as possible presidential contenders. Bradley hinted that he might run as an in-

Jesse Jackson, Jr., flanked by his family, in November wins the Democratic primary for the congressional seat vacated by Mel Reynolds. In December, Jackson was elected to Congress.

dependent. Other senators who decided to retire were David Pryor of Arkansas, Claiborne Pell of Rhode Island, Howell Heflin of Alabama, J. Bennett Johnston of Louisiana, Jim Exon of Nebraska, and Paul Simon of Illinois. The impending departures offered the GOP an opportunity to increase its 54-46 majority in the Senate.

Prominent Representative Pat Schroeder of Colorado, in her 12th House term, also announced that she would not seek reelection in 1996. Representative Norman Y. Mineta of California resigned on October 10, after 20 years in Congress. Mineta left to take a job as an executive at Lockheed Martin Corporation, the largest U.S. defense contractor.

Clinton files for reelection. Despite the GOP surge, President Clinton formally filed reelection papers on April 14, indicating that he and Vice President Albert Gore, Jr., would run again in 1996. The political picture was clouded, however, when Texas billionaire Ross Perot announced on September 25 that he would form a third party to back a presidential candidate. But at year's end, polls showed that Clinton had a positive approval rating from the American public and led Senate Majority Leader Bob Dole in the presidential race.

A few victories. Not all Democrats were dispirited in 1995, however. Chicago Mayor Richard M. Daley on April 4 won reelection to a second term with 60 percent of the vote. Illinois Attorney General Roland W. Burris, an independent running against Daley, polled 36 percent in an election marked by a record low turnout.

In Maryland, Democratic county executive Parris N. Glendening narrowly defeated his Republican opponent, Ellen Sauerbrey, in the governor's race. Official results gave Glendening a winning margin of 5,993 votes out of 1.4 million ballots cast. Sauerbrey's legal challenge of the election results was rejected by a Maryland circuit judge on January 13.

Scandal touched some prominent Democrats in 1995. Illinois Representative Mel Reynolds was convicted on August 22 of having a sexual relationship in 1992 with a 16-year-old campaign volunteer, soliciting a minor for pornography, and obstructing justice. Reynolds resigned from Congress and was sentenced to five years in prison.

Former Ohio Representative Mary Rose Oakar was indicted on February 22 on federal felony charges of filing false financial reports and lying to the Federal Election Commission about her campaign practices. Oakar pleaded not guilty to the charges and was awaiting trial at year-end.

California Representative Walter Tucker III in December resigned from Congress after he was convicted of extortion and tax evasion. He had engaged in those activities while he was mayor of Compton, California. □ William J. Eaton

See also **Clinton, Bill; Congress; Elections; Republican Party.** In *World Book,* see **Democratic Party.**

Denmark continued to enjoy one of Europe's strongest economies in 1995. The economics ministry forecast growth of 3.8 percent for the year, which was weaker than the exceptionally strong 4.5 percent rate recorded in 1994 but still more than the 2.7 percent average growth of the 15-nation European Union (EU). Strong increases in consumer spending, corporate investment, and exports fueled the economy. The buoyant growth led to the first sustained fall in the unemployment rate since before the recession of the early 1990's. The government estimated that the jobless rate averaged 10.2 percent for 1995, down from 12.1 percent in 1994.

Welfare cuts. The government in 1995 introduced cuts in social welfare programs designed to reduce the government deficit, sustain economic growth over the long term, and encourage people on benefits to seek work. Before the cutbacks, unemployed people were allowed to receive up to 11,000 crowns ($2,000) per month for up to nine years and were under no obligation to accept job offers. The measures, which Danish Prime Minister Poul Nyrup Rasmussen proposed on October 3, would limit unemployment benefits to six months for people under age 25, require youths and the long-term unemployed to accept government-generated jobs or enter educational programs after their benefits expire, and limit eligibility for early retirement. The Danish parliament approved the cuts in December.

Nuclear debate. Rasmussen in 1995 was one of Europe's fiercest critics of France's decision to resume nuclear testing. Some observers suggested that his critical stance undermined the bid by Uffe Ellemann-Jensen, leader of Denmark's opposition Liberal Party, to become secretary-general of NATO, because France did not support the bid. Foreign Minister Javier Solana Madariaga of Spain became NATO's secretary-general on December 20.

Outspoken commissioner. Ritt Bjerregaard, Denmark's representative on the EU Commission, one of the EU's five governing bodies, attracted notoriety in 1995 by criticizing several European leaders in a book concerning her life on the commission. Bjerregaard withdrew the book from publication, but several newspapers published its contents anyway. Among her comments was that Jacques Chirac was unfit to be president of France.

Minister convicted. Erik Ninn-Hansen, a former justice minister, received a four-month suspended sentence on June 22 after undergoing the country's first impeachment trial in 85 years. Ninn-Hansen was found guilty of illegally preventing Tamil refugees in Denmark from bringing their families to join them. The refugee scandal had brought down the government of Poul Schlueter in 1993. □ Tom Buerkle

See also **Europe** (Facts in brief table). In *World Book,* see **Denmark; European Union.**

Detroit. In 1995, Detroit's battered image finally saw some improvement. The city leapfrogged on *Money* magazine's annual list of America's 300 best places to live, jumping from 295 to 56. The magazine cited Detroit's lower unemployment rate and better income tax collection rate as examples of an improved quality of life.

Economic development projects. Detroit Mayor Dennis W. Archer, in the second year of his first term, achieved some success in pitching economic development projects for the city's federal empowerment zone. The empowerment zone designation, awarded by President Bill Clinton's Administration in late 1994, qualified Detroit for $100 million in grants for social service projects and $225 million in tax breaks for business owners in an 18-square-mile (47-square-kilometer) area of the city. Industrial powerhouses like the Chrysler Corporation and General Motors Corporation announced plans to either create or expand operations in Detroit.

The violent death of a Detroit woman made front-page headlines around the world. In the early morning hours of August 19, as a crowd looked on, a Detroit man beat motorist Deletha Word, 33, after a traffic altercation on the Belle Isle bridge. Apparently frightened that her attacker would continue the brutal beating, Word jumped from the bridge into the Detroit River, where she drowned.

The death, and the fact that dozens of spectators did nothing to stop the beating, sparked local and international outrage and embarrassed Detroit. Word's alleged assailant, Martell Welch, Jr., 19, was charged with second-degree murder. At a rally held near the bridge weeks after the attack, Detroit leaders promoted community activism and lauded two men who jumped into the Detroit River in an attempt to save Word's life.

Newspaper strike. On July 13, more than 2,500 employees of Detroit's daily newspapers went on strike. Members of six unions walked away from their jobs at *The Detroit News* and the *Detroit Free Press* after talks with the papers broke down. The papers' owners said the unions wanted the companies to continue outmoded and ineffective business practices. But union officials accused management of union busting and filed a complaint with the National Labor Relations Board. In a preliminary finding, the board supported some contentions of the union's unfair labor practices complaint.

Several of the papers' journalists crossed the picket line, and the papers hired replacement workers for many of the workers who took part in the bitter strike, which quickly turned violent. Police officers clashed with striking workers on picket lines at the papers' downtown Detroit and suburban printing plants, resulting in injuries to both parties. Mayor Archer and a suburban mayor strongly called for a resolution of the labor dispute, but at year's end little progress had been made.

Casino rejected. Michigan Governor John Engler in June rejected a proposal that would have established an American Indian-run downtown Detroit casino. Engler questioned casino gambling's effectiveness as a tool for economic development and said that he believed the process for establishing the casino was flawed. He said he also feared that approving casino gambling for Detroit would open the floodgates for other Michigan cities that wanted to open gambling outlets.

Detroit voters blasted Engler for his decision. Supporters of the casino project staged a boycott of the Michigan lottery in retaliation, but state officials said the boycott had little impact on lottery sales.

Sports. In June, the Detroit Red Wings went to the National Hockey League's Stanley Cup finals for the first time since 1966. They lost the championship to the New Jersey Devils in four straight games.

Long-stalled plans to build a new major league baseball stadium in downtown Detroit inched closer to reality in 1995. State officials approved a $55-million grant to help construct the proposed ballpark, which would be built closer to the city's center than the Tigers' current home. The Detroit City Council also approved plans to build the $240-million stadium. In other Tigers news, Sparky Anderson retired after 17 years as the team's manager.

☐ Kimberly Trent

See also **City.** In *World Book,* see **Detroit.**

Dini, Lamberto (1931-   ), a banker with no political party affiliation, was appointed prime minister of Italy by its president, Oscar Scalfaro, on Jan. 13, 1995. The year before, Dini had been appointed treasury minister in the government of Prime Minister Silvio Berlusconi, who resigned in December 1994 after his governing coalition broke down amid corruption charges. Dini inherited a troubled economy, with a weakening lira and a budget deficit of nearly $100 billion, one of Europe's highest. He pledged to pass legislation to trim Italy's huge pension system, reduce the budget deficit, and reform the election process. Dini ran into growing political opposition in 1995 and resigned at year-end.

Dini, a native of Florence, was born on March 1, 1931. He earned a degree in economics and commerce from Florence University and went on to study at the University of Michigan and the University of Minnesota. He joined the staff of the International Monetary Fund (IMF), an agency of the United Nations, as an economist in 1959. In 1976, he became the Italian representative on the IMF's executive committee, and in 1979 he became director-general of the Bank of Italy. Dini continued in 1995 to hold the post of treasury minister concurrently with his duties as prime minister.

Dini and his wife, Donatella, have one child.

☐ Lisa Klobuchar

Dinosaur. See Paleontology.

Disabled. Actor Christopher Reeve, best known for the title role in the movie *Superman,* was thrown from his horse on May 27, 1995, during a riding competition in Culpeper, Virginia. The accident shattered his first and second vertebrae, located at the base of the skull, paralyzing him from the neck down. On June 5, he underwent surgery to fuse the vertebrae, and a few days later he could sit up in bed with assistance and move his head slightly. Nevertheless, he depended upon a ventilator to breathe. Over the following months, he regained only slight movement in his neck and shoulders.

But on October 16, Reeve was able to make a short speech at his first public appearance, a dinner honoring fellow actor Robin Williams, who had visited him in the hospital shortly after the accident. Reeve appeared in an automated wheelchair that he controlled by blowing through a tube. Doctors said he would spend the rest of his life in a wheelchair.

Memorial controversy. After decades of delay, construction began in October 1994 on a memorial in Washington, D.C., to Franklin Delano Roosevelt, America's 32nd President. But in 1995, the National Organization on Disability (NOD) and some historians objected that none of the 10 memorial sculptures of the President would show him in a wheelchair, with crutches, braces, or a cane. He used the devices throughout his presidency because he had been paralyzed by polio years before his first inauguration in 1933. NOD wanted the memorial redesigned so at least one of the three free-standing statues would reflect the President as he was in life. They said they wanted future generations to know that Roosevelt was disabled and that it would be historically inaccurate to do otherwise.

But members of the Roosevelt family, the Memorial Commission, and the designer, Lawrence Halprin of San Francisco, disagreed. They said that to depict him in a wheelchair or with leg braces would be a disservice to his memory. Roosevelt, the only U.S. President elected to four terms, died in office in 1945. Curtis Dall Roosevelt, the President's oldest grandson and a commission member said, "He was a very private person and went to great lengths to avoid any discussion or comment on any illness that might be plaguing him."

Congress began planning for a memorial in 1955, but did not appropriate any funds until 1990. The memorial cost $52 million, but the commission had to raise $10 million in private donations. The memorial was scheduled for completion by spring 1997.

Defining disability. Genetic test results that reveal a potential for developing a disease cannot be used to deny a person employment, according to a new manual released on March 15, 1995, by the Equal Employment Opportunity Commission. Doing so, it said, would be discriminatory under the 1990 Americans With Disabilities Act.   □ Carol L. Hanson

In *World Book,* see **Disabled.**

Disasters. The natural disaster that claimed the most lives in 1995 was an earthquake that struck the city of Kobe, Japan, on January 17, killing more than 5,400 people and injuring about 26,000. Disasters that resulted in 25 or more deaths in 1995 included the following:

Aircraft crashes

January 11—Near Cartagena, Colombia. A 9-year-old girl was the sole survivor of an airplane crash that killed 52 people.

March 31—Near Bucharest, Romania. A Romanian airliner reportedly exploded in midair after taking off from Bucharest, the capital, killing all 49 passengers and 10 crew members.

August 9—Near San Salvador, El Salvador. A Guatemalan airliner crashed into the Chichontepec volcano, killing all 65 people on board.

September 13—Near Colombo, Sri Lanka. A military transport plane crashed into the sea, killing all 75 troops and crew members on board.

September 15—Tawau, Borneo. An airliner overshot the runway while attempting to land and burst into flames, killing 34 of the 53 people on board.

November 8—Central Argentina. All 53 people aboard an Argentine air force plane died when the plane crashed head-on at night into a hill and exploded in flames.

November 13—Kaduna, Nigeria. A Nigerian Air-

An injured passenger is carried from the wreckage of one of two trains that collided in Firozabad, India, on August 20, killing more than 300 people.

Disasters

ways plane crashed while landing at Kaduna airport. Sources at the airport reported that as many as 80 of the 138 people aboard died, but the government insisted that the death toll was much lower.

December 6—Near Khabarovsk, Russia. A plane en route from Sakhalin Island off the Pacific coast of Russia crashed, killing 97 people aboard.

December 18—Zaire, Africa. An old Lockheed Electra crashed in Zaire, killing 139 people.

December 20—near Cali, Colombia. An American Airlines jet flew into a mountain as it approached Cali, killing all but 4 of the 164 people aboard.

Earthquakes

January 17—Kobe, Japan. A devastating earthquake struck Kobe, Japan, a port city of 1.5 million people, killing more than 5,400 people and injuring more than 26,000 others. More than 300,000 people were left homeless. It was the most lethal quake to strike Japan since a 1923 quake destroyed Tokyo.

May 28—Sakhalin Island, Russia. A magnitude-7.5 earthquake flattened the town of Neftegorsk and killed about 2,000 people.

June 15—Egion, Greece. At least 25 people were killed when an earthquake with a magnitude of 6.1 hit the town of Egion, Greece.

October 1—Dinar, Turkey. A magnitude-6.0 earthquake damaged or destroyed nearly half of the city's 4,000 buildings, killing at least 73 people.

October 7—Sumatra, Indonesia. An earthquake with a magnitude of 7.0 killed at least 80 people and injured more than 2,000.

October 9—Manzanillo, Mexico. A 7.6-magnitude quake rocked Manzanillo and other cities and towns in the Pacific coast states of Colima and Jalisco. At least 51 people were killed.

October 24—Yunnan Province, China. A magnitude-6.6 earthquake killed more than 50 people and seriously injured at least 800. An estimated 170,000 people were left homeless.

Explosions and fires

February 15—Taichung, Taiwan. A fire broke out in a night club-restaurant complex in the central Taiwan city of Taichung. At least 64 people were killed. Police said a locked back door and the absence of a fire escape contributed to the death toll.

April 28—Taegu, South Korea. At a subway construction site, a welding torch in use near a leaking gas main touched off an explosion that killed at least 100 people and injured more than 200 others. At least half of those killed were students who were on their way to school.

August 21—Yongin, South Korea. Police said that female inmates of a correctional facility in Yongin, South Korea, set fire to a dormitory room in a bid to escape, but barred windows and locked exits trapped the inmates, killing 37 people and injuring about 20 others.

Apartment buildings in Neftegorsk, Russia, lie in total ruin after the town was struck by an earthquake on May 28 that killed nearly 2,000 people.

October 28—Baku, Azerbaijan. More than 300 people died and about 200 were injured when an electrical malfunction caused a subway train in Baku to catch fire.

December 23—Mandi Dabwali, India. More than 500 people, many of them mothers and their children, died when a fire broke out at a school ceremony. The victims were trapped by a high brick wall.

Mine disasters

March 26—Sorgun, Turkey. At least 36 miners were killed by an explosion and cave-in in a coal mine in the town of Sorgun.

May 10—Near Orkney, South Africa. More than 100 gold miners were crushed to death in one of South Africa's largest gold mines when safety mechanisms reportedly failed and a train plunged into an elevator shaft, crushing an elevator that held the miners. The accident was one of the worst mining disasters in South Africa's history.

Shipwrecks

March 2—Near Sumbe, Angola. More than 100 people drowned after an Angolan ship sailing along the coast ran aground in high winds and sank.

June 18—Off western Bangladesh. About 50 people drowned after a passenger ferry collided with a car ferry and sank.

July 1—Off the coast of Cameroon. More than 100 people drowned when a passenger ship sank in rough waters.

August 15—Off eastern Bangladesh. At least 50 people died when an overcrowded river ferry sank.

August 28—Off the coast of Eritrea. Eighty people drowned and another 51 were missing after a ferry sank in the Red Sea.

August 30—Off the coast of Yemen. Ninety-two people were reported drowned after a wooden boat sank in bad weather.

September 11—Bararighat, India. At least 40 people died when a ferry in the Ganges River hit a bridge pillar and sank.

Storms and floods

January 29-February 1—Northwestern Europe. Floodwaters triggered by heavy rains and melting snow killed 29 people.

May 17—Bay of Bengal, Bangladesh. A monsoon storm caused flooding that killed at least 41 people.

July 5—Hunan province, China. Chinese officials reported that the worst flooding in 40 years claimed the lives of about 400 people.

August 20—Near Marrakesh, Morocco. Moroccan officials said 141 people died in flash floods in areas south of Marrakesh.

August 27—Boryong County, South Korea. Typhoon Janis lashed the southern half of the Korean peninsula, killing 41 people in landslides and floods.

Train wrecks

March 13—East of Addis Ababa, Ethiopia. At least 25 people died when a train carrying about 300 passengers ran off a damaged bridge and plunged into a ravine.

May 14—Near Salem, India. More than 50 people were killed and dozens injured when an express train collided with a cargo train.

August 20—Firozabad, India. More than 300 people were killed and more than 400 others were injured when an express train crashed into a stopped train.

December 21—near Cairo, Egypt. A high-speed commuter train slammed into a passenger train in early-morning fog, killing at least 75 people. It was Egypt's worst train wreck in more than 15 years.

Other disasters

April 15—Near Cairo, Egypt. A bus collided with a train about 36 miles (58 kilometers) north of Cairo, the capital of Egypt, killing 42 bus passengers and injuring 45 others.

June 29—Seoul, South Korea. A five-story shopping mall in Seoul, the capital of South Korea, collapsed, killing more than 500 people and injuring more than 900 others.

July—Chicago. A near-record heat wave contributed to the deaths of at least 733 people, according to the Chicago Public Health Department.

Dornan, Robert K. (1933-   ), Republican congressman from California, announced his candidacy for the Republican presidential nomination in April 1995. Dornan, a fiery and outspoken ultraconservative who has expressed opposition to abortion and civil rights for homosexuals, said his campaign would stress moral issues. Throughout his political career, Dornan has been an advocate of a strong military. On Jan. 25, 1995, he was censured by House Republicans for saying that President Clinton "gave aid and comfort to the enemy" by protesting the Vietnam War and avoiding military service.

Dornan was born in New York City on April 3, 1933, and moved with his family to California at the age of 10. He attended Loyola University in Westchester, California, but left to join the Air Force in 1953. He became a fighter pilot and has flown nearly every type of plane in the U.S. arsenal.

Dornan was active in the civil rights movement in the 1960's. From 1965 to 1976, he produced and hosted public affairs shows on radio and television, winning Emmy Awards in 1968 and 1969. In 1973, he ran for mayor of Los Angeles but lost. He was elected to Congress in 1976. Dornan serves on the Armed Services Committee and has been a member of the Permanent Select Committee on Intelligence.

Dornan and his wife, Sallie, have five children and nine grandchildren.   □ Lisa Klobuchar

Drought. See Water; Weather.

Drug abuse

Drug abuse. On Aug. 10, 1995, United States President Bill Clinton said that the Food and Drug Administration (FDA) can and should regulate tobacco products. Clinton's call for new federal regulation of the tobacco industry came in response to increased smoking among teen-agers and the nearly unanimous opinion of medical researchers that nicotine is a powerfully addictive drug.

The percentage of teen-agers who smoke rose sharply after 1991, according to a 1995 report issued by the Centers for Disease Control and Prevention in Atlanta, Georgia. Smoking jumped 22 percent among 8th graders between 1991 and 1994; 16 percent among 10th graders; and 5 percent among 12th graders. The National Cancer Institute reported in April, however, that smoking by black teen-agers dropped from 27 percent in the 1970's to 4.4 percent in 1993. Among white teen-agers, 23 percent reported smoking in 1993.

Drug use rising. Illicit drug use has been growing, especially marijuana use among young people. The early results of the 1995 National Household Survey on Drug Abuse (NHSDA) confirmed that marijuana use among teen-agers nearly doubled from 1992 to 1994 in the 12 to 17 age group. The Office of National Drug Control Policy (ONDCP) also reported marijuana use more than doubling since 1991 among 8th graders. Experts attribute the rise in marijuana use to teens' belief that the drug is harmless.

Americans who used marijuana in 1995, including teens, totaled 10 million, according to the ONDCP. It said that in 1994, 7.5 million people used the drug.

The ONDCP reported a more than triple increase in the number of "hard-core" drug abusers since 1990. Heroin was more potent in the 1990's and was cheaper and easier to buy than cocaine. Rehabilitation centers and hospitals reported treating more professionals and college students for heroin addiction, and emergency rooms saw a steady increase in heroin overdoses. Because of fears of contracting AIDS from dirty needles, most people snorted and smoked heroin rather than injecting it.

Speed kills. Once called speed, now called meth, crank, or ice, methamphetamine was back in 1995, its use rising in West Coast cities and among young people. The drug, a powerful stimulant, is smoked or injected. Medical examiners reported a 144 percent rise in meth-related deaths between 1992 and 1994.

The U.S. policy toward drug abuse continued to rely heavily on punishment. The Department of Justice reported in August 1995 that, by late 1994, the nation's jails and prisons had reached a high of 1.5 million inmates, nearly doubling since 1985. Drug offenders made up 60 percent of federal prison inmates in 1993. Out of a $13.2-billion federal budget to combat drugs, about $8.8 billion went to law enforcement. Only $4.4 billion went to the treatment and prevention of drug abuse.   □ David C. Lewis

In *World Book,* see **Drug abuse.**

Drugs. A new drug therapy for stroke may prevent long-term disabilities if administered promptly, according to a five-year study reported in December 1995 by the National Institutes of Health in Bethesda, Maryland. The study found that patients who received the clot-dissolving drug TPA within three hours of experiencing stroke symptoms regained full use of their faculties 30 percent more often than did untreated patients. But the researchers cautioned that the drug, which awaits FDA approval, carries the risk of increased bleeding in the brain.

Acid indigestion. The Food and Drug Administration (FDA) in 1995 approved several new nonprescription medicines for treating heartburn and indigestion. The drugs, previously available only with a doctor's prescription, were the first fundamentally new nonprescription stomach remedies since antacids came into wide use more than 100 years ago.

The first of the heartburn drugs, Pepcid AC Acid Controller received FDA approval in April. It is a lower-strength formulation of famotidine, a prescription ulcer medication sold as Pepcid. Pepcid AC blocks the stomach's production of hydrochloric acid, which aids in digestion. When produced in abnormally large amounts, the acid irritates the stomach lining, causing a burning sensation and other symptoms of indigestion. Pepcid AC can block further production of stomach acid and relieve indigestion. It also can be taken before meals to prevent symptoms. Antacids, by contrast, neutralize excess acid but do not keep it from being produced.

Tagamet HB, approved by the FDA in June, works in much the same way as Pepcid AC and contains the same active ingredient, cimetidine, as the prescription-strength ulcer drug Tagamet. An FDA advisory panel in August recommended that the agency also approve nonprescription sales of a third, similar medication, ranitidine, to be sold as Zantac 75.

Sickle cell drug. Federal health officials in January 1995, announced the success of the first drug treatment for preventing painful attacks associated with sickle cell anemia. In the United States, this hereditary blood disorder affects an estimated 72,000 African Americans.

Claude Lenfant, director of the National Heart, Lung, and Blood Institute, said the results of a government-funded study at 21 medical centers established the effectiveness of the drug, which is called hydroxyurea. The medication already was in use for the treatment of another blood disorder.

About 1 African American in 12 carries a defective gene for sickle cell anemia. People who inherit two defective genes, one from each parent, develop the disease, in which red blood cells assume a rigid, sickle shape. These cells can clog small blood vessels, causing pain and, in severe cases, life-threatening damage to organs. Hydroxyurea prevents red blood cells from sickling but does not cure the disease, and patients must take it for the rest of their lives.

New vaccines. The FDA in March approved a vaccine for chickenpox, a highly contagious viral disease that infects about 3.7 million Americans each year. The FDA said that the vaccine, called Varivax, is 70 percent to 90 percent effective in preventing chickenpox. The vaccine is intended primarily for children over 1 year of age who have never had chickenpox. It can be given at the same time as other childhood shots.

Chickenpox is widely regarded as a childhood nuisance. But each year, about 9,600 Americans experience complications of chickenpox that require hospitalization, and from 50 to 100 of them die. Complications are more common in adults, who account for about 10 percent of all chickenpox cases. Adults who have never had chickenpox are thus also candidates for the vaccine.

Some physicians expressed concern that the vaccine may lose its effectiveness over time. Children who receive the vaccine might thus be vulnerable to the virus when they become adults. A study of the vaccine's long-term effectiveness was planned.

The FDA in February approved America's first vaccine for hepatitis A, a highly contagious viral disease of the liver. At least 40 countries had approved the vaccine before the FDA acted. The vaccine, Havrix, is intended for travelers to areas where Hepatitis A is widespread. These areas include Mexico, parts of the Caribbean, Central and South America, Africa, Asia (except Japan), Eastern Europe, and the Middle East.

About 143,000 cases of hepatitis A occur in the United States each year. The virus is spread through close personal contact with an infected person or in water and food contaminated by sewage. It attacks the liver, causing fever, vomiting, diarrhea, and other symptoms. Immunization requires an initial injection that protects against hepatitis A for as long as one year and a booster dose to prolong immunity.

Diabetes drug. A new drug for treating diabetes was approved by the FDA in September. The drug, Precose, is intended for people with Type II, or noninsulin-dependent, diabetes. Precose slows the digestion of starches and sugars and thereby helps control a rise in blood sugar levels that occurs after eating. Because people with Type II diabetes cannot process blood sugar properly, abnormally high levels can accumulate and lead to long-term complications.

Bone builder. In August, the FDA gave marketing approval for a nasal spray used in treating osteoporosis. Osteoporosis is a thinning of the bones that occurs primarily in older women, leaving the women vulnerable to fractures. The medication, Miacalcin Nasal Spray, contains a hormone, calcitonin, that increases bone density. The FDA said studies showed that Miacalcin increased spinal bone density but had no apparent benefit for bones in the forearm or hip. All these bones are especially vulnerable to fracture in women with osteoporosis. □ Michael Woods

See also **Medicine.** In *World Book,* see **Drug.**

Eastern Orthodox Churches. Many Orthodox churches expressed concern over continued fighting in Bosnia-Herzegovina during 1995. On August 7, Patriarch Pavle of Serbia's Orthodox Church appealed for a peaceful resolution of the war. He condemned the Serbian government's military policy of aiding Bosnian Serbs against the Muslim-dominated Bosnian government.

Patriarch Alexei II, head of the Russian Orthodox Church, and Pope John Paul II, leader of the Roman Catholic Church, expressed their mutual desire for peace in the region. They blessed two *icons* (religious paintings) of St. Anastasia prior to their being installed in the Russian space station Mir on July 25. The saint, who lived in the A.D. 300's, is revered by Serb, Croat, and Bosnian Christians alike. In June, Alexei II also traveled to Geneva, Switzerland, to discuss Bosnian issues with United Nations officials.

Interfaith tensions. While in Geneva, Alexei II met with officials of the World Council of Churches to discuss ways of easing tensions between the Russian Orthodox Church and Roman Catholics and Protestants. Those tensions stemmed from the appointment of Roman Catholic bishops to Russia, where relatively few people are Catholic, and increased missionary activity of Protestant denominations in Russia since Communism collapsed in 1991.

Prayers for unity. Ecumenical Patriarch Bartholomew I of Constantinople (Istanbul, Turkey) and Pope John Paul II prayed together in St. Peter's Basilica in Rome on June 29. They urged God's blessings on increased efforts to end the nearly 1,000-year division of the two ancient Christian churches. In 1054, disagreements over the pope's authority in the East produced a s*chism* (split) between the Eastern and Western Christian churches that still endures.

New African metropolitan. In Africa, Bishop Theodoros Nankyamas was elected the first black African Metropolitan of Kampala and All Uganda on April 30, 1995. In Africa, the Ugandan church ranks second to the Patriarchate of Alexandria in Egypt. Nankyamas helped found the Orthodox Church of Uganda.

The Ukrainian government refused to allow Patriarch Volodymyr of the Ukrainian Autocephalous (independent) Orthodox Church to be buried in St. Sophia's Cathedral in Kiev after the patriarch died on July 14. The cathedral, which was confiscated when Ukraine was a member of the Soviet Union, has long been a state museum. Mourners defiantly dug a makeshift grave in the sidewalk outside the cathedral and buried the patriarch there. Riot police quickly attacked the mourners with clubs and tear gas. More than 70 people were reported injured. On October 20, when Metropolitan Filaret was elected the new patriarch of the independent church, Volodymyr was still buried outside the cathedral. □ Stanley S. Harakas

In *World Book,* see **Eastern Orthodox Churches.**

Economics. The growth pace of the United States economy suddenly slowed in 1995, though the nation avoided an outright economic downturn or recession. By the year's end, the economy seemed to be heading toward sustained moderate growth.

Key economic events in 1995 included a shift in policy by the Federal Reserve System, known as the Fed or central bank, from raising interest rates in order to prevent inflation. At midyear, as the economy slowed and the threat of inflation cooled, the Fed began to cut interest rates. Also in 1995, a Republican-controlled U.S. Congress set out to enact vast economic changes. Their program included wiping out the government's annual budget deficit in seven years, curbing the growth of government programs, and cutting some taxes. But Democratic President Bill Clinton opposed many parts of their program.

The budget fight. Conflict over resolving the nation's budget reached historic proportions in 1995 because of a huge shift toward a more conservative thrust in economic programs.

The new Republican Congress, elected in November 1994, installed Representative Newt Gingrich (R., Ga.) as Speaker of the House of Representatives. Gingrich framed a legislative agenda based on his Contract with America, which included a tax cut, deep cuts in future spending, curbs on government regulation, and a balanced budget in the year 2002. Senator Robert J. Dole (R., Kans.), equally conservative on fiscal matters and waging a campaign for President in 1996, was Senate Majority Leader. Although Clinton also offered a tax cut, welfare reforms, and cuts in government entitlements, the Republican proposals granted a larger tax cut and made deeper spending cuts.

The battle left the federal government without a permanent budget at the start of its new fiscal year in October and led to a shutdown of nonessential government offices in November and again in December. At one point, it raised fears the government might even default on Treasury securities payments for the first time in history, but default was averted. Budget negotiations continued at year's end.

Economic growth. The government reported that the economy grew an unexpectedly fast 4.2 percent in the third quarter of 1995. The fourth quarter, however, was marked by weak Christmas sales and signs of a new economic slowdown. The economy seemed to be growing more slowly than in any fourth quarter since since the 1990-1991 recession.

Federal Reserve Chairman Alan Greenspan and other Fed officials suggested the Fed could further cut interest rates if a budget deal between Congress and President Clinton shrank federal spending so sharply that the economy would need help to grow and if inflation remained subdued.

On December 18, stock and bond prices staged a sharp one-day fall amid worries over the still-simmering federal budget fight and fears that the Fed might not cut interest rates further to help the economy. The next day, the Fed cut rates another one-fourth of a point to 5.5 percent, and Clinton met with Republican leaders to resume budget talks.

The government's main economic gauge, the *gross domestic product (GDP),* measures the total value of all goods and services produced within the country. The U.S. GDP ended 1994 growing at a 5.1 percent annual rate, much stronger than the 2.5 percent pace desired by the Fed to contain inflation. Fearful that the economy might be threatening to overheat and stir up a rising cycle of inflation, the Fed on Feb. 1, 1995, raised short-term interest rates from 5.5 percent to 6 percent. This was the seventh consecutive increase since about a year earlier.

Because of the rate hikes and the decline in exports, GDP growth slowed to 2.7 percent in the first quarter of 1995, and abruptly braked to 1.3 percent in the second quarter, when the economy nearly stalled out. Most government and private economists had not expected such a slowdown.

Economic growth was slow or uneven among many major U.S. trading partners, including Canada—the biggest U.S. trading partner—Japan, Mexico, and much of Europe. Slow growth abroad meant less American production of export goods.

Fed strategy works. Although the Fed kept short-term interest rates steady well into the summer—while watching inflation signals as well as economic growth—on July 6 it lowered rates by one-fourth of a point, to 5.75 percent. That minor cut, economists said, would do little by itself to stimulate the economy, but it sent an important signal to financial markets: the Fed had ended its cycle of rate increases and the threat of inflation was over.

In subsequent months, as the Fed held short-term rates steady, the economy kept growing with no sign that inflation was picking back up. Long-term interest rates, set by the markets, edged downward, and the stock market rose. Economists credited the Fed for achieving a rare "soft landing" that let the economy cool its inflationary fires without a recession. Some in the Fed system wanted to go even further and bring inflation down to almost zero.

Financial markets began 1995 reeling from a severe monetary crisis in Mexico, which is a major market for U.S. exports and a partner with the United States and Canada in the North American Free Trade Agreement (NAFTA). The peso, Mexico's currency, had plunged in value in December 1994, triggering a national recession and threatening large losses for U.S. banks with loans to Mexico. In early 1995, the United States and international lending agencies bailed Mexico out with loans to make debt payments, thus averting a more serious international crisis.

The financial markets performed strongly in 1995. The Dow Jones Industrial Average, a benchmark for U.S. stock-market strength, rose to record

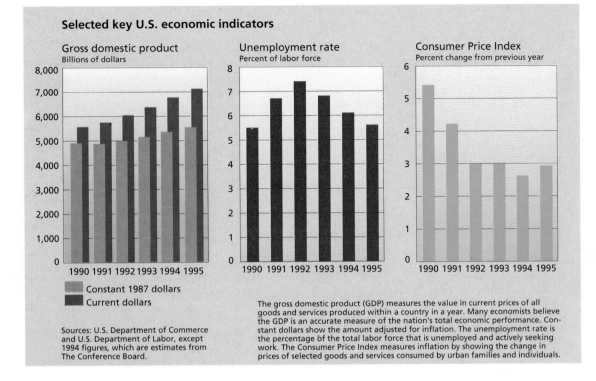

Selected key U.S. economic indicators

Gross domestic product
Billions of dollars

Unemployment rate
Percent of labor force

Consumer Price Index
Percent change from previous year

■ Constant 1987 dollars
■ Current dollars

Sources: U.S. Department of Commerce and U.S. Department of Labor, except 1994 figures, which are estimates from The Conference Board.

The gross domestic product (GDP) measures the value in current prices of all goods and services produced within a country in a year. Many economists believe the GDP is an accurate measure of the nation's total economic performance. Constant dollars show the amount adjusted for inflation. The unemployment rate is the percentage of the total labor force that is unemployed and actively seeking work. The Consumer Price Index measures inflation by showing the change in prices of selected goods and services consumed by urban families and individuals.

levels many times during the year. On November 22, the Dow closed above the 5,000 mark for the first time, and later it kept rising. (See **Stocks and bonds.**)

Unemployment edged up to 5.8 percent in April, but the jobless rate subsided to 5.6 percent in June. However, weekly levels of unemployment insurance claims kept rising. Inflation, meanwhile, did not ignite, due to both the Fed's policies and relatively flat wage gains, as large-scale layoffs from major corporations continued.

The Consumer Price Index (CPI), which measures cost changes for consumer goods, rose at a 3.2 percent pace in early 1995. But then the rate of increase began to decline along with the economy. The overall CPI for 1995 was expected to be below 3 percent.

New GDP measure. The U.S. Commerce Department in 1995 began to use a new GDP measure. The old system adjusted for inflation by measuring the GDP in *constant dollars.* This means economists determined each year's GDP based on the value of the dollar in a certain prior year, called the *base year.*

The new system, called *chain-weighted GDP,* links each year's dollar values together. One expected result was that quarterly growth rates would probably average about a half point lower than with the old method. □ John D. Boyd

In *World Book,* see **Economics.**
Ecuador. See **Latin America.**

Education. Over 51 million students entered the nation's elementary and secondary schools in autumn 1995—the largest number in United States history. But parents, politicians, and others were troubled by the quality of the education that many of those students received.

A public opinion study on education released in October found widespread dissatisfaction with the performance of the nation's public schools. The study's sponsor, a New York-based group called Public Agenda, reported that nearly 60 percent of parents with students in public schools said they would send their children to a private school if they could afford it. Nearly half of the participants in the study doubted that all students graduating from their local high schools had a good grasp of basic subjects.

A report card on the nation's schools issued in November gave credence to such doubts. The National Assessment of Educational Progress, an independent organization that measures the achievement of the nation's students, reported that only 43 percent of high school seniors had a "basic" grasp of history. A majority of the seniors taking a national history exam, for example, did not know that containing Communism was the main goal of U.S. foreign policy after World War II (1939-1945).

The National Education Goals Panel, a bipartisan body of state and federal officials, also issued a discouraging report in November. The slow pace of school reform, the panel warned, threatened the achievement of "world class standards" in core subjects and other national education goals.

Big-city trouble. The nation's big-city school systems made headlines in 1995. In March, a federal judge turned over control of the schools in Cleveland to state officials after declaring the schools to be in a state of financial crisis. In May, the Illinois legislature abolished Chicago's school board and gave Chicago's mayor, Richard M. Daley, the power to appoint a corporate-style board of trustees to run the beleaguered school district, where student achievement was low and the dropout rate was high.

In New York City, Ramon C. Cortines, the popular head of the New York City public school system—the nation's largest school district—resigned in June. His resignation came after a long fight with Mayor Rudolph W. Giuliani over control of the school system's budget. At the year's end, the U.S. Congress was debating legislation imposing a number of reforms on the schools of the District of Columbia.

School reform. The Carnegie Foundation for the Advancement of Teaching, a highly regarded school-reform group, in April released a report called *The Basic School* on the nation's elementary schools. In the report, the foundation proposed that schools limit their total number of students to 500 and their classrooms to 20 students to help foster a more intimate teaching environment. It also proposed that schools teach civic responsibility and such key values as honesty and respect. It further suggested that parents and communities become more involved in school life.

Another respected group, the Carnegie Council on Adolescent Development, in October issued a report on the nation's so-called young adolescents—those between the ages of 10 and 14. In its report, titled *Great Transitions,* the council emphasized that young adolescence is a significant growth stage and that young adolescents are not receiving the support and guidance they need. It urged that schools, parents, and the media provide much more support and guidance to the nation's young adolescents.

Many sought to improve the nation's schools in 1995 by helping them take advantage of new technology. In September, at a ceremony in San Francisco, United States President Bill Clinton called for educators, technology companies, and governments to join in improving schools' use of technology for education. The President called on public-private partnerships to equip schools with up-to-date computers, train teachers how to use computer technology in the classroom, create top-notch computer software for schools, and link every school in the United States to the Internet by the year 2000.

Several high-tech corporations, eager to introduce their products to school-age children, took up the President's challenge in 1995. Pacific Bell,

a regional phone company, and several other California-based technology firms pledged to help connect California's schools to the Internet by the end of the 1995-1996 school year. AT&T Corp., the world's largest long-distance telephone company, announced plans in October to spend $150 million over the next five years to link schools to the Internet, train teachers to use computer technology, and connect schools and homes via voice mail without charge for three months.

Schooling for profit. A controversial reform effort called *privatization*—the administration of public schools by private companies for profit—produced mixed results in 1995. A growing number of companies were interested in running public schools for profit because of a strong demand for school reform and because the nation spends $300 billion annually on public education.

One company leading the privatization effort was The Edison Project, launched in 1991 by entrepreneur Christopher Whittle. After struggling to survive in 1994, Edison in 1995 opened public elementary schools under contract with local school systems in Texas, Michigan, and Kansas. It also opened a state-funded school in Boston as a subcontractor.

Approximately 2,200 students attended the Edison schools in 1995. Under the program, the school day was an hour and a half longer than the national average, and the school year was 30 days longer. Students and teams of teachers were to work together for two or three years in small units. Their schedules called for daily 90-minute blocks of reading instruction. Several schools also had daily classes in music or art, Spanish, and physical education. Edison schools were also equipped with new technology, including lap-top computers for teachers and home computers for students.

Parents and local school officials were attracted to Edison's school design. More than 2,000 students applied for 630 spaces in the firm's Boston school, for instance. But it was too early to tell by year's end whether Edison would achieve its ambitious goal of creating a top-flight curriculum for the same amount of money school systems spend per student, while making a profit.

Educational Alternatives Incorporated (EAI), another company in the business of running public schools, stumbled badly in 1995. The company had managed public schools since 1990, and in 1995 it ran schools in Miami, Florida; Baltimore; and Hartford, Connecticut.

But in June, the Dade County school board refused to renew EAI's Miami contract. In Hartford, the company became embroiled in a conflict with the school system over contract requirements. And in Baltimore, where EAI had run nine schools since 1992, the board of education in November voted to terminate its contract with EAI. Baltimore's school superintendent said the cancellation was related to unresolved differences with the company over fee negotiations.

Another privatization project opened under a legal cloud in September. Alternative Public Schools, a small company based in Nashville, Tennessee, began running a public elementary school in the western Pennsylvania town of Wilkinsburg. But the local teacher's union challenged the school system's right to contract the running of its schools to a private firm. In late 1995, the case was awaiting a ruling by the Pennsylvania Supreme Court.

Voucher programs, through which public money is spent to educate students in private schools, suffered a setback in 1995. In August, the Wisconsin Supreme Court forced a temporary halt to a state law passed in June which permitted low-income Milwaukee residents to attend private religious schools at public expense. In June, Ohio lawmakers passed a similar law for low-income students in Cleveland. At year's end, the Wisconsin Supreme Court and an Ohio court were weighing the constitutionality of the so-called voucher programs, which critics charged violated the constitutional separation of church and state.

Cuts from Congress. The Republican-led Congress sought to reduce the federal role in education in 1995. Republicans introduced legislation to cut millions of dollars from programs for preschool and disadvantaged students; to eliminate several federal education initiatives, including one to encourage higher standards in the nation's schools; and to abolish the U.S. Department of Education. Throughout the year, President Clinton decried the congressional education proposals, and by year's end the Education Department was spared. But the budget cuts were still pending, as was the fate of the federal plan to foster higher academic standards.

Supreme Court rules on desegregation. In a June decision, the U.S. Supreme Court reduced the role of the federal courts in improving the racial balance of the nation's schools. By a 5-4 vote, the court ruled that a federal judge overstepped his authority in ordering the school system of Kansas City, Missouri, to spend heavily to improve its facilities and curriculum to attract white students from surrounding suburbs. The court also ruled that low scores on national tests by Kansas City's black students were not, by themselves, a sufficient reason for the state of Missouri to continue funding efforts to desegregate the city's schools.

Affirmative action revisited. Race was also a major issue in higher education in 1995. In May, the Supreme Court upheld a ruling that dismantled a University of Maryland scholarship program for black students, removing an incentive that many colleges used to increase their minority enrollments. The governing body of the nine-campus University

Civil rights activist Jesse Jackson speaks at a demonstration in Berkeley, California, in July against a proposal to end affirmative action in the University of California system.

of California voted in July to end by January 1996 the preferential treatment of minorities in their hiring practices. The move was part of a widespread debate over *affirmative action* on college campuses. Affirmative action policies are intended to benefit groups thought to have suffered from past discrimination. Such policies, enacted over the previous 30 years, had made the 162,000-student California university one of the nation's most ethnically diverse universities.

Citadel admits woman. In August, Shannon Faulkner became the first woman admitted to The Citadel, a public military college in Charleston, South Carolina. Faulkner had waged a highly publicized legal battle to enter the school.

In April, a federal appeals court ruled that The Citadel had to admit Faulkner unless it created a comparable program at a women's college. Faulkner withdrew from the academy on August 18, a few days after entering the academy. She cited stress and feelings of isolation as her reasons for leaving.

Cost of college. Paying for college became tougher for many students in 1995. The College Board, an organization of schools and colleges, reported in September that the average cost of college rose 6 percent during the previous year—twice the rate of inflation. □ Thomas Toch

In *World Book,* see **Education.**

Egypt. Muslim militants machine-gunned the motorcade of Egypt's President Hosni Mubarak on June 26, 1995, as he arrived in Addis Ababa, Ethiopia, to attend an Organization of African Unity meeting. Mubarak escaped unscathed, but the attack renewed concern that Mubarak had no successor or vice president to take control in an emergency.

Mubarak blamed the attack on the government of neighboring Sudan, which denied involvement in the plot. He later sent troops to reassert authority over a large, remote wedge of desert territory bordering the two countries and the Red Sea. The area had been contested by the two nations, though Sudan was administering it.

Islamic extremism. The ambush and killing of at least eight police officers by Muslim militants at four locations in the city of Mallawi shocked Egyptians on January 2. The deaths of 80 people that same month made it the bloodiest since 1992 when Muslim militants began their violent campaign to unseat Mubarak. Mubarak responded by using even more repressive measures. By September, at least 67 militants had been sentenced to death since 1992.

Mubarak also moved against the outlawed Muslim Brotherhood, arresting 28 of its leaders in late January 1995, including some former members of Egypt's People's Assembly. Authorities also acted against some unions, since members of the Muslim Brotherhood also served on various union boards. In

February, for instance, a court disbanded the leadership of the 220,000-member engineers' union. Another 15 brotherhood members were arrested in July, including prominent clergyman Sheik Sayed Askar. Mubarak claimed the Muslim Brotherhood supported militants, though for years it had been considered peaceful. About 80 brotherhood leaders were being tried in military courts by October.

Although it remained unclear whether terrorism was under control, tourism in Egypt during 1995 rose about 20 percent from 1994. Tourism, providing a major source of Egypt's income, had suffered after militants began targeting foreign visitors.

Elections. Analysts believed that the many 1995 arrests were partly aimed at controlling the results of November 29 elections for Egypt's 444-member People's Assembly. These were the first elections in eight years in which all opposition parties, excluding banned Islamic parties, participated. Opposition groups had in prior years boycotted elections to protest what they believed were fraudulent results.

Although Mubarak's supporters won the vote, human rights groups and election monitors heavily criticized the elections as being fraudulent and violent. The government reportedly arrested more than 700 Muslim activists on November 26 to curtail their influence on the elections. □ Christine Helms

See also **Middle East** (Facts in brief table). In *World Book,* see **Egypt.**

Elections. Embattled Democrats showed scattered signs of a political comeback in 1995 as they won the governor's race in Kentucky and staved off a strong Republican drive for control of the Virginia legislature. Democrats also regained a majority in one branch of the Maine legislature and narrowed the Grand Old Party (GOP) majority in the New Jersey Assembly. Democrats repulsed well-financed GOP efforts, especially in Virginia and Mississippi, to take control of state legislatures and continue the "Republican revolution" begun in Congress. The outcome, while mixed, reversed a series of election disasters for the Democrats in the past three years.

Democratic Lieutenant Governor Paul Patton narrowly won the Kentucky governor's race. He defeated GOP challenger Larry Forgy, a lawyer. Democrats won all statewide offices in Kentucky.

In Virginia, Republican Governor George F. Allen failed in an effort to take control of the General Assembly from the traditionally dominant Democrats, who held a 52-47 majority. GOP gains left the Virginia Senate deadlocked, 20-20, but Democratic Lieutenant Governor Donald S. Beyer, Jr., held the tie-breaking vote. Democrats hailed the results as a rejection of Allen's hardline politics and a sign of voter disenchantment with GOP congressional leadership.

Kirk Fordice, the first Republican Governor of Mississippi since 1874, was reelected in 1995. He defeated Democrat Dick Molpus, the secretary of state.

But a GOP effort to win a state senate majority fell far short. Also, Democrat Ronnie Musgrove defeated incumbent GOP Lieutenant Governor Eddie Briggs.

In Louisiana, conservative Republican Mike Foster defeated an African American liberal, United States Representative Cleo Fields, on November 18 in the governor's race. Foster became the state's first GOP governor in over a century.

Democrats won two special elections in Maine to regain control of the House, 76-75. Maine voters also rejected an antigay-rights proposal. In New Jersey, Democrats gained three seats in the State Assembly, but Republicans retained a 50-30 majority.

In other referenda, voters in Mississippi rejected a proposal to limit elected and appointed state officials to two consecutive terms. In Washington state, voters defeated a proposal that would have required the state to pay property owners for value lost because of government regulation.

Texas voters abolished the state treasurer's office, turning its duties over to the state comptroller. Washington state turned down a plan to allow slot machines at casinos operated by American Indians. And Pennsylvania voters approved televised and videotaped testimony of children at criminal trials, overriding a state constitutional requirement for accusers to face defendants in court.

Mayoral contests in 1995 yielded some surprising results. Dallas on May 6 elected its first African American mayor, Ron Kirk, who took 62 percent of the vote in a three-way race. Kirk, former Texas secretary of state, was supported by the white business community. In Gary, Indiana, Democrat Scott King became the city's first white mayor since 1967, though the population is about 90 percent black. King defeated three black opponents.

In San Francisco, former California Assembly Speaker Willie Brown won a December 12 runoff election against Mayor Frank Jordan. Neither had obtained a majority in November 7 balloting, but Roberta Achtenberg, who finished third, gave her support to Brown.

Chicago Mayor Richard M. Daley breezed to a second term in April with 60 percent of the vote in a record-low turnout. He defeated a black challenger, former Illinois Attorney General Roland Burris. Daley was endorsed by many prominent black politicians, including U.S. Senator Carol Moseley-Braun.

Several big-city mayors were reelected, including Kurt Schmoke in Baltimore; Bob Lanier in Houston; Steve Goldsmith in Indianapolis; Edward G. Rendell in Philadelphia; Joseph P. Riley, Jr., in Charleston, South Carolina; Roxanne Qualls in Cincinnati; Greg Lashutka in Columbus, Ohio; and Deedee Corradini in Salt Lake City. □ William J. Eaton

See also **Congress of the United States; Democratic Party; Republican Party; State government.** In *World Book,* see **Election; Election campaign.**

Electric power. See **Energy supply.**

Electronics. New technologies were responsible for one new electronic product in 1995 as well as updated versions of two existing products. The new product, a hand-held radar device to detect steel reinforcing inside concrete, went on sale in June. The device, which uses a technology called "radar-on-a-chip," was manufactured by the Zircon Corporation of Campbell, California, and was expected to be followed by many similar products.

Radar-on-a-chip uses *micropower impulse radar (MIR)* technology. Ordinary radar works by sending radio waves toward an object and receiving the waves that are reflected back from the object. Information carried by the waves tells what kind of object they were reflected from and the position of the object. MIR uses a computer microchip to emit and receive waves over short distances. Because of its small size and low cost, experts predicted that MIR will have many uses, including home security, baby monitoring devices, police work, and in automobiles to aid drivers.

Digital technology, which captures and stores data in a series of 0's and 1's, gave rise to the two updated products. The first of those was music compact discs (CD's) using High Definition Compatible Digital (HDCD) technology, which went on sale in June. HDCD technology captures sound missed by other recording processes and reduces noise and distortion. The new CD's can be played on existing CD machines, but they sound better on CD players with a special decoder chip. Pacific Microsonics Inc., of Berkeley, California, developed HDCD technology.

In July, the Sony Corporation and the Matsushita Electric Industrial Company said they would begin selling a new digital camcorder video camera that produces a sharper, clearer picture.

Zenith Electronics Corporation, of Glenview, Illinois, the last American-owned television manufacturer, was bought in July by LG Electronics Inc., a South Korean firm. LG Electronics, which makes Goldstar products, said it would continue making products with the Zenith brand name.

Nintendo of America Inc. announced in May that its long-awaited Ultra 64 video-game player would not be available until April 1996. This machine will use advanced computer technology to create superior images, sounds, and special effects. Nintendo said the delay was necessary to give software companies time to develop compatible games.

American electronics manufacturers sold $179.3 billion worth of products during the first half of 1995, 15 percent more than during the same period in 1994. Those figures were reported in July by the Electronics Industries Association, based in Arlington, Virginia. □ Michael Woods

See also **Computer.** In *World Book,* see **Computer; Electronics; Television.**

Employment. See **Economics; Labor.**

Endangered species. See **Conservation.**

El Salvador. On April 28, 1995, the United Nations (UN) withdrew most of the remaining members of its peacekeeping forces in El Salvador. The observers had been in place as part of a UN-mediated peace accord that ended the civil war that ravaged El Salvador during the 1980's, killing 75,000 people. A handful of UN observers were expected to remain in El Salvador until October 1995. As part of the 1991 accord, El Salvador's army was cut in half, the nation's judicial system was reformed, and a new civilian police force was created.

Many observers expected that the country's new-found stability would encourage economic growth. Economists predicted that El Salvador's 1995 growth rate would be about 6.5 percent, but outside financial assistance was still needed, government leaders said. In an interview on January 3, Vice President Enrique Borgo Bustamante and Salvador Sánchez Cerén, secretary-general of the Farabundo Martí National Liberation Front, the political party of the former rebels, pleaded for additional funding of $137-million to complete the work of reconstruction.

In the worst air crash in Salvadoran history, a Boeing 737 Guatemalan jetliner crashed into a dormant volcano 37 miles (60 kilometers) east of San Salvador on August 9. All 65 passengers and crew were killed. □ Nathan A. Haverstock

See also **Latin America** (Facts in brief table). In *World Book,* see **El Salvador.**

Energy supply. The Nuclear Energy Institute (NEI), a nuclear power industry organization based in Washington, D.C., reported in March 1995 that nuclear power plants in the United States set a performance record in 1994. The NEI said the average capacity factor of nuclear power plants reached 75.1 percent, up from 72.5 percent in 1993. Capacity factor is a measure of the efficiency of an electric generating station. It is the percentage of time during which a plant is able to operate at maximum power output. NEI's annual survey found that 69 percent of American nuclear power plants had a capacity factor of 70 percent or more, and 29 plants performed at 90 percent or higher.

The global use of nuclear power continued to increase in 1994. Eight new plants went into operation and 2 existing plants shut down, bringing the world total to 432 operating plants, the NEI reported in February 1995. Four new nuclear plants began operation in Japan, two in China, one in Mexico, and one in South Korea. Electric utilities shut down one plant in France and another in Scotland.

The world's largest users of electricity generated by nuclear power plants included the United States with 109 plants, France with 56, Japan with 49, the United Kingdom with 34, Russia with 29, Canada with 22, and Germany with 21. The NEI said that 3 additional nuclear power plants were expected to begin operation in 1995.

Energy production. America produced 34.0 quadrillion British thermal units (Btu's), or "quads," of energy during the first half of 1995, compared to 33.0 quads during the same period in 1994, the United States Department of Energy (DOE) reported in September. A Btu is the amount of heat needed to raise the temperature of 1 pound (0.45 kilogram) of water by 1 degree Fahrenheit (0.56 degree Celsius).

Most of the energy came from coal, followed by natural gas, crude oil, nuclear power, hydroelectric, and geothermal power. Americans consumed 43.6 quads of energy in the first half of 1995, compared to 43.4 in 1994. Imported oil made up most of the difference between production and consumption.

Coal production. In its annual forecast issued in January, the National Coal Association (NCA), an industry organization based in Washington, D.C., predicted that the United States would produce a record 1.031 billion tons (935 million metric tons) of coal in 1995. That amount would be about 0.05 percent more than the 1.030 billion tons produced in 1994. Coal consumption in the United States also was expected to reach a record 1.029 billion tons (933 million metric tons), a 1.08 percent increase from the 1.018 billion tons (923 million metric tons) consumed in 1994.

Most of the increase in coal consumption resulted from a greater demand by electric utility companies, which burn coal to generate about 56 percent of the electricity produced in the United States. Utilities used about 838 million tons (760 million metric tons) of coal in 1995, 0.6 percent more than the 833 million tons (756 million metric tons) used in 1994. NCA said coal exports would total 77 million tons (70 million metric tons), up 7 percent from the 72 million tons (65 million metric tons) exported in 1994. The rest of the coal mined in 1995 would go into utility company stockpiles, or be used to make coke for manufacturing steel, or other purposes.

Clean-coal research. A National Research Council (NRC) study in February recommended that the DOE expand its clean-coal research and development programs. The programs, which began in the 1970's, were intended to develop new combustion techniques and other technologies for reducing the amount of air pollution associated with coal. The NRC is an agency of the National Academy of Sciences, which advises the federal government on science and technology.

The NRC concluded that coal would continue to be a major fuel source in the United States for some years, providing over 50 percent of the nation's electricity. The United States has abundant supplies of coal that can be extracted inexpensively. But the study cautioned that the coal boom will increase the need for improved methods of converting coal into

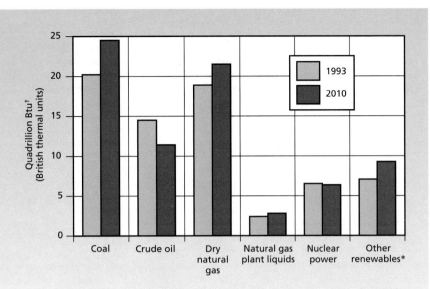

Energy production forecast

Energy experts in 1995 predicted that crude oil production would continue to decline until at least the year 2010. But, they said, the production of coal, gas, and other renewable resources would increase.

*Includes electricity from hydroelectric, geothermal, wood, municipal solid waste, wind, photovoltaic and solar, and other sources, and a number of non-electricity energy sources.

†A Btu is the amount of heat needed to raise the temperature of 1 pound (0.45 kilogram) of water by 1 degree Fahrenheit (0.56 degree Celsius).

Source: *Annual Energy Outlook 1995,* Energy Information Administration.

clean-burning gas and liquid fuels so as to reduce its impact on the environment.

Oil and gas reserves underestimated. In its first assessment of domestic oil and gas reserves since 1989, the U.S. Geological Survey (USGS) reported in February that America had more crude oil and natural gas left in the ground than previously believed.

The USGS estimated that the reserves known to exist in established oil fields totaled about 20 billion barrels, about the same amount estimated by the 1989 study. But the USGS said that intensive drilling in those fields could yield another 60 billion barrels. The agency concluded that the oil would be too expensive to extract now but could be profitably extracted in the future when prices rise. The new study also tripled estimates of *inferred reserves* (those believed to exist) of natural gas to 322 trillion cubic feet (9.1 trillion cubic meters).

High-efficiency washing machine. The Electric Power Research Institute (EPRI) in June announced an effort to speed marketing of a high-efficiency washing machine that uses substantially less energy than conventional machines. The EPRI, which is based in Palo Alto, California, manages research and development programs for the electric utility industry. The machine, a horizontal-axis clothes washer, has long been used in Europe. But it is almost unknown in the United States, where vertical-axis,

top-loading machines account for more than 98 percent of home washer sales.

In the traditional American machines, the wash tub surrounds a vertical, paddlelike agitator. A horizontal-axis machine tumbles clothes in a wash tub that spins on its side without an agitator. The machine requires less water and therefore less energy to heat the water. Higher spin speeds with the horizontal axis also remove more water from clothes so that they require less energy to dry. The EPRI said the high-efficiency machine could save an average family $50 to $120 per year and could substantially reduce national consumption of water and electricity.

New superconducting material. Scientists at Los Alamos National Laboratory in New Mexico in April announced a major advance in the development of practical high-temperature superconducting materials. Superconducting materials lose resistance to the flow of electricity and are thus energy efficient. Scientists said their new superconductor, made from layers of ceramic and nickel, could carry three times more electric current than existing superconductors and was flexible enough to be wound into coils used in magnets and other electric devices.

☐ Michael Woods

In *World Book,* see **Energy supply.**
Engineering. See **Building and construction.**
England. See **United Kingdom.**

Environmental pollution. Once again in 1995, a "hole" emerged above Antarctica in the upper atmosphere's ozone layer—the thick layer of oxygen molecules that protects life against the sun's damaging ultraviolet radiation. As spring comes to this area of the globe in September each year, a short-lived thinning of ozone occurs. This thinning has worsened nearly every year since the late 1970's.

Scientists believe that chemicals containing chlorine and bromine contribute to chemical reactions in the upper atmosphere that break down ozone molecules, which are made up of three oxygen atoms. The most common of these chemicals are chlorofluorocarbons (CFC's), which are widely used in refrigeration and air-conditioning systems.

Though the 1995 thinning spanned an area almost the size of the United States, it was not quite as large as the record ozone hole of 1993. But the World Meteorological Organization, an agency of the United Nations (UN), said in November 1995 that the year's ozone thinning lasted longer than in any previous recorded year. Atmospheric scientists believe that the hole will continue to expand somewhat each year until about 2000. International laws prohibit the manufacture of CFC's in industrialized countries after 1995, and scientists think that this ban will help diminish the size of the ozone hole.

On December 7, some 110 nations took action to further strengthen ozone-preservation strategies. At a meeting in Vienna, Austria, concerning the Montreal Protocol—the UN's ozone-protection treaty—industrial nations agreed to phase out by 2010 their use of methyl bromide, a pesticide used to treat soil and agricultural products for pests. Industrial nations account for about 80 percent of methyl bromide use.

Like the chlorine in CFC's, bromine can destroy ozone. Yet bromine is about 50 times more effective at destroying ozone than chlorine is. Though methyl bromine accounts for just 6 to 9 percent of stratospheric ozone loss, scientists believed that it could become the dominant source of seasonal ozone thinning if its use was allowed to grow.

Global warming. In July 1995, an international group of scientific experts began circulating a draft report among government leaders warning that human activities in recent decades had contributed to a warming of Earth's atmosphere. The report represented the first time a major scientific body had said that the world is getting warmer and that humans appear to be contributing to, if not causing, the change.

According to the United Nations-sponsored team—the Intergovernmental Panel on Climate Change (IPCC)—the chief culprit was the burning of *fossil fuels.* Fossil fuels are coal, oil, wood, and other fuels that release *greenhouse gases* (gases that trap the sun's heat in the atmosphere). The most important greenhouse gas is carbon dioxide.

As a greenhouse gas, carbon dioxide traps some of the *infrared* (heat) energy from sunlight as it radiates back from the Earth. Such heat-trapping helps keep Earth warm enough to support life, but scientists fear that too much carbon dioxide in the atmosphere could warm Earth to dangerous levels. Excessive warming could lead to the melting of large portions of the polar ice caps, an increase in the spread of infectious disease, and the death of some forests and agricultural crops.

Records show that Earth's average temperature has been rising steadily since the 1960's—with 1990, 1991, and 1994 the three warmest years since global temperature recording began in the late 1800's. Throughout this same period, carbon-dioxide concentrations have increased to a level 25 percent higher than before the Industrial Revolution began in the 1700's.

One event that supported suspicions that global warming had begun was the January 1995 breakup of major portions of the Larsen Ice Shelf in Antarctica. An ice shelf is an extension into the sea of a sheet of ice that begins on land. An iceberg about the size of Rhode Island—50 miles (80 kilometers) long, 23 miles (37 kilometers) wide, and 670 feet (200 meters) thick—broke off and floated away. Scientists reported that ice shelves throughout Antarctica were thinning as temperatures rose there.

During the Earth Summit in Rio de Janeiro, Brazil, in 1992, diplomats set tentative timetables for reducing greenhouse-gas emissions after the year 2000. At a climate summit in Berlin during March and April 1995, however, negotiators conceded that the Rio timetables would damage participating nations' economies. Summit participants agreed to put off setting new timetables until 1997.

Heart disease and dust. In the early 1990's, scientists linked some deaths from respiratory disease to concentrations of very fine dust-sized particles in the air. In July 1995, epidemiologist Joel Schwartz of the Harvard School of Public Health in Boston, Massachusetts, and Robert Morris of the Medical College of Wisconsin, in Madison, reported findings that link exposure to airborne dust with heart disease.

The researchers focused on Detroit, the largest city that collects daily measurements of the smallest dust particles—those 0.0003937 inch (10 microns) in diameter or smaller. Such particles are known as PM-10. The researchers correlated every admission for heart disease emergencies in area hospitals over a four-year period with data on PM-10 levels.

The researchers found that even slight increases in PM-10 levels could boost hospital admissions for heart emergencies. Moreover, they found no threshold level of pollution below which this trend disappeared. They concluded that in Detroit alone, nearly 1,200 hospitalizations for heart disease annually may be due to respiratory problems aggravated by inhaling too much dust.

Morris and his colleagues found an even more unexpected link between heart disease and another air pollutant, carbon monoxide. They extended their four-year analysis of hospital admissions for heart disease to six additional cities. And in October, they reported that hospital admissions for congestive heart failure rose and fell daily in almost exact proportion with outdoor carbon monoxide levels.

Forest declines. A team of ecologists led by Ernst-Detlef Schulze at Bayreuth University in Germany reported in February that most nitrogen—an important plant nutrient—can pass through the soils of apparently healthy forests without being taken up by trees or other plants. Previously, most foresters had assumed trees would sop up all the nitrogen they could get. The German data suggested that acid rain had overfertilized these forests to the point where they were saturated with nitrogen. This new finding signaled a silent crisis in the affected forests.

The form of nitrogen delivered by air pollution, nitrate, cannot move through soil without dragging along some calcium, magnesium, and other soil minerals essential to forest health. So if the trees aren't using the nitrogen, rainwater would wash the nitrate—and these other essential nutrients—away.

Schulze's data was collected in the Fictelgebirge, a range of mountains near the Czech border. The data suggested that even trees that had appeared healthy were in fact quite malnourished and at risk of becoming too weak to survive even normal, periodic attacks by insects, fungal blights, and extreme weather. Noted forest ecologist Lars O. Hedin of Cornell University in Ithaca, New York, said in February that U.S. forests were experiencing a similar, though less intense rain of nitrate pollution.

The Brent Spar controversy. On June 9, after years of studies and meeting with critics, Shell U.K. Ltd., a subsidiary of the Royal Dutch Shell Group oil conglomerate, began towing its Brent Spar, a floating oil-storage platform, toward a burial site 150 miles (240 kilometers) off the coast of Scotland. But the environmental group Greenpeace stirred up controversy over the proposed sinking and prompted the oil company to change its mind.

The Brent Spar had been used to store oil from North Sea drilling rigs. Shell had argued that at about $16 million, burial at sea was the most cost-effective way to dispose of the obsolete 20-year-old platform. But Greenpeace argued that the platform contained some 130 tons (118 metric tons) of sludge, toxic metals, and naturally occurring radioactive materials that should not be released into the ocean.

Shell initially challenged the Greenpeace charges but eventually gave in to public pressure. On June 20, Shell announced it would tow the Brent Spar to Norway so that the facility could be cleaned and taken apart for disposal on shore. □ Janet Raloff

In *World Book*, see **Environmental pollution.**
Equatorial Guinea. See Africa.

Estonia. Estonia's ruling coalition in 1995 broke apart amid scandal. In March elections, the Coalition Party and Rural Alliance won 41 of 101 seats in Estonia's parliament, soundly defeating the governing right-of-center coalition. Coalition Party leader Tiit Vahi became prime minister after forming a coalition with the smaller Centrist Party.

That coalition collapsed in October, when Centrist Party Chairman Edgar Savisaar was implicated in a bugging scandal that involved secret recordings of conversations between him, Vahi, and other political leaders. Savisaar was forced to resign as interior minister, and Vahi formed a new alliance with the Reform Party.

Tension over policy toward Estonia's ethnic Russians simmered. In January, the Estonian parliament adopted a citizenship law that extended the residency requirement for obtaining citizenship from two to five years and barred dual citizenship. Parliament also made Estonian the country's sole official language. Russia criticized the moves as discrimination against ethnic Russians, who make up 30 percent of Estonia's 1.6 million people.

In March, Estonia nearly concluded its privatization of large state-owned enterprises. Since 1994, more than 330 large concerns had been sold, raising more than $110 million. □ Steven L. Solnick

See also **Europe** (Facts in brief table). In *World Book*, see **Estonia.**

Ethiopia. The country's recovery from the civil war that ended in 1991 continued in 1995. Elections in 1994 for a constituent assembly led to a new Constitution, but strong controversy remained over the federal system. Ethiopia has about 80 ethnic groups, which the new Constitution allowed to become independent. Many people, particularly among the previously dominant Amhara group, believed that such independence would cause Ethiopia to dissolve.

Multiparty elections were held on May 7 to determine the new Parliament and regional councils. There was a massive turnout and most observers declared the elections fair. However, several national political parties disagreed and boycotted the elections. The ruling Ethiopia People's Revolutionary Democratic Front (EPRDF), dominated by the minority Tigrayan group, won easily. The new government came to power on August 22 and Meles Zenawi of the EPRDF became premier.

In April, the governments of Ethiopia and Eritrea, once a northern province of Ethiopia, signed an economic cooperation agreement that could lead to an economic and customs union between the nations.

Ethiopia received world attention on June 26, when terrorists attempted to assassinate Egyptian President Hosni Mubarak during his visit to Ethiopia's capital, Addis Ababa. □ Mark DeLancey

See also **Africa** (Facts in brief table). In *World Book*, see **Ethiopia.**

Large crowds of demonstrators march through the streets of Paris in December 1995 to protest the government's decision to make cuts in welfare programs.

Europe

The worst war in Europe in 50 years came to a close in 1995 as warring factions in Bosnia-Herzegovina negotiated a partition of the former Yugoslav republic. Also in 1995, the North Atlantic Treaty Organization (NATO), the Western defense alliance, outlined plans to accept Eastern European countries as members and to develop closer security ties with Russia. And currency devaluations once again upset the European economy, slowing the pace of growth and casting new doubt on the ability of the 15-nation European Union (EU) to achieve a common currency in 1999.

Bosnian war. The bloody ethnic conflict between Serbs, Muslims, and Croats in Bosnia-Herzegovina (often called Bosnia) risked spreading out of control in early 1995. But strong diplomatic and military initiatives by France and the United States led all three factions to accept a cease-fire and a settlement of the war. The war, which lasted nearly four years, caused more than 250,000 deaths and drove some 2 million people from their homes.

The events leading to a resolution of the conflict began in May after NATO launched air strikes against the Bosnian Serbs on May 25 and 26 in an attempt to end the siege of the Bosnian capital of Sarajevo. Bosnian Serbs retaliated by taking more than 300 United Nations (UN) peacekeeping troops hostage. The hostage situation prompted France and Britain, which had many among the hostages, to send more soldiers to strengthen Sarajevo's defense. All the hostages were released by June 18, but the Bosnian Serbs then captured two UN-protected Muslim safe havens in eastern Bosnia: Srebrenica on July 11 and Zepa on July 25. On August 4, Croatian troops launched a four-day offensive that recaptured Krajina, a region of eastern Croatia that had been taken by Serb forces in 1991. Croatian forces also helped the Muslims regain Serb-held territory in eastern Bosnia.

On Aug. 28, 1995, a mortar attack by Bosnian Serb forces on a market in Sarajevo killed 38 people. Two days later, NATO responded to the attack with sustained air attacks on Bosnian Serb military barracks, ammunition dumps, and other targets. The air attacks were intended to force the Serbs to remove their artillery 12 miles (19 kilometers) from Sarajevo. The bombing, which included the use of cruise missiles, was the biggest military action taken by NATO since the alliance was founded in 1949. NATO halted the bombing on September 14 when the Bosnian Serbs agreed to pull back their weapons.

After weeks of mediation by Richard C. Holbrooke, the senior U.S. negotiator, the warring parties agreed to a cease-fire, which went into effect on October 12. Settlement of the war came at negotiations in the United States on November 21 with Bosnian president Alija Izetbegovic representing the Muslim-dominated Bosnian government, Croatian president Franjo Tudjman representing the Bosnian Croats, and Serbian president Slobodan Milošević representing the Bosnian Serbs.

The settlement called for a single Bosnian state encompassing two self-governing entities: a republic under Bosnian Serb control with 49 percent of the land, and a Muslim-Croat federation in the remaining 51 percent. A central government with a parliament and a presidency would be located in Sarajevo. Both sides would have to hold elections under international supervision and allow people displaced by war to return to their homes or otherwise receive compensation. The agreement took effect on December 14 after it was formally signed in Paris by the warring parties. NATO agreed to send some 60,000 troops to supervise the implementation of the peace settlement. About a third of those troops were to be from the United States.

War crimes tribunal. The International Criminal Tribunal for the former Yugoslavia in July indicted two Serb leaders, Radovan Karadzic and General Ratko Mladic, on charges of genocide, crimes against humanity, and war crimes. The tribunal, established by the UN to investigate allegations of atrocities, also charged 21 Bosnian Serb officers and soldiers, as well as Milan Martic, who led Croatian Serbs in the region of Krajina.

NATO expansion. On September 20, NATO approved a document that spelled out commitments expected of prospective members in Eastern Europe. Among NATO's expectations was that prospective members participate in their collective defense and in peacekeeping operations. The document also said that enlargement of NATO would not require the alliance to station troops or nuclear weapons in new member countries, a measure intended to reassure Russia that expansion was not directed against its security interests.

NATO's relations with Russia improved substantially in 1995. Though Russia had refused closer ties with NATO in December 1994 in protest of the alliance's expansion plans, on May 31, 1995, Russian Foreign Minister Andrei Kozyrev signed two agreements with NATO ministers. One of the agreements established a political dialogue between the two sides, and the other identified areas in which Russia would participate in the Partnership for Peace program, which allows Eastern nations to work with the alliance on peacekeeping and military exercises. On December 5, NATO foreign ministers approved a plan to allow up to 2,000 Russian combat troops to participate in the alliance's implementation force to police the peace agreement in Bosnia. The troops were to work under the military control of an American general and a Russian deputy, while NATO and Russia set up a joint committee to oversee political control of the operation.

New NATO secretary-general. The alliance suffered internal turmoil after Willy Claes of Belgium resigned as secretary-general on October 20 amid allegations of financial wrongdoing. European members were angered when the United States vetoed their preferred candidate, Ruud Lubbers, a former Dutch prime minister. The allies then united behind Javier Solana Madariaga, the Spanish foreign minister, who was approved as secretary-general by NATO foreign ministers on December 5.

EU expansion. The EU increased its membership to 15 nations when Austria, Sweden, and Finland entered the union on January 1. Disillusionment with membership grew quickly in Austria and Sweden because of budget cuts required of countries that wanted to be part of a single European currency and because prices of food and other consumer goods failed to decline as much as EU supporters had promised.

EU leaders agreed at a summit meeting in Madrid, Spain, on December 16 to begin membership negotiations with some of the 12 candidate countries from Eastern and Southern Europe in early 1998. The future talks were made conditional, however, on the EU reforming its institutions to cope with more members. The existing members agreed to begin reform negotiations in March 1996.

One of the most divisive issues within the EU was the proposal to curb national veto power and broad-

Country	Population	Government	Monetary unit*	Foreign trade (million U.S.$) Exports†	Imports†
Albania	3,429,000	President Sali Berisha; Prime Minister Aleksander Gabriel Meksi	lek (93.30 = $1)	112	621
Andorra	59,000	Co-sovereigns bishop of Urgel, Spain, and the president of France; Prime Minister Marc Forne	French franc & Spanish peseta	30	not available
Austria	7,884,000	President Thomas Klestil; Chancellor Franz Vranitzky	schilling (9.81 = $1)	44,941	55,231
Belarus	10,320,000	President Alexander Lukashenko	C.I.S. ruble (4,504.00 = $1)	715	747
Belgium	10,042,000	King Albert II; Prime Minister Jean-Luc Dehaene	franc (28.65 = $1)	119,530 (includes Luxembourg)	112,255
Bosnia-Herzegovina	4,476,000	President Alija Izetbegovic	dinar (6,000.00 = $1)	no statistics available	
Bulgaria	8,417,000	President Zhelyu Zhelev; Prime Minister Zhan Videnov	lev (68.55 = $1)	3,582	4,315
Croatia	4,801,000	President Franjo Tudjman	kuna (5.18 = $1)	3,903	4,667
Czech Republic	10,464,000	President Václav Havel; Premier Václav Klaus	koruna (25.98 = $1)	14,318	14,789
Denmark	5,203,000	Queen Margrethe II; Prime Minister Poul Nyrup Rasmussen	krone (5.41 = $1)	41,422	35,443
Estonia	1,572,000	President Lennart Meri	kroon (11.15 = $1)	1,308	1,672
Finland	5,059,000	President Martti Ahtisaari; Prime Minister Paavo Lipponen	markka (4.21 = $1)	29,690	23,254
France	57,971,000	President Jacques Chirac; Prime Minister Alain Juppe	franc (4.88 = $1)	235,385	229,005
Germany	81,524,000	President Roman Herzog; Chancellor Helmut Kohl	mark (1.39 = $1)	414,729	372,602
Greece	10,386,000	President Konstandinos Stephanopoulos; Prime Minister Andreas Papandreou	drachma (230.27 = $1)	9,839	23,232
Hungary	10,518,000	President Arpad Goncz; Prime Minister Gyula Horn	forint (133.76 = $1)	8,604	12,520
Iceland	271,000	President Vigdis Finnbogadóttir; Prime Minister David Oddsson	krona (64.20 = $1)	1,623	1,472
Ireland	3,462,000	President Mary Robinson; Prime Minister John Bruton	pound (punt) (0.62 = $1)	34,295	25,353
Italy	57,956,000	President Oscar Scalfaro; Prime Minister Lamberto Dini	lira (1,591.75 = $1)	189,263 (includes San Marino)	167,292
Latvia	2,643,000	President Guntis Ulmanis; Prime Minister Maris Gailis	lat (0.53 = $1)	990	1,241
Liechtenstein	31,000	Prince Hans Adam II; Prime Minister Mario Frick	Swiss franc	no statistics available	

en the use of majority voting to adopt policies, which had been reserved mainly for matters of internal trade. Germany campaigned for extending majority voting to issues of foreign policy, crime, and immigration. But the United Kingdom insisted that national governments should retain veto rights on such sensitive matters.

Currency turmoil returns. Sharp swings in exchange rates among European currencies, and between those and the U.S. dollar, slowed economic recovery and strained political relations in Europe. In early 1995, the global weakness of the dollar drove up the value of the German mark against other European currencies. On March 5, Spain was forced to devalue the peseta by 7 percent, and Portugal had to devalue the escudo by 3.5 percent.

The devaluations fanned political tensions as European nations with strong currencies feared a loss of exports and jobs to countries with weak currencies. French president Jacques Chirac criticized Prime Minister Lamberto Dini of Italy for the weakness of the Italian lira at a meeting of EU leaders in Paris on June 9. Meanwhile, French, Belgian, and some German companies appealed for financial compensation or trade protection to cope with the devaluations. Partly as a result of the currency turmoil, the EU scaled back its forecast for economic growth in 1995 to 2.7 percent from 3.1 percent.

Country	Population	Government	Monetary unit*	Foreign trade (million U.S.$)	
				Exports†	Imports†
Lithuania	3,782,000	President Algirdas Brazauskas	litas (4.00 = $1)	700	515
Luxembourg	398,000	Grand Duke Jean; Prime Minister Jean-Claude Juncker	franc (28.65 = $1)	119,530	112,255 (includes Belgium)
Macedonia	2,253,000	President Kiro Gligorov	denar (36.87 = $1)	1,055	1,199
Malta	370,000	President Ugo Mifsud Bonnici; Prime Minister Eddie Fenech Adami	lira (0.35 = $1)	1,531	2,461
Moldova	4,350,000	President Mircea Ivanovich Snegur; Prime Minister Andrei Sangheli	leu (not available)	174	181
Monaco	30,000	Prince Rainier III	French franc	no statistics available	
Netherlands	15,612,000	Queen Beatrix; Prime Minister Willem Kok	guilder (1.56 = $1)	145,825	130,512
Norway	4,382,000	King Harald V; Prime Minister Gro Harlem Brundtland	krone (6.18 = $1)	34,660	27,280
Poland	38,891,000	President Lech Walesa; Prime Minister Jozef Oleksy	zloty (2.44 = $1)	17,240	21,383
Portugal	9,894,000	President Mário Alberto Soares; Prime Minister Aníbal Cavaço Silva	escudo (147.45 = $1)	17,524	26,608
Romania	23,611,000	President Ion Iliescu; Prime Minister Nicolae Vacaroíu	leu (2,217.00 = $1)	5,997	6,291
Russia	150,638,000	President Boris Yeltsin	C.I.S. ruble (4,504.00 = $1)	63,243	38,650
San Marino	23,000	2 captains regent appointed by Grand Council every 6 months	Italian lira	189,263	167,292 (includes Italy)
Slovakia	5,381,000	President Michal Kovac; Prime Minister Vladimir Meciar	koruna (29.18 = $1)	6,583	6,554
Slovenia	2,016,000	President Milan Kucan; Prime Minister Janez Drnovsek	tolar (120.22 = $1)	6,819	7,247
Spain	39,347,000	King Juan Carlos I; Prime Minister Felipe González Márquez	peseta (121.50 = $1)	73,285	92,490
Sweden	8,813,000	King Carl XVI Gustaf; Prime Minister Ingvar Carlsson	krona (6.58 = $1)	49,864	42,687
Switzerland	6,995,000	President Kaspar Villiger	franc (1.13 = $1)	66,172	64,014
Turkey	63,204,000	President Süleyman Demirel; Prime Minister Tansu Ciller	lira (51,024.00 = $1)	15,409	29,065
Ukraine	52,498,000	President Leonid Kuchma	karbovanet (176,400.00 = $1)	9,708	9,989
United Kingdom	58,733,000	Queen Elizabeth II; Prime Minister John Major	pound (0.63 = $1)	204,197	226,380
Yugoslavia	10,931,000	President Zoran Lilic; Prime Minister Radoje Kontic	new dinar (1.39 = $1)	no statistics available	

*Exchange rates as of Oct. 27, 1995, or latest available data.   †Latest available data.

Single-currency doubts. The continued currency turbulence and the slow progress by the 15 EU member countries in cutting their budget deficits cast uncertainty on plans to create a common currency among some EU members by 1999. Germany's finance minister, Theo Waigel, created a political storm on September 20 by stating that Italy would fail to join a single currency in 1999 because of its high budget deficit and national debt. Waigel also suggested that the 1999 deadline could be delayed if too many countries failed to reduce their deficits. His comments also reflected Germany's doubts about whether France would meet economic expectations with its high unemployment rate and growing labor unrest. But many Europeans wondered whether Ger-

many, where polls had shown that roughly two-thirds of the citizens opposed giving up the German mark for a single currency, might be losing enthusiasm for a European monetary union.

Despite the doubts, EU leaders reaffirmed their commitment to the 1999 deadline at a summit meeting in Madrid in December. They also agreed to call their future currency the *euro* and introduce it in stages between 1999 and 2002.

Foreign initiatives. The EU launched plans in 1995 to develop closer relations with its Mediterranean neighbors in North Africa and the Middle East. The initiative sought to address the concerns of such Mediterranean EU members as France, Italy, and Spain, who have more business and diplomatic

Explosion

presence in North Africa than in Eastern Europe, and who feared the union might ignore their regional interests in pursuing expansion into Eastern Europe.

EU leaders, meeting in Cannes, France, on June 26 and 27, agreed to devote 4.685 billion European currency units, or Ecu's, ($3.584 billion) in aid to 12 Middle Eastern and North African countries over five years, compared with 6.6983 billion Ecus ($5.125 billion) to Eastern Europe. The EU also held its first meeting with the North African and Middle Eastern countries in Barcelona in November. Both sides agreed to seek closer political relations and establish a free-trade agreement.

The EU on December 3 also agreed at a meeting in Madrid to seek closer ties with the United States, including the elimination of trade barriers.

Corruption scandals. Many of Europe's past and current leaders in 1995 faced allegations of corruption or other illicit activities. In Italy, two former prime ministers—Silvio Berlusconi and Bettino Craxi, who was living in exile in Tunisia—were charged with corruption. A warrant was issued for Craxi's arrest. Italian prosecutors also put another former prime minister, Guilio Andreotti, on trial on charges of working with the Mafia.

In Spain, prosecutors began investigating Prime Minister Felipe González Márquez on allegations of authorizing an antiterrorist group. The group had been accused of assassinating Basque terrorists.

In France, Prime Minister Alain Juppé was nearly forced to resign after it was revealed that he had obtained city-owned apartments in Paris for himself and members of his family while serving as deputy mayor of Paris.

Border holdup. Seven EU nations—Belgium, France, Germany, Italy, Luxembourg, the Netherlands, and Spain—agreed in 1995 to eliminate passport controls at their shared borders and to strengthen security at other borders. The elimination of passport controls would enable people to move about freely within those countries. But France postponed its involvement on June 29, claiming that border controls were needed to deter drug trafficking from the Netherlands. Chirac on September 19 said border controls would remain in effect indefinitely, citing the security threat posed by a recent wave of terrorist bombings in France as his reason.

Channel Tunnel struggles. Eurotunnel, the company that operates the 31-mile (50-kilometer) tunnel under the English Channel between England and France, announced on September 14 that it was suspending for 18 months interest payment on $12.4 billion in loans. The financial woes were a product of huge cost overruns and lengthy delays in completing the tunnel. □ Tom Buerkle

See also the various European country articles. In *World Book,* see **Europe; European Union;** and the various country articles.

Explosion. See **Disasters.**

Farm and farming. United States farmers in 1995 were plagued by a wet spring, followed by a hot, dry summer. The weather problems and insect infestations delivered a double blow to the nation's crops, particularly corn. The dramatic decline in U.S. corn production, coupled with strong domestic demand and record exports, reduced supplies to a record low. Meanwhile, the U.S. Congress considered dramatic new farm legislation that would eliminate a 60-year-old program that paid farmers not to cultivate land in order to maintain high prices for certain crops. But the farm bill was folded into a congressional budget proposal, which President Bill Clinton vetoed on December 6. At year-end, the impasse was unresolved, which left farmers uncertain as to the rules for producing crops in 1996.

U.S. farm production falls. The hot, dry summer slashed the corn harvest by 27 percent. Corn dropped from 1994's record high of 10.1 billion bushels to 7.4 billion bushels in 1995, causing reserve stocks to plunge to their lowest levels since the 1970's, when the former Soviet Union's need for corn virtually emptied U.S. grain reserves.

The soybean harvest amounted to 2.2. billion bushels, a 13 percent drop from the 1994 record of 2.52 billion bushels. The wheat harvest fell by 6 percent to 2.2 billion bushels, and the cotton harvest dropped 5 percent over 1994. Oats declined by 29 percent, and rice by 12 percent.

The crop losses in 1995 greatly strained the new federal crop insurance program, which was enacted in 1994 in the aftermath of the previous year's disastrous flooding. Under the new program, farmers were required to buy federally subsidized catastrophic crop insurance in order to qualify for federal commodity price supports and other government benefits. More than 2 million policies were sold for 1995. When poor weather arrived, the U.S. Department of Agriculture (USDA) was forced to broaden coverage for farmers already insured.

The small crops also translated into higher feed costs for meat and poultry producers. As financially stressed producers sold off animals, beef production rose by 3 percent, pork rose by 1 percent, and poultry was up 4 percent.

World production. In 1995, global wheat production rose by 2 percent and cotton by 4 percent. However, corn fell 10 percent; soybeans, 9 percent; and rice, 1 percent.

Low grain supplies worldwide raised fears of a shortage that could have devastating consequences for nations that must import grain to feed their growing populations. In October 1995, the USDA predicted a widening gap between available food aid and the needs of 2.2 billion people in 60 developing nations, especially in sub-Saharan Africa. The USDA predicted that by 2005, these nations would need 27 million tons (24.5 million metric tons) of annual food aid, nearly double the 1995 aid.

A California farm worker stands among ruined lettuce plants nearly buried in mud. Torrential rains flooded huge areas of California farmland in March.

Yet donor nations were changing their agricultural policies to reduce surpluses and trim food aid budgets. Food aid shipments from all donor nations fell from 13.9 million tons (12.6 million metric tons) of grain in 1993-1994 to 9.3 million tons (8.4 million metric tons) in 1994-1995. Australia, Canada, many countries in the European Union, and the United States were among the top donors.

U.S. export boom. However, sales of U.S. farm products to other nations took off dramatically, hitting a new record of $54 billion in 1995. The previous record of $43.8 billion was set in 1981. Asian countries were the primary markets for American farm exports.

One reason that Asia turned to the United States was China's reduced ability to supply Asian needs. In 1995, China produced a record corn crop, but even that was insufficient to meet domestic demand. In only two years, China had gone from being the world's second largest corn exporter to a nation needing to import corn—15.5 million tons (14.1 million metric tons) in 1995-1996, according to the USDA.

Unlike the export boom of the 1970's, which was fueled by sales of raw (unprocessed) commodities to the Soviet Union, the 1990's boom was divided among raw commodities and meats, produce, and processed food products. Business also was spread among more countries than in the 1970's.

The United States in 1995 exported more pork than it imported for the first time in 43 years. And record beef exports narrowed the difference between imports and exports of food products to only 300 million pounds (136 million kilograms) in 1995. Poultry and egg exports, led by sales to Russia, grew rapidly to $2 billion, and beef and pork exports hit $3 billion.

A decline in the value of the Mexican peso weakened U.S. farm trade with that nation. Exports of beef, pork, and other commodities to Mexico failed to meet expectations raised by the North American Free Trade Agreement (NAFTA), signed by Canada, Mexico, and the United States in 1993. NAFTA was to gradually eliminate trade barriers among the three countries, and in 1993 a U.S. agricultural coalition had predicted that the pact would result in a fourfold increase in beef and corn exports. However, corn was a bright spot in 1995, as the United States shipped 3.2 million tons (2.9 million metric tons) to Mexico, up from 2.5 million tons (2.3 million metric tons) in 1994.

New farm policy proposal. In August 1995, Representative Pat Roberts (R., Kans.), chairman of the House Agriculture Committee, introduced a revolutionary "Freedom to Farm Act" that, if passed, would end 60 years of government management of agriculture. For years, farmers had left some acreage unplanted in return for federal price and income supports. But with the development of global markets for agricultural products, idle acreage meant U.S. farmers were losing out to other nations in the competition for markets. Ending the program for idle acreage was a key goal of a coalition of American agribusiness.

The Roberts proposal was also shaped by pressure to cut farm spending as part of a comprehensive Republican package to balance the federal budget by the year 2002. Roberts's proposal offered grain and cotton farmers seven-year contracts under which they would receive guaranteed but declining payments based on what they had historically received. Payments would no longer be tied to a specific crop, which formerly had formed the basis for federal payments. Under Freedom to Farm, farmers would have the flexibility to grow the crops the market needed.

However, Roberts had difficulty moving his proposal through the House Agriculture Committee. Four Southern Republicans representing rice and cotton farmers and all Democrats voted it down on September 20. But House Speaker Newt Gingrich (R., Ga.) inserted the Roberts proposal into the budget reconciliation bill, which passed the House.

The House and Senate worked out differences between their bills in November. They cut a $50,000-per-farm limit to $40,000, but permitted farmers to receive an additional $40,000 if they owned half-shares in two other farms. They scaled back a Conservation Reserve Program created in 1985 that had idled millions of acres of highly erodible land. They created a new Livestock Environmental Assurance Program to provide $100 million a year for livestock producers to improve manure management. And they trimmed the Export Enhancement Program, which had subsidized U.S. farm exports since 1985. High grain prices made the program unnecessary. In December, President Bill Clinton vetoed the entire budget package, including the farm provisions.

In Canada, budget pressures and new global trading rules forced the government to scrap its 98-year-old rail freight subsidy of grain and oilseeds bound for export markets. Canada announced a 30 percent cut in programs that provided a safety net for farmers. But the government also agreed to compensate cropland owners $1.6 billion for reductions in the value of cropland, and it planned to spend $300 million over six years to help agriculture become less dependent on government programs.

In September, the United States lifted a one-year tariff that helped limit the flow of Canadian wheat to the United States in 1994. The temporary ceiling had been imposed after U.S. imports jumped dramatically following the poor U.S. wheat harvest of 1993. Wheat had been hard-hit by 1993 floods.

New agriculture secretary. On March 31, 1995, Daniel R. Glickman, a former Democratic congressman from Kansas, was sworn in as secretary of agriculture. He replaced Mike Espy, who resigned in December 1994 in the midst of an investigation of allegations that he had improperly used his travel privileges and had received gifts from firms that did business with the Agriculture Department. Glickman stopped the USDA from making decisions regarding the designation of land as wetlands, a controversial issue among farmers because such a designation prohibits using the land for agricultural purposes.

Antitrust probe. On July 10, *The Wall Street Journal* reported that the U.S. Department of Justice had launched a criminal investigation in 1992 of alleged price fixing of high fructose corn syrup and citric acid, two ingredients of soft drinks, and lysine, a livestock feed ingredient. The major target of the investigation was Archer Daniels Midland Co. (ADM), the world's largest corn processor. A high-ranking official of the firm had been an undercover agent for the Federal Bureau of Investigation and had secretly videotaped officials of ADM and other companies having conversations regarding prices.

Ethanol. The U.S. Treasury Department in August 1995 exempted ETBE from part of the federal tax on gasoline. ETBE is an ethanol (alcohol) derivative used as an additive to make gasoline burn cleaner, and ethanol is usually made from corn. Corn farmers haled the tax break as a signal that the demand for corn should increase. □ Sonja Hillgren

See also **Weather.** In *World Book,* see **Agriculture; Farm and Farming.**

Fashion. Men and women did not slavishly follow the dictates of powerful fashion designers in 1995. They dressed up for special events, like weddings and proms, but for the most part they wore casual clothes. The T-shirt was worn everywhere.

Women increasingly ignored the regular tidal rise and fall of hemlines, wearing miniskirts when they felt like it and long skirts at other times, ignoring provocative see-through clothes in sheer fabrics, towering heels, and restrictive corsetry. The push-up bra, however, had a following as some women sought figure-enhancing curves.

Designers contributed to America's waning interest in fashion. They paid more attention to the introduction of their styles in mammoth fashion shows presented by supermodels, such as Claudia Schiffer, Shalom Harlow, Kate Moss, Cindy Crawford, Christy Turlington, Linda Evangelista, and about a dozen others. Top models commanded huge fees to parade down a runway. For example, Crawford reportedly earned $5 million a year. And Evangelista was widely criticized for saying it would not pay her to get out of bed for less than $10,000 a day.

By getting a top model, a designer was assured that newspaper photographers and television camera crews would cover his or her fashion show. As designers made their styles more extravagant to attract the media, their fashion shows contributed to the declining interest in fashion. Women were

Italian designer Gianni Versace presents models wearing haute couture gowns from his 1995 spring and summer collections shown in Paris in January.

amused to look at extravagantly dressed models, but they were not interested in wearing the clothes.

High prices also squelched high-fashion sales, as the cost of fabrics, labor, and transportation continued to shoot past the roof in 1995. An elaborately beaded evening dress, for example, could cost as much as a small car, especially if it had a Paris label. Most women—and men—were unwilling to spend money on such extravagantly priced clothing.

Expensive labels with snob appeal gave way to utilitarian clothes from The Gap and other moderately priced shops. The Gap also experimented with stores that sold even lower-priced apparel. Many women shopped for casual clothing at mass-volume stores, like WalMart, K-Mart, and Caldor, bypassing more expensive specialty shops and department stores. However, "cross shopping" arose, which meant people bought one or two pieces in an upscale fashion store and supplemented them with sweaters, jeans, and T-shirts bought at discount shopping malls or mass-volume stores.

With the disappearance of some up-scale department store chains, such as Bonwit Teller and I Magnin, high-priced designers with pricey ready-to-wear lines, such as Pauline Trigère, Bob Mackie, and Arnold Scaasi, closed their businesses. However, Scaasi kept his made-to-order operation. Designers Bill Blass, Oscar de la Renta, Calvin Klein, and Donna Karan focused on moderately priced collections in

addition to their designer lines. Geoffrey Beene made lower-priced styles for men and women that were sold in 135 shopping malls.

The "casual" workplace. The "dress for success" formula of tailored suit, blouse, and ribbon tie, so prominent during the 1970's, became virtually obsolete in 1995. Increasingly, companies introduced "casual Fridays," which enabled employees to wear to work the jeans and sweaters or sweatshirts they usually donned only on weekends. The move proved so popular that some companies made Mondays casual days as well, and some went so far as to allow casual dress throughout the week.

The casual look was not born in 1995. Sportswear, as it was often called, was developed as an American tradition more than 50 years ago by such designers as Bonnie Cashin and Claire McArdell. Sportswear lines were characterized by jackets, shirts, and skirts or pants that could be assembled in different ways. It also involved simple cuts of clothes without elaborate decoration.

The 1995 designers who worked within this tradition were Calvin Klein, Donna Karan, and Ralph Lauren. By year-end, all of them were planning to expand their operations to Europe and the Far East by opening their own boutiques, selling to established stores, and introducing their own cosmetics and perfume lines. ☐ Bernadine Morris

In *World Book,* see **Clothing; Fashion.**

223

Finland. A broad, five-party coalition led by the Social Democratic Party took control of the Finnish government in 1995 after general elections held on March 19. Social Democratic Party leader Paavo Lipponen was named prime minister, replacing Prime Minister Esko Aho, whose Center Party came in a distant second in the elections. Other coalition members included the Conservative Party, the Green Party, and the Leftist Alliance.

The coalition instituted sharp cuts in public spending in 1995. It agreed to cut spending by $4.6-billion—about 4 percent of gross domestic product—over four years. The cuts were designed to help Finland meet the strict economic guidelines for joining the European monetary union in 1999.

Finland's economy grew at an estimated rate of 6 percent, the highest in Western Europe. The strong economy and an estimated drop of more than 8 percent in food prices as a result of Finland's entry into the European Union (EU) on Jan. 1, 1995, sustained widespread public support for EU membership.

Lipponen in May reaffirmed Finland's policy of neutrality and ruled out membership in the North Atlantic Treaty Organization. □ Tom Buerkle

See also **Europe** (Facts in brief table). In *World Book,* see **European Union; Finland.**

Fire. See Disasters.

Flood. See Disasters.

Florida. See State government.

Food. The United States Food and Drug Administration (FDA), the U.S. Department of Agriculture (USDA), and other federal agencies continued in 1995 to move toward a system in which the agencies establish performance standards and monitor the food industry's compliance. Under the new system, the food industry was being allowed greater flexibility in designing its own programs and procedures to meet federal performance standards. Farmers, food retailers, and food service operations were brought under the regulatory umbrella as part of a new farm-to-table approach to regulation.

Safety. The USDA continued its efforts to replace its outdated visual inspection system for ensuring the safety of the nation's meat and poultry supply with a scientific approach that detects microscopic contamination. On February 3, the USDA's Food Safety and Inspection Service (FSIS) proposed a mandatory Hazard Analysis Critical Control Points (HACCP) system for meat and poultry inspection. Such a system was due to take effect for the U.S. seafood industry in 1996. Under the HACCP system, food processors are responsible for developing safety plans that identify points in the process where problems are likely to arise. They must also specify preventive measures at those points and establish strict monitoring requirements.

The meat and poultry industry strongly supported the HACCP approach. However, it complained to the USDA and to Congress that the FSIS proposal imposed HACCP requirements on top of existing visual inspection regulations. The American Meat Institute (AMI) wanted the USDA to repeal obsolete visual inspection regulations. The AMI called for a single, uniform statute for meat, poultry, and seafood. In August 1995, Agriculture Secretary Dan Glickman announced that the FSIS would review its inspection regulations and eliminate or revise those that were inconsistent with the HACCP system. Congress must enact new legislation to eliminate other visual inspection requirements in existing law.

Nutrition labeling. Edward Scarborough, director of the FDA's office of food labeling, said in September 1995 that nutrition labels on foods had a high acceptance rate among American consumers. Furthermore, he said, many Americans were basing their purchasing decisions on label information.

The Nutrition Labeling and Education Act went into effect in May 1994. The act required the FDA to impose strict controls on health and nutrition claims for foods and dietary supplements. The act also required foods to carry labels listing certain facts about nutrition. In 1995, the FDA analyzed 300 products to verify the nutritional claims on the labels. The agency found that 94 percent of the figures for calories and fat were accurate and 87 percent of all nutrient claims were accurate.

Scarborough said the FDA would continue to refine and expand food labeling regulations. The FDA intended to include complex carbohydrates on the nutrition label once a satisfactory definition was developed. The FDA also considered the labeling of organic produce and information on pesticide use. Some consumer groups attacked the FDA's policy of not requiring labeling of genetically altered foods if they were indistinguishable from foods produced naturally.

Milk labeling. The Milk Industry Foundation (MIF) and the Center for Science in the Public Interest (CSPI), a Washington, D.C.-based consumer-advocate group, petitioned the FDA in May 1995 to change the rules for labeling milk. Currently, the FDA required a milk label to read "2 percent lowfat milk" when it contained 2 percent milkfat and 5 grams (0.18 ounce) of fat in an 8-ounce (237-milliliter) serving. But the Nutrition Labeling and Education Act defined lowfat milk as containing 3 grams (0.11 ounce) or less of fat per 8-ounce serving. The MIF and CSPI wanted the label to read "2 percent reduced-fat milk." The MIF also asked the FDA to establish the term "skim" as synonymous with "nonfat." In November, the FDA proposed the changes to Congress.

Demographic trends. According to the U.S. Bureau of the Census, the number of people age 45 years and older would account for approximately 40 percent of the U.S. population by the year 2010. By 2050, the population would include 80 million people over age 65, up from an estimated 33 million in 1995. The graying of America will have significant influence on the nation's food industry.

Surveys conducted in 1995 by the Food Marketing Institute, a trade association of supermarkets, found that nutrition and safety factors concerned 90 percent of senior Americans, a higher rate than for younger respondents. Salt and sugar content and spoilage also ranked high on their list of concerns. The surveys indicated older Americans were more likely than other age groups to eat a balanced diet and to choose low-cholesterol foods.

Ethnic foods appeared on grocery shelves in growing numbers in 1995, and industry analysts said the trend would continue, in part because of the growing diversity of the U.S. population. For example, the Census Bureau projected that Hispanics would rise from 11.9 percent of the population in 1995 to 15.2 percent in 2020. A 1995 survey by Peter D. Hart Research for the Grocery Manufacturers of America, a trade association of food firms, found that 21 percent of shoppers bought frozen burritos and 10 percent bought salsa.

Irradiation. The Beef Promotion and Research Board in 1995 sponsored a study of irradiation on raw and cooked beef patties. Bacterial counts were lower in irradiated meat than in untreated samples.   □ Bob Gatty

In *World Book*, see **Food; Food supply.**

Football. For the first time ever, major colleges had an actual, if not official, national championship game to determine the top team of 1995, and it was won by the University of Nebraska. At the professional level, the National Football League (NFL) attracted the most attention not with football games but with the games club owners played in moving or threatening to move their teams.

College. For years, the unofficial national championship was settled, or sometimes not settled, by separate media and coaches' polls. The major colleges played in the National Collegiate Athletic Association's (NCAA) Division I-A, and many wanted to establish a postseason tournament like the ones used by smaller colleges in Divisions I-AA, II, and III.

Major-college presidents resisted a play-off, but most of the major colleges worked out a bowl alliance that, ideally, matched the teams ranked first and second in the two polls. The Big Ten and the Pacific 10 spurned the alliance and continued to send their champions to the Rose Bowl.

By offering more than $8 million to each team that played, the Fiesta, Orange, and Sugar bowls got the best teams on an annual rotating basis. For its game on Jan. 2, 1996, in Tempe, Arizona, the Fiesta Bowl drew the two highest-ranked teams in the Associated Press poll of sportswriters and broadcasters and the *USA Today*/CNN poll of coaches. Those two teams were Nebraska and Florida.

The 1995 college football season

College conference champions

Conference	School
American West	California State-Sacramento
Atlantic Coast	Florida State—Virginia (tie)
Big East	Miami (Fla.)—Virginia Tech (tie)
Big Eight	Nebraska
Big Sky	Montana
Big Ten	Northwestern
Big West	Nevada
Gateway	Eastern Illinois—Northern Iowa (tie)
Ivy League	Princeton
Metro Atlantic	Duquesne
Mid-American	Toledo
Mid-Eastern	Florida A&M
Ohio Valley	Murray State
Pacific Ten	Southern California—Washington (tie)
Patriot	Lehigh
Pioneer	Drake
Southeastern	Florida
Southern	Appalachian State
Southland	McNeese State
Southwest	Texas
Southwestern	Jackson State
Western Athletic	Air Force—Brigham Young—Colorado State—Utah (tie)
Yankee	Delaware

Major bowl games

Bowl	Winner	Loser
Alamo	Texas A&M 22	Michigan 20
Aloha	Kansas 51	UCLA 30
Amos Alonzo Stagg (Div. III)	Wisconsin-La Crosse 36	Rowan 7
Blue-Gray	Blue 26	Gray 7
Carquest	North Carolina 20	Arkansas 10
Copper	Texas Tech 55	Air Force 41
Cotton	Colorado 38	Oregon 6
Fiesta	Nebraska 62	Florida 24
Florida Citrus	Tennessee 20	Ohio State 14
Gator	Syracuse 41	Clemson 0
Heritage	Southern 30	Florida A&M 25
Holiday	Kansas State 54	Colorado State 21
Independence	LSU 45	Michigan State 26
Las Vegas	Toledo 40	Nevada 37
Liberty	East Carolina 19	Stanford 13
Orange	Florida State 31	Notre Dame 26
Outback	Penn State 43	Auburn 14
Peach	Virginia 34	Georgia 27
Rose	Southern California 41	Northwestern 32
Sugar	Virginia Tech 28	Texas 10
Sun	Iowa 38	Washington 18
NCAA Div. I-AA	Montana 22	Marshall 20
NCAA Div. II	North Alabama 27	Pittsburg State (Kans.) 7
NAIA Div. I	Central State (Ohio) 37	Northeastern State (Okla.) 7
NAIA Div. II	Central Washington 21	Findley (Ohio) 21

All-America team (as picked by AP)

Offense
Quarterback—Tommie Frazier, Nebraska
Running backs—Eddie George, Ohio State; Troy Davis, Iowa State
Wide receivers—Terry Glenn, Ohio State; Keyshawn Johnson, Southern California
Tight end—Marco Battaglia, Rutgers
Center—Aaron Graham, Nebraska
Other linemen—Jonathan Ogden, UCLA; Jason Odom, Florida; Orlando Pace, Ohio State; Heath Irwin, Colorado
All-purpose—Leeland McElroy, Texas A&M
Place-kicker—Michael Reeder, Texas Christian

Defense
Linemen—Tedy Bruschi, Arizona; Cornell Brown, Virginia Tech; Marcus Jones, North Carolina; Jared Tomich, Nebraska
Linebackers—Ray Lewis, Miami (Florida); Pat Fitzgerald, Northwestern; Zach Thomas, Texas Tech; Kevin Hardy; Illinois
Backs—Chris Canty, Kansas State; Lawyer Milloy, Washington; Greg Myers, Colorado State
Punter—Brad Maynard, Ball State

Player awards
Heisman Trophy (best player)—Eddie George, Ohio State
Lombardi Award (best lineman)—Orlando Pace, Ohio State
Outland Trophy (best interior lineman)—Jonathan Ogden, UCLA

Northwestern (NU) tailback Darnell Autry evades tacklers in October as the Wildcats beat Illinois. NU went to the 1996 Rose Bowl—its first time there since 1949.

The Fiesta Bowl got help from Michigan. When the Wolverines upset previously unbeaten Ohio State, 31-23, on Nov. 25, 1995, Florida took over second place behind Nebraska. Ohio State, a Big Ten team, could not have gone to the Fiesta Bowl.

When the regular season ended a week later, the final coaches' poll ranked Nebraska (11-0) first, Florida (12-0) second, Northwestern (10-1) third, Tennessee (10-1) fourth, and Ohio State (11-1) fifth. The media poll was the same except that Tennessee and Ohio State tied for fourth.

With opponents Nebraska and Florida, the Fiesta Bowl matched two offensive powerhouses and the only major teams that finished the season undefeated and untied. Nebraska demolished Florida, 62-24, and was ranked number one in the post-bowl-game polls. Nebraska, which was also the top-ranked team the year before, had its third consecutive undefeated regular season in 1995. Its option attack averaged 52 points per game during the 1995 season, the highest in the nation.

The college football story of 1995 was the return of Northwestern University as a football power after years as a gridiron laughingstock. Northwestern's Wildcats compiled a 10-1 record and went to the Rose Bowl for the first time since 1949. But the Cats lost the bowl game to Southern California, 41-32.

Honors. Eddie George, an Ohio State senior running back, won the Heisman Trophy, the Maxwell award, and the Walter Camp Trophy as the player of the year. George rushed for 1,826 yards in 12 games, averaging 6.0 yards per carry, and led the nation with 24 touchdowns.

In the Heisman Trophy voting, the leaders were George with 1,460 points, quarterback Tommy Frazier of Nebraska with 1,196, quarterback Danny Wuerffel of Florida with 987, and running back Darnell Autry of Northwestern with 535.

Frazier, who missed most of the 1994 season with a life-threatening blood clot in a leg, returned healthy for the 1995 season. He passed for 17 touchdowns, ran for 14, and gained 1,966 yards in total offense. Wuerffel passed for 3,266 yards and 35 touchdowns, and his quarterback efficiency rating of 178.4 was the highest ever in Division I-A. Troy Davis of Iowa State, playing for a team with a 3-8 record, became only the fifth player in Division I-A history to rush for 2,000 yards in one season.

Although Grambling State University in Louisiana finished with a 5-6 record, it was a memorable season for 76-year-old Eddie Robinson, its coach since 1941. He became the first college head coach to win 400 games.

Professional. The franchise stability that helped make the NFL such a popular television and box-office attraction was badly shaken in 1995. It started before the season when Los Angeles, the nation's number-two television market, lost both of its teams.

The Raiders, unhappy with their stadium, the ancient Memorial Coliseum, returned to Oakland, the city they left in 1982. The Rams, who played in Anaheim, moved to St. Louis, Missouri, where they had been assured of a $20-million annual profit and where a $260-million domed stadium was being built for them. More moves were planned for 1996, pending approval of the other club owners. The Cleveland Browns, dissatisfied with aging Cleveland Stadium, agreed in November 1995 to move to Baltimore and play in a new $200-million stadium rent free for 30 years. The Houston Oilers, unhappy with the Astrodome, agreed to move to Nashville, where a $292-million stadium would be built. The Chicago Bears were also reportedly planning a move, most likely to a suburban stadium.

The NFL was involved in more than $1 billion in lawsuits involving the Raiders against the league, the league against owner Jerry Jones of the Dallas Cowboys, and Jones against the league, his fellow club owners, and NFL Properties, the league's marketing arm. Jones, contending that NFL Properties did not get the best commercial deals for the teams, signed sponsorship agreements with Nike, Coca-Cola, and American Express, none of which had sponsorship deals with the league, but whose rivals did.

The unrest spread to the public, which already had mixed feelings about the salary cap, instituted

National Football League final standings

American Conference

Eastern Division
	W.	L.	T.	Pct.
Buffalo Bills*	10	6	0	.625
Indianapolis Colts*	9	7	0	.563
Miami Dolphins*	9	7	0	.563
New England Patriots	6	10	0	.375
New York Jets	3	13	0	.188

Central Division
	W.	L.	T.	Pct.
Pittsburgh Steelers*	11	5	0	.689
Cincinnati Bengals	7	9	0	.438
Houston Oilers	7	9	0	.438
Cleveland Browns	5	11	0	.313
Jacksonville Jaguars	4	12	0	.250

Western Division
	W.	L.	T.	Pct.
Kansas City Chiefs*	13	3	0	.813
San Diego Chargers*	9	7	0	.563
Denver Broncos	8	8	0	.500
Seattle Seahawks	8	8	0	.500
Oakland Raiders	8	8	0	.500

*Made play-off.

Individual statistics

Leading scorers, touchdowns
	TD's	Rush	Rec.	Ret.	Pts.
Carl Pickens, Cincinnati	17	0	17	0	102
Chris Warren, Seattle	16	15	1	0	96
Curtis Martin, New England	15	14	1	0	92
Marshall Faulk, Indianapolis	14	11	3	0	84
Anthony Miller, Denver	14	0	14	0	84
Bill Brooks, Buffalo	11	0	11	0	66
Tim Brown, Oakland	10	0	10	0	60
Bernie Parmalee, Miami	10	9	1	0	60

Leading scorers, kicking
	PAT	FG	Longest	Pts.
Norm Johnson, Pittsburgh	39/39	34/41	50	141
Jason Elam, Denver	39/39	31/38	56	132
Steve Christie, Buffalo	33/35	31/40	51	126
Doug Pelfrey, Cincinnati	34/34	29/36	51	121
Pete Stoyanovich, Miami	37/37	27/34	51	118

Leading quarterbacks
	Att.	Comp.	Yds.	TD's	Int.
Jim Harbaugh, Indianapolis	314	200	2,575	17	5
Dan Marino, Miami	482	309	3,668	24	15
Vinny Testaverde, Cleveland	392	241	2,883	17	10
Chris Chandler, Houston	356	225	2,460	17	10
Neil O'Donnell, Pittsburgh	416	246	2,970	17	7
Dan Elway, Denver	542	316	3,970	26	14
Mark Brunell, Jacksonville	346	201	2,168	15	7
Jeff Hostetler, Oakland	286	172	1,998	12	9
Jeff Blake, Cincinnati	567	326	3,822	28	17
Jim Kelly, Buffalo	458	255	3,130	22	13

Leading receivers
	Number caught	Total yards	Avg. gain	TD's
Carl Pickens, Cincinnati	99	1,234	12.5	17
Tony Martin, San Diego	90	1,224	13.6	6
Tim Brown, Oakland	89	1,342	15.1	10
Yancey Thigpen, Pittsburgh	85	1,307	15.4	5
Ben Coates, New England	84	915	10.9	6
Brian Blades, Seattle	77	1,001	13.0	4
Adrian Murrell, N.Y. Jets	71	465	6.5	2
Joey Galloway, Seattle	67	1,039	15.5	7
Vincent Brisby, New England	66	974	14.8	3
Wayne Chrebet, N.Y. Jets	66	726	11.0	4
Terry Kirby, Miami	66	618	9.4	3

Leading rushers
	No.	Yards	Avg.	TD's
Curtis Martin, New England	368	1,487	4.0	14
Chris Warren, Seattle	310	1,346	4.3	15
Terrell Davis, Denver	237	1,117	4.7	7
Harvey Williams, Oakland	255	1,114	4.4	9
Marshall Faulk, Indianapolis	289	1,078	3.7	11
Thurman Thomas, Buffalo	267	1,005	3.8	6
Rodney Thomas, Houston	251	947	3.8	5
Marcus Allen, Kansas City	207	890	4.3	5
Bernie Parmalee, Miami	236	878	3.7	9
Erric Pegram, Pittsburgh	213	813	3.8	5

Leading punters
	No.	Yards	Avg.	Longest
Rick Tuten, Seattle	83	3,735	45.0	73
Darren Bennett, San Diego	72	3,221	44.7	66
Louie Aguiar, Kansas City	91	3,990	43.8	65
Bryan Barker, Jacksonville	82	3,591	43.8	63

National Conference

Eastern Division
	W.	L.	T.	Pct.
Dallas Cowboys*	12	4	0	.750
Philadelphia Eagles*	10	6	0	.615
Washington Redskins	6	10	0	.375
New York Giants	5	11	0	.313
Arizona Cardinals	4	12	0	.250

Central Division
	W.	L.	T.	Pct.
Green Bay Packers*	11	5	0	.688
Detroit Lions*	10	6	0	.625
Chicago Bears	9	7	0	.563
Minnesota Vikings	8	8	0	.500
Tampa Bay Buccaneers	7	9	0	.438

Western Division
	W.	L.	T.	Pct.
San Francisco 49ers*	11	5	0	.688
Atlanta Falcons*	9	7	0	.563
St. Louis Rams	7	9	0	.438
Carolina Panthers	7	9	0	.438
New Orleans Saints	7	9	0	.438

Individual statistics

Leading scorers, touchdowns
	TD's	Rush	Rec.	Ret.	Pts.
Emmitt Smith, Dallas	25	25	0	0	150
Jerry Rice, San Francisco	17	1	15	1	104
Cris Carter, Minnesota	17	0	17	0	102
Herman Moore, Detroit	14	0	14	0	84
Isaac Bruce, St. Louis	13	0	13	0	80
Derek Loville, San Francisco	13	10	3	0	80
Robert Brooks, Green Bay	13	0	13	0	78
Curtis Conway, Chicago	12		12	0	72
Barry Sanders, Detroit	12	11	1	0	72
Ricky Watters, Philadelphia	12	11	1	0	72

Leading scorers, kicking
	PAT	FG	Longest	Pts.
Jason Hanson, Detroit	48/48	28/34	56	132
Chris Boniol, Dallas	46/48	27/28	45	127
Morten Andersen, Atlanta	29/30	31/37	59	122
Fuad Reveiz, Minnesota	44/44	26/36	51	122
Kevin Butler, Chicago	45/45	23/31	47	114

Leading quarterbacks
	Att.	Comp.	Yds.	TD's	Int.
Brett Favre, Green Bay	570	359	4,413	38	13
Troy Aikman, Dallas	432	280	3,304	16	7
Eric Kramer, Chicago	522	315	3,838	29	10
Steve Young, San Francisco	447	299	3,200	20	11
Scott Mitchell, Detroit	583	346	4,338	32	12
Warren Moon, Minnesota	606	377	4,228	33	14
Jeff George, Atlanta	557	336	4,143	24	11
Jim Everett, New Orleans	567	345	3,970	26	14
Chris Miller, St. Louis	405	232	2,623	18	15
Dave Brown, N.Y. Giants	456	254	2,814	11	10

Leading receivers
	Number caught	Total yards	Avg. gain	TD's
Herman Moore, Detroit	123	1,686	13.7	14
Jerry Rice, San Francisco	122	1,848	15.1	15
Cris Carter, Minnesota	122	1,371	11.2	17
Isaac Bruce, St. Louis	119	1,781	15.0	13
Michael Irvin, Dallas	111	1,603	14.4	10
Brett Perriman, Detroit	108	1,488	13.8	9
Eric Metcalf, Atlanta	104	1,189	11.4	8
Robert Brooks, Green Bay	102	1,497	14.7	13
Larry Centers, Arizona	101	962	9.5	2

Leading rushers
	No.	Yards	Avg.	TD's
Emmitt Smith, Dallas	377	1,773	4.7	25
Barry Sanders, Detroit	314	1,500	4.8	11
Terry Allen, Washington	338	1,309	3.9	10
Ricky Watters, Philadelphia	337	1,273	3.8	11
Errict Rhett, Tampa Bay	332	1,207	3.6	11
Rodney Hampton, N.Y. Giants	306	1,182	3.9	10
Craig Heyward, Atlanta	236	1,083	4.6	6
Rashaan Salaam, Chicago	296	1,074	3.6	10
Garrison Hearst, Arizona	284	1,070	3.8	1
Edgar Bennett, Green Bay	316	1,067	3.4	3

Leading punters
	No.	Yards	Avg.	Longest
Sean Landeta, St. Louis	83	3,679	44.3	63
Jeff Feagles, Arizona	72	3,150	43.8	60
Tommy Hutton, Philadelphia	85	3,682	43.3	63
Reggie Roby, Tampa Bay	77	3,296	42.8	61

in 1993, because it led teams to cut loose older favorite players. Ticket prices increased 9.3 percent in 1995 after an 8.3 percent rise in 1994. Television ratings were down.

Season. Although the San Francisco 49ers (11-5), the Super Bowl defending champions, lost cornerback Deion Sanders, tailback Ricky Watters, and both offensive and defensive coordinators, they won their fourth consecutive National Conference Western Division title. Dallas (12-4), led by tailback Emmitt Smith, quarterback Troy Aikman, and the newly signed Deion Sanders, gained its fourth consecutive Eastern Division title. The Green Bay Packers (11-5) won their first Central Division title since 1972. The American Conference champions were the Kansas City Chiefs (13-3) in the Western Division, the Pittsburgh Steelers (11-5) in the Central, and the surprising Buffalo Bills (10-6) for the sixth time in eight years in the Eastern.

The Carolina Panthers (7-9) and the Jacksonville Jaguars (4-12) started playing as the 29th and the 30th teams in the league. Carolina became the first expansion team ever to win four consecutive games.

Stars. Quarterback Dan Marino of the Miami Dolphins in 1995 broke four of Fran Tarkenton's all-time passing records (47,003 yards, 342 touchdowns, 3,686 completions, and 6,467 attempts). Warren Moon of the Minnesota Vikings and John Elway of the Denver Broncos became the sixth and seventh NFL quarterbacks to pass for 40,000 career yards, and Drew Bledsoe of the New England Patriots, at age 23, became the youngest to reach 10,000 yards.

Joe Montana of Kansas City, the most successful quarterback of his era, retired in April at 38 after 16 seasons. Jerry Rice of San Francisco, Montana's favorite receiver when he played there, broke James Lofton's all-time record of 14,004 receiving yards. Steve Largent, once a record-breaking receiver, was voted into the Pro Football Hall of Fame with tight end Kellen Winslow, defensive end Lee Roy Selmon, defensive tackle Henry Jordan, and Jim Finks, a league and club executive.

Canadian. The Canadian Football League added teams in Birmingham, Alabama, and Memphis, Tennessee, and the Sacramento, California, team moved to San Antonio. The Memphis team folded after the season, however, and the Birmingham team announced that it was for sale.

The league realigned into one division with eight Canadian teams and another with five American teams. The Baltimore Stallions and the Calgary Stampeders won the division titles with 15-3 records and advanced to the Grey Cup championship game November 19 in Regina, Saskatchewan. Baltimore won, 37-20, and then looked for a new home because it expected the NFL's Cleveland Browns to play in Baltimore in 1996.   □ Frank Litsky

In *World Book,* see **Football.**

France. Voters in 1995 ushered in a change in French politics by electing the leader of the Rally for the Republic (RPR) party, Jacques Chirac, as president on May 7. Chirac, the former mayor of Paris, replaced Socialist leader François Mitterrand, ending Mitterrand's 14-year reign. But Chirac's popularity plunged in late 1995 after he changed the economic priorities that had ushered him into office.

Election results. Chirac won 52.6 percent of the vote, defeating the Socialist candidate, Lionel Jospin, who polled 47.4 percent. The victory marked a stunning comeback for Chirac in his third presidential campaign. Chirac began the campaign trailing far behind his rival RPR candidate, Edouard Balladur, the prime minister at that time. But his standing rose after he campaigned on promises of healing social inequalities and reducing unemployment, which at about 12 percent, stood at its highest level since the end of World War II (1939-1945).

Far Right advances. Jean-Marie Le Pen, the leader of the ultraconservative National Front Party, won 15.3 percent of the vote in the first round of the presidential election on April 23. Le Pen was known for advocating the deportation of foreign workers to fight unemployment. In elections on June 18, the Front won its first mayoral races in three cities. Also in June, another far-right candidate, Jacques Peyrat, became mayor of the city of Nice.

Policy change provokes strikes. In late 1995, after European doubts about France's ability to meet the strict economic requirements for participating in a single European currency in 1999 weakened the franc on currency markets, Chirac made a dramatic change in his economic policies. On October 26, he announced that reducing the deficit had become the government's top priority. To shore up support for the change in policy, France's prime minister, Alain Juppé, on November 7 formed a new cabinet.

Juppé proposed eliminating the large social security deficit by imposing new taxes and lengthening the number of years civil servants must work before drawing retirement benefits to 40 from 37.5. The austerity measures triggered a wave of strikes. Beginning on November 24, striking public workers shut down the national railway and the Paris subway and crippled the postal service. The unions called off the strikes in mid-December after Juppé dropped the retirement changes, promised a moratorium on most tax increases, and proposed new measures to boost growth and create jobs.

Furor over nuclear testing. Chirac provoked a storm of international protest when he announced on June 13 that France would resume underground nuclear tests in the South Pacific. The move, which ended France's three-year moratorium on nuclear testing, prompted an immediate furor. French goods were boycotted in Australia, and riots broke out in the French territory of Tahiti after the first test in September. Chirac reacted to the criticism by promis-

Smoke fills a Paris subway in July after a terrorist bomb exploded on a train, killing 7 people and injuring more than 80.

ing to support a total ban on tests when a global test-ban treaty went into effect in 1996. He also offered to extend France's nuclear prowess to a future pan-European defense system. On December 6, Chirac announced that he would end the testing in February 1996, three months earlier than planned. (See also **Pacific Islands.**)

Terror strikes. A bomb exploded on a Paris subway train on July 25, killing seven people. The government sent troops into major cities on September 8 as a security measure after two more bombs injured people in Paris and Lyon. The bombing campaign was believed to be aimed at ending French support for the military regime in Algeria.

On September 29, French police killed Khaled Kelkal, an Algerian-born immigrant, in a shootout outside Lyon. Kelkal was suspected of trying to bomb a Paris-Lyon high-speed train and of participating in the assassination of a moderate Algerian opposition leader in Paris on July 11.

Citing security concerns raised by the bombing as well as the spread of international drug trafficking, the government delayed plans to lift border controls with six other European countries. Those nations went ahead with the plan without France on July 1.

Holocaust apology. Chirac on July 16 acknowledged that France bore responsibility for the deportation of tens of thousands of Jews to Nazi death camps during World War II. The admission was a dra-

matic break from the stance taken by former President Mitterrand, who claimed that France could not be blamed for actions conducted by the Vichy government, which collaborated with Nazi Germany during the war.

Bank bailout. The government won approval from the European Commission on July 26 for the biggest bank bailout in European history. Under the plan, state-owned Credit Lyonnais, which was devastated by excessive lending in the late 1980's and early 1990's, would receive up to $9.2 billion in aid. But the commission ordered the bank to sell off at least 35 percent of its foreign assets.

Tour de France. The world's premier cycling race was marred on July 18 when 24-year-old Fabio Casartelli of Italy died of head injuries after crashing with six other riders on a descent in the Pyrenees Mountains. It was only the third death of a cyclist since the Tour was first held in 1903.

Miguel Indurain of Spain captured the tour five days later in Paris, becoming the first man to win the race for five consecutive years.   □ Tom Buerkle

See also **Europe** (Facts in brief table). In *World Book,* see **European Union; France.**

Gabon. See Africa.

Gambia. See Africa.

Gas and gasoline. See Energy supply; Petroleum and gas.

Genetic engineering. See Biology; Medicine.

Geology

Geology. Geological research during 1995 continued a trend toward nontraditional, interdisciplinary studies, which provided some startling discoveries. New insights were gained from the relatively recent geologic record of the last 1,000 years, as well as from the very distant past of 3.5 billion years ago.

Climate clues in human teeth. Fossils of human teeth can be used to learn about past changes in climate, according to an October report by geologists Henry C. Fricke and James R. O'Neil at the University of Michigan in Ann Arbor and anthropologist Niels Lynnerup at the University of Copenhagen in Denmark. The team found that the forms of oxygen in human tooth enamel vary according to the oxygen composition of local rain water and surface fresh water, the most common sources of drinking water in past times. The water's chemical makeup is related to its temperature, so the teeth can provide a permanent record of the climate at the time the person was alive. The scientists' analysis of fossil teeth found in Greenland supported a theory that there was a time of rapid global climate cooling during the period known as the Little Ice Age, about A.D. 1400 to 1700.

Climate change and the Maya. In approximately A.D. 800, the Maya civilization, which had flourished for hundreds of years in Central America and Mexico, collapsed. Although the civilization was known to have been stressed by civil war and other

factors, the precise reason for its collapse has remained a mystery. In June 1995, however, geologist David A. Hodell and his colleagues at the University of Florida in Gainesville proposed that the end of the civilization may have been prompted by an abrupt climate change.

Hodell analyzed the chemical composition of layers of sediment from a Yucatán lake and discovered that the period between A.D. 800 to 1000 was the driest interval of the past 11,000 years in Central America. The scientists proposed that the drought helped cause the decline of the Maya.

First evidence of tectonics. During the 1960's, scientists established the theory of plate tectonics, which explains that the outer shell of the Earth is divided into about 30 rigid plates that slowly move on a bed of hot rock. But for 30 years, a fundamental question has remained unanswered: Exactly when did plate tectonics begin to operate on Earth? A June 1995 report by geophysicist Andrew Calvert of the Polytechnic School of Montreal in Canada and his colleagues attempted to answer that question.

Using a technique that maps features underground using reflected sound waves, the researchers mapped a distinct zone up to 50 miles (30 kilometers) under the surface of much of Ontario and Quebec. The scientists estimated that 2.7 billion years ago, the area was a surface *subduction zone,* a boundary where one tectonic plate was drawn un-

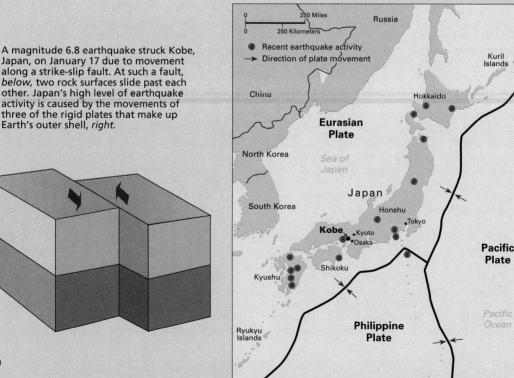

A magnitude 6.8 earthquake struck Kobe, Japan, on January 17 due to movement along a strike-slip fault. At such a fault, *below,* two rock surfaces slide past each other. Japan's high level of earthquake activity is caused by the movements of three of the rigid plates that make up Earth's outer shell, *right.*

der another. The finding pushed back the earliest known evidence of plate tectonics by some 800 million years.

How old are the continents? Exactly when the continents first appeared, and what fraction of the early Earth's surface they covered, have been hotly debated topics among geologists. In June, geologist Roger Buick of the University of Western Australia in Nedlands and his colleagues reported that they had discovered features of continental crust in 3.5-billion-year-old rocks in the Pilbara region of Australia. The finding indicated that continents existed during the early Archean Eon, which began about 3.8 billion years ago. Buick's discovery also supported a theory that large areas of continental crust existed within Earth's first billion years.

If continents were abundant during the early Archean, why are there so few remnants of the ancient crust visible on Earth's surface today? Geologists Samuel A. Bowring at the Massachusetts Institute of Technology in Cambridge and Todd Housh at the University of Texas in Austin addressed that issue in a September report. Drawing on data from chemical analyses, these researchers argued that continental crust has been continually recycled through tectonics and other natural processes. Only those fragments that escaped geologic recycling are detectable as ancient crust today.   □ Henry T. Mullins

In *World Book,* see **Geology; Plate tectonics.**

Georgia. On August 24, the Georgian parliament adopted a new Constitution, creating the office of an elected president to serve a five-year term. The leading presidential candidate, Parliament Chairman Eduard Shevardnadze, narrowly escaped assassination on August 29, when a car bomb exploded outside the parliament building in the capital, Tbilisi.

Shevardnadze, who survived the attack without serious injury, had no shortage of enemies. Talks with the breakaway regions of Abkhazia and South Ossetia were stalled. Georgia was lobbying for the construction of a pipeline to carry Caspian Sea oil, a plan strongly opposed by Russia. (In October, a compromise allowed both Georgian and Russian routes to be used.) Shevardnadze's enemies within Georgia included the opposition political group Mkhedrioni, long linked with organized crime and paramilitary activity. Shevardnadze cracked down on Mkhedrioni activities and banned its paramilitary arm.

On November 5, Shevardnadze was elected president with more than 70 percent of the popular vote.

Georgia's economy in 1995 remained highly dependent on Western aid, which accounted for more than half the nation's budget. In September, Georgia introduced a new currency, the lari.

□ Steven L. Solnick

See also **Asia** (Facts in brief table). In *World Book,* see **Georgia.**

Georgia (state of). See **State government.**

Germany. Chancellor Helmut Kohl and his Christian Democratic Party maintained a firm grip on power in 1995 despite the continued weakening of their coalition partner, the Free Democratic Party (FDP). In local elections on May 14, the FDP failed to achieve the minimum 5 percent of the vote required to hold parliamentary seats in the states of Bremen and North Rhine-Westphalia. Four days later, German Foreign Minister Klaus Kinkel resigned as party leader. Wolfgang Gerhardt, FDP leader in the state of Hesse, became the new party leader on June 11.

Criticism of party leader Rudolf Scharping led to a decline in the popularity of the opposition Social Democratic Party (SDP) in 1995. Scharping, whom party members felt provided ineffective leadership, was replaced on November 16 at the party's annual congress by Oskar Lafontaine, a long-time leader of the party's left wing. Lafontaine was expected to seek closer ties with the Green Party and the former Communists in Eastern Germany. He also questioned his party's support for establishing a single European currency in 1999 and suggested a delay in the target date to give EU governments more time to cut public spending.

The economy. Germany in 1995 pushed its European allies to agree to a pact enforcing tighter controls on government deficit spending among countries that participate in a single European currency. Finance Minister Theo Waigel said the deficit controls would reassure German citizens that the future currency would be as stable as the German mark. But the German campaign to impose tighter controls raised fears in other European countries that Germany might use its economic weight to dominate its partners or try to undermine the single currency.

The strength of the mark hurt major German companies and raised fears that the high cost of German labor and goods would drive jobs abroad and diminish long-term prosperity. Daimler-Benz AG, the country's largest industrial company, reported a loss of $1.06 billion in the first half of 1995, and predicted more losses for the entire year. It blamed losses at its aerospace division on the mark's strength against the United States dollar. A weaker dollar meant that airplanes and jet engines produced in the United States would be cheaper than those produced in Germany. The division in November won approval from Daimler-Benz to make major job cuts.

The tough economic climate persuaded some unions to agree to concessions on working hours and wages in return for job security. Adam Opel AG, the German subsidiary of the General Motors Corporation of Detroit, reached a landmark agreement with unions on September 6 that enabled Opel to vary working hours between 30 and 38.75 hours a week, as orders for cars rise and fall, without an increase in pay. Volkswagen AG reached a similar agreement with its workers on September 12.

Germany's most-wanted fugitive, real-estate

developer Juergen Schneider, was arrested in Miami, Florida, on May 18 and held pending extradition. Schneider and his wife, Claudia, who was also arrested, had been sought on fraud charges since April 1994 when his company, Juergen Schneider AG, went bankrupt with debts of about $3.5 billion.

Drawing a curtain on the Cold War. The Constitutional Court issued a landmark decision on May 23 that intelligence officials of the former East Germany could not be prosecuted for espionage. The court ruled that the former officials were acting properly under the laws of their nation at the time. The court's decision outraged many western German conservatives as well as some former East German dissidents, who believed the decision denied justice for the victims of the former Communist regime.

German troops to the Balkans. The German government in 1995 sent troops to Bosnia-Herzegovina in the country's first military deployment since World War II (1939-1945). Germany sent 1,500 troops in June to reinforce United Nations peacekeepers in Bosnia-Herzegovina, and in December it agreed to send 4,000 troops there to help enforce a peace settlement among Serbs, Muslims, and Croats.

Controversy on social issues. The Constitutional Court ruled in August that a law in the state of Bavaria requiring crucifixes to be displayed in public school classrooms violated the constitution's provisions on religious liberty. After strong criticism by state officials, the law was modified to allow crosses to be removed from classrooms if students' parents objected to their presence.

The parliament passed an abortion law on July 14 that declared the practice illegal except in cases of rape or where pregnancy endangers a mother's life. But the law would not punish doctors who perform abortions or women who seek them. The measure sought to strike a compromise between the laws of the former West Germany, which were restrictive, and the former East Germany, which made abortion free and available on demand.

Plutonium smuggling. A German court on July 17 found two Spaniards and a Colombian guilty of trying to smuggle plutonium—a highly radioactive element used in making nuclear weapons—out of Russia to the West. German police had confiscated the plutonium in 1994. The three men were sentenced to up to five years in prison. The men claimed that Germany's intelligence service set them up. Their charges led to calls for the resignation of the service's chief, Bernd Schmidbauer.

Reichstag under wraps. The Bulgarian-born artist Christo wrapped the Reichstag in Berlin with more than 1 million square feet (93,000 square meters) of silver cloth for two weeks in June and July. (See Art; Christo.) ☐ Tom Buerkle

See also **Europe** (Facts in brief table). In *World Book,* see **European Union; Germany.**
Ghana. See Africa.

Gingrich, Newt (1943-), a Republican congressman from Georgia, in 1995 began serving as the first Republican Speaker of the U.S. House of Representatives since the mid-1950's. He was one of the chief architects of the Contract with America, the 10-point program of conservative reforms that the Republican Party promised to bring to a vote within the first 100 days of the 104th Congress. And in December, he was named *Time* magazine's Man of the Year.

Gingrich is an energetic spokesman for what he calls "positive, dynamic conservatism." Chief among his goals are balancing the budget, cutting taxes, and radically reducing the federal government.

Newton Leroy Gingrich was born in Harrisburg, Pennsylvania, on June 17, 1943, the son of a career army officer. He graduated from Emory University in Atlanta, Georgia, in 1965, and earned a Ph.D. in modern European history from Tulane University in 1971. He took a teaching post at West Georgia College in Carrollton in 1970.

Gingrich was elected to the House in 1978. Fellow Republican members of Congress elected him minority whip in 1989.

Gingrich has coauthored several books, including *To Renew America* (1995), a collection of his views based partly on college lectures he delivered in 1994.

Gingrich has been married twice. He has two daughters. ☐ Lisa Klobuchar

Golf. On the course and off, Greg Norman of Australia dominated the sport in 1995. Jim Colbert was the major winner on the seniors' tour, and 24-year-old Annika Sorenstam of Sweden was the top golfer on the women's tour.

Norman was number one in the world rankings at year-end. In the United States, he won three tournaments on the Professional Golfers' Association (PGA) Tour. He led the tour in earnings with $1,654,959 to $1,543,192 for runner-up Billy Mayfair. Norman also won the point competition for PGA Player of the Year.

Steve Elkington of Australia won the Vardon Trophy for lowest average score per 18-hole round with 69.62 strokes. Norman averaged 69.06 strokes but became ineligible for the award when he dropped out of an April tournament.

Off the course, Norman was the organizer and spokesman for the projected World Golf Tour. Tour backers had a television commitment from the Fox network and had planned eight $3-million tournaments in the United States, Europe, Australia, and Japan in 1995. Four of those tournaments, all in the United States, would have conflicted with the PGA Tour, and when no American professional committed to the new tour, the plan evaporated.

Grand slam. The first tournament was the Masters from April 6 to 9 in Augusta, Georgia. That week, Harvey Penick, the celebrated golf teacher,

Emotion overcomes Ben Crenshaw after he sank a putt on the final hole to win the Masters tournament in April at the Augusta National Golf Club in Augusta, Georgia.

died at age 90. The day before the Masters began, Ben Crenshaw and Tom Kite, two of Penick's star pupils, flew from Augusta to Austin, Texas, to be pallbearers at the funeral. They flew back in time to play, and Crenshaw, sinking every key putt on the last round, won with a 72-hole score of 274 to beat Davis Love III by a stroke.

On the last hole of the United States Open from June 15 to 18 in Southampton, New York, Corey Pavin of the United States hit a 209-yard (191-meter) number-4 wood to within 5 feet (1.5 meters) of the hole. He finished with a 280 and won by two strokes over Norman.

In the British Open from July 20 to 23 in St. Andrews, Scotland, John Daly of the United States was a 66-to-1 long shot in legal betting. Costantino Rocca of Italy sank a 65-foot (20-meter) birdie putt from off the green on the last hole, and he and Daly finished at 282. Daly won the tournament's first-ever four-hole play-off by four strokes.

In the PGA championship from August 10 to 13 in Los Angeles, Steve Elkington rallied from six strokes back for a final-round 64. Colin Montgomerie of Scotland tied him at 267, the two breaking the PGA championship record and equaling the lowest score ever for a grand-slam tournament. Elkington won with a birdie on the first play-off hole.

Seniors. Colbert won the season-ending Senior Tour Championship, and his season earnings were $1,444,386. Raymond Floyd was second in earnings with $1,419,545. Colbert won four tournaments to Floyd's three. In the major tournaments, Floyd won the PGA Seniors in April, Tom Weiskopf the United States Seniors Open in July, and J.C. Snead the Senior Players Championship, also in July.

Women. Sorenstam was named Rolex Player of the Year on the Ladies Professional Golf Association (LPGA) Tour. She won three LPGA tournaments, including the United States Open and the World Championship of Women's Golf in October. She was the leading money winner on the LPGA Tour with $666,533, and she won the Vare Trophy for lowest scoring average (71.0). In the majors, Nanci Bowen won the Nabisco Dinah Shore, Kelly Robbins the LPGA championship, Sorenstam the United States Open, and Jenny Lidback the du Maurier Classic. Betsy King won her 30th career victory on June 25, giving her automatic entry into the LPGA Hall of Fame.

Other. The European team upset the United States, 14½ to 13½, in the biennial Ryder Cup professional matches September 22 to 24 in Rochester, New York. The amateur team from the United Kingdom and Ireland defeated the United States, 14 to 10, in the Walker Cup matches September 9 and 10 in Porthcawl, Wales. At 19, Tiger Woods won his second consecutive United States amateur title in August. □ Frank Litsky

In *World Book,* see **Golf.**

Gore, Albert, Jr. Vice President Albert Gore, Jr., carried out several foreign and domestic assignments for President Bill Clinton in 1995 and was assured of the second spot on the Democratic Party's national ticket in 1996.

Clinton credited Gore with leading the Administration's program to restructure the federal government, with claimed savings of $63 billion. The Vice President also led the United States delegation to the first United Nations World Summit on Social Development at Copenhagen, Denmark, March 6 to 13. Gore asserted that the United States would not abandon efforts to aid the world's poor, despite attempts by the Republican Congress to cut back foreign assistance. But he added that more aid would be provided by private groups in the future.

Gore on June 30 signed bilateral agreements with Russian Premier Viktor S. Chernomyrdin in Moscow. One pact provided for a $15-billion investment by the Exxon Corporation to explore and develop oil fields near Sakhalin Island, off Russia's Pacific coast. Another called for the sale of 500 metric tons of weapons-grade uranium to the United States over the next 20 years, for an estimated $12 billion.

Clinton and Gore formally opened their reelection campaign on April 14 by filing documents with the Federal Election Commission to allow them to begin raising funds for 1996. □ William J. Eaton

In *World Book*, see Gore, Al.

Graf, Steffi (1969-), a German tennis player, in 1995 became the second-all-time highest-paid woman tennis player (after Martina Navratilova) when her prize winnings topped $15 million. Graf's 1995 Wimbledon victory gave her 16 career grand-slam titles. As of mid-1995, she had won a total of 92 singles and 11 doubles tournaments. For six of the years since 1987, she ranked as the year's number-one woman tennis player.

Graf was born in Mannheim, West Germany, on June 14, 1969. Her parents were both semiprofessional tennis players, and her father began teaching her to play tennis when she was 4. She turned professional at age 13 and moved steadily up in the rankings, reaching number three in 1986.

After that, her extraordinary tennis abilities—a powerful forehand, a punishing serve, and remarkable speed—led to a 24-match winning streak and four titles in a row. Her defeat of Navratilova at the 1987 French Open gave Graf her first grand-slam victory. In 1988, Graf won what has become known as "the Golden Slam," winning the Australian, French, and United States opens and Wimbledon, and taking the gold medal at the Summer Olympics in Seoul, South Korea.

In August 1995, Graf's father was arrested in Germany on suspicion of tax evasion. At the time of his arrest, German authorities said that Steffi was under investigation as well. □ Lisa Klobuchar

Gramm, Phil (1942-), a senator from Texas, on Feb. 24, 1995, announced his candidacy for the 1996 Republican presidential nomination. Gramm became known as a fiscal conservative, a supporter of free trade, and an outspoken critic of President Bill Clinton. He began his campaign with promises to reduce the size of the federal government, cut taxes, and halt further reductions in military spending.

William Philip Gramm was born on July 8, 1942, in Fort Benning, Georgia. He studied economics at the University of Georgia, receiving a bachelor's degree in 1964 and a doctorate in 1967. He joined the faculty of Texas A&M University the same year.

Gramm first served in public office as a Democrat, winning a seat in the House of Representatives in 1978. He was reelected in 1980 and—after switching to the Republican Party as a result of a falling-out with his Democratic colleagues—again in 1982.

Gramm won his Senate seat in 1984 and quickly established himself as a powerful leader, especially in the area of deficit reduction. He was coauthor of the Gramm-Rudman balanced-budget bill of 1985, which initiated automatic across-the-board spending cuts if specified deficit ceilings were exceeded.

Gramm and his wife, Wendy Lee, married in 1970. They have two sons. Gramm has written several books, including *The Role of Government in a Free Society*. □ Lisa Klobuchar

Great Britain. See United Kingdom.

Greece in 1995 reached an interim agreement to resolve a four-year-old border dispute with the former Yugoslav republic of Macedonia. Greece had refused to recognize the republic since it declared its independence during the breakup of Yugoslavia in 1991. The disagreement had threatened to trigger a broader conflict in the Balkans.

Under the agreement, which was signed at the United Nations on September 13 by Foreign Minister Karolos Papoulias of Greece and his Macedonian counterpart, Stevo Crvenkovski, the two countries agreed to establish diplomatic relations and recognize their existing common border. Macedonia changed its flag to eliminate the 16-pointed Star of Vergina, an important symbol of the Greek cultural heritage, and pledged that its Constitution, which vows to protect all ethnic Macedonians, would not be used to justify claiming territory beyond its borders. Greece considered the Constitution and the flag as threats to its security because Greece has a large ethnic Macedonian population.

In return, Greece agreed to lift its trade embargo against landlocked Macedonia, which relies on Greek ports as its lifeline to the world economy. The agreement removed a major source of conflict between Greece and its allies in the European Union (EU), who had attempted for the previous two years to send aid to the former Yugoslav republic to prevent any spread of the Balkan war. The accord did not resolve a dispute over the name Macedonia, however. Greece's northernmost province is also called Macedonia, and Greece refused to permit any use of the name by its neighbor. As a result, the international community usually referred to the former Yugoslav republic of Macedonia by its awkward acronym, *Fyrom*.

Internal politics. Disputes over economic policy and the successor of Andreas Papandreou, the country's frail 76-year-old prime minister, dominated the Greek political scene in 1995. Papandreou resisted pressure from within his ruling Panhellenic Socialist Movement party, or PASOK, to designate a successor despite suffering from health problems. His ailments forced him to limit meetings with his own government ministers and caused him to be hospitalized in late November and December. At year-end, he was not expected to be able to return to work full-time.

Natural disasters. An earthquake with a magnitude of 6.1 destroyed a hotel and an apartment building in the southwest port town of Egion on June 15. Twenty-seven people were killed.

A fierce three-day fire destroyed over 10,000 acres (4,050 hectares) of forest around Athens in late July. Anarchist groups claimed responsibility for the fire, saying they wanted to punish the rich landowners of the area. ☐ Tom Buerkle

See also **Europe** (Facts in brief table). In *World Book,* see **European Union; Greece.**

Guatemala. Alvaro Arzú Irigoyen of the conservative National Advancement Party took a commanding share of the votes in presidential elections held Nov. 12, 1995. Arzú, 49, former Guatemalan foreign minister and mayor of Guatemala City, won 42 percent of the votes but fell short of the majority he needed by law to avoid a runoff.

Alfonso Portillo of the right wing Guatemalan Republican Front finished second in balloting and was to be Arzú's opponent in the runoff, which was scheduled for Jan. 7, 1996. The Guatemalan Republican Front was led by Efraín Ríos Montt, who consistently topped public opinion polls of possible presidential candidates. But as a former military dictator of the country, Ríos Montt was banned by the Guatemalan Constitution from running for president.

On Aug. 22, 1995, the Guatemalan National Revolutionary Union, a coalition of four guerrilla groups, announced a two-week cease-fire—the first in 30 years. But an army massacre on October 5 in the village of Aurora 8 de Octubre in the northern province of Alta Verapaz put the cease-fire in doubt. The soldiers killed at least 11 peasants and wounded 17 others. ☐ Nathan A. Haverstock

See also **Latin America** (Facts in brief table). In *World Book,* see **Guatemala.**

Guinea. See **Africa.**

Guyana. See **Latin America.**

Haiti. Haitians went to the polls on Dec. 17, 1995, to elect a new president to succeed Jean-Bertrand Aristide. The winner in the election, René Préval of the Lavalas Party, was due to become Haiti's next president on Feb. 7, 1996, when Aristide's term was scheduled to expire. Préval had served briefly as Haiti's prime minister under Aristide before Aristide was overthrown in a military coup in September 1991.

United Nations takes over. On March 31, United States President Bill Clinton visited Haiti to mark the withdrawal of the remaining 6,000 U.S. troops from a force of 20,000 that had entered the country in September 1994 in a successful effort to restore Aristide to power. The responsibility for keeping the peace was transferred in 1995 to a much smaller United Nations force of 6,900 soldiers and police officers from more than 30 countries.

Army purge. Aristide reduced the size of Haiti's armed forces from 7,000 to 1,500 during his first four months in office. On February 21, he purged the armed forces of virtually all senior officers, including all army generals, as plans moved ahead to create a new national police force.

Tainted elections. Haitians went to the polls on June 25 to choose 18 senators and 83 deputies for a new Parliament. Aristide's Lavalas Party won a majority of the seats, but international observers described the elections as chaotic. According to the U.S.-based Carter Center of Atlanta, Georgia, which monitored the elections, much of the voting was tainted by fraud. Makeup elections for seats that observers determined had been obtained fraudulently were held on August 13, resulting in a landslide for the Lavalas Party.

Paramilitary chief deported. On September 1, a U.S. judge ordered the deportation of Haitian paramilitary chief Emmanuel Constant to stand trial in Haiti on charges of rape, torture, and murder. Constant was the former head of the Front for the Advancement and Progress of Haiti, a paramilitary organization involved in human rights abuses under the military dictatorship that ruled the country from 1991 to 1994. Constant entered the United States in 1994, and agents of the U.S. Immigration and Naturalization Service captured him in New York City on May 10, 1995.

Aristide stirs up trouble. Speaking at the funeral of his slain cousin, Jean-Hubert Feuille, on November 11, Aristide urged his supporters to "go to neighborhoods where there are big houses and heavy weapons" and disarm "thugs" in retaliation for what many considered a political murder. Aristide's supporters lynched seven people in response. ☐ Nathan A. Haverstock

See also **Latin America** (Facts in brief table). In *World Book,* see **Haiti.**

Harness racing. See **Horse racing.**

Hawaii. See **State government.**

Health-care issues

Health-care issues. Republicans, who won control of the United States Congress in 1994, went to work in 1995 on their announced priorities. Those priorities differed strikingly from those of the Democrats, especially in terms of health-care policy.

Most Republican members of the House of Representatives and many Republican senators were committed to balancing the federal budget within seven years and thus limiting the growth of the national debt. To accomplish that goal, they believed that many federal programs had to be cut significantly. The programs they wished to cut included Medicare, which covers the cost of most hospital stays and physicians' visits for people over age 65, and Medicaid, which covers some health-care costs for the very poor, those with disabilities, and many residents of nursing homes. The Republicans also wanted to use some of the money saved by these cuts to roll back various federal taxes.

The Republicans' cause received a boost in April, when the trustees of the fund that pays for Medicare reported that, at the current rate of spending, the fund would be bankrupt by the year 2002. Saving Medicare from bankruptcy thus joined balancing the budget and the tax cut as a reason for reducing Medicare and Medicaid spending. In June 1995, the House and Senate agreed on the level of reduction: $270 billion would be cut from Medicare over seven years, and $180 billion would be taken from Medicaid. The latter figure could rise as high as $420 billion if the states, which pay for part of Medicaid, reduced their spending on the program as well.

Clinton's response. Although President Bill Clinton criticized the size of the proposed cuts, he concurred with balancing the budget in seven years, and offered to reduce Medicare spending by $124-billion and Medicaid by $54 billion in that time. He also said he would veto any legislation containing what he considered to be "unacceptable" cuts.

The President was not willing to go along with other parts of the Republican plan, however, especially with a proposal to end certain guarantees that had been part of Medicaid from its beginnings in 1965. The program had promised health-care coverage, known as entitlements, to certain groups: people (mostly mothers and children) receiving welfare payments, low-income residents of nursing homes, and those considered disabled under federal guidelines. The House and Senate leadership wanted to end the entitlements and most federal involvement in Medicaid. To do so, they proposed to turn the program over to the states as a single grant from the federal government with few strings attached.

Clinton also opposed a Republican plan to raise the amount of money Medicare beneficiaries paid as premiums to obtain Medicare coverage for their physicians' bills. The House and Senate bills also called for the enrollment of more Medicare beneficiaries in managed-care plans and for the introduc-

Boston senior citizens in June protest Medicare cuts proposed by Republicans to achieve the balanced budget promised in the Contract with America.

tion of so-called medical savings accounts that would allow potential beneficiaries to "opt out" of Medicare. Even so, much of the money to be saved would come from reduced payments to hospitals, physicians, nursing homes, and other health-care providers. Not surprisingly, most provider organizations eventually opposed most aspects of the bills.

The battle over Medicare and Medicaid went on for all of 1995, with each side accusing the other of trying to destroy the programs. The debate came to symbolize the much larger issue of how much the federal government should spend and on what.

At year's end, the matter had still not been settled, despite the fact that the lack of a federal budget had already caused a six-day suspension of most federal government activities in November. Another shutdown occurred in December. There were indications that the two sides might simply agree to disagree and retain current formats and funding levels until after the 1996 election.

Given the bitterness of the health-care debate and the uncertain future of the programs, it was ironic that both the White House and Congress held celebrations marking the 30th anniversary of the creation of Medicare and Medicaid on July 30, 1995. The congressional event failed to mention Medicaid, however. ☐ Emily Friedman

See also **Medicine.** In *World Book,* see **Health.**
Hobbies. See **Toys and games.**

Hockey. Labor troubles almost wiped out the National Hockey League's 1994-1995 season before it began. Owners of the 26 teams, unable to reach a labor agreement with the players, locked them out for 103 days. When the season was finally played, the New Jersey Devils won the Stanley Cup play-offs, the first title ever for the Devils, who played in Kansas City and Denver before moving in 1982 to East Rutherford, New Jersey.

Collective bargaining. When contract talks between owners and players stalled in 1994, the owners feared that the coming season would be interrupted by a strike. So, despite assurances by the players that they would not strike, the owners locked them out on Oct. 1, 1994.

On Jan. 11, 1995, the owners and players reached an agreement that gave the owners most of their major demands, but not a payroll tax to control salaries. After a week of practice to get the players in condition, the season began with 48-game rather than 84-game schedules for each team. However, the four rounds of the play-offs were preserved.

Season and play-offs. The Devils struggled during the regular season, but their 22-18-8 record for 52 points easily made them one of the 16 teams in the play-offs. They finished fifth in the Eastern Conference, which the Quebec Nordiques won with 65 points. The Detroit Red Wings won the Western Conference title with 70 points.

Scott Niedermayer of the New Jersey Devils scores a goal in June in the Stanley Cup finals against the Detroit Red Wings, a series the Devils won, 4-0.

National Hockey League standings

Western Conference

Central Division

	W.	L.	T.	Pts.
Detroit Red Wings*	33	11	4	70
St. Louis Blues*	28	15	5	61
Chicago Blackhawks*	24	19	5	53
Toronto Maple Leafs*	21	19	8	50
Dallas Stars*	17	23	8	42
Winnipeg Jets	16	25	7	39

Pacific Division

Calgary Flames*	24	17	7	55
Vancouver Canucks*	18	18	12	48
San Jose Sharks*	19	25	4	42
Los Angeles Kings	16	23	9	41
Edmonton Oilers	17	27	4	38
Anaheim Mighty Ducks	16	27	5	37

Eastern Conference

Northeast Division

Quebec Nordiques*	30	13	5	65
Pittsburgh Penguins*	29	16	3	61
Boston Bruins*	27	18	3	57
Buffalo Sabres*	22	19	7	51
Hartford Whalers	19	24	5	43
Montreal Canadiens	18	23	7	43
Ottawa Senators	9	34	5	23

Atlantic Division

Philadelphia Flyers*	28	16	4	60
New Jersey Devils*	22	18	8	52
Washington Capitals*	22	18	8	52
New York Rangers*	22	23	3	47
Florida Panthers	20	22	6	46
Tampa Bay Lightning	17	28	3	37
New York Islanders	15	28	5	35

*Made play-off.

Stanley Cup winner—
New Jersey Devils (defeated Detroit Red Wings, 4 games to 0)

Scoring leaders	Games	Goals	Assists	Pts.
Jaromir Jagr, Pittsburgh	48	32	38	70
Eric Lindros, Philadelphia	46	29	41	70
Alexei Zhamnov, Winnipeg	48	30	35	65
Joe Sakic, Quebec	47	19	43	62
Ron Francis, Pittsburgh	44	11	48	59
Theoren Fleury, Calgary	47	29	29	58
Paul Coffey, Detroit	45	14	44	58
Mikael Renberg, Philadelphia	47	26	31	57
John LeClair, Mtl.-Phi.	46	26	28	54
Mark Messier, N.Y. Rangers	46	14	39	53
Adam Oates, Boston	48	12	41	53

Leading goalies (13 or more games)	Games	Goals against	Avg.
Dominik Hasek, Buffalo	41	85	2.11
Rick Tabaracci, Wsh.-Cgy.	13	21	2.11
Jim Carey, Washington	28	57	2.13
Chris Osgood, Detroit	19	41	2.26
Ed Belfour, Chicago	42	93	2.28

Awards
Calder Trophy (best rookie)—Peter Forsberg, Quebec
Hart Trophy (most valuable player)—Eric Lindros, Philadelphia
Lady Byng Trophy (sportsmanship)—Ron Francis, Pittsburgh
Masterton Trophy (perseverance, dedication to hockey)—
    Pat LaFontaine, Buffalo
Norris Trophy (best defenseman)—Paul Coffey, Detroit
Ross Trophy (leading scorer)—Jaromir Jagr, Pittsburgh
Selke Trophy (best defensive forward)—Ron Francis, Pittsburgh
Smythe Trophy (most valuable player in Stanley Cup)—
    Claude Lemieux, New Jersey
Vezina Trophy (most valuable goalie)—Dominik Hasek, Buffalo

Quebec, which had missed the play-offs in six of the seven previous years, was a favorite this time, but the Nordiques lost in the first round, 4 games to 2, to the New York Rangers, the defending Stanley Cup champions. The Philadelphia Flyers then eliminated the Rangers, 4 games to 0.

Detroit and New Jersey advanced to the finals, where Detroit was favored because of its offensive talent. But the Red Wings could not overcome New Jersey's suffocating defense. The Devils won the first two games of the finals at Detroit and the next two at home to sweep the finals in four games.

Center Eric Lindros of Philadelphia was voted the Hart Trophy as the Most Valuable Player in the regular season, and forward Claude Lemieux of New Jersey the Conn Smythe Trophy as the Most Valuable Player in the play-offs. Forward Jaromir Jagr of the Pittsburgh Penguins won the Art Ross Trophy as the regular-season scoring champion.

World. On May 6, Finland won its first world title by beating Sweden, 4-1, in the final of the world hockey championships in Stockholm. The United States surprisingly won its preliminary group with a 3-0-2 record. However, the Americans lost to Canada, 4-1, in the quarterfinals. Canada lost to Sweden, 3-2, in the semifinals but took third place with a 4-1 victory over the Czech Republic.   □ Frank Litsky

In *World Book,* see Hockey.

Honduras. See Latin America.

Horse racing. Cigar, a 5-year-old thoroughbred, went undefeated in 1995, winning 10 stakes races and evoking comparisons to such all-time greats as Secretariat, Spectacular Bid, and Cigar's grandfather, Seattle Slew. The best harness horses were 3-year-olds—the pacing colt Jenna's Beach Boy and the trotting filly CR Kay Suzie.

Cigar. Cigar's winning year began and Holy Bull's career ended in the Donn Handicap on February 12 in Hallandale, Florida. Holy Bull, the 1994 3-year-old champion and Horse of the Year, broke down in the race and was retired to stud duty.

After that, Cigar won big races in California, Florida, Maryland, Massachusetts, and New York with ease. In the Hollywood Gold Cup in July, he ran away from such winners of million-dollar races as Concern, Best Pal, and Urgent Request as if they were refugees from claiming races. Cigar's earnings of $4,819,800 were the most ever won by a race horse in one year.

He ended his season by winning the $3-million Breeders' Cup Classic on October 28 at Elmont, New York, over a muddy track and from a bad post position. His time of 1 minute 59⅗ seconds for the 1¼ miles was the first sub-2-minute race in Classic history, and his margin of 2½ lengths was the largest ever.

Triple Crown. Trainer D. Wayne Lucas entered three horses in the $957,400 Kentucky Derby on May 6 in Louisville, Kentucky—Timber Country, the filly

Major horse races of 1995

Race	Winner	Value to winner
Arlington Million	Awad	$600,000
Belmont Stakes	Thunder Gulch	$415,440
Breeders' Cup Classic	Cigar	$1,560,000
Breeders' Cup Distaff	Inside Information	$520,000
Breeders' Cup Juvenile	Unbridled's Song	$520,000
Breeders' Cup Juvenile Fillies	My Flag	$520,000
Breeders' Cup Mile	Ridgewood Pearl	$520,000
Breeders' Cup Sprint	Desert Stormer	$520,000
Breeders' Cup Turf	Northern Spur	$1,040,000
Derby Stakes (England)	Lammtarra	$789,038
Hollywood Gold Cup Handicap	Cigar	$550,000
Irish Derby (Ireland)	Winged Love	$528,458
Japan Cup (Japan)	Lando	$1,708,304
Jim Beam Stakes	Serena's Song	$360,000
Jockey Club Gold Cup	Cigar	$450,000
Kentucky Derby	Thunder Gulch	$707,400
King George VI and Queen Elizabeth Diamond Stakes (England)	Lammtarra	$435,981
Molson Export Million	Peaks and Valleys	$600,000
Oaklawn Handicap	Cigar	$450,000
Pacific Classic Stakes	Tinners Way	$550,000
Pimlico Special Handicap	Cigar	$360,000
Preakness Stakes	Timber Country	$446,810
Prix de l'Arc de Triomphe (France)	Lammtarra	$745,560
Rothmans International (Canada)	Lassigny	$653,250
Santa Anita Handicap	Urgent Request	$550,000
Super Derby	Mecke	$450,000
Travers Stakes	Thunder Gulch	$450,000

Major U.S. harness races of 1995

Race	Winner	Value to winner
Cane Pace	Mattgilla Gorilla	$192,187
Hambletonian	Tagliabue	$500,000
Little Brown Jug	Nick's Fantasy	$132,111
Meadowlands Pace	David's Pass	$500,000
Messenger Stakes	David's Pass	$164,412
Woodrow Wilson	A Stud Named Sue	$292,750

Sources: *The Blood-Horse* magazine and U.S. Trotting Association.

Serena's Song, and Thunder Gulch. The least regarded, Thunder Gulch, won by 2¼ lengths.

Timber Country won the $687,400 Preakness on May 20 in Baltimore, with Thunder Gulch third. Thunder Gulch also won the $692,400 Belmont Stakes on June 10 in Elmont.

Lucas achieved two firsts in 1995. He became the first trainer to sweep the Triple-Crown series with two horses and the first to win five consecutive Triple Crown races. But his triumphs were tempered by leg injuries to Thunder Gulch and Timber Country that forced them into retirement by October.

Harness. The year's best horses were Jenna's Beach Boy, with 13 victories in 15 races; CR Kay Suzie (10 of 13); Pacific Rocket, a 4-year-old pacing horse (16 of 27); and Ellamony, a 5-year-old pacing mare (18 of 22).

Among 3-year-old pacers, Jenna's Beach Boy set a world record of 1 minute 48⅘ seconds for the mile on September 30 in Lexington. David's Pass captured the $1-million North America Cup in June, the $1-million Meadowlands Pace in July, and the first Triple Crown race, the Messenger, in July. The other Triple Crown winners were Mattgilla Gorilla in the Cane Pace in August and Nick's Fantasy in the Little Brown Jug in September.   □ Frank Litsky

In *World Book,* see Horse racing.

Hospital. See Health-care issues.

Housing. See Building and construction.

Houston gave itself the nickname "Two-ston" after winning another National Basketball Association (NBA) championship in 1995—the city's second in a row. The Houston Rockets, led by superstar center Hakeem Olajuwon and his former University of Houston teammate Clyde Drexler, on June 14 completed a four-game sweep of the Orlando Magic. The Rockets on June 16 were treated to a downtown victory parade, where an estimated 400,000 fans screamed their approval.

Oveta Culp Hobby, former editor and publisher of *The Houston Post* and a pioneer among women in business and government, died on August 16 at age 90. Hobby organized the Women's Auxiliary Army Corps in 1941 and was awarded the Distinguished Service Medal in 1944.

President Dwight D. Eisenhower in 1953 appointed Hobby the first secretary of the new Department of Health, Education and Welfare (now Health and Human Services). She resigned her cabinet post in 1955 after her husband, former Texas Governor William P. Hobby, became ill. Their son, William P. (Bill) Hobby, Jr., was a long-time lieutenant governor of Texas.

Farewell to the *Post*. After over a century of publication, *The Houston Post* printed its final edition on April 18, putting about 1,500 employees out of work. The *Post* had struggled with debt incurred in William Dean Singleton's $150-million buyout of the paper in 1987. Singleton blamed the paper's demise on the rising cost of newsprint. From about $400 a metric ton in 1994, the price of newsprint had risen to about $675 a metric ton.

The closure left Houston with only one newspaper, the *Houston Chronicle*. The Hearst Corporation, which owned the *Chronicle,* paid about $120 million for the *Post*'s building, presses, and list of about 300,000 subscribers. Adding *Post* subscribers gave the *Chronicle* a circulation of about 540,000 daily and 740,000 Sundays, ranking the paper in the top 10 nationwide.

The Oilers look east. After failing to persuade Houstonians to build a new domed stadium for his football team, Houston Oilers owner Bud Adams appeared ready to relocate the team to Nashville. He insisted as the 1995 season began that the Astrodome was not a fit stadium for big-time football.

On October 4, Adams signed a contract with Nashville Mayor Philip Bredesen in which they agreed that the Oilers would start playing in Nashville in 1998 if the city meets every step in a financing plan worth $292 million. Experts estimated that the Oilers' value would increase from about $157-million to at least $200 million if the team moved to Nashville. Many fans hoped the deal would fall through, but others were ready to let the Oilers go, tired of Adams' repeated threats to leave town. The Oilers on October 1 became the first team to lose to the Jacksonville Jaguars expansion team.

Violent crime in Houston continued to decline in 1995, following a trend that began earlier in the decade. Through the first half of the year, the police recorded a 27 percent drop in homicides from the same period in 1994, 21 percent fewer rapes, and 12 percent fewer robberies. Overall, violent crime had decreased by over 6 percent from the previous year.

Compaq Computer Corporation, based in Houston, was the world's top seller of personal computers as 1995 began. Compaq outsold both IBM and Apple, surpassing chief executive Eckhard Pfeiffer's goal of achieving the top spot by 1996. The company's management set a goal of making $30-billion in annual sales by the year 2000, almost triple the $10.9 billion in sales the company made in 1994.

Selena. A Houston jury on October 26 sentenced Yolanda Saldivar, 35, to life in prison for the murder of 23-year-old Tejano music star Selena. Saldivar was the founder and former president of Selena's fan club. She was convicted of shooting Selena in a motel room in Corpus Christi, Texas, in March 1995 after the singer reportedly confronted her with allegations of embezzlement.

Mayor Bob Lanier was reelected in November 1995 to a third and final term. He defeated by a large margin challengers Elizabeth Spates, a former school board member, and David B. Wilson, the owner of a sign company. □ Burke Watson

See also **City.** In *World Book,* see **Houston.**

Hungary. Economic issues dominated the government's agenda as it fought a $4-billion budget deficit in 1995. In March, Prime Minister Gyula Horn's socialist-liberal government unveiled an austerity plan that raised taxes, reduced the number of civil servants and teachers, cut social benefits, linked such benefits as family allowances to financial need, and introduced fees for university tuition for the first time. The Constitutional Court later ruled that some of these measures, including the transfer of responsibility for maternity leave and sick pay to employers, were unconstitutional. The court also delayed means-testing for family allowances.

University students and the National Association of Large Families staged demonstrations to protest the changes. In April, railway workers struck for 84 hours to protest against the government's economic policies. By August, the opposition Smallholders Party led other political parties in opinion polls.

In addition, the government raised the price of electricity, heating, transportation, and many basic foods. Inflation rose to about 30 percent. The Hungarian currency, the forint, was devalued by 13.4 percent in the first three months of 1995.

Industrial production rose by 11 percent in the first quarter of 1995. Foreign investment increased significantly, as did Hungarian exports. Unemployment fell, reaching 10.2 percent in May.

In January, the sale of the government-owned

Ice skating

hotel chain HungarHotels to a United States buyer, American General Hospitality Group, fell through. The deal stalled when the Hungarian government demanded an additional $10 million above the agreed-upon price of $57.5 million. In May, the government passed a bill to speed up privatization. In July, the government sold 20 percent of the Hungarian National Bank and announced plans to privatize the state oil and gas company.

Politics. In June, Hungarian President Arpad Goncz was reelected by the legislature for another five-year term. In January, two former Communist militiamen who had shot unarmed civilians during the uprising of 1956 were sentenced to five years in prison. At least 47 people died in the 1956 incident.

Foreign policy. As a condition of applying for membership in the North Atlantic Treaty Organization (NATO) and the European Union (EU), Hungary moved to improve relations with its neighbors. On March 19, Hungarian and Slovak leaders agreed to a bilateral treaty that had been stalled by disagreements over the treatment of the Hungarian minority in Slovakia.

Negotiations for a similar treaty with Romania broke off in July amid concern over the reported mistreatment of the Hungarian minority in the Romanian region of Transylvania. □ Sharon L. Wolchik

See also **Europe** (Facts in brief table). In *World Book,* see **Hungary.**

Ice skating. Figure skating was so popular among Americans in 1995 that many made-for-television competitions were held, each with its own rules and few with the blessing of the International Skating Union (ISU), the sport's world governing body. As a result, such outstanding skaters as Nancy Kerrigan, Kristi Yamaguchi, and Brian Boitano of the United States and Oksana Baiul and Viktor Petrenko of Ukraine competed only as professionals.

The ISU, hoping to keep the best skaters under its wing, announced it would pay prize money in future world championships and create a Grand Prix circuit with prize money. Meanwhile, none of those professionals competed in the 1995 world championships, held from March 5 to 11 in Birmingham, England.

In that competition, Elvis Stojko of Canada retained his men's title. Despite pain from a torn ligament above the right ankle, he landed seven clean triple jumps and almost landed a quadruple toe loop. In second place was Todd Eldredge of Chatham, Massachusetts, who had won four major competitions earlier in the season. Philippe Candeloro of France took third place.

The women's champion was 18-year-old Chen Lu, the first Chinese skater to win a world title. Surya Bonaly of France, who had won her fifth consecutive European title a month earlier, finished second; Nicole Bobek of Chicago, third; and 14-year-old

Michelle Kwan of Torrance, California, fourth. Bobek had led after the short program.

Radka Kovarikova and Rene Novotny won the pairs and became the first world champions from the Czech Republic. Oksana Grichtchuk and Yevgeny Platov of Russia retained their title in ice dancing.

Eldredge and Bobek, both coached by Richard Callaghan in Detroit, won the United States titles February 8 to 11 in Providence, Rhode Island. Bobek had gone through eight coaches in eight years.

Speed. Bonnie Blair of Champaign, Illinois, who won five gold medals in the last three Winter Olympic Games, retired in March at age 31. In the world sprint championships February 18 and 19 on her home ice in Milwaukee, she swept the two races at 500 meters, and the two at 1,000 meters and won the title easily. She also won the World Cup season-long titles at 500 and 1,000 meters.

Sergei Grinkov dies. Sergei Grinkov of Russia, 28, collapsed and died on November 20 during practice at Lake Placid, New York. He died of a heart attack caused by undetected heart disease. Grinkov and his wife, Ekaterina Gordeeva, won two Olympic gold medals and four world pairs figure skating titles. □ Frank Litsky

In *World Book,* see **Ice skating.**

Iceland. See Europe.

Idaho. See State government.

Illinois. See Chicago; State government.

Immigration. Both legal and illegal immigration came under increasing attack in 1995 as United States lawmakers moved to restrict entry to the country. Federal budget cutbacks and job losses by Americans spurred calls for tighter control over U.S. borders and fewer benefits for immigrants.

Federal moves. President Bill Clinton early in 1995 asked the U.S. Congress for measures to speed deportation of illegal aliens convicted of crimes and to establish a national identification system to prevent employment of people who enter the United States illegally. In June, the Commission on Immigration Reform, a federal advisory body, urged a one-third reduction in the number of legal immigrants— from 675,000 to 550,000 a year. The group also proposed denying automatic admission to siblings and adult children of legal immigrants. The panel recommended a ceiling of 50,000 refugees a year, half the existing quota, as well as a cutback in admission of foreign workers with needed skills from 140,000 to 100,000. The President endorsed the commission's proposed changes.

The Republican-controlled Congress shared these inclinations, introducing legislation to tighten border security against illegal crossings and to ban all benefits other than emergency medical care for people in the country illegally. Other bills proposed penalizing employers who hire illegal immigrants and expediting the deportation of convicted criminals.

Political asylum for women who fled their homelands because they feared violence such as rape or beatings became the rare exception to stricter immigration policies in 1995. The Immigration and Naturalization Service in May decided to grant this new type of asylum. They were responding to such concerns as mass rapes by soldiers in the Bosnian war.

Cubans. On May 2, Clinton finalized the reversal of a 30-year-old policy of automatically admitting all refugees from Cuba. He said that Cubans arriving in the United States would be sent back to Cuba, and any Cubans seeking to immigrate in the future would have to apply as other nationals do. But the Clinton Administration also agreed with Cuba to admit at least 20,000 Cuban immigrants each year.

On August 11, U.S. officials chose by lottery who of the more than 10,000 Cubans remaining at the U.S. naval base at Guantánamo Bay, Cuba, would be allowed to enter the United States. Thousands of Cubans who sailed for the United States in 1994 on makeshift boats were sent to camps on the base.

Haitians. On Jan. 5, 1995, U.S. officials sent 4,000 Haitians back home from Guantánamo. Officials said the Haitians no longer risked political persecution since Jean-Bertrand Aristide had been restored to the Haitian presidency. ☐ William J. Eaton

In *World Book,* see **Immigration.**

Income tax. See **Taxation.**

India. The Congress Party, which had governed India for most of the years since it gained independence from the United Kingdom in 1947, grew weaker in 1995. The party still controlled the national Parliament, but it held power in only a few state governments.

The party's losing trend began in December 1994 with its defeat in elections for state legislatures in Andhra Pradesh, Karnataka, and Sikkim. In March 1995, the Congress Party lost control of Gujarat and Maharashtra, two industrialized states of western India, despite the benefits its economic policies had produced there. In Gujarat, the Bharatiya Janata Party (BJP), whose popularity was based on Hindu nationalism, won two-thirds of the state assembly seats. And in Maharashtra, the BJP and a more extremist Hindu party, the Shiv Sena, won just enough seats to form a coalition government.

Most state elections reflected the splintering of Indian politics, though most parties followed the Congress Party's path away from socialism and toward free-market principles. Votes were won on local issues and appeals to differences within the Hindu caste system. For example, voters in Bihar retained a bankrupt government that could not maintain law and order but catered to lower caste hostility toward the long-dominant upper castes. In Uttar Pradesh, India's most populous state, a coalition of lower castes and *untouchables* (people considered by Hindus to be below the caste system) broke up on June 1, when an untouchable, Mayawati, became head of the state government. Mayawati (she uses just one name) was the first untouchable woman ever to head an Indian state.

Rao challenged. The erosion of the Congress Party's strength stimulated challenges to its leader, Prime Minister P. V. Narasimha Rao. Arjun Singh, a former education minister, publicly criticized Rao and was expelled from the party on February 7. On May 19, Singh and Narain Dutt Tiwari, another former Congress Party minister, led a rally in the capital, New Delhi, that named Tiwari to head a dissident faction seeking to replace Rao as party leader and prime minister. Rao expelled Tiwari from the party, and the dissidents did not demand a vote in parliament to defeat Rao's government.

Another challenge came from Sonia Gandhi, the Italian-born widow of Rajiv Gandhi. Rajiv was the son of Indira Gandhi—both of them prime ministers of India who were assassinated. Many Congress Party members looked to Sonia to continue the dynasty of India's independence leader, Jawaharlal Nehru, who was Indira's father and Rajiv's grandfather.

On August 24, in her first public political statement, Sonia said Rao's government was abandoning the Nehru-Gandhi ideals. She accused the government of delaying a probe into the 1991 murder of her husband by a suicide bomber. However, she did not indicate an intention to enter politics.

Kashmir aflame. The death toll in the Himalayan state of Jammu and Kashmir continued to climb. Separatist fighting claimed at least 13,000 lives since 1989. India accused Muslim-dominated Pakistan of supporting the attacks on its rule. Kashmir had been the center of a dispute between India and Pakistan since 1947, and each country claimed Kashmir as part of its territory.

About 150,000 Indian troops and police clashed with Muslims in the valley around the Kashmir capital, Srinagar. Fighting between the Indian army and Muslim rebels led to a fire on May 11, 1995, that destroyed one of the valley's most important shrines, revered by both Muslims and Hindus. The crisis forced the government to postpone June elections.

In early July, a shadowy Muslim militant group, Al-Faran, kidnapped five Western tourists hiking in Kashmir. India refused to comply with the group's demand that India release 15 jailed comrades. On August 13 the militants decapitated one of the tourists, a Norwegian. A massive search failed to find the other hostages.

Separatist strife elsewhere. Another separatist movement by a Sikh religious group in the state of Punjab flared in 1995, two years after the government had brought the state under control. Beant Singh, the state's chief minister, had played a key role in subduing the Sikhs. On August 31, Singh was killed by a car bomb that also killed 15 other people.

In northeast India, where tribes of people known as Nagas had fought for independence since the 1950's, officials blamed an outlawed Naga group for bombing a troop train on February 25. The attack killed 27 soldiers. Officials said Burma was cooperating in military operations against Nagas and other Indian insurgents based along the Burmese border.

India's economy grew by about 6 percent in 1995 as Rao's government continued to loosen state controls. Even the Communist-led government of West Bengal state encouraged private investment.

Efforts to increase foreign investment were set back, however, by Maharashtra's newly elected government. On August 3, it announced the cancellation of the previous Congress Party government's contract for a Texas-based company to build a $2.8-billion electrical power plant. The government said contract negotiations had been unfair and involved corruption. The company claimed to have spent $300 million on the project and denied any illegal activities in negotiating the contract. On October 5, the government said an expert committee was working to revive the project.

Two trains collided at Firozabad on August 20, killing more than 300 people. It was one of the worst rail disasters in India's history

□ Henry S. Bradsher

See also **Asia** (Facts in brief table). In *World Book,* see **India**.

Indian, American.
Gambling on Indian lands, permitted by a 1987 Supreme Court ruling, continued to grow in 1995. But it also met with resistance.

After gaining official recognition as a tribe in 1994, the 3,000-member Pokagon Potawatomis of Michigan had by mid-September 1995 signed agreements with major casino developers. Their casino was planned for the southwestern Michigan town of Dowagiac and would be the 12th Indian casino in Michigan. The tribes paid 8 percent of their slot-machine revenues to the state and 2 percent to local governments. In 1994, Michigan received about $20-million in revenue from the tribes. Another Michigan tribe, the Huron Band of Potawatomis, obtained federal recognition on Dec. 19, 1995.

In March 1995, the Coeur d'Alene Indians of northern Idaho announced plans for a weekly national lottery with an initial jackpot of $50 million. The tribe would accept credit card payments for lottery tickets though a toll-free phone number, available in the 36 states that allowed such gambling. The 1,300-member tribe would pay a percentage of the revenues to the states. However, the plan was blocked by some of the states, which said the lottery could take lottery business away from them.

In the fall, the U.S. House of Representatives Ways and Means Committee approved a bill to tax income from Indian-owned casinos and limit the construction of new ones. Indians did not pay feder-al taxes on tribally owned businesses, and opponents said the bill would violate years of treaties and laws favorable to Indian autonomy. People who favored the taxation of Indian gambling said Indian-owned casinos were competing unfairly against state and private gambling operations.

Budget cuts. In August, the Senate approved a 15 percent budget cut for the Bureau of Indian Affairs (BIA) for fiscal 1996, giving the BIA 23 percent less money than President Bill Clinton had asked for. The BIA prepared to drop about 3,000 staff positions, and another 2,500 contract employees could also lose jobs. On September 11, tribal leaders held a protest vigil on the Mall in Washington, D.C., and began lobbying to restore funding.

Michigan Governor John Engler in July ended funding for a tuition-waiver program that about 2,500 American Indians used to attend the state's public universities. Michigan had committed to the waivers in a treaty by which Indians gave up lands that were then used as sites for public schools.

A senator changes sides. On March 3, U.S. Senator Ben Nighthorse Campbell (R., Colo.) shocked many Indians and Democratic colleagues when he announced his change from Democrat to Republican. He is a Northern Cheyenne and the only Native American in the U.S. Congress. □ Donald L. Fixico

In *World Book,* see **Indian, American**.

Indiana. See State government.

Indonesia.
President Suharto in 1995 celebrated the nation's 50th anniversary of declaring independence from the Netherlands by removing a special stamp from the identity cards of 1.35 million Indonesians. The stamp indicated that they had been accused of involvement in a 1965 Communist attempt to seize power. On Aug. 16, 1995, Suharto released three prominent political prisoners, including former deputy prime minister Subandrio. They had been sentenced to death for participating in the 1965 failed coup, but the sentences were later commuted to life in prison.

Other political prisoners remained behind bars, and the government continued to prosecute critics of the Suharto regime. A government minister, Siswono Yudohusodo, said in July that corruption, collusion, and manipulation within the bureaucracy, the business sector, and even social organizations were growing as fast as the economy.

Megawati Sukarnoputri, a daughter of former President Sukarno, led the only real opposition, the Indonesian Democratic Party. In May, she was barred from attending party functions in East Java in what was widely seen as an effort to limit her appeal to voters. Parliamentary elections were due in 1997.

Timor trouble. In January 1995, black-hooded gangs rampaged through East Timor, a former Portuguese colony of mainly Roman Catholics that Indonesia, a Muslim nation, seized in 1975. East Timor dissidents called the attacks an attempt by Muslim government officials to intimidate them into quitting their struggle for independence. In June 1995, a military court sentenced two soldiers to jail for killing six unarmed villagers in the January violence.

In March, a United Nations investigator found that the Indonesian army had planned the 1991 massacre of 150 to 270 Timor demonstrators at an independence rally. The army had insisted that troops fired spontaneously to defend themselves. The United Nations did not recognize Indonesia's sovereignty over East Timor and regarded Portugal as the legitimate administrative power.

On Sept. 8, 1995, rioting erupted in Dili, the regional capital of East Timor. Muslim government officials reportedly had insulted the Roman Catholic faith. Youths burned Dili's central market, which was dominated by Muslim merchants from other islands.

The economy. The government had to import rice to feed a growing population in 1995, and officials worried that oil exports were stagnating while domestic consumption rose. Still, overall economic trends were good.

Queen Beatrix of the Netherlands visited Indonesia in August. Despite improved relations, Indonesia refused development aid because the Dutch criticized its human rights record. ☐ Henry S. Bradsher

See also **Asia** (Facts in brief table). In *World Book,* see **Indonesia.**

Indurain, Miguel (1964-   ), a Spanish cyclist, won the Tour de France, an international bicycle race, for a record fifth straight time on July 23, 1995. The Tour de France covers about 2,500 miles (4,000 kilometers) through southern Europe, over grueling mountainous terrain.

In the 1995 Tour, Indurain finished a 2,270-mile (3,650-kilometer) course in 92 hours, 44 minutes, and 59 seconds over 23 days. He finished 4 minutes, 35 seconds ahead of the second-place cyclist. Only three other cyclists—Jacques Anquetil and Bernard Hinault of France, and Eddy Merckx of Belgium—have won the Tour five times, none of them in succession. Indurain's 1995 victory was somewhat overshadowed by the death on July 18 of Italian cyclist Fabio Casartelli, who crashed in the Pyrenees Mountains.

Indurain was born on July 16, 1964, in the region of Navarre in Spain. He lived with his parents in their farmhouse near the city of Pamplona until 1993, when he married his long-time girlfriend, Marisa, and moved with her to a house nearby.

Indurain was a professional cyclist for about seven years before he won a major race. He won his first Tour de France in 1991 by 3 minutes, 30 seconds. In his 1994 victory, over a course that was one of the Tour's most difficult, he won by 5 minutes, 39 seconds. Indurain is known as a gracious sportsman who allows other cyclists to win segments of the 20-stage race. ☐ Lisa Klobuchar

International trade. A newly elected Republican majority ruling the United States Congress stymied some international trade initiatives by the Democratic Administration of President Bill Clinton in 1995. Despite these setbacks, important trade negotiations moved forward during 1995.

Fast-track negotiating. A major setback for Clinton was Congress's refusal to grant his Administration's request for fast-track negotiating authority. This privilege, used in the past, allows U.S. officials to negotiate trade agreements with the understanding that a time limit can be set for congressional debate over the new agreement. In addition, the fast-track power means that Congress cannot add amendments to an agreement. This quick process assures trade partners that an agreement will be enacted quickly and will not be changed by Congress.

Congress and Clinton locked horns on the fast-track issue throughout 1995. The President insisted that environmental issues and workers' rights should be allowed in fast-track agreements. The Republicans argued that the Administration could negotiate agreements on the environment and workers' rights, but should allow Congress to amend them.

NAFTA. Clinton's lack of fast-track authority slowed and then stalled ongoing talks to make Chile, with its robust economy, a member of the North American Free Trade Agreement (NAFTA). Canada, Mexico, and the United States were the existing partners in NAFTA, a 1994 pact that united them as one of the world's largest free-trade zones.

The final negotiations that were expected to lead to Chile's membership in NAFTA by early 1996 never took place in 1995. Chile refused to offer significant changes in its own trade practices without assurances that the United States would do the same, unimpeded by congressional scrutiny.

APEC. Heads of state of the 18 nations of the Asia-Pacific Economic Cooperation (APEC) forum met on November 19 in Osaka, Japan. The APEC nations include most of East and Southeast Asia, Canada, Chile, Mexico, and the United States. The meeting resulted in a comprehensive draft plan to reach total free trade among the APEC nations by the year 2010 for the more advanced nations and 2020 for the still-developing countries. The 18 leaders accepted a 15-point plan of action that included commitments to reduce tariffs and do away with burdensome regulatory barriers to trade and investment. President Clinton was unable to attend the APEC summit because of a government shut-down that resulted from his dispute with Congress over balancing the budget. Vice President Albert Gore, Jr., went in his place.

EU. On Dec. 3, 1995, Clinton met in Madrid with Spanish Prime Minister Felipe González Márquez, who held the six-month, rotating presidency of the European Union (EU). The EU is an organization of 15 Western European countries that promotes cooperation among its members. Clinton met with

American and Chinese negotiators finalize an accord in February to end Chinese pirating and manufacturing of copyrighted and patented goods.

González to pledge closer economic ties between the United States and the EU. The meeting resulted in a "Transatlantic Agenda" that addressed matters from keeping peace in the Balkans to encouraging business ties on both sides of the Atlantic.

Japan. On June 28, after the Clinton Administration threatened to impose 100 percent *duties* (import taxes) on 13 makes of luxury Japanese automobiles, U.S. and Japanese negotiators finally signed an agreement. American trade officials and executives of the Big Three automakers—Chrysler Corporation, Ford Motor Company, and General Motors Corporation—had long been upset that the Japanese bought few American autos while sales of Japanese autos in the United States continued to climb to record numbers. Japan had built up its strong U.S. sales niche for 40 years. Since 1970, the Japanese had sold about 40 million autos to Americans, but only 400,000 American cars were shipped to Japan.

The five-year accord reached in June 1995 called for increased showroom space in Japan for U.S. autos and increased efforts by Japanese industry to purchase American auto parts. Japan pledged to reduce heavy regulation of its auto repair and replacement parts business. At the end of 1995, U.S. Trade Representative Mickey Kantor gave Japan high marks for opening the auto parts sector as agreed, but he expressed continued disappointment with lackluster results of selling new American cars there.

The U.S.-Japan auto accord led to a similar resolution with South Korea, which had also used regulations to block sales of foreign cars and car parts in its growing market. Koreans had bought only a handful of imported cars in prior years, but the nation's exports were significant.

China. On February 26, China and the United States barely averted a trade war. But they reached an accord just hours after U.S. officials moved to raise duties on $1 billion worth of Chinese goods coming into the United States. Although Chinese and U.S. leaders had signed a memorandum of understanding in 1992 on the protection of intellectual property rights, the Chinese had enforced little of that agreement. In late 1994, the two parties began discussions aimed at resolving the trouble.

American copyright and patent holders—mainly makers of compact disc recordings, movies, and computer software—were losing more than $800 million annually to Chinese piracy. Increasing amounts of the illegally made products were shipped to other countries, even to the United States. The February 1995 accord committed China to a number of specific initiatives to ensure that copyright and patent holders in the United States and other nations were protected against piracy. The accord included shutting down 29 manufacturers identified as pirates. However, by autumn 1995 U.S. officials suggested that China had not kept the bargain. Although

American officials credited Chinese authorities with raiding thousands of retail outlets suspected of selling pirated goods, hardly any manufacturing facilities were shut down.

China's lack of cooperation on product piracy was one issue that stalled its bid to rejoin the World Trade Organization (WTO) until at least 1996. For WTO entry, members must agree to follow the trade rules of the 1994 rewritten General Agreement on Tariffs and Trade (GATT), which also created the WTO. American trade representatives vowed to continue blocking China's WTO entry until matters like piracy enforcement were straightened out and China further liberalized market access in other areas.

Trade deficit. Economists expected 1995 to set another record for trade imbalance for the United States—with imports outstripping exports by some $27.5 billion by October. As in recent years, weak economies abroad and American consumers' appetite for imports increased the U.S. deficit.

However, by late in the year, both Kantor and U.S. Commerce Secretary Ronald H. Brown spoke of a turnaround. Brown said figures released through September showed a turning point in reversing the trade and services deficit. Kantor noted that the rate of increase in exports began to exceed that of imports.   □ Jim Berger

In *World Book,* see **International trade.**

Iowa. See **State government.**

Iran. United States President Bill Clinton, whose Administration has called Iran the worst sponsor of global terrorism, took steps in 1995 to isolate Iran economically. But his efforts met with mixed success.

In March, Clinton pressed the Dutch subsidiary of U.S.-based Conoco Inc. petroleum company to withdraw from a $1-billion deal to develop two oil fields offshore of Iran. He also announced in May the ban of all U.S. trade with Iran and encouraged other countries to join the embargo. Only Israel agreed, but it already had banned trade with Iran.

American exports to Iran made up only $326 million yearly, but U.S. oil companies were the largest buyers of Iranian crude, buying about 20 percent of Iran's petroleum exports annually at about $4 billion. This oil had to be resold outside of the United States. Clinton's ban forced Iran to find new buyers, but may have hurt the United States. Iranian President Ali Akbar Hashemi Rafsanjani said the United States lost an opportunity to improve relations when it canceled the Conoco deal. Iran invited oil and gas investors in on nearly $7 billion in new projects.

Weapons. The United States also pressured Russia and China not to sell nuclear reactors to Iran in 1995, fearing Iran intended to develop nuclear weapons. Russia, however, signed an $800-million deal in January to complete a nuclear power plant south of Iran's capital, Teheran. Although Russia agreed not to sell a gas centrifuge that could be used to build a nuclear bomb, Russian officials said in August that they would supply nuclear fuel to Iran for 10 years in return for $30 million yearly.

China said in September that it would temporarily suspend the planned sale of two nuclear reactors to Iran but was believed to be helping Iran produce intermediate-range ballistic missiles. United States officials in March also expressed concern about the increase of Iranian armed forces near the Strait of Hormuz, through which 20 percent of the world's oil leaves the Persian Gulf.

Economy. The Iranian rial lost half its value against the American dollar after the U.S. announcement of trade sanctions in May, but it recovered by September. Iran's biggest financial challenge, however, lay in making its more than $5-billion debt payment for 1996. Economists expected exports of 2.6 million barrels of oil daily to bring Iran about $13.5-billion for the fiscal year which began in March 1995, but they expected about half of that to be used to repay loans. Imports of luxury goods virtually ceased in 1995, and annual inflation was expected to be nearly 50 percent.

Drugs. Iran is part of a major route for the movement of drugs from Asia to Europe. Iranian authorities announced in June that they would place land mines along Iran's borders with Afghanistan and Pakistan to prevent drug smuggling. In the 12-month period ending on March 20, the police confiscated 135 tons (122 metric tons) of illegal drugs and arrested 39,000 people for drug-related crimes and 63,700 for drug addiction. Iran also lost 58 police officers killed in clashes with smugglers. Iran has up to 1 million drug addicts, and its laws allow execution for possessing slightly more than an ounce (28 grams) of heroin.

Population. Iranian officials said in July that the population growth rate had fallen from 3.9 percent in 1988 to 1.75 percent in 1995. Iran, unlike many Islamic countries, has had family planning programs since 1987. With its burgeoning population overtaxing national resources, Iran has been concerned about the fact that some 26 million young people are approaching childbearing age.

Mehdi Bazargan, the first prime minister after Iran's Islamic revolution in 1979, died on Jan. 20, 1995. Although a devout Muslim, Bazargan had resigned only nine months after being appointed because he thought the new government too radical.

Rushdie. The Iranian government verbally assured European Union ambassadors in September that it would not seek the death of British author Salman Rushdie, but Iran refused to sign a document to that effect. The late Iranian spiritual leader, Ayatollah Ruhollah Khomeini, issued an edict against the author's life after Rushdie wrote a book deemed blasphemous to Islam.   □ Christine Helms

See also **Middle East** (Facts in brief table). In *World Book,* see **Iran.**

Iraq. The defection to Jordan on Aug. 8, 1995, of Iraqi President Saddam Hussein's two sons-in-law and their wives presented the most serious crisis Hussein had faced since his defeat by a United States-led coalition in the 1991 Persian Gulf War. The defections confirmed that United Nations (UN) sanctions, imposed in August 1990 after Iraq invaded Kuwait, had weakened support for Hussein among both his ruling power elite and his family. The departure of one son-in-law, Hussein Kamel Hassan, struck a special blow since he had headed Iraq's programs to develop weapons of mass destruction.

Hassan speaks out. After the defection, Hassan called for the overthrow of his father-in-law. He said Hussein had intended to invade Kuwait again and that Iraq had produced more biological weapons than it had earlier claimed. He also said that Iraq had sought to divert nuclear fuel used for civilian purposes into weapons programs. Iraq was supposed to allow its weapons systems, including chemical and ballistic-missile programs, to be dismantled and monitored by the UN as a condition for international economic sanctions being lifted.

Hussein, who reportedly survived several internal threats to his regime in 1995, reacted swiftly to discredit the defectors. Within a week, the Iraqi media charged that Hassan had absconded with $35 million and that he had been a key architect of Iraq's invasion and occupation of Kuwait, the action that led to the Gulf War. Iraq also invited Rolf Ekeus, head of the UN weapons monitoring of Iraq, to its capital, Baghdad. In mid-August, Iraqi officials produced for Ekeus some 150 boxes of documents related to weapons programs that they alleged had been hidden by Hassan in an attempt to deceive the UN.

Defection aftermath. The United States, hoping that pressure could oust Hussein's regime, sent envoys to the Middle East in August to convince Jordan's King Hussein I to sever Iraq's major economic link to the outside world. In addition to other trade, Jordan bought over 70,000 barrels of Iraqi oil daily. Jordanian and U.S. forces also held joint military maneuvers in case Iraq retaliated for the defections.

Saddam Hussein's strategy, however, had some success. Iraqi opposition groups, who initially considered cooperating with the defectors, disavowed them. Kuwaiti officials, who could have offered oil to Jordan, became angry that Jordan granted asylum to men responsible for the invasion and who might know the fate of more than 600 missing Kuwaitis. Some analysts suggested that Kuwait and Saudi Arabia preferred Hussein's continued rule. As long as Iraq remained sidelined as an oil-producing rival, oil prices would remain higher.

King Hussein, under domestic pressure, finally said in late August that he would not sever economic ties with Iraq, though he condemned the Iraqi regime. A national vote for Saddam Hussein, the only name on the ballot, approved him by the expected overwhelming majority on October 15.

Sanctions impact. The UN, which initially praised Iraq's cooperation after the defections, announced in October that its weapons inspectors had indeed been duped and that a date for the lifting of sanctions had been indefinitely postponed. Even so, Hussein continued to reject UN-approved sales of oil to alleviate grave economic conditions, saying that they infringed on Iraq's sovereignty.

The UN World Food Program said in September that food shortages put nearly 20 percent of Iraqis at severe health risk. This figure included more than 2 million children under age 5 and 600,000 pregnant women and nursing mothers. The UN children's fund, UNICEF, announced that some 30 percent of Iraqi children suffered from malnutrition.

Relief agencies also said they expected the situation to worsen catastrophically for many reasons. Iraq's agricultural production declined in 1995, and donor nations had given only 25 percent of a planned $183 million in aid. Fighting among Kurdish factions in northern Iraq caused relief agencies to cut back or depart. And staggering inflation affected poor and middle-class Iraqis, all of whom received only enough food rations to cover 50 percent of their nutritional needs. Critics said that the ruling elite still lived lavishly.   □ Christine Helms

See also **Middle East** (Facts in brief table). In *World Book,* see **Iraq.**

Ireland. The coalition government of Ireland, led by Prime Minister John Bruton and with the help of Foreign Minister Dick Spring, devoted most of its energy in 1995 to the search for a peace settlement in Northern Ireland. Throughout the year, the Irish government maintained contact with Sinn Féin, the political wing of the Irish Republican Army (IRA), and objected to the insistence of the British government that the IRA should begin to lay down its weapons before the start of full-scale peace talks.

In November, the Irish and British governments set a target of February 1996 for the start of full-scale negotiations between the two governments and the political parties representing the Protestants and Catholics of Northern Ireland. The governments in November also decided to create an international commission to study the weapons issue. The commission was to make its recommendations to Britain and Ireland before the start of the negotiations. (See **Northern Ireland** Special Report: **The Pursuit of Peace in Northern Ireland.**)

Economic news. Ireland had one of the fastest growth rates in western Europe in 1995. The gross domestic product rose by about 6.5 percent. However, the unemployment rate in Ireland remained well above 14 percent and was one of the highest in the European Union (EU).

Information on abortion permitted. On May 12, Ireland's Supreme Court approved a law permitting doctors to provide women seeking information on abortion with the addresses and phone numbers of abortion clinics abroad. Abortion remained illegal in Ireland, however. The law was bitterly opposed by the Roman Catholic Church, a powerful voice in Ireland, where the vast majority of people are Catholic. The amendment of Ireland's abortion law stemmed from a 1992 court case involving a 14-year-old rape victim, who had been initially forbidden from going to Britain for an abortion. The court case led to a referendum on the issue in November 1992 in which 60 percent of voters said women should have the right to information about abortion.

Divorce made legal. The Irish people voted on November 25 to remove Ireland's constitutional ban on divorce. The change allowed couples who had been separated for four years to remarry, a right previously denied them without the intervention of the Roman Catholic Church. Couples seeking divorce were required to show in court that there was no reasonable prospect of a reconciliation and that proper provision would be made for their children. Ireland previously allowed Irish couples to get a legal separation, but the separation was not recognized as a divorce. Opponents of divorce threatened to challenge the referendum's constitutionality.

☐ Ian J. Mather

See also **Northern Ireland.** In *World Book,* see **Ireland.**

Islam. Social and demographic trends began to influence even the most conservative Muslim societies in 1995. The changes were subtle, but they held promise of transforming Islam's image in the world.

Women in Iran. The Women's Society of Iran was one of more than 30 nongovernmental organizations (NGO) chartered in 1995 to promote women's rights in Iran. Zahra Mustafavi, a daughter of the Ayatollah Khomeini—the fundamentalist Muslim leader who overthrew Shah Mohammed Reza Pahlavi in 1979—led the group. Faezeh Hashemi, the daughter of Iran's President Ali Akbar Hashemi Rafsanjani, also advocated women's rights. Although conservative Muslims blocked many of the women's rights initiatives, some groups capitalized on the United Nations Fourth World Conference on Women in Beijing in October to advance gender equality at home.

Iran's parliament, the Majlis, had 9 female representatives out of 270 members. The small, but influential bloc succeeded in 1995 in enacting a law requiring men who divorce unemployed wives to pay them for services given during the marriage.

A higher percentage of Iranian women could read and write in 1995 than in the time of Shah Pahlavi, enabling many to join the work force. But education was only part of the reason why more women were working—Iran's poor economy was forcing many women to find jobs.

Women in Saudi Arabia. Observers believed that the growing economic power of Saudi women would be more effective than political action in promoting gender equality. Many Saudi women had amassed major fortunes since the end of the 1991 Persian Gulf War, according to Mai Yamani, the daughter of former oil minister Ahmed Zaki Yamani. She said as much as 40 percent of Saudi private wealth was in female hands in 1995. Women owned a quarter of the property in Riyadh, the capital, and half the property in Jeddah, Saudi Arabia's second-largest city. The number of women in Riyadh's Chamber of Commerce rose from 500 in 1990 to more than 2,000 in 1995. Women dominated many professions, and female teachers were being sent to distant posts formerly reserved for men.

American Islam. Nation of Islam leader Louis Farrakhan organized a Million Man March in October 1995, calling on black men to take more responsibility for their families. About one-third of the 4 million to 5 million Muslims in the United States were African American, but only about 20,000 belonged to the Nation of Islam.

Recognizing the rise of Islam in America, the Administration of President Bill Clinton said in 1995 that Islam was compatible with Western ideals. The Administration said only Muslim extremists posed threats to world peace. ☐ Vincent J. Cornell

In *World Book,* see **Muslim; Islam.**

Israel. Prime Minister Yitzhak Rabin, the man who spearheaded the nation's historic peacemaking effort with its Arab neighbors, died by a Jewish assassin's bullets on Nov. 4, 1995, as he left a peace rally in Tel Aviv, Israel. Rabin's slaying stunned the world and especially shocked Israelis, who had never had a head of state assassinated in their 47 years as a nation. The 25-year-old assassin, Yigal Amir, showed no remorse and said he killed Rabin in order to stop the Arab-Israeli peace process. Although Amir claimed to have acted alone, by mid-December Israeli authorities had charged three others. Those charged included Amir's brother, who belonged to the same right wing Jewish militant group as Amir.

A hero is mourned. At least 5,000 people attended Rabin's funeral in Jerusalem on November 6. United States President Bill Clinton as well as heads of state and dignitaries from 80 countries came to honor Rabin. Most remarkably, two Arab leaders who had not visited Jerusalem since the Arab-Israeli war of 1967 eulogized Rabin. They were Jordan's King Hussein I, who had forged a peace with Israel in 1994, and Egyptian President Hosni Mubarak, whose country made peace with Israel in 1979.

Rabin, who won the Nobel Peace Prize in 1994, had reached the height of his career of service to Israel. He had headed Israel's defense forces when they won the 1967 war and served as prime minister from 1974 to 1977 and defense minister from 1984

Freedom fighter turned military strategist and politician, Yitzhak Rabin brought Israel to the brink of a lasting peace with its long-time enemies.

Yitzhak Rabin:
Death of a Peacemaker

By Crispin Hawes

The author

Crispin Hawes is an analyst specializing in Middle East affairs.

Yitzhak Rabin, the prime minister of Israel, was shot and killed by an Israeli extremist, Yigal Amir, in a central Tel Aviv square on November 4, 1995. Rabin had been attending a peace rally to mark the redeployment of Israeli troops from population centers in the West Bank and the transfer of control over the towns and villages of the area to the Palestine Liberation Organization (PLO). For any other Israeli politician, negotiating a peace agreement with the PLO would have marked the high point of a career. For Rabin it was one of many high points.

Born in Jerusalem in 1922, the first Israeli prime minister to be born in the Holy Land, Rabin quickly distinguished himself as a leader. At the age of 21, he joined the Palmach, the elite arm of the outlawed Haganah Jewish defense force. During the 1948 Israeli war of independence, serving as deputy commander of the Palmach, he kept open the vital supply line between Jerusalem and Tel Aviv. After independence, Rabin moved quickly up the ranks of the Israeli Defense Forces (IDF), becoming chief of staff in 1964. In that capacity in June 1967, he was one of the main architects of Israel's comprehensive victory in the Six-Day War, which left the Jewish nation in control not only of the West Bank and Gaza Strip but also of the Sinai Peninsula and the Golan Heights.

On retirement from the IDF in 1968, Rabin became Israel's ambassador to the United States. It was in Washington, D.C., that he developed his reputation as a politician impatient with diplomatic niceties. Through his blunt manner he succeeded in convincing the skeptical Republican Administration of President Richard M. Nixon that Israel was an important strategic ally in the Middle East. Back home in Israel in 1974 and untainted by any responsibility for Israel's near-defeat in the 1973 Yom Kippur War, Rabin became chairman of the Labor Party and replaced Golda Meir as prime minister. His resignation as party head and prime minister in 1977 coincided with the Labor Party's fall from power.

Without Rabin leading the party, Labor failed to win power outright until 1992, although it gained a share in the 1984-1990 National Unity government, in which Rabin served as defense minister. In that post, Rabin had responsibility for suppressing the *intifada* (uprising) in the occupied territories, which broke out in 1987. Among the Palestinians, Rabin is remembered as the man who instructed IDF troops to break the bones of protesters, but it was his experience with the intifada that led him to conclude that Israel could no longer hold onto the territories by force.

The Labor Party's success in the 1992 election—a victory that returned Rabin to the prime minister's post—was due in great part to Rabin's image in Israel as a tough leader who could be trusted to safeguard national security. That was an image his rival for the party leadership, Shimon Peres, lacked. As the commander who had engineered the capture of the West Bank and Gaza Strip, Rabin had the moral authority to negotiate the relinquishment of Israeli control of the area. Although Peres, who was named foreign minister, played a vital role in establishing a framework for Israeli-Palestinian cooperation, it was Rabin's curb on Peres's optimism which helped secure peace terms most Israeli people could accept. It was Rabin's tenacity that forced the negotiations with Jordan through to completion in 1994; it was his initiative that won him a share of the Nobel Peace Prize in the same year; and it was his authority that would be missed in future talks with Syria and the PLO.

Yitzhak Rabin's death deprived Israel of one of its greatest figures and one of the last links to the generation which won its independence, but it also left the country in a precarious position. Rabin was unable to complete the peace process he had set in motion, and the Israeli public's faith in Peres as a guarantor of security was less than wholehearted. If Peres failed to maintain popular support for the deal with the PLO, the entire process might stall.

Rabin's legacy in Israeli politics was also less than completely positive. In dismissing the entire right wing of Israeli politics, some political analysts believe, he fostered a schism wherein his opponents felt no loyalty toward the elected administration. Under Rabin, Israeli solidarity, once such an important element in Israel's survival in a hostile region, ceased to be a national characteristic. ■ ■ ■

to 1990. Elected prime minister again in 1992, he directed secret negotiations with the Palestine Liberation Organization (PLO) that led to the historic Palestinian-Israeli peace agreement of 1993.

The peace process. Palestinian leader Yasir Arafat, who had worked with Rabin for peace, visited Tel Aviv on November 9 to express his condolences to Rabin's widow, Leah. The visit was his first to Israel since 1968. Arafat chose not to attend Rabin's funeral in order to avert more violence.

Arafat and Rabin had just signed the most significant affirmation of peace yet on Sept. 28, 1995, at a ceremony hosted by President Clinton at the White House. The accord detailed how the Israeli military would withdraw from 6 Israeli-occupied West Bank cities and some 450 towns by March 30, 1996, eventually transferring power to a Palestinian council to be elected by March 1996. Also outlined was a partial withdrawal from Hebron, a city of 100,000 Arabs, though some soldiers would stay to protect 400 Jewish settlers.

Opposition. Although world leaders lauded Rabin and his partner in peace, Israeli Foreign Minister Shimon Peres, the peace agreement polarized Israel. The accord won parliamentary approval by only 61 out of 120 votes in October. Right wing Jewish extremists launched a virulent campaign against Rabin, accusing him of being a "traitor" who had abandoned the Biblical Israel. Extremist Arabs opposed to peace added to a climate of fear in 1995 with four suicide bombings that killed 39 people and injured several hundred. On August 23, Israeli security forces said they had rounded up a terrorist network of 30 Arabs responsible for much of the violence.

Rabin also found himself at odds with American-Jewish rabbis opposed to the peace process. He criticized some who tried to delay or stop a U.S. loan to improve the living standards of Palestinians. Some U.S. rabbis had also supported a ruling by several Israeli rabbis in July that Israeli soldiers should refuse on religious grounds to evacuate the West Bank.

Shimon Peres became the acting Israeli prime minister upon Rabin's death. He decided not to change the November 1996 date for elections of a new parliament and prime minister. Observers believed that Peres, considered to be the visionary architect of the peace, wanted to prove his leadership credentials.

Peres's main rival was considered to be Benjamin Netanyahu, leader of the opposition Likud bloc. However, after Rabin's assassination, many people accused Netanyahu and the Likud of tolerating the inflammatory rhetoric of right wing groups that they believed had created a climate of violence.

Lebanon. Israel imposed a naval blockade along Lebanon's southern coast in February. The primary intention of the blockade was to pressure Syria, which controls Lebanese politics, to curtail the militant activities of the pro-Iranian group Hezbollah

(Party of God). Hezbollah launched more than 80 attacks against Israel in February, the highest monthly total since 1988. They killed 15 Israeli soldiers in 1995 in the 9-mile (14-kilometer) wide "security zone" Israel maintains in southern Lebanon.

Israeli people. According to Israel's Central Bureau of Statistics, Israel's population in 1995 was made up of about 81 percent Jews, 14 percent Muslims, 3 percent Christians, and 2 percent Druses, an Arabic-speaking people who practice a religion related to Islam. In a year ending in September, Israel accepted 78,000 immigrants, 86 percent of whom were from the former Soviet Union, the bureau said.

In February, the Yemenite Jewish Federation of America accused Israel of covering up the disappearance of more than 500 Yemeni Jewish children during an airlift that took about 50,000 Jews from Yemen to Israel from 1948 to 1950. Israel denied the charge, but Rabin reportedly called the issue "one of the most painful in the history of the Jewish state."

War atrocities. A retired Israeli general said in August that he and another soldier had killed 49 unarmed Egyptian prisoners of war in 1956. In September, Egypt said it had found two mass graves that held remains of about 60 Egyptian soldiers from the 1967 Arab-Israeli War. □ Christine Helms

See also **Middle East** (Facts in brief table); **Terrorism** Special Report: **The Terrorist Agenda**. In *World Book*, see **Israel**.

Italy. The country's political turmoil deepened in 1995. A government of nonelected technocrats moved hesitantly to reform the country's debt-ridden economy, while corruption allegations continued to undermine the credibility of the major political parties. The leadership vacuum threatened to marginalize the country economically as the lira tumbled, and top European officials ruled Italy out of contention for participation in a single European Union (EU) currency.

Interim government. Lacking any stable political majority in parliament following the resignation of Silvio Berlusconi as prime minister in December 1994, President Oscar Scalfaro on Jan. 15, 1995, appointed Lamberto Dini, a former director-general of the Bank of Italy, to head an interim government. It was the country's first government composed entirely of unelected officials.

Dini concentrated his efforts on reining in Italy's massive budget deficit and national debt. On March 16, the Italian parliament narrowly approved Dini's interim budget of tax increases and spending cuts intended to reduce the deficit for 1995 by about $12.5-billion. On December 22, parliament approved a budget for 1996 aimed at reducing the deficit by about another $20 billion.

Conservative parties said the package failed to reduce spending enough, and German Finance Minister Theo Waigel, a senior official of the EU, declared in September that Italy would fail to qualify for a single European currency in 1999 because of its huge debt. Italy's debt amounted to more than 120 percent of its gross domestic product—more than double the stipulated EU ceiling of 60 percent.

Dini also moved to reform Italy's system of retirement pensions, which was running a deficit of $40-billion a year. On August 4, parliament approved a law to base pensions on lifetime payroll contributions rather than the amount of salary at retirement and to require workers to make contributions for 35 years to get a full pension.

Conservative opponents led by Berlusconi sharply criticized Dini's policies and introduced a motion of no confidence against the government in October. But Dini survived the vote on October 26 after promising to step down at the end of the year—which he did.

Corruption investigations. Berlusconi's efforts to regain power were haunted by corruption allegations that forced him to resign as prime minister in December 1994. On July 4, 1995, a Milan judge ordered 22 officials of Publitalia, the advertising arm of Berlusconi's Fininvest media empire, to stand trial on corruption charges. On October 14, another judge ordered Berlusconi to stand trial on charges of involvement in bribes of $235,000 paid by Fininvest to government tax inspectors for lenient audits between 1989 and 1991. Five other Fininvest associates, including Berlusconi's brother Paolo, were also ordered to stand trial with him in January 1996. Berlusconi denied the charges.

On Oct. 27, 1995, a Milan court sentenced a group of 22 senior politicians, including former prime ministers Bettino Craxi and Arnaldo Forlani and former Foreign Minister Gianni De Michelis, to prison terms for taking part in $94 million in bribes paid by the Ferruzzi industrial group.

Former prime minister goes on trial. In the most notorious case brought by the country's anti-corruption investigators, Giulio Andreotti, a seven-time prime minister, went on trial in September on charges of collaborating with the Mafia while in power. He was charged November 5 with complicity in the 1979 murder of a journalist who investigated Mafia links to the government. Andreotti denied the charges, saying he was a victim of the Mafia seeking revenge for his stance against organized crime.

Regional elections. A center-left coalition led by the Democratic Party of the Left, the former Communist Party, won control of nine regional governments in elections on April 23. The center-right coalition led by Berlusconi won six regions.

□ Tom Buerkle

See also **Europe** (Facts in brief table). In *World Book,* see **European Union; Italy.**

Ivory Coast. See **Africa.**

Jamaica. See **West Indies.**

Japan was battered by major problems in 1995. A January earthquake in Kobe killed thousands of people, and in March members of a religious sect released poisonous gas in the Tokyo subway system, sending thousands of commuters to the hospital. The nation's troubled economy entered the fourth year of recession, causing financial upheaval and upsets in political parties.

The earthquake struck on the morning of January 17. The quake was centered 20 miles (32 kilometers) from downtown Kobe, a major industrial city and one of Japan's most important seaports. The 6.8-magnitude earthquake destroyed or damaged more than 56,000 buildings and put the port out of commission. Experts estimated reconstruction would cost $120 billion.

More than 5,400 people were counted among the dead, many crushed under falling tile roofs, and more than 300,000 people were left homeless. Most houses had heavy roofs on fairly light wooden frames, a design that had withstood the region's typhoon rains but proved deadly in the earthquake. Some elevated highways and modern buildings also collapsed. The severe damage raised doubts about the adequacy of Japan's building code provisions, which were supposed to ensure that structures could withstand earthquakes.

Kobe residents faced the disaster in an orderly manner. However, the public criticized the national government for its slow reaction to the crisis. Bureaucrats bickered for two days over the wording of a request for aid before sending 13,000 troops to help with relief work. The government ignored, or held up, offers of help from abroad. Criminals handed out food long before Tokyo sent help, but then took a cut of aid funds. Late in the year, the official death toll was upped to more than 6,000.

Nerve gas spread through the Tokyo subway system on March 20, killing 12 people and sickening more than 5,500. Investigators found cannisters of the gas, called sarin, on five subway trains. The gas was released when the trains converged at a station where police officials detrained for work.

On May 16, the police went to the headquarters of a fanatical religious sect, Aum Shinrikyo (Supreme Truth), near Mount Fuji, where they arrested the sect's 40-year-old leader, Shoko Asahara. Asahara and 40 of his followers were charged with murder. Investigators found laboratories, equipment, and chemicals to make sarin in buildings that belonged to the sect. The trial was to begin on October 26, but Asahara abruptly fired his lawyer in an attempt to delay proceedings. The trial was postponed, but the court appointed nine lawyers to prevent another such delay. The trial was rescheduled for early 1996.

Asahara had founded Aum Shinrikyo in 1987, after failing in two business careers. He was a known admirer of Nazi dictator Adolf Hitler. His sect was under suspicion of carrying out other attacks in addition to the Tokyo subway gassing, among them a poison gas attack in the city of Matsumoto in June 1994 that killed seven people.

The police also were investigating some members for the kidnapping and killing of critics of the sect and of people who had tried to recover relatives from Aum Shinrikyo's fanatical grip. The sect was implicated in the serious wounding of the chief of the National Police Agency, Takaji Kunimatsu, on March 30. The masked gunman escaped. Police suspected the sect of planting a gas-releasing device in another Tokyo subway station on May 5. A cleaning woman defused the device before it could spread deadly cyanide gas through the ventilating system.

Recession continued in 1995 for the fourth straight year. On September 11, the government said the stagnant economy might start to contract. Unemployment, officially pegged at only 3.2 percent, was actually closer to 10 percent, according to a government agency that used Western standards for its calculation. Japan's second-largest car manufacturer, the Nissan Motor Company, closed a factory on March 23—the first time a car factory closed in Japan since World War II (1939-1945).

In what the Japanese call *kakaku hakai* (price destruction), Japan became the first industrial country to experience a significant fall in prices since the Great Depression of the 1930's. The decline began with falling prices for commercial property, then residential property, and finally consumer prices started downward, falling 0.5 percent for the year. In April, McDonald's franchises cut the prices of some hamburgers by 40 percent.

Banking woes. As the price—and thus the value—of real estate fell, Japanese banks were stuck with nonperforming loans, those on which interest was not being paid. The outstanding loans carried a paper value higher than the resale value of the property. Officials estimated the total of such loans at $570 billion, but unofficial estimates put it at $1-trillion. The government put off making banks restate their paper assets to the true value for fear some banks would collapse.

In fact, five savings institutions did collapse during the summer because of bad real estate loans. In July, the government closed the country's fifth-largest credit union because 73 percent of its loans were in default. And on August 30, the government closed Japan's largest credit union as panicky depositors tried to withdraw their money. On the same day, authorities shut down a commercial bank for the first time since World War II.

What went wrong? After decades of economic success, Japan began to question whether in 1995 it needed a radical restructuring of its economy. The Ministry of International Trade and Industry said in May that government regulations and restrictive business practices had created a high-cost structure that Japan could no longer afford. The economy

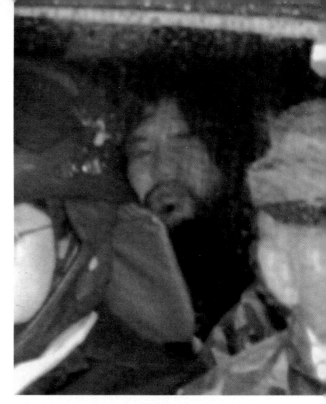

Police in August arrest the leader of a radical cult suspected of ordering a poisonous-gas attack in a Tokyo subway that killed 12 and sickened 5,500.

was being squeezed by an aging population in need of expensive social services and by newly developing countries whose dynamic economies captured an ever larger share of Japan's world trade. The trade ministry called for "economic liberalization," which meant a wider use of free-market principles. Japan's Economic Planning Agency said on July 25 that the economy would not revive unless the government instituted a policy of deregulation.

Politics. The realignment of Japan's political parties that began in 1993 remained muddled in 1995. On April 9, voters rejected traditional political parties in electing local governors (mayors) in Tokyo and Osaka, but in other local elections, old-line politicians held on to power.

Only 44.5 percent of the voters—a record low—cast ballots on July 23 to elect half of the 252-member upper house. The Social Democratic Party of Prime Minister Tomiichi Murayama won only 16 seats. The poor showing prompted the party to disband in September to form a more liberal party, the Democratic League.

The largest party in the governing coalition, the Liberal-Democratic Party (LDP), also did poorly in the upper house elections, winning only 49 seats. A small reformist group in the coalition won 3. Nevertheless, the coalition's total of 68 seats enabled it to retain control of the upper house. But the weak support for the ruling coalition intensified calls by

Japan's leading newspapers for new elections for the more important lower house of parliament before the scheduled date in mid-1997.

New LDP leader. The LDP decided to retain Murayama as prime minister, despite his party's election setback. But the LDP also prepared for future elections by installing Ryutaro Hashimoto as its new president on September 25. As minister of trade and industry, Hashimoto had negotiated with the United States in the summer of 1995 over reducing Japanese obstacles to American trade. His tough position led to a compromise agreement that made him popular with the Japanese and helped him defeat other candidates for the LDP leadership.

War apologies. On August 15, Murayama officially admitted to his country's "colonial rule and aggression" during World War II. Previous, less official apologies had not satisfied many Asian nations that had suffered under Japanese rule. Still, many Japanese opposed any apology.

Okinawa outrage. Three U.S. servicemen stationed on Okinawa were arrested September 11 on charges of raping a 12-year-old Okinawan girl. They were turned over to Japanese authorities for trial. Angry Japanese demonstrators demanded that local authorities be given more legal authority over American troops in Japan.   □ Henry S. Bradsher

See also **Asia** (Facts in brief table). In *World Book,* see **Japan.**

Jordan. King Hussein I of Jordan granted asylum on Aug. 10, 1995, to two powerful Iraqis, sons-in-law of Iraq's President Saddam Hussein who fled Iraq with their wives and families. Observers speculated that the king hoped to strengthen his ties with the United States and to reduce his isolation among the oil-rich states of the Persian Gulf, which resented his sympathy toward Iraq during the 1991 Gulf War. United States President Bill Clinton promised to protect Jordan if Iraq retaliated, and he sent 4,000 U.S. troops to Jordan for joint military exercises.

But the king's actions also received criticism. Jordanian businessmen, who had earned $450 million annually exporting goods to Iraq, argued that they might lose trade with Iraq. Some Arabs even accused King Hussein of seeking to reassert his family's power in Iraq. Relatives of King Hussein ruled in Iraq until being overthrown in a 1958 coup.

Kuwaiti officials expressed displeasure with Jordan's grant of asylum to men associated with Iraq's 1990 invasion of Kuwait. But they offered to consider selling petroleum to Jordan, which depended completely upon Iraq for oil. In a speech on Aug. 23, 1995, King Hussein condemned the Iraqi leadership and said that he would consider buying oil from alternative suppliers. However, he also said that Jordan would not sever diplomatic ties with Iraq.

Arab-Israeli peace efforts continued to receive mixed reviews in 1995. Israel's plan in May to seize

Arab land in East Jerusalem prompted more than 60 of Jordan's 80 parliament members to condemn the action and demand that Jordan's peace envoy to Israel be recalled. Many Jordanians complained that the peace process was going too slowly.

On the plus side of peace, Jordan on January 30 took control of a 125-square-mile (324-square-kilometer) piece of land that Israel seized in the 1967 Arab-Israeli war. Also, Jordanian-Israeli negotiating teams made progress on more than 24 agreements.

In February 1995, for example, Israel and Jordan, which established telephone links in 1994, agreed to also exchange mail. A $5-million, 2-mile (3.2-kilometer) pipeline to carry water from Israel's Sea of Galilee to Jordan opened on June 20, 1995. And officials of the two nations signed accords in August to support joint research on projects, including some related to oil, gas, and renewable energy sources.

In response to these peace efforts, the U.S. government agreed in September to write off the remaining $420 million of Jordan's $700-million debt to the United States.

Economy. The International Monetary Fund (IMF), an agency of the United Nations, stated in June that Jordan's economy was improving. The IMF noted that inflation stayed below 4 percent, exports and capital investment had increased, and the gross domestic product—the total amount of goods and services produced within a nation—for 1995 was growing by over 5 percent. The IMF also lauded Jordan's moves to pass legal reforms needed to protect private business and encourage economic growth.

Jordanian officials predicted in July that money sent home by Jordanians working in foreign countries would rise by 8.8 percent in 1995, bringing $1.32 billion into Jordan. In November, Jordan hosted the second annual Middle East Economic Summit. The summits, an outgrowth of the Arab-Israeli peace process, are intended to encourage economic integration throughout the Middle East.

Tourism flourished in Jordan after the October 1994 Jordanian-Israeli peace accord, with an increase of 43 percent by July 1995. The number of tourists from Western nations increased by 65 percent. At least 44,000 Israeli tourists also visited Jordan. Officials expected receipts from tourism in 1995 to be double those of 1993.

Government. The king named former general Sharif Zaid Bin Shakir as prime minister on Jan. 8, 1995. On July 11, more than half of Jordan's 800,000 eligible voters turned out to elect local councils. Jordanian officials proclaimed the results a defeat for Islamic activists, who opposed the Arab-Israeli peace accord. The activists, though, won control of some major councils. They also accused the government of unfairly influencing elections in the city of Az Zarqa.   □ Christine Helms

See also **Middle East** (Facts in brief table). In *World Book,* see **Jordan.**

Judaism. Orthodox, Conservative, and Reform congregations—the three major branches of Judaism in the United States—were concerned with six major issues during 1995. Those issues were the celebration of Jerusalem 3000; the growth of armed militias in America; *anti-Semitism* (prejudice against Jews); Jewish missionary activity; a new rabbinical school; and the announcement of a new Torah commentary.

Jerusalem 3000. Religious and secular Jewish organizations launched programs and celebrations in honor of the 3,000th anniversary of the establishment of Jerusalem as the capital city of the united Israelite tribes. Jerusalem was already ancient when King David made it his capital about 1000 B.C. Art, music, lectures, courses, tours, and archaeological exhibits featuring Jerusalem began in September 1995 and were to continue throughout 1996.

Armed militias. Jewish organizations as well as the U.S. Treasury Department's Bureau of Alcohol, Tobacco, and Firearms noted the growth of the national militia movement in 1995. The militia became an even greater concern after the bombing of a federal building in Oklahoma City, Oklahoma, in April that killed 168 people. The leaders of many militia groups in the movement allegedly had long histories of racial and religious bigotry and distrust of the federal government. Many groups used desktop publishing to produce newsletters for their members. Groups also communicated by shortwave radio, citizens access television, computer bulletin boards, and the Internet. Some militants issued strong calls for a white homeland using neo-Nazi rhetoric that included anti-Semitic statements.

Anti-Semitism. Although Jews and blacks in numerous communities worked together for better interracial and interreligious understanding, some black leaders used rhetoric that heightened tensions between blacks and Jews. Louis Farrakhan, leader of the Nation of Islam, which organized a "Million Man March" on Washington, D.C., in October, was on the defensive for making remarks against Jews. The news media accused the organization of subtly creating an atmosphere conducive to the expression of hatred of all kinds.

In a positive development, black students began to work as guides at the Holocaust Memorial Museum in Washington, D.C. Many young black people toured the museum exhibits of Nazi Germany's extermination program during World War II (1939-1945), which killed about 6 million Jews.

Missionary activity. Synagogue members of American Judaism began modest outreach efforts to non-Jews. Combining the biblical tradition of welcoming the stranger with the reality that the Jewish population in the United States was in decline, Conservative and Reform rabbis launched advertising campaigns to inform non-Jews about Judaism. The Commission on Reform Jewish Outreach placed advertisements to "come explore Jewish spirituality" in several New Jersey newspapers. The Rabbinical Assembly, representing Conservative Judaism, established a toll-free telephone number to help answer questions regarding Judaism and supported outreach programs for non-Jews married to Jews. Orthodox groups in major cities welcomed unaffiliated Jews and non-Jews to study groups and Jewish holiday celebrations.

New school. The University of Judaism in Los Angeles announced plans in September for opening in 1996 the first four-year rabbinical school west of the Mississippi River, thanks to a $22-million gift from anonymous donors. The University of Judaism had long offered two years of rabbinical course work. The expanded program was expected to place the institution in a position to challenge the preeminence of the 100-year-old Conservative Jewish Theological Seminary in New York City, the parent school.

New Torah commentary. The Women of Reform Judaism announced in September 1995 that it was underwriting a new commentary on the Torah, the first five books of the Hebrew Bible. In the commentary, scholars would for the first time address women's needs and concerns.   □ Marc Lee Raphael

In *World Book,* see **Jews; Judaism.**

Kampuchea. See **Cambodia.**

Kansas. See **State government.**

Kazakhstan. President Nursultan Nazarbayev moved during 1995 to consolidate his power. In March, he dissolved the parliament that had been elected a year earlier.The first round of elections to the new parliament, held in December, were dominated by Nazarbayev supporters.

On March 28, Nazarbayev had asked for a referendum to extend his term in office to the year 2000. The plan was called undemocratic by domestic opponents and international observers. On April 29, 91 percent of all eligible voters officially turned out to vote. The government reported that 95 percent supported Nazarbayev's proposal. The president then held an August referendum on a new Constitution that would strengthen his power. According to the government, 90 percent of the electorate defied an opposition boycott and voted 89 percent in favor of the new Constitution.

In April, Kazakhstan transferred to Russia the last of the Soviet-era nuclear missiles on its territory and became nuclear-free. Kazakhstan thus satisfied important treaty obligations with both the United States and Russia.

In September, Kazakhstan joined a customs union with Russia and Belarus and lifted controls on the Kazakh-Russian border.   □ Steven L. Solnick

See also **Europe** (Facts in brief table). In *World Book,* see **Kazakhstan.**

Kentucky. See **State government.**

Korea, North. The heaviest rains in 100 years caused widespread flooding in July and August 1995. The floods killed 70 people and left 500,000 homeless, according to government reports addressing internal problems—a rarity for North Korea. The government said the floods affected 5.2 million people and caused an estimated $15 billion in damage. However, despite North Korea's request to the United Nations (UN) for 10 million doses of cholera vaccine, the government denied reports that a major cholera epidemic had begun in May and worsened as a result of the floods.

The flooding hit the main grain-producing region of western North Korea. A UN inspection team found severe food shortages at evacuation centers. The team said North Korea's grain shortage for 1995 was expected to be 4.3 million tons (3.9 million metric tons), half the nation's normal needs.

Economic problems. Even before the floods, North Korea suffered from food shortages. The isolated Communist government urged people to eat only two meals a day, but many visitors reported that only one meal was common and malnutrition was widespread.

Thus, after decades of emphasizing self-reliance, North Korea appealed to other nations for food and financial aid. On May 26, North Korea asked Japan for rice, saying bad weather had damaged its crops. Japan agreed to give 150,000 tons (136,000 metric tons) of free rice and sell another 150,000 tons to North Korea. After the floods, Japan promised an additional 200,000 tons (181,000 metric tons).

In June, North Korea asked South Korea for rice, despite ongoing cross-border tensions. The South gave the North 150,000 tons of rice, but when the North accused a southern delivery ship of spying, the aid ceased. Further aid discussions bogged down over southern demands for the North to return eight fishermen who had been seized, along with their vessel, in May. Five surviving fishermen (the other three had died of injuries or illness) were released in December.

Still, North Korea agreed in May to the first joint venture with a South Korean company. Southern technicians would live at Nampo in the north, where they would supervise work at a garment factory using southern machinery.

Unclear leadership. North Korea in 1995 remained without an official president or leader of its ruling Communist Party. The last leader, dictator Kim Il-song, died in 1994, after ruling since 1948. The national media praised his son, Kim Chong-il, as North Korea's leader and savior, but he made few public appearances. Meetings of the government and party officials who would confer the leadership titles were reportedly postponed several times.

Rumors circulated that Kim Chong-il was in poor health, that he was not psychologically capable of running the country, and that army generals were unwilling to let him have supreme power. Most observers thought, however, that Kim was in charge. Still, when Kim appointed a new defense minister, Choe Kwang, on Oct. 8, 1995, the media referred to him only by his one official title, chairman of the National Defense Commission. The minister's predecessor, O Chin-u, died of cancer on February 25.

Nuclear issues. North Korea and the United States held difficult talks in 1995 over a program intended to reduce the North's ability to make nuclear weapons. They had agreed in October 1994 that an American-led consortium would build, at a cost of $4 billion, two nuclear power stations in North Korea that would be difficult to use in making nuclear weapons material. North Korea had such a facility and had obstructed attempts by the International Atomic Energy Agency to inspect it in 1994. The consortium of South Korea, Japan, and other countries had agreed to provide fuel oil to North Korea as compensation for keeping the reactor shut down.

But in 1995 the North sought $1 billion in additional equipment and concessions not in the agreement, and it objected to South Korea's building the power stations. There were also problems with the financing of the project. Still, American inspectors visiting the North's nuclear facilities found dangerous materials under control.   ☐ Henry S. Bradsher

See also **Asia** (Facts in brief table). In *World Book,* see **Korea.**

Korea, South. Widespread bribery of officials to allow construction of buildings that failed to meet safety standards in 1995 resulted in the worst peacetime disaster in the nation's modern history. On June 29, a five-story shopping complex in Seoul, the capital, collapsed, killing more than 500 people. The building owners were charged with criminal negligence, and five government officials were indicted for taking bribes to allow illegal changes in the design. In all, 25 people were charged, and all were found guilty of various charges in December. The longest sentence, 10½ years in prison, was given to the building's primary owner, Lee Jun.

The economy, expanding at an annual rate of more than 8 percent, ranked 10th in the world, according to the World Bank, an agency of the United Nations. Growing prosperity enabled South Korea to apply in March 1995 for membership in the World Bank's Organization for Economic Cooperation and Development. Wealthy member nations help finance projects in developing nations.

Growth raised living standards, but it also increased the nation's trade deficit. The government wanted to discourage South Korean companies from making foreign investments, so on October 9, it passed measures making such investment more expensive. The government also issued guidelines ordering employers to pay foreign workers the same minimum wage of $330 a month that Koreans got.

Pink walls and rubble mark the site of a Seoul, South Korea, retail complex that collapsed in June, killing more than 500. Officials blamed the accident on shoddy construction.

Election rout. Local offices had been filled by appointment since martial law was declared in 1961. That changed on June 27, 1995, when elections were held for 5,700 positions. But the elections backfired on President Kim Yong-sam. Opposition and independent candidates won 10 contests for mayor and governor, while Kim's Democratic Liberal Party (DLP) won only five. The DLP lost the important race for mayor of the capital to Cho Soon of the Democratic Party (DP). In 1993, Kim had fired Cho as head of the central bank for trying to make the institution independent of national control.

The DP also won in the southwest, traditionally an area of government opposition. Its victory led to the return of Kim Dae Jung, a veteran opponent of military rule who had retired from politics after losing the 1992 presidential election to Kim Yong-sam. On Sept. 5, 1995, he launched a new party, the National Congress of New Politics.

Former presidents indicted. Former South Korean presidents Roh Tae Woo and Chun Doo Hwan were indicted on Dec. 21, 1995, on charges of mutiny in connection with a 1979 coup that brought Chun to power. Both men faced a possible death sentence if convicted. Earlier in the month, Roe had been indicted on charges that he accepted $370 million in bribes while in office.　　□ Henry S. Bradsher

See also **Asia** (Facts in brief table). In *World Book*, see **Korea.**

Kuwait. Failure to curtail yearly budget deficits since the 1991 Persian Gulf War eroded Kuwait's $100-billion prewar reserves to only $35 billion in 1995. On August 19, Kuwait's opposition-dominated parliament rejected a 1995-1996 $14-billion budget, hoping to pressure the government to develop a five-year economic plan. Government revenues for 1995-1996 were projected to be only $9.6 billion. Kuwait, which has promised every citizen a job, devotes about 50 percent of its revenues to wages.

In August 1995, parliament eased the repayment terms of a $20-billion debt that came from the 1982 crash of an unregulated stock exchange. The debt was owed to the government by Kuwait's wealthiest people, including members of the ruling Sabah family. In January, Kuwait wrote off a $2.7-billion debt owed by Egypt and $130 million owed by Syria as repayment for their help against Iraq in the Gulf War.

A government investigation into abuse of some of Kuwait's foreign workers, especially 200,000 domestic servants, began in September. More than 500 Filipino maids, claiming physical and mental abuse, returned to the Philippines in 1995. Two Kuwaiti women were jailed in September for beating their maids to death. Some workers also said their salaries had been withheld.　　□ Christine Helms

See also **Middle East** (Facts in brief table). In *World Book*, see **Kuwait.**

Kyrgyzstan. See Asia.

Labor. The United States economy in 1995 lost some of its 1994 bloom as unemployment inched up in spring 1995. Some analysts feared that steady increases in short-term interest rates by the Federal Reserve System, the nation's central bank, were slowing U.S. economic expansion. But the economy picked up in the summer, and the year ended with unemployment again trending slowly downward.

The economy continued to boast strong job growth, but the 2 million new jobs created in 1995 lagged behind the more than 3 million created in 1994, and workers continued to fear job loss. Medium-sized and small firms spurred job growth, while large multinational companies continued to cut staff and unprofitable products and services to improve their position in a fiercely competitive market.

Employment and compensation. Unemployment fell from 6.1 percent of the U.S. labor force (about 8 million workers) at the beginning of 1995 to 5.6 percent (about 7.4 million workers) in November. Pay and benefits increased 2.7 percent during the year, the smallest rise since the data were first compiled in 1981. White-collar workers in 1995 received 2.8 percent; blue-collar workers, 2.3 percent; and service workers, 2.6 percent. Overall, wages and salaries rose an average of 2.8 percent, while benefits increased 2.2 percent.

Heavy equipment. In the first of two settlements in the heavy-equipment industry that did not include guaranteed wage increases, the United Automobile Workers union (UAW) ratified a three-year agreement with Deere and Company, Incorporated, of Moline, Illinois, on March 6, 1995. The agreement came at the end of a five-month deadlock.

The contract, which covered 10,500 workers in six states, provided a $500 bonus per employee and annual bonuses equal to 4 percent of wages in the first year and 3 percent in each of the last two years. It also provided for cost-of-living increases based on changes in the federal Consumer Price Index and some improvements in pensions. The Deere management won a conversion of the worker incentive plan to a system that linked wages to productivity. The bargainers also made major changes in the health care program, including a provision that newly hired employees must enroll in managed-care plans if they live in an area covered by a particular plan.

One of the longest-running major labor disputes ended on Dec. 2, 1995, when the UAW admitted defeat in a four-year battle with Caterpillar Inc. of Peoria, Illinois. The union gave in even though union members had just voted down the company's final 1995 offer. Caterpillar had continued to operate with temporary workers and some 4,000 strikers who crossed picket lines.

The terms imposed on the workers in 1995 were little changed from those the union had first rejected in April 1992. Similiar to the Deere and Company agreement, the Caterpillar contract replaced guaran-teed annual wage hikes with annual lump-sum payments. The pact also provided a *two-tier pay system*—a pay scale that would provide less compensation for newly hired workers than for veteran employees. The proposal to institute a two-tier pay system had been a crucial factor in triggering the strike.

Rubber industry. Unions also came up short in a bitter 10-month strike by 2,300 members of the United Rubber Workers Union against five U.S. plants owned by Bridgestone/Firestone, Incorporated. That strike fizzled in May when workers agreed to return to work without a contract. At issue in the strike, which began in July 1994, were proposed cutbacks in health benefits and the elimination of paid holidays such as the Fourth of July and Thanksgiving.

But the strike began losing steam almost as soon as it began, when the company hired permanent workers and some union members began crossing picket lines. On May 21, 1995, the Rubber Workers Union called off the strike after several local unions voted to return to work. Contributing to the collapse of the strike was a concern that the company would hire additional replacement workers. Another worry was that plant workers, including some of the 300 union members who crossed picket lines, would vote to decertify the union as their sole bargaining agent. The company accepted the returning strikers but insisted on retaining the 2,000 replacement employees. Striking workers not immediately rehired were placed on preferential hiring lists.

In contrast to the turmoil at Bridgestone/Firestone, rubber workers in Freeport, Illinois, voted on May 26 to accept an agreement with Kelly-Springfield Tire Company of Akron, Ohio. The pact boosted wages, provided bonuses, and continued cost-of-living adjustments. The company also agreed to invest $17 million in radial tire production at the plant. In return, the union agreed to extended work shifts.

Automobile industry. Worker complaints about excess overtime and the use of outside contractors caused strikes in the auto industry in 1995. The strikes, by local affiliates of the UAW, mainly targeted the General Motors (GM) Corporation, which had the highest labor costs of the "Big Three" automakers—GM, Ford Motor Company, and Chrysler Corporation—and had tried to boost productivity by increasing assembly line speeds and overtime.

On January 22, workers at a GM parts plant in Flint, Michigan, overwhelmingly approved an agreement ending a four-day strike of 6,800 workers. GM agreed to hire 700 workers to ease overtime demands and to return to the plant some work that had been contracted out. Similar issues led UAW workers at a GM truck plant in Pontiac, Michigan, to stage a six-day strike from March 31 to April 5, the seventh by local GM unions since January 1994.

Aircraft industry. The UAW in April 1995 ratified a five-year agreement with the McDonnell

The leaders of the United Auto Workers union, the International Association of Machinists, and the United Steelworkers announce their unions' merger in July.

Douglas Corporation of St. Louis, Missouri, that covered 8,000 workers in three states. The agreement improved pension benefits but called for modest salary increases in the first two years and bonuses in the last three years. McDonnell Douglas had sought to hold wages steady in the face of cuts in federal defense spending that threatened production.

On October 6, more than 32,000 members of the International Association of Machinists and Aerospace Workers struck the Boeing Company of Seattle over job security, health insurance, pensions, and the use of outside contractors. On November 21, union members rejected a three-year contract negotiated by federal mediators and recommended by union representatives.

Professional sports. On January 20, the National Hockey League (NHL) Players Union formally ratified a six-year pact with the NHL. On March 31, a federal district judge in New York ended a 234-day strike-lockout that had knocked out the last two months of the 1994 professional baseball season, including the World Series. On Sept. 7, 1995, the National Basketball Association (NBA) and the NBA Players Association approved a new six-year contract. (See **Baseball; Basketball; Hockey; Sports.**)

Suit settled. In February, J. P. Stevens & Company of West Point, Georgia, settled a 24-year-old lawsuit filed by the Amalgamated Clothing and Textile Workers Union by agreeing to pay $20 million to nearly 3,000 black workers. The company had been accused of refusing to hire and promote blacks.

Communications. In June, the AT&T Corp. approved separate three-year contracts with the Communication Workers of America (CWA) and the International Brotherhood of Electrical Workers. The pacts, which covered 110,000 workers, boosted top salaries, offered cash bonuses, and provided improved pension benefits.

The CWA and the Electrical Workers on August 11 also reached separate agreements with the Ameritech Corporation. The pacts provided for 3.5 percent annual wage hikes over three years and included improved pension benefits and health care coverage. In negotiations, the unions prevailed in their opposition to company proposals to hire temporary workers and introduce a two-tier pay system.

A proposed two-tier pay scale was also the focus of contract talks between the CWA and Southwestern Bell Telephone Company. On November 3, the CWA approved a pact with Southwestern Bell covering 38,000 workers in five states. Wages were to rise by 11.2 percent over three years, with an additional increase for some workers. The union had rejected a previous offer in September because it contained a more stringent two-tier pay scale than had been included in the November agreement.

Bell Atlantic Telephone Company and the CWA engaged in a bitter strike over wages and the company's desire to shift some health costs to workers. In mid-August, the union mounted a $5-million advertising campaign against the company, and in late September rejected the company's fourth offer.

The airline industry, troubled by continued revenue losses, experienced labor peace in 1995. In August, American Airlines, Incorporated, and the Transport Workers Union agreed to a wage freeze for three years, then modest increases in 1998 and 1999. American had sought to limit wages for the 27,000 union workers as part of a plan by the AMR Corporation, its parent company, to cut expenses.

The Independent Association of Continental Pilots voted in August 1995 to accept an agreement with Continental Airlines, Incorporated, offering a multimillion-dollar bonus package and an 18.5-percent wage increase by 1997. The contract was the first since 1983 between the Continental Airlines and its pilots, who were among the lowest-paid in the industry.

Union membership held steady at 16.7 million during 1994 (the most recent year for which data were available). But the proportion of U.S. workers represented by unions fell slightly, from 15.8 to 15.5 percent of the work force.

Kirkland to Sweeney. Lane Kirkland, president of the American Federation of Labor and Congress of Industrial Organizations (AFL-CIO) since 1979, announced his early retirement from the 13.3-million-member organization on June 9, 1995. Kirkland left under pressure from union dissidents led by John J. Sweeney, president of the Service Employees Union. Kirkland's opponents blamed him for declines in union membership and argued that a more dynamic, forceful leader was needed to revive union fortunes.

On August 1, the AFL-CIO executive council named Thomas R. Donahue, the union's secretary-treasurer, as interim president. Donahue was Kirkland's choice to serve out the former president's term, which expired in October. The council also chose Barbara Easterling, vice president of the CWA, to replace Donahue as AFL-CIO secretary-treasurer.

On October 25, however, in the first contested election in the union's 40-year-history, Sweeney won the presidency, defeating Donahue by 7.3 million to 5.7 million votes. Richard L. Trumka, president of the United Mine Workers, defeated Easterling by a similar margin for AFL-CIO secretary-treasurer.

Replacement ban. On March 8, President Bill Clinton issued an executive order banning companies from holding federal contracts worth more than $100,000 if they hire permanent replacements for striking workers. Republicans in Congress attempted but failed to bar funding to carry out the policy. In July, a federal district court judge upheld Clinton's authority to issue the order. ☐ Robert W. Fisher

See also **Economics; Manufacturing.** In *World Book,* see **Labor force; Labor movement.**

Changes in the United States labor force

	1994	1995
Civilian labor force	131,056,000	132,334,000
Total employment	123,060,000	124,919,000
Unemployment	7,996,000	7,415,000
Unemployment rate	6.1%	5.6%
Changes in real weekly earnings of production and nonsupervisory workers (private nonfarm sector)*	+0.4%	−0.3%
Change in output per employee hour (private nonfarm sector)†	1.9%	3.4%

*Constant (1982) dollars. 1994 change from December 1993 to December 1994; 1995 change from October 1994 to October 1995 (preliminary data).

†Annual rate for 1994; for 1995, change is from third quarter 1994 to third quarter 1995 (preliminary data).

Source: U.S. Bureau of Labor Statistics.

Lange, Jessica (1949-   ), an American motion-picture actress, won the best-actress award in 1995 for her role as Carly, a troubled military wife, in the movie *Blue Sky.* Lange starred in two other films in 1995, playing the wife of the Scottish hero Rob Roy in the movie of the same name and a social worker fighting for custody of an African American child in *Losing Isaiah.*

Lange was born in rural Minnesota on April 20, 1949. She briefly attended the University of Minnesota but dropped out to travel with and later marry Paco Grande, a Spanish photographer. She separated from Grande in 1971 and moved to Paris, where she danced and studied mime. In 1973, she settled in New York City and began to study acting.

Lange's first movie role was as Dawn, the heroine in a 1976 remake of *King Kong.* Lange's career took off in the 1980's. She won the first of her five Oscar nominations for her impassioned portrayal of the actress Frances Farmer in the film *Frances* (1982). She received her first Oscar in 1983 for her supporting role in the comedy *Tootsie.* She was nominated for best actress for her co-starring role in *Country* (1984) and for her portrayal of country singer Patsy Cline in *Sweet Dreams* (1985).

Lange and Grande divorced in 1980. She has three children and lives with her companion, playwright and actor Sam Shepard. ☐ Lisa Klobuchar

Laos. See **Asia.**

Latin America

Business occupied center stage in Latin America during 1995 as local and foreign companies scrambled to position themselves for what many observers believed was a coming economic boom. Politicians and governments played a supporting role with efforts to enhance the climate for business and persuade skeptical trade unions, whose ranks had been decimated by the privatization of state-run companies, that the good times lay just ahead.

Mexico bailout. As a result of a failed December 1994 devaluation of the peso, Mexico suffered through a severe financial crisis in 1995. The country came perilously close to defaulting on its financial obligations, and only a huge international loan package arranged in January 1995 enabled Mexico to continue paying its debts. (See **Mexico** Special Report: **Crisis in Mexico.**) Fearing opposition in Congress to a Mexican aid package, United States President Bill Clinton used special emergency authority on January 31 to provide Mexico with assurances of up to $20 billion in U.S. loans. Other sources, including the International Monetary Fund, a lending agency associated with the United Nations, pledged an additional $30 billion. Clinton argued that the assistance was vital to Mexico's economic stability and the viability of the North American Free Trade Agreement (NAFTA), the tariff-reducing accord between the United States, Mexico, and Canada that took effect in January 1994. Many observers saw the U.S. participation in the Mexican bailout as a sign of deep commitment to achieving hemisphere-wide free trade by 2005, a goal all leaders of the Americas, except Cuba's Fidel Castro, had adopted at a December 1994 summit meeting in Miami, Florida.

Elections in Argentina and Peru. Two of the presidents in the forefront of the drive toward free trade won easy reelection in 1995. In Peru, President Alberto Fujimori, whose administration had overseen one of the highest economic growth rates in the world, scored a victory on April 9 with a 2-to-1 margin over his closest rival. Despite record unemployment, President Carlos Saúl Menem of Argentina won reelection to a second term on May 14 .

Denver trade parley. On June 30, U.S. Secretary of Commerce Ronald H. Brown quantified the U.S. stake in free trade in the Western Hemisphere at a meeting of trade ministers from 34 countries of the Americas in Denver, Colorado. Exports from the United States to Latin America had doubled since 1989 and would nearly equal U.S. exports to Europe in 1995, he said. Further, Brown predicted that the United States would export more to Latin America by 2010 than to Europe and Japan combined.

Reflecting widespread business optimism, U.S. airlines developed a blueprint to increase their share

of the Latin American market from 56 percent in 1995 to 73 percent by the year 2010. As part of that effort, American Airlines began taking bids in 1995 for the construction of a $1-billion, 47-gate terminal at Miami International Airport. Construction was set to begin in early 1996.

Big business deals. Scarcely a week went by in 1995 without news of significant outside investment in Latin America. On January 9, the Colgate-Palmolive Company announced that it would spend more than $1 billion to acquire a competitor that dominated the toothpaste markets of Brazil, Argentina, and Peru. The deal would make Colgate-Palmolive the toothpaste supplier to half the people on Earth.

Other big deals in 1995 involved foreign multina-

Cuban leader Fidel Castro reviews troops in Paris during a visit to France in March. The visit was one of only a few Castro had made to a Western country since he came to power in 1959.

tional companies in partnership with Latin American counterparts to compete for business in markets that had been dominated by state-run companies. MCI Communications, the giant U.S. telecommunications company, teamed up on September 6 with Grupo Financiero Banamex-Accival, Mexico's largest business conglomerate, to win the first license to provide long-distance service when the current government monopoly of Telmex ends on Jan. 1, 1997.

In late October 1995, six large Japanese corporations—Nissho Iwai, Mitsubishi, Marubeni, Itochu, Sumitomo, and Tomen—formed a consortium to finance a $1.5-billion refinery in northeast Brazil for Petróleo Brasileiro, the government-owned oil company. On November 20, Australian-born media mogul Rupert Murdoch's News Corp. Ltd. announced a $500-million investment with Tele-Communications Inc. of Englewood, Colorado, Globo of Brazil, and Grupo Televisa of Mexico. The funding will enable the companies to transmit 150 channels of entertainment, news, and sports to Latin America, beginning in May 1996.

Cross-border trade. On Jan. 1, 1995, a common market called Mercosur, involving Argentina, Brazil, Uruguay, and Paraguay took effect. Tariffs on 90 percent of goods traded among the four countries were eliminated. On January 2, Chile and Bolivia announced that they would also seek membership in the group. As impediments to regional commerce fell, trade among Latin American countries account-

Facts in brief on Latin America

Country	Population	Government	Monetary unit*	Foreign trade (million U.S.$)	
				Exports†	Imports†
Antigua and Barbuda	69,000	Governor General James B. Carlisle; Prime Minister Lester Bird	dollar (2.70 = $1)	22	225
Argentina	35,298,000	President Carlos Saúl Menem	peso (1.00 = $1)	15,659	21,527
Bahamas	281,000	Governor General Orville Turnquest; Prime Minister Hubert Ingraham	dollar (1.00 = $1)	1,517	1,801
Barbados	262,000	Governor General Dame Nita Barrow; Prime Minister Owen Arthur	dollar (2.01 = $1)	179	574
Belize	213,000	Governor General Sir Colville Young; Prime Minister Manuel Esquivel	dollar (2.00 = $1)	144	258
Bolivia	8,256,000	President Gonzalo Sánchez de Lozada Bustamante	boliviano (4.86 = $1)	728	1,206
Brazil	163,577,000	President Fernando Henrique Cardoso	cruzeiro real (0.96 = $1)	43,558	35,997
Chile	14,436,000	President Eduardo Frei Ruíz-Tagle	peso (427.35 = $1)	11,575	11,825
Colombia	35,624,000	President Ernesto Samper Pizano	peso (993.68 = $1)	8,408	11,894
Costa Rica	3,495,000	President José Maria Figueres Olsen	colón (188.51 = $1)	2,233	3,089
Cuba	11,172,000	President Fidel Castro	peso (1.00 = $1)	2,050	2,185
Dominica	71,000	President Crispin Anselm Sorhaindo; Prime Minister Edison James	dollar (2.70 = $1)	56	111
Dominican Republic	8,050,000	President Joaquín Balaguer Ricardo	peso (13.74 = $1)	565	2,689
Ecuador	12,063,000	President Sixto Durán-Ballén Cordovez	sucre (2,646.50 = $1)	3,717	3,642
El Salvador	5,893,000	President Armando Calderon Sol	colón (8.76 = $1)	734	1,919
Grenada	92,000	Governor General Reginald Palmer; Prime Minister Keith Mitchell	dollar (2.7 = $1)	20	107
Guatemala	10,919,000	President Ramiro De León Carpio	quetzal (5.95 = $1)	1,291	2,599
Guyana	843,000	President Cheddi Jagan	dollar (142.90 = $1)	293	382
Haiti	7,328,000	President Jean-Bertrand Aristide; Prime Minister Claudette Werleigh	gourde (19.00 = $1)	103	374
Honduras	6,132,000	President Carlos Roberto Reina Idiáquez	lempira (9.84 = $1)	843	1,056
Jamaica	2,572,000	Governor General Howard Cooke; Prime Minister P. J. Patterson	dollar (36.00 = $1)	1,057	2,118
Mexico	95,365,000	President Ernesto Zedillo Ponce de León	new peso (7.24 = $1)	60,833	79,375
Nicaragua	4,569,000	President Violeta Barrios de Chamorro	gold córdoba (7.80 = $1)	267	746
Panama	2,704,000	President Ernesto Pérez Balladares	balboa (1 = $1)	533	2,404
Paraguay	4,576,000	President Juan Carlos Wasmosy	guaraní (1,966.00 = $1)	694	1,698
Peru	24,314,000	President Alberto Fujimori	new sol (2.25 = $1)	4,507	6,752
Puerto Rico	3,522,000	Governor Pedro Rosselló	U.S. dollar	21,800	16,700
St. Christopher and Nevis	44,000	Governor General Clement Athelston Arrindell; Prime Minister Denzil Douglas	dollar (2.70 = $1)	28	111
St. Lucia	144,000	Governor General Sir Stanislaus James; Prime Minister John Compton	dollar (2.70 = $1)	123	313
St. Vincent and the Grenadines	113,000	Governor General David Jack; Prime Minister James F. Mitchell	dollar (2.70 = $1)	58	134
Suriname	470,000	President Ronald R. Venetiaan	guilder (459.00 = $1)	472	472
Trinidad and Tobago	1,317,000	President Noor Hassanali; Prime Minister Basdeo Panday	dollar (5.71 = $1)	1,612	1,448
Uruguay	3,204,000	President Julio Maria Sanguinetti	peso (6.79 = $1)	1,913	2,773
Venezuela	20,490,000	President Rafael Caldera Rodríguez	bolívar (170.00 = $1)	14,378	10,979

*Exchange rates as of Oct. 27, 1995, or latest available data.
†Latest available data.

ed for more than 25 percent of all regional trade by mid-1995 compared with 10 percent in 1985.

By 1995, more than 400 Brazilian and Argentine companies had entered into joint ventures. Hourly shuttle flights between São Paulo and Buenos Aires were filled to capacity, and airline officials expected the flights to exceed the record 1.3 million passengers that they carried in 1994. To accommodate its Common Market partners, Brazil opened express lanes in 1995 at its airports, where customs officials merely waved regional business travelers through. Not to be outdone, Bolivia, Colombia, Ecuador, Peru, and Venezuela, partners in the Andean Common Market, introduced a regional passport for the convenience of their entrepreneurs.

Avon calling. Several U.S. companies reported huge profits in 1995 from their Latin American operations. The New York-based Avon cosmetics firm, for example, ranked Argentina as its fourth-largest market. In Brazil, where Avon expected its sales to top the $1-billion mark in 1995, the company said it had recruited 478,000 beauty consultants—a marketing force that, as Brazilians joked, was more than double the size of the country's army.

Putting progress in perspective. Despite the rosy business outlook, joblessness still affected many Latin Americans in 1995. Mexico's entry into the North American Free Trade Agreement in January 1994 could not prevent another 1 million Mexicans from joining the jobless ranks by July 1995. When several small businesses in Mexico City sponsored a job fair in September, 60,000 unemployed white-collar workers applied for a handful of positions.

In Argentina, unemployment hit a record 18.6 percent in August. The country's trade unions were angry at the government for selling state-run enterprises and causing hundreds of thousands of union members to lose their jobs.

Benefits from economic progress were also slow to filter down to workers in Brazil. In a March report, Brazil's Catholic bishops estimated that some 64.5 million Brazilians earned the minimum wage or less. Half of the nation's workers were without any form of social security, the report said. In addition, the bishops found, 45 million Brazilian youngsters lived in subhuman conditions, and 500,000 children supported themselves through prostitution.

Resurgence of dengue fever. The worst epidemic of dengue fever since 1981 struck Latin America in 1995. Dengue fever is a mosquito-transmitted disease characterized by headache, fever, and pain in the joints. According to the World Health Organization in Geneva, Switzerland, more than 140,000 cases of dengue fever struck 12 Latin American and Caribbean countries between January and September. In that time, 88,000 cases were reported in Brazil, 35,000 in Central America, and 15,000 in Venezuela. Thirty-eight people had died from the disease.

Preserving the environment. Environmentalists were outraged when Suriname's government invited bids in 1995 from three Asian companies to log 12 million acres (4.9 million hectares) of virgin rain forest. The area comprised some 40 percent of Suriname's national territory. Many environmentalists saw the case as a critical test in the fight against tropical deforestation worldwide. The government said the logging would create needed jobs.

Elsewhere, the people of Tepoztlán, Mexico, seized the town hall in August in a successful challenge to a joint venture by Mexican and American corporations to build an industrial park and golf course on lands set aside as an ecological reserve.

Drug trafficking. On March 1, the U.S. State Department announced that it was unhappy with the antinarcotics efforts of Colombia, Peru, Bolivia, and Paraguay. The State Department issues annual ratings of the antinarcotics efforts of 29 countries in which heavy drug traffic occurs. Countries receiving unfavorable ratings face the possibility of losing certain trade benefits and nonhumanitarian U.S. aid.

The U.S. dissatisfaction carried serious consequences in Bolivia. In March, The United States threatened to cut off aid to Bolivia unless it destroyed 4,300 acres (1,750 hectares) of coca plants—the raw material for cocaine. The Bolivian government began a coca plant eradication program, but it drew mass protests from coca farmers. In response to the protests, Bolivian President Gonzalo Sánchez de Lozada Bustamante put the country under a state of siege on April 18.

Corruption. The former Bolivian dictator General Luis Garcia Meza Tejada, who was overthrown in 1981, was extradited from Brazil on March 14, 1995, to serve a life sentence for crimes he committed while in office. Meza had been tried in absentia and convicted of human rights violations.

In Chile in May, two generals were sentenced to jail for complicity in the 1976 assassination of an outspoken opponent of military rule. In neighboring Argentina, the army chief of staff confessed in April 1995 that the nation's armed forces had indeed, as everybody had long known, been involved in assassination and torture during the so-called "Dirty War" against dissidents from 1976 to 1983.

Despite such admissions, the perpetrators went largely unpunished. In Peru, the Congress wiped the slate clean by passing a wide-ranging amnesty for violators of human rights. Of more than 100 prominent Venezuelan businessmen indicted for their roles in the 1994 collapse of the nation's banks, none had faced trial as 1995 ended. In Brazil, people seemed disposed to forget altogether the culprits from the previous administration, including a former president who was impeached for stealing huge sums of money.

CIA disciplinary actions. On September 27, the U.S. Central Intelligence Agency (CIA) announced

Guatemalan army Colonel Julio Roberto Alpírez in March denies any role in the deaths of a U.S. innkeeper and the Guatemalan husband of an American lawyer.

States, Argentina, Brazil, and Chile. The two sides reported 73 deaths during the conflict.

A similar flare-up of border tensions, involving Colombia and Venezuela, occurred in a remote Amazonian region along their common boundary in late February. It was precipitated by a cross-border raid by Colombian-based guerrillas three weeks previously that left eight Venezuelan marines dead and four wounded.

Oldest Hondurans? Archaeologists announced in January 1995 that human skeletal remains discovered in a remote cave along the Talgua River in Honduras were the oldest known evidence of civilization in Honduras. According to archaeologist James E. Brady of George Washington University in Washington, D.C., the unknown people lived about 3,000 years ago. Brady oversaw the study of the 100 to 200 skulls found in the cave in 1994.

Brady said that mounds found near the cave were probably the remains of a city inhabited by "an advanced, complex civilization" that flourished in the Mosquitia region of Honduras. Calcium crystals encrusted the skulls, causing them to glow in the light of searchers' flashlights and leading to the cave's nickname—Cave of the Glowing Skulls.

□ Nathan A. Haverstock

See also articles on the individual nations. In *World Book*, see **Latin America** and articles on the individual nations.

Latvia. On Oct. 1, 1995, Latvia held its first general election since passing a new citizenship law in 1994. Under the new law, citizens of the former Soviet Union who desire Latvian citizenship must satisfy a five-year residence requirement and pass tests in Latvian history and language. Of Latvia's ethnic Russians, who constitute about a third of the population, about 60 percent failed to meet the requirements and were ineligible to vote.

The newly elected parliament was split evenly between a coalition of two new populist parties—the Democratic Owner's Party (Saimnieks) and the Movement for Latvia—and a rival bloc organized around a former governing party, Latvian Way. In November, Latvian President Guntis Ulmanis said he considered Movement for Latvia's leader Joachim Siegerist an extremist and would oppose his inclusion in a government. Siegerist, who lived most of his life in Germany, belonged to a far-right political party there and was charged with incitement to racial hatred. In November, the parliament rejected a cabinet formed by Latvian Way, and Ulmanis invited Saimnieks to form a government without Siegerist.

During the summer, about one-third of Latvia's 67 commercial banks collapsed. Neverthless, the Latvian economy remained strong.   □ Steven L. Solnick

See also **Europe** (Facts in brief table). In *World Book,* see **Latvia.**

Law. See **Courts; Supreme Court of the U.S.**

that it would demote or discipline nearly a dozen operatives involved in a cover-up in Guatemala. The move had been prompted by the revelation that a Guatemalan officer, Colonel Julio Roberto Alpírez, who was allegedly involved in the 1992 assassination of an American citizen's Guatemalan husband, was a paid CIA informant at the time of the crime.

Border clashes. On Jan. 26, 1995, violence erupted along the Cenepa River in a border area between Ecuador and Peru that the two countries had long disputed. A cease-fire went into effect on February 14, but fighting soon broke out again. It was not until July 25 that Peru and Ecuador agreed to demilitarize the disputed area, with compliance to be monitored by peacekeepers from the United

Lebanon. The failure of Lebanon's neighbors Israel and Syria to reach a peace agreement in 1995 hurt Lebanon's recovery from its long civil war (1975-1991). In February 1995, Israel imposed a naval blockade along Lebanon's southern coast, idling more than 1,500 fishermen. Israel's action was aimed at Syria, which has more than 30,000 troops stationed in Lebanon. Syria has strong control over Lebanese politics and Lebanon's militant Hezbollah (Party of God), which opposes the Arab-Israeli peace process. In early 1995, Hezbollah had stepped up attacks against Israeli targets and the pro-Israeli South Lebanon Army.

Lebanon's Prime Minister Rafik Hariri began a second term in May 1995 and won Syrian approval to appoint his own cabinet. He also obtained Syrian support for extending the six-year term of his ally President Elias Hrawi rather than holding presidential elections. But Hariri and his allies received public criticism, and protests broke out in July. Many people blamed the government for the nation's worsening economic conditions and corruption.

Samir Geagea, former head of the Christian militia Lebanese Forces, was found guilty in June of the 1990 murder of Christian warlord Dani Chamoun and his family. □ Christine Helms

See also **Middle East** (Facts in brief table). In *World Book*, see **Lebanon**.

Lesotho. See Africa.

Liberia. As 1995 came to a close, the prospects of an end to Liberia's six-year civil war were better than at any time in recent years. While prior peace negotiations had ended in disappointment, an agreement reached in 1995 seemed to be holding. However, economic conditions remained bleak.

Lengthy discussions held in Ghana and Nigeria led to the peace agreement, signed in Nigeria on August 20. A six-member Council of State, including representatives of the major warring Liberian factions, was expected to rule until democratic elections could be held sometime in 1996. One of the council members was Charles Taylor, head of the National Patriotic Front of Liberia, who instigated the civil war in 1989 when he led rebel forces against dictator Samuel K. Doe. The council met for the first time on September 1 amid widespread celebration in a country devastated by years of war.

Despite political progress, Liberia faced tremendous economic difficulties in 1995. Food was in short supply, disease and malnutrition were rampant, and plantations and mines—the country's major sources of income—were not operating. In addition to severely damaging Liberia's economy, the civil war was responsible for the death of 150,000 people and turned 80 percent of the population into refugees. □ Mark DeLancey

See also **Africa** (Facts in brief table). In *World Book,* see **Liberia**.

Library. In 1995, millions of people in the United States took part in a renaissance of the urban public library that began in the early 1990's. Stunning new central library buildings opened in Denver, Colorado; Phoenix; and San Antonio. New buildings were being constructed in Alexandria, Virginia; Cincinnati, Columbus, and Cleveland, Ohio; Portland, Oregon; and San Francisco.

New buildings raised civic pride and generated dramatic increases in the use and support of libraries. This encouraging trend seemed to show that, in the face of governmental budget cuts, people placed high value on the services that a public library can provide families and communities.

San Francisco's new library, scheduled to open in April 1996, promised to be the most technologically advanced public library in the nation. All of the library's holdings were to be accessible through 200 computer catalog terminals. Over a dozen multimedia stations would allow patrons to see and hear a large variety of images and sounds. For blind patrons, there were to be workstations equipped with scanners to turn written material into sound. A huge children's center was to contain children's books in 40 languages, a live performance center, and an electronic center with multimedia terminals.

Festivities. The controversial new San Antonio library, designed by a Mexican architect, appeared to some more a monument to the imagination than a traditional temple of learning. A contest to name the color of the building awarded the prize to "enchilada red." On dedication day, a crowd of more than 20,000 cheered a parade that ended with four children moving the last book to the library in a little red wagon. The Denver library's opening celebration inspired a local microbrewery to create a tribute—a bottled brew labeled "Intellectu-ale."

France. In Paris, four L-shaped skyscrapers, meant to represent open books, made up the new National Library (Bibliothèque Nationale) of France, which was dedicated in the spring of 1995. The huge library, containing 3 million square feet (280,000 square meters) of space, was still being finished inside. The new complex will hold the nation's collection of more than 25 million items begun by France's King Charles V in 1367. Since the 1500's, the collection has included every book printed in France.

The 100th birthday celebration of the New York (City) Public Library (NYPL) in 1995 included a series of programs and special events. A Centennial Day celebration on May 20 included readings on the freedom of speech by noted journalists and authors. Twenty bands and dance companies from around the world performed in Bryant Park behind the 42nd Street branch. The day concluded with a sound and light show. The NYPL also prepared to open its Science, Industry, and Business Library, where computer services will be extensive.

Nobel Prize-winning author Toni Morrison spoke

Library

at the festivities. She said, "The glory of the library is not only that it has lasted . . . but that its leadership, its staff, its board, its supporters, its users, have for 100 years refused to give up the essence of the mission of the urban intellectual experience: cared-for public space, genuinely public service, and a refusal to accept less than the best for its constituency."

Funding problems continued in 1995 to challenge public, school, and university libraries. Following the 1994 elections that brought a Republican majority to the U.S. Congress, and the subsequent public debate about lessening the role of the federal government, such groups as the American Library Association (ALA) worked hard to maintain and build the programs that support libraries. The ALA

also worked to represent the public interest on issues such as telecommunications regulations that could ensure reduced rates for school and library access to the computer network called the Internet.

Award. The first annual National Information Infrastructure Award, sponsored by more than 70 organizations, had five winners in 1995. The Utah Library Network won top honors in the government category for being "the best government-sponsored, high-tech networking project in the nation." Accepting the award, director Amy Owen remarked, "Connectivity is transforming each community's library into a gateway to the world." □ Peggy Barber

In *World Book,* see **Bibliothèque Nationale; Library.**

The Bibliothèque Nationale de France, France's new national library, which opened in March, is made up of four buildings shaped like open books.

Libya. Political turbulence, mass deportations, and economic troubles marred the 26th year of leadership of Libya's Muammar Muhammad al-Qadhafi in 1995. Confrontations between Libyan security forces and Islamic militants erupted in June in Benghazi, Libya's second-largest city. About 30 people were reported killed on September 6 and 7. However, a September 1 speech by Qadhafi, in which he blamed "infiltrators" for the violence, seemed to point to more unrest than was officially reported.

Qadhafi ordered the deportation in 1995 of thousands of Libya's 2.5 million Arab and African laborers and their families. They included Palestinian workers who were expelled in September, an action that Qadhafi protrayed as a protest against the Arab-Israeli peace process. Libyan officials claimed that some deportees carried diseases such as AIDS, but major reasons for the deportations were a weak ecomomy and growing unemployment.

Libya's economy suffered from United Nations (UN) sanctions that Libyan officials said had cost $10-billion in lost revenues by early 1995. The UN imposed economic and travel sanctions against Libya in 1992 after Qadhafi refused to turn over suspects accused of the bombings of two airplanes, in 1988 and 1989, that killed 441 people.   □ Christine Helms

See also **Africa** (Facts in brief table). In *World Book*, see **Libya**.

Liechtenstein. See Europe.

Literature. British and Irish writers produced some fine literature in 1995. *Felicia's Journey,* by William Trevor, an Irishman who lives in England, was a witty novel about an Irish girl's search for the man who made her pregnant. *How Late It Was, How Late,* by Scottish author James Kelman, was a black comedy written in a salty Scottish dialect. It won England's top literary award, the Booker Prize. *East, West,* was a collection of short stories by Salman Rushdie, a British Indian living in hiding under a death sentence from Iranian clerics. Japanese-British Kazuo Ishiguro's *The Unconsoled* was a dense novel about a few days in the life of a concert pianist.

Canadian writer Robertson Davies, who died in December, contributed *The Cunning Man,* about a doctor who reflects on a priest's death. Australian Peter Carey's *The Unusual Life of Tristan Smith* was about a mutant being living in a futuristic world.

Novels in translation included *A Void,* written entirely without using the letter *e,* by the now deceased French author Georges Perec, and French author Albert Camus's posthumous novel, *The First Man.* Other notable translations were Czech Ivan Klima's *Waiting for the Dark, Waiting for the Light;* Chilean Isabel Allende's *Paula,* Colombian Gabriel Garcia Márquez's *Of Love and Other Demons,* and Japanese Shusaku Endo's *Deep River.*   □ Henry Kisor

See also **Canadian literature; Literature, American; Literature for children.**

Irish poet Seamus Heaney, known for the lyrical beauty of his poems and the powerful imagery of his words, won the 1995 Nobel Prize for literature.

Literature, American. No new American novel stood out during 1995 as an undisputed masterpiece. Nonetheless, much excellent work did appear, especially from veteran novelists and short-story writers.

Three writers in their 80's turned out notable books in 1995. Henry Roth's *A Diving Rock on the Hudson* was a sprightly novel of immigrant life in New York in the 1920's. Roth, who first won fame for his work in the 1930's, died in October.

Dorothy West, the last survivor of the literary renaissance of New York City's Harlem of the 1920's, produced two fine books in 1995. Her novel *The Wedding* told of a union between the daughter of an upper-class black family on Martha's Vineyard and a white jazz musician. *The Richer, the Poorer* was West's engaging volume of stories, sketches, and reminiscences of middle-class African American life. *All the Days and Nights* was William Maxwell's lifetime collection of splendid short stories.

Other older writers also produced noteworthy literature in 1995. William H. Gass's *The Tunnel* was the writer's long-awaited major novel about the fevered thoughts of a bigoted history professor who digs a tunnel from his basement to try to escape his misery.

Mrs. Ted Bliss, by Stanley Elkin, was a lustrous novel about an indomitable 80-year-old Jewish widow living in Miami Beach. Elkin died in March.

267

Philip Roth's *Sabbath's Theater,* a novel about a 64-year-old drama teacher and ex-puppeteer whose behavior becomes increasingly outrageous, won widespread praise for its comic inventiveness.

Other writers also turned out important work. Pete Dexter's *The Paperboy* vividly explored two American male psyches: one of a journalist and the second of the feral backwoodsman he helps free from a death sentence. James Ellroy's *American Tabloid* was a satire of the assassination of President John F. Kennedy in 1963. Jane Smiley's *Moo* lampooned Midwestern academic pretensions. And Mark Helprin's *Memoir from Antproof Case* concerned an eccentric hiding out in Brazil, who composes his memoir for his stepson.

Richard Ford's *Independence Day* continued the story of a man whose extraordinary gifts for social observation contrast with his ordinary life. Elmore Leonard won high critical praise for his experiments with spoken language in *Riding the Rap,* a comic crime thriller.

Significant work in 1995 also included Geoffrey Wolff's *The Age of Consent,* Michael Chabon's *Wonder Boys,* Scott Spencer's *Men in Black,* Russell Banks's *Rule of the Bone,* Anne Tyler's *Ladder of Years,* Sue Miller's *The Distinguished Guest,* and Clyde Edgerton's *Redeye: A Western.* Other noteworthy titles included Reynolds Price's *The Promise of Rest,* Lee Smith's *Saving Grace,* David Lodge's *Therapy,* Richard Powers's *Galatea 2.2,* Mary McGarry Morris's *Songs in Ordinary Time,* T. Coraghessan Boyle's *The Tortilla Curtain,* Joyce Carol Oates's *Zombie,* Ann Beattie's *Another You,* and Amy Tan's *The Hundred Secret Senses.*

A number of African American writers produced notable fiction during the year. Among them were Ntozake Shange, Maxine Clair, and Walter Mosley.

New novelists. Among the better first novels of the year were *Hanging Up,* by Delia Ephron, a comic tale of an unpleasant life with an alcoholic father. The black memoirist Lorene Cary's *The Price of a Child* was a story of an escaped slave's life in pre-Civil War Philadelphia.

Biography. Several important books explored the lives of Westerners who were spies for the Soviet Union during the Cold War. Anthony Cave Brown's *Treason in the Blood* was the story of British intelligence agent H.A.R. (Kim) Philby, who worked secretly for the Soviets, and his father H. St. John Philby, an expert on Arabia, who openly rebelled against his former country. Aldrich Ames, the C.I.A. official who betrayed his nation to the Soviet Union, was the subject of several books in 1995. Among them was Peter Maas's *Killer Spy,* Tim Weiner's *Betrayal,* and David Wise's *Nightmover.*

Notable literary biographies were Deirdre Bair's *Anaïs Nin,* a life of the poet and diarist; Thomas Kunkel's *Genius in Disguise,* about Harold Ross, founder of the *New Yorker* magazine; Judith Mor-

gan and Neil Morgan's *Dr. Seuss & Mr. Geisel,* which examined the career of children's author Ted Geisel, better known as Dr. Seuss; David S. Reynolds's *Walt Whitman's America,* which told how the poet transformed the culture surrounding him into art; and Gail Levin's *Edward Hopper,* which focused on the life of a major American artist.

Fine biographies of celebrities included Barbara Leaming's *Katharine Hepburn;* Marion Meade's *Buster Keaton,* and Carolyn G. Heilbrun's *The Education of A Woman: The Life of Gloria Steinem.*

Historical biographies were led by David Herbert Donald's magisterial *Lincoln,* the first major one-volume biography of the President in many years. Another excellent book, *Tom Paine* by John Keane, covered the life of a famous American Revolutionary War (1775-1783) thinker.

Autobiography. Among the year's notable personal testaments were the posthumous *Revelations,* by the black dancer and choreographer Alvin Ailey. *In the Arena* was a sprightly reminiscence of a Hollywood career by actor Charlton Heston. Ben Bradlee's *A Good Life* covered the life of the former *Washington Post* editor celebrated for his political exposés. *Palimpsest,* by Gore Vidal, was the novelist's crisp memoir of a life in literature and politics.

My Old Man and the Sea, by David Hays and Daniel Hays, was an engaging account of a father and son sailing around Cape Horn and getting to know each other. *Where White Men Fear to Tread* was the autobiography of Russell Means, a controversial leader of the American Indian Movement.

Growing up in difficult circumstances was the subject of several excellent memoirs. Among them were *Dreaming,* novelist Carolyn See's memoir of her childhood in a dysfunctional family. *In Love with Daylight* was Wilfrid Sheed's account of his battles with alcohol, drugs, and cancer. *The Liars' Club* was Mary Karr's haunting memoir of growing up in east Texas with a brilliant, but alcoholic, mother. *Moving Violations* was John Hockenberry's candid recollection of life in a wheelchair as a National Public Radio correspondent. *Secret Life* was Michael Ryan's astonishing account of an addiction to sex.

Letters. *Always, Rachel,* a volume of intimate letters exchanged by ecologist Rachel Carson and her friend Dorothy Freeman, was ably edited by Freeman's granddaughter Martha Freeman. *Closest Companion,* edited by Geoffrey C. Ward, revealed the startling closeness of President Franklin D. Roosevelt and his friend and distant cousin Margaret Suckley.

Criticism. Jack Miles's provocatively titled *God: A Biography* was a fascinating exploration into the multiple personalities of the deity over the ages. Elaine Pagels's *The Origin of Satan* imaginatively investigated the grip the concept of evil symbolized in Satan has held on Western culture.

Contemporary nonfiction. Two much-heralded political books swiftly rose to the top of best-seller lists. *To Renew America,* by Newt Gingrich, Speaker of the U.S. House of Representatives, outlined Gingrich's solutions for the country. *My American Journey,* by Colin Powell, was the autobiography of the retired black general, which led to a brief but intense flurry of interest in him as a possible presidential candidate.

Several interesting books about the world of crime appeared in 1995. Among them were Michelle Slatalla and Joshua Quittner's *Masters of Deception,* which concerned a group of teen-agers who broke into corporate computers. Nicholas Pileggi's *Casino,* probably the year's best true-crime book, explored Las Vegas gambling enterprises under the influence of the crime syndicate.

Free speech was the subject of a number of notable books in 1995, including *Defending Pornography: Free Speech, Sex and the Fight for Women's Rights,* in which author Nadine Strossen warned against a blanket censorship of sexual material.

Peter Howard's best-selling *The Death of Common Sense* attacked what the author called legal trivia that were hobbling American life. Robert S. McNamara's *In Retrospect* was a controversial self-accusing memoir of the events of the Vietnam War (1957-1975) by one of its major architects.

Comrade Criminal, by Stephen Handelman, discussed how organized crime had penetrated Russian society since the fall of the Soviet Union. *The Haunted Land,* by Tina Rosenberg, examined how several former Soviet satellite countries coped with the legacy of their actions under the old regimes.

Norman Mailer's *Oswald's Tale* synthesized all that was known about Lee Harvey Oswald, the assassin of John F. Kennedy. Michael Gross's *Model* was a best-selling exposé of the seamy side of the fashion-modeling industry.

Coming of Age was a book from the master interviewer, Studs Terkel. It was a collective portrait of the 1900's as seen and heard through the eyes and voices of 70 Americans, aged 70 to 99 years.

Two notable books dealt with troubled African American families in 1995. Jonathan Kozol's *Amazing Grace* was a revealing account of black children living in the New York City slums. *All God's Children,* by Fox Butterfield, outlined the disturbing record of a black criminal's family and linked it to the long history of violence in America.

History. The 50th anniversary of the dropping of the atomic bomb on Hiroshima and Nagasaki during World War II (1939-1945) was marked by the publication of those events. Among them were Gar Alperovitz's *The Decision to Use the Atomic Bomb,* Thomas B. Allen and Norman Polmar's *Code-Name Downfall,* Robert Jay Lifton and Greg Mitchell's *Hiroshima in America,* Ronald Takaki's *Hiroshima,* and Richard Rhodes's *Dark Sun.* The authors were divided on whether the bombings were necessary or morally defensible.

The Spoils of World War II, by Kenneth D. Alford, told how American soldiers stole and brought home art treasures that the Nazis had looted from countries during World War II. David Reynolds' *Rich Relations* was an entertaining study of how American soldiers peacefully flooded Britain before the invasion of German-occupied France in 1944.

Robert K. Massie's *The Romanovs* and Peter Kurth's *Tsar* were two excellent popular studies of the search for the bones of Tsar Nicholas II of Russia and his family, who were murdered in 1918 by Communist revolutionaries.

Best sellers. Robert James Waller, author of the best-selling novel *The Bridges of Madison County,* turned out two popular romance novels in 1995: *Border Music* and *Puerto Vallarta Squeeze.* Michael Crichton followed his phenomenal best seller, *Jurassic Park* (1991), with another dinosaur-adventure novel, *The Lost World.* Other best-selling novels were John Grisham's *The Rainmaker,* Pat Conroy's *Beach Music,* and Anne Rice's *Memnoch the Devil.*

The emergence of an epidemic of a deadly Ebola virus in Africa revived the best-selling fortunes of a 1994 book, *The Hot Zone,* by Richard Preston. It told how one strain of the virus nearly escaped from an animal facility in Virginia in 1989. ☐ Henry Kisor

See also **Canadian literature; Literature; Literature for children; Poetry.** In *World Book,* see **American literature.**

Literature for children.

Literature for children. Many children's books published in 1995 were multicultural, a trend that was also notable in 1994. Picture books in 1995 included many in Spanish/English or Spanish, talking beast tales, folk tales, and books about the environment. For preteens and teenagers, books contained more humor even in serious fiction. Much nonfiction was published, but less poetry. Outstanding books of 1995 included the following:

Picture Books. *Isla* by Arthur Dorros, illustrated by Elisa Kleven (Dutton). Rosalba and her grandmother, outfitted with wings, travel to the island where the grandmother was raised. Ages 5 to 8.

Ragsale by Artie Ann Bates, illustrated by Jeff Chapman-Crane (Houghton Mifflin). A girl tells of going to Appalachian rag sales abounding with clothes, books, toys, and more. Ages 4 to 8.

Swami on Rye: Max in India by Maira Kalman (Viking). Max the dog is whisked to India to find the meaning of life. All ages.

Passover Magic by Roni Schotter, illustrated by Marylin Hafner (Little, Brown). A family's preparations unfold for the Jewish holiday celebrating freedom. Ages 4 to 8.

The Moonglow Roll-O-Rama by Dav Pilkey (Orchard Bks.). All kinds of animals don rollerskates in the moonlight in this magical tale. Ages 3 to 6.

Feliciana Feydra LeRoux: A Cajun Tall Tale by Tynia Thomassie, illustrated by Cat Bowman Smith (Lit-

And there is the fire fighter who was at our building. He is standing in the open door, with the smoky night behind him, and I see that he's carrying a cat under each arm. That was how Mr. Ramirez carried Lissa and the baby. The cats are howling, too.

"Jasmine!" The blanket's caught on my foot and I'm trailing it. "Oh, thank you! Thank you for finding her!"

"The other cat is mine." Mrs. Kim takes her big, fat, mean old orange cat and holds him close. I'm kissing Jasmine. She smells of smoke.

Smoky Night, a story by Eve Bunting about people who learn to get along when two cats disappear during a night of rioting, won a Caldecott Medal in January for illustrator David Diaz.

tle, Brown). This Cajun tale has Feliciana saving the day in a confrontation with an alligator. Ages 4 to 8.

Okino and the Whales by Arnica Esterl, illustrated by Marek Zawadski (Harcourt Brace). A tale about a mother who goes to the undersea kingdom of whales to get her daughter back. Ages 5 to 8.

The Faithful Friend by Robert D. San Souci, illustrated by Brian Pinkney (Simon & Schuster). A supernatural tale of friendship told in the setting of the island of Martinique. Ages 5 to 10.

The Gifts of Wali Dad: A Tale of India and Pakistan retold by Aaron Shepard, illustrated by Daniel San Souci (Atheneum). In this comic folk tale, Wali Dad buys a bracelet, gives it to a queen, and finds that his gesture has surprising results. Ages 5 to 8.

Do the Whales Still Sing? by Dianne Hofmeyr, illustrated by Jude Daly (Dial). A whaler tells of a night that ended his whaling days. Ages 5 and up.

It's for You: An Amazing Picture-Puzzle Book by John Talbot (Dutton). Mirror-image messages, mazes, and puzzles of all kinds await the reader. Ages 10 and up.

Call Me Ahnighito by Pam Conrad, illustrated by Richard Egielski (Laura Geringer/HarperCollins). A meteorite is brought to New York City, but years pass before it finds a home. Ages 5 to 9.

The Song of Mu Lan by Jeanne M. Lee (Front Street). In this translation of a Chinese folk poem from the A.D. 500's, Mu Lan goes to war disguised as a man and returns home a hero. Ages 5 to 8.

Her Stories: African American Folktales, Fairy Tales, and True Tales by Virginia Hamilton, illustrated by Leo and Diane Dillon (Blue Sky/Scholastic). This collection of stories about women includes comments by the author about the tales. Ages 8 and up.

The Tooth Fairy by Peter Collington (Knopf). In this story told through pictures, a child's tooth is retrieved by the fairy for a special reason. Ages 3 to 7.

On the Road with Poppa Whopper by Marianne Busser and Ron Schroder, illustrated by Hans de Beer (North-South Bks.). When Poppa and Frannie must move, they go in an unusual vehicle with comical results. Ages 7 to 9.

Down the Road by Alice Schertle, illustrated by

E. B. Lewis (Browndeer/Harcourt Brace). Hetty feels big enough to go to the store, but her errand goes awry on her return trip home. Ages 4 to 8.

Kashtanka by Anton Chekhov, adapted and translated by Ronald Meyer, illustrated by Gennady Spirin (Gulliver/Harcourt Brace). A dog is separated from its master, taught tricks for the circus, and dramatically reunited with its master. Ages 5 to 9.

Zin! Zin! Zin! a Violin by Lloyd Moss, illustrated by Marjorie Priceman (Simon & Schuster). Starting with a trombone, the reader learns about numbers, instruments, and musical groups. All ages.

Dandelions by Eve Bunting, illustrated by Greg Shed (Harcourt Brace). A resettled pioneer woman is cheered by a gift of dandelions from her daughter. Ages 6 to 9.

The Story of the Three Kingdoms by Walter Dean Myers, illustrated by Ashley Bryan (HarperCollins). The rulers of the three kingdoms—sky, earth, and water—insist that each is more powerful, until they are captured. Ages 4 to 8.

MedioPollito/Half-Chicken by Alma Flor Ada, illustrated by Kim Howard (Doubleday). In this folk tale in Spanish and English, a vain chicken—born with only one wing, leg, and eye—goes to Mexico City to see the viceroy. Ages 5 to 9.

Re-Zoom by Istvan Banyai (Viking). Colorful illustrations reveal themselves as part of larger artworks. All ages.

Math Curse by Jon Scieszka, illustrated by Lane Smith (Viking). When the math teacher says that almost all problems are math problems, the zany fun begins. Ages 6 and up.

Fiction. *The Eagle Kite* by Paula Fox (Orchard Bks.). Liam must come to terms with his feelings about AIDS and how his father got the illness. Ages 11 to 14.

The Killick: A Newfoundland Story by Geoff Butler (Tundra Bks.). A boy, stranded with his grandfather on a melting ice slab, learns courage. Ages 8 to 11.

Tomorrow, When the War Began by John Marsden (Houghton Mifflin). Seven young people return from camping to find their dogs dead on their chains and their families captured. Ages 12 and up.

Some of the Kinder Planets by Tim Wynne-Jones (Orchard Bks.). This collection of unusual stories won Canada's 1993 Governor General's Award for Children's Literature. Ages 8 to 12.

The Midwife's Apprentice by Karen Cushman (Clarion Bks.). A homeless girl becomes a midwife's helper and learns truths about life. Ages 12 and up.

The Middle Passage by Tom Feelings (Dial). The Atlantic slave trade is described and shown in haunting black-and-white paintings. Ages 8 and up.

Music from a Place Called Half Moon by Jerrie Oughton (Houghton Mifflin). When Edie Jo's father opens the vacation Bible school to Indians, the family is ostracized and tragedy strikes. Ages 10 to 14.

Tusk and Stone by Malcolm Bosse (Front Street). Arjun, kidnapped and sold, becomes an elephant driver and seeks his lost sister. Ages 12 and up.

Prejudice: Stories About Hate, Ignorance, Revelation, and Transformation edited by Daphne Muse (Hyperion). Short stories and excerpts from novels reveal that prejudice arises for many reasons and people react to it in many ways. Ages 10 and up.

Fantasy. *Thwonk* by Joan Bauer (Delacorte). When Cupid grants A. J. a wish, she gets more than she bargained for. Ages 12 and up.

Fall-out by Gudrun Pausewang, translated by Patricia Crampton (Viking). A German literature award-winner, this novel shows people's reactions to a nuclear power station disaster. Ages 12 and up.

The Arkadians by Lloyd Alexander (Dutton). Lucian escapes the wrath of the wicked soothsayers and encounters unusual characters. Ages 12 and up.

Shadow of the Red Moon by Walter Dean Myers, illustrated by Christopher Myers (Scholastic). A tale set in a post-apocalyptic world. Ages 12 and up.

The Van Gogh Cafe by Cynthia Rylant (Harcourt Brace). Strange things happen at a cafe in Flowers, Kansas, that has magic in its walls. All ages.

Here There Be Witches by Jane Yolen, illustrated by David Wilgus (Harcourt Brace). Stories and poems about various witches have imaginative twists. Ages 8 and up.

Truly Grim Tales by Priscilla Galloway (Delacorte). Eight traditional folk tales are given original twists and perspectives. Ages 14 and up.

Elfsong by Ann Turner (Harcourt Brace). When Maddy goes to stay with Grandpa, she becomes involved with a group of elves in their struggle against a marauding owl. Ages 8 to 11.

Poetry. *Small Talk: A Book of Short Poems* selected by Lee Bennett Hopkins (Harcourt Brace). Poems rich in imagery offer a range of subjects and poets. All ages.

The Birthday ABC by Eric Metaxas, illustrated by Tim Raglin (Simon & Schuster). Elegantly costumed animals highlight alphabet birthday rhymes. Ages 3 to 6.

The Ballad of the Pirate Queens by Jane Yolen, illustrated by David Shannon (Harcourt Brace). This book of poetry describes the fates of two famous pirates and their crew. Ages 8 to 11.

Dance with Me by Barbara Juster Esbensen, illustrated by Megan Lloyd (HarperCollins). These poems capture children's feelings and play. Ages 7 to 10.

Runaway Opposites by Richard Wilbur, illustrated by Henrik Drescher (Harcourt Brace). Zany illustrations accompany poems on opposites. All ages.

Ridicholas Nicholas: More Animal Poems by J. Patrick Lewis, illustrated by Victoria Chess (Dial). Funny poems with animal illustrations. Ages 4 to 8.

Sad Underwear and Other Complications by Judith Viorst, illustrated by Richard Hull (Atheneum). Funny rhymes about the trials of childhood, and more. Ages 7 and up.

Nonfiction books. *Nights of the Pufflings* by Bruce McMillan (Houghton Mifflin). Each year in Iceland, puffin hatchlings leave their nests for the ocean, but some need help. Superb photos. All ages.

Walt Whitman by Catherine Reef (Clarion). This fine biography contains quotes from Whitman's writings. Ages 12 and up.

The Book of North American Owls by Helen Roney Sattler, illustrated by Jean Day Zallinger (Clarion Bks.). Fascinating details about owls, with maps, index, bibliography, and more. Ages 9 and up.

Galapagos: Islands of Change by Lynn Born Mayers and Christopher A. Myers, illustrated by Nathan Farb (Hyperion). Striking images help show how the islands developed. Ages 8 to 11.

Rosie the Riveter: Women Working on the Home Front in World War II by Penny Colman (Crown). This text reveals how women worked during the war, how they were treated, and what happened to them when the war ended. Ages 10 and up.

Children Just Like Me by Barnabas and Anabel Kindersley/UNICEF (Dorling Kindersley). This book features children from around the world and their families and traditions. Ages 8 to 11.

The Sea King: Sir Francis Drake and His Times by Albert Marrin (Atheneum). This biography brings Drake's life and times into focus. Ages 10 and up.

The American Eye: Eleven Artists of the Twentieth Century by Jan Greenberg and Sandra Jordan (Delacorte). Illuminating biographies include color examples of each artist's work. Ages 10 and up.

Awards. Sharon Creech won the 1995 Newbery Medal for her novel *Walk Two Moons*. The Newbery Medal is given by the American Library Association (ALA) for outstanding children's literature published the previous year. The ALA's Caldecott Medal for "the most distinguished American picture book for children" was awarded to David Diaz, the illustrator of *Smoky Night* by Eve Bunting.

☐ Marilyn Fain Apseloff

In *World Book,* see **Caldecott Medal; Newbery Medal; Literature for Children.**

Lithuania. For most of 1995, Lithuanian citizens focused on threats to their health-care and banking systems, while politicians looked ahead to a parliamentary election scheduled for 1996. In June 1995, the government announced that it could no longer afford to provide free health care to all Lithuanian citizens, despite a constitutional guarantee of universal medical care. That same month, several of Lithuania's largest commercial banks were revealed to have engaged in dubious or illegal lending practices and were forced into bankruptcy.

In October, a long-standing dispute between Lithuania and Latvia over claims to offshore oil deposits in the Baltic Sea became more heated. On October 31, Latvia signed an agreement with two Western firms to develop oil deposits in territory partially claimed by Lithuania. The two states had been negotiating the borders of their economic zones in the Baltic Sea since 1993. Lithuanian officials charged that the Latvian deal violated an agreement to postpone commercial development until the border negotiations were concluded. Lithuania protested the Latvian deal by recalling its ambassador to Latvia, but Lithuanian President Algirdas Brazauskas called for a settlement that would take into account "the interests of both sides."

◻ Steven L. Solnick

See also **Europe** (Facts in brief table). In *World Book,* see **Lithuania.**

Los Angeles. In the spellbinding climax to the most-watched media event of 1995, a Los Angeles jury on October 3 found former football star and sportscaster O. J. Simpson not guilty of murder. Although the presentation of evidence had lasted over eight months, the jury reached its verdict in less than four hours. The trial set a record for the longest *sequestration* (isolation) of a jury in California history.

Simpson, 47, had been charged with killing his second ex-wife, Nicole Brown Simpson, 35, and a male friend of hers, Ronald L. Goldman, 25. The two were stabbed to death on the night of June 12, 1994, outside the doorway of Nicole Simpson's condominium in Los Angeles. Simpson insisted that he had not been involved in the crime in any way.

The trial, which began on Jan. 31, 1995, was marked by defense charges that the police had mishandled key evidence and had tried to frame Simpson, an African American. Defense lawyers attacked the testimony of Los Angeles Police Department (LAPD) detective Mark Fuhrman, a key prosecution witness who said he found a bloody glove outside Simpson's home. The defense charged that Fuhrman was a racist and had planted the glove.

Simpson was represented by a "dream team" of more than a dozen attorneys. The prosecution team was headed by Deputy District Attorney Marcia Clark. Superior Court Judge Lance A. Ito presided over the frequently raucous trial, in which more than 100 witnesses testified. Much of the testimony involved comparing the genetic makeup of blood specimens gathered at the crime scene with that of a sample of Simpson's blood. The prosecution argued that the tests proved Simpson had been at the scene.

The trial, which was televised in the United States and abroad, sparked debate on race relations, police procedures, and the state of the American legal system. Critics of the Simpson verdict argued that the defense team directed the emphasis away from the evidence by charging the LAPD with racism. Many of the people who agreed with the verdict contended that the evidence itself was inconclusive, due in large part to police bungling. (See also **Courts.**)

Orange County. On June 27, voters in affluent Orange County, south of Los Angeles, rejected a proposed increase in the county sales tax to get the county back on its feet financially. The county had stunned the business world in December 1994 by filing for bankruptcy. It was the largest municipal bankruptcy filing in United States history.

The bankruptcy was the result of a $1.7-billion collapse of the county's investment pool, managed by Orange County treasurer and tax collector Robert L. Citron. Citron admitted that he had gambled on the success of high-risk investments while managing the pool, a total of about $7.5 billion contributed by nearly 200 cities, school districts, and agencies throughout Orange County and the West. Citron resigned from his post immediately after the bankruptcy was announced and later pleaded guilty to misappropriation of funds.

The tax initiative, which called for raising the county sales tax from 7.75 percent to 8.25 percent, was proposed by Orange County's chief executive, William Popejoy. On July 12, Popejoy resigned.

Aiming to emerge from bankruptcy by June 1996, the county was weathering the crisis with the help of Wall Street. A $520-million bond recovery plan, similar to a large equity loan, allowed the county to mortgage many of its remaining real estate assets, such as landfills and county buildings.

City and county governments. On May 15, the Los Angeles City Council approved most of Mayor Richard J. Riordan's $3.9-billion budget. The council also approved an additional $30 million, adding 32 traffic officers and expanding a domestic violence unit in the city attorney's office.

Police Chief Willie L. Williams came under fire in 1995 for allegedly accepting free Las Vegas hotel accommodations. He filed, then dropped, a $10-million lawsuit against the city for invasion of privacy.

A crisis in the county's public health system, the second largest in the nation, was averted in September when the federal government returned $364-million in accelerated federal Medicaid reimbursement funds.

◻ Margaret A. Kilgore

See also **City.** In *World Book,* see **Los Angeles.**

Louisiana. See State government.

Lugar, Richard G. (1932–   ), a Republican senator from Indiana, on April 19, 1995, announced his candidacy for the Republican presidential nomination. He promised that if elected, he would focus on ways to keep chemical and nuclear weapons out of the hands of terrorists. He also advocated replacing the federal income tax with a national sales tax, giving the President line-item veto power, and passing a balanced-budget amendment.

Lugar was born on April 4, 1932, in Indianapolis. He graduated from Denison University in Granville, Ohio, in 1954 and went on to earn two graduate degrees as a Rhodes scholar at Oxford University in England. He held an intelligence post in the Navy from 1957 to 1960, when he returned to Indiana to help run the family farm and business.

Lugar served as mayor of Indianapolis from 1968 to 1975. His chief accomplishment was Unigov, a program that united the administrative functions of the city of Indianapolis and the surrounding suburbs.

Lugar won a seat in the U.S. Senate in 1976. He served as chairman of the Foreign Relations Committee, the Intelligence Committee, and the Agriculture Committee. In 1991, he collaborated with Senator Sam Nunn of Georgia on a plan to finance the dismantling of the Soviet nuclear arsenal.

Lugar and his wife, Charlene, have four sons and seven grandchildren. □ Lisa Klobuchar

Luxembourg. See Europe.

Magazine. After months of speculation, John F. Kennedy, Jr., on Sept. 7, 1995, unveiled the first issue of *George*, his thick, glossy feature magazine about politics. The introduction was a full-scale media event, but not necessarily because of the merits of the magazine. Kennedy is the famous son of former United States President John F. Kennedy, who was assassinated in 1963.

A namesake of George Washington, *George* the magazine was launched at Federal Hall in New York City, where George the statesman and soldier was inaugurated in 1789 as the first U.S. President. The cover of the premier issue featured a photo of supermodel Cindy Crawford wearing a powdered wig and Continental Army uniform—with a bare midriff. The photo set the irreverent tone for the nonpartisan magazine, which received mixed reviews. Described by many critics as glitzy and gossipy but poorly rendered, *George* nonetheless drew praise for tapping into the popular belief that politicians had lost the public's respect, political parties had lost meaning, and voters were clamoring for a rethinking of the entire political process.

A conservative tilt. Another political magazine—this one with a definite conservative bent—was launched in Washington, D.C., on Sept. 11, 1995. *The Weekly Standard,* bankrolled by Rupert Murdoch, the media entrepreneur, and edited by William Kristol, one of the Republican Party's top strat-

John F. Kennedy, Jr., in September introduces the premier issue of *George,* an irreverent feature magazine about politics.

egists, was aimed at opinion leaders in Washington.

New titles. In August, the Hearst Corporation launched *ESPN Total Sports Magazine*, a series of magazines on individual sports aimed at men aged 18 to 54. The four issues scheduled for 1995 were to cover professional football, professional basketball, college basketball, and the year in review.

Seizing on the widespread interest in renovating and remodeling houses, Time Warner Inc. on May 1 introduced *This Old House*, based on the highly rated television program of the same name. Like the program, the magazine tells people how to fix up and make additions to their houses.

Redesigns. Two well-known magazines, *Sassy* and *Mirabella*, were revamped in 1995. *Sassy*, a teen magazine, was reintroduced in August by Petersen Publishing Company, which acquired the publication from Lang Communications in 1994. Some readers, however, complained that the new *Sassy* had lost its cheeky edge.

Mirabella returned to its origins, repositioning itself as a fashion magazine for intelligent women. *Mirabella* was launched in 1989 by Murdoch Magazines under the editorial direction of Grace Mirabella, former editor of *Vogue*, and Amy Gross. But the magazine never got on its feet financially. In March 1995, Murdoch sold *Mirabella* to Hachette Filipacchi Magazines, which suspended publication for six months for retooling. The September issue was the first under new editor in chief Amy Gross, who had moved to Hachette's *Elle* magazine.

A major freedom-of-the-press case involving *Business Week* erupted in September. A federal district judge in Cincinnati, Ohio, ordered that magazine not to print information obtained from documents that had been sealed in court and should not have been available to the press. The documents were part of a case involving Bankers Trust, an investment firm, and the Procter & Gamble Company.

Business Week immediately appealed the judge's restraining order. It argued that the government may forbid the press to publish information only if the publication of that information poses an immediate and extreme risk to the security of the United States—but not if the case involves ordinary trade. A U.S. appeals court and Associate Supreme Court Justice John Paul Stevens refused to hear the case and sent it back to the district court for resolution.

On October 3, the federal district judge unsealed the documents, and *Business Week* published the information on October 6. The judge, however, reaffirmed the original restraining order. Even though the order could no longer have any effect, *Business Week* filed another appeal with the court of appeals in an effort to prevent the restraining order from setting a precedent. ☐ Deirdre Carmody

In *World Book,* see **Magazine.**
Maine. See **State government.**
Malawi. See **Africa.**

Malaysia. Prime Minister Mahathir bin Mohamad called for parliamentary elections in April 1995, six months ahead of schedule, giving opponents of his United Malays National Organization (UMNO) little time to prepare. The UMNO dominated a 14-party coalition, called the National Front, that claimed the most sweeping victory since Malaysia gained independence from Great Britain in 1957. The coalition won 162 out of 192 parliamentary seats. The Front's majority in the new Parliament meant the UMNO could govern without an effective opposition.

The largest opposition party, the Democratic Action Party (DAP), dropped from 20 seats in the old Parliament to 9. It campaigned on allegations of widespread corruption in the government that Mahathir had headed since 1981. The DAP also complained it had been denied access to the government-controlled media, and it argued that political boundaries were redrawn to produce majorities of Malay-speaking people, the UMNO's power base.

The UMNO controlled 12 of Malaysia's 13 state governments. The All-Malaysian Islamic Party kept control of the state of Kelantan, despite the UMNO's promise of development money for a UMNO victory.

New Cabinet. On May 3, 1995, Mahathir announced he would retain the powerful post of home affairs, and he gave most of the other Cabinet posts to his loyal supporters. He said his UMNO deputy, Anwar Ibrahim, would continue as finance minister, despite Anwar's well-known ambition to succeed the 70-year-old prime minister in the future. Mahathir reduced Anwar's power by giving Anwar's close political allies less important posts than they had held before the elections.

New capital. On August 29, the government unveiled plans for a new federal city, Putrajaya, to be built south of the capital, Kuala Lumpur. Mahathir said Putrajaya would be the nation's administrative capital, and Parliament would stay in Kuala Lumpur.

The last jury trial. A law abolishing jury trials went into effect on February 1 while a court was in the midst of a juried trial, the nation's last. The three defendants were found guilty by a seven-member jury and sentenced to hang. They could appeal.

English restored. In June, Malaysian newspapers reported that the government would allow colleges and universities to teach science and technical subjects in English, effective immediately. A 1971 law made it compulsory for schools and colleges to use Bahasa Malaysia, a form of the Malay language, as a means of building a national identity. But Mahathir said that the competitive world of 1995 required proficiency in English. ☐ Henry S. Bradsher

See also **Asia** (Facts in brief table). In *World Book,* see **Malaysia.**
Maldives. See **Asia.**
Mali. See **Africa.**
Malta. See **Europe.**
Manitoba. See **Canadian provinces.**

Manufacturing

Manufacturing. In 1995, the United States economy continued a manufacturing-led recovery from recession that began in March 1991. But unlike the rapid growth of 1994, the expansion of 1995 kept a moderate pace, slowed in part by seven interest rate hikes by the Federal Reserve System, the nation's central bank. The rate hikes seemed to achieve the goal of a "soft landing" for the economy, maintaining steady growth while keeping inflation low.

In 1994's fourth quarter, the gross domestic product (GDP), the total value of goods and services produced within the United States, had roared ahead to a 5.1 percent annual pace. But in 1995, the GDP advanced only 2.7 percent in the first quarter, crawled to 1.3 percent in the second, and spurted to 4.2 percent in the third quarter.

Factory output. Factories in early 1995 ran at near full capacity to satisfy the brisk demand that had begun with the high economic growth rate in the fourth quarter of 1994. Manufacturing started 1995 at a high rate, but slowed somewhat by the fall. Much of that drop in output was due to sharp drops in automobile production.

Factory output declines in March and April were the first consecutive monthly declines since December 1991 and January 1992. In September 1995, output increased by only 0.1 percent and fell by 0.3 percent in October, as consumers cut their spending and producers subsequently cut back on production.

Factory orders for durable goods—products meant to last three years or more, such as automobiles, appliances, and business equipment—were stronger in 1995 than nondurables, which include such products as food, tobacco, textiles, and chemicals. But after a good start in January, with orders up 0.6 percent, durable-goods orders declined and then plunged 4 percent in April, as consumers and businesses cut spending. This was the largest drop since December 1991. Higher interest rates in early 1995 meant that consumers spent less on cars, houses, furniture, and appliances. Orders for motor vehicles and industrial, electrical, and transportation equipment all declined.

As interest rates fell in the summer and autumn, consumers again bought homes, and demand for durable goods grew. The business climate improved in the third quarter of 1995, with factory orders roaring back with a 5.1 percent gain in August and a 3 percent rise in September. But orders dropped 1 percent in October.

In 1994, consumer spending drove the gains in manufacturing. In 1995, business spending on computer equipment, manufacturing plants, and construction supplies fueled economic gains. In order to remain competitive in a global economy, companies in the 1990's had to become more efficient by controlling their costs and streamlining their production processes. Investing in technology equipment helped them do that, and many corporations posted record

profits in 1995. Their profits allowed them to devote funds to investing in new plants and equipment.

Capital spending, as investments in new plants and equipment are called, had been on the rise since 1991 and added heavily to economic growth in 1995. Manufacturers accounted for 30 percent of planned capital goods purchasers, according to *Business Week* magazine. Also, manufacturers planned to increase their capital expenditures by 26.1 percent in 1995, compared with a 7.5 percent hike in 1994. The Commerce Department's quarterly survey of capital spending plans among 22,500 companies found in late summer that businesses forecast spending increases of 9.4 percent in 1995. That figure was up from early 1995, when spending increases were forecast at 6.6 percent.

Manufacturing survey. A closely watched indicator of health in the manufacturing sector is the monthly National Association of Purchasing Management (NAPM) survey. The NAPM surveys purchasing managers at more than 300 industrial companies about new orders, employment levels, inventories, buying intentions, and more. A reading below 50 percent indicates that manufacturing is contracting; a reading below 44.5 percent indicates an economic slowdown. In January 1995, the NAPM reading was a healthy 57.9 percent. It hovered in the low 50's in the spring and plunged to 45.7 percent in June. After a brief jump to 50.5 percent in July, the index fell again, leveling out at 46.8 percent in October and 46.5 percent in November.

Productivity is measured by output per hours worked, and experts use it as a measure of business efficiency. From the mid-1980's, manufacturers modernized plants, purchased computer equipment, cut employees, and gave work to outside contractors. As a result, they became efficient producers. Investments in technology and reduced cost structures enabled companies to absorb higher costs for materials without charging higher prices to their customers. That helped keep inflation in check.

Productivity grew by 2.5 percent in the first quarter of 1995, surged 4.9 percent in the second, and advanced 2.0 percent in the third, according to the U.S. Department of Labor. Manufacturers led the way with a 6.2 percent annual rate. The gains in productivity of the early 1990's came after the decade of the 1980's that averaged less than 1 percent annual gains.

Exports. American manufacturers continued to do well exporting their products in 1995. These gains were led in part by a weak U.S. dollar, which made U.S. goods cheaper overseas. New emerging markets provided many outlets for U.S. goods. Exports to Asia, for example, were up more than 20 percent in 1995. Even exports to nations with mature economies, such as Germany and Japan, were up. Overall U.S. exports rose just 10 percent in 1995, however, while imports grew more than 13.4 percent from early 1994 to mid-1995. Thus, the nation's persistent trade deficit continued.

Orders for machine tools, which are used to cut and shape metal parts for other machines, are a barometer of future economic activity. The Association of Manufacturing Technology said in 1995 that 1994 was the second-best year on record for machine tool orders. And for the first 10 months of 1995, orders were up 12 percent from 1994.

Employment. The U.S. unemployment rate remained low in 1995, around 5.6 percent, but the manufacturing sector did not create many new jobs. In 1994, manufacturers had started adding workers after a period of cutting their payrolls. But in 1995, manufacturers let more than half of these employees go, cutting 234,000 jobs from May to October.

Wages grew slowly for manufacturing workers, who averaged 2 to 3 percent raises in 1994 and 1995. The Labor Department reported in 1995 that wages for American factory workers rose 2.2 percent in 1994 to $17.10 an hour. In Germany, hourly compensation was $27.37, and in Japan it was $21.38. In comparison, Mexico's manufacturing workers made an average of $2.57 an hour.　　☐ Ronald Kolgraf

In *World Book,* see **Manufacturing.**

Maryland. See **State government.**

Massachusetts. See **State government.**

Mauritania. See **Africa.**

Mauritius. See **Africa.**

Medicine. Researchers in Texas announced in November 1995 that a gene dubbed BRCA1 was responsible for nearly all breast cancers. The gene, first identified in October 1994, was previously linked only with hereditary breast cancers, which account for about 5 percent of the 180,000 breast cancers diagnosed each year in the United States. In hereditary breast cancers, BRCA1 appears to produce a faulty protein. In nonhereditary breast cancers, the team at the University of Texas at San Antonio determined, the protein is absent or located outside the cell nucleus, where it is normally found. Researchers believe the protein plays a role in regulating cell division and that the uncontrolled cell division of cancer results when the protein functions abnormally.

Obesity research. Three scientific teams reported in July 1995 that a protein produced in mice by a gene linked with obesity can cause dramatic weight loss in the mice. In one set of experiments, specially bred obese mice lost 40 percent of their body weight after one month of injections with the protein. A similar gene exists in human beings, raising hope that its protein product could mean salvation for millions of people with weight problems. United States government statistics show that 1 American in 3 is overweight and that some 58 million Americans face an increased risk of diabetes, heart disease, and other conditions as the result of obesity. Obesity is defined as weighing 20 percent or more above

Obese mice become lean with the aid of a protein that may also help people, scientists at Rockefeller University in New York City reported in July.

the recommended weight for one's height and age.

Geneticist Jeffrey M. Friedman and his associates at Rockefeller University in New York City were the first to isolate and *clone* (make copies of) the gene, which is called *ob* for *obesity*. Researchers then were able to insert the gene into bacteria, which used the gene to produce sufficient *ob* protein for the tests. The other reports came from teams at Amgen, Incorporated, a biotechnology firm in Thousand Oaks, California, and Hoffmann-La Roche Incorporated, a drug company in Nutley, New Jersey. Amgen hoped to begin testing the protein in people in 1996.

All three teams injected the *ob* protein, which Friedman called *leptin* after the Greek word for *thin*, into mice that were grossly obese. After receiving an injection, the mice ate less and quickly shed large amounts of body fat. Normal mice also ate less and lost weight when injected with the protein. Friedman further found that the human *ob* protein had the same effect in mice, suggesting that both animals have a similar weight-regulating mechanism.

Scientists theorize that fat cells produce the *ob* protein, releasing it into the blood as a weight-regulating signal read by the brain. Low *ob*-protein levels tell the body it needs more fat, stimulating the appetite so that people eat more and gain weight. High levels signal the body to reduce food intake, burn more calories, and lose weight.

Scientists cautioned, however, that the human weight-regulating system may be far more complex, making it difficult to produce a weight-loss drug from *ob*. They also noted that the protein must be injected daily to sustain weight loss. The mice quickly regained weight once the injections stopped. Furthermore, researchers do not know whether the *ob* protein would be safe for long-term use.

Genes for Alzheimer's disease. Canadian researchers in June 1995 announced the identification of a gene that may cause as many as 80 percent of cases of an aggressive, inherited form of Alzheimer's disease that strikes in middle age or earlier. Alzheimer's disease involves a severe loss of memory and other mental faculties, and most cases occur after age 65. The early-onset form, which accounts for about 10 percent of Alzheimer's cases, is especially devastating because it can strike people as early as their 30's. Geneticist Peter St. George-Hyslop at the University of Toronto headed the research team, which located the gene on chromosome 14. (Chromosomes, of which there are 23 pairs in the nucleus of a human cell, are tiny structures that carry the genes.) Researchers said the discovery could lead to a better understanding of the genetic defects that cause Alzheimer's disease and to new methods for diagnosing and treating the condition.

In August, another group of researchers reported the discovery of a gene on chromosome 1 that is responsible for most of the remaining cases of inherited, early-onset Alzheimers's disease. The researchers were with the Veterans Affairs Medical Center and the University of Washington, both in Seattle, and the Massachusetts General Hospital in Boston.

Eye surgery ineffective. In January, the National Eye Institute (NEI) alerted physicians that an operation once regarded as a sight-saver is ineffective and may even be harmful. The NEI, which is part of the National Institutes of Health in Bethesda, Maryland, said a new study found that the operation, known as optic nerve decompression, no longer should be used to treat a disease of the optic nerve called nonarteritic anterior ischemic optic neuropathy, which causes a sudden loss of vision. Each year about 6,000 Americans develop the disease.

The study found that 33 percent of patients who underwent the procedure experienced a significant improvement in vision after six months, compared with 43 percent of patients who received no treatment. A worsening of vision was reported by 24 percent of patients who had the surgery, compared with 12 percent of the untreated group.

Bone repair. Researchers in March announced the development of a pastelike material that can repair severe bone fractures without the metal screws, plates, and other hardware now used. The material consists of calcium and phosphate that can be injected into broken bone without major surgery. It quickly hardens into a substance similar to natural bone and strong enough to allow a patient to begin rehabilitation earlier than was previously possible. Clinical tests in Europe showed that the body gradually replaces the artificial bone with natural bone.

The developer of the artificial bone material, Norian Corporation in Cupertino, California, said it may enable patients with fractures to leave the hospital several days earlier than they now do. Shorter hospital stays could reduce the costs of treating hip and other fractures. The company said it had begun testing the artificial bone material in several medical centers in the United States.

Folic acid and heart disease. The American Heart Association (AHA) announced in September that researchers had discovered a new risk factor for coronary artery disease (CAD), the underlying cause of most heart attacks. The AHA, which is based in Dallas, Texas, said people with high levels of the substance homocysteine in their blood are 14 times more likely to have CAD—blockage of arteries that supply the heart with blood—than are people with normal homocysteine levels.

Homocysteine is an amino acid, one of a family of chemical compounds that the body uses to make proteins. Researchers have found evidence that abnormally high homocysteine levels can injure the lining of blood vessels. The injury promotes the accumulation of fat, cell debris, and other material that hinders blood flow through arteries. Most heart attacks occur when a blood clot forms in an artery narrowed by CAD, cutting off blood flow to the heart.

A wireless mobile unit, introduced in May by the Hewlett-Packard Company, enables physicians to receive a patient's electrocardiogram, blood pressure, and other vital signs at a remote location. In an emergency, the physician can respond by phoning in a diagnosis and instructions for treatment.

The AHA said people can lower their homocysteine levels simply and inexpensively by consuming more of the B-complex vitamin known as folic acid. Folic acid is found in spinach, asparagus, beans, peas, and other fresh vegetables. Orange juice and certain fortified breakfast cereals also contain folic acid.

Fish tales. Eating large amounts of fish has no benefit in reducing the risk of heart disease, a study conducted by researchers at the Harvard School of Public Health in Boston concluded in April. It was the largest study ever conducted on the health benefits of a diet rich in fish.

Smaller, earlier studies suggested that oils in certain fish protect people against heart attacks. The Harvard group monitored the number of heart attacks and the occurrence of severe CAD in 44,895 men over a six-year period. They found that men who ate fish several times a week were just as likely to suffer a heart attack or need bypass surgery as men who ate fish only once a month.

But a smaller study reported in November by researchers at the University of Washington found that people who ate the equivalent of 3 ounces (85 grams) of salmon weekly had half the risk of cardiac arrest as those who ate no fish. The researchers noted that their study, unlike the Harvard study, looked at just one form of heart disease.   □ Michael Woods

See also **AIDS, Drugs, Public Health.** In *World Book,* see **Medicine.**

Mental health. A severe but largely unrecognized epidemic of mental illness and behavioral problems is occurring in the world's poorest countries, according to a study presented to the United Nations (UN) on May 15, 1995. The study, which involved researchers from 30 countries, was directed by Arthur Kleinman, a psychiatrist and anthropologist at the Harvard Medical School in Boston.

Kleinman said the study's findings contradict a widespread belief that mental illness is not a problem in developing countries. The study identified sharp increases in chronic psychiatric conditions such as schizophrenia and depression. Moreover, it found that many people who are mentally ill go untreated because of a lack of medication, counseling, and other services. Suicide rates also are rising in many poor countries, and suicide ranks among the top three causes of death for younger people in almost all developing countries that keep suicide statistics.

Social problems contribute to psychiatric illness, the study noted. It estimated that some 40 million refugees, displaced by wars and political turmoil, face a high risk of clinical depression, anxiety disorders, and other mental illnesses. A growing trend toward urbanization, in which people leave villages and flock to urban slums, also causes mental distress.

The study found an increasing prevalence of behavioral problems such as drug and alcohol abuse and violence against women, children, and elderly

279

people. It estimated that from 25 percent to 75 percent of married women in developing countries are victims of domestic violence. It also found that unwanted children increasingly are being abandoned by parents, used in the commercial sex industry, or abused in other ways.

The researchers urged the UN to place more emphasis on improving mental health in developing countries. They cited an immediate need for establishing or expanding community mental health programs and training programs for health professionals. The study also asked the UN to declare a "Year of Mental Health" to promote concerted worldwide action on mental illness in poor countries.

A long-standing effort by psychologists to gain the right to prescribe medication was formally endorsed in August by the American Psychological Association (APA), the largest professional organization of psychologists. Unlike psychiatrists, psychologists are not medical doctors and thus lack the authority to prescribe drugs in treating mental illness. The APA's governing council said the group would support efforts by psychologists to convince state legislators to pass laws granting them permission to prescribe drugs. The APA also said it would help develop educational programs to qualify psychologists for prescribing medication.

Manic-depressive illness. The U.S. Food and Drug Administration (FDA) in June approved the use of an existing drug, now used against epilepsy, for the treatment of manic-depressive illness, a serious mood disorder that affects an estimated 2 million Americans. The drug, divalproex sodium, is sold under the trade name Depakote.

People with manic-depressive illness, also known as bipolar disorder, experience wide mood swings in which periods of elation alternate with periods of depression and interfere with normal life. During manic episodes, patients become overactive, have grandiose ideas and poor judgment, and sometimes exhibit aggression or extreme irritability.

Psychiatrists reported in March that Depakote may be better for some patients than lithium, the only drug previously approved for the illness, because it causes fewer side effects. The drugs were compared in a study of 179 patients conducted by the University of Texas Health Science Center at San Antonio. Experts estimate that lithium is ineffective in 30 to 40 percent of manic-depression patients.

Lithium may have another use in treating children with a conduct disorder marked by aggressive behavior so extreme that they often require psychiatric hospitalization. A study of 50 children with the disorder found that 40 percent of those taking lithium showed significant improvement in their symptoms, the National Institute of Mental Health reported in May.   □ Michael Woods

See also **Psychology.** In *World Book,* see **Mental illness.**

Mexico. His country gripped suddenly and unexpectedly by a severe economic crisis, newly inaugurated President Ernesto Zedillo Ponce de León called on the Mexican people for sacrifice on Jan. 3, 1995. But even as he spoke of harsh measures to right the battered Mexican economy, the situation was getting worse as Mexican and foreign investors pulled massive amounts of money out of Mexico because of their lack of confidence in Zedillo.

The crisis began on Dec. 20, 1994, when the Mexican government devalued its currency, the peso, by 13 percent on international markets. The peso's fall continued the next day, and within weeks it had lost nearly 40 percent of its value. (See also **Mexico** Special Report: **Crisis in Mexico.**)

U.S. bailout. On Jan. 31, 1995, United States President Bill Clinton announced that he would invoke special emergency powers to lend Mexico $20-billion. A group of international lending institutions, including the International Monetary Fund, an agency associated with the United Nations, pledged an additional $30 billion. As collateral against default, Mexico pledged its oil revenues and agreed to bank them at the Federal Reserve Bank in New York City.

Unemployment and social unrest. Price hikes on basic necessities ravaged the nation's poor in 1995. By September, the cost of corn meal was 50 percent higher than before the crisis. Inflation for 1995 was expected to top 40 percent, compared with 7 percent for 1994. Unemployment doubled between December 1994 and June 1995 and affected more than 9 million people.

PAN gubernatorial victories. On February 12, the opposition, center-right National Action Party (PAN) won almost every major elective office in the state of Jalisco by a wide margin. Two days later, the long-dominant Institutional Revolutionary Party (PRI) was forced to replace the governor of the state of Chiapas, where a peasant rebellion smoldered. Opposition parties had accused the PRI of massive vote fraud during the state's 1994 gubernatorial election. On May 28, 1995, PAN candidate Vicente Fox won a landslide victory in the state of Guanajuato. That same day, PAN militants joined demonstrations to protest cheating at the polls in the Yucatán, where the PRI had claimed victory in the governor's race. In a further demonstration of its growing strength, PAN retained its hold on the governorship of Baja California on August 6.

PRI infighting. The string of three gubernatorial losses plus unanswered charges of massive vote fraud in at least three other states created turmoil within the PRI. To add to the party's problems, Mexican authorities on February 28 charged Raúl Salinas, the older brother of former President Carlos Salinas de Gortari, with having ordered and paid for the September 1994 assassination of José Francisco Ruíz Massieu, secretary-general of the PRI. The indictment fueled suspicions among many Mexicans of a

Mexican rebels of the Zapatista National Liberation Army review documents
to present to government negotiators during April peace talks.

cover-up involving federal police, prosecutors, and perhaps even the former president himself.

On March 1, 1995, Salinas blamed his successor, Zedillo, for Mexico's financial crisis. In speaking out, Salinas broke the long-standing unwritten code of Mexican politics whereby former presidents remain silent on political matters. In retaliation, President Zedillo arranged to have Salinas and his family deported to the United States on March 11. In June, Salinas moved to Canada.

On November 26, Salinas expressed "amazement" when he learned that his brother Raúl had $84 million in Swiss bank accounts under a false name. The matter came to light November 15 when Swiss police arrested Raul's wife and her brother as they attempted to withdraw most of the money using false documents.

Subcommandante Marcos unmasked. On February 10, the government announced the identity of the Zapatista National Liberation Army rebel leader known as Subcommandante Marcos. According to the government, Marcos was really Rafael Sebastián Guillén, 37, the Jesuit-trained son of a furniture salesman from the Gulf Coast city of Tampico. The Zapatistas had waged a sporadic rebellion against the government since January 1994. As Marcos, Guillén had attained international notoriety, partly as a result of the dashing figure he presented with his trademark ski mask and the pipe that he

smoked during his public statements. A national poll conducted in August indicated that more than half of Mexicans believed the Zapatistas should become a peaceful political party, but Marcos said in October that the rebels would not join mainstream politics.

Drug corruption. On March 3, 1995, U.S. authorities arrested Mario Ruíz Massieu, Mexico's former deputy attorney general and the brother of the assassinated PRI leader, at the Newark International airport in New Jersey. Ruíz had been preparing to board a plane for Spain with $46,000 in cash. On March 6, the Mexican government asked the United States to extradite Ruíz and announced that it was investigating him for impeding the investigation into the assassination of his brother. On June 22, a U.S. magistrate refused to extradite Ruíz, however, calling the charges against him "flimsy."

In March, Mexican authorities said they had uncovered evidence that Ruíz had deposited $9 million in several U.S. banks from March to November 1994 when he served both as attorney general and head of Mexico's antinarcotics task force. Existence of the U.S. bank accounts led to suspicions among many Mexicans that Ruíz had taken bribes from drug cartels to protect their operations.

☐ Nathan A. Haverstock

See also **Latin America** (Facts in brief table). In *World Book*, see **Mexico**.

Michigan. See State government.

Crisis in Mexico

By Sidney Weintraub

Mexico's financial crisis of 1995 added to the burdens of a country already deeply troubled by poverty and political corruption.

The Mexican financial system was on the brink of ruin in January 1995. Days away from defaulting on billions of dollars in foreign loans and other debts, Mexican President Ernesto Zedillo Ponce de León turned to the United States and the international community for help. On February 21, Mexico and the United States signed the formal agreement that underlined the two countries' fragile but critical relationship. The agreement finalized a $20-billion loan package to Mexico designed to stabilize that country's economy and prevent an economic catastrophe that could have dragged down the U.S. financial structure, as well as much of the world's. Other sources contributed $30 billion to the loan package.

Little more than a year before, Mexico had been the darling of the international economic community. Investors had poured large amounts of money into productive plants and equipment and into Mexican stocks and bonds. Then, in 1994, this admiration turned to deep concern about the future of the country. A peasant uprising erupted in Chiapas on January 1, and a year of horrors followed, bringing political assassinations and a rise in lawlessness stimulated partly by drug trafficking.

Sensing political instability, investors began drawing money out of Mexico in mid-1994—money that Mexico needed to help pay its debts and finance its imports. Because Mexico had run out of foreign exchange, President Zedillo devalued the peso on international markets. The government hoped the reduced value of the peso would make exports less expensive and spur sales of Mexican goods to other countries. Increased exports would, in turn, bring in more foreign currency.

But the devaluation backfired. The peso's value compared with the U.S. dollar fell 50 percent between late December 1994 and March 1995, a loss nearly four times greater than government economists had planned.

In a near panic, investors pulled even more money out of Mexico, leaving the country unable to pay its debts.

As a result of the crisis, life became harder for nearly every person in Mexico. Hardship came in the form of an emergency government plan to help save the country from financial ruin. The plan, instituted in March 1995, raised interest rates sharply on short-term loans and drastically increased taxes on nearly all goods and services. Such price increases were a staggering blow to a nation where, according to the World Bank, an international lending agency based in Washington, D.C., about 33 percent of the population lacked the money to properly feed and clothe themselves. Nearly 1 million people lost their jobs after March 1995, and the country headed into recession.

Problems underlying progress

How did things become so critical in Mexico? After struggling with debt problems through much of the 1980's, Mexico seemed to have turned its economy around as the decade ended. It had opened its national markets more to imports and expanded the role of private enterprise. These actions transformed the economy into an emerging powerhouse by the early 1990's.

Mexican authorities had expected 1994 to be a year of continued economic and political accomplishments. Mexico had signed the North American Free Trade Agreement (NAFTA), which took effect on Jan. 1, 1994. NAFTA proponents claimed the treaty would increase trade between Mexico, Canada, and the United States by gradually reducing trade barriers between the countries. In August 1994, the Mexican people elected Zedillo, the ruling Institutional Revolutionary Party's (PRI) candidate, to carry on the changes that had revitalized the economy. Economic forecasters projected high economic growth and continued flows of capital into Mexico.

Despite the progress, Mexican authorities made major errors in economic policy. In addition, painfully familiar problems of poverty and corruption tainted Mexico's gains. Progress was not deep enough to transform a society where more than 30 million people lived in wrenching poverty. In the southern state of Chiapas, a rural area inhabited largely by Maya Indians who rely on farming for a living, nearly 60 percent of workers in 1994 earned either no income or less than the Mexican minimum wage of about $3 a day. Peasants in Chiapas had other long-standing complaints against the government, including restrictions on land ownership, government failure to provide them with roads, water, and credit to grow and sell their agricultural crops, as well as neglect of their health and educational needs.

On Jan. 1, 1994, Chiapas peasants calling themselves the Zapatista National Liberation Army rebelled against the authorities. The rebels chose their name to establish a connection with Emiliano Zapata, the leader of the Mexican Revolution of 1910, who emphasized the need for a change in land ownership patterns. Negotiations between the rebels and the government ceased several times but were still active in mid-1995.

The author

Sidney Weintraub is the William E. Simon Chair at the Center for Strategic and International Studies in Washington, D.C.

Political assassinations and drug trafficking

No sooner had the Chiapas rebellion quieted down than events that would lead to evidence of massive political corruption erupted. In March 1994, a gunman assassinated Luís Donaldo Colosio Murrieta, the presidential candidate of the PRI, in the city of Tijuana during a campaign trip. A young factory worker named Mario Aburto Martínez confessed to the murder, but in February 1995, police arrested a second man, Othon Cortes Vazquez, and charged him with participating in the killing.

Government prosecutors made little progress in their investigation, however, and the on-and-off investigation made many Mexicans wonder whether there had been an official cover-up. In May 1995, a poll published in a leading Mexico City newspaper, *El Universal*, showed that nearly half of Mexicans polled believed that former President Carlos Salinas de Gortari and old-guard members of the PRI had ordered the assassination to prevent the reform-minded Colosio from purging the PRI of corruption.

A second high-level political assassination occurred in September 1994, when the number-two official of the PRI, José Francisco Ruíz Massieu, was murdered in Mexico City. Police arrested Raúl Salinas, the brother of President Salinas, for alleged complicity in this murder. Ruíz had once been married to Salinas's sister, and prosecutors were investigating possible personal, business, or political motivations in the murder.

Mario Ruíz Massieu, José Francisco's brother, resigned as attorney general in November 1994, charging that the PRI was impeding his investigation of his brother's murder. Prosecutors later charged Mario Ruíz himself with covering up Raúl Salinas's involvement in the murder. Police in the United States arrested Ruíz at the Newark, New Jersey, airport in February 1995 as he was about to board a plane to Europe. Police charged him with breaking a U.S. law that requires travelers entering or leaving the country to declare whether they are carrying more than $10,000. Mexican authorities asked the United States to send Ruíz back to Mexico to be tried for covering up Salinas's links to the murder. But a U.S. judge rejected the plea in June on the grounds of insufficient evidence. Authorities also found about $10 million in Ruíz's name in U.S. bank accounts, leading to suspicions that drug traffickers had bribed him to protect their operations while he was in office.

Ruíz's arrest further undermined the integrity of Mexican political leadership. His alleged cover-up in his brother's murder investigation combined with the government's ineptitude in retrieving him from the United States heightened public suspicions that the government was unable to solve its most pressing problems.

Evidence mounted throughout 1994 and 1995 that much of the corruption within the government stemmed from drug money. Reports surfaced in mid-1995 of Raúl Salinas's close relationship with Juan García Abrego, the king of Mexico's increasingly powerful cocaine cartels. News reports alleged that Raúl Salinas attended García's parties, helped protect his drug smuggling operations, and even collaborated in

Political Unrest in Mexico

High-level corruption

Political assassinations and corruption rocked Mexico during 1994 and 1995. An assassin killed Luis Donaldo Colosio Murrieta, a leading presidential candidate, in March 1994. Several top-level government leaders had either been charged with involvement in murder or were being investigated for involvement in murder as 1995 ended. Mexico's attorney general under former President Carlos Salinas de Gortari was in jail in the United States waiting to be sent back to Mexico to stand trial for hindering the murder investigation of a top government official, and Salinas's brother, Raúl, had been arrested and charged with planning the murder of the same government leader.

Presidential candidate Colosio
A gunman killed Institutional Revolutionary Party (PRI) presidential candidate Luis Donaldo Colosio Murrieta on March 23, 1994, in Tijuana.

PRI secretary general Ruíz
The secretary general of the PRI, José Francisco Ruíz Massieu, was murdered in Mexico City in September 1994.

Attorney general Ruíz
In March 1995, prosecutors charged Mario Ruíz Massieu, Mexico's former attorney general and brother of the slain PRI leader, with hiding information on who may have masterminded his brother's murder.

President Salinas's brother
Police arrested Raúl Salinas de Gortari, brother of the former president, in March 1995 on charges of ordering and helping plan Ruíz's murder.

Former President Salinas
Many people blamed Salinas's policies for the peso crisis. Amid rumors and speculation about his possible involvement in the country's political murders, Salinas fled Mexico in early 1995 and entered Canada in June.

Current President Zedillo
In 1995, Zedillo tried to distance himself from the evident corruption of the former administration. Zedillo's approval of Raúl Salinas's arrest broke a tradition of impunity from prosecution enjoyed by Mexico's former presidents and their families.

Signs of political change

The Institutional Revolution Party (PRI), in power since 1929, began losing its total hold on Mexican politics in the late 1980's and early 1990's. The PRI lost its first governorship, that of the state of Baja California Norte, in 1989 to a candidate from the National Action Party (PAN). By 1995, PAN had won 4 of 31 state governorships. The PRI's loss of state governorships mirrored its loss of votes in national elections since the mid-1970's. Meanwhile, a political uprising flared during 1994 in the state of Chiapas.

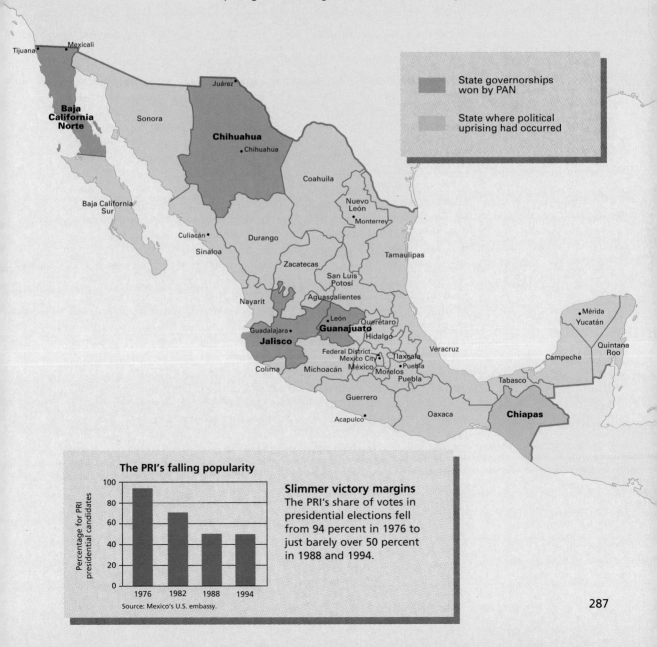

State governorships won by PAN

State where political uprising had occurred

The PRI's falling popularity

Percentage for PRI presidential candidates

1976 1982 1988 1994

Source: Mexico's U.S. embassy.

Slimmer victory margins

The PRI's share of votes in presidential elections fell from 94 percent in 1976 to just barely over 50 percent in 1988 and 1994.

some of them. Arrests of federal police for protecting drug traffickers became common in 1995, and U.S. drug enforcement authorities claimed that the freedom drug smugglers enjoyed in Mexico in the late 1980's and early 1990's had turned Mexico into the main route for shipments of Colombian cocaine into the United States. In June 1995, President Zedillo acknowledged the seriousness of the trafficking problem when he said, "Drug trafficking is the most serious threat to our national security."

Striving for fair elections

Corruption extended into the electoral process as well. In the 1994 election, Zedillo and the PRI struggled to overcome allegations of past election fraud. In the 1988 presidential election, for instance, Cuauhtémoc Cárdenas Solórzano of the Party of the Democratic Revolution lost after holding a comfortable lead over Salinas. As the vote count neared its end, the election computers mysteriously went down. Government officials blamed the crash on "atmospheric conditions." When the computers came back on several days later and election officials announced the final count, Salinas had made a miraculous comeback to win. Most observers concluded that the PRI had simply stolen the election after it became apparent that they were about to lose the presidency.

After Colosio's murder, President Salinas had anointed Zedillo as the PRI presidential candidate in the traditional manner, known as *dedazo*, which refers to the outgoing President pointing his finger to designate his successor. Because the PRI had not lost a presidential election since taking power in 1929, dedazo had essentially conferred power to the next president. Yet the power Zedillo would need to clean up Mexican politics would have to be anything but traditional.

Some changes did come in the electoral process to make the election more democratic, however. Largely as a result of the 1988 election, several features of the 1994 presidential election were new. For the first time, there was a national television debate among the three leading candidates. Mexicans saw the debate as a sign that the PRI had at least acknowledged the existence of other parties. Second, foreign visitors and Mexican observers from all parties for the first time monitored the voting to make sure the election results were credible. Third, and perhaps most important, while Zedillo won the election, his winning percentage of slightly more than 50 percent of the final valid votes was in line with the forecasts of reputable pollsters. The PRI had won most previous presidential elections by ridiculously large margins. Most observers concluded that the 1994 election had been fair.

Reforming the PRI

Faced with such apparently deep-rooted corruption, Zedillo took an unprecedented step after he assumed office in December 1994. He appointed the first cabinet secretary from outside the PRI since the party took power in 1929. Political observers saw his choice of Fernando Antonio Lozano Gracia of PAN to be attorney general as a significant sign that Zedillo was serious about pursuing justice and rooting

Rebellion in Chiapas

Maya Indian rebels in the state of Chiapas display their weapons in a show of defiant protest. The peasants in Chiapas began an armed rebellion against the Mexican government in 1994 to protest poor living conditions, lack of education, and evictions from communal farmlands. The rebellion highlighted sharp class differences in Mexico and shook many investors' confidence in Mexico's economy.

out corruption. But as 1995 ended, the political benefit from this appointment appeared to fade because the country's assassination investigations remained unresolved.

Opposition to Zedillo's reform efforts demonstrated the difficulty of his task. Any serious transformation of political practices in Mexico had to involve deep changes within the PRI, and because of this, many party members resisted Zedillo's efforts.

Yet Zedillo still attempted other reform measures. He promised to permit more local autonomy in choosing PRI candidates for local and state offices. He promised to end the practice of dedazo. During his first week in office, he announced a proposal to overhaul the Mexican justice system, put limits on the Supreme Court, and get rid of corrupt officers in the national police force.

Some observers thought the PRI's loosening of the reins of power might simply be a recognition of reality as electoral democracy gained ground. Zedillo's slim margin of victory combined with Salinas's dubious 1988 victory illustrated the PRI's falling popularity. It remained Mexico's dominant party, but the PRI in 1995 did not dominate the way it once had. In 1995, opposition members held 33 seats in the 128-member federal Senate, compared with none as recently as 1988. The PAN held governorships in 4 of Mexico's 31 states (Baja California Norte, Chihuahua, Guanajuato, and Jalisco) in 1995. There were no governors outside the PRI until 1989.

Financial problems

Financial problems were layered on top of Mexico's problems with political corruption and inefficiency. One of the biggest financial problems the country faced as 1994 ended was a large balance-of-payments deficit of $29 billion. A deficit occurs when a country imports more than it exports. Mexico's deficit in 1994 was 8 percent of its gross domestic product (GDP)—the total value of all the goods and services a country produces. This was a level that economists considered too high, because it forces the government to borrow to pay for imports. By comparison, the U.S. deficit was about 2 percent of its GDP in 1994.

In order to deal with a deficit, a country must either have currency reserves or attract foreign funds to pay for its imports. Mexico started 1994 with about $29 billion in reserves. And enough investments were entering the country to enable Mexico to finance its deficit without dipping into its reserves.

Devaluing the peso

But when investors began removing their money because of political uncertainty in 1994, the Mexican government had to use its reserves to pay for imports. These reserves had practically disappeared by mid-December. Under these circumstances, the Mexican authorities felt it necessary to devalue the country's currency, the peso, in order to discourage imports by making them more expensive and to encourage exports by making them less expensive. Government planners hoped in this way to drastically reduce the deficit and restore the confidence of investors.

The government devalued the peso from 3.5 pesos to 4.0 pesos to the dollar on December 20, but many international economists and investors were not satisfied. These investors believed other budgetary and monetary measures were also necessary to carry Mexico through its crisis. Many investors had wanted the government to announce a plan to eliminate its public-sector deficit—debt produced by Mexico's many state-run companies. They also wanted the government to sell money-losing state companies. International investors also expected the government to work out a plan to hold down price increases that would likely result from the devaluation. Many analysts believed that the devaluation backfired due to the government's failure to simultaneously adopt these extra measures.

The rescue package

Mexico devalued its currency because it was unable to meet its immediate payments. At this point, in December 1994, Mexico was close to defaulting on its obligations. Skirting opposition in Congress, U.S. President Bill Clinton organized a rescue package for Mexico. This was formalized on Feb. 21, 1995, when the United States loaned Mexico $20 billion. The International Monetary Fund (IMF) contributed $17.8 billion, and central banks from other industrial countries added $10 billion. The World Bank and the Inter-American Development Bank, another international development bank, also pledged funds to bring the total loan to more than $50 billion. The lenders mainly wanted to give private holders of Mexican government debt confidence that funds existed to repay them.

Falling peso, falling market

The value of Mexico's peso fell dramatically after the Mexican government devalued its currency in late December 1994, *below*. The peso's fall also sent the country's stock market into a three-month slide in which it lost more than 40 percent of its value, *bottom*.

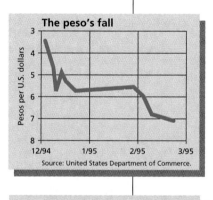

The peso's fall

Pesos per U.S. dollars

Source: United States Department of Commerce.

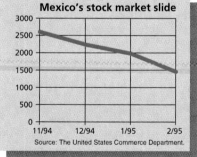

Mexico's stock market slide

Source: The United States Commerce Department.

Rising inflation in Mexico

Percentage of annual increase

	1994 total	1995*

Values on y-axis: 0, 10, 20, 30, 40, 50

* Through July.
Source: Mexico's United States embassy.

Rise in Mexican unemployment

Percentage of unemployed workers

	December 1994	June 1995

Values on y-axis: 0, 1, 2, 3, 4, 5, 6, 7

Source: Mexico's U.S. embassy.

EL BANCO
DE MEXICO
B 7724150

VEINTE NUEVOS PE
A LA VISTA AL PORTA

Working class woes

Unemployed workers advertise their skills in Mexico City in January 1995, *top*. The Mexican financial crisis and the government's stringent measures to solve it helped fuel a big jump in inflation during 1995, *above left*. Unemployment doubled in Mexico after the financial crisis in December 1994, throwing nearly 1 million people out of work, *above right*.

The foreign rescue package prevented Mexican bankruptcy. The financial situation, while not fully resolved, was under control, at least in the absence of further political shocks. By mid-1995, the value of the peso settled at about 6 to the dollar, a devaluation of more than 40 percent from the initial rate of 3.5 to the dollar. The stabilization also calmed fears that the Mexican crisis would spread to other countries, such as Argentina and Brazil, where stock markets fell by as much as 30 percent immediately following the December 1994 peso devaluation.

The large loans to Mexico carried severe economic conditions, however. Mexico promised to eliminate its public-sector deficit. Many public companies were sold to private investors. Economists agreed that the remaining state-run companies would have to streamline operations to produce profits, a move that could cost many jobs. Economists conceded that the combination of state-run company reform and restrictive economic policy would decrease Mexico's GDP by about 5 percent in 1995.

The government's emergency economic plan to help resolve the peso crisis added to the burdens of the international loan conditions. So that banks could maintain profits on loans in the face of inflation, the plan led to an increase in interest rates, at one point to more than 100 percent for credit cards. Consumer prices, which rose by only 7 percent in 1994, were projected to increase by some 50 percent during 1995. Gasoline prices rose 35 percent, electricity prices rose 20 percent, and inflation soared toward a yearly rate of 40 percent. Wage increases averaged 11 percent, much less than price increases.

Consequences in the United States

Because trade between Mexico and the United States has always been strong, the potential consequences of Mexico's crisis extended beyond its own borders. More than 70 percent of Mexico's exports go to the United States, and Mexico, in 1994, was the largest market for U.S. exports after Canada and Japan. Because of the decline in purchasing power of Mexicans, the U.S. trade deficit with Mexico grew 10.5 percent in May 1995 to $1.6 billion. Exports from the United States to Mexico from January through June 1995 dropped 11.9 percent compared with the same period the previous year, while Mexican exports to the United States soared 29 percent, according to the U.S. Commerce Department.

Many Americans feared that worsening economic conditions in Mexico would cause an increase in illegal immigration to the United States as unemployed Mexicans sought jobs. Illegal immigration had become a political issue, especially in California, where voters in November 1994 had approved Proposition 187, which would deny many public services to illegal immigrants, including education and non-emergency health care. But according to the U.S. Immigration and Naturalization Service, a federal agency that enforces immigration laws and tracks illegal immigration into the United States, no clear increase in illegal Mexican immigration occurred after the peso crisis. The crisis did little to ease Americans' concerns over the impacts of illegal immigration, however.

Most economists agreed that by late summer 1995 the international rescue package had worked. The country had significantly rebuilt its for-

More illegal entry?
Mexicans cross the Rio Grande River on the Texas border to enter the United States illegally, *below.* Some experts had predicted that Mexico's financial crisis would increase that country's unemployment and create more illegal immigration to the United States. But U.S. border agents had not recorded such an increase by late 1995.

eign reserves, the peso had stabilized, the stock market had recovered, and Mexico had a trade surplus. Serious problems of unemployment and falling wages remained, but most observers acknowledged that Mexico was no longer on the brink of ruin.

Yet the Mexican people wanted more than promises that conditions wouldn't get worse. Mexicans were much more concerned about creating jobs, raising incomes, providing universal and quality education for their children, and obtaining adequate health care. Only restored growth in the GDP could effectively deal with these inequalities.

President Zedillo's six-year economic plan that he presented to the country on May 31, 1995, stated that economic recovery would take place in 1996 and that sustained growth in the GDP of 5 percent a year would follow. Most economists thought this projection was not out of the question.

The future of the PRI and all effective leadership would depend largely on the continued success of the economic program, but the PRI was not likely to regain the monopoly it held before the 1980's. The PAN's success in the 1995 governors' elections showed that Mexico was developing a three-way political line-up of right, left, and center within a more vibrant democratic structure than existed before. Regardless of the ruling party, however, the most critical tasks facing Mexico's rulers were cleaning up political corruption, stopping drug trafficking, and providing equal justice to everyone. The Zedillo administration had pledged such reforms and taken measures to implement them, but it had not yet convinced the public that it could accomplish them. These were nonpartisan issues, but observers believed that the way the government handled them would affect the fortunes of all political parties.

Mexico's first six months of 1995 included financial collapse, economic austerity, political turmoil, and social unrest. But as 1995 ended, it appeared that the worst of Mexico's political shocks had subsided, and the nation's future seemed cautiously optimistic. ■ ■ ■

Immigration battle
California voters rally against Proposition 187, which called for denying schooling, welfare benefits, and nonemergency medical care to illegal immigrants in the state. Voters approved the measure in November 1994, and political and economic upheaval in Mexico during 1995 continued to make many Americans uneasy about illegal immigration.

Mourners in Jerusalem gather at a candlelit shrine to Israeli Prime Minister Yitzhak Rabin outside the prime minister's official residence in November after Rabin was assassinated.

Middle East

The Arab-Israeli peace process sustained a tragic blow on Nov. 4, 1995, when a Jewish extremist hoping to halt the process assassinated Israeli Prime Minister Yitzhak Rabin at a rally in Tel Aviv, Israel. The act shook the Israeli nation to its core and showed that Jews as well as Arabs were deeply polarized about peace. But Israeli Foreign Minister Shimon Peres, who assumed the post of prime minister, vowed that he would continue along the road toward peace upon which Rabin had embarked.

The presence at Rabin's funeral in Jerusalem of Jordan's King Hussein I and Egypt's President Hosni Mubarak, who both eulogized the slain Israeli leader, showed how far peace had progressed in only two years. It was their first trip to Jerusalem since the Arab-Israeli Six-Day War (1967). Leaders and emissaries from 80 countries, including United States President Bill Clinton, also came to pay homage and show solidarity for the peace process. Yasir Arafat, chairman of the Palestine Liberation Organization (PLO), made his own historic trip to Israel to pay condolences to Rabin's widow, Leah. She told him that he had been her husband's "partner" in peace.

Peace. Rabin and Arafat, who stunned the world in 1993 when they agreed to pursue peace, signed perhaps an even more significant peace accord on Sept. 28, 1995, in Washington, D.C. The 460-page

The 1995 Israeli withdrawal, which began in October, set the stage for January 1996 elections of a president and an 82-member Palestinian Council, who were to gradually assume legislative and executive powers over the 1.3 million West Bank Palestinians. In addition to the right to establish courts, the council was to have jurisdiction over such matters as health, electricity, sewage, zoning, and taxation.

Unsettled issues. By May 1996, assuming no disruptions of the peace process, Israel and the Palestinians were to begin discussing some of their most difficult unresolved issues. These issues included final borders and the sharing of water and other resources. Yet to be decided was whether the Palestinian self-rule authority would lead to the founding of an independent state. Also, the future status of the Jewish settlements in the West Bank, where about 110,000 Jewish people lived, remained to be decided. The question of whether and how many Palestinian refugees who left the West Bank and Gaza Strip before 1967 would be allowed to return also remained. Many of those Arabs had since settled in neighboring countries.

The city of Jerusalem remained one of the most sensitive unresolved issues that both sides agreed to discuss. The Palestinians have claimed East Jerusalem, which Israel captured from Jordan in the 1967 war, as their capital. Israel also called Jerusalem its capital and insisted the city would not be divided.

The United States added to the dilemma on Oct. 24, 1995, when Congress overwhelmingly voted to move the American embassy in Israel from Tel Aviv to Jerusalem by May 31, 1999. Israel welcomed the idea, but Arab leaders condemned the acknowledgement of Jerusalem as Israel's capital and accused the United States of forfeiting its role as a neutral peacemaker. American allies, such as the United Kingdom, France, and Germany, said they would not move their embassies to Jerusalem. The congressional bill, however, included a face-saving option for delaying the move indefinitely.

Land seizure. On May 22, 1995, Rabin was forced to back down from a plan to confiscate 135 acres (55 hectares) of mostly Arab-owned land in disputed East Jerusalem. The potential seizure of land, to be used for Jewish housing, prompted a storm of international protest that threatened to derail the peace process and bring down Rabin's government. On May 17, Oman had introduced a resolution to the United Nation Security Council to condemn Israel for the plan. The United States was the only nation that vetoed the resolution, embittering Arabs who accused the United States of favoring Israel.

The Palestinian people showed greater optimism in 1995 about prospects for peace and expressed more confidence in Arafat's leadership. Polls showed that popular support for Hamas (Islamic Resistance Movement), which uses violence to pursue its goal of replacing Israel with an Islamic Palestinian

document outlined the second phase of the move toward Palestinian self-government. It provided a blueprint for the withdrawal of Israeli troops from more than 450 towns and 7 cities in the Israeli-occupied West Bank by late March 1996. The West Bank is an area that Israel captured from Jordan in the 1967 war. Palestinian police were to take over the duties of the Israeli troops, except for within Jewish settlements. Although Israel recognized Hebron as a Palestinian city, some Israeli troops were to remain there to protect a Jewish enclave considered by many to be the spiritual heart of right wing Jewish extremists. The Palestinians and Israelis also agreed to cooperate against terrorism, drug smuggling, and crime. Israel also said it would gradually release some 5,000 jailed Palestinians, and in early October it set 900 free.

Facts in brief on Middle Eastern countries

Country	Population	Government	Monetary unit*	Foreign trade (million U.S.$) Exports†	Imports†
Bahrain	592,000	Amir Isa bin Salman Al Khalifah; Prime Minister Khalifa bin Salman Al Khalifah	dinar (0.38 = $1)	2,656	3,744
Cyprus	742,000	President Glafcos Clerides (Turkish Republic of Northern Cyprus: President Rauf R. Denktas)	pound (0.45 = $1)	960	3,013
Egypt	59,713,000	President Hosni Mubarak; Prime Minister Atef Sedky	pound (3.40 = $1)	2,243	8,176
Iran	64,073,000	Leader of the Islamic Revolution Ali Hoseini Khamenei; President Ali Akbar Hashemi Rafsanjani	rial (3,000.00 = $1)	16,000	18,000
Iraq	21,882,000	President Saddam Hussein	dinar (2,600.00 = $1)	10,400	6,600
Israel	5,971,000	President Ezer Weizman; Prime Minister Shimon Peres	new shekel (3.03 = $1)	16,437	23,776
Jordan	4,234,000	King Hussein I; Prime Minister Zayd bin Shakir	dinar (0.71 = $1)	1,424	3,382
Kuwait	1,626,000	Amir Jabir al-Ahmad al-Jabir Al Sabah; Prime Minister & Crown Prince Saad al-Abdallah al-Salim Al Sabah	dinar (0.30 = $1)	10,491	7,042
Lebanon	3,082,000	President Ilyas Harawi; Prime Minister Rafik Hariri	pound (1,605.50 = $1)	925	4,100
Oman	2,239,000	Sultan Qaboos bin Said Al Said	rial (0.39 = $1)	5,545	3,915
Qatar	500,000	Amir and Prime Minister Hamid bin Khalifa Al Thani	riyal (3.64 = $1)	3,181	1,891
Saudi Arabia	18,171,000	King & Prime Minister Fahd bin Abd al-Aziz Al Saud	riyal (3.75 = $1)	30,203	28,224
Sudan	27,061,000	President Umar Hasan Ahmad al-Bashir	pound (800.00 = $1)	509	1,060
Syria	15,283,000	President Hafiz al-Asad; Prime Minister Mahmud Zubi	pound (41.95 = $1)	3,146	4,140
Turkey	63,204,000	President Süleyman Demirel; Prime Minister Tansu Ciller	lira (51,024.00 = $1)	15,409	29,065
United Arab Emirates	1,820,000	President Zayid bin Sultan Al Nuhayyan; Prime Minister Maktum bin Rashid Al Maktum	dirham (3.67 = $1)	15,837	6,422
Yemen	14,361,000	President Ali Abdallah Salih; Prime Minister Abd al-Aziz Abd al-Ghani	rial (12.00 = $1)	101	1,378

*Exchange rates as of Oct. 27,1995, or latest available data.
†Latest available data.

state, had dropped to 11 percent in 1995 from 40 percent in 1993. Hamas suicide bombings against Israeli targets in 1995 had created a serious problem for Palestinians who depended upon employment in Israel. Their access to Israel and work had been restricted by Israeli officials due to the bombings.

The Palestinians also enjoyed growing freedom in 1995. The departure of Israeli troops in October ended nearly three decades of occupation. Arafat also lifted curfews in 1995 and moved elections for the Palestinian Council forward from March 1996 to January. Economic improvements, including a construction boom, also added to Palestinian optimism.

Arafat, bolstered by the mood shift, detained a number of Hamas leaders during 1995 and ordered Islamic prayer leaders to submit their sermons to be censored for inflammatory rhetoric. Arafat aimed to split militant Hamas members from more moderate ones who could be persuaded to support the peace. He also offered to release jailed Hamas members in return for a commitment to cease their attacks against Israel and accept the leadership of the Palestine Authority, which he headed. By October, some Hamas members were reported to be considering running for the council elections.

Another sign of the changing mood of Palestinians occurred in early November when Israel hinted that it might have been responsible for the assassination of an Muslim extremist leader, Fathi Shiqaqi, in Malta on October 26. Although Muslim militants vowed revenge, most Arabs paid it little attention.

Palestinians received news of Rabin's death with mixed emotions. While few mourned, many feared that Peres, who lacked Rabin's credentials, would be unable to deliver further concessions for peace, which they had begun to value.

Jewish militants loomed in 1995 as a potentially greater threat to the peace process than Arab militants, as the assassination of Rabin painfully pointed out. The confessed murderer, Yigal Amir, 25, claimed he was carrying out God's will and Jewish religious law in killing Rabin. This drew praise from some right wing Jewish extremists who had vowed to end the peace process. On December 6, officials charged Amir with murder and charged his brother and a friend with conspiring to commit the murder.

Most Israelis expressed revulsion about the murder and the bitter anti-Rabin campaign by right wing extremists that seemed to have led to it. Israeli moderates had tolerated the threatening talk prior to Rabin's murder, which led to national soul-searching when he died. This bolstered support for Peres, but many feared that both the peace process and the murder would polarize the nation further.

Economic summit. The second Middle Eastern economic summit was held in Amman, Jordan, in late October. The first summit had been in Casablanca, Morocco, in 1994. The three-day affair, which drew representatives from more than 60 countries, was intended to improve trade and investment in the region, following the success of the Arab-Israeli peace process. Many obstacles to economic integration still remained, but the conference was an opportunity for Israel, the Arab nations, and others to make contacts.

Fundamentalist violence in Europe. On Feb. 9, 1995, ambassadors to the North Atlantic Treaty Organization (NATO), a military alliance of Western nations, announced that NATO would seek talks with Egypt, Israel, Mauritania, Morocco, and Tunisia on the threat posed by Muslim extremism. The ambassadors said that Muslim violence posed a serious threat to European and Western security.

Although some NATO members, as well as other nations, criticized the announcement as inflammatory, violence in Europe during 1995 seemed to support NATO's call for action. Between July 25 and October 17, eight bombs killed 7 people and wounded more than 170 in France. The Algerian Armed Islamic Group (GIA) claimed responsibility for these acts. The GIA accused France of supporting Algeria's military-backed government, which had been waging a bloody civil war since 1992 against militants who wanted to establish an Islamic government in Algeria. French officials arrested an Algerian suspected in

the bombings on November 1 and sought to extradite another young Algerian detained by the British on November 4. Swedish courts refused to extradite a third Algerian suspect to France for lack of evidence. In Germany, at least 11 Algerians received jail sentences in 1995 for charges that included hostage taking and arson. Most of the suspects had unsuccessfully sought political asylum in Germany.

Americans and terrorism. On January 24, President Clinton froze the American financial assets of 12 Middle Eastern groups and 18 individuals said to support terrorism. The frozen assets included funds of some charitable organizations believed to be fronts for funneling money to Middle Eastern terrorist groups. Not only Muslim extremist groups, such as Hamas and Hezbollah (Party of God), but also the Jewish extremist groups of Kach and Kahane Chai were affected. United States officials also said that they would increase investigations of terrorist suspects and speed their deportation. These actions were intended to aid the Arab-Israeli peace process and avert terrorist incidents in the United States.

On October 1, a federal court in New York City found Egyptian Sheik Omar Abdel Rahman and nine other Muslims guilty of conspiring to commit murders and to bomb New York City landmarks and a U.S. military installation. The conspirators allegedly wanted to force the United States to help establish a fundamentalist Islamic government in Egypt. They also wanted an end to American support of Israel and the Arab-Israeli peace process.

Bahrain. The rise of Muslim extremism caused increasing concern in 1995 among Arab nations in the Persian Gulf. Some of the most serious incidents occurred in Bahrain, where demonstrations close to the capital, Manama, resulted in the death of at least 10 civilians and 3 policemen in early 1995. By late in the year, many people had been sentenced or detained for political dissent. (See **Bahrain.**)

Argentine bombing. Confusion arose in 1995 about who was responsible for a 1994 bombing that killed up to 100 people at a Jewish center in Buenos Aires. Iran had been blamed for the bombing. However, in November 1995, a former Argentine army sergeant turned himself in to police who were investigating the case. Speculation arose that anti-Semitic members of Argentina's police and security forces may have orchestrated the bombing.

By early December 1995, a dozen soldiers and civilians were being held for questioning about the bombing. A bomb blast in 1992 that killed about 30 people at the Israeli embassy in Buenos Aires also remained unsolved.

Qatar. Qatar's crown prince, Hamad bin Khalifa Al Thani, peacefully ousted his father, Khalifa bin Hamad Al Thani, to become the new emir on June 27. The new leader, who had essentially run the country since 1992, gained quick recognition by the international community.

Foreign workers. The plight of foreign workers in Persian Gulf nations continued to be a focus of international concern in 1995. The workers, many of whom had replaced Palestinians and other Arabs who returned home during the Persian Gulf War (1991), complained of physical abuse and garnished wages. On Sept. 16, 1995, a 16-year-old Filipino maid was sentenced to death in the United Arab Emirates for killing her employer, whom she said had raped her. After much international criticism, the girl's sentence was reduced to 100 lashes, a year in jail, and deportation. In Kuwait, where two Arab women beat their foreign maids to death in 1995, an investigation began into the treatment of foreign workers.

The Roman Catholic Church announced on June 22 that it was establishing a Joint Liaison Committee to promote understanding between Christians and Muslims.   □ Christine Helms

See also articles on the various Middle Eastern countries. In *World Book,* see **Middle East** and individual Middle Eastern country articles.

Mining. See **Energy supply.**

Minnesota. See **State government.**

Mississippi. See **State government.**

Missouri. See **State government.**

Moldova. See **Commonwealth of Independent States.**

Mongolia. See **Asia.**

Montana. See **State government.**

Montreal. Some 260,000 people from across Canada came together in downtown Montreal on Oct. 27, 1995, as part of a Stand Up for Canada rally held three days before a referendum on independence for Quebec. It was the largest political gathering in Montreal's history. Voters in the province narrowly defeated the Quebec independence initiative.

Gang violence. An 11-year-old Montreal schoolboy in August 1995 became the first innocent victim in an escalating turf war between criminal motorcycle gangs for Montreal's multimillion-dollar illegal drug trade. The bloody battle, pitting the Quebec chapter of the Hell's Angels against the rival Rock Machine—a front for a coalition of Montreal crime families—claimed at least 25 lives in 1994 and 1995. The boy, Daniel Desrochers, died on August 13 of head injuries he suffered four days earlier when the booby-trapped Jeep of a neighborhood drug dealer exploded. The drug dealer was killed in the blast.

The youngster's murder sparked a petition, signed by more than 12,000 people, demanding a federal antigang law. On September 23, Quebec's public security minister, Serge Ménard, announced that he was launching a special antibiker squad consisting of Montreal Urban Community (MUC) police, the provincial police force, and the Royal Canadian Mounted Police. On the same day, MUC Police Chief Jacques Duchesneau vowed to crack down on gangs by deploying all 4,000 of his officers to assist the department's existing 40-member antigang squad.

Barnabé case. In 1995, MUC police came under renewed fire by community groups protesting police brutality. On June 26, a jury found four MUC police officers guilty of assault causing bodily harm in the Dec. 14, 1993, beating of taxi driver Richard Barnabé. Barnabé remained in a coma as a result of his injuries. The four policemen were acquitted of the more serious charge of aggravated assault and the lone female officer charged with both offenses was found not guilty. Three of the officers were sentenced to 60 to 90 days in jail on weekends, while the fourth was required to perform 180 days of community service.

Protests also erupted on May 31 when MUC police fatally shot a suspected shoplifter named Martin Suazo. The two cases led about 20 Montreal community and special interest groups in June to form the Concerned Citizens Against Police Brutality. The group planned to create a civilian tribunal that was to begin hearing complaints in December. On September 13, Public Security Minister Ménard confirmed there would be two inquiries—one into the Suazo case and another into police practices.

Lengthy labor disputes hit several sectors of Montreal in 1995. A 15-month strike at Canada's biggest flour mill, ADM Milling, in the Port of Montreal ended on September 18, after unionized workers accepted a mediator-assisted contract offer from United States-based Archer Daniels Midland—one of the world's largest agricultural conglomerates. During the strike, which began on June 6, 1994, replacement workers kept the plant operating.

A series of strikes and lockouts involving 900 longshoremen closed the Port of Montreal for 2½ weeks in March 1995, stranding about $300 million worth of cargo and forcing shippers to divert their goods to other Canadian ports. A settlement was reached on June 22.

Pressure tactics by the city's 4,000 blue-collar workers closed the Biodôme ecological museum from March 29 until June 24. And a contract dispute between 2,000 unionized casino employees and the provincial government shut down the Montreal Casino for 45 days during the peak summer season. Quebec lost an estimated $40 million in revenues while the casino was closed, from June 29 to August 15.

Health-care workers and Montreal citizens alike were shocked on May 12, when the Montreal Regional Health Board announced that nine hospitals would be closed due to budget cuts in the Quebec Health Department. But in June, Quebec Health Minister Jean Rochon said two of the targeted facilities—one English and one French rehabilitation hospital—would be spared the ax. Staff and supporters of the other seven establishments held numerous demonstrations in an ultimately unsuccessful effort to keep them operating.   □ Mike King

See also **Canada.** In *World Book*, see **Montreal.**

Morocco. Severe drought for three of the previous four years brought on what Morocco's King Hassan II declared a "national disaster" in 1995. Agricultural output fell by more than 50 percent. Inflation rose as the government was forced to buy grain overseas, and unemployment rose to about 22 percent as farm workers lost work. Interest on Morocco's $21-billion foreign debt ate up 35 percent of the budget.

Hassan excluded opposition parties from power when he reneged on a 1994 pledge to name someone from their four-party alliance as prime minister. Instead, on Jan. 31, 1995, he reappointed Abdellatif Filali. A public vote to decide if Western Sahara would be part of Morocco was put off until 1996.

A dispute over coastal fishing rights between Morocco and the European Union remained unresolved by late 1995. European officials also worried that Morocco, Europe's major supplier of marijuana, expected a bumper crop of the drug in 1995.

Three men received death sentences and 11 others were sent to jail for up to 10 years on January 28 for terrorist attacks in Morocco during 1993 and 1994. Because several of the terrorists were Algerian, the attacks had soured relations between Morocco and neighboring Algeria, whose civil war threatened to spill over its borders. ☐ Christine Helms

See also **Africa** (Facts in brief table). In *World Book,* see **Morocco.**

Motion pictures. Giant mergers dominated the United States entertainment industry in 1995, including motion pictures. In July, the Walt Disney Company announced that it had purchased Capital Cities/ABC Inc. for $19 billion—the world's largest entertainment company merger. In September, Time Warner Inc. agreed to buy Turner Broadcasting System, Incorporated, which owns New Line Cinema, for $7.5 billion. Although the mergers attracted heavy media attention, they were expected to have little effect on filmmaking.

American movies dominated the world film market in 1995, with comedies and dramas showing unprecedented strength in non-English-speaking countries. In past years, action films proved the biggest American money-makers worldwide. The international grosses of *While You Were Sleeping*, for example, topped that movie's U.S. receipts.

'95 notables. Tom Hanks continued his formidable winning streak, collecting his second consecutive Academy Award for best actor (for 1994's *Forrest Gump*) and starring as astronaut James A. Lovell, Jr., in *Apollo 13*, one of 1995's most popular films. Ed Harris and Gary Sinise also turned in strong performances. Under Ron Howard's direction, the film wrenched suspense from a familiar story—the April 1990 flight of the Apollo 13 spacecraft, which was crippled by an explosion as it headed toward the moon and barely made it safely back to Earth.

Martin Scorsese's *Casino*, a portrayal of 1970's Las Vegas, earned mixed reviews, but its stars, Sharon Stone—previously dismissed by critics—and Robert De Niro, won praise. Jim Carrey's return as the wild-haired pet detective in *Ace Ventura 2: When Nature Calls* again proved the rubber-faced actor's popularity. Bryan Singer's clever *The Usual Suspects* proved a solid art-house favorite. The intellectual crime caper was peppered with idiosyncratic performances, including those by Kevin Spacey and Gabriel Byrne.

One of the most surprisingly successful romantic pairs of 1995 was Meryl Streep and Clint Eastwood who starred in the film version of Robert James Waller's 1992 novel *The Bridges of Madison County*. Eastwood, best known for his action films, directed the story of a romance between a lonely Iowa housewife and a magazine photographer.

Films about women. In a trend welcomed by many people, more movies emphasized the bond between women. *Waiting to Exhale*, about four single black women, was an eagerly anticipated year-end attraction. *How to Make an American Quilt, Pocahontas, A Little Princess, Now and Then, The Baby-Sitters Club,* and *Gold Diggers: The Secret of Bear Mountain* all made impressions in 1995. Although none of these movies were particularly popular with men, the new emphasis on strong female leads promised to continue in 1996.

Classics. In 1995, filmmakers paid fresh attention to the classics. *The Scarlet Letter*, a revisionist version of Nathaniel Hawthorne's 1856 novel starring Demi Moore, was scorned by both the public and critics. But *Persuasion,* an adaptation of British author Jane Austen's 1818 novel, found a more receptive audience. Also receiving lavish praise was an adaptation of Austen's 1811 novel, *Sense and Sensibility,* with Emma Thompson and Hugh Grant. Two Shakespeare adaptations attracted critical praise: *Othello*, with Kenneth Branagh, Laurence Fishburne, and Irene Jacob; and *Richard III* with Patrick Stewart of television's "Star Trek" and Annette Bening.

Animation continued to flourish. Compared with Disney's *The Lion King*, probably the most profitable animated film ever made, *Pocahontas* was disappointing, though it still found favor with young audiences. In contrast, Disney's *Toy Story* not only won critical praise but also showed signs of becoming one of the most popular animated films ever. The animation was created entirely by computer.

Stellar salaries. The salaries of American stars skyrocketed in 1995, raising concerns about their effect on production costs—which averaged $50.4 million per movie in 1995—and film quality, as producers cut scenes and characters to stay within budget.

In September, Sylvester Stallone negotiated a three-movie deal with Universal Pictures for $60 million. Although Stallone's *Judge Dredd* was a summer flop and his *Assassins* a fall box-office disappointment, Stallone had high international appeal. Other

Motion pictures

stars with greater U.S. appeal who hired out for $20-million per film were Harrison Ford for *The Devil's Own*, Jim Carrey for *Cable Guy,* and Mel Gibson for *Ransom* (all due out in 1996).

John Travolta's asking price soared to $21 million. Travolta, a late-1970's star, regained public favor with 1994's *Pulp Fiction*, and 1995's *Get Shorty*, in which he played a Miami loan shark who goes to Hollywood and discovers that the motion-picture business is more treacherous than racketeering. Travolta also collected favorable notices for *The White Man's Burden*, a poorly received film about an alternate world in which black people make up the majority and white people are an oppressed minority.

Actresses, however, continued to be paid lower salaries than their male counterparts. Demi Moore drew the top female salary—$12.5 million for *Striptease,* and then mainly because she appeared nude.

Some industry observers blamed the soaring salaries on the ferocious competition among studios for proven box-office draws, especially in the international market. The inflated salaries also trickled down to second-level actors, who were able to demand increasingly lucrative contracts in 1995.

Pushing the envelope, please. Director Paul Verhoeven's *Showgirls* was the first mainstream

Tom Hanks won his second consecutive Academy Award for best actor in March, for his title role in *Forrest Gump*.

Academy Award winners in 1995

The following winners of the 1994 Academy Awards were announced in March 1995:

Best Picture, *Forrest Gump.*
Best Actor, Tom Hanks, *Forrest Gump.*
Best Actress, Jessica Lange, *Blue Sky.*
Best Supporting Actor, Martin Landau, *Ed Wood.*
Best Supporting Actress, Dianne Wiest, *Bullets Over Broadway.*
Best Director, Robert Zemeckis, *Forrest Gump.*
Best Original Screenplay, Quentin Tarantino and Roger Avary, *Pulp Fiction.*
Best Screenplay Adaptation, Eric Roth, *Forrest Gump.*
Best Cinematography, John Toll, *Legends of the Fall.*
Best Film Editing, Arthur Schmidt, *Forrest Gump.*
Best Original Score, Hans Zimmer, *The Lion King.*
Best Original Song, Elton John and Tim Rice, "Can You Feel the Love Tonight" from *The Lion King.*
Best Foreign-Language Film, *Burnt by the Sun* (Russia).
Best Art Direction, Ken Adam and Carolyn Scott, *The Madness of King George.*
Best Costume Design, Lizzy Gardiner and Tim Chappel, *The Adventures of Priscilla, Queen of the Desert.*
Best Sound, Gregg Landaker, Steve Maslow, Bob Beemer, and David R. B. MacMillan, *Speed.*
Best Sound Effects Editing, Stephen Hunter Flick, *Speed.*
Best Makeup, Rick Baker, Ve Neill, and Yolanda Toussieng, *Ed Wood.*
Best Animated Short Film, *Bob's Birthday.*
Best Live-Action Short Film, *Franz Kafka's It's a Wonderful Life* and *Trevor* (tie).
Best Feature Documentary, *Maya Lin: A Strong Clear Vision.*
Best Short Subject Documentary, *A Time for Justice.*
Honorary Award, Michelangelo Antonioni.
Irving G. Thalberg Memorial Award, Clint Eastwood.

movie to welcome the dreaded "NC-17" rating (No children under 17 admitted) from the Motion Picture Association of America (MPAA). (Filmmakers generally try to avoid an NC-17 rating—the MPAA's most restrictive—because many theaters are reluctant to show such movies and many video chains refuse to rent or sell them.) *Showgirls*, a variation of the 1950 classic *All About Eve* transplanted to Las Vegas, overflowed with nudity, sexual promiscuity, and rough language. After a reasonably successful opening weekend, *Showgirls* flopped. Most observers felt that *Showgirls'* poor performance would dissuade filmmakers from making "NC-17" movies.

Rather than accept an "NC-17" rating for director Larry Clark's controversial *Kids*, Miramax Films released the movie without a rating at all. Produced on a modest budget, *Kids*, which unblinkingly depicted the sexual habits of a group of contemporary teen-agers, proved a critical success and a box-office hit at art theaters. Miramax's controversial R-rated *Priest*, in which the title character is gay, was a solid success at U.S. art houses.

Action flicks. *Batman Forever* was the summer's biggest hit. Director Joel Schumacher approached the latest in the Batman series in a lighter vein than had Tim Burton, who directed *Batman* (1989) and *Batman Returns* (1992). As a result, the film drew the most positive response of the three. Val Kilmer was well-received as Batman and his alter ego, Bruce Wayne—previously played by Michael Keaton—and Chris O'Donnell made a strong impression as his sidekick, Robin. Jim Carrey added to his box-office prowess as the Riddler.

The James Bond series continued with Pierce Brosnan, best known as television's Remington Steele, assuming the role of Agent 007 in *GoldenEye*. The film attempted to bring a 1990's sensibility to the secret agent's well-known male chauvinism.

Awash in yawns. The most publicized film of 1995 was *Waterworld*, starring Kevin Costner as a part-man, part-fish survivor of a postapocalyptic world in which land is only a rumor. *Waterworld* was also the most expensive movie in history, with an estimated cost of at least $175 million. The huge cost resulted, in part, because of creative differences between Costner and director Kevin Reynolds, who left the production during its editing stages. Ultimately, the film was neither disaster nor blockbuster.

Holiday openings. Year-end releases collecting favorable notices included *Jumanji*, a comedy-fantasy in which Robin Williams plays a man who escapes from a board game where he had been imprisoned for 25 years; *The American President*, with Michael Douglas as a widowed chief executive and Annette Bening as the lobbyist he falls in love with; and *Sabrina*, a remake of the 1954 romantic comedy, with Harrison Ford and Julia Ormond assuming roles originated by Humphrey Bogart and Audrey Hepburn.

One of 1995's most anticipated films was director

Oliver Stone's *Nixon*, which offered a sympathetic view of America's most controversial modern President. Anthony Hopkins played the title role, while Bob Hoskins (as J. Edgar Hoover), Paul Sorvino (as Henry Kissinger) and James Wood (as H.R. Haldeman) gave strong supporting performances.

Hot properties. Brad Pitt emerged as the hottest new star of 1995. *Legends of the Fall*, an old-fashioned melodrama in which Pitt played a tormented loner, opened in a few cities late in 1994 but played most of the world in 1995. It was a box-office hit, as was the grim, overly stylized *Seven*, in which Pitt and Morgan Freeman played cops trying to catch a sadistic and imaginative serial killer.

Sandra Bullock emerged as one of the year's biggest female stars, largely because of her performance in the romantic comedy *While You Were Sleeping*. Bullock's *The Net* was the only "cyberflick"—a movie focusing on computers—to score a modest success in 1995. In that film, she played a computer nerd whose political enemies erase her identity via computer. The year's other cyberflicks—*Virtuosity*, *Strange Days*, *Hackers*, and *Johnny Mnemonic*—crashed and burned at the box office.

Italian renaissance. Although American movies remained the focus of the international movie industry, Italian filmmaking was on the upswing, an encouraging sign as 1994 had marked the lowest production schedule in that country in 10 years. Director Bernardo Bertolucci shot his first film in Italy in 16 years—the intimate drama *Stealing Beauty*, starring Jeremy Irons. Italy's Tuscany region was the setting for Paolo and Vittorio Taviani's *Elective Affinities*, adapted from German writer Johann Wolfgang von Goethe's 1809 novel and starring Isabelle Huppert. Michelangelo Antonioni and Wim Wenders went to Italy to complete their codirection of *Beyond the Clouds*, based on Antonioni's journal and a collection of his short stories. John Malkovich, Jeremy Irons, and Fanny Ardant starred.

Foreign films. Director Jean-Paul Rappeneau of France, whose *Cyrano de Bergerac* (1990) was a worldwide success, returned to the screen with the most expensive film in French history—the $35-million *The Horseman on the Roof*. The film tells of a young military officer's romance with an aristocratic woman in the midst of a cholera epidemic in the 1800's. *Shanghai Triad*, the Chinese director Zhang Yimou's version of a 1930's Hollywood gangster film, won raves at its U.S. premiere at the New York Film Festival in September. ☐ Philip Wuntch

See also **Lange, Jessica.** In *World Book*, see **Motion pictures.**

Mozambique. See Africa.

Music. See Classical music; popular music.

Myanmar. See Burma.

Namibia. See Africa.

Nebraska. See State government.

Nepal. See Asia.

Floodwaters from the Waal River in February threaten a farmhouse near the Dutch town of Tiel in the worst flooding to hit the Netherlands in 40 years.

Role in Bosnia questioned. A debate over the performance of Dutch peacekeeping troops in the former Yugoslavia gripped the Netherlands in 1995 after Dutch troops abandoned the Muslim safe haven of Srebrenica to Bosnian Serb forces on July 11. Western governments and human rights groups said that after the town fell, several thousand civilian Muslim men and boys were slaughtered by the Bosnian Serbs. The massacre led some members of parliament to question whether the 450 lightly armed Dutch peacekeepers should have resisted the Bosnian Serbs. An investigation by the ministry of defense concluded in October that the troops had no option but to surrender because of the overwhelming number of attackers and the failure of UN commanders to order sufficient air strikes to support the Dutch troops.

Winter floods. Heavy rains triggered the country's worst flooding in 40 years as the Rhine, Meuse, and Waal rivers overflowed their banks in late January and early February. The government evacuated nearly 250,000 people from their homes, mostly in southeastern regions of the country, when saturated dikes along the rivers threatened to collapse. The dikes held, but the government quickly launched a program to reinforce and renovate the earthen barriers.   □ Tom Buerkle

See also **Europe** (Facts in brief table). In **World Book,** see **European Union; Netherlands.**

Netherlands. Netherlands in 1995 had one of the strongest economies in Europe as consumer demand and corporate investment increased at a brisk pace. The output of goods and services grew an estimated 3 percent, the highest growth rate in the Netherlands since 1990.

The main thrust of the economic policy in the Netherlands continued to be restraint in public spending. The goal was to reduce the budget deficit enough to qualify for participation in a single European currency in 1999.

Controversy over drugs. The lenient drug policy of the Netherlands, which includes tolerance toward *soft drugs* (marijuana and hashish) and the licensing of coffee shops to sell such drugs, sparked tension between the Dutch and other members of the European Union (EU) in 1995. In June, President Jacques Chirac of France reproached Dutch Prime Minister Willem Kok over the drugs issue at a meeting of EU leaders in Paris. Also in June, Chirac suspended France's participation in an agreement to lift border controls with six other EU countries, citing a rise in international drug trafficking among his reasons. In response, the Dutch government in September instituted measures to tighten the nation's drug policy. It limited the number of licenses available and the amounts of drugs that shops could sell, and it announced its intention to step up measures in the fight against international drug trafficking.

New York City. Rudolph F. Crew, superintendent of the Tacoma, Washington school system, was appointed chancellor of New York City schools on Oct. 7, 1995. The appointment ended a long search that was complicated by a feud between City Hall and the Board of Education.

On September 29, Daniel A. Domenech, district superintendent for Western Suffolk County, Long Island, had been narrowly elected chancellor. But the next day, under pressure from the administration of Mayor Rudolph W. Giuliani, the board reversed itself and voted to withdraw Domenech's contract. Crew, 45, New York City's second African American chancellor, had the support of both the board and the mayor.

Crew was the third chancellor to be appointed in New York City in 1995 and the seventh since 1983. As head of the nation's largest school system, his domain included 1.1 million students, compared with Tacoma's 31,500; nearly 1,100 schools, many in need of repair; and 60,000 teachers.

Crew succeeded Ramon C. Cortines, who resigned effective October 15 following a prolonged dispute with Giuliani over diminished school funding and control of school security. The mayor had sought to gain more control over the $8-billion education budget and Board of Education operations, arguing that school reform was being hampered by a surplus of administrators at school board headquarters.

Muslim radicals convicted. Egyptian cleric Sheik Omar Abdel-Rahman and nine other Muslim radicals were convicted on October 1 of a plot to assassinate Egyptian President Hosni Mubarak and to bomb the United Nations, the Federal Bureau of Investigation (FBI) headquarters, the George Washington Bridge, and two Hudson River tunnels. The nine-month federal trial was the second to result from the bombing of the World Trade Center on Feb. 26, 1993, which left six people dead and more than 1,000 injured. Abdel-Rahman had been implicated in that bombing.

Among the others convicted was Sayyid Nosair, who was found guilty of killing Rabbi Meir Kahane in a Manhattan hotel in 1990. A state jury had previously acquitted Nosair. Abdel-Rahman and Nosair were expected to be sentenced in January 1996 to life in prison. The other conspirators were expected to receive 20- to 30-year sentences.

Rockefeller Center purchase. An investment group including Goldman, Sachs, and Company and David Rockefeller announced on November 7 that it would buy Rockefeller Center. The Goldman group offered Rockefeller Center Properties $306 million and agreed to assume over $800 million in debt.

On May 11, the Mitsubishi Real Estate Company, which owned an 80 percent share of the building, and the Rockefeller family trusts, which owned 20 percent, had filed for bankruptcy. The two partnerships in September transferred ownership of the building to Rockefeller Center Properties, an investment trust that was also financially unstable.

The agreement between the trust and the Goldman group ended months of negotiations by potential investors. Mitsubishi had bought Rockefeller Center in 1989 at the peak of New York City's real estate market. The company blamed its financial difficulties in the 1990's on the real estate market's decline.

Fulton Fish Market. Mayor Giuliani took steps in 1995 to clean up the historic Fulton Fish Market, often described as one of the last strongholds of organized crime. City officials proposed on February 1 to license vendors and workers at the nation's largest fish market—and to end a so-called "mob tax" that has driven away fish dealers, caused a two-thirds loss in business, and led to higher fish prices.

The violent death of 6-year-old Elisa Izquierdo on November 23, a victim of the city's child welfare system as well as of her accused murderer—her mother—prompted demands in New York and around the nation for a review of child custody policies. The city's Child Welfare Administration had allowed Elisa to live with her biological mother, Awilda Lopez, despite complaints from neighbors, relatives, and teachers that the girl was being abused at home. □ Owen Moritz

See also **City.** In *World Book,* see **New York City.**
New York State. See State government.

New Zealand. The economy of the nation continued to expand vigorously in 1995. There were signs, however, that the annual rate of economic growth was slowing to around 3 percent from more than 6 percent in 1994.

One economic problem was the growing trade deficit, the gap between the value of imports and a lesser value of exports. By October 1995, the deficit of $3.3 billion (New Zealand dollars, equal to U.S $1.98 billion) was the worst since 1986. Economists believed that much of the surge in imports was due to purchases of machinery and materials needed to meet increased production. The gap was expected to close, and most experts predicted positive trade balances for the remainder of the 1990's.

The nation's reduced economic activity had the positive side-effect of reversing a rising inflation rate. In the 12 months ending in June 1995, the annual rate was 2.2 percent, but by September, it had fallen to 2 percent. As a result, banks cut their mortgage interest rates.

Politics. New Zealand's political system, traditionally dominated by two parties, became highly fragmented in the lead-up to the 1996 election under a new voting system based on proportional representation. Political experts predicted that the new system would result in a greater number of parties in Parliament. The most significant move of 1995 was the formation in June of the United Party by seven members of the 97-seat Parliament. Those defectors represented a voting block that the ruling National Party could not afford to ignore if it expected to continue holding a majority.

Foreign affairs during the year were dominated by protests against the resumption of nuclear testing by France in the South Pacific Ocean. The New Zealand government tried unsuccessfully to stop the testing by asking the World Court at The Hague in the Netherlands to reopen a 1974 challenge to French nuclear tests. But the court ruled on Sept 22, 1995, that the 1974 challenge had dealt exclusively with stopping atmospheric testing, while the 1995 tests—which began on September 5—were being conducted underground at an ocean atoll. France said testing would end in the first half of 1996.

Tragedy struck in an isolated section of New Zealand's South Island on April 28, 1995, when 13 students and a guide fell 100 feet (30 meters) to their death after a viewing platform collapsed at Cave Creek in Paparoa National Park. Another four people were seriously hurt and five others who had been on the platform escaped injury.

America's Cup. The yacht *Black Magic 1* won the America's Cup yacht race off San Diego in May. It was just the second time in the 144-year history of the race that a United States team lost. □ Gavin Ellis

See also **Asia** (Facts in brief table). In *World Book,* see **New Zealand.**
Newfoundland. See Canadian provinces.

Newsmakers of 1995

Newsmakers of 1995 included the following people and events:

Cowpokes ride again. Thirty modern cowboys, 300 longhorn cattle, 82 horses, and 2 covered wagons set out from Fort Worth, Texas, on March 5 on a 1,600-mile (2,575-kilometer), six-month journey into the past. The cowboys on the "Great Amer- ican Cattle Drive of '95" had saddled up to recapture the spirit of the Old West during the golden age of cattle herding in the late 1800's. The event marked the first large-scale cattle drive since 1886.

Bud McCasland, a former telephone company executive from Fort Worth, organized the event. McCasland picked the most experienced cowpunchers he could find from more than 3,000 applicants. The wranglers traveled 12 to 15 miles (19 to 24 kilometers) a day, slept in tepees or in the open, sang cowboy songs to the herd, and ate the trail cook's grub twice a day.

The drive ended in Miles City, Montana, on September 1. The cowboys arrived with their herd intact and, presumably, some tender backsides. Trail bosses reported that the cattle stampeded only four times. In one unfortunate instance, six steers charged down the middle of a Texas highway, stomped over the top of a stopped car, then turned and stomped over it again.

Korean War Memorial opens. The United States honored its Korean War (1950-1953) veterans in July with the dedication of the Korean War Memorial in Washington, D.C. More than 54,000 U.S. soldiers died in the conflict, and total deaths were more than 1.5 million. The $18-million memorial shows 19 U.S. soldiers from all branches of the military and all ethnic groups that served in the conflict. The 7-foot (213-centimeter) cast-steel soldiers are depicted in patrol formation wearing foul-weather ponchos. There is also a black granite monument depicting the faces of Korean War veterans, as well as other images from the war.

President Bill Clinton dedicated the memorial on July 27 along with South Korean President Kim Yong-Sam. About 50,000 people attended the ceremony.

So you think you're a high roller? A picture of Australian media mogul Kerry Packer should be in the dictionary next to the word *high roller*. Kerry won $20 million playing blackjack in Las Vegas, Nevada, on May 14. Packer reportedly wagered $250,000 per hand during his spree and handed out $2,500 tips to about 40 people who had worked the tables as he gambled. The casino described Packer as a "recreational gambler" with a "very good basic strategy" at blackjack.

The windfall reversed a bit of misfortune for Packer. Sometime between April 28 and May 1, a thief stole $4 million in gold from a secret safe in one of Packer's office buildings, according to Australian police. Packer's personal fortune had also reportedly fallen by half in 1995 to a mere $2.2 billion.

Unsolvable equation solved—for certain. The math world celebrated the final solution of a 350-year mystery in May. That was when Princeton University mathematician Andrew Wiles's solution to Fermat's Last Theorem passed the critical review of his peers and appeared in the journal *Annals of Mathematics*. Wiles spent seven years working on a proof that the equation $x^n + y^n = z^n$ has no solutions in positive integers x, y, and z if the exponent

n is greater than 2. The French mathematician Pierre de Fermat made this claim in the 1630's in the margins of a mathematics text, including a note in Latin that he had a proof to the equation but that the margin was too small to include it. Wiles had announced his 200-page proof in 1993, but colleagues found a mistake in his work that he corrected for the 1995 review.

Over Niagara Falls on a jet ski. Robert Overacker of Camarillo, California, plunged to his death on October 1 when he tried to ride a jet ski over Niagara Falls. Overacker, 39, a car salesman and stock car racer, died when his parachute failed to open. According to the police, Overacker apparently planned his stunt to draw attention to the plight of the homeless. His jet ski bore stickers with the slogan "Save the Homeless," and he videotaped a message decrying homelessness before his ill-fated jump.

***Roe v. Wade* pioneer changes mind.** The woman whose appeal to the United States Supreme Court in 1973 launched legal abortions in the United States joined her opposition in August 1995. Norma McCorvey, the "Jane Roe" of the *Roe v. Wade* case that overturned bans on abortion—it was an anonymous name, equivalent to John Doe—said in August that she had been baptized by Flip Benham, head of the antiabortion group Operation Rescue. McCorvey quit her job at a Dallas abortion clinic and began working for Benham's group. McCorvey reportedly was still in favor of abortions performed during the first three months of a woman's pregnancy, however.

Searching for Jesse James. Jesse James—or at least someone reputed to be the infamous Western outlaw—was buried for the third time on Oct. 28, 1995. In July, investigators had exhumed the remains of an individual buried in Kearney, Missouri, under a tombstone declaring the grave to be James's. Seventeen of James's known descendants had sought a court order to exhume the body in order to resolve questions

Cowboys bring their herd of longhorn cattle through Fort Worth, Texas, in March at the start of the "Great American Cattle Drive of '95," *left*. The cowboys drove the cattle for six months, ending in Montana, *above*. The cattle drive was meant to capture the spirit of the Old West during the heyday of cattle drives in the late 1800's.

about where James is buried and how many descendants he has. A judge ruled that scientists could dig up the body to collect tissue samples in order to compare genetic material in the tissue with genetic material in blood samples from James's confirmed descendants. The results were not expected to be ready until February 1996. Scientists said, however, that they had recovered silver coffin handles and a gold tooth from the grave. James's coffin was known to have had silver handles, and the outlaw reportedly had a gold tooth.

From the 1860's until his death in 1882, James and his gang of outlaws robbed banks, stagecoaches, and trains. Historians have also attributed as many as 32 murders to James and his gang. According to a long-accepted account of James's death, a fellow gang member, Robert Ford, shot him to death in St. Joseph, Missouri. Some people claimed, though, that James faked his death, living many years longer under assumed names and fathering more children. The body said to be that of James was moved from a grave in his mother's yard near Kearney to a cemetery in Kearney in

1902 so that James would be buried next to his wife. About 450 spectators filled the hall where James's latest funeral was held.

Globetrotters lose. These guys weren't clowning around. A team of professionals and former college players led by former National Basketball Association great Kareem Abdul-Jabbar defeated the Harlem Globetrotters, 91-85, in Vienna, Austria, on Sept. 12, 1995. It was the Globetrotters' first defeat in 24 years and 8,829 games. The Globetrotters last lost on Jan. 15, 1971, to the New Jersey Reds, 100-99. "It's a strange feeling to lose a game," said Globetrotter Reggie (Regulator) Phillips.

First woman to fly U.S. spaceship. Air Force Lieutenant Colonel Eileen M. Collins, 38, in February 1995 became the first woman to pilot a National Aeronautics and Space Administration spaceship. Collins was second in command aboard the space shuttle Discovery on its mission February 2 to 11 to practice docking maneuvers with the Russian space station Mir.

During the mission, Collins fired rockets to help steer the shuttle. She also called out distances and other data to keep track of various navigation systems and make sure Discovery commander James D. Wetherbee was maneuvering safely on the approach to Mir.

Balloonist sets distance record. For relaxation, some people garden, do crossword puzzles, or play tennis. Chicago stockbroker Steve Fossett breaks daredevil world records. Not content to set a world solo ballooning record in 1995, Fossett also broke a sailing record for crossing the Pacific Ocean. On February 18, Fossett, 50, set out from Seoul, South Korea, to accomplish something no one else had— fly a balloon solo across the Pacific Ocean. He had planned to fly to San Francisco, but winds blew him off course and pushed him instead toward Canada.

On February 21, Fossett crossed into Canada over British Columbia and kept going. He landed on February 22 in a farmer's field near Leader, Canada, having traveled about 5,430 nautical miles (10,000 kilometers). The previous distance record was 5,208 nautical miles (9,650 kilometers).

Fossett experienced freez-

Justin T. Carroll of Wynne, Arkansas, exults in June after spelling xanthosis to win the National Spelling Bee in Washington, D.C.

ing temperatures after his propane heaters went out on the first night of his trip. Temperatures dropped to -4 °F (-20 °C), and to keep his drinking water from freezing, Fossett said, he had to hold it next to his body. The cold "made the flight rather uncomfortable, to say the least," he said.

In August, Fossett and three crew members broke the world record for sailing across the Pacific Ocean. The sailors piloted their trimaran *Lakota* from Yokohama, Japan, to Tiburon, California, in 16 days, 16 hours, and 23 minutes, cutting almost five days off the previous record set by the clipper ship *James Stafford* in 1885.

Mystery kisser identified. He's not the kiss-and-tell type, but his secret is out now. Following Japan's surrender to the United States, which ended World War II (1939-1945), a *Life* magazine photographer captured a nation's sense of joy and celebration on Aug. 15, 1945, in New York City's Times Square. In the now-famous *Life* photo, a tall, dark-haired sailor kisses a nurse, bending her backward in his arms. The nurse, dressed in a white uniform, lifts one foot off the ground.

In 1980, *Life* identified the nurse as Edith Shain of Santa Monica, California, but the sailor's identity remained a mystery. Several men had claimed to be the mystery kisser, but either Shain or *Life* had rejected them. Then, in August 1995, Carl Muscarello, a former New York City police detective who is now retired and living in Florida, said he was the one, and Shain agreed. Muscarello was 19 when the photo was taken.

Muscarello said that when he called Shain and identified himself, she was skeptical. But he passed her acid test consisting of two questions: What was the kiss like and what did you say afterwards?

Shain said that all of the imposter kissers failed the question about what was said after the kiss. Some of the would-be kissers claimed that they

Shannon Faulkner speaks to reporters in August after announcing that she had withdrawn from The Citadel, a military college in Charleston, South Carolina. Faulkner had waged a two-year battle to become the first female cadet at The Citadel.

asked for Shain's phone number, or for a date, she said. But according to Muscarello, he said nothing at all after the famous smooch, and Shain confirmed it. And what was the kiss like? "Thrilling," Shain said.

Religion prize goes to physicist. A scientist won the world's major religion prize—the $1-million Templeton Prize for Progress in Religion—in March. But ironically the winner, theoretical physicist Paul Davies of the University of Adelaide in Australia, is not religious in the traditional sense. He doesn't go to church, and he says the Bible is "not God's manifesto."

Davies said, however, that through his study of physics, he has developed a conviction that the laws of nature offer a hopeful message in a chaotic world. The more people understand about the universe, he said, the more they will see how "wonderfully organized everything seems to be, the greater evidence of some underlying meaning or purpose." The prize committee cited Davies's books, including *The Mind of God,* for raising questions "that fall within religion in general and humanity's quest for meaning in God."

1995 Kennedy Center honorees. On September 5, the Kennedy Center for the Performing Arts in Washington, D.C., announced the recipients of the Kennedy Center Honors. The award is presented each year to five individuals who have had outstanding careers in the performing arts. The 1995 honorees were dancer Jacques d'Amboise, singer Marilyn Horne, blues musician Riley B. (B.B.) King, actor Sidney Poitier, and playwright Neil Simon.

Historic rebel submarine found. Divers searching near Sullivans Island off the coast of Charleston, South Carolina, claimed in May 1995 to have found the Confederate submarine *Hunley*, the first submarine in history to sink a warship. Searchers claimed the submarine was several miles offshore in only 18 feet (5.5 meters) of water.

Statues in the Korean War Memorial in Washington, D.C., stare out from their ghostly procession. The memorial, dedicated in July, contains 19 figures representing all branches of the United States military and all ethnic groups that served during the Korean War (1950-1953).

The *Hunley* went to the bottom on Feb. 17, 1864, after sinking the U.S.S. *Housatonic* with an explosive device attached to a pole. The *Housatonic* was one of a group of Union warships blockading Charleston harbor. The *Hunley*'s crew tried to escape by working the hand-cranked propeller shaft—the submarine's only method of locomotion—but the craft sank. The submarine was made from an iron boiler, had no periscope, and used only a candle for interior illumination. The vessel had also sunk on three trial runs, killing all crew members each time, but salvagers repeatedly raised the submarine to sail again.

Clive Cussler, author of *Raise the Titanic* (1984) and other adventure novels, funded the successful search for the *Hunley*. The *Hunley*'s feat was not repeated until World War I (1914-1918), when German U-boats sank many allied ships.

Ice woman found. In October 1995, archaeologists reported finding the 500-year-old frozen remains of a young woman high atop a peak in the Andes Mountains of southern Peru. According to the scientists, the woman's body was wrapped in fine wool, and she wore an elaborate feather headdress.

According to Johan Reinhard, the U.S. archaeologist who found the body, the young Incan woman was probably killed as a sacrifice to the gods. The Inca were a South American Indian people who ruled one of the largest and richest empires in the Americas during the 1400's. Researchers also found two other frozen bodies—one woman and the other likely a man—near the first body. The three bodies were discovered at the 20,700-foot (6,300-meter) summit of Mount Ampato. Rare ceramics, statuettes, and other artifacts surrounded the bodies, the scientists said.

Lost Mantle bust recovered. Investigators got help in October from the Internet—a global collection of computer networks—in recovering a bronze bust of New York Yankee baseball legend Mickey Mantle, commemorating Mantle's 500th Major League home run, that had disappeared from Yankee Stadium. On October 30, authorities arrested a former Yankee Stadium security guard after he placed an offer on the Internet to sell the bust for $27,500.

Investigators said that Robert Pagani, 43, of Hyattsville, Maryland, arranged to meet agents from the Federal Bureau of Investigation, who posed as buyers. After they settled the deal, the agents arrested Pagani.

Mantle died on Aug. 13, 1995, at age 63. He had received a transplant on June 8 to replace his liver, which had been ravaged by cancer, hepatitis, and heavy drinking. Mantle had revealed on August 1 that he also had lung cancer.

☐ Mark Dunbar

Newspaper. The biggest problem newspapers faced in 1995 came from the paper they were printed on. After enjoying low newsprint prices since the late 1980's, United States publishers suddenly confronted tight supplies at a time when rising advertising volumes meant they were printing fatter newspapers. As a result, newsprint prices soared from as low as $420 per metric ton (a metric ton is equal to 0.9 short ton) in 1994 to $675 by May 1995 and nearly $800 by the end of the year.

The New York Times alone uses some 300,000 tons (270,000 metric tons) of newsprint each year. Knight-Ridder Incorporated, publisher of 28 daily papers, estimated in January that its 1995 newsprint bill would increase by about $100 million over 1994.

Unabomber. *The New York Times* and *The Washington Post* faced an ethical dilemma when a terrorist called the Unabomber on June 29 sent them a 35,000-word, antitechnology manifesto and suggested that if either paper published the full text within 90 days he would stop sending people mail bombs. After much debate and at the urging of top law enforcement authorities, *The Washington Post* published the manifesto on September 19.

Walkout. About 2,500 union workers walked off their jobs July 13 at the *Detroit Free Press* and the *Detroit News,* which share business and production operations. The papers continued publishing, though the strike continued through the fall.

The final issue of the 111-year-old *Houston Post* lies on a lunch counter in April as a Houston cafe owner and a customer discuss the paper's closing.

Changes. The owners of the *Houston Post* blamed newsprint prices for the April 18, 1995, closing of the 111-year-old newspaper. Houston thus became the largest U.S. city with only one major daily. Milwaukee became a one-paper city when the 113-year-old afternoon *Milwaukee Journal* merged with the 158-year-old morning *Milwaukee Sentinel* on April 2 to become the *Milwaukee Journal Sentinel.*

New York City lost one of its four major daily newspapers when the tabloid *New York Newsday* closed July 16 after racking up a reported $100 million in losses during its 10-year existence. Its owner, the Times Mirror Company, also closed Baltimore's 85-year-old *Evening Sun* on September 15, leaving the sister *Baltimore Sun* as the city's only daily. Providence, Rhode Island, also became a one-newspaper city June 5 when the 132-year-old *Evening Bulletin* merged with the *Providence Journal* to become the *Providence Journal-Bulletin.*

On July 24, the Gannett Company, the nation's largest newspaper chain, agreed to buy Multimedia Incorporated, owner of 60 newspapers and five television stations. McClatchy Newspaper, publisher of the *Sacramento Bee* and 11 other papers, said on May 17 it would buy *The News & Observer* of Raleigh, North Carolina. Knight-Ridder agreed on August 29 to buy Lesher Communications Incorporated, a California news publisher. ☐ Mark Fitzgerald

In *World Book,* see **Newspaper.**

Nicaragua. On June 15, 1995, President Violeta Barrios de Chamorro ended four months of political paralysis by reluctantly yielding to extensive changes in Nicaragua's Constitution that had been approved by Nicaragua's National Assembly in November 1994. The amended Constitution strengthened the powers of the National Assembly at the expense of those of the president.

The new Constitution prohibited consecutive presidential terms, barring Chamorro from running again in national elections scheduled for 1996. It also banned any relatives of presidents in power from seeking the presidency. This provision blocked the path of Chamorro's son-in-law and chief adviser, Antonio Lacayo Oyangurén, who had harbored presidential ambitions. Lacayo Oyangurén resigned his post as presidency minister on June 20, 1995.

The political stand-off during 1995 hampered the delivery of an estimated $600 million in international grants and loans. It also retarded action to settle some 3,000 claims, many by citizens of the United States, for properties seized when the Sandinista National Liberation Front seized power in 1979. Among the claimants were three Somoza brothers who belonged to the family that ruled Nicaragua from 1933 to 1979. ☐ Nathan A. Haverstock

See also **Latin America** (Facts in brief). In *World Book,* see **Nicaragua.**

Niger. See Africa.

Nigeria. Nigeria's authoritarian rule continued in 1995, becoming so repressive it stirred international protests. By year's end, Nigeria's political and economic future was the bleakest since 1960, when the nation achieved its independence. Petroleum production was down, and not enough capital was being invested to increase production. Nigeria's foreign debt had reached almost $40 billion, and the per capita annual income had declined to $290.

Human rights abuses. The regime of General Sani Abacha, in power for two years, had brought Nigeria a bad reputation in world affairs. Many people, including Randall Robinson, director of TransAfrica, a foreign-policy lobbying group, called for economic *sanctions* (bans) against Nigeria. Countries were urged to stop purchasing Nigerian petroleum, the country's largest source of income.

Early in March, numerous people were arrested for planning a coup to overthrow Abacha. General Olusegun Obasanjo, a former military ruler well-known internationally for his efforts to bring better governance to Africa, was one of those arrested. After brief military-dominated trials, some 40 accused plotters were convicted and 14 sentenced to death. The sentences were later commuted, and Obasanjo was expected to be released.

But Moshood Abiola, elected president in 1993, remained in prison under harsh conditions at year's end. Abiola had been charged with treason for demanding that he be allowed to assume the office to which he had been elected.

Activists executed. On November 10, the regime hanged noted playwright Ken Saro-Wiwa and eight other human rights activists who had been hastily convicted by a military court for the murder of four rural progovernment chiefs. The convictions were widely seen as politically motivated. The executions prompted an international outcry, and some nations took actions—albeit minor ones—to punish Abacha. Several countries recalled their ambassadors from Nigeria, the country's Commonwealth membership was suspended, and the United States forbade military equipment sales to Nigeria. But no country invoked the sanction that would have produced the greatest effect—a cutoff of petroleum purchases. A few days after the executions, the Shell Oil Company announced that it would go ahead with a $3.8-billion natural gas project in Nigeria.

Hopes for political improvement were raised on June 27 when General Abacha unveiled a new Constitution aimed at reinstating civilian rule. But on October 1, Abacha announced that he planned to stay in office for three more years. Many observers believed that Abacha, widely seen as a dictator with more interest in gaining wealth than in helping the country, would not give up power even after the three years had elapsed. □ Mark DeLancey

See also **Africa** (Facts in Brief table). In *World Book,* see **Nigeria.**

Nobel Prizes in literature, peace, sciences, and economics were awarded in October 1995 by the Norwegian Storting (parliament) in Oslo and by the Royal Swedish Academy of Sciences, the Karolinska Institute, and the Swedish Academy of Literature in Stockholm. The value of each prize was $1 million.

The literature prize went to Irish poet Seamus Heaney, 56, whose poems, said the Nobel committee, display "lyrical beauty and ethical depth, which exalt everyday miracles and the living past." The committee also praised Heaney, a Roman Catholic, for discussing the violence in Northern Ireland without resorting to "conventional terms."

Born to a farming family, Heaney had often compared his poetic excavations of hidden memories and secrets to his ancestors' toil in Ireland's peat bogs. Heaney's first collections of poetry, *Death of a Naturalist* (1966) and *Door into the Dark* (1969) brought him immediate recognition as a talented lyric poet. He later published nine more volumes, including the highly lauded *Station Island* (1984), a powerful reworking of the Italian poet Dante that dramatized Ireland's tortured history.

The peace prize went to Joseph Rotblat, 86, a Polish-born British physicist who helped develop the first atomic bomb in the 1940's, and to the Pugwash Conferences on Science and World Affairs, an antinuclear group he helped found. In awarding the prize, the committee said it wanted to protest nuclear tests conducted in 1995 by France and China.

Rotblat left the United States government's project to develop an atomic bomb before the U.S. atomic attack on Hiroshima, Japan, in August 1945. He later said he quit after learning that Nazi Germany had abandoned its atomic bomb project, which, he believed, made the development of a U.S. bomb unnecessary. In 1955, Rotblat and 10 other prominent scientists signed a declaration by British philosopher Bertrand Russell and German-born physicist Albert Einstein that nuclear weapons imperiled human survival. From that statement grew a series of annual conferences on the dangers of nuclear war, the first held in Pugwash, Canada, in 1957.

The prize for physiology or medicine was shared by Americans Edward B. Lewis, 77, of the California Institute of Technology in Pasadena; and Eric F. Wieschaus, 48, of Princeton University in Princeton, New Jersey; and German Christiane Nüesslein-Volhard, 52, of the Max Planck Institute for Developmental Biology in Tübingen, Germany. Their research on fruit flies helped explain how genes control the earliest development of human embryos.

Lewis's work, which began in the 1940's, focused on master genes or groups of genes that control the development of organs in specific segments of the fruit fly's body. Lewis correlated flaws in certain genes to such mutations as extra wings or legs. Wieschaus and Nüesslein-Volhard, building together on Lewis's work, identified other genes that enable a fertilized fruit fly egg to develop into a segmented embryo. Scientists have since found human counterparts to the fruit fly genes. The Nobel committee noted that flaws in the genes identified by the three scientists are probably responsible for about 40 percent of birth defects for which no cause is known.

The economics prize went to American Robert E. Lucas, Jr., of the University of Chicago for originating the "rational expectations" school of economic theory. Lucas's work, begun in 1976, challenged Keynesian economics, a then-prevailing economic theory which stated that governments could fine-tune the economy using interest rates, spending, and taxes. Lucas's theory, which has since gained wide acceptance, argues that people learn to anticipate such governmental actions and behave in ways that thwart the government's intended outcome. Lucas was the fifth University of Chicago professor in six years to win the economics prize.

The chemistry prize was shared by Americans F. Sherwood Rowland, 68, of the University of California (UC) at Irvine and Mario Molina, 52, of the Massachusetts Institute of Technology in Cambridge and by Dutch-born Paul Crutzen of the Max Planck Institute for Chemistry in Mainz, Germany. The scientists were cited for their pioneering research explaining the chemical processes that lead to the depletion of the ozone layer in the atmosphere, which screens out much of the sun's harmful ultraviolet rays.

In 1970, Crutzen discovered that ozone molecules, created by the action of sunlight on oxygen, are naturally destroyed in reactions with chemicals called nitrogen oxides. In the early 1970's, Rowland and Molina discovered that chemicals known as chlorofluorocarbons (CFC's), then widely used in refrigerants and aerosol propellants, could remain in the atmosphere for about 100 years. They also identified the process by which CFC's destroy ozone. Their prediction in 1974 that continued emissions of CFC's would seriously erode the ozone layer came under severe attack by the chemical industry.

The physics prize went to Americans Martin L. Perl, 68, of the Stanford Linear Accelerator Center in Palo Alto, Calif., and Frederick Reines, 77, of UC Irvine. The scientists won the prize for their separate discoveries of two types of leptons, a class of subatomic particles believed, along with quarks and bosons, to make up all the matter in the universe.

In the 1950's, Reines and Clyde L. Cowan, Jr., then at the Los Alamos National Laboratory in New Mexico, detected the neutrino, whose existence had been predicted. Neutrinos have no measurable mass and no electric charge. In contrast, Perl's discovery of the tau lepton in 1977 was unanticipated. Taus are heavy, unstable particles that quickly break down into lighter particles.   □ Barbara A. Mayes

In *World Book*, see Nobel Prizes.

North Carolina. See State government.
North Dakota. See State government.

Northern Ireland. The British government proceeded in 1995 with steps toward normalizing life in Northern Ireland, as the cease-fire announced by the Irish Republican Army (IRA) in August 1994 continued to hold. The suspension of violence in the region offered the hope of increased foreign investment and new jobs. By mid-1995, the tourist industry had already benefited from the cease-fire, seeing a 56 percent increase in the number of visitors in the first half of 1995 over the same period in 1994. However, attempts to work out the region's political future ran into difficulties.

The peace process. On February 22, the British and Irish governments issued a "Framework Document," which laid a course for all-party talks to determine the region's future. But the Ulster Unionist Party, the Protestant political party favoring union with Britain, was highly suspicious of such talks, and it threatened to boycott them.

In March, United States President Bill Clinton lifted a ban on U.S. fund-raising by Sinn Féin, the political wing of the IRA. He also invited Gerry Adams, president of Sinn Féin, to the White House for a St. Patrick's Day reception. The gestures were made in return for Sinn Féin's commitment to make IRA disarmament part of the peace talks. Clinton's actions infuriated British Prime Minister John Major, who wanted to see the IRA disarm before it was granted any favors.

On May 10, landmark talks took place between Sinn Féin and Michael Ancram, the junior British minister for Northern Ireland. It was the first public meeting between a British minister and Sinn Féin since 1972. Ancram restated Britain's insistence that the IRA should begin to disarm before Sinn Féin could be admitted to all-party talks. Britain's precondition to talks with Sinn Féin later led to the cancellation of a crucial summit scheduled for September 6 between Major and Irish Prime Minister John Bruton. Talks between Britain and Ireland were rescheduled for February 1996. (See **Northern Ireland** Special Report: **The Pursuit of Peace in Northern Ireland**.)

Clegg parole sparks violence. On July 3, riots began in Belfast and Londonderry after Britain freed Lee Clegg, a British soldier jailed for life for the 1990 shooting of a Belfast teen-ager who had been riding in a stolen car. It was the worst violence in the region since the start of the cease-fire. Government officials said Clegg was paroled after only two years because an appeals court ruled that he should have been tried for manslaughter rather than murder.

Gibraltar killing condemned. On September 27, the European Court of Human Rights in Strasbourg, France, condemned Britain for the 1988 killing of three unarmed IRA guerrillas by British soldiers in the British colony of Gibraltar.   □ Ian Mather

In *World Book*, see **Northern Ireland**.
Northwest Territories. See Canadian territories.

311

The Pursuit of Peace in Northern Ireland

The cessation of paramilitary activities in Northern Ireland marked the beginning of a peace process that could lead to the end of an age-old conflict in the region.

By Ian Mather

The scene at the White House on March 17, 1995—St. Patrick's Day—was a bit unusual. For the first time in history, an American President greeted the leader of Sinn Féin, the legal political wing of the outlawed Irish Republican Army (IRA), at a White House ceremony. The historic encounter between President Bill Clinton and Gerry Adams, president of Sinn Féin, was controversial, however. In London, the British government headed by Prime Minister John Major voiced strenuous objections to the meeting.

But only a year earlier, such an event would have been unthinkable because Adams had been banned from the United States as a supporter of terrorism. Then in August 1994, the IRA announced a cease-fire in its 25-year struggle to end British rule of Northern Ireland. And in December of that year, peace negotiations began. The White House decision to invite Adams was dramatic proof of the impact of the peace process that followed the cease-fire in Northern Ireland. Yet Clinton chose to meet Adams out of sight of the cameras, illustrating just how sensitive and fragile the peace process still was.

Peace in Northern Ireland would mean an end to a conflict that has wracked the region for decades. Since the 1960's, disputes between the Roman Catholic minority and the Protestant majority in Northern Ireland have openly divided the country politically, economically, and socially. The continuing dispute has led to riots, bombings, kidnappings, and other acts of terrorism by extremist groups on both sides. And the violence these groups meted out against one another was at the expense of thousands of civilian lives.

Northern Ireland's flag has a six-pointed star and the ancient Ulster symbol of a red hand. The flag is often flown by private citizens, but the official flag is the British Union flag.

313

History of the conflict in Northern Ireland

The origins of the conflict in today's Northern Ireland go back many centuries. In 1541, England's King Henry VIII, a Protestant, forced Ireland's Parliament to declare him king of Ireland, a largely Catholic country since the 400's. In the late 1500's, revolts against English rule began in Ulster, a large province in northern Ireland. In an attempt to quell the revolts, King James I seized land in Ulster in the early 1600's and gave it to Protestant English and Scottish settlers. Protestants then became the majority group in Ulster and have been ever since.

Irish Catholics suffered discrimination at the hands of Protestant English rulers. In the late 1500's, Queen Elizabeth I outlawed Roman Catholic services and executed a number of bishops and priests. When King James II, a Catholic, became the ruler of England in 1685, however, he abolished many of the anti-Catholic laws. But the English people were mainly Protestant, and they forced James from the throne in 1688. He fled to Ireland to raise an army that would help him reclaim the throne from William III, a Protestant, also known as William of Orange. But Protestants in Ulster supported William and in 1690 helped him defeat James's forces at the Battle of the Boyne near Dublin, Ireland.

Following William's victory, Catholics were forbidden to purchase or inherit land, and their rights to practice their religion were restricted. Catholics also were excluded from Ireland's Parliament. In the late 1700's, Ireland's all-Protestant Parliament restored the right of Catholics to hold land, and religious rights were restored, but Parliament still refused to give Catholics any political rights.

In 1801, Ireland officially became part of the United Kingdom of Great Britain and Ireland, and Ireland's Parliament was dissolved. Instead, Ireland elected representatives to the British Parliament. In the late 1800's, some Irish began to demand home rule, which would have given Ireland its own parliament to rule over domestic affairs. Ulster Protestants opposed this policy, because it would have made them a minority in a largely Catholic country.

The British Parliament passed a home rule bill in 1914, but the bill never took effect because of the outbreak of World War I (1914-1918). Militant members of the Irish Republican Brotherhood (IRB), a secret organization that wanted an independent Irish republic, believed the British distraction with the war would give Ireland a chance to gain independence. On Easter Monday in 1916, they staged a rebellion in Dublin. British troops defeated the rebels and executed 15 IRB leaders. These executions and the mass arrests that accompanied the rebellion won popular support for the rebels.

In 1918, the IRB gained control of the political organization called Sinn Féin, a Gaelic term meaning *We Ourselves*, and won a majority of Ireland's seats in the British Parliament. But instead of meeting in London, the seat of the British government, the new members met in Dublin. There, they declared all Ireland an independent republic on Jan. 21, 1919. The declaration sparked fighting between Irish rebels and British forces. The rebels were part of the IRA, which was formed in 1919 as an unofficial military force that aimed to gain independence from Britain.

Ian Mather

is Diplomatic Editor for *The European*.

In 1920, in an effort to appease the largely Irish Catholic desire for sovereignty without caving into demands for complete independence, the British Parliament passed the Government of Ireland Act, which divided Ireland into two political units. Both units would remain a part of Britain but would have some powers of self-government. Ulster Protestants accepted the act and formed Northern Ireland in Ulster. But the Irish leaders in Dublin rejected the division, and southern Ireland began fighting for complete independence.

In 1921, southern Irish leaders and the United Kingdom signed a treaty creating the Irish Free State in the south as a *dominion* (self-governing country) within the British Commonwealth. The division of Ireland was bitterly opposed by many Roman Catholics in Northern Ireland as well as groups in the south. And fighting against the British by armed groups continued. In 1949, the Irish Free State declared itself the independent Republic of Ireland.

Over the years, economic and political grievances festered in the Roman Catholic neighborhoods of Northern Ireland. Catholics were denied a fair share of political power in election districts set up to ensure that Unionists—who favored union with the United Kingdom—won control of local councils even when they were in the minority. Catholics also faced discrimination in employment by Protestants, who retained a monopoly on positions in commerce and industry. Protestant control of local government also guaranteed that decent public housing went to Protestants, leaving many Catholics in overcrowded, substandard tenement buildings.

Resentment toward Protestants simmered among Catholics. The members of the Orange Order, a militant Protestant organization, which claimed the right to march through Catholic neighborhoods and celebrate Protestant domination in the region, were a particular source of irritation.

Northern Ireland is a political division of the United Kingdom of Great Britain and Northern Ireland. It occupies the northeastern corner of the island of Ireland.

The Troubles begin

Violence in Northern Ireland, often called *the Troubles*, began in 1968 when Catholic protesters clashed with police. The rioting worsened, and in August 1969, British troops were sent to Northern Ireland to restore order—and they have been there ever since. The IRA, which had long opposed the separation of Ireland and Northern Ireland, reactivated a campaign of violence both in Northern Ireland and on the British mainland. In the 25 years that followed, over 3,000 people were killed in the three-way struggle between British security forces, the IRA, and the Protestant terrorist groups that sprang up to fight the IRA. Protestant paramilitary groups were responsible for about a third of the deaths and the IRA for most of the others, according to the British government.

In the early 1970's, the British government became increasingly frustrated with the inability of Stormont, the parliament of Northern Ireland, to deal with the escalating violence. In 1972, Britain abolished Stormont and began ruling Northern Ireland directly from the British Parliament in London. Soldiers and armored tanks patrolling city streets

The history of conflict in Northern Ireland

The conflict between Catholics and Protestants in Northern Ireland goes back to the 1600's, when Protestants from England and Scotland settled in the northern part of Ireland. Since then, the Catholic Irish have revolted against Protestant economic and political control of the region. Frequently, the tensions flared into violence, and extremists on both sides committed acts of terrorism. But in the 1990's, increasing weariness over the violent conflict led to a breakthrough in relations between Catholics and Protestants and a hope for peace in troubled Northern Ireland.

1607

King James I of England gave land in northern Ireland to English and Scottish Protestants.

This settlement led to a Protestant majority in the region.

1641-1649

Irish Catholics revolted against England

in an effort to prevent further Protestant settlement. After the Irish were put down in 1649, the English gave more land in Ireland to Protestants and deprived Irish Catholics of many political rights.

1690

The Battle of the Boyne

marked the beginning of Protestant political and economic control in Ireland. In the battle, former King James II, a Roman Catholic, failed in his attempt to regain the English throne from Protestant William of Orange, who had become king of England in 1689.

1886

Irish home rule

was proposed by the British Liberal Party to give Ireland its own parliament for domestic affairs. But Protestants in Ulster, a province in northern Ireland, feared an Irish Catholic parliament, and the British Parliament defeated the plan.

in Northern Ireland became commonplace. Virtual war zones existed where Protestant and Catholic neighborhoods bordered each other.

But in the early 1990's, there were signs of weariness over a conflict that clearly no one was winning. Then, on Aug. 31, 1994, a dramatic breakthrough came when the IRA announced a "complete cessation of military operations"—the cease-fire that set the stage for peace negotiations. Protestant paramilitary groups of Northern Ireland also announced a cease-fire on October 13. The peace process had begun.

Players in the peace process

Although the cease-fire was a crucial step, it only marked the beginning of a long and delicate process that involved appeasing the demands of a number of different groups. Key players in the process included the Protestant and the Catholic political parties, the IRA, Sinn Féin, the British government, and the Republic of Ireland.

Protestants made up a little over half of Northern Ireland's population of about 1.6 million people, according to 1991 census figures. They also owned most of the property and ran most of the businesses. Most Protestants were anxious that Northern Ireland should remain part of the United Kingdom. They feared becoming a minority in a united, Catholic Ireland, because their livelihood was largely dependent upon British financial support. The United Kingdom provides an annual subsidy of nearly $8 billion to Northern Ireland, most of it going to support jobs in the public sector, which constitutes nearly half the work force.

Of the two mainstream Protestant political parties, the larger one, the Ulster Unionist Party (UUP), did not condemn the peace process but remained cautious about it. However, its rival, the smaller Democratic Unionist Party (DUP), headed by firebrand preacher Ian Paisley, was deeply suspicious of the peace process and was totally opposed to any dealings with the Irish government or with Sinn Féin. But in 1995, the UUP had one strong card that the DUP lacked—it had 11 members in the British House of Commons, one of the two houses of Parliament. This representation gave it influence over the British government headed by the Conservative Party and Prime Minister Major. For the Conservatives to maintain their increasingly diminishing parliamentary majority, they needed the votes of the UUP.

There were also three Protestant terrorist groups fighting the IRA: the Ulster Defence Association, the Ulster Volunteer Force, and the Red Hand Commandos. Among them, they had carried out some of the worst atrocities in Northern Ireland.

Most Catholics in Northern Ireland saw themselves as underdogs in the conflict. They believed they had only to gain from union with the Republic of Ireland. Their unemployment rate was twice that of Protestants. Northern Ireland's unemployment rate of 15 percent was the highest in the British Isles. Housing conditions for Catholics in Northern Ireland were also among the worst in the United Kingdom.

The IRA was fighting for a united Ireland. Although it had only a few hundred active fighters, it was well armed and organized. But its support from the Catholic population was lukewarm. Many Catholics opposed the IRA's terrorism. The IRA was notorious for setting off bombs in large public spaces, such as shopping districts. It was also known for the ruthless punishments it imposed on informers and others who threatened their interests. The IRA was outlawed in Ireland, and there were agreements between the governments in Dublin and London for cross-border police cooperation against such terrorists.

Sinn Féin represented only 10 percent of the voters in Northern Ireland, but because of its close links with the IRA, its influence was far greater than its electoral strength. In the peace talks, Sinn Féin demanded the removal of British troops from Northern Ireland, the release of prisoners jailed for terrorist offenses, and the disbandment of the mainly Protestant police force, the Royal Ulster Constabulary.

1921

Southern Ireland became a self-governing country

of the British Commonwealth called the Irish Free State. Twenty-eight years later it renounced this status and became the independent Republic of Ireland.

1919

Ireland was declared independent

by 73 members of the political party Sinn Féin, who won seats in the British Parliament. Following the declaration, fighting broke out between Irish rebels and British forces. Also that year, the Irish Republican Army formed as an unofficial military force that aimed to gain independence for Ireland.

1920

Northern Ireland formed in Ulster

after the British Parliament passed the Government of Ireland act and separated Ireland into two distinct political units. Southern Catholics who rejected the act began fighting for complete independence.

Not all Northern Irish nationalist groups were committed to violence, however. Ulster's biggest nationalist party, the Social Democratic and Labour Party (SDLP), advocated a united Ireland through the democratic process. The SDLP was supported by most northern Catholics, and its leader, John Hume, was one of the architects of the peace process.

The British government had long held onto Northern Ireland in support of the Unionist majority, who wanted to remain British citizens. But in the mid-1990's, Britain declared that it would support the rights of the people of Northern Ireland to determine their own future, whether that meant that they would remain a part of the United Kingdom or not. Through the peace process, Britain also hoped to negotiate for the IRA's disarmament.

The Republic of Ireland was interested in Northern Ireland becoming a part of Ireland. It had a formal claim to the territory of the whole island of Ireland written into its Constitution in 1937. And because Roman Catholicism was the official religion, the Irish government also felt obliged to support the Catholic minority in the North—though not through the extremist measures of the IRA.

Although it was not a key player, the United States government also played a role in the peace process. The Clinton Administration was sensitive to the interests of Irish Americans, many of whom sympathized with the northern Catholics. On Oct. 3, 1994, the Administration lifted its ban on official contacts with Sinn Féin, and later gave Sinn Féin permission to raise funds in the United States, despite strong objections from the British government. But the United States also applied pressure on Sinn Féin to persuade the IRA to give up its arms. It further initiated a drive for industrial investment in Northern Ireland that could bring economic opportunities to the region. The Clinton Administration recog-

1968

Bloody riots broke out in Northern Ireland

after the government tried to stop a civil rights demonstration. Demonstrators had been protesting discrimination against Catholics in housing, employment, and other areas.

1969

British troops were sent to restore order in Northern Ireland

after recurring riots. The IRA took up the cause of the Catholics and began fighting British soldiers and committing terrorist acts.

1985

Anglo-Irish Agreement was signed

by the United Kingdom and the Republic of Ireland, giving the Irish government an advisory role in Northern Ireland's affairs. The IRA and the Unionists, mostly Protestants in favor of maintaining union with the UK, opposed the agreement.

nized that economic growth was central to the peace effort. If people had steady jobs and home ownership, the Administration contended, they would be less likely to resort to violence.

Determining the path to peace

Even before the cease-fires by the IRA and the loyalist terrorists had gone into effect, the weary parties involved in the conflict had begun to search for a settlement that would bring about peace. In 1993, the British government had secret contacts with the IRA. Secret talks between Adams and Hume led to an announcement in September 1993 of a set of principles for peace, in which the IRA would give up its terrorist tactics and Sinn Féin would be included in future peace talks.

On Dec. 14, 1993, in the Downing Street Declaration, the British and Irish governments announced their own set of principles for peace talks. They stated that it was for the people of Ireland alone to determine their political future. Britain declared that it had no strategic or economic interest in Northern Ireland, and Dublin announced it would drop its claim to Northern Ireland if there were an overall settlement.

A framework document launched on Feb. 22, 1995, contained the British and Irish governments' joint proposals for all-party talks on the future of Northern Ireland. Among the key elements to be discussed was the proposal for joint Irish and Northern Irish bodies

1995

The British and Irish governments proposed a framework for peace talks,

by which the British and Irish governments and various political parties would try to determine the region's future. The results of these talks would be put to the people of Northern Ireland and of Ireland in separate referendum votes. In the meantime, tourists who had avoided the area during *the Troubles* flocked to Northern Ireland in 1995, and citizens of the region enjoyed a taste of peace.

1994

The IRA announced a cease-fire,

and Protestant paramilitary groups followed suit. Negotiations for the peace process began between the British and Irish governments and various political parties.

1993

The Downing Street Declaration,

a set of principles for peace talks, was announced by Britain and Ireland. It was designed to bring about peace talks that would include Sinn Féin if the IRA agreed to renounce violence. Sinn Féin was considered the political wing of the IRA.

late 1980's-early 1990's

Terrorist bombings by the IRA intensified

in Northern Ireland and mainland Britain and spread to continental Europe, where British military personnel and their families were targeted. Protestant terrorist groups countered the attacks with violent action.

An imbalance of power and prosperity

For many years, the rate of unemployment among Catholics has been at least twice that of Protestants. And of the 17 people representing Northern Ireland in the British parliament, only 4 are Catholic, even though Catholics make up more than a third of the population.

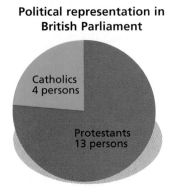

Political representation in British Parliament

Catholics 4 persons

Protestants 13 persons

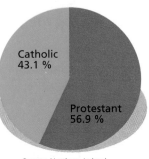

Population of Northern Ireland

Catholic 43.1 %

Protestant 56.9 %

Source: Northern Ireland Census 1991.

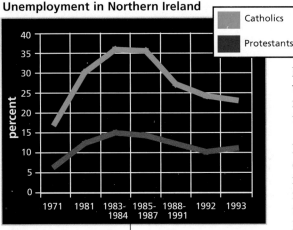

Unemployment in Northern Ireland

Catholics

Protestants

Sources: Northern Ireland Census, Northern Ireland Continuous Household Survey.

known as "cross-border" institutions that would be set up to boost trade and investment and to oversee such areas as agriculture, tourism, and health.

A three-phase process was envisaged. First, there would be talks among the political parties of Northern Ireland to agree on a form of regional self-government—perhaps in the form that Northern Ireland had before the British government began to rule from London. The next round of talks would take place between the Irish government and the political parties of Northern Ireland. And finally, negotiations would be held between the British and Irish governments. The results of these talks would be put to referendums in Northern Ireland and the Republic of Ireland.

But the peace process moved painfully slow. Initially, the British government refused to allow Sinn Féin to take part in peace talks until the IRA had announced that the cease-fire was permanent. Britain argued that it could not conduct negotiations with a party that retained the means to revert to violence. But the IRA refused to disarm. Then in October 1994, Britain dropped this condition, and announced that it accepted as a "working assumption" that the cease-fire was permanent.

On Dec. 9, 1994, the first officially sanctioned, publicly announced talks took place between Sinn Féin and British officials. Sinn Féin said problems in Northern Ireland would not be solved until Britain pulled out of the region. Britain argued that the IRA must give up its weapons before Sinn Féin would be allowed to negotiate on the same basis as the other parties. This British position also was gradually changed, and on May 10, 1995, the first open talks in 73 years between a British minister and Sinn Féin took place when Michael Ancram, the deputy minister for Northern Ireland, met a Sinn Féin delegation headed by Martin McGuinness, one of Adams's senior aides. The talks were described as "exploratory," and Britain said they would remain at this level until some or all IRA and Protestant paramilitary weapons were handed over.

A political settlement remained elusive. The British government was walking a tightrope. It had to avoid antagonizing the Unionists without whose support a settlement was impossible, and it had to include Sinn Féin in peace talks or any negotiations would be meaningless. The British government hoped to get around the IRA's unwillingness to disarm by suggesting a "token" surrender of weapons or by handing the matter over to an international commission.

The Ulster Unionists also presented a roadblock in the peace process. In early February, the Unionists, who had denounced the cross-border proposals as a "dishonorable blueprint for a united Ireland," threatened to boycott the proposed first phase of the negotiations because they felt Britain had made too many concessions to Sinn Féin. Then, in August 1995, the head of the UUP, James Molyneaux, regarded as an influential moderate among Northern Irish Protestants, unexpectedly resigned. Molyneaux had come under attack for failing to resist British pressures to speed up contacts with Sinn Féin. His successor, David Trimble, was expected to take a harder line toward the peace process.

Political uncertainties in the British Parliament also complicated matters. The peace process was closely identified with Major personally, and although he was widely praised for his boldness, his popularity was the lowest of any British prime minister since popularity polls began in the 1930's.

Meanwhile, the people of Northern Ireland began to enjoy a peace dividend. The British government introduced measures to bring about a return to normalcy. In September 1994, it lifted a broadcasting ban on Sinn Féin, and in February 1995, it allowed Sinn Féin leaders to travel to the British mainland. A gradual withdrawal of the security apparatus of 30,000 police and troops also began, and the British army ended street patrols.

The peace in the north produced an upturn in business confidence. Foreign tourists and many southern Irish who had avoided the area during *the Troubles* flocked to Northern Ireland in 1995. These developments helped build popular support for the peace process. After years of strife, many leaders in the north and south hoped that this taste of peace would prove to be a durable foundation for the long and difficult negotiations to come. ■ ■ ■

What's at stake in the peace process

- **The Protestants** want the region to remain a part of the United Kingdom. They fear losing economic subsidies from Britain and becoming a minority in a united Catholic Ireland.

- **The Catholics** seek a unified Ireland. After centuries of economic and political discrimination, many Catholics in Northern Ireland think they will only achieve their civil rights through unity with the Republic of Ireland.

- **Sinn Féin**, the political arm of the IRA, supports a unified Ireland. Among its chief goals in the peace process are the removal of British troops from Northern Ireland, the release of prisoners jailed for terrorist offenses, and the disbandment of the Royal Ulster Constabulary, a police force dominated by Protestants.

- **The British government** wants an end to terrorism in Northern Ireland and against British citizens throughout Europe. Britain has declared that it will support the rights of the people of Northern Ireland to determine their own future, even if they decide to secede from the United Kingdom.

- **The Republic of Ireland** is interested in a unified Ireland. But to achieve a final peace in the region, it is willing to remove from its constitution a claim to Northern Ireland. The Irish Republic also seeks an end to the terrorist activities of the IRA and the Protestant paramilitary groups.

Norway. The government of Norway in 1995 worked to maintain its economic and political links with the rest of Western Europe in the wake of the rejection by voters in November 1994 of membership in the European Union (EU). The country's main ties with Europe, through its trading partners in the European Free Trade Association (EFTA), were greatly diminished when Sweden, Finland, and Austria left the group to enter the EU on Jan. 1, 1995. Norway continued to work with its remaining EFTA partners—Iceland, Switzerland and Liechtenstein—to manage economic relations with the EU. It also agreed to hold periodic meetings with EU officials.

Norwegians themselves showed little regret about their decision to opt out of EU membership. An opinion poll in May showed that 56 percent of Norway's citizens opposed EU membership. That compared with an opposition vote of about 52 percent in November 1994.

Economic growth continues. The country's oil-rich economy continued to boom in 1995. Economic output grew at an estimated rate of more than 4 percent. On October 4, Finance Minister Sigbjorn Johnsen presented a draft budget that projected a budget surplus of $1.55 billion in 1996. He said the money would be put into a savings fund for when the country's North Sea oil runs out.

Far right makes gains in election. The right-wing Progress Party captured about 12 percent of the vote in municipal elections on Sept. 11, 1995, up from 7 percent in 1991. The governing Labor Party of Prime Minister Gro Harlem Brundtland polled 31.4 percent of the vote, up one point from 1991.

Immigration was a dominating issue in the campaign, though only about 1 percent of the population is of non-European origin. The Progress Party accused immigrants of bringing a number of social ills to Norway, including AIDS and organized crime. Among their goals was the deportation of any foreigner sentenced to more than three months in prison and the abolition of free legal advice to foreigners seeking asylum in Norway.

Flood damage. Heavy rains and a late snow runoff combined in early June to produce the country's worst flooding in more than 200 years. The floods, which hit hardest in rural areas northeast of Oslo, caused at least $350 million in damage.

Oil rig finds a home. Norway in July agreed to house the North Sea oil platform, the Brent Spar, for one year in one of its fiords to give oil company Shell U.K. Limited time to figure out how to dispose of the rig. Shell had abandoned plans to dump the platform in the North Atlantic after strong opposition from environmental groups.   □ Tom Buerkle

See also **Europe** (Facts in brief table). In *World Book,* see European Union; Norway.

Nova Scotia. See **Canadian provinces.**

Nuclear energy. See **Energy supply.**

Nutrition. See **Food.**

Ocean. The area of ocean covered with ice at Earth's poles appears to be shrinking. That finding was announced in October 1995 by oceanographer Ola Johannessen and his colleagues at the Nansen Remote Sensing Center in Bergen, Norway. The researchers based their finding on satellite data collected between 1978 and 1994.

According to the researchers, Arctic ice appears to be shrinking at a greater rate than Antarctic ice. Arctic ice, they said, decreased by about 2.5 percent from 1978 through 1987 and at a rate equal to 4.3 percent per decade from 1987 to 1994. Antarctic sea ice decreased by about 1.4 percent per decade during the same periods.

The researchers noted that the observed difference between the rate of ice loss at the two polar regions was consistent with some computer model projections of *global warming* (a predicted rise in Earth's average temperature as a result of an increase in heat-trapping gases in the atmosphere). The scientists cautioned, however, that it is too early to tell whether the declines in polar sea ice represent a long-term trend.

Ocean fertilization. In June 1995, for the second time in two years, scientists succeeded in fertilizing a large patch of the Pacific Ocean by dumping iron into the water. The first such experiment was conducted in October 1993 near the Galapagos Islands. The latest experiment took place between Tahiti and the Galapagos Islands.

In both experiments, scientists wanted to determine why algae grow so poorly in the sunny, nutrient-rich waters of the equatorial Pacific. They suspected that algae in those waters might be deficient in iron, a mineral important for cell growth. To test that theory, investigators dumped a dilute iron solution into a patch of ocean several square miles in extent.

They found that the iron produced a "stupendous" increase in the growth of algae. The scientists theorized that ocean fertilization might help limit the buildup of carbon dioxide in the atmosphere by increasing the amount of algae in the sea. The algae, through the process of *photosynthesis*—in which plants use sunlight, water, and carbon dioxide to make food—would take in some of the millions of tons of heat-trapping carbon dioxide that spew into the atmosphere each year from the combustion of *fossil fuels* (coal, oil, and natural gas). Many scientists believe that the continued buildup of carbon dioxide in the atmosphere could be contributing to global warming.

Fishing treaty. More than 90 nations in August 1995 agreed to the first-ever treaty to regulate fishing in international waters. The United Nations-sponsored Straddling Fish Stocks and Highly Migratory Fish Stocks Treaty was to become effective when the national legislatures of 30 of the signatories ratified it.

A New Zealander watches as an underwater volcano erupting in the Tonga islands of the South Pacific Ocean in June forms a new island.

The treaty set fishing quotas on sought-after species such as turbot and tuna when they migrate into international waters from the territorial waters of individual nations. The quotas were designed to preserve such species from overfishing. (See also **Conservation** Special Report: **Have We Fished Out the Sea?**) The treaty also mandated a minimum mesh size for nets to keep undersized fish from getting snared by accident and established procedures to resolve fishing disputes on the high seas.

Gold-laden submarine found. On May 2, a search team lead by Paul Tidwell, an American oceanic researcher, found a treasure-laden Japanese submarine, the *I-52*. A United States Navy bomber had torpedoed the submarine on June 23, 1944, about 1,100 miles (1,800 kilometers) west of the Cape Verde Islands in the Atlantic Ocean. The *I-52* sank carrying 2.2 tons (2 metric tons) of gold to Nazi-held France to trade for German war technology.

Salvagers located the *I-52* at a depth of 17,000 feet (5,200 meters). Tidwell's team used newly de-classified notes from the U.S. National Archives on the *I-52*'s position, along with military sonars aboard the Russian research ship *Yuzhmorgeologiya*, to locate the sunken vessel. ☐ Arthur G. Alexiou

In *World Book,* see **Ocean.**

Ohio. See State government.
Oklahoma. See State government.
Old age. See Social security.

Olympic Games. In June 1995, the International-al Olympic Committee (IOC) awarded the Winter Olympics for the year 2002 to Salt Lake City, Utah. Salt Lake City won on the first ballot, receiving 54 votes to 14 for Ostersund, Sweden; 14 for Sion, Switzerland; and 7 for Quebec City, Canada. In 1991, Salt Lake City lost to Nagano, Japan, for the 1998 Winter Games, and it had bid unsuccessfully for the Winter Games three other times since 1965.

Seven weeks after Salt Lake City's successful bid, the National Broadcasting Company (NBC) won the U.S. television rights to two Olympics—the 2000 Summer Games in Sydney, Australia, and the 2002 Winter Games in Salt Lake City—for a total of $1.27-billion. While other networks awaited the formal bidding process, NBC made a preemptive offer, which the IOC accepted. NBC agreed to pay $715-million for the Sydney rights and $555 million for the Salt Lake City rights.

On Dec. 12, 1995, the IOC accepted NBC's $2.3-billion bid to televise the 2004 Summer, 2006 Winter, and 2008 Summer Olympics. The deal was the richest in television sports history and preempted bidding from any other networks. ☐ Frank Litsky

In *World Book,* see **Olympic Games.**

Oman. See Middle East.
Ontario. See Canadian provinces.
Opera. See Classical music.
Oregon. See State government.

Pacific Islands

Pacific Islands. On June 13, 1995, French President Jacques Chirac announced that France would resume nuclear testing in its territory of French Polynesia in the Pacific Ocean. France had conducted 175 nuclear tests in French Polynesia between 1966 and 1991, but beginning in April 1992, it had observed a self-imposed moratorium on nuclear testing. Chirac said the first of a series of eight tests would begin on Mururoa Atoll in September 1995 and the last would be conducted in May 1996 at the latest. He said computer simulations were not a satisfactory alternative for France to be assured of its nuclear deterrent capability. At once, environmentalists and antinuclear activists worldwide protested.

The first weapon was detonated deep in the ocean floor at Mururoa Atoll on Sept. 5, 1995. The test triggered rioting in Papeete, Tahiti, the capital of French Polynesia. Antinuclear activists and members of the territory's independence movement were joined by large numbers of disgruntled, unemployed youths. Eventually, 2,000 rioters vandalized much of Papeete's commercial center, looting and destroying shops and burning cars. The international airport suffered heavy damage and was shut down. Authorities brought in French Foreign Legionnaires to quell the disturbance. Tourism, Tahiti's most important industry, came to a standstill. Elsewhere, Australia and New Zealand recalled their ambassadors from Paris. The Pacific Island nations of Kiribati, Nauru, and Tuvalu severed diplomatic relations with France.

The South Pacific Forum, the most influential organization in the region, unanimously condemned France during its meeting in Papua New Guinea in September. Chirac was undeterred, however, and announced that France would agree to a comprehensive nuclear test-ban treaty only after the completion of the tests. In October, France set off two more nuclear devices—one at Mururoa and the other at a neighboring atoll.

The Republic of Palau celebrated the first anniversary of its independence on October 1. Palau, the last of the four members of the U.S. Trust Territory of the Pacific Islands, became a self-governing nation in free association with the United States on Oct. 1, 1994. People from a state in free association with America can freely enter the United States to live and work. Palau joined the United Nations on Dec. 15, 1994, and became the 16th member of the South Pacific Forum at its September meeting.

Papua New Guinea celebrated the 20th anniversary of its independence from Australia while it hosted the South Pacific Forum meeting. However, it could not celebrate a solution to the long-standing problem of separatists on Bougainville, a copper-rich island 500 miles (800 kilometers) northeast of the nation's capital, Port Moresby.

Bougainville has resisted being a part of Papua New Guinea since the nation's independence in 1975. In 1988, disputes over copper royalties and

France's nuclear tests in the Pacific

France resumed nuclear testing in its overseas territory of French Polynesia in September 1995, breaking a self-imposed test ban in effect since 1992. The first test touched off demonstrations in Papeete, Tahiti, the capital of French Polynesia. Riot police rounded up protesters at the international airport in Papeete in August, prior to the test, *right.* The airport later suffered heavy damage and was shut down when post-test demonstrations turned into rioting. The violence destroyed much of Papeete's commercial district and brought tourism to a standstill.

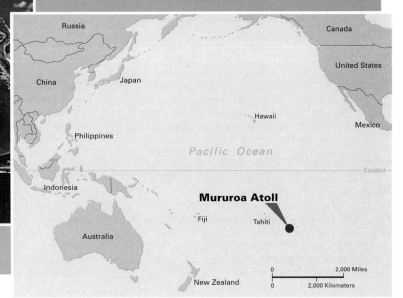

The first test of 1995 occurred on Mururoa Atoll, *left,* one of French Polynesia's more than 120 islands scattered over an area in the Pacific Ocean about the size of Western Europe, *below.* The nuclear device, reportedly with an explosive force equal to that of the atomic bomb the United States dropped on Hiroshima in 1945, was detonated in the deep ocean bed at the atoll. France set off two more nuclear devices in early October, the largest on an atoll near Mururoa. France said the testing would end in early 1996.

Russia

Canada

China

Japan

United States

Hawaii

Mexico

Philippines

Pacific Ocean

Equator

Indonesia

Mururoa Atoll

Fiji

Tahiti

Australia

0   2,000 Miles

New Zealand

0   2,000 Kilometers

Facts in brief on Pacific Island countries

Country	Population	Government	Monetary unit*	Foreign trade (million U.S.$)	
				Exports†	Imports†
Australia	18,058,000	Governor General Bill Hayden; Prime Minister Paul Keating	dollar (1.32 = $1)	47,556	53,414
Fiji	769,000	President Ratu Sir Kamisese Mara; Prime Minister Sitiveni Rabuka	dollar (1.42 = $1)	544	822
Kiribati	81,000	President Teburoro Tito	Australian dollar	5	37
Marshall Islands	57,000	President Amata Kabua	U.S. dollar	4	63
Micronesia, Federated States of	126,000	President Bailey Olter	U.S. dollar	3	91
Nauru	11,000	President Bernard Dowiyogo	Australian dollar	93	73
New Zealand	3,583,000	Governor General Dame Catherine Tizard; Prime Minister James B. Bolger	dollar (1.52 = $1)	12,184	11,902
Palau	17,000	President Kuniwo Nakamura	U.S. dollar	1	25
Papua New Guinea	4,443,000	Governor General Sir Wiwa Korowi; Prime Minister Sir Julius Chan	kina (1.32 = $1)	2,484	1,299
Solomon Islands	390,000	Governor General Moses Pitakaka; Prime Minister Solomon Mamaloni	dollar (3.46 = $1)	96	101
Tonga	100,000	King Taufa'ahau Tupou IV; Prime Minister Baron Vaea	pa'anga (1.26 = $1)	17	61
Tuvalu	13,000	Governor General Manuella Tulaga; Prime Minister Kamuta Latasi	Australian dollar	1	4
Vanuatu	173,000	President Jean Marie Leye; Prime Minister Maxime Carlot Korman	vatu (112.25 = $1)	24	82
Western Samoa	160,000	Head of State Malietoa Tanumafili II; Prime Minister Tofilau Eti Alesana	tala (2.51 = $1)	4	80

*Exchange rates as of Oct. 27, 1995, or latest available data. †Latest available data.

other grievances finally erupted in an armed revolt by the Bougainville Revolutionary Army. Papua New Guinea's defense force has occupied Bougainville ever since. Ongoing armed conflicts with a considerable loss of life continued in 1995, despite attempts by Australia to mediate the dispute. The government of Prime Minister Sir Julius Chan feared that any major success by Bougainville secessionists would trigger separatist movements in other island provinces of Papua New Guinea, including Manus, New Ireland, and New Britain.

Cultural and linguistic diversity remained one of Papua New Guinea's major problems in building a viable nation. Its 4.4 million people spoke more than 800 different languages, and loyalties remained at the village or local level. Approximately 80 percent of the people grew their own food and sold what little they did not need. Rural areas stopped receiving the most basic services from the 19 provincial governments. The governments, created at the time of independence to decentralize authority, finally proved too costly and inefficient, and the system was dismantled by mid-1995.

Port Moresby and other urban centers were also beset with problems. Increasing differences in wealth separated the business and political elite from the majority of the population. Migrant workers from rural areas clustered in squatter settlements around cities, and everywhere crime and unemployment rates were high. Violence and the threat of violence were common, and at times during 1995 the government imposed nighttime curfews.

Despite being rich in natural resources, Papua New Guinea was on the verge of financial collapse in 1995. Years of government overspending and corruption had taken its toll, and earnings from mineral and oil extraction were not used to develop sustainable industries in timber, fishing, and agriculture. In September, the government sought loans and other financial assistance from the World Bank and the International Monetary Fund for an economic recovery plan that extended to 1997. But by the end of 1995, Chan's administration had not shown the political will needed to address the nation's ills. Papua New Guinea's very existence as a nation was at stake.

Fiji. In June, Fiji's President Ratu Sir Kamisese Mara swore in a three-member commission to review the nation's racially biased 1990 Constitution. The controversial document guaranteed indigenous Fijians political supremacy over ethnic Indians, who made up 46 percent of Fiji's population. The Constitution required the head of state to be a Fijian chief. The commission was scheduled to submit its recommendations for change to President Mara by June 1996. □ Robert C. Kiste

In *World Book,* see **Pacific Islands.**
Painting. See Art.

Pakistan. Military authorities arrested at least 36 high-ranking officers—including a major general and a brigadier general—for plotting to overthrow the government of Prime Minister Benazir Bhutto in September 1995. The officers wanted to replace Bhutto's secular, democratic regime with an Islamic fundamentalist state, according to media reports. In October, the Lahore High Court banned further reporting of court proceedings involving the officers.

The army had ruled Pakistan for 25 of the 48 years since the Muslim nation was created out of sections of India in 1947. Over the 48 years, a growing number of officers supported an Islamic revolution to solve Pakistan's social and economic problems. Many Muslims had received military training, and in 1995 sects clashed violently.

Turmoil in Karachi. Ethnic and religious groups fought in Karachi, Pakistan's largest city. More than 1,600 people were killed in lawless chaos there during 1995. More than 900 had been killed in 1994.

The violence started in 1992, when the Mohajir Qaumi Movement (MQM) had been elected to govern the city, but the national government ousted it. The MQM united Muslims who had migrated to Pakistan from India in 1947, when Pakistan was created out of sections of northern India. Many of Karachi's 12 million people were mohajirs, but they said they were discriminated against in employment and education. Young mohajirs had turned to violence, and other groups struck back. The government accused the MQM of using terrorism against officials in an effort to gain political control of the city. Militant mohajirs killed more than 200 police and paramilitary troops in 1995. In turn, the MQM accused the government of trying to eliminate their influence.

Negotiations on giving the MQM a political role in Karachi made little headway in 1995. The situation was complicated by Pakistani accusations that India encouraged the violence. India believed Pakistan was backing guerrillas who fought in the two-thirds of Jammu and Kashmir state that India controlled. Pakistan controlled the remaining third. Each nation had claimed Kashmir since 1947.

Death sentence for blasphemy. A 14-year-old Christian boy and his uncle were convicted on Feb. 9, 1995, of writing blasphemous graffiti against Muhammad, the founder of Islam, on a mosque wall. They were given the mandatory sentence of hanging. But on February 23, a court dismissed the charge, saying there was no evidence to support it. In 1994, Muslim militants had killed a third person charged in the case who was out on bail.

Americans killed. On March 8, 1995, two Americans working at the United States consulate in Karachi were killed in a well-planned ambush of their commuter van. The killers and the motive remained unclear at year-end. □ Henry S. Bradsher

See also **Asia** (Facts in brief). In **World Book,** see **Pakistan.**

A boy and his uncle, both Christians, leave a Pakistani court in February after receiving death sentences—later dismissed—for writing blasphemous graffiti on a mosque wall.

Paleontology. Research in 1995 provided missing details about the transition between the Permian and Triassic periods, some 250 million years ago. This interval, called the Permo-Triassic (P-T) boundary, was the time of the greatest mass extinction in the history of marine life. Unfortunately, in most parts of the world, the geologic record is marked by gaps at the P-T boundary, so details of the mass extinction have been obscured. In November 1994, however, paleontologists had described fossils from near the boundary in China indicating that up to 80 percent of marine species were killed off at the end of the Permian. The scientists also documented a short-lived mass extinction that occurred 5 million years earlier.

In January 1995, paleontologist Gregory Retallack of the University of Oregon in Eugene reported evidence that the Permo-Triassic extinctions affected *terrestrial* (land-dwelling) plants as well as marine life. Retallack observed in Australia that fossils of a diverse array of seed-bearing ferns suddenly disappeared at the boundary. They were replaced by a relatively small number of conifer and moss species.

Scientists have proposed several hypotheses to account for the P-T extinctions. One possibility is that intense volcanic activity raised clouds of ash that blocked the sun, abruptly cooling the climate. Support for this theory came in September, when geologists Paul Renne of the Berkeley Geochronolo-

327

Paleontology

gy Center in California and Asish R. Basu of the University of Rochester in New York reported that massive outpourings of volcanic rock in Siberia date to the time of the P-T extinctions. Volcanic ash beds in China at the P-T boundary yield precisely the same age of 250 million years. The injection of immense quantities of volcanic ash and gases into the atmosphere may have darkened the globe and lowered temperatures, driving many species to extinction.

Clams and the K-T extinction. Another study in 1995 focused on the more famous, though less severe, mass extinction of the Cretaceous-Tertiary (K-T) boundary, about 65 million years ago. In April, David Jablonski and David M. Raup, paleontologists at the University of Chicago, published the results of a statistical comparison of clams that became extinct 65 million years ago versus those that survived the mass extinction. Surprisingly, they found that clams did not follow the expected patterns regarding which species were more susceptible to extinction. For example, clam species that lived in a wide range of environments were just as likely to become extinct as species that could survive in only one environment.

Thus, characteristics that normally protect species from extermination may be less effective in times of global catastrophe. In the case of the K-T extinctions, many paleontologists believe that catastrophe was an asteroid impact with the Earth.

Evolution and mountain building. The upheaval of mountains may have helped diversify marine animal species, according to studies summarized in April by Arnold Miller and Shuguang Mao, paleontologists at the University of Cincinnati. Miller and Mao surveyed marine fossils from different environments of the Ordovician Period (about 500 million to 435 million years ago). They demonstrated that fossils were more diverse in shallow muddy seas next to active mountain belts than in cleaner limestone deposits in geologically stable areas. The researchers speculated that certain factors related to geologic activity stimulate evolution. For example, the release of nutrients from eroding mountains or the disruption of environments due to mountain building may trigger the rapid rise of new species.

Gigantic *Giganotosaurus*. *Tyrannosaurus rex,* probably the most famous of all dinosaurs, was long considered the largest land-dwelling predator of all time. But a somewhat older dinosaur discovered in 1995 now holds that title. In September, Argentinian paleontologists described the partial skeletal remains of the huge dinosaur, called *Giganotosaurus carolinii,* found in Patagonia in southern Argentina.

The sediments containing the skeleton date from the middle Cretaceous Period, about 100 million years ago. The new meat-eater is the largest known predatory dinosaur, with an estimated length of 41 feet (12.5 meters) and a weight of 7 to 9 tons (6 to 8 metric tons). □ Carlton E. Brett

In *World Book,* see **Paleontology.**

Pan American Games. The United States, which had dominated this Western Hemisphere Olympic-style competition since it began in 1951, broke the records for gold medals and total medals in 1995. The quadrennial games March 8 to 26 in Mar del Plata, Argentina, attracted more than 7,000 athletes from 42 nations. The United States sent the most athletes, 746, but some of its teams were weak. Its baseball team, from St. John's University in Jamaica, New York, lost all six games. Its soccer team lost its three games and did not score a goal.

Still, the United States won 169 gold medals, 146 silver, and 109 bronze for a total of 424. Next were Cuba with 238 (112-66-60), and Canada with 177 (48-60-69). The U.S. women's basketball team might have won a medal, but the competition was canceled because only four nations entered (the rules required at least five).

The gold medalists from the United States included Roger Kingdom, Lance Deal, and Kim Batten in track and field; Tom Jager, Jeff Rouse, and Angel Martino in swimming; Shannon Miller in gymnastics, and Bruce Baumgartner in wrestling. □ Frank Litsky

In *World Book,* see Pan American Games.

Panama. See Latin America.

Papua New Guinea. See Asia; Pacific Islands.

Paraguay. See Latin America.

Pennsylvania. See Philadelphia; State government.

Peru. On April 9, 1995, Peruvian President Alberto Fujimori, 56, of the Change 90/New Majority coalition was elected to a second five-year term. He was inaugurated on July 28. Fujimori's success in guiding Peru's 1994 economic growth to a rate of 12 percent—the highest in the world—bolstered his political standing. He also gained high marks for his skillful handling of a brief but bloody border conflict with Ecuador in January and February 1995.

On June 16, Fujimori enacted a sweeping law providing amnesty for military, police, and civil officials accused of past human-rights abuses. The national Congress had approved the law two days earlier. Those pardoned included nine members of the military who had been convicted in 1994 of participating in the 1992 murder of nine students and a professor at Enrique Guzmán y Valle University east of Lima, the capital.

The Shining Path rebels, whose leader was jailed for life in 1992, proved that they were still capable of terrorist acts in 1995. The police said they suspected the Shining Path of planting a car bomb that went off on May 24 in Lima, killing 4 people and wounding 60 others. On July 20, members of the same guerrilla force killed 16 Peruvian soldiers in the Upper Huallaga Valley in northern Peru.

□ Nathan A. Haverstock

See also **Latin America** (Facts in brief table). In *World Book,* see **Peru.**

Petroleum and gas. The world's thirst for petroleum continued to grow in 1995. That growth was expected to continue for a third straight year in 1996, barring a major economic slump. Until 1994, demand for oil had been flat because oil prices escalated during the Persian Gulf War (1991), which threatened the prolific oil fields of that region.

The world demand for oil rose more than 1.6 percent in 1995, pushing total consumption to nearly 70 million barrels a day. That amount exceeded 1994's level by more than 1 million barrels a day, and experts projected 1996 consumption to reach more than 71 million barrels a day.

The fast-growing nations of Asia accounted for much of the growth in world oil demand. In some Asian countries, fuel needs shot up by as much as 10 percent a year because of booming economies. Petroleum consumption also grew, though at more modest rates, in some European nations.

Low fuel prices. After adjusting for taxes and inflation, 1995 prices in the United States for fuels such as gasoline were the cheapest on record. Low prices came about mainly because the world's oil production kept pace with the rising demand for oil. Prices of West Texas Intermediate crude oil, the U.S. grade used as a benchmark, ranged between $17 and $18 a barrel for much of 1995. There are 42 gallons (159 liters) in a barrel.

Natural gas prices in most of 1995 were well below the $1.83 per 1,000 cubic feet (28 cubic meters) that U.S. producers had averaged in 1994, dropping at one point to $1.50 at the wellhead. But late in 1995, prices moved up to $2.00 as weather experts forecast a colder-than-average winter.

Industry officials generally did not expect much change in prices of oil and gas for 1996. "We are forecasting an $18 [a barrel] flat oil price for the next couple of years," Kenneth T. Derr, chairman of Chevron Corp. of San Francisco, told reporters at the November 1995 meeting of the American Petroleum Institute in Houston. Derr, who headed the institute, estimated an average of $1.80 to $1.85 per 1,000 cubic feet for 1996 natural gas prices.

OPEC versus the world. Frustrated by their inability to obtain a targeted price of $21 a barrel for their oil, member nations of the Organization of Petroleum Exporting Countries (OPEC) continued holding down their output of crude oil in hopes of forcing up petroleum prices. However, some OPEC nations cheated on the voluntary production quotas, and although analysts estimated 1995 demand for OPEC's oil at about 25 million barrels a day, the organization's total output exceeded that amount. Seven Middle Eastern nations plus Gabon, Indonesia, Libya, Nigeria, and Venezuela make up the 12 member nations of OPEC.

Meanwhile, non-OPEC oil supplies surged in 1995, despite slowing American and Russian production. The United States and Russia—the world's second- and third-largest oil producers—kept output down in 1995. Those two countries ranked behind only Saudi Arabia, the OPEC top producer.

Record volumes of oil from drilling facilities in the North Sea, and rising output from parts of South America and other new finds, contributed to the overflow. These non-OPEC supplies were more than enough to satisfy the world's high oil demand, keeping a lid on petroleum prices and adding to the gloomy outlook for OPEC.

Oil ministers of the OPEC nations agreed at their winter meeting in November 1995 to maintain the ceiling on production levels in 1996. However, even their own economists joined with other oil experts in projecting that there would be further rises in non-OPEC oil supplies.

One member nation, Iraq, cast another shadow over OPEC in 1995. Iraq wanted to resume oil exports that had been banned by the United Nations (UN) after Iraq invaded Kuwait in 1990. Some oil analysts insisted that Iraqi oil was unlikely to reenter world oil markets for yet another year. But late in 1995, it seemed that Iraq might be moving to accept UN conditions for an emergency sale of oil in 1996. Because of deteriorating economic conditions within Iraq, the UN had offered several times to permit the Iraqis to hold a one-time oil sale to finance the purchase of food and medicine.

Within OPEC, the oil ministers insisted that once

Peruvian President Alberto Fujimori shakes hands with supporters after voting in presidential balloting in April. Fujimori was easily reelected.

the UN lifted its sanctions against Iraq, they would immediately hold an emergency meeting to reallocate production quotas and make room for Iraqi oil. In any event, if oil consumption continued to grow as expected, Iraqi oil eventually would be needed to meet world demand.

American gas guzzlers. Demand for oil remained high among the world's leading oil consumers as American motorists continued using gasoline in record volumes. Gas consumption in the United States averaged 7.7 million barrels a day in the first 10 months of 1995, up 1.6 percent from the same months of 1994. By November 1995, gasoline use had climbed to nearly 8.5 million barrels a day, an unusually high level of demand for that late in the year. Normally, gasoline use declines after Labor Day, which marks the end of the heavy American driving season.

The escalating use of gasoline came despite controversies over a new type of fuel, required by the U.S. Clean Air Act of 1990, meant to reduce pollution from automobile emissions. In January 1995, refiners introduced the cleaner-burning fuel, called "reformulated" gasoline. Gas companies had been reluctant to produce the fuel because it meant costly modifications to refineries. But they made the changes and complied with the Clean Air Act.

Reformulated gasoline generally drew little attention, even though drivers got fewer miles per gallon with it and paid as much as 15 cents a gallon more for it. But in some cities, people complained that the gas had an unpleasant odor and cost too much. Some people also claimed that the fumes given off by the gas had made them ill.

The biggest controversy erupted in the Milwaukee area, where reformulated gasoline was required for six Wisconsin counties, and several hundred complaints were made to state and federal agencies. The number of complaints dwindled, however, as the year progressed and prices leveled out.

Natural gas, a clean-burning fuel, continued to gain in use around the world. Supplies of natural gas remained ample as new fields were developed in Asian nations and other areas. These fields provided the fuel required for use in the generation of electricity to feed the world's growing power needs.

In the first eight months of 1995, according to the U.S. Department of Energy, Americans consumed 14.5 trillion cubic feet (410.6 billion cubic meters) of gas. That was up from 14.1 trillion cubic feet (399.2 billion cubic meters) in the same period of 1994.

United States gas production reached nearly 12.7 trillion cubic feet (359.6 billion cubic meters) in the first eight months of 1995. That compared to 12.5 trillion cubic feet (353.9 billion cubic meters) in the same months of 1994. Gas imports from Canada made up the supply difference, as the U.S. demand for gas continued to rise. □ James Tanner

In *World Book*, see Gas; Petroleum.

Philadelphia. One of the worst police scandals in Philadelphia history occurred in 1995. Six officers of the 39th District in North Philadelphia, a neighborhood of poor and mostly black residents, pleaded guilty during the year to faking evidence, framing innocent people, and stealing drugs and money. Federal indictments charged the six officers with offenses including searching homes with phony warrants, planting drugs, holding guns to suspects' heads, falsifying arrests in order to get overtime pay for court testimony, and lying in court.

As a result of the indictments, authorities began a review of 1,400 arrests made by the six officers, and by year-end more than 40 drug convictions had been thrown out. In addition, 23 supervisors were transferred during the probe, and more arrests of police officers were expected. The investigation spread to the Philadelphia police force's elite unit, the Highway Patrol, where officials believed that officers stole drugs from dealers and then sold the drugs back to them.

The investigation that led to the arrest of the officers was a joint effort of the police department, the United States attorney's office, and the Federal Bureau of Investigation. The investigation was spurred by a complaint filed in 1991 by Arthur Colbert, a student at Temple University. According to Colbert, the police arrested him as a suspected drug dealer, took him to a house where crack cocaine was sold, threatened to kill him, and then locked him up at district headquarters while they illegally searched his apartment.

Police misconduct also occurred in other areas of the city. An officer was sentenced in September to 7 to 22 years in prison for stopping motorists for minor infractions and forcing them to give him money. A decorated Highway Patrol veteran was fired in August after he was charged with attacking a couple who said they discovered him having sex with a boy in a van. And investigators were trying to determine whether a group of policemen had beaten a man who died in May shortly after he was arrested.

Charity bankruptcy. One of the nation's largest charities, the Foundation for New Era Philanthropy, based in the Philadelphia suburb of Radnor, filed for bankruptcy on May 15. The charity, run by its founder, John G. Bennett, Jr., had received donations from churches and schools around the nation, and from many Philadelphia cultural institutions. Investors had been led to believe that New Era would find wealthy donors to match their donations. Instead, the original investors were paid off with money from newer investors. Unable to match funds for the new investors, the charity collapsed. On September 26, U.S. Bankruptcy Court released documents showing that institutions filed over $725 million in claims against the charity. New Era's assets were estimated at about $30 million. Bennett denied any wrongdoing and no charges were filed against him.

Mob trial. The trial of reputed Philadelphia mob boss John Stanfa and seven associates began on September 27. Among the charges were murder, kidnapping, extortion, loan-sharking, and arson. Several mobsters, including former hit men, were among informants to federal prosecutors, who secretly recorded over 100 conversations involving mob business in the Philadelphia area. Stanfa and his associates were convicted on November 21. Stanfa was expected to be sentenced to life in prison.

John Wanamaker, the main department store named for the man who founded it in 1876, was purchased on August 28 in bankruptcy court by the May Department Stores Company, with an offer of $460 million. The Wanamaker stores had been owned since 1986 by Woodward & Lothrop, Incorporated, a Washington, D.C., department store company. The May Company changed the name of the 14 Wanamaker stores it purchased to Hecht's, the name of one of its store chains.

Democratic Mayor Edward G. Rendell was elected in November to a second term. Rendell easily defeated Republican challenger Joseph Rocks.

The heat wave that spread over much of the Northeastern United States in 1995 was responsible for the death of 71 Philadelphians and 16 suburban residents. On July 15, the temperature in Philadelphia reached 103 °F (39 °C).   □ Howard S. Shapiro

See also **City.** In *World Book,* see **Philadelphia.**

Philippines. Voters in the May 1995 midterm elections for Congress gave President Fidel V. Ramos a weak vote of confidence. In the Senate, 12 of 24 seats were up for election, and Ramos candidates won 9. In the House of Representatives, all 204 seats were up for election, and Ramos held on to his two-thirds majority.

Ramos's party, Lakas-National Union of Christian Democrats, and the party of Senate President Edgardo Angara, Laban ng Demokratikong Pilipino (Struggle of Filipino Democrats—LDP), had signed an agreement in 1994 to share a slate of Senate seats in the 1995 elections. By this means, Ramos could prevent the LDP from continuing to block his economic program in the Congress. However, on Aug. 29, 1995, the Senate ousted Angara from its presidency, and many Filipinos believed that Ramos had engineered it. They thought he planned to amend the Constitution so he could run for a second presidential term, which the Constitution prohibited. Ramos said on September 6, however, that he would step down at the end of his term in 1998.

Fighting crime. Ramos personally took over the government's faltering anticrime campaign from Vice President Joseph Estrada in September 1995. Ramos began to prosecute criminal charges against some of the country's elite who previously appeared to be exempt from the law. The Philippines had a major crime problem that included kidnappings,

murders, and drug trafficking that involved members of the police and military.

The economy grew by about 6 percent during 1995, up from 5.1 percent in 1994, but the growth brought concerns over rising inflation. Ramos cut business restrictions and broke up monopolies in order to encourage foreign investment, which helped the nation produce electronics, textiles, and other products for export. Nevertheless, agricultural output remained low, and poverty was widespread.

Migrant workers trials. A 42-year-old Filipino maid was hanged in Singapore on March 17, 1995, after being convicted of a double murder committed in 1991. The woman had been charged with killing another Filipino maid and a 4-year-old boy in the murdered woman's care. Protesters in Manila who believed the condemned woman had been framed caused months of tension between the two countries. Then, on September 16, a 16-year-old Filipino maid working in the United Arab Emirates was sentenced to death for murdering her employer. A local court said he raped her before she stabbed him to death. The sentence was later reduced to a flogging and a year in jail. The trials called attention to the abuse migrant workers faced in wealthy nations that employed some 4.2 million Filipinos.

Civil war flared again in 1995 between government forces and Muslims seeking to form a separate religious state in the southern Philippines. The radical Moro Islamic Liberation Front (MILF) refused to quit fighting while the Moro National Liberation Front (MNLF) negotiated with the government for regional autonomy under a cease-fire agreement Ramos had signed with the MNLF in 1994. The MILF built up a jungle army estimated at 30,000 men, mostly in the central part of Mindanao island.

On April 4, 1995, about 200 radical Muslims of a splinter group called Abu Sayyaf (Sword of the Father) attacked Ipil, a town of 50,000 people, mostly Christian, on Mindanao. The men killed at least 47 people, burned buildings, and looted banks before escaping into the jungle. MNLF leader Nur Misuari said the attack was intended to disrupt peace talks.

Military spending increased after the Philippines in January 1995 discovered a Chinese naval garrison on Mischief Reef in the South China Sea. The reef is part of the Spratly Islands, which six nations, including the Philippines and China, were feuding over because of potential oil and natural gas deposits in the nearby seabed. (See **Asia.**) The Philippine's few naval vessels and jet fighter planes were obsolete. Thus, in February, Congress voted nearly $2 billion for the first five years of a 15-year plan to modernize the military.

Typhoon. The worst typhoon in a decade struck the Philippines in early November. The storm killed more than 700 people.   □ Henry S. Bradsher

See also **Asia** (Facts in brief table). In *World Book,* see **Philippines.**

Physics. The year 1995 saw two long-awaited discoveries in physics. In March, physicists at the Fermi National Accelerator Laboratory (Fermilab) near Batavia, Illinois, confirmed the existence of the top quark, the last of the 12 fundamental building blocks of matter to be discovered. Then in June, researchers affiliated with the National Institute of Standards and Technology and the University of Colorado at Boulder created a new phase of matter, the Bose-Einstein condensate.

Top quark confirmed. In April 1994, a team of scientists at Fermilab revealed that they had seen examples of what looked like top quarks, but they could not yet be sure. By March 1995, they had enough additional evidence to remove all doubt.

Top quarks belong to one of the two related families of matter particles, quarks and leptons. An atom, which consists of one or more electrons orbiting a central core of protons and neutrons, contains both kinds of fundamental particles. The electrons are leptons, while the protons and neutrons in the atomic nucleus are each made up of three quarks.

There are six kinds of quarks and six leptons. Only the lightest of these particles make up ordinary matter, because the heavier quarks and leptons are extremely unstable. But these particles can be created in *particle accelerators,* devices that accelerate particles to high speeds and then cause them to collide. The collision produces a shower of new particles as

the energy of the impact is converted to matter.

In March, Fermilab scientists reported that in their experiments, about one collision in a billion had produced top quarks. The physicists said that the top quark's mass was about 190 atomic mass units, making it by far the heaviest fundamental particle. Other experiments had suggested that there were no more quarks or leptons to be discovered, so the top quark closed the book on a quest that began in 1897, with the discovery of the electron.

A new phase of matter. In 1924, German-born physicist Albert Einstein, building on the work of Indian physicist Satyendranath Bose, predicted that a new state of matter could form at extremely low temperatures. Physicists named the predicted new phase of matter the Bose-Einstein condensate (BEC), and in June 1995, scientists finally achieved it.

Matter exists in only three phases under ordinary conditions—solid, liquid, and gas. According to Einstein's theory, the BEC is a peculiar consequence of the laws of quantum mechanics, which in part say there are restrictions to the energy of motion of atoms confined to a limited area.

At very low temperatures—less than a millionth of a degree above *absolute zero* (the lowest possible temperature)—there is little energy available, and a large fraction of the atoms will all have exactly the same small amount of energy. If there are enough atoms present, they then lose their individual identi-

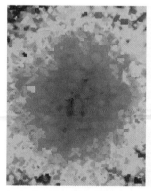

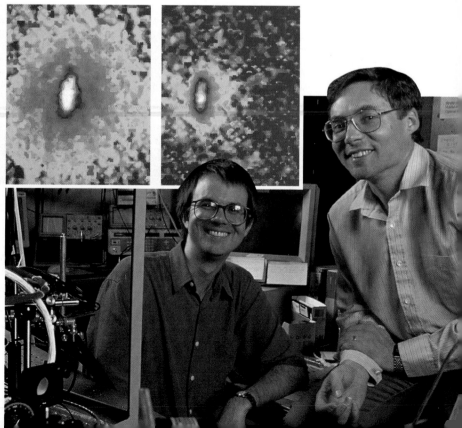

In June, two Colorado scientists, *right,* achieved a new state of matter called a Bose-Einstein condensate. Cooling rubidium atoms to nearly the lowest possible temperature caused them to form a single entity somewhat like a large "superatom." Video images, *above,* documented the appearance of the superatom.

ties and become part of a single unified entity somewhat like a large "superatom." That state is the BEC.

Temperature is a measure of the motion of atoms or molecules, so the Boulder team was able to cool rubidium atoms by holding them still in a magnetic trap, which makes particles hover in a vacuum between six poles of electromagnets. The atoms were further hemmed in by six converging laser beams. This procedure cooled the atoms to one-millionth of a degree above absolute zero.

To get the atoms even colder, the team created a leak in the magnetic trap that allowed the fastest atoms to escape, leaving the slower ones behind. When the overall temperature dropped to 20-billionths of a degree above absolute zero, a concentration of matter formed in the center of the trap. With further cooling, the concentration grew.

To prove that the central region was a BEC, the experimenters turned off the magnetic trap. Video images taken a few thousandths of a second after the release showed that atoms formed the pattern predicted by theory. Within weeks, the finding was confirmed by two other scientific groups.

The discovery opened a new field of research. While Einstein's theory predicted the existence of the BEC, it had little to say about its properties. Experts said that much more research would be required before the BEC is fully understood.   □ Robert H. March

In *World Book,* see **Physics.**

Poetry. The death of James Merrill at age 68 in February 1995 saddened poetry lovers. With the completion of his book-length poem *The Changing Light at Sandover* (1983), Merrill had established himself as the best-known and most admired poet in the United States. His final book, *A Scattering of Salts* (1995), was written with his usual style and wit, though reviewers detected, in some works, premonitions of his death.

New collections. John Ashbery's *Can You Hear, Bird* was welcomed by critic David Lehman as Ashbery's finest volume since *A Wave* (1984). Consider "My Philosophy of Life": "I'd sort of let things be what they are while injecting them with the serum of the new moral climate I thought I'd stumbled into, as a stranger accidentally presses against a panel and a bookcase slides back, revealing a winding staircase with a greenish light somewhere down below, and he automatically steps inside and the bookcase slides shut, as is customary on such occasions."

Stanley Kunitz, age 90, had long been the dean of American poetry, but *Passing Through: The Later Poems, New and Selected* made clear that he had not retired to a fireplace and mug of hot cocoa. Here, for instance, are the last lines of "Touch Me," ablaze with a lust for life: "What makes the engine go? Desire, desire, desire. The longing for a dance stirs in the buried life. One season only and it's done. So let the battered old willow thrash against the windowpanes and the house timbers creak. Darling, do you remember the man you married? Touch me, remind me who I am."

James Laughlin, well known as the founder-publisher of *New Directions* magazine, is also a poet of love and wit and memory. His 1995 volume, *The Country Road: New Poems,* included among its paeans to love numerous easygoing conversation poems, sips from what James Merrill once called Laughlin's "cool, unflavored spring."

William Bronk possesses an even more severe simplicity, and many of his best poems are only a few lines long. His *Selected Poems* covered a career ranging from 1949 to the present. Here is the opening of "Weathers We Live In": "One makes a poem as little as one makes the weather. One goes to the window and looks out and sees it there, outside. Read! We go out into it if we dare."

Jorie Graham's *The Dream of the Unified Field: Selected Poems 1971-1994* made a fit companion volume to critic Helen Vendler's *The Breaking of Style,* which reflected on the variety and depth of Graham's poetry (as well as that of Seamus Heaney, the winner of the 1995 Nobel Prize in literature). Although Graham's poems are philosophically serious, they are touched with rapture and horror.

Where Graham flies high toward the philosophical, Louis Simpson stays simple, earthy, and direct. In *There You Are,* Simpson told delicious stories of illicit romance, wistful memory, and funny speculation. In "An Academic Story," a professor has an affair that costs him tenure: "That was why he was at the MLA [Modern Language Association]. He was being interviewed at five by a man from upstate New York. They had a place for a lost soul somewhere in the Finger Lakes teaching rhetoric."

Other collections. In *Dark Fields of the Republic: Poems 1991-1995,* Adrienne Rich reflected on American history and culture—what it means, ultimately, to be an American. Her lines are loose and prosy, but her poems take their political and poetic inspiration not only from life but also from such diverse sources as jazz, German revolutionary Rosa Luxemburg, and the execution of convicted American spy Ethel Rosenberg. Roberto Polito's *Doubles* was an inviting book by a new young poet. Peter Davison, one of the best editors of modern poetry, is also an amiable, diverting poet. In the amazingly various *The Collected Poems of Peter Davison,* he explored identity, love, and religious conflict.

As fine as they were, these collections paled next to Donald Justice's *New and Selected Poems.* In each of the poems, the voice that rises is formal, elegant, perfectly cadenced. In his pages are poems with titles like "On a Painting by Patient B of the Independence State Hospital for the Insane," and even a poem about an unflushed urinal. Out of all these subjects, Justice created beauty.   □ Michael Dirda

In *World Book*, see **Poetry.**

Poland. On Nov. 5, 1995, President Lech Walesa, whose popular support had been slipping all year, was defeated by Alexander Kwasniewski, 41, a former Communist. After Poland's Communist government was ousted in 1989, Kwasniewski had helped form a new political organization, the Democratic Left Alliance. Along with the Polish Peasant Party, it had gained control of parliament in 1993. Kwasniewski's election represented a complete take-over of Poland's government by former Communists.

During much of the year, politics in Poland was dominated by conflict between Walesa and the parliament and within the governing coalition. In January, Walesa threatened to dissolve the parliament amid disagreements over who should control appointments to key Cabinet posts. The president and parliament also clashed over a new tax law and the budget. On March 1, parliament used a "constructive no-confidence vote" to replace Prime Minister Waldemar Pawlak with Jozef Oleksy, the speaker of the *Sejm* (the lower house of parliament). Walesa approved Oleksy's government on March 6 and the country's budget on March 7, resolving the crisis.

Relations with the Catholic Church remained troubled as parliament debated ratification of a 1993 agreement between the Vatican and the Walesa government, outlining the church's role in Polish society. This was one factor that prevented the completion of a draft of a new constitution in 1995.

Poland's economy continued to be among the strongest in the region. The country's gross domestic product was expected to grow by 6.5 percent and exports by 20 percent by year-end. Industrial production increased by 13 percent in the first half of 1995. Still, unemployment remained high, at more than 15 percent. In May, Polish leaders allowed the country's currency, the zloty, to find its own value relative to foreign currencies. Foreign investment in Poland increased by $1.07 billion during the first half of 1995.

Consumer prices rose by 113 percent in the first five months of 1995, and inflation was expected to average 28 percent for the year. In May, tractor and arms workers went on strike to protest economic hardships. Activists from the union Solidarity, which Walesa once led, staged protests in Silesia calling for more economic assistance to the region.

Walesa on July 17 vetoed a bill, passed by parliament on June 30, that would have given parliament a decisive role in the sale of state-owned companies to private buyers. Walesa said the measure would hinder the move toward the privatization of industry. But parliament overrode the veto on July 21.

In February, Polish leaders signed an agreement with Russia allowing a gas pipeline to be constructed across Poland, linking Russia and Western Europe.

☐ Sharon L. Wolchik

See also **Europe** (Facts in Brief table). In *World Book,* see **Poland.**

Pollution. See **Environmental pollution.**

Popular music once again became a target for public criticism in 1995, when Senate Majority Leader Robert J. Dole attacked the entertainment industry in a speech in Los Angeles on May 31 for "bombarding our children with destructive messages of casual violence and even more casual sex." Dole aimed most of his criticism of popular music at the musical style called "gangsta" rap, which often deals with stories of inner-city life, including boasts of involvement with violent crime.

Rock and Roll Hall of Fame. The Rock and Roll Hall of Fame opened on September 1 in Cleveland. The $92-million building was designed by architect I. M. Pei. Cleveland was chosen as the museum's site because it was there in 1952 that disc jockey Alan Freed popularized the term "rock and roll."

The hall displays a variety of exhibits, including stage costumes, sheet music, staging fixtures, and other artifacts that give a sense of the historical progression of rock music. Tributes will honor annual inductees into the Hall of Fame.

The opening of the Hall of Fame was accompanied by a concert on September 2 at Cleveland Stadium. The show featured cross-generational acts and lasted more than six hours. Highlights of the concert included Bruce Springsteen performing with both Chuck Berry and Bob Dylan, Soul Asylum backing Iggy Pop and Lou Reed, and Sheryl Crow paying tribute to the Rolling Stones.

Pearl Jam versus Ticketmaster. The popular Seattle band Pearl Jam in 1995 continued the campaign it began in 1994 against the powerful ticketing service Ticketmaster. The band charged that Ticketmaster used its monopoly position within the concert industry to add excessive service charges—typically about $3.50 to $7.50—to ticket prices. For its 1995 summer tour, Pearl Jam attempted to bypass the ticketing service, which had exclusive contracts with most major concert sites throughout the country, by scheduling 15 concerts in a variety of alternative locations. The band then sold tickets by phone through a smaller ticket service. It subsequently canceled the final nine tour dates because its lead singer, Eddie Vedder, became ill on tour and because of all the difficulties the band experienced with non-Ticketmaster concert sites.

An investigation begun in late 1994 by the United States Department of Justice into possible antitrust violations by Ticketmaster continued in 1995. But in July, after a series of hearings at which members of Pearl Jam testified, the Justice Department announced that it was dropping the investigation.

Death of Jerry Garcia. On August 9, Grateful Dead guitarist Jerry Garcia died in his sleep at a drug-treatment center in California. His death was attributed to natural causes. The 53-year-old musician had been battling a variety of physical ailments in recent years.

The veteran San Francisco band had become the

most successful touring act of the 1990's, despite the fact that it often went years between album releases and had only one Top 40 hit—1987's "Touch of Grey"—over the course of three decades. As news of Garcia's death spread, the band's legions of loyal fans known as "Deadheads," who followed the group from concert to concert, mourned what they feared was the end of the band as well as the loss of Garcia. In December, the band announced that it was breaking up.

Murder of Selena. On March 31, 23-year-old Selena Quintanilla Perez, the world's most popular singer of *Tejano* music (dance-oriented music recorded by Texans of Mexican descent) was murdered in Corpus Christi, Texas. News of the murder stunned the Mexican-American community and the world of music at large. Selena was in the process of recording an album of English-language pop music which was predicted to win her new fans. Yolanda Saldivar, founder of Selena's fan club and manager of two of her boutiques, was arrested and charged with shooting the singer at a Corpus Christi motel, where the two had reportedly met to discuss some irregularities in financial records. On October 23, a Houston jury convicted Saldivar of murdering Selena. On October 26, Saldivar was sentenced to life in prison.

The July release of *Dreaming of You*, which combined tracks in English with some of Selena's Spanish-language Tejano hits, became an immediate chart-topper. Music industry sources reported that it was the fastest-selling album by a female artist in American recording history.

Beatlemania was revived at the year's end with the broadcast of *The Beatles Anthology*, a six-hour documentary on the ABC television network. Also in late November was the release of the first of three double-CD sets of Beatles music. The first, called *The Beatles Anthology 1*, contains previously unreleased Beatles material, including the "new" Beatles song "Free as a Bird." The song was originally recorded by John Lennon in 1977. George Harrison, Paul McCartney, and Ringo Starr added their voices and lyrics to the track for the release of the album.

Michael Jackson, the self-proclaimed "King of Pop" returned to action with *HIStory: Past, Present and Future, Book 1,* a two-volume album featuring one disc of greatest hits and one of new material. After a media blitz to launch the album, including a widely televised interview with his wife, Lisa Marie, the album was considered a commercial disappointment when, contrary to expectations, it failed to dominate the sales charts.

Concert tours. The first tour in five years by R.E.M. highlighted the year's concert activity. But a series of health problems, including a brain aneurysm suffered by drummer Bill Berry, caused the

Yoko Ono, left center, and Little Richard, right center, celebrate at the gala opening of the Rock and Roll Hall of Fame in Cleveland in September.

Grammy Award winners in 1995

Record of the Year, "All I Wanna Do," Sheryl Crow.

Album of the Year, *MTV Unplugged,* Tony Bennett.

Song of the Year, "Streets of Philadelphia," Bruce Springsteen.

New Artist, Sheryl Crow.

Pop Vocal Performance, Female, "All I Wanna Do," Sheryl Crow.

Pop Vocal Performance, Male, "Can You Feel the Love Tonight," Elton John.

Pop Performance by a Duo or Group with Vocal, "I Swear," All-4-One.

Traditional Pop Vocal Performance, *MTV Unplugged,* Tony Bennett.

Pop Instrumental Performance, "Cruisin'," Booker T & the MG's.

Rock Vocal Performance, Female, "Come to My Window," Melissa Etheridge.

Rock Vocal Performance, Male, "Streets of Philadelphia," Bruce Springsteen.

Rock Performance by a Duo or Group with Vocal, "Crazy," Aerosmith.

Hard Rock Performance, "Black Hole Sun," Soundgarden.

Metal Performance, "Spoonman," Soundgarden.

Rock Instrumental Performance, "Marooned," Pink Floyd.

Rock Song, "Streets of Philadelphia," Bruce Springsteen, songwriter.

Alternative Music Performance, *Dookie,* Green Day.

Rhythm-and-Blues Vocal Performance, Female, "Breathe Again," Toni Braxton.

Rhythm-and-Blues Vocal Performance, Male, "When Can I See You," Babyface.

Rhythm-and-Blues Performance by a Duo or Group with Vocal, "I'll Make Love to You," Boyz II Men.

Rhythm-and-Blues Song, "I'll Make Love to You," Babyface, songwriter.

Rap Solo Performance, "U.N.I.T.Y.," Queen Latifah.

Rap Performance by a Duo or Group, "None of Your Business," Salt-N-Pepa.

New-Age Album, *Prayer for the Wild Things,* Paul Winter.

Contemporary Jazz Performance, *Out of the Loop,* Brecker Brothers.

Jazz Vocal Performance, *Mystery Lady (Songs of Billie Holiday),* Etta James.

Jazz Instrumental Solo, "Prelude to a Kiss," Benny Carter.

Jazz Instrumental Performance, Individual or Group, *A Tribute to Miles,* Ron Carter, Herbie Hancock, Wallace Roney, Wayne Shorter, and Tony Williams.

Large Jazz Ensemble Performance, *Journey,* McCoy Tyner Big Band.

Latin Jazz Performance, *Danzon (Dance on),* Arturo Sandoval.

Country Vocal Performance, Female, "Shut Up and Kiss Me," Mary Chapin Carpenter.

Country Vocal Performance, Male, "When Love Finds You," Vince Gill.

Country Performance by a Duo or Group with Vocal, "Blues for Dixie," Asleep at the Wheel with Lyle Lovett.

Country Vocal Collaboration, "I Fall to Pieces," Aaron Neville and Trisha Yearwood.

Country Instrumental Performance, "Young Thing," Chet Atkins.

Bluegrass Album, *The Great Dobro Sessions,* various artists.

Country Song, "I Swear," Gary Baker and Frank J. Myers, songwriters.

Rock Gospel Album, *Wake-Up Call,* Petra.

band to postpone its tour in April. The tour resumed to positive reviews in the summer and fall.

The annual Lollapalooza tour drew smaller crowds in 1995 than it had in previous years. The tour featured acts that had not yet received much mainstream exposure. Headlining the 1995 tour was the dissonant-art-rock group Sonic Youth. Another band that gained a lot of attention during the tour was Hole, featuring Courtney Love, widow of Nirvana's Kurt Cobain, who committed suicide in 1994.

Another package tour known as *H.O.R.D.E.* (Horizons of Rock Developing Everywhere) demonstrated the increasing popularity of jam sessions and hippie revivalism. In its fourth year, the package had its strongest lineup to date, including tour founders Blues Traveler joined by the Southern classic rockers the Black Crowes, Grammy-winner Sheryl Crow, reggae's Ziggy Marley, and country rockers Wilco.

Country. The year's major country breakthrough was Canadian musician Shania Twain, whose *The Woman in Me* album topped the country charts throughout the summer and into the fall. It featured the hit "Any Man of Mine." Music industry sources say the album benefited from the collaboration of Twain's husband, Robert "Mutt" Lange, a producer-songwriter who had previously worked with such top-selling rock acts as Def Leppard.

The year also saw the rise of vocalist and blue-grass fiddler Alison Krauss. Her album retrospective, *Now That I Found You: A Collection,* established her as one of country's finest female vocalists.

Amid indications that country's popular boom through the 1990's had begun to level off, country singers Alan Jackson and Travis Tritt both released greatest hits collections. Popular honky-tonk singer and songwriter Garth Brooks announced plans to follow his hits collection of late 1994 with an album of new material by the end of 1995.

Rhythm and blues. Atlanta's hip-hop trio TLC was one of the year's biggest acts with their *Crazysexycool* album and its "Waterfalls" hit. Rap music also continued to score in 1995. Cleveland's Bone Thugs-N-Harmony topped the charts with their *E. 1999 Eternal* album, which was followed to the top by the multiartist soundtrack to the rap documentary film *The Show.*

Jazz. The blend of instrumental improvisation with rap's rhythms and rhymes continued to win new adherents to jazz, while vocalists such as Cassandra Wilson and Holly Cole brought jazz interpretations to contemporary popular favorites. Alto saxophonist Ornette Coleman's *Tone Dialing* album highlighted the year's jazz activity. It was Coleman's first new recording in seven years. Multivolume anthologies of such innovative masters as saxophonist John Coltrane and trumpeter Miles Davis also came out in 1995. ☐ Don McLeese

In *World Book,* see **Country music; Jazz; Popular music; Rock music.**

Population. Investing in individuals will be the key to containing world population growth, according to the annual State of the World Population report, issued in July 1995 by the United Nations Population Fund (UNPF). The report drew largely on ideas and activity generated by the UN's third International Conference on Population and Development, held in Cairo, Egypt, in 1994.

The Cairo conference placed women and their reproductive needs at the top of the international health agenda. The UNPF followed this lead by stressing the importance of meeting the needs of individuals in order to stabilize the world's population. In particular, it said, women should have access to education, health care, and family planning services.

The agency's report expressed alarm over evidence that, though fewer women were dying during pregnancy and childbirth, those mortality rates were 15 to 50 times higher in developing countries than in most developed nations. Also, one-third of all disease in women in the developing world was related to pregnancy, childbirth, abortion, AIDS, and reproductive-tract infections. Contraceptive use, though, had quadrupled worldwide since the late 1960's.

Progress since Cairo. The 1995 report reviewed the progress made in the year since the Cairo conference, where a commitment had been made to gender equality; expansion of educational opportunities for girls; reduction of infant, child, and maternal mortality; and creation of universal access to family planning and reproductive-health services. A 20-year program of action, based on these commitments, had been developed in order to stabilize the world's population at about 7.27 billion by the year 2015.

The program had called for financial backing by governments, and delegates at the conference set a goal of $17 billion a year in spending for population control by the year 2000. However, on Nov. 1, 1995, UN Secretary-General Boutros Boutros-Ghali said that UN funds for all activities were dwindling. "The mobilization of resources to the level of $17 billion over the next five years is a formidable challenge," he said. In 1995, member nations were $3.4 billion behind in making required contributions and repaying debts to the UN.

Status and projections. The UN said the world's population stood at 5.7 billion by mid-1995 and would grow by more than 86 million annually until 2015. By that year, the UN projected, the world would have between 7.1 billion and 7.8 billion people. Experts then expect the population to stabilize, but without planning and education, it could rise as high as 11.9 billion by 2050. The most populous countries in 1995 remained China, with about 1.2 billion people; India, with 931 million; the United States, with 263 million; Indonesia, with 201 million; and Russia, with 149 million.   □ J. Tuyet Nguyen

See also **Census**. In *World Book*, see **Food supply; Population**.

Portugal. Portugal's Socialist Party returned to power in 1995 after an absence of 10 years by winning 44 percent of the vote and 112 seats in the general election held on October 1. The governing, center-right Social Democratic Party won 88 seats, the anti-European Union coalition led by the Popular Party took 15 seats, and the Communist-led coalition won 15 seats. Socialist party leader Antonio Guterres became prime minister. He replaced Aníbal Cavaço Silva, who had held the post since 1985 and was known for bringing political and economic stability to Portugal. Political analysts say the Socialist victory reflected more of a desire for new leadership after a decade of Social Democratic control than a mandate for major policy changes.

Political analysts say the campaign of the Social Democrats, led by Defense Minister Fernando Nogueira, was hampered by allegations of corruption under the party's rule. The allegations stem from the investigation of more than 1,600 companies suspected of avoiding about $190 million in tax payments in 1991 and 1992 and of using some of the money to bribe officials for government contracts.

The government continued with its privatization program in 1995. On June 1, it sold a 26.3 percent stake in Portugal Telecom, the state-owned telephone company.   □ Tom Buerkle

See also **Europe** (Facts in brief table). In *World Book*, see **European Union; Portugal**.

Postal Service, United States. The Postal Service in August 1995 proposed a policy that would allow advertisers to send mail to addresses in certain areas by putting only "Postal Patron" or "Neighbor" on the mailing label. Previous guidelines required a specific address for each piece of mail. Critics charged that the policy, scheduled to be tested in four cities, would vastly increase the amount of "junk mail" and would allow the Postal Service to compete unfairly for advertising dollars.

The Postal Service Board of Governors, responding to violent incidents at post offices in recent years, announced on August 1 that any postal employee carrying a gun to work would be fired immediately. In the previous 10 years, 34 postal workers had been killed by gunfire on the job.

President Bill Clinton on August 10 proposed to ban the sale of cigarettes by mail as part of regulations designed to discourage underage smoking. The Republican-controlled House of Representatives on January 5 abolished the Post Office and Civil Service committee in an effort to reduce the number of congressional committees.   □ William J. Eaton

In *World Book,* see **Post office; Postal Service, United States**.

President of the United States. See **Clinton, Bill; United States, Government of the**.

Prince Edward Island. See **Canadian provinces**.

Prison. As 1995 began, federal and state prisons in the United States held 1,053,738 inmates, according to an August 1995 report by the U.S. Department of Justice's Bureau of Justice Statistics (BJS). The BJS said the prison population grew 8.6 percent—83,294 more inmates—in a year, the second largest increase ever. In addition, the nation's jails held 504,324 inmates in mid-1994, 6.7 percent more than a year earlier. (Jails hold people awaiting trial and those serving sentences of less than one year.)

In most years since 1980, the rate that women entered prison rose faster than the rate for men. For example, between 1980 and 1993, the number of white men imprisoned (not those in jails) grew by 163 percent. But for the same time period, the number of white women rose 327 percent and the number of black women by 343 percent. This trend continued through 1994, when the number of women prisoners grew by 10.6 percent, in contrast to the 8.5 percent rise for men.

Crowding. The prison population nationwide grew by more than 1,600 inmates a week during 1994, which translated to a need for three new prisons each week. But prison construction was not proceeding at that pace. As a result, American prisons overall were operating at 125 percent of their capacity in 1994. California's prisons, an extreme case, housed 84 percent more prisoners than they were designed to accommodate.

Racial disparities. More than half of the inmates in U.S. prisons in 1993 were black, though blacks made up less than 13 percent of the U.S. population. The primary reason was recent drug-control policies that emphasized lengthy sentences for anyone convicted of a charge involving crack cocaine, a drug used and sold mostly by blacks. For example, under federal law, anyone convicted of possessing or selling 0.18 ounce (5 grams) of crack cocaine got a five-year prison sentence. On the other hand, a conviction for possessing or selling the same amount of powder cocaine was a misdemeanor with a prison sentence of less than one year. Powder cocaine was sold and used mostly by whites.

The U.S. Department of Justice wanted to keep the current penalties. U.S. Attorney General Janet Reno said in September that she was opposed to any measure that failed "to reflect the harsh and terrible impact of crack on communities across America." Congress in October 1995 rejected a proposal by the U.S. Sentencing Commission to equalize the penalties for crack and powder-cocaine convictions.

AIDS. The BJS reported in August 1995 that 2.4 percent of federal and state prison inmates were infected with HIV, the virus that causes AIDS. More women (4.5 percent) than men (2.5 percent) were infected. □ Michael Tonry

See also **Crime.** In *World Book,* see **Prison.**

Prizes. See **Nobel Prizes; Pulitzer Prizes.**

Alabama corrections officers in May shackle prison inmates into a chain gang to do hard roadside labor, as the state introduces several stiff measures to deter crime.

Protestantism. Both mainstream and evangelical Protestant groups were beset by financial scandals during 1995. The Episcopal Church suffered the most embarrassing setback, when on February 15 presiding Bishop Edmond Browning announced that former denominational treasurer Ellen Cooke would be investigated for mishandling church money. She allegedly diverted $2.2 million in church funds to her personal accounts. The Episcopal Church began cutting staff and services in 1991, as a result of declining financial support from its membership. Some Episcopal leaders called for Browning to step down, as the scandal had occurred "on his watch."

A second major financial scandal involved dozens of evangelical churches and church-related colleges. They stood to lose millions of dollars that they had invested with a nonprofit organization called the Foundation for New Era Philanthropy, which had started up in 1992 with headquarters in Philadelphia. New Era asked investors for large sums, assuring them their money would double in six months, thanks to a "matching grant" program in which anonymous philanthropists would contribute like amounts. But, according to investigators, New Era used new deposits to pay off earlier depositors. The scheme continued until May 15, 1995, when the organization filed for bankruptcy protection. A few days later, the Securities and Exchange Commission filed suit against New Era founder John G. Bennett, Jr., alleging he fraudulently diverted $4.2 million of New Era funds into his private businesses. New Era then was put into the hands of a liquidator, who said creditors were owed $175 million to $225 million. Bennett admitted there were no anonymous donors.

Leadership changes in mainstream denominations reflected a prevailing desire for moderation in order to bring together liberal and conservative factions. The Evangelical Lutheran Church in America at its August meeting in Minneapolis, Minnesota, elected H. George Anderson to its top position. The Presbyterian Church (U.S.A.) meeting in Cincinnati, Ohio, in July, elected retired journalist Marj Carpenter as president.

Christian Coalition. In May, Ralph Reed, the executive director of the conservative and largely Protestant Christian Coalition, unveiled the group's "Contract with the American Family." The document, modeled after the Contract with America that the Republican Party used in the 1994 congressional election campaign, outlined 10 legislative goals the coalition wanted the U.S. Congress to pass.

Most Republican Party candidates for the 1996 presidential election spoke to the 4,000 delegates attending the Christian Coalition's annual convention in Washington, D.C., in September 1995. The group had demonstrated its political power in the 1994 elections, when it was widely credited for conservative victories at the local level. By year-end, religious

In May, Ralph Reed, director of the Christian Coalition, introduces the "Contract with the American Family," 10 proposals the conservative group wants Congress to pass.

and political leaders considered the coalition, which claimed to have 1.7 million members, to be a major player in 1996 political campaigns.

More moderate Protestants organized to counter the Christian Right. On May 23, 1995, moderate evangelical, mainline Protestant, Orthodox, and Roman Catholic leaders issued "The Cry for Renewal," in which they said the Christian Right was erroneously claiming its programs had biblical sanctions. A nonpartisan group of mainstream religious leaders, called the Interfaith Alliance, also met in Dallas in late May to discuss ways to counteract the influence of the Christian Coalition.

The Southern Baptist Convention (SBC), the largest Protestant denomination in the United States, won praise for officially repenting its historical support of slavery at its June meeting in Atlanta. Northern and Southern Baptists had split in 1845 because Southern Baptist missionaries were allowed to keep slaves, which Northern Baptists opposed.

The SBC leadership continued its strong support of conservative causes. In March, Albert G. Mohler, president of the Southern Baptist Theological Seminary in Louisville, Kentucky, fired Diana Garland, dean of the Carver School of Church Social Work, located on the seminary campus. She had publicly criticized him for not a hiring a professor known for his support of women ministers.   □ Martin E. Marty

In *World Book,* see **Protestantism.**

Psychology. The brains of men and women work differently during an important step in understanding language, according to a study published in February 1995. The difference appears in a frontal area of the brain that helps regulate the perception and use of speech.

A research team directed by neurologist Bennett A. Shaywitz of Yale University School of Medicine in New Haven, Connecticut, used a technique called functional magnetic resonance imaging, which creates images of blood-flow changes in the brain, to measure the brains of 19 men and 19 women. The subjects performed a task in which they looked at pairs of nonsense words and decided if they rhymed. Images taken while they performed the task showed more brain activity on the left side in men, while in women, both left and right sides of the frontal region displayed increased activity. In other tests of letter recognition and word comprehension, no sex differences emerged. Both men and women performed equally well on all the tasks.

Shaywitz and his coworkers emphasized that their study seemed to show a sex difference in only one facet of language abilities. He said that other parts of the brain that make sense of speech may work in the same way for both sexes.

Phantom limbs. People who have an arm or leg amputated often report sharp, sometimes severe pains from the area where the limb was. This condition is known as phantom-limb pain. Researchers reported in June 1995 that the pain may be caused by an extensive rewiring of the brain area that formerly handled sensations from the severed body part.

Psychologist Herta Flor of Humboldt University in Berlin, Germany, and her colleagues studied 12 men and 1 woman who had had an arm amputated at least a year before the study. Flor's team applied light pressure to the volunteers' intact thumbs and fifth fingers and to the left and right sides of either the upper lip or chin. With a special device, they measured the resulting magnetic activity in the volunteers' brains and mapped the activity in each participant's somatosensory cortex, a strip of brain tissue that regulates sensations in various parts of the body.

The left and right halves of the brain control opposite sides of the body, and the researchers found that brain regions that had previously been devoted to the amputated fingers now responded to stimulation of the opposite side of the face. This showed a great deal of brain reorganization. These changes occurred most strongly in the eight participants who suffered from phantom-limb pain.

Flor's team theorized that cells in the somatosensory cortex may strengthen their connections and forge new ones after an amputation. This process may result in an excess of pain messages in the area, leading to phantom-limb pain. Or nerve fibers from reorganized somatosensory areas may accidentally intrude into nearby pain centers and thus foster this eerie and disturbing form of pain.

Infant memory. Babies develop the ability to recall simple events in their first year of life, psychologists reported in August 1995. But it is unknown if they realize where and when such memories were acquired, said study director Laraine McDonough of the University of California at San Diego.

The researchers observed 11-month-old babies accurately imitating an adult's actions up to three months after witnessing them. That finding indicated that infants possess *declarative memory,* the capacity for intentionally calling to mind specific facts and events. In the experiment, the infants watched several causal actions, such as making a rattle by putting a button in a box and shaking it, as well as a few arbitrary actions, such as putting a bracelet on a teddy bear and then brushing the bear.

When given the same objects the next day and again three months later, infants imitated the causal actions with few errors. However, they had largely forgotten the arbitrary actions. The same ability to remember causal chains of events, but not arbitrarily ordered events, had been seen in other experiments with adults, McDonough noted. If babies can indeed consciously recall at least one category of simple events, it is unclear why people usually have no memories of their infancy, she said. ☐ Bruce Bower

In *World Book,* see **Psychology.**

Public health. People with a weakened immune system should ask their physicians about the safety of their drinking water before drinking any more of it, two federal government agencies said on June 15, 1995. The agencies made the recommendation after studies suggested that a parasite found in some municipal water systems is more dangerous than previously believed. Some 6 million Americans have weakened immune systems as a result of cancer therapy, infection with the AIDS virus, organ transplants, or hereditary deficiencies.

The suspect microbe, cryptosporidium, caused more than 100 deaths and 400,000 illnesses in Milwaukee in 1993. Cryptosporidium is present in the feces of cows and other farm animals, and heavy rainfall can wash it from fields into reservoirs, rivers, and other drinking-water sources. Water may still contain the microbes after being treated in purification plants.

Experts had thought that a person must consume large numbers of the microbes before developing nausea, vomiting, diarrhea, and other digestive-tract symptoms. But in March 1995, researchers reported that people can become ill from consuming as few as 30 cryptosporidium organisms. Although symptoms often are relatively minor in people with a fully functioning immune system, they can prove fatal in people with a weakened immune system. The agencies suggested several protective measures for those

Tracking Lyme disease

The number of Lyme disease cases reported in the United States rose by 58 percent in 1994, largely because of an increase in the number of ticks that transmit the disease, the Centers for Disease Control and Prevention announced in June 1995. The agency said that a total of 13,083 cases of Lyme disease were reported in 1994, compared with 8,257 cases in 1993.

Number of reported Lyme disease cases per state in 1994

- Over 1,000
- 101 to 1,000
- 21 to 100
- 1 to 20
- None

Source: Centers for Disease Control and Prevention.

with weakened immune systems, including boiling tap water for at least one minute before drinking it, using home water filters capable of removing microorganisms, or drinking bottled water.

More water-safety questions. More than 25 percent of all drinking-water systems in the United States violated federal purity standards at least once in 1993 and 1994, the Environmental Working Group reported in a June 1995 study. The group, a research and advocacy organization based in Washington, D.C., analyzed reports on water quality that local water systems must submit to the government. It found that 53 million Americans had received tap water that violated government safety standards.

Smoking and teens. President Bill Clinton in August authorized the U.S. Food and Drug Administration (FDA) to begin a new program to stop the sale and marketing of cigarettes and smokeless tobacco to youngsters. Clinton endorsed the FDA's conclusion that the ingredient nicotine in cigarettes is an addictive drug and announced his decision to let the FDA regulate cigarettes and snuff as drug-delivery systems. Clinton said the goal was to reduce smoking among young people by 50 percent. American tobacco companies argued that voluntary measures would be more effective in curbing teen smoking and filed a lawsuit to block any FDA action.

Blood screening test. A government advisory panel on January 11 recommended that blood banks

discontinue use of a screening test that had unnecessarily excluded about 1 million Americans from donating blood. The panel was organized by the National Institutes of Health in Bethesda, Maryland.

The test in question, the liver alanine aminotransferase test, was introduced in 1987 to identify people infected with the hepatitis C virus. The panel concluded that the test was ineffective and caused blood banks to needlessly discard 200,000 units of healthy blood each year. Other tests, the panel said, could now protect the blood supply from hepatitis.

America's infant mortality rate dropped to a record low 7.9 deaths per 1,000 births in 1994, researchers at the National Center for Health Statistics (NCHS) said in July 1995. Although the rate measures deaths during the first year of life, it is seen as a key indicator of a population's overall health.

The NCHS said the 1994 rate represented a significant drop from a rate of 8.3 in 1993 and 8.5 in 1992. But it expressed concern about a widening gap between mortality rates for black babies and white babies. Black babies had a mortality rate 1.6 times as high as white babies in 1950 and 2.2 times as high in 1991, the latest year for which complete data were available. The NCHS said the higher mortality rate for black babies was due mainly to low birth weight and premature birth. ☐ Michael Woods

See also **AIDS; Medicine.** In *World Book,* see **Public health.**

Deadly new infections and old diseases once thought to have been conquered are breaking out in many places around the world.

Emerging Diseases

By Mary Elizabeth Wilson

The first reports of an epidemic of disease causing severe bleeding and death began to come out of the African nation of Zaire in April 1995. Scientists quickly identified the culprit as an organism called the Ebola virus. The frightening epidemic peaked in late May, and the last person to contract the illness was hospitalized a month later. In its brief attack, Ebola struck 315 people, killing 244.

The epidemic alarmed public health officials worldwide. It was frightening for many reasons. The virus often killed the person it infected; no one knew where the virus came from; no effective treatment was available for it; and the virus could spread from one person to another. But scientists were concerned about the Ebola outbreak for another important reason. It was one more example of a growing public health threat: newly emerging infectious diseases.

All infectious diseases are caused by various kinds of organisms. Most are microbes, or germs, too

Glossary

Antibiotic: A drug used to treat bacterial infections.

Drug resistance: The ability of some disease-causing microbes to survive contact with drugs. Sometimes they multiply and, over time, become the dominant strain.

Microbes: Microscopic organisms, including bacteria, fungi, and viruses, that live in water, soil, plants, animals, and human beings. A small percentage cause disease in humans.

Preceding pages:

Staff members from a hospital in Kikwit, Zaire, carry the coffin of a fellow worker who died in Zaire's Ebola epidemic of 1995.

small to be seen without a microscope. This germ theory of disease was developed in the late 1800's.

Microbes—such as bacteria, fungi, protozoa, and viruses—are everywhere in the world. They live in plants, soil, water, animals, and even human beings. Most microbes are harmless to humans. Indeed, some are essential for human life. The small percentage that cause disease typically enter the body through the skin, the lining of the eyes, or the genital, respiratory, or gastrointestinal tracts. People can pass some infectious microbes to one another through coughs, sneezes, and contact with body fluids. Other microbes need an insect or animal, called a vector, to help transmit them to human hosts.

There have always been outbreaks of infectious disease. However, since the late 1960's, public health scientists have begun to detect a change in the pattern of infectious disease outbreaks around the world. They have seen infections that are common in one region of the world appear for the first time in distant geographic areas. They have discovered that some organisms once controlled by antibiotics and other drugs can become resistant to the treatments. They have found that *mutations* (genetic changes) in disease-causing organisms can result in more severe cases of common infections. And they have found infectious diseases resulting from organisms never before known to cause human disease—some of them from organisms that appear to be entirely new. Public health experts call all of these newly recognized and changing infections emerging infectious diseases.

Tracking mysterious new diseases

At the first sign of a mysterious disease outbreak, public health scientists investigate everything in the environment that people had contact with prior to falling ill. They want to find out what organism is responsible for the disease, where it came from, and how it is transmitted. One such outbreak occurred in 1967 among laboratory workers in Germany and Yugoslavia, who were conducting research on tissue from African green monkeys. The monkeys had been trapped in Uganda and shipped to Europe. Thirty-one workers developed *hemorrhagic disease* (severe bleeding), and seven died. Investigators found that the workers had been infected with a virus present in the monkey tissue. The virus, unrelated to any other known at the time, was named Marburg after the city in Germany where it was first identified. A few cases of Marburg virus infection occurred among the medical personnel who cared for the sick workers. Rather than spreading further to the general population, however, the outbreak ended as suddenly as it began.

Then, in 1976, epidemics of severe hemorrhagic disease occurred in Zaire and the Sudan. More than 430 persons died. Investigators found a virus that appeared similar to the Marburg virus, but it had some clear differences. They named it Ebola, after a river near the site of the Zaire outbreak. And they found one way it could spread. Nurses in a missionary clinic had reused needles and syringes without sterilizing them. One report describing the epidemic noted that the nursing staff was issued only five syringes and needles each morning for use on some 300 patients that came to the hospital daily. Once health workers began to wear protective clothing, isolate the patients, and use clean needles, the epidemic ended. But, unlike the Marburg virus, researchers could find no sign of the Ebola virus in any animals or insects of the region. After the outbreak, Ebola went into hiding.

Ebola did not appear in Zaire again until 1995. This epidemic centered in Kikwit, a city of about 150,000 residents. The first patient may have been a charcoal maker who perhaps came in contact with the virus as he cut wood in the forest outside Kikwit. Family members who cared for him while he was ill became infected, as did some people who attended his funeral. In keeping with local tradition, there was an open casket, and mourners touched the body. Unsanitary hospital procedures worsened the epidemic, as they had in 1976. Then the Ebola epidemic again ended suddenly.

Scientists working to find where the Ebola virus survives between epidemics have examined thousands of tissue samples from bats, rodents, snakes, spiders, and other creatures. Investigators believe the Ebola virus may have been around for decades, even centuries, perhaps occasionally causing human infections that were mistaken for one of the many infections common in tropical Africa.

Epidemics of newly emerging diseases have not been confined to tropical regions, however. Eleven people in the Southwestern United States died in the spring of 1993, when a mysterious respiratory disease caused their lungs to fill rapidly with fluid. Researchers identified the infectious agent as a type of microbe called a hantavirus. They knew of related hantaviruses in Asia and parts of Europe, but this was the first ever found to cause outbreaks in North America and the first to cause fatal respiratory infection. Further investigations found that rodents acted as vectors for the hantavirus without becoming sick themselves. People became sick after inhaling dust that contained virus-laden particles of dried urine, saliva, and feces of infected deer mice.

Studies conducted since the outbreak indicate that there had been isolated cases of hantavirus infection in the Southwest before 1993. But the large 1993 outbreak was related to the weather. In the early 1990's, severe drought followed by heavy rains in the Southwest provided abundant food for deer mice. Their population jumped more than tenfold between 1992 and 1993, which increased the likelihood of human contact.

The appearance of AIDS

The most devastating of the newly emerging infections is the worldwide epidemic of AIDS, caused by the human immunodeficiency virus (HIV). AIDS was first recognized in the United States as a distinctive disease in the early 1980s. By 1993, AIDS had become the leading cause of death among Americans aged 25 to 44 years, according to the Centers for Disease Control and Prevention (CDC) in

The author

Mary Elizabeth Wilson is an assistant professor at the Harvard School of Public Health in Boston and heads the Division of Infectious Diseases at Mount Auburn Hospital in Cambridge, Massachusetts.

345

Hantavirus

A potentially fatal lung infection that broke out in the Southwestern United States in 1993 was caused by the microscopic hantavirus, *right* (red spots), carried in airborne particles of urine, saliva, and feces from infected deer mice. The disease outbreak, in which 11 people died, followed a population explosion of deer mice that resulted from heavy rains, which had greatly increased their food supply.

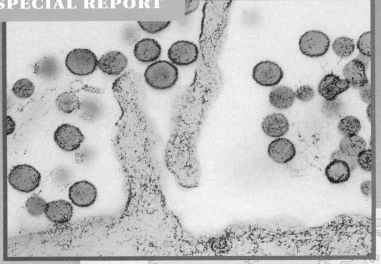

A new worldwide perspective on infectious diseases

Doctors and medical scientists have known since the late 1800's that infectious diseases are caused by organisms, most of which are too small to see with the naked eye. But other factors are involved in outbreaks of new diseases and diseases that were once under control. These factors include international travel, environmental and climatic changes, and breakdowns in public health services.

Coccidioidomycosis, a disease caused by a fungus found in soil, was on the rise in California in 1995, perhaps aided by recent earthquakes that have shifted soil, helping the fungus to become airborne.

North America

Guanarito, a virus that causes severe bleeding, was first identified in Venezuela in 1989, when 100 cases were diagnosed. The virus's reservoir is a species of rat that dwells in forests, which rural Venezuelans were starting to clear for agriculture. They inhaled the virus in dust contaminated with rat excrement.

South America

Machupo, a virus that causes severe bleeding, killed dozens of people in San Joaquin, Bolivia, during the 1950's. Extermination of the vesper mice that carry the virus quelled the disease until 1994, when Machupo resurfaced in the same location.

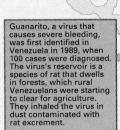

Cholera

A cholera epidemic began in Peru in 1991 and spread rapidly to other areas of Latin America, where cholera had not been seen for almost 100 years. The cholera bacterium, *left*, which is transmitted by contaminated food or water, had infected a million Latin Americans by 1995. Scientists believe the bacterium was released into Latin American waters from the ballast water of an Asian ship. Cholera is widespread in parts of Asia and Africa.

Diphtheria

A diphtheria outbreak in the former Soviet Union in 1994 infected almost 48,000 people, of whom nearly 2,000 died. The diphtheria bacterium, *Corynebacterium diphtheriae, left* (red spot), infects the mucous membranes of the upper breathing passages. Although a vaccine exists to prevent diphtheria, the social upheaval that followed the collapse of the Soviet Union in 1991 disrupted the public health services that administered vaccinations. In a brief period of time, this once-controlled disease reached epidemic proportions.

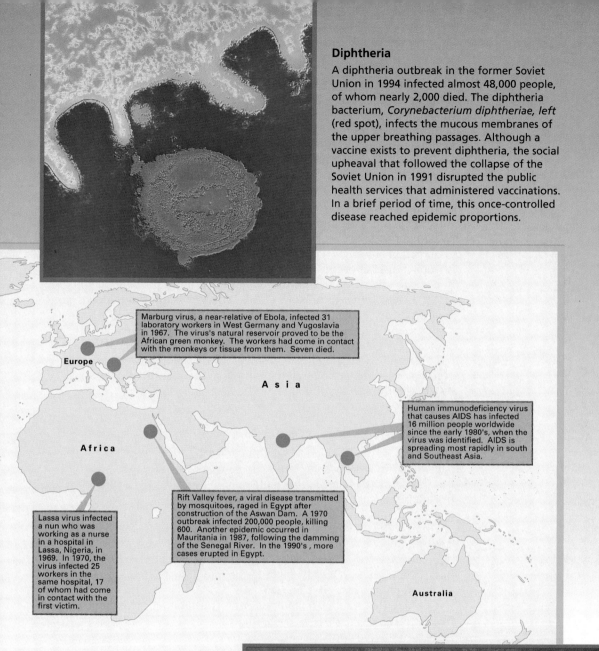

Marburg virus, a near-relative of Ebola, infected 31 laboratory workers in West Germany and Yugoslavia in 1967. The virus's natural reservoir proved to be the African green monkey. The workers had come in contact with the monkeys or tissue from them. Seven died.

Europe

Asia

Africa

Human immunodeficiency virus that causes AIDS has infected 16 million people worldwide since the early 1980's, when the virus was identified. AIDS is spreading most rapidly in south and Southeast Asia.

Lassa virus infected a nun who was working as a nurse in a hospital in Lassa, Nigeria, in 1969. In 1970, the virus infected 25 workers in the same hospital, 17 of whom had come in contact with the first victim.

Rift Valley fever, a viral disease transmitted by mosquitoes, raged in Egypt after construction of the Aswan Dam. A 1970 outbreak infected 200,000 people, killing 600. Another epidemic occurred in Mauritania in 1987, following the damming of the Senegal River. In the 1990's , more cases erupted in Egypt.

Australia

Ebola

A new disease, first recognized in Africa in 1976, is caused by the Ebola virus, *right.* That first Ebola outbreak killed more than 430 people in Zaire and Sudan. A 1995 Ebola epidemic killed 244 people in Zaire. Ebola is spread through contact with blood and other body fluids, but where the virus came from and where it resides in nature between human outbreaks remains a mystery.

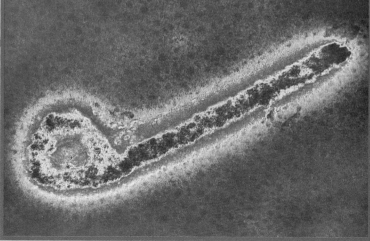

Atlanta, Georgia. An estimated 13 million people worldwide were infected with HIV as of 1994, and the number of people with AIDS could reach 40 million by the year 2000, according to the World Health Organization (WHO). HIV infection weakens a person's immune system, the body's defense against disease. People with weakened immune systems can become infected with microbes that cannot cause disease in people with normal immune systems.

How HIV is transmitted helps to explain the extraordinary rise of AIDS. The virus can spread as a result of certain sexual behaviors and by contact with infected blood. Having multiple sex partners carries great risk of coming in contact with HIV. Contact with infected blood now usually occurs among drug abusers who share contaminated needles to inject drugs. Transfusions from contaminated blood supplies caused a number of cases in the early 1980's. But since 1985, routine testing has made the U.S. blood supply virtually HIV-free.

Scientists who have studied HIV think that the virus most likely came from a related virus in a nonhuman primate. They have found related viruses in chimpanzees, mangabeys, macaques, and African green monkeys. The research has led most scientists to think that HIV probably originated in one of these primates and jumped to the human species.

The return of old diseases

Other infections classified as emerging diseases have long-established histories. They are alarming because outbreaks have erupted after decades of absence. For example, cholera, a bacterial infection that causes severe diarrhea and sometimes death, reappeared in South America in 1991 after an absence from that region of nearly 100 years. The first cases began in shantytowns in Peru. The disease spread rapidly to eight other Latin American countries, and by August 1991, more than 300,000 people were infected and 3,000 died, according to WHO. By 1995, cholera had infected more than 1 million people in Latin America.

Cholera is caused by a bacterium that contaminates water and marine life. In the intestinal tract, the bacterium produces toxins that cause severe diarrhea and vomiting. Without fluid replacement, patients die of dehydration. Scientists believe the bacterium arrived from Asia in a ship's ballast water, which was discharged in South American waters. Lack of clean water and adequate sanitation permitted rapid spread of the disease.

Another old disease migrating to new regions is dengue fever, a viral infection spread by mosquitoes. Dengue has spread rapidly from its home territory of Southeast Asia to the Caribbean, Mexico, Central and South America, and Texas. Health experts believe that rising mosquito populations and people migrating to crowded urban areas in the tropics have placed more people at risk. International travel and trade has helped spread the disease to the Western Hemisphere. No vaccine against the disease is yet available.

A vaccine is available, however, against deadly diphtheria. Yet this infection has been on the rampage in countries of the former Soviet Union since 1990. Like most industrialized nations, the Soviet Union had controlled diphtheria through vaccination programs. But as Communism began to crumble and finally collapse in 1991, health services disintegrated as well. By 1993, WHO said the disease had reached epidemic proportions in the former Soviet Union. Almost 48,000 cases occurred in 1994 alone, and almost 2,000 people died. This showed how rapidly a previously controlled disease could reappear and spread.

Drug-resistant bugs

Paradoxically, the widespread use of drugs, not a lack of treatment, has caused some conquered diseases to threaten people anew. Antibiotics, used against bacterial infections since the 1940's, are losing their effectiveness because the bacteria are becoming drug resistant. Although most attention has focused on bacteria's growing resistance, viruses, fungi, protozoa, and insects also are becoming resistant to drugs, pesticides, and other chemicals used to control them.

The mechanism responsible for this resistance is similar to the natural selection of evolution. When bacteria are exposed to antibiotics, most are killed. However, some have genes that allow them to survive contact with the drug and multiply. Over time, the drug-resistant strain sometimes takes over. The widespread use of antibiotics has both hastened and spread resistance to the drugs.

In 1994, the CDC found that 25 percent of the strains of a bacterium that causes ear infections, meningitis, and pneumonia had become resistant to penicillin, the drug that has been the mainstay of treating these infections. Many staphylococcal infections are resistant to penicillin, as well.

Drug resistance also has played a role in the rise of tuberculosis (TB). Worldwide, in 1993, almost 3 million people died of TB, mainly in developing countries. But since the 1980's, TB also has become a growing health problem in the United States. The AIDS epidemic has contributed to its spread. People with immune systems weakened by HIV infection are more likely to contract TB. Also crowded living conditions in homeless shelters and in prisons foster the spread of TB from one person to another. To be cured, patients usually must take three or four drugs

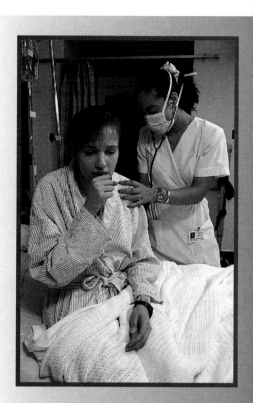

The growing threat of drug resistance

Many disease-causing organisms are becoming resistant to the drugs and chemicals used to control them. One of the most serious public health threats involves drug-resistant bacteria. Most infection-causing bacteria are killed by a dose of antibiotics. But a few are able to survive and multiply. Over time, the drug-resistant bacteria become the dominant strain. Infections that have or are developing drug resistance include:

- Tuberculosis
- Gonorrhea
- Malaria
- Meningitis
- Staphylococcal infections
- Streptococcal infections
- Bacterial pneumonia
- Bacterial diarrhea

The human factor

International airports can jet people and disease to all parts of the globe, *below*. Clearing land in tropical rain forests, *right*, brings human beings in contact with a vast unknown world of animals, plants, and deadly microbes.

for six months or longer to kill off the bacterium that causes TB. If they take too few drugs or quit taking them early, patients increase the chances that their disease will become drug resistant.

In some ways, malaria has reemerged for reasons similar to those responsible for the rise in TB cases. The protozoan that causes the recurrent chills and fever of malaria is becoming resistant to such drugs as chloroquine, used to combat malaria attacks. In addition, the mosquitoes that spread malaria are showing increased resistance to the pesticides used to control them. Human activity has played a role in the spread of malaria as well. For example, clearing tropical forests for agriculture brings people in contact with the mosquitoes that carry malaria. New irrigation systems create reservoirs of standing water that become breeding grounds for mosquitoes.

Environmental changes also affect mosquito populations, and hence the incidence of malaria. Mosquitoes thrive in warm, rainy weather, and this type of weather may increase and spread to other regions if Earth's climate becomes warmer. Such global warming could be brought on by increased carbon dioxide and other gases sent into Earth's atmosphere by automobile exhausts, industry, and other human activities. Forecasters are predicting that malaria will increase if the climate warms, and it now kills millions each year.

Poverty has driven thousands of people to seek a better life in cities. The migrations, however, have created crowded slums, *left*, where inadequate water supplies and poor sanitation can lead to the spread of infectious diseases, such as cholera. The overprescribing of antibiotics, *below,* has contributed to the development of strains of bacteria that are resistant to common antibiotic drugs.

More than simply germs at work

Clearly, worldwide travel and trade, along with various social factors, have many complex effects on infectious diseases. Civil wars and crop failures trigger mass migrations of people seeking safety in temporary refugee camps or jobs in urban areas. In crowded camps or slums, infested with insects and rodents and lacking basic sanitary facilities and fresh water, infection can spread quickly.

When humans explore remote areas or clear new lands, they may come into contact with microbes unknown to science. Tropical rain forests, where development is occurring at a rapid pace, contain the world's greatest diversity of life, no doubt including millions of microbes, many capable of causing infections as deadly as Ebola.

The building of dams also alters the balance of microbes, plants, and animals that constitute the ecology of the area, sometimes leading to epidemics. After the Aswan Dam was constructed in Egypt, the Rift Valley fever virus infected 200,000 people, killing 600. The dam had raised the water table and provided irrigation, but the new water supplies also enabled virus-carrying mosquitoes to multiply.

Natural disasters can play a role in the patterns of infectious disease. Hurricanes disrupt the ecological balance of a region, allowing disease-carrying insects to infest the rotting debris left behind. Flood-

Health scientists fight back

Public health scientists are using a combination of biotechnology and careful surveillance to combat newly emerging diseases, such as drug-resistant tuberculosis. A visiting nurse, *right,* makes sure that a tuberculosis patient takes the full course of drugs needed to cure the disease. Several drugs must be taken for up to six months or else the patient's tuberculosis can become drug resistant.

A hospital worker in Zaire, *left,* disinfects people who may have been exposed to the Ebola virus. World Health Organization scientists in Nigeria collect the larvae of malaria-carrying mosquitoes to determine the effectiveness of pesticide-spraying efforts, *below.*

ing can spread bacteria-laden raw sewage over wide areas. Strong winds also can spread disease. In 1977, a severe windstorm in California carried soil aloft and dispersed it over an area about the size of the state of Maine. The soil harbored a fungus that when inhaled by humans causes an infection called coccidioidomycosis. In the 1990's, infection rates increased in California. One factor may have been earthquakes that shifted the soil, sending the fungus aloft again.

The technologic advances that make life easier can also aid in the spread of infection. Municipal water systems carry clean water to large populations, but when parasites get into the system, the same technology menaces the public it was designed to serve. The mass processing of food and the transportation systems that distribute the food to distant locations have a potential for danger. Processed foods such as meats and milk can occasionally become contaminated with bacteria and infect thousands of people in a short period of time.

The need for worldwide vigilance

Outbreaks of newly emerging diseases have focused scientific and public attention on the need for an improved worldwide surveillance system to monitor epidemics. When an outbreak occurs, teams of experts must be able to rush to the site anywhere in the world. A global network of laboratories must be ready to analyze specimens of blood and tissue and rapidly identify new or unusual microbes.

Many tools are now available to help scientists better understand the spread of infections and even anticipate where they are most likely to emerge. Satellites can provide images of conditions on Earth that could lead to an outbreak of disease, such as masses of algae in coastal regions that could become breeding grounds for cholera bacteria. Powerful laboratory tests and techniques can help scientists trace the spread of a particular strain of microbe. This biotechnology might also help in the race to develop new antibiotics.

For more than 100 years, the germ theory has played a fundamental role in our understanding of infectious disease. However, public health experts now believe that our future understanding, treatment, and prevention of infections requires not only looking into a microscope, but also at the environment and the human activities that are contributing to newly emerging diseases. ■ ■ ■

For further reading:

Dixon, B. *Power Unseen: How Microbes Rule the World.* W. H. J. Freeman, 1994.

Garrett, L. *The Coming Plague: Newly Emerging Diseases in a World Out of Balance.* Farrar, Straus, and Giroux, 1994.

Lederberg J., Shope R. E., and Oaks S. C., eds. *Emerging Infections: Microbial Threats to Health in the United States.* Report of the Institute of Medicine. National Academy Press, 1992.

Levy, S. B. *The Antibiotic Paradox: How Miracle Drugs Are Destroying the Miracle.* Plenum Press, 1992.

Puerto Rico. Puerto Ricans were increasingly angry in 1995 that their commonwealth had become a place of violence, beset by drug trafficking, gangs, and a growing murder rate. In an attempt to stem drug trafficking and the crime that goes with it, authorities increased the number of police on the streets in 1995, enacted harsher prison sentences for drug offenders, conducted island-wide arms and drug raids, and deployed units of the National Guard in about 70 public housing projects. By mid-year, authorities reported that homicides had fallen 18 percent compared with 1994.

As part of the crime crackdown, police conducted predawn raids on June 1, 1995, in and around San Juan that resulted in nearly 1,000 arrests. Police arrested more than 150 children and teenagers and confiscated stashes of heroin, cocaine, and marijuana. In addition, the raids netted dozens of weapons, ammunition, and 60 cars used in drug operations.

In an attempt to generate extra revenue, the United States Congress in 1995 proposed eliminating tax breaks for U.S. companies with manufacturing plants in Puerto Rico. At a time when Puerto Rico's unemployment rate stood at 14 percent—double the U.S. average—islanders feared that an end to the tax breaks could spell trouble for the economy.

□ Nathan A. Haverstock

See also **Latin America** (Facts in brief table). In **World Book**, see **Puerto Rico**.

Pulitzer Prizes in journalism, letters, drama and music were awarded on April 18, 1995, by Columbia University in New York City, on the recommendation of the Pulitzer Prize Board.

Journalism. The public service award went to the *Virgin Islands Daily News* of St. Thomas for a series on corruption in the islands' criminal justice system. *The Washington Post* collected the explanatory journalism prize for "Rosa Lee's Story," a series on an inner-city family's struggle with drug addiction, crime, and poverty by writer Leon Dash and photographer Lucian Perkins. *Post* photographer Carol Guzy won the spot-news photography award for pictures of Haiti taken before, during, and after the 1994 United States military intervention there.

New York Newsday also took two prizes: commentary, for Jim Dwyer's columns about New York City; and investigative reporting, for reporters Stephanie Saul and Brian Donovan's exposure of attempts by some Long Island police officers to defraud the state's disability pension system. *The Wall Street Journal* won the national reporting prize, for reporter Tony Horwitz's articles on the oppressive working conditions in some low-paying jobs; and the feature writing award, for reporter Ron Suskind's articles on achievers at a crime-ridden high school. Coverage of the 1994 ethnic conflict and mass slaughter in the central African country of Rwanda earned the Associated Press two prizes: feature pho-

tography, for pictures by four staff photographers; and international reporting, for pieces by reporter Mark Fritz.

The spot-news reporting award went to the *Los Angeles Times* for its coverage of the January 1994 earthquake in that city. *The Boston Globe* won the beat reporting prize for David M. Shribman's coverage of events in Washington, D.C. Jeffrey Good of the *St. Petersburg* (Florida) *Times* received the editorial writing award for exposing abuses by dishonest estate executors. The editorial cartooning prize went to Mike Luckovich of the *Atlanta* (Georgia) *Constitution*. Margo Jefferson of *The New York Times* won the criticism award for various cultural reviews.

Letters, drama, and music. The fiction award went to Carol Shields for her novel *The Stone Diaries*. Playwright Horton Foote won the drama award for *The Young Man from Atlanta*. The history prize was awarded to Doris Kearns Goodwin for *No Ordinary Time: Franklin and Eleanor Roosevelt: The Home Front in World War II*. Joan D. Hedrick won the biography award for *Harriet Beecher Stowe: A Life*. The general nonfiction prize went to Jonathan Weiner for *The Beak of the Finch: A Story of Evolution in Our Time*. Philip Levine won the poetry award for *Simple Truth*. The music award went to Morton Gould for *Stringmusic*. □ Barbara A. Mayes

In **World Book**, see **Pulitzer Prizes**.

Quebec. See **Canadian provinces**.

Reeves, Keanu (1964-), an American motion-picture actor, whose roles range from a goofy party guy in *Bill and Ted's Excellent Adventure* (1989) to a pumped-up action hero in *Speed* (1994), had by 1995 earned a reputation as one of Hollywood's most talented and versatile young actors. His body of work was the subject of a film class at the Art Center College of Design in Pasadena, California.

Reeves was born in Beirut, Lebanon, on Sept. 2, 1964. His father was an American geologist of Hawaiian and Chinese descent. Keanu (*KEE ah noo*) was named after his paternal grandfather; *Keanu* is Hawaiian for "cool breeze over the mountains."

Reeves grew up in Toronto, where he attended the High School of Performing Arts. After studying acting at theaters in the Toronto area and Moylan, Pennsylvania, he moved to Los Angeles in 1984.

In 1987, Reeves delivered his first noteworthy performance, a supporting role in *River's Edge*, a disturbing, fact-based story of a teen-ager who murders his girlfriend. His other film roles include the street-hustler Scott in *My Own Private Idaho* (1991), the treacherous Don John in *Much Ado About Nothing* (1993), and Siddhartha Gautama in *Little Buddha* (1994). In 1995, he played the lead role in the stage production of *Hamlet* at the Manitoba Theatre Centre in Winnipeg, Canada.

Reeves, unmarried, spends his free time playing bass guitar and motorcycle riding. □ Lisa Klobuchar

Religion. Many religious groups in the United States were involved in politics in 1995. The Religious Right, a loose coalition of Protestant conservatives, had played a key role in the 1994 election of a Republican majority to the U.S. Congress. In 1995, the Religious Right supported the congressional Republican agenda to reduce the size of the federal government. The Religious Right also favored school prayer and opposed homosexuality and abortion.

About 18 percent of American adults considered themselves members of the Religious Right movement, according to a Gallup Poll reported in late 1994. The best-known and largest group—claiming 1.7 million members—was the Christian Coalition. It mobilized strong support for the "Contract with America" set forth by the Republican members of the House of Representatives and in May 1995 unveiled its own "Contract with the American Family." The latter document contained 10 legislative proposals for Congress, including proposals for a constitutional amendment to affirm the role of religion in America and for an end to funding for organizations that offer abortion.

Debate over federal role. Many religious groups debated proposals in Congress that would shrink federal programs for the poor. Proponents of reduced spending said that the government help created a dependence that prevents people from breaking out of poverty. They also said that the religious charitable community could take up the slack.

But many groups involved in programs for the poor disagreed. A bill sent to the president in November proposed $82 billion in welfare cuts over the next seven years. Bread for the World, the largest Christian antihunger organization, said that each of the 350,000 churches in the United States would have to provide an additional $235,000 in charitable contributions over the seven years to fill that vacuum. The U.S. Catholic Bishops Conference, the National Council of Churches, and more than 1,000 Conservative Jewish rabbis mounted protests against congressional actions they thought would hurt the poor.

Million Man March. Hundreds of thousands of African American men joined Louis Farrakhan, the Nation of Islam leader, in Washington, D.C., on October 16 for a peaceful gathering he called the Million Man March. Farrakhan and other black organizers held the march to promote racial unity and restore a sense of responsibility among black men. However, Farrakhan was noted for his anti-Semitic statements, and his call for black separatism prompted some African American Christian leaders to oppose the march.

The Promise Keepers. An integrated, but largely white male, evangelical organization called the Promise Keepers held 13 rallies in football stadiums across the nation in 1995. The rallies, attended by 720,000 men, were held to reinforce the role men

Religious groups with 150,000 or more members in the United States*

Group	Members
African Methodist Episcopal Church	3,500,000
African Methodist Episcopal Zion Church	1,200,000
American Baptist Association	300,000
American Baptist Churches in the U.S.A.	1,516,505
Antiochian Orthodox Christian Archdiocese of North America	350,000
Armenian Apostolic Church of America	350,000
Armenian Church of America, Diocese of the	650,000
Assemblies of God	2,271,718
Bahá'í Faith	260,000
Baptist Bible Fellowship International	1,500,000
Baptist Missionary Association of America	230,747
Buddhists	240,000
Christian and Missionary Alliance	302,414
Christian Church (Disciples of Christ)	958,017
Christian Churches and Churches of Christ	1,088,000
Christian Methodist Episcopal Church	876,000
Christian Reformed Church in North America	214,545
Church of God (Anderson, Ind.)	216,117
Church of God (Cleveland, Tenn.)	700,517
Church of God in Christ	5,499,875
Church of God in Christ, International	200,000
Church of Jesus Christ of Latter-day Saints	4,520,000
Church of the Nazarene	591,134
Churches of Christ	1,651,103
Conservative Baptist Association of America	200,000
Coptic Orthodox Church	180,000
Episcopal Church	2,504,682
Evangelical Free Church of America	226,391
Evangelical Lutheran Church in America	5,212,785
General Association of Regular Baptist Churches	154,943
Greek Orthodox Archdiocese of North and South America	1,500,000
International Church of the Foursquare Gospel	217,515
Hindus	600,000
International Council of Community Churches	500,000
Jehovah's Witnesses	926,614
Jews	5,950,000
Liberty Baptist Fellowship	150,000
Lutheran Church—Missouri Synod	2,598,935
Muslims	4,600,000
National Association of Free Will Baptists	207,576
National Baptist Convention of America	3,500,000
National Baptist Convention, U.S.A., Inc.	8,200,000
National Missionary Baptist Convention of America	2,500,000
National Primitive Baptist Convention, Inc.	500,000
Orthodox Church in America	600,000
Pentecostal Assemblies of the World	500,000
Presbyterian Church in America	260,885
Presbyterian Church (U.S.A.)	3,796,766
Progressive National Baptist Convention, Inc.	2,500,000
Reformed Church in America	316,553
Roman Catholic Church	59,858,042
Salvation Army	442,246
Seventh-Day Adventist Church	761,703
Southern Baptist Convention	15,398,642
United Church of Christ	1,530,178
United Methodist Church	8,646,595
United Pentecostal Church International	450,000
Wisconsin Evangelical Lutheran Synod	416,886

*A majority of the figures are for the years 1993 and 1994. Includes only groups with at least 150,000 members within the United States.
Sources: Representatives of individual organizations; David B. Barrett, Editor, *The World Christian Encyclopedia*; *Yearbook of American and Canadian Churches 1995.*

play in nurturing their families. The Promise Keepers' message included ways to build relationships with other men, reach across racial lines, and tell others about Jesus Christ.

Baptist apology. As part of its 150th anniversary celebration in June in Atlanta, Georgia, the Southern Baptist Convention (SBC) passed a resolution denouncing racism and lamenting its "historic acts of evil such as slavery." Northern and Southern Baptists split in 1845 over the issue of slavery. Southern Baptist missionaries were allowed to keep slaves, which Northern Baptists opposed.

However, E. Edward Jones, head of the National Baptist Convention of America (NBCA), said at the denomination's September 1995 convention that the apology for racism was belated. The NBCA's 3.5 million members are African American.

The U.S. Supreme Court, in a 5-to-4 decision, ruled in June that the University of Virginia had to subsidize *Wide Awake*, an evangelical student magazine. The issue, the court said, was not the constitutional prohibition against establishing religion, but discrimination in funding. The university paid to print all 15 of the other student publications, but withheld funds from *Wide Awake* because it was a religious publication. □ Leon Howell

See also **Eastern Orthodox Churches; Islam; Judaism; Protestantism; Roman Catholic Church.** In *World Book,* see **Religion.**

Republican Party. Emboldened by their control of both houses of Congress for the first time in 40 years, Republican party leaders in 1995 translated their electoral "revolution" into legislation designed to slash taxes and federal spending. Grand Old Party (GOP) majorities in the House of Representatives and the Senate radically rewrote traditionally untouchable programs such as Medicare and Medicaid in hopes of balancing the budget by 2002. The federal government came under attack as Republicans moved to shift funds and responsibility to the states for welfare, health care, and other social programs.

Sensing that President Bill Clinton would be vulnerable in 1996, a dozen Republicans, including Senate Majority Leader Robert J. Dole of Kansas, announced that they would seek the GOP presidential nomination. Clinton alternately negotiated with the Republicans and threatened to veto key legislation, raising the stakes for the 1996 presidential race.

Gingrich flexes his muscles. Speaker of the House Newt Gingrich dominated Congress in 1995 as few other Speakers have. Gingrich was widely credited for writing the controversial Contract with America that was embraced by GOP candidates, who stunned the Democrats by capturing control of the House in the 1994 elections. When the new Congress convened on Jan. 4, 1995, Gingrich and his supporters began making changes. They abolished three standing committees, fired over 600 committee staff

aides, and set term limits for the tenure of committee and subcommittee chairs.

But Gingrich became embroiled in controversy in 1995. He was criticized for his acceptance of a $4.5-million advance from publishing baron Rupert Murdoch for writing a book on political philosophy and editing an anthology on politics. Democrats accused him of a conflict of interest, noting that Murdoch was pushing for telecommunications legislation to benefit his media empire. The controversy intensified when it was revealed that Gingrich had met with Murdoch to discuss regulatory issues affecting Murdoch's broadcasting interests. Gingrich initially defended the agreement, but later agreed to accept only royalties, payable as books were sold.

In another setback, Gingrich on January 9 called for the resignation of Christina Jeffrey, whom he had appointed as House historian. Gingrich acted after the media disclosed that Jeffrey had criticized a school history program for failing to present the Nazi point of view on mass extermination of Jews.

And in early December, the House Ethics Committee voted to appoint a special counsel to investigate whether Gingrich violated tax laws in financing a course he taught at a Georgia state college. Supporters of Gingrich were concerned that the investigation would be broadened to include other matters, such as an examination of the fundraising activities of GOPAC, a political action committee formerly headed by Gingrich.

GOP political momentum continued in 1995 as several Democratic members of Congress switched to the Republican Party and some leading Democratic senators decided on early retirement. Senator Ben Nighthorse Campbell of Colorado, the only Native American in Congress, defected to the GOP on March 3, raising the Republican majority to 54-46. In the House, Democratic Representatives Nathan Deal of Georgia, Greg Laughlin of Texas, and W.J. (Billy) Tauzin of Louisiana all switched to the GOP. That gave the Republicans a margin of 233 to 199 over the Democrats in the House, with one independent and two vacancies.

Presidential candidates. Several Republicans rushed to enter the 1996 presidential race. Senator Phil Gramm of Texas announced his candidacy on February 24, followed quickly by former Tennessee Governor Lamar Alexander. Senator Dole, widely regarded as the front-runner, announced his third try for the White House on April 10. Dole, 72, was seen as a centrist at a time when the GOP appeared to be moving rapidly to the right, but he led all other Republicans in the polls.

Other entrants were Senator Richard G. Lugar of Indiana, Representative Robert K. Dornan of California, and television commentator Patrick J. Buchanan.

Two African Americans—Alan Keyes, a former State Department official, and Arthur A. Fletcher, a former member of the United States Civil Rights

Commission—also declared for the party's nomination. Multimillionaire business executives Malcolm S. (Steve) Forbes, Jr., of New York City and Maurice Taylor of Des Moines, Iowa, also entered the contest.

Republicans were jolted when Ross Perot, who took 19 percent of the vote when he ran for president in 1992 as an independent candidate, announced in September that he would form a third party to back a White House contender in 1996. Perot founded the Reform Party, which at year's end was on the ballot in Maine, Ohio, and California, and there was speculation about whether Perot himself would be the party's presidential candidate. General Colin L. Powell, widely expected to seek the GOP presidential nomination, announced on November 8 that he would not be a candidate.

GOP scandals. Oregon Senator Bob Packwood resigned on October 1 after the Senate Ethics Committee unanimously recommended his expulsion. Packwood, chairman of the Senate Finance Committee, was accused of sexual misconduct, influence peddling, and obstruction of the Senate investigation into his conduct. And former Senator David Durenberger of Minnesota pleaded guilty on August 22 to five misdemeanor charges of cheating on his Senate expense account.   □ William J. Eaton

See also **Democratic Party; Elections.** In *World Book,* see **Republican Party.**

Rhode Island. See **State government.**

Ripken, Cal, Jr. (1960-   ), shortstop with the Baltimore Orioles baseball team, on Sept. 6, 1995, played his 2,131st consecutive game, setting a new record. The old record of 2,130 consecutive games had been set in 1939 by Lou Gehrig of the New York Yankees. Ripken also held a number of other major league records in 1995, including most consecutive games without an error by a shortstop, with 95. He was named the American League's Most Valuable Player in 1983 and 1991 and won Gold Glove awards in 1991 and 1992.

Ripken's streak began on May 30, 1982, and he played in every Orioles game in the 13 years since. On his way to smashing Gehrig's record, Ripken also set the record for most consecutive innings played, with 8,243.

Calvin Edward Ripken, Jr., was born on Aug. 24, 1960 in Havre de Grace, Maryland. His father, Cal Ripken, Sr., a baseball player, coach, and manager, spent his entire career with the Orioles organization. In his senior year, Cal Junior led his high school baseball team to a state championship. Ripken joined the Orioles in 1978 and played in the minor leagues until being called to the majors late in the 1981 season. In his second season, he batted .264, with 28 homers and 93 runs batted in and was named the American League rookie of the year.

Ripken lives with his wife, Kelly, and two children in Reisterstown, Maryland.   □ Lisa Klobuchar

Roman Catholic Church. In October 1995, Pope John Paul II visited the United States for the fourth time since 1978, when he was elevated to the papacy and became the spiritual leader of the world's Roman Catholics. The main purpose of his five-day visit was to address the United Nations (UN) during its 50th anniversary celebrations.

In his Oct. 5, 1995, address to the UN General Assembly, the pope pleaded for the rights of nations to be protected against powerful neighbors. "No one, neither a state nor another nation nor an international organization, is ever justified in asserting that an individual nation is not worthy of existence," he said. He appealed for the United Nations to become a true family of nations that could usher in a "new springtime of the human spirit."

John Paul II celebrated several large outdoor masses, including one at Camden Yards in Baltimore. He repeatedly called on Americans to help those in need: the poor, the hungry, the homeless, and the ill, including victims of AIDS. His remarks came in the midst of an emotional public debate in the United States over reduced welfare spending and restrictions on immigration. His views put him at odds with leaders of the Republican Party, who were heading a movement to cut back social spending. His forceful restatement of the church's position against legalized abortion likewise put him at odds with many leaders of the Democratic Party, who favor keeping abortion legal in the United States.

Several opinion polls taken during the pope's visit showed that a large majority of American Catholics had enormous respect for him as a charismatic world leader and a man of peace. But the polls also revealed that many Catholics disagreed with his stands opposing abortion, birth control, divorce, the admittance of women into the priesthood, and the right of priests to marry.

The Pope's opposition to the ordination of women was affirmed on November 18 by the Vatican Congregation for the Doctrine of Faith. The congregation decreed that the church's teaching that women cannot be ordained priests had been taught "infallibly" by Pope John Paul II.

Gospel of Life. Pope John Paul II issued his 11th *encyclical* on March 30. An encyclical is a letter considered to be a major church teaching that is distributed to all Roman Catholic churches. In the encyclical, called *Evangelium Vitae (The Gospel of Life),* the pope called abortion and *euthanasia* (mercy killing) serious crimes against God.

French bishop ousted. The Vatican removed a French bishop from his diocese on January 13. The Vatican said Bishop Jacques Gaillot of Evreux, a town in Normandy, had not upheld church teachings against homosexuality and priests marrying. Gaillot had urged the use of condoms to prevent AIDS and spoke in favor of allowing priests to marry. His ouster touched off protests in parts of France, ac-

tions intended to pressure the Vatican to reinstate Gaillot.

The Society of Jesus, the world's largest male religious order—often called the Jesuits—concluded its 34th General Congregation in Rome on March 22. The congregation, the Jesuits' highest decision-making body, meets less than once every 10 years. After six weeks of deliberations, it issued documents committing the order to work more boldly for social justice, including furthering the "essential equality" between men and women. The Jesuits also committed themselves to giving lay people a greater role in the order's mission.

Yves Cardinal Congar, a highly regarded Roman Catholic theologian, died June 22 in Paris at the age of 91. Conger became one of the leading voices in Vatican Council II (1962-1965), which was a major effort to renew and reform the church. Pope John Paul II named him a cardinal in October 1994.

Beijing women's conference. The Vatican chose Mary Ann Glendon, a professor of law at Harvard University in Cambridge, Massachusetts, to head its delegation to the United Nations Fourth World Conference on Women in Beijing, China, in September. Glendon voiced the Vatican's opposition to abortion and its support for the advancement of women throughout the world.   □ Thomas C. Fox

See also **Religion.** In *World Book,* see **Roman Catholic Church.**

Romania experienced tensions with its Hungarian minority in 1995. On June 22, Romania applied for European Union (EU) membership, but strained relations between the Romanian government and ethnic Hungarians, who constitute about 8 percent of the population, prevented the signing of a political treaty with Hungary. The treaty was necessary for Romania to advance to the next stage in its application for EU membership. In September, President Ion Iliescu called for a reconciliation with Hungary.

Romania's economy improved in 1995. Inflation fell to an average of 1.4 percent monthly early in the year. By May, unemployment had fallen slightly to 10.3 percent and wages were rising. Nonetheless, workers organized numerous strikes and demonstrations to protest economic hardships. In July, the government, labor unions, and employers signed a pact to increase wages in return for an end to strikes.

The International Monetary Fund and the World Bank, agencies of the United Nations, withheld loans to Romania in 1995 pending economic reforms, though the World Bank approved a $55.4-million loan to improve the Romanian social safety net. In March, Romanian leaders passed a law allowing the privatization of 3,000 state enterprises by spring 1996.   □ Sharon L. Wolchik

See also **Europe** (Facts in brief table). In *World Book,* see **Romania.**

Rowing. See **Sports.**

Pope John Paul II celebrates mass in October at New York City's Central Park, an event attended by an estimated 50,000 people.

Russia. Two events dominated Russian politics for most of 1995: the Russian invasion of the separatist region of Chechnya and preparations for the parliamentary elections that were held on December 17. Despite the turmoil caused by these events and by Russian President Boris Yeltsin's precarious health, the Russian economy began to show signs of a turnaround after four years of steady decline.

Chechnya. The Russian invasion of Chechnya in December 1994 cast a long and dark shadow over the first half of 1995. Chechen President Dzhokhar Dudaev had declared the oil-rich autonomous region in southern Russia to be independent in 1991. Criminal gangs had taken advantage of weakened Russian control to establish operations in the region. On Dec. 11, 1994, Yeltsin dispatched about 40,000 Russian troops to Chechnya to restore Russian control and arrest Dudaev.

Russian military planners had underestimated the skill and tenacity of the Chechen rebel forces, as well as the substantial cache of arms they had accumulated. The poorly trained Russian troops, who had been expecting a quick victory, instead were mired in a protracted war against guerrilla forces in the mountainous region. They faced formidable military forces in Grozny, the capital of Chechnya. In an attempt to overwhelm the rebels, the Russian air force began saturation bombing of Grozny, a city of 400,000 Chechens and ethnic Russians. More than 100,000 residents fled the fighting. Thousands of civilians were killed before Russian troops captured Grozny in late January 1995. The city was left in ruins.

The capture of Grozny did not end the fighting, which dragged on for months in the mountains south of the capital. On June 14, a group of Chechens led by a man named Shamil Basaev stormed a hospital in Budennovsk, a small Russian city north of Grozny. The Chechens took more than 1,000 patients and doctors hostage. As many as 100 hostages were killed in the initial assault and in two ill-fated attempts by Russian troops to retake the building. With President Yeltsin in Canada for a G-7 economic summit—a meeting of seven leading Western industrialized countries—Russian Prime Minister Viktor Chernomyrdin took charge of the hostage negotiations. After two days of tense talks, which were televised live to a mesmerized public, Chernomyrdin agreed to Basaev's chief demands, including the immediate commencement of peace talks to end the Chechen war.

On June 20, peace talks between Russian and Chechen negotiators opened in Grozny, and on July 30 they signed a military accord. But even after the agreement took effect, sporadic fighting continued. Fighting became intense in December, when Russian troops battled Chechen rebels for a week in Gudermes, Chechnya's second-largest city.

Yeltsin and parliament. The bloody and expensive conflict with Chechnya damaged Yeltsin's already-waning popularity with Russian citizens. The war was bitterly opposed by groups all across the political spectrum. Soldiers' mothers traveled to Grozny amid great fanfare to bring their sons back from the fighting. Pro-Western politicians, such as former First Deputy Prime Minister Yegor Gaidar, condemned the use of force against Russian citizens. Nationalist politicians condemned the army's inability to wage an effective and decisive campaign. The Russian *Duma* (lower house of parliament) became a forum for regular and heated denunciation of Yeltsin and his handling of the Chechen war.

On June 21, Duma opponents of the Chechen war united with long-standing opponents of Yeltsin's economic reforms to pass a vote of no confidence in Chernomyrdin's government. Under the Russian Constitution, however, two consecutive votes of no confidence are required to topple the government. Chernomyrdin fought back by threatening to call early elections if a second vote succeeded. Parliamentary deputies, who were expecting elections in December and had no wish to contest them sooner, backed down on July 1. After Chernomyrdin agreed to shuffle some of the cabinet officials responsible for the Budennovsk fiasco, a second no-confidence measure was defeated.

The Communists advance. When the summer's constitutional confrontation was over, most Russian politicians began to focus on the upcoming December 17 elections for seats in the Duma. Under the Russian electoral system, half of the Duma's 450 seats are filled by proportional representation—the voters cast their ballots for political parties rather than for individual candidates. The Communist Party ran strongly in the December elections. On December 25, Russia's Central Election Commission announced that Communists would control 158 of the Duma's seats in 1996.

Election prelude. By autumn 1995, more than 40 parties had registered to participate in the December elections. Some, such as the Beer Lovers Party, were curiosities. The others tended to cluster into three groups.

One group included reform parties, such as Russia's Democratic Choice, headed by the economic reformer Gaidar and Yabloko, led by economist Grigorii Yavlinskii. This group supported market-oriented reforms and close ties with the West. The reform parties did well in 1993 elections, but squabbling among themselves and the unpopularity of economic reforms in much of the country made their task difficult in 1995.

Communists and nationalists composed a second group. The Communist Party made a comeback from the brink of extinction following the collapse of the Soviet Union in 1991. The Communist revival owed much to the leadership of Gennadii Zyuganov, who stripped away much of the party's Communist-era sloganeering, and to the persistence of strong or-

Russia

ganizational structures in the countryside. Right-wing nationalists, on the other hand, capitalized on the anger and resentment unleashed by the fall of the Soviet Union. Nationalist politicians such as Vladimir Zhirinovsky made flamboyantly populist appeals for law and order, the redistribution of wealth, and a restoration of the Soviet Union. In 1995, many liberal politicians feared that a coalition of Communists and nationalists could win enough seats to dominate the new Duma.

Finally, a large group of centrist parties appealed to specific segments of the population or served as platforms for individual politicians. One of these was the Women of Russia party, which won 8 percent of the vote in 1993. Another, Our Home Is Russia, was formed by Chernomyrdin to consolidate his control over the government. And the Congress of Russian Communities showed significant strength as a vehicle for Alexander Lebed, a popular former general who became a harsh critic of Yeltsin over Chechnya.

Yeltsin's future. Many Russians viewed the December 1995 Duma elections chiefly as a prelude to the presidential election scheduled for June 1996. The Duma elections were considered the best guide to the leanings of the Russian electorate. Many observers speculated that if those leanings proved extreme, Yeltsin would seek a pretext for canceling or postponing the presidential election.

Yeltsin's own intentions remained unclear. The Chechen war and four years of painful economic reforms pushed his approval rating among voters below 10 percent, according to midyear polls. In addition, Yeltsin was twice hospitalized for heart disease: first on July 11 and again on October 26. Concern over the health of Yeltsin, who was 64 in 1995, fueled speculation that he would not seek reelection.

Economic reforms. The Russian economy showed signs in 1995 of ending its punishing decline. Russia's gross domestic product—the total value of goods and services produced by the nation—had declined by more than 50 percent since the Soviet collapse. In 1995, more than 45 million Russians lived in poverty. The effects of economic hardship were dramatic: Rising alcoholism, a deteriorating diet, and a disintegrating health-care system helped push the average life expectancy of Russian men below 58 years, down from 65 years in 1987.

Despite these gloomy indicators, Russian industrial output in 1995 showed the first signs of growth in five years. Russian officials predicted that the economy as a whole would begin to grow again in 1996. The monthly inflation rate remained at around 5 percent for most of the year, well below 1994 levels.

The second stage of privatizing state-owned companies proceeded slowly. The first stage, which involved distributing property vouchers to all Russian citizens, concluded successfully in 1994. The vouchers could be used to buy shares in enterprises released

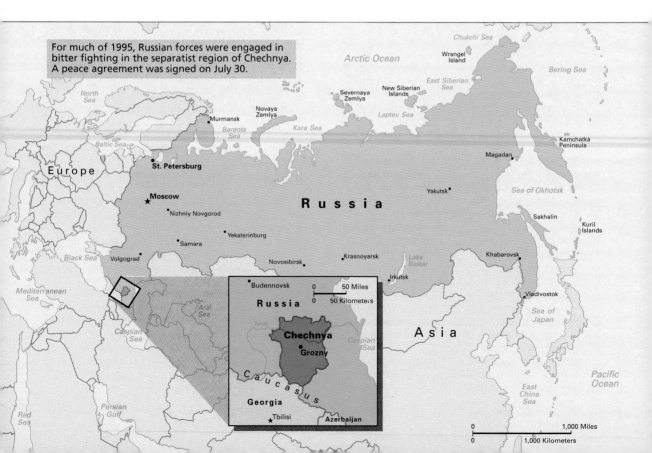

For much of 1995, Russian forces were engaged in bitter fighting in the separatist region of Chechnya. A peace agreement was signed on July 30.

A Chechen woman refugee rests in front of a demolished block of apartment buildings in Grozny in February after fierce fighting left the city in ruins.

from state control. The second stage, which involved cash sales of state-held shares and companies, was more disappointing. A long stock market slump lowered the value of the state's remaining property. At the same time, managers in such lucrative sectors as the oil and gas monopolies maneuvered to keep valuable assets under their direct control.

Poor regulation of emerging markets wreaked havoc with novice Russian investors. Many banks and investment schemes were mismanaged or fraudulent, and the steadily declining stock market pushed many such operations into insolvency. Investors lobbied the government to compensate them for their losses. During the 1995 Duma campaign, some candidates promised investor bailouts.

Crime. Assassinations became increasingly common in 1995, with bankers and businessmen the chief targets. Several politicians and journalists also were assassinated.

Perhaps the most prominent victim was Vladislav Listev, a popular television journalist who had been appointed director of a Russian television network. Listev, who was gunned down outside his home on March 1, had imposed a temporary ban on all network advertising until ethical guidelines could be implemented. The ban had significant financial consequences—advertising revenues had skyrocketed in recent years—and was thought to be the reason for his murder. Listev's funeral in Moscow was attended by thousands of mourners and led to renewed calls for harsh measures against organized criminal activity. No suspects were arrested for the murder.

Russian-American relations swung between warm cooperation and chilly confrontation throughout 1995. Russian nationalists were highly critical of NATO-led air strikes on Serb positions in Bosnia-Herzegovina in August, since the Russians have a long-standing alliance with the Slavic Serbs. Yeltsin condemned NATO activity in the former Yugoslavia in increasingly strident terms during 1995.

Yeltsin also criticized NATO plans to expand the alliance eastward to include the former Soviet allies of Eastern Europe. Addressing the Duma on August 8, Yeltsin warned that NATO expansion would "light the fires of war all over Europe." On September 13, a rocket grenade hit the American Embassy in Moscow. No embassy personnel were hurt in the attack.

An October 23 meeting between Yeltsin and U.S. President Bill Clinton in New York state was surprisingly amicable, however. The two presidents announced agreement on an approach to the Bosnian situation and ridiculed the international media for exaggerating the rift between Russia and America. But three days later, Yeltsin's hospitalization in Moscow again threw into doubt the direction of Russian foreign policy.   ☐ Steven L. Solnick

See also **Europe** (Facts in brief table). In **World Book,** see **Russia.**

Rwanda. The terrible conditions that emerged in Rwanda in 1994 did not significantly improve during 1995. There were many indications that fighting between the country's two major ethnic groups, the Hutu and the Tutsi, would continue, and the economy continued to perform miserably. Reports from the World Bank, an agency of the United Nations (UN), indicated that even with foreign aid returning, there was almost no money in Rwanda to spur the economy, and little income was being generated.

The relationship between the majority Hutu and the minority Tutsi has often been violent. Civil war between the exiled Tutsi Rwandan Patriotic Front (RPF) and the Hutu-led government in 1994 caused at least 500,000 deaths, and left the Tutsi in power with millions of Hutu refugees in neighboring countries. But the Tutsi-led government had difficulty maintaining stability in 1995. At the end of August, President Pasteur Bizimungu fired the prime minister and four members of the cabinet.

At year's end, about 30,000 prisoners were being held by the government on suspicion of acts of genocide against the Tutsi. The prisoners awaited trial by a UN tribunal that was slowly moving toward hearing its first cases.

The refugee question was a major concern of the Rwandan government in 1995. Most of the refugees were Hutu, many of whom had been involved in the slaughter of thousands of Tutsi at the start of the civil war. Refugees feared that if they left the refugee camps they would be charged with crimes or subjected to other retribution. In addition, they faced the knowledge that many of their homes and material goods had been taken by Tutsi.

Many camps had become training sites for a Hutu army preparing to take back control of the government, in what many observers feared would be a bloodbath like that of 1994. With this in mind, the government began disbanding camps within Rwanda's borders at the end of April 1995. Tutsi troops forced as many as 250,000 Hutu to leave the camps and return home to an uncertain future. On April 22, according to the UN, over 2,000 Hutu were killed. It was reported that some were shot by troops and others were trampled to death as panic ensued.

Refugees outside of Rwanda also faced difficult conditions. Host countries found the refugees a burden, politically and economically, and were eager to have them go home. Western governments, fearing that the refugees would become a long-term burden on international relief, agreed.

The refugee problem became a divisive political issue in Zaire, and to appease domestic complaints, Zairian troops in August began to force Hutu to return to Rwanda. After a powerful outcry from the international community, Zaire agreed to stop the pressure. The UN then agreed to hasten the peaceful return of the refugees.

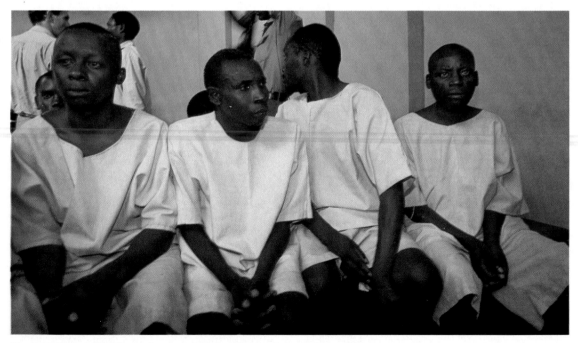

The first of some 30,000 people accused of participating in acts of genocide during Rwanda's 1994 civil war are brought to court in April.

Arming the militia. France and Zaire, allies of the previous Hutu regime, appeared to want some delay in the return of refugees—until the Hutu militia was better prepared to reconquer Rwanda. The U.S.-based organization Human Rights Watch reported in late May that France and Zaire were arming the militia. Weapons shipments were reported to have continued at least until March 1995. Zaire's government was accused of aiding in the training as well as the arming of the Hutu.

The threat of war. By October, it was clear that not all returning Hutu had peace in mind. Numerous cross-border attacks by small groups of Hutu militia were reported, and the number of incidents seemed to be increasing at year's end. Rwandan officials predicted that a major attack, probably backed by Zaire, would soon occur and threatened war with Zaire in retaliation. Burundi, with the same ethnic mix of Tutsi and Hutu, could easily join in such a war, as could Uganda, a supporter of the Tutsi.

Pact reached on refugee issue. In late November, a meeting of the leaders of Rwanda, Burundi, Zaire, Uganda, and Tanzania resulted in an agreement on a plan for the safe and voluntary return of almost 2 million refugees to Rwanda. The agreement called for the return of refugees at an eventual rate of 10,000 per day.   □ Mark DeLancey

See also **Africa** (Facts in brief table). In *World Book,* see **Rwanda.**

Safety. The American Academy of Pediatrics (AAP) in May 1995 warned parents that infant walkers are dangerous. The AAP, an organization of 48,000 pediatricians, urged a government ban on the manufacture and sale of walkers—wheeled devices that a baby sits in and can propel across the floor while the baby is learning to walk. Walkers cause about 25,000 serious injuries and several infant deaths each year, the AAP said. Most of these injuries occur when unattended babies tumble down stairways. Americans buy about 3 million new walkers each year, and millions of second-hand walkers also are in use.

Crib safety. Parents should be cautious about using hand-me-down cribs, the United States Consumer Product Safety Commission (CPSC) urged in August. Cribs are responsible for about 50 infant deaths annually, and most of the deaths involve cribs made before the mid-1970's that do not meet current safety standards. Rails, hardware, and other components on these cribs can trap an infant's head or neck, causing strangulation or suffocation. The CPSC urged local community groups to sponsor "crib roundups" to collect and destroy unsafe older cribs.

The CPSC in February announced new evidence that pillows, comforters, sheepskins, and other soft bedding may contribute to as many as 1,800 deaths annually from sudden infant death syndrome (SIDS). SIDS is a mysterious condition in which infants stop breathing while asleep. It kills about 6,000 infants each year.

In their study, CPSC researchers determined that about 30 percent of infants who died from SIDS in 1992 and 1993 had been found with their noses and mouths covered by soft bedding. Parents had put most of these infants to sleep stomach-down on the bedding. The researchers used mechanical models to re-create the death scenes and test the bedding for its ability to accumulate carbon dioxide, which is exhaled during breathing. The CPSC speculated that the infants may have suffocated by rebreathing their own carbon dioxide that collected in the soft bedding. To avoid this hazard, the CPSC recommended that parents put healthy infants to sleep on their backs in a crib with a firm, flat mattress.

Adultproof caps. In June 1995, the CPSC approved new rules to make it easier for senior citizens and other adults to open childproof caps on drugs, household cleaners, and other potentially dangerous products. The CPSC acted after years of complaints, especially from older people with arthritis, muscle weakness, and other disabilities who find it difficult to open child-resistant packaging. The new rules do not specify any particular type of packaging. Rather, they require the inclusion of adults aged 60 to 75 on consumer panels that test child-resistant packaging.

Road safety. A recall of 8 million automobiles and trucks with defective seat belts was announced in May by the National Highway Traffic Safety Administration (NHTSA), a government agency. It was the largest auto safety recall since 1980. The NHTSA said the defect could cause the belts to become unbuckled in an accident. The belts were installed in dozens of 1986 to 1991 models sold by Honda, Nissan, Mitsubishi, Mazda, Suzuki, Subaru, Isuzu, Daihatsu, Chrysler, General Motors, and Ford. A Japanese firm, Takata Corporation, made the belts.

In August 1995, the NHTSA announced new regulations that require improved protection against head injury in all cars and light trucks, starting with 1999 models. The rules will help prevent injuries that occur during accidents when occupants strike their heads on the roof or other hard interior surfaces. Manufacturers can meet the regulations by installing additional padding in the interior. The NHTSA said the regulations could save more than 1,000 lives and prevent thousands of severe head injuries each year.

The development of a new airbag that could improve auto safety was announced in June 1995 by researchers at Sandia National Laboratories in Albuquerque, New Mexico, and Precision Fabrics Group, Incorporated, in Greensboro, North Carolina. The airbag inflates to the same size as existing devices but can be packed into half the space. It would enable automakers to install airbags in door panels, back seats, and other areas.   □ Michael Woods

In *World Book,* see **Safety.**

Sailing. See Boating.

San Diego police pursue a tank that was stolen from an armory and taken on a rampage in a residential area. Minutes later, the police shot and killed the driver.

San Diego. Two sports milestones dominated the news in San Diego in 1995. The San Diego Chargers played their first Super Bowl game on January 29 in Miami's Joe Robbie Stadium. The Chargers, American Football Conference league champions, lost to the San Francisco 49ers, 49-26.

Women made sports news in the waters off San Diego in the spring. The America's Cup sailing competition included an all-female team for the first time in the competition's history. *Mighty Mary's* 16 team members came from such divergent disciplines as weightlifting and rowing. After a highly successful run, the team replaced one woman with a man before ultimately losing to Dennis Conner's *Stars and Stripes* in a series of races that determined who would represent the United States against Team New Zealand. Conner's team lost the cup on May 13 as the New Zealanders completed a five-race sweep over *Stars and Stripes.*

Tank rampage. On May 23, Shawn Nelson, a 35-year-old unemployed plumber, stole a tank from a National Guard armory and went on a 23-minute rampage. Nelson, who first drove the huge combat vehicle through a residential neighborhood, flattened at least 19 cars, trucks, and recreational vehicles before entering state Route 163. When the tank became stuck on the freeway's concrete center divider, San Diego police stormed the vehicle and shot and killed Nelson. Nelson had allegedly been a chronic abuser of drugs and alcohol and was discharged from the U.S. Army in 1980 for drug use.

San Diego to host Republican convention. San Diego was selected in January to host the Republican National Convention in August 1996. Planners said they expected the event to attract 25,000 visitors and bring in as much as $100 million.

Education. The faculty of the University of California (UC) at San Diego drew high ratings in 1995 in a National Research Council Report on doctoral programs at U.S. universities. Fourteen of the university's programs were listed in the top 10 for their fields, while two, oceanography and neuroscience, were ranked the best in the nation. The university was tied with three other universities for 10th place in the number of programs ranked in the top 10. The council report covered more than 3,600 doctoral programs in 41 fields at 169 public and 105 private universities. It was the organization's first comprehensive assessment of research-doctorate programs since 1982 and took four years to complete.

The university's chancellor of 15 years, Richard C. Atkinson, was selected by the University of California Board of Regents on August 18 to succeed Jack W. Peltason as president of the nine-campus system. Atkinson, an experimental psychologist, became the 17th president of the University. Prior to becoming chancellor of UC San Diego in 1980, Atkinson was affiliated with the National Science Foundation for five years, having been appointed first by President Gerald Ford and then by President Jimmy Carter.

In other education news, on March 13, La Jolla High School senior Irene Ann Chen won first place in the Westinghouse Science Talent Search, considered the most prestigious high school science competition in the United States. The 17-year-old Chen's biochemistry project on lymphoma cancer earned her a $40,000 college scholarship. Classmate Franz Edward Boas won the 10th-place prize and Elaine Wei-Yin Yu, another La Jolla High School senior, was among the top 40 finalists out of a field of 1,667. No other high school had more than two finalists.

Deaths. San Diego lost three prominent residents in 1995. Physician and researcher Jonas Salk, who created the first polio vaccine and was at work on an AIDS vaccine, died on June 23 at age 80. On July 12, UC San Diego scientist George Glenner, who conducted landmark research on Alzheimer's disease and established a network of day-care centers for Alzheimer's patients and their families, died at age 67. Finally, popular popcorn entrepreneur Orville Redenbacher died at age 88 on September 19. The amiable Redenbacher, who had lived in Coronado for the past 20 years, was known for handing out lapel stickers reading, "I met Orville Redenbacher, the popcorn king" to well-wishers.   □ Caron Golden

See also **City.** In *World Book,* see **San Diego.**
Saskatchewan. See **Canadian provinces.**

Saudi Arabia, the world's largest petroleum producer and one of the biggest welfare states, took steps in 1995 to correct an economic crisis caused by sagging oil prices and more than a decade of overspending. On January 1, the kingdom released a $40-billion budget for 1995. Although it projected a $4-billion deficit, the budget called for a 6-percent spending cut, cuts in subsidies, and measures to raise other revenue by creating or increasing charges for gasoline, utilities, and air travel.

By September, Saudi officials and international bankers expressed cautious optimism that the kingdom could resolve its crisis. On May 22, the government made its last $900-million payment on a $4.5-billion loan from international lenders. The loan, the kingdom's first ever, was taken out after the 1991 Persian Gulf War, which cost the Saudis an estimated $55 billion to $60 billion. However, economic experts noted that rising oil prices in 1995 gave the Saudis a boost that allowed them to make up $2.5 billion in revenue. The Saudi government owed another $20 billion in 1995 to Saudi banks and contractors.

Regional relations. Saudi Arabia and Yemen moved to defuse tensions after a 60-year-old border dispute erupted in skirmishes in early January in which several soldiers were killed. In early June, Yemeni President Ali Abdallah Salih made his first trip to Saudi Arabia in five years to meet with King Fahd. Until the Gulf War, Yemen had received some

$100 million in annual aid from Saudi Arabia, but relations cooled after Yemen supported Iraq during the war. Yemen had also resented Saudi support for South Yemen, which tried to break away in 1994. Saudi relations with Jordan and Sudan improved in 1995, and the Saudis clearly marked their mutual border with Oman.

Human rights. Despite international criticism, the kingdom had beheaded 192 suspects by mid-October for crimes ranging from murder to drug smuggling. That total far exceeded the number for all of 1994, when 53 people were beheaded. About 60 percent of those executed were African, Asian, and non-Saudi Arab workers. Turkish leaders expressed outrage at the executions of four Turks in August for drug offenses. In August, the Committee for the Defense of Legitimate Rights, a Saudi group based in London, accused Saudi authorities of torturing to death a member of their group. On June 5, the committee said the Saudis had arrested a 75-year-old Muslim scholar who had called for democratic reforms in Saudi Arabia.   □ Christine Helms

See also **Middle East** (Facts in brief table). In *World Book,* see **Saudi Arabia.**
School. See **Education.**
Senegal. See **Africa.**
Sierra Leone. See **Africa.**
Singapore. See **Asia.**
Skating. See **Hockey; Ice skating; Sports.**

Skiing. Alpine skiers from the United States, notably Picabo Street, enjoyed wide success in 1995. In the World Cup international series from November 1994 to March 1995, held mostly in Europe, the 23-year-old Street, from Sun Valley, Idaho, won six of the nine women's downhill races. With those victories, Street became the first U.S. skier ever to win the World Cup downhill title. Hilary Lindh of Juneau, Alaska, won two of the three downhill races Street did not.

In the 28 previous years of World Cup competition, Americans Phil Mahre (1981-83), Tamara McKinney (1981-84), and Marilyn Cochran (1969) had won season overall or individual-event titles. But no American had won a season downhill title.

In the men's downhill, Kyle Rasmussen of Angels Camp, California, won two races, and A.J. Kitt of Rochester, New York, apparently won another on March 5 in Aspen, Colorado. But the International Ski Federation later nullified the race results because heavy snow and poor visibility had prevented some of the skiers from racing.

Alberto Tomba of Italy won 11 races during the year and gained his first overall title. The men's individual-event champions were Tomba in slalom and giant slalom, Luc Alphand of France in downhill, and Peter Runggaldier of Italy in super giant slalom.

Vreni Schneider of Switzerland barely won her third women's overall title with 1,248 points to 1,242

Picabo Street of the United States races toward her World Cup downhill crown in March at the season finale in Bormio, Italy.

for Katja Seizinger of Germany. Schneider won the slalom and giant slalom titles, and Seizinger won the super giant slalom title. Schneider then retired.

A lack of snow in Granada, Spain, forced the postponement of the world championships, which are normally held in odd-numbered years. They were rescheduled for February 1996 at the same site.

United States Skiing, the sport's national governing body, reported a $2-million budget deficit in 1995. After the season, four skiers said they would leave the national team to join a professional circuit.

Nordic. In March 1995 in Thunder Bay, Canada, Larissa Lazutina of Russia became the first woman to win three individual gold medals in a Nordic world championship. Vladimir Smirnov of Kazakhstan won three gold medals and a bronze.

Freestyle. The United States won four of the eight gold medals in the freestyle World Championships in February in La Clusaz, France, and five of the eight championships in the World Cup series. Trace Worthington of Park City, Utah, swept the World and World Cup titles in men's aerials and combined, and Nikki Stone of Westborough, Massachusetts, did the same in women's aerials. Kriste Porter of Greenland, New Hampshire, won the World Cup women's overall title, and Johnny Mosley of Tiburon, California, won the men's overall crown.

□ Frank Litsky

In *World Book,* see **Skiing.**

Slovakia. Political life in Slovakia was full of conflict in 1995. The coalition government that formed in December 1994, made up of Prime Minister Vladimir Mečiar's Movement for a Democratic Slovakia, the Peasant Party, the Slovak National Party, and the Association of Slovak Workers, took steps to consolidate its power. By forming the coalition, Mečiar had regained the post of prime minister after being ousted the previous March. Through personnel changes in state supervisory bodies, the government reoriented the media in its favor and replaced many state workers with its own supporters.

Power struggle. Mečiar and President Michal Kovac were at odds throughout 1995. In May, the parliament passed a nonbinding motion of no confidence in the president over his alleged failure to control the activities of the Slovak Intelligence Service. The president's staff and budget were drastically reduced. His control over the Slovak Intelligence Service was transferred to Mečiar under a law signed in April.

Two attacks on opposition figures were widely seen as politically motivated. In August, the son of President Kovac was kidnapped and taken across the border to Austria. And in September, František Miloško, deputy chairman of the Christian Democratic Movement, was beaten outside his home.

Opposition fears. In April, Slovak National Party leaders introduced amendments to the penal code providing five-year prison terms for injuring the interests of Slovakia at home or abroad. Opposition activists feared that the bill could be used to silence opposition to the ruling coalition.

Ethnic relations. Relations between Slovaks and the 600,000 ethnic Hungarians in Slovakia deteriorated in 1995. The signing of a treaty between Hungary and Slovakia in March paved the way for a possible reconciliation between the two groups. The treaty recognized the rights of minorities within states. However, a decision to allow the minister of education to appoint local school principals brought protests from Hungarians. They also objected to a plan to introduce "alternative education" in the Slovak language in schools that previously used only the Hungarian language.

In May, the government proposed a law that would severely restrict the use of languages other than Slovak. Under the proposed law, a Central Linguistic Inspectorate would be established in the Ministry of Culture and language inspectors would enforce the law. Leaders of the Hungarian minority expressed outrage at that proposal.

The privatization of state-owned companies slowed in 1995. In June, Slovak leaders announced a new program for privatizing property worth 40 billion Slovak korunas (about $1.36 billion in November 1995), which would give citizens bonds that could be redeemed in five years. An additional 73 billion korunas (about $2.48 billion in November) worth of property was to be sold by direct sales. Many enterprises, including agricultural properties, were excluded from the privatization plan.

Inflation reached an annual rate of 9.8 percent by August. Unemployment ranged from 15 percent in February to 13.3 percent at the end of August. Foreign assistance to Slovakia's sizable nongovernmental sector continued in 1995, as the European Union (EU) and the United States government sought to support the development of democratic values and voluntary associations.

Foreign relations. Slovakia formally applied for membership in the EU in June, and Mečiar reaffirmed Slovakia's desire to join NATO.

Relations with Hungary improved after the two countries signed a state treaty in March. The Hungarian parliament ratified the treaty on June 13, but the Slovak parliament delayed ratification.

Relations with Austria were complicated by Austrian concern over the safety of Slovak nuclear power plants and by Slovak plans to build a new nuclear power plant near the Austrian border. Slovak, Hungarian, and Austrian leaders met in July to discuss ways to increase cooperation among the three countries on economic and security issues.

□ Sharon L. Wolchik

See also **Czech Republic; Europe** (Facts in brief table). In *World Book,* see **Slovakia.**

Slovenia. See **Europe.**

Soccer. In the summer of 1995, the United States national team enjoyed its best six-week stretch ever. In that span, it won the U.S. Cup by defeating three of the world's 10 highest-ranked teams and reached the semifinals of the South American championship.

In the four-nation competition June 11 to 25 for the U.S. Cup, the United States allowed only two goals. It beat Nigeria, 3-2, and Mexico, 4-0. In the final game in Piscataway, New Jersey, the United States tied Colombia, 0-0.

The field for the South American championship for the Copa American July 5 to 23 in Uruguay comprised 10 South American nations and 2 guests—the United States and Mexico. The United States won its preliminary group, qualifying for the semifinals. There, it lost to Brazil's World Cup champions, 1-0. In the championship game, Uruguay defeated Brazil, 5-3, on penalty kicks. In the game for third place, Colombia beat the United States, 4-1.

The United States excelled with a new attacking style under coach Steve Sampson. He was the team's assistant coach who became interim coach April 14 when Bora Milutinovic left the team. On August 2, Sampson become the permanent coach.

In his four years as coach, Milutinovic had transformed the United States into a competitive team. But he left his job after refusing the U.S. Soccer Federation's requests to develop a youth program in addition to coaching. Carlos Queiroz of Portugal and

Carlos Alberto Parreira of Brazil turned down offers to replace him.

U.S. league. The debut of the Major Soccer League, a proposed outdoor professional league scheduled for 1995, was put off to April 1996. The 10 franchises were awarded to New York/New Jersey; Washington, D.C.; Boston; Columbus, Ohio; Tampa, Florida; Los Angeles; Dallas; Denver, Colorado; Kansas City, Missouri; and San Jose, California. The new league signed such stars as Alexi Lalas and Tab Ramos from the U.S. national team.

Women. Twelve nations took part in the 1995 Women's World Cup June 5 to 18 in Sweden. The defending champions from the United States won their preliminary round. They shut out Japan, 4-0, in the quarterfinals before losing to Norway, 1-0, in the semifinals. In the final, Norway defeated Germany, 2-0. The United States won the bronze medal with a 2-0 victory over China. The Americans gained some revenge by beating Norway, 2-1 in overtime, to win the U.S. Women's Cup August 6 in Washington, D.C.

European. Ajax Amsterdam won the European Cup by defeating AC Milan of Italy, 1-0, in the final. Arsenal of England lost two major finals—to AC Milan by 2-0 for the European Super Cup and 2-1 to Real Zaragoza of Spain for the European Cup Winners Cup. Parma of Italy won the UEFA Cup.

□ Frank Litsky

In *World Book,* see **Soccer.**

Social security. Basic social security benefits were protected in 1995 from federal budget cuts that affected nearly every other United States government agency. Both President Bill Clinton and the Republican-controlled Congress, fearing a political backlash from the 43 million Americans who receive social security payments, agreed to shield the popular program. In fact, social security spending would increase under the Republican budget plan.

Strong bipartisan support emerged, however, for legislation to reduce annual cost-of-living increases for social security. This would be accomplished by adjusting the Consumer Price Index (CPI), the government's primary measure of inflation, on the theory that the CPI overstates the rate of inflation. Both the House of Representatives and the Senate approved this approach. If enacted, the legislation could save an estimated $52 billion by the year 2000.

On April 5, the House approved a bill that would allow some social security recipients to earn more money without losing benefits. This bill would also repeal a 1993 law requiring individuals with incomes over $34,000 and couples with incomes over $44,000 to pay taxes on 85 percent of their social security payments. The bill was sent to the Senate, where its prospects were uncertain.

□ William J. Eaton

See also **Social security** Special Report: **Social Security's Insecure Future.**

In *World Book*, see **Social security.**

As a large group of Americans nears retirement age, those who administer social security say it needs reform to avoid going broke in the next century.

Social Security's Insecure Future

By Peter Diamond

Glossary

Social security: A government program that pays monthly cash benefits to former workers and their families.

COLA's: Cost of living adjustments, or automatic annual increases, made to social security benefits. COLA's are tied to increases in the Consumer Price Index.

FICA tax: The payroll tax that helps fund social security. In 1995, 12.4 percent of a worker's pay went toward social security.

Normal retirement age: The age at which a worker can retire and receive full social security benefits. Workers who retire before the normal retirement age receive lower benefits; those who retire after it receive higher benefits.

The author

Peter Diamond is a professor of economics at the Massachusetts Institute of Technology.

It may be the most popular program ever offered by the United States government. In 1994, it paid $316.8 billion to 42.9 million people. Despite the number of people who depend on it, those who administer it say it needs reform to avoid going broke in the next century. In 1995, with growing concern over the federal budget deficit, it became a topic of debate. Its name, of course, is social security.

Social security is a government program that pays monthly cash benefits to former workers and their families. These benefits help replace the money families lose when workers retire, become disabled, or die. Although social security is separate from the U.S. budget for accounting purposes, surpluses in the social security fund are sometimes included when economists calculate the federal deficit—the gap between money the government collects and money it spends. Thus, balancing the budget without including social security would be difficult. But because the program is extremely popular, cutting social security would be difficult from a political standpoint.

Despite its importance, the fate of social security is murky. Its funds will run out in 2030, the board of trustees that administers them warned in April 1995. Public confidence in the program's future is low. In a 1991 survey conducted for the Advisory Council on Social Security, only 40 percent of Americans said they were very or somewhat confident that social security will continue. Yet, the same survey showed that more than 90 percent expected to receive social security benefits. This ambivalence reflects the status of social security today.

Beginnings and growth of social security

Among industrialized nations, the United States was late in providing benefits for retired workers. Germany led the way with the first compulsory old-age and disability insurance program in 1889. The Social Security Act of 1935 created social security in the United States. The new U.S. program covered workers under the age of 65 in commerce and industry, except railroads, which had their own pension system. Over the years, social security broadened to cover more and more workers. Today, the only significant group of workers not covered by social security are some state and local government employees.

At first, benefits went only to retired workers over age 65. In 1939, payments started going to some survivors of deceased workers, such as widows older than 65 and children younger than 18. In 1950, benefits were extended to dependent widowers over the age of 65. Women between the ages of 62 and 65 became eligible for reduced benefits in 1956, and men of those ages in 1961. Benefits were extended to disabled workers over the age of 50 in 1956, and to insured disabled workers of all ages in 1960. In 1965, workers' divorced wives became eligible for benefits provided the marriage had lasted at least 10 years, and the same became true of divorced husbands in 1983. The total amount going to a particular worker's family was limited by a maximum monthly benefit that varied with the workers' earnings.

Until 1972, it took an act of Congress to increase monthly benefits. In that year, Congress introduced automatic annual increases, called

cost of living adjustments (COLA's), which were tied to consumer price increases. Because of a flaw in the plan, benefits rose much faster than wages. This flaw, known as *overindexing*, increased benefits so sharply that the financing of social security was endangered.

In 1977, Congress moved to restore social security's finances. It corrected the indexing flaw and raised the payroll taxes that fund social security. But in the late 1970's, prices rose much faster than wages. Hence, social security payments rose faster than tax revenues. With the program facing a shortfall in funds in 1983, Congress tackled its financial problems. The most notable change was to gradually increase the normal retirement age. Normal retirement age starts increasing by two months a year for workers who turn 62 in the year 2000, progresses to age 66 for those who turn 62 in 2005, and eventually reaches age 67 for workers who turn 62 in 2022 or later.

Funds for social security benefits come from three sources: payroll taxes, earned interest, and taxes on some social security benefits. The major source of money is the payroll tax, called the Federal Insurance

A program to fight poverty

The spread of poverty during the Great Depression, a worldwide economic slump in the 1930's, led to the introduction of social security in 1935.

Contribution Act (FICA) tax. Under FICA, 12.4 percent of a worker's earnings in 1995 went toward social security. An additional 2.9 percent went toward Medicare, a government-run health insurance program for retired and disabled workers. The worker paid half of this 15.3 percent tax, and his or her employer paid the other half.

High-earning workers do not pay FICA tax on all of their wages. In 1995, the 12.4 percent payroll tax for social security applied only to the first $61,200 a worker earned. The 1995 base used to calculate benefits was also limited to $61,200, no matter how much the worker actually earned. This limit rises every year. Employers deduct the FICA tax from workers' pay, add an equal contribution, and send the money to the Department of the Treasury, which sends the money on to the Social Security Administration.

Social security's second source of income is interest earned on U.S. Treasury bonds, in which surplus social security funds are invested. The third source is taxes on part of social security benefits that go to people with high incomes from other sources.

Claiming benefits

Americans can claim benefits from three separate parts of the social security program. Old-age insurance pays benefits to retired workers and their dependents, survivors insurance pays benefits to survivors of workers, and disability insurance pays benefits to disabled workers and their dependents. In all cases, a worker must have worked long enough to be insured before receiving benefits.

Retired workers can claim retirement benefits anytime after they turn 62. The government in 1995 regarded 65 as the normal retirement age, however, and workers who retire earlier receive lower payments than those who wait until they are 65. While claiming social security, retirees can only earn a set amount of money from other sources or their benefits will be cut. In 1995, retirees could earn up to $8,160 a year from other sources if they were between ages 62 and 65; up to $11,280, between ages 65 and 70. Retirees between 62 and 65 lose $1 of social security for each $2 they earn above this limit, and those between 65 and 70 lose $1 for every $3 earned above this limit. Those over 70 could earn any amount and still receive social security.

How benefits are calculated

When a worker retires, the government calculates his or her benefits by *wage indexing* that worker's covered earnings. That is, it adjusts the person's earnings to reflect the rise in wages over his or her working lifetime. The government's second step is to select the 35 years in which that worker earned the largest indexed wage. These 35 best years are averaged out and divided by 12 to obtain the worker's Average Indexed Monthly Earnings (AIME).

The next step is to apply a formula to the worker's AIME in order to calculate his or her monthly primary insurance amount (PIA). The actual payment is adjusted from the PIA depending on the age at which benefits were first claimed. In 1995, a worker who retired at

How social security works

Social security is a U.S. government program that pays monthly cash benefits to former workers and their families. In 1994, social security paid $316.8 billion to 42.9 million people, or about one-sixth of all Americans.

Social security is funded primarily through a payroll tax. In 1995, 12.4 percent of a worker's earnings went toward social security. An additional 2.9 percent went to fund Medicare, a government-run health insurance program for former workers.

A worker's employer contributes half the payroll tax.

Half the payroll tax that funds social security is deducted from a worker's paycheck.

The payroll tax goes to the U.S. Department of the Treasury, which distributes it among the trust funds that pay the three kinds of social security benefits.

Social Security Trust Fund

Old Age Insurance

Old age insurance pays benefits to retired workers. Retirees can claim social security after their 62nd birthday. But in 1995, the government regarded 65 as the normal retirement age, and workers who retired at an earlier age received lower benefits.

Survivors Insurance

Survivors insurance pays benefits, in some cases, to the family members of deceased workers. Those eligible for such benefits include dependent spouses over the age of 65 and children younger than 18.

Disability Insurance

Disability insurance pays benefits to workers who become disabled after they become fully insured under social security. These workers must have a severe physical or mental condition that has lasted at least a year, or is expected to last that long or result in death.

The threat to social security

Population trends are driving social security toward insolvency. The retirement of the baby boom generation, the large group of Americans born between 1946 and 1964, is expected to drain the program's funds.

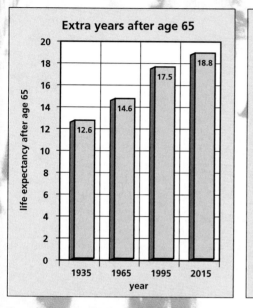

Extra years after age 65

life expectancy after age 65

12.6 · 14.6 · 17.5 · 18.8

1935 · 1965 · 1995 · 2015

year

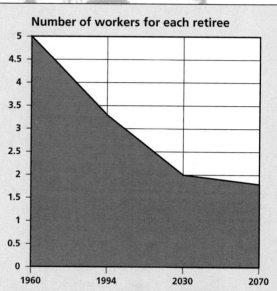

Number of workers for each retiree

1960 · 1994 · 2030 · 2070

Population explosion of the elderly

The life expectancy of Americans over age 65 will rise steadily. Great numbers of aging baby boomers living longer will result in an ever-increasing number of people drawing funds from social security.

Drop in workers paying social security

As the number of social security recipients grows, there will be fewer workers to support them. In 1994, 3.3 American workers paid into social security for every worker drawing out money. By 2030, this ratio is expected to slip to 2 workers per recipient.

age 62 saw benefits reduced by 20 percent. A worker who retired after 65 saw benefits increase. The increase is 3 percent per year worked beyond 65 for those born in 1924. This rate rises in the future, reaching 8 percent for those born in 1943 and after. Due to COLA's, the worker's payment increases as the cost of living rises.

How successful is social security in delivering economic security? One way to answer that question is to compare a retiree's benefits in the first year of retirement with his or her wage in the last year of work. This comparison is called a *replacement rate.* For a worker with no dependents who retired at age 65 in 1995 and had earnings that grew as fast as the average earnings in the economy, reaching $15,000 in 1994, the replacement rate is 50 percent. This means the retiree's yearly benefits total $7,500. If that worker with similar earnings growth had earned $45,000 in 1994, however, the replacement rate would be only 30 percent. He or she would receive $13,500.

Important income for the poor

Another way to assess social security benefits is to compare them with other sources of income for the elderly. In 1992, elderly people as a group received 40 percent of their total income from social security. But social security is more important for people with low incomes. Indeed, 63 percent of aged families received 50 percent or more of their income from social security; 26 percent received 90 percent or more of their income from social security.

Social security benefits are particularly important for poor retirees and help hold down the poverty rate among the elderly. In 1993, the federal government regarded an individual as poor if he or she earned less than $7,356. In 1992, the poverty rate for Americans over 65 was 13 percent, compared with 12 percent for adults under 65. Poverty was considerably higher among some elderly people than others: 16 percent among women, 22 percent among Hispanic Americans, and 33 percent among African Americans. By contrast, poverty rates among the elderly in other industrial countries were much lower—less than 5 percent in Australia, Canada, France, Germany, and the United Kingdom. In these countries, a combination of social security, private pensions, and guaranteed minimum incomes help hold down poverty, economists say.

Will the boomers bring a bust?

Social security will be hard pressed financially when the baby boom generation—the large group of Americans born between 1946 and 1964—retires. After 2013, social security will pay out more than it receives in taxes. After 2020, it will pay out more than it receives in taxes plus interest on invested funds. Social security's trust fund is expected to empty out in 2030.

This drain will occur because a larger number of people will be drawing from social security as a relatively smaller number of people pay in. In 1994, for every American receiving money from social security, 3.3 workers paid in. By 2030, this ratio is expected to slip to about 2 workers for every claimant, and by 2070 to 1.8 workers.

Each year, the Social Security Administration's Office of the Actuary projects social security's spending and earnings for the next 75 years and calculates whether they balance. Social security is now out of balance. If the FICA payroll tax were raised immediately to 14.57 percent, up from the 12.4 percent that Americans now pay for social security, balance would be restored for the next 75 years.

Another way to assess social security's financial woes is to ask how big a payroll tax we would need every year to collect just enough money to pay that year's benefits. As the population ages, this number steadily rises. In 75 years, it would be about 18 percent. That is, if nothing is done to hold down social security benefits, a payroll tax that grows steadily to 18 percent would finance social security. This is a higher tax than Americans pay now, but many countries function well with such taxes. For example, Switzerland funds its pensions with a 23.4 percent payroll tax.

Americans in 1995 appeared to have little taste for most tax increases. Yet polls found the country behind tax increases specifically for social security. In a 1994 EBRI/Gallup poll, 64 percent of people responding favored raising taxes now to lessen future tax increases.

Because social security is so popular, Congress has avoided announcing benefit cuts—even when it has, in fact, cut benefits. In 1983 Congress tackled social security's financial problems with legislation that included a one-time delay in the yearly COLA's. Economists say this effectively reduced benefits, but Congress preferred to describe its action as a "delay on COLA" rather than a "cut in benefits." Also, by gradually raising the normal retirement age from 65 to 67, the amount of benefits a retiree receives will shrink. For example, a worker retiring at the age of 62 in 2022 (when the normal retirement age hits 67), will receive 70 percent of the benefits he or she would have received at normal retirement age. This is down from the 80 percent an early retiree would receive in 1995. Future benefit cuts are usually included in proposals to balance social security.

Ideas for saving social security

Social security could save money if there is a change in the way the U.S. inflation rate is calculated. The inflation rate measures the rise of prices, and is used to set social security COLA's. Many economists say this rate of inflation is overstated by the Consumer Price Index, the chief statistical measure of U.S. inflation and the basis for COLA's. Congress could wait for improvements in the Consumer Price Index. If Congress simply guessed the true rate of inflation and tied the COLA's to that figure, it would run the risk that the COLA's could be too small and retirees' real benefits would shrink. That shortfall would compound over time. Thus, the benefit cut would especially hurt those who live a long time after retirement, mostly elderly women who already have a very high poverty rate. Indeed, many analysts want to *raise* benefits for elderly widows.

Other proposals to balance social security center around how the funds are invested. In 1995, all of social security's funds were invested in U.S. Treasury bonds. Some economists and members of Congress suggested investing part of these funds in stocks and corporate bonds, keeping a portion in Treasury bonds as a cushion against the risk of investing in stocks and bonds. This would imitate the investment practices of private pension funds. Some analysts think that social security should invest in mutual funds, which use investors' money to buy stocks and other securities. The kind of mutual fund that economists favor is called an index fund, in which the money is invested in equal proportions in all of the firms in some group, such as all of the firms listed on a stock exchange. This means the government is not picking the individual firms to invest in.

Proposals to save social security

Suggestions for saving social security range from stealth cuts in benefits to investing its funds in the stock market. But all proposals aim to bring the program's long-term expenses in line with its long-term earnings.

Proposal	Pros	Cons
Cut benefits Ideas that effectively cut benefits are part of many proposals. These include raising the normal retirement age to 68 or 70, and changing the way in which benefits are calculated so that workers receive less money.	Such changes would reduce social security's expenses in a practical and straightforward way. Since people are expected to live longer, they will collect benefits for a longer time after retirement.	Workers who paid into social security over their working lifetime would receive fewer benefits relative to their wages than those of the previous generation.
Raise the payroll tax In 1995, social security's finances could be balanced for the following 75 years if it were funded by an additional 2.17 percent payroll tax, on top of the 12.4 percent already paid by Americans.	A higher payroll tax would bring more money into social security's funds, ensuring that the rise in claims when baby boomers retire would not bankrupt the program.	In 1995, Americans had little taste for most tax hikes, although polls showed support for raising taxes specifically for social security. Some saw the idea of raising the payroll tax as politically unwise.
Recalculate the rate of inflation Social security benefits rise every year in line with the rate of inflation. Some experts say that the way the government measures inflation exaggerates the true cost of living, and should be changed.	If the rate of inflation is calculated to be lower, social security payments would rise less quickly. This would ease some of the program's financial strain.	In 1995, there was no other precise way to measure inflation. Congress could not simply guess the rate of inflation because, if it guessed wrong, the real incomes of retirees would fall.
Invest in stocks and bonds Social security now invests its surplus funds in safe, but low-earning, U. S. Treasury bonds. Some experts say some of this money should be invested in stocks and bonds.	Stocks and bonds usually earn more money than U.S. Treasury bonds.	Investing in stocks and bonds is riskier than investing in Treasury bonds. There is no guarantee of how much money such investments might earn—or lose.
Privatize social security One proposal calls for diverting part of a worker's payroll tax away from social security trust funds and toward IRA's. Others call for investing all of the worker's payroll tax in IRA's.	IRA investments would allow individuals to control their own retirement savings program and perhaps earn higher rates of interest. Some individuals, however, would earn a lower rate of interest.	Partial or full privatization would require social security to collect more money than it does now, so that it could put money in IRA's while continuing to pay checks to retirees and other beneficiaries.

Such investments look very attractive because, on average, private bonds and equities earn more than U.S. Treasury bonds. However, one reason for this higher return is that the risks also are higher. Economists wonder if it would be good for social security to take on these risks. If investments in the stock market yielded poor returns in one year or one decade, how would this affect future beneficiaries, future workers, or the government's general revenues? There is no way to know how Congress might react to this in the future. However, in calculating risk, it is worth noting that in times of rapid inflation, an investment in low-earning Treasury bonds could also be risky. Some countries, such as Chile, have seen inflation wipe out most of the value of their social security funds.

Is privatization the cure?

A more radical change was discussed in 1994 by the Entitlements Commission, a bipartisan group appointed to study balancing the federal budget. The commission considered permitting part of the FICA payroll tax to go into individual accounts. The worker would have some choice over how the money was invested, and the earnings of the account would accumulate tax-free until withdrawn. Benefits would depend on the return on the worker's individual account. Partial or full privatization would require social security to collect more money than it does now in order to free up money for individual accounts while continuing to pay monthly checks to retirees.

Chile privatized its social security system in 1981. Workers there are required to save 10 percent of their earnings in individual mutual fund accounts. They also pay for survivor and disability insurance and fees associated with the mutual funds. On average, they devote 13 percent of earnings toward retirement savings and insurance. The retirement funds have earned very high returns—averaging about 14 percent a year higher than inflation. These high returns were caused by rapid growth and high interest rates in the Chilean economy.

The privatization of Chile's social security helped foster this rapid economic growth. The government financed the phase-out of the old social security system by spending less money than it collected in taxes. This led to an accumulation of money, or capital, that could be invested in the economy, and this added investment fueled growth.

The Chilean system has two drawbacks. Economists believe that the best retirement benefit is an annuity, a sum of money paid in installments at regular times as long as the retiree lives. But retired Chileans had to purchase their own annuities and found them to be very expensive. So instead, many Chilean retirees withdraw some of their retirement savings each month. They risk outliving their money and falling back on a guaranteed minimum pension from the government. Secondly, individual accounts are expensive to run, especially compared with the low administrative costs of U.S. social security.

What can be learned from this Chilean experience about the pros and cons of investing U.S. social security money in individual accounts? For a start, analysts say, these accounts would cost more to administer than social security. Also, there would be no guarantees that all retirees would invest in annuities. Insurance companies would be eager to sell annuities to some people and reluctant to sell to others, especially low-wage earners and those likely to live long.

The United States also would be unlikely to reap such gains as Chile did by privatizing social security. The United States would get the level of investment that helped fuel Chile's economic growth only if Congress raised taxes or cut spending to replace the money diverted from social security into individual accounts.

Dangers posed by the deficit

Social security may be affected as lawmakers struggle to end the federal budget deficit. In 1990, Congress largely exempted social security from procedures for controlling the budget. Speaker of the House Newt Gingrich (R., Georgia) in 1995 said that social security should be off the table as Congress wrestles with the budget deficit. But an antideficit advocacy group, the Concord Coalition, wants social security benefits cut for those who have high incomes from any source.

Surplus social security funds are included in some, but not all, measures of the deficit. They were included in the proposed balanced budget amendment that almost passed Congress in March 1995. This proposal—to change the U.S. Constitution to force the federal government to balance its budget—eventually failed in the Senate. If those social security surpluses were not counted, it would make balancing the budget even more difficult in the near future.

When the baby boomers retire, however, social security will pay out more money than it takes in. Including social security then would make it harder to satisfy a balanced budget amendment. Do Americans want social security—an important source of income for so many elderly—to be subject to annual budget battles, rather than continuing to be treated as a separate entity?

Many economists believe that social security income should be protected from political maneuvering. Some protection would be provided by keeping social security a separate entity, rather than part of the official budget. Many observers believe that Congress is likely to take its time in grappling with social security's financial problem because the crisis is not immediate and the political consequences could be severe. Delay, however, will make it harder to eventually close the looming shortfall. ■ ■ ■

For further reading:

Social Security Bridging the Centuries: Issues, Answers, and Challenges. Ed. by Eric Kingson and James Schulz. Oxford University Press, 1996.

Social Security: What Role for the Future? Ed. by Peter Diamond and others. The Brookings Institution, 1996.

World Bank. *Averting the Old Age Crisis: Policies to Protect the Old and Promote Growth.* Oxford University Press, 1994.

Somalia

Somalia faced political difficulties in 1995, but events were not as bloody or chaotic as many observers had predicted. The decision of the United Nations (UN) in 1994 to remove its peacekeeping forces from the country in March 1995 did not lead to an immediate outbreak of widespread fighting between rival warlords. However, no central governing body had emerged by the end of the year, and there were indications that warfare would resume.

By late January, UN forces were concentrated in Mogadishu, the country's capital, having been withdrawn from all other locations. Skirmishes broke out as militias and individuals fought for control of materials and property abandoned by the UN.

To prevent militias from attacking the departing UN forces in attempts to take hostages or capture weapons and supplies, a special international force, comprised mainly of United States Marines, gathered offshore. In late February, the troops went ashore to guard the remaining UN personnel as they departed from Mogadishu's airports and seaports.

The last UN forces were withdrawn from Somalia on March 3. While there was no last-minute attack on UN troops, immediately upon their departure, the militia of General Mohamed Farah Aideed, a major clan leader, seized control of the airport.

Violence in the next few months was limited, and small numbers of UN and voluntary-agency workers continued relief work. However, talks between clan leaders on the establishment of a new government made little progress. General Aideed and his Somali National Alliance controlled southern Mogadishu, while Ali Mahdi Mohammad and his Somali Salvation Alliance were in control in the northern part of the city. Both leaders had declared themselves president of Somalia.

Open fighting broke out in September as General Aideed suddenly moved some of his forces from Mogadishu, capturing the southwestern city of Baidoa on September 17. For the remainder of 1995, large areas of the country were peaceful, while the warring clans concentrated their activities in the cities. Some observers suggested that a new form of rule, a cooperation between clans without a central government, was being established.

In the so-called Somaliland Republic, the northern region that declared its independence from Somalia in May 1991, stability of a sort prevailed and some reconstruction was underway. The president of Somaliland, Mohammed Ibrahim Egal, maintained control of Hargeisa, the capital of the "republic," and much of the region's countryside. But clan conflict led to fighting in October 1995 as forces loyal to Egal clashed with allies of Aideed over control of Jidhi, a village about 35 miles (56 kilometers) northwest of Hargeisa. It was the first time Aideed had moved his forces into Somaliland.   □ Mark DeLancey

See also **Africa** (Facts in brief table). In *World Book,* see **Somalia.**

South Africa continued to make progress in 1995 in solving the many political, economic, and social problems that had resulted from decades of *apartheid* (racial separation). In local elections held on November 1, the African National Congress (ANC), headed by South African State President Nelson R. Mandela, won the majority of seats and kept control in most areas. The white population apparently felt reassured that enough of their representatives were elected to protect their interests.

Important issues in 1995 included writing a new constitution and integrating various population groups and military organizations. A particular problem was bringing peace to the KwaZulu-Natal province, home of the Inkatha Freedom Party, which had long been at odds with the ANC, and integrating the province into the new constitutional system. Inkatha had withdrawn in April from the Constitutional Assembly.

Political crimes. Bringing to justice those who committed crimes either in fighting or defending apartheid was another crucial problem. The Promotion of National Unity and Reconciliation Bill, which became law in July, included provisions for granting amnesty to those who confessed to their crimes and for punishing those who failed to come forward. But the announcement that key apartheid military officers were to be arrested, including former Minister of Defense Magnus Malan, led to a strong outcry among whites. In November, President Mandela named Nobel Peace Prize winner Archbishop Desmond M. Tutu to head the Truth Commission, a 17-member multiracial panel created to investigate political crimes committed by both the apartheid government and antiapartheid groups.

Resignations. Winnie Mandela—the estranged wife of President Mandela—resigned under pressure on April 17 from her position as minister of arts, culture, science, and technology. Her reputation had been tainted by corruption scandals, and her public conduct had been harshly criticized.

Allan Boesak, a long-time ally of Mandela's, on February 13 resigned from his post as South Africa's ambassador-designate to United Nations offices in Geneva, Switzerland. Boesak was accused of misappropriating funds. An investigation commissioned by Mandela cleared him of the charges in April, but investigations into his actions continued.

Two important visitors in 1995 recognized South Africa's progress. On March 20, Queen Elizabeth II arrived in Cape Town for a week's stay. And on September 16, Pope John Paul II made his first official visit to the newly democratic country.

□ Mark DeLancey

See also **Africa** (Facts in brief table). In *World Book,* see **South Africa.**

South America. See Latin America.

South Carolina. See State government.

South Dakota. See State government.

Members of a new, racially mixed Constitutional Court take the oath of office in February as South Africa ends its system of justice based on apartheid.

Space exploration. Two historic dockings took place in 1995 between a United States space shuttle and the Russian space station Mir. A U.S. astronaut was carried into space aboard a Russian Soyuz spacecraft for the first time and spent nearly four months on Mir. And crews on the 7 shuttle missions flown in 1995 conducted experiments to study the commercial use of space, made scientific observations of the universe, and prepared for the building of a U.S. space station.

Missions to Mir. The shuttle Discovery, which was launched on February 3, flew within 40 feet (12 meters) of Mir, 200 miles (320 kilometers) over the Pacific Ocean. It was the first U.S.-Russian meeting in space since an Apollo spacecraft and a Soyuz spacecraft docked with each other on July 17, 1975. Discovery made its closest approach to Mir on February 6. The crew included the first woman to serve as pilot on a shuttle mission, Air Force Lieutenant Colonel Eileen M. Collins, 38. Discovery landed at the Kennedy Space Center (KSC) in Florida on February 11.

On March 14, Norman E. Thagard, a 51-year-old astronaut and physician, became the first American to be launched aboard a foreign spacecraft. Thagard rode a Russian Soyuz spacecraft to a docking with the space station Mir on March 16. By June 6, Thagard had completed 84 days aboard Mir, breaking the U.S. record for the longest stay in space. On March 22, Valery Polyakov returned to Earth from Mir after setting a new record of 439 days in space.

Historic meetings. On June 29, the shuttle Atlantis, launched on June 27, docked with Mir. Joined together, the two spacecraft formed the largest structure ever assembled in space, measuring more than 230 feet (70 meters) long, weighing 225 tons (200 metric tons), and housing 10 people.

Norman Thagard, who had been conducting medical experiments on the effects of spending long periods in space, returned to Earth aboard Atlantis with Mir crewmen Vladimir N. Dezhurov and Gennady M. Strekalov. Atlantis landed at KSC on July 7.

Atlantis docked with Mir again on November 15, during an eight-day shuttle mission. The shuttle landed at KSC on November 20.

Longest shuttle flight. Endeavour went into orbit on March 2 with a crew of seven. Once in space, the crew focused ASTRO 2, a battery of three ultraviolet telescopes, on the moon, white dwarf stars, supernovas, and quasars. The views provided by the telescopes cannot be seen from Earth because the air and clouds absorb ultraviolet radiation. After a flight lasting 16 days, 15 hours, Endeavour landed at Edwards Air Force Base (EAFB) in California on March 18. It was the longest flight in the shuttle program's history. The seven astronauts aboard Endeavour, plus the three each aboard Soyuz and Mir, added up to the largest number of people ever in space at one time.

Space exploration

Delayed missions. Discovery went into orbit again on July 13 after a six-week delay caused by two woodpeckers that drilled holes into the foam insulation covering the shuttle's main fuel tank. The shuttle's crew launched a tracking and data-relay satellite, used for communications between spacecraft and ground controllers. The satellite replaced one that was being carried into orbit by the shuttle Challenger on Jan. 28, 1986, and was destroyed when the shuttle exploded. Discovery returned to KSC on July 22, 1995.

A postflight inspection of Discovery revealed that hot gas from burning fuel had damaged rubber seals on one of the two booster rockets used in shuttle launches. The National Aeronautics and Space Administration (NASA) concluded that failure of such a seal, called an O-ring, had caused the Challenger explosion. A damaged seal was also found on an Atlantis booster after its July flight. Seal damage, together with a faulty fuel-cell valve, delayed the lift-off of Endeavour for about a month.

On September 7, Endeavour took five astronauts into orbit to release and then retrieve two research satellites. But problems arose with both satellites. One of them, designed to measure the *solar wind* (charged particles blowing from the sun), went into a spin and faced the wrong way. The other, a 12-foot (3.7 meter) disk on which ultrathin semiconductor films were to be grown, overheated, wobbled, and tilted. Also during the mission, two crew members, James S. Voss and Michael L. Gernhardt, took a 6-hour spacewalk to test heated gloves and thermal clothing designed to keep astronauts warm in temperatures below −100 °F (−73 °C). Endeavour landed at KSC on September 18.

The shuttle Columbia roared into space on October 20 with a crew of seven, after repeated delays caused by a fuel leak, a hurricane, a faulty hydraulic system, and a computer malfunction. During the 16-day flight, the crew studied the effects of low gravity on plants, protein-crystal growth, fire, and various fluids. Columbia landed at KSC on November 5.

Shuttle operations shift. NASA announced plans in 1995 to transfer space shuttle operations to private industry. The switch could take three years, and could cut as much as $1 billion a year from the shuttle program's current $3.1-billion annual budget. NASA also endorsed a plan to develop a new generation of reusable rockets for launching shuttles and other payloads. The rockets would be built, owned, and operated by private companies.

Jupiter probe. On July 12, the Galileo spacecraft began a 2-year reconnaissance of Jupiter and its four largest moons. While still millions of miles from the planet, the spacecraft released a 750-pound (340-kilogram) probe that entered Jupiter's atmosphere on December 7. During its descent, the probe transmitted data on the clouds of the planet's atmosphere back to Galileo. After about 75 minutes of

Russian cosmonaut Valery Polyakov toasts his return to Earth in March. Polyakov spent 439 days in space aboard the space station Mir, setting a new record.

data relay, the probe was destroyed by extreme heat and pressure. Galileo, which was launched from a shuttle in October 1989, then continued its orbit.

The Ulysses spacecraft flew above the sun's north pole on July 31. The craft carried nine instruments used for measuring solar wind, magnetic fields, interplanetary dust and gas, and cosmic rays. It was launched from a shuttle in 1990.

International missions. A Chinese Long March 2 rocket blew up during a launch on January 26, killing 6 people. The Apstar 2 communications satellite, built by the United States for television broadcasts to Asia, was destroyed in the explosion.

In March, Japan launched a platform containing instruments used to search for sources of infrared light in the universe. By late April, more than 50,000 objects that cannot be seen by ground-based telescopes had been detected, including galaxies, stars, and asteroids.

An Israeli communications satellite was lost on March 28 when the converted Russian missile carrying it crashed into the sea off the east coast of Siberia. Two Russian satellites also were destroyed, dealing a blow to Russia's plans to use SS-25 long-range missiles for launching commercial missions. Israel used its own rocket to orbit a spy satellite, Ofek-3, on April 5.　　　　□ William J. Cromie

See also **Astronomy**. In *World Book*, see **Space exploration**.

Spain. The government of Spain in July 1995 was shaken by allegations that Prime Minister Felipe González Márquez in the 1980's had authorized death squads to hunt down members of the Basque separatist group ETA (the initials stand for Basque Homeland and Freedom in the Basque language). González denied the allegations and rejected opposition calls to resign but agreed to call elections by March 1996, more than a year ahead of schedule. His decision to call elections came in July after the Catalán Convergence and Union Party withdrew its support from his government.

Spain's supreme court in August began considering whether to lift González's parliamentary immunity after an investigating judge named the prime minister as a suspect in the campaign against the ETA. The death squads were reported to have killed 27 people between 1983 and 1987 in an effort to destroy the safe havens of the ETA in southern France. ETA violence had claimed about 800 lives since the late 1960's. The judge also named three other senior members of the ruling Socialist Party, including the former deputy prime minister, Narcis Serra. Spain's Senate began its own inquiry into the affair on October 18.

Phone tap scandal. Serra and Defense Minister Julian Garcia Vargas resigned on June 28 following revelations that the military intelligence service, CESID, had taped telephone conversations of many prominent citizens, including King Juan Carlos I, from 1985 to 1994. The two ministers and the government denied having ordered the wiretaps. Two former CESID officials were arrested on charges of illegal telephone monitoring.

Right makes gains. In local elections on May 29, the conservative Popular Party captured control of five regional governments from the Socialists, including the capital region of Madrid. The results put the Popular Party in control of 10 of the country's 17 regions, and reduced the Socialists' regions to four. Independent parties took the other three regions.

Terrorist attacks. José Maria Aznar, leader of the Popular Party, escaped assassination in Madrid on April 20, when a bomb set by the ETA damaged his car. In August, the police arrested three ETA guerrillas on the island of Majorca and charged them with plotting to assassinate King Juan Carlos.

EU presidency. Spain in the second half of 1995 launched several diplomatic initiatives during its six-month tenure as head of the European Union (EU). In November, it held a conference between 15 EU countries and a dozen countries in the Middle East and North Africa. And in December, it sponsored a transatlantic summit between the United States and the EU to remove trade barriers and coordinate efforts on foreign aid and the fight against international crime. ☐ Tom Buerkle

See also **Europe** (Facts in brief table). In *World Book,* see **European Union; Spain.**

Specter, Arlen (1930-   ), Republican senator from Pennsylvania, on March 30, 1995, announced his candidacy for the Republican nomination for President of the United States. Specter, a fiscal conservative, advocated a flat tax and deficit reduction. But as a liberal on social issues, he supported policies favoring labor unions and opposed cuts in abortion funding. But on November 21, Specter announced that he was dropping out of the race.

Specter was born in Wichita, Kansas, on Feb. 12, 1930, the son of Jewish immigrants from Russia. He earned a B.A. from the University of Pennsylvania in 1951 and a law degree from Yale University in 1956.

Specter served as assistant district attorney for the city of Philadelphia from 1959 to 1963, when he joined the Warren Commission, the body that investigated the assassination of President John F. Kennedy. He is credited with creating the so-called single-bullet theory—the theory that the bullet that passed through Kennedy's throat was the same one that wounded Texas Governor John B. Connally.

In 1965, Specter was elected district attorney for Philadelphia. He was reelected in 1969 but lost in 1974.

Specter won a seat in the United States Senate in 1980 and was reelected in 1986 and 1992.

Specter is married to Joan Lois Levy, a businesswoman and member of the Philadelphia city council. They have a son and a daughter. ☐ Lisa Klobuchar

Sports. Harsh business realities in the form of strikes, lockouts, franchise moves and threats to move nearly took the fun out of sports in 1995. Just one year after labor peace was achieved in the National Football League (NFL), the three other major professional team-sports leagues endured severe problems in negotiating contracts with their players.

A 234-day players' strike delayed the start of the major league baseball season three weeks, and the 162-game season was trimmed to 144 games. The players and owners had begun tentative negotiations again by year's end, but there was still no labor agreement. The National Hockey League (NHL) locked out its players for 103 days in late 1994 and early 1995, and its 84-game season was cut to 48 games, with the season opening delayed until January 20. After the 1994-1995 season, the National Basketball Association (NBA) owners locked out players from June 30 to September 18. The lockout ended when the two sides agreed on a new six-year contract.

With average player salaries escalating into the millions of dollars, team owners wanted more luxury boxes and more club, or premium-priced, seats to increase income and ensure profits. Owners wanted modern stadiums and arenas to replace the outmoded ones built in the 1960's and before, and they wanted local governments to build, or at least help build, the facilities.

Sports

About half of the 111 teams in the four sports were getting new or significantly renovated facilities in 1995. Such historic arenas as the Boston Garden and the Montreal Forum were replaced by new buildings.

New cities lured NFL teams with new or modernized stadiums and multimillion-dollar incentive packages. Before the 1995 season, the Los Angeles Rams moved to St. Louis, Missouri, and the Los Angeles Raiders moved back to their old home in Oakland, California. The Cleveland Browns signed an agreement to move to Baltimore in 1996, subject to approval from club owners. The Houston Oilers signed an agreement on Nov. 16, 1995, to move the team to Nashville, Tennessee.

In the NHL, the owners of the Quebec Nordiques sold the team for $75 million on May 25, 1995, and the team moved to Denver, Colorado, where they became the Colorado Avalanche. The Winnipeg Jets were sold for $68 million and seemed likely to move to Phoenix for the 1996-1997 season.

There was expansion, too. The Carolina Panthers and the Jacksonville Jaguars started playing in the NFL in 1995 and won more games than previous expansion teams. The Toronto Raptors and the Vancouver Grizzlies began play in the NBA in the 1995-1996 season. On March 9, 1995, team owners awarded new baseball franchises to Phoenix and Tampa Bay, Florida, to debut in 1998.

Drugs. International swimming officials tightened drug-testing procedures in 1995, especially in China, where 10 swimmers, including two world champions, tested positive in 1994 for illegal bodybuilding anabolic steroids. However, there were two startling cases in 1995 of girls who tested positive at age 14—Liza de Villiers, a South African runner, in April and October, and Jessica Foschi, an American swimmer, in August. Foschi denied using drugs.

Awards. Dan Jansen, an Olympic and world champion speed skater, won the Sullivan Award as America's outstanding amateur athlete of 1994. The other finalists were Michael Johnson and Leroy Burrell (track and field), Shannon Miller and Dominique Dawes (gymnastics), Nancy Kerrigan (figure skating), Tiger Woods (golf), Bruce Baumgartner (wrestling), Tommy Moe (skiing), and Glenn Robinson (basketball).

Other speed skaters who won major awards were Bonnie Blair, an American, and Johann Olaf Koss of Norway, both 1994 Olympic champions. In April 1995, Jansen and Blair were named Sportsman and Sportswoman of the Year by the United States Olympic Committee. Blair and Rebecca Lobo, the University of Connecticut basketball player, were chosen as Sportswomen of the Year by the Women's Sports Foundation in October. In February, Koss received the Jesse Owens International Trophy Award from the International Amateur Athletic Association in recognition of his sportsmanship.

Miguel Indurain of Spain, foreground, heads toward the Paris finish line in the Tour de France, which he won for a record fifth straight time in July.

Among the winners in 1995 were:

Cycling. Miguel Indurain of Spain won the 23-day, 2,270-mile (3,650-kilometer) Tour de France in July and became the first rider to capture the world's most prestigious cycling-race title for five consecutive years. In the world championships in October in Colombia, Indurain won the 26-mile (42-kilometer) time trial but finished second in the 165-mile (266-kilometer) road race, won by Abraham Olano of Spain. Jeannie Longo of France won world championships in the women's road race and the road time trial.

Diving. China won 7 of the 10 events in the major competition of 1995, the World Cup, held September 5 to 9 in Atlanta, Georgia. The only American winners were Brian Earley of Irvine, California, and Kevin McMahon of Fort Lauderdale, Florida, in the men's 3-meter synchronized, a new event. David Pichler won three of the six United States titles for men.

Gymnastics. China won the most medals (10) and tied Romania for the most gold medals (3) in the world championships held from October 1 to 10 in Sabae, Japan. China won the men's team title, and Romania won the women's team title. Li Xiaoshuang of China won the men's all-around title, and Lilia Podkopayeva of Ukraine took the women's all-around crown. The United States won only two medals—a silver by 14-year-old Dominique Moceanu in the women's balance beam and a bronze by the women's team.

Marathon. The major international winners were Martin Fiz of Spain (world men), Manuela Machado of Portugal (world women), Douglas Wakiihuri of Kenya (World Cup men), and Anuta Catuna of Romania (World Cup women). In April, Cosmas Ndeti of Kenya won his third straight Boston Marathon, and Uta Pippig of Germany won the women's race.

Rowing. In the 24 events of the world championships, which ended August 27 in Tampere, Finland, the United States and Italy led with five gold medals each. In total medals, Germany won nine, Italy eight, and the United States and Denmark seven each. The eight-oared champions were the German men and the American women.

Wrestling. With four gold and two bronze medals in the 10 weight classes, the United States won the world free-style team championship in August in Atlanta. The American individual champions were Bruce Baumgartner in super heavyweight (286 pounds [130 kilograms]), Kurt Angle (220 pounds [100 kilograms]), Kevin Jackson (180.5 pounds [82 kilograms]), and Terry Brands (125.5 pounds [57 kilograms]).

Other champions

Archery, world recurve-bow champions: men, Kyung Chui Lee, South Korea; women, Natalya Valeyeva, Moldova.

Badminton, world champions: men, Heryanto Arbi, Indonesia; women, Ye Zhaoying, China.

Biathlon, world champions: men's 20-kilometer, Tomasz Sikora, Poland; women's 15-kilometer, Corinne Niogret, France.

Billiards, world three-cushion champion: Sang Chun Lee, New York City.

Bobsledding, world champions: two-man, Christoph Langen, Germany; four-man, Wolfgang Hoppe, Germany.

Canoeing, world 500-meter champions: men's canoe, Nikolai Buchalov, Bulgaria; men's kayak, Piotr Markiewicz, Poland; women's kayak, Rita Koban, Hungary.

Cricket, World Series champion: Australia.

Croquet, U.S. open champion: Wayne Rodoni, San Mateo, California.

Cross-country, world champions: men, Paul Tergat, Kenya; women, Derartu Tulu, Ethiopia.

Curling, world champions: men, Kerry Burtnyk, Canada; women, Elizabet Johansson-Gustafson, Sweden.

Equestrian, World Cup champions: jumping, Nick Skelton, England; dressage, Anky van Grunsven, Netherlands.

Fencing, world foil champions: men, Dmitri Chevchenko, Russia; women, Laura Badea, Romania.

Field hockey, Atlanta Cup Challenge champions: men, Germany; women, Australia.

Handball, U.S. four-wall champions: men, Dave Chapman, Long Beach, California; women, Anna Engele, St. Paul, Minnesota.

Hang gliding, world champion: Tomas Suchanek, Czech Republic.

Horseshoe pitching, world champions: men, Alan Francis, Blythedale, Missouri; women, Sue Snyder, Madisonville, Kentucky.

Lacrosse, U.S. college champions: men, Syracuse; women, Maryland.

Luge, world champions: men, Armin Zoggeler, Italy; women, Gabi Kohlisch, Germany.

Modern pentathlon, world champions: men, Dmitri Svatkovski, Russia; women, Kristin Danielson, Sweden.

Motorcycle racing, world 500-cc champion: Michael Doohan, Australia.

Orienteering, world classic champions: men, Jorgen Martensson, Sweden; women, Katalin Olah, Hungary.

Racquetball, U.S. champions: men's pro, Cliff Swain, Boston; women's pro/amateur, Michelle Gould, Boise, Idaho.

Rhythmic gymnastics, world all-around champion: Maria Petrova, Bulgaria, and Yekaterina Serebryanskaya, Ukraine (tie).

Roller skating, U.S. freestyle champions: men, Eric Anderson, El Cajon, California; women, Patricia Houle, Convent Station, New Jersey.

Rugby, World Cup men's champion: South Africa.

Shooting, world trap champions: men, Giovanni Pelleilo, Italy; women, Frances Strodtman-Royer, Jackson, Montana.

Short-track speed skating, world overall champions: men, Chae Ji Hoon, South Korea; women, Chun Lee Kyung, South Korea.

Snowboarding, World Cup slalom champions: men, Peter Pichler, Italy; women, Marcella Boerma, the Netherlands.

Soap Box Derby, masters champion: Johnathon Fensterbush, Kingman, Arizona.

Softball, ISC world men's champion: Toronto Gators.

Squash racquets, world men's champions: open, Jansher Khan, Pakistan; team, England.

Surfing, world champions: men, Kelly Slater, Sebastian Inlet, Florida; women, Lisa Anderson, Ormond Beach, Florida.

Synchronized swimming, World Cup champion: Becky Dyroen-Lancer, San Jose, California.

Table tennis, world champions: men, Kong Linghui, China; women, Deng Yaping, China.

Team handball, men's world champion: France.

Triathlon, Ironman champions: men, Mark Allen, Boulder, Colorado; women, Karen Smyers, Lincoln, Massachusetts.

Volleyball, World Cup champions: men, Italy; women, Cuba.

Water polo, FINA World Cup champions: men, Hungary; women, Australia.

Water skiing, world overall champions: men, Patrice Martin, France; women, Judy Messer, Canada.

Weightlifting, world heavyweight champions: men, Andrei Chemerkin, Russia; women Erika Takacs, Hungary. ☐ Frank Litsky

See also articles on the various sports. In *World Book*, see articles on the sports.

Are Professional Team Sports Striking Out?

Fans are growing frustrated with the labor unrest that has been plaguing professional baseball, basketball, football, and hockey.

By Andrew Zimbalist

Sports fans love records, but not the kind that were broken in 1994 and 1995. On Aug. 12, 1994, major league baseball players began a strike that was to last for 234 days. The strike led to an aborted 1994 season and the cancellation of the play-offs and World Series, the first time the World Series had not been played since 1904. Then, on Oct. 1, 1994, National Hockey League (NHL) team owners locked out their players and shut down the sport for 103 days. These simultaneous work stoppages were the longest in the history of professional sports in the United States and Canada.

Many angry fans wondered why seemingly profitable sports with wealthy players and even wealthier owners could not resolve their labor disputes. Many questioned in particular why baseball, often regarded as the national pastime, had endured eight work stoppages from 1972 to 1994.

Labor unrest has pushed the business side of team sports into the foreground. Since the early 1970's, the growing popularity of professional team sports and the spread of team franchises to new cities have accompanied a dramatic rise in player salaries. These salary increases were primarily due to the gradual introduction of free agency, which allowed players who had been in a league for a specified number of years to switch to other teams after their contracts expired. Although attendance and television ratings have grown steadily since the 1970's, problems within leagues and growing tension between owners and players are threatening the continuing success of the sports industry.

However fiercely sports teams may compete with one another on the field, economics requires them to cooperate as businesses. The prosperity of individual teams depends on the overall health of the leagues they play in. Fans often lose interest when one team takes the championship year after year or when teams have such differing abilities that games are virtually decided in advance. Intense or long-standing rivalry between teams, on the other hand, can help boost ticket sales. The Ford Motor Company might not mind if General Motors

Glossary

Free Agency: The right of players to switch teams after their contracts expire.

Lockout: When team owners refuse to let players work until their terms are accepted.

Reserve Clause: A contract provision giving a sports team owner perpetual rights to the services of a player.

Salary Cap: A ceiling on the amount a team can spend on player salaries.

The author

Andrew Zimbalist is Robert A. Woods Professor of Economics at Smith College, the author of *Baseball and Billions* (Basic Books, 1994), cofounder of the United Baseball League, and a sports consultant.

went out of business, but the New York Yankees would definitely be hurt if the Boston Red Sox folded.

Therefore, owners of rival teams tend to cooperate in matters of business. For example, throughout most of the history of team sports in the United States, owners cooperated in maintaining reserve clauses. These clauses gave team owners perpetual rights over a player's services. In baseball, a reserve clause was enacted in 1879, three years after the founding of the National League in 1876. For the next 100 years, the reserve clause remained the focus of resentment among players, who did not receive the salaries they would have earned in a free labor market because teams were prohibited from bidding competitively for their services. The system ensured that players were paid less than the value they produced for team owners.

Evidence of this undervaluing of player services can be found in the rapid rise of salaries after baseball players won the right to limited free agency. In 1976, the last year the old reserve clause was in effect, the average player earned $51,500. By 1994, the average salary was nearly $1.2 million. Increases in other sports were almost as dramatic after the piecemeal introduction of free agency, starting in the late 1970's.

Reserve clauses, though, functioned only within leagues. Thus, when challenges to the National Football League (NFL), National Basketball Association (NBA), and the NHL were made by the American Football League (AFL), American Basketball Association (ABA), and World Hockey Association (WHA) respectively in 1960, 1967, and 1972, players were able to receive competitive bids from the rival leagues. This weakened the effect the reserve clause had in lowering salaries until each of the original leagues subsequently arranged a merger with its new competitor.

Baseball's antitrust exemption

Major league baseball, however, has not had a competitor since 1914–1915. Baseball has been protected from such competition by a unique legal decision. The last league to challenge major league baseball was the Federal League, which folded in 1915 after two seasons. In 1922, the United States Supreme Court decided in a lawsuit by the owners of a Federal League team that baseball was exempt from antitrust laws (laws designed to protect competition by prohibiting monopolies). Justice Oliver Wendell Holmes, Jr., wrote that since baseball is unrelated to production, it is not "trade or commerce in the commonly-accepted use of the words." This ruling has allowed baseball to remain the only professional team sport and the only industry in the United States to exist as an unregulated, legal monopoly.

One important consequence of baseball's antitrust exemption is that franchises can sign amateur players to contracts that bind the players for up to seven years in the minor leagues. This practice, a clear violation of free labor markets, would be illegal without the exemption. Because the minor leagues are the best alternative source of players for a prospective rival league to major league baseball, the exemption has helped prevent competition in the baseball industry.

Work stoppages in professional team sports

Football

1956 The NFL Players Association is founded.

1974 A strike called on June 30 disrupts training camp. Six weeks later, the strike collapses. The regular season starts on schedule.

1982 The players go on strike for 57 days, canceling 8 weeks of the season. The clubs lose $240 million and the players lose $72 million as a result of the strike.

1987 NFL owners field replacement teams after the players call a strike on Sept. 22. The union returns to work on Oct. 15 without a contract and files a federal antitrust suit against the NFL.

Baseball

1953 The Major League Baseball Players Association is founded.

1969 The players strike during spring training.

1972 The players strike April 1–13.

1973 The owners lock out the players prior to the regular season

1976 The owners lock out the players during spring training.

1980 The players strike during the preseason.

1981 The players strike June 12 to July 31.

1985 The players strike August 6–7.

1990 The owners lock out the players prior to spring training.

1994– 1995 MLB players strike for 234 days, canceling the play-offs and World Series.

Basketball

1962 The National Basketball Players Association is founded.

1995 NBA owners institute an off-season lockout. The lockout ends Sept. 18 after players and owners approve a new 6-year labor agreement.

Hockey

1967 The National Hockey League Players Association is founded.

1992 The players strike for 10 days.

1994– 1995 NHL owners lock out the players for 103 days.

The exemption also prevents the baseball players' union from defending itself in court against the owners' efforts to place constraints on the labor market. When owners in other sports attempt to unilaterally impose constraints on salaries, players can claim a violation of antitrust laws in court. For example, instead of continuing a three-week strike in 1987, football players sued the NFL over its refusal to accept a real free-agency plan. In 1994, basketball players sued the NBA over its salary cap (a ceiling on the total amount a team can spend on salaries) and amateur-draft policies. Deprived of a legal recourse to defend their interests, baseball players have resorted to strikes much more often than football, basket-

How Sports Teams Make Money

Ticket sales, arena revenue, radio and television contracts, and licensing agreements are the main sources of team income. But these revenue sources differ in importance among the various sports.

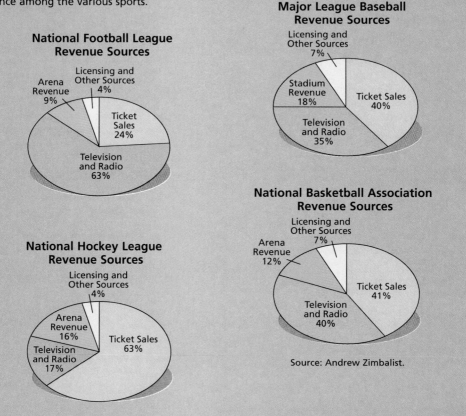

National Football League Revenue Sources

Arena Revenue 9%
Licensing and Other Sources 4%
Ticket Sales 24%
Television and Radio 63%

Major League Baseball Revenue Sources

Licensing and Other Sources 7%
Stadium Revenue 18%
Ticket Sales 40%
Television and Radio 35%

National Hockey League Revenue Sources

Licensing and Other Sources 4%
Arena Revenue 16%
Television and Radio 17%
Ticket Sales 63%

National Basketball Association Revenue Sources

Licensing and Other Sources 7%
Arena Revenue 12%
Television and Radio 40%
Ticket Sales 41%

Source: Andrew Zimbalist.

Attractive new stadiums such as Oriole Park at Camden Yards, where the Baltimore Orioles have played since 1992, can increase team revenues by as much as 40 percent.

Enclosed luxury suites for entertaining and other types of special seating arrangements at newer stadiums generate higher income for sports teams.

ball, or hockey players. Significantly, prior to the 1994 strike, the baseball players' union pledged not to strike in exchange for a partial lifting of the antitrust exemption that would allow it to challenge a salary cap in court.

Because there were no rival leagues to compete for their skills, baseball players fought especially hard to abolish the reserve clause. In 1975, a three-man arbitration panel, ruling in the case of pitchers Andy Messersmith of the Los Angeles Dodgers and Dave McNally, who had been with the Montreal Expos, decided that the reserve clause bound a player for only one year after the expiration of his prior contract. The owners appealed this decision, but it was upheld in federal courts. In 1976, the owners and the players reached a settlement on a modified reserve clause that would allow players with more than six years of major league experience to become free agents and receive competitive bids from other teams.

Free agency developed more slowly in other team sports. Following lawsuits by players, the NFL and NBA introduced versions of free agency during the late 1970's. These concessions, however, were limited by burdensome provisions. Teams signing free agents had to compensate the player's former team, and teams had the right of first refusal, which allows them to retain a free agent by matching a contract offer from another team. Although these two sports have since adopted more open free-agency systems, they both operate under a salary cap, limiting player payrolls to a percentage of overall league revenues. In hockey, free-agency rights are extremely limited and conditional.

With the development of free agency, the economic challenges of operating a professional sports team have grown more complicated. Revenues from television networks or from local stations for rights to telecast games, revenues from licensing merchandise, and special stadium revenues such as luxury boxes have become increasingly important. Exact figures on revenues, however, are difficult to obtain. Almost

Superstar Salaries

The salaries of top players sometimes inspire bigger headlines than their athletic accomplishments and focus attention on the business side of sports.

12-year, $84-million contract

Earnings exceed $6 million a year

Larry Johnson, basketball
Charlotte Hornets, forward

Troy Aikman, football
Dallas Cowboys, quarterback

5-year, 29.5-million contract

3-year, $25.5-million contract

Bobby Bonilla, baseball
Baltimore Orioles, right fielder

Wayne Gretzky, hockey
Los Angeles Kings, center

The average salaries of all professional team sport athletes increased greatly between 1984 and 1994. Basketball players enjoyed the largest 10-year average increase.

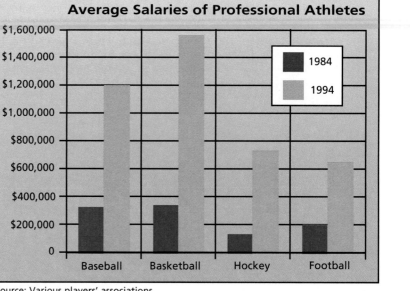

Average Salaries of Professional Athletes

	1984	1994

Vertical axis: $1,600,000 / $1,400,000 / $1,200,000 / $1,000,000 / $800,000 / $600,000 / $400,000 / $200,000 / 0

Horizontal axis: Baseball, Basketball, Hockey, Football

Source: Various players' associations.

all teams keep their finances closely guarded secrets. Except for the NBA's Boston Celtics and the NFL's Green Bay Packers, teams are either privately owned or are subdivisions of larger corporations. In their annual reports, corporations rarely give detailed financial data on a division, making it difficult to learn about the financial performance of a team owned by a corporation. Nevertheless, one can build a general picture of team finances in each of the leagues from information provided through congressional inquiries, newspaper and magazine articles, and documents stemming from lawsuits.

Team income sources

According to these sources, in a typical year the average major league baseball team earns approximately $66 million in total revenues, with the poorest club bringing in about $40 million a year and the richest club around $115 million a year. About 40 percent of team revenues come from ticket sales. National, local, and cable television, along with radio, provide 35 percent of revenues. Luxury boxes, stadium advertising, concession sales, and parking fees provide another 18 percent. Most of the remaining 7 percent comes from licensing merchandise such as trading cards, caps, and clothing. Since 1994, the share of media revenue coming from national television has diminished, while local media income, particularly from cable channels, has grown. Because national television revenue is shared equally among all the clubs and most local media revenue goes to the local team, this trend has led to increased revenue imbalance among the 28 baseball franchises.

Another trend contributing toward revenue inequality in baseball and other sports is the growing importance of stadium and arena revenues, which are retained by the local team. Newer stadiums are more profitable than older ones because they can generate higher income from luxury boxes, semiprivate club seating, improved concessions facilities, and increased stadium advertising. In some cases, the construction of new stadiums has increased team revenues by over 40 percent.

Many owners of teams that play in older stadiums are pressuring cities to provide new facilities. Because sports teams are perceived to be economically important to a city, city officials often scramble to accommodate owners who threaten to move their teams.

Annual team revenues in the NFL range from approximately $53 million to $100 million, with the average team earning $64 million. Since each team has only eight regular-season home

Basketball star Scottie Pippin departs from the Chicago Bulls airplane. Team travel along with stadium or arena rental and player payrolls are among the expenses that must be born by a franchise.

games—as opposed to 81 in baseball—ticket sales account for a relatively small share of revenues (24 percent). Lucrative national television contracts take up the slack, providing 63 percent of total revenues. Revenue imbalance among teams is less of a problem in the NFL than in the other sports because all national television income is shared equally and because home teams share 40 percent of ticket revenues with visiting teams. The only local television income comes from broadcasts of a few preseason games. Stadium revenues apart from ticket sales account for around 9 percent of all income.

In the NBA, annual team revenues range from about $32 million to $84 million, with the average team earning $50 million. About 41 percent of revenues come from ticket sales; 40 percent from television and radio; 12 percent from arena revenue, including luxury suites; and 7 percent from licensing and other sources.

Annual team revenues in the NHL range from $15 million to $55-million, with the average team earning about $35 million. Hockey has low television ratings and small national television contracts. Only 17 percent of team income comes from radio and television. Many observers believe that hockey does not broadcast well on television because the pace of the action and the small puck size make the game difficult to follow. Ticket sales account for 63 percent of revenue, and another 16 percent comes from arena income. Team revenue imbalance is a serious problem in the NHL due to a low level of national revenue and large differences in market size among NHL cities.

Team expenses

Along with the economic challenges of generating revenue for a sports team comes the challenge of meeting team expenses. Player payrolls are the largest expense in every major team sport, so it is not surprising that player salaries have inspired so much conflict in the sports industry. But also figured into payroll costs are such other benefits as bonuses, deferred payments, insurance, taxes, and pensions.

NFL teams with active rosters of 45 players have a *mean salary* of $650,000 (half the players earn more; half, less). The average payroll is about $40 million (62 percent of team revenues). Major league baseball teams, with active rosters of 25 players and a mean salary of $1.2 million, have an average payroll approaching $36 million (55 percent of team revenues). NHL teams, with active rosters of 20 players and a mean salary of $733,000, have an average payroll of $14 million (40 percent of team revenues). NBA teams, with active rosters of 12 players and a mean salary of $1,558,000, have an average payroll near $20 million. NBA payrolls are 40 percent of team revenues.

Other team expenses include stadium or arena rental and maintenance; team travel; front-office operations such as administration, marketing, and ticketing; and payments to the central league office. In addition, owners often pay themselves or family members substantial salaries or consulting fees. For example, the antitrust suit of Freeman McNeil v. the NFL revealed that in 1990 Ralph Wilson, owner of the NFL's Buffalo Bills, paid himself nearly $3.5 million, and Norman

Braman, former owner of the Philadelphia Eagles, paid himself $7.5-million. These kinds of salaries inflate team operating costs and reduce reported profits.

The profitability of sports teams is a contentious issue. Many owners claim that high player salaries have made it difficult for teams in smaller markets to stay competitive without losing money. This problem is particularly acute in baseball and hockey, where the relatively small share of income from national television has helped increase revenue imbalance among teams.

Players often argue that owners give a misleading account of their profits. The high salaries that some owners pay themselves are one example of how sports team owners take their investment return in a form other than explicit profits. Another example can be found in the undervaluing of local television and radio rights. If the same person or company owns both a sports team and a local television or radio station, the owner can underpay the sports franchise for broadcast rights, in effect transferring revenue from the team to the broadcast station. The Tribune Company, for instance, owns both the superstation WGN and the Chicago Cubs. WGN broadcasts 140 Cubs games per season to about 38 million households across the United States. Based on standard spot advertising prices, the annual broadcast rights for Cubs games should be worth more than $40 million to WGN, but the superstation only pays the Cubs about $10 million. The team's reported revenues may be artificially reduced by the $30-million difference. This common accounting technique, known as transfer pricing or related party transactions, can also be used when a person or company owns both a sports team and its stadium or arena.

The prevalence of such practices suggests that revenue figures for many sports teams may be understated. In general, professional sports teams are thought to be profitable investments. According to *Financial World*, the average NBA team earned $10.5 million in operating profits during the 1993–1994 season. NHL teams averaged $3.8 million in operating profits during the 1993–1994 season, and NFL teams averaged $3.1 million during the 1994 season. *Financial World* estimated that if the entire 1994 baseball season had been played, total team profits would have amounted to $150 million, though some teams in smaller markets would have shown losses.

Another profitable aspect of owning a

Empty seats at Shea Stadium in New York City, during a game between the Mets and the San Diego Padres on Memorial Day 1995, provide an example of the decrease in attendance that followed the previous season's baseball players' strike and cancellation of the 1994 World Series.

sports team derives from the public exposure and business ties the owners reap. Such exposure and relationships can be helpful for an owner's other business interests. Some team owners also receive tax sheltering opportunities and interest income.

But the largest returns for owners have come in the form of rapidly growing franchise values. For example, Eli Jacobs purchased the Baltimore Orioles in 1989 for $70 million. He sold the team four years later to a group of investors for $173 million. It is certainly possible for teams to lose money due to the small size of their market, unattractive stadiums or arenas, poor competitive performance, inadequate promotion, and faulty management. The average franchise, however, seems to be profitable in all four sports.

Labor unrest in the world of sports

Each of the major sports has experienced labor unrest since 1972. Revenue imbalance is a central problem underlying troubled labor relations. Teams in large markets with attractive facilities can earn up to three times as much revenue as teams in smaller markets, but to remain competitive the small-market team must pay the same high player salaries as the large-market team. Without some means of compensating for this imbalance, poorer teams find it difficult to retain highly paid players.

Baseball and hockey, the two sports hit by work stoppages in 1994 and 1995, have the greatest revenue imbalances. Instead of sharing more revenue among themselves, baseball and NHL owners tried to prop up weaker franchises by reducing player costs, either through a proposed salary cap or a so-called "luxury tax," whereby any team that exceeded a set payroll amount would have to pay a punitive tax.

The hockey players, already deprived of effective free-agency rights and with the lowest average salaries in the major team sports, refused to accept additional restrictions on their labor market. On Oct. 1, 1994, the owners locked out the players, postponing the start of the season until the players accepted their terms. On Jan. 11, 1995, the owners and players agreed on a six-year contract that did not include salary controls except for a cap on rookie salaries.

Each side made compromises. The owners allowed players over 32 years old (31 years beginning in 1998) to become unrestricted agents. The players agreed to some weakening of salary arbitration by allowing the owners to release players if they disagree with the arbitration award and if the award is above the league average salary. The regular 1995 NHL season was reduced from 84 to 48 games.

Baseball owners demanded a salary cap in June 1994, claiming that free agency had driven player salaries too high and needed to be restrained. The players argued that free agency was already limited to those who played six years in the majors, and that the owners themselves were to blame for high salaries. After negotiations stalled during the summer, the players went on strike on August 12. Finally, on March 31, 1995, a complaint that the players had filed with the National Labor Relations Board led to a federal court injunction that prevented the owners from implementing unilateral changes in the labor contract. The union immediately called off the strike. The owners, facing massive legal damages if they ordered a lockout, agreed on April 2 to accept the players back without a new labor agreement.

On Jan. 6, 1993, NFL owners and players agreed on a new seven-year labor contract that introduced unrestricted free agency and a salary cap. The league had been operating without a collective-bargaining agreement since 1987. Negotiations between the two sides gained momentum after running back Freeman McNeil of the New York Jets and seven other players won an antitrust suit against the NFL in 1992.

Basketball has had a salary cap since 1983. The basketball players' union sued the NBA owners on two occasions, claiming that they were hiding important revenue sources by excluding them from the definition of revenues used to limit team payrolls. The first suit was settled for $60 million in favor of the players. The second suit was still pending in 1995. The 1994–1995 season was played without a labor agreement but with a moratorium on the signing of free agents and on contract adjustments. In August 1995, the team owners and the basketball players' union negotiated a new agreement. After a group of players failed in their attempt to decertify the union, the players ratified the agreement in September. Even after labor disputes are resolved, the damage from a work stoppage may continue. Prior to the most recent baseball strike, all of the major team sports were experiencing record attendance levels. Midway through the 1995 season, however, the average attendance at National League baseball games was 24,224 fans per game, down from 30,694 in 1994. Average attendance at American League games was 23,624, down from 28,755 in 1994, and revenues in both leagues were down because of this drop-off in attendance. A vibrant industry just two years ago, major league baseball may now be financially fragile. By staying away from games, fans have issued a clear warning that their allegiance to a sport can no longer be taken for granted.

Like all industries, the professional leagues face change and uncertainty. New revenue sources, including luxury suites and cable television, are increasingly important to the financial health of teams. The major team sports must compete for audiences not only with other professional sports, such as tennis, but also with college sports and other forms of entertainment.

The immediate challenge facing each of the leagues, however, is internal. Owners have tried to alleviate the problems of small-market franchises by restraining player salaries and pressuring cities for new stadiums and arenas. These efforts have led to increased tension between owners of big-market and small-market teams, between owners and city officials, and most importantly between owners and players. If the sports leagues find a way to resolve their ownership rifts and labor instability soon, their games will continue to flourish. But if they fail to do so, players, owners, and fans may have a rough schedule ahead of them. ■ ■ ■

Sri Lanka. Fighting escalated in 1995 between the government, which is controlled by Sinhalese Buddhists, the nation's ethnic majority, and a guerrilla army of Tamil Hindus, a minority group seeking an independent state in north and northeast Sri Lanka. Between 35,000 and 50,000 had died in the civil war since it began in 1983.

Chandrika Kumaratunga became president in 1994 on a platform to end the war. She reached a truce agreement on Jan. 5, 1995, with Velupillai Prabhakaran, head of the guerrilla army, the Liberation Tigers of Tamil Eelam (LTTE). The government then loosened its blockade of the Jaffna Peninsula at Sri Lanka's northern tip where the LTTE had its headquarters. But in peace talks, the LTTE sought more concessions and refused to discuss a political solution.

Breaking the truce, LTTE divers sank two navy gunboats on April 19, killing 12 sailors. Prabhakaran wrote to Kumaratunga that he was withdrawing from the peace talks, which he claimed the government was dragging out in order to build up the army. Kumaratunga reinstated the blockade.

In late April, the LTTE used missiles for the first time to shoot down two planes carrying army troops toward the Jaffna Peninsula, killing 97 men. In July, the army captured large areas of LTTE-held territory in a major offensive. But accidental bombings took a toll of civilians, including 121 killed in a Roman Catholic church. The LTTE used women and children in counterattacks, and in one battle alone more than 300 were killed.

Peace plan. On August 3, as the offensive began to slow, Kumaratunga proposed changes in the constitution that she hoped would end the war. She offered to turn Sri Lanka into a federal state of eight regions. Parts of the north and east provinces, having Tamil majorities, would be joined to create a Tamil self-governing region. The LTTE signaled its rejection of the plan with a suicide bomb attack on a government building on August 7, killing 22 people.

New offensive. On October 17, the army launched the biggest offensive of the war against the LTTE, using more than 35,000 infantrymen and other forces. In an effort to relieve Jaffna, LTTE forces attacked Sinhalese villages in eastern Sri Lanka, hacking to death more than 120 men, women, and children, and on October 20 an LTTE commando squad blew up two major oil depots in the national capital, Colombo. But on December 5, the army captured Jaffna city and raised the national flag, though fighting continued.

Economic growth. Despite the war and military spending, Sri Lanka's economy continued to grow at more than 5 percent a year. On November 17, the Parliament passed a 1996 budget that included large increases for the military.　　□ Henry S. Bradsher

See also **Asia** (Facts in brief table). In **World Book**, see **Sri Lanka**.

State government. The year 1995 saw the enactment of a conservative agenda in many of the largest states in the Union. With Republicans in charge of 31 of the 50 governorships, many states adopted welfare reforms, enacted tougher criminal laws, and limited the damages awarded in lawsuits.

Some of the most dramatic policy changes took place in New York, where voters replaced Governor Mario M. Cuomo, a liberal Democrat, with conservative Republican George E. Pataki. Aided by a Republican Senate, Pataki cut the personal income tax rate by 25 percent and reduced spending from the general fund to below the 1994 level. In addition, Pataki signed a bill reinstating the death penalty, which Cuomo had vetoed for the past 18 years, and enacted a law requiring able-bodied welfare recipients to work or lose their welfare benefits.

Crime and punishment. States continued to fund more prisons and push for tougher sentences for people convicted of crimes, as they have done for the last several years. Texas approved a $2-billion prison-building program and moved the state's prisoners out of county jails and into state prisons. As a result, Texas counties lost some $200 million in funding from the state government, and some Texas counties began accepting out-of-state inmates on a paying basis. Virginia, for example, contracted to send 700 inmates to Newton County, Texas.

Florida, Illinois, Minnesota, Nebraska, and New York were among the states that in 1995 passed laws lengthening prison sentences for violent offenders. Ohio enacted a so-called truth-in-sentencing law, which required violent criminals to serve out 85 percent of their sentence before being eligible for *parole* (early conditional release from prison).

Nebraska and New Jersey in 1995 joined the growing number of states that have enacted "three-strikes" laws, which require life imprisonment without parole after the third conviction for a violent crime. An Associated Press survey found, however, that only California had sentenced a significant number of offenders under a three-strikes law. The state imprisoned some 700 repeat offenders for life from March 1994 to August 1995.

To ensure the safety of runaway teen-agers, a new law in Washington state gave police the power to pick up runaway youths and detain them in a locked facility. The law was passed after Rebecca Hedman, a chronic runaway, was murdered in Spokane. Georgia authorized state counties and cities to establish holding facilities for youths who violate local curfews.

The New Jersey Supreme Court in July upheld the constitutionality of a state law that requires convicted sex offenders to register with local police after their release. The police, in turn, must notify the community of the offender's release. The law was passed in 1994 following the murder of 7-year-old Megan Kanka by a convicted sex offender who lived across the street from her home in Hamilton. Similar laws were passed in 1995 by Iowa, Maryland, New York, and New Mexico. By year-end, more than 40 states required the registration of released sex offenders with police, and half the states required police to notify neighbors of the person's presence.

The Supreme Court of the United States on April 26 struck down a 1990 federal law that banned the possession of guns within 1,000 feet (300 meters) of a school. The high court said that Congress does not have authority over such matters and that states should regulate school safety. Some 40 state laws restricting guns near schools remained in effect.

Welfare reforms. Congress in 1995 proposed to turn over more authority to state governments for allocating welfare benefits. The proposal called for the federal government to make a single lump-sum payment to each state, which could then decide how to use the funds. (Existing laws allowed the federal government to specify how certain federal funds are spent.) Congress also sought to end certain guaranteed welfare benefits known as entitlements. Among those entitlements was access to health care for welfare recipients under the Medicaid program.

A number of states in 1995 sought and received waivers from the federal government, allowing them to make changes in welfare programs that receive federal funding. The program most often targeted was Aid to Families with Dependent Children

(AFDC). Although each state made its own reforms, there were some common threads. Most reforms required AFDC recipients to work or to seek education or job training that would enable them to find work. Many reforms placed a time limit on the payment of welfare benefits—typically two years. Some states also required teen-age mothers to live with a parent, and some states adopted a "family cap" that would deny additional benefits to women who conceived a child while on welfare.

Limiting lawsuits. In a determined effort to hold down insurance costs, at least 18 states passed some type of reform restricting consumers' rights to file lawsuits against manufacturers of faulty products and against physicians for malpractice. The most comprehensive and far-reaching laws were pushed through state legislatures by Republican governors in Illinois, Michigan, New Jersey, Texas, and Wisconsin.

State health reforms. In an effort to save money, several states sought or received federal waivers allowing them to enroll Medicaid recipients in managed-care programs—health-care plans that provide comprehensive care for a fixed fee. Some states used the savings produced by managed care to expand coverage to more low-income families. By year-end, more than half the states had used federal waivers to move Medicaid patients into managed care.

Not all the states achieved a smooth transition to

Toward an official language

In 1995, laws in 22 states made English the official language. Proponents said such laws serve to facilitate communication in an ethnically diverse nation. Critics said the laws send a message that immigrants are unwelcome.

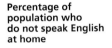
States where English is the official language

Percentage of population who do not speak English at home

Alabama	2.9%
Arizona	20.8%
Arkansas	2.8%
California	31.5%
Colorado	10.5%
Florida	17.3%
Georgia	4.8%
Illinois	14.2%
Indiana	4.8%
Kentucky	2.5%
Louisiana	10.1%
Mississippi	2.8%
Montana	5.0%
Nebraska	4.8%
New Hampshire	8.7%
North Carolina	3.9%
North Dakota	7.9%
South Carolina	3.5%
South Dakota	6.5%
Tennessee	2.9%
Virginia	7.3%

* Hawaii has two official languages, English and Hawaiian.

Sources: English First, U.S. Census Bureau.

Selected statistics on state governments

State	Resident population*	Governor†	House (D)	House (R)	Senate (D)	Senate (R)	State tax revenue‡	Tax revenue per capita‡	Public school expenditures per pupil§
Alabama	4,062,608	Fob James, Jr. (R)	73	32	23	12	$ 4,640,000,000	$1,110	$4,460
Alaska	551,947	Tony Knowles (D)	17	22#	8	12	2,227,000,000	3,720	9,980
Arizona	3,677,985	Fife Symington (R)	22	38	11	19	5,282,000,000	1,340	4,300
Arkansas	2,362,239	Jim Guy Tucker (D)	88	12	28	7	2,943,000,000	1,210	4,110
California	29,839,250	Pete Wilson (R)	39	41	21	17**	48,738,000,000	1,560	4,650
Colorado	3,307,912	Roy Romer (D)	24	41	16	19	3,789,000,000	1,060	5,500
Connecticut	3,295,699	John G. Rowland (R)	91	60	17	19	6,675,000,000	2,040	8,600
Delaware	688,696	Tom Carper (D)	14	27	12	9	1,340,000,000	1,910	7,150
Florida	13,003,362	Lawton Chiles (D)	63	57	18	22	16,407,000,000	1,200	5,680
Georgia	6,508,419	Zell Miller (D)	112	66††	35	21	8,150,000,000	1,180	4,980
Hawaii	1,115,274	Ben Cayetano (D)	44	7	23	2	2,748,000,000	2,340	6,140
Idaho	1,011,986	Phil Batt (R)	13	57	8	27	1,560,000,000	1,420	4,230
Illinois	11,466,682	Jim Edgar (R)	54	64	27	32	14,500,000,000	1,240	5,260
Indiana	5,564,228	Evan Bayh (D)	44	56	20	30	6,915,000,000	1,210	5,620
Iowa	2,787,424	Terry E. Branstad (R)	36	64	27	23	3,902,000,000	1,390	5,440
Kansas	2,485,600	Bill Graves (R)	44	81	13	27	3,276,000,000	1,290	5,900
Kentucky	3,698,969	Paul E. Patton (D)	62	37‡‡	21	17	5,277,000,000	1,390	5,610
Louisiana	4,238,216	Murphy J. (Mike) Foster (R)	78	27	26	13	4,366,000,000	1,020	4,930
Maine	1,233,223	Angus King (I)	76	75	16	18#	1,764,000,000	1,420	6,370
Maryland	4,798,622	Parris N. Glendening (D)	100	41	32	15	7,175,000,000	1,450	6,720
Massachusetts	6,029,051	William F. Weld (R)	125	34#	30	10	10,383,000,000	1,730	6,940
Michigan	9,328,784	John Engler (R)	54	56	16	22	13,177,000,000	1.390	6,780
Minnesota	4,387,029	Arne H. Carlson (R)	69	65	43	24	8,137,000,000	1,800	5,800
Mississippi	2,586,443	Kirk Fordice (R)	85	34§§	34	18	2,983,000,000	1,130	3,700
Missouri	5,137,804	Mel Carnahan (D)	87	76	19	15	5,480,000,000	1,050	5,000
Montana	803,655	Marc Racicot (R)	33	67	19	31	1,130,000,000	1,350	5,620
Nebraska	1,584,617	E. Benjamin Nelson (D)	unicameral (49 nonpartisan)				1,981,000,000	1,230	5,300
Nevada	1,206,152	Bob Miller (D)	21	21	8	13	2,207,000,000	1,590	5,170
New Hampshire	1,113,915	Steve Merrill (R)	112	280##	6	18	993,000,000	880	6,390
New Jersey	7,748,634	Christine Todd Whitman (R)	30	50	16	24	13,026,000,000	1,650	9,890
New Mexico	1,521,779	Gary E. Johnson (R)	46	24	27	15	2,777,000,000	1,720	5,410
New York	18,044,505	George E. Pataki (R)	94	56	25	36	31,291,000,000	1,720	9,300
North Carolina	6,657,630	James B. Hunt, Jr. (D)	52	68	26	24	9,757,000,000	1,400	5,070
North Dakota	641,364	Edward T. Shafer (R)	23	75	20	29	877,000,000	1,380	4,640
Ohio	10,887,325	George V. Voinovich (R)	42	56#	13	20	12,788,000,000	1,150	5,910
Oklahoma	3,157,604	Frank Keating (R)	65	36	35	13	4,166,000,000	1,290	4,330
Oregon	2,853,733	John Kitzhaber (D)	26	34	11	19	3,658,000,000	1,210	6,230
Pennsylvania	11,924,710	Tom J. Ridge (R)	101	101††	21	29	16,601,000,000	1,380	7,570
Rhode Island	1,005,984	Lincoln C. Almond (R)	84	16	40	10	1,433,000,000	1,430	7,350
South Carolina	3,505,707	David Beasley (R)	54	66***	25	20#	4,289,000,000	1,180	4,730
South Dakota	699,999	William J. Janklow (R)	24	46	16	19	589,000,000	820	4,920
Tennessee	4,896,641	Don Sundquist (R)	59	40	16	17	5,117,000,000	1,000	4,540
Texas	17,059,805	George W. Bush (R)	86	64	17	14	18,241,000,000	1,010	5,490
Utah	1,727,784	Michael O. Leavitt (R)	20	55	10	19	2,212,000,000	1,190	3,630
Vermont	564,964	Howard Dean (D)	86	61†††	12	18	793,000,000	1,380	7,170
Virginia	6,216,568	George Allen (R)	52	47#	20	20	7,572,000,000	1,170	5,660
Washington	4,887,941	Mike Lowry (D)	37	61	25	24	8,904,000,000	1,690	5,960
West Virginia	1,801,625	Gaston Caperton (D)	69	31	26	8	2,475,000,000	1,360	6,010
Wisconsin	4,906,745	Tommy G. Thompson (R)	48	51	15	17‡‡	7,956,000,000	1,580	6,990
Wyoming	455,975	Jim Geringer (R)	13	47	10	20	662,000,000	1,410	5,940

*1990 Census (source: U.S. Bureau of the Census).
†As of December 1995 (source: state government officials).
‡1993 figures (source: U.S. Bureau of the Census).
§1994-1995 figures for elementary and secondary students in average daily attendance (source: National Education Association).
#One independent.
**Two independents.

††Two vacancies.
‡‡One vacancy.
§§Three independents.
##One libertarian; one independent; six vacancies.
***Four independents.
†††Two independents; one progressive.

managed care, however. New York state, for example, in July stopped managed-care programs from enrolling Medicaid patients directly after several of the programs failed to deliver on their promises.

Some states started their own programs to make health insurance more widely available to those without it. New Jersey poured $50 million into a new Health Access program to subsidize health insurance for at least 30,000 uninsured state residents. Kentucky in July began operating a Health Purchasing Alliance, created by a 1994 law, to make health insurance more affordable. Other states enacting similar reforms included Montana, New York, North Dakota, Utah, and Wyoming.

Other states backed off earlier health-care reforms. Washington repealed most of its ground-breaking 1993 Health Services Act, which required employers to pay for half the insurance coverage of employees. Oregon scaled down an innovative 1994 health plan that limited Medicaid coverage to 587 medical procedures in order to expand Medicaid eligibility to more low-income families. And Minnesota repealed portions of a landmark 1993 law that included a mandate to provide every state resident with health insurance by July 1997.

Education. Support grew in 1995 for the establishment of public schools that are not under the control of local school districts. Parents, teachers, and other groups operate such schools under a charter granted by the state. Freed from most of the regulations other public schools face, the charter schools can create their own curriculum and policies. Arizona and Massachusetts opened their first charter schools during the year, and laws passed in 8 states during 1995 brought to 19 the number of states authorizing these innovative schools.

In a blow to affirmative action, the University of California Board of Regents voted on July 20 to end preference in admissions given to members of racial minorities. California Governor Pete Wilson, who heads the regents, supported a policy that required all campuses in the system to admit from 50 percent to 75 percent of their students solely on the basis of academic achievement. The policy was to take effect Jan. 1, 1997.

Taxes and finance. No state raised its income or sales tax rates in 1995, and nearly half the states reduced taxes. Among the largest reductions was a $240-million tax cut pushed through the state legislature by Pennsylvania Governor Tom J. Ridge, a Republican who took office in January. In New Jersey, Republican Governor Christine Todd Whitman completed a 30 percent tax cut she had promised in her 1994 election campaign. In North Carolina, Democratic Governor James B. Hunt, Jr., signed $300 million in tax cuts aimed primarily at the middle class and at businesses.   □ Elaine Stuart

In *World Book,* see **State government** and the articles on the individual states.

Stocks and bonds. United States stock and bond markets boomed in 1995, as shrinking inflation and expanding corporate profits gave investors a powerful incentive to buy. After a strong finish to 1994, the economy settled into what came to be known as a "soft landing." This meant that inflation stayed low while the economy grew moderately. The result was a near-perfect climate for stocks and bonds. The popularity of *mutual funds* (publicly sold pools of stocks and bonds) provided a steady source of cash for 1995's market rally.

The daily Dow Jones Industrial Average, a composite of the stock prices of 30 major companies, recorded 69 record-high closes in 1995 and only one downturn of more than 100 points. The Dow closed above 4,000 for the first time on February 23 and kept rising to close above 5,000 on November 22. At year-end, it closed at 5,117.12, up 33 percent for the year and well above the average annual return on stocks of about 10 percent.

Broader stock market indexes, including Standard & Poor's (S&P) 500-Stock Index and the National Association of Securities Dealers Automated Quotation (NASDAQ) system, rose virtually in lockstep with the 30 Dow industrials. By the end of 1995, the S&P 500 index was up 34 percent for the year. The NASDAQ composite index, which is dominated by major computer technology companies, had gained 40 percent.

After peaking at 8.16 percent in early November 1994, the yield on the 30-year U.S. Treasury bond fell to less than 6 percent by the end of 1995. The yield on three-month U.S. Treasury bills peaked at just over 6 percent on February 1 and fell to 5.08 percent at year-end.

Winners and losers. Computer-related technology stocks, especially speculative new stocks related to the global web of computer networks called the Internet, advanced strongly in 1995. For example, the stock of Netscape Communications Corporation, which makes software for browsing the Internet, more than doubled in price on its first day of trading August 9. It began at $28 a share and closed the year at $139 a share.

More-traditional sectors of the market also boomed, with airline stocks winning big. Stocks of the employee-owned parent company of United Airlines, UAL Inc., soared 140 percent in 1995 to $210 a share on November 30. Banking stocks also did well, such as Citicorp's nearly 80 percent gain.

Among stocks that did poorly were those of companies unable to benefit from little or no inflation. For example, USX-U.S. Steel Group Inc. closed 1994 at $35.50 a share and traded at about $30 a share at the end of 1995. Gold mining stocks also did poorly.

Investors poured money into mutual funds at a rate of about $10 billion a month. New public offerings of stock also rose to record levels. Companies issuing stock for the first time raised nearly $30 billion in 1995, up from $23 billion in 1994.

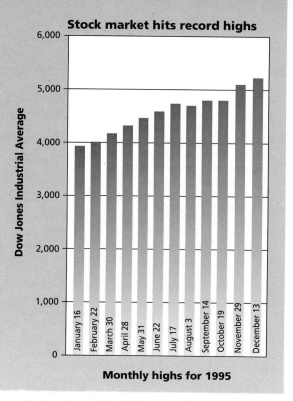

Stock market hits record highs

Dow Jones Industrial Average

Monthly highs for 1995

6,000
5,000
4,000
3,000
2,000
1,000
0

January 16
February 22
March 30
April 28
May 31
June 22
July 17
August 3
September 14
October 19
November 29
December 13

The Dow Jones Industrial Average hit more than 70 record highs in 1995, closing for the first time above 4,000 in February and rising over 5,000 in November.

International stock markets. Many U.S. investors bailed out of international stocks after the 1994 Mexican peso devaluation severely eroded stock prices throughout Latin America. Despite continued political and economic uncertainties, though, the Mexican stock market rallied in November 1995 to levels not seen in over a year. In early December, the IPC Bolsa index at the Mexican Stock Exchange was up nearly 17 percent for the year.

The other major comeback story occurred on the Tokyo Stock Exchange. The Nikkei Index of 225 major Japanese companies fell 26 percent from the end of 1994 to the middle of 1995 but recovered to break above the 20,000 mark in late December. The United States and Japan helped rescue the troubled Japanese banking system, which was plagued by bad loans and sharply declining real estate values.

In London, hopes for lower interest rates and a resurgent economy in Europe kept share prices rising in line with Wall Street stocks. The London Financial Times-Stock Exchange index of 100 stocks climbed 20 percent by year-end. Canadian stocks rallied in the first half of the year but slipped during debate on a referendum on whether to make Quebec an independent nation. After the proposal lost in October, stocks resumed their rally. By the end of December, the Toronto Stock Exchange index of 300 stocks had gained 12 percent for 1995.   □ Bill Barnhart

In *World Book,* see **Bond; Investment; Stock.**

Sudan. Tensions rose between Egypt and Sudan when Egypt accused Sudan's President Umar Hasan Ahmad al-Bashir of supporting an assassination attempt against Egyptian President Hosni Mubarak on June 26, 1995. Sudan denied the charges. Mubarak called for Bashir's overthrow, and he reasserted control of a remote wedge of desert territory bordering the two countries and the Red Sea. The area, believed to be rich in oil, had been contested by the two nations for decades, though Sudan had been administering it.

Former United States President Jimmy Carter brokered a truce in March between the factions in Sudan's 12-year-old civil war. But real chances for peace remained slim as sporadic fighting continued during 1995 between the north's mainly Arab and Islamic governmental forces and the south's mainly Christian rebels. The war had killed more than 1 million people since 1983, either through fighting or related famines. The neighboring states of Uganda, Kenya, and Eritrea were accused by Sudan in 1995 of aiding the rebels.

The war had hurt Sudan financially, costing at least $1 million daily, but in 1995 officials announced renewed efforts to find and exploit oil deposits. Sudan's most promising deposits, however, lay south where the war raged.   □ Christine Helms

See also **Middle East** (Facts in brief table). In *World Book,* see **Sudan.**

Supreme Court of the United States.

During its 1994-1995 term, the Supreme Court of the United States issued important rulings on gun possession near schools, term limits for politicians, the racial redrawing of voting districts, and affirmative action. The term was also marked by the death of retired Chief Justice Warren E. Burger at age 87.

Burger, who died on June 25, headed the court from 1969 until 1986. Although President Richard M. Nixon nominated Burger to stem the liberal tide of the court under the previous chief justice, Earl Warren, Burger presided during a period when the court established a woman's right to an abortion, granted public schools the right to bus students to achieve racial desegregation, and upheld some applications of racial preferences in hiring practices and college admissions. In July 1974, Burger joined a unanimous court in ruling that Nixon had to turn over secret tape recordings of White House conversations concerning the Watergate scandal—an attempted burglary of the headquarters of the Democratic National Committee and a subsequent cover-up. Nixon resigned two weeks later, after the tapes revealed his participation in the cover-up.

Voting rights. In possibly the most explosive ruling of the term, the court said on June 29, 1995, that redrawing the boundaries of electoral districts strictly on the basis of voters' race was unconstitutional. The 5-to-4 ruling involved a Georgia congressional district that had been drawn in 1992 to increase minority voting strength. In 1993, the court ruled that bizarrely drawn districts designed to boost minority representation might violate constitutional guarantees of equal rights. But in the Georgia case, the justices said that they had based their decision on the constitutionality of using race as the main consideration in setting boundaries, not on the bizarre shape of the district—a 250-mile (400-kilometer) corridor.

In an effort to increase minority representation in the U.S. Congress, a number of voting districts were redrawn in 1992 to reflect population shifts revealed by the 1990 U.S. census. Largely because of such redistricting, the number of blacks in the 435-member House of Representatives grew from 24 to 39 after the 1992 elections. Critics of the court's ruling said the decision threatened many of these districts.

Term limits. The court, ruling in an Arkansas case, said states may not place limits on the number of terms that members of the U.S. Congress may serve. In a 5-to-4 decision on May 22, 1995, the justices said a constitutional amendment would be needed to grant states the right to impose term limits. The U.S. Constitution lists age, citizenship, and residency requirements for members of Congress, but it does not restrict the number of terms they may serve. A constitutional amendment would require approval by two-thirds of both the House and the Senate and ratification by 38 of the 50 states.

The ruling effectively overturned laws adopted by 23 states that limit congressional service.

Affirmative action. On June 12, the court limited Congress's power to require federal agencies to give special preferences to minorities and women in awarding contracts for work on publicly funded projects. Voting 5 to 4 in a Colorado case, the court said preference programs must be narrowly designed to remedy clear cases of past discrimination. To assume that someone is a victim of discrimination simply by virtue of belonging to a certain population group is unwarranted, the court said, and basing federal preferences on such an assumption is unconstitutional. The restriction has applied to state and local government programs since 1989. In the Colorado ruling, the justices said federal agencies should follow the same standard.

The Colorado case involved a Federal Highway Administration program, but the decision threatened the continuation of many other affirmative action efforts. On July 19, 1995, U.S. President Bill Clinton directed federal agencies to make sure their affirmative action programs complied with the new guidelines set by the court.

Desegregation. Ruling 5 to 4 on June 12, the Supreme Court reversed a ruling by a federal appeals court that required Missouri to continue funding pay raises and educational improvements as a means of promoting desegregation in a Kansas City,

Demonstrators march in front of the Supreme Court building in Washington, D.C., in January to urge the court to preserve minority hiring preferences.

Missouri, school district. The improvements were intended to make predominantly black schools in the district so outstanding that white students from surrounding areas would enroll voluntarily in them.

In their ruling, the justices also rejected the argument that court-ordered school desegregation plans cannot be ended if students' test scores have not reached national norms. The court said that below-normal scholastic achievement by a school district's minority students is relevant to the continuation of a desegregation plan only if the students' performance is clearly related to past discrimination.

Firearms. The justices on April 26 struck down a federal law banning the possession of firearms within 1,000 feet (300 meters) of a school. Voting 5 to 4, the court said that Congress does not have authority over such local matters and that states should regulate school safety. By late 1995, more than 40 states had made it a crime to have a gun on or near school grounds. A high school student in San Antonio challenged the federal law after he was convicted and sentenced to six months in prison for bringing a loaded gun to school.

Drug testing. The court ruled on June 26 that public schools can require student athletes to take tests for possible drug use even if school authorities have no reason to believe the students are using illegal substances. The 6-to-3 ruling came in the case of an Oregon seventh-grader who was banned from his school's football team for refusing to agree to a urine test. The justices said that because schools have a responsibility to safeguard students' health and safety, the school district's testing policy did not violate the Constitution's Fourth Amendment guarantee against unreasonable searches and seizures.

Free speech. Public universities that subsidize student-run journals cannot deny funding to religious publications because of their content, the court ruled on June 29. The justices voted 5 to 4 that the University of Virginia violated First Amendment free-speech protections by refusing to fund a student magazine called *Wide Awake: A Christian Perspective at the University of Virginia.* The court said that giving the magazine a share of a student activities fund financed by student fees did not amount to an unconstitutional endorsement of religion. The decision was the first in the Supreme Court's history in which the court supported the funding of a religious activity by a government body.

The court on June 19 said the South Boston Allied War Veterans Council should have been allowed to exclude homosexuals from participating in its annual St. Patrick's Day parade. The court's unanimous ruling said previous state-court rulings forcing the council to include homosexuals in the parade in 1992 and 1993 violated the group's free-speech rights under the First Amendment. State courts had ruled that the parade was an open event and that excluding homosexuals would violate a Massachusetts law

prohibiting bias in public accommodations. The parade's sponsor canceled the event in 1994 rather than allow a homosexual group to participate.

In a ruling on Feb. 22, 1995, the justices struck down a federal ethics law that made it illegal for federal employees to receive payment for speeches and written articles that were unrelated to their work. The court's 6-to-3 decision said the ban on accepting honorariums violated the free-speech rights of government workers. The court said Congress could write a narrower law that bans fees only in clear cases of conflict of interest. The decision left intact a ban on honorariums for senior officials in the executive branch and for employees of the legislative and judicial branches.

On June 21, the court said states do not violate free-speech rights by requiring lawyers to wait 30 days before writing to accident victims asking for their business. Voting 5 to 4, the court reinstated a 30-day restriction in Florida that had been struck down by a federal appeals court. The court said that the restriction was a valid limitation on free-speech rights because it protects victims from intrusions by attorneys. □ Geoffrey A. Campbell and Linda P. Campbell

See also **Courts.** In *World Book,* see **Supreme Court of the United States.**

Surgery. See **Medicine.**

Suriname. See **Latin America.**

Swaziland. See **Africa.**

Sweden. Swedes voiced growing misgivings about the 15-nation European Union (EU) within months of joining, even though a faster-than-expected economic recovery raised the prospect that Sweden could join a common EU currency in 1999. The anti-Union sentiment surfaced most notably in September 17 elections for the country's 22 seats in the European Parliament. The Green Party and the Left Party, which opposed Sweden's membership in the 15-nation Union, polled roughly one-third of the votes combined and won four and three seats, respectively. The Social Democratic Party, which swept to power in national elections in September 1994 with 45 percent of the vote, received just 28 percent of the vote and seven seats. It was the party's worst showing in a nationwide ballot, but government officials attributed the poor showing in part to a low turnout of some 40 percent of voters. Opinion polls showed that if Swedes were given another chance to vote on EU membership, roughly two-thirds would oppose it.

Economy. The drop in popularity for the Social Democrats came as the government announced in January 1995 a series of tax increases and spending cuts to reduce its budget deficit, which at about $21.8 billion, was one of Europe's biggest. The measures, which included cuts in benefits for the unemployed, the sick, and parents taking family leave, were to reduce the deficit by about $16 billion.

In spite of the cuts, the economy grew at a strong rate of 3.5 percent. Buoyant exports aided by the roughly 25 percent devaluation of the Swedish krona since 1992 fueled the economy. The combined impact of good growth and a sharp reduction in the deficit increased the chances that Sweden would be able to join in a single European currency in 1999. The government predicted that the budget deficit would disappear in 1998 and that the national debt would begin declining as a percentage of economic output in 1996, one year ahead of schedule.

The government in June announced plans to sell some $6.8 billion worth of state-owned assets by the year 2000 to help reduce the national debt. It began its privatization campaign in late 1995 by selling a 30 percent stake in Nordbanken for about $820 million.

Carlsson to step down. Prime Minister Ingvar Carlsson announced on August 18 that he would resign in March 1996, citing personal reasons. Carlsson had led the Social Democrats since the 1986 assassination of his predecessor, Olof Palme. Mona Salhin, the deputy prime minister, appeared likely to succeed Carlsson until she was forced to resign in November 1995 amid allegations that she had misused a government credit card. On December 5, the Social Democrats chose Finance Minister Goran Persson as Carlsson's successor.   □ Tom Buerkle

See also **Europe** (Facts in brief table). In *World Book,* see **Europe; European Union; Sweden.**

Swimming. Four of the world's major swimming powers—the United States, Australia, Germany, and Russia—did well in major competitions in 1995. A fifth—China—made a few appearances internationally but, because so many of its swimmers had tested positive for illegal drugs, was not invited to the Pan Pacific championships in August, one of the year's two major meets.

China. In September 1994, Chinese swimmers won 12 of the 16 women's events in the world championships in Rome. Later that year, seven Chinese swimmers, including two world champions, tested positive for illegal bodybuilding drugs and were suspended.

Several other nations accused the Chinese swimming federation of supplying illegal drugs to its swimmers, an allegation the Chinese denied. Still, the United States, Australia, and Canada, three of the four founding nations of the Pan Pacific championships, voted in February 1995 not to invite China to the competition in August in Atlanta, Georgia.

The World Swimming Coaches Association implored the International Swimming Federation to exclude Chinese swimmers from the 1996 Summer Olympics in Atlanta. The federation declined, but said it might test every potential Olympic swimmer for drugs in early 1996.

Pan Pacific. The field for the Pan Pacific meet, once restricted to nations that border the Pacific

Germany's Franziska van Almsick was one of the most dominant female swimmers of 1995, following her world-record performance in the 200-meter free-style at the world championships in Rome in September 1994, *below.*

Ocean, was expanded to 24 nations. The United States won 15 of the 34 events, and Australia won 13. Of the 102 total medals, the United States won 42 and Australia 34.

Gary Hall, Jr., of Phoenix won four gold medals, and the U.S. 4x100-meter free-style relay team set a world record of 3 minutes 15.11 seconds. Six swimmers won two individual events each—Hall; Tom Dolan of Arlington, Virginia; and Dan Kowalski and Scott Miller of Australia among the men; and Brooke Bennett of Brandon, Florida, and Susan O'Neill of Australia among the women.

In the European championships from August 22 to 27 in Vienna, Austria, Russia led in gold medals with 17 to Germany's 13. But Germany led in total medals with 37 to Russia's 23. Franziska van Almsick of Germany dominated the women's races with five gold medals and a silver. Alexsandr Popov of Russia won two gold medals in free-style sprints and two in relays. On August 23, Denis Pankratov of Russia set a world record of 52.32 seconds for the 100-meter butterfly to go with his 200-meter world record of 1 minute 55.22 seconds June 14 in Canet, France.

United States. Janet Evans won the 400-, 800-, and 1,500-meter free-styles in the United States spring championships in March, leaving her three short of Tracy Caulkins's record of 48 national titles.

□ Frank Litsky

In *World Book*, see **Swimming**.

Switzerland.

Switzerland. The four governing parties of Switzerland won a majority in the lower house of parliament in an election held on Oct. 11, 1995. The Social Democratic Party, which campaigned in favor of eventual entry into the European Union (EU), became the biggest party by gaining 12 seats for a total of 54. The anti-EU Swiss People's Party picked up four new seats for a total of 29. The Radical Democrats and the Christian Democrats showed little change, with 45 seats and 34 seats, respectively.

Swiss voters exhibited their isolationist tendency again in 1995. In a referendum on June 25, they rejected a proposal that would have made it easier for foreigners to buy real estate in Switzerland.

Switzerland witnessed its first public takeover battle ever in 1995 when Holvis Holzstoff AG, a textile and paper company, attracted the attention of United States and British bidders. BBA Group PLC of Britain, an industrial engineering group, won control of Holvis in July with an offer of $385 million.

The Swiss Bankers' Association announced on September 12 that its members had found $34 million in their vaults that had been deposited before 1945, presumably by Jews and other people who later became victims of Nazi Germany. The banks said they would make it easier for relatives of the depositers to trace lost funds. □ Tom Buerkle

See also **Europe** (Facts in brief table). In *World Book*, see **Switzerland**.

Syria stood as the main Arab holdout to the Arab-Israeli peace process in 1995. Although both Syria and Israel seemed in 1994 to have accepted the principle of Syrian recognition of Israel as a nation in return for Israel's withdrawal from the occupied Golan Heights, they disagreed on the details. The Golan Heights is a region on the Syrian-Israeli border that Israel seized during the Six-Day War (1967).

After suspending negotiations with Israel in December 1994, Syrian President Hafiz al-Asad resumed talks on June 27, 1995. The talks were conducted near Washington, D.C., between the Syrian and Israeli army chiefs of staff. However, Asad canceled a meeting slated for late July. Asad, who was said to have accepted Israeli aerial surveillance of the border, opposed Israeli ground troops there. Both sides also disagreed on a timetable for Israel's military withdrawal from the Golan Heights. The two sides resumed talks in late December.

Despite Asad's avowed commitment to peace, he continued to support radical Arab groups, such as Hamas and Hezbollah (Party of God), that opposed the Arab-Israeli peace process. In August, the United States warned it would hold Syria accountable for terrorist acts against Americans by such groups. In July, a Hamas leader was found in the United States and held for extradition to Israel. □ Christine Helms

See also **Middle East** (Facts in brief table). In *World Book*, see **Syria**.

Taiwan in 1995 resisted China's pressure for reunification. The two had separated in 1949, when Communists took over the mainland, but China still regarded Taiwan as its province. In 1995, Taiwan sought world prominence for itself. On June 26, Taiwan President Li Teng-hui offered to donate $1 billion to the United Nations (UN) if Taiwan were granted UN membership. But in September, the UN decided not to consider Taiwan's application.

The United States granted Li a visa for a "private" visit to Cornell University in Ithaca, New York, to attend an alumni reunion in June 1995. The move angered China because it saw the visit as a reversal of a U.S. policy that prohibited official visits by Taiwan's leaders. That policy had been followed since 1979, after America withdrew recognition of Taiwan and established official ties with the Communist mainland. China also said the visit meant that Li was abandoning a commitment to unification in order to lead Taiwan to independence. China renewed old threats to regain control of the island state by force if necessary and postponed talks that had been scheduled with Taiwan for July.

Pressure mounts. In July, China fired six unarmed missiles from an inland base to an ocean test area 85 miles (140 kilometers) north of Taiwan. In August, China conducted military exercises near Taiwan. Political observers interpreted both actions as attempts to intimidate Taiwan. China's militant

Senator Jesse Helms (R., N.C.) greets Taiwan's President Li Teng-hui, *right,* in Syracuse, New York, in June. Li received an alumni award from Cornell University in Ithaca.

actions triggered a temporary drop in the stock market in Taipei, Taiwan's capital, and prompted Taiwan to plan for increased defense spending. However, in October, China's President Jiang Zemin said he would welcome a meeting with Li.

Politics. On July 20, Taiwan's parliament cleared the way for the first direct election for president, scheduled for March 1996. Li had been elected in an indirect procedure. On Aug. 31, 1995, the ruling Kuomintang (KMT) party nominated Li as its presidential candidate for 1996. The main opposition, the Democratic Progressive Party (DPP), selected Peng Ming-min. The DPP sought an independent Taiwan.

In parliamentary elections on December 2, seen as a reflection of Taiwanese views on the unification issue, the KMT lost 5 seats, and the DPP gained 4, though most of its strongest proindependence candidates lost. The right wing New Party (NP) tripled its seats, from 7 to 21. The NP advocated immediate unification with China. Political analysts said China's intimidation influenced Taiwanese voters.

The economy continued to grow in 1995. By the end of May, foreign exchange reserves had climbed to $100 billion. □ Henry S. Bradsher

See also **Asia** (Facts in brief table). In *World Book,* see **Taiwan.**

Tajikistan. See **Commonwealth of Independent States.**

Tanzania. See **Africa.**

Taxation. President Bill Clinton and the Republican-led Congress both favored major tax cuts in 1995 but clashed over the size of the reductions and who should receive them. The President vetoed a budget bill that included a seven-year, $245-billion package of tax cuts—far more than his own plan to reduce taxes by $63 billion in five years. Clinton and Republican congressional leaders agreed to work out a compromise.

A child tax credit was the main feature of both the bill approved by Congress and the President's proposal. The Republican bill would give families a $125-a-child tax credit for 1995 and a $500 credit in later years. The credit for each child under 18 would go to married couples earning less than $110,000. One-parent households with incomes under $75,000 would also qualify. The revenue loss of $147.6 billion over the next seven years would make the credit the most costly part of the Republicans' tax package.

Clinton proposed a five-year plan that would provide a tax credit of $300 for each child under 13 in families with income up to $60,000. Families with incomes from $60,000 to $75,000 would receive smaller credits for each child. The price tag of Clinton's proposal would be $35.4 billion.

IRA eligibility. Both the President and Congress favored expanded eligibility for Individual Retirement Accounts (IRA's). In addition, Clinton proposed tax deductions of up to $5,000 a year for college ex-

407

penses, rising to $10,000 after 1999. The Republican-backed bill would provide a tax deduction of up to $2,500 for interest on student loans.

The congressional bill would also lower taxes on profits from the sale of assets, known as *capital gains,* for individuals and corporations. The top rate for individuals would drop from 28 percent to 19.8 percent under the GOP bill. The President did not include any such provision in his plan.

Clinton strongly opposed a provision of the Republican bill that would reduce tax breaks for the working poor by $32.5 billion over seven years. The benefit, known as an Earned Income Tax Credit, was increased in 1993 at Clinton's request.

Tax deductions. In April 1995, President Clinton signed a bill to restore a tax deduction for part of the health insurance premiums paid by people who are self-employed. This allowed the self-employed to deduct 30 percent of their health insurance premiums for 1995 and raised the deduction to 50 percent after 1995.

The same bill contained a tax break for media baron Rupert Murdoch in the sale of broadcast properties to minority group owners in Chicago. But a provision to close a loophole for multimillionaires who avoid taxes by renouncing their U.S. citizenship was dropped from the final version of the bill.

□ William J. Eaton

In *World Book,* see **Taxation.**

Telecommunications. The big players in the communications world opened up their wallets in 1995 in hopes of positioning themselves for a new competitive order. Barriers separating broadcasting, cable, and telephone companies continued to break down after the expiration in late 1994 of the regulations that had prohibited television networks from producing, distributing, and profiting from syndicated programming. And the United States Congress in 1995 inched toward a major reworking of the Telecommunications Act. The result of these changes produced some of the biggest and most important mergers in communications history.

Merger mania. On April 9, the Seagram Company, Limited, of Canada, agreed to buy 80 percent of MCA Incorporated, owner of the Universal Pictures motion-picture studio, from the Japanese consumer electronics giant Matsushita Electric Industrial Company. The deal was worth $5.7 billion.

On May 10, MCI Communications Corporation, the nation's second-largest long-distance telephone company, said it would invest up to $2 billion in News Corporation, the global media empire controlled by Rupert Murdoch. News Corporation includes television stations, newspapers, a movie studio, and the Fox television network. The deal enabled MCI to hook into Murdoch's extensive communications network and gave Murdoch a large infusion of cash to invest in media acquisitions.

The Republican-led U.S. Congress in 1995 planned to reduce the tax rate for America's wealthy, already one of the lowest rates among industrialized nations.

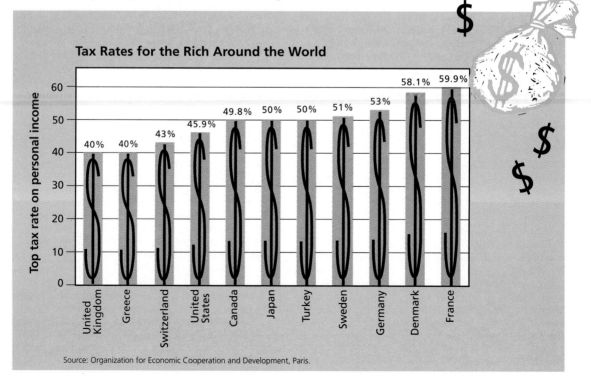

Tax Rates for the Rich Around the World

Top tax rate on personal income

United Kingdom	40%
Greece	40%
Switzerland	43%
United States	45.9%
Canada	49.8%
Japan	50%
Turkey	50%
Sweden	51%
Germany	53%
Denmark	58.1%
France	59.9%

Source: Organization for Economic Cooperation and Development, Paris.

The number of cellular phone subscribers around the world continued to climb in 1995. According to estimates by telecommunications experts, the number of cellular users worldwide would double by the year 1999.

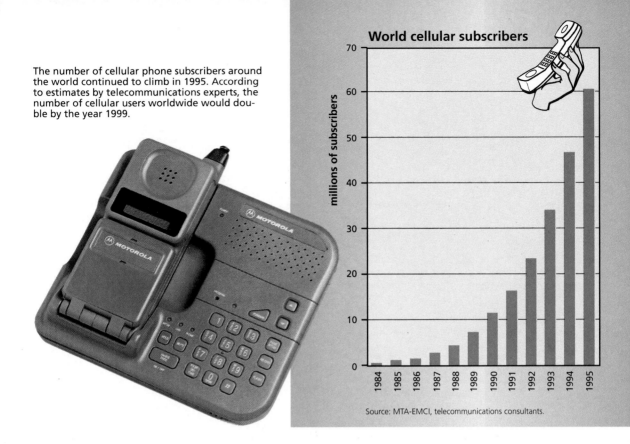

World cellular subscribers

millions of subscribers

Source: MTA-EMCI, telecommunications consultants.

The Gannett Company, the nation's largest newspaper company, on July 24 announced its purchase of Multimedia Incorporated for $1.7 billion. Multimedia's businesses included syndicated talk shows, such as "Donahue," "Sally Jessy Raphael," and "Rush Limbaugh." Gannett also picked up 11 daily newspapers and 5 television stations in the deal.

On July 31, the Walt Disney Company and Capital Cities Communications/ABC Incorporated, two giants in the entertainment industry, stunned Wall Street with a $19-billion merger announcement. The merger would bring together the nation's most profitable TV network and the popular sports network ESPN with Disney's Hollywood film and television studios.

On August 1, the Westinghouse Electric Corporation said it had agreed to pay $5.4 billion for CBS Incorporated. The network was considered by many media experts to be the crown jewel of broadcasting despite its rapid decline in the television ratings.

Time Warner weds Turner. Ted Turner, the founder and chairman of Atlanta-based Turner Broadcasting System Incorporated (TBS), spent much of the year trying to buy NBC, the television network owned by the General Electric Company. By August, however, Turner had become the object of Time Warner Incorporated's desires, and on September 22 the two companies announced that Time Warner would purchase TBS for $8 billion in stock. The merger created the world's largest enter-

tainment company. The new company combined Time Warner's television, studio, cable, and publishing assets with Turner's cable networks, including CNN, and his studio and film-library operation.

On October 31, Murdoch and John Malone, chairman of Tele-Communications Incorporated, the nation's largest cable company, announced a joint venture to create a new sports network rivaling ESPN.

Great expectations. The expectation that Congress would finally approve a telecommunications reform bill sent ripples throughout the communications industry and created a veritable gold rush in the television business in 1995. Although Disney, Time Warner, and other large companies grabbed the most headlines, there was a furious, year-long auction for television stations. By early November, more than $3 billion in television station sales had been announced or finalized, a new record for one year. Several factors contributed to the seller's market, including the successful launches of two new television networks in January: the WB, created by Warner Brothers, and UPN, a joint venture between Paramount Communications Incorporated and Chris-Craft Industries Incorporated. The anticipated lifting of television station ownership limits and a continued strong advertising market that boosted profits also contributed to the interest in television stations.

☐ Tim Jones

In *World Book,* see **Cable; Telecommunications.**

409

TELECOMMUNICATIONS: A SPECIAL REPORT

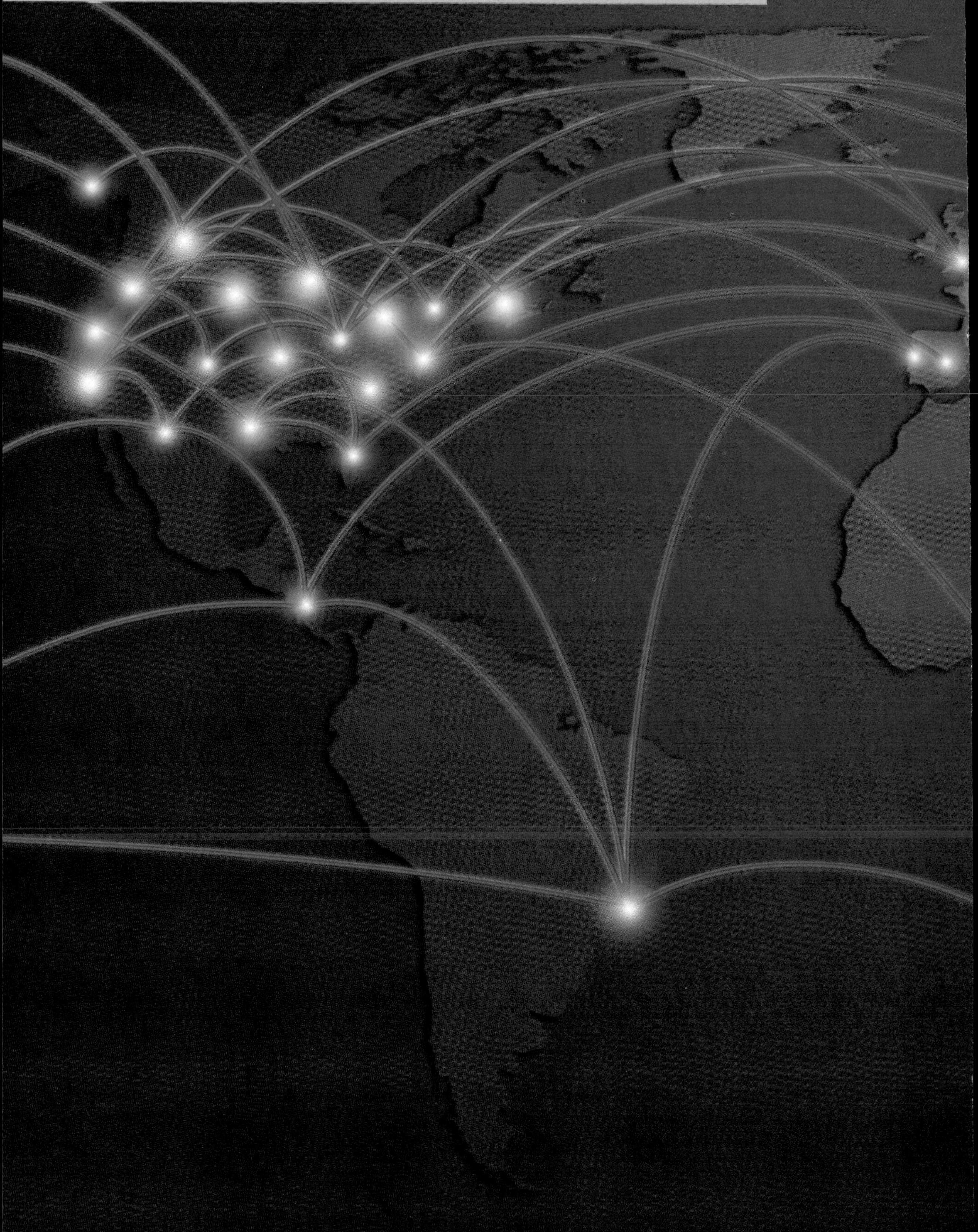

The explosive growth of the Internet has brought a wealth of information to homes, businesses, and institutions around the world.

Wired to the World

By Herb Brody

FAQ's

Frequently asked questions

What is the Internet?

The Internet is a global web of computer networks linked through the telephone system.

What does the Internet offer?

Popular features of the Internet include ways to send and receive messages; copy and retrieve information from remote databases; join discussion groups on a wide range of topics; and browse information databases from a vast collection of resources.

The author

Herb Brody is a senior editor at *Technology Review* magazine.

Imagine a place where people gather to exchange ideas, conduct business, shop, do research, or play games. Now imagine that this place has no buildings, no roads, no schools, no government, and no real physical location. This "place" exists, and it's called the Internet—a global web of computer networks connected through telephone lines.

This complex web of interlinked databases supports a wide range of activities. It's a place where people from all over the world view documents and images held in government and corporate databases, conduct intense discussions about topics ranging from the serious to the inane, exchange messages, publish articles, pass along jokes and rumors, buy and sell goods and services, and even commit crimes. And on the "Net," as it's known, distance is no object. You can send a message from Canada to Malaysia as easily and inexpensively as sending a message to your next-door neighbor.

By early 1995, more than 20 million people were tapping into this worldwide collection of computers, according to Internet analysts. And those numbers have grown at a phenomenal rate. According to some industry estimates, use of the Internet in 1995 grew at a monthly rate of 20 percent.

The attraction of the Internet lies in its vast and ever-changing offerings and its growing commercial potential. Among its many features is the simple exchange of ordinary text messages through a system called electronic mail, or e-mail. Another popular feature is Usenet, a collection of more than 9,000 electronic bulletin boards that feature discussions on just about every topic imaginable. Not all of the Internet is devoted to written exchanges, however. It also hosts a rich depository of information put on-line by universities, government agencies, businesses, and individuals around the world.

E-mail is the most commonly used feature of the Internet. This inexpensive and efficient communication system can deliver messages to one or many people around the world within a matter of minutes. Large computer files can also be sent through e-mail, giving the recipient the ability to work on those files upon their delivery.

Usenet consists of electronic bulletin boards, or discussion centers, called *newsgroups*. Each newsgroup has a special interest, such as child rearing, politics, or perhaps proper care of tropical fish. People participate by reading and responding to the messages posted by others. Conversations in newsgroups range from arcane intellectual discussions to verbal brawls marked by vicious interchanges of insults. Some Usenet groups have moderators who determine what gets posted, edit messages, and often compile answers to frequently asked questions (FAQ's). Others are unmoderated. Newsgroups are organized by broad families—such as comp. for computer-related discussions; sci. for science; rec. for exchanges of messages about such recreational activities as sports, hobbies, and the arts; and alt. for alternative or miscellaneous material, an area that is home to much of the Net's x-rated material.

The treasure trove of information available on the Internet has become one of its most valued features. On the Net, you can browse such resources as dictionaries, encyclopedias, library catalogs, compilations of famous quotations, the complete works of William Shakespeare and the Irish poet W. B. Yeats, and an index to the lyrics of popular songs. Government databases offer news about space exploration, the text of pending legislation from the U.S. Congress, and other up-to-date information about the work of government agencies. A variety of interactive games also flourish on the Internet.

Much of the information on the Internet can be *downloaded* (copied and retrieved) at no cost. For example, when the planet Jupiter was struck by a comet in 1994, the Jet Propulsion Laboratory of the National Aeronautics and Space Administration (NASA) in Pasadena, California, posted photos of the event that anyone on the Internet could download free of charge.

For universities and research institutions, the Internet has become an invaluable communications tool and resource. Scientists post theories and experimental results on the Internet. Colleagues all over the world can read them and offer comments quickly. College students use the Net's messaging system to communicate with fellow students around the world. A growing number of elementary, middle, and high schools have also plugged into the Net, both to let students and teachers communicate with their peers and to tap the network's proliferating educational resources. School children can consult on-line experts from a variety of fields. In 1994, for example, NASA operated a "Live from Antarctica" program that let students and teachers pose questions to scientists working on the southernmost continent.

Navigating the Net

Getting around on the Internet has been simplified since the early 1990's. It once featured stark, text-only screenfaces and required knowledge of complex computer addresses and codes. However, the application of a number of recently developed software programs helped improve the Internet's ease of use. One of these programs was Gopher, an Internet tool that organized searches through a hierarchical series of lists called menus. Shortly after Gopher was introduced in 1991, another system was released on the Internet that brought a whole new way of viewing information. This system was called the World Wide Web, and rather than text-only screens, it featured graphical representations of commands that linked documents to other documents on the Web. These links dramatically improved the Internet's ease of use. The system ran on the Internet standard called *hypertext transfer protocol* (*http*).

The Web soon became the most popular part of the Internet. All the computer files on the Web are formatted with hypertext, electronic links that whisk the user to a related section of a document or to a linked Web document. Hypertext consists of highlighted words that function as cross-references. Using a computer mouse, a person clicks on the highlighted word, and a new screen will appear with more information related to that word. Pictures may also have links.

What is the World Wide Web?

The multimedia part of the Internet, in which documents are interlinked by a system called *hypertext*, is called the World Wide Web. It contains embedded electronic links to other Web documents, which, in addition to text, might contain pictures, sounds, or even video.

What is a Web browser?

A Web browser is software that helps the user navigate the World Wide Web and that allows easy retrieval of text, images, and sound. Examples include Netscape Navigator and Mosaic.

What is a home page?

A home page describes the nature of an organization or individual. As such, it functions as the face of a group or individual on the World Wide Web. Like all pages on the Web, it has links to related documents on the Internet.

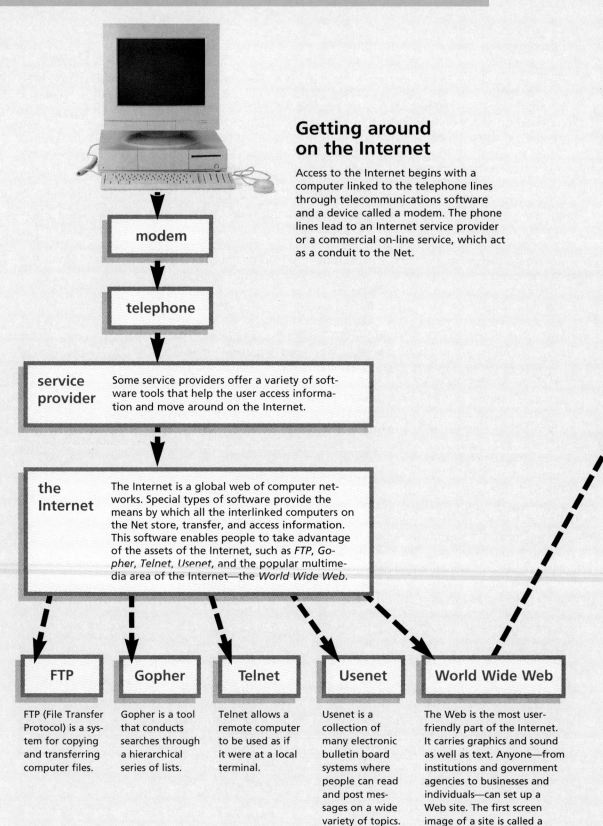

Getting around on the Internet

Access to the Internet begins with a computer linked to the telephone lines through telecommunications software and a device called a modem. The phone lines lead to an Internet service provider or a commercial on-line service, which act as a conduit to the Net.

modem

telephone

service provider

Some service providers offer a variety of software tools that help the user access information and move around on the Internet.

the Internet

The Internet is a global web of computer networks. Special types of software provide the means by which all the interlinked computers on the Net store, transfer, and access information. This software enables people to take advantage of the assets of the Internet, such as *FTP*, *Gopher*, *Telnet*, *Usenet*, and the popular multimedia area of the Internet—the *World Wide Web*.

FTP

FTP (File Transfer Protocol) is a system for copying and transferring computer files.

Gopher

Gopher is a tool that conducts searches through a hierarchical series of lists.

Telnet

Telnet allows a remote computer to be used as if it were at a local terminal.

Usenet

Usenet is a collection of many electronic bulletin board systems where people can read and post messages on a wide variety of topics.

World Wide Web

The Web is the most user-friendly part of the Internet. It carries graphics and sound as well as text. Anyone—from institutions and government agencies to businesses and individuals—can set up a Web site. The first screen image of a site is called a home page.

The home page of Netscape, a popular *Web browser* (software used to search the Web), has a variety of features that help the user find information and get around on the Web.

URL (Uniform Resource Locator) identifies a document and its location. By typing a URL into the location bar, the user can go to different documents.

Directories serve as electronic "phone books" to help the user find topics of interest. Favorite sites can be stored in a menu called Bookmarks.

What's New? What's Cool? are pull-down menus of interesting home pages that have been reviewed and selected from among the hundreds of thousands of home pages on the Web.

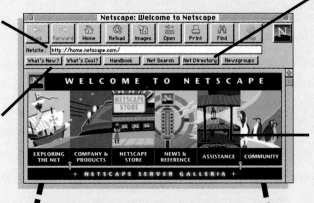

Hyperlinked areas within a home page can also provide guidance and assistance to the user, even allow for on-line shopping.

Other home pages are a simple mouse click away once they have been found using the navigation tools. All the sites on the Web are interlinked by means of a system called hypertext.

Shakespeare home page

Hubble Space Telescope home page

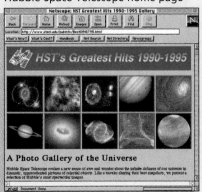

Using the URL or clicking on a hyperlink brings up the Shakespeare home page, *above*, which includes a list of the Bard's plays. Clicking on the title *Julius Caesar*, brings up a listing of the acts and scenes of the play. Clicking on Act III, Scene 2 brings up Mark Antony's famous speech, *below*.

The Hubble Space Telescope home page has many graphics. It includes a photo gallery, *above*, of some spectacular Hubble shots of celestial objects. Clicking on the representation of a black hole brings up a tutorial on that object, *below*.

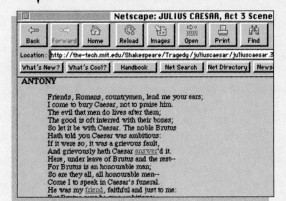

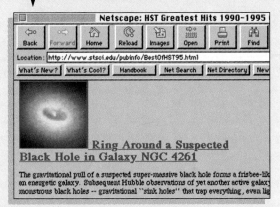

What is e-mail?

E-mail is electronic mail that people use to send and receive messages and documents on computers.

Is e-mail private?

E-mail is as private as a postcard. Just as anyone who comes across the postcard can read it, an e-mail may be seen by people other than the intended recipient. Privacy is not guaranteed.

What is a mailing list?

A mailing list is an electronic conference on a topic of interest to which a person can subscribe. All messages posted to the conference are delivered directly to a subscriber's electronic mailbox.

What is a protocol?

A protocol is a special format that enables computers to communicate with one another. It can specify such things as how two programs will transfer a file across the Internet and the syntax of a message.

Computers that provide information to the Web are known as Web servers. A Web server typically holds any of a number of home pages —screens that function as electronic front doors to greet people and convey a sense of what the home page is all about. Home pages are also called Web sites. Many companies, universities, political organizations, and a growing number of individuals have created home pages on the Web. Every week, dozens of new Web pages appear.

To navigate the databases of the World Wide Web, a person needs a special software program called a Web browser. Although several Web browsers were available in 1995, Netscape Navigator became the most popular browser on the Web. Other special software programs available on the Net allow the user to access images, sounds, or video. The Web sites Yahoo and WebCrawler function as tools to help users find information.

The location of information stored on the Internet is specified by a *Uniform Resource Locator*, or *URL*. A URL basically consists of three parts: the protocol used to access the information, the host name of the computer that holds the information, and the path name to the file where the information is stored. The following URL: http://stardust.jpl.nasa.gov/planets, says that the document is a World Wide Web hypertext document on a host computer called *stardust*, which is owned by the Jet Propulsion Laboratory of NASA, a government agency. The path name *planets* at this site takes the user to a file on a collection of images from NASA's planetary exploration program. A URL is also the standard way to refer to an Internet document.

The Web's ease of use and graphics capability has encouraged a tremendous influx of commercial activity. In 1993, Web traffic increased more than 300,000 percent over 1992. Companies were flocking to set up home pages, where they could display their wares, show pictures of their top officials and facilities, announce new products, and provide a means for customers to order products.

Having the right connection

Anyone with a computer, the right software, a telephone line, and a *modem*, which connects the computer to the phone line, can partake of the Net's rich feast of information. Computers around the world store this information in digital format—a series of 1's and 0's referred to as bits. When strung together, these bits represent everything from text to pictures, sounds, or programming code. Telecommunications software makes it possible to send this digital information over the telephone lines by changing it into tones. These tones are launched into the telephone system through a modem. To connect to the Internet, these transmissions must adhere to a prescribed protocol, which structures the form, order, and content of transmissions. Some people use special communications software to structure their transmissions for Internet usage. Others rely on a commercial on-line service—such as America Online, Compuserve, or Prodigy—to convert their transmissions into the suitable protocol.

Every computer on the Internet is connected through an Internet service provider. Some providers are small and local to a city or town. Others are national, with offices in all major metropolitan areas and 800-numbers that traveling subscribers can use to connect to the Net anywhere in the country without having to pay for a long-distance connection. Small service providers buy their Internet connections from larger providers who deal with even larger providers. The largest providers are national in scope. They exchange communications with other national providers and with providers in other countries. A transmission sent through the Net moves through progressively larger service providers—up to the national level—and then progressively smaller providers until it reaches its destination.

Data sent over the Internet travel in packets—clusters of 40 to around 1,500 characters. Each packet, individually marked with its destination address, is routed through a series of computers. At each network junction, a special computer called a router examines the packet to see where it is headed and sends it along the best path to its destination. If a packet sent by one computer does not reach the next computer, the first computer re-sends the packet, possibly on another route. The packets eventually all arrive at the same place and are pieced back together into the original text message or image. Packet switching thus makes the Internet nearly impossible to disrupt. If any single computer or transmission line fails, the network slows down but remains operational because swarms of packets continue to search for the links that remain in good working order.

Packet-switching is a legacy of the Net's origins as a military communication system during the Cold War, when planners wanted to make sure communications could continue even after a nuclear attack. With this system, if an enemy attack disrupted a communication link between Washington, D.C., and a military post, information could still flow between the two points via a different pathway.

Issues of quality and control

Control over the content of the Internet belongs to no one. Unlike such mass media as television, radio, and motion pictures, the Internet is not owned by a corporation or regulated by a central government authority. Net citizens cherish this lack of supervision because it exists nowhere else in the world and it lets the people who use the system decide its content.

But with no person or organization regulating the Internet, some problems have developed. Among them are lack of quality control, the access of pornography to children, the lingering threat of censorship, the question of how to fund the growth of the Net, and how to ensure that the Internet is available to everyone.

Quality control is virtually nonexistent. Because much of the Net is free of editors and fact-checkers, the reliability of information is often suspect. Searching the Internet can also become an exercise in frustration. Long search paths can lead to dead ends or blocked sites so deluged with phone-line traffic that it becomes impossible to get through. Directories to Internet resources remain incomplete. And

What is a node?

A node is a computer attached to a network. It is also called a host. The Internet is made up of nodes.

What is a URL?

URL (Uniform Resource Locator) is the standard way to refer to an Internet document. A URL specifies the protocol used to access the document, the host name of the computer that holds the document, and the path name to the file where the document is stored.

What is "netiquette?"

Netiquette is the set of customs followed by veteran users of the Internet. It includes the following:

- Get to know a newsgroup before posting a message and keep your message brief.

- Don't type in all capitals. It's like shouting.

- Courtesy is important for effective communication.

- Send advertisements to only specified newsgroups or mailing lists, not to everyone on the Net.

A Most-Wanted Cyberthief Is Caught in His Own Web

By JOHN MARKOFF
Special to The New York Times

go Supercomputer Center.
Mr. Shimomura then made a
usade of tracking down the in-
a pursuit that led to to-
[Page D17.]
working from
can Jose,
day

3 Software Makers Propose Rating System for Internet

By LAWRENCE M. FISHER

Hoping to provide an alternative
to legislation that would censor material posted on the Internet, three
software companies yester-
posed a voluntary ra-
an electronic
parents

on the Internet origin-
countries.
The n-
other

Writer Arrested After Sending Violent Fiction Over Internet

stuff," and that he had never spoken
to the woman whose name he used.
The Michigan Daily newspaper re-
that Mr. Baker's story in-
ring a woman with a
mutilating and
eagged

SENATE SUPPORTS SEVERE PENALTIES ON COMPUTER SMUT

FINES AND PRISON TERMS

84-to-16 Vote on Amendment to Telecommunications Bill — Free Speech Is Issue

Making the Net a safe place

The rising tide of crime on the Internet has made headlines. Information theft and an increasing amount of pornography and violent material on the Net have raised concerns that the Internet is not a safe place for commercial activity or for children. But law enforcement officials have improved ways to track criminals on the Net. And software developers have created programs that can block access to adult material. A proposed rating system for the Net could also help parents choose which Net sites they would allow their children to access.

because people who communicate electronically tend to discard social courtesies, Internet discourse can appear shallow and mean-spirited.

A small but increasing amount of pornography has also become available on the Net. This problem stems from the ease with which a person can read and contribute material anonymously. Pornography is accessible to anyone—including minors—who can navigate the Net with minimal competence.

The issue of adult material on the Net has been the subject of a heated debate between those who want to preserve the unregulated nature of the Internet and those who seek ways to guarantee that the Net is suitable for both adults and children to roam. In 1995, the battle gained momentum with the passage in June in the U.S. Senate of the Communications Decency Act (CDA), an amendment to a bill designed to deregulate the nation's telecommunications system. If enacted, the CDA would impose stiff penalties on anyone convicted of distributing "indecent" material through a telecommunications device. The law would penalize both the transmitter of the material and the service provider.

Such efforts to censor the Internet have raised fierce opposition from civil libertarians, who argue that the CDA's target of "indecency" is unconstitutionally vague and could make any owner of a computer that simply relays an obscene message subject to prosecution. Besides, they say, the solution to pornography on the Net lies not in censorship but in the use of services that block access to Web sites with sexually explicit material.

Companies concerned about censorship have banded together to create another means of filtering pornography from the Internet. A number of leading firms in the computer industry have formed the Platform for Internet Content Selection (PICS) to develop technology standards for labeling Net content. Such technology could enable parents to select the Internet sites to which their children have access.

Yet another subject under debate is how to fund the rapid growth of the Internet. The National Science Foundation (NSF), an independent agency of the U.S. government designed to promote science and engineering research, underwrote much of the cost of building and maintaining the Net's high-speed backbone lines. Because of these subsidies, users of the Internet have received a tremendous bargain. Individuals typically pay a flat monthly fee to a commercial Internet service provider rather than a usage fee for each message sent or Web page viewed. But in April 1995, the NSF ceased funding the backbone service and transferred financial and managerial responsibility to three commercial telecommunications carriers—Sprint, Ameritech, and Pacific Bell. Over the next four years, NSF will withdraw its support for the regional networks as well. Without the public subsidy, additional sources of revenue will be needed to keep the Internet up and running. Some experts believe that revenue will eventually be generated by a metered usage system, such as that used for long-distance telephone service, or a usage fee system.

Usage-based pricing could have an important ramification. As the Web grows and more people send pictures and sound across the networks, the Internet is in danger of sagging under an information overload. A system that charged users extra for the privilege of sending video signals or other large digital files might deter frivolous use of the Internet and help prevent network congestion.

But the idea of charging for each use of the Internet angers many in the on-line community. The value of the Net, contend some of its devotees, lies in the ability to wander from site to site and tap into the Net's resources without the inhibition of cost. This value will be lost if people have to start watching a meter instead of following a trail of information wherever it may lead.

Tapping into the Internet's range of offerings requires relatively expensive computers and modems. Many schools and individuals in the United States lack the financial means to acquire such technology. This barrier to participation has raised fears that the Internet may drive a wedge between information "haves" and "have-nots."

Fortunately, the declining cost of computers should help level the playing field, especially because the cost of connection to the Net is generally cheaper than that of cable TV. Still, some industry experts believe other measures will be needed to narrow the information gap. One such measure might be taxing Internet service fees to fund community centers that offer free Internet access.

In the 1960's, telecommunications visionary Marshall McLuhan coined the term "global village" to describe a world in which electronic media would break down cultural and linguistic barriers among people. With the continued growth of the Internet around the world, that village may soon become a reality. ▪ ▪ ▪

What is Netspeak?

Netspeak is a vocabulary commonly used on the Internet. For example, "flaming" is jeering at someone; "spamming" is sending unsolicited advertising through the Net; and a "newbie" is someone new to the Internet.

What is ;-)?

The symbol ;-) is one of many used in netspeak to express a user's mood. By looking at the symbol sideways, one can see a winking smiley face, which when used, indicates that the user is only joking.

What does IMHO mean?

IMHO is an acronym that means *in my humble opinion*. It is typically used in Internet communications. Other such acronyms include: CMIIW (correct me if I'm wrong), BTW (by the way), and LOL (laugh out loud).

For further reading:

Hahn, Harley. *Internet Yellow Pages*. 2nd ed. Osborne McGraw-Hill, 1994.

Krol, Ed. *Whole Internet User's Guide & Catalog*. O'Reilly & Associates, Inc., 1992.

LaQuey, Tracy. *The Internet Companion: A Beginner's Guide to Global Networking*. 2nd ed. Addison-Wesley, 1994.

Levine, John. *The Internet for Dummies*. 3rd ed. IDG Books Worldwide, 1995.

Television. The most memorable television event of 1995 may have been the murder trial of football star-turned-actor O. J. Simpson. Simpson was accused of the stabbing deaths of his ex-wife Nicole Brown Simpson and her friend Ronald L. Goldman on June 12, 1994. Almost all the networks provided live coverage of the trial's opening arguments, which began on Jan. 24, 1995, and cable channels Court TV and the Cable News Network (CNN) aired nearly every minute of the courtroom events thereafter. The three major networks—the American Broadcasting Companies (ABC), the National Broadcasting Company (NBC), and CBS Inc.— as well as the Fox Broadcasting Company rarely let an edition of the nightly news go by without a major story on the case. And many TV newsmagazine programs devoted segments to issues raised by the trial, ranging from wife battering to the validity of *DNA fingerprinting* (the use of genetic material to identify individuals).

On Tuesday, October 3, more than 107 million viewers tuned in to see the Simpson jury return a verdict of not guilty. Eight days later, Simpson agreed to a live interview on the "Dateline NBC" program. But he canceled just hours before the broadcast, in part because of thousands of protest calls to NBC and its affiliate stations from people who believed Simpson was guilty. In addition, Simpson's lawyers advised him not to do the interview.

Mergers. On July 31, the Walt Disney Company acquired Capital Cities/ABC Inc. for $19 billion in the second largest corporate takeover in United States history. Several Disney shows, such as the durable hit "Home Improvement," were already being shown on ABC. One day later, the Westinghouse Electric Corporation announced its purchase of CBS, the last independent network, for $5.4 billion. The merger would create a company controlling a record 15 television stations.

On September 22, Time Warner Inc. agreed to buy the Turner Broadcasting System (TBS) outright for $7.5 billion. In 1987, Time Warner, the world's largest communications company, had acquired an 18-percent stake in TBS, which owns several cable networks, including TNT and CNN.

Tobacco companies conflicts. In August, ABC settled a $10-billion libel case filed by the Philip Morris Companies and R. J. Reynolds Tobacco Company in spring 1994. At issue was a story aired by "Day One," an ABC newsmagazine show in February 1994 that asserted that the tobacco companies "spiked" cigarettes with extra nicotine in order to addict smokers. ABC issued an on-air apology to the companies and agreed to pay their legal expenses.

A second furor over press reporting on tobacco company activities erupted in November 1995 when CBS's "60 Minutes" canceled an interview with a former executive of the Brown & Williamson Tobacco

Ted Turner of Turner Broadcasting, left, and Gerald Levin of Time Warner do a "high five" in September to celebrate Time Warner's agreement to purchase Turner Broadcasting.

Corporation that was to have been part of a November 12 story on efforts by tobacco companies to silence critics. CBS denied that fear of a libel suit by Brown & Williamson had motivated its decision. Instead, network executives said they feared a liability suit charging the network with inducing the executive to break a contract he had signed with his former employer not to disclose confidential corporate information.

Many media analysts criticized the network for dropping the interview. They argued that the legal theory on which the decision was based had never been tested in cases involving freedom of the press. Some analysts also accused the network of backpedaling in order to avoid jeopardizing its pending multibillion-dollar merger with Westinghouse.

Advertising gains, viewer losses. Financially, 1995 was a strong year for the three major networks as well as for Fox Broadcasting. Network advertising revenues reached a record $5.6 billion for the 1995-1996 season, up 27 percent from the previous year. At the same time, however, cable television continued to siphon off network viewers. In October 1995, Nielsen Media Research, a TV rating service, reported that cable viewership had jumped by more than 24 percent since October 1994, while viewership for the four major networks fell by 7 percent. Cable was particularly attractive to viewers younger than 18 and older than 49, who fell outside advertisers' primary target group.

Although all the networks had strong advertising sales, NBC emerged as the leader in programs and ratings. Several of its 1994-1995 situation comedies, such as "Friends," "Seinfeld," and "Frasier," proved solid hits, as did "E.R.," a hospital drama. Throughout most of 1995, ratings for NBC's "Tonight Show with Jay Leno" began catching up to—and then surpassing—those of its archrival, CBS's "Late Night with David Letterman." NBC also bought the rights to broadcast both the 2000 Summer and the 2002 Winter Olympics for a hefty $1.27 billion.

Aiming for the middle. Many of the record 42 series that debuted in fall 1995 on the four established networks aimed at capturing viewers in the 18- to 34-year-old group. Several new shows were situation comedies featuring unmarried urban professionals: "The Single Guy," with Jonathan Silverman as a novelist; "Caroline in the City," with Lea Thompson as a cartoonist; and "Can't Hurry Love," featuring two love-hungry women.

Unusual new dramas included "Murder One," created by Steven Bochco, the producer of "Hill Street Blues" and "L.A. Law." "Murder One" was a courtroom serial that followed the twists and turns of a single murder case over the entire season. "American Gothic" was a surrealistic, nightmarish melodrama about a diabolic small-town sheriff. Nighttime soap operas returned with "Central Park West" (steamy scheming among chic Manhattanites)

Top-rated U.S. television series

The following were the 25 most-watched television series for the 30-week 1994-1995 regular season, which ended on April 16, 1995.

1. "Seinfeld" (NBC)
2. "E.R." (NBC)
3. "Home Improvement" (ABC)
4. "Grace Under Fire" (ABC)
5. "NFL Monday Night Football" (ABC)
6. "60 Minutes" (CBS)
7. "N.Y.P.D. Blue" (ABC)
8. "Friends" (NBC)
9. "Roseanne" (ABC)
10. "Murder, She Wrote" (CBS)
11. "Mad About You" (NBC)
12. "Madman of the People" (NBC)
13. "Ellen" (ABC)
14. "Hope & Gloria" (NBC)
15. "Frasier" (NBC)
16. "Murphy Brown" (CBS)
17. "20/20" (ABC)
18. "CBS Sunday Movie" (CBS)
19. "NBC Monday Night Movie" (NBC)
20. "Dave's World" (CBS)
21. "Me and the Boys" (ABC)
22. "Cybill" (CBS)
23. "ABC Sunday Night Movie" (ABC)
24. (tie) "Full House" (ABC)
         "Nanny" (CBS)

Source: American Broadcasting Companies.

and "The Monroes" (the trials of a rich and famous political family in Washington, D.C.).

Specials and documentaries on both cable and broadcast stations commemorated the 50th anniversary of the end of World War II (1939-1945). Several programs debated whether the atomic bomb attacks on the Japanese cities of Hiroshima and Nagasaki were necessary to end the war.

Cable channels showed several daring programs in 1995. The irreverent British sitcom "Absolutely Fabulous," about two female fashion plates who drink, party, and shop their way through life, ran and reran on Comedy Central. The Arts & Entertainment Network presented *The Boys of St. Vincent*, a Canadian film that portrayed child molestation in a Catholic orphanage. The Discovery Channel adapted *The Promised Land*, a 1991 best-selling nonfiction book. The five-part miniseries movingly depicted the migration of 5 million African Americans from the rural South to the urban North from 1940 to 1970.

Mixed signals. After months of wrangling over a bill that would overhaul the telecommunications industry, the U.S. Senate and the House of Representatives on Oct. 14, 1995, appointed a conference committee to reconcile the differences between competing versions of the bill. Offering the biggest changes in communications law in 61 years, the bill deregulated cable TV prices and lifted most restrictions on the number of stations a single company

Muppets Bert, left, and Ernie of "Sesame Street" appear at the Capitol in March to urge Congress to support the Public Broadcasting System, which airs their show.

Emmy Award winners in 1995

Comedy
Best Series: "Frasier"
Lead Actress: Candice Bergen, "Murphy Brown"
Lead Actor: Kelsey Grammer, "Frasier"
Supporting Actress: Christine Baranski, "Cybill"
Supporting Actor: David Hyde Pierce, "Frasier"

Drama
Best Series: "N.Y.P.D. Blue"
Lead Actress: Kathy Baker, "Picket Fences"
Lead Actor: Mandy Patinkin, "Chicago Hope"
Supporting Actress: Julianna Margulies, "E.R."
Supporting Actor: Ray Walston, "Picket Fences"

Other awards
Drama or Comedy Miniseries or Special: *Joseph*
Variety, Music, or Comedy Series: "The Tonight Show with Jay Leno"
Made for Television Movie: *Indictment: The McMartin Trial*
Lead Actress in a Miniseries or Special: Glenn Close, *Serving in Silence: The Margarethe Cammermeyer Story*
Lead Actor in a Miniseries or Special: Raul Julia, *The Burning Season*
Supporting Actress in a Miniseries or Special: (tie) Judy Davis, *Serving in Silence: The Margarethe Cammermeyer Story;* Shirley Knight, *Indictment: The McMartin Trial*
Supporting Actor in a Miniseries or Special: Donald Sutherland, *Citizen X*

may own (though it stipulated that no one owner's stations may reach more than 35 percent of U.S. households). The bill also required new TV sets to be equipped with a "V-chip" that can be used by parents to block programs they consider unsuitable.

Two new cable networks with limited broadcast hours debuted in January 1995—Time Warner's WB and Viacom's United Paramount Network (UPN). WB concentrated on families and young viewers, with programming heavily weighted to cartoons and half hour comedies. UPN, in contrast, targeted male viewers in their 20's with science-fiction and action dramas. One of UPN's four evening shows, "Star Trek: Voyager," was a hit, but the network replaced the rest of its line-up in the fall.

Departures. CBS removed Connie Chung as coanchor of the "CBS Evening News" on May 20, 1995—two years after she had been hired. Chung and coanchor Dan Rather had failed to attract viewers for the program, which had fallen to third place among the "Big Three" evening news shows.

Robert MacNeil departed from the Public Broadcasting System's "The MacNeil/Lehrer Newshour" on October 20, the 20th anniversary of the program he created with Jim Lehrer. The show was renamed "The Newshour with Jim Lehrer." □ Troy Segal

See also **Telecommunications**. In *World Book*, see **Television**.

Tennessee. See State government.

Tennis. Steffi Graf and Monica Seles provided the most significant tennis stories of 1995, not only for what they accomplished on the court, but for surviving trials off the court. In the four Grand Slam tournaments, the major winners were Graf among the women and Pete Sampras among the men.

Graf. During the winter, the 25-year-old Graf missed three months, including the Australian Open, because of back and calf injuries. Then her father, Peter Graf, was arrested on August 2 in their native Germany. The government said he was in charge of her finances and had failed to file tax returns for her for four years on income of $25 million. The police interrogated Graf herself but did not charge her.

The tennis courts proved a partial refuge for Graf. She lost in the first round of two tournaments, but she won the year's last three grand slams. She began the year ranked number one in computerized rankings and traded the top spot with Arantxa Sánchez Vicario of Spain several times until regaining it for the remainder of the year in June.

Seles. During a 1993 tournament in Germany, a deranged spectator stabbed Seles in the back, saying he wanted Graf to regain the number-one ranking that Seles had won from her. A German court sentenced the man—Guenter Parche—to probation, but no prison time. Seles appealed, but in April 1995 a German appeals court upheld the sentence.

After the stabbing, Seles, who had become an American citizen, was physically and psychologically devastated. It was not until July 1995, 27 months after the stabbing, that she returned to public competition, playing in an exhibition match in Atlantic City, New Jersey.

The Women's Tennis Association (WTA) told Seles that when she rejoined the tour, she would share the number-one ranking for at least six tournaments or 12 months, whichever came first. Seles returned in August and won the Canadian Open in Toronto. She reached the finals of the United States Open in September, but she missed the WTA's season-ending championship because of an injured knee.

Grand slam. The four grand-slam tournaments were the Australian Open, ending January 29 in Melbourne; the French Open, ending June 11 in Paris; the Wimbledon championships, ending July 9 outside London; and the U.S. Open, ending September 10 in New York City. The Australian and United States opens were played on hard courts, the French Open on clay, and Wimbledon on grass.

In the Australian Open final for women, Mary Pierce, an American playing for France, defeated Sánchez Vicario, 6-3, 6-2. Then Graf returned from injury and swept the other grand-slam finals—7-5, 4-6, 6-0 over Sánchez Vicario in the French Open; 4-6, 6-1, 7-5 over Sánchez Vicario at Wimbledon; and 7-6, 0-6, 6-3 over Seles in the United States Open.

Sampras, an American, won the two richest tournaments of the year—the $9.8-million United States

Germany's Steffi Graf returns a shot on the way to winning her sixth Wimbledon singles championship in July.

Open and the $9.6-million Wimbledon. He defeated Boris Becker of Germany, 6-7, 6-2, 6-4, 6-2, for his third consecutive Wimbledon title and took the U.S. Open title from Andre Agassi, the defending champion, 6-4, 6-3, 4-6, 7-5. In the other grand-slam finals, Agassi beat Sampras, 4-6, 6-1, 7-6, 6-4, in Australia, and Thomas Muster of Austria defeated Michael Chang of the United States, 7-5, 6-2, 6-4, in France.

Other. In Davis Cup competition for men, with Sampras and Agassi as the key players, the United States eliminated France (4-1) in February, Italy (5-0) in April, and Sweden (4-1) in September. With Agassi out for the final with an injury, Sampras nearly single handedly beat Russia, 3-2, for the U.S. win December 1 to 3 in Moscow. Sampras won two singles matches and paired with Todd Martin to win a doubles match. In the women's Fed Cup (formerly Federation Cup) final, Spain defeated the United States, 3-2, from November 24 to 26 in Valencia, Spain.

The low point of the year may have come on July 1 at Wimbledon when Jeff Tarango, a short-fused American, quit in midmatch after accusing veteran chair umpire Bruno Rebeuh of showing favoritism to certain players. As Tarango walked off, his wife slapped Rebeuh twice. Tarango was fined $63,756 and suspended from two grand-slam tournaments.

☐ Frank Litsky

In *World Book,* see **Tennis.**

The terrorist agenda

Terrorists around the world use random acts of violence in an attempt to achieve political, national, or religious aims through fear and intimidation.

By Richard E. Rubenstein

On April 19, 1995, an ordinary Wednesday morning, few workers going to their jobs at the Alfred P. Murrah Federal Building in Oklahoma City, Oklahoma, probably paid much attention to a large Ryder rental truck at the curb in front of the building. More than 500 men and women went to offices housing the United States Social Security Administration, the Department of Housing and Urban Development, the Bureau of Alcohol, Tobacco, and Firearms (ATF), and the Department of Veterans Affairs. Twenty-four preschool children went to the day-care center on the second floor.

Everything seemed normal until 9:30 a.m. Then their world exploded. A blinding flash lit the air, followed by a sound so loud that, according to survivors, it was like silence: a noise literally too loud to hear. The explosion tore a hole from the first floor of the nine-story building to its roof. Seconds later, the entire front of the structure collapsed, each floor smashing through the floor below it. The death toll eventually reached 168 people, including many of the children.

Investigators quickly identified the source of the explosion: the truck parked in front of the building had been filled with a lethal combination of fuel oil and fertilizer. But who had committed this most destructive terrorist attack in American history? Some people hastily concluded that radical Muslims had done it, since a similar truck bomb had blown up part of the World Trade Center in New York City

Opposite page: Death and rubble remain after the nine stories of the Alfred P. Murrah Federal Building in Oklahoma City collapsed upon each other in April 1995 in the worst terrorist bombing in U.S. history.

in 1993, and a group of Muslim extremists were on trial for that crime. However, investigators considered another possibility. They realized that the date of the Oklahoma bombing was the second anniversary of an event that some Americans considered a watershed episode in their imagined showdown between the federal government and the American people. Far right extremists, the investigators theorized, might have bombed the Murrah building to mark the anniversary of a violent confrontation that took place near Waco, Texas, on April 19, 1993, between U.S. law enforcement agents and a group of Christian fundamentalists known as Branch Davidians.

The Davidians, led by a man named David Koresh, believed that the end of the world was near, and they were reported to be stockpiling illegal weapons. After a standoff that began in February, federal agents on April 19 drove tanks into the Davidians' building. A huge fire erupted, killing over 80 adults and children. The government agencies involved in the incident were the Federal Bureau of Investigation (FBI) and the ATF, agents already considered violent and dictatorial by certain groups on the far right. Could the Oklahoma City bombing have been some sort of "payback" for Waco?

A coincidental arrest of a man known to espouse some of these anti-government theories, Timothy J. McVeigh, and reports from several witnesses soon led officials to charge McVeigh and an alleged accomplice, Terry Nichols, with blowing up the federal building. A third suspect who agreed to testify against those two received lesser charges. According to federal prosecutors, McVeigh and Nichols acted alone and not as part of any larger terrorist organization. But their ideas had apparently been formed as a result of extensive contact with certain people who belong to groups known as "militias."

These militias are groups of men and women who believe in arming themselves and who meet regularly to practice military-style maneuvers. Many militia members fear and distrust the federal government. Some think there is a conspiracy on the part of the federal government and the United Nations to form a dictatorship over the United States. They believe that gun control laws are part of this conspiracy to disarm and enslave white Christian Americans. Many militia members and members of allied groups believed that the Waco incident was a step toward establishing full control over the American people.

Most Americans consider these beliefs unfounded. But the Oklahoma City bombing raised a number of important questions:

- What is political terrorism, and why do people sometimes engage in apparently senseless acts of violence?
- Has America experienced outbreaks of terrorism before? If so, what have been the results?
- What sorts of people become terrorists?
- What conditions breed terrorist movements, and how can these conditions be changed?

Political terrorism is the use of violence by individuals or small groups to make a political statement or to change a political situation. Terrorists use or threaten to use violence in order to create fear and

The author

Richard E. Rubenstein is Professor of Conflict Resolution and Public Affairs at George Mason University, Fairfax, Virginia. He is the author of several books including *Alchemists of Revolution: Terrorism in the Modern World* (1987).

alarm and to draw attention to their grievances. Some terrorists are nationalists, seeking their own homeland. Others are part of a religious movement that may also have a political or nationalist agenda.

The long history of terrorism

Political terrorism is an old practice. In the year 167 B.C., a Jewish priest named Mattathias unleashed a holy war against Judea's Greek overlords by assassinating two government officials. Assassination through the years has often been a tool of terrorists. In fact, the killing of evil tyrants, *tyrannicide*, was a practice approved both by ancient authorities and—with strong qualifications—by later European thinkers. In Swiss history, legendary hero William Tell was a skilled marksman who shot an arrow through a tyrant's heart, an act that led to the Swiss revolt for independence from the Austrian Habsburgs in the 1300's. The American revolutionary, Patrick Henry, even threatened tyrannicide against King George III of England during the Revolutionary War (1775-1783).

The term "terrorism" first appeared during the French Revolution (1789-1799). Some of the revolutionaries who took power in France adopted a policy of violence that included sending their opponents to a beheading instrument called a guillotine. The period of their rule became known as the Reign of Terror. Antigovernment terrorism grew in Russia in the 1800's, when a succession of small groups used assassination and sabotage in attempts to overthrow the czars, Russia's kings. A terrorist group called the People's Will employed a new weapon—the dynamite bomb—to kill Czar Alexander II in 1881. Terrorists associated with a group called the Social Revolutionary Party killed hundreds of important government officials in the first decade of the 1900's. A member of the Social Revolutionary Party even shot Russian leader V. I. Lenin in 1918 after the Communists had taken control of Russia. Lenin survived, and the terrorist was executed.

The period between World War I (1914-1918) and World War II (1939-1945) was a time of political confusion, giving rise to a host of terrorist activities. In Germany, right-wing nationalists assassinated scores of liberal and Socialist officials. Germany's Jewish foreign minister, Walter Rathenau, was killed in 1922 by anti-Semitic nationalists. In Romania, the Iron Guard became a strong authoritarian movement in the early 1930's. Its followers were *fascists* who sought to establish a dictatorship. Features of fascism include extreme patriotism, warlike policies, and persecution of minorities. The Iron Guard used terror against its political opponents and blamed Communists, Jews, and liberals for Romania's problems. They murdered two prime ministers.

Other fascist groups, such as Hungary's Arrow Cross, Croatia's Ustase, the French CSAR, and Japan's Terrorist League of Blood also gained support in the late 1930's. They helped weaken governments, creating a demand for law and order and preparing the way in Germany and other nations for takeover by Nazis or other fascists. These historical experiences helped demonstrate that violence by small groups is most effective when societies are divided and people are dis-

American terrorists
The Molly Maguires, *above,* meet secretly during a Pennsylvania coal strike in 1874. They took part in violent labor conflicts between mine owners and workers. Members of the Ku Klux Klan, *right,* parade through a Southern city in 1923. The Klan often used terror and violence in their opposition to minority groups.

organized. Without this instability, acts of terrorism lose their impact.

The years following World War II brought great political change around the world. Terrorism also became global. In many areas, armed groups seeking to free their nations from colonial powers or foreign domination used terrorist tactics against rulers. In East Africa and Palestine, terrorists helped drive British occupiers out, while in Algeria and Vietnam, small-group violence against the French quickly developed into large-scale wars for independence. From the 1960's onward, establishing an independent nation became a primary motive for terrorist activity among such diverse groups as the Palestinians in the Middle East, the Roman Catholics of Northern Ireland, the Croatians of southeastern Europe, and the Kurds of Turkey and Iraq.

The 1970's and early 1980's featured terrorism based on extreme left political ideologies, particularly in Western Europe and Latin America. Leftist terrorist groups of those decades included the Communist-based Red Brigades of Italy and Sendero Luminoso (Shining Path) of Peru, known as the world's most ruthless terrorists. In the 1990's, religious beliefs spawned terrorist violence by militant groups of Muslim fundamentalists in the Middle East, white supremacists in the United States, Sikhs in India, and Buddhists in Japan.

Terrorism in America

Of all the terrorist campaigns in history, however, one of the most effective thrived on American soil. The racist Ku Klux Klan, formed in the 1860's, launched a terrorist campaign to prevent African Americans from achieving a share of political power in the South. After the Civil War (1861-1865), masked Klansmen dressed in white sheets terrorized blacks and their white supporters, lynching those who would not yield to their threats. By 1872, most Southern states were back under the control of white supremacists—a victory made secure in 1877, when remaining federal troops were withdrawn from the South. Klan-style terrorism continued, with more than 5,000 African Americans falling victim to racist violence in the years from 1880 to 1940.

In the late 1800's, America experienced another kind of terrorism in the North. Workers trying to form labor unions faced police and private armies hired by their employers, often with violent results. The era's most notorious act of violence took place in Chicago on May 4, 1886. A group of *anarchists*, people who want to abolish government authority, had gathered a crowd of workers in Haymarket Square to protest a shooting of strikers at the McCormick Reaper plant. When two companies of police appeared and ordered the crowd to disperse, someone hurled a bomb into the midst of the police, killing seven policemen and one civilian. Although there was no evidence implicating the rally's anarchist organizers in the crime, seven organizers were sentenced to death, four of whom were quickly hanged. Seven years later, the Illinois governor pardoned the remaining prisoners.

Labor-management terrorism persisted into the 1900's. In 1920, a bomb demolished J. P. Morgan's bank on Wall Street in New York City, killing more than 30 people and wounding more than 200. The perpetrators were never discovered, but the incident caused a "Red Scare" in which the government deported thousands of alleged left wing radicals from the country without due process of law.

Organized terrorism in the 1970's stemmed from divisions among Americans over the nation's involvement in the Vietnam War (1957-1975) and the struggle of African Americans for equality. From 1970 to 1974, a radical group of ex-students calling themselves the Weathermen, after a Bob Dylan song, bombed about 25 corporate and government offices in an attempt to hamper the U.S. war effort. During these same years, the Black Liberation Army robbed banks and stores to finance its activities and engaged in a shooting war with police.

Meanwhile, a small group calling itself the Symbionese Liberation Army (SLA) achieved brief fame by killing Marcus A. Foster, the Oakland, California, school superintendent, and kidnapping the newspaper heiress, Patricia Hearst. When the FBI attacked the SLA's Los Angeles hideout, most of the terrorists died. Agents captured Hearst and she was convicted for her part in a 1974 bank robbery. The jury believed that, at some point, she had become a willing SLA member. During this same period, groups favoring Puerto Rico's independence from the United States set off a series of bombs in major American cities. Militants of the Jewish Defense League, led by Rabbi Meir

Terrorist aims

Political terrorism is used to make a statement or to change a situation. Some terrorists are nationalists, seeking a homeland. Others are part of a religious movement that may also be political or nationalistic.

Nationalistic

The Irish Republican Army (IRA) seeks to unite independent Ireland with Northern Ireland, which is part of the United Kingdom. Members of an IRA faction that uses terrorism to achieve its goals attend a member's funeral.

Political

The extreme leftist Red Brigades opposed all political parties in Italy. They bombed public places and shot and kidnapped public figures. Red Brigade suspects, considered very dangerous, were kept caged during their trial in 1978.

Religious

Hamas (Islamic Resistance Movement) members pause for ritual prayer. Hamas uses violence to pursue its goal of replacing Israel with an Islamic Palestinian state. The group has claimed responsibility for many attacks in Israel.

Kahane and seeing themselves as defenders of Jews against anti-Semites, also committed bombings.

However, terrorist activity in America remained at a fairly low level until the mid-1990's, when violence seemed to escalate sharply. Militant opponents of abortion firebombed dozens of abortion clinics and shot and killed eight doctors and clinic workers. Militant Muslim extremists exploded a truck bomb in the garage of New York City's World Trade Center, killing six people and causing heavy damage. And then, in April 1995, terrorists destroyed the building in Oklahoma City.

Who becomes a terrorist and why?

For years, experts have tried to develop a personality profile of the typical terrorist, but most have concluded that there is no such thing as a terrorist personality. In terms of mental health, terrorists are generally like other people. Some are well balanced and others are unstable. Some come from harmonious families and others from dysfunctional homes. Some are addicts of risk and danger, but most consider themselves "soldiers" and avoid unnecessary risks to themselves.

Terrorists are often young male adults, aged 20 to 35, according to various studies. Many terrorists, but certainly not all, come from middle class backgrounds and have had more than the average amount of education. Beyond those attributes, most terrorists share certain attitudes toward government and society. They are often idealists, people who want society to be much better than it is. Often, they have worked through normal political channels to bring about the changes they advocate. But events have convinced them that things are changing for the worse and that "politics as usual" will lead only to disaster.

Therefore, experts say, terrorists feel powerless to reform society through normal political methods. They feel isolated, as if no one is listening to them or recognizing the dangers that they perceive. Often, they feel betrayed both by the authorities and by the common people who refuse to rally to their cause. Sometimes they are responding to the use of excessive force by authorities or to violence by other groups.

The result of these attitudes and emotions is a turn away from words and toward violent acts that will make the terrorists feel powerful, capture public attention, and punish evildoers. Sometimes vengeance is the terrorist's primary motive. For example, John Wilkes Booth and his co-conspirators assassinated President Abraham Lincoln in 1865 in order to avenge the honor of the defeated South. But most terrorist acts are also what experts call *instrumental*. They are intended to whip up popular support for some political program, to incite further violence against the government or another group, to tempt the authorities to overreact, or to make some territory ungovernable. The alleged Oklahoma City bombers, for example, may have sought both vengeance and popular support: revenge for the "Waco massacre" and support for their antigovernment philosophy.

Terrorist movements appear to grow most rapidly and to become most destructive under certain economic, cultural, political, or historical conditions. For example, when a nation or region experiences a

Profiles in terror

Most of history's worst terrorist acts are the work of a group. Although little is known about the leaders of many of these groups, some individual terrorist leaders have become notorious.

• Illich Ramirez Sanchez, a.k.a. Carlos (b. 1950)
When Carlos was captured in August 1994 in Sudan, a 20-year hunt for one of the world's most notorious terrorists ended. Carlos, a native of Venezuela, had operated with a variety of guerrilla groups, but his primary affiliations were with Arab groups. In 1975, Carlos masterminded the kidnapping of 11 oil ministers attending a major oil meeting in Vienna, Austria. He and his group killed three people in the incident but escaped to Algeria. During a visit to Sudan, he was captured and extradited to France to stand trial for terrorist acts committed there. Officials suspect Carlos of killing 83 people in his years of assassinations and bombings. Carlos was married to Magdalena Kopp, a German terrorist, and has a daughter.

• Sabri al Banna, a.k.a. Abu Nidal (b. 1943)
Abu Nidal was born to a wealthy Palestinian family that lived near present-day Jaffa, Israel. He split off from the Palestine Liberation Organization (PLO) in 1974, forming an organization violently opposed to reconciliation between Israel and the Arab states. Abu Nidal received a death warrant from the PLO after he attempted to assassinate PLO leader Yasir Arafat. The Abu Nidal organization received support from Iraq, Libya, and Syria. They are blamed for killing almost 900 Arab, Israeli, and Western civilians in 20 countries from 1974 through 1994.

period of rapid economic growth and development, the benefits of prosperity are often unevenly distributed. Some groups shoot ahead in economic power and status, while others fall far behind. Those left behind may feel powerless to change their economic circumstances without resorting to violence. Terrorism may arise when members of a particular nation, race, ethnic group, or religion feel increasingly insecure. These people may feel that their existence as a group—their cultural identity—is seriously threatened either by the government or by other groups more powerful than them.

Certain political situations may convince people that they are not able to participate in making important decisions. Some nations have only one political party. In other countries, the major political parties resemble each other quite closely. These conditions leave members of dissenting groups with the feeling that they have no sig-

• Abimael Guzman Reynoso (b. 1934)
Guzman was a philosophy professor in a small Peruvian town before he founded Sendero Luminoso (Shining Path), a terrorist group committed to replacing Peru's government with a regime based on Communist teachings. Hoping to inspire a mass uprising against the government, Guzman and his followers began a campaign of terror in 1980. By 1992, according to Peruvian officials, they had killed over 25,000 people and caused over $22 billion in property damage. In 1992, President Alberto Fujimori took dictatorial control of Peru, allegedly to stop the Shining Path. That September, Guzman and 10 other Shining Path leaders were arrested and sentenced to life in prison.

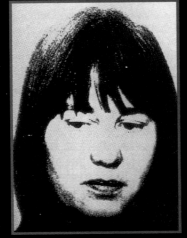

• Andreas Baader (1943-1977) and Ulrike Meinhof (1934-1976)
Baader and Meinhof were leaders of a leftist German terrorist group called the Red Army Faction, which was formed in 1968 and often called the Baader-Meinhof gang. The gang robbed banks and other businesses. They also bombed and burned West German corporations and German and American military installations in Germany. The group operated in the early 1970's but most of them were jailed by 1972. Meinhof hanged herself in prison in 1976, and Baader was found shot in his cell in 1977, presumed to be a suicide. People using the name Red Army continued terrorist activities until 1992, when it was revealed that the former East Germany had backed the group at the peak of its terrorist activities.

nificant voice. Dramatic historical changes, such as a sudden increase in violence by other groups or by the government, often increase people's sense of powerlessness, humiliation, and anger, leading to terrorist activity.

In the long run, understanding how these conditions impact people could help root out the causes of terrorism. One challenge is to discover methods of distributing the benefits of economic growth more evenly. A second is to recognize each group's cultural identity and to teach people to live peacefully in a diverse society. A third is to open up political systems to participation by a wide spectrum of groups and philosophies, and a fourth is to discover methods of solving problems without using force or violence. America's long-term ability to avert the threat of increased terrorism may well depend upon how its citizens respond to these difficult challenges. ■ ■ ■

Thailand. In April 1995, Chuan Likphai set a record for coup-plagued Thailand by serving 32 months as a democratically elected prime minister. He was credited with liberalizing the nation's financial system and other reforms.

But on May 19, Chuan's five-party parliamentary coalition fell apart over a land scandal, despite his own reputation for integrity. Chuan called for parliamentary elections, held on July 2, in which his Democrat Party increased its number of seats from 79 to 86. However, the main opposition Chart Thai party captured 92 seats, more than any other party in the new parliament.

New prime minister. Banharn Silapa-archa, the Chart Thai leader, became prime minister at the head of a seven-party coalition. Banharn had served as interior minister in a Cabinet the armed forces had ousted for rampant corruption in 1991. He had been investigated for being "unusually rich," but later cleared of corruption charges. Still, Banharn was known as "Mr. ATM" for his tactic of dispensing money like a human automatic teller machine to win supporters. Newspapers in the capital, Bangkok, said presents and cash had influenced voters.

New Cabinet. Banharn named a Cabinet of veteran politicians, but few had any experience running complex departments at the national level. Some had been accused of corruption. After Banharn announced the appointments, the Thai stock market fell 5 percent. Bangkok newspapers said the politicians had sought Cabinet posts with the aim of recouping their huge investments in the July election.

Banharn did not give Cabinet posts to Chart Thai's deputy leader or its chief adviser. Allegations arose in 1994 that they had been involved in international drug trafficking, which had prevented them from getting visas to the United States. In 1995, a U.S. spokesman warned that drug-tainted politicians in the Thai Cabinet could strain relations with America. The warning angered Chart Thai members, but in September, Banharn named former Foreign Minister Thanat Khoman to head a commission to look into drug charges against politicians.

Royal criticism. Usually silent on government matters, Thailand's king, Phumiphon Adunyadet, publicly chastised the government on August 17, saying Bangkok's traffic jams, widely known as being among the world's worst, discouraged other nations from investing in the city and deterred tourists from visiting. On September 19, the 67-year-old monarch appeared on television to criticize officials for failing to help flood victims. The interior ministry said that between July 27 and October 12, floods affected 3.7 million people, and 180 people died.

Inflation rose after Banharn took power. This raised doubts that Thailand's 8 percent rate of economic growth could continue.   □ Henry S. Bradsher

See also **Asia** (Facts in brief table). In *World Book*, see **Thailand.**

Theater. The punishing economics of Broadway continued to define New York City theater in 1995. New musicals, Broadway's traditional mainstay, found the Great White Way a difficult environment. Classic plays, however, proved surprisingly popular.

In late December 1994, Neil Simon, the most-produced playwright in America, announced plans to open his latest comedy off-Broadway for financial reasons. It would have cost $1.6 million to open on Broadway, while opening it at a small off-Broadway theater cost only $660,000. The play, *London Suite,* opened in April 1995 at the Union Square Theatre and closed in September. That a writer who is all but guaranteed a Broadway run opted for a less financially risky alternative sent a clear message to the Broadway establishment that its future was in jeopardy. But was that message heard?

A musical stands alone. Many observers thought not, given two events that unfolded during the year. The first was the decision in May by the American Theater Wing to give *Sunset Boulevard* two Antoinette Perry (Tony) awards, including best musical, without going through the usual process of nominating and voting. Because *Sunset Boulevard* was the only new musical to open on Broadway during the 1994-1995 season, there were no other productions to nominate for best score and best book and lyrics. Several other organizations that confer annual theater awards chose to suspend these two categories. Some insiders felt that the Theater Wing awarded these prizes rather than suspend the categories because it was reluctant to call attention to the scarcity of new musicals on Broadway. *Sunset Boulevard* ended up winning four awards.

Sunset Boulevard's solitary status on Broadway was dismaying because musicals had long been a vital and truly American art form. Some critics also expressed dismay that this musical retelling of the classic 1950 Billy Wilder film of the same name was actually more English than American, since it was composed by Andrew Lloyd Webber of Great Britain.

The fall season brought only one new musical to Broadway, a stage version of the film *Victor/Victoria,* starring Julie Andrews.

Union contracts. The second event was the outcome of negotiations for new union contracts between Broadway producers and backstage workers and musicians. Many people in the New York City theater community attributed a large part of Broadway's economic problems to a long-standing union contract clause requiring producers to employ a set number of backstage workers and musicians no matter what a production's needs. This often forced producers to hire many more staff for a production than was necessary. Unions defended the clause as a rightful protection of the interests of their members. Theater owners historically dominated contract negotiations and kept the clause in place rather than cause a strike. A coalition of producers formed in late 1994 in an effort to counter the owners' dominance. But the coalition weakened in 1995, and the new union contracts maintained the status quo.

The British keep coming. The British dominance of the American theatrical arena continued in 1995. The revolutionary British production of Rodgers and Hammerstein's *Carousel* (1945) mounted by Lincoln Center Theatre's Vivian Beaumont Theater closed in January, earlier than expected. But in April, Tom Stoppard's intelligent, time-warping drama *Arcadia* opened at the Vivian Beaumont. That play, in turn, was followed by another British production in November—*Racing Demon*, David Hare's portrayal of the Anglican Church.

One of the most talked-about dramatists in New York City in 1995 was the ultimate English playwright, William Shakespeare. Three successful productions of the Bard's works indicated that audiences were eager for classic fare—particularly if it featured a pop culture star. A British-originated production of *Hamlet* starring Ralph Fiennes, best known for his work in the motion picture *Schindler's List* (1993), enlivened the late spring and summer on Broadway. And the New York Shakespeare Festival's production of *The Tempest,* with Patrick Stewart of TV's "Star Trek" as Prospero, proved so popular in its summer run at the Delacorte Theater in Central Park that it was transferred to Broadway in November. The Shakespeare Festival also mounted a provocative off-Broadway production of *The Merchant of Venice,* featuring Ron Leibman as Shylock.

Season of the divas. Several legendary actresses returned to Broadway in autumn 1995, some after long absences. Julie Andrews won plaudits for her performance as a woman impersonating a man impersonating a woman in a stage version of her hit 1982 film *Victor/Victoria.* Carol Channing reprised the role that made her famous—matchmaker Dolly Levi in *Hello, Dolly!* (1964). Comedian Carol Burnett made her first stage appearance in 30 years in Ken Ludwig's comedy *Moon over Buffalo.* And Zoe Caldwell played that supreme diva, opera star Maria Callas, in Terrence McNally's *Master Class.*

Musicals. Nostalgia shows proved popular. *Smokey Joe's Cafe*, a revue of rock classics by songwriters Jerry Leiber and Mike Stoller, including "Hound Dog" and "Yakety Yak," appeared in February 1995. *Swinging on a Star*, which opened in October at the Music Box Theater, paid tribute to lyricist Johnny Burke, whose songs included "Pennies from Heaven" and "Moonlight Becomes You."

Comedy. McNally's warm comedy of gay life and death in the 1990's, *Love! Valour! Compassion!,* picked up the Tony for best play of 1995. The play at first appeared to be one of the year's success stories, but it closed in September at a financial loss. Although McNally's play was favored for the Pulitzer Prize for drama, the award went instead to Horton Foote's nostalgic family drama *The Young Man from Atlanta.* Mounted by the tiny but acclaimed Signature Theatre Company, it was scheduled for a Broadway run in early 1996.

An imagined meeting of scientist Albert Einstein and artist Pablo Picasso in a Paris bar provided comedian and playwright Steve Martin with the setting for his comedy, *Picasso at the Lapin Agile.* Martin's *Wasp and Other Plays,* opened at the Joseph Papp Public Theater in November 1995.

Drama. Cherry Jones's luminous performance in the stage revival of the 1947 classic film *The Heiress* at Lincoln Center Theatre's Mitzi E. Newhouse Theater won her the Tony for best actress and the public recognition she had long worked for. One of the most warmly received plays of 1995 was Emily Mann's *Having Our Say,* based on the lives of Bessie and Sadie Delaney, centenarian sisters whose lives were a living history of African American culture.

Macabre humor was an emerging theme in 1995. The Broadway success of the British import *Indiscretions*—a renamed version of Jean Cocteau's 1948 film *Les Parents Terrible*—which makes sport of incestuous tensions within a French family, set the tone. Playwright Nicky Silver followed suit with his off-Broadway hits *Raised in Captivity*, about an estranged brother and sister reunited when their mother is killed by a flying shower head, and *The Food Chain*, about the interlocking lives of a group of neurotic New Yorkers.

Tony Award winners in 1995

Best Play, *Love! Valour! Compassion!* Terrence McNally.

Best Musical, *Sunset Boulevard.*

Best Play Revival, *The Heiress.*

Best Musical Revival, *Show Boat.*

Leading Actor in a Play, Ralph Fiennes, *Hamlet.*

Leading Actress in a Play, Cherry Jones, *The Heiress.*

Leading Actor in a Musical, Matthew Broderick, *How to Succeed in Business Without Really Trying.*

Leading Actress in a Musical, Glenn Close, *Sunset Boulevard.*

Featured Actor in a Play, John Glover, *Love! Valour! Compassion!*

Featured Actress in a Play, Frances Sternhagen, *The Heiress.*

Featured Actor in a Musical, George Hearn, *Sunset Boulevard.*

Featured Actress in a Musical, Gretha Boston, *Show Boat.*

Direction of a Play, Gerald Gutierrez, *The Heiress.*

Direction of a Musical, Harold Prince, *Show Boat.*

Book of a Musical, Don Black and Christopher Hampton, *Sunset Boulevard.*

Original Musical Score, Music by Andrew Lloyd Webber and lyrics by Don Black and Christopher Hampton, *Sunset Boulevard.*

Scenic Design, John Napier, *Sunset Boulevard.*

Costume Design, Florence Klotz, *Show Boat.*

Lighting Design, Andrew Bridge, *Sunset Boulevard.*

Choreography, Susan Stroman, *Show Boat.*

Regional Theater, Goodspeed Opera House, East Haddam, Connecticut.

One of 1995's biggest off-Broadway successes was a trio of one-act plays by David Mamet, Elaine May, and Woody Allen called *Death Defying Acts*, whose uniting theme was death. And the season's underground discovery was the brother-and-sister writing team of David and Amy Sedaris, whose barbed satire *One Woman Shoe* at La Mama's Experimental Theater Club told the story of a group of witless female welfare recipients forced to work as performance artists to earn their benefits.

Touring theater. The national touring circuit of professional shows continued to be one of the few flourishing arenas for theater. The League of American Theatres and Producers reported gross ticket sales of $695 million in the 1994-1995 season, up from $621 million in 1993 and $503 million in 1992.

The regional theater circuit, like Broadway, struggled for economic health. Theatre Communications Group, the national organization of regional theaters, reported deficit budgets and continuing declines in attendance among the 68 theaters surveyed for its 1993-1994 report, the latest available in 1995. These sample theaters had ended 1994 with a combined deficit of $5.1 million. More than half the theaters surveyed reported an operating fund deficit, and total attendance figures dropped to a five-year low of 8.6 million. □ Karen Fricker

In *World Book*, see **Theater.**

Togo. See Africa.

Toronto. Known in the 1970's as "the city that works" and during the 1980's as a "world-class city," Toronto in 1995 became a city painfully trying to chart a future course. The year was marked by a sensational murder trial, the worst subway accident in the city's history, and the beginning of a massive reorganization of government for the Greater Toronto Area (GTA)—an urban region that sprawls over 2,800 square miles (7,300 square kilometers) and is home to 4.2 million people.

Restructuring. In February, Ontario's Premier Bob Rae appointed a task force headed by Anne Golden, a historian and the president of the United Way of the GTA, to propose a new system of government for the GTA. Rae was responding to complaints that the GTA, which encompasses five regional governments as well as the governments of 30 cities and towns, included too many ruling bodies and had become too expensive to operate. In a November 1994 referendum, 58 percent of voters in the city of Toronto had indicated they would like to abolish the metropolitan federation that has governed Toronto and its suburbs since 1954.

Rae gave the Golden commission 18 months to prepare a report, but his New Democratic Party government was soundly defeated in provincial elections by the Progressive Conservatives on June 8, 1995. Ontario's new premier, Mike Harris, asked the Golden commission to issue a confidential report by the end of 1995 and promised to release the report and act on the proposed reforms to the GTA in 1996.

Bernardo trial. The trial of Paul Bernardo, a 31-year-old accountant accused of kidnapping, raping, torturing, and murdering two teen-age girls in 1991 and 1992, opened on May 18, 1995, in Toronto. The crimes took place in the quiet city of St. Catharines, 80 miles (130 kilometers) away, but the trial was moved to Toronto because of publicity.

The proceedings drew intense local as well as international media coverage, in part because Bernardo's accomplice was a woman—his wife, Karla Homolka. She videotaped the assaults, and the tapes were used as evidence. Homolka became a *crown witness* (a witness for the prosecution) in return for a 12-year sentence for the lesser crime of manslaughter. On September 1, the jury found Bernardo guilty of first-degree murder. He was later sentenced to life imprisonment with no eligibility of parole for 25 years.

Subway accident. The Toronto Transit Commission (TTC), which had long prided itself on its reputation for safety, suffered the worst disaster in its 74-year history on August 11. A subway train coming down a steep incline in the Spadina Subway line went through two red lights, rounded a corner, and smashed into the back of a train waiting at a station. Three people were killed. An inquest was begun in November and continued at year-end.

The TTC experienced other difficulties as well. In late February, the Metropolitan Council, which provides most of Metropolitan Toronto's services, decided it could afford to build only two new subways—on Eglinton Avenue and Sheppard Avenue—instead of the four that had been in the planning stages since 1990. Municipalities in Ontario pay 25 percent of subway construction costs, with provincial governments providing the balance. Premier Rae had urged the council to create new jobs by building all four lines, including a northwest extension of the Spadina line and a northeast extension of the Scarborough rapid transit line.

But in July 1995, after the new Harris government cut back on funding for the TTC, the transit agency raised fares by 20 cents and canceled the Eglinton line. That left only the Sheppard line in the works, and even that project was in jeopardy.

Raptors' debut. On October 18, the Raptors, the new National Basketball Association franchise in Toronto, played their first game before a hometown audience. The Raptors lost, 99-95, to the Atlanta Hawks in an exhibition game but drew a crowd of 17,814 to a temporary court set up in the SkyDome stadium, which is home to the Blue Jays baseball team in summer. In August, the Toronto City Council had given the Raptors permission to build an arena of their own. Work on it was expected to begin early in 1996. □ David Lewis Stein

In *World Book,* see **Toronto.**

Toys and games. Retail toy sales in the United States were somewhat disappointing in 1995, rising just slightly more than 3 percent over 1994 sales, despite a relatively stable economy. Some industry analysts theorized that cautious consumer spending throughout the year and during the holiday season—when approximately 65 percent of toy sales are made each year—was related to Americans' fear of job layoffs. Industry analysts estimated that consumers in the United States purchased about 2.7 billion toys in 1995.

Games in cyberspace. Hasbro Interactive Worldwide of Beverly, Massachusetts, in 1995 introduced a CD-ROM version of the board game Monopoly, the popular real-estate-trading game that first came out in 1935. The game featured music from the 1930's and more than 800 computer animations, including graphic displays of Depression-era real-estate properties. Up to six players could play on one computer or over a computer network.

Hasbro's Monopoly CD-ROM also had an Internet feature, allowing players all over the world to compete. The game automatically made language translations, real estate translations, and currency conversions. Up to six players with the game software could play together on the Internet. The first copies of the Monopoly CD-ROM were made available in the United States and Europe in late 1995. It was available in three languages: English, French, and German. Hasbro Interactive also announced in 1995 that it would develop CD-ROM versions of some of its other classic games, including Risk and Candy Land.

Action figures still popular. The announcement of plans for a new series of *Star Wars* films, the movie blockbusters of the late 1970's and early 1980's, inspired Hasbro Incorporated of Pawtucket, Rhode Island, in 1995 to reissue action figures from the original movie, including Luke Skywalker, Darth Vader, and R2D2. The growing popularity of collectible toys and memorabilia made these reissued items a hit for the 1995 holiday season.

Across all cultures. Ethnic themes in toys flourished in 1995. Walt Disney Company's *Pocahontas,* one of the year's most successful animated motion pictures, launched a craze for Pocahontas dolls and other related toy products.

Toy Biz Incorporated of New York City in 1995 introduced the Gerber Talking Baby, a Hispanic American doll with olive skin and dark hair. This electronic, soft-bodied doll speaks both Spanish and English. When different parts of its body are pressed, the doll responds with the corresponding Spanish and English words.

Tyco Toys, Incorporated, of Mount Laurel, New Jersey, came out with a Spanish-speaking version of its Magic 8 Ball in 1995. Players could ask the ball a question and turn it over to see 1 of 20 possible predictions appear in the mystery window.

The Dream Doll House from Fisher-Price of East Aurora, New York, was a Victorian-styled house complete with a Caucasian or African American family of dolls. Asian American or Hispanic families were available for other Fisher-Price dollhouse sets. Another notable feature of the dollhouse was that the house and its accessories folded up for easy storage.

Flying dancers. Sky Dancer, a flying doll from Lewis Galoob Toys, Incorporated, of South San Francisco, California, made its debut in 1995. A pull-string mechanism sent Sky Dancer into the air from a special launcher. Once aloft, the doll pirouetted to the ground.

The "yuck" factor. Some of 1995's new toys were designed to appeal to many children's fascination with the grotesque. Earthworm Jim action figures from Playmates Toys, Incorporated, of La Mirada, California, were one of the year's hottest hero collections. The figures were based on the best-selling video game of the same name. Earthworm Jim was a worm who inherited a magical spacesuit that gave him power to fight such evil characters as Professor Monkey-for-a-Head and Major Mucus.

Pressman Toy Corporation of New Brunswick, New Jersey, addressed the yuck factor with its Gooey Louie. Players pulled plastic "gooeys" from Louie's nose until someone got the gooey that made Louie's head explode.

Also new for 1995 was Big John, manufactured by Parker Brothers of Beverly, Massachusetts. Players took turns tossing plastic playing pieces called "ickeys" into the plastic toilet bowl. When a player tossed in one ickey too many, the bowl exploded, and the ickeys shot out of the bowl.

Video wars. The next generation of video games was unveiled in 1995 with the debut of 32-bit-microprocessor systems, having twice the power of earlier video games. The two most prominent new games were PlayStation from Sony Corporation of America of Park Ridge, New Jersey, and Sega Saturn from Sega of America, Incorporated, of Redwood City, California. Both systems offered more realistic characters and higher quality graphics, sound, and colors than older video games.

Nintendo of America of Redmond, Washington, in 1995 premiered Virtual Boy, a handheld, portable video system offering three-dimensional images in its games. Industry analysts believe such virtual reality game systems are the future of video systems.

Toys make Hollywood. Toys were the stars of the Walt Disney Company's 1995 animated hit *Toy Story,* which was billed as the first animated feature film produced entirely by computer. The film spawned a series of new action figures and brought back the popularity of old favorites featured in the film, including Mr. Potato Head, Etch-a-Sketch, and the coiled wire dog called Slinky Dog.

☐ Diane P. Cardinale

In *World Book,* see **Doll; Game; Toy.**

Track and field

Track and field. The outstanding athletes in 1995 were three African distance and middle-distance runners (Haile Gebrselassie of Ethiopia, Moses Kiptanui of Kenya, and Noureddine Morceli of Algeria); a British triple jumper (Jonathan Edwards); and an American sprinter (Michael Johnson). The United States won the most medals in the world outdoor championships.

Stars. The 22-year-old Gebrselassie decimated the world records for 5,000 meters and 10,000 meters. On June 5 in Hengelo, the Netherlands, he ran the 10,000 in 26 minutes 43.53 seconds, breaking the record by almost 9 seconds. On August 16 in Zurich, Switzerland, he ran the 5,000 in 12 minutes 44.39 seconds, eclipsing the record by almost 11 seconds.

In the 3,000-meter steeplechase, an event in which no one else had broken 8 minutes 5 seconds, Kiptanui twice bettered 8 minutes and lowered his world record to 7 minutes 59.18 seconds.

In a 10-day span in July, Morceli set world records for 1,500 meters (3 minutes 27.37 seconds) and 2,000 meters (4 minutes 47.88 seconds). He also ran a mile (1.6 kilometers) in 3 minutes 45.19 seconds, the second-fastest time ever.

Edwards broke the world record for the triple jump three times in three weeks. On July 18, he jumped 59 feet (17.98 meters), one-half inch (1 centimeter) better than Willie Banks's 10-year-old record. On August 7, in the world outdoor championships in Göteborg, Sweden, Edwards jumped 59 feet 7 inches (18.16 meters) on his first attempt and 60 feet ¼ inch (18.29 meters) on his second.

In the United States championships June 16 to 18 in Sacramento, California, Johnson became the first man in the 1900's to win both the 200 meters (19.83 seconds, wind aided) and 400 meters (43.66 seconds). In the world championships, he achieved the same double, winning the 200 in 19.79 seconds, a meet record, and the 400 in 43.39 seconds.

Ivan Pedroso of Cuba apparently broke the world record for the long jump on July 29 in Sestriere, Italy. His jump of 29 feet 4¾ inches (8.96 meters) bettered U.S. jumper Mike Powell's 1991 record by a quarter-inch (1 centimeter). However, the Italian national track federation did not submit Pedroso's jump for recognition to international track and field authorities because an Italian coach, apparently anxious to watch from close range, had blocked the wind gauge.

The drought of women's world records continued in 1995. The only major records during the year were set by Kim Batten of the United States (52.61 seconds for the 400-meter hurdles) and Inessa Kravets of Ukraine in the triple jump—50 feet 10¼ inches (15.50 meters)—both during the world championships. Since 1988, only eight women's records had fallen in running and field events in world-championship or Olympic programs, and Chinese women

World outdoor track and field records established in 1995

Men

Event	Holder	Country	Where set	Date	Record
1,500 meters	Noureddine Morceli	Algeria	Nice, France	July 12	3:27.37
2,000 meters	Noureddine Morceli	Algeria	Paris	July 3	4:47.88
3,000-meter steeplechase	Moses Kiptanui	Kenya	Zurich, Switzerland	August 18	7:59.18
5,000 meters	Haile Gebrselassie	Ethiopia	Zurich, Switzerland	August 16	12:44.39
10,000 meters	Haile Gebrselassie	Ethiopia	Hengelo, the Netherlands	June 5	26.43.53
Triple jump	Jonathan Edwards	United Kingdom	Göteborg, Sweden	August 7	60 ft. ¼ in. (18.29 m)

Women

Event	Holder	Country	Where set	Date	Record
1,000 meters	Maria Mutola	Mozambique	Brussels, Belgium	August 25	2:29.34
5,000 meters	Fernanda Ribeiro	Portugal	Hechtel, Belgium	July 22	14:36.45
400-meter hurdles	Kim Batten	U.S.A.	Göteborg, Sweden	August 11	52.61
Pole vault	Emma George	Australia	Melbourne, Australia	December 17	14 ft. ½ in. (4.30 m)
Triple jump	Inessa Kravets	Ukraine	Göteborg, Sweden	August 8	50 ft. 10¼ in. (15.50 m)
Hammer throw	Olga Kuzenkova	Russia	Moscow	June 18	223 ft. 7 in. (68.16 m)

m = meters

Jonathan Edwards of the United Kingdom sets a world record of 60.25 feet (18.29 meters) in the triple jump in August at the world outdoor championships in Göteborg, Sweden.

widely suspected of using illegal bodybuilding drugs set five of those.

World. The outdoor championships from August 6 to 13 attracted 1,959 men and women from a record 192 nations. The medal leaders were the United States with 19 (12 gold, 2 silver, 5 bronze) and Russia with 12 (1 gold, 4 silver, 7 bronze).

The American men who won gold medals were Michael Johnson in the 200 and 400 meters, Allen Johnson in the 110-meter hurdles, Derrick Adkins in the 400-meter hurdles, Dan O'Brien in the decathlon, John Godina in the shot-put, and the 1,600-meter relay team.

The American women's winners were Gwen Torrence in the 100 meters, Gail Devers in the 100-meter hurdles, Batten in the 400-meter hurdles, and the 400-meter and 1,600-meter relay teams. Torrence also finished first in the 200 meters, but was disqualified for running out of her lane.

Sergei Bubka, the pole vaulter from Ukraine, became the only athlete to win a title in all five world outdoor championships. Gebrselassie won the 10,000 meters, and Pedroso won the long jump. Donovan Bailey and Bruny Surin finished 1-2 in the 100-meter dash and helped Canada win the 400-meter relay. Ana Quirot of Cuba won the women's 800 meters.

☐ Frank Litsky

In *World Book*, see **Track and field.**
Transit. See **Transportation.**

Transportation. Railway companies in the Western United States took steps in 1995 toward consolidating the five major railroads into just two. After a bidding war broke out in late 1994 over control of the Atchison, Topeka, and Santa Fe railway, the Burlington Northern Railroad, based in Fort Worth, Texas, merged with the Santa Fe Pacific Corporation of Schaumburg, Illinois, which operates the Santa Fe railway. The $4-billion deal produced the nation's largest railroad, with a 30,500-mile (49,000-kilometer) network of track. The Union Pacific Corporation of Bethlehem, Pennsylvania, had been part of the bidding war and later opposed Burlington Northern's proposed deal on the grounds that it violated antitrust laws. But on March 29, 1995, Union Pacific dropped its opposition in exchange for track rights on a Santa Fe line in Kansas and Nebraska.

Union Pacific in March purchased the Chicago and North Western Transportation Company, based in Chicago, for $1.2 billion. Then on August 3, it made a $5.4-billion bid to acquire the Southern Pacific Rail Corporation of San Francisco. The combination would restore Union Pacific's former status as the nation's largest railroad, giving it 36,400 miles (58,600 kilometers) of track. On September 26, the Burlington Northern Santa Fe Corporation dropped its opposition to the acquisition in return for access to 3,800 miles (6,100 kilometers) of track, mostly along the Mexican border.

Federal reform. On November 28, President Bill Clinton signed into law a bill to repeal the national speed limit of 55 miles (90 kilometers) per hour on most roads and 65 miles (105 kilometers) per hour on rural interstate highways. Under the new law, states were allowed to set their own speed limits. Congress also eliminated the federal mandate that states require motorcycle riders to wear helmets. The law became effective on December 8.

Congress also in 1995 cut by 20 percent the $800-million annual U.S. subsidy for Amtrak, the semipublic corporation that operates intercity passenger trains. Amtrak responded by making service cuts in April and September. The latter cuts included terminating the famous "Broadway Limited," which had provided daily service between New York City and Chicago by way of Philadelphia and Pittsburgh, Pennsylvania, since 1902. In its heyday, the train provided the ultimate in speed and luxury, including barbers, valets, and a library.

Federico Peña, U.S. secretary of transportation, in early 1995 proposed a reorganization of the Department of Transportation aimed at slimming the agency. Part of his plan included the consolidation of a number of federal transportation agencies into one operation. President Bill Clinton's federal budget included the elimination of the 108-year-old Interstate Commerce Commission, which used to regulate transportation laws across state lines.

Canadian railway news. In an effort to improve financial viability, the Canadian government introduced legislation to permit the country's two major railways, the Montreal-based Canadian National Railway Co. (CN) and Canadian Pacific Limited's CP Rail System, to sell off money-losing lines to small independent railroads. In August, the government issued a prospectus for privatizing the state-owned CN in a stock offering totaling $1.5 to $2 billion. On July 31, both CN and CP Rail lost a $415-million, century-old subsidy of grain shipments. Canada discontinued the payments in an effort to reduce agricultural subsidies.

Channel Tunnel financial problems. Eurotunnel, the operator of the 31-mile (50-kilometer) rail tunnel between Britain and France, announced on September 14 that it would suspend payment of interest on its $12.4-billion debt for 18 months pending financial restructuring.

Philadelphia transit strike. Philadelphia's commuters faced 14 days without bus and subway services in late March and early April when the city's transit union went on strike. The union struck to demand a pay hike and better benefits. The transit employees returned to work on April 10 after reaching an agreement with the city. ☐ Ian Savage

See also **Automobile; Aviation**. In *World Book*, see **Bus; Electric railroad; Subway; Transportation**.
Trinidad and Tobago. See **West Indies**.
Tunisia. See **Middle East**.

Turkey. Prime Minister Tansu Ciller's True Path Party lost to a Muslim group, the Welfare Party, in general elections held on Dec. 24, 1995. The next day, Ciller resigned, along with her cabinet, though she was expected to stay in office until a new government was formed.

Ciller's problems had been mounting through the year. On Sept. 20, 1995, civil servants nationwide went on strike to protest government austerity measure. Ciller resigned the same day after Deniz Baykal and his Republican People's Party withdrew from her coalition government. Baykal, whose party represents mainly workers and civil servants, was critical of Ciller's economic austerity program.

The strike, the largest in decades, spread to 650,000 workers and civil servants. The strikers demanded a wage increase large enough to help offset the nation's 70 percent inflation rate.

In October, President Süleyman Demirel asked Ciller to form a new government, but she failed to form a coalition. Even members within the True Path Party withheld their support, and she lost a parliamentary vote of confidence on October 15. As a result, elections that had been slated for October 1996 were rescheduled for December 1995.

As prime minister, Ciller had sought democratic reforms and the privatization of state-owned companies. She also secured Turkey's entrance into a trade alliance with the European Union (EU), and won collective-bargaining rights for civil servants.

Economy. Ciller opposed a pay increase for the strikers because it would hurt economic reforms she began in July 1994, which the International Monetary Fund (IMF), an agency of the United Nations, had stated as a condition for a loan of nearly $1 billion. By June 1995, Turkey had exceeded some IMF goals for its recovery, including holding its budget deficit to $2.9 billion, $1.7 billion below IMF's target figure. Turkey had hoped to earn $5 billion by selling off state-owned companies in 1995, but that figure went down to about $1 billion by November.

Kurds. Turkey launched three military incursions into Iraq in 1995 to destroy bases of the militant Kurdish Workers Party (PKK). The largest offensive began March 20 with 35,000 troops. Although Ciller said her troops were to stay indefinitely, international pressure forced her to withdraw in April. In early July, Turkey sent 6,000 troops into Iraq after the PKK ambushed and killed Turkish soldiers in two attacks. Troops also briefly entered Iraq in October. More than 19,000 people have died since Kurdish rebels began fighting in 1984 to establish an independent homeland in the Kurdish region of Turkey and Iraq.

Human rights. Turkey came under international criticism in 1995 for having a poor human rights record. The EU said Turkey's admission to the trade alliance depended on an improved human rights record, though it later softened its stance. The EU particularly criticized 1994 jail sentences for six Kurdish members of parliament for allegedly supporting the PKK.

Ciller failed in 1995 to win parliamentary approval to abolish Article 8, a harsh antiterrorist constitutional amendment adopted in 1982. Article 8 had led to the 1995 arrests of many intellectuals and writers, some of whom had only suggested that the Kurdish problem be resolved peacefully by broadening Kurdish rights. In November, Turkish officials reformed the amendment and ordered the release of dozens of prisoners convicted under the law.

Terrorism. Dozens of deadly bombings of public and private facilities disrupted Turkey's major cities in 1995. The PKK was blamed for most of them, though leftists and the Iranian-backed Hezbollah, a Muslim extremist group, were also suspected. On June 7, the leader of Ankara's small Jewish community survived a car-bomb attack, allegedly by Muslim extremists.

Drug traffickers have used Turkey as a major transit point for moving drugs into Europe. In January, Turkey announced that it had seized more than 19 tons (17 metric tons) of illegal drugs in 1994. European officials in mid-1995 noted a decline in drug smuggling and credited Turkey's clampdown on the PKK. The PKK allegedly funds itself partly through illicit drug trafficking.   □ Christine Helms

See also **Middle East** (Facts in brief table). In *World Book,* see **Kurds; Turkey.**

Turkmenistan. Turkmenistan's President Saparmurad Niyazov consolidated single-party authoritarian rule in 1995. In a February 1994 referendum, Niyazov's presidential term had been extended to the end of the century. In 1995, every seat in the new 50-member *Majlis* (assembly) was occupied by one of Niyazov's allies—members of his Turkmen Democratic Party, the former Communist Party and Turkmenistan's only legal political organization. The Majlis members were all elected without opposition in December 1994.

Niyazov's rule became increasingly autocratic in 1995. His portrait was displayed in public places, and streets were named in his honor. No opposition political activity was allowed, and critics of the regime were jailed. The national press and radio and television stations were closely controlled.

Turkmenistan had to contend with serious economic problems in 1995. Although Turkmenistan possessed one of the world's largest natural gas reserves, all of its gas pipeline routes passed through Russia. Russian energy officials restricted Turkmenistan's access to lucrative West European markets, so gas revenues were disappointing. Turkmen officials explored alternative pipeline routes through China or Iran, but meanwhile the economy declined steeply. In 1995, the average monthly income in the country was about $15.   □ Steven L. Solnick

Uganda. See **Africa.**

Ukraine. Ukrainian President Leonid Kuchma expanded his powers at the expense of the *Rada* (parliament) in 1995. Kuchma's economic reforms began to bear fruit, and the long-awaited recovery of the Ukrainian economy appeared within grasp. A potential conflict with Russia over the autonomous region of Crimea subsided, while another over the former Soviet Union's Black Sea fleet simmered.

Power sharing with parliament. Frustrated with parliamentary efforts to curtail his economic reforms, Kuchma introduced a special bill redefining the separation of government powers. Kuchma sought enhanced powers, including the right to appoint a Cabinet without parliamentary approval.

Confrontation burst into the open in April, when the Rada passed a vote of no confidence in the government. Kuchma demanded the right to name a new government unilaterally, and he stormed out of parliament on April 12 when his separation-of-powers bill again stalled. On May 31, Kuchma announced that a national referendum would be held on his version of the bill. The following day, parliament declared Kuchma's act unconstitutional.

Rada members soon realized that Kuchma had sufficient popularity with Ukrainian voters to prevail if the referendum took place. On June 7, parliament backed down and approved Kuchma's "constitutional accord" by 240 votes to 81. The agreement called for a new constitution to be written within a year.

Economic reform. Kuchma's victory over the Rada left him in a stronger position to continue promoting comprehensive economic reforms. In the new government, Kuchma appointed former security chief Yevhen Marchuk prime minister, and reappointed leading reformer Viktor Pynzenyk deputy prime minister for economic affairs.

Ukrainian officials vowed to continue the tight monetary and fiscal policies that won Ukraine praise from the International Monetary Fund (IMF)—and massive loans to stabilize its weak economy. That commitment to reform was questioned in August, when the government reinstated subsidies for some large state farms and failing manufacturers. The resulting spike in the budget deficit triggered a run on the Ukrainian transitional currency, the coupon, which plunged down 15 percent in one day. The government rushed to renew its commitment to fiscal austerity.

Economic reforms that Kuchma introduced in October 1994 bore fruit in 1995. Inflation decreased to less than 5 percent a month, a dramatic improvement over the hyperinflation of 1994. Real wages doubled over nine months, and foreign exchange reserves rose for the first time since Ukraine became independent in 1991. Privatization of large state-owned enterprises proceeded slowly, however, and land privatization stalled.

Crimea. Ukrainian officials moved to defuse a volatile situation in Crimea, an autonomous region

Unemployment

within Ukraine that has a large ethnic Russian population and was part of Russia until 1954. In January 1994, Crimean voters elected Yuri Meshkov president, responding to his platform of separating from Ukraine and reunifying with Russia. In March 1995, the Ukrainian parliament suspended the Crimean Constitution, brought Crimea under its direct rule, and removed Meshkov from office. Elections held in the region during the summer failed to reflect any sympathy for the ousted separatists.

The Black Sea fleet. A dispute between Russia and Ukraine over dividing the Soviet Black Sea fleet proved insoluble in 1995. The fleet was based at Sevastopol, in Crimea. Ukraine claimed it was entitled to half the fleet as well as to the Sevastopol naval base. In June, Kuchma and Russian President Boris Yeltsin agreed that the fleet should be evenly split, after which Russia would buy back 30 percent of the ships from Ukraine. The deal would thus have left Ukraine with only 20 percent of the Black Sea vessels and would have allowed Russia to continue using the Sevastopol naval base. Conflicting interpretations of the deal caused it to unravel over the summer. The dispute remained the chief roadblock to the signing of a comprehensive friendship treaty between Russia and Ukraine.   □ Steven L. Solnick

See also **Commonwealth of Independent States.** In *World Book,* see **Ukraine.**

Unemployment. See Economics, Labor.

In August, Mark Campbell became the first black soldier to join the Household Cavalry, which guards the Queen of England on official occasions.

United Kingdom. Government leadership by the Conservative Party in the United Kingdom (U.K.) faced challenges in 1995, as attacks on the prime minister, scandals, and infighting rocked the nation's ruling party. Britain's Labour Party, however, gained strength under its new leader, Tony Blair, who was elected party leader in mid-1994. Labour membership increased by one-third under Blair, partly due to his continued efforts to reform the party.

Attacks on Major. Prime Minister John Major threw down the gauntlet to critics who for months had been attacking his ability to lead the nation. He announced in June 1995 that he was resigning as Conservative Party leader and was calling a fresh leadership contest with himself as a candidate.

Major's government had become the most unpopular government since public opinion polling began in the late 1930's. His Conservative Party also suffered increasingly from dissension within its ranks as right-wing members of the party doggedly expressed opposition to certain aspects of the United Kingdom's integration with the European Union (EU). Many in the party also wanted Britain to come down harder on criminals and to lower taxes.

On June 26, 1995, John Redwood, secretary of state for Wales, whose political views were well to the right of Major's, resigned from the Cabinet and announced his candidacy. Redwood, known as a fiscal conservative, promised to lower taxes, strength-

en the military, and halt the transfer of powers from Britain to Brussels, Belgium, the seat of the European Union. He also felt that Britain should never take part in a common European currency, an important issue on the EU agenda. Major had refused to commit himself on the issue because he felt it important to remain a part of EU discussions on a common currency. In the election on July 4, of the 329 Conservative Party members, Major took 218 votes to Redwood's 89, with 22 abstentions.

Local election results. British citizens registered their disapproval of the ruling party in the year's local elections. In Scotland's elections on April 6, Conservative candidates won only 11 percent of the vote and failed to win a majority on any of Scotland's 29 councils. The Labour Party garnered 47 percent of the vote and won control of 20 of the councils, and the Scottish National Party took 26 percent of the vote and held a majority in three districts. Liberal Democrats and independent candidates took the rest of the vote.

Then on May 4, in their worst-ever electoral showing, the Conservatives won only 25 percent of the vote and gained control of only 8 of the 346 local councils in England and Wales, down from 67. Labour took 46 percent of the vote and won control of 155 councils, and the Liberal Democrats won 24 percent of the vote and dominated 45 councils. Independent candidates won majorities in 18 councils.

Conservative scandals continue. On April 9, Richard Spring, private secretary to Patrick Mayhew, secretary for Northern Ireland, was forced to step down after a tabloid newspaper alleged that he had engaged in sexual relations with a Sunday school teacher and her tycoon boyfriend. Spring was the 17th Conservative to leave Major's government after sexual or financial scandals.

On April 10, a newspaper made allegations that Jonathan Aitken, chief secretary of the treasury, was guilty of misconduct in business dealings. Among its allegations was that Aitken, who had Middle East business contacts, had procured prostitutes for wealthy Arab friends in the 1980's. Aitken instituted legal action against the newspaper, becoming the first Cabinet minister under Major to sue for libel. Aitken later resigned when Major reshuffled his Cabinet on July 5 following his leadership triumph.

Labour Party news. Labour leader Blair sought to reform his party in 1995 and give it a more centrist image that would have greater appeal to middle-class voters than Labour's traditional socialist leanings. One of Blair's most notable reforms came on March 13, when Labour voted for a major revision of the Marxist precepts upon which the party had been founded in the early 1900's. By a 21 to 3 vote, the party's National Executive Committee (NEC) supported Blair's plan to scrap "Clause Four" of the party's constitution, which for 77 years had committed Labour to state ownership of all industry.

Barings bank collapses. Financial markets reeled when Baring Brothers, one of Britain's oldest and most venerable merchant banks, collapsed on February 27 with debts of 827 million pounds (U.S. $1.32 billion). The 233-year-old bank, which had financed the Napoleonic Wars of the early 1800's and listed Queen Elizabeth II among its clients, was reportedly brought down by a single employee.

Nicholas W. Leeson, a 28-year-old Singapore-based trader, was suspected of causing the debacle with high-stakes gambles on Far East stock markets. German authorities arrested him on March 1, 1995, in Frankfurt after he had fled Singapore. Singapore requested Leeson's extradition, but he fought to stand trial in Britain, fearing a heavier sentence in Singapore. But after a lengthy delay, Britain refused to seek Leeson's extradition, and Germany returned him to Singapore on November 23. On December 1, Leeson pleaded guilty in a Singapore court to two charges against him and was sentenced to 6½ years in prison. Barings was acquired in March by ING Group (Internationale Nederlanden Groep), a large Dutch financial services company.

Outcry over animal exports. Protesters trying to stop the export of live calves and sheep from Britain clashed repeatedly with police at British ports and airports in early 1995. The demonstrators protested the exportation of animals to places where they could be raised for slaughter under inhumane conditions that are outlawed in Britain. One practice activists protested was the raising and force feeding of veal calves in dark, narrow crates, which supposedly produced a better quality meat.

Britain's agriculture minister, William Waldegrave, who himself had come under fire when it was disclosed that calves from his farm had been sold in Europe for raising in crates, asked the EU in January to ban that method of raising veal calves. British ports decided to ban animal traffic. But on April 12, the British High Court overturned the ban.

Environmental victory. Environmentalists scored a victory in June when Shell U.K., Limited, gave in to pressure from the environmental group Greenpeace and abandoned its plans to dump an aging oil storage rig in the Atlantic Ocean. The rig supposedly contained toxic sludge and radioactive waste that could have harmed marine life. Customer boycotts inspired by Greenpeace protests helped persuade Shell to give up its plans for dumping the rig and to search for other means of disposal.

Bishop of London. In a public statement on March 13, David Hope, the Bishop of London, said that his sexuality was a "greyer" area than that of most people, and that he had chosen to live a "single, celibate life." Hope made the statement after receiving what he called an intimidating letter from OutRage!, a gay group widely known for its militant methods of exposing homosexuals in prominent positions. The Church of England supported Hope through the media blitz surrounding his statement and on April 11 promoted him to Archbishop of York, the Church of England's second highest post, subordinate only to Archbishop of Canterbury.

Banned in the military. Britain's High Court on June 7 upheld a ban on homosexuals in the military, following the first legal challenge to the ban by four former military personnel dismissed for being homosexual. In his landmark verdict, one of the presiding judges, Lord Justice Simon Brown, called on parliament to review the ban, and he said that its days may be numbered because the policy was outdated.

Churchill papers retained. On April 26, the British government announced that it would pay 13.25 million pounds (U.S. $21 million) to the family of Winston Churchill, Britain's prime minister in World War II (1939-1945) for his pre-1945 writings. Most of the payment would come from lottery funds. The more than 1.5 million papers included drafts of Churchill's most famous speeches, which contained such historic statements as "We shall fight them on the beaches" and "This was their finest hour." Critics condemned the sale, saying that the papers already belonged to the nation. The government had launched an earlier campaign to prevent the sale of the papers outside the country.

Royal activities. Queen Elizabeth II arrived in South Africa on March 19, 1995, for a six-day visit, her first to the African nation since she had gone

Britain's Prime Minister John Major smiles for the press in July just prior to winning a resounding victory in a Conservative Party leadership contest.

there as a princess in 1947. Elizabeth and her husband, Prince Philip, were greeted by some of the biggest crowds of her reign, though there was some hostility from South Africa's Afrikaner nationalists.

On May 7, 1995, Queen Elizabeth attended the greatest celebration of reconciliation in British history in London to mark the 50th anniversary of the end of World War II. Fifty-four foreign heads of state attended the event, which was part of a three-day observance of the end of the war in Europe.

Prince Charles arrived in Dublin, Ireland, on May 31 for the first British royal visit to the Irish Republic since it became a self-governing country in 1921. Charles was well received, though there were protests against him relating to his leadership of a regiment of British soldiers that shot and killed 13 people in Northern Ireland in 1972 in what became known as Bloody Sunday.

Britannia for sale. The royal yacht *Britannia,* Queen Elizabeth's luxury oceangoing ship, was officially put up for sale on Aug. 3, 1995. The floating palace, which was costing Britain 10 million pounds (U.S. $16 million) a year to run, was expected to stay in the country, probably as a tourist attraction or conference center.   □ Ian Mather

See also **Ireland; Northern Ireland; Northern Ireland** Special Report: **The Pursuit of Peace in Northern Ireland.** In *World Book,* see **European Union; United Kingdom.**

United Nations. The largest gathering ever of government leaders celebrated the 50th anniversary of the founding of the United Nations (UN) at UN Headquarters in New York City in October 1995. A total of 91 presidents, 8 vice presidents, 37 prime ministers, at least 2 kings, and dozens of foreign ministers and heads of organizations addressed the anniversary session held in the UN General Assembly.

The session ended on the UN's birthday, October 24, called United Nations Day. Member nations adopted a declaration to reaffirm their commitment to the *Charter of the United Nations,* which went into effect on Oct. 24, 1945. The members vowed that the "United Nations of the future will work with renewed vigor and effectiveness in promoting peace, development, equality and justice, and understanding among the peoples of the world."

Before the world leaders met in New York, many of them gathered on June 26, 1995, in San Francisco's War Memorial Opera House to celebrate the 50th anniversary of the actual signing of the charter. The establishment of the United Nations came at the end of World War II (1939-1945).

The Pope visits. On Oct. 5, 1995, Pope John Paul II, head of the Roman Catholic Church, paid his first visit to the UN Headquarters since 1979 and gave a speech to a packed UN General Assembly. He said the world is facing "enormous challenges," and it needs the UN more than ever. But he also admonished the UN to reform itself. "Now is the time for new hope, which calls us to expel the paralyzing burden of cynicism from the future of politics and of human life," he said. He urged nations to work together to overcome "our fear of the future."

Big debts. As the UN turned 50, it was financially crippled because its members were $3.4 billion behind in making required contributions and repaying debts to the organization. Secretary-General Boutros Boutros-Ghali said the severe cash shortage hampered UN activities worldwide.

The United States, which formerly made the largest contributions to the UN budget and peace-keeping operations, owed the United Nations more than $1.3 billion in 1995. Russia followed the United States, with a debt of close to $600 million, and scores of other countries had smaller debts.

Former Yugoslav republics, led by President Slobodan Milošević of Serbia, President Franjo Tudjman of Croatia, and President Alija Izetbegovic of Bosnia-Herzegovina (often called Bosnia), agreed to peace terms on November 21 after negotiating at Wright-Patterson Air Force Base near Dayton, Ohio, since November 1. The agreement ended fighting between Bosnian Muslims and Croats and the Bosnian Serbs that began in 1992. Bosnia would retain its borders, but it would be divided into a Bosnian-Croat federation and a Bosnian Serb republic.

While the talks progressed, the UN had monitored a shaky cease-fire agreement that the leaders signed on Oct. 11, 1995. Members of the U.S.-led military alliance, the North Atlantic Treaty Organization (NATO), promised to send about 60,000 peacekeeping troops to Bosnia to help keep order as the peace treaty was implemented. About 20,000 American troops were to be part of the peace mission.

Another year of violence. Peacemakers won their bid that the negotiations in Ohio would end the bloodletting that had continued through most of 1995 in the Balkan region. In the first week of May, Croatian forces had attacked the Serb-held Krajina region of central Croatia. Serb forces immediately retaliated with rocket attacks on Zagreb, the capital of Croatia, that killed 6 people and injured 175 others. On May 28, Bosnian Serb forces shot down a helicopter carrying Bosnia's foreign minister, who was killed in the attack. The Serbs also took 41 UN peacekeepers as hostage, bringing the number of peacekeepers held hostage to more than 300.

On July 11, Bosnian Serbs captured the town of Srebrenica, a Muslim enclave under UN protection, in one of the worst defeats for UN forces in their three years as peacekeepers in Bosnia. The Serbs seized men of military age but let women and children be evacuated. United States officials later said they had evidence that 6,000 Muslim men reported missing after the fall of Srebrenica were massacred by the Serbs.

On August 4, the Croation government launched an all-out offensive against rebel Croation Serbs in the self-proclaimed Serb Republic of Krajina, a region of Croatia bordering Bosnia-Herzegovina that the Serbs took over in 1991. By Aug. 7, 1995, the Croatian forces had recaptured all of the Krajina region. The UN high commissioner for refugees said more than 100,000 Serbian people had to flee the area, where many had lived for years.

Climactic events in late August finally led the fighting factions to November's peace table in Ohio. On August 28, in the worst attack on Bosnia's capital city since February 1994, two mortar shells landed in Sarajevo's central market, killing 38 people. Blaming Bosnian Serbs for the attack, NATO began a massive retaliation against Bosnian Serb positions on Aug. 30, 1995. Intense bombings continued for about two weeks, destroying ammunition depots and weapons sites under Serb control.

On September 8, U.S. officials brokered an agreement with the Serbs, who were to remove their weapons from direct firing range of Sarajevo and reopen the Sarajevo airport for humanitarian flights. NATO agreed on September 14 to suspend bombings for three days but threatened to resume them if the Serbs did not live up to their agreement. Between September 16 and 20, the Serbs removed 250 heavy weapons from the designated zone, meeting the NATO deadline. The bombings were called off and the peace process began.

Lighted office windows in the United Nations (UN) Secretariat Building in New York City proclaim the UN's 50th anniversary in October.

Libya. In March, a sanctions panel of the UN Security Council relaxed travel sanctions against Libya to allow some 6,000 Libyans to fly to Saudi Arabia for the *hajj,* the annual Islamic pilgrimage to the city of Mecca. This was the first instance of easing the economic and travel sanctions against Libya that the UN imposed in 1992. The sanctions were ordered because Libya refused to turn over suspects accused of the bombings of two airliners, in 1988 and 1989, that killed 441 people.

Iraq. On April 14, 1995, the 15-member UN Security Council voted to allow Iraq to sell $2 billion worth of oil over a six-month period and to use the revenues for relief aid for many Iraqis suffering severely from the nation's food shortages. However, Iraq's President Saddam Hussein rejected the offer. He wanted the council to entirely lift the crippling economic sanctions that the UN imposed after Iraq invaded Kuwait in 1990, leading to the Persian Gulf War.

The World Summit for Social Development met in Copenhagen, Denmark, in March 1995 to draw up a program of action aimed at eliminating inequalities within and among countries of the world. Representatives from 117 countries and major organizations dealing with social and development issues attended the summit. The American delegation included Vice President Albert Gore, Jr., and First Lady Hillary Rodham Clinton. Many other world leaders came to the UN summit.

Summit participants adopted a declaration containing 10 commitments intended to emphasize strong action rather than mere promises in eradicating poverty and promoting social equality. The commitments aimed at solving the "profound social problems" of poverty, unemployment, and social exclusion, which were called the core issues of the summit. This was the first UN summit devoted to the subject of social inequities.

In the spirit of the summit, some governments declared forgiveness of debts owed them by developed countries. Denmark forgave about $200 million, and Austria wrote off $100 million. South Korea pledged to give technical training to 30,000 people, the United States pledged 40 percent of its development assistance funds to nongovernmental organizations, and France and Norway called for an international taxation system to finance social development programs.

The development of Africa's sub-Saharan region, where at least 31 countries ranked as being least developed in 1995, became an important topic of the summit, as did 16 other least-developed countries outside of Africa. In addition, the summit put particular emphasis on helping poor women around the world. United Nations studies in 1994 said that 40 percent of the world's women were illiterate and that 70 percent of the world's poor people were women.

The Fourth World Conference on Women, held in China's capital, Beijing, from Sept. 4 to Sept. 15, 1995, resulted in the "Beijing Platform of Action," calling for programs to deal with 12 critical areas of concern considered obstacles to the advancement of women. The platform offered specific five-year objectives for governments and the private sector to remove those obstacles. The 12 critical areas were poverty, education, health care, violence against women, armed conflicts, gender equality in work, sharing in decision making, advancement of women in government, human rights, mass media, the environment, and discrimination against girls.

Conference organizers said that more than 6,000 delegates from 189 governments attended the conference, while another 30,000 women, representing nongovernmental organizations, attended a parallel conference outside of Beijing. The previous UN conferences on women took place in Stockholm, Sweden, in 1975, Mexico City in 1980, and Nairobi, Kenya, in 1985.

Refugees. The UN High Council on Refugees reported on Nov. 15, 1995, that the number of people assisted by their agency grew from 17 million in 1990 to 27 million in early 1995. This number included both refugees and *displaced persons*, people who must leave their homes but who remain within their own country. ☐ J. Tuyet Nguyen

In *World Book,* see **United Nations.**

United States, Government of the.

A political standoff between Democratic President Bill Clinton and the Republican-controlled Congress led to a partial shutdown of federal operations for six days in mid-November 1995. Clinton vetoed a bill to continue spending beyond November 13, contending that it was loaded with unrelated and undesirable amendments. The government furloughed 800,000 nonessential workers the following day. Republicans accused the White House of refusing to negotiate their differences.

Earlier, Clinton had vetoed a bill to raise the United States debt limit, also on grounds that the bill included irrelevant provisions. Treasury Secretary Robert E. Rubin managed to avoid a default on United States payments by borrowing from a government workers' pension fund.

The shutdown, which closed such tourist attractions as Grand Canyon National Park and the Washington Monument, was the longest interruption of federal services in U.S. history. Stoppages in the past had been so brief that few people noticed. Polls suggested that most Americans blamed the Republicans in Congress for provoking the shutdown rather than Clinton for refusing to accept Grand Old Party (GOP) conditions for the temporary spending authority.

The White House reached agreement with Speaker of the House Newt Gingrich and Senate Majority Leader Bob Dole on November 19, ending the im-

Federal spending
United States budget for fiscal 1995*

	Billions of dollars
National defense	272.2
International affairs	16.4
General science, space, technology	17.6
Energy	5.1
Natural resources and environment	23.3
Agriculture	9.8
Commerce and housing credit	– 18.7
Transportation	38.6
Community and regional development	11.0
Education, training, employment, and social services	52.7
Health	114.8
Social security	335.8
Medicare	159.9
Income security	220.2
Veterans' benefits and services	37.9
Administration of justice	16.3
General government	13.9
Interest	232.2
Undistributed offsetting receipts	– 44.5
Total budget outlays	**1,514.5**

*Oct. 1, 1994, to Sept. 30, 1995.
Source: U.S. Department of the Treasury.

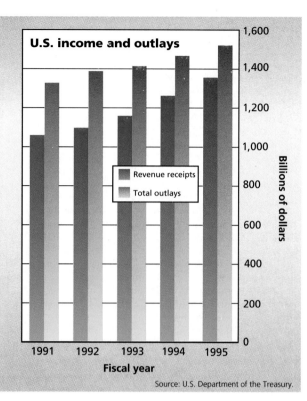

U.S. income and outlays

Revenue receipts
Total outlays

Billions of dollars

1991   1992   1993   1994   1995

Fiscal year

Source: U.S. Department of the Treasury.

passe and sending federal employees back to work. Clinton accepted the Republicans' proposed seven-year target for balancing the U.S. budget, on the condition that Medicare, Medicaid, and other popular programs would be protected from heavy cuts. Spending was authorized until December 15 at 75 percent of current outlays, to allow time for passage of regular appropriations bills.

On December 6, President Clinton rejected a Republican-backed plan to wipe out the deficit by 2002, saying it was too harsh. The next day, Clinton offered his own seven-year plan, but it came under immediate fire from Republican leaders, who said that it would not lead to a balanced budget.On December 16, with no agreement reached, a second partial government shut-down began, this one involving about 265,000 workers. At year-end, the two sides had still not agreed on a budget.

Relations with Congress. The deadlock reflected the increasing animosity between the President and Republican leaders in Congress over the Republican drive to impose tax cuts and massive spending reductions to eliminate federal deficits in seven years. Armed with his veto pen, Clinton vowed to protect Medicare, education, and environmental programs against the onslaught from Capitol Hill. Buoyed by their control of both the House and the Senate for the first time in 40 years, Republicans pushed for radical changes they said were essential

to balance the budget. Outnumbered Democrats hoped for a backlash in the 1996 elections to counter the GOP campaign.

Relations between President Clinton and the GOP Congress steadily deteriorated as the year progressed. Clinton on Jan. 23, 1995, signed a broadly supported bill that would apply most federal laws to Congress and its employees, including wage-hour laws and antidiscrimination measures. He also approved a bill to deter Congress from imposing costly requirements on states and cities without providing the funds to pay for them. Clinton made few new policy proposals in his January 24 State of the Union message, however. He asked for an increase in the $4.25-an-hour federal minimum wage, but most political analysts said there was little chance of its passage in the Republican-led Congress.

Clinton and Congress in September agreed to accept recommendations from a federal commission to close 79 major military bases and consolidate 26 others to eliminate 43,742 military and civilian jobs. The moves were expected to save $19.3 billion over a 20-year period. This was the last of four rounds of base closings, which by late 1995 had resulted in the shutdown of 60 major bases and 104 smaller facilities since 1991.

Terrorism in the U.S. The federal government became a target of terrorists in 1995. On April 19 in Oklahoma City, a massive car bomb exploded, shattering the Alfred P. Murrah federal office building in the deadliest terrorist attack on American soil in U.S. history. The death toll mounted to 168, including 19 children in a child care center. Federal officials tightened security at other government buildings. Police arrested Timothy J. McVeigh, a 27-year-old Army veteran with extreme antigovernment views, and charged him with the crime. Two days after the blast, two brothers, Terry Lynn Nichols and James Nichols, were taken into custody. Terry Nichols, 40, had served in the same Army unit as McVeigh. All three were charged with conspiring to produce explosives.

A federal grand jury on August 10 indicted McVeigh and Terry Nichols on charges of conspiring to blow up the federal building. Both men pleaded innocent. A third man, Michael Fortier, pleaded guilty to separate charges of conspiring to steal firearms and agreed to testify about the bombing. Charges against James Nichols were dropped.

In another terrorist incident, an Amtrak train was derailed on October 9 as it passed over a remote desert ravine near Hyder, Arizona. One person was killed and 100 were injured when cars of the *Sunset Limited*, en route from Los Angeles to Miami, fell into the ravine. Federal Bureau of Investigation (FBI) investigators concluded that the wreck was caused by sabotage of the tracks by someone with knowledge of railroad operations. Copies of a note signed by an unknown group calling itself the "Sons of Gestapo" were found near the site.

A federal jury in New York City on October 1 convicted 10 militant Muslims, including Egyptian cleric Sheik Omar Abdel Rahman, in the most prominent terrorism trial in U.S. history. The men were found guilty of plotting to bomb the United Nations (UN) headquarters and other New York landmarks and to kill political leaders. The sheik was accused of leading a "war of urban terrorism" in retaliation for U.S. support for Israel and Egypt's secular government. Siddig Ibrahim Siddig Ali, an alleged ringleader of the group, pleaded guilty prior to the trial.

Abdel Rahman was also accused of leading the group allegedly responsible for the 1993 bombing of the World Trade Center in New York City. He was not charged with that crime, however.

The FBI on Aug. 2, 1995, in Jordan arrested the alleged driver of a van in the World Trade Center bombing and brought him to New York for trial. The suspect, Eyad Ismail, pleaded innocent to bombing and conspiracy charges. The man believed to be the mastermind of the World Trade Center blast—Ramzi Ahmed Yousef—was arrested on February 7 in Pakistan and flown to the United States. Yousef had left the United States shortly after the bombing.

FBI and CIA under fire. In an unusual twist, the FBI itself was investigated during Senate hearings into the death of two people during an armed standoff in 1992 at Ruby Ridge, Idaho. Government

Investigators survey the remains of a federal building in Oklahoma City that was bombed in April by antigovernment extremists. The blast killed 168 people.

Executive Office of the President
President, Bill Clinton
Vice President, Albert Gore, Jr.
White House Chief of Staff, Leon E. Panetta
Presidential Press Secretary, Michael McCurry
Assistant to the President for Domestic Policy, Carol H. Rasco
Assistant to the President for National Security Affairs, W. Anthony Lake
Assistant to the President for Science and Technology, John H. Gibbons
Council of Economic Advisers—Joseph E. Stiglitz, Chairman
Office of Management and Budget—Alice M. Rivlin, Director
Office of National Drug Control Policy—Lee P. Brown, Director
U.S. Trade Representative, Mickey Kantor

Department of Agriculture
Secretary of Agriculture, Daniel R. Glickman

Department of Commerce
Secretary of Commerce, Ronald H. Brown
Bureau of Economic Analysis—J. Steven Landefeld, Director
Bureau of the Census—Martha F. Riche, Director

Department of Defense
Secretary of Defense, William J. Perry
Secretary of the Air Force, Sheila E. Widnall
Secretary of the Army, Togo D. West, Jr.
Secretary of the Navy, John H. Dalton
Joint Chiefs of Staff—
General John Shalikashvili, Chairman
General Ronald R. Fogleman, Chief of Staff, Air Force
General Dennis J. Reimer, Chief of Staff, Army
Admiral Jeremy M. Boorda, Chief of Naval Operations
General Charles C. Krulak, Commandant, Marine Corps

Department of Education
Secretary of Education, Richard W. Riley

Department of Energy
Secretary of Energy, Hazel R. O'Leary

Department of Health and Human Services
Secretary of Health and Human Services, Donna E. Shalala
Public Health Service—Philip R. Lee, Assistant Secretary
Centers for Disease Control and Prevention—David Satcher, Director
Food and Drug Administration—David A. Kessler, Commissioner
National Institutes of Health—Harold Varmus, Director
Surgeon General of the United States, Audrey F. Manley

Department of Housing and Urban Development
Secretary of Housing and Urban Development, Henry G. Cisneros

Department of the Interior
Secretary of the Interior, Bruce Babbitt

Department of Justice
Attorney General, Janet Reno
Bureau of Prisons—Kathleen M. Hawk, Director
Drug Enforcement Administration—Thomas A. Constantine, Administrator
Federal Bureau of Investigation—Louis J. Freeh, Director
Immigration and Naturalization Service—Doris M. Meissner, Commissioner
Solicitor General, Drew S. Days III

Department of Labor
Secretary of Labor, Robert B. Reich

Department of State
Secretary of State, Warren Christopher
U.S. Ambassador to the United Nations, Madeleine K. Albright

Department of Transportation
Secretary of Transportation, Federico F. Peña
Federal Aviation Administration—David R. Hinson, Administrator
U.S. Coast Guard—Admiral Robert E. Kramek, Commandant

*As of Dec. 31, 1995.

Department of the Treasury
Secretary of the Treasury, Robert E. Rubin
Internal Revenue Service—Margaret Milner Richardson, Commissioner
Treasurer of the United States, Mary Ellen Withrow
U.S. Secret Service—Eljay B. Bowron, Director
Office of Thrift Supervision—Jonathan L. Fiechter, Acting Director

Department of Veterans Affairs
Secretary of Veterans Affairs, Jesse Brown

Supreme Court of the United States
Chief Justice of the United States, William H. Rehnquist
Associate Justices—
John Paul Stevens
Sandra Day O'Connor
Antonin Scalia
Anthony M. Kennedy
David H. Souter
Clarence Thomas
Ruth Bader Ginsburg
Stephen G. Breyer

Congressional officials
President of the Senate pro tempore, Strom Thurmond
Senate Majority Leader, Bob Dole
Senate Minority Leader, Thomas A. Daschle
Speaker of the House, Newt Gingrich
House Majority Leader, Dick Armey
House Minority Leader, Richard A. Gephardt
Congressional Budget Office—June E. O'Neill, Director
General Accounting Office—Charles A. Bowsher, Comptroller General of the United States
Library of Congress—James H. Billington, Librarian of Congress

Independent agencies
Central Intelligence Agency—John M. Deutch, Director
Commission on Civil Rights—Mary Frances Berry, Chairperson
Commission of Fine Arts—J. Carter Brown, Chairman
Consumer Product Safety Commission—Ann Winkelman Brown, Chairman
Corporation for National Service—Harris Wofford, Chief Executive Officer
Environmental Protection Agency—Carol M. Browner, Administrator
Equal Employment Opportunity Commission—Gilbert F. Casellas, Chairman
Federal Communications Commission—Reed E. Hundt, Chairman
Federal Deposit Insurance Corporation—Ricki Helfer, Chairman
Federal Election Commission—Danny Lee McDonald, Chairman
Federal Emergency Management Agency—James Lee Witt, Director
Federal Reserve System Board of Governors—Alan Greenspan, Chairman
Federal Trade Commission—Robert Pitofsky, Chairman
General Services Administration—Roger W. Johnson, Administrator
International Development Cooperation Agency—J. Brian Atwood, Acting Director
Interstate Commerce Commission—Linda J. Morgan, Chairman
National Aeronautics and Space Administration—Daniel S. Goldin, Administrator
National Endowment for the Arts—Jane Alexander, Chairman
National Endowment for the Humanities—Sheldon Hackney, Chairman
National Labor Relations Board—William B. Gould IV, Chairman
National Railroad Passenger Corporation (Amtrak)—Thomas M. Downs, Chairman
National Science Foundation—Neal F. Lane, Director
National Transportation Safety Board—James E. Hall, Chairman
Nuclear Regulatory Commission—Shirley A. Jackson, Chairman
Peace Corps—Mark D. Gearan, Director
Securities and Exchange Commission—Arthur Levitt, Jr., Chairman
Selective Service System—Gil Coronado, Director
Small Business Administration—Phillip Lader, Administrator
Smithsonian Institution—I. Michael Heyman, Secretary
Social Security Administration—Shirley S. Chater, Commissioner
U.S. Arms Control and Disarmament Agency—John D. Holum, Director
U.S. Information Agency—Joseph D. Duffey, Director
U.S. Postal Service—Marvin T. Runyon, Postmaster General

agents under FBI direction killed the wife and son of Randy Weaver, a white separatist, in an exchange of gunfire. A deputy U.S. marshall was also killed. The U.S. government agreed on Aug. 15, 1995, to pay $3.1-million to the Weaver family to settle a lawsuit. At the same time, four FBI agents were suspended while the Justice Department investigated whether there was a cover-up of the FBI's actions at Ruby Ridge.

The Central Intelligence Agency (CIA) also came under fire in 1995. In March, the agency settled a series of sex discrimination charges filed between 1986 and 1994 by several hundred women in its clandestine-operations division. Payments totaling about $1 million were authorized and 25 women received retroactive promotions. Agreement on a plan to end sex bias was approved on June 9 by U.S. Judge Albert V. Bryan, Jr. But many of the women felt that the settlement was inadequate, given the extent of the discrimination they had experienced.

In another crackdown, new CIA Director John M. Deutch in September fired two CIA officers and reprimanded eight others for mishandling covert operations in Guatemala. The actions followed disclosures that a CIA-paid informant was linked to the murders of a U.S. citizen and a Guatemalan married to an American woman. Deutch also ordered a review of spending by the National Reconnaissance Office after receiving reports that it had hoarded $1.5 billion in a secret fund that was concealed from Congress.

Foreign policy. On December 3, President Clinton approved the deployment of the first of 20,000 American troops to Bosnia-Herzegovina, a former republic of Yugoslavia, to help establish peace between warring Serbian and Croatian forces. The American troops were part of a North Atlantic Treaty Organization (NATO) peacekeeping force of 60,000 troops. Clinton promised that the U.S. troops would remain in Bosnia-Herzegovina for no more than a year.

President Clinton in January announced an international rescue package for Mexico to bolster the sinking peso. The package included a loan of $20 billion from the United States, and $29.5 billion in backing from the International Monetary Fund and the Bank of International Settlements.

In Haiti, the United States in late March turned over security duties to a UN peacekeeping force, following the return to power, with American support, of Haitian President Jean-Bertrand Aristide. Also in March, U.S. forces pulled out of Somalia without having ended a civil war there. American troops had gone to Somalia in December 1992 to try to restore order and to protect food supplies for the starving population.

President Clinton in January eased a trade embargo against North Korea, in an attempt to prevent that country from taking steps to acquire nuclear weapons. But he issued an executive order to bar all trade with Iran, citing that nation's efforts to obtain nuclear weapons and its promotion of terrorism. The President in March blocked a $1-billion contract, awarded by Iran to Conoco, Incorporated, to develop two oil fields and build a natural gas pipeline.

The United States threatened to impose punitive tariffs on Japan and China in separate trade disputes, but last-minute agreements made the penalties unnecessary. China agreed on February 26 to shut down factories accused of making copies of U.S. goods without payment and to enforce international copyright laws. Japan's major auto producers agreed on June 28 to increase purchases of U.S. auto parts and raise production at their auto plants in the United States.

Factory raids. Agents of the Department of Labor and the Immigration and Naturalization Service raided three garment factories in the Los Angeles area on August 23 to check on alleged sweatshop conditions. They arrested 55 people, including 39 Thai workers. The raids came shortly after state officials shut down a garment factory in El Monte, California, where 70 Thai immigrants had been held against their will and forced to work under slavelike conditions. A federal grand jury in Los Angeles on August 17 indicted nine Thai nationals whom they accused of running the El Monte operation.

Radiation experiments. Expanding on earlier disclosures, the Department of Energy in February announced that about 9,000 people had been used as subjects in 154 radiation experiments conducted by the federal government during the Cold War era. The President on October 3 received a report from the Committee on Human Radiation Experiments that said federal agencies had sponsored about 4,000 experiments involving tens of thousands of people, many of whom were not aware of the possible consequences.

Photos declassified. The Clinton Administration announced on February 24 that it had declassified hundreds of thousands of photos taken by U.S. spy satellites between 1960 and 1972. Up to 800,000 photos could be approved for release for use by scientists and others studying the global environment.

Chicago Housing Authority takeover. The Department of Housing and Urban Development on May 30 took over the Chicago Housing Authority (CHA), the second-largest public housing agency in the nation. The CHA was accused of allowing crime and drug dealing to flourish in many of its projects.

Auto recall. The Department of Transportation announced on May 23 that nine U.S. and Japanese automakers had agreed to recall over 8 million cars sold between 1986 and 1991 to repair or replace faulty seat-belt buckles. It was the second largest recall in 30 years. □ William J. Eaton

See also **Clinton, Bill; Congress of the United States.** In *World Book,* see **United States, Government of the.**

Uruguay. On March 1, 1995, Julio María Sanguinetti of the Colorado Party was sworn for a second five-year term as Uruguay's president. He had also served from 1985 to 1990.

Sanguinetti pledged to reform the nation's social security system, which was consuming some 37 percent of the federal budget. In late August 1995, the General Assembly took the first step in that direction by increasing from 30 to 35 the number of years Uruguayans must work to qualify for a pension, raising the retirement age for women from 55 to 60, and offering incentives for men to keep working until age 65.

Protests stymied Sanguinetti's attempts to reform Uruguay's economy. On April 7, the day after the government imposed measures to reduce the deficit, inflation, and unemployment, workers in Uruguay's confederation of trade unions went on strike. The strike was called to protest tax increases that accompanied the economic package.

On May 3, Sanguinetti ruled out conducting investigations of past human rights abuses in Uruguay during military rule from 1973 to 1985. He reportedly believed that any such offenses had not been serious enough for the government to investigate. ☐ Nathan A. Haverstock

See also **Latin America** (Facts in brief table). In *World Book,* see **Uruguay.**

Utah. See State government.

Uzbekistan. On March 26, 1995, Uzbekistan's President Islam Karimov held a referendum on extending his term of office by three years, to the year 2000. Karimov ignored international objections to voting procedures, such as restrictions on opposition campaigning, a lack of secret ballots, and the absence of international monitors. A stunning 99.3 percent of eligible voters were reported to have turned out to cast ballots, and Karimov officially won 99.6 percent of the vote.

During an April visit to Tashkent, the capital, U.S. Secretary of Defense William J. Perry expressed concern about reported political and human-rights abuses in Uzbekistan. Nevertheless, he called the republic "an island of stability in a troubled area." Karimov said the United States had a "distorted picture" of Uzbek affairs and said he needed to guard against a return of Russian imperialism.

In July, Russian Prime Minister Viktor S. Chernomyrdin visited Tashkent and signed agreements allowing for closer Russian-Uzbek economic relations. Included in the agreements was a commitment by Uzbekistan to join the emerging customs union within the Commonwealth of Independent States, a loose organization of states formerly part of the Soviet Union. The visit illustrated the continuing influence of Russia in Uzbek affairs. ☐ Steven L. Solnick

In *World Book,* see **Uzbekistan.**

Vanuatu. See Pacific Islands.

Venezuela. Venezuelans continued in 1995 to feel the impact of the 1994 collapse of most of the nation's banks due to corruption and mismanagement. By October 1995, inflation was running at 52.7 percent, creating widespread havoc among all the nation's social classes.

Although the government had restored some of the constitutional freedoms that it suspended in June 1994, there were repeated arrests in 1995. In mid-March, government security forces cracked down on alleged subversives, arresting 150 people in the capital, Caracas, and three other cities—Maracaibo, Valencia, and Cumaná.

The government claimed that those arrested had planned to provoke violence at an antigovernment demonstration in Caracas on March 16. Only about 200 people participated in the demonstration, but public opinion polls indicated a deep dissatisfaction with the government.

Venezuela and Brazil signed an agreement on July 4 to create a joint oil company. The new company, Petroamérica, would launch projects to improve oil exploration and refining capabilities in both countries. ☐ Nathan A. Haverstock

See also **Latin America** (Facts in brief table). In *World Book,* see **Venezuela.**

Vermont. See State government.

Vice President of the United States. See **Gore, Albert, Jr.**

Vietnam. United States President Bill Clinton announced full diplomatic recognition of Vietnam on July 11, 1995, 20 years after the Vietnam War (1957-1975) ended. Some American political leaders as well as veterans' groups opposed the move because many U.S. military personnel who fought in the war were still officially listed as missing in action (MIA)—1,621, according to the U.S. government.

However, Vietnam's Prime Minister Vo Van Kiet welcomed the decision. On nationwide television the day of the announcement, he promised continued efforts to account for missing Americans.

Clinton had set the stage for diplomatic recognition by lifting a trade embargo on Vietnam in 1994. In January 1995, the United States opened a liaison office in Hanoi, the national capital, to work for the fullest possible accounting of prisoners of war and MIA's. American officials on June 18 visited an underground site where Americans reputedly were being held prisoner, but the site was a military depot.

Embassy opens. Upon arriving at Hanoi's airport on August 5, U.S. Secretary of State Warren Christopher participated in a military ceremony at which flag-draped coffins containing the remains of four U.S. servicemen were being transported back to the United States. The next day, he formally opened the American Embassy.

Economic issues. Christopher also discussed with Vietnamese officials their need to develop

Secretary of State Warren Christopher watches marines raise an American flag at the opening of the United States Embassy in Vietnam in August.

trade and investment laws and to institute other reforms in order to encourage economic ties. Vietnam wanted trade and investment to alleviate poverty. The World Bank, an agency of the United Nations, said 27 percent of Vietnam's urban population and 57 percent of its rural population lived in poverty, unable to obtain a diet of 2,100 calories a day.

The economy grew about 9 percent, but most growth occurred in Hanoi and Ho Chi Minh City (formerly Saigon). A building boom in Hanoi, which is on the Red River Delta, led to illegal construction on dikes. Authorities feared that the dikes would weaken under the load, so they ordered some of the buildings torn down.

Economic growth led to corruption in the ruling Communist Party. In May, the head of the party, Do Muoi, denounced "debauchery, abuse of power, and embezzlement of public funds" by party members.

Human rights. The government continued a two-year crackdown on leaders of the dissident United Buddhist Church of Vietnam. On August 15, five church leaders were given sentences ranging from two to five years in prison. Most had been convicted of organizing an unofficial mission to help flood victims. □ Henry S. Bradsher

See also **Asia** (Facts in brief table). In *World Book,* see **Vietnam.**

Virginia. See State government.

Vital statistics. See Census; Population.

Washington, D.C. Faced with a ballooning budget deficit, serious erosion in city services, and finally bankruptcy, Washington in 1995 also faced a takeover of District finances by an oversight board created by the United States Congress on April 7. The creation of the board, which was given near-total control over the District's fiscal affairs, was the most significant change to District government since 1973, when Congress granted District voters the right to elect their own officials.

The action by Congress followed years of steadily worsening financial problems. They were the result, in part, of the city's inability to tax its sizable commuter population and its fiscal responsibility for services that, in other cities, are generally paid for by state government. District critics also blamed the city's dismal financial condition on mismanagement, corruption, and a too-large municipal work force.

The move toward the creation of a review board began on Feb. 1, 1995, when D.C. Mayor Marion S. Barry, Jr., reported that the city's budget deficit for fiscal year 1995, which ended on September 30, would total $722 million, up from the $490 million projected in 1994. On Feb. 2, 1995, Barry announced a city bailout plan that included wage and job cuts for city employees and reductions in city services. He also proposed that the U.S. government pay the District's $267-million bill for Medicaid (government-funded health care for the poor).

Congress, however, which has final authority over all District affairs, rejected Barry's plan. Instead, a bipartisan group that included Eleanor Holmes Norton, the District's nonvoting delegate to the House of Representatives, began considering a plan for a review board. Support for the board picked up in March when Barry presented the District's 1996 budget. The mayor, who had also endorsed the congressional plan, refused to trim spending, arguing that more cuts would eliminate essential services.

The oversight legislation passed by Congress gave the review board the authority to cut District spending, eliminate city jobs and services, and reject District-negotiated contracts. The board, whose five members were appointed by President Bill Clinton, was to remain in existence until the District had produced four consecutive balanced budgets—the first due in 1999. On May 1, 1995, Clinton appointed Andrew F. Brimmer, a former member of the Federal Reserve Board, as the chairman of the review board.

Million Man March. Hundreds of thousands of African American men from across the United States converged on Washington on October 16 for the Million Man March. The National Park Service estimated attendance at 400,000, but other sources put attendance at more than 800,000. Organized by Louis Farrakhan, leader of the Nation of Islam, the march was promoted as a day of reconciliation and unity during which African American men would atone for past neglect of their families and communities and vow to take more responsibility for their lives. (See **Civil rights.**)

Health problems. Mayor Barry revealed on November 15 that he had been diagnosed with prostate cancer during his annual physical examination in October. He underwent surgery on December 9, and his doctors gave him a favorable prognosis.

New sports arena. Groundbreaking ceremonies for the new MCI sports arena were held on October 18. The 20,600-seat arena, scheduled to open in fall 1997, was to be the home of the Washington Bullets basketball team and the Washington Capitals hockey team. The District agreed to spend $56 million to prepare a site for the arena in northwest Washington. The main cost of the $175-million project, however, was to be borne by Abe Pollin, the owner of the Bullets and Capitals. The project ran into stiff opposition from community groups and architectural preservationists, who argued that the arena would alter the character of the neighborhood.

Fauntroy sentenced. Walter E. Fauntroy, who represented the District in Congress from 1971 to 1991, was sentenced on Aug. 9, 1995, to two years' probation, a $1,000 fine, and 300 hours of community service for falsifying a financial disclosure report to Congress. □ Barbara A. Mayes

See also **City.** In *World Book*, see **Washington, D.C.**

Washington. See **State government.**

Skaters and pedestrians take over Pennsylvania Avenue in front of the White House in May after fears of terrorist attacks led to the street's closing.

Water. Several studies released in the United States during the summer of 1995 by various federal agencies and private environmental groups warned Americans about drinking water contamination. Some studies were released to counter the Republican Party's proposals in the U.S. Congress for the relaxation of regulations in the 1974 Safe Drinking Water Act. The act authorized the Environmental Protection Agency (EPA) to set standards for municipal water systems to reduce contamination in reservoirs that supply tap water. Critics said the studies were alarmist and exaggerated the risk of trace amounts of contaminants.

Parasite contamination. A study released on June 1, 1995, by the Natural Resources Defense Council, an environmental group, found that 1 in every 5 American water systems contained the parasite cryptosporidium. The parasite is commonly found in rivers and streams contaminated by animal wastes or sewage. In 1993, cryptosporidia entered Milwaukee's water supply through an intake plant. Ultimately, the parasite infected 400,000 people, and at least 100 died.

On June 15, 1995, the EPA and the Centers for Disease Control and Prevention (CDC) in Atlanta, Georgia, recommended boiling drinking water to kill any cryptosporidia or filtering it through special devices that remove particles less than one *micron* (millionth of a meter) in diameter. The guidelines were intended for people with weakened immune systems, such as those with AIDS.

Toxic chemical contamination. Two other studies in 1995 warned of drinking water contamination by toxic chemicals. A June 1 report by the Environmental Working Group (EWG), a private environmental organization, listed American cities with potentially hazardous water supplies. New York City was on the list because its water supply contained sediment and coliform bacteria, organisms associated with sewage. Another report by the EWG, released on August 17, stated that the group found chemical weed killers in the drinking water of almost all the 29 Midwestern cities tested.

Zebra mussels in California. In June, for the fourth time in six months, state agricultural inspectors at California border points discovered zebra mussels on the bottom of recreational boats being towed into the state from the Great Lakes area. The finding raised fears that the pest would soon invade California's water distribution systems.

The zebra mussel originated in the Caspian Sea in Europe. It can attach itself to almost any surface and has larvae that can swim, traits that enable it to spread quickly. The mollusk colonized the Great Lakes region and Eastern United States in the 1980's. It reproduces rapidly and clogs the intake pipes and pumps of water systems.   □ Iris Priestaf

In *World Book,* see **Water.**

Weather. The first few days of 1995 featured cold weather in the Northeastern United States and warm dry weather in the Southwest. A string of Pacific storms from January 8 to 15 dropped torrential rains on coastal areas in California and up to 10 feet (3 meters) of snow in the mountains. Rising waters and mud slides closed highways and railroads and forced tens of thousands of people from their homes. The storms left 11 people dead and caused more than $300 million in damage. The United States government declared 34 of the state's 58 counties federal disaster areas.

Meanwhile, a storm traveled through the Eastern states and brought the season's first snowstorm and an outbreak of severe cold. However, warm weather quickly spread over the East and set all-time high temperatures for January in parts of the northeastern United States.

In early February, a strong flow of cold air from the Northwest brought heavy snows and low temperatures to the Central and Eastern states, while much drier conditions developed in the West. A particularly severe storm developed in eastern Virginia on February 3 and brought snowfalls of 8 inches (20 centimeters) to Washington, D.C.; 16 inches (41 centimeters) to Princeton, New Jersey; 10 inches (25 centimeters) to New York City; and 8 inches to Boston. In an ensuing outbreak of cold weather, gale-force winds accompanied snow accumulations

of up to 40 inches (100 centimeters) along Lake Ontario in New York, and caused wind chill temperatures to fall below –40 °F (–40 °C) in many areas of the Northeast.

In contrast, record-breaking high temperatures hit the Southwest in February. Los Angeles tied a February record of 94 °F (34 °C) twice on the 2nd and 3rd, then set a new February record with 95 °F (35 °C) on the 20th. On February 19, San Diego observed its first 90 °F (32 °C) reading for a winter season.

Temperatures also soared in Alaska, with readings of 52 °F (11 °C) at Healy in south-central Alaska and 38 °F (3 °C) at Bettles in north-central Alaska—its 2nd warmest February reading in recorded history. For the contiguous United States, it was the 15th warmest February in the past 101 years of record keeping. Five of these warm months occurred between 1984 and 1995. Some weather specialists believed the warm winters were part of a warming trend of the 1900's that has brought unusually warm temperatures to the whole world.

Winter floods in Europe. An extended period of exceptionally warm weather over central and southern Europe came to a climax in late January and early February when excessive runoff from melted snow in the Swiss Alps, augmented by several heavy rainfalls, caused the Rhine River to go over its banks in northern Germany and caused the Rhine, Waal, and Meuse rivers to flood areas of the Netherlands. Hundreds of thousands of people in the lowlands evacuated these areas in fear that the region's extensive network of dikes, which were saturated by floodwaters, would crumble. However, no serious breaches occurred.

Heavy spring precipitation in U.S. The 1994-1995 winter season's snowfall reached a record 110 inches (2.8 meters) at Nome, Alaska, by summer, surpassing Nome's previous record of 107.5 inches (2.7 meters) in the winter of 1931-1932. Meanwhile, heavy precipitation returned to California. For the second time in three months, the Russian River at Guerneville flooded severely, rising 33 feet (9.9 meters) in a 24-hour period on March 8 and 9. On March 10, raging floodwaters destroyed a bridge on Interstate Highway 5 near Coalingua. By the end of the month, the water content in the snows blanketing the California mountains was 165 to 180 percent of normal, and water reservoirs stood at levels averaging 112 percent of normal.

Above-normal rain persisted on the West Coast into April, but the heaviest rains shifted to the Great Plains, where many areas received nearly 200 percent of their normal April rainfall. In Missouri, the May total at St. Louis reached 12.9 inches (32.8 centimeters) and at Kansas City, 12.8 inches (32.4 centimeters)—both totals the highest on record. In late May and early June, the Missouri River between Miami, Missouri, and the Missouri-Mississippi confluence stood at 10 to 16 feet (3 to 5 meters) above flood

Hurricane Marilyn, 1 of the 11 Atlantic hurricanes of 1995, tossed sailboats onto a busy street on Saint Thomas in the Virgin Islands in September.

stage, and some levies failed near the confluence. At St. Louis, the Mississippi reached 11.8 feet (3.6 meters) above flood stage, the third greatest flood on record. The Big Muddy River at Murphysboro in southern Illinois crested at 21.1 feet (6.4 meters) above flood stage on May 22.

A hot, dry summer. The wet spring in the central part of the United States brought fears of severe flooding. However, the wet months of April and May were followed by a relatively dry summer. Fourteen states across the Northeast, deep South, Central Plains, and Southwest had 1 of their 10 driest summers ever. The Northeast was especially hard hit, receiving a mere 64 percent of its normal rainfall. In addition, temperatures approached record highs east of the Great Lakes. The Northeast experienced its third hottest summer and some North Central states had their fifth hottest.

Though the western half of the nation had below-normal summer temperatures, the nation as a whole averaged 0.6 °F (0.3 °C) above normal. A brief intense heat wave hit the Midwest and East in the middle of July and was responsible for more than 700 deaths in Chicago alone. High temperatures continued through much of August.

Tropical storms and hurricanes. Tropical Storm Allison formed in the northwest Caribbean Sea on June 3 and briefly reached hurricane strength before it weakened to tropical storm intensity and struck the northwest coast of Florida on June 5. The storm weakened and just two days later moved back out to sea through eastern North Carolina.

Tropical Storm Dean hit land near Galveston, Texas, on July 30. Its moisture spread a band of heavy rain from Texas to New England. Hurricane Erin followed on the heals of Dean and struck Vero Beach, Florida, on August 2. After crossing Florida, Erin restrengthened over the eastern Gulf of Mexico, and then hit Pensacola with gusts up to 98 miles (158 kilometers) per hour. One week later, Tropical Storm Gabrielle hit the Mexican state of Tamaulipas, about 200 miles (320 kilometers) south of Brownsville, Texas.

In mid-August, as the eastern half of the United States was sweltering in heat, Hurricane Felix moved northward out of the eastern Caribbean and came to a halt 150 miles (240 kilometers) east of Cape Hatteras, North Carolina, bringing gale-force winds and a heavy surf that eroded beaches over the entire mid-Atlantic coastline.

On August 23, Tropical Storm Jerry came ashore at West Palm Beach. After crossing the state, it reentered Georgia as a tropical depression and moved across South Carolina. Spectacular rainfall from this storm included a 24-hour total of 9.9 inches (25 centimeters) at West Palm Beach, and 12.3 inches (31 centimeters) at Greenville, South Carolina, with the latter breaking its former August monthly record by

Weightlifting

over 3 inches (7.6 centimeters). As Jerry moved eastward and fizzled, no fewer than four other tropical storms—Humberto, Iris, Karen, and Luis—dotted the Atlantic Ocean.

Moving northward from near Barbados on September 15, Hurricane Marilyn then battered the Virgin Islands and St. Croix with winds up to 127 miles (204 kilometers) per hour. A week later, Tropical Storm Opal formed near Mexico's Yucatán Peninsula and set its sights on Pensacola, Florida, where Erin had wrought its havoc just two months earlier. Accompanied by gusts up to 144 miles (232 kilometers) per hour and a 15-foot (4.6-meter) high surge of water, Opal damaged up to 120 miles (193 kilometers) of Florida coastline, causing at least $2.1 billion in damages, the third highest insured loss in history, after Andrew in 1992 and Hugo in 1989.

Four more storms rounded out the season's spectacular total. One was Pablo, which ran its course over the central Atlantic. The other was Hurricane Roxanne, which crossed the Yucatán Peninsula, killing at least nine people. A total of 19 named Atlantic storms—11 of which were hurricanes—occurred in 1995, the second highest number of storms in the history of record-keeping.

☐ Alfred K. Blackadar

See also **Disasters**. In *World Book*, see **Weather**.

Weightlifting. See **Sports**.

Welfare. The Republican-led United States Congress clashed with President Bill Clinton in 1995 over his campaign promise to "end welfare as we know it." Clinton's rejection of an interim spending bill on November 14 and his vow to veto legislation that would slash projected spending on welfare and turn the federal program over to the states led to a deadlock with Republican congressional leaders. The impasse resulted in a six-day shutdown of all nonessential government services.

Clinton opposes Republican plan. The President's opposition came after months of conflicting signals from the White House on what changes would be acceptable. Clinton strongly objected to a bill passed by the House of Representatives in March, but voiced support for milder legislation approved by the Senate in September.

Senate-House compromise. Projected welfare spending would be reduced by $81.5 billion over seven years under a Senate-House compromise plan. Spending in 2002 for welfare, child care and nutrition, and food stamps would be about 15 percent lower than projected. The plan would give the states vast power to fashion their own welfare programs with a minimum of federal oversight. States would be required to spend only 75 percent of the amount they currently spend on welfare.

The Senate-House plan would require adult welfare recipients to work after two years of receiving

Demonstrators outside the office of Massachusetts Governor William Weld in February protest legislation proposed to reduce welfare benefits.

benefits and would cut off benefits after five years. It would also deny food stamps and Supplemental Security Income to legal immigrants who have not become U.S. citizens and would allow states to decide whether to bar legal immigrants from other social welfare programs.

Studying the consequences. Opponents of the legislation within the Administration and on Capitol Hill charged that a Senate-House compromise bill would push 1 million children into poverty and eliminate the federal food stamp program. A study issued on Nov. 9, 1995, by the White House Office of Management and Budget estimated that the Senate bill would add 1.2 million children to the poverty rolls, compared to 2.1 million for the House measure. Critics also said the measure would repeal a federal guarantee—enacted in 1935—to assist poor families with dependent children.

After studying the outlines of the compromise plan, White House Chief of Staff Leon Panetta said on November 12 that the President would veto the legislation because of unacceptable cuts in child care and school lunches. Republicans accused Clinton of reneging on his commitment to reform the welfare system. Panetta said Clinton would have signed the Senate bill, which was supported by 35 of 46 Democratic senators, if the final version had not moved so close to the House position.   ☐ William J. Eaton

In *World Book,* see **Welfare.**

West Indies. The 25 nations of the Association of Caribbean States (ACS) held their first meeting on Aug. 17 and 18, 1995, in Port of Spain, Trinidad and Tobago. The newly formed ACS includes all the Caribbean nations, including Cuba, together with the Latin American nations that border the Caribbean Sea. The organization vowed to expand regional trade and support "the right of their peoples to self-determination, the rule of law, the adherence to democratic principles, human rights, and peaceful resolution of disputes."

Devastating hurricanes. In one of the worst hurricane seasons on record, two vicious storms caused widespread damage to islands in the eastern Caribbean. Hurricane Luis scored a direct hit September 5 and 6 on the island of St. Martin, a colony owned jointly by France and the Netherlands, where it devastated homes, downed power lines, and ruptured water mains. The storm also struck the French islands of Guadeloupe and seriously damaged or destroyed some 75 percent of the structures on the twin-island nation of Antigua and Barbuda. Luis killed more than 50 people on St. Martin, Antigua, and Guadeloupe.

A second hurricane, Marilyn, struck the U.S. Virgin Islands on September 15. More than half of the structures on St. Thomas were destroyed, and another 30 percent were seriously damaged. Marilyn also devastated the islands of Guadeloupe.

Montserrat volcano. The island of Montserrat experienced a natural disruption in July, when the volcano Chances Peak began to rumble and spew ash. By August 21 the ash was so thick over the island's capital, Plymouth, that the government evacuated 6,000 of the island's 11,000 residents.

Dominican unrest. With national elections scheduled for May 1996, the Dominican Republic was once again gripped by frequent protests and demonstrations. On July 31, 1995, Ramón Julián Peña, a founder of the island's Communist party, was murdered by unknown assailants.

Trinidad and Tobago. The ruling People's National Movement Party (PNM) of Prime Minister Patrick Manning lost its majority in Parliament in elections on November 6. The United National Congress Party took control of the legislature and elected Basdeo Panday as the new prime minister. Except for 1986 to 1991, the PNM had ruled Trinidad and Tobago since the nation's independence in 1962.

Dominica. Edison James of the center-left United Workers Party (UWP) was sworn in as Dominica's prime minister on June 12. The UWP victory ended nearly 15 years of rule by Dame Eugenia Charles of the conservative Dominica Freedom Party.

☐ Nathan A. Haverstock

See also **Latin America** (Facts in brief table); **Weather.**

West Virginia. See **State government.**

Wilson, Pete (1933-   ), the governor of California, in 1995 was briefly a candidate for the 1996 Republican presidential nomination. Wilson joined the presidential race on June 22, 1995, despite his promising the California voters in 1994 that if elected governor he would serve his entire four-year term. However, he dropped out of the presidential campaign on Sept. 29, 1995, citing lack of support from Republican voters and insufficient funds.

Wilson was born in Lake Forest, Illinois, on Aug. 23, 1933, and grew up in St. Louis, Missouri. After graduating from Yale University in 1955, he served in the U.S. Marine Corps. He earned a law degree from the University of California at Berkeley in 1962.

In 1966, Wilson won a seat in the California legislature, and in 1971, he was elected mayor of San Diego. He was mayor until 1982, when he was elected to the U.S. Senate. He was reelected in 1988 but left the Senate in 1991, when he became governor of California. That year, inheriting a huge budget deficit, Wilson passed a $7-billion tax increase. Wilson also supported a controversial ballot initiative to restrict social services for illegal aliens and in 1995 was a major force behind a decision to end affirmative action in the University of California system.

Wilson married his second wife, Gayle Edlund Graham, in 1983. He has no children.   ☐ Lisa Klobuchar

Wisconsin. See **State government.**

Wyoming. See **State government.**

Remembering

Fireworks explode over Moscow's Kremlin in May, *left,* as Russia celebrates the 1945 Allied victory over Nazi Germany in the Second World War. Events in the United States commemorating the last year of the war included a controversial exhibit at the Smithsonian Institution in Washington, D.C., displaying a section of the B-29 that dropped an atomic bomb on the Japanese city of Hiroshima, *above.* American observances of the war culminated on September 2—the day in 1945 when Japan formally surrendered—with ceremonies at Pearl Harbor in Hawaii, where President Bill Clinton spoke, *facing page.*

World War II

By David Dreier

Looking back 50 years to 1945, the United States and its Allies celebrate a great victory.

In early 1945, Germany's armies were being pushed back on all fronts. In April of that year, American and Soviet troops advancing into Germany from the west and east meet on a wrecked bridge over the Elbe River and join hands.

The author

David Dreier is managing editor of the *Year Book.*

In 1995, Americans who had found little to celebrate in recent years looked back in pride to the triumphant year of 1945, when America and its Allies won the final victory in World War II. Their defeat of the Axis nations—Germany, Japan, and Italy—ended the most devastating conflict in human history.

Despite being over for 50 years, the war continued to stir passions in 1995. United States President Bill Clinton was widely criticized in May when he skipped a Victory in Europe Day (V-E Day) commemoration in London on May 8, opting instead to observe the anniversary in Moscow. Although the United Kingdom was America's closest ally in the war, Clinton calculated that showing solidarity with Russia's faltering democracy by attending its V-E Day celebrations was the most prudent course of action. The Soviet Union, the now-defunct nation to which Russia belonged until 1991, was the third major partner in the Allied powers. The Soviets suffered more than 20 million civilian and military deaths in the war.

During 1995, Germans continued to face up to their nation's Nazi past. It was Germany, guided by its fanatical *Führer* (leader), Adolf Hitler, that launched the war in September 1939 with an attack on Poland. A controversial exhibit that opened in May in Berlin, Germany's capital, asserted that the German army had been involved in the Holocaust, the systematic extermination of 11 million people, including 6 million Jews and 5 million Gypsies, Poles, Soviet prisoners, and others. Previously, blame for the Holocaust had rested solely with the Nazi Party and its elite corps, the SS.

On the opposite side of the globe, the government of Japan continued in 1995 to resist pressures to apologize for atrocities and acts of aggression committed by Japan during the war in the Pacific. In June, the lower house of the Japanese parliament issued a weakly worded resolution expressing "remorse" but refused to make an actual apology. Finally, on August 15, in connection with an observance of the 50th anniversary of Japan's surrender, Japanese Prime Minister Tomiichi Murayama formally apologized for Japan's actions in the war.

America had a controversy of its own as the Smithsonian Institution in Washington, D.C., prepared an exhibit on the atomic bombings of the Japanese cities of Hiroshima and Nagasaki in August 1945. Veterans groups were outraged by what they saw as an attempt by the institution to portray Japan as the victim of an unnecessary act of vengeance. In May, Martin Harwit, director of the Smithsonian's Air and Space Museum, resigned, and the following month a smaller and much toned-down exhibit opened. Proponents of the original exhibit charged that the institution had caved in to political pressure.

The observances of the war's end were brought to a satisfying closure with V-J Day (Victory over Japan) ceremonies on September 2 in Honolulu, Hawaii. It was in Honolulu that the United States was brought into the war with the Dec. 7, 1941, Japanese sneak attack on Pearl Harbor. And it was on Sept. 2, 1945, that representatives of Japan signed articles of surrender aboard the U.S. battleship *Missouri* in Tokyo Harbor.

Speaking at the Honolulu gathering, President Clinton praised the sacrifices of the World War II generation and said that "in order to succeed, we must remain true to the spirit of that brilliant time." It was a time, he said, "when our nation stood united in purpose and mighty in spirit as never before."

Crushing the Nazis

Everything was going the Allies' way by early 1945. Italy had surrendered in September 1943, and there was no longer any doubt that Germany and Japan would be defeated. But both those nations, dominated by fanatics and military hard-liners, were determined to fight on to the bitter end.

In Europe, Hitler's decimated armies retreated steadily, with

The advancing Allies liberated many Nazi concentration camps as they swept through Germany. At a camp in Eselheide, Germany, Russian prisoners hoist an American soldier on their shoulders as they rejoice over their freedom.

Adolf Hitler's Third Reich came to an end in May 1945 with the fall of Berlin. In the final days of fighting in late April, a Soviet soldier places the flag of the Soviet Union atop the Reichstag, the German parliament building.

the Allies closing in relentlessly from east and west. And in the air, Germany's once-formidable air force, the *Luftwaffe,* had been shattered, giving Allied planes a free hand to pound German targets. On February 13 and 14, in one of the most devastating air attacks of the war, U.S. and British bombers fire-bombed Dresden, a center of art and culture that had been known as Florence on the Elbe. The raid killed as many as 35,000 people and left the city a smoldering ruin.

The last German defenses began collapsing in March after forces under Supreme Allied Commander Dwight D. Eisenhower captured an important bridge at Remagen, Germany, over the Rhine River. Eisenhower's troops then rolled almost unimpeded into the heart of Germany, linking up with the Soviets at the Elbe River in late April. Everywhere, German soldiers were surrendering by the thousands.

As they swept through Germany, the Allies liberated one Nazi concentration camp after another and were appalled to find piles of emaciated corpses and groups of sickly, starving inmates—staggering evidence of the crimes committed by Hitler's Third Reich.

Hitler escaped being tried for his atrocities and for the horrible war he had precipitated. On April 30, as the Soviet army battled its way into Berlin, Hitler and his long-time mistress, Eva Braun, committed suicide in his underground command bunker in Berlin. Outside, the Führer's insanely loyal SS, refusing to concede that the end had come, was executing anyone it judged to be guilty of "defeatism." A week later, on May 7, Germany surrendered. Hitler's self-proclaimed Thousand-Year Reich had lasted just 12 years.

In the United States, jubilation over the Allied victory in Europe was tempered by the death of President Franklin D. Roosevelt. The man who had guided the nation through the Great Depression and

The war in the Pacific Ocean saw months of vicious fighting in 1945 as U.S. forces captured one Japanese-held island after another, moving ever closer to Japan itself. One of the year's fiercest battles was fought on the barren volcanic island of Iwo Jima in February and March. On February 23, four days into the month-long battle, U.S. Marines raise the American flag over Mount Suribachi, a volcano that marked the highest point of the island.

The dropping of atomic bombs on Japan in August 1945 brought the war to a swift end. On August 6, less than two hours after much of Hiroshima had been obliterated by an A-bomb, survivors of the bombing gather on the outskirts of the city, *below*. On August 9, a mushroom cloud rises over Nagasaki, the second Japanese city to be devastated by an atomic bomb, *right*.

most of World War II died on April 12 of a stroke. It fell to his successor, President Harry S. Truman, to bring the long war to a conclusion.

Fierce fighting in the Pacific

With the defeat of Germany, the United States could focus its full attention on the war in the Pacific. There, American forces had been waging a bloody campaign against the Japanese, taking one enemy-held island after another and pushing ever closer to Japan itself. The fighting had been terrible, as the Japanese contested every square foot of the islands they held, dying almost to the last man. On Iwo Jima in February and March, 21,000 Japanese defenders inflicted about 25,000 casualties, including nearly 7,000 dead, on the Marine invasion force.

In early 1945, the United States also stepped up its air war against Japan, sending long-range B-29 bombers to hammer Japanese cities. On the night of March 9 and 10, more than 300 B-29's carried out the single most destructive raid in the history of aerial warfare, a fire-bombing attack on Tokyo. The city was reduced to ashes and 100,000 people died.

The last stop in the island-hopping campaign was the large island of Okinawa, where 120,000 Japanese soldiers were dug in and waiting. Okinawa turned out to be the most vicious battle of the Pacific war. From April 1 to June 21, some 300,000 U.S. soldiers and Marines slugged it out with the fanatical defenders, who continued to fight to the death even when all hope of victory was gone. By the end of the battle, U.S. forces had suffered about 50,000 casualties, including 13,000 dead. Only about 10,000 Japanese soldiers survived. About 80,000 Okinawans, mostly civilians, also died; many committed suicide by jumping off cliffs.

Of the American dead at Okinawa, close to 5,000 were naval personnel on ships that were under heavy attack by Japanese planes, including hundreds piloted by the suicide pilots known as kamikazes. More than 30 American ships were sunk and at least 350 damaged.

U.S. military leaders now began firming up plans for an invasion of the Japanese mainland, the first phase of which was slated to begin on November 1 under the joint command of General Douglas MacArthur and Admiral Chester W. Nimitz. Estimates of probable American and Japanese casualties were in the hundreds of thousands.

On August 15, hearing that Japan had agreed to surrender, Americans celebrated in the streets. In New York City's Times Square, a sailor grabs a nurse on the street and gives her a kiss.

The long war came to its official conclusion on Sept. 2, 1945, with Japan's formal surrender at a ceremony aboard the U.S. battleship *Missouri* in Tokyo Harbor. U.S. Army General Douglas MacArthur, *above*, at microphone, presides as representatives of Japan sign the surrender document.

Bringing the war to an end

By now, the United States possessed an awesome new weapon capable of ending the war at a single stroke—the atomic bomb. The bomb, developed by a top-secret program code-named the Manhattan Project, had been successfully tested in New Mexico on July 16. In the summer of 1945, some members of Japan's government favored surrender. But others, especially the military leaders, wanted to fight on, and their views prevailed. President Truman gave the order to use the bomb.

On August 6, the B-29 bomber *Enola Gay* dropped an atomic bomb on the Japanese city of Hiroshima. Never before had one bomb inflicted such a terrible toll. The city's central area was laid waste, and an estimated 70,000 to 100,000 people died. Three days later, another B-29, *Bock's Car*, destroyed the city of Nagasaki with a second A-bomb, killing about 40,000 people. Thousands of others in both cities would die later of burns and radiation poisoning. On August 14, facing the specter of total annihilation, Japan agreed to surrender.

The final end of the war came on September 2 with the solemn surrender ceremony on the deck of the battleship *Missouri*, presided over by General MacArthur. "Let us pray that peace be now restored and that God will preserve it always," MacArthur said at the conclusion of the proceedings.

In less than five years, caught up in a new struggle against the threat of expanding Communism, the United States would be at war in Korea. ■ ■ ■

465

Young, Steve (1961-), star quarterback for the San Francisco 49ers football team, on Jan. 29, 1995, led the 49ers to a 49-to-26 victory over the San Diego Chargers in Super Bowl XXIX and was named the Super Bowl's Most Valuable Player (MVP). Young was the leading passer in the National Football League (NFL) for the 1994 season and the league's MVP. Young, the NFL's highest-rated quarterback in each of his four years as a starter, had a win/loss record of 38 and 11 from 1991 through the end of the 1994 season. He won the first of his two league MVP awards at the end of the 1992 season.

Young's rise to football superstardom was somewhat slow because he spent four years as backup to the 49ers' former starting quarterback, Joe Montana. Young became the starting quarterback in 1991 when Montana was benched for most of the season after undergoing elbow surgery.

Jon Steven Young was born in Salt Lake City, Utah, on Oct. 11, 1961. He is a great-great-great-grandson of Brigham Young, one of the founders of the Mormon Church. Young was a star quarterback at Brigham Young University and runner-up for the Heisman Trophy in his senior year. He signed with the Tampa Bay Buccaneers of the NFL in 1985 and two years later was traded to the 49ers.

Young, who is unmarried, earned a law degree from Brigham Young in 1994. He is active in a number of charitable organizations.   □ Lisa Klobuchar

Yugoslavia. The presidents of Bosnia-Herzegovina, Croatia, and Serbia (one of two republics making up the nation of Yugoslavia) sat down together at the peace table on Nov. 1, 1995, to seek an end to the war that had torn apart the Balkan region since 1992. U.S. Secretary of State Warren Christopher presided at the opening of the conference, held at Wright-Patterson Air Force Base near Dayton, Ohio. Christopher warned the three leaders—Alija Izetbegovic of Bosnia-Herzegovina, Franjo Tudjman of Croatia, and Slobodan Milošević of Serbia—that failure of the talks would mean a resumption of war and atrocities. On November 21, the three leaders signed an agreement calling for Bosnia-Herzegovina to be divided into a Bosnian-Croat federation and a Serb republic. The peace was to be enforced by 60,000 North Atlantic Treaty Organization (NATO) troops, including 20,000 from the United States.

A tense and violent year. In 1995, Yugoslavia continued to deal with the impact of United Nations (UN) trade sanctions, ethnic tension, and war in Bosnia-Herzegovina (often called Bosnia) and Croatia, both former republics of Yugoslavia. Leaders of Yugoslavia sought unsuccessfully to persuade the international community to lift remaining economic *sanctions* (bans). The sanctions were imposed by the UN Security Council in May 1992 to pressure Yugoslavia into ending support for Bosnian Serbs fighting the Muslim government of Bosnia.

On Aug. 30, 1995, NATO launched a massive bombing attack against Serb positions in Bosnia. The bombing was in retaliation for a Serb shelling on August 28 that killed 38 people in a market in Sarajevo, a city that had been declared a safe area by the UN. The bombing prompted Serbia's President Milošević to announce on August 30 that Yugoslavia and the Bosnian Serbs would form a negotiating team to discuss a peace plan for Bosnia. In September, Yugoslav leaders agreed with those of Bosnia and Croatia on a cease-fire and a plan to end the war. The plan called for keeping Bosnia's existing borders but dividing the country into two regions, one run by Muslims and Croats, the other by Bosnian Serbs. That proposal was incorporated into the formal peace plan drawn up for the Dayton conference.

Relations with Croatia were tense earlier in the year. Conflict between Croatia's government and ethnic Serbs seemed likely when, on January 12, President Tudjman demanded that UN forces leave Croatia after their mandate expired on March 31. About 12,000 UN troops had been stationed there to oversee an uneasy truce reached when a war between Serbia and Croatia ceased in 1992. Croatia agreed on March 12, 1995, to renew the UN mandate, though for a smaller force of 5,000 troops. The renewal helped defuse tensions with Yugoslavia. In August, leaders of Yugoslavia deplored a Croatian offensive that recaptured the self-declared Serbian Republic of Krajina in Croatia, but they did not provide military support to the Krajina Serbs.

Economic conditions remained difficult in Yugoslavia. Inflation—which in 1994 fell sharply after the creation of a new unit of currency called the superdinar—rose again. Yugoslav leaders blamed their economic difficulties on UN trade sanctions. In February 1995, the UN approved a Yugoslav trade agreement with Russia in which Russia agreed to sell Yugoslavia kerosene and natural gas.

Ethnic unrest. Approximately 650,000 refugees from the Balkan war lived in Yugoslavia in 1995. Yugoslav leaders planned to settle many of the newcomers in Kosovo, a Serbian province where about 90 percent of the population is Albanian.

The resettlement plan added to tension between the government and Kosovo, an autonomous province until Milošević took control of it in 1989. In April 1995, three ethnic Albanian leaders in the province were convicted of planning secession and received two-year prison terms. In May, seven former police officers of Albanian descent were charged with creating an unofficial interior ministry in Kosovo. In September, 38 police officers received prison sentences of up to 6½ years for conspiring against the Yugoslav state.   □ Sharon L. Wolchik

See also **Bosnia-Herzegovina; Croatia; Europe** (Facts in brief table); **United Nations.** In *World Book*, see **Yugoslavia.**

Yukon Territory. See Canadian territories.

Zaire. President Mobutu Sese Seko remained in power in 1995, more securely than in previous years. Prime Minister Kengo wa Dondo achieved some success in bringing Zaire's inflation problem under control. But the impasse between Mobutu and opposition leader Etienne Tshisekedi continued, in spite of attempts in January to resolve their differences. No real progress in moving toward a more democratic society took place.

On May 11, the World Health Organization and the United States Centers for Disease Control and Prevention reported an outbreak of Ebola hemorrhagic fever in the city of Kikwit. The often fatal disease spread rapidly, causing symptoms such as severe bleeding and high fever. Zairian officials cordoned off the region, and the disease was geographically contained after several weeks.

On August 19, the government of Zaire began to *repatriate* (send home) Rwandan refugees. Zaire had become frustrated by the inability of international organizations to repatriate the refugee population, which totaled nearly 1.8 million. The world was shocked by images of thousands of people being moved at gunpoint. Forced removal of refugees ceased on August 24, and the government of Zaire agreed to a program of voluntary repatriation.

☐ Mark DeLancey

See also **Africa** (Facts in brief table). In **World Book,** see **Zaire.**

Zoos and aquariums from Florida to Nebraska in 1995 opened a variety of blockbuster exhibits that realistically reproduced wild habitats. The aquatic world continued to be a popular focus of exhibits.

The Florida Aquarium. The biggest splash was the March opening of a completely new institution, Tampa's Florida Aquarium. More than 4,300 animals and plants representing 550 species native to Florida are housed in exhibits based on the state's freshwater and marine habitats. The aquarium is organized so that visitors follow the path of a drop of water from a subterranean limestone spring through four ecosystems, each in a large gallery.

The first gallery is an array of wetland habitats beneath an enormous shell-like dome. Under a forest canopy where birds fly freely, visitors explore a sawgrass marsh where they encounter lively alligator hatchlings and playful river otters. After walking through a cypress swamp and a tangled mangrove forest, visitors reach the Bays and Beaches gallery, where waves ripple in grassy shallows that are home to seahorses, shrimp, stingrays, and flounder.

From there, visitors "plunge" into the aquarium's signature exhibit, a 500,000-gallon (1.9 million-liter) tank containing a full-scale replica of a coral reef. A winding ramp snakes down below the water, with viewing ports angled to show various aspects of the reef and its inhabitants. Visitors then enter an acrylic tunnel that leads through an elkhorn coral forest

swarming with a watery rainbow of angelfish, butterfly fish, parrot fish, triggerfish, sergeant majors, and other brilliantly colored reef-dwellers.

Last stop is the Florida Offshore gallery, which provides views of an open-ocean ecosystem, where moon jellyfish and sea wasps drift about. The Florida Current, a massive oceanic tank, opens on a world of sharks, a 100-pound (45-kilogram) jewfish, barracudas, sting rays, and other dramatic specimens.

Arctic theme park. Another Sunshine State institution, Sea World of Florida in Orlando, opened "Wild Arctic," a combination theme-park ride and animal exhibit, in May. Visitors board a jet helicopter—actually a flight simulator like those used to train pilots—that "flies" them to the Arctic through a raging blizzard and an avalanche.

After landing safely, visitors trek over facsimile frozen tundra to encounter animals living in or near an Arctic "sea." Beluga whales—white, melonheaded creatures with perpetual smiles—glide through the sparkling, fish-filled waters, while harbor seals frolic nearby. Walruses dive into the huge tank and haul themselves out onto ice floes. Polar bears prowl among rocky outcroppings carpeted with snow. Throughout the exhibit, touch screens and other interactive devices enable visitors to learn about Arctic animals' behavior and biology.

Prairie seas. In April, the Henry Doorly Zoo in Omaha, Nebraska, brought the ocean to the prairies with the opening of "Kingdoms of the Seas." At 71,000 square feet (6,600 square meters), the aquarium is the largest aquatic facility in an American zoo.

The aquarium introduces visitors to a spectrum of aquatic habitats from polar to tropical. Just inside the entrance is an Arctic scene with above- and below-water views of puffins diving from tall cliffs and zipping through icy water. Around the corner is an Antarctic panorama, complete with 40 king and gentoo penguins toddling about snow-covered shores.

The aquarium's centerpiece exhibit immerses visitors in a Caribbean coral reef as they travel through a 70-foot (21-meter) acrylic tunnel in a 450,000-gallon (1.7 million-liter) tank. Viewers are surrounded by thousands of fish, including parrot fish, angelfish, and butterfly fish decked out in vivid colors; and a variety of shark species, including a tiger shark.

Another gallery depicts a South American forest flooded by the Amazon River. The murky waters are alive with redtail catfish, arapaimas, and other river fish. In the mangrove trees rising from the water, tiny monkeys called tamarins and small Amazonian birds bound and flit about the branches.

The Omaha aquarium also contains special-focus tanks. These are exhibits featuring such extraordinary creatures as a giant Pacific octopus, its relative the chambered nautilus, exotic moon jellyfish drifting in a simulated ocean current, and a collection of small sharks—zebra, bamboo, blacktip reef, and bonnetheads.

Eleven-month-old lowland gorilla twins make their first appearance at New York City's Bronx Zoo in July. The pair were the sixth known set born in captivity.

Out of Africa, into Kansas City. On June 17, the Kansas City (Missouri) Zoo opened "Africa," a $32-million complex that sprawls over 95 acres (38 hectares). More than 400 animals occupy naturalistic replicas of habitats in Kenya, Zaire, Tanzania, and Uganda.

The Nairobi Wildlife Reserve exhibit is a savannah populated with Masai giraffes, Chapman's zebras, ostriches, and antelope. Surrounding the plains are separate areas for other large savannah species such as lions, black rhinos, cheetahs, warthogs, and hippos. In rocky outcroppings live smaller animals such as *meerkats* (a type of mongoose), bat-eared foxes, leopard tortoises, and gopherlike rock hyraxes.

In the Tanzanian section, a raucous troop of chimpanzees romps on a woody hillside. A nearby island is home to jackals, African porcupines, and guinea baboons. A dense forest simulating one in Zaire is the refuge of a family of lowland gorillas and a variety of monkeys. In this wooded setting, leopards lurk among the trees, and forest antelopes scurry through the shadows.

Asheboro zoo grows. The North Carolina Zoological Park in Asheboro expanded its North American complex with five new exhibits in August. One contains bison and elk in a capsule version of the Old West. A new Alaskan seabird exhibit is the first in America to contain horned puffins, thick-billed murres, and parakeet auklets. ☐ Eugene J. Walter, Jr.

In *World Book,* see Zoo.

1995

DICTIONARY SUPPLEMENT

A list of new words added to the 1996 edition of **The World Book Dictionary** because they have been used enough to become a permanent part of our ever-changing language.

word

(wėrd), *n.*, *v.* – *n.* ...nd or a group of ...s that has meaning ...an independent ...speech; vocable: ...*ak words when* ... *A free form which* ... *phrase is a word.* ..., *then, is a free form which does not consist entirely of . . . lesser free forms; in brief, a word is a minimum free form* (Leonard Bloomfield).

spell | ing

dictionary

dic|tion|ar|y (dik´shə ner´ē), *n., pl.* –ar|ies.
1. a book that explains the words of a language, or some special kind of words. It is usually arranged alphabetically. One can use a dictionary to find out the meaning, pronunciation, or spelling of a word.

1. a way of pronouncing:
a foreign pronunciation.

pro|nun|ci|a|tion

sup|ple|ment

(sup´lə mənt), *n.* 1. Something added to complete a thing, or to make it larger or bett...

A a

ACE (no periods), angiotensin-converting enzyme, an enzyme that converts one form of angiotensin into another, which contracts blood vessels and causes blood pressure to rise.

acid jazz, music written in the style of jazz with rock rhythms and acid rock sound: *Far from the smoke-filled rooms, pulsating acid jazz music . . . [she] tries to translate urban counter-culture into marketable sneaker ideas* (New York Times).

adaptive optics, mirrors whose shape can be altered to compensate for the distortion of light by the atmosphere: *Adaptive optics, . . . would enable telescopes to get crisp pictures . . . but would also help improve mirrors used on spy satellites* (Wall Street Journal).

adoption fair, an event where groups of orphaned children can be seen by prospective adoptive parents: *Today . . . in their determination to provide a home for every child [social workers] sometimes resort to "adoption fairs"* (Mary-Lou Weisman).

aer|o|brak|ing (âr″ō brā′king), *n.* the use of atmospheric friction to slow a moving space vehicle: *a technique known as "aerobraking," in which a light-weight shield slows down a vehicle as it zooms through a planetary atmosphere* (William J. Broad).

all-court press (ôl′kôrt, -kōrt), an all-out effort: *"We still don't have the other passports," he said. So I flew back to Bujumbura for an all-court press* (Alex Shoumatoff).

Am|bu|lo|ce|tus na|tans (am″byə lō sē′təs nā′tanz), an ancestor of modern whales that lived in the Eocene period and hunted on both land and sea: *Ambulocetus . . . still had four limbs for walking on land . . . It could also hunt in the sea, probably swimming by kicking its big feet* (John Noble Wilford).

B b

Basic Law or **basic law**, **1** a written statement of the fundamental organization of the government of a nation or state: *[Yeltsin] convened a constitutional conference to draft a new Basic Law for Russia, which would enshrine a powerful new presidency and a much-weakened parliament* (Jonathan Steele). **2** the organization of the government of Hong Kong: *[Patten] said his ideas did not contradict the Basic Law, China's stated plan for Hong Kong after 1997* (World Book Year Book).

beta amyloid, a protein found in Alzheimer patients in deposits that accumulate in the regions of the brain that control memory and learning: *Beta amyloid destroys a brain cell's ability to regulate potassium, the chemical that triggers signals governing memory* (Time).

bi|o|ger|on|tol|o|gy (bī″ō jer″on tol′ə jē), *n.* the study of the biology of aging: *[Leonard] Hayflick delineates the field of biogerontology, . . . provides statistical data on aging, shows how humans age . . . and explores the possibilities for manipulating the life span* (Science News).

blame game, an effort to escape responsibility by assigning blame or finding fault in other people or circumstances: *By not playing a blame game, the film confers a greater dignity on the dead. It doesn't leave us arguing over the bodies* (James Wolcott).

blue-sky|ing (blū′skī′ing), *n. Informal.* the act of engaging in imagination or unrealistic speculation: *On North Korea, a Mondale-inspired policy would probably avoid any further "public blue-skying about U.S. options"* (Michael Kramer).

breakdown lane, **1** a lane at the side of a highway for emergency stops. **2** *Figurative.* the condition of being disabled or unable to function properly: *He's heading in the only direction that might lead the city out of the breakdown lane* (Eric Pooley).

C c

chal|lenged (chal′ənjd), *adj.* handicapped or disabled: *The range of victims . . . has now expanded to include . . . the short, or, to put it correctly, the vertically challenged* (Robert Hughes).

che|mo|cline (kē′mō klīn″), *n.* the boundary between the dense noncirculating layer and the top circulating layer of water in a stratified lake: *A chemocline separates freshwater at the surface from deeper, denser fluids containing dissolved minerals and gases* (Science News).

cher|ry-pick|ing (cher′ē pik′ing), *n.* the act or practice of selecting only the best or most desirable: *Chief among the forces . . . was cherry-picking, the practice used by for-profit insurers to lure away Empire's young and healthy customers* (New York Times).

clean-down (klēn′doun″), *n., adj.*—*n.* an agreement requiring a company to reduce its debt and renegotiate the terms of its loans.—*adj.* of or related to a clean-down: *Mr. Ullman said such "clean-down" requirements were standard in most working capital agreements* (Stephanie Strom).

Clipper chip or **Clipper Chip**, a computer chip designed to scramble electronic messages according to a code known only by the user and the United States government.

compassion fatigue, loss of pity or sympathy due to overexposure to human suffering: *Wihan is encountering a phenomenon known . . . , in the case of Bosnia, [as] "compassion fatigue"—people . . . numbed by the spectacle of Croats, Serbs, and Muslims slaughtering one another* (Timothy W. Ryback).

course|pack (kôrs′pak″, kōrs′-), *n.* a collection of readings from a variety of sources selected for a specific academic course and sold in place of a principal textbook: *Somewhere between lugging thick tomes to class and using a notebook computer . . . a new era of textbooks has taken hold: the coursepack* (Joshua Mills).

cyber-, *combining form.* **1** of or having to do with computers, as in *cyberphobia.* **2** created by or existing only on computer; virtual, as in *cyberspace.* **3** involved with or using computers, as in *cyberpunk.*

D d

digital compact cassette, a digitally recorded tape cassette which reproduces sound as clearly as a compact disk.

E e

E|bo|la virus (i bō′lə), a thread virus that causes hemorrhagic fever, first identified in Zaire and Sudan.

G g

Generation X, people in their twenties, born in the 1970's: *Maybe it's the pandemic shrug of Generation X, the futility felt by the young when analyzed to death by self-styled experts* (Rolling Stone).

gold-card (gōld′kärd′), *adj.* having an elevated rank; elitist; privileged: *How can those already holding gold-card membership of the nuclear club convincingly object to a country aspiring to junior league status* (Manchester Guardian Weekly).

gut renovation, repair or restoration of a building that involves removal and reconstruction of the interior; gut rehabilitation: *Maintenance fees are usually set at lower levels than in buildings that undergo gut renovation* (New York Times).

H h

han|ta|vi|rus (han′tə vī″rəs), *n.* a virus carried by rodents that is known to cause kidney and respiratory infections, which are often fatal in humans: *Hantavirus . . . has so far afflicted 42 people in the U.S., killing 26 of them* (Time). [< *Hanta* genus name, originally river in Korea]

heavy lifting, **1** a demanding task; difficult or hard work: *Mr. Milosevic still has a lot of heavy lifting to do to be convincing* (Manchester Guardian Weekly). **2** serious or sustained effort; complete dedication: *It's sad to think that so much heavy lifting is now required to deliver a package as ordinary as this* (Terence Rafferty). **3** the capacity for hard work: *She sent a message of both traditional femininity and career-woman heavy lifting* (New Yorker).

hydrophobic pocket, a water-repellent, pocketlike fold on the surface of a protein that repels water and affects the protein's shape: *One leading idea is that anaesthetics bind to proteins at sites called hydrophobic pockets* (New York Times).

hypertext fiction, an interactive computer program which provides the user with a basic story and various options for altering it: *Hypertext fiction [is] a new computer-based format . . . affording the reader the opportunity to skip from place to place in the text creating his own story* (Sarah Lyall).

I i

inner child, those qualities of an adult's personality considered to be childlike and often repressed, fashionably viewed as pure, innocent, and creative: *The newest . . . feminism . . . puts a popular feminist spin on deadeningly familiar messages about . . . liberating one's inner child, and restoring one's self-esteem* (Wendy Kaminer).

intermediate punishment, punishment for a criminal offense, that does not involve a sentence of confinement in prison: *Concern for prison crowding . . . has led many states to develop intermediate punishments . . . [including] community service, restitution . . . and boot camps* (World Book Year Book).

J j

just-in-time (just′in tīm′), *adj.* supplying goods and services to customers as they are needed: *Just-in-time manufacturing operations match railroad timetables with the scheduling requirements of their customers* (World Book Year Book).

K k

keiret|su (kī ret′sü), *n. Japanese.* an association of Japanese companies, such as banks and industrial corporations or suppliers and manufacturers, in which members hold shares in associated firms and make loans and engage in joint ventures with each other: *Nor would Japanese keiretsu be allowed to exclude foreign suppliers from their production systems* (Akio Morita).

M m

man|aged (man′ijd), *adj.* involving centralized planning and regulation, especially by government: *managed currency. The Clinton plan . . . managed trade. It seeks to make the free market abide by government-set rules with a system called "managed competition"* (Martin Walker).

med|i|cide (med′ə sīd), *n.* physician-assisted suicide: *But this ninth "medicide" since 1990 offered some new twists: Miller was the first male to die . . . outside [Dr.] Kevorkian's former home territory* (Time). [< *medi*(cal) + *-cide*²]

mega|store (meg′ə stôr″, -stôr″), *n.* a very large store that sells goods in the manner of a supermarket: *The protests have grown in proportion to the relentless expansionary march of behemoth retailers. Hundreds of new megastores are opening annually* (Time). [< *mega-* + *store*]

meta-a|nal|y|sis (met″ə ə nal′ə sis), *n., pl.* **-ses** (-sēz). a type of statistical analysis that is based on the combined results of many smaller related studies: *Meta-analysis promises to play an increasingly important role in determining health risks . . . and national policy on payment for medical care* (Lawrence K. Altman).

mi|cro|in|sem|i|na|tion (mī″krō in sem″ə nā′shən), *n.* a technique for external fertilization in which a single sperm is injected directly into an egg cell: *Customers could opt for a standard . . . in vitro fertilization . . . or newer techniques like microinsemination, which has proved successful in . . . helping sperm penetrate the egg* (A.L. Cowan).

mon|do (mon′dō), *adj. Slang.* absolute, complete, unalloyed, or quintessential: *The film was so raw and assaultive in its mondo-trasho fashion . . . that it made viewers feel it was made by those crude people onscreen* (Time). [< English *mondo* totally, very, probably < Spanish *mondo* plain, unadulterated]

mu|ta|tor gene (myü tā′tər), a gene that, if defective, can cause cancer by allowing mutations to accumulate in a person's DNA: *The extensive research on bacteria and yeast . . . that showed how mutator genes work* (Gina Kolata).

N n

net|i|quette (net′ə ket), *n.* customary rules for use of a computer network, especially the Internet: *One clear breach of netiquette is . . . putting the same message in different places on the net* (James Barron). [< *Net* + (et)*iquette*]

Pronunciation Key: hat, āge, cãre, fär; let, ēqual, tėrm; it, īce; hot, ōpen, ôrder; oil, out; cup, pùt, rüle; child; long; thin; ᴛʜen; zh, measure; ə represents **a** in about, **e** in taken, **i** in pencil, **o** in lemon, **u** in circus.

---

no-fly zone (nō′flī″), an area where certain kinds of flights are prohibited: *The United States will again press the U.N. Security Council to enforce a "no-fly zone" over Bosnia* (Manchester Guardian Weekly).

O o

o|pen-mike (ō′pən mīk′), *adj.* available to anyone who wants to perform: *Expectations ran exceptionally high for this show . . . hardly . . . an average Greenwich Village open-mike session* (Ann Powers).

o|ver|den|si|ty (ō′vər den′sə tē), *n., pl.* **-ties.** an area with a greater than average concentration of matter, often dark matter: *Astronomers have tried to reconstruct how [the universe's] structure evolved, based on the assumption . . . of unseen cold dark matter and random overdensities acting as seeds* (New York Times).

P p

pa|le|o|cap|i|tal|ism (pā″lē ō kap′ə tə liz″əm), *n.* capitalism based on a return to earlier practices and forms of free-market economy.

pa|le|o|con|serv|a|tism (pā″lē ō kən sėr′və tiz″əm), *n.* extreme or reactionary form of conservatism.

pas|sive-ag|gres|sive (pas′iv ə gres′iv), *adj.* appearing to yield or be a victim of events while actively pursuing a goal or objective; manipulative: *Her husband before Gabe describes her as "passive-aggressive"—a quiet manipulator* (Peter Travers).

pa|thol|o|gize (pə thol′ə jīz), *v.t.,* **-gized, -giz|ing.** to treat or explain as a disease or as evidence of a diseased condition: *There is now an attempt to pathologize what was once considered the normal range of behavior of boys* (New York Times).

phy|si|cian-as|sist|ed suicide (fə zish′ən ə sis′təd), suicide accomplished with the help of a physician: *[A] panel has recommended, unanimously, that the state resist pressure to legalize physician-assisted suicide for the terminally ill* (Elisabeth Rosenthal).

post-po|li|o sequelae (pōst″pō′lē ō), the return of polio symptoms to former polio patients: *Polio survivors are reporting new symptoms, including weakness, pain and respiratory problems, grouped under the name post-polio sequelae* (Science News).

pub|lic-ac|cess (pub′lik ak′ses), *adj.* available for public use, especially of cable television: *By law, only programs that are obscene or call for the commission of crimes can be banned from public-access cable* (New Yorker).

Q q

Q rating, a numerical rating of a product or celebrity's popularity based on consumer surveys: *The New Yorker credits his new Q rating to four appearances this year on* Late Show with David Letterman (People). [< *q*(ualitative)]

R r

re|cov|ered-mem|o|ry (ri kuv′ərd mem′ər ē, -mem′rē), *adj.* of or relating to the repression and subsequent recovery of a person's recollection of a traumatic experience, such as violence or sexual abuse: *"Recovered-memory therapy will come to be recognized as the quackery of the 20th century,"* predicts Richard Ofshe (Time).

S s

safe haven, **1** a place free from harm or danger, especially by attack of military forces or prosecution by civilian authorities: *They would create safe havens for noncombatants, and corridors to let supplies in* (New York Times). **2** a place or an investment protected from financial risk: *Switzerland, with its tradition of secret banking, is always a popular safe haven* (Christian Science Monitor). **—safe′-ha′ven,** *adj.*

sports utility or **sports-u|til|i|ty vehi|cle** (spôrts′yü til′ə tē, spôrts′-), a van or light truck, usually with four-wheeled drive, that has the interior design of a sports or passenger car: *Auto manufacturers . . . are finding that sports-utility vehicles . . . have replaced luxury cars* (Time).

su|per|ma|jor|i|ty (sü″pər mə jôr′ə tē, -jôr′-), *n., pl.* **-ties.** a majority of at least three-fifths of votes cast: *Supermajorities are required for passing Constitutional amendments and for ratifying treaties* (New Yorker).

su|per|mod|el (sü′pər mod″əl), *n.* a very successful fashion model: *Never content to amass fortunes ambling down runways in leather bikinis . . . supermodels like to diversify* (Ginia Bellafonte).

T t

thread virus, one of various viruses causing hemorrhagic fever, such as the Ebola virus or Marburg virus: *The virulent thread viruses may in a day or two kill one in four, or up to nine in 10, depending on the filovirus subtype* (Scientific American).

trans|vest (trans vest′), *v.t., v.i.* to change into the character or appearance of the opposite sex: *Sharpe . . . even transvests Charles I into a baroque Margaret Thatcher* (Perry Anderson).

U u

un|plugged (un plugd′), *adj.* not using or featuring electronically amplified musical instruments: *In this unplugged performance, he is sure to unearth some wonderful vintage gems* (New Yorker).

ur|ban-edge (ėr′bən ej″), *adj.* bordering an urban area: *Much of the land threatened by this urban sprawl is . . . urban-edge agricultural land* (Ken Wilbecan).

W w

warm fuzz|ies (fuz′ēz), *occasionally sing.* **warm fuzzy.** anything that reassures or produces a sympathetic or affectionate response: *Even "gambling" . . . has been buffed with warm fuzzies. We call it "gaming" these days* (Gerri Hirshey).

working poor, people who work at low-paying jobs: *The U.S. job-creation machine of the 1980s produced millions of "working poor" in service jobs* (Bruce W. Nelan).

Z z

Za|pa|tis|ta (zä″pä tēs′tä), *n., adj.* **—n.** a member of a group of Mexican revolutionaries located chiefly in the state of Chiapas: *The Zapatistas also wanted the leftist candidate for Governor . . . to be recognized as the winner* (Anthony De Palma). **—adj.** of or relating to the Zapatistas.

AFRICA ■ AIDS ■ ALBANIA ■ ALBERTA ■ ALGERIA ■ ANTHROPOLOGY ■ AR

SIA ■ ASTRONOMY ■ AUSTRALIA ■ AUSTRIA ■ AUTOMOBILE ■ AUTOMOBILE

ELGIUM ■ BIOLOGY ■

BULGARIA ■ BURM

CITY ■ CIVIL RIGHTS

ONSERVATIO

DENM

YPT ■ EL S   DOR

FASHION ■ FINLAN

1995

WORLD BOOK
SUPPLEMENT

NE ■ MA

NETHERL

NIGERIA

OCEAN

A ■ PER

RVICE ■

To help World Book owners keep their encyclopedias up to date, the following articles are reprinted from the 1996 edition of the encyclopedia.

The Inuit live farther north than any other people in the world. They have developed many ways to survive in their harsh Arctic climate. For example, a traditional type of Inuit house, such as the one pictured, is built of snow. The Inuit also depend on animal products for many necessities. This photograph shows Inuit rugs and clothing made from animal skins and a fire fueled by animal blubber.

P. H. Cornut, Tony Stone Images

Inuit

Inuit, *IHN yoo iht,* are a people who live in and near the Arctic. Their homeland stretches from the northeastern tip of Russia across Alaska and northern Canada to Greenland. Many Inuit live farther north than any other people in the world.

In this article, the word *Inuit* refers to the people formerly called Eskimos. The term *Eskimo* comes from a Native American word that may have meant *eater of raw meat, netter of snowshoes,* or *speaker of a foreign language.* Many Inuit consider this term insulting. They prefer the name Inuit, which means *the people* or *real people,* and comes from a language called Inuit-Inupiaq. The singular of Inuit is *Inuk,* which means *person.* Dialects of the Inuit-Inupiaq language are spoken by the Inuit in Canada, Greenland, and northern Alaska.

Another group of Arctic people, the Yuit, are often called Inuit as well. Their culture resembles that of other

James A. Tuck, the contributor of this article, is Professor of Archaeology at the Memorial University of Newfoundland. Professor Tuck has written several books on northern peoples. These works include Newfoundland and Labrador Prehistory *and* Ancient People of Port au Choix.

Inuit, but they speak a different language called Yupik. The Yuit live in western and southern Alaska and in Siberia in Russia.

Inuit culture developed more than 1,000 years ago in what is now the Bering Sea region of Alaska and Siberia. Most Inuit have always lived near the sea, which has provided much of their food. The first Inuit hunted bowhead whales and other mammals. As the Inuit spread eastward, they modified their way of life to suit the Arctic environments they encountered. They caught fish and hunted seals, walruses, and whales. On land, they hunted a type of deer called *caribou,* musk oxen, polar bears, and many smaller animals. The Inuit used the skins of these animals to make clothes and tents. They crafted tools and weapons from the animals' bones, antlers, horns, and teeth. In summer, they traveled in boats covered with animal skin and, in winter, on sleds pulled by dog teams. Most Inuit lived in tents in the summer and in large sod houses during winter. When traveling in search of game in winter, they built snowhouses as temporary shelters.

The Inuit way of life began to change in the 1800's. At that time, European whalers and traders began arriving in the Arctic in large numbers. The Inuit eventually adopted many aspects of European culture and permanently altered their traditional way of life.

Today, there are more than 100,000 Inuit in Russia, Alaska, Canada, and Greenland. Most live in towns or small settlements scattered along the Arctic coast. The Inuit retain a considerable knowledge of their ancient culture. Many Inuit still spend much of their time in traditional activities, such as hunting and fishing.

The land of the Inuit

The Inuit live in one of the coldest and harshest regions of the world. Most kinds of plants and animals cannot live as far north as the Inuit do.

Inuit lands include the northeastern tip of Siberia, the islands of the Bering Sea, and the coastal regions of mainland Alaska. They also include the north coast and islands of the Canadian Arctic and most of the west coast and part of the east coast of Greenland. The region is often called the Land of the Midnight Sun because the sun shines all day and all night for part of each summer. During part of each winter, however, some areas are continuously dark. See **Midnight sun.**

Climate. Most of the Far North has long, cold winters and short, cool summers. Average temperatures in the region rise above freezing for only two or three months each year. During the coldest months, temperatures average between −20 and −30 °F (−29 and −34 °C). Annual snowfall averages between 15 and 90 inches (38 and 229 centimeters). Little of the snow melts until spring, and winter storms of wind-driven snow can force people to remain inside for days at a time. However, because snow contains much less water than rain, average *precipitation* (rain, melted snow, and other forms of moisture) totals only about 6 to 10 inches (15 to 25 centimeters) per year. Such scarce precipitation makes the Arctic technically a desert.

Thick sheets of ice cover parts of some northern Canadian islands and most of Greenland throughout the year. Rivers, lakes, and the sea itself remain frozen for much of the year. Even in summer, large pieces of ice float in the sea. When the wind blows toward the shore, it often piles this ice on beaches.

Plants and animals. The land area of the Arctic consists mainly of huge treeless plains called *tundra*. In most places, only the top 1 to 10 feet (30 to 300 centimeters) of ground thaws in summer. Below that level, the ground remains permanently frozen in a condition called *permafrost*. During the summer, melted ice or snow creates many ponds, small lakes, and swamps.

The Arctic has no forests. Tundra vegetation consists of low shrubs, mosses, grasslike plants called *sedges,* and tiny flowering plants. Rootless, plantlike organisms known as *lichens* grow on many rocks. For a short time each summer, colorful flowers bloom in great abundance in the tundra.

Seals, walruses, whales, and polar bears live in the sea, on the sea ice, and along the Arctic shores. The tundra supports populations of caribou, musk oxen, wolves, foxes, and hares. Many of these animals migrate south annually and are available to Inuit hunters for only a few months each year. Numerous ducks and geese summer in the Arctic, where they build their nests and raise their young. Some birds, such as the ptarmigan (pronounced *TAHR muh guhn*), are year-round residents. Fish include Arctic char, Arctic cod, lake trout, salmon, and whitefish.

Traditional way of life

From the earliest beginnings of their culture, the Inuit lived a way of life different from that of most other peo-

Inuit lands

The Inuit have lived in the Arctic for thousands of years. Some areas formerly occupied by the Inuit are no longer inhabited. But most of the groups named on this map have inhabited the areas for centuries. Most groups are named for the areas in which they live. In Russia and parts of Alaska, the Inuit are called Yuit.

Land inhabited by the Inuit today

Land formerly inhabited by the Inuit

WORLD BOOK map

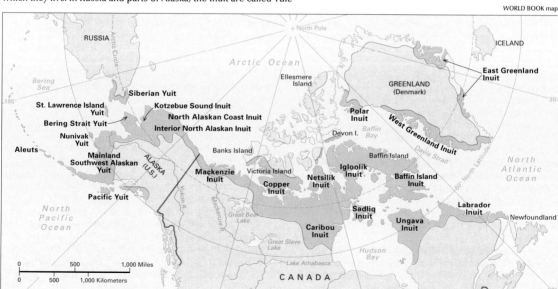

An Inuit family in Canada relaxes inside a hunting lodge. Traditionally, the Inuit lived in small groups that sometimes consisted of only one family. Each member of a family had to help in the activities that ensured the group's survival.

Bryan & Cherry Alexander

ple. The Inuit had little contact with other cultures for most of their history. Some occasionally met with other northern peoples that lived south of Inuit country. Such meetings were often hostile. Over time, however, strong trade relationships developed between these peoples.

The Inuit have always lived in small groups scattered over a huge region. Many differences developed among the cultures of the widespread Inuit groups. These differences make it impossible to describe a general way of life for all Inuit. The following sections chiefly discuss the traditional way of life of Canadian Inuit before the arrival of Europeans. Inuit people no longer follow many of these ways.

Group life. The Inuit lived in groups that varied in size from a single family to several hundred people. The size of the groups depended on the amount of food available in different seasons. During the spring and fall in Alaska, the largest groups gathered where they could hunt migrating caribou. On the coast of Labrador, Inuit groups often formed large winter villages to share the food and other necessities provided by the killing of a bowhead whale. Many of these larger communities split up during the rest of the year. Small Inuit groups moved about the countryside in search of fish, seals, birds, and other game. These local groups were the most important social units for the Inuit.

In most regions, an Inuit household consisted of a married couple, their unmarried children, and the married sons or daughters and their families. Some households also included one or more parents or unmarried siblings of the couple. Inuit groups governed themselves by traditional rules of conduct rather than written laws. The most important rule was that each individual help in the day-to-day activities that ensured the group's survival.

When disputes arose, Inuit societies often settled them by contests of strength or some other peaceful means. Conflicts sometimes resulted in groups splitting off from one another. If an individual's conduct threatened the safety or harmony of a group, that person was

banished. Banishment usually meant death, because an individual could not survive alone in the Arctic.

Food. The Inuit diet varied according to location and the seasons of the year. On the Alaskan coast and the coast of Labrador, the kill of a single bowhead whale provided tons of meat for an Inuit community. In other parts of Alaska, the fall caribou hunt supplied communities for the entire winter. Many Inuit obtained food from smaller animals, including hares and foxes.

The Inuit also caught fish in the sea, lakes, and rivers. They ate berries and other plant foods when they were available. Delicacies included such items as the skin of beluga whales and fat from the backs of caribou.

The Inuit often ate meat raw or frozen. When they cooked meat, they used pots made from a soft stone called soapstone. Soapstone lamps, which were fueled by blubber or oil from seals and whales, provided heat. Inuit cooks used a curved knife called the *ulu* (pronounced *OO loo*) to prepare much of their food. The ulu was made in the form of a half moon. It had a blade of slate or metal and a handle of bone, ivory, or wood. The Inuit ate from wooden plates and bowls, using forks made of bone. They drank from cups made of the horns of musk oxen.

Clothing. The Inuit made their clothing from the skins of animals. Styles varied from region to region, but in all regions men, women, and children wore the same general outfit. It consisted of a hooded jacket called a *parka,* trousers or leggings, socks, boots, and mittens. The Inuit often wore goggles of wood, bone, or ivory to reduce glare from the sun. The goggles had small holes or narrow slits through which to see.

The Inuit preferred caribou skin as a material for clothing. The skin was lightweight, and the inner hairs of the skin made it warm. Skins from seals, foxes, polar bears, and other animals served as substitutes for caribou. The Inuit often decorated their clothing with furs, beads, and good luck charms such as carvings or parts of animals.

The parka fit loosely over the head, neck, and shoulders. It hung in varying lengths from above the waist to below the knees. Women often carried young children in the backs or hoods of their parkas. Most Inuit wore two layers of clothing in winter: an inner suit with the fur next to the skin and an outer suit with the fur on the outside. The air between the two layers provided insulation, and the fur allowed perspiration to evaporate. In warmer weather, the Inuit wore only the inner suit of caribou or a suit of sealskin. The Inuit used sealskin to make their tightly sewn boots.

Shelter. Most Inuit families had both a summer and a winter dwelling. During the summer months, almost all Inuit lived in tents framed with wood and covered with seal or caribou skins. Some tents had raised platforms at the rear where people slept.

To build a winter house, the Inuit first dug a large hole in the ground. The builders then piled rocks and sod around the outer boundary of the hole to form walls. Rafters of wood or whalebone topped the walls and were covered with sod. Often, the Inuit excavated a sod-covered entrance passage below the level of the house floor. This passage kept warm air inside the house and cold air outside. Cold air became warmer as it flowed through the passage, and it then rose into the house. The Inuit usually stored food in this entrance passage or in storage areas off of the passage. Inside the house, the Inuit built sleeping platforms that filled most of the rear section. They also constructed platforms to hold oil lamps that provided heat and light. In addition, Inuit in some regions built a kitchen area near the entrance passage.

People often imagine that the Inuit lived in snowhouses for much of the year. In fact, only the Inuit of central Canada and the northern Canadian Arctic islands lived in snowhouses all winter. Most Inuit built snowhouses only as temporary shelters when traveling.

Inuit builders could construct a snowhouse in about two hours. First, they cut blocks of hard snow using a *snow knife,* a long, straight knife made from whalebone. They then stacked the blocks in a continuous, circular row that wound upward in smaller and smaller circles to form a dome-shaped house.

The Inuit who used snowhouses as permanent winter dwellings built much more elaborate structures. They attached storage rooms to the snowhouse and excavated entrance passages similar to those in sod houses. Sometimes, a series of passages connected a group of snowhouses occupied by several families. The Inuit arranged the interiors of permanent winter snowhouses in much the same fashion as sod houses. These interiors included both sleeping platforms and lamp platforms.

Transportation. During winter months, most Inuit traveled on sleds. In summer, they walked over land and traveled by boat over water.

The Inuit made two basic types of sleds: plank sleds and frame sleds. The plank sled was mostly used in Canada and Greenland and looked like a long ladder. It consisted of two long runners with a series of crosspieces lashed between them. The Inuit preferred wood as the material to make plank sleds. In areas where wood was not available, the Inuit used whalebone and even frozen animal skins. Frame sleds, used often in Alaska and Siberia, had a basketlike frame built on the runners. The frame slanted upward from the front to the back of the sled. For both kinds of sleds, the Inuit fastened sled shoes of whalebone to the bottoms of the runners. These shoes were both durable and slippery.

Both types of sleds were pulled by dogs. The Inuit of Canada and Greenland usually hitched each dog to the sled by a separate line. In this kind of hitch, the dogs fanned out in front of the sled as they pulled it. The Inuit of Alaska and Siberia hitched their dogs in pairs along a central line.

The Inuit kept as many dogs as they could feed. Northern Canadian Inuit, who lived in a particularly harsh climate, usually had only 1 or 2 dogs. However, teams of 10 or more dogs were common in eastern Canada. During the summer, many Inuit used dogs to carry packs as they moved from place to place.

The Inuit used two types of boats: the *kayak* (pronounced *KY ak*) and the *umiak* (*OO mee ak*). The kayak resembled a canoe with a deck. It had a narrow body pointed at both ends. The body consisted of a carefully fitted wood frame covered with seal or caribou skin. Be-

Bryan & Cherry Alexander

Building a snowhouse involves cutting blocks of hard snow and stacking them in a continuous coil. This coil winds upward in smaller and smaller circles to form a dome-shaped house.

Bryan & Cherry Alexander

Building a kayak begins with constructing a sturdy wooden frame, like the one above. Traditionally, the Inuit covered the frame with animal skin. Most kayaks carry only one person.

cause the Inuit normally used kayaks for hunting, they fitted harpoon rests to the deck. Most kayaks carried only one person, who sat in a hole in the deck. Some carried two people and had two holes. The design of the kayak remains popular today. Modern boatbuilders commonly make fiberglass boats that copy the kayak's design.

To propel a kayak, the Inuit used either a long paddle with a blade at each end or a short paddle with a single blade. A kayaker often wore a special waterproof jacket made from seal intestine. The boater fitted the edge of the jacket around the edge of the kayak opening and tied the jacket in front to form a waterproof seal. A person could tip over in a kayak, roll back up, and continue to float.

The umiak was a large open boat that usually carried 8 to 10 people. Like kayaks, umiaks consisted of a wooden frame covered with skin. The Inuit propelled these boats with single-bladed paddles. Umiaks were used for long-distance travel. The Inuit hauled their belongings in umiaks when they moved camp, and they used the boats for hunting walruses and whales.

Hunting and fishing provided almost all of the Inuit's food and many of the raw materials for their tools, weapons, clothing, and shelter. The Inuit most commonly hunted seals and caribou, but they also killed whales, musk oxen, polar bears, hares, and birds.

The Inuit hunted seals by different methods in different seasons. In winter, they hunted at the breathing holes that the seals kept open in the ice. Hunters used long bone tools called probes to find the angle of the holes. They then waited by these holes and killed the

Traditional Inuit clothing, transportation, and shelter

WORLD BOOK illustrations by Marion Pahl

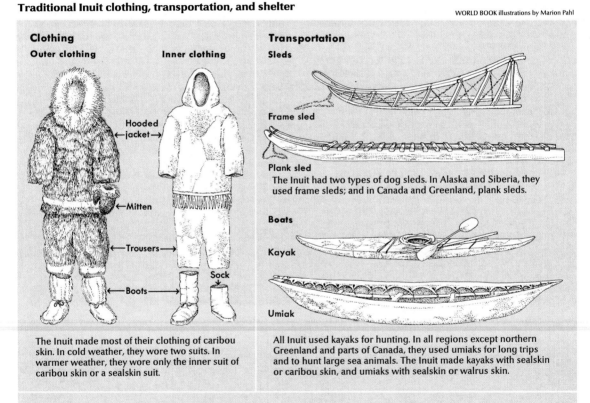

Clothing

Outer clothing

Inner clothing

Hooded jacket

Mitten

Trousers

Boots

Sock

The Inuit made most of their clothing of caribou skin. In cold weather, they wore two suits. In warmer weather, they wore only the inner suit of caribou skin or a sealskin suit.

Transportation

Sleds

Frame sled

Plank sled

The Inuit had two types of dog sleds. In Alaska and Siberia, they used frame sleds; and in Canada and Greenland, plank sleds.

Boats

Kayak

Umiak

All Inuit used kayaks for hunting. In all regions except northern Greenland and parts of Canada, they used umiaks for long trips and to hunt large sea animals. The Inuit made kayaks with sealskin or caribou skin, and umiaks with sealskin or walrus skin.

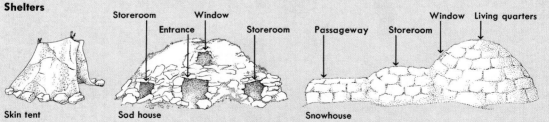

Shelters

Storeroom   Window   Window   Living quarters
Entrance   Storeroom   Passageway   Storeroom

Skin tent   Sod house   Snowhouse

Almost all Inuit lived in animal-skin tents in summer. In winter, most Inuit lived in sod houses. They also built snowhouses as temporary shelters when they traveled. Only the Inuit of central Canada and the northern Canadian islands used snowhouses as permanent winter homes.

seals when the animals surfaced to breathe. Some Inuit used tools that indicated when a seal was using a breathing hole. These tools often consisted of feathers or of a long, thin sliver of wood or bone called an *idlak* (*IHD lak*). A hunter would stick the indicator into the breathing hole. When a seal swam over to the hole, its breath would cause the indicator to vibrate. The Inuit would then kill the seal.

The Inuit killed seals with harpoons. They made harpoon heads from bone or ivory and tipped the heads with a stone or iron point. After the harpoon struck the animal, the harpoon head detached from its shaft. A sealskin line fastened to the head held the animal securely. When hunting through the ice, the Inuit held a handle at the end of the harpoon line.

In the spring, the Inuit hunted seals as the animals climbed out onto the ice. The hunters stalked seals slowly and carefully. Many hunters approached their prey by imitating the seals' movements as the animals awoke every minute or so to watch for danger. Other hunters stalked while hiding behind a movable hunting screen. The Inuit also hunted seals from the ice edge during spring and from kayaks during the open water months of summer. When hunting from the ice edge or from kayaks, the Inuit attached an inflated sealskin float to the other end of the harpoon line. This technique slowed the seal down and prevented the loss of the harpoon.

Inuit hunters used special bone plugs to close wounds in dead seals. These plugs held in the seal's blood, which was a common part of the Inuit diet. Hunters then pulled the seals home using large pins or handles of bone, wood, ivory, or antler.

Most Inuit hunted caribou by shooting them with arrows from small, stout bows. Hunters could also spear caribou from kayaks when the animals crossed lakes or rivers. The Inuit sometimes built rows of stone piles, which directed the caribou toward water crossings or other spots where hunters could spear them.

Inuit hunters also killed a variety of other animals. For example, many Inuit hunted whales by shooting them with *darts*—long, spearlike weapons that were tipped with poison. After shooting a whale, the Inuit would wait a few days for the animal to die and wash up on shore. Hunters trapped foxes in stone traps. These traps had small holes at the top through which the fox could not escape. A few Inuit caught polar bears in huge stone traps. Usually, a hunter's dogs surrounded the bear and kept it at bay until the hunter could kill it with a lance. In some other areas, the Inuit set snares to catch birds and hares. They also killed birds by throwing multipronged spears into the flocks.

The Inuit usually fished with a three-pronged spear called a *leister* (*LEES tuhr*). For much of the year, they fished through holes in the ice. In summer, the Inuit often fished in shallow streams. Sometimes, they placed lines of rocks in the streams to channel the fish toward them.

Religion. The Inuit believed that all people, animals, things, and forces of nature had spirits. The spirits of people and animals lived in another world after they died. Other spirits included those of the wind, the weather, the sun, and the moon. One of the most important spirits to many groups was a goddess who gov-

erned the sea. In some areas, she was called Sedna (*SEHD nuh*). She lived at the bottom of the ocean and controlled the seals, whales, and other sea mammals.

The Inuit followed special rules to please the spirits. They believed that if they ignored the rules, the spirits might punish them by causing sickness or other misfortune. In many communities, the wife of a hunter might offer a drink of water to an animal that had been killed. She would do this to satisfy its spirit. In Alaska, the Inuit saved the bladders of the seals they killed. They believed a seal's spirit rested within its bladder. In a special ceremony each year, the community returned the bladders to the sea to ensure good hunting in the year to come.

The death of an Inuk required certain observances. In many regions, the Inuit wrapped the body in skins and

Bryan & Cherry Alexander

Catching fish in Inuit culture involves spearing the fish through holes in the ice. The Inuk fisherman shown above uses a three-pronged spear called a *leister* to catch his fish.

Michio Hoshino, Minden Pictures

Drying fish helps preserve the food for many months. The Inuit catch fish the year around. They often fish on frozen lakes in winter and in shallow streams during summer.

Skin drums are traditional instruments in Inuit music. The Inuit often use such drums to accompany dancers. These three drummers are Russian Inuit performing at a festival.

Norm Stelfox, Tony Stone Images

left it on the tundra, covered by an arrangement of stones. They often placed tools, weapons, and other items with the body for use in the otherworld.

Inuit communities usually had an individual who they believed had special powers to communicate with the spirit world. Such a person was called an *angekok* (*ANG guh kahk*) by the Inuit and a *shaman* by Europeans. These individuals could be either men or women. They healed the sick and tried to influence aspects of life over which people had little control. For example, they attempted to communicate with spirits to bring good weather and to ensure a steady supply of game.

Recreation. The long Arctic winter was the time for storytelling and for passing the Inuit's unique traditions and mythology from one generation to the next. During winter, darkness and storms often kept people indoors for long periods. The Inuit performed traditional dances to the beat of a large skin drum. Other activities included song contests and tests of strength such as wrestling and tug-of-war.

One of the most popular Inuit games was the *blanket toss*. A dozen or more people held a round blanket made of walrus hides sewn together. When they all pulled the blanket tight, a person on the blanket was tossed into the air. The one being tossed tried to land on his or her feet and often did somersaults in the air. Another popular game was *ajegaq* (*AJ uh gahk*), in which a bone drilled with holes was tossed in the air and caught on a pin or spike. Inuit children played with toy bows and arrows, leather balls, and dolls made of wood, skins, or ivory.

Arts and crafts. The Inuit elaborately carved or decorated many of the objects they used every day. These objects included needle cases, snow goggles, combs, pins, and many other items made from antler, bone, or walrus ivory. The Inuit often carved pins and buttons into the forms of animals, such as seals and fish. They decorated clothing with some of these carvings and with the dyed skins of seals and the furs of foxes,

wolves, and other animals.

Language. The Inuit included speakers of two related language groups. Most Inuit communities spoke dialects of the Inuit-Inupiaq language. These communities stretched from northwest Alaska to Greenland and southward into Hudson Bay and the Labrador coast. The other language, Yupik, was spoken in far eastern Siberia and along portions of the Alaskan coast.

The Inuit formed many of their words by adding one or more suffixes to a root word. Such words could have five or more syllables. For example, the Inuit word *igdlo* means *house,* while the word *igdlorssualiorpoq* means *he who builds a large house.* Inuit languages included numerous words that reflected their own way of life. For example, the Inuit used many terms for the seal. Different names depended upon the kind of seal, whether the animal was young or old, whether it was on land or in the water, and other circumstances.

History

Inuit origins. People have lived in the Arctic for thousands of years. The earliest Arctic peoples were not closely related to modern Inuit. They did not hunt large whales or use dogs to pull their sleds, and their tools and weapons were different from those of the Inuit.

Inuit culture developed in what is now the Bering Sea region about 1,000 years ago. The people there, who were of Asian origin, developed the technology to hunt huge bowhead whales. This culture spread eastward and is called the Thule (*THOO lee*) culture, after the place in northern Greenland where archaeologists first discovered it.

The Thule people, the ancestors of the Inuit, had reached present-day northern Alaska by A.D. 1000. There, they hunted bowhead whales along the shore during the whales' annual migrations. About A.D. 1000, Thule people began to spread eastward into what are now the Canadian Arctic and Greenland. They also moved southward into what are now Hudson Bay and the coast of Labrador. The Thule people displaced or absorbed earlier residents that lived in many of these regions. Archaeological evidence indicates that this expansion occurred rapidly. For example, scientists have found remarkably similar tools, weapons, and house types at Thule archaeological sites from the Bering Sea region in the west to Greenland in the east. Scientists think that warming climates may have been partly responsible for this rapid spread.

As the Thule people moved throughout this vast Arctic region, they modified their culture to suit the different environments they found. The Caribou Inuit of the west coast of Hudson Bay, for example, lived on caribou and fish. The Inuit of the Labrador coast hunted large whales.

In time, the Inuit in each region of the Arctic came to recognize themselves as distinct cultural groups with their own individual dialects. The members of these groups usually called themselves after the places where they lived. These names end with the suffix -*miut,* which means *the people of.* For example, *Aivilingmiut* means *the people of the village Aivilik.*

The arrival of Europeans. The first Europeans to meet Inuit people were Norse settlers in what is now northern Newfoundland, Canada. These settlers lived there for a short time in about A.D. 1000. Beginning in the 1500's, European whalers, fishing crews, and explorers met many Inuit along the coast of Labrador. The English explorer Martin Frobisher visited an Inuit village in the Baffin Islands in the 1570's. He and his party wrote descriptions of the village and made paintings and drawings of some Inuit people. Russians and other Europeans first met Alaskan Inuit in the 1700's. In the later 1700's, Moravian missionaries from what is now Germany traded with Labrador Inuit and converted many of them to Christianity.

In the mid-1800's, whalers began to hunt in the Arctic. Some Inuit worked for whalers and traded with them. The Inuit received firearms, ammunition, wood, iron, and other European goods. Unfortunately, European diseases often accompanied the whalers and traders. These diseases, which included smallpox and measles, completely wiped out some Inuit populations.

The Inuit way of life changed as a result of contact with Europeans. For example, many Inuit began trapping animals only for their furs, which they traded to Europeans for rifles and other goods. Because of the trapping, many animals the Inuit hunted became scarce. This scarcity, in turn, made the Inuit more dependent upon European goods and permanently altered their traditional way of life. Nevertheless, many Inuit continued to follow their traditional ways well into the 1800's.

New ways of life began for most Inuit in the early and middle 1900's. During that time, the impact of European societies on the Inuit increased greatly. The industrialized cultures of Europe were extremely different from traditional Inuit societies, and many Inuit had difficulty adopting European lifestyles. The Inuit way of life changed in different ways in Russia, Alaska, Canada, and Greenland.

In Russia, the Communist government of the Soviet Union took control of all Inuit communities during the 1920's. Russia was part of the Soviet Union from 1922 until 1991, when the Soviet Union was dissolved. The Soviet Communists provided improved health care, housing, and education for the Inuit. However, they also forcibly relocated many Inuit groups from their traditional lands to other areas. The Inuit were grouped with other Siberian peoples into economic units called *collectives.* The purpose of the collectives was to produce goods for sale throughout the country. Since the Inuit could no longer hunt sea mammals for food, they began to sell walrus tusks and such handicrafts as bone and soapstone carvings.

In Alaska, hunting with rifles and widespread trapping greatly reduced the quantity of game animals by the late 1800's. As a result, many of the Inuit became unable to survive independently. The United States government brought reindeer from Siberia in an attempt to start a reindeer herding industry. However, the industry failed. The Inuit of Alaska became United States citizens in 1924.

Joe Rychetnik, Van Cleve Photography

Inuit communities changed greatly in the 1900's. Wooden homes largely replaced sod houses, snowhouses, and tents. The Inuit also modified some of their traditional ways. For example, many began to use snowmobiles instead of dog teams to pull their sleds.

During World War II (1939-1945), many Inuit worked at U.S. military bases in Alaska. After the war, some Inuit found part-time work in commercial fishing, construction, or other businesses run by the rapidly growing white population. But most Inuit could not find jobs. The U.S. government established programs to improve living conditions of the Inuit, but many of them still lived in poverty.

In Canada, the Inuit way of life changed little until the 1950's. At that time, the fur trade declined and the number of caribou decreased sharply after the animals had been hunted with rifles for many years. These developments led more and more Inuit to move to communities that had developed around trading posts, government administrative offices, radar sites, and mission churches. The Inuit could find construction jobs and other temporary work in these communities. But there was not enough work for all the Inuit. As a result, many of them began to receive housing and other assistance from the Canadian government.

In Greenland, many Inuit began fishing commercially during the early 1900's. This development resulted from a change in climate that warmed Greenland's coastal waters. The warm water drove the seals north and attracted cod, salmon, and other fish from the south.

Greenland was a colony of Denmark from 1380 until 1953, when it became a Danish province. At that time, the Inuit became Danish citizens. During the early 1900's and mid-1900's, the Danish government established programs to aid the Greenland Inuit. These programs provided improved education, housing, and health care. In addition, the Danish government helped train the Inuit for jobs in manufacturing, service industries, and other fields.

The Inuit today. The traditional way of life has ended for most Inuit. They live in wooden homes rather than in snowhouses, sod houses, or tents. They wear modern clothing instead of animal skin garments. Most Inuit speak English, Russian, or Danish in addition to their native language. The kayak and umiak have given way to the motorboat, and the snowmobile has replaced the dog team. Christianity has taken the place of most traditional Inuit beliefs.

Today's Inuit must compete in the modern economic world instead of the world of nature. While some Inuit have adjusted to their new ways of life, many suffer from unemployment and other problems. In addition, industrial and nuclear pollution are poisoning their traditional homelands and food sources.

Altogether, more than 100,000 Inuit live in Russia, Alaska, Canada, and Greenland. The Inuit population almost doubled between 1950 and 1970, and it continues to grow rapidly. This growth has resulted chiefly from improved health care and better living conditions.

Russia. About 1 percent of all Inuit live on the northeastern tip of Siberia. They hunt walruses, whales, seals, and other animals and produce carvings and other handicrafts for sale. They receive education, housing, and other benefits from the government.

Alaska has about 34 percent of the world's Inuit. Some Alaskan Inuit live in towns and cities. But the majority live in small settlements and hunt and fish for most of their food. Some Inuit work in the petroleum or mining industries. However, there is little other industry, so most of the state's Inuit are either unemployed or can find only temporary jobs. They depend on the U.S. government for housing and other assistance. The government has greatly expanded the educational programs for the Inuit, and more than half of the young people complete high school.

In 1971, the United States Congress passed a bill that gave $962½ million and 44 million acres (18 million hectares) of Alaskan land to the state's native peoples. These peoples are the Inuit, the *Aleuts* (a people native to Alaska's Aleutian Islands), and American Indians. Congress passed the bill in response to long-standing land claims made by the Inuit and Indians.

Canada has about 29 percent of the world's Inuit. Most of them live in towns in housing provided by the government. They also receive financial aid, health care, and other help from the government. About half of all Canadian Inuit cannot find permanent employment. To combat this problem, the government has helped the Inuit establish commercial fishing and handicraft cooperatives. These organizations have been especially successful in selling soapstone sculpture and prints, which have become increasingly popular in Canada and the

Bryan & Cherry Alexander

Inuit children listen to a story at a school in the Northwest Territories in Canada. Educational opportunities have increased greatly for the Inuit people since the mid-1900's.

Ken Graham

An Inuk technician uses a computer to regulate activity in a lead and zinc mine in Alaska. Mining and petroleum industries provide jobs for many of Alaska's Inuit people.

Wolfgang Kaehler

Frank Mayrs, Tony Stone Images

Inuit artists, such as this printmaker, *left,* and sculptor in soapstone, *right,* have found a growing demand for their work. Many Inuit artists belong to organizations called *cooperatives,* which collect the artwork of their members and sell it throughout the world.

United States. Educational opportunities have increased greatly for the Canadian Inuit since the 1950's, but most Inuit students do not finish high school.

In 1993, Canada's government passed legislation to create a vast new territory that will be controlled by the Inuit. The territory, called Nunavut, will cover a large part of northern Canada and will come into being in 1999. At that time, the government will also give Canada's Inuit title to much of Nunavut's land.

Greenland has about 36 percent of all Inuit. Almost all these people have mixed Inuit and European ancestry. But most experts classify them as Inuit. In 1979, Denmark granted Greenland *home rule* status. This allows Greenlanders to control the internal affairs of the province, including Inuit affairs.

Most Greenland Inuit work in towns, chiefly in the fishing industry. Only the Inuit in northern Greenland still live mainly by hunting seals and continue many of their traditional ways. Most Greenland Inuit do not complete high school. Greenland's government provides them with housing, health care, and other assistance.

James A. Tuck

Related articles in *World Book* include:

Alaska (Visitor's guide; picture)	Kayak
Aleuts	Northwest Territories
Arctic	Seal
Caribou	Sled dog
Clothing (pictures)	Tundra
Greenland	Walrus
Igloo	

Outline

I. The land of the Inuit
   A. Climate
   B. Plants and animals
II. Traditional way of life
   A. Group life
   B. Food
   C. Clothing
   D. Shelter
   E. Transportation
   F. Hunting and fishing
   G. Religion
   H. Recreation
   I. Arts and crafts
   J. Language
III. History
   A. Inuit origins
   B. The arrival of Europeans
   C. New ways of life
   D. The Inuit today

Questions

In what countries do the Inuit live today?
Who were the first Europeans to meet the Inuit?
What two types of boats did the Inuit use?
What traditional methods have the Inuit used to hunt seals?
Why did the Inuit prefer caribou skin as a material for clothes?
In what types of houses did the Inuit live?
Why has the Inuit population grown so rapidly since 1950?
What foods have been part of the traditional Inuit diet?
Why is Inuit country called the Land of the Midnight Sun?
Where did Inuit culture originate?

Reading and Study Guide

See *Inuit* in the Research Guide/Index, Volume 22, for a *Reading and Study Guide.*

Additional resources

Level I
Alexander, Bryan and Cherry. *Inuit.* Steck-Vaughn, 1993.
Ekoomiak, Normee. *Arctic Memories.* 1988. Reprint. Holt, Rinehart, 1990.
Hoyt-Goldsmith, Diane. *Arctic Hunter.* Holiday Hse., 1992.
Osborn, Kevin. *The Peoples of the Arctic.* Chelsea Hse., 1990.
Smith, J. H. Greg. *Eskimos.* Rourke, 1987.

Level II
Brody, Hugh. *Living Arctic: Hunters of the Canadian North.* 1987. Reprint. Douglas & McIntyre, 1990.
Burch, Ernest S., Jr. *The Eskimos.* Univ of Oklahoma Pr., 1988.
Chance, Norman A. *The Inupiat and Arctic Alaska.* Holt, Rinehart, 1990.
Fienup-Riodan, Ann. *Eskimo Essays.* Rutger, 1990.

Oil painting on wood (1503); The Louvre, Paris (Giraudon/Art Resource)

Leonardo da Vinci's *Mona Lisa* is probably the most famous portrait ever painted. Its blurred outlines, graceful figure, dramatic contrasts of dark and light, and overall feeling of calm are characteristic of Leonardo's style.

Unfinished oil painting on wood (early 1500's);
The Louvre, Paris (Erich Lessing for Art Resource)

The Virgin and Child with Saint Anne is arranged in a pyramid shape. Leonardo often used this arrangement.

Leonardo da Vinci

Leonardo da Vinci, *lee uh NAHR doh duh VIHN chee* or *lay uh NAHR doh duh VIHN chee* (1452-1519), was one of the greatest painters and most versatile geniuses in history. He was one of the key figures of the Renaissance, a great cultural movement that had begun in Italy in the 1300's. His portrait *Mona Lisa* and his religious scene *The Last Supper* rank among the most famous pictures ever painted.

Leonardo, as he is almost always called, was trained to be a painter. But his interests and achievements spread into an astonishing variety of fields that are now considered scientific specialties. Leonardo studied anatomy, astronomy, botany, geology, geometry, and optics, and he designed machines and drew plans for hundreds of inventions.

Because Leonardo excelled in such an amazing number of areas of human knowledge, he is often called a universal genius. However, he had little interest in literature, history, or religion. He formulated a few scientific laws, but he never developed his ideas systematically. Leonardo was most of all an excellent observer. He con-

cerned himself with what the eye could see, rather than with purely abstract concepts.

Leonardo's life

Early career. Leonardo was probably born outside the village of Vinci, near Florence in central Italy. The name *da Vinci* simply means *from Vinci*. At that time, Florence and its surrounding villages and farms made up a nearly independent area called a *city-state*. Florence was also a commercial and cultural center. Leonardo was the illegitimate son of Ser Piero da Vinci, a legal specialist, and a peasant woman named Caterina. Ser Piero's family raised the boy in Vinci.

During the late 1460's, Leonardo became an apprentice to Andrea del Verrocchio, a leading painter and sculptor in Florence. He remained with Verrocchio as an assistant for several years after completing his apprenticeship. Verrocchio and Leonardo collaborated on the painting *The Baptism of Christ* about 1472.

From about 1478 to 1482, Leonardo had his own studio in Florence. During this period, he received an important commission to paint a church altarpiece now known as the *Adoration of the Kings.*

Years in Milan. Leonardo never finished the *Adoration of the Kings* because he left Florence about 1482 to become court artist for Ludovico Sforza, the Duke of

Adoration of the Kings, intended as an altarpiece, was left unfinished after Leonardo worked on it in 1481 and 1482. The artist drew the scene in pen and ink. He used a technique called *metal point* to add precise details with a metal rod much like a pencil. He also brushed on a fine layer of color called a *wash* to give the scene shading and volume.

Uffizi Gallery, Florence, Italy (SCALA/Art Resource)

Milan. Leonardo lived in Milan until 1499. He had a variety of duties in the duke's court. As a military engineer, he designed artillery and fortresses. As a civil engineer, he devised a system of locks for Milan's canals and designed revolving stages for pageants. As a sculptor, he planned a huge monument of the duke's father mounted on a horse.

About 1483, Leonardo painted the *Madonna of the Rocks.* This painting is his earliest major work that survives in complete form. During his years in Milan, he also created his famous wallpainting *The Last Supper.*

Return to Florence. In 1499, the French overthrew Ludovico Sforza and forced him to flee Milan. Leonardo also left the city. He visited Mantua, where he made a famous drawing of Isabella d'Este, the wife of the Duke of Mantua. He also visited Venice briefly before returning to Florence.

Leonardo's paintings during his stay in Milan had made him famous, and the people of Florence received him with great respect. The early work Leonardo had done in Florence before he left for Milan had strongly influenced a number of young artists, including Sandro Botticelli and Piero di Cosimo. These artists had become the leaders of the next generation of Florentine painters. The work Leonardo was to create after his return to Florence would inspire yet another generation of artists. This generation included Andrea del Sarto, Michelangelo, and Raphael.

When Leonardo returned, Florence was building a

new hall for the city council. The Florentine government hired Leonardo and Michelangelo to decorate the walls of the hall with scenes of the city's military victories. Leonardo chose the Battle of Anghiari, in which Florence had defeated Milan in 1440. His painting showed a cavalry battle, with tense soldiers, leaping horses, and clouds of dust.

In painting the *Battle of Anghiari,* Leonardo tried an experimental technique that did not work. The paint began to run, and he never finished the project. The painting no longer exists. Its general appearance is known from Leonardo's sketches and from copies made by other artists. About 1503, while working on the *Battle of Anghiari,* Leonardo painted the *Mona Lisa,* probably the most famous portrait ever painted.

Last years. In 1513, Pope Leo X gave Leonardo rooms for his use in the Vatican Palace. Leonardo did little painting during his later years. However, about 1515, he completed *The Deluge,* a series of drawings in which he portrayed the destruction of the world in a tremendous flood. These drawings are the climax of Leonardo's attempts to visualize the forces of life and nature.

Renaissance rulers competed to surround themselves with great artists and scholars. In 1516, Francis I, the king of France, invited Leonardo to become "first painter and engineer and architect of the king." He provided Leonardo a residence connected to the Palace of Cloux at Amboise, near Tours. Leonardo devoted his time to doing anatomical drawings, drafting architectural plans,

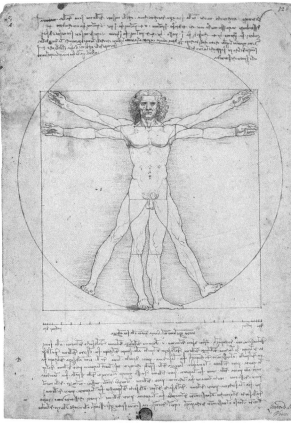

Pen and ink (about 1492); Accademia, Venice, Italy (SCALA/Art Resource)

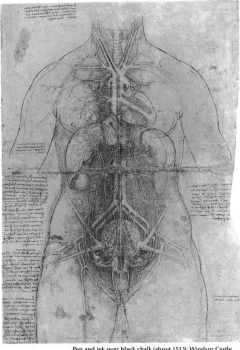

Pen and ink over black chalk (about 1513); Windsor Castle
(The Royal Collection © Her Majesty Queen Elizabeth II)

Leonardo's scientific drawings include his famous study of human proportions called *Vitruvian man, left,* and an anatomical drawing of a female, *above,* in which Leonardo illustrated the body's circulatory and other systems. Leonardo produced more drawings than any artist before him.

and designing sets for court entertainments. He died on May 2, 1519.

Leonardo's works

Drawings and scientific studies. Leonardo used drawings both as a tool of scientific investigation and as an expression of artistic imagination. He changed forever the art of drawing. He made drawings in much greater numbers than any artist before him, and he was one of the first artists to use sketches to work out his artistic and architectural compositions. Drawing was indispensable to Leonardo's processes of observation, creation, and invention.

Physical sciences. Leonardo was interested in *mechanics* (the science of motion and force), and many of his ideas and designs were far ahead of their time. For example, he drew plans for aircraft, including a helicopter, and for a parachute. Like many Renaissance artists, Leonardo sometimes worked as an engineer or military architect. He produced designs for a variety of war machines, among them tanks, machine guns, and movable bridges.

Life sciences. Leonardo studied anatomy by dissecting human corpses and the bodies of animals. He made scientific drawings that clarify not only the appearance of bones, tendons, and other body parts, but also their function. These drawings are considered the first accurate portrayals of human anatomy.

Leonardo tried to understand the human body as a mechanism. As his studies progressed, he also tried to understand the forces of life that animated the body. His drawings of anatomy, for example, extended to investigations of human reproduction and embryology and the circulation of the blood. None of these things were understood at the time. His anatomical drawing of a female, which he made about 1508, is his attempt, partly erroneous in detail, to illustrate the body's circulatory and other systems in a single image.

Like other artists, Leonardo was interested in the proportions of the human body. He drew a famous study of human proportions based on the statement of the Roman architect Vitruvius that the "well-shaped man" fits into the perfect shapes of the square and circle. According to Vitruvius, the parts of the body are related to one another in ratios of whole numbers, and these ratios should be used in the design of architecture. Leonardo's drawing of the *Vitruvian man,* done about 1487, is one of the most famous images in European art.

Leonardo also worked to understand the relation between the life of the human body and that of the larger world. For Leonardo, principles of proportion similar to those that shaped the human body also governed the growth of trees, the flight of birds, and the flow of water. When Leonardo drew the leaves of a plant, he intended the lines to show living energy responding to light, water, and soil. The mystery of life was the unifying theme of his work.

Leonardo's notebooks. Leonardo planned to write

books on many subjects, including painting, human movement, and the flight of birds, but he never completed any of them. The writings exist in partial drafts and fragments in notebooks. Leonardo's notebooks also include his scientific observations and ideas for inventions, as well as detailed drawings. Most of the notebooks were not published until nearly 400 years after Leonardo's death. By the time his scientific and technical investigations became widely known, other people had come up with the same ideas.

Paintings. For much of his life, Leonardo was interested in optics, which is concerned with the properties of light. Leonardo carefully analyzed such things as the pattern of light and shadow on a sphere before a window. The understanding he gained from such study is evident in the rich effects of light, dark, and color in such paintings as the *Mona Lisa* and *The Virgin and Child with Saint Anne* (early 1500's).

Leonardo also explored the techniques of perspective, which painters use to create an illusion of depth on a flat surface. Florentine artists began to use these techniques in the early 1400's. *Linear perspective* is based on the optical illusion that parallel lines seem to converge as they recede toward one point, called a *vanishing point. Aerial perspective* is based on the fact that light, shade, and color change with an object's distance from the viewer.

Early paintings. Verrocchio and Leonardo shared the work of painting *The Baptism of Christ.* Leonardo painted the left angel, the distant landscape, and possibly the skin of Christ. Leonardo's parts of the painting, with their soft shadings and shadows concealing the edges, are an early example of the *sfumato* (smoky) quality of his paintings. Verrocchio's figures, on the other hand, are defined by hard lines typical of early Renaissance painting. Leonardo's more graceful approach marked the beginning of the High Renaissance style, which did not become popular in Italy until about 25 years later.

Leonardo's *Adoration of the Kings* exists today in an unfinished form, with the figures visible only as outlines of contrasting light and dark areas. This kind of composition is called *chiaroscuro,* a word which combines the Italian words for *light* and *dark.* Chiaroscuro is characteristic of the High Renaissance style.

The *Adoration of the Kings* shows three kings worshiping the newborn Christ child. Leonardo abandoned the traditional treatment of this popular subject. Earlier versions showed the figures in profile, with the Virgin Mary and Jesus on one side of the painting and the kings on the other. To give the Holy Family more emphasis, Leonardo placed them in the center, facing the viewer. The kings and other figures form a semicircle around Mary and Jesus. Leonardo sharply contrasted foreground and background. Strong light-dark contrasts and simple geometric forms were basic features of Leonardo's mature style as a painter.

In the *Adoration of the Kings,* Mary and the Christ child are arranged in a pyramid shape. Leonardo also used this arrangement in other paintings, including the

Pen and ink over black chalk (1514-1516); Windsor Castle (The Royal Collection © Her Majesty Queen Elizabeth II)

Hurricane is part of a series of drawings called *The Deluge,* which Leonardo produced near the end of his life. In the series, Leonardo attempted to visualize the forces of life and nature.

Red chalk (about 1514); Biblioteca Reale, Turin, Italy (SCALA/Art Resource)
Leonardo's self-portrait was drawn when he was about 60 years old. It is the only existing likeness of the artist.

Madonna of the Rocks and *The Virgin and Child with Saint Anne*. In *The Virgin and Child with Saint Anne,* pictured with this article, the gazes of all the figures are concentrated on one side of the pyramid, giving it a new psychological and dramatic unity.

The Last Supper. Leonardo finished painting *The Last Supper* about 1497. He created the famous scene on a wall of the dining hall in the monastery of Santa Maria delle Grazie. The painting shows the final meal of Jesus Christ and His 12 apostles. Jesus has just announced that one of them will betray him.

When painting *The Last Supper,* Leonardo rejected the *fresco* technique normally used for wallpaintings. The technique requires an artist to mix dry pigments with water and brush them onto damp, freshly laid plaster. An artist who uses the fresco method must work quickly. But Leonardo wanted to paint slowly, to revise his work, and to use shadows—all of which would have been impossible in fresco painting. He developed a new technique that involved coating the wall with a compound he had created. But the compound, which was supposed to hold the paint in place and protect it from moisture, did not work. Soon after Leonardo completed the picture, the paint began to flake away. *The Last Supper* still exists, but in poor condition, though many attempts have been made to restore it.

Leonardo also changed the traditional arrangement of the figures. Christ and His apostles are usually shown in a line, with Judas, the betrayer, set apart in some way. Leonardo painted the apostles in several small groups. Each apostle responds in a different way to Christ's announcement that one of them will betray Him. Jesus sits in the center of the scene, apart from the other figures. Leonardo's composition creates a more active and centralized design than earlier artists had achieved. The composition, in which the space recedes to a point behind the head of Christ, is one of the great examples of one-point perspective in Italian Renaissance painting. Leonardo used linear perspective to focus attention on the painting's religious and dramatic center, the face of Jesus Christ.

Mona Lisa, shown in this article, is probably a portrait of the young wife of a rich Florentine silk merchant, Francesco del Giocondo. *Mona Lisa* is a shortened form of *Madonna Lisa* (my lady, Lisa). The woman is also often called *La Gioconda,* which is the feminine form of her husband's last name.

The portrait shows a young woman seated on a balcony high above a landscape. Leonardo used a pyramid design to place the woman simply and calmly in the space of the painting. Her folded hands form the front corner of the pyramid. Her breast, neck, and face glow in the same light that softly models her hands. The light gives the variety of living surfaces to an underlying geometry of spheres and circles, which includes the arc of her famous smile. Behind the figure, a vast landscape recedes to icy mountains. Winding paths and a distant bridge give only the slightest indications of human presence. The landscape reflects Leonardo's studies of geology. He was one of the first people to grasp that geological time is revealed in rock layers and to understand such processes as erosion.

Leonardo's importance

Leonardo had one of the greatest scientific minds of the Italian Renaissance. He wanted to know the workings of what he saw in nature. Many of his inventions and scientific ideas were centuries ahead of his time. For example, he was the first person to study the flight of birds scientifically. Leonardo's importance to art was even greater than his importance to science. He had a strong influence on many leading artists, including Raphael and Michelangelo. Leonardo's balanced compositions and idealized figures became standard features of later Renaissance art. Painters also tried to imitate Leonardo's knowledge of perspective and anatomy, and his accurate observations of nature.

What most impresses people today is the wide range of Leonardo's talent and achievements. He turned his attention to many subjects and mastered nearly all. His inventiveness, versatility, and wide-ranging intellectual curiosity have made Leonardo a symbol of the Renaissance spirit.   David Summers

Related articles in *World Book* include:

Aerodynamics (Pioneers of aerodynamics)
Airplane (picture: An early design)
Heart (picture: Leonardo da Vinci)

Painting (The 1400's)
Parachute (picture: Leonardo da Vinci)
Renaissance (The fine arts; picture: The drawings of Leonardo da Vinci)

Additional resources

Bramly, Serge. *Leonardo.* HarperCollins, 1991.
Clark, Kenneth. *Leonardo da Vinci.* Rev. ed. 1959. Reprint. Penguin, 1989.
McLanathan, Richard B. *Leonardo da Vinci.* Abrams, 1990.
Mühlberger, Richard. *What Makes a Leonardo a Leonardo?* Viking, 1994. Younger readers.

Fresco (1511); © Nippon Television Network Corporation 1990

The Sistine Chapel was probably Michelangelo's greatest achievement as a painter. A detail of the ceiling fresco, *above,* shows God creating the sun, the moon, and vegetation.

Michelangelo

Michelangelo, *MY kuhl AN juh LOH* or *MIHK uhl AN juh LOH* (1475-1564), was one of the most famous artists in history. He was mainly interested in creating large marble statues, but his endless creative energy also led him to become a great painter and architect as well as a poet. He was also one of the most famous people of his time and a great leader of the Italian Renaissance, a period marked by a rebirth of interest in the art and learning of ancient Greece and Rome.

Michelangelo is best known for his treatment of the human body in painting and sculpture. His figures convey a sense of grandeur and power, and arouse strong emotions in many spectators. In size, strength, and emotional intensity, these figures go beyond real people. Michelangelo's figures are both animated and restrained, and seem to possess great spiritual energy. His work presses toward the extremes of heroism and tragedy but is never false or artificial.

Early life. Michelangelo was born on March 6, 1475. His full name was Michelangelo Buonarroti. He came from a respectable Florence family and was born in the village of Caprese, where his father was a government agent. Michelangelo had a brief classical education that dealt with the literature, art, and life of ancient Greece and Rome. When he was 12 years old, Michelangelo became an apprentice to the most popular painter in Florence, Domenico Ghirlandajo.

Before his apprenticeship was completed, Michelangelo stopped painting and began working as a sculptor under the guidance of a pupil of the sculptor Donatello. Michelangelo attracted the support of the ruler of Florence, Lorenzo de' Medici, who invited the young artist to stay at his palace. Michelangelo's earliest surviving sculpture is a small unfinished relief of a battle, done when he was about 16. This work shows the obvious influence of ancient Roman marble sculpture belonging to Lorenzo. But the relief also shows the force and movement that became typical of Michelangelo's style. During these years, he began the study of anatomy.

After the Medici family lost power in 1494, Michelangelo began traveling. He lived in Rome from 1496 to 1501. There he had his first marked success when he carved in marble a life-sized statue of the Roman wine god Bacchus. At 23, Michelangelo carved a version of the traditional Pietà subject, the dead Christ in the lap of the mourning Virgin Mary. Both figures are larger than life-sized. This statue, now in St. Peter's Basilica in Rome, established him as a leading sculptor. The work was plainer and less decorative than most statues of the time, and thus looked stronger and more solemn.

Michelangelo returned to Florence in 1501 and remained there until 1505. He may have gone there to compete for the right to work on a large piece of marble that had been abandoned by earlier sculptors working on the Cathedral of Florence. The marble became Michelangelo's *David* (1504), one of the most famous works in the history of art.

Michelangelo's *David* portrays the Israelite king partly as an ideal man, partly as an adolescent youth. The young figure faces his foe tensely but confidently, with a bold scowl and his sling at the ready.

The Florentines had planned to put the statue high in the air on the Cathedral of Florence. But they decided instead to place this great work of art at eye level in their main public square, and it became a symbol of the new republic that had replaced Medici rule.

The new democratic government of Florence then asked Michelangelo and the city's other outstanding artist, Leonardo da Vinci, to create large battle scenes for the walls of the city hall. Michelangelo probably never started to paint the wall, but his design for the work is known to us through his sketches and through copies by other artists. It displayed his expert ability to render

Marble sculpture (about 1550); Duomo, Florence (SCALA/Art Resource)

The Florentine *Pietà* was intended for Michelangelo's own tomb. The hooded figure helping to hold the body of Christ is a self-portrait of the sculptor when he was about 75 years old.

human anatomy. It was during these years that Michelangelo formed the basis of the style in which he would work for the rest of his life.

From about 1505 on, Michelangelo devoted nearly all his time to large projects. In his enthusiasm for creating grand and powerful works of art, he accepted projects that were far too large for him to complete. The first one was a tomb ordered by Pope Julius II that was to include 40 marble statues. The artist accepted the job in 1505 and ended the project unsuccessfully 40 years later.

The Sistine Chapel. Julius II was a patron of the arts with a sweeping imagination equal to Michelangelo's. Julius gave Michelangelo a more practical commission, painting the *vault* (arched ceiling) of the Sistine Chapel in the Vatican. This project became Michelangelo's most famous work.

The Sistine Chapel is where major papal ceremonies take place. The chapel was built by Pope Sixtus IV, Julius II's uncle, and was decorated during the 1480's with paintings by some of the greatest artists of the time, including Sandro Botticelli, Luca Signorelli, and Perugino. All of its decoration together shows the history of the world according to the Bible. The earlier painters showed the lives of Moses and Jesus Christ and the sequence of the popes. Michelangelo's contribution to the project was the grandest of all.

On the lowest part of the vault of the Sistine Chapel as well as on the upper walls, over the arched windows, Michelangelo painted *The Ancestors of Christ.* In the corners, he portrayed stories of the salvation of the Jewish people, such as *David and Goliath.*

The highest part of the vault was originally painted blue with gold stars, symbolizing heaven. Michelangelo changed this treatment. Above the *Ancestors,* he painted great thrones in which are seated prophets believed to have foretold the coming of a *Messiah* (savior). Male prophets of the Old Testament or Hebrew Bible alternate with *sibyls,* female prophets of ancient times. The series of prophets ends above the high altar of the chapel with Jonah, who survived after three days inside a whale, an event that foretells Christ's death and his Resurrection.

Above the thrones of the prophets are nude figures, called *ignudi,* who hold bronze-colored disks with stories taken mostly from the Books of Kings. Michelangelo covered the very top of the vault with nine scenes from the Book of Genesis, including three scenes portraying the creation of the universe, three showing the creation of Adam and Eve and their fall from grace, and three illustrating the story of Noah. The most famous scene is *The Creation of Adam.*

Michelangelo, forced against his own wishes by Julius to undertake the huge task, began the ceiling in 1508 and completed it in 1512. He used a technique called *fresco,* applying the paint to damp, freshly laid plaster and working quickly before the plaster dried. He began at the entrance and worked toward the altar, starting with the scenes from Noah's life and working backward in time to the beginning of creation. Michelangelo painted the ceiling from a scaffolding, standing up, not lying on his back as historians once thought. During this period, he wrote a satirical poem in which he complained of a stiff neck and of paint dripping into his eyes. In the margin of the page, he drew a caricature of himself reaching up to paint.

At first, Michelangelo approached the task in a style resembling his earlier works. But he soon gained confidence and developed new ways of showing tension and power. The last frescoes he painted, which include *The Separation of Light from Darkness* and the portrait of Jonah, are much richer and more active compositions. The figures in these last paintings are also larger and freer in execution.

When the frescoes of the Sistine ceiling were cleaned in the 1980's, restorers found that Michelangelo had painted in much brighter colors than had been realized. The brilliance of the colors makes the paintings visible from a great distance. The top of the vault is about 70 feet (21 meters) above the floor.

The tomb of Julius II. After he had finished the ceiling, Michelangelo resumed work on the pope's tomb. He carved three famous figures that resemble the painted prophets and decorative figures on the Sistine ceiling. These figures are Moses and two prisoners, sometimes called *The Heroic Captive* and *The Dying Captive,* completed by 1516. The figure of Moses, who seems to be filled with terrible anger, was later used as the centerpiece of the tomb. This statue was finally placed in the Church of St. Peter in Chains in Rome. The figures of the two captives may symbolize lands conquered by Julius II or arts and sciences left without support after his death. One of them struggles violently against his bonds as the other languishes and seems to submit to defeat.

The Medici Chapel. Michelangelo spent the years

Fresco (1550); The Vatican Museums (SCALA/Art Resource)

The Crucifixion of Saint Peter, left, was completed by Michelangelo when he was 75. This fresco and a companion work, *The Conversion of Saint Paul,* were his last paintings. They were commissioned by Pope Paul III for a chapel in the Vatican.

from 1515 to 1534 working mainly for the Medici family, who had regained control of Florence. He designed and carved tombs for two Medici princes and also designed the Medici Chapel, in which the tombs are placed. Michelangelo left the chapel incomplete when he moved away from Florence in 1534.

Along with the statues of the two young princes, the tombs include the figures of *Night* and *Day* on one tomb and *Evening* and *Dawn* on the other. The figures recline on curving lids, conveying a sense of fate or individual tragedy. They make a great impact on spectators as a significant observation about human destiny. Some read the parts of the monument from floor to ceiling as a symbol of the rising of the soul after its release from the body. Others see the four statues on the curved lids as a sign of the endless movement of time, in which life is only an incident.

Michelangelo also designed the architecture of the Medici Chapel. He planned the walls like a carved relief, with projections and hollows and long, narrow shapes to give an elongated effect. This approach, resembling carved architecture, is carried further in the entrance hall and staircase to the Laurentian library in Florence, which he designed between 1524 and 1559.

The Last Judgment. Michelangelo was sometimes torn between loyalty to the Florentine republic and loyalty to the Medici family, his patrons. In the late 1520's, the Medici family once more lost power in Florence. The city fortified itself against an attempt by the family to regain control. Michelangelo served as director of fortifications. In 1530, the Medici family took the city by

force, and Michelangelo went into hiding to avoid arrest. However, Pope Clement VII, himself a member of the Medici family, sent word to Florence that Michelangelo was to be treated well and allowed to continue working on the Medici tombs. Michelangelo resumed his work, but he left Florence in 1534. He never returned to the city, though he was buried there.

Michelangelo settled in Rome, where he worked for Pope Paul III. From 1536 to 1541, Michelangelo painted the fresco of *The Last Judgment* for the altar wall of the Sistine Chapel, destroying some of his earlier *Ancestors of Christ* to do so. In a single scene covering the entire wall, Michelangelo showed the resurrection and judgment of humanity.

At the top of *The Last Judgment* are wingless angels with the cross upon which Christ died. Beneath them, the blessed gather in heaven. In the center, Christ raises His right arm. The Virgin Mary, who intercedes for souls, sits beside Him. In response to Christ's commanding gesture, the world below comes to life. On the left, tombs open and the dead—some skeletons, others in grave shrouds—rise toward heaven. To the right, the damned tumble or are dragged into hell. Hell is filled with demons and is ruled over by Minos, the mythical king of Crete who imprisoned a monster known as the Minotaur. A large snake coils around Minos. The depiction of hell is based on *The Divine Comedy* (1321), a famous poem by the Florentine writer Dante Alighieri. Michelangelo is supposed to have known the lengthy poem by heart.

The Last Judgment caused great controversy, and Mi-

Marble sculpture (1498-1499); St. Peter's Basilica, Vatican City (SCALA/Art Resource)

Marble sculpture; Castello Sforzesco, Milan (SCALA/Art Resource)

Two Pietàs span Michelangelo's career. The *Pietà, above,* was the most important work of his youth and established his reputation. The stark, unfinished Rondanini *Pietà, right,* dates from 1564, the year of his death.

chelangelo was very disturbed by the reaction to his work. Some critics objected that Christ was shown inappropriately. The fresco was bitterly criticized for its display of nudity. In fact, draperies were later added to many of the figures by one of Michelangelo's followers. In the early 1990's, when the fresco was cleaned and repaired, restorers removed some of the draperies that had been added.

Later years. The small amount of sculpture in Michelangelo's later years includes works to complete old commissions and two unfinished Pietà groups. He created both Pietàs for his own satisfaction and not for a patron. One of the Pietàs is now in the Cathedral of Florence and is called the Florentine *Pietà* (1555). It was meant for Michelangelo's own tomb. It is designed as a massive pyramid, with Christ's body slumping down on the ground. In the other Pietà, known as the Rondanini *Pietà* (1564), now in Milan, the marble limbs are reduced to a ghostlike thinness. The bodies seem to lack substance, while the material of the stone is emphasized by the hacking chisel marks left on the unfinished surface. Because of this technique, many modern sculptors, including Henry Moore, admire this work above all others Michelangelo produced.

Michelangelo devoted much time after 1546 to architecture and poetry. In 1546, Pope Paul III appointed him supervising architect of St. Peter's Basilica, one of Julius II's unfinished projects. Michelangelo worked on the church without salary. By the time he died in 1564, construction had reached the lower part of the dome, which was finished by another architect. After 1538, he planned a square for the Civic Center of Rome and the buildings facing it. The square is shaped like a trapezoid, a four-sided figure with two parallel sides of unequal length. The square and the oval design at its center symbolize Rome as the center of the world.

Michelangelo's last paintings, finished when he was 75 years old, were frescoes in the Pauline Chapel in the Vatican. They show *The Conversion of Saint Paul* (1545) and *The Crucifixion of Saint Peter* (1550). Although they are large, complicated designs like the Sistine Chapel paintings, they are graver, more still and inward. Michelangelo became deeply religious in his last years, during which he made devotional drawings comparable to the Rondanini *Pietà.* He also wrote some of his finest poetry during his old age.   David Summers

Related articles in *World Book* include:

Italy (picture: Renaissance sculpture)	Saint Peter's Basilica (History)
Painting (The High Renaissance)	Sculpture (Michelangelo)
Renaissance (The fine arts)	Sistine Chapel

Reading and Study Guide

See *Michelangelo* in the Research Guide/Index, Volume 22, for a *Reading and Study Guide.*

Additional resources

Hall, Marcia. *Michelangelo: The Sistine Ceiling Restored.* Rizzoli, 1993.

Hibbard, Howard. *Michelangelo.* 2nd ed. Harper, 1985.

Lace, William W. *Michelangelo.* Lucent Bks., 1993. Younger readers.

McLanathan, Richard. *Michelangelo.* Abrams, 1993. Younger readers.

Murray, Linda. *Michelangelo.* 1980. Reprint. Thames & Hudson, 1985.

Richmond, Robin. *Introducing Michelangelo.* Little, Brown, 1992. Younger readers.

Ken Cole, Earth Scenes

A national park is an area set aside to protect natural beauty or other notable features. The magnificent scenery of Banff National Park in Canada includes snow-covered Mount Victoria and sparkling Lake Louise, *above*. Such beauty makes Banff one of the favorite parks in North America.

National park

National park is an area set aside by a nation's government to protect natural beauty, wildlife, or other remarkable features. National parks also preserve places of cultural, historical, or scientific interest. In addition, some parks protect entire environments, such as coral reefs, deserts, grasslands, mountain ranges, or rain forests. Governments create national parks to guard their natural treasures from the harmful effects of farming, hunting, logging, mining, and other economic development.

National parks serve important purposes. Many parks allow us to enjoy and appreciate majestic peaks, sparkling lakes, spectacular waterfalls, and other scenic wonders. Others let us see fascinating wild animals in their natural settings. Still others provide opportunities for boating, camping, hiking, and other forms of recreation. As a means of attracting tourism, national parks are vital to the economies of many nations.

In addition, many national parks foster education by preserving important buildings, battlegrounds, and other features of a nation's cultural and historical heritage. Parks help save endangered animals and plants, and they provide natural laboratories for scientists seek-

Craig W. Allin, the contributor of this article, is Professor of Political Science at Cornell College and the editor of International Handbook of National Parks and Nature Reserves.

ing to understand relationships of animals and plants to their environment. Another goal of many parks is to protect the area's *biodiversity* (variety of plant and animal species). In this way, parks help maintain a healthy balance among species and help preserve the natural processes that support life on the earth.

National parks face a number of challenges. Many park managers must deal with pressures to develop park resources. They also are concerned about *poaching* (illegal hunting), the collection of rare plants, pollution, and overcrowding. Other concerns include the rights of the people who were the parks' original inhabitants, and the wise management of natural forces such as fire and wildlife.

The world's first national park, Yellowstone National Park, was established in the United States in 1872. National parks gradually spread throughout the world. Today, about 1,500 national parks protect about $1\frac{1}{2}$ million square miles (3.9 million square kilometers) in more than 120 countries. Many countries use the term *nature reserves* for areas similar to national parks. There are about 6,000 of these areas. Together, the world's national parks and nature reserves cover an area about the size of the mainland United States.

Notable national park systems

A number of countries have developed important national park systems. These countries include Argentina, Australia, Canada, Japan, Kenya, New Zealand, South Africa, and the United States.

Argentina has about 20 national parks. The parks cover a total of about 10,000 square miles (26,000 square kilometers). The country's first national park, the National Park of the South, was established in 1922 to preserve an area of scenic mountains.

Argentina's national parks are known for protecting an enormous range of geographical features, plants, and animals. The most notable parks include Nahuel Huapi, Los Glaciares, and Iguazú. Nahuel Huapi was originally called National Park of the South. It took its present name in 1934. It is Argentina's largest national park, covering about 3,000 square miles (7,800 square kilometers). Only slightly smaller is Los Glaciares, which has nine major glaciers. Together, Iguazú National Park in Argentina and Iguaçu National Park in Brazil protect the magnificent Iguaçu Falls and about 900 square miles (2,300 square kilometers) of tropical rain forest. The waterfall actually consists of about 275 separate falls. The combined falls measure about 2 miles (3 kilometers) wide and drop 237 feet (72 meters).

Australia has about 500 national parks. The first one, established in 1879, was National Park (now called Royal National Park). Today, the system extends over 100,000 square miles (275,000 square kilometers).

Australia's history makes its parks especially important to scientists. About 200 million years ago, Australia broke apart from a huge land mass that is now Africa and South America. As a result, Australia's wildlife developed differently from the wildlife on the other continents. Kangaroos, koalas, wombats, and thousands of other animals and many native plants are unique to Australia.

Australia's Great Barrier Reef Marine Park and Kakadu National Park are of exceptional interest. Great Barrier Reef, a large group of coral reefs in the South Pacific Ocean, is the largest marine reserve in the world. It extends about 1,250 miles (2,000 kilometers) along Australia's northeast coast. The park is home to about 400 species of coral, 200 kinds of birds, and thousands of different species of fish and shellfish.

Kakadu National Park protects evidence of human life from about 30,000 years ago. This evidence includes one of the world's greatest collections of prehistoric cave paintings. Kakadu is a pioneer in cooperative management. Most of the park belongs to groups of Aborigines, whose members are descendants of hunting and gathering people who were Australia's earliest inhabitants. The Aborigines have leased their lands to the federal government with the understanding that the park will be managed to preserve their traditional ways of life.

Michael Fogden, Oxford Scientific Films from Earth Scenes

The spectacular Iguaçu Falls lies on the border between Brazil and Argentina and forms a part of national parks in each country. The waterfall actually consists of about 275 separate falls. The combined falls measure about 2 miles (3 kilometers) wide and drop 237 feet (72 meters).

Kelvin Aitken, Peter Arnold, Inc.

The Great Barrier Reef Marine Park stretches about 1,250 miles (2,010 kilometers) along Australia's coast. Its approximately 400 species of colorful coral attract many divers.

Canada has about 35 national parks that occupy a total of about 85,000 square miles (220,000 square kilometers). The Canadian system of national parks began in 1885, with land near Banff, Alberta. This area became part of what is now Banff National Park.

Canada has pioneered an *ecosystem* approach to park planning. An ecosystem consists of all the living and nonliving things in a given area and the relationships among them. An area's air, climate, soil, and water are part of its ecosystem. Under the ecosystem approach, Canada's park service has divided the country into about 70 areas, each with a different combination of land, water, plants, and animals. National parks are developed around the relationships among the natural features in each area.

The Canadian park system is exceptionally diverse. Banff, Jasper, Kootenay, and Yoho national parks protect almost 8,000 square miles (20,700 square kilometers) of mountain ecosystem. These four adjacent Rocky Mountain parks have rugged peaks, active glaciers, glistening lakes, thundering waterfalls, and boiling hot springs. The parks are home to grizzly and black bears, bighorn sheep, deer, elk, moose, mountain goats, and dense forests of evergreen trees.

In addition, Canada has begun to develop a system of marine parks to protect underwater environments in the Atlantic, Pacific, and Arctic oceans and in the Great Lakes. Its first national marine park, Fathom Five, was established in 1987 in Lake Huron's Georgian Bay. The bay's cold, clear waters preserve several historic shipwrecks and provide opportunities for recreational divers. For a complete listing of Canada's national parks and historic sites, see **Canada** (National park system).

Japan has about 80 national parks. The parks cover about 13,000 square miles (34,000 square kilometers). The national parks of Japan are rooted in both religion and recreation. Japan's major religions, Buddhism and Shintoism, stress harmony with nature and deep respect for living things. The Japanese people regard forests, islands, mountains, and other places of special beauty as sacred. For centuries, they treated such places as shrines and left them unspoiled. To protect the beauty of Japan's scenic mountains, the government created the country's first national park in 1934. In the mid-1900's, the growing popularity of mountain climbing led to the expansion of Japan's national park system.

Japan's park planners have been challenged by the country's huge population and small area. Japan is one of the most densely populated nations in the world. As a result, little unused land is available for the creation of national parks. Japan's solution has been to establish national parks that include private lands. The government then works with the landowners to save the natural beauty of each area. About a fourth of Japan's parkland is privately owned.

Japan's best-known scenic treasure is Mount Fuji, a beautifully shaped volcano in Fuji-Hakone-Izu National Park. This park lies near Tokyo and other large cities and attracts about 100 million visitors each year.

Kenya has about 30 national parks and reserves. Its national park system covers about 14,000 square miles (36,000 square kilometers) and protects a spectacular variety of wild animals. The national parks of Kenya date to the early 1900's, when colonial governments set aside wildlife reserves mainly to provide sightseeing and hunting opportunities for Europeans. Today, the money spent by tourists visiting the national parks is a major source of Kenya's national income.

Kenya's most famous protected areas include Tsavo National Park and Masai Mara Game Reserve. Both lie in the grasslands of East Africa. Tsavo is Kenya's largest park. It covers about 8,000 square miles (20,700 square kilometers) and is known for its elephants and rhinocer-

D. & J. Heaton, West Light

Mount Fuji, long considered a sacred place by the Japanese people, stands in Fuji-Hakone-Izu National Park. The beautifully shaped volcano attracts about 100 million visitors each year.

oses. Masai Mara lies next to the Serengeti National Park in Tanzania. It is home to antelopes, buffaloes, cheetahs, elephants, giraffes, hippopotamuses, hyenas, jackals, leopards, lions, rhinoceroses, and many kinds of birds. Between August and October, hundreds of thousands of migrating zebras and wildebeests from the Serengeti Plain cross into Masai Mara.

New Zealand has about 15 national parks. These parks cover about 9,000 square miles (23,000 square kilometers). New Zealand's national park system grew from the beliefs and vision of its original inhabitants, the Maoris. The Maoris feared that Europeans settling in the country in the late 1800's would not respect their sacred volcanoes. In 1887, a Maori chief gave land to the government for a park. The area was expanded and became Tongariro National Park in 1894.

Saving nature has special importance in New Zealand, an island country. Like Australia, New Zealand separated from the other continents about 200 million years ago. When Europeans began arriving in the 1800's, more than half of New Zealand's native plants and animals were unique to the island. But European settlers introduced many new plants and animals to New Zealand. The results have been disastrous for the native species. In many parts of the country, most native plants and animals have been destroyed.

Fiordland, New Zealand's largest national park, has about 15 *fiords* (narrow inlets from the sea) that extend up to 27 miles (43 kilometers) long and about 1,600 feet (500 meters) deep. This park also includes evergreen forests and Sutherland Falls, which drops 1,904 feet (580 meters) and ranks as one of the world's highest waterfalls. The national parks have helped make tourism and outdoor recreation major industries in New Zealand.

South Africa has about 15 national parks. The parks occupy about 12,000 square miles (31,000 square kilometers). The country's first national park, Kruger National Park, was established in 1926. Nature observers have called South Africa's animal population "the greatest wildlife show on earth." Not surprisingly, the history of South Africa's national park system has focused on wildlife protection. Kruger National Park and Kalahari Gemsbok National Park stand out for their enormous size and great variety of wildlife.

Kruger covers about 7,500 square miles (19,500 square kilometers) and may have the largest variety of mammals in any African park or reserve. It has thousands of buffaloes, elephants, impalas, and zebras, as well as hundreds of species of birds and plants. The park's grasslands are home to antelopes, cheetahs, giraffes, hyenas, jackals, leopards, and lions. Crocodiles and hippopotamuses live in the rivers. Kruger has become a world center for wildlife research.

Kalahari Gemsbok National Park was established in 1931 to protect herds of migrating animals. It covers about 3,700 square miles (9,600 square kilometers) and lies next to Gemsbok National Park in Botswana. These parks are famous for their various species of antelopes, including elands, gemsboks, springboks, steenboks, and wildebeests, as well as for cheetahs, hyenas, jackals, and lions.

The United States has about 50 national parks. These parks and over 300 other protected areas in the country's National Park System occupy about 125,000 square miles (325,000 square kilometers). The U.S. government's work in establishing and managing national parks has

Gerald Cubitt

The sprawling Kruger National Park in South Africa is home to thousands of mammals, including impalas and waterbucks, *above.* The park covers about 7,500 square miles (19,500 square kilometers) and ranks as one of the leading centers of wildlife research in the world.

served as a model for countries around the world. The opening of Yellowstone National Park in 1872 was soon followed by the creation of many other important national parks. To preserve recreational opportunities in natural settings, the government set aside more than 400 wilderness areas, mostly within national parks, national forests, and national wildlife refuges. For more information on U.S. parks, see **National Park System.**

Other interesting national parks

More than 120 countries have established national parks. A number of these parks are famous throughout the world and attract millions of visitors annually. Tourists are often drawn by the variety of wildlife in a country's national parks. Costa Rica's parks are especially popular because they have more species of birds— about 850—than do the United States and Canada combined. This small country's national parks also protect about 9,000 species of plants.

Many people are attracted by the outstanding features of individual parks as well. Some of these parks are considered world treasures. For example, Nepal's Sagarmatha National Park includes "the peak whose head touches the sky," according to local peoples. Westerners know this majestic, snow-capped peak as Mount Everest, which rises to 29,028 feet (8,848 meters) and is the highest peak in the world. Guatemala's Tikal National Park protects pyramids of the ancient Maya civilization.

Another famous protected area, Ecuador's Galapagos National Park, preserves the natural laboratory that influenced the British biologist Charles Darwin. Darwin's studies there contributed to his famous theory of evolution. England's Lake District inspired the British poet

David Woodfall, NHPA

The scenic Lake District National Park in England is one of Europe's natural treasures. About 15 lakes in the region, including Ullswater, *above,* attract writers, artists, and other visitors.

D. Donne Bryant

Tikal National Park in Guatemala protects ruins of pyramids and temples of the ancient Maya Indian civilization. This civilization flourished in Guatemala between A.D. 300 and 900.

Interesting national parks throughout the world

By the 1990's, there were about 1,500 national parks in the world. These parks protect about 1½ million square miles (3.9 million square kilometers) in over 120 countries. Examples of interesting national parks throughout the world are described below and on page 499.

Name	Location	Outstanding features
AFRICA		
Amboseli	Kenya	Views of nearby Mt. Kilimanjaro; elephants, leopards, and vervet monkeys
Chobe	Botswana	Giraffes, zebras, elephants, lions, and hippopotamuses
Comoe	Ivory Coast	Elephants
Dzanga-Ndoki/	Central African Republic/	Gorillas, chimpanzees, elephants; rain forest
Nouabalé-Ndoki	Congo	
Etosha	Namibia	Savanna and woodland surrounding a shallow depression that fills with water in the rainy season; large elephant population, zebras, wildebeests, springboks, other wildlife
Garamba	Zaire	Habitat for white rhinoceroses and buffaloes
Hwange	Zimbabwe	Woodland and scrub savanna; elephants, buffaloes, giraffes, and zebras
Kabalega Falls	Uganda	Murchison Falls, crocodiles, hippopotamuses, other wildlife
(Murchison Falls)		
Kalahari Gemsbok/Gemsbok	South Africa/Botswana	Desert area with migrating groups of springboks and gemsboks; lions and cheetahs
Kilimanjaro	Tanzania	Trails to the summit of Mt. Kilimanjaro for mountaineers, elands and leopards
Kruger	South Africa	Savanna home to vast wildlife, including buffaloes, giraffes, elephants, and zebras
Lake Malawi	Malawi	Deep-water lake with hundreds of species of fish
Montagne d'Ambre	Madagascar	Volcanic area with crater lakes and waterfalls; tropical forests, lemurs and butterflies
Ngorongoro	Tanzania	Rim of ancient volcanic crater surrounds flat savanna; diverse wildlife
Niokolo-Koba	Senegal	River habitat, bordered by forest and savanna; crocodiles, buffaloes, and gazelles and other antelopes
Ranomafana	Madagascar	Rugged area of rain forest; endangered aye-ayes and ruffed lemurs
Ruwenzori (Queen Elizabeth)	Uganda	Two large lakes; chimpanzees and colobus monkeys, many antelopes
Selous	Tanzania	Elephants, buffaloes, other species
Serengeti/Masai Mara	Tanzania/Kenya	Migrating zebras and wildebeests; diverse savanna wildlife
South Luangwa	Zambia	Woodland savanna for elephants, giraffes, leopards, other wildlife
Tsavo	Kenya	Largest park in Kenya; major elephant and rhinoceros populations
Victoria Falls/	Zimbabwe/Zambia	Magnificent Victoria Falls
Mosi oa Tunya		
Virunga/Volcanoes	Zaire/Rwanda	Wide variety of habitats, including home of mountain gorillas
ASIA		
Angkor	Cambodia	Protected area for the ancient temples of Angkor
Bandipur/Mudumalai	India	In western Ghat mountains; one of the last strongholds for the Asian elephant
Corbett	India	Forest and grasslands provide habitat for Bengal tigers
Daisetsuzan	Japan (Hokkaido)	Mountainous habitat for the brown bear and other wildlife; ski areas and hot springs
Fuji-Hakone-Izu	Japan	Scenic Mount Fuji; lakes; rocky coastline
Gunung Leuser	Indonesia (Sumatra)	Rain forest; rhinoceroses, tigers, orangutans, and the world's largest flower, the rafflesia
Kanha	India	Forests and bamboo thickets in central India; home to much wildlife, including tigers, swamp deer
Karatepe-Aslantas	Turkey	Archaeological site of former Hittite settlement; museum
Kaziranga	India	Elephants, rhinoceroses, wild buffaloes, birds
Keoladeo	India	Wetland for migrating waterfowl
Khao Yai	Thailand	Tropical, evergreen, and deciduous forests, as well as grassland; elephants, deer, and numerous bird species
Kinabalu	Malaysia (Borneo)	Jungle at the base of Mt. Kinabalu; tree-level walkway through rain forest
Komodo	Indonesia	Habitat for the endangered Komodo dragon
Manas/	India/	Foothills of the Himalaya; diverse forests, many bird species; tigers, rhinoceroses, golden langur monkeys
Royal Manas	Bhutan	
Mount Apo	Philippines (Mindanao)	Sanctuary for the Philippine eagle
Nikko	Japan	Historic shrines and temples, mountainous scenery, rivers, and waterfalls
Royal Chitwan	Nepal	Grassland and forest; diverse animal and bird population, including tigers and rhinoceroses
Ruhuna (also called Yala)	Sri Lanka	Scrub woodland; elephants, spotted deer, and water buffaloes
Sagarmatha	Nepal	Includes Mount Everest, highest peak in the world
Sorak	South Korea	High peak of Mt. Sorak; lush valleys and forests; Buddhist temples, waterfalls, and hiking trails
Stolby	Russia (Siberia)	Coniferous forests; granite hills; hiking and climbing
Taman Negara	Malaysia	Ancient tropical rain forest; kingfishers, hornbills, buffaloes, tapirs
Ujung Kulon	Indonesia (Java)	Wilderness for Javan rhinoceroses, leopards, Javan gibbons, and leaf monkeys
Wilpattu	Sri Lanka	Jungle habitat for spotted deer, sloth bears, leopards, other wildlife
Wolong	China	Rugged mountainous area of Sichuan province; forests, bamboo, rhododendrons; endangered giant pandas, red pandas, golden monkeys, takins
Yushan	Taiwan	Remote park, home to Taiwan serows, Taiwan black bears, Formosan macaques, and emperor pheasants
AUSTRALIA AND NEW ZEALAND		
Blue Mountains	Australia (New South Wales)	River-eroded gorges, waterfalls, eucalyptus forests
Cradle Mountain/Lake St. Clair	Australia (Tasmania)	Native plants, including pandanus; highlands, temperate rain forest, alpine moors, with glacial lakes
Daintree	Australia (Queensland)	Tropical rain forest, waterfalls, and diverse wildlife
Fiordland	New Zealand	New Zealand's largest park; includes coastal fiords, rain forests, and Sutherland Falls
Great Barrier Reef	Australia (Queensland)	World's largest marine reserve; coral reefs and underwater species
Kakadu	Australia (Northern Territory)	Aboriginal cave paintings; includes tropical tidal flats, mangrove swamps, floodplains, woodlands, and sandstone escarpments
Mount Cook	New Zealand	High mountains, Tasman Glaciers, native wildlife
Tongariro	New Zealand	Active volcanoes; ancestral land of the Maori
Uluru	Australia (Northern Territory)	Includes Ayers Rock and the Olgas, rock domes in the desert; ancient cave paintings
EUROPE		
Askaniya Nova	Ukraine	Steppe wilderness and wetlands; summer home for migrating ducks and geese; spawning site for fish
Bayerischer Wald	Germany	Bavarian forest
Bialowieza	Poland	Lowland forests, hundreds of species of flowering plants, virgin woodlands, European bison
Doñana	Spain	Wetland reserve for migrating waterfowl
Gran Paradiso/Vanoise	Italy/France (Alps)	Alpine landscape; ibex, chamois

Name	Location	Outstanding features
Greenland	Greenland	Arctic wildlife habitat
Lake District	United Kingdom	Mountains, valleys, and glacial lakes, picturesque scenery
Padjelanta/Sarek/ Stora Sjofallet	Sweden	Meadows, glacial peaks, and rugged valleys; grazing herds of reindeer, other wildlife
St. Kilda	United Kingdom	National scenic area; breeding ground for puffins, gannets, other marine birds
Swiss	Switzerland	Coniferous forests, alpine meadows, slopes, and outcrops
Tatransky/Tatra	Czech Republic/Poland	Mountainous area with alpine plants and trees
Teberdinskiy	Russia (Caucasus)	Mountainous forests and meadows, glaciers and glacial lakes; home to ibex, deer, wild boars, pheasants, partridges, and grouse

NORTH AMERICA

Name	Location	Outstanding features
Banff/Jasper	Canada (Alberta)	Rocky Mountain scenery with glaciers and hot springs
Darien	Panama	Rain forest, mangrove swamps, white sand beaches
Denali	USA (Alaska)	Mount McKinley, highest mountain in North America; spectacular wildlife
Everglades	USA (Florida)	Subtropical wilderness with plentiful wildlife
Fundy	Canada (New Brunswick)	Rugged Bay of Fundy shoreline with coves and cliffs; world's highest tides
Glacier	USA (Montana)	Glaciers and lakes among towering Rocky Mountain peaks
Grand Canyon	USA (Arizona)	Deep canyon with brightly colored walls and rock shapes
Great Smoky Mountains	USA (North Carolina/ Tennessee)	High mountains; large hardwood and evergreen forests
Gros Morne	Canada (Newfoundland)	Scenic Long Range Mountains; fiordlike lakes, waterfalls, and rugged seacoasts
Isle Royale	USA (Michigan)	Island wilderness with large moose herd and wolves
Ixtacihuatl-Popocatepetl	Mexico	Mountain peaks, climbing and hiking trails
La Amistad	Costa Rica/Panama	Virgin forest; great biological diversity; dormant volcano
Mammoth Cave	USA (Kentucky)	Huge cave with several hundred miles of corridors
Mesa Verde	USA (Colorado)	Ancient Indian cliff dwellings
Olympic	USA (Washington)	Mountain wilderness, wild coastline, and rain forest; elk
Pacific Rim	Canada (British Columbia)	Beaches, rocky shore, islands, and forests; sea lions, whales
Redwood	USA (California)	World's tallest known tree in coastal redwood forest
Sian Ka'an	Mexico	Tropical forest, mangrove swamps, white sand beaches
Tikal	Guatemala	Ruins of the ancient Mayan civilization
Tortuguero	Costa Rica	Nesting area for the Atlantic green turtle; lowland rain forest
Wood Buffalo	Canada (Alberta/Northwest Territories)	Largest buffalo herd in North America and nesting grounds of rare whooping cranes
Yellowstone	USA (Wyoming/Montana/Idaho)	World's greatest geyser area; canyons and waterfalls; wide variety of wildlife
Yosemite	USA (California)	Mountain scenery with deep gorges and high waterfalls; sequoia forests

SOUTH AMERICA

Name	Location	Outstanding features
Amazonia	Brazil	Variety of ecosystems; spider and howler monkeys, anteaters, capybaras, caimans, parrots, and toucans
Canaima	Venezuela	Angel Falls, the world's highest waterfall; grassland with flat-topped mountains, rain forests
Galapagos	Ecuador	Island ecosystems with unique wildlife
Iguaçu/Iguazú	Brazil/Argentina	Magnificent Iguaçu Falls; tropical rain forests; diverse bird and mammal species
Itatiaia	Brazil	Rugged area between Rio de Janeiro and São Paulo; diverse habitats ranging from rain forests to high plateaus with unique rock formations
Kaieteur	Guyana	Tropical rain forest, savannas; Kaieteur Falls; jaguars, ocelots, tapirs, and many species of birds
Los Glaciares	Argentina	Major glaciers from the southern Patagonian ice field
Manu	Peru	Undisturbed rain forest, with diverse plant and animal life; many species of birds and monkeys
Nahuel Huapi	Argentina	Mountains, glaciers, and glacial lakes and streams; hiking trails
Noel Kempff Mercado	Bolivia	Rain forest; jaguars, tapirs, monkeys, and the endangered giant otter
Pantanal	Brazil	Freshwater wetland near border with Bolivia; dense wildlife, including capybaras and hyacinth macaws
Raleighvallen-Voltzberg	Suriname	Rain forest along the Coppename River, Raleigh Falls; macaws and toucans, armadillos, sloths, and pumas
Rapa Nui	Chile (Easter Island)	Archaeological monuments and local cultural heritage
Torres del Paine	Chile	Dramatic peaks of southern Andes; Andean condors, eagles, rheas, and wild guanacos

Patrick Fagot, NHPA

Keith & Liz Laidler, Animals Animals

Wildlife preservation is a key goal of national parks throughout the world. Indonesia's Komodo National Park protects the endangered Komodo dragon, *above left,* and China's Wolong Natural Reserve shelters the rare giant panda, *above right.*

William Wordsworth long before it became a national park in the 1950's. Victoria Falls National Park in Zimbabwe and Mosi oa Tunya National Park in Zambia share protection of Africa's most famous waterfall. This landmark, the magnificent Victoria Falls, drops 355 feet (108 meters).

Many of the world's national parks are vital to wildlife preservation. Wolong Natural Reserve in China shelters rare giant pandas. Indonesia's Komodo National Park provides a habitat for the endangered Komodo dragon, a lizard that may grow over 10 feet (3 meters) long and weigh up to 300 pounds (135 kilograms). India's national parks, such as Ranthambhore, have probably saved the Indian tiger from extinction. The marshlands of Doñana National Park in Spain provide food and shelter to nearly half the bird species in Europe.

Challenges for the parks

People often think of the world's national parks as islands of unspoiled nature. We assume these parks are safely separated from a world rapidly becoming more urban, more industrial, and more artificial. The world's national parks, however, are part of the world in which we all live. What we do affects the parks and may threaten their existence.

Today, national parks face several major challenges. Major threats come from pressures to develop park resources, from environmental change, and from overcrowding. Park managers also struggle to guarantee the rights of the land's original inhabitants and to ensure sound management of fire and wildlife.

Development of park resources. Many national parks were set aside in the belief that they had little or no commercial value. Later, however, people discovered that many of the parks contain valuable resources. There are trees that might be cut, minerals that might be mined, grass that might be grazed, and land that might be farmed. There are also animals that might be captured or killed for sport or financial gain. The resources inside the parks will become increasingly valuable as resources outside the parks are exhausted. The commercial development of park resources often will produce more jobs and economic growth in the short term than will preservation of the parks.

Pressures to develop park resources generally cause only minor problems for governments of rich nations, where economic growth is strong. These governments have more ways to protect their national parks than do governments of developing nations. People of wealthy nations also do not need to use park resources for survival.

In developing nations, however, the situation is different. In such countries, especially in Africa and South America, governments may be forced to sacrifice parks in favor of economic development. Large corporations may acquire the right to use park resources by paying public officials for their cooperation. Many landless peasants seek park resources for survival. They may view the parks as the only lands available for collecting firewood, for building homes, for hunting food, or for raising crops.

Poachers also invade many parks. Many of these illegal hunters seek profits by killing animals for valuable body parts. For example, poachers slaughter leopards

Belinda Wright, DRK Photo

Poaching is a major problem in a number of national parks that provide homes for endangered wildlife. The leopard and tiger skins shown above were seized from poachers in India.

for their skin, elks for their antlers, elephants for their tusks, and rhinoceroses for their horns. Poachers also collect live animals for illegal sale, especially small birds that can be sold as pets. Some people also take rare plants from the parks. Where all or most of these pressures on park resources are severe, the parks may not survive.

Changes in the environment also endanger the parks. Various forms of pollution—especially air and water pollution—present major threats because they easily cross park boundaries. For example, the scenic views of Grand Canyon National Park in the United States are often reduced due to air pollution from Los Angeles, which lies about 300 miles (480 kilometers) away. In addition, the park's environment has suffered from the construction of dams upstream on the Colorado River, which flows through the Grand Canyon. Changes in the flow of water have harmed water birds and other wildlife in the park.

Worldwide environmental problems also threaten national parks. These problems include an increase in the so-called *greenhouse effect* and the rapid reduction of tropical rain forests. The greenhouse effect is a warming at the earth's surface that results when the earth's atmosphere traps the sun's heat. The heat is trapped when it is absorbed by carbon dioxide and other gases in the atmosphere.

The amount of carbon dioxide in the atmosphere has grown because of the increased burning of such fuels as coal, gas, and oil. Rain forests absorb large amounts of carbon dioxide. But the forests can handle less and less carbon dioxide because developers and farmers continue to cut down or burn the trees.

Some scientists are concerned about the effect of higher temperatures on the earth's surface. They warn that global warming may produce mass extinction of plants and animals and other harmful effects.

Overcrowding. The world's national parks have experienced dramatic growth in tourism during the 1900's. However, some popular parks are actually endangered by their admiring visitors, especially in the United States, Japan, and other wealthy nations with large populations. Too many visitors can harm the natural environments that national parks are set aside to protect. In some popular national parks, for example, visitors' automobiles create traffic jams, kill wildlife, and pollute the air. In addition, overcrowded campgrounds increase the level of litter and destroy the unspoiled beauty of scenic areas.

Overcrowding creates a difficult choice for park managers. Tourist spending demonstrates that park preservation has economic as well as spiritual value. In fact, income from tourists visiting the national parks in Africa is vital to the economies of many nations there. Nevertheless, managers have had to limit the number of cars and campers, and to establish other restrictions to protect park resources for future generations.

The rights of original inhabitants. The peoples who live in and near national parks are especially concerned about who benefits from tourism in the parks. In some countries, the benefits have gone to political officials who control the parks and to large foreign-based corporations. The original inhabitants may then see the parks as a foreign idea and one damaging to their lives. As a result, they may oppose the establishment and preservation of national parks.

Some park managers concerned for the rights of local peoples look to New Zealand and Australia for solutions. In those countries, the Maoris and the Aborigines support the creation of national parks as a way to preserve their sacred places and traditional ways of life. The cooperation of the Aboriginal groups and the Australian National Park and Wildlife Service at Kakadu National Park, for example, may serve as a model for other countries.

Management of fire and wildlife. Fire and wildlife often cause problems for park managers. Both fire and wild animals must behave naturally to preserve a park's ecosystem. If allowed to burn freely, fire destroys old and diseased trees and shrubs and helps nourish the soil. These conditions promote new growth. Allowing animals to hunt and roam freely helps parks maintain a balanced and varied wildlife community.

However, fire and wild animals may threaten neighboring crops, livestock, property, and people. Neither fire nor animals recognize park boundaries. As a result, park managers must find ways to prevent fire and wildlife from passing over park boundaries. Solving this problem is difficult because some solutions can lead to

The Grand Canyon of the Yellowstone cuts across Yellowstone National Park in the United States for about 20 miles (32 kilometers). The Yellowstone River flows through the canyon, creating two waterfalls. Yellowstone, the world's first national park, was established in 1872.

Tom Till, DRK Photo

other problems. For example, park officials can use modern techniques to extinguish fires, and they can build fences to prevent animals from roaming outside the parks. But such actions can upset the delicate balance required for healthy wildlife populations and damage the ecosystem.

Park managers also must maintain an adequate amount of vegetation in the parks for plant-eating animals. Overgrazing can lead to starvation for such animals. This problem may result if a park lacks animals that prey on the plant-eating animals. Overgrazing has developed in Yellowstone National Park in the United States, partly because of an elk population unchallenged by natural predators. Park managers have added wolves, a natural enemy of elk, to the park's wildlife.

History

Throughout history, people have preserved and protected places they considered special. But it was not until the 1800's that governments became active in establishing national parks.

The early national parks. The United States pioneered the development of national parks. Americans became interested in protecting the nation's wilderness as the country expanded westward during the 1800's. In 1832, the artist George Catlin became one of the first noted Americans to publicly call for the creation of a national park. In 1858, the writer Henry David Thoreau also promoted the idea. Both Catlin and Thoreau also saw national parks as places where American Indians could preserve their vanishing cultures. The dream of a great national park became a reality in 1872, when President Ulysses S. Grant signed a law creating Yellowstone National Park.

The national park idea spread to other countries. In 1885, the Canadian government established a park around the hot springs at Banff, Alberta. During the next 40 years, national parks opened in Australia, Germany, Italy, New Zealand, South Africa, Spain, Sweden, and Switzerland. Also during this period, Belgium and France established national parks in their colonial possessions in Africa.

International concern for national parks. The growth of national parks around the world led to the formation of international conservation organizations. In 1948, the International Union for the Protection of Nature was founded. In 1956, it was renamed the International Union for the Conservation of Nature and Natural Resources and became known as the IUCN. In 1960, the IUCN established the International Commission on National Parks. The commission became the Commission on National Parks and Protected Areas in 1975. This commission has taken the lead in organizing world conferences on national parks.

The United Nations Educational, Cultural, and Scientific Organization (UNESCO) established two other important conservation programs. It founded the Man and the Biosphere Program in 1971 to preserve ecosystems throughout the world for scientific and educational purposes. In 1978, UNESCO released the first World Heritage List, which recognized areas of unique natural or cultural importance.

The national park movement today. By the 1990's, the idea of establishing national parks had proved popular and had spread to most of the world's countries. Planners put more emphasis on creating parks to preserve the full range of a nation's plants, animals, and landscapes. They stressed the value of establishing parks in areas of scientific and environmental importance even if those parks might not be particularly popular with tourists.

People also increasingly recognized that national parks are not natural islands that can be maintained separately from the world around them. Now we know that the survival of national parks depends on what we do both inside and outside the parks.   Craig W. Allin

Related articles in *World Book.* See the political maps in many country articles for locations of national parks. See also:

Audubon Society, National	National Wildlife
Balance of nature	Federation
Biodiversity	National Wildlife
Conservation	Refuge System
Ecology	Nature Conservancy
Elephant (Protecting	Park
elephants)	Poaching
Endangered species	Sierra Club
Greenhouse effect	Tropical rain forest
National Park System	Wildlife conservation

Outline

I. Notable national park systems

A. Argentina	E. Kenya
B. Australia	F. New Zealand
C. Canada	G. South Africa
D. Japan	H. The United States

II. Other interesting national parks

III. Challenges for the parks
    A. Development of park resources
    B. Changes in the environment
    C. Overcrowding
    D. The rights of original inhabitants
    E. Management of fire and wildlife

IV. History

Questions

What are some purposes of national parks?

Why does Australia's history make its parks especially important to scientists?

What is Canada's ecosystem approach to park planning?

Why are Japan's national parks rooted in both religion and recreation?

What is the Man and the Biosphere Program? The World Heritage List?

Which park was the world's first national park?

What problems does overcrowding cause in some popular parks?

Why may the peoples who live in or near national parks oppose the establishment of parks?

What have people increasingly recognized about national parks?

What worldwide environmental problems threaten national parks?

Additional resources

Allin, Craig W., ed. *International Handbook of National Parks and Nature Preserves.* Greenwood, 1990.
Burton, Robert, ed. *Nature's Last Strongholds.* Oxford, 1991. Discusses national parks of the world.
Lowry, William R. *The Capacity for Wonder: Preserving National Parks.* Brookings, 1994.
McNamee, Kevin. *The National Parks of Canada.* Key Porter, 1994.
Nature's Wonderlands: National Parks of the World. National Geographic Soc., 1989.
Taylor, Christopher J. *Negotiating the Past: The Making of Canada's National Historic Parks and Sites.* McGill-Queens Univ. Pr., 1990.

Olympic Games

Olympic Games are the most important international athletic competition in the world. The Olympics bring together thousands of the world's finest athletes to compete against one another in a variety of individual and team sports. Millions of people have attended the games, and more than 1 billion people throughout the world watch the Olympics on television.

The Olympic Games originated in ancient Greece and were held from 776 B.C. to A.D. 393. The modern games began in 1896. The organizers revived the games to encourage world peace and friendship and to promote healthy sporting competition for young athletes throughout the world.

The Olympic Games consist of the Summer Games and the Winter Games. From 1896 to 1992, the Olympics were held every four years, except in 1916 during World War I, and in 1940 and 1944 during World War II. The Winter Games, which were established in 1924, took place the same year as the Summer Games. Beginning in 1994, the Winter and Summer Games were divided and scheduled on four-year cycles two years apart. For the years and locations of the games, see the table *Sites of the Olympic Games* in this article.

Olympic ceremonies and symbols

Colorful ceremonies combine with thrilling athletic competition to create the special feeling of excitement in the Olympics. The opening ceremony is particularly impressive. The Olympic athletes of Greece march into the stadium first, in honor of the original games held in ancient Greece. The athletes of the other countries follow in alphabetical order by country according to the spelling in the language of the host country. The athletes of the host country enter last. The president or other head of state of the host country opens the games. The Olympic flag is raised, trumpets play, and cannons boom in salute. Hundreds of doves are released as a symbol of peace.

The most dramatic moment of the opening ceremony is the lighting of the Olympic flame. The flame symbolizes the light of spirit, knowledge, and life, and it is a messenger of peace. The fire is ignited in Olympia, Greece, by using a mirror to concentrate the rays of the sun. Runners transport the flame in a torch relay from Greece to the site of the games. Most runners carry the flame on foot. However, many other kinds of transportation, including airplanes, horses, and skis, have also been used. The final runner carries the torch into the stadium, circles the track, and lights a huge *caldron* (kettle). The flame burns throughout the games and then is extinguished during the closing ceremony.

The Olympic symbol, created in 1913, consists of five interlocking rings that represent the continents of Africa, Asia, Australia, Europe, and the Americas. The colors of the rings, from left to right, are blue, yellow, black, green, and red. The flag of every nation competing in the games has at least one of these colors. Under the rings is the Olympic motto, the Latin words *Citius, Altius, Fortius.* The words are translated as *Swifter, Higher, Stronger.*

The International Olympic Committee

The International Olympic Committee (IOC) is the governing body of the Olympic Games. The IOC has headquarters in Lausanne, Switzerland. The committee approves the sports and events to be included in the games. The IOC also selects the host cities for the Summer Games and Winter Games, seven years in advance. The cities bidding for the games must prove they can provide athletic facilities for the games and housing for the athletes, coaches, officials, and visiting spectators. Host cities provide a special housing compound called the Olympic Village for the athletes and coaches. The prospective hosts must also convince the IOC that they can furnish adequate transportation, food service, and cultural activities. Host cities are chosen by a majority vote of the IOC.

Originally, members of the IOC were elected for life. However, according to a rule change in 1995, all members must retire before they reach the age of 81. The members of the IOC are not allowed to accept instructions on voting from any government or other group or individual. New members of the IOC are elected by current members. There are no rules setting the size of the IOC or what countries should be represented.

Olympic competition

Every country or territory competing in the Olympic Games is represented by a national Olympic committee. In the mid-1990's, about 195 nations and territories had such groups. Each committee is responsible for selecting its national team, providing uniforms and equipment, and furnishing transportation to the Olympic site. Most countries use government funds to pay their

Sites of the Olympic Games

Year	Summer	Winter
1896	Athens, Greece	Not held
1900	Paris, France	Not held
1904	St. Louis, U.S.	Not held
1908	London, England	Not held
1912	Stockholm, Sweden	Not held
1916	Not held	Not held
1920	Antwerp, Belgium	Not held
1924	Paris, France	Chamonix, France
1928	Amsterdam, the Netherlands	St. Moritz, Switzerland
1932	Los Angeles, U.S.	Lake Placid, U.S.
1936	Berlin, Germany	Garmisch-Partenkirchen, Germany
1940	Not held	Not held
1944	Not held	Not held
1948	London, England	St. Moritz, Switzerland
1952	Helsinki, Finland	Oslo, Norway
1956	Melbourne, Australia	Cortina, Italy
1960	Rome, Italy	Squaw Valley, U.S.
1964	Tokyo, Japan	Innsbruck, Austria
1968	Mexico City, Mexico	Grenoble, France
1972	Munich, West Germany	Sapporo, Japan
1976	Montreal, Canada	Innsbruck, Austria
1980	Moscow, Soviet Union	Lake Placid, U.S.
1984	Los Angeles, U.S.	Sarajevo, Yugoslavia
1988	Seoul, South Korea	Calgary, Canada
1992	Barcelona, Spain	Albertville, France
1994		Lillehammer, Norway
1996	Atlanta, U.S.	
1998		Nagano, Japan
2000	Sydney, Australia	
2002		Salt Lake City, U.S.

Paul J. Sutton, Duomo

The opening ceremonies of the Olympic Games feature the entry of the athletes into the stadium. Athletes from Greece enter first, followed by teams from the other countries.

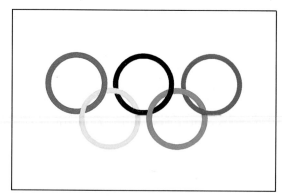

The Olympic symbol consists of five interlocking rings that represent Africa, Asia, Australia, Europe, and the Americas.

Olympic expenses. The IOC also provides financial aid. The United States is the only large nation whose government does not give its team financial support. The U.S. team is largely financed by contributions from private corporations and individuals.

Selection of the athletes. In many countries, athletes qualify for the Olympics by winning or finishing high in competitions called *selection trials*. In most cases, athletes are invited to the trials based on their performance in national and international competitions.

An athlete representing a country must be a citizen of that country. For many years, only amateur athletes competed in the games. This gave an advantage to wealthy athletes who could devote all their time to training without worrying about earning money. Professional athletes are now eligible to compete in most Olympic sports. Exceptions include baseball and boxing.

Entries. In most Olympic sports, a nation may enter as many as three competitors in each event as long as the athletes meet a minimum standard set by the international governing body of that sport. Team sports are limited to 8 to 16 teams per sport. National teams must win or place high in qualifying tournaments to make the final competition. The host country is allowed to enter a team in every team event.

Medals. The top three finishers in each event receive a medal and a diploma. The next five finishers get only a diploma. Each first-place winner receives a gold medal, which is actually made of silver and coated with gold. The second-place medal is made of silver, and the third-place medal is bronze. The design for the medal changes for each Olympics. All members of a winning relay team get a medal, including those who participated only in qualifying rounds. In team sports, all the members of a winning team who have played in at least one of the games during the competition receive a medal.

The top three finishers receive their medals in a ceremony after the event. The medal winners stand at attention on a platform, with the gold medalist in the middle.

Manny Millan, *Sports Illustrated*

The Olympic flame is lit during the opening ceremonies. The fire is ignited in Olympia, Greece, and transported by relay to the site of the games. The flame symbolizes the light of spirit, knowledge, and life, and it is a herald of peace.

David Black

The medal ceremony takes place after the finals of each event. The top three finishers receive a medal and a diploma. They stand at attention on a platform while the flags of their countries are raised and a band plays the national anthem of the country of the gold medal winner.

The silver medalist stands on the gold medalist's right and the bronze medalist on the left. The flags of their countries are raised, and a band plays the national anthem of the country of the gold medal winner.

Olympic competition is intended to test the skill of individuals and teams, not nations. Therefore, the IOC does not keep an official score among the nations. No country "wins" the Olympics. However, unofficial medal totals are compiled for the press and the public.

The Summer Games

The Summer Games are held during the summer season of the host city, usually between July and October, and last 16 days. Athletes compete in more than 270 separate events during the Summer Games. A sport must be played in at least 75 countries on four continents before it can be considered for men's competition. To be eligible for women's competition, a sport must be played in 40 countries on three continents.

The Summer Games have grown enormously. In the first modern games in 1896, about 311 male athletes representing 13 nations competed. Today, more than 10,000 male and female athletes representing over 190 nations participate.

The closing ceremonies come after the end of the athletic competition. The ceremonies are marked by spectacle and conclude with the extinguishing of the Olympic flame.

Nathan Bilow, All Sport

The Winter Games

The Winter Games are usually held in February and last 16 days. A sport must be played in at least 25 countries on three continents to be considered. The Winter Olympics include over 60 events. The games attract approximately 2,000 athletes from about 60 countries.

The ancient games

Athletics played an important role in the religious festivals of ancient Greece. Historians believe the ancient Greeks first organized athletic games as part of funeral ceremonies for important people. This practice probably existed by the 1200's B.C. Later, games became part of religious festivals honoring the gods. Many Greek cities held festivals every two or four years.

Over time, four great religious festivals developed that brought together people from throughout the Greek world. These festivals were the Isthmian, Nemean, Pythian, and Olympic games. The Olympic Games, which ranked as the most important, honored Zeus, the king of the gods.

The first recorded Olympic contest took place in 776 B.C. at Olympia in western Greece. The first winner was Koroibos (also spelled Coroebus), a cook from Elis. The Olympic Games were held every four years. They were so important to the ancient Greeks that time was measured in *Olympiads,* the four-year intervals between games. The only event in the first 13 games was the *stadion,* a running race of 192 meters (210 yards). Through the years, longer running races were added.

Other types of competition became part of the ancient Olympics. In 708 B.C., wrestling and the pentathlon were added. The pentathlon was a combination of jumping, running, the discus throw, the javelin throw, and

wrestling. Boxing joined the program in 688 B.C., and the four-horse chariot race was added in 680 B.C. Horse racing was included in 648 B.C., as was the *pancratium* (also spelled *pankration*), a combination of boxing, wrestling, and kicking. Some unusual events were included in the Olympics, such as a race in armor, a chariot race called the *apene* in which two mules pulled the chariot, and a competition for trumpeters.

The ancient Olympics produced several famous champions. Milo of Kroton won the wrestling competition five times between 532 and 516 B.C., and Leonidas of Rhodes won three running races in each of four Olympics from 164 to 152 B.C.

The Romans conquered Greece during the 140's B.C., and the games soon lost their religious meaning. In A.D. 393, Emperor Theodosius I banned the games.

The modern games

The modern games begin. In 1875, a group of German archaeologists began to excavate the ruins of the stadium and temples of Olympia, which had been destroyed by an earthquake and buried by a landslide and floods. Their discoveries inspired Baron Pierre de Coubertin, a French educator, to organize a modern international Olympics. He first proposed the idea publicly in 1892. In 1894, the first IOC was formed.

The first modern Olympic Games were held in Athens, Greece, in 1896. The athletes competed in nine sports: (1) cycling, (2) fencing, (3) gymnastics, (4) lawn tennis, (5) shooting, (6) swimming, (7) track and field, (8) weightlifting, and (9) wrestling. James B. Connolly of the United States became the first modern Olympic champion, winning the triple jump (then known as the *hop, step, and jump*).

The games of 1900 and 1904 attracted little attention.

The 1900 Olympics were held as part of the Universal Exposition, a world's fair in Paris. Competition was spread out over five months. Attendance was poor, and some athletes did not even realize they had participated in the Olympics. The 1900 Olympics included the first competitions involving women, in lawn tennis and golf. The first women gold medalists were British tennis player Charlotte Cooper and American golfer Margaret Abbott. Poor attendance and other problems also plagued the 1904 Olympics, held as part of the Louisiana Purchase Exposition in St. Louis, Missouri.

In the early years of the Olympics, competitions were held in several sports that were later dropped. They included polo, croquet, tug of war, live pigeon shooting, the high jump on horseback, and a swimming obstacle race.

The Olympic movement might have died except for the *Intercalated,* or *Interim,* Games held in Athens in 1906. The IOC did not consider these games official. However, they were popular and held the movement together until the next official games in London in 1908. The most dramatic moment of the 1908 games came in the marathon. Dorando Pietri of Italy entered the stadium in first place but collapsed before reaching the finish line. Officials dragged Pietri across the finish line and declared him the winner, but he was later disqualified because he did not finish under his own power.

The 1912 Olympics in Stockholm, Sweden, were the first well-organized Olympic Games. The hero of Stockholm was Jim Thorpe, an American Indian who easily won the 10-event decathlon and the 5-event pentathlon. Thorpe's medals were taken away after it was discov-

ered that he had played baseball for a small salary before the games, making him a professional athlete and therefore ineligible for the Olympics. In 1982, the IOC voted to return the medals to Thorpe's family and put his name back in the record books as an Olympic champion.

Between the wars. The 1916 games were canceled because of World War I (1914-1918). The 1920 Olympics in Antwerp, Belgium, marked the first appearance of the great Finnish distance runner Paavo Nurmi. He competed in all three Olympics of the 1920's, winning nine gold medals.

Figure skating was included in the 1908 games, and both figure skating and ice hockey were part of the 1920 games. The first separate Winter Games took place in Chamonix, France, in 1924, with 281 men and 13 women representing 16 countries.

The 1924 Summer Games were held in Paris. One of the stars was American swimmer Johnny Weissmuller, who later became famous portraying Tarzan in motion pictures. Other famous athletes included British sprinters Harold Abrahams and Eric Liddell, later portrayed in the film *Chariots of Fire* (1981).

The 1928 Summer Games, held in Amsterdam, the Netherlands, were the first in which women competed in track and field. In the Winter Games in St. Moritz, Switzerland, Sonja Henie of Norway won her first gold medal in women's figure skating. She repeated as champion in the 1932 and 1936 Winter Games before becoming a star of Hollywood musicals.

The 1932 Summer Games were held in Los Angeles. These games introduced automatic timing for races and

Black-figure painting (about 530 B.C.) on a Greek vase; The Metropolitan Museum of Art, New York City, Rogers Fund, 1914

The ancient Olympic Games were held every four years in Olympia in western Greece. The first recorded games took place in 776 B.C. For the first 13 competitions, the only event was a running race for male athletes, *above,* of 192 meters (210 yards). Other events were added over the years.

the photo-finish camera. The first Olympic Village was also erected. The games produced the first U.S. female Olympic star, Babe Didrikson (later Babe Didrikson Zaharias). She qualified for five track and field events but was allowed to enter only three. She won the javelin throw and the hurdles race and finished second in the high jump.

In 1931, the IOC chose Berlin, Germany, as the site for the 1936 Summer Games and Garmisch-Partenkirchen, Germany, for the Winter Games. Two years later, Adolf Hitler and his Nazi Party rose to power in Germany. As Hitler's policies became known, there were pleas to move the Summer Games, but the IOC refused.

The Berlin games were the first to be preceded by a torch relay of the Olympic flame from Greece, and they were the first games to be shown on television. But the 1936 Summer Olympics are best remembered for Hitler's failed attempt to use them to prove his theory of racial superiority. The Nazis glorified the Germans and other northern European peoples, while claiming that Jews, blacks, and other groups were inferior. But the most successful athlete in the Summer Games was Jesse Owens, an African American who won four gold medals in track and field. The German spectators, ignoring Hitler's speeches against black people, treated Owens as their favorite hero of the games.

The postwar games. The Olympics scheduled for 1940 and 1944 were canceled because of World War II (1939-1945). The first postwar Summer Games were held in London in 1948 and the Winter Games again in St. Moritz. The most popular athlete in the Summer Games was Fanny Blankers-Koen of the Netherlands, a home-

Hulton Deutsch from All Sport

Jim Thorpe of the United States won the decathlon and pentathlon at the 1912 Summer Games. His medals were taken away after he was declared ineligible, but they were restored in 1982.

AP/Wide World

All Sport

Early women Olympic stars included Babe Didrikson of the United States and Sonja Henie of Norway. Didrikson, *running second from the left,* won the hurdles in the 1932 Summer Games. She also won the javelin throw and finished second in the high jump. Henie, *right,* won the gold medal in figure skating in 1928, 1932, and 1936, the only woman to win the event three times.

maker who won four gold medals in track and field. A star of the Winter Games was Dick Button of the United States, who won the gold medal in figure skating, an achievement he repeated in the 1952 games. Barbara Ann Scott of Canada won the women's figure-skating title, becoming the first Canadian figure skater to win an Olympic gold medal.

Athletes from the Soviet Union made their first Olympic appearance in the 1952 Summer Games in Helsinki, Finland. By the 1956 games, Soviet athletes were winning more medals than the athletes of any other country. In Helsinki, Emil Zátopek of Czechoslovakia became the only runner to win the 5,000 meters, 10,000 meters, and marathon races in the same Olympics.

The 1956 Summer Games were held in Melbourne, Australia, the first to be held in the Southern Hemisphere. Because of Australian quarantine laws concerning horses, the equestrian events were staged separately in Stockholm. In the weeks preceding the Melbourne games, Israel invaded Egypt and Soviet troops invaded Hungary. These actions led to the first boycotts of the modern Olympics. Egypt, Iraq, and Lebanon withdrew to protest the Israeli take-over of the Suez Canal. The Netherlands and Spain boycotted to protest the Soviet invasion.

The 1960 Winter Games at Squaw Valley in California and the Summer Games in Rome were the first to be televised to the United States. The track and field stars of the Summer Games included American sprinter Wilma Rudolph and marathon winner Abebe Bikila of Ethiopia, the first black African to win a gold medal. American boxer Cassius Clay won the light heavyweight gold medal. He later gained international fame as professional boxer Muhammad Ali.

In 1964, the Summer Games were held in Tokyo, the first Asian city to serve as host. Ukrainian gymnast Larissa Latynina won six medals. In her career, she won a record 18 Olympic medals. The Tokyo games were the last Summer Games for more than 20 years to be free of major controversy.

The 1968 games. The 1968 Summer Games were held in Mexico City during a period of political turmoil throughout the world. The most controversial episode took place during the medal ceremony for the men's 200-meter dash. The gold and bronze medals were won by African American sprinters Tommie Smith and John Carlos. To protest what they considered to be racism in the United States, both athletes bowed their heads and raised clenched fists during the playing of the U.S. national anthem. At the insistence of the IOC, the U.S. Olympic Committee suspended both men from the Olympic team and ordered them to leave the Olympic Village.

Mexico City's high altitude was disastrous for athletes in long-distance races and other endurance events, but it contributed to world records in many other contests. The most famous record was 29 feet $2\frac{1}{2}$ inches (8.90 meters) in the long jump, set by Bob Beamon of the United States. The jump became a new world record that lasted for 23 years.

The 1968 Winter Games in Grenoble, France, produced one of the great Olympic heroes of the 1960's. French skier Jean-Claude Killy won three gold medals and became an international celebrity.

Wide World

Jesse Owens of the United States was the hero of the 1936 Summer Games. Owens won four gold medals in track and field.

Terrorism in Munich. The 1972 Summer Games were held in Munich, in what was then West Germany. The Munich Olympics are remembered for the events of September 5. Eight Palestinian terrorists broke into the Olympic Village and entered the dormitory of the Israeli team. They killed two Israelis and took nine hostages, demanding the release of more than 200 Arab prisoners in Israel. During a battle with West German sharpshooters, all the Israeli hostages were killed, along with five terrorists and one policeman.

The highlight of the competition was swimmer Mark Spitz of the United States, who won seven gold medals. The Soviet Union also won a controversial victory over the U.S. men's basketball team in the championship game. The Americans led by 1 point when the buzzer sounded to end the game. But the officials twice ordered the game to continue, first for 1 second and then for 3 seconds more, enabling the Soviet team to score the winning basket.

Boycotts. The 1976 Summer Games, held in Montreal, Canada, were hit by a boycott led by Tanzania. More than 20 African nations and 2 other countries refused to compete. The boycotters demanded that New Zealand be banned from competition because a New Zealand rugby team had toured South Africa. At that time, South Africa had a white-controlled government that enforced a policy of rigid racial segregation called *apartheid*. South Africa was barred from the Olympics because of its racial policies, but the IOC said it had little control over the travel of rugby teams because rugby was not an Olympic sport.

In spite of the absence of hundreds of top athletes, the 1976 games were filled with outstanding performances. A 14-year old gymnast from Romania named Nadia Comaneci caused a sensation by earning the first perfect score of 10 ever awarded in the Olympics. She eventually earned seven scores of 10 and won three gold medals.

AP/Wide World

Controversy erupted in 1968 when American sprinters Tommie Smith, *center,* and John Carlos raised clenched fists at a medal ceremony to protest what they considered to be racism.

The 1980 Summer Games in Moscow were disrupted by another boycott, this one led by U.S. President Jimmy Carter. The boycott protested the Soviet Union's 1979 invasion of Afghanistan. Carter urged other nations to join the boycott, and about 55 nations stayed away as part of the protest.

The 1980 Winter Games in Lake Placid, New York, were among the most exciting in history. Eric Heiden won all five speed-skating races, setting an Olympic or world record in each race. He became the first athlete to win five individual gold medals in one Olympics. Mark Spitz had won three of his seven gold medals as a member of a winning relay team.

Also at the 1980 Winter Games, the United States ice hockey team won an unexpected gold medal in that effort. The American team upset the Soviet Union team in an emotional semifinal match and then defeated Finland in the finals.

The games returned to Los Angeles in 1984. With the games being held in the United States, the Soviet Union launched a revenge boycott. Only 13 countries joined the boycott, but they included such sports powers as Bulgaria, East Germany, Cuba, and Hungary. Among the sports that lost most of their medal favorites were weightlifting, wrestling, gymnastics, women's swim-

ming, and women's track and field. However, China competed in the Olympics for the first time in more than 30 years. China was led by the popular gymnast Li Ning, who won six medals. United States track and field star Carl Lewis matched Jesse Owens's 1936 feat of winning four gold medals.

Charges of steroid use. The 1988 Summer Games were held in Seoul, South Korea, and were boycotted by North Korea and Cuba. Instead of political controversy, disputes over the use of drugs called *anabolic steroids* marked the 1988 games. Anabolic steroids are artificial forms of male hormones used to increase strength and weight. Their use is banned in Olympic competition. Since 1968, the IOC has tested athletes for steroids and other performance-enchancing drugs.

In the 1988 Olympics, Ben Johnson of Canada defeated Carl Lewis in the 100-meter dash and set a world record. Three days later, the IOC announced that Johnson had tested positive for steroids and was disqualified. Lewis was awarded the gold medal, thus becoming the first man to win the 100-meter dash twice. He also won the long jump for the second time. Other notable performers were swimmers Matt Biondi of the United States, who won five gold medals, and Kristin Otto of East Germany, who won six.

In the 1988 Winter Games in Calgary, Canada, Katarina Witt of East Germany won the women's figure-skating title. Witt also had won the event in 1984. She was the first woman to repeat as champion since Sonja Henie.

The recent games. The 1992 Summer Games in Barcelona, Spain, reflected the breakup of the Soviet Union and the collapse of Communist governments in Eastern Europe. Germany entered a unified team representing the former countries of East and West Germany. The Baltic states of Estonia, Latvia, and Lithuania, previously part of the Soviet Union, competed as separate nations. Russia and other former Soviet republics competed as the Unified Team. However, when athletes from the Unified Team won a medal, they were honored by the raising of the flag of their own republic and by the playing of their own national anthem. South Africa, which had ended apartheid, rejoined the Olympics and competed for the first time since 1960.

The 1992 Olympics also marked the first time that professional basketball players were eligible for the competition. This rule change led to the creation of a U.S. "Dream Team" that included Magic Johnson, Larry Bird, Michael Jordan, Charles Barkley, and other stars of the National Basketball Association. The American team easily won the gold medal.

Speed-skater Bonnie Blair was a star of the Winter Games of 1988, 1992, and 1994. She won five gold medals and a bronze medal in the three games. She became the first American woman to win gold medals in consecutive Winter Games.   David Wallechinsky

Related articles. *World Book* has separate articles on many Olympic sports, including gymnastics, ice skating, swimming, and track and field. See also the following:

Blair, Bonnie	Olympiad
Comaneci, Nadia	Owens, Jesse
Horse (Horse shows and sports)	Rudolph, Wilma
Joyner-Kersee, Jackie	Scott, Barbara Ann
Lewis, Carl	Thorpe, Jim
Olympia	Zaharias, Babe Didrikson

Ron Garrison, Zoological Society of San Diego

A zoo gives people a chance to see many kinds of animals they might never see otherwise. Many zoos keep their animals in spacious outdoor and indoor exhibits, and offer visitors guided tours. At the San Diego Zoo, *above,* zoogoers can tour the zoo in special double-decker buses.

Zoo

Zoo is a place where people keep and display animals. Visiting zoos is a popular recreational and educational activity throughout the world. Almost every large city has at least one zoo, and many smaller communities also have one. Many zoos have beautiful gardens and tree-lined paths leading from one animal display to another. The word *zoo* is short for *zoological garden.*

Zoos vary in the type of animals they keep. Many large zoos keep mammals, birds, reptiles, and fish from all over the world. Some even have collections of inter-esting insects. Smaller zoos may have animals from just one part of the world, or just one type of animal. Zoos that have only fish and *aquatic mammals,* which live in water, are called *aquariums.* Some zoos display only ani-mals from the region where the zoo is located.

Jack Hanna, the contributor of this article, is the Director of the Columbus Zoological Gardens in Ohio and the author of several children's books about animals and zoos. He frequently appears on television shows to increase public awareness of wildlife and conservation.

Zoos range in size from hundreds of acres or hec-tares to only a few. But size alone does not determine the quality or importance of a zoo. The best zoos are those that have healthy, well-tended animals and dis-plays that help visitors learn about each animal's natural behavior and its role in the environment.

Modern zoos have become refuges for some *species* (types) of animals that are in danger of *extinction* (dying out) in the wild. Many human activities threaten the sur-vival of wild species, especially the destruction of *habi-tats* (natural environments). Most animals are specially suited to live in a certain environment and cannot sur-vive when their habitat is destroyed. Zoos are becoming increasingly active in the struggle to save the world's vanishing wildlife.

The importance of zoos

Zoos are important centers for (1) recreation and edu-cation, (2) wildlife conservation, and (3) scientific studies.

Recreation and education. People of all ages enjoy viewing animals they would probably never see other-

Michael Nichols, Magnum

At a children's zoo, youngsters can touch and sometimes even feed a variety of animals. Two girls pet a reptile in the children's zoo at the Audubon Park Zoo, *above,* in New Orleans.

wise. In the United States and Canada, zoos attract millions of visitors every year. Zoos also help people understand how animals live. In addition, zoos teach people about the problems facing wildlife and about conservation.

In many zoos, trained workers give visitors brief talks and provide guided tours. Many zoos have education departments that conduct lectures, classes, and group programs for children and adults. Some zoos offer summer day camps and junior zookeeper programs that give youngsters opportunities to help care for the animals. In addition, zoos publish magazines, pamphlets, and other materials that describe their activities. Some zoos even produce television programs.

Wildlife conservation has become one of the most important jobs of zoos. Zoos breed many endangered species to increase their numbers. Such captive breeding in zoos has helped save several species from extinction, including the European bison; the *nene,* also known as the Hawaiian goose; and the Arabian *oryx,* a type of antelope.

Zoos throughout the world trade and lend animals to one another to avoid *inbreeding* (breeding animals that are closely related to each other). Inbreeding can produce birth defects and can eventually weaken an entire population. A number of zoo associations share breeding information through the International Species Information System (ISIS), a computerized inventory of more than 200,000 animals cared for by zoos throughout the world. ISIS also maintains records on the ancestors of the animals to more accurately track the genetic background of the living animals.

The American Zoo and Aquarium Association sponsors the Species Survival Plan (SSP), a long-term plan to save some of the most seriously endangered species. Many major zoos in the United States and other countries participate in the SSP. There are dozens of SSP programs, each focusing on a different species or group of species. Participating zoos keep careful records of each animal's family lines and physical characteristics. Zoos use this information to determine which males and females to breed together. The goal is to develop healthy

populations of animals that can someday be returned to the wild.

Zoos also participate in conservation projects outside their walls. For example, many zoos sponsor efforts to preserve the natural habitats of threatened species, such as the Asian bamboo forests of the giant panda and the South American tropical rain forests of the *lion tamarin,* a species of small monkey.

Scientific studies. Zoos provide scientists with living laboratories in which to study animals. By treating diseased animals and by studying animals that have died, zoo veterinarians and other scientists have developed and improved medical equipment, drugs, and surgical techniques for animals.

Scientists called *zoologists* study animals in zoos, as well as in the wild, to learn about animal behavior, such as hunting, eating, breeding, and caring for the young. Such research helps zoos know how to better care for their animals and how to make their exhibits as natural as possible. This knowledge is especially important for breeding because many animals will only reproduce if they are healthy and living in natural surroundings.

Scientific progress in breeding techniques has greatly reduced the need to move animals from zoo to zoo for mating. Researchers can freeze the sperm and embryos of various species. The frozen material can be shipped to another zoo for use in *artificial insemination,*

WORLD BOOK photo

Tigers and deer at the Milwaukee County Zoo live in areas that are side-by-side. A deep moat, which visitors cannot see, prevents the tigers from attacking the deer.

embryo transfer, and other breeding techniques (see **Breeding** [Animal breeding]).

Displaying animals

In the past, zoos kept their animals in rows of mostly bare cages made of concrete and steel bars. Often, the cages were arranged in no particular order.

Today, animal displays are far different. Zoos have replaced most old-fashioned cages with natural-looking enclosures that give animals greater liberty to lead normal lives. Both the layout of the zoo and the design of the exhibits teach visitors about animals.

Layout of a zoo. Many zoos group their animals mostly by type. For example, lions, tigers, and other large cats may be kept in the same building or in nearby outdoor exhibits. Animals from similar climates, such as warm tropical areas or chilly polar regions, are often housed together. Zoos also group animals by the continent where they naturally live, such as Africa or Asia. Another grouping method is by the animals' natural habitat, such as the East African *savanna* (grassland with scattered trees) or the Australian desert. In habitat groupings, many animals appear to be living together. However, animals that would attack each other are kept apart by empty *moats* (deep, wide pits) or by hidden fences.

Many zoos contain a *children's zoo,* where boys and girls can pet and even feed tame animals. Some children's zoos give city youngsters an opportunity to see farm animals. Many children's zoos feature baby animals.

Exhibits. Most modern exhibits, both indoors and outdoors, are *naturalistic*—that is, they resemble the animal's natural habitat. Such exhibits contain rock formations, pools, grass, trees, shrubs, and places for the animals to take shelter or hide. Heating coils may be concealed in artificial rocks or trees to attract the animals to locations where they can be seen by visitors.

Many animals become bored if they have nothing to do. To combat boredom, exhibits may provide climbing structures and toys that encourage active behavior. Giant ice cubes keep polar bears occupied. Rhinoceroses and elephants seem to enjoy rolling in shallow pools of mud. In addition, keepers often hide meals in shrubs, trees, and other places so that the animals must search for the food just as they would in the wild. A stimulating environment is especially important to apes, elephants, and other intelligent species. In some zoos, chimpanzees may keep busy for hours probing artificial termite mounds filled with honey, cereal, or other treats.

Barriers. Zoos use a variety of barriers to keep animals in their exhibits. One widely used naturalistic barrier is a moat surrounding the display area. Moats enable zoos to safely keep bears, lions, tigers, and other large animals in spacious outdoor settings.

Zoos also use barriers that are almost invisible, such as glass or a net of thin wire. Through underwater viewing windows, visitors can watch such animals as polar bears and hippopotamuses swimming or observe beavers building a dam. A zoo may cover a huge bird shelter, complete with trees and plants, with a wire net.

Controlled environments. Indoor exhibits enable zoos to reproduce the environmental conditions that some animals need to stay healthy. For example, pen-

Interesting facts about zoo animals

A polar bear's coat sometimes looks green instead of white. Each hair of a polar bear's coat is hollow. The air in the middle of each hair helps keep the bear warm. Sometimes, green *algae* (simple plantlike organisms) grow in the hollows and the green color shows through.

A giraffe's tongue is up to 21 inches (53 centimeters) long. A giraffe uses its tongue to reach high into trees for leaves and tender branches. The outer part of the tongue is purplish-blue. The dark pigment may help protect the tongue from sunburn.

WORLD BOOK illustration by Colin Newman, Bernard Thornton Artists

The fierce-looking gorilla is actually a gentle, peaceful animal. A gorilla will not hurt a human being unless the gorilla or its family is threatened or attacked. The animal's ferocious "King-Kong" reputation is just a movie myth.

An elephant uses its trunk as a human being uses hands and arms. An elephant's trunk has about 40,000 muscles. It is strong enough to lift a 600-pound (270-kilogram) log. Yet the tip of the trunk has enough flexibility to grasp a single peanut.

Snakes in zoos sometimes eat only once a month. Their meals last a long time because snakes, which are cold-blooded, do not use much food energy to maintain a steady body temperature. The bodies of cold-blooded animals are warm when their surroundings are warm, and cool when their surroundings are cool. Also, snakes use little energy because they stay inactive for long periods and live off their body fat.

Flamingos need a special diet to maintain the bright pink and red colors of their feathers. In zoos, these birds may receive reddish foods such as shrimp and sometimes even liquid red dye.

When a dolphin dives, its lungs collapse and its heart beats slower. These actions allow the animal's body to adjust to the increasing pressure of the water as the dolphin dives deeper.

WORLD BOOK illustration by Colin Newman, Bernard Thornton Artists

guins from the Antarctic need cold air. Other creatures may require moist air, dry air, or regular rain showers.

One special indoor exhibit is for *nocturnal* animals, which are active at night. Zoos display such nocturnal animals as owls, bats, and raccoons under a blue light or other dim light, which seems like darkness to the animals. But visitors can clearly see the animals going about their normal nighttime activities. At night, a bright light causes the animals to sleep as if it were day.

With modern technology, a number of zoos have created vast enclosures that imitate scorching deserts, frigid polar regions, and other natural habitats. Such exhibits house a variety of mammals, fish, birds, reptiles,

An underwater viewing window enables zoogoers to observe the activities and graceful movements of fish and aquatic mammals beneath the water. At the left, a woman meets a nurse shark close-up in a viewing tunnel at the Sydney Aquarium in Australia.

Sydney Aquarium

and insects that would naturally live in the environment. A number of zoos, for example, have large indoor exhibits that reproduce steamy tropical rain forests. These exhibits house trees, cliffs, and waterfalls in structures several stories tall. Machines produce a foglike mist. Elevated walkways allow zoogoers to stroll among the treetops and view several types of primates, birds, and other animals that live in the trees.

Cageless zoos. Drive-through zoos keep their animals in outdoor settings without cages, though predators and prey are kept apart. Visitors view the animals while riding through the zoo in their automobile or aboard a bus or a train.

Wild-animal parks resemble drive-through zoos because the animals are not caged. But these parks are larger than most drive-through zoos and are more interested in breeding animals, especially endangered species, than in exhibiting them. Such parks provide the natural surroundings many animals need to mate successfully and raise offspring. The San Diego Wild Animal Park, the first such establishment in the United States, opened in 1972. In this enormous zoo, which covers about 2,200 acres (900 hectares), groups of rhinoceroses, giraffes, deer, antelope, zebras, and many other species roam over large areas under the close watch of zoo workers. Visitors ride a special train that travels through the park. The train's route skirts the areas where animals live, thus disturbing the herds as little as possible.

Caring for zoo animals

Zoo animals receive daily care, special diets, and regular medical attention.

Daily care. Trained workers called *keepers* take care of the animals' daily needs. In large zoos, each keeper usually looks after just one type of animal. The keepers clean the animals' enclosures. They feed the animals and watch for changes in behavior, eating habits, and overall appearance that may be signs that an animal is sick or injured. Keepers also provide companionship for the animals. Many types of animals, including monkeys and apes, become fond of their keepers and develop special relationships with them.

Diet. An appropriate diet is vital in keeping zoo animals healthy. The kinds and amounts of food different creatures require vary greatly.

Zoo kitchens stock a wide assortment of basic foods, including fruits, vegetables, meat, fish, dairy products, cereals, seeds, grains, and hay. They also have such unusual items as rats, mice, brine shrimp, crickets, worms, and snakes. Many animals enjoy grazing on the leaves of freshly cut branches. In addition, zoos use large quantities of prepared pellets, seed mixes, and other foods made especially for animals. Zoos also use vitamins and mineral supplements to ensure a nutritious diet for each animal.

Some animals require exactly the type of food they would eat in the wild. For example, koalas will eat only certain kinds of eucalyptus leaves. Giant pandas must have bamboo. Zoos ship in these foods from wherever they are grown or grow the foods themselves.

In zoo kitchens, keepers, nutritionists, and other trained workers prepare balanced meals for each animal in whatever form the animal will eat. Some animals eat their food just as it comes. But for many animals, zoo workers must peel, chop, combine, and even cook foods. Some animals, including certain birds and small mammals, eat several meals each day. Other animals, such as some species of snakes, eat only once every few weeks.

A zoo animal's diet varies under certain circumstances. For example, pregnant females and mothers nursing their young require special food. Animals may also need special diets for gaining or losing weight, for breeding, or for health problems.

Some zoos sell food pellets that visitors may distribute to certain animals. The zoo controls the amount of food provided so the animals are not overfed. Except for such pellets, visitors should not feed zoo animals. Candy, popcorn, and similar foods can make an animal sick. Thoughtless visitors often throw wrappers or other trash to the animals. If an animal swallows this trash, it could become ill and might even die.

Medical care. Most large zoos employ one or more full-time veterinarians. Smaller zoos often have part-time veterinarians. The doctor visits regularly and treats sick or injured creatures. Many animals receive routine vaccinations to protect them from diseases.

Before examining or treating an animal, the doctor may inject the animal with tranquilizers or drugs that temporarily paralyze the patient. After the drugs take effect, the doctor can examine and treat the animal without danger of injury to either the doctor or the animal.

Many large zoos have their own hospitals with operating rooms, X-ray machines, and laboratories. Some zoos have *quarantine* areas where newly acquired animals or those with contagious diseases are kept apart from the other animals to prevent the spread of disease.

How zoos operate

Many zoos are owned and operated by local governments. Some zoos are owned by individuals or nonprofit corporations. In the United States, zoos must be licensed by the U.S. Department of Agriculture.

In the United States and Canada, a number of zoos are members of the American Zoo and Aquarium Association. The association requires its members to maintain high standards of animal care and management. All member institutions must pass an inspection every five years.

Funding. Zoo operations are funded by several sources. Many zoos receive funds from local governments. Most zoos charge admission fees. Other money comes from food and gift shop sales, fund-raising events, donations, "adopt-an-animal" programs, membership fees, and grants from foundations and corporations.

Zoo workers. A zoo is similar to a small town and needs many types of workers to operate smoothly. A *director* is the head of the zoo. A *curator* manages the care of zoo animals and supervises the people who work with the animals. Large zoos may have more than one curator, each overseeing a particular group of animals. Keepers take care of the animals, and veterinarians provide medical care. Zoo scientists study the animals and do research.

Most zoo jobs that involve working with animals require a college degree. Keepers and curators often study biology or zoology. Zoo scientists usually have training in such fields as animal behavior, genetics, anthropology, nutrition, reproductive science, or veterinary technology. Some veterinary schools offer training

Michael Nichols, Magnum

An indoor rain forest exhibit at the Henry Doorly Zoo in Omaha, Nebraska, re-creates the vegetation and humid climate of a tropical rain forest inside an eight-story structure. Visitors stroll among the treetops on elevated walkways and view primates, birds, and other animals.

in wild-animal medicine. Some zoos provide internships for students at the graduate and undergraduate levels.

Many people who have jobs at zoos do not work directly with the animals. Large numbers of employees are involved in administration, office work, fund-raising, security, and maintaining the grounds and buildings. In addition, zoos may rely on volunteer workers to sweep sidewalks, help keepers watch animals, guide tours, and perform many other important jobs.

Obtaining animals. Most zoo animals are born in captivity. An increasingly small number of zoo animals are captured in the wild by hunters.

A zoo's director and curators usually decide which animals the zoo needs. Zoos often get animals to fill a gap in their collection, such as when an animal dies. To obtain animals, zoos deal directly with one another, buying, trading, or lending stock. Zoos also buy animals from professional animal dealers. The American Zoo and Aquarium Association and animal dealers circulate lists of what each zoo needs and what species are available.

The United States government severely restricts the importing of many animals, especially endangered species and those that may transmit diseases. Animals that enter the United States from zoos outside the country or from the wild must be *quarantined* (kept in isolation) for a time to be sure they are disease-free.

When an animal first comes to a zoo, it must adjust to its new keepers, its exhibit mates, and its surroundings. Keepers watch the newcomers carefully so that they do not hurt themselves or harm other animals.

History

Early zoos. People have put wild animals on display since ancient times. One of the earliest known zoos was established by Queen Hatshepsut of Egypt about 1500 B.C. About 500 years later, the Chinese emperor Wen Wang founded the Garden of Intelligence, an enormous zoo that covered nearly 1,500 acres (610 hectares). Between 1000 and 400 B.C., rulers in northern Africa, India, and China established many small zoos that were designed to display their wealth and power.

In ancient Greece, rulers and nobles kept private zoos for their own enjoyment. Scholars visited such zoos to study the animals. The Romans also had many private zoos. In addition, the Romans kept a large collection of wild animals used in bloody fights in large outdoor theaters such as the Colosseum. During the Middle Ages, from about A.D. 400 to 1500, many European rulers and nobles maintained private zoos.

By the end of the 1400's, global exploration and an increased interest in learning promoted the popularity of zoos in Europe. Explorers returned from the New World with strange creatures for European zoos. In 1519, Spanish explorers discovered a huge zoo built by the Aztec Indians in what is now Mexico.

During the next 250 years, several zoos were established in Europe. Some of them were merely small exhibits called *menageries.* These consisted of a few bears, lions, or tigers kept in small, gloomy cages or in pits. Only the nobility were allowed to visit most of these exhibits.

The first modern zoos. Over the years, menageries were replaced by larger collections of animals that received better care. These facilities not only displayed animals but also served as centers of research. They developed into the first modern zoos.

The oldest zoo still in existence is the Schönbrunn Zoo, which was founded in Vienna, Austria, in 1752. The Madrid Zoo in Spain was established in 1775. The Paris Zoo, the third oldest zoo in continuous operation, dates from 1793. The Berlin Zoo, which became a leader in research on animal behavior, opened in Germany in 1844.

The development of zoos in the United States began

Jim Tuten, Earth Scenes

Inside a zoo kitchen, trained workers peel, chop, combine, and even cook foods for the animals. Zoo kitchens stock a wide variety of fruits, vegetables, seeds, and many other types of foods. Each animal receives nutritionally balanced meals.

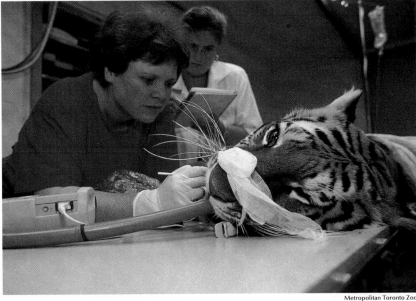

Regular medical treatment helps keep zoo animals healthy. At the left, a veterinarian gives a Siberian tiger a dental checkup. Before an examination, doctors often tranquilize the animal to eliminate the danger of injury to either the medical personnel or the animal.

Metropolitan Toronto Zoo

with the chartering of the Philadelphia Zoological Society in 1859. But the American Civil War (1861-1865) delayed construction of the zoo, which did not open until 1874. In 1889, Congress established the National Zoological Park in Washington, D.C. This zoo is the only one that is operated by the United States government. In Canada, the first zoo opened in Halifax, Nova Scotia, in 1847.

The evolution of zoos. In 1907, Karl Hagenbeck, a German animal dealer and zoo owner, developed the moat technique of displaying animals. The idea gradually spread to zoos throughout the world, improving the life of zoo animals and the experiences of visitors. Zoos began replacing barred cages with larger, more natural enclosures. The first children's zoo in the United States opened at the Philadelphia Zoo in 1938.

By the 1940's, zoologists recognized that many species of animals faced extinction in the wild. Zoos realized they could help preserve some of these species and began developing the first breeding programs. Before this time, most zoos had tried to display at least one member of as many different species as possible. Few zoos owned more than one or two animals of a rare species. Today, many zoos keep family groups and breeding populations.

Current issues. Some animal welfare groups criticize the treatment of animals in zoos. Some people are especially opposed to keeping large sea mammals, such as whales and dolphins, in captivity. They claim that these creatures fare poorly even under the best zoo conditions. Some animal rights activists call for all zoos to be shut down. They believe people have no right to keep animals in captivity.

Zoo officials stress the importance of zoos in conservation and science. They agree that substandard zoos should improve their treatment of animals but point out that many zoos meet high standards of care.

Jack Hanna

Related articles in *World Book* include:

Aquarium (Public aquariums)	Veterinary medicine
Endangered species	Wildlife conservation
National Zoological Park	Zoology

Outline

I. The importance of zoos
    A. Recreation and education
    B. Wildlife conservation
    C. Scientific studies

II. Displaying animals
    A. Layout of a zoo   C. Cageless zoos
    B. Exhibits

III. Caring for zoo animals
    A. Daily care   C. Medical care
    B. Diet

IV. How zoos operate
    A. Funding   C. Obtaining animals
    B. Zoo workers

V. History

Questions

What is an aquarium?
What are some ways that zoos help conserve wildlife?
Why do zoos try to prevent inbreeding among their animals?
How have zoos changed in the way they display their animals?
How do zoos help keep their animals amused?
What is the job of a zoo *curator*? Of a *keeper*?
What are some ways that zoos keep animals in their exhibits?
What is the oldest zoo in the United States?
What are some animals that zoos have saved from extinction?
Where does a zoo get new animals?

Additional resources

Benyus, Janine M. *Beastly Behaviors: A Zoo Lover's Companion.* Addison-Wesley, 1992.
Bostock, Stephen S. *Zoos and Animal Rights: The Ethics of Keeping Animals.* Routledge, 1993.
Curtis, Patricia. *Animals and the New Zoos.* Lodestar, 1991. Younger readers.
Nyhuis, Allen W. *The Zoo Book: A Guide to America's Best.* Carousel Pr., 1994.
Smith, Roland. *Inside the Zoo Nursery.* Cobblehill, 1993. Younger readers.

Index

How to use the index

This index covers the contents of the 1994, 1995, and 1996 editions of *The World Book Year Book.*

Each index entry gives the edition year and the page number or numbers—for example, **Nuclear energy, 96:** 212. This means that information on this topic may be found on page 212 of the 1996 *Year Book.*

When there are many references to a topic, they are grouped alphabetically by clue words under the main topic. For example, the clue words under **Nuclear weapons** group the references to that topic under numerous subtopics.

When a topic such as **OCEAN** appears in all capital letters, this means that there is a *Year Book* Update article entitled Ocean in at least one of the three volumes covered by this index. References to the topic in other articles may also appear after the topic name.

When only the first letter of a topic, such as **Okinawa, Japan,** is capitalized, this means that there is no article entitled Okinawa, Japan, but that information on this topic may be found in the edition and on the pages listed.

An index entry followed by *WBE* refers to a new or revised *World Book Encyclopedia* article in the supplement section, as in **OLYMPIC GAMES, 96:** 503. This means that a *World Book Encyclopedia* article on the Olympic Games begins on page 503 of the 1996 *Year Book.*

The indication (il.) means that the reference on this page is to an illustration only, as in the **Ono, Yoko** picture on page 335 of the 1996 edition.

The "see" and "see also" cross references—for example, **Opera.** See **Classical music**—refer the reader to other entries in the index.

Index

Index

Index

Index

Index

Index

Index

Index

Index

Acknowledgments

The publishers acknowledge the following sources for illustrations. Credits read from top to bottom, left to right, on their respective pages. An asterisk (*) denotes illustrations and photographs that are the exclusive property of *The Year Book*. All maps, charts, and diagrams were prepared by *The Year Book* staff unless otherwise noted.

6 Sovfoto/Eastfoto; AP/Wide World
7 A. B. Dowsett/Science Source from Photo Researchers; AP/Wide World
8 Chris & Sam K.; Markel, Gamma/FSP; AP/Wide World
9 Reuters/Archive Photos; Noboru Hashimoto, Sygma
10 AP/Wide World
12 Noboru Hashimoto, Sygma; AP/Wide World
13 Focus on Sports
14 Wim Ruigrok, Sygma
15 Reuters/Bettmann
16-17 AP/Wide World
18 Chris & Sam K.
20 Patrick Landmann, Gamma/Liaison
21 D. Aubert/Sygma
22 Reuters/Bettmann
23 AFP/Bettmann; NASA
24-29 AP/Wide World
30 Larry Downing, Sygma
31 AP/Wide World
32 Andy Hernandez, Gamma/Liaison
34 Ron Haviv, Saba
36 AP/Wide World
39 Frank Spooner, Gamma/Liaison
41 Louise Gubb, NYT Pictures
47 Agence France-Presse
48 R. J. Clarke; Dan Swanson, Van Garde Imagery*
49 AP/Wide World
50 Barry Iverson, *Time* Magazine; AP/Wide World
51 AP/Wide World
53 Hiroshi Ueda
54 Reuters/Bettmann
56 Agence France-Presse
59 Reuters/Bettmann
60 Reuters/Bettmann
64 Space Telescope Science Institute/NASA
67-76 AP/Wide World
78 John Biever, *Sports Illustrated*
81 California Polytechnic State University
82 Art Zamur, Gamma/Liaison
85 Reuters/Bettmann
87 Gilles Bassignac, Gamma/Liaison
88 Noboru Hashimoto, Sygma; Gary Williams, Gamma/Liaison; Dan Swanson, Van Garde Imagery*
91 Dan Swanson, Van Garde Imagery*
92 AP/Wide World; Dan Swanson, Van Garde Imagery*
93 Chitrakar, Sipa Press; Dan Swanson, Van Garde Imagery*
94 Noboru Hashimoto, Sygma; *Modern Steel Construction*; Dan Swanson, Van Garde Imagery*
95 Joe Samberg
97 Earthquake Engineering Research Institute; Dan Swanson, Van Garde Imagery*
98 Su Brodsky, Southern Stock Photo; Dan Swanson, Van Garde Imagery*

99-100 Dan Swanson, Van Garde Imagery*
102-106 AP/Wide World
109 Canapress
112 Reuters/Bettmann
114 Gerard Kwiatkowski
116 *Halifax Daily News*
118 Canapress
122 Bob Horsch Gallery Ltd.
123-130 AP/Wide World
132 Matt Herron, Black Star
133 Louis Mematteis, JB Pictures
136 UPI/Bettmann; Sygma
142 Andy Sacks, Tony Stone Images
146 Reuters/Bettmann
148 *Calvin & Hobbes*© 1922 Watterson. Dist. by Universal Press Syndicate. Reprinted with permission. All rights reserved.
149 Richard D. Olson Collection, Ohio State University Cartoon Research Library
150-157 ©King Features Syndicate. Reprinted with special permission
158 Reprinted by permission of Tribune Media Services
159 ©King Features Syndicate. Reprinted with special permission.
160 Reprinted with permission of Scott Daley
161 *Doonesbury*© 1995 G. B. Trudeau. Reprinted with permission of Universal Press Syndicate. All rights reserved.
162 *Peanuts* reprinted by permission of United Feature Syndicate, Inc.
163 *Calvin & Hobbes*© 1922 Watterson. Dist. by Universal Press Syndicate. Reprinted with permission. All rights reserved.
171 AP/Wide World
172 Jeff Rotman
180 Michael Kaufman, Impact Visuals
182 Kaku Kurita, Gamma/Liaison
185 Reuters/Bettmann
186 AP/Wide World
188 Reuters/Archive Photos
190 AP/Wide World
192 Beatrice Schiller
193 AP/Wide World; AP/Wide World; AP/Wide World; Cynthia Johnson, Gamma/Liaison
194 AP/Wide World; Pam Francis, Gamma/Liaison; AP/Wide World; Archive Photos
195 Bettmann; UPI/Bettmann; Swann, Gamma/Liaison; AP/Wide World;
196 AP/Wide World; AP/Wide World; AP/Wide World; Archive Photos
197 UPI/Bettmann; UPI/Bettmann; Cynthia Johnson, Gamma/Liaison; UPI/Bettmann
198 AP/Wide World
201 Reuters/Bettmann
202-208 AP/Wide World
216 G. Korganow, Gamma/Liaison

221 Reuters/Bettmann
223 Barthelemy, Sipa Press
226 AP/Wide World
229 Tongo, Gamma/Liaison
230 Sarah Figlio*
233 Focus on Sports
236 AP/Wide World
237 Lou Cappozzola, *Sports Illustrated*
244 Reuters/Bettmann
248 Markel, Gamma/FSP
252 Yamashi Nichinich, Gamma/Liaison
256-258 AP/Wide World
260 Villard-Witt-Haley, Sipa Press
264 Nancy McGirr, Black Star
266 Adenis, Sipa Press
267 AP/Wide World
270 Reprinted by permission of American Library Association; Illustration from *Smoky Night* by Eve Bunting. Text©1994 Eve Bunting, Illustrations© 1994 David Diaz. Reprinted by permission of Harcourt Brace & Company. All rights reserved.
274 AP/Wide World
277 Benali, Gamma/Liaison
279 Ed Quinn, NYT Pictures
281 Reuters/Bettmann
283 Dan Groshong, Sygma
286 AP/Wide World; Sergio Dorantes; Reuters/Bettmann; Jorge Nunez, Sipa Press; Porter Gifford, Gamma/Liaison; Dante Busquets-Sordo, Gamma/Liaison
289 Reuters/Bettmann
291 Stephen Ferry, Gamma/Liaison
292 Tom Keck, Gamma/Liaison
293 Ted Soqui, Sygma
294 AP/Wide World
300 Paramount from Shooting Star
302 AP/Wide World
304 Danny Deen
306 AP/Wide World
307 Bill Jordan, *Charleston Post and Courier* from Sipa Press
308 AP Wide World
309 *Houston Chronicle*
313 Michael J. Philippot, Sygma
316 Bettmann Archive
318 UPI/Bettmann
319 Michael J. Philippot, Sygma; Northern Ireland Tourist Board
323 AP/Wide World
324 Reuters/Bettmann
325-329 AP/Wide World
332 JILA Research team; Ken Abbott, University of Colorado
335-338 AP/Wide World
339 Jeffrey Markowitz, Sygma
342 Reuters/Bettmann
346 Center for Disease Control from Photo Researchers; CNRI from Photo Researchers
347 Kari Lounatanaa, Photo Researchers; A. B. Dowsett, Photo Researchers
349 Richard Falco, Black Star

350 Rafael Macia, Photo Researchers; Claus Meyer, Black Star
351 David R. Frazier, Photo Researchers; Jeff Guerrant*
352 Malcolm Linton, Black Star; World Health Organization; Richard Falco, Black Star
358 Reuters/Archive Photos
361 Reuters/Bettmann
362 Anne Nosten, Gamma/Liaison
364 Shannon Hill, Gamma/Liaison
366 Tim Hancock, Sports File
368 Leland Bobbe, Tony Stone Images
371 UPI/Bettmann
373 David Oliver, Tony Stone Images; David Young-Wolff, Tony Stone Images; Pascal Crapet, Tony Stone Images; Barros & Barros from The Image Bank
374-377 David Oliver, Tony Stone Images
382-384 Reuters/Bettmann
386 Reuters/Bettmann
390 Jerry Wachter, The Baltimore Orioles
391 Jerry Wachter
392 Focus on Sports; C. Melvin, SportsChrome; Focus on Sports; Focus on Sports
393 Bill Smith
395 Reuters/Bettmann
403 Jay Mallin, Impact Visuals
405 Simon Bruty, Allsport
407 Michael J. Okoniewski, Gamma/Liaison
409 Motorola Corporation
410 Dan Swanson, VanGarde Imagery*
415 Reprinted with permission of Netscape Communications Corp. ©1995 Netscape Communications Corp.
418 *The New York Times*
420 AP/Wide World
422 Reuters/Bettmann
423 Bill Frakes, *Sports Illustrated*
424 AP/Wide World
428 Granger Collection; AP/Wide World
430 UPI/Bettmann; Ginsanti, Sygma; Esaias Baitel, Gamma/Liaison
432 Ammar Adb Rabbo, Sipa Press; Reuters/Bettmann
433 Reuters/Bettmann; AP/Wide World; UPI/Bettmann
439 Reuters/Bettmann
442 AP/Wide World
444 Reuters/Bettmann
445 Sygma
448 Les Stone, Sygma
452 Jason Bleibtreu, Sygma
453 Reuters/Bettmann
455-456 AP/Wide World
458 Sovfoto/Eastfoto; AP/Wide World
459 Reuters/Bettmann
460-461 UPI/Bettmann
462 Sovfoto/Eastfoto
463 AP/Wide World; AP/Wide World; Bettmann Archive
464 Alfred Eisenstaedt, *Life* Magazine ©1945, Time Inc.
465 Bettmann Archive
468 AP/Wide World
472 Michael Fogden, Oxford Scientific Films from Earth Scenes

A Preview of 1996

JANUARY

Sun	Mon	Tue	Wed	Thur	Fri	Sat
	1	2	3	4	5	6
7	8	9	10	11	12	13
14	15	16	17	18	19	20
21	22	23	24	25	26	27
28	29	30	31			

1 **New Year's Day.**
Rose Bowl and other bowl games played by top college football teams.

4 **100th Anniversary of Utah's** admission as the 45th state.

5 **Twelfth Night,** marking the traditional end of Christmas celebrations.

6 **Epiphany,** 12th day after Christmas celebrates visit of the Three Wise Men.
Carnival season begins in traditionally Roman Catholic countries.

8 **Birth Anniversary of Elvis Aaron Presley** (1935-1977)

15 **Blessing of the Animals Day** in Mexico.

15 **Martin Luther King, Jr., Day.**

19 **Robert E. Lee's Birthday,** celebrated as a legal holiday in most Southern states.

20 **Senior Bowl,** featuring the best college seniors.

21 **Ramadan,** a Muslim holiday, beginning a month of fasting.

28 **Super Bowl XXX.**

FEBRUARY

Sun	Mon	Tue	Wed	Thur	Fri	Sat
				1	2	3
4	5	6	7	8	9	10
11	12	13	14	15	16	17
18	19	20	21	22	23	24
25	26	27	28	29		

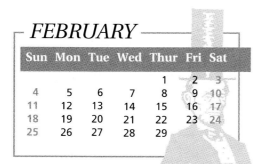

1 **African American History Month,** also known as Black History Month, begins.
American Heart Month begins.

2 **Ground-Hog Day;** according to legend, if the ground hog emerges and sees its shadow, six weeks of winter weather will follow.

3 **175th Birth Anniversary of Elizabeth Blackwell,** first woman awarded U.S. medical degree.

4 **Boy Scouts of America Anniversary Week** begins.

5 **Tu B'Shebat, a Jewish arbor day;** Jews donate funds to plant trees in Israel.

12 **Abraham Lincoln's Birthday,** celebrated in many states.

14 **Valentine's Day.**

19 **Presidents' Day,** honoring Lincoln, Washington, and other past U.S. Presidents.
Chinese New Year.

20 **Mardi Gras,** last celebration before Lent, observed in New Orleans and many Roman Catholic countries.

21 **Ash Wednesday,** first day of Lent.

22 **George Washington's Birthday.**

29 **Leap Year Day.**

MARCH

Sun	Mon	Tue	Wed	Thur	Fri	Sat
					1	2
3	4	5	6	7	8	9
10	11	12	13	14	15	16
17	18	19	20	21	22	23
24	25	26	27	28	29	30
31						

1 **National Women's History Month** begins, to celebrate the contributions and achievements of women.
World Day of Prayer.

2 **Iditarod Dog-Sled Race** from Anchorage to Nome, Alaska, begins.

3 **Save Your Vision Week** begins, to promote awareness of the importance of eye health.

5 **Purim,** commemorates the saving of ancient Persian Jews from a plot to kill them.

7 **World's Largest Concert,** on PBS stations nationwide, to draw attention to Music in Our Schools Month.

8 **United Nations' International Women's Day.**

10 **Girl Scout Week** begins.

11 **Commonwealth Day in Canada.**

16 **Freedom of Information Day.**

17 **St. Patrick's Day,** honoring the patron saint of Ireland.
Campfire Boys' and Girls' Week begins.
National Poison Prevention Week begins.

20 **Spring begins** with the Vernal Equinox at 3:03 a.m. (E.S.T.).

31 **Palm Sunday,** marking Jesus's final entry into Jerusalem along streets covered with palm leaves.

APRIL

Sun	Mon	Tue	Wed	Thur	Fri	Sat
	1	2	3	4	5	6
7	8	9	10	11	12	13
14	15	16	17	18	19	20
21	22	23	24	25	26	27
28	29	30				

1 **April Fools' Day.**
4 **Maundy Thursday.**
   Passover, or Pesah, begins, celebrating deliverance of the ancient Israelites from Egypt.
   Total eclipse of the moon, visible over eastern North and South America as well as parts of Europe, Africa, Antarctica, Australia, and Asia.
5 **Good Friday,** marks the death of Jesus.
7 **Easter Sunday.**
   Daylight-Saving Time begins at 2:00 a.m. in most areas of the United States.
12 **35th Anniversary of First Manned Space Fight** in 1961, by Soviet Cosmonaut Yuri Gagarin.
14 **National Library Week** begins.
16 **Day of Remembrance** commemorating victims of the Nazi Holocaust.
17 **Partial Solar Eclipse** visible over New Zealand and Antarctica.
21 **Boys' and Girls' Club Week** begins.
22 **Earth Day.**
24 **Professional Secretaries Day.**
25 **Take Our Daughters to Work Day.**
28 **National Day of Mourning in Canada** for workers killed or injured on the job.
   Canadian-U.S. Goodwill Week begins.

MAY

Sun	Mon	Tue	Wed	Thur	Fri	Sat
			1	2	3	4
5	6	7	8	9	10	11
12	13	14	15	16	17	18
19	20	21	22	23	24	25
26	27	28	29	30	31	

1 **May Day; Law Day** in the United States.
   Older Americans Month begins.
2 **National Day of Prayer.**
3 **United Nations' World Press Freedom Day.**
4 **Kentucky Derby,** famed horse race.
5 **Be Kind to Animals Week** begins.

Cinco de Mayo, commemorating an 1862 battle in which Mexican forces defeated invading French troops.
8 **World Red Cross Day.**
12 **Mother's Day.**
   National Police Week begins.
15 **Canadian Tulip Festival** in Ottawa, Ontario, billed as the world's largest tulip festival.
   Peace Officer Memorial Day.
   United Nations' International Day of Families.
18 **Armed Forces Day.**
20 **Victoria Day in Canada.**
22 **Immigrant's Day in Canada,** recognizing the contributions made by immigrants to Canada.
25 **African Freedom Day** in Organization of African Unity countries.
26 **Indianapolis 500-Mile Race,** the world's largest single-day sporting event.
   Pentecost.
27 **Memorial Day** celebrated.

JUNE

Sun	Mon	Tue	Wed	Thur	Fri	Sat
						1
2	3	4	5	6	7	8
9	10	11	12	13	14	15
16	17	18	19	20	21	22
23	24	25	26	27	28	29
30						

1 **70th Birth Anniversary of Marilyn Monroe,** legendary American actress.
2 **National Safe Boating Week** begins.
3 **National Fishing Week** begins.
5 **United Nations' World Environment Day.**
7 **Donut Day,** on which the Salvation Army raises funds by selling paper donuts.
8 **Euro '96: European Football (Soccer) Championships** begin at various sites around England, the host country.
9 **Children's Sunday,** observed by many Christian congregations.
10 **National Little League Baseball Week** begins.
14 **Flag Day,** commemorates the adoption in 1777 of the Stars and Stripes as the U.S. flag.
   Father's Day.
20 **Summer begins** in the Northern Hemisphere with the summer solstice that occurs at 10:24 p.m. (E.D.T.). Winter begins at the same time in the Southern Hemisphere.
29 **Gettysburg Civil War Heritage Days** begin, featuring battle reenactment.

JULY

Sun	Mon	Tue	Wed	Thur	Fri	Sat
	1	2	3	4	5	6
7	8	9	10	11	12	13
14	15	16	17	18	19	20
21	22	23	24	25	26	27
28	29	30	31			

1 **Canada Day,** commemorates the confederation of Upper and Lower Canada with certain Maritime provinces to form the Dominion of Canada in 1867.

4 **Independence Day in the United States.**

7 **Newport Music Festival** begins its 28th season of concerts in the mansions of Newport, Rhode Island.
75th Birthday of Nancy Reagan, second wife of former U.S. President Ronald Reagan.

11 **United Nations' World Population Day,** calling attention to issues involving population growth.

13 **Festival of Lanterns** begins in Japan, with religious rites in memory of the dead.

14 **Bastille Day,** France's Independence Day.

19 **The Summer Olympic Games** begin in Atlanta, an event that marks the 100th anniversary of the modern Olympic Games.
Pro Football Hall of Fame Festival begins, to honor new inductees.

20 **Festival of the American South** begins in Atlanta, designed by the Smithsonian Institution as part of its Festival of American Folklife.

AUGUST

Sun	Mon	Tue	Wed	Thur	Fri	Sat
				1	2	3
4	5	6	7	8	9	10
11	12	13	14	15	16	17
18	19	20	21	22	23	24
25	26	27	28	29	30	31

4 **Coast Guard Day,** celebrates the founding of the U.S. Coast Guard in 1790.

5 **Canadian Civic Holiday** observed in Alberta, British Columbia, Manitoba, New Brunswick, Ontario, Saskatchewan, and the Northwest Territories.

6 **Colt League World Series,** for baseball players ages 15 and 16, begins in Lafayette, Indiana.

7 **Mustang League World Series,** for ages 9 and

10, begins in Washington, Pennsylvania.

8 **Bronco League World Series,** for ages 11 and 12, begins in Monterey, California.

9 **Little League Baseball World Series** begins in Fort Lauderdale, Florida.

10 **Republican National Convention** begins in San Diego, California.
150th Anniversary Celebration of the founding of the Smithsonian Institution.

14 **Palomino League World Series,** for baseball players ages 17 and 18, begins in Greensboro, North Carolina.

16 **Paralympic Games** begin in Atlanta for athletes with physical disabilities.

17 **Pony League World Series,** for ages 13 and 14, begins in Washington, Pennsylvania.

19 **National Aviation Day.**

26 **Democratic National Convention** begins in Chicago.
Women's Equality Day.

SEPTEMBER

Sun	Mon	Tue	Wed	Thur	Fri	Sat
1	2	3	4	5	6	7
8	9	10	11	12	13	14
15	16	17	18	19	20	21
22	23	24	25	26	27	28
29	30					

1 **National Literacy Month** begins.

2 **Labor Day** in the United States and Canada.

8 **National Grandparents Day.**
75th Anniversary of the Miss America pageant.

10 **Miss America** pageant begins in Atlantic City.

14 **Rosh Hashanah,** celebrating the Jewish New Year, 5757.

15 **National Hispanic Heritage Month** begins and continues through October 15.

17 **National Constitution Day** commemorates signing of the U.S. Constitution in 1787.

22 **Autumn begins** with the autumnal equinox at 2:00 p.m. (E.D.T.).
Religious Freedom Week begins.

23 **Yom Kippur,** the Jewish Day of Atonement.

26 **Total eclipse of the moon** visible over North and South America, Europe, and Africa.

27 **Sukkot,** Jewish Feast of Tabernacles, begins.

28 **Banned Books Week begins,** emphasizing the right to read and the importance of freedom from censorship.

OCTOBER

Sun	Mon	Tue	Wed	Thur	Fri	Sat
		1	2	3	4	5
6	7	8	9	10	11	12
13	14	15	16	17	18	19
20	21	22	23	24	25	26
27	28	29	30	31		

1 **National Disability Employment Awareness Month** begins to encourage integration of people with disabilities into the workplace.
6 **Fire Prevention Week** begins.
7 **Child Health Day** in the United States.
9 **Leif Ericson Day.**
11 **General Pulaski Memorial Day,** recognizing the role of Polish cavalry officer Casimir Pulaski in the American Revolutionary War.
12 **Partial eclipse of the sun** visible over parts of northeastern Canada, Greenland, Iceland, Europe, and northern Africa.
14 **Columbus Day** in the United States.
  Canadian Thanksgiving Day.
18 **Canadian Persons' Day** commemorates a 1929 court ruling that women in Canada are persons with rights and privileges.
19 **Sweetest Day.**
24 **United Nations' Day.**
27 **Daylight-Saving Time ends** and Standard Time resumes at 2:00 a.m.
31 **Halloween.**
  National UNICEF Day to raise awareness about the lives of children in the developing world.

NOVEMBER

Sun	Mon	Tue	Wed	Thur	Fri	Sat
					1	2
3	4	5	6	7	8	9
10	11	12	13	14	15	16
17	18	19	20	21	22	23
24	25	26	27	28	29	30

1 **All Saints' Day.**
  National Alzheimer's Disease Month begins.
  National Diabetes Month begins.
  National Epilepsy Awareness Month begins.
2 **All Souls' Day.**
3 **National Chemistry Week** begins, to promote public awareness of the importance of chemistry in everyday life.

5 **General Election Day.**
  New York City Marathon, which draws about 25,000 runners and 2 million spectators.
11 **Veterans Day in the United States.**
  Remembrance Day in Canada.
14 **100th Birth Anniversary of Mamie Doud Eisenhower,** wife of former President Dwight D. Eisenhower.
17 **American Education Week** begins, calling attention to the importance of public education in the United States.
18 **National Children's Book Week,** begins.
20 **United Nations' Universal Children's Day.**
21 **Great American Smokeout,** urging smokers to quit for at least a day.
22 **John F. Kennedy,** 35th President of the United States, assassinated in Dallas in 1963.
28 **Thanksgiving Day in the United States.**

DECEMBER

Sun	Mon	Tue	Wed	Thur	Fri	Sat
1	2	3	4	5	6	7
8	9	10	11	12	13	14
15	16	17	18	19	20	21
22	23	24	25	26	27	28
29	30	31				

1 **United Nations' World AIDS Day,** focusing on efforts to prevent and control AIDS.
  Advent begins.
6 **St. Nicholas Day,** when children in parts of Europe receive gifts.
  Hanukkah, the eight-day Jewish Feast of Lights, begins.
7 **Pearl Harbor Day,** commemorating the 1941 bombing of the U.S. fleet in Hawaii by the Japanese.
8 **Lailat al Miraj,** Muslim holy day commemorating the ascent of the Prophet Muhammad into heaven.
  5th Anniversary of the breakup of the Soviet Union.
10 **Nobel Prize Awards Ceremony** in Norway and Stockholm, Sweden.
21 **Winter begins** in the Northern Hemisphere with the winter solstice at 9:06 a.m. (E.S.T.).
25 **Christmas Day.**
26 **Kwanzaa,** an African American family observance based on African harvest festivals, begins and continues through Jan. 1, 1997.
  Boxing Day, observed in England, Canada, and other Commonwealth nations.
31 **New Year's Eve.**